Hippocrene
Practical Dictionaries

English – Français
French – Anglais

Rosalind Williams BA

HIPPOCRENE BOOKS, New York

First Hippocrene Edition, 1983

© Laurence Urdang Associates, 1982

Glossary of Menu Terms and special American
usage entries © Hippocrene Books, 1983

ISBN 0-88254-928-6 (h.c.)
ISBN 0-88254-815-8 (pbk)

Printed in the United States of America

Abbreviations/Abréviations

adj adjective, adjectif
admin administration
adv adverb, adverbe
aero aeronautics
aéro aéronautique
anat anatomy, anatomie
arch architecture
art article
astrol astrology, astrologie
astron astronomy, astronomie
auto automobile
aux auxiliary, auxiliaire
bot botany, botanique
chem chemistry
chim chimie
coll colloquial
comm commerce
conj conjunction, conjonction
derog derogatory
econ economics
écon économie
elec electricity
élec électricité
f feminine, féminin
fam familiar, familier
geog geography
géog géographie
geol geology

géol géologie
gramm grammar, grammaire
impol impolite, impoli
interj interjection
invar invariable
m masculine, masculin
math mathematics,
      mathématiques
med medicine
méd médicine
mil military, militaire
n noun, nom
naut nautical, nautique
péj péjoratif
phone telephone
phot photography, photographie
pl plural, pluriel
pol politics, politique
prep preposition, préposition
pron pronoun, pronom
psych psychology, psychologie
rail railways
rel religion
sing singular, singulier
tech technical, technique
v verb, verbe
V vide (see, voir)
zool zoology, zoologie

French pronunciation

ɑ pate [pɑt]
a rame [ram]
ɛ baie [bɛ]
e pré [pre]
i fiche [fiʃ]
ɔ col [kɔl]
o pot [po]
u route [rut]
y vue [vy]
ə me [mə]
ø deux [dø]
œ jeune [ʒœn]
ɑ̃ vent [vɑ̃]
ɛ̃ fin [fɛ̃]
ɔ̃ ton [tɔ̃]
œ̃ brun [brœ̃]
' hibou ['ibu] (no liaison)
b bière [bjɛr]
d dame [dam]

f faîte [fɛt]
g gant [gɑ̃]
h hola [hɔla]
j pierre [pjɛr]
k conte [kɔ̃t]
l lieu [ljø]
m mon [mɔ̃]
n nid [ni]
p poli [pɔli]
r rage [raʒ]
s sein [sɛ̃]
t tube [tyb]
v vite [vit]
w oui [wi]
z zone [zon]
ɥ lui [lɥi]
ʃ chou [ʃu]
ʒ neige [nɛʒ]
ɲ ligne [liɲ]
ŋ parking [parkiŋ]

In French, the stress always falls on the final syllable of a word or group of words.

Prononciation de l'anglais

a hat [hat]
e bell [bel]
i big [big]
o dot [dot]
ʌ bun [bʌn]
u book [buk]
ə alone [ə'loun]
a: card [ka:d]
ə: word [wə:d]
i: team [ti:m]
o: torn [to:n]
u: spoon [spu:n]
ai die [dai]
ei ray [rei]
oi toy [toi]
au how [hau]
ou road [roud]
eə lair [leə]
iə fear [fiə]
uə poor [puə]
b back [bak]
d dull [dʌl]
f find [faind]

g gaze [geiz]
h hop [hop]
j yell [jel]
k cat [kat]
l life [laif]
m mouse [maus]
n night [nait]
p pick [pik]
r rose [rouz]
s sit [sit]
t toe [tou]
v vest [vest]
w week [wi:k]
z zoo [zu:]
θ think [θiŋk]
ð those [ðouz]
ʃ shoe [ʃu:]
ʒ treasure ['treʒə]
tʃ chalk [tʃo:k]
dʒ jump [dʒʌmp]
ŋ sing [siŋ]

Le signe ' est placé devant la syllabe qui porte l'accent tonique.
Le signe ˌ est placé devant la syllabe qui porte l'accent secondaire.

Guide to the dictionary

Irregular plural forms are shown at the headword and in the text. The following categories of French plural forms are considered regular:

main	mains
prix	prix
cheval	chevaux
feu	feux
seau	seaux

Irregular feminine forms of adjectives are shown at the headword and in the text. The following categories are considered regular:

brun	brune
digne	digne
précieux	précieuse
vif	vive
artificiel	artificielle
ancien	ancienne
premier	première

Irregular verbs marked with an asterisk in the headword list are listed in the verb tables, with the following exceptions:

For verbs ending in **-aindre, -eindre**, or **-oindre** see **atteindre**.
For verbs ending in **-aître** (except **naître**) see **connaître**.
For verbs ending in **-cevoir** see **apercevoir**.
For verbs ending in **-clure** see **conclure**.
For verbs ending in **-crire** see **écrire**.
For verbs ending in **-entir** (also **dormir, partir, servir, sortir**) see **mentir**.
For verbs ending in **-quérir** see **acquérir**.
For verbs ending in **-uire** (except **luire, nuire**) see **conduire**.

Adverbs are shown only if their formation is irregular. English adverbs are considered regular if they are formed by adding -*ly* to the adjective. French adverbs are considered regular if they are formed by adding -*ment* to the feminine form of the adjective.

Guide au dictionnaire

Les formes irrégulières au pluriel sont indiquées après le mot cherché et dans le texte. Les catégories suivantes des formes plurielles sont considérées régulières en anglais:

cat	cats
glass	glasses
fly	flies
half	halves
wife	wives

Les formes irrégulières des adjectifs au féminin sont indiquées après le mot cherché et dans le texte. Les catégories suivantes des formes féminines sont considérées régulières:

brun	brune
digne	digne
precieux	précieuse
vif	vive
artificiel	artificielle
ancien	ancienne
premier	première

Les verbes irréguliers se trouvant dans la liste des verbes sont marqués d'un astérisque dans la liste des mots du dictionnaire.

Les adverbes se construisant régulièrement ne sont pas indiqués. Les adverbes anglais sont considérés réguliers s'ils sont construits en ajoutant -*ly* à l'adjectif. Les adverbes français sont considérés réguliers s'ils sont construits en ajoutant -*ment* à la forme féminine de l'adjectif.

French irregular verbs

Infinitive	Present	Imperfect	Past Participle	Future
absoudre	absous	absolvais	absous	absoudrai
acquérir	acquiers	acquérais	acquis	acquerrai
aller	vais	allais	allé	irai
apercevoir	aperçois	apercevais	aperçu	apercevrai
assaillir	assaille	assaillais	assailli	assaillirai
asseoir	assieds	asseyais	assis	assiérai
atteindre	atteins	atteignais	atteint	atteindrai
avoir	ai	avais	eu	aurai
battre	bats	battais	battu	battrai
boire	bois	buvais	bu	boirai
bouillir	bous	bouillais	bouilli	bouillirai
braire	brais	brayais	brait	brairai
circoncire	circoncis	circoncisais	circoncis	circoncirai
clore	clos		clos	clorai
conclure	conclus	concluais	conclu	conclurai
conduire	conduis	conduisais	conduit	conduirai
confire	confis	confisais	confit	confirai
connaître	connais	connaissais	connu	connaîtrai
coudre	couds	cousais	cousu	coudrai
courir	cours	courais	couru	courrai
couvrir	couvre	couvrais	couvert	couvrirai
croire	crois	croyais	cru	croirai
croître	croîs	croissais	crû	croîtrai
cueillir	cueille	cueillais	cueilli	cueillerai
devoir	dois	devais	dû	devrai
dire	dis	disais	dit	dirai
dissoudre	dissous	dissolvais	dissous	dissoudrai
échoir	il échoit		échu	il échoira
écrire	écris	écrivais	écrit	écrirai
envoyer	envoie	envoyais	envoyé	enverrai
être	suis	étais	été	serai
faillir			failli	faillirai
faire	fais	faisais	fait	ferai
falloir	il faut	il fallait	fallu	il faudra
foutre	fous	foutais	foutu	foutrai
frire	fris		frit	frirai
fuir	fuis	fuyais	fui	fuirai

Infinitive	Present	Imperfect	Past Participle	Future
gésir	gis	gisais		
haïr	hais	haïssais	haï	haïrai
importer	il importe			
lire	lis	lisais	lu	lirai
luire	luis	luisais	lui	luirai
maudire	maudis	maudissais	maudit	maudirai
mentir	mens	mentais	menti	mentirai
mettre	mets	mettais	mis	mettrai
moudre	mouds	moulais	moulu	moudrai
mourir	meurs	mourais	mort	mourrai
mouvoir	meus	mouvais	mû	mouvrai
naître	nais	naissais	né	naîtrai
nuire	nuis	nuisais	nui	nuirai
offrir	offre	offrais	offert	offrirai
ouïr	ois	oyais	ouï	oirrai
ouvrir	ouvre	ouvrais	ouvert	ouvrirai
plaire	plais	plaisais	plu	plairai
pleuvoir	il pleut	il pleuvait	plu	il pleuvra
pouvoir	peux or puis	pouvais	pu	pourrai
prendre	prends	prenais	pris	prendrai
résoudre	résous	résolvais	résolu	résoudrai
rire	ris	riais	ri	rirai
savoir	sais	savais	su	saurai
seoir	il sied	il seyait		
souffrir	souffre	souffrais	souffert	souffrirai
suffire	suffis	suffisais	suffi	suffirai
suivre	suis	suivais	suivi	suivrai
surseoir	sursois	sursoyais	sursis	surseoirai
taire	tais	taisais	tu	tairai
tenir	tiens	tenais	tenu	tiendrai
traire	trais	trayais	trait	trairai
tressaillir	tressaille	tressaillais	tressailli	tressaillirai
vaincre	vaincs	vainquais	vaincu	vaincrai
valoir	vaux	valais	valu	vaudrai
venir	viens	venais	venu	viendrai
vêtir	vêts	vêtais	vêtu	vêtirai
vivre	vis	vivais	vécu	vivrai
voir	vois	voyais	vu	verrai
vouloir	veux	voulais	voulu	voudrai

Verbes irréguliers anglais

Infinitif	Prétérit	Participe Passé	Infinitif	Prétérit	Participe Passé
abide	abode	abode	**deal**	dealt	dealt
arise	arose	arisen	**dig**	dug	dug
awake	awoke	awoken	**do**	did	done
be	was	been	**draw**	drew	drawn
bear	bore	borne	**dream**	dreamed	dreamed
		or born		*or* dreamt	*or* dreamt
beat	beat	beaten	**drink**	drank	drunk
become	became	become	**drive**	drove	driven
begin	began	begun	**dwell**	dwelt	dwelt
behold	beheld	beheld	**eat**	ate	eaten
bend	bent	bent	**fall**	fell	fallen
bet	bet	bet	**feed**	fed	fed
beware			**feel**	felt	felt
bid	bid	bidden	**fight**	fought	fought
		or bid	**find**	found	found
bind	bound	bound	**flee**	fled	fled
bite	bit	bitten	**fling**	flung	flung
bleed	bled	bled	**fly**	flew	flown
blow	blew	blown	**forbid**	forbade	forbidden
break	broke	broken	**forget**	forgot	forgotten
breed	bred	bred	**forgive**	forgave	forgiven
bring	brought	brought	**forsake**	forsook	forsaken
build	built	built	**freeze**	froze	frozen
burn	burnt	burnt	**get**	got	got
	or burned	*or* burned	**give**	gave	given
burst	burst	burst	**go**	went	gone
buy	bought	bought	**grind**	ground	ground
can	could		**grow**	grew	grown
cast	cast	cast	**hang**	hung	hung
catch	caught	caught		*or* hanged	*or* hanged
choose	chose	chosen	**have**	had	had
cling	clung	clung	**hear**	heard	heard
come	came	come	**hide**	hid	hidden
cost	cost	cost	**hit**	hit	hit
creep	crept	crept	**hold**	held	held
cut	cut	cut	**hurt**	hurt	hurt

Infinitif	Prétérit	Participe Passé	Infinitif	Prétérit	Participe Passé
keep	kept	kept	**say**	said	said
kneel	knelt	knelt	**see**	saw	seen
knit	knitted	knitted	**seek**	sought	sought
	or knit	or knit	**sell**	sold	sold
know	knew	known	**send**	sent	sent
lay	laid	laid	**set**	set	set
lead	led	led	**sew**	sewed	sewn
lean	leant	leant			or sewed
	or leaned	or leaned	**shake**	shook	shaken
leap	leapt	leapt	**shear**	sheared	sheared
	or leaped	or leaped			or shorn
learn	learnt	learnt	**shed**	shed	shed
	or learned	or learned	**shine**	shone	shone
leave	left	left	**shoe**	shod	shod
lend	lent	lent	**shoot**	shot	shot
let	let	let	**show**	showed	shown
lie	lay	lain	**shrink**	shrank	shrunk
light	lit	lit	**shut**	shut	shut
	or lighted	or lighted	**sing**	sang	sung
lose	lost	lost	**sink**	sank	sunk
make	made	made	**sit**	sat	sat
may	might		**sleep**	slept	slept
mean	meant	meant	**slide**	slid	slid
meet	met	met	**sling**	slung	slung
mow	mowed	mown	**slink**	slunk	slunk
must			**slit**	slit	slit
ought			**smell**	smelt	smelt
pay	paid	paid		or smelled	or smelled
put	put	put	**sow**	sowed	sown
quit	quitted	quitted			or sowed
	or quit	or quit	**speak**	spoke	spoken
read	read	read	**speed**	sped	sped
rid	rid	rid		or speeded	or speeded
ride	rode	ridden	**spell**	spelt	spelt
ring	rang	rung		or spelled	or spelled
rise	rose	risen	**spend**	spent	spent
run	ran	run	**spill**	spilt	spilt
saw	sawed	sawn		or spilled	or spilled
		or sawed	**spin**	spun	spun

Infinitif	Prétérit	Participe Passé	Infinitif	Prétérit	Participe Passé
spit	spat	spat	**swim**	swam	swum
spilt	split	split	**swing**	swung	swung
spread	spread	spread	**take**	took	taken
spring	sprang	sprung	**teach**	taught	taught
stand	stood	stood	**tear**	tore	torn
steal	stole	stolen	**tell**	told	told
stick	stuck	stuck	**think**	thought	thought
sting	stung	stung	**throw**	threw	thrown
stink	stank	stunk	**thrust**	thrust	thrust
	or stunk		**tread**	trod	trodden
stride	strode	stridden	**wake**	woke	woken
strike	struck	struck	**wear**	wore	worn
string	strung	strung	**weave**	wove	woven
strive	strove	striven	**weep**	wept	wept
swear	swore	sworn	**win**	won	won
sweep	swept	swept	**wind**	wound	wound
swell	swelled	swollen	**wring**	wrung	wrung
		or swelled	**write**	wrote	written

Glossary of menu terms

France is the home of the most elegant cooking in the world. French-speaking people take eating seriously, and visitors can find a great variety of good food in many different kinds of eating establishments. **Cafés, restaurants, bistros, charcuteries** (delicatessens), and that popular import from the United States, **le drugstore,** can provide nourishment almost around the clock. French meals are **petit déjeuner** (breakfast), **déjeuner** (lunch), and **diner** (dinner). Breakfast is usually only coffee and a roll; if you need more sustenance, stock up on fruit and cheese from a food store the night before. Lunch and dinner are both large meals. If you aren't up to both, eat from a delicatessen or market for one of them.

Menus will list **hors d'oeuvre** (appetizers); **potages** or **soupes** (soups); **entrées** (main courses) including **poissons** (fish), **volailles** (poultry), **oeufs** (eggs), and **viandes** (meats); **légumes** (vegetables); and **entremets** (desserts). **Volailles** usually means chicken (**poulet**) but may include duck (**canard**), or quail (**cailles**) or one of many other birds; if you're fussy, ask. Desserts may also include cheeses (**fromages**) and fruits and so on (**fruits et les autres**).

A complete meal (not including drinks and tip) at a set price is **prix fixe.** A tip is called **service** and is either **compris** (included on the check) or **pas compris** (not included). Look at the menu or the sign on the café wall to see which way the establishment works. In a restaurant serving both ways, you must pay extra for drinks on the **à la carte** menu, but the **service** is usually **compris.**

Hors d'Oeuvre (Appetizers, but sometimes served as main courses as well)

artichaut entier whole artichoke

assiette de charcuterie cold cuts that most Americans will recognize in the Italian version as antipasto, but meat only in France

assiette de crudités raw sliced vegetables, often served with an oil and vinegar sauce or dip

caviar sturgeon caviar; expensive

céleri remoulade celery with a mayonnaise sauce (anything *remoulade* is in a mayonnaise sauce)

champignons à la greque mushrooms with an oil, vinegar, and herb dressing

coeur de palmier hearts of palm

coquilles au crabe, or **colin,** or **langouste,** or **saumon** medallions of crab, or hake, or spiny lobster, or salmon garnished with mayonnaise

coquilles St. Jacques bay scallops in creamy sauce served in large scallop shells

escargots snails, usually dressed in herb or butter or cognac sauce and served in their shells

feuilles de vigne vine leaves stuffed with rice

filets de hareng de la baltique crème herring in sour cream

moules remoulade mussels in mayonnaise sauce

oeufs de lumps lumpfish caviar; less expensive than **caviar**

pâté finely chopped meat cooked with a variety of other ingredients and spices

pâté imperial egg roll in the Vietnamese style (Vietnamese food is to French as Chinese is to American)

quiche non-sweet custard in a pastry shell with any of many ingredients: spinach, bacon, onion

salade niçoise anchovies, eggs, black and green olives, peppers, tomatoes, green beans, and usually tuna; a very

popular dish, ubiquitous in **charcuteries**
salade piemontaine like salade niçoise except with radishes instead of anchovies
salade verte green salad; also served as a side dish with the main course or, more rarely, as a last course
sardines à l'huile sardines in oil (**huile** is oil)
saucissons sausages: **à l'ail,** with garlic; **sec,** dry (actually rather moist and tender)
saucissons chaud lyonnais hot sausages Lyonnais style, which means they are usually white
saumon fumé smoked salmon or lox, very popular and expensive
terrine de canard sauvage wild smoked duck pâté
le thon mayonnaise tuna with mayonnaise, or, tunafish salad

Potages or Soupes (Soups)

bisque shellfish soup
bouillabaisse fish and shellfish stew
bouillon any clear soup stock
consommé de volaille chicken soup (clear)
consommé madrilène chicken stock flavored with tomato juice, lemon rind, and spices
petite marmite hearty soup of chicken, beef, and vegetables
potage crème Saint-Germain cream of pea soup
sorbet tomate gazpacho-type soup
soup à l'oignon onion soup
vichyssoise cream of leek and potato soup, usually served cold; pronounce the last ''s''

Entrées (Main Courses)

Poissons (Fish)

bar bass
crevettes shrimp
daurade gilthead bream, a popular fish with white flesh and a delicate taste

filet de maquerreaux mackerel filet
filet de sole the one and only
grenouilles frogs' legs
homard lobster
limande meunière lemon sole or flounder sautéed in oil and butter
poire d'avocat au crabe avocado stuffed with crab meat
raie skatefish: **au beurre noir** (browned butter and vinegar sauce); **au beurre blanc** (butter sauce with shallots and spices)
truite au bleu de meunière trout in oil and butter
turbot also called turbot in English, but not usually available in the U.S.; light, white-fleshed salt-water fish

Volailles (Poultry)

cailles aux raisins quail with raisins, a popular recipe for these tiny birds, usually served two to an order
caneton aux cerises duckling with cherries
coq au vin chicken with vegetables in red wine sauce
coquelet sauté sautéed baby rooster
fricassé de volailles aux cepes wings and backs of a bird cooked with mushrooms
pardix partridge
poulet à la Kiev chicken Kiev
poulet imperial Vietnamese chicken
poulet rôti au froid chicken roasted on a rotisserie and served cold

Oeufs (Eggs)

oeufs à la coque boiled eggs; **brouillé** (scrambled); **en gelée** (in aspic, often a first course); **sur le plat** (fried)

Viandes (Meats)

bifteck steak: **entrecôte** (usually a good cut); **pavé** (a thick steak often served **au poivre,** with pepper and very spicy);

filet mignon (same as in English); **à l'échalote** (with shallots); **chateau briant frite** (chateaubriand with French-fried potatoes — most steaks are served with French-fried potatoes automatically in France); **steak tartare** or **cru** (raw chopped steak); **steak frites** (fried) is the national dish; **bleu** means meat is still almost raw, just heated up; **saignant** is rare; **au point** is medium; **bien cuit** is well done; French restaurants have difficulty cooking **au point** steaks

boeuf burguignonne stew of beef chunks, vegetables and burgundy wine sauce

boeuf en gelée sliced beef in a jelled sauce

boeuf Stroganoff same as in English

boudin blood sausage

brochette de mouton shish kebab: mutton on a skewer, broiled

carre de porc florentine ribs of pork in the Italian style with spinach and cheese

jambon ham: **Parme** (red and uncooked); **de Prague** (Polish); other varieties are named for the place they were made, such as Virginia, York, and various French provinces

jarret de veau veal knuckles, sometimes **au citron** (with lemon)

l'andouillette intestines of pork, often mixed with other parts of the animal — liver, heart — and chopped and wrapped into a sausage

l'escalope panne spaghetti filet, rib, or leg of an animal with spaghetti

lapin en papilotte rabbit cooked wrapped in paper or foil

osso bucco Italian dish of braised chucks of meat

pieds de porc pigs' feet

tournedos de veau medallions of veal, usually broiled or sautéed

les tripes au vin blanc tripe (usually pork) in white wine

vol au vent de ris de veau veal sweetbreads served in pastry shell

Légumes (Vegetables)

asperges fraiches fresh asparagus

choux blanc; choux rouge white or red cabbage

concombres cucumbers

girolles one of many varieties of mushrooms

haricots rouges; haricots verts kidney beans and string beans

maïs corn

petits pois tiny green peas

poireaux leeks, often served **vinaigrette** as an appetizer

pommes mayonnaise potato salad

radis beurre radishes with butter and salt

vapeur riz steamed or boiled rice

Entremets (Desserts)

crème caramel caramel custard

crème chantilly whipped cream lightly sweetened

crème fraiche slightly soured sweet cream

crème de marrons pureed chestnuts in cream

gâteau cake

glaces ice creams

meringue glaces chantilly meringue filled with chocolate ice cream and topped with whipped cream

omelette norvegienne baked Alaska

pêche ou banane melba poached peach or banana with vanilla ice cream, raspberry puree, and kirsch

poire belle Hélène pear with ice cream, a cookie, and hot chocolate sauce

profiterolles au chocolate cream puffs filled with ice cream and covered with chocolate sauce; supposedly Napoleon's favorite dessert

salade au citron green salad dressed with sliced lemon dressing; refreshing after a big meal

sorbets sherbets

tarte aux fruits fruit tarts: small pastries filled with custard and topped with glazed fruits

Fromages (Cheeses)

Cheeses are almost always offered as dessert in cafés and restaurants. Among the great varieties of cheeses commonly offered are: Camembert, Cantal, Gruyère, St. Paulin, Pont l'Eveque, Gorgonzola, Munster, Brie de Meaux, and a special favorite with the French, goat cheese under the blanket name of Chèvre. **Fromage aux herbes** is mild white cheese with various herbs.

Fruits

ananas pineapple; **l'ananas au sirop** (pineapple in syrup)
fraises strawberries
framboises raspberries
melon nature plain melon in season

pamplemousse grapefruit
plum au rhum plum in rum sauce
poire au vin rouge pear poached in red wine
prunneaux au sirop prunes in syrup

Boissons (Drinks)

Restaurants have a variety of **vin** (wine), usually including house liters and demi-liters of Beaujolais, côte de Rhone, and others. After-dinner **liqueurs** are also called **digestifs** and **plus cafés.** Ask for **de l'eau** for a glass or carafe of water. **De l'eau mineral** is mineral water, a popular alternative to wine with dinner. Common French brands include Perrier, Vittel, Vichy, and Evian.

Note: Sometimes you will see a cooking style noted on a menu that puzzles even the French. Some regions of France are used to connote a style known primarily to the chef. Or there are simply esoteric designations, such as **Limousin** (done with onions, shallots, mushrooms, and seasonings). If you know some of the basic words for French foods, you will be able to understand an explanation by restaurant employees.

English–Français

A

a [ə], **an** *art* un, une.
aback [ə'bak] *adv* **be taken aback** être déconcerté.
abandon [ə'bandən] *v* abandonner; (*hope, etc.*) renoncer à.
abashed [ə'baʃt] *adj* décontenancé, confus.
abate [ə'beit] *v* (*storm*) s'apaiser; (*fever*) baisser; (*courage*) diminuer. **abatement** *n* suppression *f*; réduction *f*.
abattoir ['abətwaɪ] *n* abattoir *m*.
abbey ['abi] *n* abbaye *f*. **abbess** *n* abbesse *f*. **abbot** *n* abbé *m*.
abbreviate [ə'briːvieit] *v* abréger. **abbreviation** *n* abréviation *f*.
abdicate ['abdikeit] *v* (*king, etc.*) abdiquer; (*give up*) renoncer à. **abdication** *n* abdication *f*; renonciation *f*.
abdomen ['abdəmən] *n* abdomen *m*. **abdominal** *adj* abdominal.
abduct [ab'dʌkt] *v* enlever. **abduction** *n* enlèvement *m*.
aberration [abə'reifən] *n* aberration *f*. **aberrant** *adj* aberrant.
abet [ə'bet] *v* encourager. **abettor** *n* complice *m*, *f*.
abeyance [ə'beiəns] *n* **be in abeyance** rester en suspens. **fall into abeyance** tomber en désuétude.
abhor [ab'hoɪ] *v* abhorrer. **abhorrence** *n* horreur *f*. **abhorrent** *adj* odieux.
***abide** [ə'baid] *v* (*tolerate*) supporter. **abide by** (*rule*) se conformer à; (*promise*) rester fidèle à.
ability [ə'biləti] *n* capacité *f*; talent *m*. **to the best of one's ability** de son mieux.
abject [abd3ekt] *adj* abject; misérable; (*apology*) servile. **in abject poverty** dans la misère noire.

ablaze [ə'bleiz] *adv*, *adj* en feu.
able ['eibl] *adj* capable. **be able** pouvoir; (*know how to*) savoir. **able-bodied** *adj* robuste.
abnormal [ab'nɔɪml] *adj* anormal. **abnormality** *n* anomalie *f*; malformation *f*.
aboard [ə'bɔɪd] *adv* à bord. *prep* à bord de. **go aboard** s'embarquer.
abode [ə'boud] *V* **abide**. *n* demeure *f*; (*law*) domicile *m*.
abolish [ə'boliʃ] *v* abolir; supprimer. **abolition** *n* abolition *f*; suppression *f*.
abominable [ə'bominəbl] *adj* abominable. **abomination** *n* abomination *f*.
Aborigine [abə'ridʒini] *n* aborigène *m*, *f*.
abort [ə'bɔɪt] *v* avorter. **abortion** *n* avortement *m*. **have an abortion** se faire avorter. **abortive** *adj* manqué.
abound [ə'baund] *v* abonder.
about [ə'baut] *adv* (*approximately*) vers, environ; (*here and there*) ça et là; (*around*) autour. *prep* (*concerning*) au sujet de; (*around*) autour de. **about to** sur le point de. **what is it about?** de quoi s'agit-il?
above [ə'bʌv] *adv*, *prep* au-dessus (de). **above all** surtout. **above-mentioned** *adj* ci-dessus.
abrasion [ə'breiʒən] *n* frottement *m*; (*med*) écorchure *f*. **abrasive** *nm*, *adj* abrasif.
abreast [ə'brest] *adv* de front. **keep abreast of** se tenir au courant de.
abridge [ə'bridʒ] *v* abréger. **abridgment** *n* résumé *m*.
abroad [ə'brɔɪd] *adv* à l'étranger.
abrupt [ə'brʌpt] *adj* soudain; brusque; (*slope*) abrupt.
abscess ['abses] *n* abscès *m*.
abscond [ab'skond] *v* s'enfuir.
absent ['absənt] *adj* absent. **absent-minded** *adj* distrait. **absent-mindedness** *n* distraction *f*. **absence** *n* absence *f*. **in the**

absence of faute de. **absentee** *n* absent,
-e *m, f.*

absolute ['absəluːt] *adj* absolu; complet,
-ète. **absolutely** *adv* absolument, tout à
fait.

absolve [əb'zolv] *v* absoudre; (*law*)
acquitter. **absolution** *n* absolution *f.*

absorb [əb'zoːb] *v* absorber. **absorbent** *adj*
absorbant. **absorbing** *adj* (*book, etc.*)
passionnant. **absorption** *n* absorption *f.*

abstain [əb'stein] *v* s'abstenir. **abstention**
n abstention *f.* **abstinence** *n* abstinence *f.*

abstract ['abstrakt; *v* ab'strakt] *adj*
abstrait. *n* abstrait *m*; résumé *m*. *v* isoler.
abstraction *n* (*removal*) extraction *f*;
(*absent-mindedness*) distraction *f*; (*concept*) abstraction *f.*

absurd [əb'səːd] *adj* absurde.

abundance [ə'bʌndəns] *n* abondance *f.*
abundant *adj* abondant. **abundantly** *adv*
abondamment; (*grow*) à foison; (*completely*) tout à fait.

abuse [ə'bjuːz; *n* ə'bjuːs] *v* (*misuse*) abuser
de; (*insult*) injurier, insulter. *n* abus *m*;
insultes *f pl.* **abusive** *adj* abusif;
injurieux.

abyss [ə'bis] *n* abîme *m.*

academy [ə'kadəmi] *n* académie *f.* **academic** *adj* académique; théorique; (*studies*) scolaire, universitaire.

accede [ak'siːd] *v* accede to agréer.

accelerate [ək'seləreit] *v* accélérer. **acceleration** *n* accélération *f.* **accelerator** *n*
accélérateur *m.*

accent [ak'sənt] *n* accent *m.* *v also* **accentuate** accentuer.

accept [ək'sept] *v* accepter. **acceptable** *adj*
acceptable. **acceptance** *n* acceptation *f*;
approbation *f.*

access ['akses] *n* accès *m.* **accessible** *adj*
accessible. **accession** *n* accession *f*; (*to
throne*) avènement *m.*

accessory [ək'sesəri] *nm, adj* accessoire.

accident ['aksidənt] *n* accident *m.* **by accident** par hasard. **accidental** *adj*
accidentel.

acclaim [ə'kleim] *v* acclamer. *n also* **acclamation** acclamation *f.*

acclimatize [ə'klaimətaiz] *v* acclimater;
habituer.

accolade ['akəleid] *n* accolade *f.*

accommodate [ə'komədeit] *v* loger;
(*adapt*) accommoder. **accommodating** *adj*
obligeant. **accommodation** *n* logement *m*,
chambres *f pl.*

accompany [ə'kʌmpəni] *v* accompagner.
accompaniment *n* accompagnement *m.*
accompanist *n* accompagnateur, -trice *m,
f.*

accomplice [ə'kʌmplis] *n* complice *m, f.*

accomplish [ə'kʌmpliʃ] *v* accomplir; réaliser. **accomplished** *adj* (*skilled*) doué;
accompli. **accomplishment** *n* accomplissement *m*; talent *m.*

accord [ə'koːd] *v* (s')accorder. *n* accord *m.*
of one's own accord de son plein gré.
accordance *n* conformité *f.* **in accordance
with** conformément à. **according to** selon.

accordion [ə'koːdiən] *n* accordéon *m.*

accost [ə'kost] *v* accoster.

account [ə'kaunt] *n* compte *m*; (*report*)
exposé *m.* **on account of** à cause de. **on
no account** en aucun cas. **take into
account** tenir compte de. *v* **account for**
justifier; expliquer. **accountant** *n* comptable *m, f.*

accrue [ə'kruː] *v* revenir; s'accumuler.
accrued interest intérêt couru *m.*

accumulate [ə'kjuːmjuleit] *v*
(s')accumuler. **accumulation** *n* accumulation *f.*

accurate ['akjurət] *adj* exact, précis. **accuracy** *n* exactitude *f*, précision *f.*

accuse [ə'kjuːz] *v* accuser. **accusation** *n*
accusation *f.* **accusing** *adj* accusateur,
-trice.

accustom [ə'kʌstəm] *v* habituer.

ace [eis] *n* as *m.*

ache [eik] *v* faire mal. *n* douleur *f.*

achieve [ə'tʃiːv] *v* (*task*) accomplir; (*aim*)
atteindre. **achievement** *n* (*feat*) exploit
m; (*completion*) exécution *f.*

acid ['asid] *nm, adj* acide.

acknowledge [ək'nolidʒ] *v* reconnaître;
(*letter, etc.*) accuser réception de, répondre à. **acknowledgment** *n* reconnaissance
f; (*of error*) aveu *m*; (*receipt*) reçu *m.*

acne ['akni] *n* acné *f.*

acorn ['eikoːn] *n* gland *m.*

acoustic [ə'kuːstik] *adj* acoustique. **acoustics** *pl n* acoustique *f sing.*

acquaint [ə'kweint] *v* (*inform*) aviser.
acquaint with mettre au courant de. **be
acquainted with** (*a fact*) savoir; (*a place
or person*) connaître. **become acquainted
with** faire la connaissance de. **acquaintance** *n* connaissance *f*, relation *f.*

acquiesce [akwi'es] *v* acquiescer. **acquiescence** *n* consentement *m.*

acquire [ə'kwaiə] v acquérir; prendre.
acquired taste goût qui s'acquiert m.
acquisition n acquisition f. **acquisitive** adj âpre au gain.

acquit [ə'kwit] v acquitter. **acquittal** n acquittement m.

acrid ['akrid] adj âcre; (biting) acerbe.

acrimony ['akriməni] n acrimonie f. **acrimonious** adj acrimonieux.

acrobat ['akrəbat] n acrobate m, f. **acrobatic** adj acrobatique. **acrobatics** pl n acrobatie f sing.

across [ə'kros] prep en travers de, à travers; de l'autre côté. adv (width) de large. **go across** traverser.

acrylic [ə'krilik] adj acrylique.

act [akt] n acte m, action f; (law) loi f; (theatre) acte m. **in the act of** en train de. v agir; (theatre) jouer. **act the fool** faire l'idiot. **acting** adj (temporary) suppléant, par intérim. **actor** n acteur m. **actress** n actrice f.

action ['akʃən] n action f; (law) procès m; (mil) combat m. **out of action** hors d'usage.

active ['aktiv] adj actif. **activate** v activer. **activity** n activité f.

actual ['aktʃuəl] adj réel; (factual) positif. **actually** adv effectivement; à vrai dire.

actuary ['aktjuəri] n actuaire f.

acumen [ə'kjumen] n perspicacité f.

acupuncture n ['akjupʌŋktʃə] n acupuncture f.

acute [ə'kjuit] adj aigu, -guë; (mind) pénétrant; (pain, etc.) vif.

adamant ['adəmənt] adj inflexible.

Adam's apple [adəm'zapl] n pomme d'Adam f.

adapt [ə'dapt] v (s')adapter. **adaptable** adj adaptable. **adaptation** n adaptation f. **adaptor** n (elec) prise multiple f.

add [ad] v ajouter; (numbers) additionner. **addition** n addition f. **in addition** de plus. **in addition to** en plus de. **additional** adj additionnel; supplémentaire.

addendum [ə'dendəm] n addendum m invar.

adder ['adə] n vipère f.

addict ['adikt; v ə'dikt] n (drugs) toxicomane m, f; fanatique m, f. v **become addicted to** s'adonner à. **addiction** n (med) dépendance f.

additive ['aditiv] nm, adj additif.

address [ə'dres] n adresse f; (talk) discours m. v (s')adresser (à).

adenoids ['adənoidz] pl n végétations adénoïdes f pl.

adept [ə'dept] adj expert, versé.

adequate ['adikwət] adj suffisant.

adhere [əd'hiə] v adhérer. **adherent** n adhérent, -e m, f. **adhesion** n adhérence f. **adhesive** nm, adj adhésif.

adjacent [ə'dʒeisənt] adj adjacent, contigu, -guë.

adjective ['adʒiktiv] n adjectif m.

adjoin [ə'dʒoin] v être contigu à. **adjoining** adj voisin.

adjourn [ə'dʒəin] v ajourner; (meeting) suspendre la séance; (move) se retirer.

adjudicate [ə'dʒuidikeit] v juger. **adjudication** n jugement m. **adjudicator** n juge m.

adjust [ə'dʒʌst] v ajuster; (s')adapter; (correct) régler. **adjustment** n réglage m.

ad-lib ['ad'lib] adv à volonté. v improviser.

administer [əd'ministə] v administrer; (business, etc.) gérer. **administration** n administration f; gestion f. **administrative** adj administratif. **administrator** n administrateur, -trice m, f.

admiral ['admərəl] n amiral m. **Admiralty** n ministère de la Marine m.

admire [əd'maiə] v admirer. **admirable** adj admirable. **admiration** n admiration f. **admiring** adj admiratif.

admit [əd'mit] v (let in) laisser entrer; (acknowledge) admettre. **admission** n admission f.

adolescence [adə'lesns] n adolescence f. **adolescent** n, adj adolescent, -e.

adopt [ə'dopt] v adopter. **adopted** adj (child) adoptif. **adoption** n adoption f.

adore [ə'doi] v adorer. **adorable** adj adorable. **adoration** n adoration f.

adorn [ə'doin] v orner, parer.

adrenalin [ə'drenəlin] n adrénaline f.

adrift [ə'drift] adv à la dérive. **come adrift** (wire, etc.) se détacher.

adroit [ə'droit] adj adroit.

adulation [adju'leiʃən] n adulation f.

adult ['adʌlt] n(m+f), adj adulte.

adulterate [ə'dʌltəreit] v adultérer, falsifier.

adultery [ə'dʌltəri] n adultère m. **adulterer** n adultère m, f.

advance [əd'vains] v (s')avancer. n avance f. **advance booking office** location f. **book in advance** retenir à l'avance. **luggage in advance** bagages enregistrés m pl.

advantage [əd'vɑːntidʒ] *n* avantage *m*. **take advantage of** profiter de. **advantageous** *adj* avantageux.

advent ['advənt] *n* venue *f*. **Advent** *n* (*rel*) Avent *m*.

adventure [əd'ventʃə] *n* aventure *f*. **adventurer** *n* aventurier, -ère *m, f*. **adventurous** *adj* aventureux.

adverb ['advɜːb] *n* adverbe *m*.

adversary ['advəsəri] *n* adversaire *m, f*.

adverse ['advɜːs] *adj* défavorable, hostile. **adversity** *n* adversité *f*.

advertise ['advətaiz] *v* (*comm*) faire de la publicité (pour); (*newspaper, etc.*) insérer une annonce. **advertisement** *n* (*comm*) réclame *f*, publicité *f*; (*newspaper*) annonce *f*. **advertising** *n* publicité *f*.

advise [əd'vaiz] *v* conseiller; recommander; (*inform*) aviser. **advice** *n* conseils *m pl*; avis *m*. **advisable** *adj* recommandable. **adviser** *n* conseiller, -ère *m, f*. **advisory** *adj* consultatif.

advocate ['advəkeit] *v* recommander.

aerial ['eəriəl] *adj* aérien. *n* antenne *f*.

aerodynamics [eərədai'namiks] *n* aérodynamique *f*.

aeronautics [eərə'nɔːtiks] *n* aéronautique *f*.

aeroplane ['eərəplein] *n* avion *m*.

aerosol ['eərəsɒl] *n* bombe *f*; (*perfume*) atomiseur *m*.

aesthetic [iːs'θetik] *adj* esthétique.

affair [ə'feə] *n* affaire *f*. **have an affair with** avoir une liaison avec.

affect[1] [ə'fekt] *v* (*influence*) affecter, toucher.

affect[2] [ə'fekt] *v* (*feign*) affecter, feindre. **affected** *adj* affecté, maniéré.

affection [ə'fekʃən] *n* affection *f*. **affectionate** *adj* affectueux.

affiliate [ə'filieit] *v* affilier. **affiliated company** filiale *f*. **affiliation** *n* affiliation *f*.

affinity [ə'finəti] *n* affinité *f*.

affirm [ə'fɜːm] *v* affirmer. **affirmative** *nm, adj* affirmatif.

affix [ə'fiks; *n* 'afiks] *v* apposer; (*stick*) coller. *n* (*gramm*) affixe *m*.

afflict [ə'flikt] *v* affliger. **affliction** *n* affliction *f*; infirmité *f*.

affluent ['afluənt] *adj* abondant; riche. **affluence** *n* abondance *f*; richesse *f*.

afford [ə'fɔːd] *v* avoir les moyens d'acheter; (*provide*) fournir.

affront [ə'frʌnt] *v* insulter. *n* affront *m*.

afield [ə'fiːld] *adv* **far afield** très loin. **farther afield** plus loin.

afloat [ə'fləut] *adv* à flot.

afoot [ə'fut] *adv* **there's something afoot** il se prépare quelque chose.

aforesaid [ə'fɔːsed] *adj* susdit.

afraid [ə'freid] *adj* effrayé. **be afraid** avoir peur; (*polite regret*) regretter.

afresh [ə'freʃ] *adv* de nouveau. **start afresh** recommencer.

Africa ['afrikə] *n* Afrique *f*. **African** *adj* africain; *n* Africain, -e *m, f*.

aft [ɑːft] *adv* sur *or* à l'arrière.

after ['ɑːftə] *prep, conj* après. *adv* après; ensuite. **after all** après tout.

after-effect *n* suite *f*.

aftermath ['ɑːftəmɑːθ] *n* conséquences *f pl*.

afternoon [ɑːftə'nuːn] *n* après-midi *m*.

afterthought ['ɑːftəθɔːt] *n* pensée après coup *f*.

afterwards ['ɑːftəwədz] *adv* ensuite.

again [ə'gen] *adv* de nouveau, encore. **again and again** à plusieurs reprises.

against [ə'genst] *prep* contre. **against the law** contraire à la loi.

age [eidʒ] *n* âge *m*; (*historical*) époque *f*. **for ages** pendant une éternité. **of age** majeur, -e. **under age** mineur, -e. *v* vieillir. **aged** *adj* âgé.

agency ['eidʒənsi] *n* agence *f*, bureau *m*.

agenda [ə'dʒendə] *n* ordre du jour *m*.

agent ['eidʒənt] *n* agent, -e *m, f*; représentant, -e *m, f*.

aggravate ['agrəveit] *v* aggraver; (*increase*) augmenter; (*annoy*) agacer. **aggravation** *n* aggravation *f*; agacement *m*.

aggregate ['agrigət] *n* ensemble *m*. *adj* collectif.

aggression [ə'greʃən] *n* agression *f*. **aggressive** *adj* agressif.

aghast [ə'gɑːst] *adj* atterré.

agile ['adʒail] *adj* agile. **agility** *n* agilité *f*.

agitate ['adʒiteit] *v* (*shake*) agiter; (*worry*) troubler. **agitated** *adj* inquiet, -ète. **agitation** *n* agitation *f*; émotion *f*. **agitator** *n* agitateur, -trice *m, f*.

agnostic [ag'nɒstik] *n* (*m*+*f*), *adj* agnostique.

ago [ə'gəu] *adv* il y a: *il y a deux mois*.

agog [ə'gɒg] *adj, adv* en émoi. **be all agog** être impatient.

agony ['agəni] *n* (*mental*) angoisse *f*; (*med*) agonie *f*. **be in agony** souffrir le martyre. **agonizing** *adj* angoissant.

agree [əˈgriː] v être d'accord; consentir; (*concur*) convenir, s'accorder. **agreeable** *adj* agréable. **agreement** *n* accord *m*.

agriculture [ˈagrikʌltʃə] *n* agriculture *f*. **agricultural** *adj* agricole.

aground [əˈgraund] *adv* échoué. **run aground** s'échouer.

ahead [əˈhed] *adv* en avant; (*time*) en avance.

aid [eid] v aider. **aid and abet** être complice de. *n* aide *f*. **in aid of** au profit de.

aim [eim] v viser; aspirer. *n* (*purpose*) but *m*. **take aim (at)** viser. **aimless** *adj* (*person*) sans but; (*action*) futile.

air [eə] *n* air *m*. **by air** par avion. v aérer; (*opinion*) faire connaître. **airy** *adj* bien aéré.

airbed [ˈeəbed] *n* matelas pneumatique *m*.

airborne [ˈeəbɔin] *adj* aéroporté. **become airborne** (*aircraft*) décoller.

air-conditioned *adj* climatisé. **air-conditioning** *n* climatisation *f*.

aircraft [ˈeəkraift] *n* avion *m*. **aircraft-carrier** *n* porte-avions *m invar*.

airfield [ˈeəfiild] *n* terrain d'aviation *m*.

air force *n* armée de l'air *f*.

air-hostess *n* hôtesse de l'air *f*.

airing cupboard *n* placard-séchoir *m*.

air lift *n* pont aérien *m*.

airline [ˈeəlain] *n* ligne aérienne *f*.

airmail [ˈeəmeil] *n* poste aérienne *f*. **airmail letter** lettre par avion *f*. **by airmail** par avion.

airport [ˈeəpɔit] *n* aéroport *m*.

air-raid *n* attaque aérienne *f*. **air-raid shelter** abri antiaérien *m*.

airtight [ˈeətait] *adj* hermétique.

aisle [ail] *n* (*church*) allée centrale *f*, bas-côté *m*; (*theatre*) passage *m*; (*train*, etc.) couloir central *m*.

ajar [əˈdʒɑi] *adj*, *adv* entrouvert.

akin [əˈkin] *adj* **be akin to** (*resemble*) tenir de, ressembler à; (*family*) être parent de.

alabaster [ˈaləbaistə] *n* albâtre *m*.

alarm [əˈlɑim] *n* alarme *f*. **alarm clock** *n* réveil *m*. v alarmer. **alarmist** *n* alarmiste *m*, *f*.

alas [əˈlas] *interj* hélas!

Albania [alˈbeinjə] *n* Albanie *f*. **Albanian** *nm*, *adj* albanais; *n* (*people*) Albanais, -e *m*, *f*.

albatross [ˈalbətrɒs] *n* albatros *m*.

albino [alˈbiinou] *n* albinos *m*, *f*.

album [ˈalbəm] *n* album *m*.

alchemy [ˈalkəmi] *n* alchimie *f*. **alchemist** *n* alchimiste *m*.

alcohol [ˈalkəhol] *n* alcool *m*. **alcoholic** *n*(*m+f*), *adj* alcoolique. **alcoholism** *n* alcoolisme *m*.

alcove [ˈalkouv] *n* (*room*) alcôve *f*; (*wall*) niche *f*.

alderman [ˈɔildəmən] *n* conseiller municipal *m*.

ale [eil] *n* bière *f*.

alert [əˈlɔit] *adj* alerte; vigilant. *n* alerte *f*. **on the alert** sur le qui-vive. v alerter, éveiller l'attention de.

algebra [ˈaldʒibrə] *n* algèbre *f*. **algebraic** *adj* algébrique.

Algeria [alˈdʒiəriə] *n* Algérie *f*. **Algerian** *n* Algérien, -enne *m*, *f*; *adj* algérien.

Algiers [alˈdʒiəz] *n* Alger.

alias [ˈeiliəs] *adv* alias. *n* faux nom *m*.

alibi [ˈalibai] *n* alibi *m*.

alien [ˈeiliən] *n*, *adj* étranger, -ère. **alien to** contraire à. **alienate** v aliéner. **alienation** *n* aliénation *f*; éloignement *m*.

alight[1] [əˈlait] v descendre; (*bird*) se poser.

alight[2] [əˈlait] *adj* allumé; en feu. **set alight** mettre le feu à.

align [əˈlain] v (s')aligner. **alignment** *n* alignement *m*.

alike [əˈlaik] *adj* semblable. *adv* pareillement, de la même façon. **be alike** se ressembler.

alimentary canal [aliˈmentəri] *n* tube digestif *m*.

alimony [ˈaliməni] *n* pension alimentaire *f*.

alive [əˈlaiv] *adj* vivant.

alkali [ˈalkəlai] *n* alcali *m*. **alkaline** *adj* alcaline.

all [ɔil] *pron*, *adj* tout, toute (*pl* tous, toutes). *adv* tout, complètement. **all right** ça va. **All Saints' Day** le Toussaint. **all the same** tout de même. **not at all** pas du tout.

allay [əˈlei] v apaiser; (*suspicion*) dissiper.

allege [əˈledʒ] v alléguer. **allegation** *n* allégation *f*. **alleged** *adj* prétendu, allégué; présumé.

allegiance [əˈliːdʒəns] *n* fidélité *f*.

allegory [ˈaligəri] *n* allégorie *f*. **allegorical** *adj* allégorique.

allergy [ˈalədʒi] *n* allergie *f*. **allergic** *adj* allergique.

alleviate [əˈliːvieit] v soulager.

alley [ˈali] *n* ruelle *f*.

alliance [ə'laiəns] *n* alliance *f*.
alligator ['aligeitə] *n* alligator *m*.
alliteration [əlitə'reiʃən] *n* allitération *f*.
allocate ['aləkeit] *v* (*allot*) allouer; (*share*) répartir. **allocation** *n* allocation *f*; (*share*) part *f*.
allot [ə'lot] *v* assigner. **allotment** *n* (*land*) parcelle de terre *f*.
allow [ə'lau] *v* permettre; (*give*) accorder. **allow for** tenir compte de. **allowance** *n* allocation *f*; (*subsistence*) indemnité *f*, pension *f*; (*comm*) rabais *m*.
alloy ['aloi; *v* ə'loi] *n* alliage *m*. *v* allier; faire un alliage de.
allude [ə'luːd] *v* faire allusion. **allusion** *n* allusion *f*.
allure [ə'ljuə] *v* attirer. *n* charme *m*. **alluring** *adj* séduisant.
ally ['alai; *v* ə'lai] *n* allié, -ée *m*, *f*. *v* allier. **allied** *adj* allié; (*connected*) apparenté.
almanac ['oːlmənak] *n* almanach *m*.
almighty [oːl'maiti] *adj* tout-puissant; (*coll*) fameux.
almond ['aːmənd] *n* (*nut*) amande *f*; (*tree*) amandier *m*.
almost ['oːlmoust] *adv* presque, à peu près.
alms [aːmz] *n* aumône *f*. **almshouse** *n* hospice *m*.
aloft [ə'loft] *adv* en haut.
alone [ə'loun] *adj*, *adv* seul. **leave alone** laisser tranquille. **let alone** sans parler de.
along [ə'loŋ] *prep* le long de. **alongside** *prep* à côté de.
aloof [ə'luːf] *adj* distant. *adv* à l'écart.
aloud [ə'laud] *adv* (*reading*) à voix haute; (*think*) tout haut.
alphabet ['alfəbit] *n* alphabet *m*. **alphabetical** *adj* alphabétique. **in alphabetical order** par ordre alphabétique.
already [oːl'redi] *adv* déjà.
Alsatian [al'seiʃən] *n* (*dog*) chien-loup *m*.
also ['oːlsou] *adv* aussi.
altar ['oːltə] *n* autel *m*.
alter ['oːltə] *v* changer; (*dress, etc.*) retoucher. **alteration** *n* changement *m*; retouchage *m*.
alternate [oːl'təːnət; *v* 'oːltəneit] *adj* alternatif, alterné; (*every other*) tous les deux. *v* alterner. **alternating current** courant alternatif *m*. **alternator** *n* alternateur *m*.
alternative [oːl'təːnətiv] *n* (*of two*) alterna-

tive *f*; (*of several*) choix *m*; autre solution *f*. *adj* autre, alternatif.
although [oːl'ðou] *conj* bien que, quoique.
altitude ['altitjuːd] *n* altitude *f*.
alto ['altou] *n* (*male*) haute-contre *f*; (*female*) contralto *m*; (*instrument*) alto *m*.
altogether [oːltə'geðə] *adv* (*completely*) entièrement; (*including everything*) en tout.
altruistic [altru'istik] *adj* altruiste.
aluminium [alju'miniəm] *n* aluminium *m*.
always ['oːlweiz] *adv* toujours.
am [am] *V* **be**.
amalgamate [ə'malgəmeit] *v* (*companies*) fusionner; (*metals*) amalgamer. **amalgamation** *n* fusionnement *m*; amalgamation *f*.
amass [ə'mas] *v* amasser.
amateur ['amətə] *n* amateur *m*.
amaze [ə'meiz] *v* stupéfier. **amazed** *adj* stupéfait. **amazement** *n* stupéfaction *f*. **amazing** *adj* stupéfiant, ahurissant.
ambassador [am'basədə] *n* ambassadeur *m*.
amber ['ambə] *n* ambre; (*traffic lights*) feu orange *m*.
ambidextrous [ambi'dekstrəs] *adj* ambidextre.
ambiguous [am'bigjuəs] *adj* ambigu, -guë. **ambiguity** *n* ambiguïté *f*.
ambition [am'biʃən] *n* ambition *f*. **ambitious** *adj* ambitieux.
ambivalent [am'bivələnt] *adj* ambivalent. **ambivalence** *n* ambivalence *f*.
amble ['ambl] *v* marcher d'un pas tranquille; (*horse*) ambler. *n* pas tranquille *m*; (*horse*) amble *m*.
ambulance ['ambjuləns] *n* ambulance *f*.
ambush ['ambuʃ] *n* embuscade *f*. **in ambush** en embuscade. *v* attirer dans une embuscade.
ameliorate [ə'miːliəreit] *v* (s')améliorer. **amelioration** *n* amélioration *f*.
amenable [ə'miːnəbl] *adj* (*cooperative*) maniable; (*answerable*) responsable.
amend [ə'mend] *v* (s')amender; (*revise*) modifier; (*correct*) corriger. **amendment** *n* amendement *m*; modification *f*.
amenity [ə'miːnəti] *n* agrément *m*. **amenities** *pl n* commodités *f pl*.
America [ə'merikə] *n* Amérique *f*; (*United States*) Etats-Unis *m pl*. **American** *n* Américain, -e *m*, *f*; *adj* américain.

amethyst ['aməθist] *n* améthyste *f*.

amiable ['eimiəbl] *adj* aimable.

amicable ['amikəbl] *adj* amical; (*law*) à l'amiable.

amid [ə'mid] *prep* au milieu de.

amiss [ə'mis] *adv* de travers. *adj* mal à propos. **something is amiss** quelque chose ne va pas.

ammonia [ə'mouniə] *n* (*gas*) ammoniac *m*; (*liquid*) ammoniaque *f*.

ammunition [amju'niʃən] *n* munitions *f pl*.

amnesia [am'niːziə] *n* amnésie *f*.

amnesty ['amnəsti] *n* amnistie *f*.

amoeba [ə'miːbə] *n* amibe *f*.

among [ə'mʌŋ] *prep* entre, parmi.

amoral [ei'morəl] *adj* amorale.

amorous ['amərəs] *adj* amoureux.

amorphous [ə'moːfəs] *adj* amorphe; (*ideas, etc.*) sans forme.

amount [ə'maunt] *n* quantité *f*; (*total*) montant *m*. *v* **amount to** s'élever à; (*be equivalent to*) revenir à, équivaloir à.

ampere ['ampeə] *n* ampère *m*.

amphetamine [am'fetəmiːn] *n* amphétamine *f*.

amphibian [am'fibiən] *nm, adj* amphibie. **amphibious** *adj* amphibie.

amphitheatre ['amfiθiətə] *n* amphithéâtre *m*.

ample ['ampl] *adj* (*plenty*) bien assez de; (*large*) ample.

amplify ['amplifai] *v* amplifier; développer. **amplifier** *n* amplificateur *m*.

amputate ['ampjuteit] *v* amputer. **amputation** *n* amputation *f*.

Amsterdam [amstə'dam] *n* Amsterdam.

amuse [ə'mjuːz] *v* (*cause laughter*) faire rire; (*entertain*) distraire. **amuse oneself** s'amuser. **amused** *adj* amusé. **amusement** *n* amusement *m*; distraction *f*.

an [ən] *V* **a**.

anachronism [ə'nakrənizəm] *n* anachronisme *m*. **anachronistic** *adj* anachronique.

anaemia [ə'niːmiə] *n* anémie *f*. **anaemic** *adj* anémique.

anaesthetic [anəs'θetik] *nm, adj* anesthésique. **under anaesthetic** sous anesthésie. **anaesthetist** *n* anesthésiste *m, f*. **anaesthetize** *v* anesthésier.

anagram ['anəgram] *n* anagramme *f*.

anal ['einl] *adj* anal.

analogy [ə'nalədʒi] *n* analogie *f*.

analysis [ən'aləsis] *n* analyse *f*. **analyse** *v*

analyser, faire l'analyse de. **analytical** *adj* analytique.

anarchy ['anəki] *n* anarchie *f*. **anarchist** *n* anarchiste *m, f*.

anathema [ə'naθəmə] *n* anathème *m*. **it is anathema to me** je l'ai en abomination.

anatomy [ə'natəmi] *n* (*med*) anatomie *f*; structure *f*.

ancestor ['ansestə] *n* ancêtre *m*, aïeul, -e *m, f*. **ancestral** *adj* ancestral. **ancestry** *n* ascendance *f*; ancêtres *m pl*, aïeux *m pl*.

anchor ['aŋkə] *n* ancre *f*. *v* (*naut*) (se) mettre à l'ancre; (*fasten*) ancrer.

anchovy ['antʃəvi] *n* anchois *m*.

ancient ['einʃənt] *adj* antique; ancien.

ancillary [an'siləri] *adj* auxiliaire.

and [and] *conj* et.

Andorra [an'dorə] *n* Andorre *f*.

anecdote ['anikdout] *n* anecdote *f*.

anemone [ə'neməni] *n* anémone *f*.

anew [ə'njuː] *adv* de nouveau.

angel ['eindʒəl] *n* ange *m*. **angelic** *adj* angélique.

angelica [an'dʒelikə] *n* angélique *f*.

anger ['aŋgə] *n* colère *f*. *v* mettre en colère.

angina [an'dʒainə] *n* angine de poitrine *f*.

angle ['aŋgl] *n* angle *m*; aspect *m*.

angling ['aŋliŋ] *n* pêche à la ligne *f*. **angler** *n* pêcheur, -euse *m, f*.

angry ['aŋgri] *adj* en colère; furieux. **become angry** se fâcher.

anguish ['aŋgwiʃ] *n* angoisse *f*.

angular ['aŋgjulə] *adj* anguleux.

animal ['animəl] *nm, adj* animal.

animate ['animət; *v* 'animeit] *adj* animé. *v* animer. **animation** *n* animation *f*.

animosity [ani'mosəti] *n* animosité *f*.

aniseed ['anisiːd] *n* graine d'anis *f*; (*as modifier*) à l'anis.

ankle ['aŋkl] *n* cheville *f*.

annals ['anlz] *pl n* annales *f pl*.

annex [ə'neks; *n* 'aneks] *v* annexer. **annexe** *n* annexe *f*.

annihilate [ə'naiəleit] *v* (*mil*) anéantir; annihiler. **annihilation** *n* anéantissement *m*.

anniversary [ani'vəːsəri] *n* anniversaire *m*.

annotate ['anəteit] *v* annoter. **annotation** *n* annotation *f*.

announce [ə'nauns] *v* annoncer. **announcement** *n* annonce *f*; (*official*) avis *m*; (*of birth, etc.*) faire-part *m*. **announcer** *n* (*radio, TV*) speaker, -erine *m, f*.

annoy [ə'noi] v ennuyer, agacer. **annoyance** n mécontentement m; (*nuisance*) tracas m. **annoyed** adj mécontent. **annoying** adj agaçant, ennuyeux.
annual ['ɑnjuəl] adj annuel. n (*bot*) plante annuelle f; (*children's book*) album m.
annul [ə'nʌl] v (*marriage*) annuler; (*law*) abroger. **annulment** n annulation f; abrogation f.
anode ['anoud] n anode f.
anomaly [ə'noməli] n anomalie f. **anomalous** adj anormal.
anonymous [ə'noniməs] adj anonyme. **anonymity** n anonymat m.
anorak ['anərak] n anorak m.
another [ə'nʌðə] pron, adj (*different*) un autre; (*extra*) encore un. **one another** l'un l'autre, les uns les autres.
answer ['ɑinsə] n réponse f; solution f. v répondre (à). **answerable** adj responsable.
ant [ant] n fourmi f. **anthill** n fourmilière f.
antagonize [an'tagənaiz] v contrarier. **antagonism** n antagonisme m. **antagonist** n antagoniste m, f. **antagonistic** adj opposé.
antecedent [anti'siidənt] adj antérieur, -e. n antécédent m.
antelope ['antəloup] n antilope f.
antenna [an'tenə] n antenne f.
anthem ['anθəm] n (*national*) hymne m; motet m.
anthology [an'θolədʒi] n anthologie f.
anthropology [anθrə'polədʒi] n anthropologie f. **anthropological** adj anthropologique. **anthropologist** n anthropologiste m, f.
anti-aircraft [anti'eəkrɑift] adj antiaérien.
antibiotic [antibai'otik] nm, adj antibiotique.
antibody ['anti,bodi] n anticorps m.
anticipate [an'tisipeit] v (*foresee*) prévoir; (*act in advance*) prévenir, anticiper. **anticipation** n attente f; appréhension f. **in anticipation** par anticipation, d'avance.
anticlimax [anti'klaimaks] n chute f.
anticlockwise [anti'klokwaiz] adj dans le sens inverse des aiguilles d'une montre.
antics ['antiks] pl n singeries f pl, cirque m sing.
anticyclone [anti'saikloun] n anticyclone m.

antidote ['antidout] n antidote m.
antifreeze ['antifriiz] n antigel m.
antihistamine [anti'histəmin] n antihistaminique m.
antipathy [an'tipəθi] n antipathie f. **antipathetic** adj antipathique.
antique [an'tiik] adj ancien; antique. n (*ornament*) objet d'art ancien m; (*furniture*) meuble ancien m. **antique dealer** n antiquaire m, f. **antique shop** n magasin d'antiquités m. **antiquated** adj vieilli. **antiquity** n antiquité f.
anti-Semitic [antisə'mitik] adj antisémite. **anti-Semite** n antisémite m, f. **anti-Semitism** n antisémitisme m.
antiseptic [anti'septik] nm, adj antiseptique.
antisocial [anti'souʃəl] adj antisocial.
antithesis [an'tiθəsis] n antithèse f.
antlers ['antləz] pl n bois m pl, ramure f sing.
antonym ['antənim] n antonyme m.
anus ['einəs] n anus m.
anvil ['anvil] n enclume f.
anxious ['aŋkʃəs] adj (*worry*) anxieux; (*desire*) impatient. **anxiety** n anxiété f; grand désir m. **anxiously** adv avec inquiétude; avec impatience.
any ['eni] adj (*interrogative*) du, de la, des; (*negative*) de; (*whichever*) n'importe quel. pron en: je n'en ai pas; aucun; n'importe lequel. **anybody** or **anyone** pron n'importe qui; (*somebody*) quelqu'un; (*negative*) personne. **anyhow** or **anyway** adv en tout cas; quand même. **any more** encore (de); (*negative*) plus. **anything** pron n'importe quoi; (*something*) quelque chose; (*negative*) rien. **anywhere** adv n'importe où; (*somewhere*) quelque part; (*negative*) nulle part. **at any rate** en tout cas. **in any case** de toute façon.
apart [ə'pɑit] adv à part; à distance; séparément; en pièces. **apart from** en dehors de. **come apart** se défaire. **take apart** démonter. **tell apart** distinguer l'un de l'autre.
apartment [ə'pɑitmənt] n (*room*) pièce f; (*flat*) appartement m.
apathy ['apəθi] n apathie f, indifférence f. **apathetic** adj apathique.
ape [eip] n singe m, f. v singer, imiter.
aperture ['apətjuə] n (*phot*) ouverture f; orifice m.

apex ['eipeks] *n* sommet *m*.
aphid ['eifid] *n* aphidé *m*.
aphrodisiac [afrə'diziak] *nm, adj* aphrodisiaque.
apiece [ə'piːs] *adv* chacun; par personne; la pièce.
apology [ə'polədʒi] *n* excuses *f pl*; (*defence*) apologie *f*. **apologize** *v* s'excuser. **be apologetic** se répandre en excuses.
apoplexy ['apəpleksi] *n* apoplexie *f*. **fit of apoplexy** coup de sang *m*.
apostle [ə'posl] *n* apôtre *m*.
apostrophe [ə'postrəfi] *n* apostrophe *f*.
appal [ə'poːl] *v* (*shock*) consterner; (*frighten*) épouvanter. **appalling** *adj* consternant; épouvantable.
apparatus [apə'reitəs] *n* appareil *m*, dispositif *m*.
apparent [ə'parənt] *adj* (*not real*) apparent; (*obvious*) évident, manifeste. **apparently** *adv* apparemment; paraît-il.
apparition [apə'riʃən] *n* apparition *f*.
appeal [ə'piːl] *v* faire (un) appel. **appeal to** (*please*) plaire à; (*request*) s'adresser à. **appealing** *adj* (*moving*) attendrissant; (*attractive*) attirant.
appear [ə'piə] *v* (*be seen*) apparaître, se montrer; (*seem*) paraître. **appearance** *n* apparition *f*; (*aspect*) apparence *f*.
appease [ə'piːz] *v* apaiser. **appeasement** *n* apaisement *m*.
appendix [ə'pendiks] *n* appendice *m*. **appendicitis** *n* appendicite *f*.
appetite ['apitait] *n* appétit *m*. **appetizer** *n* apéritif *m*. **appetizing** *adj* appétissant.
applaud [ə'ploːd] *v* applaudir. **applause** *n* applaudissements *m pl*.
apple ['apl] *n* (*fruit*) pomme *f*; (*tree*) pommier *m*.
apply [ə'plai] *v* appliquer; (*paint, etc.*) mettre; (*ask*) s'adresser; (*refer*) s'appliquer. **appliance** *n* appareil *m*. **applicable** *adj* applicable. **applicant** *n* candidat, -e *m, f*. **application** *n* application *f*; (*job*) demande *f*.
appoint [ə'point] *v* désigner, nommer. **at the appointed time** à l'heure convenue. **appointment** *n* (*meeting*) rendez-vous *m*; (*job*) poste.
apportion [ə'poːʃən] *v* partager, répartir; assigner.
appraise [ə'preiz] *v* estimer, évaluer. **appraisal** *n* évaluation *f*; appréciation *f*.
appreciate [ə'priːʃieit] *v* (*value*) apprécier; (*be aware of*) se rendre compte de; (*be grateful for*) être reconnaissant de; (*rise in value*) prendre de la valeur. **appreciation** *n* appréciation *f*; reconnaissance *f*.
apprehend [apri'hend] *v* (*arrest*) arrêter, appréhender; (*understand*) comprendre. **apprehension** *n* (*fear*) appréhension *f*; arrestation *f*. **apprehensive** *adj* inquiet, -ète; appréhensif.
apprentice [ə'prentis] *v* placer *or* mettre en apprentissage (chez); *n* apprenti, -e *m, f*. **apprenticeship** *n* apprentissage *m*.
approach [ə'prəutʃ] *v* (s')approcher (de). *n* approche *f*, accès *m*.
appropriate [ə'prəuprieit; *adj* ə'prəupriət] *v* s'approprier. *adj* (*name, etc.*) juste, bien choisi; (*correct*) approprié.
approve [ə'pruːv] *v* approuver. **approval** *n* approbation *f*. **on approval** à l'essai.
approximate [ə'proksimeit; *adj* ə'proksimət] *v* se rapprocher (de). *adj* approximatif.
apricot ['eiprikot] *n* (*fruit*) abricot *m*; (*tree*) abricotier *m*.
April ['eiprəl] *n* avril *m*. **April fool** *n* poisson d'avril *m*.
apron ['eiprən] *n* tablier *m*; (*aero*) aire de manœuvre *f*.
apt [apt] *adj* (*fitting*) juste, convenable; (*inclined*) enclin, porté. **aptly** *adv* à propos.
aptitude ['aptitjuːd] *n* aptitude *f*.
aqualung ['akwəlʌŋ] *n* scaphandre autonome *m*.
aquarium [ə'kweəriəm] *n* aquarium *m*.
Aquarius [ə'kweəriəs] *n* Verseau *m*.
aquatic [ə'kwatik] *adj* aquatique.
aqueduct ['akwidʌkt] *n* aqueduc *m*.
Arab ['arəb] *n* Arabe *m, f. adj* arabe. **Arabia** *n* Arabie *f*. **Arabian** *or* **Arabic** *adj* arabe.
arable ['arəbl] *adj* arable.
arbitrary ['aːbitrəri] *adj* arbitraire.
arbitrate ['aːbitreit] *v* arbitrer, juger. **arbitration** *n* arbitrage *m*. **arbiter** *n* arbitre *m*.
arc [aːk] *n* arc *m*. **arc lamp** lampe à arc *f*. **arc light** arc voltaïque *m*.
arcade [aː'keid] *n* arcade *m*; (*shopping*) passage.
arch [aːtʃ] *v* (s')arquer. *n* (*church, etc.*) voûte *f*, cintre *m*; (*bridge*) arche *f*.
archaeology [aːki'olədʒi] *n* archéologie *f*. **archaeological** *adj* archéologique. **archaeologist** *n* archéologue *m, f*.

archaic [aɪˈkeiik] *adj* archaïque. **archaism** *n* archaïsme *m*.

archbishop [aɪtʃˈbiʃəp] *n* archevêque *m*.

archduke [aɪtʃˈdjuɪk] *n* archiduc *m*. **archduchess** *n* archiduchesse *f*.

archery [ˈaɪtʃəri] *n* tir à l'arc *m*. **archer** *n* archer *m*.

archetype [ˈaɪkitaip] *n* archétype *m*.

archipelago [aɪkiˈpeləgou] *n* archipel *m*.

architect [ˈaɪkitekt] *n* architecte *m*. **architecture** *n* architecture *f*.

archives [ˈaɪkaivz] *pl n* archives *f pl*. **archivist** *n* archiviste *m*, *f*.

ardent [ˈaɪdənt] *adj* ardent.

ardour [ˈaɪdə] *n* ardeur *f*.

arduous [ˈaɪdjuəs] *adj* ardu.

are [aɪ] *V* **be**.

area [ˈeəriə] *n* aire *f*; (*region*) étendue *f*, région *f*.

arena [əˈriːnə] *n* arène *f*.

argue [ˈaɪgjuɪ] *v* se disputer, discuter. **argument** *n* dispute *f*; (*debate*) discussion *f*; (*reasons*) argument *m*.

arid [ˈarid] *adj* aride. **aridity** *n* aridité *f*.

Aries [ˈeəriːz] *n* Bélier *m*.

*****arise** [əˈraiz] *v* s'élever; (*question*) se présenter; résulter.

arisen [əˈrizn] *V* **arise**.

aristocracy [ariˈstokrəsi] *n* aristocratie *f*. **aristocrat** *n* aristocrate *m*, *f*. **aristocratic** *adj* aristocratique.

arithmetic [əˈriθmətik] *n* arithmétique *f*, calcul *m*.

arm[1] [aɪm] *n* bras *m*. **armchair** *n* fauteuil *m*. **arm in arm** bras dessus bras dessous. **armpit** *n* aisselle *f*.

arm[2] [aɪm] *n* arme *f*. **be up in arms against** s'élever contre. *v* armer.

armistice [ˈaɪmistis] *n* armistice *m*.

armour [ˈaɪmə] *n* armure *f*. **suit of armour** armure complète *f*. **armoured** *adj* cuirassé, blindé. **armoury** *n* arsenal *m*.

army [ˈaɪmi] *n* armée *f*.

aroma [əˈroumə] *n* arome *m*; (*wine*) bouquet.

arose [əˈrouz] *V* **arise**.

around [əˈraund] *prep* autour de; (*approximately*) à peu près. *adv* autour, à l'entour.

arrange [əˈreindʒ] *v* arranger; (*meeting, etc.*) fixer; (*make plans*) s'arranger. **arrangement** *n* arrangement *m*. **make arrangements** faire des préparatifs, prendre des mesures.

array [əˈrei] *v* (*adorn*) orner; (*mil*) ranger. *n* (*display*) étalage *m*; (*mil*) ordre *m*.

arrears [əˈriəz] *pl n* arriéré *m sing*. **in arrears** arriéré; en retard.

arrest [əˈrest] *v* arrêter. *n* arrestation *f*. **under arrest** en état d'arrestation.

arrive [əˈraiv] *v* arriver. **arrival** *n* arrivée *f*; (*person*) arrivant, -e *m*, *f*.

arrogant [ˈarəgənt] *adj* arrogant. **arrogance** *n* arrogance *f*.

arrow [ˈarou] *n* flèche *f*.

arse [aɪs] *n* (*vulgar*) cul *m*.

arsenal [ˈaɪsənl] *n* arsenal *m*.

arsenic [ˈaɪsnik] *n* arsenic *m*.

arson [ˈaɪsn] *n* incendie criminel *m*.

art [aɪt] *n* art *m*; (*painting, etc.*) beaux-arts *m pl*; (*cunning*) artifice *m*. **art gallery** musée d'art *m*. **arts and crafts** artisanat *m sing*. **art school** école des beaux-arts *f*. **Arts degree** licence ès lettres *f*. **artful** *adj* rusé.

artefact [ˈaɪtifakt] *n* objet fabriqué *m*.

artery [ˈaɪtəri] *n* artère *f*.

arthritis [aɪˈθraitis] *n* arthrite *f*.

artichoke [ˈaɪtitʃouk] *n* artichaut *m*.

article [ˈaɪtikl] *n* article *m*; objet *m*.

articulate [aɪˈtikjuleit; *adj* aɪˈtikjulət] *v* articuler. **articulated lorry** semi-remorque *m*. *adj* bien articulé; net, nette. **be articulate** s'exprimer bien. **articulation** *n* articulation *f*.

artifice [ˈaɪtifis] *n* artifice *f*, stratagème *m*.

artificial [aɪtiˈfiʃəl] *adj* artificiel; synthétique; (*affected*) factice, forcé. **artificial respiration** respiration artificielle *f*.

artillery [aɪˈtiləri] *n* artillerie *f*.

artisan [aɪtiˈzan] *n* artisan *m*.

artist [ˈaɪtist] *n* artiste *m*, *f*. **artistic** *adj* artistique.

as [az] *conj* (*while*) comme, tandis que, à mesure que; (*because*) puisque; (*like*) comme, en. *adv* aussi. **as . . . as . . .** aussi . . . que . . . . **as for** quant à. **as if** comme si. **as it were** pour ainsi dire. **as usual** comme d'habitude. **as well** aussi.

asbestos [azˈbestos] *n* amiante *f*.

ascend [əˈsend] *v* monter. **ascension** *n* ascension *f*. **Ascension Day** jour de l'Ascension *m*. **ascent** *n* ascension *f*; montée *f*.

ascertain [asəˈtein] *v* établir; vérifier.

ascetic [əˈsetik] *adj* ascétique. *n* ascète *m*, *f*.

ash[1] [aʃ] *n* cendre *f*. **ashtray** *n* cendrier *m*. **Ash Wednesday** mercredi des cendres *m*.

ash² [aʃ] *n* (*tree*) frêne *m.*

ashamed [ə'ʃeimd] *adj* honteux. **be ashamed** avoir honte.

ashore [ə'ʃɔ:] *adv* à terre. **go ashore** débarquer.

Asia ['eiʃə] *n* Asie *f.* **Asian** *n* Asiatique *m, f; adj* asiatique.

aside [ə'said] *adv* de côté, à part. *n* aparté *m.*

ask [a:sk] *v* demander; inviter. **ask about** s'informer de. **ask after** demander des nouvelles de. **ask a question** poser une question. **ask for** demander.

askew [ə'skju:] *adv* de travers.

asleep [ə'sli:p] *adj* endormi. **be asleep** dormir. **fall asleep** s'endormir.

asparagus [ə'spærəgəs] *n* asperge *f.*

aspect ['æspekt] *n* aspect *m;* (*of house*) orientation *f.*

asphalt ['æsfælt] *n* asphalte *m. v* asphalter.

asphyxiate [əs'fiksieit] *v* (s')asphyxier. **asphyxia** *or* **asphyxiation** *n* asphyxie *f.*

aspire [ə'spaiə] *v* aspirer, ambitionner. **aspirate** *adj* aspiré. **aspiration** *n* aspiration *f.* **aspiring** *adj* ambitieux.

aspirin ['æspərin] *n* aspirine *f.*

ass [æs] *n* âne, -esse *m, f;* (*coll*) imbécile *m.*

assail [ə'seil] *v* assaillir. **assailant** *n* agresseur *m.*

assassinate [ə'sæsineit] *v* assassiner. **assassin** *n* assassin *m.* **assassination** *n* assassinat *m.*

assault [ə'sɔ:lt] *n* attaque *f;* (*mil*) assaut *m;* (*law*) voies de fait *f pl. v* attaquer.

assemble [ə'sembl] *v* (*things*) (s')assembler; (*people*) (se) rassembler; (*put together*) monter. **assembly** *n* assemblée *f;* rassemblement *m;* montage *m.* **assembly line** chaîne de montage *f.*

assent [ə'sent] *n* assentiment *m. v* consentir.

assert [ə'sə:t] *v* (*declare*) affirmer; (*rights, etc.*) revendiquer. **assertion** *n* affirmation *f;* revendication *f.*

assess [ə'ses] *v* évaluer; (*payment, etc.*) fixer le montant de; (*property*) calculer la valeur imposable de. **assessment** *n* évaluation *f;* calcul *m.*

asset ['æset] *n* avantage *m.* **assets** *pl n* biens *m pl;* (*comm*) actif *m sing.*

assiduous [ə'sidjuəs] *adj* assidu. **assiduity** *n* assiduité *f.*

assign [ə'sain] *v* (*job, etc.*) assigner; (*meaning*) attribuer; (*person*) nommer.

assignation *n* (*meeting*) rendez-vous *m.*

assignment mission *f;* (*school*) devoir *m.*

assimilate [ə'simileit] *v* (s')assimiler. **assimilation** *n* assimilation *f.*

assist [ə'sist] *v* aider. **assistance** *n* aide *f,* secours *m.* **assistant** *n* auxiliaire *m, f;* (*school*) assistant, -e *m, f;* (*shop*) vendeur, -euse *m, f;* (*as modifier*) adjoint, sous-.

associate [ə'sousiət; *v* ə'sousieit] *n* associé, -e *m, f,* collègue *m, f. v* associer. **be associated with** (*things*) être associé à; (*people*) s'associer avec. **association** *n* association *f.*

assorted [ə'sɔ:tid] *adj* assorti. **assortment** *n* assortiment *m;* mélange *m.*

assume [ə'sju:m] *v* supposer, présumer; (*take on*) assumer, adopter. **assumption** *n* supposition *f.*

assure [ə'ʃuə] *v* assurer. **assurance** *n* assurance *f.*

asterisk ['æstərisk] *n* astérisque *m. v* marquer d'un astérisque.

asthma ['æsmə] *n* asthme *m.* **asthmatic** *n*(*m+f*), *adj* asthmatique.

astonish [ə'stoniʃ] *v* étonner. **astonishment** *n* étonnement *m.*

astound [ə'staund] *v* stupéfier, abasourdir.

astray [ə'strei] *adv* **go astray** s'égarer.

astride [ə'straid] *adv* à califourchon. *prep* à califourchon sur.

astringent [ə'strindʒənt] *nm, adj* astringent.

astrology [ə'strolədʒi] *n* astrologie *f.* **astrologer** *n* astrologue *m.* **astrological** *adj* astrologique.

astronaut ['æstrənɔt] *n* astronaute *m, f.*

astronomy [ə'stronəmi] *n* astronomie *f.* **astronomer** *n* astronome *m.* **astronomical** *adj* astronomique.

astute [ə'stju:t] *adj* fin, astucieux. **astuteness** *n* finesse *f,* astuce *f.*

asunder [ə'sʌndə] *adv* (*in two*) en deux; (*in pieces*) en morceaux.

asylum [ə'sailəm] *n* asile *m.*

at [æt] *prep* à; chez: *chez le docteur;* (*towards*) vers. **at first** d'abord. **at last** enfin. **at least** au moins. **at once** tout de suite.

ate [et] *V* **eat**.

atheism ['eiθiizəm] *n* athéisme *m.* **atheist** *n* athée *m, f.* **atheistic** *adj* athée.

Athens ['æθinz] *n* Athènes. **Athenian** *adj* athénien; *n* Athénien, -enne *m, f.*

athlete ['æθliːt] *n* athlète *m, f.* **athlete's foot** *n* mycose *f.* **athletic** *adj* sportif, athlétique. **athletics** *n* athlétisme *m.*

Atlantic [ət'læntik] *adj* atlantique. **the Atlantic (Ocean)** l'(océan) Atlantique *m.*

atlas ['ætləs] *n* atlas *m.*

atmosphere ['ætməsfiə] *n* atmosphère *f*; ambiance *f.* **atmospheric** *adj* atmosphérique.

atom ['ætəm] *n* atome *m*; (*tiny part*) grain *m.* **atom bomb** bombe atomique *f.* **atomic** *adj* atomique. **atomizer** *n* atomiseur *m.*

atone [ə'toun] *v* **atone for** expier; réparer. **atonement** *n* expiation *f*; réparation *f.*

atrocious [ə'trouʃəs] *adj* atroce. **atrocity** *n* atrocité *f.*

attach [ə'tætʃ] *v* attacher, joindre. **attached** *adj* (*letter, etc.*) ci-joint; (*fond*) attaché. **attachment** *n* accessoire *m*; affection *f.*

attaché [ə'tæʃei] *n* attaché, -e *m, f.* **attaché case** mallette *f.*

attack [ə'tæk] *n* attaque *f*; (*med*) accès *m*, crise *f. v* attaquer, combattre. **attacker** *n* attaquant *m.*

attain [ə'tein] *v* atteindre (à). **attainments** *pl n* résultats *m pl.*

attempt [ə'tempt] *v* tenter (de), essayer (de). *n* tentative *f*, essai *m.*

attend [ə'tend] *v* (*meeting*) assister à; (*school*) aller à; servir; faire attention. **attend to** s'occuper de. **attendance** *n* présence *f*; (*number present*) assistance *f*; service *m.* **attendant** *n* gardien, -enne *m, f.* **attendants** *pl n* suite *f sing.*

attention [ə'tenʃən] *n* attention *f*; (*mil*) garde-à-vous *m.* **pay attention** faire attention. **attentive** *adj* (*caring*) prévenant; (*listening*) attentif.

attic ['ætik] *n* grenier *m.* **attic room** mansarde *f.*

attire [ə'taiə] *v* parer (de). *n* habits *m pl*; (*ceremonial*) tenue *f.*

attitude ['ætitjuːd] *n* attitude *f.*

attorney [ə'tɜːni] *n* mandataire *m*; (*US*) avoué *m.* **Attorney General** Procureur Général *m.*

attract [ə'trækt] *v* attirer. **attract attention** éveiller l'intérêt. **attraction** *n* attraction *f*; (*charm*) attrait *m.* **attractive** *adj* attrayant; (*price, etc.*) intéressant.

attribute [ə'tribjuːt] *n* ['ætribjuːt] *v* attribuer; (*crime, etc.*) imputer. *n* attribut *m.* **attribution** *n* attribution *f*; imputation *f.*

attrition [ə'triʃən] *n* usure *f.*

atypical [ei'tipikl] *adj* atypique.

aubergine ['oubəʒiːn] *n* aubergine *f.*

auburn ['ɔːbən] *adj* auburn *invar*; roux, rousse.

auction ['ɔːkʃən] *n* vente aux enchères *f. v* vendre aux enchères. **auctioneer** *n* commissaire-priseur *m.*

audacious [ɔː'deiʃəs] *adj* (*brave*) audacieux; (*impudent*) effronté. **audacity** *n* audace *f*; effronterie *f.*

audible ['ɔːdəbl] *adj* audible, distinct.

audience ['ɔːdjəns] *n* spectateurs *m pl*, auditeurs *m pl*; (*interview*) audience *f.*

audiovisual [ɔːdiou'viʒuəl] *adj* audiovisuel. **audiovisual aids** support audiovisuel *m sing.*

audit ['ɔːdit] *v* vérifier. *n* vérification *f.* **auditor** *n* expert-comptable *m.*

audition [ɔː'diʃən] *n* audition *f. v* auditionner.

auditorium [ɔːdi'tɔːriəm] *n* salle *f.*

augment [ɔːg'ment] *v* (s')augmenter.

August ['ɔːgəst] *n* août *m.*

aunt [ɑːnt] *n* tante *f.*

au pair [ou 'peə] *adv* au pair. *n* jeune fille au pair *f.*

aura ['ɔːrə] *n* aura *f*; ambiance *f.*

auspicious [ɔː'spiʃəs] *adj* favorable, de bon augure.

austere [ɔː'stiə] *adj* austère. **austerity** *n* austérité *f.*

Australia [o'streiljə] *n* Australie *f.* **Australian** *n* Australien, -enne *m, f*; *adj* australien.

Austria ['ɔːstriə] *n* Autriche *f.* **Austrian** *n* Autrichien, -enne *m, f*; *adj* autrichien.

authentic [ɔː'θentik] *adj* authentique. **authenticity** *n* authenticité *f.*

author ['ɔːθə] *n* auteur *m.*

authority [ɔː'θɔriti] *n* (*power*) autorité *f*; (*permission*) autorisation *f.* **authoritative** *adj* (*source, etc.*) autorisé; (*person*) autoritaire.

authorize ['ɔːθəraiz] *v* autoriser. **authorization** *n* autorisation *f*; (*legal*) mandat *m.*

autobiography [ɔːtoubai'ogrəfi] *n* autobiographie *f.* **autobiographical** *adj* autobiographique.

autocratic [ɔːtou'krætik] *adj* autocratique. **autocracy** *n* autocratie *f.* **autocrat** *n* autocrate *m.*

autograph ['ɔːtəgraːf] *v* dédicacer, signer. *n* autographe *m.*

automatic [ɔːtə'mætik] *adj* automatique. *n* (*car*) voiture automatique *f.* **automation** *n* automatisation *f.*

automobile ['ɔɪtəməbiɪl] *n* automobile *f*.
autonomous [ɔɪ'tɒnəməs] *adj* autonome.
  autonomy *n* autonomie *f*.
autopsy ['ɔɪtɒpsɪ] *n* autopsie *f*.
autumn ['ɔɪtəm] *n* automne *m*.
auxiliary [ɔɪg'zɪljərɪ] *n(m+f)*, *adj* auxiliaire.
avail [ə'veɪl] *v* **avail oneself of** utiliser;
  profiter de. *n* **to no avail** sans résultat.
available [ə'veɪləbl] *adj* disponible. **availability** *n* disponibilité *f*.
avalanche ['avəlɑɪnʃ] *n* avalanche *f*.
avarice ['avərɪs] *n* avarice *f*. **avaricious** *adj*
  avare.
avenge [ə'vendʒ] *v* venger. **avenge oneself**
  prendre sa revanche.
avenue ['avɪnjuɪ] *n* avenue *f*.
average ['avərɪdʒ] *n* moyenne *f*. *adj* moy-
  en.
aversion [ə'vɜɪʃən] *n* aversion *f*. **averse**
  adj adversaire (de). **be averse to** avoir
  horreur de.
avert [ə'vɜɪt] *v* (*avoid*) prévenir; (*turn
  away*) écarter; (*eyes, etc.*) détourner.
aviary ['eɪvɪərɪ] *n* volière *f*.
aviation [eɪvɪ'eɪʃən] *n* aviation *f*.
avid ['avɪd] *adv* avide. **avidity** *n* avidité *f*.
avocado [avə'kɑɪdoʊ] *n* (*pear*) avocat *m*;
  (*tree*) avocatier *m*.
avoid [ə'vɔɪd] *v* éviter. **avoidable** *adj* évitable.
await [ə'weɪt] *v* attendre.
***awake** [ə'weɪk] *v* (s')éveiller. *adj* éveillé.
  awake to conscient de.
award [ə'wɔɪd] *v* décerner; (*damages*)
  accorder. *n* récompense *f*, prix *m*.
aware [ə'weə] *adj* conscient; au courant.
  be aware of savoir. **awareness** *n* conscience *f*.
away [ə'weɪ] *adv* au loin, à une distance
  de; absent. *adj* (*sport*) à l'extérieur.
awe [ɔɪ] *n* crainte révérentielle *f*. **awe-
  inspiring** *adj* impressionnant. **awe-struck**
  adj stupéfait. **be in awe of** être intimidé
  par.
awful ['ɔɪful] *adj* affreux, épouvantable.
  awfully *adv* (*very*) vraiment.
awkward ['ɔɪkwəd] *adj* (*difficult*) peu
  commode; (*situation*) délicat; (*inconvenient*) inopportun; (*clumsy*) maladroit.
  awkwardness *n* maladresse *f*; embarras
  m.
awning ['ɔɪnɪŋ] *n* (*shop*) banne *f*; (*tent*)
  auvent *m*; (*naut*) taud *m*.
awoke [ə'woʊk] *V* **awake**.

awoken [ə'woʊkn] *V* **awake**.
axe [aks] *n* hache *f*.
axiom ['aksɪəm] *n* axiome *m*.
axis ['aksɪs] *n* axe *m*.
axle ['aksl] *n* axe *m*; (*mot*) essieu *m*.

B

babble ['babl] *v* bredouiller; (*baby*) babiller; (*stream*) gazouiller. *n* babil *m*;
  (*noise*) rumeur *f*.
baboon [bə'buɪn] *n* babouin *m*.
baby ['beɪbɪ] *n* bébé *m*. **babyish** *adj* enfantin.
bachelor ['batʃələ] *n* célibataire *m*. **Bachelor of Arts/Science** licencié, -e ès let-
  tres/sciences *m*, *f*.
back [bak] *n* dos, derrière *m*; (*reverse
  side*) revers *m*, verso *m*; (*furthest part*)
  fond *m*. *adj* arrière. *adv* en arrière. *v*
  renforcer; financer; (*bet on*) parier sur.
  back away se reculer. **back out** (*car, etc.*)
  sortir en marche arrière; (*duty, etc.*) se
  dérober (à).
backache ['bakeɪk] *n* mal aux reins *m*.
backdate [,bak'deɪt] *v* (*cheque*) antidater.
  backdated to avec rappel à.
backfire [,bak'faɪə] *v* (*mot*) pétarader;
  (*plan, etc.*) échouer.
backgammon ['bak,gamən] *n* trictrac *m*.
background ['bakgraund] *n* fond *m*,
  arrière-plan *m*; (*social*) milieu *m*. **background music** musique de fond *f*.
backhand ['bakhand] *adj*, *adv* (*sport*) en
  revers. *n* revers *m*.
backlog ['baklɒg] *n* arriéré *m*.
backside ['baksaɪd] *n* arrière *m*; (*coll*)
  derrière *m*.
backstage ['baksteɪdʒ] *adv* derrière la
  scène. **go backstage** aller dans la coulisse.
backstroke ['bakstroʊk] *n* dos crawlé *m*.
backward ['bakwəd] *adj* en arrière;
  (*retarded*) arriéré. **backwardness** *n* arrié-
  ation mentale *f*.
backwards ['bakwədz] *adv* en arrière;
  (*back first*) à rebours, à reculons; (*in
  reverse order*) à l'envers.
backwater ['bakwɔɪtə] *n* (*place*) trou perdu *m*; (*pool*) eau stagnante *f*.

bacon ['beikən] *n* bacon *m*. **bacon and eggs** œufs au jambon *m pl*.

bacteria [bak'tiəriə] *pl n* bactéries *f pl*.

bad [bad] *adj* mauvais; (*naughty*) méchant; (*serious*) grave; (*decayed*) gâté, carié. **bad-mannered** *adj* mal élevé. **bad-tempered** *adj* acariâtre. **badly** *adv* mal; (*seriously*) grièvement; (*very much*) absolument.

badge [badʒ] *n* insigne *m*; (*scouting*) badge *m*; (*police, etc.*) plaque *f*.

badger ['badʒə] *n* blaireau *m*. *v* harceler.

badminton ['badmintən] *n* badminton *m*.

baffle ['bafl] *v* déconcerter.

bag [bag] *n* sac *m*. **baggage** *n* bagages *m pl*. **baggy** *adj* bouffant; trop ample.

bagpipes ['bagpaips] *pl n* cornemuse *f sing*.

bail¹ [beil] *n* (*law*) caution *f*. **on bail** sous caution. **stand bail for** se rendre garant de. *v* **bail out** faire mettre en liberté provisoire sous caution.

bail² *or* **bale** [beil] *v* **bail out** (*flooded boat*) écoper; (*from aircraft*) sauter en parachute.

bailiff ['beilif] *n* (*law*) huissier *m*; (*of estate*) régisseur *m*.

bait [beit] *n* (*fishing*) amorce *f*; (*lure*) appât *m*. *v* amorcer; (*annoy*) tourmenter.

bake [beik] *v* (faire) cuire au four. **baked beans** haricots blancs à la sauce tomate *m pl*. **baker** *n* boulanger, -ère *m, f*. **bakery** *n* boulangerie *f*.

balance ['baləns] *n* equilibre *m*; (*scales*) balance *f*; (*comm*) solde *m*. **balance of payments** balance des paiements *f*. *v* (se) tenir en équilibre; (*equal*) équilibrer; (*comm*) balancer, solder. **balance the books** dresser le bilan.

balcony ['balkəni] *n* balcon *m*; (*theatre*) fauteils de deuxième balcon *m pl*.

bald [boːld] *adj* chauve; (*tyre*) lisse; (*style*) plat.

bale¹ [beil] *n* ballot *m*; (*hay*) balle *f*. *v* emballotter.

bale² *V* **bail²**.

ball¹ [boːl] *n* balle *f*, boule *f*; (*football*) ballon *m*; (*wool, etc.*) pelote *f*; (*of foot*) plante *f*. **ball bearings** roulement à billes *m sing*. **ball-point pen** stylo bille *m*.

ball² [boːl] *n* (*dance*) bal *m*. **ballroom** *n* salle de danse *f*.

ballad ['baləd] *n* ballade *f*; (*music*) romance *f*.

ballast ['baləst] *n* (*naut*) lest *m*; (*rail*) ballast *m*. *v* lester; ballaster.

ballet ['balei] *n* ballet *m*. **ballerina** *n* ballerine *f*.

ballistic [bə'listik] *adj* balistique. **ballistic missile** engin balistique *m*.

balloon [bə'luːn] *n* ballon *m*. **balloonist** *n* aéronaute *m, f*.

ballot ['balət] *n* scrutin *m*; (*paper*) bulletin de vote *m*. **ballot box** urne électorale *f*. *v* voter au scrutin secret.

bamboo [bam'buː] *n* bambou *m*.

ban [ban] *v* interdire. *n* interdit *m*. **put a ban on** interdire.

banal [bə'naɪl] *adj* banal. **banality** *n* banalité *f*.

banana [bə'naːnə] *n* (*fruit*) banane *f*; (*tree*) bananier *m*.

band¹ [band] (*group*) bande *f*; (*music*) orchestre *m*; (*mil*) fanfare *f*. **bandstand** *n* kiosque à musique *m*. **jump on the bandwagon** prendre le train en marche.

band² [band] *n* (*strip*) bande *f*.

bandage ['bandidʒ] *n* pansement *m*, bandage *m*. *v* mettre un pansement sur.

bandit ['bandit] *n* bandit *m*.

bandy ['bandi] *adj* *also* **bandy-legged** bancal, arqué. *v* échanger. **bandy about** faire circuler. **bandy words** discuter.

bang [baŋ] *n* (*noise*) claquement *m*, détonation *f*; (*blow*) coup *m*. *interj* pan! *v* (*hit*) frapper, cogner; (*door*) claquer; (*gun, etc.*) détoner.

bangle ['baŋgl] *n* bracelet *m*, jonc *m*.

banish ['baniʃ] *v* bannir; exiler. **banishment** *n* bannissement *m*, exil *m*.

banister ['banistə] *n* rampe *f*.

banjo ['bandʒou] *n* banjo *m*.

bank¹ [baŋk] *n* (*edge*) bord *m*; (*river*) rive *f*; (*sand*) banc *m*; (*earth, etc.*) talus *m*.

bank² [baŋk] *n* banque *f*. **bank account** compte en banque *m*. **bank holiday** jour férié *m*. **bank statement** relevé de compte *m*. *v* mettre en banque. **bank on** compter sur. **bank with** avoir un compte à. **banker** *n* banquier *m*. **banker's order** ordre de virement bancaire *m*.

bankrupt ['baŋkrʌpt] *adj* failli, en faillite. **go bankrupt** faire faillite. *n* failli, -e *m, f*. *v* mettre en faillite. **bankruptcy** *n* faillite *f*.

banner ['banə] *n* bannière *f*.

banquet ['baŋkwit] *n* banquet *m*.

banter ['bantə] *v* plaisanter. *n* badinage *m*.

baptize [bap'taiz] *v* baptiser. **baptism** *n* baptême *m*. **Baptist** *n(m+f)*, *adj* baptiste.

bar [baː] *n* (*rod*) barreau *f*, barre *f*; obstacle *m*; (*law*) barreau *m*; (*chocolate*) tablette *f*; (*for drinks*) bar *m*, comptoir *m*; (*music*) mesure *f*. *v* barrer; défendre. *prep* sauf.

barbarian [baː'beəriən] *n(m+f)*, *adj* barbare. **barbaric** *or* **barbarous** *adj* barbare. **barbarism** *or* **barbarity** *n* barbarie *f*.

barbecue ['baːbikjuː] *n* barbecue *m*. *v* griller au charbon de bois.

barbed wire [baːbd] *n* fil de fer barbelé *m*.

barber ['baːbə] *n* coiffeur pour hommes *m*.

barbiturate [baː'bitjurət] *n* barbiturique *m*.

bare [beə] *v* mettre à nu. **bare one's teeth** montrer les dents. *adj* nu; dénudé. **barefaced** *adj* éhonté. **barefoot** *adv* nu-pieds. **the bare necessities** le strict nécessaire *m*. **barely** *adv* à peine.

bargain ['baːgin] *n* (*transaction*) marché; (*offer*) occasion. **into the bargain** par-dessus le marché. *v* négocier. **bargain for** (*expect*) s'attendre à. **bargain with** marchander avec.

barge [baːdʒ] *n* chaland *m*, péniche *f*. *v* **barge in** faire irruption, entrer sans façons. **barge through** traverser comme un ouragan.

baritone ['baritoun] *n* baryton *m*.

bark¹ [baːk] *v* (*dog*) aboyer. *n* aboiement *m*.

bark² [baːk] *n* (*tree*) écorce *f*.

barley ['baːli] *n* orge *f*. **barley sugar** sucre d'orge *m*. **barley water** orgeat *m*.

barn [baːn] *n* grange *f*.

barometer [bə'romitə] *n* baromètre *m*.

baron ['barən] *n* baron *m*. **baroness** *n* baronne *f*. **baronet** *n* baronnet *m*.

barracks ['barəks] *n* (*mil*) caserne *f*, quartier *m*.

barrage ['baraːʒ] *n* barrage *m*; (*of questions*) pluie *f*; (*of words*) flot *m*.

barrel ['barəl] *n* (*cask*) tonneau *m*; (*gun*, *etc.*) canon *m*.

barren ['barən] *adj* stérile; aride. **barrenness** *n* stérilité *f*; aridité *f*.

barricade [bari'keid] *n* barricade *f*. *v* barricader.

barrier ['bariə] *n* barrière *f*; (*rail*) portillon *m*.

barrister ['baristə] *n* avocat *m*.

barrow ['barou] *n* voiture de quatre saisons *f*.

barter ['baːtə] *v* troquer, faire un troc. *n* troc *m*.

base¹ [beis] *n* base *f*. *v* baser. **baseless** *adj* sans fondement.

base² [beis] *adj* bas, basse; ignoble. **baseness** *n* bassesse *f*.

baseball ['beisboːl] *n* base-ball *m*.

basement ['beismənt] *n* sous-sol *m*.

bash [baʃ] *v* cogner. *n* coup *m*. **have a bash** (*try*) essayer un coup.

bashful ['baʃful] *adj* timide.

basic ['beisik] *adj* fondamental; (*salary*, *etc.*) de base; (*chem*) basique.

basil ['bazl] *n* basilic *m*.

basin ['beisin] *n* cuvette *f*; (*bowl*) bol *m*; (*bathroom*) lavabo; (*geog*) bassin *m*.

basis ['beisis] *n* base *f*.

bask [bask] *v* (*in the sun*) se dorer; (*in glory*, *etc.*) jouir (de).

basket ['baːskit] *n* (*shopping*) panier *m*; (*linen*, *etc.*) corbeille *f*. **basketball** *n* basket *m*.

bass¹ [beis] *n* (*voice*) basse *f*.

bass² [bas] *n* (*freshwater*) perche *f*; (*sea*) bar *m*.

bassoon [bə'suːn] *n* basson *m*.

bastard ['baːstəd] *n* bâtard, -e *m*, *f*; (*derog*) salaud *m*; (*coll*) type *m*.

baste [beist] *v* (*cookery*) arroser.

bastion ['bastjən] *n* bastion *m*.

bat¹ [bat] *n* (*sport*) batte *f*. **off one's own bat** de sa propre initiative. *v* frapper; manier la batte. **bat an eyelid** sourciller.

bat² [bat] *n* chauve-souris *f*.

batch [batʃ] *n* (*loaves*) fournée *f*; (*letters*) paquet *m*; (*goods*) lot *m*.

bath [baːθ] *n* bain *m*; (*tub*) baignoire *f*. **bathchair** *n* fauteuil roulant *m*. **bathroom** *n* salle de bains *f*. **baths** *pl n* (*swimming*) piscine *f* *sing*. *v* baigner; prendre un bain.

bathe [beið] *v* (se) baigner; (*wound*) laver. **bather** *n* baigneur, -euse *m*, *f*. **bathing** *n* baignade *f*. **bathing costume** maillot *m*. **bathing trunks** slip de bain *m*.

baton ['batn] *n* bâton *m*; (*police*) matraque *f*; (*race*) témoin *m*.

battalion [bə'taljən] *n* bataillon *m*.

batter¹ ['batə] *v* battre. **battered** *adj* délabré.

batter² ['batə] *n* pâte à frire *f*; (*pancakes*) pâte à crêpes *f*.

battery ['batəri] *n* (*elec*) pile *f*; (*mot*) batterie *f*; (*mil*) batterie *f*.

battle ['batl] *n* bataille *f*. **battlefield** *n* champ de bataille *m*. **battlements** *pl n* remparts *m pl*. **battleship** *n* cuirassé *m*. *v* se battre, lutter.

bawl [bɔːl] *v* brailler.

bay¹ [bei] *n* (*geog*) baie *f*.

bay² [bei] *v* aboyer. *n* aboi *m*. **at bay** à distance.

bay³ [bei] *n* laurier *m*. **bay leaf** feuille de laurier *f*.

bayonet ['beiənit] *n* baïonnette *f*.

bay window *n* fenêtre en saillie *f*.

bazaar [bə'zɑː] *n* (*charity sale*) vente de charité *f*; (*eastern*) bazar *m*.

*be [biː] *v* être.

beach [biːtʃ] *n* plage *f*. *v* échouer.

beacon ['biːkən] *n* phare *m*; (*naut*) balise *f*.

bead [biːd] *n* perle *f*; (*rosary*) grain *m*.

beak [biːk] *n* bec *m*.

beaker ['biːkə] *n* gobelet *m*.

beam [biːm] *n* (*arch*) poutre *f*; (*light*) rayon *m*, faisceau *m*; (*smile*) sourire épanoui *m*. *v* rayonner.

bean [biːn] *n* haricot *m*; (*coffee*) grain *m*. **full of beans** en pleine forme.

*bear¹ [beə] *v* (*carry*) porter; (*support*) soutenir; (*tolerate*) supporter; (*give birth*) donner naissance à. **bear right/left** prendre à droite/gauche. **bearable** *adj* supportable. **bearing** *n* (*behaviour*) maintien *m*; (*relation*) rapport *m*; (*direction*) relèvement *m*. **lose one's bearings** être désorienté.

bear² [beə] *n* ours *m*.

beard [biəd] *n* barbe *f*. **bearded** *adj* barbu.

beast [biːst] *n* bête *f*; (*person*) brute *f*. **beastly** *adj* abominable; (*unkind*) sale.

*beat [biːt] *v* battre. *n* battement *m*; rythme *m*; (*police*) ronde *f*. **beating** *n* (*as punishment*) rossée *f*; (*defeat*) défaite *f*.

beaten ['biːtn] *V* **beat**.

beauty ['bjuːti] *n* beauté *f*. **beautician** *n* esthéticien, -enne *m*, *f*. **beautiful** *adj* beau, belle; magnifique. **beautify** *v* embellir.

beaver ['biːvə] *n* castor *m*.

became [bi'keim] *V* **become**.

because [bi'koz] *conj* parce que. **because of** à cause de.

beckon ['bekən] *v* faire signe (à).

*become [bi'kʌm] *v* devenir; (*suit*) aller à. **becoming** *adj* convenable; (*clothes*) seyant.

bed [bed] *n* lit *m*; (*coal, etc.*) couche *f*; (*flowers*) parterre *m*. **bedclothes** *pl n* literie *f sing*. **bedridden** *adj* alité. **bedroom** *n* chambre *f*. **bedside** *n* chevet *m*. **bed-sitter** *n* studio *m*. **bedspread** *n* couvre-lit *m*. **go to bed** se coucher.

bedraggled [bi'dragld] *adj* débraillé.

bee [biː] *n* abeille *f*. **beehive** *n* ruche *f*. **have a bee in one's bonnet** avoir une marotte. **make a beeline for** filer droit sur.

beech [biːtʃ] *n* hêtre *m*.

beef [biːf] *n* bœuf *m*.

been [biːn] *V* **be**.

beer [biə] *n* bière *f*.

beetle ['biːtl] *n* coléoptère *m*.

beetroot ['biːtruːt] *n* betterave *f*.

before [bi'foː] *prep* avant; (*in front of*) devant. *adv* auparavant, avant. *conj* avant de, avant que. **beforehand** *adv* à l'avance.

befriend [bi'frend] *v* traiter en ami; (*help*) venir en aide à.

beg [beg] *v* mendier; (*entreat*) supplier, demander. **beggar** *n* mendiant, -e *m*, *f*.

began [bi'gan] *V* **begin**.

*begin [bi'gin] *v* commencer. **to begin with** pour commencer. **beginner** *n* novice *m*, *f*. **beginning** *n* commencement *m*, début *m*; origine *f*.

begrudge [bi'grʌdʒ] *v* envier. **begrudge doing** faire à contre-cœur.

begun [bi'gʌn] *V* **begin**.

behalf [bi'hɑːf] *n* part *f*. **on behalf of** de la part de; en faveur de.

behave [bi'heiv] *v* se conduire. **behave yourself!** sois sage! **behaviour** *n* conduite *f*.

behead [bi'hed] *v* décapiter.

behind [bi'haind] *adv, prep* derrière, en arrière (de); (*late*) en retard. *n* (*coll*) postérieur *m*. **behindhand** *adv, adj* en retard.

*behold [bi'hould] *v* voir.

beige [beiʒ] *nm, adj* beige.

being ['biːiŋ] *n* existence *f*; être *m*. **for the time being** pour le moment.

belated [bi'leitid] *adj* tardif.

belch [beltʃ] *v* roter; (*smoke, etc.*) vomir. *n* renvoi *m*.

belfry ['belfri] *n* beffroi *m*; (*church*) clocher *m*.

Belgium ['beldʒəm] *n* Belgique *f*. **Belgian** *n* Belge *m*, *f*; *adj* belge.

Belgrade ['belgreid] *n* Belgrade.

believe [bi'liːv] *v* croire. **believe in** (*God*) croire en; (*ghosts, etc.*) croire à; (*approve of*) être partisan de. **belief** *n* croyance *f*; (*rel*) credo m, foi *f*; opinion *f*. **believable** *adj* croyable. **believer** *n* partisan, -e *m*, *f*; (*rel*) croyant, -e *m*, *f*.

bell [bel] *n* cloche *f*, clochette *f*; (*door*) sonnette *f*; (*telephone*) sonnerie *f*; (*bicycle*) timbre *m*.

belligerent [bi'lidʒərənt] *n*, *adj* belligérant, -e. **belligerence** *n* belligérance *f*.

bellow ['belou] *v* mugir; (*cow*) beugler; (*person*) brailler. *n* mugissement *m*; beuglement *m*; (*person*) hurlement *m*.

bellows ['belouz] *pl n* (*organ*) soufflerie *f* sing; (*fire*) soufflet *m* sing.

belly ['beli] *n* ventre *m*.

belong [bi'lon] *v* appartenir; (*club*) être membre (de). **belongings** *pl n* affaires *f pl*.

beloved [bi'lʌvid] *adj* bien aimé. *n* bienaimé, -e *m*, *f*.

below [bi'lou] *prep* sous, au-dessous de. *adv* en bas, en dessous; (*letters, etc.*) cidessous. **hit below the belt** porter un coup bas (à).

belt [belt] *n* ceinture *f*; (*land*) zone *f*, région *f*; (*tech*) courroie *f*. *v* (*slang: hit*) flanquer un gnon à; (*slang: rush*) se carapater.

bench [bentʃ] *n* banc *m*; (*workshop*) établi *m*; (*law*) tribunal *m*.

***bend** [bend] *n* coude *m*; (*road*) virage *m*; (*arm, knee*) pli *m*. *v* (se) courber; plier. **bend over** se pencher. **bend over backwards** se mettre en quatre.

beneath [bi'niːθ] *prep* sous, au-dessous de; (*unworthy*) indigne de. *adv* au-dessous, en bas.

benefactor ['benəfaktə] *n* bienfaiteur *m*. **benefactress** *n* bienfaitrice *f*.

benefit ['benəfit] *n* avantage *m*; (*money*) allocation *f*. **for the benefit of** dans l'intérêt de. **the benefit of the doubt** le bénéfice du doute. *v* faire du bien à; gagner (à). **beneficial** *adj* salutaire.

benevolent [bi'nevələnt] *adj* (*kindly*) bienveillant; (*charitable*) bienfaisant. **benevolence** *n* bienveillance *f*; bienfaisance *f*.

benign [bi'nain] *adj* (*med*) bénin, -igne; (*kindly*) bienveillant.

bent [bent] *V* **bend**. *adj* courbé; (*slang: dishonest*) véreux; (*slang: homosexual*) homosexuel. **be bent on** vouloir absolument. *n* aptitude *f*, disposition *f*.

bequeath [bi'kwiːð] *v* léguer. **bequest** *n* legs *m*.

bereaved [bi'riːvd] *adj* endeuillé. **bereavement** *n* deuil *m*.

beret ['berei] *n* béret *m*.

Berlin [bəː'lin] *n* Berlin.

Bern [bəːn] *n* Berne.

berry ['beri] *n* baie *f*.

berserk [bə'səːk] *adj* fou furieux, folle furieuse. **go berserk** devenir fou furieux; (*with anger*) se mettre en rage.

berth [bəːθ] *n* couchette *f*; (*naut*) mouillage *m*. **give a wide berth to** éviter. *v* (*naut*) mouiller, amarrer.

beside [bi'said] *prep* à côté de. **beside oneself** (*with anger*) hors de soi. **besides** *adv* (*as well*) de plus; (*moreover*) d'ailleurs.

besiege [bi'siːdʒ] *v* (*town*) assiéger; (*pester*) assaillir.

best [best] *adj* le meilleur, la meilleure. **best man** garçon d'honneur *m*. *adv* le mieux. *n* mieux *m*. **at best** au mieux. **do one's best** faire de son mieux. **make the best of** s'accommoder de; profiter de.

bestow [bi'stou] *v* accorder; (*title*) conférer.

bet [bet] *v* parier. *n* pari *m*. **betting shop** bureau de paris *m*.

betray [bi'trei] *v* trahir. **betrayal** *n* trahison *f*.

better ['betə] *adj* meilleur. *nm*, *adv* mieux. **be better** (*after illness*) aller mieux. **get the better of** triompher de. *v* améliorer, dépasser.

between [bi'twiːn] *prep* entre.

beverage ['bevəridʒ] *n* boisson *f*.

***beware** [bi'weə] *v* prendre garde. *interj* attention (à)!

bewilder [bi'wildə] *v* dérouter, abasourdir. **bewilderment** *n* confusion *f*; abasourdissement *m*.

beyond [bi'jond] *prep* au delà de; (*exceeding*) au-dessus de. *adv* au delà. **be beyond** dépasser.

bias ['baiəs] *n* tendance *f*; préjugé *m*; (*sewing*) biais *m*. *v* influencer; (*prejudice*) prévenir. **biased** *adj* partial. **be biased** avoir un préjugé.

bib [bib] n bavoir m; (of apron) bavette f.
Bible ['baibl] n Bible f. **biblical** adj biblique.
bibliography [bibli'ografi] n bibliographie f. **bibliographer** n bibliographe m, f. **bibliographical** adj bibliographique.
biceps ['baiseps] n biceps m.
bicker ['bikǝ] v se chamailler. **bickering** n chamailleries f pl.
bicycle ['baisikl] n bicyclette f, vélo m.
*bid [bid] n offre f; (auction) enchère f; (cards) demande f; (attempt) tentative f. v faire une offre or enchère (de); (cards) demander; (command) ordonner; (greeting) dire, souhaiter. **bidder** n offrant m. **bidding** n enchères f pl; ordre m.
bidet ['biːdei] n bidet m.
biennial [bai'eniǝl] adj biennal.
bifocals [bai'foukǝlz] pl n lunettes bifocales f pl.
big [big] adj grand; gros, grosse.
bigamy ['bigǝmi] n bigamie. **bigamist** n bigame m, f. **bigamous** adj bigame.
bigot ['bigǝt] n fanatique m, f. **bigoted** adj fanatique.
bikini [bi'kiːni] n bikini m.
bilingual [bai'lingwǝl] adj bilingue.
bilious ['biljǝs] adj bilieux. **bilious attack** crise de foie f. **biliousness** n affection hépatique f.
bill¹ [bil] (hotel, shop) note f; (restaurant) addition f; (fuel, etc.) facture f; (pol) projet de loi m; (poster) affiche f.
bill² [bil] n bec m.
billiards ['biljǝdz] n billard m.
billion ['biljǝn] n (10^{12}) billion m; (10^9) milliard m.
billow ['bilou] n flot m; (sail) gonflement m. v (sail) se gonfler; (smoke) tournoyer.
bin [bin] n (rubbish) poubelle f; (coal) coffre m; (wine) casier m.
binary ['bainǝri] adj binaire.
*bind [baind] v lier; (book) relier; (neaten edge) border; (force) obliger. n (coll) barbe f.
binding ['baindiŋ] n (book) reliure f; (tape) extra-fort m; (skis) fixation f. adj obligatoire.
binoculars [bi'nokjulǝz] pl n jumelles f pl.
biography [bai'ografi] n biographie f. **biographer** n biographe m, f. **biographical** adj biographique.
biology [bai'olǝdʒi] n biologie f. **biological** adj biologique. **biologist** n biologiste m, f.

birch [bǝːtʃ] n bouleau m; (punishment) verge f.
bird [bǝːd] n oiseau m.
birth [bǝːθ] n naissance f; (confinement) accouchement m. **birth certificate** acte de naissance m. **birth control** contrôle des naissances m. **birthday** n anniversaire m. **birthmark** n tache de vin f. **birthplace** n lieu de naissance m. **birth rate** natalité f. **give birth to** donner naissance à.
biscuit ['biskit] n petit gâteau sec m; biscuit m.
bishop ['biʃǝp] n évêque m.
bison ['baisǝn] n bison m.
bit¹ [bit] V **bite**. n (horse) mors m; (drill) mèche f.
bit² [bit] n morceau m, bout m, brin m. **a bit** adv un peu. **bit by bit** petit à petit. **do one's bit** fournir sa part d'effort.
bitch [bitʃ] n (dog) chienne f; (slang) garce f.
*bite [bait] v mordre; (insect) piquer. n morsure f; piqûre f; (mouthful) bouchée f. **biting** adj (remark, etc.) mordant; (wind) cinglant; (cold) âpre.
bitten ['bitn] V **bite**.
bitter ['bitǝ] adj amer; (cold) glacial. **to the bitter end** jusqu'au bout. **bitterness** n amertume f.
bizarre [bi'zaː] adj bizarre.
black ['blak] adj noir. n noir m; (person) Noir, -e m, f. v (comm) boycotter. **blacken** v noircir. **blackness** n noirceur f; (darkness) obscurité f.
blackberry ['blakbǝri] n (fruit) mûre f; (bush) mûrier m.
blackbird ['blakbǝːd] n merle m.
blackboard ['blakbɔːd] n tableau (noir) m.
blackcurrant [,blak'kʌrǝnt] n cassis m.
black eye n œil poché m.
blackhead ['blakhed] n point noir m.
black ice n verglas m.
blackleg ['blakleg] n jaune m.
blackmail ['blakmeil] n chantage m. v faire chanter. **blackmailer** n maître-chanteur m.
black market n marché noir m.
blackout ['blakaut] n (med) étourdissement m; (war) black-out m; (power cut) panne d'électricité f.
blacksmith ['blaksmiθ] n (iron) forgeron m; (horses) maréchal-ferrant m.
bladder ['bladǝ] n vessie f.

blade [bleid] *n* lame *f*; (*oar*) plat *m*; (*grass*) brin *m*; (*propeller*) pale *f*.

blame [bleim] *v* attribuer (à), rejeter la responsabilité (sur); (*censure*) blâmer. *n* responsabilité *f*; blâme *m*.

blank [blaŋk] *adj* blanc, blanche; (*cheque*) en blanc; (*empty*) vide; (*puzzled*) déconcerté. *n* blanc *m*, vide *m*; (*gun*) cartouche à blanc *f*.

blanket ['blaŋkit] *n* couverture *f*. *v* recouvrir; (*muffle*) étouffer.

blare [bleə] *n* vacarme *m*; (*trumpet*) sonnerie *f*. *v* retentir; (*radio, etc.*) beugler.

blaspheme [blas'fiːm] *v* blasphémer. **blasphemous** *adj* blasphématoire. **blasphemy** *n* blasphème *m*.

blast [blaːst] *n* explosion *f*; (*noise, wind*) coup *m*; (*trumpet*) fanfare *f*; (*steam*) jet *m*. *v* (*rocks*) faire sauter; (*hopes, etc.*) détruire. *interj* la barbe!

blatant ['bleitənt] *adj* (*obvious*) flagrant; (*shameless*) éhonté.

blaze [bleiz] *n* (*flare*) flambée *f*; (*large fire*) incendie *m*; (*sun*) flamboiement *m*; (*anger*) explosion *f*. *v* flamber; flamboyer; (*light*) resplendir. **blazing** *adj* en flammes; (*sun*) éclatant; (*coll*) furibond.

bleach [bliːtʃ] *n* blanchir; (*hair*) décolorer. *n* décolorant *m*; (*household*) eau de Javel *f*.

bleak [bliːk] *adj* (*landscape*) morne, désolé; (*bare*) austère; (*prospect*) triste; (*weather*) froid.

bleat [bliːt] *v* bêler. *n* bêlement *m*.

bled [bled] *V* **bleed**.

*****bleed** [bliːd] *v* saigner. **bleeding** *n* saignement *m*, hémorragie *f*.

blemish ['blemiʃ] *n* défaut *m*; (*reputation*) souillure *f*; (*fruit*) tache *f*. *v* gâter; (*reputation*) ternir.

blend [blend] *v* (se) mélanger; (*ideas*) fusionner; (*colours*) (se) fondre, aller bien ensemble. *n* mélange *m*.

bless [bles] *v* bénir. **bless you!** à vos souhaits! **blessed** (*rel*) béni, bienheureux; (*coll*) sacré. **blessing** *n* bénédiction *f*; (*at meal*) bénédicité; (*benefit*) bien *m*. **what a blessing!** quelle chance!

blew [bluː] *V* **blow²**.

blind [blaind] *adj* aveugle. **blind spot** (*mot*) angle mort *m*. *v* aveugler. *n* (*window*) store *m*; (*mask*) feinte *f*. **the blind** les aveugles *m pl*. **blindness** cécité *f*.

blindfold ['blaindfould] *v* bander les yeux à. *n* bandeau *m*. *adv* les yeux bandés.

blink [bliŋk] *v* cligner des yeux. *n* clignotement *m*. **blinkers** *pl n* œillères *f pl*.

bliss [blis] *n* bonheur suprême *m*. **blissful** *adj* merveilleux, divin.

blister ['blistə] *n* ampoule *f*; (*paint*) boursouflure *f*. *v* se couvrir d'ampoules; se boursoufler.

blizzard ['blizəd] *n* tempête de neige *f*.

blob [blob] *n* goutte *f*.

bloc [blok] *n* (*pol*) bloc *m*.

block [blok] *n* bloc *m*; (*wood*) billot *m*; (*flats*) immeuble *m*; (*houses*) pâté *m*; obstruction *f*. **block letters** majuscules *f pl*. *v* (*obstruct*) bloquer, boucher; (*hinder*) gêner. **blockage** *n* obstruction *f*.

bloke [blouk] *n* (*coll*) type *m*.

blond [blond] *adj* blond. **blonde** *nf, adj* blonde.

blood [blʌd] *n* sang *m*. **bloody** *adj* sanglant, ensanglanté; (*slang*) foutu.

bloodcurdling ['blʌdkəːdliŋ] *adj* à figer le sang.

blood donor *n* donneur, -euse de sang *m*, *f*.

blood group *n* groupe sanguin *m*.

bloodhound ['blʌdhaund] *n* limier *m*.

blood poisoning *n* empoisonnement du sang *m*.

blood pressure *n* tension *f*. **have high/low blood pressure** faire de l'hypertension/hypotension.

bloodshed ['blʌdʃed] *n* effusion de sang *f*.

bloodshot ['blʌdʃot] *adj* injecté de sang.

bloodstream ['blʌdstriːm] *n* système sanguin *m*.

bloodthirsty ['blʌdθəːsti] *adj* sanguinaire.

bloom [bluːm] *v* fleurir. *n* floraison *f*; (*single flower*) fleur *f*. **in full bloom** en pleine floraison.

blot [blot] *n* tache *f*; (*ink*) pâté *m*. *v* tacher; (*dry*) sécher. **blot out** effacer. **blotting paper** papier buvard *m*.

blouse [blauz] *n* chemisier *m*.

blow¹ [blou] *n* (*hit*) coup *m*. **come to blows** en venir aux mains.

*****blow²** [blou] *v* souffler; (*trumpet*) sonner; (*whistle*) siffler. **blow away** chasser. **blow off** (faire) s'envoler. **blow one's nose** se moucher. **blow out** (s')éteindre. **blow up** (*explode*) (faire) sauter; (*inflate*) gonfler.

blown [bloun] *V* **blow²**.

blubber ['blʌbə] *n* blanc de baleine *m. v* pleurer comme un veau.

blue [bluː] *adj* bleu; (*coarse*) grivois. *n* bleu *m.* **bluebell** *n* jacinthe des bois *f.*

blueprint *n* bleu *m*; plan *m.*

bluff [blʌf] *n* bluff *m. v* bluffer.

blunder ['blʌndə] *n* bévue *f*; (*coll*) gaffe *f*; (*social*) impair *m. v* faire une bévue.

blunt [blʌnt] *adj* (*blade*) émoussé; (*point*) épointé; (*frank*) carré, brusque. *v* émousser; épointer.

blur [bləː] *n* tache floue *f. v* estomper. **blurred** *adj* flou.

blush [blʌʃ] *v* rougir. *n* rougeur *f.*

boar [boː] *n* sanglier *m.*

board [boːd] *v* (*ship, plane*) monter à bord de; (*train, bus*) monter dans; (*lodge*) prendre en pension. *n* (*wood*) planche *f*; (*meals*) pension *f*; (*officials*) conseil *m*; (*naut*) bord *m.* **above board** régulier. **across the board** de portée générale. **boardroom** *n* salle du conseil *f.* **go on board** (s')embarquer. **on board** à bord. **boarder** *n* pensionnaire *m, f.* **boarding card** carte d'embarquement *f.* **boarding house** pension *f.* **boarding school** pensionnat *m.*

boast [boust] *v* se vanter. *n* fanfaronnade *f.* **boastful** *adj* vantard.

boat [bout] *n* bateau *m.* **all in the same boat** tous logés à la même enseigne. **boater** *n* (*hat*) canotier *m.* **boating** *n* canotage *m.*

bob[1] [bob] *v* (*up and down*) sautiller; (*curtsy*) faire une révérence. *n* révérence *f.*

bob[2] [bob] *v* (*hair*) couper court; (*tail*) écourter. *n* (*hairstyle*) coiffure à la Jeanne d'Arc *f.*

bobbin ['bobin] *n* bobine *f.*

bodice ['bodis] *n* corsage *m.*

body ['bodi] *n* corps *m*; (*corpse*) cadavre *m.* **bodyguard** *n* garde du corps *m.* **bodywork** *n* (*mot*) carrosserie *f.*

bog [bog] *n* marais *m.* **get bogged down** s'embourber. **boggy** *adj* marécageux.

bogus ['bougəs] *adj* faux, fausse.

bohemian [bə'hiːmiən] *n(m+f), adj* (*artist*) bohème; (*gipsy*) bohémien, -enne.

boil[1] [boil] *v* (faire) bouillir; (*vegetables, etc.*) cuire à l'eau. **boil down to** revenir à. **boil over** déborder. **boiled egg** œuf à la coque *m.* **boiler** *n* chaudière *f.* **boiler suit** bleus *m pl.* **boiling point** point d'ébullition *m.*

boil[2] [boil] *n* furoncle *m.*

boisterous ['boistərəs] *adj* (*person*) turbulent; (*sea*) tumultueux.

bold [bould] *adj* hardi. **boldness** *n* hardiesse *f.*

bolster ['boulstə] *n* (*pillow*) traversin *m. v* **bolster up** soutenir.

bolt [boult] *n* (*door*) verrou *m*; (*for nut*) boulon *m*; (*dash*) bond *m. v* verrouiller; (*food*) engouffrer; (*run away*) se sauver.

bomb [bom] *v* bombarder. *n* bombe *f.* **bomber** *n* (*aircraft*) bombardier *m.*

bombard [bəm'baːd] *v* bombarder. **bombardier** *n* (*mil*) caporal d'artillerie *m.* **bombardment** *n* bombardement *m.*

bond [bond] *n* (*agreement*) engagement *m*; (*tie*) lien *m*; (*comm*) bon *m*; (*glue*) adhérence *f.* **bondage** *n* esclavage *m.*

bone [boun] *n* os *m*; (*fish*) arête *f.* **bone china** porcelaine tendre *f.* **bone-dry** *adj* absolument sec, absolument sèche. **have a bone to pick with** avoir un compte à régler avec. **boned** *or* **boneless** *adj* désossé. **bony** *adj* osseux; (*person*) anguleux.

bonfire ['bonfaiə] *n* feu de joie *m.*

Bonn [bon] *n* Bonn.

bonnet ['bonit] *n* (*hat*) capote *f*; (*mot*) capot *m.*

bonus ['bounəs] *n* prime *f.*

booby trap ['buːbi] *n* traquenard *m*; (*mil*) objet piégé *m.*

book [buk] *n* livre *m*; (*writing*) cahier *m*; (*tickets*) carnet *m. v* retenir, réserver. **booked up** complet, -ète. **bookcase** ['bukkeis] *n* bibliothèque *f.* **booking** ['bukiŋ] *n* réservation *f.* **booking office** location *f.* **book-keeper** ['buk,kiːpə] *n* comptable *m, f.* **book-keeping** *n* comptabilité *f.* **booklet** ['buklit] *n* brochure *f.* **bookmaker** ['bukmeikə] *n* bookmaker *m.* **bookmark** ['bukmaːk] *n* marque *f.* **bookseller** ['bukselə] *n* libraire *m, f.* **bookshop** ['bukʃop] *n* librairie *f.* **bookstall** ['bukstoːl] *n* kiosque à livres *m.*

boom [buːm] *v* (*noise*) gronder; (*comm*) prospérer. *n* grondement *m*; (*comm*) forte hausse *f*; (*econ*) boom *m.*

boost [buːst] *v* (*confidence*) renforcer; (*comm*) faire monter; (*publicize*) faire de la réclame pour.

boot [buːt] *n* (*shoe*) botte *f*; (*mot*) coffre *m.*

booth [buːð] n cabine f; (voting) isoloir m.

booze [buːz] (coll) n boissons alcoolisées f pl. v biberonner. **booze-up** n beuverie f.

border ['bɔːdə] n (edge) bord m; (boundary) frontière f; (garden) bordure f. **borderline** n ligne de démarcation f. **borderline case** cas limite m. v border. **border on** (be adjacent) avoisiner; (be almost) frôler.

bore[1] [bɔː] v (hole) percer; (well) creuser; (rock) forer. n (gun) calibre m.

bore[2] [bɔː] n (person) raseur, -euse m, f; (situation) corvée f. v ennuyer. **be bored** s'ennuyer (à). **boredom** n ennui m. **boring** adj ennuyeux.

bore[3] [bɔː] V **bear**[1].

born [bɔːn] adj né. **be born** naître.

borne [bɔːn] V **bear**[1].

borough ['bʌrə] n circonscription électorale f; (London) arrondissement m.

borrow ['borou] v emprunter (à).

bosom ['buzəm] n (woman) seins m pl; (of family, etc.) sein m. **bosom friend** ami, -e intime m, f.

boss [bos] n chef m; patron, -onne m, f. v régenter. **bossy** adj tyrannique.

botany ['botəni] n botanique f. **botanical** adj botanique. **botanist** n botaniste m, f.

both [bouθ] adj les deux. pron tous les deux.

bother ['boðə] v (annoy) ennuyer; (make effort) se donner la peine (de). n ennui m. interj zut!

bottle ['botl] n bouteille f; (beer) canette f; (perfume) flacon m; (baby's) biberon m. **bottle-neck** n (road) rétrécissement de la chaussée m; (traffic) embouteillage m. **bottle-opener** n ouvre-bouteilles m. v (fruit) mettre en bocal; (wine) mettre en bouteilles. **bottle up** contenir.

bottom ['botəm] n fond m, bas m; (buttocks) derrière m. **bottomless** adj sans fond.

bough [bau] n rameau m.

bought [bɔːt] V **buy**.

boulder ['bouldə] n rocher m.

bounce [bauns] v (faire) rebondir; (cheque) être sans provision. n bond m.

bound[1] [baund] v (leap) bondir. n bond m.

bound[2] [baund] v (limit) borner. **bounds** pl n limites f pl, bornes f pl.

bound[3] [baund] V **bind**. adj obligé; sûr; (tied) lié.

bound[4] [baund] adj **bound for** en route pour; à destination de.

boundary ['baundəri] n limite f, frontière f.

bouquet [buːkei] n bouquet m.

bourgeois ['buəʒwaɪ] n, adj bourgeois, -e.

bout [baut] n (illness) accès m; (fight) combat m; (period) période f.

bow[1] [bau] v (bend) (se) courber; (greeting) saluer. n salut m.

bow[2] [bou] n (archery) arc m; (music) archet m; (ribbon) nœud m. **bow-legged** adj aux jambes arquées. **bow tie** nœud papillon m. **bow window** fenêtre en saillie f.

bow[3] [bau] n (naut) avant m.

bowels ['bauəlz] pl n (anat) intestins m pl; (of earth, etc.) entrailles f pl.

bowl[1] [boul] n bol m; (for water) cuvette f.

bowl[2] [boul] v (cricket, etc.) lancer; (bowls) faire rouler. n jeu de boules m. **bowler** n (cricket) lanceur m; (hat) chapeau melon m. **bowling alley** bowling m. **bowling green** terrain de boules m.

box[1] [boks] n boîte f; (theatre) loge f. **box number** boîte postale f. **box office** guichet m.

box[2] [boks] v (sport) boxer. **boxer** n boxeur m. **boxing** n boxe f.

Boxing Day n le lendemain de Noël m.

boy [boi] n garçon m; (son) fils m; (pupil) élève m. **boyfriend** n petit ami m. **boyhood** n enfance f.

boycott ['boikot] v boycotter. n boycottage m.

bra [braː] n soutien-gorge m.

brace [breis] n (dental) appareil m; (tool) vilebrequin m; (pair) paire f. **braces** pl n bretelles f pl. v soutenir. **brace oneself** se préparer. **bracing** adj fortifiant.

bracelet ['breislit] n bracelet m.

bracken ['brakən] n fougère f.

bracket ['brakit] n support m; (writing) parenthèse f. v mettre entre parenthèses; (group together) accoler.

brag [brag] v se vanter.

braille [breil] nm, adj braille.

brain [brein] n cerveau m. **brains** pl n intelligence f sing; (cookery) cervelle f sing. adj cérébral. **brain-child** n invention personnelle f. **brainwashing** n lavage de cerveau m; (coll) bourrage de crâne m.

brainwave n inspiration f. **brainy** adj intelligent.

braise [breiz] v braiser.

brake [breik] n frein m. v freiner.

bramble ['brambl] n roncier m; (blackberry bush) ronce des haies f.

branch [braɪntʃ] n branche f; (road) embranchement m, bifurcation f; (comm) succursale f. v (road) bifurquer.

brand [brand] v marquer. n marque f. **brand-new** adj tout neuf, toute neuve.

brandish ['brandiʃ] v brandir.

brandy ['brandi] n cognac m.

brass [braɪs] n cuivre jaune m. **brass band** fanfare f.

brassière ['brasiə] V **bra**.

brave [breiv] adj courageux. v braver. **bravery** n courage m.

brawl [broɪl] n rixe f. v se quereller.

brawn [broɪn] n (cookery) fromage de tête m; (strength) muscle m.

brazen ['breizn] adj effronté.

breach [briɪtʃ] n (gap) brèche f; (violation) infraction f; (promise) violation f; (contract) rupture f. **breach of the peace** attentat à l'ordre public m.

bread [bred] n pain m; (slang: money) fric m. **breadcrumbs** pl n chapelure f sing. **bread-winner** n soutien de famille m.

breadth [bredθ] n largeur f.

*break [breik] v (se) casser; (promise, law, etc.) violer. **break down** (cease functioning) tomber en panne; (cry) fondre en larmes. **breakdown** n panne f; (mental) depression nerveuse f; analyse f. **break into** (house) entrer par effraction; (safe, etc.) forcer. **breakthrough** n découverte sensationnelle f. **break up** (se) briser; (school) entrer en vacances. n pause f; rupture f; interruption f. **breakable** adj cassable, fragile. **breakage** n casse f. **breaker** n (wave) brisant m.

breakfast ['brekfəst] n petit déjeuner m.

breast [brest] n (chest) poitrine f; (woman's) sein m; (chicken) blanc m. **breast-feed** v allaiter. **breast-stroke** n brasse f.

breath [breθ] n haleine f, souffle m. **breathtaking** adj stupéfiant. **out of breath** à bout de souffle.

breathalyser ['breθəlaizə] n alcootest m.

breathe [briɪð] v respirer; (sigh) pousser. **breather** n moment de répit m. **breathing** n respiration f.

bred [bred] V **breed**.

*breed [briɪd] n espèce f. v (rear) élever; (reproduce) se multiplier; (give rise to) engendrer. **breeding** n élevage m; (manners) savoir-vivre m.

breeze [briɪz] n brise f.

brew [bruɪ] v (beer) brasser; (tea) (faire) infuser; (storm) (se) préparer. n brassage m; infusion f. **brewery** n brasserie f.

bribe [braib] n pot-de-vin m. v suborner, soudoyer. **bribery** n corruption f.

brick [brik] n brique f. **bricklayer** n maçon m. v **brick up** murer.

bride [braid] n mariée f. **bridegroom** n marié m. **bridesmaid** n demoiselle d'honneur f. **bridal** adj nuptial; de mariée.

bridge¹ [bridʒ] n pont m; (naut) passerelle m.

bridge² [bridʒ] n (cards) bridge m.

bridle ['braidl] n bride f. **bridle path** sentier m. v (horse) brider; (anger) regimber.

brief [briɪf] adj bref, brève. v donner des instructions à. n (law) dossier m. **briefcase** n serviette f. **briefly** adv brièvement.

brigade [bri'geid] n brigade f.

bright [brait] adj (shining) brillant; (well-lit) clair; (colour) vif; (clever) intelligent. **brighten** v faire briller; s'éclairer; (cheer) (s')égayer. **brightness** n éclat m; (of light) intensité f.

brilliant ['briljənt] adj (clever) brillant; (sun) éclatant. **brilliance** n éclat m.

brim [brim] n bord m. **brimful** adj plein à déborder.

brine [brain] n eau salée f; (cookery) saumure f.

*bring [briŋ] v (person) amener; (object) apporter. **bring about** causer, provoquer. **bring in** faire entrer; introduire; (comm) rapporter. **bring off** (succeed) réussir. **bring out** sortir; (colour, etc.) faire ressortir; (publish) publier. **bring up** (rear) élever; (question) soulever; (vomit) vomir.

brink [briŋk] n bord m. **on the brink of** à deux doigts de.

brisk [brisk] adj vif; (trade) actif.

bristle ['brisl] n poil m. v se hérisser. **bristly** adj aux poils durs.

Britain ['britn] n Grande-Bretagne f. **British** adj britannique. **the British** les Britanniques m pl.

Brittany ['britəni] n Bretagne f.

brittle ['britl] adj fragile.

broad [brɔːd] *adj* (*wide*) large; vaste; général; (*accent*) prononcé. **broad bean** fève *f.* **broad-minded** *adj* tolérant. **broaden** *v* (s')élargir. **broadly** *adv* en gros.

broadcast ['brɔːdkɑːst] *v* *émettre; (*rumour, etc.*) répandre. *n* émission *f. adj* radiodiffusé; télévisé. **broadcasting** *n* radiodiffusion *f.* télévision *f.*

broccoli ['brɔkəli] *n* brocoli *m.*

brochure ['brəuʃuə] *n* brochure *f.*

broke [brouk] *V* break. *adj* (*coll*) à sec.

broken ['broukn] *V* break.

broker ['broukə] *n* courtier *m.*

bronchitis [broŋ'kaitis] *n* bronchite *f.*

bronze [bronz] *n* bronze *m. v* brunir; (se) bronzer.

brooch [broutʃ] *n* broche *f.*

brood [bruːd] *v* couver; (*think*) ruminer. *n* nichée *f.*

brook [bruk] *n* ruisseau *m.*

broom [bruːm] *n* (*brush*) balai *m;* (*bush*) genêt *m.*

broth [broθ] *n* bouillon *m.*

brothel ['broθl] *n* bordel *m.*

brother ['brʌðə] *n* frère *m.* **brother-in-law** *n* beau-frère *m.* **brotherhood** *n* fraternité *f.* **brotherly** *adj* fraternel.

brought [brɔːt] *V* bring.

brow [brau] *n* (*forehead*) front *m;* (*hill*) sommet *m.*

brown [braun] *n* brun, marron; (*tanned*) bronzé. *n* brun *m. v* (*skin*) brunir; (*cookery*) (faire) dorer. **be browned off** (*coll*) en avoir marre.

browse [brauz] *v* (*book*) feuilleter; (*animal*) brouter.

bruise [bruːz] *n* bleu *m,* meurtrissure *f. v* faire un bleu à, (se) meurtrir; (*fruit*) (s')abîmer.

brunette [bruː'net] *n* brunette *f.*

brush [brʌʃ] *n* brosse *f;* (*broom*) balai *m;* (*undergrowth*) taillis *m;* (*skirmish*) accrochage *m. v* brosser; balayer. **brush against** effleurer. **brush up on** se remettre à.

brusque [brusk] *adj* brusque.

Brussels ['brʌsəlz] *n* Bruxelles. **Brussels sprouts** choux de Bruxelles *m pl.*

brute [bruːt] *n* brute *m.* **brutal** *adj* brutal; de brute. **brutality** *n* brutalité *f.*

bubble ['bʌbl] *n* bulle *f;* (*in liquid*) bouillon *m. v* bouillonner; (*champagne*) pétiller.

Bucharest [buːkə'rest] *n* Bucharest.

buck [bʌk] *n* mâle *m.* **buck-teeth** *pl n* dents de lapin *f pl. v* lancer une ruade. **buck up** (*coll: hurry up*) se remuer; (*coll: cheer up*) ravigoter.

bucket ['bʌkit] *n* seau *m.*

buckle ['bʌkl] *n* (*fastening*) boucle *f;* (*distortion*) gauchissement *m,* voilure *f. v* (se) boucler; gauchir, (se) voiler.

bud [bʌd] *n* bourgeon *m;* (*flower*) bouton *m. v* bourgeonner. **budding** *adj* (*plant*) bourgeonnant; (*talent*) en herbe.

Budapest [buːdə'pest] *n* Budapest.

budge [bʌdʒ] *v* (faire) bouger.

budgerigar ['bʌdʒərigɑː] *n* perruche *f.*

budget ['bʌdʒit] *n* budget *m. v* budgétiser. **budget for** prévoir des frais de.

buffalo ['bʌfələu] *n* buffle, -esse *m, f.*

buffer ['bʌfə] *n* tampon *m.*

buffet¹ ['bʌfit] *n* (*blow*) coup *m. v* frapper, battre; (*waves*) ballotter.

buffet² ['bufei] *n* buffet *m.* **buffet car** voiture-buffet *f.* **buffet lunch** lunch *m.*

bug [bʌg] *n* punaise *f;* (*germ*) microbe *m;* (*microphone*) micro *m. v* (*room*) poser des micros dans; (*annoy*) embêter.

bugger ['bʌgə] *n* (*vulgar*) con *m. interj* merde alors! **bugger off!** fous-moi la paix!

bugle ['bjuːgl] *n* clairon *m.*

build [bild] *v* bâtir, construire. **build up** (*land*) urbaniser; (*tension*) monter; (*develop*) se développer. *n* carrure *f.* **builder** *n* entrepreneur *m;* ouvrier du bâtiment *m.* **building** *n* construction *f;* (*thing built*) bâtiment *m;* (*offices, etc.*) immeuble *m.* **building site** chantier de construction *m.* **building society** société immobilière *f.*

built [bilt] *V* build.

bulb [bʌlb] *n* (*plant*) bulbe *m;* (*elec*) ampoule *f;* (*thermometer*) cuvette *f.*

Bulgaria [bʌl'geəriə] *n* Bulgarie *f.* **Bulgarian** *n* (*people*) Bulgare *m, f; nm, adj* bulgare.

bulge [bʌldʒ] *v* bomber; (*pocket, etc.*) être gonflé (de). *n* bombement *m,* gonflement *m;* (*increase*) poussée *f,* augmentation *f.* **bulging** *adj* (*eyes*) protubérant; (*pockets*) bourru.

bulk [bʌlk] *n* grosseur *f;* volume *m.* **in bulk** en gros. **the bulk of** la plus grande partie de. **bulky** *adj* encombrant.

bull [bul] *n* taureau *m.* **bulldog** *n* bouledogue *m.* **bulldozer** *n* bulldozer *m.* **bullfight** *n* corrida *f.* **bull's eye** (*target*) noir *m,* mille *m.*

bullet ['bulit] *n* balle *f*. **bullet-proof** *adj* pare-balles; (*car*) blindé.

bulletin ['bulətin] *n* bulletin *m*.

bullion ['buliən] *n* (*gold*) or en barre *m*; (*silver*) argent en lingot *m*.

bully ['buli] *n* tyran *m*; (*school*) brute *m*. *v* tyranniser; intimider; brutaliser.

bum [bʌm] (*coll*) *n* arrière-train *m*. *adj* moche. *v* **bum around** fainéanter.

bump [bʌmp] *n* (*blow*) heurt *m*, choc *m*; (*on road*) bosse *f*. *v* heurter; (*head, etc*.) cogner. **bump into** (*car*) tamponner; (*meet*) rencontrer par hasard. **bumpy** *adj* (*road*) bosselé; (*ride*) cahoteux.

bumper ['bʌmpə] *n* (*mot*) pare-chocs *m invar*. *adj* sensationnel.

bun [bʌn] *n* (*hair*) chignon *m*.

bunch [bʌntʃ] *n* (*flowers*) bouquet *m*; (*grapes*) grappe *f*; (*tuft*) touffe *f*; (*people*) bande *f*.

bundle ['bʌndl] *n* paquet *m*, ballot *m*. *v* empaqueter, faire un ballot de.

bungalow ['bʌŋgəlou] *n* bungalow *m*.

bungle ['bʌŋgl] *v* (*coll*) bâcler. **bungling** *adj* maladroit.

bunion ['bʌnjən] *n* oignon *m*.

bunk [bʌŋk] *n* couchette *f*.

bunker ['bʌŋkə] *n* (*coal*) coffre *m*; (*naut*) soute *f*; (*golf*) bunker *m*; (*mil*) blockhaus *m*.

buoy [boi] *n* bouée *f*. **buoyancy** *n* (*ship*) flottabilité *f*; (*liquid*) poussée *f*. **buoyant** *adj* flottable; (*mood*) gai.

burden ['bəːdn] *n* fardeau *m*. *v* charger.

bureau ['bjuərou] *n* (*desk*) secrétaire *m*; (*office*) bureau *m*.

bureaucracy [bju'rokrəsi] *n* bureaucratie *f*. **bureaucrat** *n* bureaucrate *m, f*. **bureaucratic** *adj* bureaucratique.

burglar ['bəːglə] *n* cambrioleur, -euse *m, f*. **burglar alarm** sonnerie antivol *f*. **burglary** *n* cambriolage *m*. **burgle** *v* cambrioler.

Burgundy ['bəːgəndi] *n* (*wine*) bourgogne *m*.

***burn** [bəːn] *v* brûler; (*building*) incendier. *n* brûlure *f*. **burning** *adj* brûlant; (*passion*) ardent; (*lit*) allumé.

burnt [bəːnt] *V* **burn**.

burrow ['bʌrou] *n* terrier *m*. *v* creuser.

***burst** [bəːst] *v* éclater; (*balloon, etc*.) crever. **burst in** faire irruption. *n* explosion *f*; éclat *m*.

bury ['beri] *v* enterrer. **burial** *n* enterrement *m*.

bus [bʌs] *n* autobus *m*. **bus shelter** abribus *m*. **bus station** gare routière *f*. **bus stop** arrêt d'autobus *m*.

bush [buʃ] *n* buisson *m*; (*thicket*) taillis *m*. **the bush** (*Australia*) la brousse *f*. **bushy** *adj* touffu.

business ['biznis] *n* affaires *f pl*; (*enterprise*) commerce *f*; (*matter*) affaire *f*. **businessman** *n* homme d'affaires *m*. **mind one's own business** se mêler de ses affaires. **businesslike** *adj* pratique; sérieux.

bust¹ [bʌst] *n* (*anat*) buste *m*; (*measurement*) tour de poitrine *m*.

bust² [bʌst] *adj* (*coll: broken*) fichu. **go bust** faire faillite.

bustle ['bʌsl] *v* s'affairer. *n* remue-ménage *m*.

busy ['bizi] *adj* occupé. **busybody** *n* mouche du coche *f*.

but [bʌt] *conj* mais. *adv* (*only*) seulement. *prep* (*except*) sauf. **but for** sans.

butane ['bjuːtein] *n* butane *m*.

butcher [butʃə] *n* boucher *m*. **butcher's shop** boucherie *f*. *v* massacrer; (*animal*) abattre.

butler ['bʌtlə] *n* maître d'hôtel *m*.

butt¹ [bʌt] *n* (*cigarette*) mégot *m*, bout *m*; (*gun*) crosse *f*.

butt² [bʌt] *n* victime *f*.

butt³ [bʌt] *v* (*goat*) donner un coup de corne à. **butt in** s'immiscer dans la conversation, intervenir. *n* coup de corne *m*.

butter ['bʌtə] *n* beurre *m*. *v* beurrer.

buttercup ['bʌtəkʌp] *n* bouton d'or *m*.

butterfly ['bʌtəflai] *n* papillon *m*; (*swimming*) brasse papillon *f*. **have butterflies** (*coll*) avoir le trac.

buttocks ['bʌtəks] *pl n* (*person*) fesses *f pl*; (*animal*) croupe *f sing*.

button ['bʌtn] *n* bouton *m*. **buttonhole** *n* boutonnière *f*; (*flower*) fleur *f*. *v* (se) boutonner.

buttress ['bʌtris] *n* (*arch*) arc-boutant *m*; (*support*) soutien *m*. *v* soutenir.

***buy** [bai] *v* acheter. *n* **a good/bad buy** une bonne/mauvaise affaire *f*. **buyer** acheteur, -euse *m, f*.

buzz [bʌz] *v* bourdonner. *n* bourdonnement *m*.

by [bai] *prep* par; (*near*) près de; (*before*) avant; (*per*) à. *adv* près. **by and by** bientôt. **by the way** à propos. **go by** passer.

bye-law ['bailɔɪ] *n* arrêté municipal *m*.
by-election ['baɪɪ,lekʃən] *n* election partielle *f*.
bypass ['baɪ,paɪs] *n* route de contournement *f*. *v* contourner.
bystander ['baɪ,standə] *n* spectateur, -trice *m*, *f*.

C

cab [kab] *n* taxi *m*; (*lorry*) cabine *f*.
cabaret ['kabərei] *n* cabaret *m*; (*show*) spectacle *m*.
cabbage ['kabidʒ] *n* chou (*pl* choux) *m*.
cabin ['kabin] *n* cabine *f*; (*hut*) cabane *f*.
cabinet ['kabinit] *n* cabinet *m*; (*filing*) classeur *m*; (*pol*) cabinet *m*. **cabinet-maker** *n* ébéniste *m*. **cabinet minister** membre du cabinet *m*.
cable ['keibl] *n* câble *m*. **cablecar** *n* téléphérique *m*. *v* câbler.
cackle ['kakl] *v* caqueter; (*laugh*) glousser. *n* caquet *m*; gloussement *m*.
cactus ['kaktəs] *n* cactus *m*.
caddie ['kadi] *n* caddie *m*.
cadence ['keidəns] *n* cadence *f*; (*voice*) modulation *f*.
cadet [kə'det] *n* élève officier *m*.
café ['kafei] *n* café *m*.
cafeteria [kafə'tiəriə] *n* cafétéria *f*.
caffeine ['kafiɪn] *n* caféine *f*.
cage [keidʒ] *n* cage *f*.
cake [keik] *n* gâteau *m*; (*soap, etc*) pain *m*. **cake shop** pâtisserie *f*. **it's a piece of cake** c'est du gâteau. **like hot cakes** comme des petits pains. **caked** *adj* coagulé. **caked with** raidi par.
calamine ['kaləmain] *n* calamine *f*. **calamine lotion** lotion calmante à la calamine *f*.
calamity [kə'laməti] *n* calamité *f*.
calcium ['kalsiəm] *n* calcium *m*.
calculate ['kalkjuleit] *v* calculer; (*reckon*) évaluer. **calculable** *adj* calculable. **calculated** *adj* délibéré. **calculating** *adj* (*scheming*) calculateur, -trice. **calculation** *n* calcul *m*. **calculator** *n* machine à calculer *f*, calculatrice *f*.
calendar ['kaləndə] *n* calendrier *m*. **calendar month** mois de calendrier *m*.

calf¹ [kaɪf] *n* (*animal*) veau *m*.
calf² [kaɪf] *n* (*anat*) mollet *m*.
calibre ['kalibə] *n* calibre *m*.
call [kɔɪl] *n* appel *m*; cri *m*; visite *f*. **callbox** *n* cabine téléphonique *f*. *v* appeler; (*waken*) réveiller; (*visit*) passer. **be called** s'appeler. **call for** (*need*) demander; (*person*) passer prendre. **call off** (*cancel*) annuler. **call on** (*visit*) passer voir. **call up** (*mil*) mobiliser. **caller** *n* visiteur, -euse *m*, *f*; (*phone*) demandeur, -euse *m*, *f*. **calling** *n* vocation *f*; (*job*) métier *m*.
callous ['kaləs] *adj* dur, sans pitié.
calm [kaɪm] *adj* calme. *n* calme *m*; période de tranquillité *f*. *v* calmer. **calm down** (se) calmer. **calmness** *n* calme *m*; sang-froid *m*.
calorie ['kaləri] *n* calorie *f*.
came [keim] *V* **come**.
camel ['kaməl] *n* chameau, -elle *m*, *f*. **camel-hair** *n* poil de chameau *m*.
camera ['kamərə] *n* appareil-photo *m*; (*cine*) caméra *f*.
Cameroon [kamə'ruɪn] *n* Cameroun *m*.
camouflage ['kaməflaɪʒ] *n* camouflage *m*. *v* camoufler.
camp¹ [kamp] *v* camper. **go camping** faire du camping. *n* camp *m*. **camp-bed** *n* lit de camp *m*. **campsite** *n* camping *m*.
camp² [kamp] *adj* affecté; efféminé; (*slang: homosexual*) pédé.
campaign [kam'pein] *n* campagne *f*. *v* faire campagne.
campus ['kampəs] *n* campus *m*.
camshaft ['kamʃaɪft] *n* (*mot*) arbre à cames *m*.
*can¹ [kan] *v* (*be able*) pouvoir; (*know how to*) savoir.
can² [kan] *n* (*oil*) bidon *m*; (*beer, fruit*) boîte *f*. **can-opener** *n* ouvre-boîtes *m* invar. *v* mettre en boîte.
Canada ['kanədə] *n* Canada *m*. **Canadian** *n* Canadien, -enne *m*, *f*; *adj* canadien.
canal [kə'nal] *n* canal *m*.
canary [kə'neəri] *n* serin *m*.
Canberra ['kanbərə] *n* Canberra *m*.
cancel ['kansəl] *v* annuler; (*order*) décommander; (*contract*) résilier; (*train*) supprimer; (*cheque*) faire opposition à. **cancellation** *n* annulation *f*; suppression *f*.
cancer ['kansə] *n* cancer *m*. **Cancer** *n* Cancer *m*.
candid ['kandid] *adj* franc, franche.
candidate ['kandidət] *n* candidat *m*.

candle ['kandl] *n* (*wax*) bougie *f*; (*tallow*) chandelle *f*. **candle-light** *n* lumière de bougie *f*. **candlestick** *n* bougeoir *m*; chandelier *m*. **candlewick** *n* chenille de coton *f*.

candour ['kandə] *n* franchise *f*.

candy ['kandi] *n* (*US*) bonbons *m pl*. **candied** *adj* glacé, confit.

cane [kein] *n* canne *f*; (*school*) verge *f*. *v* fouetter.

canine ['keinain] *adj* canin. *n* (*tooth*) canine *f*.

canister ['kanistə] *n* boîte *f*.

cannabis ['kanəbis] *n* (*drug*) cannabis *m*; (*plant*) chanvre indien *m*.

cannibal ['kanibal] *n*(*m+f*), *adj* cannibale. **cannibalism** *n* cannibalisme *m*.

cannon ['kanən] *n* canon *m*. **cannonball** *n* boulet de canon *m*.

canoe [kə'nuɪ] *n* canoë *m*; (*sport*) kayac *m*. *v* faire du canoë; faire du kayac.

canon ['kanən] *n* canon *m*. **canonical** *adj* canonique. **canonize** *v* canoniser.

canopy ['kanəpi] *n* baldaquin *m*, dais *m*.

canteen [kan'tiɪn] *n* (*dining place*) cantine *f*; (*flask*) bidon *m*; (*cutlery*) ménagère *f*.

canter ['kantə] *n* petit galop *m*. *v* aller au petit galop.

canton ['kantən] *n* canton *m*.

canvas ['kanvəs] *n* toile *f*.

canvass ['kanvəs] *v* (*pol*) faire du démarchage électoral; (*for orders, votes*) solliciter. **canvasser** *n* (*pol*) agent électoral *m*; (*comm*) démarcheur *m*. **canvassing** *n* démarchage *m*.

canyon ['kanjən] *n* cañon *m*.

cap [kap] *n* (*hat*) casquette *f*; (*bottle*) capsule *f*; (*pen*) capuchon *m*. *v* capsuler; surpasser.

capable ['keipəbl] *adj* capable; (*situation*) susceptible. **capability** *n* capacité *f*; aptitude *f*.

capacity [kə'pasəti] *n* capacité *f*; (*status*) qualité *f*.

cape[1] [keip] *n* (*cloak*) pèlerine *f*.

cape[2] [keip] *n* (*geog*) cap *m*.

caper ['keipə] *n* (*cookery*) câpre *f*.

capital ['kapitl] *n* (*city*) capitale *f*; (*letter*) majuscule *f*; (*money*) capital *m*. *adj* capital. **capitalism** *n* capitalisme *m*. **capitalist** *n* capitaliste *m, f*. **capitalize** *v* capitaliser; (*word*) mettre une majuscule à. **capitalize on** tirer parti de.

capitulate [kə'pitjuleit] *v* capituler. **capitulation** *n* capitulation *f*.

capricious [kə'prifəs] *adj* capricieux.

Capricorn ['kaprikoɪn] *n* Capricorne *m*.

capsicum ['kapsikəm] *n* piment *m*.

capsize [kap'saiz] *v* (*naut*) (faire) chavirer.

capsule ['kapsjuɪl] *n* capsule *f*.

captain ['kaptin] *n* capitaine *m*.

caption ['kapfən] *n* légende *f*; (*title*) sous-titre *m*.

captive ['kaptiv] *n* captif, -ive *m, f*. *adj* captif. **captivate** *v* captiver. **captivity** *n* captivité *f*.

capture ['kaptfə] *v* prendre, capturer; (*attention*) capter. *n* capture *f*. **captor** *n* ravisseur *m*.

car [kaɪ] *n* voiture *f*; (*rail*) wagon *m*. **car park** parking *m*. **car wash** lave-auto *m*.

caramel ['karəmel] *n* caramel *m*.

carat ['karət] *n* carat *m*.

caravan ['karəvan] *n* caravane *f*; (*gipsy*) roulotte *f*.

caraway ['karəwei] *n* cumin *m*, carvi *m*.

carbohydrates [kaɪbə'haidreits] *pl n* farineux *m pl*, féculents *m pl*.

carbon ['kaɪbən] *n* carbone *m*. **carbon copy** (*typing*) carbone *m*; (*identical thing*) réplique *f*. **carbon dioxide** gaz carbonique *m*. **carbon paper** papier carbone *m*.

carburettor ['kaɪbjuretə] *n* carburateur *m*.

carcass ['kaɪkəs] *n* carcasse *f*.

card [kaɪd] *n* carte *f*; (*index*) fiche *f*. **cardboard** *n* carton *m*. **card trick** tour de cartes. **it's on the cards** il y a de grandes chances. **play one's cards right** bien mener son jeu.

cardiac ['kaɪdiak] *adj* cardiaque. **cardiac arrest** arrêt du cœur *m*.

cardigan ['kaɪdigən] *n* cardigan *m*.

cardinal ['kaɪdənl] *nm, adj* cardinal.

care [keə] *v* se soucier (de). **care for** (*like*) aimer; (*tend*) soigner; (*look after*) s'occuper de. *n* soin *m*, attention *f*; (*worry*) souci *m*. **care of** chez. **take care** faire attention. **take care of** s'occuper de. **carefree** *adj* sans souci, insouciant. **careful** *adj* prudent; consciencieux. **be careful!** faites attention! **careless** *adj* négligent; (*work*) peu soigné.

career [kə'riə] *n* carrière *f*.

caress [kə'res] *v* caresser. *n* caresse *f*.

caretaker ['keəteikə] *n* gardien, -enne *m, f*; concierge *m, f*.

cargo ['kaɪgou] *n* cargaison *m*.

caricature ['karikətjuə] *n* caricature *f*. *v* caricaturer. **caricaturist** *n* caricaturiste *m, f*.

carnage ['kaɪnidʒ] *n* carnage *m*.

carnal ['kaɪnl] *adj* charnel. **carnal knowledge** (*law*) relations sexuelles *f pl*.

carnation [kaɪ'neiʃən] *n* œillet *m*.

carnival ['kaɪnivəl] *n* carnaval *m*.

carnivorous [kaɪ'nivərəs] *adj* carnivore. **carnivore** *n* carnivore *m*.

carol ['karəl] *n* chant joyeux *m*. **Christmas carol** chant de Noël *m*.

carpenter ['kaɪpəntə] *n* charpentier *m*. **carpentry** *n* charpenterie *f*.

carpet ['kaɪpit] *n* tapis *m*. **carpet-sweeper** *n* balai mécanique *m*. *v* moquetter.

carriage ['karidʒ] *n* (*horse-drawn*) voiture *f*; (*rail*) wagon *m*; (*comm*) transport *m*; (*person*) maintien *m*. **carriageway** *n* chaussée *f*. **dual carriageway** route à chaussées séparées *f*.

carrier ['kariə] *n* (*comm*) entreprise de transports *f*; (*med*) porteur, -euse *m, f*. **carrier-bag** *n* sac en plastique *m*.

carrot ['karət] *n* carotte *f*.

carry ['kari] *v* porter; transporter. **carry away** emporter. **carrycot** *n* porte-bébé *m*. **carry on** continuer. **carry out** exécuter. **get carried away** (*coll*) s'emballer.

cart [kaɪt] *n* (*horse-drawn*) charrette *f*. **cart-horse** *n* cheval de trait *m*. **turn a cart-wheel** faire la roue. *v* transporter; (*coll*) trimballer.

cartilage ['kaɪtəlidʒ] *n* cartilage *m*.

cartography [kaɪ'tɒgrəfi] *n* cartographie *f*. **cartographer** *n* cartographe *m, f*.

carton ['kaɪtən] *n* (*cream, etc.*) pot *m*; (*milk*) carton *m*.

cartoon [kaɪ'tuɪn] *n* dessin *m*; (*film*) dessin animé *m*. **cartoonist** *n* dessinateur, -trice *m, f*; animateur, -trice *m, f*.

cartridge ['kaɪtridʒ] *n* cartouche *f*; (*camera*) chargeur *m*. **cartridge paper** papier à cartouche *m*.

carve [kaɪv] *v* (*meat*) découper; (*wood, etc.*) tailler; sculpter; (*initials*) graver. **carving** *n* sculpture *f*. **carving knife** couteau à découper *m*.

cascade [kas'keid] *n* cascade *f*. *v* tomber en cascade.

case¹ [keis] *n* cas *m*; (*law*) affaire *f*; arguments *m pl*. **in any case** en tout cas. **in case** à tout hasard. **in case of** en cas de. **in that case** dans ce cas-là.

case² [keis] *n* (*luggage*) valise *f*; (*crate*) caisse *f*; (*violin, camera, etc.*) étui *m*.

cash [kaʃ] *n* (*money*) argent *m*; (*not cheque*) espèces *f pl*; (*immediate payment*) argent comptant *m*. **cash desk** caisse *f*. **cash register** caisse enregistreuse *f*. *v* encaisser.

cashier¹ [ka'ʃiə] *n* caissier *m*.

cashier² [ka'ʃiə] *v* renvoyer; (*mil*) casser.

cashmere [kaʃ'miə] *n* cachemire *m*.

casino [kə'siːnou] *n* casino *m*.

cask [kaɪsk] *n* fût *m*.

casket ['kaɪskit] *n* coffret *m*.

casserole ['kasəroul] *n* (*dish*) cocotte *f*; (*food*) ragoût en cocotte *m*. *v* cuire en cocotte.

cassette [kə'set] *n* cassette *f*.

cassock ['kasək] *n* soutane *f*.

*cast [kaɪst] *n* (*mould*) moulage *m*; (*theatre*) distribution *f*; (*throw*) coup *m*. *v* (*throw*) jeter, lancer; (*plaster, etc.*) couler; (*theatre*) distribuer les rôles (de). **cast away** rejeter. **castaway** *n* naufragé, -e *m, f*. **casting vote** voix prépondérante *f*. **cast-iron** *adj* en fonte; (*excuse, etc.*) inattaquable.

caste [kaɪst] *n* caste *f*.

castle ['kaɪsl] *n* château fort *m*.

castor oil ['kaɪstə] *n* huile de ricin *f*.

castrate [kə'streit] *v* châtrer; émasculer. **castration** *n* castration *f*.

casual ['kaʒuəl] *adj* (*chance*) fortuit, fait par hasard; (*informal*) sans-gêne, désinvolte. **casually** *adv* par hasard; avec désinvolture.

casualty ['kaʒuəlti] *n* (*injured*) blessé, -e *m, f*; (*dead*) mort, -e *m, f*; (*of accident*) victime *f*; (*hospital ward*) salle des accidentés *f*.

cat [kat] *n* chat, chatte *m, f*. **cat's eyes** (*road*) cataphotes *m pl*. **catsuit** *n* combinaison-pantalon *f*. **let the cat out of the bag** vendre la mèche.

catalogue ['katəlog] *n* catalogue *m*. *v* cataloguer.

catalyst ['katəlist] *n* catalyse *f*.

catamaran [katəmə'ran] *n* catamaran *m*.

catapult ['katəpʌlt] *n* lance-pierres *m invar*; (*aero, mil*) catapulte *f*. *v* catapulter.

cataract ['katərakt] *n* cataracte *f*.

catarrh [kə'taɪ] *n* catarrhe *m*.

catastrophe [kə'tastrəfi] *n* catastrophe *f*. **catastrophic** *adj* catastrophique.

*catch [katʃ] v attraper; (by surprise) prendre; (train, etc.) ne pas manquer; (on nail) (s')accrocher; (hear) saisir. **catch fire** prendre feu. **catch on** devenir populaire; (understand) comprendre. **catch up** (se) rattraper. n prise f; (drawback) attrape f; (window) loqueteau m. **catching** adj contagieux.
category ['katəgəri] n catégorie f. **categorical** adj catégorique. **categorize** v classer par catégories.
cater ['keitə] v **cater for** (needs) pourvoir à. **caterer** n fournisseur m, traiteur m. **catering** n restauration f.
caterpillar ['katəpilə] n chenille f.
cathedral [kə'θiːdrəl] n cathédrale f.
cathode ['kaθoud] n cathode f. **cathode ray tube** tube cathodique m.
catholic ['kaθəlik] adj (rel) catholique; (tastes, etc.) éclectique. n catholique m, f. **catholicism** n catholicisme m.
catkin ['katkin] n chaton m.
cattle ['katl] pl n bétail m sing.
catty ['kati] adj (slang) vache.
caught [kɔːt] V **catch**.
cauliflower ['koliflauə] n chou-fleur (pl choux-fleurs) m.
cause [kɔːz] v causer. n cause f.
causeway ['kɔːzwei] n chaussée f.
caustic ['kɔːstik] adj caustique.
caution ['kɔːʃən] n prudence f; (warning) avertissement m; réprimande f. v avertir. **cautious** adj prudent.
cavalry ['kavəlri] n cavalerie f.
cave [keiv] n caverne f, grotte f. v **cave in** s'effondrer; (wall) céder.
caviar ['kaviaː] n caviar m.
cavity ['kavəti] n cavité f. **cavity wall** mur creux m.
cayenne [kei'en] n cayenne m.
cease [siːs] v cesser. **cease-fire** n cessez-le-feu m invar. **ceaseless** adj incessant. **ceaselessly** adv sans cesse.
cedar ['siːdə] n cèdre m.
cedilla [si'dilə] n cédille f.
ceiling ['siːliŋ] n plafond m.
celebrate ['seləbreit] v célébrer. **celebrated** adj célèbre. **celebration** n célébration f; (occasion) festivités f pl. **celebrity** n célébrité f.
celery ['seləri] n céleri m. **stick of celery** côte de céleri f.
celestial [sə'lestiəl] adj céleste.
celibate ['selibət] n(m+f), adj célibataire. **celibacy** n célibat m.

cell [sel] n cellule f; (elec) élément m.
cellar ['selə] n cave f.
cello ['tʃelou] n violoncelle m. **cellist** n violoncelliste m, f.
cellular ['seljulə] adj cellulaire; (blanket) en cellular.
cement [sə'ment] n ciment m. **cement-mixer** n bétonnière f. v cimenter.
cemetery ['semətri] n cimetière m.
cenotaph ['senətɑːf] n cénotaphe m.
censor ['sensə] n censeur m. v censurer. **censorship** n censure f.
censure ['senʃə] v blâmer. n critique f.
census ['sensəs] n recensement m.
cent [sent] n cent m. **per cent** pour cent.
centenary [sen'tiːnəri] nm, adj centenaire.
centigrade ['sentigreid] adj centigrade.
centimetre ['sentimiːtə] n centimètre m.
centipede ['sentipiːd] n mille-pattes m invar.
central ['sentrəl] adj central. **central heating** chauffage central m. **centralization** n centralisation f. **centralize** v (se) centraliser.
centre ['sentə] n centre m. v centrer. **centre on** (thoughts) se concentrer sur; (problem) tourner autour de.
centrifugal [sen'trifjugəl] adj centrifuge.
century ['sentʃuri] n siècle m.
ceramic [sə'ramik] adj (en) céramique. **ceramics** n céramique f.
cereal ['siəriəl] n céréale f.
ceremonial [serə'mouniəl] n cérémonial m. adj cérémoniel; de cérémonie.
ceremony ['serəməni] n (event) cérémonie f; (formality) cérémonies f pl. **stand on ceremony** faire des façons. **ceremonious** adj solennel; (over-polite) cérémonieux.
certain ['sɜːtn] adj certain. **certainly** adv certainement; (willingly) volontiers. **certainty** n certitude f.
certificate [sə'tifikət] n certificat m; diplôme m. **certify** v certifier.
cervix ['sɜːviks] n col de l'utérus m.
cesspool ['sespuːl] n fosse d'aisances f.
chafe [tʃeif] v (rub) frotter; (make sore) gratter.
chaffinch ['tʃafintʃ] n pinson m.
chain [tʃein] n chaîne f. **chain smoke** fumer cigarette sur cigarette. **chain store** magasin à succursales multiples m.
chair [tʃeə] n chaise f; (university) chaire f; (meeting) présidence f. **chairlift** n télésiège m. **chairman** n président. v présider.

chalet ['ʃalei] n chalet m; (motel) bunga-low m.

chalk [tʃɔik] n craie f. **chalky** adj crayeux.

challenge ['tʃalindʒ] n défi m. n défier; (sport) inviter; (question) contester.

chamber ['tʃeimbə] n chambre f. **chambermaid** n femme de chambre f. **chamber music** musique de chambre f. **chamberpot** n pot de chambre m.

chameleon [kəmiilliən] n caméléon m.

chamois ['ʃamwai] n chamois m. **chamois leather** peau de chamois m.

champagne [ʃam'pein] n champagne m.

champion ['tʃampiən] n champion, -onne m, f. v défendre. **championship** n championnat m.

chance [tʃains] n (luck) hasard m; (possibility) chance f; (opportunity) occasion f. **by chance** par hasard. adj fortuit. v prendre le risque de.

chancellor ['tʃainsələ] n chancelier m.

chandelier [ʃandə'liə] n lustre m.

change [tʃeindʒ] n changement m; (money) monnaie f. v changer; échanger; (clothes) se changer. **changeable** adj changeant; (weather) variable. **changing-room** n vestiaire m.

channel ['tʃanl] n chenal m; (duct) conduit m; (TV) chaîne f. **the Channel Islands** les îles anglo-normandes f pl. **the English Channel** la Manche. v (efforts, etc.) canaliser.

chant [tʃaint] v (rel) psalmodier; (crowd) scander. n psalmodie f; chant scandé m.

chaos ['keios] n chaos m. adj chaotique.

chap¹ [tʃap] v (skin) (se) gercer. n gerçure f.

chap² [tʃap] n (coll) type m.

chapel ['tʃapəl] n chapelle f.

chaperon ['ʃapəroun] n chaperon m. v chaperonner.

chaplain ['tʃaplin] n aumônier m.

chapter ['tʃaptə] n chapitre m.

char¹ [tʃai] v (burn) carboniser.

char² [tʃai] v faire des ménages. **charwoman** n femme de ménage f.

character ['karəktə] n caractère m; (theatre, etc.) personnage m. **characteristic** nf, adj caractéristique. **caracterize** v caractériser.

charcoal ['tʃaikoul] n charbon de bois m.

charge [tʃaidʒ] n (law) accusation f; (mil) charge f; (cost) prix m; responsabilité f; (battery) charge f. **in charge** responsable. **take charge of** se charger de. v (law)

accuser (de); (mil) charger; (person) faire payer; (amount) demander; (battery) (se) charger. **charge in/out** entrer/sortir en coup de vent.

chariot ['tʃariət] n char m.

charity ['tʃarəti] n charité f; (society) œuvre charitable f. **charitable** adj charitable.

charm [tʃaim] n charme m; (on bracelet) breloque f. v charmer. **charming** adj charmant.

chart [tʃait] n (map) carte f; (graph, etc.) graphique m, diagramme m. v (journey) porter sur la carte; (sales, etc.) faire le graphique de.

charter ['tʃaitə] v (boat, etc.) affréter. **chartered accountant** expert-comptable m. n affrètement; (document) charte f. **charter flight** charter m.

chase [tʃeis] v chasser, poursuivre. n chasse f, poursuite f.

chasm ['kazəm] n gouffre m.

chassis ['ʃasi] n (mot) châssis m.

chaste [tʃeist] adj chaste, pur. **chastity** n chasteté f.

chastise [tʃas'taiz] v châtier. **chastisement** n châtiment m.

chat [tʃat] n causette f. v bavarder.

chatter ['tʃatə] v jacasser; (teeth) claquer. n jacassement m; bavardage m. **chatterbox** n bavard, -e m, f.

chauffeur ['ʃoufə] n chauffeur m.

chauvinism ['ʃouvinizəm] n chauvinisme m. **chauvinist** n, adj chauvin, -e. **male chauvinist** (slang) phallocrate m.

cheap [tʃiip] adj bon marché invar; (reduced) réduit. **cheapen** v baisser le prix de; (degrade) déprécier. **cheaply** adv à bon marché.

cheat [tʃiit] v (deceive) tromper; (at games) tricher; frauder. n tricheur, -euse m, f; fraude f.

check [tʃek] n contrôle m, vérification f; (restraint) arrêt m; (chess) échec m; (US: cheque) chèque m; (US: bill) addition f. **checkmate** n échec et mat. **checkpoint** n contrôle m. **checks** pl n (pattern) carreaux m pl. v vérifier; contrôler; (restrain) maîtriser. **check-in** n (aero) enregistrement m. **check-out** n (supermarket) caisse f. **check out** (hotel) régler sa note. **check-up** n (med) bilan de santé m. **check up on** (thing) vérifier; (person) se renseigner sur. **checked** adj (pattern) à carreaux.

cheek [tʃiːk] n (*anat*) joue f; (*coll: impudence*) toupet m. **cheekbone** n pommette f. **cheeky** adj effronté.

cheer [tʃiə] v (*shout*) acclamer, pousser des hourras. **cheer up** (s')égayer; prendre courage; (*comfort*) consoler. n gaieté f; (*shout*) acclamation f. **cheerio!** *interj* salut! cheers! *interj* à la vôtre! **cheerful** adj gai; (*news*) réconfortant. **cheerless** adj morne. **cheery** adj joyeux.

cheese [tʃiːz] n fromage m. **cheesecake** n tarte au fromage blanc f. **cheesecloth** n (*for clothes*) toile à beurre f.

cheetah ['tʃiːtə] n guépard m.

chef [ʃef] n chef (de cuisine) m.

chemistry ['kemistri] n chimie f. **chemist** n chimiste m, f; pharmacien, -enne m, f. **chemist's shop** pharmacie f.

cheque or US **check** [tʃek] n chèque m. **chequebook** n chéquier m. **cheque card** carte d'identité bancaire f.

cherish ['tʃeriʃ] v chérir; (*hope, etc.*) nourrir.

cherry ['tʃeri] n (*fruit*) cerise f; (*tree*) cerisier m.

chess [tʃes] n échecs m pl. **chessboard** n échiquier m. **chessman** n pièce f.

chest [tʃest] n (*anat*) poitrine f; (*box*) caisse f. **chest of drawers** commode f. **chesty** adj (*cough*) de poitrine.

chestnut ['tʃesnʌt] n (*fruit*) châtaigne f, marron m; (*tree*) châtaignier m, marronnier m. adj (*hair*) châtain.

chew [tʃuː] v mâcher. **chewing gum** chewing-gum m. **chew over** ruminer. **chew the cud** ruminer. **chew up** mâchonner.

chicken ['tʃikin] n poulet m, (*very young*) poussin m. **chicken pox** n varicelle f. v **chicken out** (*slang*) se dégonfler.

chicory ['tʃikəri] n chicorée f.

chief [tʃiːf] n chef m. adj principal; en chef. **chiefly** adv principalement; surtout.

chilblain ['tʃilblein] n engelure f.

child [tʃaild] n pl **children** enfant. **childbirth** n accouchement m. **childhood** n enfance f. **childish** adj puéril. **childless** adj sans enfants.

chill [tʃil] n fraîcheur f, froid m; (*fear*) frisson m; (*med*) refroidissement m. v (*wine*) rafraîchir; (*champagne*) frapper. **chilled to the bone** transi jusqu'aux os. **chilly** adj froid.

chilli ['tʃili] n piment m.

chime [tʃaim] v carillonner; (*hours*) sonner. n carillon m.

chimney ['tʃimni] n cheminée f. **chimney pot** tuyau de cheminée m. **chimney sweep** ramoneur m.

chimpanzee [tʃimpənˈziː] n chimpanzé m.

chin [tʃin] n menton m.

china ['tʃainə] n porcelaine f.

China ['tʃainə] n Chine f. **Chinese** nm, adj chinois. **the Chinese** les Chinois m pl.

chink[1] [tʃiŋk] n (*slit*) fente f; (*door*) entrebâillement m.

chink[2] [tʃiŋk] n (*sound*) tintement m. v (faire) tinter.

chip [tʃip] n (*fragment*) éclat m; (*in cup, etc.*) ébréchure f; (*poker, etc.*) jeton m. **chipboard** n bois aggloméré m. **chips** pl n (*cookery*) frites f pl. v (s')ébrécher. **chip in** (*interrupt*) dire son mot; (*money*) contribuer.

chiropody [kiˈropədi] n soins du pied m pl. **chiropodist** n pédicure m, f.

chirp [tʃəːp] v pépier. n pépiement m. **chirpy** adj gai.

chisel ['tʃizl] n ciseau m. v ciseler.

chivalry ['ʃivəlri] n chevalerie f. **chivalrous** adj chevaleresque.

chive [tʃaiv] n ciboulette f.

chlorine ['klɔːriːn] n chlore m. **chlorinate** v javelliser.

chloroform ['klɔrəfɔːm] n chloroforme m. v chloroformer.

chlorophyll ['klɔrəfil] n chlorophylle f.

chocolate ['tʃokələt] n chocolat m.

choice [tʃois] n choix m. adj (*fruit*) de choix *invar*; (*word*) bien choisi.

choir ['kwaiə] n chœur m; chorale f. **choirboy** n jeune choriste m. **choir-stall** n stalle f.

choke [tʃouk] v (s')étrangler, étouffer; (*block*) boucher. n (*mot*) starter m.

cholera ['kolərə] n choléra m.

*choose** [tʃuːz] v choisir.

chop[1] [tʃop] n (*meat*) côtelette f; (*blow*) coup m. v trancher; (*wood*) couper à la hache; (*vegetables, etc.*) hacher. **chop down** (*tree*) abattre. **chopper** n hachoir m.

chop[2] [tʃop] v **chop and change** changer constamment. **chop logic** ergoter. **choppy** adj (*sea*) un peu agité.

chops [tʃops] pl n (*jaws*) mâchoires f pl. **lick one's chops** se lécher les babines.

chopstick ['tʃopstik] n baguette f.

chord [kɔːd] n (*anat*) corde f; (*music*) accord m.

chore [tʃɔɪ] *n* (*unpleasant*) corvée *f.*
chores *pl n* (*household*) travaux du
ménage *m pl.*
choreography [kɔriˈɔgrɔfi] *n* chorégraphie
f. **choreographer** *n* chorégraphe *m, f.*
chorus [ˈkɔɪrɔs] *n* refrain *m*; (*singers*)
chœur *m*; (*dancers*) troupe *f.* **choral** *adj*
choral.
chose [tʃouz] *V* **choose.**
chosen [ˈtʃouzn] *V* **choose.**
christen [ˈkrisn] *v* baptiser; (*nickname*)
surnommer. **christening** *n* baptême *m.*
Christian [ˈkristʃən] *n, adj* chrétien,
-enne. **Christian name** prénom *m.* **Christianity** *n* christianisme *m.*
Christmas [ˈkrisməs] *n* Noël *m.* **Christmas
Day** le jour de Noël *m.* **Christmas Eve** la
veille de Noël *f.*
chromatic [krɔˈmatik] *adj* chromatique.
chrome [kroum] *n* chrome *m.*
chromium [ˈkroumiəm] *n* chrome *m.*
chromium-plated *adj* chromé. **chromium-
plating** *n* chromage *m.*
chromosome [ˈkroumɔsoum] *n* chromosome *m.*
chronic [ˈkronik] *adj* chronique; (*coll*)
atroce.
chronicle [ˈkronikl] *n* chronique *f.*
chronological [kronɔˈlodʒikɔl] *adj* chronologique. **in chronological order** par
ordre chronologique.
chrysalis [ˈkrisɔlis] *n* chrysalide *f.*
chrysanthemum [kriˈsanθəməm] *n*
chrysanthème *m.*
chubby [ˈtʃʌbi] *adj* potelé.
chuck [tʃʌk] (*coll*) *v* (*throw*) lancer; (*give
up*) laisser tomber. **chuck out** (*thing*) balancer; (*person*) vider.
chuckle [ˈtʃʌkl] *v* glousser. *n* petit rire *m.*
chunk [tʃʌŋk] *n* gros morceau *m*; (*bread*)
quignon *m.*
church [tʃɔɪtʃ] *n* église *f.* **churchgoer** *n*
pratiquant, -e *m, f.* **church hall** salle
paroissiale *f.* **churchyard** *n* cimetière *m.*
churn [tʃɔɪn] *n* baratte *f.* *v* baratter;
(*water*) (faire) bouillonner. **churn out**
(*coll: books, etc.*) pondre en série.
chute [ʃuɪt] *n* glissière *f.*
cider [ˈsaidɔ] *n* cidre *m.*
cigar [siˈgaɪ] *n* cigare *m.*
cigarette [sigɔˈret] *n* cigarette *f.* **cigarette
lighter** briquet *m.*
cinder [ˈsindɔ] *n* cendre *f.* **burnt to a cinder** réduit en cendres.
cine camera [ˈsini] *n* caméra *f.*

cinema [ˈsinɔmɔ] *n* cinéma *m.*
cinnamon [ˈsinɔmən] *n* cannelle *f.*
circle [ˈsɔɪkl] *n* cercle *m*; (*theatre*) balcon
m. *v* (*surround*) encercler; (*move round*)
tourner autour de; (*aircraft*) tourner. **circular** *nf, adj* circulaire.
circuit [ˈsɔɪkit] *n* tour *m*; (*law*) tournée *f*;
(*elec, sport*) circuit *m.* **circuitous** *adj* indirect.
circulate [ˈsɔɪkjuleit] *v* (faire) circuler. **circulation** *n* circulation *f*; (*newspaper*)
tirage *m.*
circumcise [ˈsɔɪkɔmsaiz] *v* circoncire. **circumcision** *n* circoncision *f.*
circumference [sɔɪˈkʌmfɔrɔns] *n* circonférence *f.*
circumflex [ˈsɔɪkɔmfleks] *adj* circonflexe.
n accent circonflexe *m.*
circumscribe [ˈsɔɪkɔmskraib] *v* circonscrire.
circumspect [ˈsɔɪkɔmspekt] *adj* circonspect.
circumstance [ˈsɔɪkɔmstans] *n* circonstance *f.* **circumstances** *pl n* (*financial*)
moyens *m pl.* **under no circumstances** en
aucun cas. **under the circumstances** vu
l'état des choses.
circus [ˈsɔɪkɔs] *n* cirque *m.*
cistern [ˈsistɔn] *n* citerne *f*; (*toilet*) chasse
d'eau *f.*
cite [sait] *v* citer. **citation** *n* citation *f.*
citizen [ˈsitizn] *n* (*town*) habitant, -e *m, f*;
(*state*) citoyen, -enne *m, f.* **citizenship** *n*
citoyenneté *f.*
citrus [ˈsitrɔs] *n* citrus *m pl.* **citrus fruits**
agrumes *m pl.* **citric acid** acide citrique
m.
city [ˈsiti] *n* ville *f,* cité *f.* **city centre** centre ville *m.*
civic [ˈsivik] *adj* (*authorities*) municipal;
(*rights*) civique. **civic centre** centre
administratif *m.*
civil [ˈsivl] *adj* civil; poli. **civil engineering**
travaux publics *m pl.* **civil rights** droits
civiques *m pl.* **civil servant** fonctionnaire
m, f. **civil service** administration *f.* **civil
war** guerre civile *f.*
civilian [sɔˈviljɔn] *n, adj* civil, -e.
civilization [ˌsiviliˈzeiʃɔn] *n* civilisation *f.*
civilize *v* civiliser.
clad [klad] *adj* habillé.
claim [kleim] *v* (*right, prize, etc.*) revendiquer; (*damages*) réclamer; (*profess*)
déclarer. *n* revendication *f*; réclamation

f; (*insurance*) déclaration de sinistre *f*; (*right*) droit *m*.

clairvoyant [kleə'voiənt] *n* voyant, -e *m, f*.

clam [klam] *n* praire *f*.

clamber ['klambə] *v* grimper en rampant.

clammy ['klami] *adj* moite.

clamour ['klamə] *n* clameur *f*. *v* vociférer.

clamp [klamp] *n* pince *f*, crampon *m*. *v* serrer, cramponner. **clamp down on** supprimer; restreindre.

clan [klan] *n* clan *m*.

clandestine [klan'destin] *adj* clandestin.

clang [klaŋ] *n* bruit métallique *m*. *v* résonner. **clanger** *n* (*coll*) gaffe *f*.

clap [klap] *v* applaudir. **clap one's hands** battre des mains. *n* (*noise*) claquement *m*; (*thunder*) coup *m*; (*applause*) applaudissements *n pl*.

claret ['klarət] *n* bordeaux *m*.

clarify ['klarəfai] *v* (se) clarifier; (*situation*) (s')éclaircir.

clarinet [klarə'net] *n* clarinette *f*.

clarity ['klarəti] *n* clarté *f*.

clash [klaʃ] *n* (*bang*) s'entrechoquer; (*conflict*) se heurter; (*colours*) jurer. *n* (*dispute*) accrochage *m*; (*personalities*) incompatibilité *f*; (*noise*) choc *m*.

clasp [klaːsp] *v* serrer. *n* (*fastening*) fermoir *m*; (*grip*) étreinte *f*.

class [klaːs] *n* classe *f*; catégorie *f*; (*school*) cours *m*. **class-room** *n* salle de classe *f*. *v* classer.

classic ['klasik] *nm, adj* classique. **classical** *adj* classique. **classics** *n* humanités *f pl*.

classify ['klasifai] *v* classifier. **classification** *n* classification *f*. **classified** *adj* classifié; secret, -ète. **classified advertisement** petite annonce *f*.

clatter ['klatə] *n* cliquetis *m*. *v* cliqueter.

clause [kloːz] *n* (*law*) clause *f*; (*gramm*) proposition *f*.

claustrophobia [kloːstrə'foubiə] *n* claustrophobie *f*. **claustrophobe** *n* claustrophobe *m, f*. **claustrophobic** *adj* claustrophobique.

claw [kloː] *n* griffe *f*; (*lobster*) pince *f*. *v* griffer.

clay [klei] *n* argile *f*.

clean [kliːn] *adj* propre; net, nette. *adv* entièrement. **clean-shaven** *adj* glabre. *v* nettoyer. **cleaner** *n* (*charwoman*) femme de ménage *f*. **cleaner's** *n* teinturerie *f*. **cleaning** *n* nettoyage *m*; (*housework*)

ménage. **cleanliness** *or* **cleanness** *n* propreté *f*.

cleanse [klenz] *v* nettoyer; purifier. **cleanser** *n* (*cosmetic*) démaquillant *m*.

clear [kliə] *adj* clair; transparent; distinct; (*without obstacles*) libre. *v* (s')éclaircir; clarifier; (*remove obstacles*) débarrasser; (*law*) disculper; (*jump*) franchir. **clearance** *n* (*space*) espace (*m*) libre; (*customs*) dédouanement *m*; (*aero*) autorisation *f*. **clearing** *n* clairière *f*. **clearness** *n* clarté *f*.

clef [klef] *n* clef *f*.

clench [klentʃ] *v* empoigner. **clench one's fists/teeth** serrer les poings/dents.

clergy ['kləːdʒi] *n* clergé *m*. **clergyman** *n* (*Protestant*) pasteur *m*; (*Catholic*) prêtre *m*.

clerical ['klerikəl] *adj* (*office*) d'employé, de bureau; (*rel*) clérical.

clerk [klaːk] *n* employé, -e *m, f*.

clever ['klevə] *adj* intelligent; (*skilful*) habile; (*smart*) astucieux. **cleverness** *n* intelligence *f*; habileté *f*; astuce *f*.

cliché ['kliːʃei] *n* cliché *m*.

click [klik] *n* déclic *m*. *v* claquer, faire un déclic.

client ['klaiənt] *n* client, -e *m, f*. **clientele** *n* clientèle *f*.

cliff [klif] *n* falaise *f*.

climate ['klaimət] *n* climat *m*. **climatic** *adj* climatique.

climax ['klaimaks] *n* apogée *m*, point culminant *m*.

climb [klaim] *v* grimper, monter; (*mountain*) gravir. *n* montée *f*. **climbing** *n* (*sport*) alpinisme *m*.

*cling [kliŋ] *v* se cramponner; (*stick*) (se) coller.

clinic ['klinik] *n* clinique *f*. **clinical** *adj* (*med*) clinique; (*attitude*) objectif.

clink [kliŋk] *v* (faire) tinter. *n* tintement *m*.

clip[1] [klip] *v* (*hedge*) tailler; (*hair*) couper; (*dog*) tondre. *n* (*coll: blow*) taloche *f*; (*cinema*) extrait *m*. **clipping** *n* (*newspaper*) coupure de presse *f*.

clip[2] [klip] *n* attache *f*. *v* attacher.

clitoris ['klitəris] *n* clitoris *m*.

cloak [klouk] *n* (*clothing*) cape *f*; (*mask*) manteau *m*. **cloakroom** *n* vestiaire *m*. *v* masquer.

clock [klok] *n* (*large*) horloge *f*; (*small*) pendule *f*. **against the clock** contre la montre. **clock-tower** *n* clocher *m*. **clock-**

wise *adj, adv* dans le sens des aiguilles d'une montre. **clockwork** *adj* mécanique. **like clockwork** comme sur des roulettes.

clog [klog] *n* sabot *m. v* boucher.

cloister ['kloistə] *n* cloître *m. v* cloîtrer.

close[1] [klous] *adj* (*near*) proche; (*friend*) intime; (*contest, etc.*) serré; (*atmosphere*) étouffant. *adv* de près. **close by** tout près. **close-fitting** *adj* ajusté. **close-up** *n* gros plan *m. n* cul-de-sac *m.* **closely** *adv* de près; attentivement.

close[2] [klouz] *n* (*end*) fin *f. v* (se) fermer; (*block*) boucher; (*finish*) (se) terminer. **close in** approcher; (*enclose*) clôturer. **close up** se rapprocher. **closing** *or* **closure** *n* fermeture *f.*

closet ['klozit] *n* placard *m*; (*room*) cabinet *m. v* enfermer.

clot [klot] *n* caillot *m. v* (se) coaguler.

cloth [kloθ] *n* (*fabric*) tissu *m*; (*linen*) toile *f*; (*cleaning*) chiffon *m.*

clothe [klouð] *v* vêtir, habiller. **clothes** *pl n* vêtements *m pl.* **clothes brush** brosse à habits *f.* **clothes horse** séchoir *m.* **clothes line** corde à linge *f.* **clothes peg** pince à linge *f.* **clothing** *n* vêtements *m pl.*

cloud [klaud] *n* nuage *m.* **cloudburst** *n* déluge de pluie *m. v* (*mind*) (s')obscurcir; (*face*) (s')assombrir. **cloud over** se couvrir de nuages. **cloudless** *adj* sans nuages. **cloudy** *adj* nuageux, couvert; (*liquid*) trouble.

clove[1] [klouv] *n* (*spice*) clou de girofle *m.* **oil of cloves** essence de girofle *f.*

clove[2] [klouv] *n* (*of garlic*) gousse *f.*

clover ['klouvə] *n* trèfle *m.*

clown [klaun] *n* clown *m.*

club [klʌb] *n* (*weapon*) massue *f*; (*cards*) trèfle; (*society*) club *m.* **club-foot** *n* pied-bot *m.* **clubhouse** *n* pavillon *m. v* matraquer. **club together** se cotiser.

clue [kluː] *n* indice *m*; (*crosswords*) définition *f.*

clump [klʌmp] *n* massif *m*; (*trees*) bouquet *m*; (*grass, flowers*) touffe *f.*

clumsy ['klʌmzi] *adj* maladroit, gauche. **clumsiness** *n* maladresse *f*, gaucherie *f.*

clung [klʌŋ] *V* **cling.**

cluster ['klʌstə] *n* (*flowers, fruit*) grappe *f*; groupe *m. v* se grouper.

clutch [klʌtʃ] *n* (*grip*) étreinte *f*; (*mot*) embrayage *m. v* empoigner, se cramponner à.

clutter ['klʌtə] *n* désordre *m. v* encombrer.

coach [koutʃ] *n* (*bus*) car *m*; (*rail*) voiture *f*; (*sport*) entraîneur *m*; (*school*) répétiteur, -trice *m, f. v* entraîner; (*for exam*) préparer. **coaching** *n* répétitions *f pl*; entraînement *m.*

coagulate [kou'agjuleit] *v* (se) coaguler. **coagulation** *n* coagulation *f.*

coal [koul] *n* charbon *m*, houille *f.* **coalman** *n* charbonnier *m.* **coalmine** *n* houillère *f.* **coalminer** *n* mineur *m.* **coalmining** *n* charbonnage *m.*

coalition [kouə'liʃən] *n* coalition *f.*

coarse [kɔːs] *adj* grossier; (*salt, etc.*) gros, grosse. **coarseness** *n* rudesse *f.*

coast [koust] *n* côte *f.* **coastguard** *n* garde maritime *m.* **coastline** *n* littoral *m.* **the coast is clear** la voie est libre. *v* (*mot*) descendre en roue libre. **coastal** *adj* côtier. **coaster** *n* (*mat*) dessous de verre *m.*

coat [kout] *n* manteau *m*; (*animal*) pelage *m*, poil *m*; (*horse*) robe *f*; (*paint, etc.*) couche *f.* **coat hanger** cintre *m. v* couvrir; (*cookery*) enrober. **coating** *n* couche *f.*

coax [kouks] *v* cajoler.

cobbler ['koblə] *n* cordonnier *m.*

cobra ['koubrə] *n* cobra *m.*

cobweb ['kobweb] *n* toile d'araignée *f.*

cocaine [kə'kein] *n* cocaïne *f.*

cock [kok] *n* coq *m*; mâle *m*; (*vulgar: penis*) bitte *f. v* (*gun*) armer; (*ears*) dresser.

cockle ['kokl] *n* coque *f.*

cockpit ['kokpit] *n* poste de pilotage *m.*

cockroach ['kokroutʃ] *n* blatte *f.*

cocktail ['kokteil] *n* cocktail *m.*

cocky ['koki] *adj* suffisant.

cocoa ['koukou] *n* cacao *m.*

coconut ['koukənʌt] *n* noix de coco *f.* **coconut palm** cocotier *m.*

cocoon [kə'kuːn] *n* cocon *m.*

cod [kod] *n* morue *f.* **cod-liver oil** huile de foie de morue *f.*

code [koud] *n* code *m. v* chiffrer.

codeine ['koudiːn] *n* codéine *f.*

coeducation [kouedju'keiʃən] *n* éducation mixte *f.* **coeducational** *adj* mixte.

coerce [kou'əːs] *v* contraindre. **coercion** *n* contrainte *f.* **coercive** *adj* coercitif.

coexist [kouig'zist] *v* coexister.

coffee ['kofi] *n* café *m.* **black/white coffee** café noir/au lait *m.* **coffee bar** café *m.* **coffee bean** grain de café *m.* **coffee pot** cafetière *f.* **coffee table** table basse *f.*

coffin ['kofin] *n* cercueil *m*.

cog [kog] *n* dent *f*.

cognac ['konjak] *n* cognac *m*.

cohabit [kou'habit] *v* cohabiter. **cohabitation** *n* cohabitation *f*.

coherent [kou'hiərənt] *adj* cohérent; (*account, etc.*) facile à suivre. **coherence** *n* cohérence *f*. **coherently** *adj* avec cohérence.

coil [koil] *n* rouleau *m*; (*elec*) bobine *f*; (*med*) stérilet *m*. *v* (s')enrouler; (*snake*) se lover.

coin [koin] *n* pièce (de monnaie) *f*. *v* (*money*) frapper; (*word, etc.*) inventer.

coincide [kouin'said] *v* coïncider. **coincidence** *n* coïncidence *f*. **coincidental** *adj* de coïncidence.

colander ['koləndə] *n* passoire *f*.

cold [kould] *adj* froid. **be cold** (*person*) avoir froid; (*weather*) faire froid. **cold-blooded** *adj* (*animal*) à sang froid; (*person*) insensible. **cold-hearted** *adj* impitoyable. **cold sore** *n* herpès *m*. *n* froid *m*; (*med*) rhume *m*. **have a cold** être enrhumé.

colic ['kolik] *n* colique *f*.

collaborate [kə'labəreit] *v* collaborer. **collaboration** *n* collaboration *f*. **collaborator** *n* collaborateur, -trice *m, f*.

collapse [ke'laps] *v* s'écrouler, s'éffondrer. *n* éffondrement *m*, écroulement *m*. **collapsible** *adj* pliant.

collar ['kolə] *n* (*on garment*) col *m*; (*dog, etc.*) collier *m*. **collarbone** *n* clavicule *f*.

collate [ko'leit] *v* collationner. **collation** *n* collation *f*.

colleague ['koliːg] *n* collègue *m, f*.

collect [kə'lekt] *v* (s')amasser; (se) rassembler; (*as hobby*) collectionner; (*pick up*) ramasser; (*gather*) recueillir; (*call for*) passer prendre. *adj, adv* (*US: phone*) en P.C.V. **collection** *n* rassemblement *m*; (*money*) quête *f*; (*stamps, etc.*) collection *f*; (*mail*) levée *f*. **collective** *adj* collectif. **collector** *n* (*stamps, etc.*) collectionneur, -euse *m, f*.

college ['kolidʒ] *n* collège *m*; (*professional*) école *f*.

collide [kə'laid] *v* se heurter. **collision** *n* collision *f*.

colloquial [kə'loukwiəl] *adj* familier. **colloquialism** *n* expression familière *f*.

colon ['koulon] *n* (*punctuation*) deux points *m invar*.

colonel ['kəːnl] *n* colonel *m*.

colony ['koləni] *n* colonie *f*. **colonial** *adj* colonial. **colonization** *n* colonisation *f*. **colonize** *v* coloniser.

colossal [kə'losəl] *adj* colossal.

colour ['kʌlə] *n* couleur *f*. **colour bar** discrimination raciale *f*. **colour-blind** *adj* daltonien. **colour scheme** combinaison de couleurs *f*. **colour television** (*set*) téléviseur couleur *m*. *v* colorer; (*picture*) colorier. **coloured** *adj* coloré; (*picture*) en couleur; (*person*) de couleur. **colourful** *adj* coloré. **colouring** *n* (*complexion*) teint *m*; coloration *f*. **colourless** *adj* incolore.

colt [koult] *n* poulain *m*.

column ['koləm] *n* colonne *f*. **columnist** *n* journaliste *m, f*.

coma ['koumə] *n* coma *m*. **in a coma** dans le coma.

comb [koum] *n* peigne *m*; (*bird*) crête *f*. *v* (*hair*) peigner; (*search*) fouiller.

combat ['kombat] *n* combat *m*. *v* combattre. **combatant** *n* combattant, -e *m, f*.

combine [kəm'bain; *n* 'kombain] *v* combiner; s'unir; association *f*. **combination** *n* combinaison *f*. **combination lock** serrure à combinaison *f*.

combustion [kəm'bastʃən] *n* combustion *f*. **combustible** *adj* combustible.

*****come** [kʌm] *n* venir; arriver. **come across** (*find*) tomber sur. **come back** revenir. **come-back** *n* rentrée *f*. **come down** descendre. **come-down** *n* déchéance *f*. **come in** entrer. **come off** se détacher; (*succeed*) réussir. **come out** sortir. **come to** (*from faint*) revenir à soi; (*total*) monter à.

comedy ['komədi] *n* comédie *f*. **comedian** *n* comique *m*.

comet ['komit] *n* comète *f*.

comfort ['kʌmfət] *n* confort *m*; consolation *f*. *v* consoler; (*soothe*) soulager. **comfortable** *adj* confortable; (*person*) à l'aise.

comic ['komik] *adj* comique. *n* (*person*) comique *m*; (*magazine*) comic *m*. **comical** *adj* drôle.

comma ['komə] *n* virgule *f*.

command [kə'maind] *v* commander ordonner; (*respect*) exiger. *n* commandement *m*; ordre *m*; (*mastery*) maîtrise *f*. **commander** *n* chef *m*; (*mil*) commandant *m*. **commandment** *n* commandement *m*.

commandeer [komən'diə] *v* réquisitionner.

commando [kə'maɪndou] *n* commando *m*.
commemorate [kə'meməreit] *v* commémorer. **commemoration** *n* commémoration *f*. **commemorative** *adj* commémoratif.
commence [kə'mens] *v* commencer. **commencement** *n* commencement *m*.
commend [kə'mend] *v* (*praise*) louer; recommander; (*entrust*) confier. **commendable** *adj* louable; recommandable. **commendation** *n* louange *f*; recommandation *f*.
comment ['koment] *n* observation *f*, commentaire *m*. *v* remarquer. **comment on** commenter, faire des remarques sur. **commentary** *n* commentaire *m*; (*sport*) reportage *m*. **commentator** *n* reporter *m*.
commerce ['koməɪs] *n* commerce *m*. **commercial** *adj* commercial; de commerce. **commercialize** *v* commercialiser.
commiserate [kə'mizəreit] *v* (*illness*) témoigner de la sympathie (à); (*bad luck*) s'apitoyer sur le sort (de). **commiseration** *n* commisération *f*.
commission [kə'miʃən] *n* commission *f*; ordres *m pl*; (*mil*) brevet *m*. *v* (*order*) commander; déléguer; (*mil*) nommer à un commandement. **commissioner** *n* commissaire *m*; (*police*) préfet *m*.
commit [kə'mit] *v* commettre; (*entrust*) confier. **commit oneself** s'engager. **commit suicide** se suicider. **commitment** *n* responsabilité *f*; (*comm*) engagement *m*.
committee [kə'miti] *n* commission *f*, comité *m*.
commodity [kə'modəti] *n* produit *m*, marchandise *f*.
common ['komən] *adj* commun; ordinaire; vulgaire. **Common Market** Marché Commun *m*. **commonplace** *adj* banal. **common-room** *n* salle commune *f*. **common sense** bon sens. **commonwealth** *n* république *f*; confédération *f*; (*British*) Commonwealth *m*.
commotion [kə'mouʃən] *n* commotion *f*; (*noise*) agitation *f*.
communal ['komjunəl] *adj* (*shared*) commun; (*of community*) communautaire.
commune¹ [kə'mjuɪn] *v* communier; converser intimement.
commune² ['komjuɪn] *n* communauté *f*; (*admin*) commune *f*.
communicate [kə'mjuɪnikeit] *v* communiquer. **communication** *n* communication *f*.

communication cord sonnette d'alarme *f*.
communicative *adj* communicatif, bavard.
communion [kə'mjuɪnjən] *n* communion *f*.
communism ['komjunizəm] *n* communisme *m*. **communist** *n*(*m+f*). *adj* communiste.
community [kə'mjuɪnəti] *n* communauté *f*; colonie *f*. **community centre** foyer socio-éducatif *m*.
commute [kə'mjuɪt] *n* (*travel*) faire la navette; échanger; (*law*) commuer. **commuter** *n* banlieusard, -e *m, f*.
compact¹ [kəm'pakt; *n* 'kompakt] *adj* compact; concis. *v* condenser. *n* (*powder*) poudrier *m*.
compact² ['kompakt] *n* (*agreement*) contrat *m*.
companion [kəm'panjən] *n* compagnon *m*, compagne *f*. **companionship** *n* camaraderie *f*.
company ['kʌmpəni] *n* compagnie *f*; (*theatre*) troupe *f*.
compare [kəm'peə] *v* (se) comparer. **comparable** *adj* comparable. **comparative** *adj* comparatif; relatif. **comparison** *n* comparaison *f*.
compartment [kəm'paɪtmənt] *n* compartiment *m*.
compass ['kʌmpəs] *n* boussole *f*; (*naut*) compas *m*; (*extent*) étendue *f*. **compasses** *pl n* (*math*) compas *m sing*.
compassion [kəm'paʃən] *n* compassion *f*. **compassionate** *adj* compatissant; (*leave, etc.*) pour raisons de famille.
compatible [kəm'patəbl] *adj* compatible. **compatibility** *n* compatibilité *f*.
compel [kəm'pel] *v* contraindre, forcer. **compelling** *adj* irrésistible.
compensate ['kompənseit] *v* compenser; (*money*) dédommager. **compensation** *n* compensation *f*.
compete [kəm'piɪt] *v* concourir; (*comm*) faire concurrence. **competition** *n* compétition *f*; (*contest*) concours *m*; (*rivalry*) concurrence *f*. **competitive** *adj* (*price*) compétitif; (*selection*) par concours. **competitor** *n* concurrent, -e *m, f*.
competent ['kompətənt] *adj* compétent; suffisant. **competence** *n* compétence *f*.
compile [kəm'pail] *v* compiler; (*dictionary*) composer; (*list*) dresser. **compilation** *n* compilation *f*.

complacent [kəm'pleisnt] *adj* content de
soi. **complacency** *n* contentement de soi
m.

complain [kəm'plein] *v* se plaindre. **complaint** *n* plainte *f*; (*comm*) réclamation *f*;
(*med*) maladie *f*.

complement ['kompləmənt] *n* complément *m.* *v* compléter. **complementary** *adj*
complémentaire.

complete [kəm'pliːt] *adj* complet, -ète;
(*finished*) achevé. *v* compléter; achever.
completion *n* achèvement *m.*

complex ['kompleks] *nm, adj* complexe.
complexity *n* complexité *f.*

complexion [kəm'plekʃən] *n* teint *m*;
aspect *m.*

complicate ['komplikeit] *v* compliquer.
complication *n* complication *f.*

complicity [kəm'plisəti] *n* complicité *f.*

compliment ['kompləmənt] *n* compliment
m. *v* complimenter (de). **complimentary**
adj flatteur, -euse; (*free*) gracieux. **complimentary copy** exemplaire offert en
hommage *m.* **complimentary ticket** billet
de faveur *m.*

comply [kəm'plai] *n* se soumettre (à);
(*wishes*) se conformer (à); (*request*)
accéder (à). **compliant** *adj* accommodant.
in compliance with conformément à.

component [kəm'pounənt] *n* (*tech*) pièce
f; (*chem*) composant *m.* *adj* constituent.

compose [kəm'pouz] *v* composer. **composed** *adj* calme. **composer** *n* compositeur, -trice *m, f.* **composition** *n* composition *f*; (*essay*) rédaction *f.*

compost ['kompost] *n* compost *m.* **compost heap** tas de compost *m.*

composure [kəm'pouʒə] *n* sang-froid *m.*

compound¹ ['kompaund; *v* kəm'paund] *n*
composé *m. adj* composé; (*number*) complexe; (*fracture*) compliqué. *v* composer;
(*make worse*) aggraver.

compound² ['kompaund] *n* enclos *m.*

comprehend [kompri'hend] *v* comprendre. **comprehensible** *adj* compréhensible.
comprehension *n* compréhension *f.* **comprehensive** *adj* compréhensif; détaillé;
(*insurance*) tous-risques. **comprehensive
school** centre d'études secondaires *m.*

compress [kəm'pres; *n* 'kompres] *v* (se)
comprimer; (se) condenser. *n* compresse
f. **compression** *n* compression *f*; concentration *f.*

comprise [kəm'praiz] *v* comprendre.

compromise ['komprəmaiz] *v* transiger;
(*risk*) compromettre. *n* compromis *m.*

compulsion [kəm'pʌlʃən] *n* contrainte *f.*
compulsive *adj* (*gambler, etc.*) invétéré;
(*psych*) compulsif; (*demand*) coercitif.
compulsory *adj* obligatoire.

compunction [kəm'pʌŋkʃən] *n* remords
m.

computer [kəm'pjuːtə] *n* ordinateur *m.*
computer science informatique *f.* **com-
puterization** *n* automatisation électronique *f.* **computerize** *v* informatiser.

comrade ['komrid] *n* camarade *m, f.* **com-
radeship** *n* camaraderie *f.*

concave [kon'keiv] *adj* concave.

conceal [kən'siːl] *v* dissimuler, cacher.
concealment *n* dissimulation *f.*

concede [kən'siːd] *v* concéder.

conceit [kən'siːt] *n* vanité *f.* **conceited** *adj*
vaniteux.

conceive [kən'siːv] *v* concevoir; (*understand*) comprendre. **conceivable** *adj* con-
cevable.

concentrate ['konsəntreit] *v* (se) concentrer. *n* (*chem*) concentré *m.* **concentration**
n concentration *f.* **concentration camp**
camp de concentration *m.*

concentric [kon'sentrik] *adj* concentrique.

concept ['konsept] *n* concept *m.*
conception [kən'sepʃən] *n* conception *f.*

concern [kən'səɪn] *v* concerner; regarder.
n (*business*) affaire *f*; (*comm*) entreprise
f; (*anxiety*) inquiétude *f.* **concerned** *adj*
inquiet, -ète; affecté; en question. **concerning** *prep* en ce qui concerne.

concert ['konsət; *v* kən'səɪt] *n* concert *m.*
v concerter.

concertina [konsə'tiːnə] *n* concertina *m.*

concerto [kən'tʃəɪtou] *n* concerto *m.*

concession [kən'seʃən] *n* concession *f*;
(*comm*) réduction *f.* **concessionary** *adj*
concessionnaire; (*cheap*) à prix réduit.

conciliate [kən'silieit] *v* (se) concilier;
apaiser. **conciliation** *n* conciliation *f*;
apaisement *m.* **conciliatory** *adj* con-
ciliant.

concise [kən'sais] *adj* concis.

conclude [kən'kluːd] *v* conclure. **conclud-
ing** *adj* final. **conclusion** *n* conclusion *f.*
conclusive *adj* définitif.

concoct [kən'kokt] *v* (*cookery*) confectionner; (*excuse*) fabriquer. **concoction** *n*
confection *f*; (*excuse*) combinaison *f.*

concrete ['koŋkriːt] *adj* (*real*) concret,

-ète. *n* béton *m*. **concrete mixer** bétonnière *f*. *v* bétonner.

concur [kən'kəː] *v* (*agree*) être d'accord; coïncider. **concurrent** *adj* simultané.

concussion [kən'kʌʃən] *n* (*med*) commotion cérébrale *f*. *v* **be concussed** être commotionné.

condemn [kən'dem] *v* condamner. **condemnation** *n* condamnation *f*.

condense [kən'dens] *v* (se) condenser. **condensation** *n* condensation *f*. **condenser** *n* (*elec*) condensateur *m*.

condescend [kondi'send] *v* condescendre, daigner. **condescension** *n* condescendance *f*.

condition [kən'diʃən] *n* condition *f*; (*state*) état *m*. *v* conditionner. **conditional** *nm*, *adj* conditionnel. **be conditional on** dépendre de.

condolences [kən'doulənsiz] *pl n* condoléances *f pl*.

condom ['kondom] *n* préservatif *m*.

condone [kən'doun] *v* pardonner; fermer les yeux sur.

conducive [kən'djuːsiv] *adj* contribuant. **be conducive to** conduire à.

conduct ['kondʌkt; *v* kən'dʌkt] *n* conduite *f*. *v* diriger; (*phys*) conduire. **conduct oneself** se conduire. **conducted tour** excursion accompagnée *f*; visite guidée *f*. **conduction** *n* conduction *f*.

conductor [kən'dʌktə] *n* (*music*) chef d'orchestre *m*; (*bus*) receveur *m*; (*phys*) conducteur *m*. **conductress** *n* (*bus*) receveuse *f*.

cone [koun] *n* cône *m*; (*ice cream*) cornet *m*.

confectioner [kən'fekʃənə] *n* (*cakes*) pâtissier, -ère *m, f*; (*sweets*) confiseur, -euse *m, f*. **confectionery** *n* confiserie *f*; pâtisserie *f*.

confederate [kən'fedərət] *n, adj* confédéré, -e. *v* (se) confédérer. **confederation** *n* confédération *f*.

confer [kən'fəː] *v* conférer. **conference** *n* conférence *f*.

confess [kən'fes] *v* confesser, avouer. **confession** *n* confession *f*; aveu *m*.

confetti [kən'feti] *n* confettis *m pl*.

confide [kən'faid] *v* confier; avouer en confidence. **confide in** (*tell*) se confier à; (*trust*) se fier à. **confidence** *n* (*trust*) confiance *f*; (*self-assurance*) assurance *f*; (*secret*) confidence *f*. **confident** *adj*

assuré. **confidential** *adj* confidentiel. **confidently** *adv* avec confiance.

confine [kən'fain] *v* (*imprison*) enfermer; limiter. **be confined** (*childbirth*) accoucher. **confinement** *n* (*childbirth*) couches *f pl*; emprisonnement *m*.

confirm [kən'fəːm] *v* confirmer. **confirmation** *n* confirmation *f*. **confirmed** *adj* (*liar, etc.*) invétéré; (*bachelor*) endurci.

confiscate ['konfiskeit] *v* confisquer. **confiscation** *n* confiscation *f*.

conflict ['konflikt; *v* kən'flikt] *n* conflit *m*. *v* être en conflit; s'opposer. **conflicting** *adj* incompatible; contradictoire.

conform [kən'foːm] *v* (se) conformer. **conformity** *n* conformité *f*.

confound [kən'faund] *v* confondre.

confront [kən'frʌnt] *v* (*present*) confronter; (*face*) affronter. **confrontation** *n* confrontation *f*.

confuse [kən'fjuːz] *v* confondre; (*mix up*) embrouiller. **confused** *adj* confus; embrouillé. **confusing** *adj* déroutant. **confusion** *n* confusion *f*; désordre *m*.

congeal [kən'dʒiːl] *v* (se) figer; (*blood*) (se) coaguler; (*freeze*) (se) congeler.

congenial [kən'dʒiːniəl] *adj* sympathique.

congenital [kən'dʒenitl] *adj* congénital.

congested [kən'dʒestid] *adj* encombré; (*med*) congestionné. **congestion** *n* encombrement *m*; (*med*) congestion *f*.

conglomeration [kən,glomə'reiʃən] *n* agglomération *f*.

congratulate [kən'gratjuleit] *v* féliciter. **congratulations** *pl n* félicitations *f pl*.

congregate ['kongrigeit] *v* (se) rassembler. **congregation** *n* assemblée *f*.

congress ['kongres] *n* congrès *m*.

conical ['konikəl] *adj* conique.

conifer ['konifə] *n* conifère *m*. **coniferous** *adj* conifère.

conjecture [kən'dʒektʃə] *v* conjecturer. *n* conjecture *f*. **conjectural** *adj* conjectural.

conjugal ['kondʒugəl] *adj* conjugal.

conjugate ['kondʒugeit] *v* (se) conjuguer. **conjugation** *n* conjugaison *f*.

conjunction [kən'dʒʌŋkʃən] *n* conjunction *f*.

conjunctivitis [kən,dʒʌŋkti'vaitis] *n* conjonctivite *f*.

conjure ['kʌndʒə; (*appeal to*) kən'dʒuə] *v* (*magic*) faire apparaître; (*appeal to*) conjurer. **conjurer** *n* prestidigitateur, -trice *m, f*. **conjuring** *n* prestidigitation *f*. **conjuring trick** tour de passe-passe *m*.

connect [kə'nekt] v (se) relier. **be connected with** avoir des rapports avec. **connection** n jonction f; (elec) connexion f; relation f; (rail) correspondance f.
connoisseur [konə'sɔː] n connaisseur, -euse m, f.
connotation [konə'teiʃən] n connotation f.
conquer ['koŋkə] v conquérir; vaincre. **conqueror** n conquérant m. **conquest** n conquête f.
conscience ['konʃəns] n conscience f.
conscientious [konʃi'enʃəs] adj consciencieux. **conscientious objector** objecteur de conscience m.
conscious ['konʃəs] adj conscient. **consciousness** n (med) connaissance f; (awareness) conscience f.
conscript ['konskript] nm conscrit. **conscription** n conscription f.
consecrate ['konsikreit] v consacrer. **consecration** n consécration f.
consecutive [kən'sekjutiv] adj consécutif.
consensus [kən'sensəs] n consensus m.
consent [kən'sent] v consentir. n consentement m.
consequence ['konsikwəns] n conséquence f; importance f. **consequent** adj résultant. **consequently** adv par conséquent.
conservative [kən'sɜːvətiv] adj (pol) conservateur, -trice; modeste; traditionnel. n (pol) conservateur, -trice m, f.
conserve [kən'sɜːv] v conserver. **conservation** n préservation f; défense de l'environnement f. **conservatoire** n (music) conservatoire m. **conservatory** n (greenhouse) serre f.
consider [kən'sidə] v considérer. **considerable** adj considérable. **considerate** adj prévenant. **consideration** n considération f. **considering** prep étant donné.
consign [kən'sain] v (goods) expédier; (entrust) confier. **consignment** n envoi m.
consist [kən'sist] v consister (en). **consistency** n (of substance) consistance f; (of behaviour, etc.) cohérence f. **consistent** adj logique; compatible.
console [kən'soul] v consoler. **consolation** n consolation f.
consolidate [kən'solideit] v (se) consolider. **consolidation** n consolidation f.
consommé [kən'somei] n consommé m.
consonant ['konsənənt] n consonne f. adj en accord.

conspicuous [kən'spikjuəs] adj remarquable; en vue. **be conspicuous** attirer les regards; se faire remarquer.
conspire [kən'spaiə] v conspirer. **conspiracy** n conspiration f. **conspirator** n conspirateur, -trice m, f.
constable ['kʌnstəbl] n agent de police m. **constabulary** n police f.
constant ['konstənt] adj (unchanging) constant; incessant. n constante f. **constancy** n constance f.
constellation [konstə'leiʃən] n constellation f.
consternation [konstə'neiʃən] n consternation f.
constipation [konsti'peiʃən] n constipation f. **constipated** adj constipé.
constituent [kən'stitjuənt] adj constituant. n élément constitutif m; (pol) electeur, -trice m, f. **constituency** n (pol) circonscription électorale f.
constitute ['konstitjuːt] v constituer. **constitution** n constitution f. **constitutional** adj constitutionnel.
constraint [kən'streint] n contrainte f.
constrict [kən'strikt] v resserrer. **constriction** n resserrement m.
construct [kən'strʌkt] v construire. **construction** n construction f; interprétation f. **constructive** adj constructif.
consul ['konsəl] n consul m. **consular** adj consulaire. **consulate** n consulat m.
consult [kən'sʌlt] v consulter. **consultant** n consultant m; (med) spécialiste m. **consultation** n consultation f.
consume [kən'sjuːm] v consommer; (fire) consumer. **consumer** n consommateur, -trice m, f. **consumer goods** biens de consommation m pl. **consumption** n consommation f.
contact ['kontakt] n contact m; (acquaintance) connaissance f. **contact lenses** verres de contact m pl. v se mettre en contact avec.
contagious [kən'teidʒəs] adj contagieux.
contain [kən'tein] v contenir. **container** n (box, etc.) récipient m; (transport) conteneur m.
contaminate [kən'tamineit] v contaminer. **contamination** n contamination f.
contemplate ['kontəmpleit] v (consider) envisager; (look at) contempler. **contemplation** n contemplation f. **contemplative** adj contemplatif.

contemporary [kən'tempərəri] *n, adj* contemporain, -e.

contempt [kən'tempt] *n* mépris *m*. **contempt of court** outrage à la Cour *m*. **contemptible** *adj* méprisable. **contemptuous** *adj* dédaigneux.

contend [kən'tend] *v* (*fight*) combattre (contre), faire face à; (*claim*) soutenir. **contention** *n* dispute *f*.

content¹ ['kontent] *n* contenu *m*. **contents** *pl n* contenu *m sing*; (*book*) table des matières *f*.

content² [kən'tent] *adj also* **contented** content, satisfait. **be content with** se contenter de. **contentment** *n* contentement *m*, satisfaction *f*.

contest [kən'test; *n* 'kontest] *v* contester; (se) disputer. *n* (*fight*) combat *m*; (*sport*) lutte *f*; (*competition*) concours *m*. **contestant** *n* concurrent, -e *m, f*.

context ['kontekst] *n* contexte *m*.

continent ['kontinənt] *n* continent *m*. **continental** *adj* continental. **continental breakfast** petit déjeuner à la française *m*. **continental quilt** couette *f*.

contingency [kən'tindʒənsi] *n* éventualité *f*. **contingent** *adj* contingent.

continue [kən'tinjuː] *v* continuer; (*after pause*) reprendre. **continual** *adj* continuel. **continuation** *n* continuation *f*; reprise *f*; (*serial*) suite *f*. **continuity** *n* continuité *f*. **continuous** *adj* continu.

contort [kən'toːt] *v* tordre. **contortion** *n* (*acrobat*) contorsion *f*; (*twisting*) torsion *f*.

contour ['kontuə] *n* contour *m*. **contour line** courbe de niveau *f*.

contraband ['kontrəband] *n* contrebande *f*.

contraception [kontrə'sepʃən] *n* contraception *f*. **contraceptive** *nm, adj* contraceptif.

contract ['kontrakt; *v* kən'trakt] *n* contrat *m*. *v* (se) contracter. **contraction** *n* contraction *f*. **contractor** *n* entrepreneur *m*.

contradict [kontrə'dikt] *v* contredire. **contradiction** *n* contradiction *f*. **contradictory** *adj* contradictoire.

contralto [kən'traltou] *n* contralto *m*.

contraption [kən'trapʃən] *n* (*coll*) machin *m*.

contrary ['kontrəri; (*perverse*) kən'treəri] *adj* contraire; (*perverse*) contrariant. *adv* contrairement. *n* contraire *m*. **on the contrary** au contraire.

contrast [kən'traːst; *n* 'kontraːst] *v* contraster. *n* contraste *m*. **contrasting** *adj* contrasté.

contravene [kontrə'viːn] *v* enfreindre. **contravention** *n* violation *f*.

contribute [kən'tribjut] *v* contribuer. **contribution** *n* contribution *f*. **contributor** *n* (*magazine, etc.*) collaborateur, -trice *m, f*; (*money*) donateur, -trice *m, f*.

contrive [kən'traiv] *v* (*invent*) combiner; (*manage*) s'arranger (pour). **contrived** *adj* artificiel.

control [kən'troul] *n* contrôle *m*; autorité *f*. **controls** *n* commandes *f pl*. *v* (*restrain*) maîtriser; (*prices, etc.*) contrôler; (*business*) diriger. **controller** *n* contrôleur *m*.

controversy [kən'trovəsi] *n* controverse *f*. **controversial** *adj* discuté; discutable.

convalesce [konvə'les] *v* se remettre. **convalescence** *n* convalescence *f*. **convalescent** *n, adj* convalescent, -e.

convector [kən'vektə] *n* radiateur à convection *m*.

convenience [kən'viːnjəns] *n* commodité *f*, convenance *f*. **convenient** *adj* commode, convenable. **be convenient** convenir (à).

convent ['konvənt] *n* couvent *m*.

convention [kən'venʃən] *n* (*meeting*) convention *f*; (*tradition*) usage *m*. **conventional** *adj* conventionnel, classique.

converge [kən'vəːdʒ] *v* converger. **convergence** *n* convergence *f*. **convergent** *adj* convergent.

converse¹ [kən'vəːs] *v* causer. **conversation** *n* conversation *f*.

converse² ['konvəːs] *nm, adj* contraire, inverse.

convert [kən'vəːt; *n* 'konvəːt] *v* convertir; (*house*) aménager. *n* converti, -e *m, f*. **conversion** *n* conversion *f*; aménagement *m*.

convertible [kən'vəːtəbl] *n* (*car*) voiture décapotable *f*.

convex ['konveks] *adj* convexe.

convey [kən'vei] *v* transmettre; transporter; communiquer. **conveyance** *n* transport *m*. **conveyor belt** tapis roulant *m*.

convict ['konvikt; *v* kən'vikt] *n* forçat *m*. *v* déclarer coupable.

conviction [kən'vikʃən] *n* (*law*) condamnation *f*; (*belief*) conviction *f*.

convince [kən'vins] *v* convaincre.

convoy ['kɒnvɔi] n convoi m.
convulsion [kən'vʌlʃən] n (med) convulsion f. **convulsive** adj convulsif.
cook [kuk] n cuisinier, -ère m, f. v (faire) cuire; faire la cuisine. **cooker** n cuisinière f. **cookery** or **cooking** n cuisine f. **cookie** n (US) petit gâteau sec m.
cool [kuːl] adj (temperature) frais, fraîche; calme; (unfriendly) froid. v (se) rafraîchir, (se) refroidir. **cooler** n glacière f. **coolness** n fraîcheur f; froideur f; (calmness) sang-froid m.
coop [kuːp] n poulailler m. v **coop up** cloîtrer.
cooperate [kou'ɒpəreit] v coopérer. **cooperation** n coopération f. **cooperative** adj coopératif.
coordinate [kou'ɔːdineit] v coordonner. adj coordonné. n coordonnée f.
cope¹ [koup] v se débrouiller. **cope with** s'occuper de; (solve) venir à bout de.
cope² [koup] n chape f.
Copenhagen [koupən'heigən] n Copenhague.
copious ['koupiəs] adj copieux; abondant.
copper¹ ['kɒpə] n (metal) cuivre m. **coppers** pl n (money) petite monnaie f sing.
copper² ['kɒpə] n also **cop** (slang) flic m.
copulate ['kɒpjuleit] v copuler. **copulation** n copulation f.
copy ['kɒpi] n copie f; (phot) épreuve f; (of book, etc.) exemplaire m. v copier. **copyright** n copyright m.
coral ['kɒrəl] n corail (pl -aux) m. **coral reef** récif de corail m.
cord [kɔːd] n cordon m; (windows) corde f.
cordial ['kɔːdiəl] nm, adj cordial. **cordiality** n cordialité f.
cordon ['kɔːdn] n cordon m. v **cordon off** interdire l'accès à.
corduroy ['kɔːdərɔi] n velours côtelé m.
core [kɔː] n (fruit) trognon m; (earth) noyau m; (problem, etc) essential m. v enlever le trognon de.
cork [kɔːk] n liège m; (of bottle) bouchon m. **corkscrew** n tire-bouchon m. v boucher.
corn¹ [kɔːn] n blé m; (US) maïs m. **cornflour** n farine de maïs f. **cornflower** n bleuet m. **corn on the cob** épi de maïs m.
corn² [kɔːn] n (med) cor m.
corner ['kɔːnə] n coin m; (mot) tournant m. v (coll) coincer; (comm) accaparer.

cornet ['kɔːnit] n cornet m.
Cornwall ['kɔːnwɔːl] n Cornouailles f.
coronary ['kɒrənəri] adj coronaire. **coronary thrombosis** infarctus (du myocarde) m.
coronation [kɒrə'neiʃən] n couronnement m.
corporal¹ ['kɔːpərəl] adj corporel.
corporal² ['kɔːpərəl] n caporal-chef m.
corporation [kɔːpə'reiʃən] n (town) conseil municipal m; (comm) société commerciale f.
corps [kɔː] n corps m.
corpse [kɔːps] n cadavre m.
correct [kə'rekt] adj correct. v corriger. **correction** n correction f.
correlate ['kɒrəleit] v correspondre; mettre en corrélation. **correlation** n corrélation f.
correspond [kɒrə'spɒnd] v correspondre. **correspondence** n correspondance f. **correspondent** n correspondant, -e m, f.
corridor ['kɒridɔː] n couloir m.
corroborate [kə'rɒbəreit] v corroborer. **corroboration** n confirmation f.
corrode [kə'roud] v (se) corroder. **corrosion** n corrosion f. **corrosive** adj corrosif.
corrugated ['kɒrəgeitid] adj ondulé. **corrugated iron** tôle ondulée f.
corrupt [kə'rʌpt] v corrompre. adj corrompu. **corruption** n corruption f.
corset ['kɔːset] n corset m.
Corsica ['kɔːsikə] n Corse f. **Corsican** n Corse m, f; adj corse.
cosmetic [kɒz'metik] adj cosmétique; (surgery) plastique. **cosmetics** pl n produits de beauté m pl.
cosmic ['kɒzmik] adj cosmique.
cosmopolitan [kɒzmə'pɒlitən] n(m+f), adj cosmopolite.
***cost** [kɒst] v coûter. n coût m; frais m pl. **cost of living** coût de la vie m. **costly** adj coûteux.
costume ['kɒstjuːm] n costume m.
cosy ['kouzi] adj douillet, -ette.
cot [kɒt] n lit d'enfant m.
cottage ['kɒtidʒ] n cottage m; petite maison f; (thatched) chaumière f. **cottage cheese** fromage maigre m.
cotton ['kɒtn] n coton m; (thread) fil m. **cotton-wool** n ouate f.
couch [kautʃ] n canapé m. v exprimer.
cough [kɒf] n toux f. v tousser.
could [kud] V **can¹**.

council ['kaunsəl] n conseil m; (of town) conseil municipal m. **councillor** n conseiller, -ère m, f.

counsel ['kaunsəl] n conseil m; (law) avocat, -e m, f. v conseiller. **counsellor** n conseiller, -ère m, f; (social) orienteur m.

count[1] [kaunt] v compter; (consider) estimer. n compte m. **countdown** n compte à rebours m. **countless** adj innombrable.

count[2] [kaunt] n comte m. **countess** n comtesse f.

counter[1] ['kauntə] n (shop, etc.) comptoir m; (bank) guichet m; (disc) jeton m.

counter[2] ['kauntə] adj contraire. v (blow) parer; (boxing, etc.) riposter. **counter to** à l'encontre de.

counteract [kauntə'rakt] v neutraliser.

counterattack ['kauntərə,tak] v contre-attaquer. n contre-attaque f.

counterfeit ['kauntəfit] adj faux, fausse. v contrefaire. n faux m.

counterfoil ['kauntə,foil] n talon m.

counterpart ['kauntə,pɑrt] n contrepartie f; équivalent m; (person) homologue m, f.

country ['kʌntri] n pays m; (not town) campagne f; (native land) patrie f. **the countryside** la campagne f.

county ['kaunti] n comté m. **county town** chef-lieu m.

coup [ku] n (pol) coup d'État m.

couple ['kʌpl] n couple m. v accoupler; (animals) s'accoupler.

coupon ['kuipon] n (comm) bon m; (advertisements, etc.) coupon m.

courage ['kʌridʒ] n courage m. **courageous** adj courageux.

courgette [kuə'ʒet] n courgette f.

courier ['kuriə] n guide m; (messenger) courrier m.

course [kots] n cours m; (naut) route f; (meal) plat m. **of course** bien entendu.

court [kott] v (woman) courtiser; (favour) solliciter; (danger) s'exposer à. n cour m; (tennis) court m; (other sports) terrain m. **court-martial** n conseil de guerre m. **court-room** n salle de tribunal f. **courtyard** n cour f.

courteous ['kɔːtiəs] adj courtois. **courtesy** n courtoisie f, politesse f.

cousin ['kʌzn] n cousin, -e m, f.

cove [kouv] n anse f.

cover ['kʌvə] n couverture f; (lid) couver-cle m; (protective) housse f; (shelter) abri m. v couvrir. **coverage** n reportage m.

covering n (wrapping) couverture f; (layer) couche f.

cow [kau] n vache f. **cowboy** n cow-boy m. **cowslip** n primevère f.

coward ['kauəd] n lâche m, f. **cowardice** n lâcheté f. **cowardly** adj lâche.

cower ['kauə] v trembler; se blottir.

coy [koi] adj timide.

crab [krab] n crabe m. **crab-apple** pomme sauvage f. **crabby** adj revêche.

crack [krak] n (split) fente f; (glass, china, etc.) craquement m. v (se) fêler; (ground) (se) crevasser; (ice) (se) craqueler; (nut) casser; (noise) (faire) craquer.

cracker ['krakə] n (biscuit) craquelin m; (firework) pétard m; (Christmas) diablotin m.

crackle ['krakl] v crépiter. n crépitement m.

cradle ['kreidl] n berceau m. v bercer.

craft [krɑtft] n (skill) art m; (job) métier m; (boat) barque f; (cunning) astuce f. **craftsman** n artisan m. **crafty** astucieux.

cram [kram] v fourrer, bourrer; (people) (s')entasser; (for exam) (faire) bachoter.

cramp [kramp] n (med) crampe f. **cramped** adj à l'étroit.

cranberry ['kranbəri] n canneberge f.

crane [krein] n grue f. **cranefly** n tipule f. v **crane one's neck** tendre le cou.

crank [kraŋk] n (tech) manivelle f. **crankshaft** n vilebrequin m.

crap [krap] n (vulgar) n merde f; (nonsense) conneries f pl. **crappy** adj merdique.

crash [kraʃ] n fracas m; (car, etc.) accident m, collision f. v (car, etc.) s'écraser; (collide) se percuter; (smash) (se) fracasser. **crash course** cours intensif m. **crash helmet** casque m. **crash landing** atterrissage forcé m.

crate [kreit] n cageot m.

crater ['kreitə] n cratère m; (bomb) entonnoir m.

cravat [krə'vat] n foulard m.

crave [kreiv] v avoir grand besoin de; (beg) solliciter. **craving** n besoin maladif m; désir insatiable m.

crawl [krɔtl] v ramper; (cars) avancer au pas; (babies) aller à quatre pattes; (with lice, etc.) grouiller. n (swimming) crawl m.

crayfish ['kreifiʃ] *n* écrevisse *f.*

crayon ['kreiən] *n* crayon de couleur *m. v* colorier au crayon.

craze [kreiz] *n* engouement *m.*

crazy ['kreizi] *adj* fou, folle. **crazy paving** dallage irrégulier *m.*

creak [kriːk] *v* grincer. *n* grincement *m.*

cream [kriːm] *nf, adj* crème. **cream cheese** fromage blanc *m. v also* **cream off** écrémer. **creamy** *adj* crémeux.

crease [kriːs] *n* pli *m.* **crease-resistant** *adj* infroissable. *v* (se) froisser.

create [kri'eit] *v* créer. **creation** *n* création *f.* **creative** *adj* créatif.

creature ['kriːtʃə] *n* créature *f.* bête *f.*

credentials [kri'denʃəlz] *pl n* références *f pl.* pièce d'identité *f sing.*

credible ['kredəbl] *adj* croyable; plausible. **credibility** *n* crédibilité *f.*

credit ['kredit] *n* crédit *m.* honneur *m.* **credit card** carte de crédit *f.* **credits** *pl n* (*cinema*) générique *m sing. v* croire, attribuer; (*banking*) créditer. **creditable** *adj* honorable. **creditor** *n* créancier, -ère *m, f.*

credulous ['kredjuləs] *adj* crédule. **credulity** *n* crédulité *f.*

creed [kriːd] *n* credo *m.*

*creep [kriːp] *v* se glisser. **creeper** *n* plante grimpante *f.* **creepy** *adj* qui fait frissonner.

cremate [kri'meit] *v* incinérer. **cremation** *n* crémation *f.* **crematorium** *n* crématorium *m.*

crêpe [kreip] *n* crêpe *m.* **crêpe paper** papier crêpon *m.*

crept [krept] *V* creep.

crescent ['kresnt] *n* croissant *m.*

cress [kres] *n* cresson *m.*

crest [krest] *n* crête *f;* (*mark*) timbre *m.* **crestfallen** *adj* découragé.

crevice ['krevis] *n* fissure *f.*

crew [kruː] *n* (*naut*) équipage *m;* (*group*) équipe *f. v* (*sailing*) être équipier. **crewcut** *n* cheveux en brosse *m pl.* **crew-neck** *n* col ras *m.*

crib [krib] *n* (*baby's*) berceau *m;* (*manger*) mangeoire *f;* (*rel*) crèche *f. v* copier.

cricket¹ ['krikit] *n* (*insect*) grillon *m.*

cricket² ['krikit] *n* (*sport*) cricket *m.*

crime [kraim] *n* crime *m.* **criminal** *n, adj* criminel, -elle.

crimson ['krimzn] *nm, adj* cramoisi.

cringe [krindʒ] *v* reculer; s'humilier.

crinkle ['kriŋkl] *v* (se) froisser. *n* fronce *f.*

cripple ['kripl] *v* estropier; (*industry, etc.*) paralyser. *n* estropié, -e *m, f.*

crisis ['kraisis] *n* crise *f.*

crisp [krisp] *adj* (*biscuit*) croquant; (*snow*) craquant; (*weather, style*) vif. **crisps** *pl n* chips *f pl.*

criterion [krai'tiəriən] *n, pl* -ria critère *m.*

criticize ['kritiˌsaiz] *v* critiquer. **critic** *n* critique *m.* **critical** *adj* critique. **criticism** *n* critique *f.*

croak [krouk] *v* (*frog*) coasser; (*crow*) croasser. *n* coassement *m;* croassement *m.*

crochet ['krouʃei] *n* travail au crochet *m. v* (*activity*) faire du crochet; (*make*) faire au crochet. **crochet hook** crochet *m.*

crockery ['krokəri] *n* vaisselle *f.*

crocodile ['krokəˌdail] *n* crocodile *m.*

crocus ['kroukəs] *n* crocus *m.*

crook [kruk] *n* (*shepherd's*) houlette *f;* (*bend*) angle *m;* (*coll*) escroc *m.* **crooked** ['krukid] *adj* (*bent*) courbé; (*path*) tortueux; (*askew*) de travers; (*dishonest*) malhonnête.

crop [krop] *n* culture *f;* (*harvest*) récolte *f;* (*cereals*) moisson *f;* (*riding*) cravache *f. v* écourter, tondre; (*graze*) brouter; (*hair*) couper ras. **crop up** survenir.

croquet ['kroukei] *n* croquet *m.*

cross [kros] *n* croix *f;* hybride *m;* biais *m. adj* (*angry*) fâché; diagonal. *v* (se) croiser; (*go across*) traverser; (*cheque*) barrer.

cross-examine [ˌkrosig'zamin] *v* interroger. **cross-examination** *n* contre-interrogatoire *m.*

cross-eyed [ˌkros'aid] *adj* louche.

crossfire ['krosˌfaiə] *n* feux croisés *m pl.*

crossing ['krosiŋ] *n* (*junction*) croisement *m;* (*for pedestrians*) passage clouté *m;* (*journey*) traversée *f.*

cross-legged [ˌkros'legid] *adj* les jambes croisées.

cross-reference [ˌkros'refərəns] *n* renvoi *m.* **cross-refer** *v* renvoyer.

crossroads ['krosˌroudz] *n* carrefour *m.*

cross section *n* coupe transversale *f;* (*sample*) échantillon *m.*

crosswind ['krosˌwind] *n* vent de travers *m.*

crossword ['krosˌwəːd] *n* mots croisés *m pl.*

crotchet ['krotʃit] *n* noire *f.* **crotchety** *adj* grognon, -onne.

crouch [kraut∫] v s'accroupir. n accroupissement m.

crow[1] [krou] n corneille f. **as the crow flies** à vol d'oiseau. **crowbar** n levier m.

crow[2] [krou] v (cock) chanter; (baby) gazouiller. n chant du coq m.

crowd [kraud] n foule f. v (gather round) s'attrouper; (fill up) (s')entasser. **crowded** adj plein (de monde).

crown [kraun] n couronne f; (road) milieu m; (hat) fond m. v couronner. **crown jewels** joyaux de la couronne m pl. **crown prince** prince héritier m.

crucial ['kru:∫əl] adj crucial.

crucify ['kru:si,fai] v crucifier. **crucifix** n crucifix m. **crucifixion** n crucifixion f, crucifiement m.

crude [kru:d] adj (materials) brut; rudimentaire; (behaviour) grossier. **crudely** adv crûment; imparfaitement.

cruel ['kru:əl] adv cruel. **cruelty** n cruauté f.

cruise [kru:z] n croisière f. v (ship) croiser; (mot) rouler. **cruising speed** vitesse de croisière f. **cruiser** n (ship) croiseur m.

crumb [krʌm] n miette f.

crumble ['krʌmbl] v (to crumbs) (s')émietter; (to dust) (s')effriter; (collapse) s'écrouler.

crumple ['krʌmpl] v (se) chiffonner.

crunch [krʌnt∫] v (food) croquer; (snow, etc.) faire craquer. n craquement m. **the crunch** (coll) l'instant critique. **crunchy** adj croquant.

crusade [kru:'seid] n croisade f. v faire une croisade.

crush [krʌ∫] v (s')écraser; (clothes) (se) froisser. n cohue f. **crushing** adj (defeat) écrasant; (remark) percutant.

crust [krʌst] n croûte f. **crusty** adj (bread) croustillant; (coll) hargneux.

crutch [krʌt∫] n béquille f; (support) soutien m.

cry [krai] n cri m. v (shout) crier; (weep) pleurer. **cry out** s'écrier, pousser un cri. **rypt** [kript] n crypte f.

rystal ['kristl] n cristal m. **crystal-clear** adj clair comme le jour. **crystallize** v (se) cristalliser.

ub [kʌb] n petit, -e m, f; (bear) ourson m; (fox) renardeau m; (lion) lionceau m. **cub scout** louveteau m.

ube [kju:b] n cube m. v (maths) cuber;

(cookery) couper en cubes. **cubic** adj cubique; (in units) cube.

cubicle ['kju:bikl] n (for changing) cabine f; (for sleeping) alcôve f.

cuckoo ['kuku:] n coucou m.

cucumber [kju'kʌmbə] n concombre m.

cuddle ['kʌdl] n étreinte f. v serrer dans les bras; (child) câliner. **cuddle up** se pelotonner.

cue[1] [kju:] n signal m; (theatre) réplique f.

cue[2] [kju:] n (billiards) queue de billard f.

cuff[1] [kʌf] n (shirt) manchette f. **cuff-link** n bouton de manchette m. **off the cuff** à l'improviste.

cuff[2] [kʌf] v gifler. n gifle f.

culinary ['kʌlinəri] adj culinaire.

culminate ['kʌlmi,neit] v culminer. **culminate in** se terminer par. **culmination** n point culminant m; (success) apogée m.

culprit ['kʌlprit] n coupable m, f; (law) accusé, -e m, f.

cult [kʌlt] n culte m.

cultivate ['kʌlti,veit] v cultiver. **cultivation** n culture f.

culture ['kʌlt∫ə] n culture f. **cultural** adj culturel. **cultured** adj cultivé.

cumbersome ['kʌmbəsəm] adj encombrant.

cunning ['kʌniŋ] adj astucieux; rusé. n astuce f; ruse f.

cup [kʌp] n tasse f; (prize) coupe f.

cupboard ['kʌbəd] n placard m.

curate ['kjuərət] n vicaire m.

curator [kjuə'reitə] n conservateur m.

curb [kə:b] v refréner; restreindre. n frein m.

curdle ['kə:dl] v (milk) (se) cailler; (blood) (se) figer.

cure [kjuə] v guérir; (salt) saler; (smoke) fumer. n remède m; (recovery) guérison f. **curable** adj guérissable.

curfew ['kə:fju:] n couvre-feu m.

curious ['kjuəriəs] adj curieux. **curiosity** n curiosité f.

curl [kə:l] v (hair) friser, boucler. **curl up** (s')enrouler; (person, animal) se pelotonner. n boucle f; spirale f. **curler** n (hair) rouleau m. **curly** adj bouclé, frisé.

currant ['kʌrənt] n (dried fruit) raisin de Corinthe m; (berry) groseille f; (bush) groseillier m.

currency ['kʌrənsi] n monnaie f; (foreign) devise f; circulation f.

current ['kʌrənt] adj courant; (fashion, etc.) actuel. **current affairs** questions

d'actualité *f pl. n* courant *m*; tendance *f.*
currently *adv* en ce moment.

curry ['kʌri] *n* curry *m*. **curry powder** poudre de curry *f*. **curried** *adj* au curry.

curse [kɜːs] *v* maudire; (*swear*) jurer. *n* malédiction *f*; juron *m*; (*bane*) fléau *m*.

curt [kɜːt] *adj* brusque.

curtail [kɜː'teil] *v* écourter; (*expenses*) réduire. **curtailment** *n* raccourcissement *m*; réduction *f.*

curtain ['kɜːtn] *n* rideau *m*. **curtain call** rappel *m*. *v* garnir de rideaux.

curtsy ['kɜːtsi] *n* révérence *f*. *v* faire une révérence.

curve [kɜːv] *n* courbe *f*. *v* (se) courber.

cushion ['kuʃən] *n* coussin *m*. *v* amortir.

custard ['kʌstəd] *n* (*pouring*) crème anglaise *f*; (*with eggs*) flan *m*.

custody ['kʌstədi] *n* garde *f*; emprisonnement *m.*

custom ['kʌstəm] *n* coutume *f*; (*comm*) clientèle *f*. **customs** *n* douane *f*. **customs officer** douanier *m*. **customary** *adj* habituel. **customer** *n* client, -e *m, f.*

*cut [kʌt] *n* (*slit*) coupure *f*; (*stroke*) coup *m*; réduction *f*; (*of clothes*) coupe *f*; (*of meat*) morceau *m*. *v* couper; (*slice*) découper; (*shape*, trim) tailler; réduire. **cutback** *n* réduction *f*. **cut down** (*tree*, *etc.*) abattre; réduire. **cut glass** cristal taillé *m*. **cut off** couper; isoler. **cut out** (*engine*) caler; (*picture*) découper; (*give up*) supprimer. **cut-price** *adv* à prix réduit.

cute [kjuːt] *adj* (*sweet*) mignon, -onne; (*clever*) rusé.

cutlery ['kʌtləri] *n* couverts *m pl.*

cutlet ['kʌtlit] *n* côtelette *f.*

cutting ['kʌtiŋ] *n* (*rail*) tranchée *f*; (*newspaper*) coupure *f*; (*plant*) bouture *f. adj* (*edge*) tranchant; (*wind*) cinglant; (*remark*) mordant.

cycle ['saikl] *n* cycle *m*; bicyclette *f*, vélo *m*. *v* faire de la bicyclette; aller à bicyclette. **cycling** *n* cyclisme *m*. **cyclist** *n* cycliste *m, f.*

cyclone ['saikloun] *n* cyclone *m.*

cylinder ['silində] *n* cylindre *m*. **cylinder head** (*mot*) culasse *f*. **cylindrical** *adj* cylindrique.

cymbal ['simbəl] *n* cymbale *f.*

cynic ['sinik] *n* cynique *m, f*. **cynical** *adj* cynique. **cynicism** *n* cynisme *m.*

cypress ['saiprəs] *n* cyprès *m.*

Cyprus ['saiprəs] *n* Chypre *f*. **Cypriot** *n* Cypriote *m, f*; *adj* cypriote.

cyst [sist] *n* (*med*) kyste *m.*

Czechoslovakia [ˌtʃekəslə'vakiə] *n* Tchécoslovaquie *f*. **Czech** *n* (*people*) Tchèque *m, f*; *nm, adj* tchèque. **Czechoslovak** *n* (*people*) Tchécoslovaque *m, f*; *nm, adj* tchécoslovaque.

D

dab [dab] *n* goutte *f*, petite touche *f*. *v* tamponner; appliquer à petits coups.

dabble ['dabl] *v* (*in water*) barboter; (*politics*, *etc.*) se mêler un peu (de).

dad [dad] *n* (*coll*) papa *m.*

daffodil ['dafədil] *n* jonquille *f.*

daft [daːft] *adj* idiot.

dagger ['dagə] *n* poignard *m.*

daily ['deili] *adj* quotidien. *n* (*newspaper*) quotidien *m*; (*cleaner*) femme de ménage *f. adv* tous les jours.

dainty ['deinti] *adj* délicat; (*small*) menu.

dairy ['deəri] *n* laiterie *f*; crémerie *f*. **dairy farming** industrie laitière *f*. **dairy produce** produits laitiers *m pl.*

daisy ['deizi] *n* marguerite *f*; (*wild*) pâquerette *f.*

dam [dam] *n* barrage *m*. *v* endiguer; construire un barrage (sur).

damage ['damidʒ] *n* dommage *m*. **damages** *pl n* (*law*) dommages-intérêts *m pl. v* endommager; (*health*, *etc.*) abîmer; (*reputation*) nuire à. **damaging** *adj* préjudiciable.

damn [dam] *v* (*rel*) damner; condamner. *interj* (*coll*) zut! *adj also* **damned** (*slang*) fichu. *adv* (*slang*) sacrément. **damn all** (*slang*) zéro. **I don't give a damn** (*slang*) je m'en fiche pas mal. **damnable** *adj* odieux. **damnation** *n* (*rel*) damnation *f.*

damp [damp] *adj* humide; (*skin*) moite. *n also* **dampness** humidité *f*. *v also* **dampen** (*moisten*) humecter; (*noise*) étouffer; (*courage*) refroidir. **damp-course** *n* couche isolante *f*. **put a damper on** jeter un froid sur.

damson ['damzən] *n* (*fruit*) prune de Damas *f*; (*tree*) prunier de Damas *m.*

dance [daːns] *v* danser. *n* danse *f*; bal *m.*

dance floor piste de danse *f.* **dancer** *n* danseur, -euse *m, f.* **dancing** *n* danse *f.*

dandelion ['dændiˌlaiən] *n* pissenlit *m.*

dandruff ['dændrəf] *n* pellicules *f pl.*

danger ['deindʒə] *n* danger *m.* **be in danger of** risquer de. **danger money** prime de risque *f.* **on the danger list** dans un état critique. **dangerous** *adj* dangereux.

dangle ['dæŋgl] *v* (*be hanging*) pendre; (*let hang*) balancer.

Danish ['deiniʃ] *nm, adj* danois. **Dane** *n* Danois, -e *m, f.*

dare [deə] *v* oser; (*challenge*) défier. **I dare say** sans doute. *n* défi *m.*

daring ['deəriŋ] *n* audace *f. adj* audacieux.

dark [daik] *adj* obscur; (*colour*) foncé; (*hair*) brun. **be dark** (*night*) faire nuit. **dark horse** quantité inconnue *f.* **darkroom** *n* (*phot*) chambre noire *f. n* obscurité *f*; nuit *f.* **in the dark** (*ignorant*) dans le noir. **darken** *v* (s')obscurcir; (*sky*) (s')assombrir; foncer. **darkness** *n* obscurité *f*, ténèbres *f pl.*

darling ['dailiŋ] *n, adj* chéri, -e.

darn [dain] *v* (*socks*) repriser; (*clothes*) raccommoder. *n* reprise *f.* **darning** *n* raccommodage *m.*

dart [dait] *n* (*game*) fléchette *f*; (*sewing*) pince *f.* **dartboard** *n* cible *f. v* s'élancer; (*rays*) darder.

dash [daʃ] *n* (*drop*) goutte *f*; (*writing*) tiret *m*; (*rush*) élan *m. v* (*rush*) se précipiter; (*throw*) (se) jeter; (*hopes*) anéantir. **dashboard** *n* (*mot*) tableau de bord *m.* **dashing** *adj* plein de panache.

data ['deitə] *n* données *f pl.* **data processing** informatique *f.*

date[1] [deit] *n* date *f*; (*meeting*) rendez-vous *m.* **out of date** (*invalid*) périmé; (*old-fashioned*) démodé. **up to date** moderne; (*books, etc.*) à jour. *v* dater; fixer la date de; (*boyfriend, etc.*) sortir avec. **dated** *adj* démodé.

date[2] [deit] *n* (*fruit*) datte *f*; (*tree*) dattier *m.*

daub [doib] *v* barbouiller.

daughter ['doitə] *n* fille *f.* **daughter-in-law** *n* belle-fille *f.*

daunt [doint] *v* décourager. **dauntless** *adj* intrépide.

dawdle ['doidl] *v* traîner.

dawn [doin] *n* aube *f*; point du jour *m. v* (*day*) poindre; (*hope*) naître. **dawn on** venir à.

day [dei] *n* jour *m*, journée *f.* **day after** lendemain *m.* **day before** veille *f.* **daylight** *n* jour *m.* **day-to-day** *adj* journalier.

daydream ['deidriim] *v* rêvasser. *n* rêvasserie *f.*

daze [deiz] *v* hébéter; (*from blow*) étourdir; (*shock*) abasourdir. *n* hébétement *m*; étourdissement *m*; stupéfaction *f.*

dazzle ['dæzl] *v* éblouir. *n* lumière aveuglante *f.*

dead [ded] *adj* mort. *adv* absolument. **dead-beat** *adj* (*coll*) claqué. **dead end** impasse *f.* **deadline** *n* date limite *f*; heure limite *f.* **deadlock** *n* impasse *f.* **deadpan** *adj, adv* sans expression. **deaden** *v* amortir; (*pain*) calmer. **deadly** *adj* mortel.

deaf [def] *adj* sourd. **deaf-mute** *n* sourd-muet, sourde-muette *m, f.* **deafen** *v* rendre sourd; (*noise*) assourdir. **deafness** *n* surdité *f.*

*deal [diil] *n* quantité *f*; (*bargain*) marché *m*; (*cards*) donne *f.* **a good deal** beaucoup. *v* (*cards*) distribuer. **deal in** être dans le commerce de. **deal with** (*comm*) négocier avec; (*handle*) se charger de; (*book, report, etc.*) traiter de. **dealer** *n* négociant *m*; (*cards*) donneur *m.* **dealings** *pl n* (*comm*) opérations *f pl*; (*people*) relations *f pl.*

dealt [delt] *V* **deal.**

dean [diin] *n* doyen *m.*

dear [diə] *n, adj* cher, chère. **oh dear!** oh là là! **dearly** *adv* cher, chèrement.

death [deθ] *n* mort *f.* **death certificate** acte de décès *m.* **death duties** droits de succession *m pl.* **death penalty** peine de mort *f.* **death toll** chiffre des morts *m.* **deathly** *adj* cadavérique; mortel.

debase [di'beis] *v* avilir; (*lower quality*) rabaisser. **debasement** *n* avilissement *m*; baisse *f.*

debate [di'beit] *v* discuter. *n* débat *m*; discussion *f.* **debatable** *adj* contestable.

debit ['debit] *n* débit *m. v* débiter; porter au débit.

debris ['deibrii] *n* débris *m pl.*

debt [det] *n* dette *f.* **get into debt** s'endetter. **debtor** *n* débiteur, -trice *m, f.*

decade ['dekeid] *n* décade *f.*

decadent ['dekədənt] *adj* décadent. **decadence** *n* décadence *f.*

decant [di'kænt] *v* décanter. **decanter** *n* carafe *f.*

decapitate [di'kapi,teit] *v* décapiter. **decapitation** *n* décapitation *f*.

decay [di'kei] *v* (*rot*) pourrir; décliner; tomber en ruines; (*tooth*) se carier. *n* pourrissement *m*; décadence *f*, carie *f*. **decaying** *adj* en pourriture; en décadence.

decease [di'siːs] *n* décès *m*. *v* décéder. **deceased** *n*, *adj* défunt, -e.

deceit [di'siːt] *n* tromperie *f*. **deceitful** *adj* trompeur, -euse. **deceitfully** *adv* faussement. **deceitfulness** *n* fausseté *f*.

deceive [di'siːv] *v* tromper.

December [di'sembə] *n* décembre *m*.

decent ['diːsənt] *adj* (*dress*) décent; (*respectable*) convenable; (*coll: nice*) chic. **decency** *n* décence *f*; convenances *f pl*; (*kindness*) gentillesse *f*.

deceptive [di'septiv] *adj* trompeur. **deception** *n* tromperie *f*; illusion *f*.

decibel ['desi,bel] *n* décibel *m*.

decide [di'said] *v* (se) décider. **decided** *adj* résolu; incontestable; marqué. **deciding** *adj* décisif.

deciduous [di'sidjuəs] *adj* à feuilles caduques.

decimal ['desiməl] *adj* décimal. *n* décimale *f*. **decimal point** virgule *f*. **decimalization** *n* décimalisation *f*. **decimalize** *v* décimaliser.

decipher [di'saifə] *v* déchiffrer.

decision [di'siʒən] *n* décision *f*. **decisive** *adj* décisif; (*manner*) décidé.

deck [dek] *n* (*naut*) pont *m*; (*records*) table de lecture *f*. **deck-chair** *n* transat *m*. *v* orner.

declare [di'kleə] *v* déclarer. **declaration** *n* déclaration *f*.

decline [di'klain] *n* déclin *m*; (*prices*) baisse *f*. *v* décliner; baisser. **declension** *n* déclinaison *f*.

decompose [,diːkəm'pouz] *v* (se) décomposer. **decomposition** *n* décomposition *f*.

decorate ['dekə,reit] *v* décorer; orner; (*room, house*) peindre et tapisser. **decorating** *n* décoration intérieure *f*. **decoration** *n* décoration *f*; ornement *m*; (*room*) décor *m*. **decorative** *adj* décoratif. **decorator** *n* décorateur *m*.

decoy ['diːkoi; *v* di'koi] *n* leurre *m*; (*person*) compère *m*. *v* leurrer.

decrease [di'kriːs] *v* diminuer, décroître. *n* diminution *f*, décroissance *f*.

decree [di'kriː] *n* décret *m*. *v* décréter.

decrepit [di'krepit] *adj* décrépit; (*building*) délabré. **decrepitude** *n* décrépitude *f*; délabrement *m*.

dedicate ['dedi,keit] *v* dédier; consacrer. **dedication** dédicace *f*; consécration *f*; dévouement *m*.

deduce [di'djuːs] *v* déduire. **deduction** *n* déduction *f*.

deduct [di'dʌkt] *v* déduire; (*numbers*) soustraire; (*from wage*) prélever (sur). **deductible** *adj* déductible. **deduction** *n* déduction *f*; prélèvement *m*.

deed [diːd] *n* action *f*; (*law*) contrat *m*. **deed poll** acte unilatéral *m*.

deep [diːp] *adj* profond; (*broad*) large; (*sound*) grave. *adv* profondément. **deep-freeze** *n* congélateur *m*. **deep-seated** *adj* profondément enraciné. **deepen** *v* (s')approfondir.

deer [diə] *n* cerf *m*, biche *f*.

deface [di'feis] *v* mutiler; (*poster, etc.*) barbouiller.

default [di'fɔːlt] *n* défaut *m*. **in default of** faute de. *v* faire défaut; être en défaut.

defeat [di'fiːt] *v* vaincre, battre. *n* défaite *f*. **defeatist** *n*(*m*+*f*), *adj* défaitiste.

defect [di'fekt; *v* di'fekt] *n* défaut *m*. *v* faire défection. **defection** *n* défection *f*. **defective** *adj* défectueux. **defector** *n* transfuge *m*, *f*.

defend [di'fend] *v* défendre. **defence** *n* défense *f*. **defenceless** *adj* sans défense. **defendant** *n* défendeur, -eresse *m*, *f*. **defending** *adj* (*champion*) en titre; (*law*) de la défense.

defensive [di'fensiv] *n* défensive *f*. *adj* défensif.

defer [di'fəː] *v* (*put off*) différer. **deferment** *n* ajournement *m*; suspension *f*.

defiant [di'faiənt] *adj* rebelle; provocant. **defiance** *n* défi *m*. **in defiance of** au mépris de. **defiantly** *adv* d'un air *or* ton de défi.

deficient [di'fiʃənt] *adj* insuffisant. **be deficient in** manquer de. **deficiency** *n* manque *f*; (*med*) carence *f*.

deficit ['desifit] *n* déficit *m*.

define [di'fain] *v* définir. **definition** *n* définition *f*; délimitation *f*; (*clearness*) netteté *f*. **definitive** *adj* définitif.

definite ['definit] *adj* certain; déterminé; manifeste; (*gramm*) défini. **definitely** *adv* sans aucun doute; catégoriquement.

deflate [di'fleit] *v* (*tyre, etc.*) dégonfler; (*person*) démonter. **deflation** *n* (*econ*) déflation *f*; dégonflement *m*.

deform [di'fɔɪm] *v* déformer. **deformation** *n* déformation *f*. **deformed** *adj* difforme. **deformity** *n* difformité *f*.

defraud [di'frɔɪd] *v* (*state*) frauder; (*person*) escroquer.

defrost [diɪ'frɒst] *v* (*refrigerator, etc.*) dégivrer; (*frozen food*) décongeler.

deft [deft] *adj* habile. **deftness** *n* habileté *f*.

defunct [di'fʌŋkt] *adj* défunt.

defy [di'fai] *v* défier.

degenerate [di'dʒenəˌreit; *n, adj* di'dʒenərit] *v* dégénérer. *n, adj* dégénéré, -e. **degeneracy** *or* **degeneration** *n* dégénérescence *f*.

degrade [di'greid] *v* dégrader. **degradation** *n* (*person*) avilissement *m*; dégradation *f*.

degree [di'griɪ] *n* degré *m*; (*university*) licence *f*. **by degrees** petit à petit.

dehydrate [diɪ'haidreit] *v* déshydrater. **dehydration** *n* déshydratation *f*.

de-icer [diɪ'aisə] *n* dégivreur *m*. **de-ice** *v* dégivrer.

deity ['diɪəti] *n* divinité *f*, déité *f*.

dejected [di'dʒektid] *adj* abattu. **dejection** *n* abattement *m*.

delay [di'lei] *v* (*make late*) retarder; (*put off*) différer. *n* délai *m*; retardement *m*; (*rail*) retard *m*. **delaying** *adj* dilatoire.

delegate ['deləgeit; *n, adj* 'deləgit] *v* déléguer. *n, adj* délégué, -e. **delegation** *n* délégation *f*; nomination *f*.

delete [di'liɪt] *v* rayer. **deletion** *n* (*act*) suppression *f*; (*word, phrase, etc.*) rature *f*.

deliberate [di'libərət; *v* di'libəreit] *adj* (*intentional*) délibéré; réfléchi; mesuré. *v* délibérer (sur). **deliberately** *adv* exprès; avec mesure. **deliberation** *n* délibération *f*.

delicate ['delikət] *adj* délicat; (*health*) fragile. **delicacy** *n* délicatesse *f*; (*food*) friandise *f*.

delicious [di'liʃəs] *adj* délicieux.

delight [di'lait] *n* grand plaisir *m*, joie *f*. *v* enchanter; se délecter (à). **delighted** *adj* ravi. **delightful** *adj* charmant, ravissant.

delinquency [di'liŋkwənsi] *n* délinquance *f*. **delinquent** *n, adj* délinquant, -e.

delirious [di'liriəs] *adj* délirant. **be delirious** (*med*) avoir le délire; (*crowd, etc.*) être en délire. **delirium** *n* délire *m*.

deliver [di'livə] *v* (*message*) remettre; (*goods*) livrer; (*letters*) distribuer; (*save*) délivrer; (*speech*) prononcer; (*woman*) accoucher. **deliverance** *n* délivrance *f*.

delivery *n* livraison *f*; distribution *f*; (*speech*) débit *m*; accouchement *m*.

delta ['deltə] *n* delta *m*.

delude [di'luɪd] *v* tromper. **delude oneself** se faire des illusions. **deluded** *adj* induit en erreur. **delusion** *n* illusion *f*; (*psych*) fantasme *m*.

deluge ['deljuɪdʒ] *n* déluge *n*. *v* inonder.

delve [delv] *v* creuser, fouiller.

demand [di'maɪnd] *v* exiger, réclamer. *n* exigence *f*; (*claim*) réclamation *f*; (*comm*) demande *f*. **be in demand** être demandé.

democracy [di'mokrəsi] *n* démocratie *f*. **democrat** *n* démocrate *m, f*. **democratic** *adj* démocratique.

demolish [di'moliʃ] *v* démolir. **demolition** *n* démolition *f*.

demon ['diɪmən] *n* démon *m*. **demoniacal** *adj* démoniaque.

demonstrate ['demənˌstreit] *v* démontrer; (*machine, etc.*) faire une démonstration de; (*pol*) manifester. **demonstration** *n* démonstration *f*; manifestation *f*. **demonstrative** *adj* démonstratif.

demoralize [di'morəˌlaiz] *v* démoraliser. **become demoralized** perdre courage. **demoralization** *n* démoralisation *f*.

demure [di'mjuə] *adj* modeste, sage.

den [den] *n* tanière *f*, repaire *m*.

denim ['denim] *n* toile de jean *f*. **denims** *pl n* (*jeans*) blue-jean *m* *sing*.

Denmark ['denmaɪk] *n* Danemark *m*.

denomination [diˌnomi'neiʃən] *n* dénomination *f*; (*money*) valeur *f*; (*rel*) secte *f*. **denominator** *n* dénominateur *f*.

denote [di'nout] *v* dénoter.

denounce [di'nauns] *v* dénoncer.

dense [dens] *adj* dense; (*coll: stupid*) bouché. **density** *n* densité *f*.

dent [dent] *n* bosselure *f*. *v* bosseler, cabosser.

dental ['dentl] *adj* dentaire. **dental surgeon** chirurgien dentiste *m*.

dentist ['dentist] *n* dentiste *m, f*. **dentistry** *n* art dentaire *m*.

denture ['dentʃə] *n* dentier *m*.

denude [di'njuɪd] *v* dénuder.

denunciation [diˌnʌnsi'eiʃən] *n* dénonciation *f*.

deny [di'nai] *v* nier; refuser. **denial** *n* dénégation *f*; (*accusation, etc.*) démenti *m*.

deodorant [diɪ'oudərənt] *nm, adj* déodorant, désodorisant.

depart [di'pɑːt] v partir. **depart from**
(*leave*) quitter; (*deviate*) s'écarter de.
departure n départ m. **departure lounge**
salle de départ f.
department [di'pɑːtmənt] n département
m; (*shop*) rayon m; (*school, university*)
section f; domaine m; (*comm*) service m.
department store grand magasin m.
depend [di'pend] v dépendre. **depend on**
dépendre de; (*rely*) compter sur. **depen-**
dant n personne à charge f. **dependence** n
dépendance f. **dependent** adj dépendant.
depict [di'pikt] v (*words*) peindre; (*pic-*
ture) représenter. **depiction** n peinture f;
représentation f.
deplete [di'pliːt] v réduire. **depletion** n
réduction f.
deplore [di'plɔː] v déplorer. **deplorable** adj
déplorable.
deport [di'pɔːt] v déporter; expulser.
deportation n déportation f; expulsion f.
deportment n maintien m.
depose [di'pouz] v déposer. **deposition** n
déposition f.
deposit [di'pozit] v déposer. n dépôt m;
(*against damage*) caution f; (*token pay-*
ment) acompte m. **deposit account**
compte de dépôt m. **depositor** n
déposant, -e m, f.
depot ['depou] n dépôt m.
deprave [di'preiv] v dépraver. **depravity** n
dépravation f.
depreciate [di'priːʃieit] v (se) déprécier.
depreciation n dépréciation f.
depress [di'pres] v déprimer; (*press down*)
appuyer sur. **depression** n dépression f;
découragement m; (*econ*) crise f.
deprive [di'praiv] v priver. **deprivation** n
privation f.
depth [depθ] n profondeur f; (*breadth*)
largeur f; intensité f.
deputy ['depjuti] n adjoint, -e m, f. **depu-**
tation n délégation f. **deputize for** assurer
l'intérim de.
derail [di'reil] v (faire) dérailler. **derail-**
ment n déraillement m.
derelict ['derilikt] adj abandonné,
délaissé.
deride [di'raid] v railler. **derision** n dérision f. **derisive** adj moqueur. **derisory** adj
(*offer, etc.*) dérisoire.
derive [di'raiv] v (*gain*) trouver, tirer. **be**
derived from dériver de, provenir de. **der-**
ivation n dérivation f.

derogatory [di'rogətəri] adj dénigrant,
désobligeant.
descend [di'send] v descendre. **descend to**
(*crime, etc.*) s'abaisser à. **descendant** n
descendant, -e m, f. **descent** n descente f;
origine f.
describe [di'skraib] v décrire. **description**
n description f. **descriptive** adj descriptif.
desert[1] ['dezət] n désert m.
desert[2] [di'zəːt] v déserter, abandonner.
deserted adj désert. **deserter** n déserteur
m. **desertion** n désertion f; abandon m.
desert[3] [di'zəːt] n dû m. **get one's just**
deserts avoir ce que l'on mérite.
deserve [di'zəːv] v mériter.
design [di'zain] n modèle m, plan m; (*pat-*
tern) dessin m; (*comm*) design m;
(*machine, etc.*) conception f; (*intention*)
dessein m. v dessiner; projeter; concevoir. **designer** n (*comm*) concepteur-
projeteur m; (*art*) dessinateur, -trice m, f.
designate ['dezigneit] v désigner. **designa-**
tion n désignation f.
desire [di'zaiə] n désir m. v désirer. **desir-**
able adj désirable.
desk [desk] n bureau m; (*school*) pupitre
m.
desolate ['desələt] adj désert; sombre;
(*person*) affligé. **desolation** n désolation f.
despair [di'speə] n désespoir m. v désespérer.
desperate ['despərət] adj désespéré.
desperation n désespoir m.
despise [di'spaiz] v mépriser.
despite [di'spait] prep malgré.
despondent [di'spondənt] adj découragé.
despondency n découragement m.
despot ['despot] n despote m. **despotic** adj
despotique.
dessert [di'zəːt] n dessert m. **dessertspoon**
n cuiller à dessert f.
destination [desti'neiʃən] n destination f.
destine ['destin] v destiner. **destiny** n
destin m.
destitute ['destitjuːt] adj indigent. **destitu-**
tion n dénuement m.
destroy [di'stroi] v détruire. **destroyer** n
(*ship*) contre-torpilleur m. **destruction** n
destruction f. **destructive** adj destructeur,
-trice; destructif.
detach [di'tatʃ] v détacher. **detachable** adj
détachable. **detached** adj détaché; (*unbi-*
ased) objectif; indifférent. **detached**
house maison individuelle f. **detachment**
n détachement m; séparation f.

detail ['diːteil] *n* détail *m*. *v* détailler; (*mil*) affecter.

detain [di'tein] *v* retenir; (*law*) détenir.

detect [di'tekt] *v* découvrir; distinguer. **detective** *n* agent de la sûreté *m*. **detective story** roman policier *m*. **detector** *n* detecteur *m*.

detention [di'tenʃən] *n* détention *f*; (*school*) retenue *f*.

deter [di'təː] *v* décourager; dissuader; (*prevent*) détourner. **deterrent** *n* force de dissuasion *f*.

detergent [di'təːdʒənt] *nm, adj* détersif.

deteriorate [di'tiəriəˌreit] *v* (se) détériorer. **deterioration** *n* détérioration *f*.

determine [di'təːmin] *v* déterminer; fixer; décider. **determination** *n* détermination *f*. **determined** *adj* déterminé; résolu.

detest [di'test] *v* détester.

detonate ['detəˌneit] *v* (faire) détoner. **detonation** *n* détonation *f*. **detonator** *n* détonateur *m*.

detour [diːtuə] *n* détour *m*. *v* faire un détour.

detract [di'trakt] *v* **detract from** diminuer.

detriment ['detrimənt] *n* détriment *m*. **detrimental** *adj* nuisible.

devalue [diː'valjuː] *v* dévaluer. **devaluation** *n* dévaluation *f*.

devastate ['devəˌsteit] *v* (*town, etc.*) dévaster; (*person*) terrasser. **devastating** *adj* (*power*) dévastateur, -trice; (*effect*) accablant. **devastation** *n* dévastation *f*.

develop [di'veləp] *v* (se) développer; contracter. **development** *n* développement *m*; exploitation *f*.

deviate ['diːviˌeit] *v* dévier. **deviation** *n* déviation *f*.

device [di'vais] *n* appareil *m*; (*scheme*) formule *f*.

devil ['devl] *n* diable *m*. **talk of the devil!** quand on parle du loup! **devilish** *adj* diabolique.

devise [di'vaiz] *v* inventer; (*plan*) combiner.

devious ['diːviəs] *adj* détourné, tortueux.

devoid [di'void] *adj* dénué.

devolution [ˌdiːvə'luːʃən] *n* (*pol*) décentralisation *f*.

devote [di'vout] *v* consacrer. **devoted** *adj* dévoué. **devotion** *n* dévouement *m*.

devour [di'vauə] *v* dévorer.

devout [di'vaut] *adj* (*person*) pieux; (*earnest*) fervent.

dew [djuː] *n* rosée *f*.

dexterous ['dekstrəs] *adj* adroit. **dexterity** *n* adresse *f*.

diabetes [ˌdaiə'biːtiːz] *n* diabète *m*. **diabetic** *n(m+f), adj* diabétique.

diagnose [ˌdaiəg'nouz] *v* diagnostiquer. **diagnosis** *n* diagnostic *m*. **diagnostic** *adj* diagnostique.

diagonal [dai'agənəl] *adj* diagonal. *n* diagonale *f*.

diagram ['daiəgram] *n* diagramme *m*; (*math*) figure *f*. **diagrammatic** *adj* schématique.

dial ['daiəl] *n* cadran *m*. *v* (*number*) faire. **dial direct** appeler par l'automatique. **dial 999** appeler Police Secours. **dialling code** indicatif *m*. **dialling tone** tonalité *f*.

dialect ['daiəlekt] *n* dialecte *m*; (*rural*) patois *m*.

dialogue ['daiəlog] *n* dialogue *m*.

diameter [dai'amitə] *n* diamètre *m*. **diametrically opposed** diamétralement opposé.

diamond ['daiəmənd] *n* (*gem*) diamant *m*; (*cards*) carreau *m*; (*shape*) losange *m*.

diaper ['daiəpə] *n* (*US*) couche *f*.

diaphragm ['daiəˌfram] *n* diaphragme *m*.

diarrhoea [ˌdaiə'riə] *n* diarrhée *f*.

diary ['daiəri] *n* (*record*) journal *m*; (*appointments*) agenda *m*.

dice [dais] *n* dé *m*. *v* couper en dés. **dice with death** jouer avec la mort.

dictate [dik'teit] *v* dicter. **dictation** *n* dictée *f*. **dictator** *n* dictateur *m*. **dictatorship** *n* dictature *f*.

dictionary ['dikʃənəri] *n* dictionnaire *m*.

did [did] *V* do.

die [dai] *v* mourir. **be dying** se mourir. **be dying to** mourir d'envie de. **be dying for** avoir une envie folle de. **die down** s'apaiser. **die out** disparaître.

diesel ['diːzəl] *n* diesel *m*. **diesel oil** gas-oil *m*. **diesel train** autorail *m*.

diet ['daiət] *n* (*restricted*) régime *m*; (*normal food*) nourriture *f*. *v* suivre un régime.

differ ['difə] *v* différer; ne pas être d'accord. **difference** *n* différence *f*. **different** *adj* différent; (*another*) autre. **differential** *adj* différentiel. **differentials** *pl n* (*salary*) écarts salariaux *m pl*. **differentiate** *v* distinguer.

difficult ['difikəlt] *adj* difficile. **difficulty** *n* difficulté *f*.

*dig [dig] v creuser; (dog) fouiller. **dig up** déterrer. n (archaeol) fouille f; (coll: remark) coup de patte m; (with elbow) coup de coude m.

digest [dai'dʒest] v digérer. **digestion** n digestion f.

digit ['didʒit] n (math) chiffre m; (finger) doigt m. **digital** adj (clock, etc.) à affichage numérique.

dignified ['dignifaid] adj digne.

dignity ['digniti] n dignité f.

digress [dai'gres] v s'éloigner. **digression** n digression f.

digs [digz] pl n chambre f sing, logement m sing.

dilapidated [di'lapideitid] adj délabré.

dilate [dai'leit] v (se) dilater. **dilation** n dilatation f.

dilemma [di'lemə] n dilemme m.

diligent ['dilidʒent] adj assidu; laborieux. **diligence** n assiduité f, zèle m.

dilute [dai'luːt] v diluer. adj dilué.

dim [dim] adj (light) faible; (sound) vague; (coll: stupid) bouché. **take a dim view of** voir d'un mauvais œil. v (light) baisser; (sound) affaiblir. **dimness** n faiblesse f; obscurité f.

dimension [di'menʃən] n dimension f. **two-/three-dimensional** à deux/trois dimensions.

diminish [di'miniʃ] v diminuer.

diminutive [di'minjutiv] adj (small) tout petit; (gramm) diminutif. n diminutif m.

dimple ['dimpl] n fossette f.

din [din] n vacarme m.

dine [dain] v dîner. **diner** n (person) dîneur, -euse m, f. **dining car** wagon-restaurant m. **dining room** salle à manger f.

dinghy ['dingi] n youyou m; (with sail) dériveur m.

dingy ['dindʒi] adj miteux.

dinner ['dinə] n dîner m; (midday meal) déjeuner m. **dinner jacket** smoking m.

dinosaur ['dainəsoɪ] n dinosaure m.

diocese ['daiəsis] n diocèse m.

dip [dip] v (into water, etc.) plonger; (go down) baisser. n (coll: bathe) baignade f; (in ground) déclivité f. **dip-stick** n jauge f.

diphthong ['difθoŋ] n diphtongue f.

diploma [di'ploumə] n diplôme m.

diplomacy [di'plouməsi] n diplomatie f. **diplomat** n diplomate m. **diplomatic** adj diplomatique; (person) diplomate.

dire [daiə] adj terrible; extrême. **in dire straits** dans une situation désespérée.

direct [di'rekt] adj direct. **direct object** complément direct m. v diriger; adresser; (instruct) charger. adv directement. **direction** n direction f; instruction f. **directly** adv directement; (immediately) tout de suite. **director** n directeur, -trice m, f; (theatre) metteur en scène m; (film, TV, etc.) réalisateur, -trice m, f. **directory** n (phone) annuaire m; (addresses) répertoire m. **directory enquiries** renseignements m pl.

dirt [dəːt] n saleté f, crasse f.

dirty ['dəːti] adj sale; (vulgar) grossier. v salir.

disability [disə'biləti] n incapacité f; infirmité f. **disabled** adj infirme, handicapé.

disadvantage [disəd'vaːntidʒ] n désavantage m. **at a disadvantage** dans une position désavantageuse.

disagree [disə'griː] v ne pas être d'accord; (be different) ne pas concorder; (food, etc.) ne pas convenir (à). **disagreeable** adj désagréable. **disagreement** n désaccord m.

disappear [disə'piə] v disparaître. **disappearance** n disparition f.

disappoint [disə'point] v decevoir. **disappointment** n déception f.

disapprove [disə'pruːv] v désapprouver **disapproval** n désapprobation f. **disapproving** adj désapprobateur, -trice m, f.

disarm [dis'aːm] v désarmer. **disarmamen** n désarmement m. **disarming** adj (smile désarmant.

disaster [di'zaːstə] n désastre m, catastrophe f. **disastrous** adj désastreux.

disband [dis'band] v (se) disperser.

disbelief [disbi'liːf] n incrédulité f.

disc or US **disk** [disk] n disque m.

discard [dis'kaːd; n 'diskaːd] v se débarrasser de; abandonner; (cards) s défausser de. n défausse f.

discern [di'səːn] v discerner. **discernible** adj perceptible. **discerning** adj judicieux **discernment** n discernement m.

discharge [dis'tʃaːdʒ] v (patient, employee renvoyer; (gun) tirer; (cargo) décharger (duty) remplir; (law, mil) libérer. n renvo m; (elec) décharge f; (med) pertes f pl. **disciple** [di'saipl] n disciple m.

discipline ['disiplin] n discipline f. v disc pliner; punir. **disciplinary** adj dis ciplinaire.

disclaim [dis'kleim] v désavouer.
disclose [dis'klouz] v divulguer, révéler.
disclosure n divulgation f, révélation f.
discolour [dis'kʌlə] v (se) décolorer; (from white) jaunir. **discolouration** n décoloration f; jaunissement m.
discomfort [dis'kʌmfət] n malaise m, gêne f.
disconcert [diskən'sɜːt] v déconcerter.
disconnect [diskə'nekt] v disjoindre; (gas, phone, etc.) couper; (television, etc.) débrancher. **disconnected** adj (thoughts, etc.) décousu.
disconsolate [dis'kɔnsələt] adj adj inconsolable.
discontented [diskən'tentid] adj mécontent. **discontent** or **discontentment** n mécontentement m.
discontinue [diskən'tinjuː] v cesser; interrompre.
discord ['diskɔːd] n discorde f; (music) dissonance f. **discordant** adj discordant; dissonant.
discotheque ['diskətek] n discothèque f.
discount ['diskaunt] n remise f, escompte m. **at a discount** au rabais. **discount store** magasin de demi-gros m. v ne pas tenir compte de.
discourage [dis'kʌridʒ] v décourager. **become discouraged** se laisser décourager. **discouragement** n désapprobation f.
discover [dis'kʌvə] v découvrir. **discovery** n découverte f.
discredit [dis'kredit] v discréditer. n discrédit m.
discreet [di'skriːt] adj discret, -ète. **discretion** n discrétion f. **use your own discretion** c'est à vous de juger. **discretionary** adj discrétionnaire.
discrepancy [di'skrepənsi] n divergence f, désaccord m.
discrete [di'skriːt] adj discret, -ète.
discriminate [di'skrimi,neit] v distinguer; (unfairly) établir une discrimination. **discrimination** n distinction f; discrimination f; discernement m.
discus ['diskəs] n disque m.
discuss [dis'kʌs] v discuter. **discussion** n discussion f.
disdain [dis'dein] n dédain m. **disdainful** adj dédaigneux. **disdainfully** adv avec dédain.
disease [di'ziːz] n maladie f. **diseased** adj malade.

disembark [disim'bɑːk] v débarquer. **disembarkation** n débarquement m.
disengage [disin'geidʒ] v dégager; (tech) débrayer. **disengaged** adj libre; débrayé.
disentangle [disin'tangl] v débrouiller.
disfigure [dis'figə] v défigurer. **disfigurement** n défigurement m.
disgrace [dis'greis] n honte f; (disfavour) disgrâce f. **in disgrace** (child, etc.) en pénitence. v faire honte à; déshonorer. **disgraceful** adj honteux, scandaleux.
disgruntled [dis'grʌntld] adj mécontent.
disguise [dis'gaiz] v déguiser. n déguisement m; masque m. **in disguise** déguisé.
disgust [dis'gʌst] n dégoûter. **disgusting** adj dégoûtant, écœurant.
dish [diʃ] n plat m. **do the dishes** faire la vaisselle. **dishcloth** n lavette f. **dishwasher** n lave-vaisselle m invar. v **dish up** servir.
dishearten [dis'hɑːtn] v décourager.
dishevelled [di'fevəld] adj échevelé.
dishonest [dis'ɔnist] adj malhonnête. **dishonesty** n malhonnêteté f.
dishonour [dis'ɔnə] n déshonneur m. v déshonorer. **dishonourable** adj déshonorant.
disillusion [disi'luːʒən] v désillusionner. n désillusion f.
disinfect [disin'fekt] v désinfecter. **disinfectant** nm, adj désinfectant. **disinfection** n désinfection f.
disinherit [disin'herit] v déshériter.
disintegrate [dis'inti,greit] v (se) désintégrer. **disintegration** n désintégration f.
disinterested [dis'intristid] adj désintéressé.
disjointed [dis'dʒointid] adj décousu.
disk V **disc**.
dislike [dis'laik] v ne pas aimer. n aversion f. **take a dislike to** prendre en grippe.
dislocate ['dislə,keit] v disloquer. **dislocation** n dislocation f.
dislodge [dis'lodʒ] v faire bouger.
disloyal [dis'loiəl] adj déloyal. **disloyalty** n déloyauté f.
dismal ['dizməl] adj morne, lugubre.
dismantle [dis'mantl] v démonter.
dismay [dis'mei] n consternation f. v consterner.
dismiss [dis'mis] v (send away) renvoyer, congédier; (meeting) dissoudre; (reject) écarter. **dismissal** n renvoi m, congédiement m.

dismount [dis'maunt] *v* descendre.
disobey [disə'bei] *v* désobéir à. **disobedience** *n* désobéissance *f*. **disobedient** *adj* désobéissant.
disorder [dis'ɔːdə] *n* désordre *m*; (*med*) trouble *m*. **disorderly** *adj* désordonné.
disorganized [dis'ɔːgənaizd] *adj* désorganisé.
disown [dis'oun] *v* renier.
disparage [di'sparidʒ] *v* dénigrer. **disparagement** *n* dénigrement *m*. **disparaging** *adj* désobligeant.
disparity [dis'pariti] *n* disparité *f*.
dispassionate [dis'paʃənit] *adj* calme; impartial. **dispassionately** *adv* sans émotion; impartialement.
dispatch [di'spatʃ] *v* expédier. *n* expédition *f*; (*report*) dépêche *f*.
dispel [di'spel] *v* dissiper.
dispense [di'spens] *v* distribuer, administrer; (*medicine*) préparer. **dispense with** se passer de. **dispensary** *n* pharmacie *f*. **dispensation** *n* (*decree*) décret *m*; (*rel*) dispense *f*.
disperse [di'spəːs] *v* (se) disperser; (se) dissiper. **dispersal** *n* dispersion *f*.
displace [dis'pleis] *v* déplacer. **displacement** *n* déplacement *m*.
display [di'splei] *v* étaler; (*courage, etc.*) faire preuve de. *n* exposition *f*; (*comm*) étalage; (*courage, etc.*) manifestation *f*.
displease [dis'pliːz] *v* déplaire à. **displeasure** *n* mécontentement *m*.
dispose [di'spouz] *v* disposer. **dispose of** se débarrasser de. **disposable** *adj* à jeter. **disposal** *n* disposition *f*; (*rubbish*) enlèvement *m*; (*bomb*) désamorçage *m*. **disposition** *n* tempérament *m*; inclination *f*.
disproportion [disprə'pɔːʃən] *n* disproportion *f*. **disproportionate** *adj* disproportionné.
disprove [dis'pruːv] *v* réfuter.
dispute [di'spjuːt] *n* dispute *f*, (*argument*) discussion *f*; (*industrial*) conflit *m*. **beyond dispute** incontestable. *v* contester; discuter. **disputable** *adj* discutable.
disqualify [dis'kwoliˌfai] *v* disqualifier. **disqualification** *n* disqualification *f*.
disregard [disrə'gaːd] *v* (*ignore*) mépriser; négliger. *n* indifférence *f*; mépris.
disreputable [dis'repjutəbl] *adj* louche; (*clothes*) miteux.
disrespect [disrə'spekt] *n* manque de respect *m*. **disrespectful** *adj* irrespec-

tueux. **be disrespectful to** manquer de respect envers.
disrupt [dis'rʌpt] *v* perturber, interrompre. **disruption** *n* perturbation *f*; interruption *f*. **disruptive** *adj* perturbateur, -trice.
dissatisfied [di'satisˌfaid] *adj* mécontent. **dissatisfaction** *n* mécontentement *m*.
dissect [di'sekt] *v* disséquer. **dissection** *n* dissection *f*.
dissent [di'sent] *v* différer. *n* dissentiment *m*. **dissension** *n* dissension *f*.
dissident ['disidənt] *n, adj* dissident, -e. **dissidence** *n* dissidence *f*.
dissimilar [di'similə] *adj* dissemblable. **dissimilarity** *n* dissemblance *f*.
dissociate [di'sousieit] *v* dissocier. **dissociation** *n* dissociation *f*.
dissolve [di'zolv] *v* (se) dissoudre.
dissuade [di'sweid] *v* dissuader. **dissuasion** *n* dissuasion *f*.
distance ['distəns] *n* distance *f*. **in the distance** au loin. **distant** *adj* lointain, éloigné; (*reserved*) distant.
distaste [dis'teist] *n* dégoût *m*. **distasteful** *adj* déplaisant.
distemper [di'stempə] *n* (*paint*) détrempe *f*. *v* peindre en détrempe.
distended [di'stendid] *adj* (*med*) dilaté; distendu. **distension** *n* dilatation *f*; distension *f*.
distil [di'stil] *v* (se) distiller. **distillery** *n* distillerie *f*.
distinct [di'stiŋkt] *adj* distinct; net, nette. **distinction** *n* distinction *f*. **distinctive** *adj* distinctif.
distinguish [di'stiŋgwiʃ] *v* distinguer; caractériser.
distort [di'stɔːt] *v* déformer. **distortion** *n* distorsion *f*; déformation *f*.
distract [di'strakt] *v* distraire. **distracting** *adj* gênant. **distraction** *n* distraction *f*; interruption *f*.
distraught [di'strɔːt] *adj* éperdu.
distress [di'stres] *n* douleur *f*, affliction *f*; (*poverty, danger*) détresse *f*. *v* affliger. **distressing** *adj* pénible.
distribute [di'stribjut] *v* distribuer; (*share*) répartir. **distribution** *n* distribution *f*; répartition *f*. **distributor** *n* (*mot*) distributeur *m*.
district ['distrikt] *n* (*of town*) quartier *m*; (*admin*) arrondissement *m*; (*of country*) région *f*. **district nurse** infirmière visiteuse *f*.

distrust [dis'trʌst] v se méfier de. n méfiance f. **distrustful** adj méfiant.

disturb [di'stəːb] v déranger; troubler. **disturbance** n dérangement m; (noise) tapage m. **disturbing** adj inquiétant.

disuse [dis'juːs] n désuétude f. **fall into disuse** tomber en désuétude. **disused** adj désaffecté.

ditch [ditʃ] n fossé m.

ditto ['ditou] adv idem.

divan [di'van] n divan m.

dive [daiv] v plonger. n plongeon m; (submarine) plongée f. **diver** n plongeur m. **diving board** plongeoir m.

diverge [dai'vəːdʒ] v diverger. **divergence** n divergence f. **divergent** adj divergent.

diverse [dai'vəːs] adj divers. **diversity** n diversité f.

divert [dai'vəːt] v détourner; (traffic) dévier; (amuse) divertir. **diversion** n déviation f; divertissement m. **create a diversion** faire une diversion.

divide [di'vaid] v (se) diviser; (se) séparer. **divided** adj (country) désuni. **dividers** pl n compas à pointes sèches m sing. **dividing** adj (wall, etc.) mitoyen. **divisible** adj divisible. **division** n division f; séparation f.

dividend ['dividend] n dividende m.

divine [di'vain] adj divin. **divinity** n divinité f; théologie f.

divorce [di'vɔːs] n divorce m. v divorcer (avec). **divorcee** n divorcé, -e m, f.

divulge [dai'vʌldʒ] v divulguer.

dizzy ['dizi] adj pris de vertige; (height) vertigineux. **dizziness** n vertige m.

***do** [duː] v faire; (suffice) suffire (à); (coll: cheat) refaire. **do away with** supprimer. **do up** (clothes) (se) fermer; (parcel) emballer; (house) remettre à neuf. **do without** se passer de. **how do you do?** (on introduction) enchanté. **that will do!** ça suffit!

docile ['dousail] adj docile.

dock¹ [dok] n (ships) dock m, bassin m. **dockyard** n chantier naval m. v mettre à quai; (space) s'arrimer. **docker** n docker m.

dock² [dok] n (law) banc des accusés m.

dock³ [dok] v écourter; (wages) rogner.

doctor ['doktə] n docteur m, médecin m; (university) docteur m. **doctorate** n doctorat m.

doctrine ['doktrin] n doctrine f.

document ['dokjumənt] n document m. v documenter. **documentary** nm, adj documentaire. **documentation** n documentation f.

dodge [dodʒ] v (s')esquiver; (tax) éviter de payer. n détour m; (sport) esquive f; (coll: trick) truc m. **dodgy** adj délicat; douteux.

dog [dog] n chien m. **dog-eared** adj écorné. **dogfish** n chien de mer m. **dog rose** églantine f. v (follow) suivre de près; (plague) harceler.

dogged ['dogid] adj tenace. **doggedly** adv avec ténacité.

dogma ['dogmə] n dogme m. **dogmatic** adj dogmatique.

do-it-yourself [ˌduːitjɔː'self] n bricolage m.

dole [doul] n allocation de chômage f. **on the dole** au chômage. v **dole out** distribuer.

doll [dol] n poupée f. v **doll up** bichonner.

dollar ['dolə] n dollar m.

dolphin ['dolfin] n dauphin m.

domain [də'mein] n domaine m.

dome [doum] n dôme m.

domestic [də'mestik] adj domestique; (not foreign) intérieur. **domestic science** arts ménagers m pl. n domestique.

dominate ['domiˌneit] v dominer. **dominance** n dominance f. **dominant** adj dominant. **domination** n domination f.

domineering [domi'niəriŋ] adj dominateur, -trice.

dominion [də'minjən] n dominion m, territoire m.

domino ['dominou] n domino m.

don [don] v revêtir.

donate [də'neit] v faire don de; (blood) donner. **donation** n don m.

done [dʌn] V do.

donkey ['doŋki] n âne, -esse m, f.

donor ['dounə] n (med) donneur, -euse m, f; (charity) donateur, -euse m, f.

doom [duːm] v condamner. n destin m. **doomed** adj voué à l'échec.

door [dɔː] n porte f; (car, train) portière f. **doorbell** n sonnette f. **doorknob** n poignée de porte f. **door-knocker** n heurtoir m. **doormat** n essuie-pieds m invar. **doorstep** n pas de porte m. **door-to-door** adj, adv à domicile. **doorway** n embrasure de porte f.

dope [doup] v doper. n dopant m; (slang: drugs) drogue f; (slang: person) andouille f.

dormant ['dɔːmənt] *adj* en sommeil.
dormitory ['dɔːmɪtəri] *n* dortoir *m*. **dormitory town** ville dortoir *f*.
dormouse ['dɔːˌmaus] *n, pl* -**mice** loir *m*.
dose [dous] *n* dose *f*. *v* administrer un médicament à. **dosage** *n* dosage *m*; (*on bottle*) posologie *f*.
dot [dot] *n* point *m*. *v* pointiller. **dotted line** pointillé *m*.
dote [dout] *v* **dote on** raffoler de. **dotage** *n* (*senility*) gâtisme *m*.
double ['dʌbl] *adj, adv* double; deux fois. *n* double *m*. *v* doubler; plier en deux.
double-barrelled [ˌdʌbl'barəld] *adj* (*coll: name*) à rallonges; (*gun*) à deux coups.
double bass [beis] *n* contrebasse *f*.
double bed *n* grand lit *m*.
double cream crème à fouetter *f*.
double-cross [ˌdʌbl'kros] *v* (*coll*) doubler.
double-decker [ˌdʌbl'dekə] *n* autobus à impériale *m*.
double dutch *n* baragouin *m*. **talk double dutch** baragouiner.
double-glazing [ˌdʌbl'gleiziŋ] *n* doubles fenêtres *f pl*.
double-jointed [ˌdʌbl'dʒointid] *adj* désarticulé.
double room *n* chambre à deux personnes *f*.
doubt [daut] *n* doute *m*. **no doubt** sans doute. *v* douter (de). **doubtful** *adj* douteux; incertain. **doubtless** *adv* sans aucun doute.
dough [dou] *n* pâte *f*; (*slang: money*) fric *m*. **doughnut** *n* beignet *m*.
dove [dʌv] *n* colombe *f*. **dovecote** *n* colombier *m*.
Dover ['douvə] *n* Douvres *f*.
dowdy ['daudi] *adj* sans élégance; démodé.
down¹ [daun] *adv* en bas; (*to ground*) par terre. *prep* en bas de; (*along*) le long de. *v* (*coll: drink*) s'envoyer. **down tools** cesser le travail.
down² [daun] *n* duvet *m*. **downy** *adj* duveté.
downcast ['daunˌkɑːst] *adj* abattu.
downfall ['daunˌfɔːl] *n* chute *f*.
downhearted [ˌdaun'hɑːtid] *adj* abattu.
downhill [ˌdaun'hil] *adj* en pente. **go downhill** descendre la pente; (*deteriorate*) être sur le déclin; (*business*) péricliter.
down payment *n* acompte *m*.
downpour ['daunˌpɔː] *n* averse *f*.

downright ['daunˌrait] *adj* catégorique. *adv* carrément; purement et simplement.
downstairs ['daunˌsteəz; *adv* ˌdaun'steəz] *adj* (*ground floor*) du rez-de-chaussée; (*below*) d'en bas. *adv* au rez-de-chaussée; en bas. **go downstairs** descendre.
downstream [ˌdaun'striːm] *adv* en aval. **go downstream** descendre le courant.
down-to-earth [ˌdauntə'əːθ] *adj* terre à terre.
downtrodden ['daunˌtrodn] *adj* opprimé.
downward ['daunwəd] *adj* vers le bas; (*glance*) baissé.
downwards ['daunwədz] *adv* vers le bas, en bas.
dowry ['dauəri] *n* dot *f*.
doze [douz] *v* sommeiller. *n* somme *m*.
dozen ['dʌzn] *n* douzaine *f*.
drab [drab] *adj* terne.
draft¹ [drɑːft] *n* (*letter*) brouillon *m*; (*sketch*) ébauche *f*; (*money*) retrait *m*; (*mil*) détachement *m*. *v* faire le brouillon de; (*plan*) esquisser; (*comm*) rédiger; (*mil*) détacher.
draft² *V* **draught**.
drag [drag] *v* traîner; (*river*) draguer. *n* résistance; (*coll: bore*) corvée *f*; (*coll: smoke*) bouffée *f*. **in drag** en travesti.
dragon ['dragən] *n* dragon *m*. **dragonfly** *n* libellule *f*.
drain [drein] *n* (*pipe*) égout *m*; (*grid*) bouche d'égout *f*. *v* drainer, vider. **draining board** égouttoir *m*. **drainpipe** *n* tuyau d'écoulement *m*. **drainage** *n* drainage *m*; (*in town*) système d'égouts *m*.
drama ['drɑːmə] *n* drame *m*; art dramatique *m*. **dramatic** *adj* dramatique; (*effect*) théâtral. **dramatist** *n* dramaturge *m*. **dramatize** *v* adapter pour la scène; (*exaggerate*) dramatiser.
drank [draŋk] *V* **drink**.
drape [dreip] *v* draper. **drapes** *pl n* (*US*) rideaux *m pl*.
draper ['dreipə] *n* marchand de nouveautés *m*. **draper's shop** magasin de nouveautés *m*. **drapery** *n* draperie *f*.
drastic ['drastik] *adj* énergique, radical.
draught *or US* **draft** [drɑːft] *n* courant d'air *m*; (*drink*) coup *m*. **draughts** *pl n* dames *f pl*. **draught beer** bière à la pression *f*. **draughtboard** *n* damier *m*. **draught excluder** bourrelet *m*. **draughtsman** *n* dessinateur *m*.
*draw [drɔː] *v* (*art*) dessiner; (*pull*) tirer; (*attract*) attirer; (*be equal*) être ex aequo.

draw back reculer. **draw near** s'approcher (de). **draw up** (*plan*) dresser. *n* (*sport*) match nul *m*; (*lottery*) tirage au sort *m*.

drawback ['drɔːbak] *n* inconvénient *m*.

drawbridge ['drɔːbrɪdʒ] *n* pont-levis *m*.

drawer ['drɔːə] *n* tiroir *m*.

drawing ['drɔːɪŋ] *n* dessin *m*. **drawing board** planche à dessin *f*. **drawing pin** punaise *f*. **drawing room** salon *m*.

drawl [drɔːl] *n* voix traînante *f*. *v* parler d'une voix traînante.

drawn [drɔːn] *V* **draw**.

dread [dred] *v* redouter. *n* terreur *f*. **dreadful** *adj* épouvantable, atroce. **dreadfully** *adv* terriblement.

*dream [driːm] *n* rêve *m*. *v* rêver; (*imagine*) songer. **dreamy** *adj* rêveur, -euse.

dreamt [dremt] *V* **dream**.

dreary ['drɪəri] *adj* morne; monotone.

dredge [dredʒ] *v* draguer. *n* drague *f*.

dregs [dregz] *pl n* lie *f sing*.

drench [drentʃ] *v* tremper.

dress [dres] *n* robe; (*clothing*) tenue *f*. **dress circle** premier balcon *m*. **dressmaker** *n* couturière *f*. **dressmaking** *n* couture *f*. **dress rehearsal** répétition générale *f*. *v* (s')habiller; (*salad*) assaisonner; (*wound*) panser. **dress up as** se déguiser en. **dressy** *adj* élégant.

dresser[1] ['dresə] *n* (*furniture*) buffet *m*.

dresser[2] ['dresə] *n* (*theatre*) habilleur, -euse *m, f*.

dressing ['dresɪŋ] *n* (*wound*) pansement *m*; (*cookery*) assaisonnement *m*. **dressing gown** robe de chambre *f*. **dressing room** (*theatre*) loge *f*; (*in house*) dressing-room *m*. **dressing table** coiffeuse *f*.

drew [druː] *V* **draw**.

dribble ['drɪbl] *v* (*child*) baver; (*liquid*) couler lentement; (*sport*) dribbler. *n* bave *f*; petite goutte *f*; dribble *m*.

dried [draɪd] *adj* séché; déshydraté; (*milk*) en poudre. **dried fruit** fruits secs *m pl*.

drier ['draɪə] *n* séchoir *m*.

drift [drɪft] *v* dériver, aller à la dérive. *n* (*heap*) amoncellement *m*; (*deviation*) dérive *f*; (*gist*) but *m*. **driftwood** *n* bois flotté *m*.

drill [drɪl] *v* (*hole*) forer; (*tooth*) fraiser. *n* foret *m*; fraise *f*; (*mil*) exercice *m*.

*drink [drɪŋk] *v* boire. *n* boisson *f*. **drinkable** *adj* potable. **drinking water** eau potable *f*.

drip [drɪp] *v* dégoutter. *n* (*drop*) goutte *f*; (*coll: person*) nouille *f*; (*med*) goutte-à-goutte *m invar*. **drip-dry** *adj* (*on label*) ne pas repasser. **dripping** *n* (*fat*) graisse *f*.

*drive [draɪv] *v* conduire; (*push*) chasser; (*nail*) enfoncer. *n* (*trip*) promenade en voiture *f*; (*to house*) allée *f*; (*energy*) dynamisme *m*. **driver** *n* conducteur, -trice *m, f*. **driving** *n* conduite *f*. **driving licence** permis de conduire *m*. **driving school** auto-école *f*. **driving test** examen du permis de conduire *m*.

drivel ['drɪvl] *v* radoter. *n* radotage *m*.

driven ['drɪvn] *V* **drive**.

drizzle ['drɪzl] *v* bruiner. *n* bruine *f*.

drone [droun] *v* ronronner, vrombir; (*bee*) bourdonner. *n* ronronnement *m*, vrombissement *m*; bourdonnement *m*.

droop [druːp] *v* s'affaisser, retomber.

drop [drop] *n* (*liquid*) goutte *f*; (*fall*) baisse *f*. *v* (*fall*) tomber; (*let fall*) laisser tomber; (*price*) baisser. **drop off** (*sleep*) s'endormir. **dropper** *n* compte-gouttes *m invar*. **droppings** *pl n* crottes *f pl*; (*bird*) fiente *f sing*.

drought [draut] *n* sécheresse *f*.

drove [drouv] *V* **drive**.

drown [draun] *v* (se) noyer.

drowsy ['drauzi] *adj* somnolent. **grow drowsy** s'assoupir. **drowsiness** *n* somnolence *f*.

drudgery ['drʌdʒəri] *n* corvée *f*.

drug [drʌg] *n* drogue *f*. **be on drugs** se droguer. **drug addict** drogué, -e *m, f*. *v* droguer.

drum [drʌm] *n* tambour *m*; (*oil*) tonnelet *m*. **drumstick** *n* baguette de tambour *f*; (*chicken*) pilon *m*. *v* tambouriner. **drummer** *n* tambour *m*.

drunk [drʌŋk] *V* **drink**. *adj* ivre. **get drunk** s'enivrer. *n also* **drunkard** ivrogne, -esse *m, f*. **drunkenness** *n* ivresse *f*.

dry [draɪ] *adj* sec, sèche; (*wit*) caustique; (*dull*) aride. **dry-clean** *v* nettoyer à sec. **dry cleaner's** teinturerie *f*. **dry rot** pourriture sèche *f*. **dry ski slope** piste artificielle *f*. *v* sécher. **dry up** se dessécher, se tarir; (*dishes*) essuyer la vaisselle.

dual ['djuəl] *adj* double.

dubbed ['dʌbd] *adj* (*film*) doublé. **dubbing** *n* doublage *m*.

dubious ['djuːbiəs] *adj* douteux.

Dublin ['dʌblin] *n* Dublin.

duchess [ˈdʌtʃis] n duchesse f.
duck¹ [dʌk] n canard m. **duckling** n
caneton, canette m. f. **duckpond** n mare
aux canards f.
duck² [dʌk] v (dodge) se baisser subitement; (submerge) plonger.
duct [dʌkt] n conduite f; (anat) conduit
m.
dud [dʌd] adj raté; faux, fausse.
due [djuː] adj dû, due; (suitable) qui convient. **be due** devoir arriver. adv droit.
dues pl n droits m pl.
duel [ˈdjuəl] n duel m. v se battre en duel.
duellist n duelliste m.
duet [djuˈet] n duo m.
dug [dʌg] V **dig**.
duke [djuːk] n duc m.
dull [dʌl] adj terne; (sound) sourd;
(weather) gris. (se) ternir; (s')assourdir;
(blunt) s')émousser.
dumb [dʌm] adj muet, muette; (slang:
stupid) bêta, -asse. **dumbbell** n haltère m.
dumbfound v confondre. **dumbness** n
mutisme m.
dummy [ˈdʌmi] n (comm) factice m;
(dressmaker's) mannequin m; (ventriloquist's) pantin m; (baby's) sucette f. **dummy run** coup d'essai m.
dump [dʌmp] n (tip) décharge f; (coll:
place) trou. **be down in the dumps** avoir
le cafard. v déposer.
dumpling [ˈdʌmpliŋ] n (savoury) boulette
de pâte f; (fruit) chausson m.
dunce [dʌns] n âne m. **dunce's cap** bonnet
d'âne m.
dune [djuːn] n dune f.
dung [dʌŋ] n crotte f; (manure) fumier m.
dungarees [ˌdʌŋɡəˈriːz] pl n salopette f
sing.
dungeon [ˈdʌndʒən] n cachot m.
Dunkirk [ˈdʌnkəːk] n Dunkerque.
duplicate [ˈdjuːplikeit; n, adj ˈdjuːplikət] v
faire un double de; (photocopy)
polycopier. n double m. adj en double;
(comm) en duplicata.
durable [ˈdjuərəbl] adj solide; durable.
duration [djuˈreiʃən] n durée f.
during [ˈdjuəriŋ] prep pendant.
dusk [dʌsk] n crépuscule m. **dusky** adj
sombre.
dust [dʌst] n poussière f. **dustbin** n
poubelle f. **dustman** n éboueur m. **dustpan** n pelle à poussière f. **dust sheet**
housse f. v épousseter. **duster** n chiffon
m. **dusty** adj poussiéreux.

Dutch [dʌtʃ] nm, adj hollandais, néerlandais. **the Dutch** les Hollandais m pl,
les Néerlandais m pl.
duty [ˈdjuːti] n devoir m; (job) fonction f;
(tax) droit m. **duty-free** exempté de
douane. **duty-free shop** magasin hors-
taxe m. **off duty** libre. **on duty** de service.
dutiful adj respectueux; consciencieux.
duvet [ˈduːvei] n couette f.
dwarf [dwoːf] n, adj nain, -e m, f. v
écraser.
*** dwell** [dwel] v habiter. **dwell on** s'arrêter
sur. **dwelling** n habitation f.
dwelt [dwelt] V **dwell**.
dwindle [ˈdwindl] v diminuer.
dye [dai] n teinture f. v teindre.
dyke [daik] n (ditch) fossé m; (barrier)
digue f.
dynamic [daiˈnamik] adj dynamique.
dynamism n dynamisme m.
dynamite [ˈdainəˌmait] n dynamite f.
dynamo [ˈdainəˌmou] n dynamo f.
dynasty [ˈdinəsti] n dynastie f.
dysentery [ˈdisəntri] n dysenterie f.
dyslexia [disˈleksiə] n dyslexie f. **dyslexic**
n(m + f), adj dyslexique.
dyspepsia [disˈpepsiə] n dyspepsie f.

E

each [iːtʃ] adj chaque. pron chacun, -e.
each other l'un l'autre, les uns les autres.
eager [ˈiːɡə] adj avide; ardent; impatient.
eagerness n désir ardent m; impatience f.
eagle [ˈiːɡl] n aigle m.
ear¹ [iə] n oreille f. **earache** n mal
d'oreille m. **eardrum** n tympan m.
earmark v réserver; (money) assigner.
earphones pl n casque m sing. **earring** n
boucle d'oreille f. **earshot** n portée de
voix f.
ear² [iə] n (grain) épi m.
earl [əːl] n comte m.
early [ˈəːli] adv de bonne heure, tôt. adj
tôt; prématuré; précoce.
earn [əːn] v gagner; mériter. **earnings** pl n
salaire m sing; profits m pl.
earnest [ˈəːnist] adj sérieux; ardent; sincère. **in earnest** sérieusement.

earth [əɪθ] *n* terre *f*; (*of fox*) terrier *m*. **earthenware** *n* faïence *f*. **earthquake** *n* tremblement de terre *m*. *v* (*elec*) mettre à la terre.

earwig ['iəwig] *n* perce-oreille *m*.

ease [iɪz] *n* aise *f*; (*easiness*) aisance *f*. **at ease** à l'aise; (*mil*) repos. **with ease** facilement. *v* (*pain*) soulager; calmer; diminuer; (*relax*) se détendre.

easel ['iɪzl] *n* chevalet *m*.

east [iɪst] *n* est *m*. *adj also* **easterly, eastern** oriental; d'est; à l'est. *adv* à *or* vers l'est. **eastbound** *adj* est *invar*.

Easter ['iɪstə] *n* Pâques *f pl*. **Easter egg** œuf de Pâques *m*.

easy ['iɪzi] *adj* facile. **easy chair** fauteuil *m*. **easy-going** *adj* accommodant. **take it easy** ne pas se fatiguer. **easily** *adv* sans difficulté; sans aucun doute. **easiness** *n* facilité *f*.

*eat [iɪt] *v* manger. **eat out** aller au restaurant. **eat up** finir. **eatable** *adj* mangeable.

eaten ['iɪtn] *V* eat.

eavesdrop ['iɪvzdrop] *v* écouter de façon indiscrète. **eavesdropper** *n* oreille indiscrète *f*.

ebb [eb] *n* reflux *m*. *v* refluer; (*courage, etc*.) décliner.

ebony ['ebəni] *n* ébène *f*.

eccentric [ik'sentrik] *n*(*m*+*f*), *adj* excentrique. **eccentricity** *n* excentricité *f*.

ecclesiastical [ikliɪzi'astikl] *adj* ecclésiastique.

echo ['ekou] *n* écho *m*. *v* répercuter; répéter; résonner.

eclair [ei'kleə] *n* éclair *m*.

eclipse [i'klips] *n* éclipse *f*. *v* éclipser.

ecology [i'kolədʒi] *n* écologie *f*. **ecological** *adj* écologique. **ecologist** *n* écologiste *m*, *f*.

economy [i'konəmi] *n* économie *f*. **economic** *adj* économique; (*profitable*) rentable. **economical** *adj* économe, économique. **economics** *n* économique *f*. **economist** *n* économiste *m*, *f*. **economize** *v* économiser.

ecstasy ['ekstəsi] *n* extase *f*. **ecstatic** *adj* extasié. **be ecstatic about** s'extasier sur.

eczema ['eksimə] *n* eczéma *m*.

edge [edʒ] *n* bord *m*; (*of blade*) tranchant *m*. **on edge** énervé. *v* border; (*move*) se glisser. **edging** *n* bordure *f*. **edgy** *adj* énervé.

edible ['edəbl] *adj* comestible.

Edinburgh ['edinbərə] *n* Edimbourg.

edit ['edit] *v* (*text*) éditer; (*film*) monter; (*magazine*) diriger. **editor** *n* rédacteur, -trice *m*, *f*, éditeur, -trice *m*, *f*; (*newspaper*) rédacteur, -trice en chef *m*, *f*. **editorial** *n* éditorial *m*. **editorial staff** rédaction *f*.

edition [i'diʃən] *n* édition *f*.

educate ['edjuˌkeit] *v* instruire. **educated** *adj* instruit; cultivé. **education** *n* éducation *f*; (*teaching*) enseignement *m*; (*studies*) études *f pl*. **educational** *adj* (*methods*) pédagogique; (*game, etc*.) éducatif.

eel [iɪl] *n* anguille *f*.

eerie ['iəri] *adj* étrange; sinistre.

effect [i'fekt] *n* effet *m*. **take effect** (*drug*) faire son effet; (*rule, etc*.) entrer en vigueur. *v* effectuer. **effective** *adj* efficace. **effectiveness** *n* efficacité *f*.

effeminate [i'feminət] *adj* efféminé.

effervescent [ˌefə'vesənt] *adj* effervescent; (*drink*) gazeux. **effervescence** *n* effervescence *f*; (*drink*) pétillement *m*.

efficient [i'fiʃənt] *adj* efficace; compétent. **efficiency** *n* efficacité *f*; compétence *f*.

effigy ['efidʒi] *n* effigie *f*.

effort ['efət] *n* effort *m*. **effortless** *adj* facile.

egg [eg] *n* œuf *m*. **egg-cup** *n* coquetier *m*. **egg-shaped** *adj* ovoïde. **eggshell** *n* coquille d'œuf *f*.

egotism ['egətizm] *n* égotisme *m*. **egotist** *n* égotiste *m*, *f*.

Egypt ['iɪdʒipt] *n* Egypte *f*. **Egyptian** *n* Egyptien, -enne *m*, *f*; *adj* égyptien.

eiderdown ['aidədaun] *n* édredon *m*.

eight [eit] *nm*, *adj* huit. **eighth** *n*(*m*+*f*), *adj* huitième.

eighteen [ei'tiɪn] *nm*, *adj* dix-huit. **eighteenth** *n*(*m*+*f*), *adj* dix-huitième.

eighty ['eiti] *nm*, *adj* quatre-vingts. **eightieth** *n*(*m*+*f*), *adj* quatre-vingtième.

either ['aiðə] *adj* l'un ou l'autre; (*each*) chaque. *pron* l'un ou l'autre. *adv* non plus. *conj* ou. **either ... or ...** ou ... ou ....

ejaculate [i'dʒakjuleit] *v* éjaculer; (*shout*) s'exclamer. **ejaculation** *n* éjaculation *f*; exclamation *f*.

eject [i'dʒekt] *v* éjecter; expulser. **ejection** *n* éjection *f*; expulsion *f*. **ejector seat** siège éjectable *m*.

eke [iɪk] *v* **eke out** (*add to*) augmenter; (*make last*) faire durer.

elaborate [i'labərət; v i'labəreit] adj compliqué, minutieux. v élaborer; donner des détails. **elaborately** adv en détail.

elapse [i'laps] v s'écouler.

elastic [i'lastik] nm, adj élastique. **elastic band** n élastique m. **elasticity** n élasticité f.

elated [i'leitid] adj transporté. **elation** n exultation f.

elbow ['elbou] n coude m. **elbow grease** (coll) huile de coude f.

elder[1] ['eldə] n, adj aîné, -e.

elder[2] ['eldə] n sureau m. **elderberry** n baie de sureau f.

elderly ['eldəli] adj âgé.

eldest ['eldist] adj aîné.

elect [i'lekt] v élire; choisir. adj futur. **election** n élection f. **electoral** adj électoral. **electorate** n électorat m.

electric [ə'lektrik] adj électrique. **electric blanket** couverture chauffante f. **electric fire** radiateur électrique m. **electric shock** décharge électrique f. **electrical** adj électrique. **electrician** n électricien m. **electricity** n électricité f. **electrify** v électriser; (rail) électrifier.

electrocute [i'lektrəkjuːt] v électrocuter. **electrocution** n électrocution f.

electrode [i'lektroud] n électrode f.

electronic [elək'tronik] adj électronique. **electronics** n électronique f.

elegant ['eligənt] adj élégant. **elegance** n élégance f.

elegy ['elidʒi] n élégie f.

element ['eləmənt] n élément m; (elec) résistance f. **elementary** adj élémentaire.

elephant ['elifənt] n éléphant m.

elevate ['eliveit] v élever. **elevation** n élévation f; altitude f. **elevator** n (US) ascenseur m.

eleven [i'levn] nm, adj onze. **eleventh** n(m+f), adj onzième.

elf [elf] n elfe m. **elfin** adj d'elfe.

eligible ['elidʒəbl] adj éligible.

eliminate [i'limineit] v éliminer. **elimination** n élimination f.

elite [ei'liːt] n élite f.

ellipse [i'lips] n ellipse f. **elliptical** adj elliptique.

elm [elm] n orme m.

elocution [elə'kjuːʃən] n élocution f.

elope [i'loup] v s'enfuir.

eloquent ['eləkwənt] adj éloquent. **eloquence** n éloquence f.

else [els] adv autre, d'autre. **or else** autrement, ou bien. **elsewhere** adv ailleurs.

elude [i'luːd] v éluder, échapper à. **elusive** adj insaisissable.

emaciated [i'meisieitid] adj émacié. **emaciation** n émaciation f.

emanate ['eməneit] v émaner. **emanation** n émanation f.

emancipate [i'mansipeit] v émanciper. **emancipation** n émancipation f.

embalm [im'baːm] v embaumer.

embankment [im'baŋkmənt] n (rail) talus m; (river) quai m; (canal) digue f.

embargo [im'baːgou] n embargo m.

embark [im'baːk] v (s')embarquer. **embark on** commencer; s'engager dans. **embarkation** n embarquement m.

embarrass [im'barəs] v embarrasser, gêner. **embarrassment** n embarras m, gêne f.

embassy ['embəsi] n ambassade f.

embellish [im'beliʃ] v embellir. **embellishment** n embellissement m.

ember ['embə] n charbon ardent m. **embers** pl n braise f sing.

embezzle [im'bezl] v détourner. **embezzlement** n détournement de fonds m. **embezzler** n escroc m.

embitter [im'bitə] v (person) aigrir; (relationship) envenimer.

emblem ['embləm] n emblème m.

embody [im'bodi] v exprimer; réunir. **embodiment** n incarnation f, personnification f.

emboss [im'bos] v (metal) repousser; (paper, etc.) gaufrer. **embossed** adj (letterhead, etc.) en relief.

embrace [im'breis] v (s')embrasser. n enlacement m.

embroider [im'broidə] v broder; (truth) broder sur. **embroidery** n broderie f. **embroidery silk** soie à broder f.

embryo ['embriou] n embryon m. **in embryo** (project, etc.) en germe.

emerald ['emərəld] n émeraude f.

emerge [i'məːdʒ] v émerger, surgir.

emergency [i'məːdʒənsi] n cas urgent m; (med) urgence f. **emergency exit** sortie de secours f. **emergency landing** atterrissage forcé m. **in case of emergency** en cas d'urgence.

emigrate ['emigreit] v émigrer. **emigration** n émigration f.

eminent ['eminənt] adj éminent. **eminence** n distinction f.

emit [i'mit] *v* émettre.

emotion [i'mouʃən] *n* émotion *f*. **emotional** *adj* (*state*) émotionnel; (*shock*) émotif.

emotionally *adv* avec émotion.

empathy ['empəθi] *n* communion d'idées *f*.

emperor ['empərə] *n* empereur *m*.

empress *n* impératrice *f*.

emphasis ['emfəsis] *n* accent *m*; importance *f*. **emphasize** *v* appuyer sur; accentuer. **emphatic** *adj* énergique.

empire ['empaiə] *n* empire *m*.

empirical [im'pirikəl] *adj* empirique.

employ [im'ploi] *v* employer. **employee** *n* employé, -e *m*, *f*. **employer** *n* patron, -onne *m*, *f*. **employment** *n* emploi *m*. **employment agency** agence de placement *f*.

empower [im'pauə] *v* autoriser.

empty ['empti] *adj* vide; vacant. **empty-handed** *adj* bredouille. *v* vider. **emptiness** *n* vide *m*.

emu ['iːmjuː] *n* émeu *m*.

emulate ['emjuːleit] *v* imiter. **emulation** *n* émulation *f*.

emulsion [i'mʌlʃən] *n* émulsion *f*.

enable [i'neibl] *v* permettre à.

enact [i'nakt] *v* (*play*) jouer; (*decree*) décréter.

enamel [i'naməl] *n* émail (*pl* -aux) *m*. *v* émailler.

enamour [i'namə] *v* enchanter. **be enamoured of** être épris de.

encase [in'keis] *v* recouvrir (de).

enchant [in'tʃaint] *v* enchanter. **enchanting** *adj* ravissant. **enchantment** *n* enchantement *m*.

encircle [in'səːkl] *v* entourer.

enclose [in'klouz] *v* enclore; (*surround*) entourer; (*in letter*) joindre. **enclosed** *adj* ci-joint. **enclosure** *n* enceinte *f*; (*document*) pièce jointe *f*.

encore ['oŋkoɪ] *nm, interj* bis. *v* bisser.

encounter [in'kauntə] *v* affronter, rencontrer. *n* rencontre *f*.

encourage [in'kʌridʒ] *v* encourager. **encouragement** *n* encouragement *m*.

encroach [in'kroutʃ] *v* empiéter. **encroachment** *n* empiétement *m*.

encumber [in'kʌmbə] *v* encombrer. **encumbrance** *n* embarras *m*.

encyclopedia [insaiklə'piːdiə] *n* encyclopédie *f*.

end [end] *n* (*tip*) bout *m*; (*finish*) fin *f*.

end product (*comm*) produit fini *m*; (*result*) résultat *m*. **make ends meet** joindre les deux bouts. *v* finir; (se) terminer. **ending** *n* fin *f*; (*of word*) terminaison *f*. **endless** *adj* interminable; incessant.

endanger [in'deindʒə] *v* mettre en danger; compromettre.

endeavour [in'devə] *n* effort *m*. *v* s'efforcer (de).

endemic [en'demik] *adj* endémique. *n* endémie *f*.

endive ['endiv] *n* endive *f*; (*curly*) chicorée *f*.

endorse [in'dois] *v* (*cheque, etc.*) endosser; approuver. **endorsement** *n* endossement *m*; sanction *f*; (*mot*) contravention *f*.

endow [in'dau] *v* doter (de); (*prize, etc*) fonder. **endowment** *n* dotation *f*; fondation *f*.

endure [in'djuə] *v* supporter; (*last*) durer. **endurance** *n* endurance *f*, résistance *f*.

enemy ['enəmi] *n* ennemi, -e *m*, *f*.

energy ['enədʒi] *n* énergie *f*. **energetic** *adj* énergique.

enfold [in'fould] *v* envelopper.

enforce [in'fois] *v* (*law*) faire obéir; (*discipline*) imposer.

engage [in'geidʒ] *v* (s')engager; (*employee*) embaucher; (*clutch*) s'embrayer. **engaged** *adj* fiancé; occupé. **get engaged** se fiancer. **engagement** *n* rendez-vous *m invar*; fiançailles *f pl*; (*actor*) engagement *m*.

engine ['endʒin] *n* machine *f*; moteur *m*. **engine driver** mécanicien *m*. **engine room** (*on ship*) salle des machines *f*.

engineer [endʒi'niə] *n* ingénieur *m*; (*mechanic*) technicien *m*. *v* machiner. **engineering** *n* ingénierie *f*.

England ['iŋglənd] *n* Angleterre *f*. **English** *nm, adj* anglais. **the English** les Anglais.

engrave [in'greiv] *v* graver. **engraver** *n* graveur *m*. **engraving** *n* gravure *f*.

engrossed [in'groust] *adj* absorbé.

engulf [in'gʌlf] *v* engouffrer.

enhance [in'hains] *v* mettre en valeur, rehausser.

enigma [i'nigmə] *n* énigme *f*. **enigmatic** *adj* énigmatique.

enjoy [in'dʒoi] *v* aimer; (*good health, etc.*) jouir de. **enjoy oneself** s'amuser. **enjoyable** *adj* agréable. **enjoyment** *n* plaisir *m*.

enlarge [in'laidʒ] *v* (s')agrandir. **enlargement** *n* agrandissement *m*.

enlighten [in'laitn] v éclairer. **enlighten-ment** n éclaircissement m.

enlist [in'list] v (s')engager; recruter. **enlistment** n engagement m.

enmity ['enmɪti] n inimitié f.

enormous [i'nɔːməs] adj énorme. **enor-mously** adv énormément.

enough [i'nʌf] adj, adv, n assez. **be enough** suffire.

enquire [in'kwaiə] V **inquire**.

enrage [in'reidʒ] v mettre en rage.

enrich [in'ritʃ] v enrichir; (soil) fertiliser.

enrol [in'roul] v (s')inscrire; (mil) (s')enrôler. **enrolment** n inscription f; enrôlement m.

ensign ['ensain] n (emblem) insigne m; (flag) drapeau m; (naut) pavillon m.

enslave [in'sleiv] v asservir. **enslavement** n asservissement m.

ensue [in'sjuː] v s'ensuivre.

ensure [in'ʃuə] v assurer.

entail [in'teil] v occasionner, comporter.

entangle [in'taŋgl] v empêtrer, emmêler.

enter ['entə] v entrer (dans); (register) inscrire. **enter for** (exam) (se) présenter à.

enterprise ['entəpraiz] n entreprise f; initiative f. **enterprising** adj entreprenant.

entertain [entə'tein] v (amuse) divertir; (guests) recevoir; (idea) considérer. **entertainer** n artiste m, f. **entertainment** n divertissement m.

enthral [in'θrɔil] v captiver.

enthusiasm [in'θuːziˌazəm] n enthousiasme m. **enthusiast** n enthousiaste m, f. **enthusiastic** adj enthousiaste, passionné.

entice [in'tais] v attirer, entraîner. **enticing** adj attrayant; (food) alléchant.

entire [in'taiə] adj entier. **in its entirety** en entier.

entitle [in'taitl] v autoriser, donner droit à; (book) intituler.

entity ['entəti] n entité f.

entrails ['entreilz] pl n entrailles f pl.

entrance[1] ['entrəns] n entrée f.

entrance[2] [in'trains] v ravir.

entrant ['entrənt] n (competition, exam) candidat, -e m, f; (race) concurrent, -e m, f; (profession) débutant, -e m, f.

entreat [in'trit] v supplier. **entreaty** n supplication f.

entrench [in'trentʃ] v (mil) retrencher. **entrenched** adj (custom) implanté; indélogeable.

entrepreneur [ˌontrəprə'nəi] n entrepreneur m.

entrust [in'trʌst] v confier; (with task) charger.

entry ['entri] n entrée f; (on list) inscription f. **entry form** feuille d'inscription f. **no entry** (road) sens interdit; (gate, etc.) défense d'entrer.

entwine [in'twain] v (s')entrelacer.

enunciate [i'nʌnsiˌeit] v articuler; (theory) énoncer. **enunciation** n articulation f; énonciation f.

envelop [in'veləp] v envelopper.

envelope ['envəˌloup] n enveloppe f.

environment [in'vaiərənmənt] n milieu m, environnement m.

envisage [in'vizidʒ] v (foresee) prévoir; (imagine) envisager.

envoy ['envoi] n envoyé, -e m, f.

envy ['envi] n envie f. v envier. **enviable** adj enviable. **envious** adj envieux. **enviously** adv avec envie.

enzyme ['enzaim] n enzyme f.

ephemeral [i'femərəl] adj éphémère.

epic ['epik] adj épique. n épopée f.

epidemic [epi'demik] n épidémie f. adj épidémique.

epilepsy ['epilepsi] n épilepsie f. **epileptic** n(m+f), adj épileptique. **epileptic fit** crise d'epilepsie f.

epilogue ['epilog] n épilogue m.

Epiphany [i'pifəni] n Epiphanie f, fête des Rois f.

episcopal [i'piskəpəl] adj épiscopal.

episode ['episoud] n épisode m. **episodic** adj épisodique.

epitaph ['epiˌtaːf] n épitaphe f.

epitome [i'pitəmi] n modèle m; quintessence f. **epitomize** v incarner.

epoch ['iːpɔk] n époque f.

equable ['ekwəbl] adj égal.

equal ['iːkwəl] adj égal, -e. v égaler. **equality** n égalité f. **equalize** v égaliser.

equanimity [ekwə'nimɪti] n sérénité f.

equate [i'kweit] v assimiler; (make equal) égaler. **equation** n équation f.

equator [i'kweitə] n équateur m. **equatorial** adj équatorial.

equestrian [i'kwestriən] adj équestre. n cavalier, -ère m, f.

equilateral [ˌiːkwi'latərəl] adj équilatéral.

equilibrium [ˌiːkwi'libriəm] n équilibre m.

equinox ['ekwinoks] n équinoxe m. **equinoctial** adj équinoxial.

equip [i'kwip] *v* équiper. **equipment** *n* équipement *m*; matériel *m*.

equity ['ekwəti] *n* équité *f*.

equivalent [i'kwivələnt] *nm, adj* équivalent.

era ['iərə] *n* ère *f*; époque *f*.

eradicate [i'radi,keit] *v* extirper, supprimer.

erase [i'reiz] *v* effacer; (*with rubber*) gommer. **eraser** *n* gomme *f*.

erect [i'rekt] *adj* droit. *v* (*statue, etc.*) ériger; (*build*) bâtir; (*tent, etc.*) dresser. **erection** *n* érection *f*; construction *f*.

ermine ['əɪmin] *n* hermine *f*.

erode [i'roud] *v* éroder, ronger. **erosion** *n* érosion *f*. **erosive** *adj* érosif.

erotic [i'rotik] *adj* érotique.

err [əɪ] *v* se tromper; (*sin*) pécher.

errand ['erənd] *n* course *f*. **errand boy** garçon de courses *m*.

erratic [i'ratik] *adj* irrégulier.

error ['erə] *n* erreur *f*.

erudite ['erudait] *adj* savant. **erudition** *n* érudition *f*.

erupt [i'rupt] *v* (*volcano*) entrer en éruption; (*quarrel*) éclater. **eruption** *n* éruption *f*.

escalate ['eskə,leit] *v* (s')intensifier. **escalation** *n* escalade *f*. **escalator** *n* escalier roulant *m*.

escalope ['eskə,lop] *n* escalope *f*.

escape [is'keip] *v* (s')échapper (à). *n* fuite *f*, évasion *f*.

escort ['eskoɪt; *v* i'skoɪt] *n* escorte *f*. *v* escorter.

esoteric [esə'terik] *adj* ésotérique.

especial [i'speʃəl] *adj* particulier. **especially** *adv* particulièrement, surtout.

espionage ['espiə,naʒ] *n* espionnage *m*.

esplanade [,esplə'neid] *n* esplanade *f*.

essay ['esei] *n* essai *m*; (*school*) rédaction *f*, dissertation *f*. **essayist** *n* essayiste *m, f*.

essence ['esns] *n* essence *f*.

essential [i'senʃəl] *adj* essentiel. **essentials** *pl n* essentiel *m sing*.

establish [i'stabliʃ] *v* établir; fonder. **establishment** *n* établissement *m*; fondation *f*.

estate [i'steit] *n* propriété *f*; (*houses*) lotissement *m*; (*law*) biens *m pl*. **estate agent** agent immobilier *m*. **estate car** break *m*.

esteem [i'stiɪm] *v* estimer. *n* estime *f*.

estimate ['estimət; *v* 'esti,meit] *n* évaluation *f*; (*comm*) devis *m*. *v* estimer. **estimation** *n* jugement *m*; (*esteem*) estime *f*.

estuary ['estjuəri] *n* estuaire *m*.

eternal [i'təɪnl] *adj* éternel. **eternity** *n* éternité *f*.

ether ['iɪθə] *n* éther *m*.

ethereal [i'θiəriəl] *adj* éthéré.

ethical ['eθikl] *adj* moral. **ethics** *pl n* morale *f sing*.

ethnic ['eθnik] *adj* ethnique.

etiquette ['eti,ket] *n* étiquette *f*.

etymology [,eti'molədʒi] *n* étymologie *f*. **etymological** *adj* étymologique.

Eucharist ['juɪkərist] *n* Eucharistie *f*.

eunuch ['juɪnək] *n* eunuque *m*.

euphemism ['juɪfə,mizəm] *n* euphémisme *m*. **euphemistic** *adj* euphémique.

euphoria [ju'foɪriə] *n* euphorie *f*. **euphoric** *adj* euphorique.

Europe ['juərəp] *n* Europe *f*. **European** *n* Européen, -enne *m, f*; *adj* européen. **European Economic Community (EEC)** Communauté Economique Européenne (CEE) *f*.

euthanasia [,juɪθə'neiziə] *n* euthanasie *f*.

evacuate [i'vakju,eit] *v* évacuer. **evacuation** *n* évacuation *f*. **evacuee** *n* évacué, -e *m, f*.

evade [i'veid] *v* éviter. **evasion** *n* fuite *f*. **evasive** *adj* évasif.

evaluate [i'valju,eit] *v* évaluer. **evaluation** *n* évaluation *f*.

evangelical [,iivan'dʒelikəl] *adj* évangélique. **evangelist** *n* évangéliste *m*.

evaporate [i'vapə,reit] *v* s'évaporer; (*fade away*) se volatiliser. **evaporated milk** lait concentré *m*. **evaporation** *n* évaporation *f*.

eve [iɪv] *n* veille *f*.

even ['iɪvən] *adj* (*surface*) uni; régulier; égal; (*number*) pair. *adv* même; (*more, etc.*) encore. **even so** quand même. **even-tempered** *adj* placide. *v* égaliser.

evening ['iɪvniŋ] *n* soir *m*, soirée *f*. **evening class** cours du soir *m*. **evening dress** (*man*) tenue de soirée *f*; (*woman*) robe du soir *f*.

evensong ['iɪvən,soŋ] *n* office du soir *m*.

event [i'vent] *n* évènement *m*; cas *m*; (*race*) course *f*. **in the event of** en cas de; au cas où. **eventful** *adj* mouvementé.

eventual [i'ventʃuəl] *adj* qui s'ensuit. **eventuality** *n* éventualité *f*. **eventually** *adv* finalement.

ever ['evə] *adv* jamais; (*always*) toujours.

evergreen ['evəgriːn] *adj* vert, à feuilles persistantes. *n* arbre vert *m*.

everlasting [ˌevə'laːstiŋ] *adj* éternel.

every ['evri] *adj* (*all*) tous les, toutes les; (*each*) chaque, tout. **everybody** *or* **everyone** *pron* tout le monde. **everyday** *adj* banal; de tous les jours. **every other day** tous les deux jours, un jour sur deux. **everything** *pron* tout. **everywhere** *adv* partout.

evict [i'vikt] *v* expulser. **eviction** *n* expulsion *f*.

evidence ['evidəns] *n* évidence *f*; (*testimony*) témoignage *m*; signe *m*. **give evidence** témoigner. **evident** *adj* évident. **evidently** *adv* évidemment; à ce qu'il paraît.

evil ['iːvl] *adj* mauvais. *n* mal *m*.

evoke [i'vouk] *v* évoquer. **evocation** *n* évocation *f*. **evocative** *adj* évocateur, -trice.

evolve [i'volv] *v* (se) développer. **evolution** *n* évolution *f*. **evolutionary** *adj* évolutionniste.

ewe [juː] *n* brebis *f*.

exacerbate [ig'zasəˌbeit] *v* exacerber.

exact [ig'zakt] *adj* exact. *v* exiger. **exacting** *adj* exigeant; (*task*) astreignant. **exactly** *adv* précisément, exactement.

exaggerate [ig'zadʒəˌreit] *v* exagérer; accentuer. **exaggeration** *n* exagération *f*.

exalt [ig'zolt] *v* élever; (*praise*) exalter.

examine [ig'zamin] *v* examiner; (*law*) interroger. **examination** *n* examen *m*. **examiner** *n* examinateur, -trice *m, f*.

example [ig'zaːmpl] *n* exemple *m*. **for example** par exemple. **set a good example** donner l'exemple.

exasperate [ig'zaːspəˌreit] *v* exaspérer. **exasperation** *n* exaspération *f*.

excavate ['ekskəˌveit] *v* excaver; (*dig*) creuser; (*archaeol*) fouiller, faire des fouilles. **excavation** *n* creusage *m*; fouille *f*.

exceed [ik'siːd] *v* dépasser. **exceedingly** *adv* extrêmement.

excel [ik'sel] *v* briller; surpasser. **excellence** *n* excellence *f*. **excellent** *adj* excellent.

Excellency ['eksələnsi] *n* Excellence *f*.

except [ik'sept] *prep* sauf, excepté; (*but*) sinon. *v* excepter. **exception** *n* exception *f*. **take exception to** s'offenser de. **exceptional** *adj* exceptionnel.

excerpt ['eksɜːpt] *n* extrait *m*.

excess [ik'ses] *n* excès *m*. **excess fare** sup-

plément *m*. **excess luggage** excédent de bagages *m*. **excessive** *adj* excessif.

exchange [iks'tʃeindʒ] *v* échanger; faire un échange (de). *n* échange *m*; (*phone*) central *m*; (*finance*) change *m*. **exchange rate** taux de change *m*.

exchequer [iks'tʃekə] *n* ministère des finances *m*.

excise ['eksaiz] *n* taxe *f*; (*department*) régie *f*. **excise duties** contributions indirectes *f pl*.

excite [ik'sait] *v* exciter. **excited** *adj* excité, agité. **get excited** s'exciter, s'agiter. **excitement** *n* excitation *f*. **exciting** *adj* passionnant.

exclaim [ik'skleim] *v* s'exclamer, s'écrier.

exclamation [ˌeksklə'meiʃən] *n* exclamation *f*. **exclamation mark** point d'exclamation *m*.

exclude [ik'skluːd] *v* exclure. **exclusion** *n* exclusion *f*. **exclusive** *adj* exclusif; select; (*dates, numbers, etc.*) exclusivement; (*price, charge*) non compris.

excommunicate [ekskə'mjuːniˌkeit] *v* excommunier. **excommunication** *n* excommunication *f*.

excrete [ik'skriːt] *v* excréter. **excrement** *n* excrément *m*. **excretion** *n* excrétion *f*.

excruciating [ik'skruːʃieitiŋ] *adj* (*pain*) atroce; (*noise*) infernal.

excursion [ik'skɜːʃən] *n* excursion *f*.

excuse [ik'skjuːz] *v* excuser. **excuse me!** excusez-moi! *n* excuse *f*. **excusable** *adj* excusable.

execute ['eksiˌkjuːt] *v* exécuter; accomplir. **execution** *n* exécution *f*; (*of duties*) exercice *m*. **executioner** *n* bourreau *m*.

executive [ig'zekjutiv] *adj* (*power*) exécutif; (*job*) administratif. *n* (*person*) cadre *m*; (*group*) bureau *m*.

exemplify [ig'zempliˌfai] *v* exemplifier.

exempt [ig'zempt] *adj* exempt. *v* exempter. **exemption** *n* exemption *f*.

exercise ['eksəˌsaiz] *n* exercice *m*. **exercises** *pl n* (*physical*) gymnastique *f sing*. **exercise book** cahier *m*. *v* exercer.

exert [ig'zɜːt] *v* exercer; (*force*) employer. **exert onself** se dépenser; s'appliquer. **exertion** *n* effort *m*; exercice *m*; emploi *m*.

exhale [eks'heil] *v* (*give off*) exhaler; (*breathe out*) expirer.

exhaust [ig'zoːst] *v* épuiser. *n* (*system*) échappement *m*; (*pipe*) tuyau d'échappement *m*. **exhaustion** *n* épuisement *m*. **exhaustive** *adj* complet, -ète. **exhaustively** *adv* à fond.

exhibit [ig'zibit] *v* exposer; (*skill, etc.*) faire preuve de. *n* objet exposé *m*. **exhibition** *n* exposition *f*. **make an exhibition of oneself** se donner en spectacle. **exhibitionist** *n*(*m+f*). *adj* exhibitionniste. **exhibitor** *n* exposant, -e *m, f*.

exhilarate [ig'zilə‚reit] *v* vivifier, stimuler. **exhilaration** *n* ivresse *f*.

exile ['eksail] *v* exiler. *n* exil *m*; (*person*) exilé, -e *m, f*. **go into exile** s'exiler.

exist [ig'zist] *v* exister; (*live*) vivre. **existence** *n* existence *f*. **existentialism** *n* existentialisme *m*. **existing** *adj* (*current*) actuel.

exit ['egzit] *n* sortie *f*.

exonerate [ig'zonə‚reit] *v* (*from blame*) disculper; (*from obligation*) exempter. **exoneration** *n* disculpation *f*; exemption *f*.

exorbitant [ig'zoːbitənt] *adj* exorbitant.

exorcise ['eksoː‚saiz] *v* exorciser. **exorcism** *n* exorcisme *m*. **exorcist** *n* exorciste *m*.

exotic [ig'zotik] *adj* exotique.

expand [ik'spand] *v* (se) dilater; (se) développer; (s')étendre. **expansion** *n* expansion *f*; développement *m*. **expansive** *adj* expansif.

expanse [ik'spans] *n* étendue *f*.

expatriate [eks'peitrieit; *n, adj* eks'peitriət] *v* expatrier. *n, adj* expatrié, -e.

expect [ik'spekt] *v* attendre; supposer; (*demand*) exiger. **expectancy** *or* **expectation** *n* attente *f*.

expedient [ik'spiːdiənt] *adj* (*convenient*) opportun; politique. *n* expédient *m*.

expedition [‚ekspi'diʃən] *n* expédition *f*.

expel [ik'spel] *v* expulser; (*school*) renvoyer.

expenditure [ik'spenditʃə] *n* dépense *f*.

expense [ik'spens] *n* frais *m pl*. **at the expense of** aux dépens de. **expense account** frais de représentation *m pl*. **expensive** *adj* cher. **be expensive** coûter cher.

experience [ik'spiəriəns] *n* expérience *f*. *v* (*encounter*) rencontrer; (*feel*) éprouver. **experienced** *adj* expérimenté.

experiment [ik'sperimənt] *n* expérience *f*. *v* faire une expérience; expérimenter. **experimental** *adj* expérimental.

expert ['ekspəːt] *nm, adj* expert.

expertise [‚ekspəː'tiːz] *n* adresse *f*.

expire [ik'spaiə] *v* expirer. **expiry** *n* expiration *f*.

explain [ik'splein] *v* expliquer. **explanation** *n* explication *f*. **explanatory** *adj* explicatif.

expletive [ek'spliːtiv] *n* (*oath*) juron *m*; exclamation *f*.

explicit [ik'splisit] *adj* explicite.

explode [ik'sploud] *v* (faire) exploser. **explosion** *n* explosion *f*. **explosive** *nm, adj* explosif.

exploit ['eksploit; *v* ik'sploit] *n* exploit *m*. *v* exploiter. **exploitation** *n* exploitation *f*.

explore [ik'sploː] *v* explorer. **exploration** *n* exploration *f*. **explorer** *n* explorateur, -trice *m, f*.

exponent [ik'spounənt] *n* interprète *m*.

export [ik'spoːt; *n* 'ekspoːt] *v* exporter. *n* exportation *f*. **exporter** *n* (*person*) exportateur, -trice *m, f*; (*country*) pays exportateur *m*.

expose [ik'spouz] *v* exposer; révéler; (*uncover*) découvrir. **exposure** *n* exposition *f*; (*phot*) pose *f*. **die of exposure** mourir de froid.

express [ik'spres] *v* exprimer. *n* (*train*) rapide *m*. *adj, adv* exprès. **expression** *n* expression *f*. **expressive** *adj* expressif.

expulsion [ik'spʌlʃən] *n* expulsion *f*; (*school*) renvoi *m*.

exquisite ['ekswizit] *adj* exquis.

extend [ik'stend] *v* (s')étendre; (se) prolonger. **extension** *n* prolongation *f*; (*flex, etc.*) rallonge *f*; (*to house*) agrandissements *m pl*; (*phone*) poste *m*. **extensive** *adj* étendu; considérable.

extent [ik'stent] *n* étendue *f*, longueur *f*; (*range*) importance *f*; (*degree*) mesure *f*.

exterior [ik'stiəriə] *nm, adj* extérieur, -e.

exterminate [ik'stəːmi‚neit] *v* exterminer. **extermination** *n* extermination *f*.

external [ik'stəːnl] *adj* externe, extérieur, -e. **for external use only** pour l'usage externe.

extinct [ik'stiŋkt] *adj* (*species*) disparu; (*volcano*) éteint. **extinction** *n* extinction *f*.

extinguish [ik'stiŋgwiʃ] *v* éteindre; (*hopes*) anéantir. **extinguisher** *n* extincteur *m*.

extort [ik'stoːt] *v* extorquer. **extortion** *n* extorsion *f*. **extortionate** *adj* exorbitant.

extra ['ekstrə] *adj* de plus; supplémentaire; de réserve. *n* supplément *m*; (*theatre, cinema*) figurant, -e *m, f*.

extract [ik'strakt; *n* 'ekstrakt] *v* extraire;
(*tooth*) arracher. *n* extrait *m*. **extraction** *n*
extraction *f*.
extradite ['ekstrə‚dait] *v* extrader. **extradition** *n* extradition *f*.
extramural [‚ekstrə'mjuərəl] *adj* (*course*)
hors faculté; (*district*) extra-muros.
extraordinary [ik'strɔːdənəri] *adj*
extraordinaire.
extravagant [ik'stravəgənt] *adj* (*person*)
dépensier; (*taste*) dispendieux; (*ideas,
dress*) extravagant. **extravagance** *n* prodigalité *f*; (*expensive thing*) folie *f*; extravagance *f*.
extreme [ik'striːm] *nm, adj* extrême.
extremist *n*(*m*+*f*), *adj* extrémiste.
extremity *n* extrémité *f*.
extricate ['ekstri‚keit] *v* dégager; tirer.
extrovert ['ekstrəvɔːt] *n, adj* extraverti, -e.
exuberant [ig'zjuːbərənt] *adj* exubérant.
exuberance *n* exubérance *f*.
exude [ig'zjuːd] *v* exsuder, suinter.
exult [ig'zʌlt] *v* se réjouir. **exultant** *adj*
triomphant. **exultation** *n* exultation *f*.
eye [ai] *n* œil (*pl* yeux) *m*. **as far as the
eye can see** à perte de vue. **keep an eye
on** surveiller. *v* regarder.
eyeball ['aibɔːl] *n* globe oculaire *m*.
eyebrow ['aibrau] *n* sourcil *m*.
eye-catching ['aikatʃiŋ] *adj* accrocheur,
-euse.
eyelash ['ailaʃ] *n* cil *m*.
eyelid ['ailid] *n* paupière *f*.
eye shadow *n* fard à paupières *m*.
eyesight ['aisait] *n* vue *f*.
eyesore ['aisɔː] *n* horreur *f*.
eyewitness ['ai‚witnis] *n* témoin oculaire
m.

F

fable ['feibl] *n* fable *f*.
fabric ['fabrik] *n* tissu *m*. **fabricate** *v* fabriquer. **fabrication** *n* fabrication *f*.
fabulous ['fabjuləs] *adj* fabuleux; (*coll:
wonderful*) formidable.
façade [fə'saːd] *n* façade *f*.
face [feis] *n* visage *m*, figure *f*. **facecloth** *n*
gant de toilette *m*. **facelift** *n* lifting *m*.
face pack masque de beauté *m*. **face-to-
face** *nm, adv* face à face. **face value** (*coin*)

valeur nominale *f*. **at face value** au pied
de la lettre. **in the face of** face à, devant.
v faire face à; (*building*) donner sur. **face
the facts** regarder les choses en face.
facet ['fasit] *n* facette *f*.
facetious [fə'siːʃəs] *adj* facétieux.
facial ['feiʃəl] *adj* facial. *n* soin de visage
m.
facilitate [fə'sili‚teit] *v* faciliter.
facility [fə'siləti] *n* facilité *f*. **facilities** *pl n*
installations *f pl*, équipements *m pl*.
facing ['feisiŋ] *n* (*sewing*) revers *m*; (*building*) revêtement *m*.
facsimile [fak'siməli] *n* fac-similé *m*.
fact [fakt] *n* fait *m*; réalité *f*. **as a matter
of fact** à vrai dire. **in fact** en fait. **factual**
adj basé sur les faits.
faction ['fakʃən] *n* faction *f*.
factor ['faktə] *n* facteur *m*.
factory ['faktəri] *n* usine *f*; (*smaller*)
fabrique *f*.
faculty ['fakəlti] *n* faculté *f*; aptitude *f*.
fad [fad] *n* marotte *f*. **faddy** *adj*
capricieux.
fade [feid] *v* (*light*) baisser; (*colour*) passer; (*flower*) se faner; (*sound*) s'affaiblir.
fag [fag] (*coll*) *n* (*cigarette*) sèche *f*; (*boring task*) barbe *f*. **fag end** (*of cigarette*)
mégot *m*. **fagged out** claqué.
fail [feil] *v* (not succeed) échouer; (*grow
weak*) faiblir, baisser; (*neglect*) manquer
(de). *n* échec *m*. **without fail** à coup sûr;
inévitablement. **failing** *n* défaut *m*. **failure**
n échec *m*; (*person*) raté, -e *m, f*; (*breakdown*) panne *f*.
faint [feint] *adj* faible; (*colour*) pâle;
(*idea*) vague. **I haven't the faintest idea** je
n'en ai pas la moindre idée. *v* s'évanouir.
n évanouissement *m*.
fair¹ [feə] *adj* juste, équitable; (*average*)
passable; (*hair*) blond; (*skin*) clair; (*fine*)
beau, belle. **by fair means or foul** par
tous les moyens. **fair copy** copie au
propre *f*. **fair-sized** *adj* assez grand. **play
fair** jouer franc jeu. **fairly** *adv* avec justice; (*reasonably*) assez. **fairness** *n* justice
f; blondeur *f*.
fair² [feə] *n* foire *f*. **fairground** *n* champ de
foire *m*.
fairy ['feəri] *n* fée *f*. *adj* féerique. **fairy
lights** guirlande électrique *f*. **fairy tale**
conte de fées *m*.
faith [feiθ] *n* foi *f*. **have faith in** avoir
confiance en. **faithful** *adj* fidèle. **faithfulness** *n* fidelité *f*.

fake [feik] *n (picture)* faux *m*; article truqué *m*; *(person)* imposteur *m*. *adj* faux, fausse; *(photo, interview, etc.)* truqué; falsifié. *v* faire un faux de; truquer; falsifier; *(illness)* faire semblant (de).

falcon ['fɔːlkən] *n* faucon *m*.

*fall [fɔːl] *v* tomber. **fall apart** tomber en morceaux; *(plans, life, etc.)* se désagréger. **fall back on** avoir recours à. **fall through** échouer. *n* chute *f*; *(US)* automne *m*; *(price, etc.)* baisse *f*.

fallacy ['faləsi] *n* erreur *f*.

fallen ['fɔːlən] *V* **fall**.

fallible ['faləbl] *adj* faillible. **fallibility** *n* faillibilité *f*.

fallow ['falou] *adj (land)* en jachère; *(idea, etc.)* en friche.

false [fɔːls] *adj* faux, fausse; artificiel. **false alarm** fausse alerte *f*. **false teeth** fausses dents *f pl*. **under false pretences** par des moyens frauduleux. **falsehood** *n* mensonge *m*. **falseness** *n* fausseté *f*. **falsify** *v* falsifier. **falsification** *n* falsification *f*.

falsetto [fɔːl'setou] *n* fausset *m*.

falter ['fɔːltə] *v* chanceler; *(voice)* hésiter.

fame [feim] *n* renommée *f*.

familiar [fə'miljə] *adj* familier. **be familiar with** bien connaître. **familiarity** *n* familiarité *f*. **familiarize** *v* familiariser.

family ['faməli] *n* famille *f*. **family allowance** allocations familiales *f pl*. **family planning** planning familial *m*. **family tree** arbre généalogique *m*.

famine ['famin] *n* famine *f*.

famished ['famiʃt] *adj* affamé. **be famished** *(coll)* avoir une faim de loup.

famous ['feiməs] *adj* célèbre; *(coll: excellent)* fameux.

fan¹ [fan] *n* ventilateur *m*; *(hand-held)* éventail *m*. **fan belt** courroie de ventilateur *f*. **fan heater** radiateur soufflant *m*. *v* éventer.

fan² [fan] *n* fan *m*, *f*, passionné, -e *m*, *f*, admirateur, -trice *m*, *f*. **fan club** club de fans *m*.

fanatic [fə'natik] *n* fanatique *m*, *f*. **fanatical** *adj* fanatique.

fancy ['fansi] *n* caprice *m*; *(desire)* envie *f*; imagination *f*. *v (imagine)* se figurer, croire; avoir envie de. **fancy oneself** se gober. *adj* de fantaisie. **fancy dress** travesti *m*. **fanciful** *adj* imaginaire; fantasque, bizarre.

fanfare ['fanfeə] *n* fanfare *f*.

fang [faŋ] *n (dog)* croc *m*; *(snake)* crochet *m*.

fantastic [fan'tastik] *adj* fantastique.

fantasy ['fantəsi] *n* fantaisie *f*.

far [faː] *adv* loin; *(much)* beaucoup. *adj* lointain; *(opposite)* autre. **as far as** jusqu'à, autant que. **far and wide** partout. **far away** *adv* au loin. **faraway** *adj* lointain. **Far East** Extrême Orient *m*. **far-fetched** *adj* tiré par les cheveux. **far-off** *adj* eloigné. **far-reaching** *adj* d'une grande portée. **so far so good** jusqu'ici ça va.

farce [faːs] *n* farce *f*. **farcical** *adj* risible, grotesque.

fare [feə] *n* prix du billet *m*. **fare stage** section *f*.

farewell [feə'wel] *nm*, *interj* adieu.

farm [faːm] *n* ferme *f*. **farmhouse** *n* ferme *f*. **farmland** *n* terres cultivées *f pl*. **farmyard** *n* cour de ferme *f*. *v* cultiver; être fermier. **farmer** *n* fermier *m*. **farmer's wife** fermière *f*. **farming** *n* agriculture *f*.

fart [faːt] *(vulgar)* *n* pet *m*. *v* péter.

farther ['faːðə] *adv* plus loin. *adj* plus lointain.

farthest ['faːðist] *adv* le plus loin. *adj* le plus lointain.

farthing ['faːðiŋ] *n* sou *m*.

fascinate ['fasi,neit] *v* fasciner. **fascination** *n* fascination *f*.

fascism ['faʃizəm] *n* fascisme *m*. **fascist** *n(m+f)*, *adj* fasciste.

fashion ['faʃən] *n* mode *f*; *(manner)* façon *f*. **after a fashion** tant bien que mal. **fashion show** présentation de collections *f*. **in fashion** à la mode. *v* façonner. **fashionable** *adj* à la mode.

fast¹ [faːst] *adj* rapide; *(colour)* bon teint *invar*. **be fast** *(clock, etc.)* avancer. *adv* vite; *(securely)* ferme. **fast asleep** profondément endormi.

fast² [faːst] *v* jeûner. *n* jeûne *m*.

fasten ['faːsn] *v* (s')attacher; *(close)* (se) fermer. **fastener** *or* **fastening** *n* attache *f*; fermeture *f*.

fastidious [fa'stidiəs] *adj* méticuleux, exigeant.

fat [fat] *n* graisse *f*; *(on meat)* gras *m*. *adj* gros, grosse; gras, grasse. **get fat** grossir. **fatten** *v* engraisser. **fattening** *adj (food)* qui fait grossir.

fatal ['feitl] *adj* fatal, mortel. **fatality** *n* mort *m*; accident mortel *m*.

fate [feit] n sort m. **fated** adj destiné;
(condemned) voué au malheur. **fateful** adj
fatal.

father ['fɑːðə] n père m. **Father Christmas**
le père Noël. **father-in-law** n beau-père
m. **fatherland** n patrie f. v engendrer.
fatherhood n paternité f. **fatherly** adj
paternel.

fathom ['faðəm] n brasse f. v **fathom out**
sonder.

fatigue [fə'tiːg] n fatigue f. v fatiguer.

fatuous ['fatjuəs] adj imbécile, stupide.

fault [fɔːlt] n (failing) défaut m; (blame)
faute f. **at fault** fautif. **faultless** adj
impeccable; irréprochable. **faulty** adj
défectueux.

fauna ['fɔːnə] n faune f.

favour ['feivə] n faveur f; service m;
avantage m. **be in favour of** être partisan
de. v favoriser; préférer. **favourable** adj
favorable; (wind, etc.) propice. **favourite**
n, adj favori, -ite.

fawn [fɔːn] n faon m. adj fauve.

fear [fiə] n peur f, crainte f. v craindre.
fearful adj (terrible) affreux; (frightened)
peureux. **fearless** adj intrépide.

feasible ['fiːzəbl] adj faisable; plausible.
feasibility n possibilité f; plausibilité f.

feast [fiːst] n festin m; (rel) fête f.

feat [fiːt] n exploit m.

feather ['feðə] n plume f. **feather bed** lit
de plume m. **feathery** adj plumeux.

feature ['fiːtʃə] n trait m, caractéristique f;
spécialité f. **feature film** grand film m. v
(faire) figurer; (make prominent) mettre
en vedette.

February ['februəri] n février m.

fed [fed] V **feed**.

federal ['fedərəl] nm, adj fédéral.

federate ['fedəˌreit] v (se) fédérer. adj
fédéré. **federation** n fédération f.

fee [fiː] n droits m pl, frais m pl; (doctor,
etc.) honoraires m pl.

feeble ['fiːbl] adj faible; (excuse) pauvre.
feebleness n faiblesse f.

***feed** [fiːd] v (se) nourrir; (machine, fire)
alimenter. **be fed up** (coll) en avoir
marre. n nourriture f; (baby's) tétée f,
biberon m. **feedback** n feed-back m.

***feel** [fiːl] v (se) sentir; (touch) palper;
(think) avoir l'impression. n toucher m;
sensation f. **feeler** n antenne f. **feeling** n
sentiment m; sensation f.

feet [fiːt] V **foot**.

feign [fein] v feindre, simuler.

feline ['fiːlain] n, adj félin, -e.

fell¹ [fel] V **fall**.

fell² [fel] v abattre.

fellow ['felou] n compagnon m; (coll) type
m; (of society) membre m. **fellowship** n
amitié f; association f.

felony ['feləni] n crime m. **felon** m
criminel, -elle m, f.

felt¹ [felt] V **feel**.

felt² [felt] n feutre m. **felt-tip pen** feutre
m.

female ['fiːmeil] adj femelle, féminin. n
femelle f; (person) femme f.

feminine ['feminin] nm, adj féminin. **femininity** n féminité f. **feminism** n féminisme
m. **feminist** n féministe m, f.

fence [fens] n clôture f; (horse-racing)
obstacle m. v clôturer; (sport) faire de
l'escrime. **fencing** n (sport) escrime f.

fend [fend] v **fend for oneself** se débrouiller. **fend off** parer; (attacker) repousser.

fender ['fendə] n garde-feu m invar; (US)
garde-boue m invar.

fennel ['fenl] n fenouil m.

ferment [fə'ment; n 'fɔːment] v (faire) fermenter. n ferment m; agitation f. **fermentation** n fermentation f.

fern [fɔːn] n fougère f.

ferocious [fə'rouʃəs] adj féroce. **ferocity** n
férocité f.

ferret ['ferit] n furet m. v fureter. **ferret
out** dénicher.

ferry ['feri] n ferry m; (smaller) bac m. v
transporter.

fertile ['fɔːtail] adj (land) fertile; (person)
fécond. **fertility** n fertilité f; fécondité f.
fertilization n fertilisation f. **fertilize** v
fertiliser; féconder. **fertilizer** n engrais m.

fervent ['fɔːvənt] adj fervent. **fervour** n
ferveur f.

fester ['festə] v suppurer; (anger, etc.)
couver.

festival ['festəvəl] n festival m; (rel) fête f.
festoon [fə'stuːn] v festonner. n feston m.

fetch [fetʃ] v aller chercher; (person)
amener; (thing) apporter; (sell for) rapporter. **fetching** adj ravissant.

fête [feit] n fête f.

fetid ['fiːtid] adj fétide.

fetish ['fetiʃ] n fétiche m.

fetter ['fetə] v entraver. **fetters** pl n
entraves f pl; (irons) fers m pl.

feud [fjuːd] n querelle f. v se quereller.

feudal ['fjuːdl] *adj* féodal.

fever ['fiːvə] *n* fièvre *f*. **feverish** *adj* fiévreux.

few [fjuː] *nm, adj* peu (de). **a few** quelques; quelques-uns, quelques-unes. **quite a few** pas mal (de). **fewer** *nm, adj* moins (de). **fewest** le moins (de).

fiancé [fiˈonsei] *n* fiancé *m*. **fiancée** *n* fiancée *f*.

fiasco [fiˈaskou] *n* fiasco *m*.

fib [fib] *n* blague *f*. *v* raconter des blagues.

fibre ['faibə] *n* fibre *f*. **fibreglass** *n* fibre de verre *f*.

fickle ['fikl] *adj* inconstant.

fiction ['fikʃən] *n* (*stories*) romans *m pl*; (*invention*) fiction *f*. **fictional** *or* **fictitious** *adj* fictif.

fiddle ['fidl] *n* violon *m*; (*coll: fraud*) combine *f*. *v* jouer du violon; (*coll: cheat*) traficoter; (*coll: falsify*) truquer. **fiddle with** tripoter. **fiddly** *adj* minutieux.

fidelity [fiˈdeləti] *n* fidélité *f*.

fidget ['fidʒit] *v* se trémousser. **fidgety** *adj* remuant.

field [fiːld] *n* champ *m*; (*sport*) terrain *m*; (*of knowledge, etc.*) domaine *f*. **field glasses** jumelles *f pl*. **field marshal** maréchal *m*. **fieldwork** *n* recherches sur le terrain *f pl*.

fiend [fiːnd] *n* démon *m*; (*coll: enthusiast*) enragé, -e *m, f*. **fiendish** *adj* diabolique.

fierce [fiəs] *adj* féroce; violent; (*struggle*) acharné. **fierceness** *n* férocité *f*; violence *f*; acharnement *m*.

fiery ['faiəri] *adj* ardent, brûlant; (*temper*) violent.

fifteen [fifˈtiːn] *nm, adj* quinze. **fifteenth** *n*(*m+f*). *adj* quinzième.

fifth [fifθ] *n*(*m+f*) *adj* cinquième.

fifty ['fifti] *nm, adj* cinquante. **fifty-fifty** *adj, adv* moitié-moitié, cinquante pour cent. **fiftieth** *n*(*m+f*). *adj* cinquantième.

fig [fig] *n* (*fruit*) figue *f*; (*tree*) figuier *m*.

*__fight__ [fait] *v* se battre, combattre; (*argue*) se disputer. *n* combat *m*; (*struggle*) lutte *f*.

figment ['figmənt] *n* création *f*. **figment of the imagination** invention *f*.

figure ['figə] *n* figure *f*; (*number*) chiffre *m*; (*slimness*) ligne *f*; (*human*) forme *f*. **figurehead** *n* figure de proue *f*; (*derog*) prête-nom *m*. **figure skating** patinage artistique *m*. *v* (*appear*) figurer; (*think*)

penser. **figure out** arriver à comprendre. **figurative** *adj* figuré.

filament ['filəmənt] *n* filament *m*.

__file__ [fail] *n* (*folder*) dossier *m*; (*card index*) fichier *m*; (*in office*) classeur *m*. **in single file** à la file. *v* classer; (*claim, etc.*) déposer, intenter. **file past** défiler; passer un à un. **filing** *n* classement *m*. **filing cabinet** classeur *m*. **filing clerk** documentaliste *m, f*.

file² [fail] *n* lime *f*. *v* limer. **filings** *pl n* limaille *f sing*.

filial ['filiəl] *adj* filial.

fill [fil] *v* (se) remplir; (*tooth*) plomber. **fill in** (*form*) remplir; (*hole*) boucher. **fill up** (*petrol tank*) faire le plein; (*cup, etc.*) remplir.

fillet ['filit] *n* filet *m*. **fillet steak** tournedos *m*. *v* désosser.

filling ['filiŋ] *n* plombage *m*; (*of pie, etc.*) garniture *f*. *adj* (*food*) substantiel. **filling station** poste d'essence *m*.

film [film] *n* film *m*; (*phot*) pellicule *f*; (*layer*) couche *f*. **film star** vedette *f*. **filmstrip** *n* film fixe *m*. *v* filmer.

filter ['filtə] *n* filtre *m*. **filter paper** papier filtre *m*. **filter-tipped** *adj* à bout filtre. *v* filtrer; purifier.

filth [filθ] *n* saleté *f*. **filthy** *adj* crasseux; (*language*) ordurier.

fin [fin] *n* nageoire *f*.

final ['fainl] *adj* (*last*) dernier; définitif. *n* finale *f*. **finalist** *n* finaliste *m, f*. **finalize** *v* mettre la dernière main à. **finally** *adv* enfin, finalement.

finance [faiˈnans] *n* finance *f*. *v* financer. **financial** *adj* financier. **financial year** année budgétaire *f*. **financier** *n* financier *m*.

finch [finʃ] *n* fringillidé *m*.

*__find__ [faind] *v* trouver. **find out** se renseigner (sur); découvrir. *n* trouvaille *f*. **findings** *pl n* conclusions *f pl*.

fine¹ [fain] *adj* fin, délicat; (*sunny, excellent*) beau, belle. *adv* bien. **fine arts** beaux arts *m pl*. **finely** *adv* magnifiquement; (*small*) menu. **finery** *n* parure *f*.

fine² [fain] *n* amende *f*. *v* **be fined** avoir une amende.

finesse [fiˈnes] *n* finesse *f*; (*cards*) impasse *f*.

finger ['fiŋgə] *n* doigt *m*. **finger bowl** rince-doigts *m invar*. **fingermark** *n* trace de doigt *f*. **fingernail** *n* ongle *m*. **finger-**

print *n* empreinte digitale *f.* **fingertip** *n* bout du doigt *m. v* toucher.

finish ['finiʃ] *v* finir, (se) terminer. **finishing line** ligne d'arrivée *f.* **finishing touch** touche finale *f. n* fin *f; (sport)* arrivée *f;* surface *f.*

finite ['fainait] *adj* fini.

Finland ['finlənd] *n* Finlande *f.* **Finn** *n* Finlandais, -e *m, f; (Finnish speaker)* Finnois, -e *m, f.* **Finnish** *adj* finlandais; *nm, adj (language)* finnois.

fir [fəː] *n* sapin *m.* **fir cone** pomme de pin *f.*

fire [faiə] *n* feu *m; (uncontrolled)* incendie *m.* **set fire to** mettre le feu à. *v (enthusiasm, etc.)* enflammer; *(pottery)* cuire; *(gun)* tirer; *(coll: dismiss)* vider.

fire alarm *n* avertisseur d'incendie *m.*

firearm ['faiəˌaːm] *n* arme à feu *f.*

fire brigade *n* pompiers *m pl.*

fire door *n* porte anti-incendie *f.*

fire drill *n* exercice anti-incendie *m.*

fire engine *n* pompe à incendie *f.*

fire escape *n (stairs)* escalier de secours *m; (ladder)* échelle d'incendie *f.*

fire exit *n* sortie de secours *f.*

fire extinguisher *n* extincteur *m.*

fire-guard ['faiəˌɡaːd] *n* garde-feu *m invar.*

firelight ['faiəˌlait] *n* lueur du feu *f.*

fireman ['faiəmən] *n* pompier *m.*

fireplace ['faiəˌpleis] *n* cheminée *f.*

fireproof ['faiəˌpruːf] *v* ignifuger. *adj* ignifuge.

fireside ['faiəˌsaid] *n* foyer *m.*

fire station *n* caserne de pompiers *f.*

firewood ['faiəˌwud] *n* bois à brûler *m.*

firework ['faiəˌwəːk] *n* feu d'artifice *m.*

firing squad *n* peloton d'exécution *m.*

firm[1] [fəːm] *adj* ferme; solide. **firmness** *n* fermeté *f;* solidité *f.*

firm[2] [fəːm] *n (comm)* compagnie *f,* firme *f.*

first [fəːst] *n, adj* premier. *adv* d'abord; pour la première fois. **at first** d'abord. **first aid** premiers secours *m pl.* **first-class** *adj (ticket)* de première classe; *(mail)* tarif normal. **first floor** premier étage *m.* **first-hand** *adj* de première main. **first name** prénom *m.* **first-rate** *adj* excellent, de premier ordre. **in the first place** en premier lieu.

fiscal ['fiskəl] *adj* fiscal.

fish [fiʃ] *n* poisson *m. v* pêcher. **fish out** extirper. **fishy** *adj (coll)* louche.

fishbone ['fiʃˌboun] *n* arête *f.*

fish cake *n* croquette de poisson *f.*

fisherman ['fiʃəmən] *n* pêcheur *m.*

fish fingers *pl n* bâtonnets de poisson *m pl.*

fishing ['fiʃiŋ] *n* pêche *f.* **fishing boat** barque de pêche *f.* **fishing line** ligne de pêche *f.* **fishing rod** canne à pêche *f.* **fishing tackle** attirail de pêche *m.* **go fishing** aller à la pêche.

fishmonger ['fiʃˌmʌŋɡə] *n* marchand de poisson *m.*

fishpond ['fiʃˌpond] *n* étang à poissons *m.*

fish shop *n* poissonnerie *f.*

fish slice *n* pelle à poisson *f.*

fish tank *n* aquarium *m.*

fission ['fiʃən] *n* fission *f.*

fissure ['fiʃə] *n* fissure *f.*

fist [fist] *n* poing *m.* **fistful** *n* poignée *f.*

fit[1] [fit] *adj (suitable)* convenable; *(competent)* capable; *(worthy)* digne; *(healthy)* en bonne santé. *v (clothes, etc.)* aller à; ajuster; *(match)* correspondre à; équiper; *(faire)* entrer. **fitness** *n* santé *f,* forme *f;* aptitudes *f pl.* **fitter** *n (tech)* monteur *m; (clothes)* essayeur, -euse *m, f.* **fitting** *adj* approprié. **fitting room** salon d'essayage *m.* **fittings** *pl n* installations *f pl.*

fit[2] [fit] *n* accès *m,* crise *f.* **fitful** *adj* intermittent; *(sleep)* troublé.

five [faiv] *nm, adj* cinq.

fix [fiks] *v* fixer; arranger; réparer. *n (coll)* embêtement *m; (slang: drugs)* piqûre *f.* **fixation** *n* fixation *f.* **fixed** *adj* fixe. **fixture** *n* installation *f; (sport)* épreuve *f.*

fizz [fiz] *v* pétiller. *n* pétillement *m.* **fizzy** *adj* pétillant.

flabbergasted ['flabəˌɡaːstid] *adj (coll)* sidéré.

flabby ['flabi] *adj* mou, molle; *(person)* flasque.

flag[1] [flaɡ] *n* drapeau *m; (naut)* pavillon *m.* **flagpole** *n* mât *m.* **flagship** *n* vaisseau amiral *m. v* **flag down** héler.

flag[2] [flaɡ] *v* languir; *(tire)* s'alanguir; *(interest)* faiblir.

flagon ['flaɡən] *n* grande bouteille *f; (jug)* cruche *f.*

flagrant ['fleiɡrənt] *adj* flagrant.

flair [fleə] *n* flair *m.*

flake [fleik] *n (snow, etc.)* flocon *m; (paint, plaster, etc.)* écaille *f. v* s'écailler; *(skin)* peler. **flake out** *(coll)* tomber dans les pommes. **flaky** *adj* floconneux; *(pastry)* feuilleté.

flamboyant [flam,bɔiənt] *adj* flamboyant.
flame [fleim] *n* flamme *f*. **burst into flames** s'enflammer. *v* flamber. **flaming** *adj* ardent; (*slang*) foutu. **flammable** *adj* inflammable.
flamingo [flə'miŋgou] *n* flamant *m*.
flan [flan] *n* tarte *f*.
flank [flaŋk] *n* flanc *m*. *v* flanquer.
flannel ['flanl] *n* (*fabric*) flanelle *f*; (*facecloth*) gant de toilette *m*. **flannels** *pl n* pantalon de flanelle *m sing*. *v* (*slang*) baratiner.
flap [flap] *v* battre; (*sails*) claquer; (*coll*) paniquer. *n* (*envelope, etc.*) rabat *m*; battement *m*; claquement *m*; (*table*) abattant *m*; (*coll*) panique *f*.
flare [fleə] *n* signal lumineux *m*; (*clothes*) évasement *m*. *v* s'enflammer; (*clothes*) (s')évaser. **flare up** (*anger, etc.*) éclater; (*person*) s'emporter; (*fire*) s'embraser.
flash [flaʃ] *n* éclat *m*, éclair *m*; (*phot*) flash *m*. **flashback** *n* flashback *m invar*. **flash bulb** ampoule de flash *f*. **flash cube** cube-flash *m*. **flashlight** *n* (*torch*) lampe électrique *f*. *v* (*light*) projeter, (*intermittently*) clignoter; (*sparkle*) étinceler; (*show off*) étaler; (*mot*) faire un appel de phares. **flashy** *adj* tapageur, -euse; tape-à-l'œil *invar*.
flask [flaɪsk] *n* flacon *m*; thermos ® *m*.
flat¹ [flat] *adj* plat; (*tyre, battery*) à plat; (*music*) faux, fausse; (*beer*) éventé. *n* (*music*) bémol *m*. **flat-fish** *n* poisson plat *m*. **flat-footed** *adj* aux pieds plats. **flat rate** taux fixe *m*. **go flat out** (*car*) être à sa vitesse de pointe. **work flat out** travailler d'arrache-pied. **flatly** *adv* carrément, catégoriquement. **flatten** *v* (s')aplatir; (*smooth*) (s')aplanir.
flat² [flat] *n* appartement *m*. **flatlet** *n* studio *m*.
flatter ['flatə] *v* flatter. **flatterer** *n* flatteur, -euse *m, f*. **flattering** *adj* flatteur, -euse. **flattery** *n* flatterie *f*.
flatulence ['flatjuləns] *n* flatulence *f*.
flaunt [flɔint] *v* étaler, faire étalage de. **flaunt oneself** poser.
flautist ['flɔitist] *n* flûtiste *m, f*.
flavour ['fleivə] *n* goût *m*; (*ice-cream, etc.*) parfum *m*. *v* parfumer; assaisonner. **flavouring** *n* parfum *m*; assaisonnement *m*.
flaw [flɔi] *n* défaut *m*. **flawed** *adj* imparfait. **flawless** *adj* parfait.

flax [flaks] *n* lin *m*. **flaxen** *adj* de lin.
flea [fliɪ] *n* puce *f*.
fleck [flek] *n* (*colour*) moucheture *f*; particule *f*. *v* moucheter.
fled [fled] *V* **flee**.
*****flee** [fliɪ] *v* fuir; s'enfuir (de).
fleece [fliɪs] *n* toison *f*. *v* (*coll*) tondre. **fleecy** *adj* (*cloud*) floconneux; (*woolly*) laineux.
fleet [fliɪt] *n* flotte *f*.
fleeting ['fliɪtiŋ] *adj* fugace, passager.
Flemish ['flemiʃ] *nm, adj* flamand. **the Flemish** les Flamands *m pl*.
flesh [fleʃ] *n* chair *f*. **flesh-coloured** *adj* couleur chair *invar*. **in the flesh** en chair et en os. **fleshy** *adj* charnu.
flew [fluɪ] *V* **fly¹**.
flex [fleks] *n* fil souple *m*; (*telephone*) cordon *m*. *v* fléchir; (*muscles*) tendre. **flexibility** *n* flexibilité *f*. **flexible** *adj* flexible, souple.
flick [flik] *v* donner un petit coup à. **flick through** (*book*) feuilleter. *n* petit coup *m*; (*with finger*) chiquenaude *f*. **the flicks** (*coll*) le ciné *m*.
flicker ['flikə] *v* danser, trembloter. *n* vacillement *m*; (*of hope, etc.*) lueur *f*.
flight¹ [flait] *n* (*of bird, etc.*) vol *m*; (*of stairs*) escalier *m*. **flight path** trajectoire *f*.
flight² [flait] *n* (*fleeing*) fuite *f*.
flimsy ['flimzi] *adj* peu solide; (*cloth, paper*) léger, mince; (*excuse*) piètre.
flinch [flintʃ] *v* broncher.
*****fling** [fliŋ] *v* lancer, jeter. **have one's fling** se payer du bon temps.
flint [flint] *n* silex *m*.
flip [flip] *v* donner un petit coup à. **flip through** (*book*) feuilleter. *n* petit coup *m*; (*with finger*) chiquenaude *f*. **flipping** *adv* (*coll*) fichu.
flippant ['flipənt] *adj* désinvolte. **flippancy** *n* désinvolture *f*.
flipper ['flipə] *n* (*seal, etc.*) nageoire *f*; (*swimmer's*) palme *f*.
flirt [flɔit] *v* flirter. *n* flirteur, -euse *m, f*. **flirtation** *n* flirt *m*.
flit [flit] *v* voleter. **do a moonlight flit** déménager à la cloche de bois.
float [flout] *v* (faire) flotter; (*swimmer*) faire la planche. *n* (*fishing*) flotteur *m*; (*in procession*) char *m*.
flock¹ [flok] *n* (*animals*) troupeau *m*; (*birds*) volée *f*; (*people*) foule *f*. *v* s'attrouper.

flock² [flok] n (*wool*) bourre de laine f; (*cotton*) bourre de coton f.

flog [flog] v flageller. **flogging** n flagellation f; (*law*) fouet m.

flood [flʌd] n inondation f; (*sudden rush*) déluge m. **open the floodgates** ouvrir les vannes. v inonder; (*river*) (faire) déborder. **flooding** n inondation f.

***floodlight** ['flʌd,lait] v illuminer; (*sport*) éclairer. n projecteur m. **floodlighting** n illumination f; éclairage m.

floor [flo:] n plancher m; (*ground*) sol m; (*storey*) étage m. **floorboard** n planche f. v terrasser; stupéfier.

flop [flop] n (*coll*) fiasco m. v s'effondrer; (*coll*) faire fiasco. **floppy** adj flottant; (*hat*) à bords flottants.

flora ['flo:rə] n flore f.

floral ['flo:rəl] adj floral.

florist ['florist] n fleuriste m, f.

flounce¹ [flauns] v **flounce in/out** entrer/sortir dans un mouvement d'humeur. n geste impatient m.

flounce² [flauns] n (*of dress*) volant m.

flounder¹ ['flaundə] v patauger.

flounder² ['flaundə] n flet m.

flour ['flauə] n farine f. **floury** adj enfariné; (*potatoes*) farineux.

flourish ['flʌriʃ] v prospérer; (*wave*) brandir. n fioriture f; (*gesture*) moulinet m. **flourishing** adj florissant.

flout [flaut] v se moquer de.

flow [flou] v couler; circuler. n écoulement m; circulation f. **flow chart** organigramme m. **flowing** adj gracieux; (*hair, etc.*) flottant.

flower ['flauə] n fleur f. **flower arrangement** composition florale f. **flower bed** plate-bande f. **flowerpot** n pot à fleurs m. **flower show** floralies f pl. v fleurir. **flowery** adj fleuri.

flown [floun] V **fly¹**.

flu [flu:] n grippe f.

fluctuate ['flʌktjueit] v fluctuer, varier. **fluctuating** n fluctuation f, variation f.

flue [flu:] n tuyau m, conduit m.

fluent ['fluənt] adj coulant. **fluency** n aisance f. **fluently** adv couramment.

fluff [flʌf] n (*on animal, bird*) duvet m; (*from fabric*) peluche f. v (*coll: fail*) louper. **fluffy** adj duveteux; pelucheux.

fluid ['fluid] nm, adj fluide.

fluke [flu:k] n coup de chance m, hasard extraordinaire m.

flung [flʌŋ] V **fling**.

fluorescent [fluə'resnt] adj fluorescent. **fluorescence** n fluorescence f.

fluoride ['fluəraid] n fluor m.

flush¹ [flʌʃ] n (*blush*) rougeur f; (*burst*) éclat m. v rougir; (*wash out*) nettoyer à grande eau; (*toilet*) tirer la chasse. **flushed** adj rouge.

flush² [flʌʃ] adj à ras (de); (*slang: rich*) plein de fric.

fluster ['flʌstə] v énerver. **get flustered** s'énerver. n agitation f.

flute [flu:t] n flûte f.

flutter ['flʌtə] v voleter; (*wings*) battre; (*heart*) palpiter. n battement m; palpitation f; agitation f.

flux [flʌks] n flux m. **be in a state of flux** changer sans arrêt.

***fly¹** [flai] v voler; (*aeroplane*) piloter; (*kite*) faire voler; (*time*) passer vite; (*flee*) fuir. **fly across** or **over** survoler. **fly away** s'envoler. **flyaway** adj (*hair*) difficile. **flyleaf** n page de garde f. **flyover** n (*mot*) autopont m. **flysheet** n feuille volante f. **flywheel** n (*tech*) volant m. n also **flies** (*on trousers*) braguette f.

fly² [flai] n mouche f.

foal [foul] n poulain m.

foam [foum] n mousse f; (*sea, animal*) écume f. **foam rubber** caoutchouc mousse m. v mousser; écumer. **foamy** adj mousseux; écumeux.

focal ['foukəl] adj focal. **focal point** foyer m; (*of attention*) point central m.

focus ['foukəs] n foyer m; (*of interest*) centre m. **in focus** au point. v (*phot, etc.*) mettre au point; (*rays*) (faire) converger; concentrer.

fodder ['fodə] n fourrage m.

foe [fou] n ennemi, -e m, f.

foetus ['fi:təs] n fœtus m. **foetal** adj fœtal.

fog [fog] n brouillard m. **fogbound** adj bloqué par le brouillard. **foghorn** n corne de brume f. **foglamp** n (*mot*) phare antibrouillard m. **foggy** adj brumeux. **it's foggy** il fait du brouillard.

foible ['foibl] n marotte f.

foil¹ [foil] v déjouer.

foil² [foil] n feuille de métal f; (*cooking*) papier d'aluminium m.

foil³ [foil] n (*fencing*) fleuret m.

foist [foist] v refiler.

fold¹ [fould] n pli m. v (se) plier. **fold one's arms** se croiser les bras. **fold up** plier; (*coll: collapse*) s'écrouler. **folder** n dossier *m.* chemise *f.* **folding** *adj* pliant. **folding door** porte en accordéon *f.*

fold[2] [fould] *n* (*sheep*) parc à moutons *m.*

foliage ['fouliidʒ] *n* feuillage *m.*

folk [fouk] *pl n* gens *f pl.* **folk dance** danse folklorique *f.* **folklore** *n* folklore *m.* **folk music** musique folk *f.* **folks** *pl n* (*coll*) famille *f sing.* **folk singer** chanteur, -euse de folk *m. f.*

follicle ['folikl] *n* follicule *m.*

follow ['folou] *v* suivre; (*result*) s'ensuivre. **follow up** exploiter; (faire) suivre. **follower** *n* disciple *m.*

folly ['foli] *n* folie *f.*

fond [fond] *adj* tendre, affectueux. **be fond of** aimer. **fondness** *n* (*for person*) affection *f*; (*for thing*) prédilection *f.*

fondant ['fondənt] *n* fondant *m.*

fondle ['fondl] *v* caresser.

font [font] *n* fonts baptismaux *m pl.*

food [fuːd] *n* nourriture *f*, aliments *m pl.* **food poisoning** intoxication alimentaire *f.* **foodstuffs** *pl n* aliments *m pl.*

fool [fuːl] *n* imbécile *m, f.* **foolproof** *adj* infaillible. *v* (*deceive*) duper. **fool around** faire l'imbécile. **foolhardy** *adj* téméraire. **foolish** *adj* idiot. **foolishly** *adv* bêtement. **foolishness** *n* bêtise *f.*

foolscap ['fuːlskap] *n* papier pot *m.*

foot [fut] *n, pl* **feet** pied *m*; (*bird, animal*) patte *f*; (*of page*) bas *m.* **get off on the right/wrong foot** être bien/mal parti. **on foot** à pied. **put one's foot in it** mettre les pieds dans le plat.

foot-and-mouth disease *n* fièvre aphteuse *f.*

football ['fut,boːl] *n* (*game*) football *m*; (*ball*) ballon *m.* **footballer** *n* footballeur *m.*

footbridge ['fut,bridʒ] *n* passerelle *f.*

foothold ['fut,hould] *n* prise de pied *f.*

footing ['futiŋ] *n* position *f*; relations *f pl.* **equal footing** pied d'égalité *m.*

footlights ['fut,laits] *pl n* rampe *f sing.*

footnote ['fut,nout] *n* note en bas de la page *f.*

footpath ['fut,paːθ] *n* sentier *m.*

footprint ['fut,print] *n* empreinte du pied *f.*

footstep ['fut,step] *n* pas *m.*

footwear ['fut,weə] *n* chaussures *f pl.*

for [foː] *prep* pour; (*exchange*) contre; (*distance*) pendant. *conj* car.

forage ['foridʒ] *v* fourrager. *n* fourrage *m.*

forbade [foːˈbad] *V* **forbid**.

*****forbear** [foːˈbeə] *v* s'abstenir. **forbearance** *n* patience *f.*

*****forbid** [foːˈbid] *v* défendre, interdire. **forbidding** *adj* menaçant; (*look*) rébarbatif.

forbidden [foːˈbidn] *V* **forbid**.

force [foːs] *n* force *f.* **in force** en vigueur. *v* forcer; imposer; (*thrust*) pousser. **forcefeed** *v* nourrir de force. **forceful** *adj* énergique, puissant. **forcibly** *adv* de force.

forceps ['foːseps] *pl n* forceps *m sing.*

ford [foːd] *n* gué *m.* *v* passer à gué.

fore [foː] *adj* antérieur, de devant. *n* (*naut*) avant *m.* **come to the fore** se faire remarquer. *adv* à l'avant.

forearm ['foːraːm] *n* avant-bras *m invar.*

forebears ['foːbeəz] *pl n* ancêtres *m pl.*

foreboding [foːˈboudiŋ] *n* pressentiment *m.*

*****forecast** ['foːkaːst] *n* prévision *f.* **weather forecast** bulletin météorologique *m.* *v* prévoir.

forecourt ['foːkoːt] *n* avant-cour *m*; (*of garage*) devant *m.*

forefathers ['foːfaːðəz] *pl n* ancêtres *m pl.*

forefinger ['foːfiŋgə] *n* index *m.*

forefront ['foːfrʌnt] *n* premier rang *m.*

foregone [foːgon] *adj* **be a foregone conclusion** être à prévoir.

foreground ['foːgraund] *n* premier plan *m.*

forehand ['foːhand] *n* (*tennis*) coup droit *m.*

forehead ['forid] *n* front *m.*

foreign ['forən] *adj* étranger. **foreigner** *n* étranger, -ère *m. f.*

foreleg ['foːleg] *n* jambe antérieure *f*; patte de devant *f.*

foreman ['foːmən] *n* contremaître *m.*

foremost ['foːmoust] *adj* principal. **first and foremost** tout d'abord.

forename ['foːneim] *n* prénom *m.*

forensic [fəˈrensik] *adj* (*medicine*) légal; (*evidence*) médico-légal.

forerunner ['foːrʌnə] *n* précurseur *m.*

*****foresee** [foːˈsiː] *v* prévoir. **foreseeable** *adj* prévisible.

foreshadow [foːˈʃadou] *v* présager.

foresight ['foːsait] *n* prévoyance *f.*

foreskin ['foːskin] *n* prépuce *m.*

forest ['forist] *n* forêt *f.* **forester** *n* forestier *m.* **forestry** *n* sylviculture *f.* **Forestry Commission** Eaux et Forêts *f pl.*

forestall [fɔrˈstɔːl] v devancer, anticiper.
foretaste [ˈfɔːteist] n avant-goût m.
***foretell** [fɔrˈtel] v prédire.
forethought [ˈfɔːθɔːt] n prévoyance.
forever [fɔrˈevə] adv toujours.
foreword [ˈfɔːwəːd] n avant-propos m.
forfeit [ˈfɔːfit] v perdre. n peine f; (game) gage m.
forgave [fəˈgeiv] V **forgive**.
forge[1] [fɔːdʒ] v (counterfeit) contrefaire; (metal) forger. n forge f. **forger** n faussaire m, f; (law) contrefacteur m. **forgery** n (act) contrefaçon f; (thing forged) faux m.
forge[2] [fɔːdʒ] v **forge ahead** pousser de l'avant.
***forget** [fəˈget] v oublier. **forget-me-not** n myosotis m. **forgetful** adj distrait.
***forgive** [fəˈgiv] v pardonner. **forgiveness** n pardon m; clémence f.
forgiven [fəˈgivn] V **forgive**.
***forgo** [fɔːˈgou] v renoncer à.
forgot [fəˈgot] V **forget**.
forgotten [fəˈgotn] V **forget**.
fork [fɔːk] n (cutlery) fourchette f; (branch) fourche f; (roads) embranchement m. v (road) bifurquer. **fork out** (slang: pay) allonger. **forked** adj fourchu.
forlorn [fəˈlɔːn] adj malheureux; abandonné.
form [fɔːm] n forme f; (document) formulaire m; (bench) banc m; (school) classe f. v (se) former. **formation** n formation f. **formative** adj formateur, -trice.
formal [ˈfɔːməl] adj (dress) de cérémonie; officiel; (person, manner) compassé; (in form only) formel. **formality** n formalité f.
format [ˈfɔːmat] n format m.
former [ˈfɔːmə] adj (previous) ancien; (first) premier. pron celui-là, celle-là. **formerly** adv autrefois.
formidable [ˈfɔːmidəbl] adj redoutable.
formula [ˈfɔːmjulə] n formule f.
formulate [ˈfɔːmjuˌleit] v formuler. **formulation** n formulation f.
***forsake** [fəˈseik] v abandonner.
forsaken [fəˈseikn] V **forsake**.
forsook [fəˈsuk] V **forsake**.
fort [fɔːt] n fort m.
forte [ˈfɔːtei] n fort m.
forth [fɔːθ] adv en avant. **and so forth** et ainsi de suite. **forthcoming** adj à venir, prochain; (person) ouvert. **forthright** adj franc, franche. **forthwith** adv sur-le-champ.

fortify [ˈfɔːtiˌfai] v fortifier. **fortification** n fortification f.
fortitude [ˈfɔːtiˌtjuːd] n courage m.
fortnight [ˈfɔːtnait] n quinzaine f. **fortnightly** adv tous les quinze jours.
fortress [ˈfɔːtris] n forteresse f.
fortuitous [fɔːˈtjuːitəs] adj fortuit.
fortunate [ˈfɔːtjunət] adj heureux. **be fortunate** avoir de la chance. **fortunately** adv heureusement.
fortune [ˈfɔːtʃən] n fortune f; (luck) chance f. **fortune-teller** n diseur, -euse de bonne aventure m, f.
forty [ˈfɔːti] nm, adj quarante. **forty winks** un petit somme. **fortieth** n(m+f), adj quarantième.
forum [ˈfɔːrəm] n forum m; (meeting) tribune f.
forward [ˈfɔːwəd] adj en avant; (impudent) effronté. **come forward** se présenter. v expédier; (send on) faire suivre. **please forward** prière de faire suivre.
forwards [ˈfɔːwədz] adv en avant.
fossil [ˈfosl] n fossile m. **fossilized** adj fossilisé.
foster [ˈfostə] v (child) élever; encourager; (idea) entretenir.
fought [fɔːt] V **fight**.
foul [faul] adj infect; (language) ordurier; (weather) sale. **foul play** acte criminel m; (sport) jeu déloyal m. n (sport) coup défendu. v infecter; (entangle) (s')emmêler.
found[1] [faund] V **find**.
found[2] [faund] v fonder. **foundation** n fondation f; base f, fondement m. **founder** n fondateur, -trice m, f.
founder [ˈfaundə] v (ship) sombrer; (collapse) s'effondrer.
foundry [ˈfaundri] n fonderie f.
fountain [ˈfauntin] n fontaine f. **fountain pen** stylo à encre m.
four [fɔː] nm, adj quatre. **foursome** n (game) partie à quatre f; deux couples m pl. **on all fours** à quatre pattes. **fourth** n(m+f), adj quatrième.
fourteen [fɔːˈtiːn] nm, adj quatorze. **fourteenth** n(m+f), adj quatorzième.
fowl [faul] n volaille f.
fox [foks] n renard m. **foxglove** n digitale f. **foxhunting** n chasse au renard f. **foxtrot** n slow m. v (coll) mystifier.
foyer [ˈfoiei] n foyer m.

fraction ['frakʃən] *n* fraction *f.* **fractionally** *adv* un tout petit peu.

fracture ['fraktʃə] *n* fracture *f.* *v* (se) fracturer.

fragile ['fradʒail] *adj* fragile. **fragility** *n* fragilité *f.*

fragment ['fragmənt] *n* fragment *m.* **fragmented** *adj* morcelé.

fragrant ['freigrənt] *adj* parfumé. **fragrance** *n* parfum *m.*

frail [freil] *adj* frêle, fragile. **frailty** *n* fragilité *f;* (*moral*) faiblesse *f.*

frame [freim] *n* cadre *m;* (*house*) charpente *f;* (*car*) châssis *m;* (*spectacles*) monture *f;* (*film*) image *f.* **frame of mind** humeur *f.* **framework** *n* charpente *f;* structure *f.* *v* encadrer.

franc [fraŋk] *n* franc *m.*

France [frains] *n* France *f.*

franchise ['frantʃaiz] *n* droit de suffrage *m.*

frank [fraŋk] *adj* franc, franche. **frankness** *n* franchise *f.*

frantic ['frantik] *adj* frénétique; (*person*) hors de soi.

fraternal [frə'tə:nl] *adj* fraternel. **fraternity** *n* fraternité *f;* (*community*) confrérie *f.* **fraternize** *v* fraterniser.

fraud [fro:d] *n* (*law*) fraude *f;* (*deception*) supercherie *f;* (*financial*) escroquerie *f;* (*person*) imposteur *m.* **fraudulent** *adj* frauduleux.

fraught [fro:t] *adj* (*tense*) tendu. **fraught with** chargé de.

fray[1] [frei] *v* (s')effilocher; (*cuff, etc.*) (s')effranger.

fray[2] [frei] *n* rixe *f.*

freak [fri:k] *n* phénomène *m;* anomalie *f.* **freak of nature** accident de la nature *m.* *adj* insolite, inattendu.

freckle ['frekl] *n* tache de son *f.* **freckled** *adj* taché de son.

free [fri:] *adj* libre; gratuit. **free-for-all** *n* mêlée générale *f.* **freehand** *adj, adv* à main levée. **freehold** *n* propriété foncière libre *f.* **freelance** *n, adj* indépendant, -e. **freemason** *n* francmaçon *m.* **freestyle** *n* nage libre *f.* **of one's own free will** de son propre gré. *v* libérer. **freedom** *n* liberté *f.*

freesia ['fri:ziə] *n* freesia *m.*

*****freeze** [fri:z] *v* geler; (*food*) congeler; (*prices, etc.*) bloquer. *n* gel *m;* blocage *m.* **freezer** *n* congélateur *m.* **freezing** *adj* glacial. **freezing point** point de congélation *m.*

freight [freit] *n* fret *m;* transport *m;* (*goods*) marchandises *f pl.* **freight train** train de marchandises *m.* *v* affréter; transporter. **freighter** *n* (*ship*) cargo *m;* (*aircraft*) avion-cargo *m.*

French [frentʃ] *nm, adj* français. **the French** les Français *m pl.* **French bean** haricot vert *m.* **French dressing** vinaigrette *f.* **French horn** cor d'harmonie *m.* **French-polish** *v* vernir à l'alcool. **french fries** *pl n* pommes frites *f pl.*

frenzy ['frenzi] *n* frénésie *f.* **frenzied** *adj* frénétique.

frequent ['fri:kwənt] *v* fri'kwent] *adj* fréquent. *v* fréquenter. **frequency** *n* fréquence *f.* **frequently** *adv* fréquemment.

fresco ['freskou] *n* fresque *f.*

fresh [freʃ] *adj* frais, fraîche; (*new*) nouveau, -elle. **freshwater** *adj* (*fish*) d'eau douce. **freshen up** faire un brin de toilette. **freshness** *n* fraîcheur *f.*

fret[1] [fret] *v* se tracasser. **fretful** *adj* agité; (*child*) pleurnicheur, -euse.

fret[2] [fret] *v* découper, chantourner. **fretsaw** *n* scie à découper *f.* **fretwork** *n* découpage *m.*

friar ['fraiə] *n* frère *m,* moine *m.*

friction ['frikʃən] *n* friction *f;* désaccord *m.*

Friday ['fraidei] *n* vendredi *m.*

fridge [fridʒ] *n* (*coll*) frigo *m.*

friend [frend] *n* ami, -e *m, f.* **make friends with** devenir ami avec. **friendliness** *n* bienveillance *f.* **friendly** *adj* amical; (*kind*) gentil, -ille. **friendship** *n* amitié *f.*

frieze [fri:z] *n* frise *f.*

frigate ['frigit] *n* frégate *f.*

fright [frait] *n* effroi *m,* peur *f.* **frighten** *v* effrayer. **be frightened** avoir peur. **frightening** *adj* effrayant. **frightful** *adj* affreux.

frigid ['fridʒid] *adj* glacial; (*manner*) froid; (*woman*) frigide. **frigidity** *n* froideur *f;* frigidité *f.*

frill [fril] *n* (*dress*) ruche *f;* (*shirt*) jabot *m.* **frilly** *adj* à fanfreluches.

fringe [frindʒ] *n* frange *f;* (*edge*) bord *m.* **fringe benefits** avantages supplémentaires *m pl.* *v* franger; border.

frisk [frisk] *v* gambader; (*search*) fouiller. **frisky** *adj* vif.

fritter[1] ['fritə] *v* **fritter away** gaspiller.

fritter[2] ['fritə] *n* (*cookery*) beignet *m.*

frivolity [fri'voliti] *n* frivolité *f.* **frivolous** *adj* frivole.

frizz [friz] v (hair) friser. **frizzy** adj crépu.
fro [frou] adv **to and fro** de long en large. **go to and fro between** aller et venir entre.
frock [frok] n robe f.
frog [frog] n grenouille f. **frogman** n homme-grenouille m. **frogs' legs** cuisses de grenouille f pl.
frolic ['frolik] v folâtrer. n ébats m pl.
from [from] prep de; (starting from) à partir de; (extract) dans, à.
front [frʌnt] n devant m, avant m; (mil, weather) front m; (promenade) front de mer m. **in front of** devant. adj de devant, en avant; (first) premier. **front view** vue de face f. **frontage** n façade f; (shop) devanture f.
frontier ['frʌntiə] n frontière f.
frost [frost] n gelée f. **frostbite** n gelure f. v geler. **frosted glass** verre dépoli m. **frosty** adj glacial.
froth [froθ] n écume f, mousse f. v écumer, mousser. **frothy** adj écumeux, mousseux.
frown [fraun] n froncement de sourcils m. v froncer les sourcils, se renfrogner. **frown on** désapprouver.
froze [frouz] V **freeze**.
frozen ['frouzn] V **freeze**. adj gelé. **frozen food** aliments congelés m pl.
frugal ['fruːgəl] adj (meal, etc.) frugal; (person) économe. **frugality** n frugalité f.
fruit [fruːt] n fruit m. **fruit cake** cake m. **fruit machine** machine à sous f. **fruit salad** salade de fruits f. **fruitful** adj fructueux. **fruition** n réalisation f. **fruitless** adj stérile.
frustrate [frʌ'streit] v frustrer; (plans, etc.) faire échouer. **frustration** n frustration f.
fry [frai] v (faire) frire. **fried** adj frit. **fried egg** œuf sur le plat m. **frying** n friture f. **frying pan** poêle f.
fuchsia ['fjuːʃə] n fuchsia m.
fuck [fʌk] (vulgar) v baiser. **fuck off!** va te faire foutre!
fudge [fʌdʒ] n fondant m.
fuel ['fjuəl] n combustible m; (mot) carburant m. **fuel gauge** indicateur de niveau de carburant m. **fuel pump** pompe à essence f. v (stove, etc.) alimenter; (aircraft) (se) ravitailler en combustible.
fugitive ['fjuːdʒitiv] n, adj fugitif, -ive.
fulcrum ['fulkrəm] n pivot m.
fulfil [ful'fil] v accomplir; exécuter; satisfaire. **fulfilment** n accomplissement m; exécution f; contentement m.

full [ful] adj plein; complet, -ète. **full blast** adv (radio, etc.) à pleines tubes. **full-length** adj (picture) en pied; (film) long métrage. **full moon** pleine lune f. **full name** nom et prénoms. **full-scale** adj de grande envergure. **full stop** point m. **full-time** adj, adv à plein temps. **fully** adv entièrement.
fumble ['fʌmbl] v (feel) tâtonner; (search) fouiller.
fume [fjuːm] v fumer; (coll: rage) être furibond. **fumes** pl n vapeurs f pl.
fun [fʌn] n amusement m. **for fun** pour rire. **funfair** n fête foraine f. **have fun** bien s'amuser. **make fun of** se moquer de.
function ['fʌŋkʃən] n fonction f; réception f. v fonctionner. **functional** adj fonctionnel.
fund [fʌnd] n fond m, caisse f. **funds** pl n fonds m pl.
fundamental [fʌndə'mentl] adj fondamental.
funeral ['fjuːnərəl] n enterrement m; (state) funérailles f pl. **funeral parlour** dépôt mortuaire m. **funeral service** service funèbre m.
fungus ['fʌŋgəs] n, pl **fungi** champignon m.
funnel ['fʌnl] n (pouring) entonnoir m; (ship) cheminée f.
funny ['fʌni] adj drôle; bizarre.
fur [fəː] n fourrure f; (kettle) incrustation f. v s'incruster. **furrier** n fourreur m. **furry** adj à poil.
furious ['fjuəriəs] adj furieux.
furnace ['fəːnis] n fourneau m.
furnish ['fəːniʃ] v (house, etc.) meubler; (supply) fournir. **furnishings** pl n mobilier m sing.
furniture ['fəːnitʃə] n meubles m pl, mobilier m.
furrow ['fʌrou] n sillon m; (brow) ride f. v sillonner; rider.
further ['fəːðə] adv (farther) plus loin; (more) davantage. adj (farther) plus lointain; additionnel. **further education** enseignement post-scolaire m. **furthermore** en outre. **until further notice** jusqu'à nouvel ordre. v avancer.
furthest ['fəːðist] adv le plus loin. adj le plus lointain.
furtive ['fəːtiv] adj furtif.

fury ['fjʊəri] *n* fureur *f*.
fuse[1] [fjuːz] *v* (*blend*) fusionner; (*melt*) fondre; (*elec*) faire sauter. **fused** *adj* (*plug*) avec fusible incorporé. *n* (*elec*) plomb *m*. **fuse box** boîte à fusibles *f*. **fuse wire** fusible *m*.
fuse[2] [fjuːz] *v* (*bomb*) amorcer. *n* amorce *f*.
fuselage ['fjuːzəˌlaːʒ] *n* fuselage *m*.
fusion ['fjuːʒən] *n* fusion *f*.
fuss [fʌs] *n* façons *f pl*; agitation *f*. **make a fuss** faire des histoires. *v* s'affairer; (*worry*) se tracasser. **fussy** *adj* tatillon, -onne; (*overelaborate*) tarabiscoté.
futile ['fjuːtail] *adj* futile, vain. **futility** *n* futilité *f*.
future ['fjuːtʃə] *n* avenir *m*; (*gramm*) futur *m*. **in future** à l'avenir. *adj* futur, à venir. **futuristic** *adj* futuriste.
fuzz [fʌz] *n* (*hair*) cheveux crépus *m pl*; (*on body*) duvet *m*; (*slang: police*) flicaille *f*. **fuzzy** *adj* crépu; (*photo*) flou.

G

gabble ['gabl] *v* brédouiller. *n* baragouin *m*.
gable ['geibl] *n* pignon *m*.
gadget ['gadʒit] *n* gadget *m*.
gag[1] [gag] *v* bâillonner. *n* bâillon *m*.
gag[2] [gag] (*coll*) *n* (*joke*) plaisanterie *f*. *v* plaisanter.
gaiety ['geiəti] *n* gaieté *f*.
gain [gein] *n* gain *m*, profit *m*. *v* gagner; (*speed, weight*) prendre; (*clock, watch*) avancer.
gait [geit] *n* démarche *f*.
gala ['gaːlə] *n* gala *m*.
galaxy ['galəksi] *n* galaxie *f*.
gale [geil] *n* coup de vent *m*.
gallant ['galənt] *adj* courageux; noble; (*to women*) galant. **gallantry** *n* courage *m*; galanterie *f*.
gall-bladder ['gɔːlˌbladə] *n* vésicule biliaire *f*.
galleon ['galiən] *n* galion *m*.
gallery ['galəri] *n* galerie *f*; (*spectators*) tribune *f*; (*theatre*) dernier balcon *m*.
galley ['gali] *n* (*ship*) galère *f*; (*kitchen*) cuisine *f*.
gallon ['galən] *n* gallon *m*.

gallop ['galəp] *n* galop *m*. *v* galoper.
gallows ['galouz] *n* gibet *m*.
gallstone ['gɔːlstoun] *n* calcul biliaire *m*.
galvanize ['galvənaiz] *v* galvaniser. **galvanize into action** donner le coup de fouet à.
gamble ['gambl] *v* jouer. **gamble on** compter sur. *n* jeu (de hasard) *m*; entreprise risquée *f*. **gambler** *n* joueur, -euse *m*, *f*. **gambling** *n* jeu *m*.
game [geim] *n* jeu *m*; (*of cards, tennis, etc.*) partie *f*; (*hunting*) gibier *m*. **gamekeeper** *n* garde-chasse *m*. **games** *n* (*school*) sport *m*. *adj* courageux. **be game for** être prêt à.
gammon ['gamən] *n* jambon salé *m*; (*smoked*) jambon fumé *m*.
gang [gaŋ] *n* bande *f*. *v* **gang up on** se liguer contre. **gangster** *n* gangster *m*.
gangrene ['gaŋgriːn] *n* gangrène *f*.
gangway ['gaŋwei] *n* passage *m*; (*naut*) passerelle *f*.
gaol *V* **jail**.
gap [gap] *n* trou *m*, vide *m*.
gape [geip] *v* (*stare*) rester bouche bée; (*open wide*) bâiller. **gaping** *adj* béant.
garage ['garaːdʒ] *n* garage *m*.
garbage ['gaːbidʒ] (*US*) *n* ordures *f pl*. **garbage can** poubelle *f*.
garble ['gaːbl] *v* déformer, embrouiller. **garbled** *adj* confus; incompréhensible.
garden ['gaːdn] *n* jardin *m*. **garden party** garden-party *f*. **gardens** *pl n* parc *m sing*, jardin public *m sing*. **gardener** *n* jardinier, -ère *m*, *f*. **gardening** *n* jardinage *m*.
gargle ['gaːgl] *v* se gargariser. *n* gargarisme *f*.
gargoyle ['gaːgoil] *n* gargouille *f*.
garland ['gaːlənd] *n* guirlande *f*. *v* enguirlander.
garlic ['gaːlik] *n* ail (*pl* aulx) *m*.
garment ['gaːmənt] *n* vêtement *m*.
garnish ['gaːniʃ] *v* garnir. *n* garniture *f*.
garrison ['garisn] *n* garnison *f*. *v* mettre en garnison.
garter ['gaːtə] *n* jarretière *f*; (*for socks*) fixe-chaussette *m*; (*US*) jarretelle *f*. **garter belt** (*US*) porte-jarretelles *m invar*.
gas [gas] *n* gaz *m*; (*US: petrol*) essence *f*. **gasmask** *n* masque à gaz *m*. **gas ring** (*cooker*) brûleur *m*. **gasworks** *n* usine à gaz *f*. *v* asphyxier. **gaseous** *adj* gazeux. **gassy** *adj* gazeux.

gash [gaʃ] n entaille f. v entailler.
gasket ['gaskit] n joint (d'étanchéité) m.
gasoline ['gasəˌliːn] n (US) essence f.
gasp [gaːsp] v haleter; (from surprise) avoir le souffle coupé. n halètement m; souffle m.
gastric ['gastrik] adj gastrique. **gastric ulcer** ulcère de l'estomac m. **gastroenteritis** n gastro-entérite f.
gastronomic [gastrə'nomik] adj gastronomique. **gastronomy** n gastronomie f.
gate [geit] n (garden) porte f; (field) barrière f; (iron) grille f; (airport) sortie f. **gatecrash** v s'introduire sans invitation. **gateway** n porte f.
gateau ['gatou] n gâteau m.
gather ['gaðə] v ramasser; (people) (se) rassembler; (sewing) froncer; (infer) déduire. **gathering** n rassemblement m, réunion f.
gaudy ['goːdi] adj criard.
gauge [geidʒ] n (instrument) jauge f; (rail) écartement m; (measurement) calibre m. v jauger, mesurer.
gaunt [goːnt] adj décharné; (face) creux; (grim) lugubre.
gauze [goːz] n gaze f.
gave [geiv] V **give**.
gay [gei] adj gai; (slang) homo. n (slang) homosexuel, -elle m, f.
gaze [geiz] n regard fixe m. v regarder.
gazelle [gə'zel] n gazelle f.
gazetteer [gazə'tiə] n index géographique m.
gear [giə] n (equipment) matériel m; (belongings) affaires f pl; (mot) vitesse f. **gearbox** n boîte de vitesses f. **gear lever** levier de vitesse m. **in gear** en prise. v adapter; préparer.
geese [giːs] V **goose**.
gelatine ['dʒeləˌtiːn] n gélatine f.
gelignite ['dʒeligˌnait] n gélignite f.
gem [dʒem] n gemme f; (delightful thing) bijou (pl -oux) m, perle f.
Gemini ['dʒemini] n Gémeaux m pl.
gender ['dʒendə] n genre m.
gene [dʒiːn] n gène m.
genealogy [dʒiːniˌalədʒi] n généalogie f. **genealogical** adj généalogique.
general ['dʒenərəl] nm, adj général. **general election** élections législatives f pl. **general hospital** centre hospitalier m. **general knowledge** connaissances générales f pl. **general practitioner** généraliste

m. **in general** en général. **generalization** n généralisation f. **generalize** v généraliser.
generate ['dʒenəreit] v engendrer; produire. **generation** n génération f; production f. **generator** n (elec) génératrice f; (steam) générateur m.
generic [dʒi'nerik] adj générique.
generous ['dʒenərəs] adj généreux. **generosity** n générosité f.
genetic [dʒi'netik] adj génétique. **genetics** n génétique f.
Geneva [dʒi'niːvə] n Genève. **Lake Geneva** le lac Léman.
genial ['dʒiːniəl] adj cordial.
genital ['dʒenitl] adj génital. **genitals** pl n organes génitaux m pl.
genius ['dʒiːniəs] n génie m.
genteel [dʒen'tiːl] adj distingué.
gentle ['dʒentl] adj doux, douce; (light) léger. **gentleman** n monsieur m (pl messieurs) m; (courteous man) gentleman m. **gentleness** n douceur f.
gentry ['dʒentri] n petite noblesse f.
gents [dʒents] n (sign) messieurs m.
genuine ['dʒenjuin] adj véritable, authentique; sincère.
genus ['dʒiːnəs] n genre m.
geography [dʒi'ogrəfi] n géographie f. **geographer** n géographe m, f. **geographical** adj géographique.
geology [dʒi'olədʒi] n géologie f. **geological** adj géologique. **geologist** n géologue m, f.
geometry [dʒi'omətri] n géométrie f. **geometrical** adj géométrique.
geranium [dʒə'reiniəm] n géranium m.
geriatric [dʒeri'atrik] adj gériatrique. **geriatrics** n gériatrie f.
germ [dʒəːm] n (med) microbe m; germe m.
Germany ['dʒəːməni] n Allemagne f. **German** nm, adj allemand; n (people) Allemand, -e m, f. **German measles** rubéole f. **Germanic** adj germanique.
germinate ['dʒəːmineit] v (faire) germer. **germination** n germination f.
gerund ['dʒerənd] n gérondif m.
gesticulate [dʒe'stikjuˌleit] v gesticuler. **gesticulation** n gesticulation f.
gesture ['dʒestʃə] n geste m. v faire signe.
*get [get] v avoir; obtenir; recevoir; (fetch) aller chercher; (go) aller; (become) devenir. **get across** (cross) traverser; communiquer. **get at** (reach) atteindre; (tease) s'en prendre à. **getaway** n fuite f.

get back (*return*) revenir; (*recover*) retrouver. **get down** descendre. **get down to** se mettre à. **get off** descendre. **get on** continuer; (*horse, etc.*) monter (*sur*); (*agree*) s'accorder. **get out** sortir. **get up** se lever.

geyser ['giːzə] n geyser m; (*water-heater*) chauffe-bain m *invar*.

ghastly ['gaːstli] adj horrible; (*pale*) blême.

gherkin ['gəːkin] n cornichon m.

ghetto ['getou] n ghetto m.

ghost [goust] n fantôme m. **ghostly** adj spectral.

giant ['dʒaiənt] nm, adj géant.

gibberish ['dʒibəriʃ] n baragouin m.

gibe [dʒaib] n raillerie f. v **gibe at** railler.

giblets ['dʒiblits] pl n abattis m pl.

giddy ['gidi] adj (*dizzy*) pris de vertige; (*height*) vertigineux; (*scatterbrained*) étourdi. **giddiness** n vertiges m pl.

gift [gift] n cadeau m; (*talent*) don m. **gift token** chèque-cadeau m. **gifted** adj doué.

gigantic [dʒaiˈgantik] adj gigantesque.

giggle ['gigl] v rire nerveusement, glousser. n gloussement m. **get the giggles** avoir le fou rire.

gill [gil] n (*fish*) branchie f; (*mushroom*) lamelle f.

gilt [gilt] n dorure f. adj doré.

gimmick ['gimik] n (*coll*) truc m.

gin [dʒin] n gin m.

ginger ['dʒindʒə] n gingembre m. **gingerbread** n pain d'épice m. adj (*hair*) roux, rousse.

gingerly ['dʒindʒəli] adv avec précaution.

gipsy ['dʒipsi] n bohémien, -enne m, f.

giraffe [dʒiˈraːf] n girafe f.

girder ['gəːdə] n poutre f.

girdle ['gəːdl] n ceinture f; (*corset*) gaine f. v ceindre.

girl [gəːl] n fille f; (*pupil*) élève f. **girlfriend** n petite amie f. **girlhood** n enfance f.

girth [gəːθ] n (*tree*) circonférence f; (*waist, etc.*) tour m; (*saddle*) sangle m.

gist [dʒist] n essentiel m.

****give** [giv] v donner; offrir; céder. **give-and-take** n concessions mutuelles f pl. **give away** faire cadeau de; révéler. **give back** rendre. **give in** se rendre. **give off** émettre. **give out** distribuer. **give up** abandonner. **give way** céder; (*collapse*) s'affaisser.

given ['givn] V **give**.

glacier ['glasiə] n glacier m. **glaciation** n glaciation f.

glad [glad] adj heureux. **gladden** v réjouir. **gladly** adv avec plaisir.

glamour [glamə] n prestige m, éclat m; (*person*) fascination f. **glamorous** adj (*life*) brillant; (*person*) séduisant; (*job*) prestigieux; (*dress*) splendide.

glance [glaːns] n coup d'œil m. v jeter un coup d'œil.

gland [gland] n glande f. **glandular** adj glandulaire. **glandular fever** mononucléose infectieuse f.

glare [gleə] v lancer un regard furieux; (*light*) éblouir. n regard furieux m; éblouissement m.

glass [glaːs] n verre m. **glasses** pl n lunettes f pl. **glassworks** n verrerie f. **glassy** adj vitreux.

glaze [gleiz] v (*window*) vitrer; (*pottery, etc.*) vernisser; (*cookery*) glacer. n vernis m; glaçage m. **glazier** n vitrier m.

gleam [gliːm] v luire. n lueur f. **gleaming** adj brillant.

glean [gliːn] v glaner.

glee [gliː] n joie f. **gleeful** adj joyeux.

glib [glib] adj désinvolte. **glibly** adv avec aisance, avec désinvolture.

glide [glaid] v (*aero*) planer; (*slide*) glisser. n vol plané m; glissement m. **glider** n planeur m.

glimmer ['glimə] v luire faiblement; miroiter. n faible lueur f; miroitement m.

glimpse [glimps] v entrevoir. n vision rapide f.

glint [glint] v étinceler. n reflet m.

glisten ['glisn] v briller.

glitter ['glitə] v scintiller. n scintillement m.

gloat [glout] v jubiler.

globe [gloub] n globe m. **globe artichoke** artichaut m. **globe-trotter** n globe-trotter m. **global** adj global; universel.

gloom [gluːm] n obscurité f; mélancolie f. **gloomy** adj sombre, lugubre.

glory ['gloːri] n gloire f; splendeur f. **glorify** v glorifier. **glorious** adj magnifique, glorieux.

gloss [glos] n lustre m; (*paint*) brillant m. **glossy** adj brillant, lustré.

glossary ['glosəri] n glossaire m.

glove [glʌv] n gant m. **glove compartment** vide-poches m *invar*.

glow [glou] v rougeoyer. n rougeoiement m. **glowing** adj rougeoyant; (words) chaleureux.

glucose ['gluːkous] n glucose m.

glue [gluː] n colle f. v coller.

glum [glʌm] adj triste.

glut [glʌt] n surplus m.

glutton ['glʌtən] n glouton, -onne m, f. **gluttonous** adj glouton. **gluttony** gloutonnerie f.

gnarled [naːld] adj noueux.

gnash [naʃ] v **gnash one's teeth** grincer les dents.

gnat [nat] n moucheron m.

gnaw [noː] v ronger. **gnawing** adj tenaillant.

gnome [noum] n gnome m.

***go** [gou] v aller; (leave) partir; (work) marcher; (become) devenir; (make sound) faire. **go away** s'en aller. **go back** retourner. **go-between** n intermédiaire m, f. **go by** passer; (judge by) se fonder sur. **go down** descendre; (temperature, etc.) baisser. **go in** entrer. **go off** (food) se gâter; (cease to like) perdre le goût de. **go on** continuer. **go out** sortir. **go up** monter. **go with** (match) s'assortir avec. **go without** se passer de. n énergie f; (try) coup m. **it's your go** c'est à toi de jouer. **on the go** sur la brèche.

goad [goud] v aiguillonner. n aiguillon m.

goal [goul] n but m. **goalkeeper** n gardien de but m. **goal post** montant de but m.

goat [gout] n chèvre f. **act the goat** (coll) faire l'imbécile.

gobble ['gobl] v engloutir.

goblin ['goblin] n lutin m.

god [god] n dieu m. **goddaughter** n filleule f. **godfather** n parrain m. **godmother** n marraine f. **godsend** n aubaine f. **godson** n filleul m. **goddess** n déesse f.

goggles ['goglz] pl n lunettes protectrices f pl.

gold [gould] n or m. **goldfinch** n chardonneret m. **goldfish** n poisson rouge m. **goldfish bowl** bocal m. **gold mine** mine d'or f. **goldsmith** n orfèvre m. **golden** adj d'or, doré. **golden opportunity** occasion magnifique f. **golden rule** règle d'or f. **golden syrup** mélasse raffinée f.

golf [golf] n golf m. **golf course** terrain de golf m. **golfer** n golfeur, -euse m, f.

gondola ['gondələ] n gondole f. **gondolier** n gondolier m.

gone [gon] V **go**.

gong [goŋ] n gong m.

gonorrhoea [ˌgonəˈriə] n blennorragie f.

good [gud] adj bon, bonne; (person) brave; (well-behaved) sage. **good afternoon** bonjour; (later) bonsoir. **goodbye** interj au revoir. **good evening** bonsoir. **good-for-nothing** nm, adj propre à rien. **Good Friday** vendredi saint m. **good-looking** adj beau, belle. **good morning** bonjour. **goodnight** interj bonsoir; (bedtime) bonne nuit. **goodwill** n bonne volonté f; (comm) incorporels m pl. n bien m. **be no good** ne servir à rien. **for good** pour de bon. **goodness** n bonté f. **goods** [gudz] pl n (comm) marchandises f pl, articles m pl; (law) biens m pl. **goods train** train de marchandises m.

goose [guːs] n, pl **geese** oie f.

gooseberry ['guzbəri] n (fruit) groseille à maquereau f; (bush) groseiller m. **play gooseberry** tenir la chandelle.

gore [goː] v encorner.

gorge [goːdʒ] n gorge f. v se gorger.

gorgeous ['goːdʒəs] adj magnifique.

gorilla [gəˈrilə] n gorille m.

gorse [goːs] n ajonc m.

gory [ˈgoːri] adj sanglant.

gospel ['gospəl] n évangile m.

gossip ['gosip] n (chat) bavardage m; (unkind) commérage m; (person) commère f. v bavarder; (unkindly) potiner.

got [got] V **get**.

Gothic ['goθik] adj gothique.

goulash ['guːlaʃ] n goulache f.

gourd [guəd] n gourde f.

gourmet ['guəmei] n gourmet m.

gout [gaut] n goutte f.

govern ['gʌvən] v gouverner; administrer; déterminer. **governess** n gouvernante f. **government** n gouvernement m. **governor** n gouverneur m; (school) administrateur, -trice m, f; (coll: boss) patron m.

gown [gaun] n robe f; (law, university) toge f.

grab [grab] v saisir. n mouvement vif pour saisir m.

grace [greis] n grâce f; (before meal) bénédicité m. **graceful** adj gracieux, élégant. **gracious** adj gracieux; courtois.

grade [greid] n catégorie f; échelon m; qualité f; (mark) note f. v classer.

gradient ['greidiənt] n (measurement) inclinaison f; (slope) pente f.

gradual ['gradjuəl] *adj* graduel.
graduate ['gradju͵eit; *n. adj* 'gradjuət] *v* graduer; (*university*) obtenir sa licence. *n. adj* licencié, -e.
graffiti [grə'fiːtiː] *pl n* graffiti *m pl*.
graft [graːft] *n* greffe *f. v* greffer.
grain [grein] *n* grain *m*; (*wood*) fibre *f.*
gram [gram] *n* gramme *m.*
grammar ['gramə] *n* grammaire *f.* **grammar school** lycée *m*. **grammatical** *adj* grammatical.
gramophone ['graməfoun] *n* phonographe *f.*
granary [granəri] *n* grenier *m.*
grand [grand] *adj* magnifique; grandiose. **grandeur** *n* splendeur *f.*
grandchild ['grantʃaild] *n* petit-enfant, petite-enfant *m. f.*
grand-dad ['grandad] *n also* **grandpa** (*coll*) pépé.
granddaughter ['grandoːtə] *n* petite-fille *f.*
grandfather ['gran͵faːðə] *n* grand-père *m.*
grandma ['granmaː] *n also* **granny** (*coll*) mémé *f.*
grandmother ['gran͵mʌðə] *n* grand-mère *f.*
grandparent ['gran͵peərənt] *n* grand-parent *m.*
grand piano *n* piano à queue *m.*
grandson ['gransʌn] *n* petit-fils *m.*
grandstand ['granstand] *n* tribune *f.*
grand total *n* somme globale *f.*
granite ['granit] *n* granit *m.*
grant [graːnt] *v* accorder; admettre. *n* subvention *f*; (*student*) bourse *f.*
granule ['granjuːl] *n* granule *m.* **granulated sugar** sucre semoule *m.*
grape [greip] *n* raisin *m*. **grapevine** *n* vigne *f*; (*coll*) téléphone arabe *f.*
grapefruit ['greipfruːt] *n* pamplemousse *m.*
graph [graf] *n* graphique *f.* **graph paper** papier quadrillé *m*; papier millimétré *m*. **graphic** *adj* graphique; (*description*) vivant.
grapple ['grapl] *v* **grapple with** affronter résolument.
grasp [graːsp] *v* saisir. *n* prise *f*; compréhension *f.* **grasping** *adj* avare.
grass [graːs] *n* herbe *f*; (*lawn*) gazon *m.* **grasshopper** *n* sauterelle *f.* **grass snake** couleuvre *f.* **grassy** *adj* herbeux.
grate¹ [greit] *n* grille de foyer *f.* **grating** *n* grille *f.*

grate² [greit] *v* (*food*) râper; (*metal*) (faire) grincer. **grater** *n* râpe *f.*
grateful ['greitful] *adj* reconnaissant.
gratify ['grati͵fai] *v* satisfaire; faire plaisir à. **gratifying** *adj* agréable.
gratitude ['gratitjuːd] *n* reconnaissance *f.*
gratuity [grə'tjuəti] *n* pourboire *m.*
grave¹ [greiv] *n* tombe *f.* **gravedigger** *n* fossoyeur *m*. **gravestone** *n* pierre tombale *f.* **graveyard** *n* cimetière *m.*
grave² [greiv] *adj* grave.
gravel ['gravəl] *n* gravier *m. v* couvrir de gravier.
gravity ['gravəti] *n* (*physics*) pesanteur *f*; (*seriousness*) gravité *f.*
gravy ['greivi] *n* jus de viande *m*; sauce *f.*
graze¹ [greiz] *v* (*scrape*) écorcher; (*touch*) frôler. *n* écorchure *f.*
graze² [greiz] *v* (*animal*) brouter, paître.
grease [griːs] *n* graisse *f.* **grease-paint** *n* fard gras *m*. **greaseproof paper** papier parcheminé *m. v* graisser. **greasy** *adj* graisseux; (*hair, road*) gras, grasse.
great [greit] *adj* grand; magnifique. **Great Britain** Grande-Bretagne *f.* **greatly** *adv* fort, très. **greatness** *n* grandeur *f.*
Greece [griːs] *n* Grèce *f.* **Greek** *nm. adj* grec, grecque; *n* (*people*) Grec, Grecque *m. f.*
greed [griːd] *n* avidité *f*; (*for food*) gourmandise *f.* **greedy** *adj* avide; (*for food*) vorace.
green [griːn] *adj* vert; naïf, naïve; (*bacon*) non fumé. *n* vert *m*; (*grass*) gazon *m*. **greenfly** *n* puceron *m*. **greengage** *n* reine-claude *f.* **greengrocer's** *n* fruiterie *f.* **greenhouse** *n* serre *f*; **green light** feu vert *m*. **greens** *pl n* légumes verts *m pl*. **have green fingers** avoir le pouce vert. **greenery** *n* verdure *f.*
Greenland ['griːnlənd] *n* Groenland *m.* **Greenlander** *n* Groenlandais, -e *m. f.*
greet [griːt] *v* saluer, accueillir. **greeting** *n* salutation *f.* **greetings card** carte de vœux *f.*
gregarious [gri'geə͵riəs] *adj* grégaire.
grenade [grə'neid] *n* grenade *f.*
grew [gruː] *V* **grow**.
grey [grei] *nm. adj* gris. **greyhound** *n* lévrier, levrette *m, f*. **go grey** (*hair*) grisonner.
grid [grid] *n* grille *f*; (*elec*) réseau *m.*
grief [griːf] *n* chagrin *m.*
grieve [griːv] *v* (*upset*) peiner; (*sorrow*) s'affliger. **grieve for** pleurer. **grievance** *n*

grief *m*; injustice *f*. **grievous** *adj* affreux; grave. **grievous bodily harm** coups et blessures *m pl*.

grill [gril] *v* (faire) griller. *n* gril *m*; (*meal*) grillade *f*. **grillroom** *n* rôtisserie *f*.

grille [gril] *n* grille *f*.

grim [grim] *adj* sinistre; (*coll*) désagréable. **grimly** *adv* d'un air mécontent.

grimace [gri'meis] *n* grimace *f*. *v* grimacer.

grime [graim] *n* crasse *f*. **grimy** *adj* crasseux.

grin [grin] *n* sourire *m*. *v* sourire.

*****grind** [graind] *v* (*coffee*, *etc*.) moudre; (*crush*) écraser; (*knife*) aiguiser; (*teeth*) grincer. *n* grincement *m*; (*coll*) boulot *m*. **grinder** *n* broyeur *m*, moulin *m*.

grip [grip] *n* (*of hand*) poigne *f*; (*hold*) prise *f*; (*bag*) trousse *f*. *v* saisir; (*hold*) serrer; (*tyres*) adhérer. **gripping** *adj* passionnant.

gripe [graip] *n* colique *f*. *v* (*coll*) rouspéter.

grisly ['grizli] *adj* macabre; horrible.

gristle ['grisl] *n* cartilage *m*. **gristly** *adj* cartilagineux.

grit [grit] *n* sable *m*; gravillon *m*; (*coll: courage*) cran *m*. *v* (*teeth*) serrer; (*road*) répandre du gravillon sur.

groan [groun] *n* (*pain*) gémissement *m*; (*dismay*) grognement *m*. *v* gémir; grogner.

grocer ['grousə] *n* épicier, -ère *m*, *f*. **grocer's** *n* (*shop*) épicerie *f*. **groceries** *pl n* provisions *f pl*.

groin [groin] *n* aine *f*.

groom [gruːm] *n* (*for horse*) palefrenier *m*; (*of bride*) marié *m*. *v* (*horse*) panser; préparer.

groove [gruːv] *n* cannelure *f*, rainure *f*; (*record*) sillon *m*. *v* canneler.

grope [group] *v* tâtonner. **grope for** chercher à tâtons.

gross [grous] *adj* (*not net*) brut; flagrant; obèse; (*coarse*) grossier. *n* grosse *f*.

grotesque [grə'tesk] *nm*, *adj* grotesque.

grotto ['grotou] *n* grotte *f*.

ground[1] [graund] *V* grind.

ground[2] [graund] *n* terre *f*; (*area*) terrain *m*. **ground floor** rez-de-chaussée *m*. **ground frost** gelée blanche *f*. **grounds** *pl n* parc *m sing*; motifs *m pl*; (*coffee*) marc *m sing*. **groundsheet** *n* tapis de sol *m*. **groundwork** *n* base *f*. *v* (*aircraft*) retenir

au sol; fonder; (*ship*) s'échouer. **groundless** *adj* sans fond.

group [gruːp] *n* groupe *m*. *v* (se) grouper.

grouse[1] [graus] *n* grouse *f*.

grouse[2] [graus] (*coll*) *v* rouspéter. *n* grief *m*.

grove [grouv] *n* bocage *m*.

grovel ['grovl] *v* ramper.

*****grow** [grou] *v* pousser; grandir; (*become*) devenir; cultiver. **grown-up** *n*(*m*+*f*). *adj* adulte. **growth** *n* croissance *f*; (*thing grown*) pousse *f*; (*med*) grosseur *f*.

growl [graul] *v* grogner. *n* grognement *m*.

grown [groun] *V* grow.

grub [grʌb] *n* larve *f*; (*slang: food*) bouffe *f*. **grubby** *adj* sale.

grudge [grʌdʒ] *v* donner à contre-cœur. *n* rancune *f*. **bear a grudge against** en vouloir à. **grudgingly** *adv* de mauvaise grâce.

gruelling ['gruəliŋ] *adj* exténuant.

gruesome ['gruːsəm] *adj* horrible.

gruff [grʌf] *adj* bourru.

grumble ['grʌmbl] *v* grommeler. *n* grognement *m*.

grumpy ['grʌmpi] *adj* maussade.

grunt [grʌnt] *v* grogner. *n* grognement *m*.

guarantee [garən'tiː] *n* garantie *f*. *n* garantir. **guarantor** *n* garant, -e *m*, *f*.

guard [gaːd] *n* garde *f*; (*rail*) chef de train *m*. **guard dog** chien de garde *m*. **guard's van** fourgon *m*. *v* garder; défendre. **guarded** *adj* (*remark*, *etc*.) prudent.

guardian *n* gardien, -enne *m*, *f*; (*of child*) tuteur, -trice *m*, *f*. **guardian angel** ange gardien *m*.

Guernsey ['gəːnzi] *n* Guernesey *m*.

guerrilla [gə'rilə] *n* guérillero *m*. **guerrilla warfare** guérilla *f*.

guess [ges] *n* conjecture *f*. **at a guess** au jugé. **guesswork** *n* conjecture *f*. *v* deviner; estimer; supposer; (*believe*) croire.

guest [gest] *n* invité, -e *m*, *f*; (*hotel*) client, -e *m*, *f*. **guesthouse** *n* pension de famille *f*. **guest room** chambre d'ami *f*.

guide [gaid] *n* guide *m*; manuel *m*; (*girl*) éclaireuse *f*. **guidebook** *n* guide *m*. **guide dog** chien d'aveugle *m*. *v* guider. **guidance** *n* conseils *m pl*. **guided** *adj* (*missile*) téléguidé. **guided tour** visite guidée *f*.

guild [gild] *n* confrérie *f*; (*craftsmen*, *etc*.) guilde *f*.

guillotine ['gilətiːn] *n* (*beheading*) guillotine *f*; (*paper*) massicot *m*. *v* guillotiner; massicoter.

guilt [gilt] *n* culpabilité *f*. **guilty** *adj* coupable.

Guinea ['gini] *n* Guinée *f*.

guinea pig *n* cochon d'Inde *m*; (*for experiment*) cobaye *m*.

guitar [gi'taː] *n* guitare *f*. **guitarist** *n* guitariste *m, f*.

gulf [gʌlf] *n* golfe *m*; (*abyss*) gouffre *m*.

gull [gʌl] *n* mouette *f*.

gullet ['gʌlit] *n* œsophage *m*; (*throat*) gosier *m*.

gullible ['gʌləbl] *adj* crédule. **gullibility** *n* crédulité *f*.

gully ['gʌli] *n* ravine *f*.

gulp [gʌlp] *v* avaler; (*food*) engloutir; (*drink*) lamper. *n* (*food*) bouchée *f*; (*drink*) gorgée *f*; (*action*) coup (de gosier) *m*.

gum[1] [gʌm] *n* (*glue*) gomme *f*. **gumboots** *pl n* bottes de caoutchouc *f pl*. *v* gommer.

gum[2] [gʌm] *n* (*mouth*) gencive *f*.

gun [gʌn] *n* pistolet *m*; (*rifle*) fusil *m*. **gunfire** *n* fusillade *f*. **gunman** *n* bandit armé *m*. **gunpowder** *n* poudre à canon *f*. **gunrunning** *n* contrebande d'armes *f*. **gunshot wound** blessure de balle *f*.

gurgle ['gəːgl] *n* gargouillis *m*. *v* gargouiller.

gush [gʌʃ] *v* jaillir. *n* jaillissement *m*. **gushing** *adj* (*person*) trop exubérant.

gust [gʌst] *n* (*wind*) rafale *f*; (*smoke*) bouffée *f*; (*laughter*) éclat *m*. *v* souffler en bourrasque.

gut [gʌt] *n* (*anat*) boyau *m*. **guts** *pl n* (*coll*) cran *m sing*. *v* vider.

gutter ['gʌtə] *n* (*roof*) gouttière *f*; (*street*) caniveau *m*.

guy[1] [gai] *n* (*coll*) type *m*.

guy[2] [gai] *n* (*rope*) corde de tente *f*.

gymnasium [dʒim'neiziəm] *n* gymnase *m*. **gymnast** *n* gymnaste *m, f*. **gymnastic** *adj* gymnastique. **gymnastics** *n* gymnastique *f*.

gynaecology [gainə'kolədʒi] *n* gynécologie *f*. **gynaecological** *adj* gynécologique. **gynaecologist** *n* gynécologue *m, f*.

gypsum ['dʒipsəm] *n* gypse *m*.

gyrate [dʒai'reit] *v* tournoyer. **gyration** *n* giration *f*.

gyroscope ['dʒairə‚skoup] *n* gyroscope *m*.

H

haberdasher ['habədaʃə] *n* mercier, -ère *m, f*. **haberdashery** *n* mercerie *f*.

habit ['habit] *n* habitude *f*; (*clothes*) habit *m*. **habitual** *adj* habituel.

habitable ['habitəbl] *adj* habitable.

habitat ['habitat] *n* habitat *m*.

hack[1] [hak] *v* hacher, tailler. *n* entaille *f*. **hacksaw** *n* scie à métaux *f*.

hack[2] [hak] *n* (*horse*) cheval de selle *m*; (*writer*) nègre *m*.

hackneyed ['haknid] *adj* usé, rebattu.

had [had] *V* **have**.

haddock ['hadək] *n* églefin *m*.

haemorrhage ['heməridʒ] *n* hémorragie *f*.

haemorrhoids ['heməroidz] *pl n* hémorroïdes *f pl*.

hag [hag] *n* (*coll*) chameau *m*.

haggard ['hagəd] *adj* hagard.

haggle ['hagl] *v* marchander, chicaner. **haggling** *n* marchandage *m*.

Hague [heig] *n* **The Hague** La Haye.

hail[1] [heil] *n* grêle *f*. **hailstone** *n* grêlon *m*. *v* grêler.

hail[2] [heil] *v* saluer; (*taxi*) héler. **hail from** être originaire de.

hair [heə] *n* cheveux *m pl*; (*single strand*) cheveu *m*; (*of body, animal*) poil *m*; (*animal coat*) pelage *m*. **hairy** *adj* velu; (*person*) hirsute.

hairbrush ['heəbrʌʃ] *n* brosse à cheveux *f*.

haircut ['heəkʌt] *n* coupe *f*. **have a haircut** se faire couper les cheveux.

hairdresser ['heə‚dresə] *n* coiffeur, -euse *m, f*. **hairdresser's** *n* salon de coiffure *m*. **hairdressing** *n* coiffure *f*.

hair-dryer ['heə‚draiə] *n* sèche-cheveux *m*.

hairnet ['heənet] *n* filet à cheveux *m*.

hair-piece ['heəpiːs] *n* postiche *m*.

hairpin ['heəpin] *n* épingle à cheveux *f*. **hairpin bend** virage en épingle à cheveux *m*.

hair-raising ['heə‚reiziŋ] *adj* horrifique.

hair spray *n* laque *f*.

hairstyle ['heəstail] *n* coiffure *f*.

Haiti ['heiti] *n* Haïti *f*.

hake [heik] *n* colin *m*.

half [haːf] *n* moitié *f*; demi, -e *m, f*. **go halves** se mettre de moitié. **in half** en deux. *adj* demi. *adv* à moitié, à demi.

half-and-half *adv* moitié-moitié.

half-baked [ˌhaːfˈbeikt] (coll) adj (idea) à la noix; (person) mal dégrossi.

half-breed [ˈhaːfbriːd] n (person) métis, -isse m, f; (horse) demi-sang m invar.

half-hearted [ˌhaːfˈhaːtid] adj (person) sans enthousiasme; (attempt) sans conviction.

half-hour [ˌhaːfˈauə] n demi-heure f.

half-mast [ˌhaːfˈmaːst] n at half-mast en berne.

half-open [ˌhaːfˈoupən] adj entrouvert.

half-price [ˌhaːfˈprais] adj, adv demi-tarif; à moitié prix.

half-term [ˌhaːfˈtəːm] n congé de demi-trimestre m.

half-time [ˌhaːfˈtaim] adv, adj à mi-temps.

halfway [ˌhaːfˈwei] adj à mi-chemin. **meet halfway** (compromise) couper la poire en deux.

half-wit [ˈhaːfwit] n idiot, -e m, f.

halibut [ˈhalibət] n flétan m.

hall [hɔːl] n vestibule m; (room) salle f; (corridor) couloir m.

hallmark [ˈhɔːlmaːk] n poinçon m; (of genius, etc.) sceau m. v poinçonner.

hallowed [ˈhaloud] adj saint, sanctifié.

Halloween [halouˈiːn] n veille de la Toussaint f.

hallucination [həˌluːsiˈneiʃən] n hallucination f.

halo [ˈheilou] n auréole f; (astron) halo m.

halt [hɔːlt] n halte f. v faire halte; (car, etc.) faire arrêter; interrompre.

halter [ˈhɔːltə] n licou m.

halve [haːv] v diviser en deux; réduire de moitié.

ham [ham] n jambon m.

hamburger [ˈhambəːgə] n hamburger m.

hammer [ˈhamə] n marteau m. v marteler. **hammer** in enfoncer. **hammer out** (disputes, etc.) démêler.

hammock [ˈhamək] n hamac m.

hamper[1] [ˈhampə] v gêner.

hamper[2] [ˈhampə] n panier m.

hamster [ˈhamstə] n hamster m.

hand [hand] n main f; (worker) travailleur, -euse m, f; (clock) aiguille f; (measure) paume f; (coll: assistance) coup de main m. **by hand** à la main. **keep one's hand in** garder la main. **on the other hand** par contre. **to hand** sous la main. v passer. **hand down** transmettre. **hand in** remettre. **hand over** céder. **handful** n poignée f.

handbag [ˈhandbag] n sac à main m.

handbook [ˈhandbuk] n manuel m; guide m.

handbrake [ˈhandbreik] n frein à main m.

handcuff [ˈhandkʌf] v mettre les menottes à. **handcuffs** pl n menottes f pl.

handicap [ˈhandikap] n handicap m. v handicaper.

handicraft [ˈhandikraːft] n artisanat m.

handiwork [ˈhandiwəːk] n œuvre f, ouvrage m.

handkerchief [ˈhaŋkətʃif] n mouchoir m.

handle [ˈhandl] n (broom, etc.) manche m; (door, drawer) poignée f; (basket) anse f. v manier; (control) manœuvrer. **handle-bars** pl n guidon m sing.

handmade [ˌhandˈmeid] adj fait main.

hand-out [ˈhandaut] n (leaflet) prospectus m; charité f. v **hand out** distribuer.

hand-pick [handˈpik] v trier sur le volet.

handrail [ˈhandreil] n rampe f.

handshake [ˈhandʃeik] n poignée de main f.

handsome [ˈhansəm] adj beau, belle.

handstand [ˈhandstand] n **do a handstand** faire l'arbre droit.

handwriting [ˈhandˌraitiŋ] n écriture f. **handwritten** adj manuscrit.

handy [ˈhandi] adj (useful) commode; accessible; (to hand) sous la main; adroit.

*****hang** [haŋ] v pendre; (picture, etc.) accrocher. **hang around** rôder. **hang fire** traîner en longueur. **hang-gliding** n vol libre m. **hangman** n bourreau m. **hang on** (coll: wait) attendre; (hold out) tenir bon; dépendre de. **hangover** n (slang) gueule de bois f. **hang up** accrocher; (phone) raccrocher. **hang-up** n (coll) complexe m. **hanger** n cintre m.

hangar [ˈhaŋə] n hangar m.

hanker [ˈhaŋkə] v **hanker for** or **after** aspirer à. **hankering** n envie f.

haphazard [ˌhapˈhazəd] adj (fait) au petit bonheur.

happen [ˈhapən] v arriver, se passer. **happening** n événement m.

happy [ˈhapi] adj heureux. **happy birthday/Christmas!** joyeux anniversaire/Noël! **happy-go-lucky** adj insouciant. **happily** adv tranquillement; joyeusement. **happiness** n bonheur m.

harass [ˈharəs] v harceler.

harbour [ˈhaːbə] n port m. v héberger (hope, suspicions, etc.) entretenir.

hard [haːd] *adj* dur; difficile. *adv* fort, ferme. **hard-and-fast** *adj* (*rule*) absolu; inflexible. **hardback** *n* livre relié *m*. **hard-boiled** *adj* (*egg*) dur. **hard-hearted** *adj* impitoyable. **hard up** (*coll*) fauché. **hardware** *n* (*ironmongery*) quincaillerie *f*; (*computers*) hardware *m*. **try hard** faire un gros effort. **work hard** travailler dur. **harden** *v* durcir. **hardness** *n* dureté *f*; difficulté *f*. **hardship** *n* épreuves *f pl*; privation *f*.

hardly ['haːdli] *adv* à peine.

hardy ['haːdi] *adj* robuste; (*plant*) résistant au gel; (*bold*) hardi.

hare [heə] *n* lièvre *m*. **hare-brained** *adj* (*person*) écervelé; (*scheme*) insensé. **harelip** *n* bec-de-lièvre *m*.

haricot ['harikou] *n* haricot blanc *m*.

harm [haːm] *n* mal *m*. *v* faire du mal à. **harmful** *adj* nuisible. **harmless** *adj* innocent; pas méchant.

harmonic [haːˈmonik] *nm*, *adj* harmonique.

harmonica [haːˈmonikə] *n* harmonica *m*.

harmonize ['haːmənaiz] *v* (s')harmoniser.

harmony ['haːməni] *n* harmonie *f*. **harmonious** *adj* harmonieux.

harness ['haːnis] *n* harnais *m*. *v* harnacher; (*power, etc.*) exploiter.

harp [haːp] *n* harpe *f*. **harpist** *n* harpiste *m, f*.

harpoon [haːˈpuːn] *n* harpon *m*. *v* harponner.

harpsichord ['haːpsiˌkoːd] *n* clavecin *m*.

harrowing ['harouiŋ] *adj* poignant; (*cry*) déchirant.

harsh [haːʃ] *adj* dur; (*texture*) rêche, rugueux; (*sound*) discordant, criard. **harshness** *n* dureté *f*; rugosité *f*; discordance *f*.

harvest ['haːvist] *n* moisson *f*; (*fruit*) récolte *f*; (*grapes*) vendange *f*. *v* moissonner; récolter; vendanger.

has [haz] *V* **have**.

hash [haʃ] *n* (*food*) hachis *m*; (*coll: mess*) gâchis *m*.

hashish ['haʃiːʃ] *n* haschish *m*.

haste [heist] *n* hâte *f*. **hasten** *v* (se) hâter. **hastily** *adv* en hâte; sans réfléchir. **hasty** *adj* hâtif; rapide.

hat [hat] *n* chapeau *m*.

hatch[1] [hatʃ] *v* (faire) éclore; (*plot*) ourdir.

hatch[2] [hatʃ] *n* (*canteen*) passe-plats *m invar*; (*naut*) écoutille *f*. **hatchback** *adj* (*car*) avec hayon arrière *m*.

hatchet ['hatʃit] *n* hachette *f*.

hate [heit] *v* haïr, détester. *n also* **hatred** haine *f*. **pet hate** (*coll*) bête noire *f*. **hateful** *adj* haïssable, odieux.

haughty ['hoːti] *adj* hautain. **haughtiness** *n* hauteur *f*.

haul [hoːl] *v* traîner; (*naut*) haler. *n* (*fish*) prise *f*; (*stolen goods*) butin *m*. **haulage** *n* (*transport*) roulage *m*; (*naut*) halage *m*.

haunch [hoːntʃ] *n* hanche *f*. **haunches** *pl n* derrière *m sing*.

haunt [hoːnt] *v* hanter. *n* repaire *m*. **haunting** *adj* obsédant.

*have [hav] *v* avoir; (*meal*) prendre; (*cause to be*) faire. **have on** (*wear*) porter; (*coll: tease*) faire marcher. **have to** devoir, être obligé de.

haven ['heivn] *n* havre *m*.

haversack ['havəsak] *n* havresac *m*, sac à dos *m*.

havoc ['havək] *n* ravages *m pl*. **play havoc with** désorganiser complètement.

hawk [hoːk] *n* faucon *m*.

hawthorn ['hoːθoːn] *n* aubépine *f*.

hay [hei] *n* foin *m*. **go haywire** (*plans*) mal tourner; (*machine*) se détraquer. **hay fever** rhume des foins *m*. **haystack** *n* meule de foin *f*.

hazard ['hazəd] *n* risque *m*; (*chance*) hasard *m*. *v* hasarder, risquer. **hazardous** *adj* hasardeux, risqué.

haze [heiz] *n* brume *f*. **hazy** *adj* brumeux; vague.

hazel ['heizl] *n* noisetier *m*. **hazel-nut** *n* noisette *f*. *adj* (*colour*) noisette *invar*.

he [hiː] *pron* il; (*emphatic*) lui. **he who** celui qui. *n* (*coll*) mâle *m*.

head [hed] *n* tête *f*; (*leader*) chef *m*; (*coin*) face *f*. *adj* principal. *v* se diriger; venir en tête de; intituler. **headed** *adj* (*paper*) à en-tête. **heading** *n* titre *m*. **heady** *adj* capiteux.

headache ['hedeik] *n* mal de tête *m*. **have a headache** avoir mal à la tête.

headfirst [ˌhedˈfoːst] *adv* la tête la première.

headlamp ['hedlamp] *n also* **headlight** (*mot*) phare *m*.

headland ['hedlənd] *n* promontoire *m*.

headline ['hedlain] *n* (*newspaper*) manchette *f*; (*news*) grand titre *m*.

headlong ['hedloŋ] *adv* la tête la première; (*rush*) à toute allure.

headmaster [ˌhedˈmɑːstə] *n* directeur *m*. **headmistress** *n* directrice *f*.
head-on *adj, adv* de plein fouet.
headphones [ˈhedfəunz] *n* casque *m sing*.
headquarters [ˌhedˈkwɔːtəz] *n* bureau principal *m*.
headrest [ˈhedrest] *n* appui-tête *m*.
headscarf [ˈhedskɑːf] *n* foulard *m*.
headstrong [ˈhedstrɒŋ] *adj* têtu.
headway [ˈhedwei] *n* progrès *m*.
heal [hiːl] *v* guérir; (*wound*) (se) cicatriser.
health [helθ] *n* santé *f*. **health foods** aliments naturels *m pl*. **healthy** *adj* sain, en bonne santé; (*appetite*) robuste.
heap [hiːp] *n* tas *m*. *v* entasser, empiler.
*hear [hiə] *v* entendre. **hear from** avoir des nouvelles de. **hear of** entendre parler de. **hearing** *n* (*sense*) ouïe *f*; audition *f*. **hearing aid** appareil acoustique *m*. **hearsay** *n* ouï-dire *m invar*.
heard [hɜːd] *V* **hear**.
hearse [hɜːs] *n* corbillard *m*.
heart [hɑːt] *n* cœur *m*. **by heart** par cœur. **set one's heart on** vouloir à tout prix. **to one's heart's content** tout son content. **hearten** *v* encourager. **heartless** *adj* cruel. **hearty** *adj* (*welcome, etc.*) chaleureux; (*meal*) copieux.
heart attack *n* crise cardiaque *f*.
heartbeat [ˈhɑːtbiːt] *n* battement de cœur *m*.
heart-breaking [ˈhɑːtbreikiŋ] *adj* navrant. **heart-broken** *adj* navré.
heartburn [ˈhɑːtbɜːn] *n* brûlures d'estomac *f pl*.
heart failure *n* arrêt du cœur *m*.
heartfelt [ˈhɑːtfelt] *adj* sincère.
hearth [hɑːθ] *n* foyer *m*. **hearthrug** *n* devant de foyer *m*.
heart-throb [ˈhɑːtθrɒb] *n* (*coll*) idole *f*.
heart-to-heart *adj, adv* à cœur ouvert. *n* **have a heart-to-heart** parler à cœur ouvert.
heartwarming [ˈhɑːtwɔːmiŋ] *adj* réconfortant.
heat [hiːt] *n* chaleur *f*; (*sport*) épreuve éliminatoire *f*. *v* chauffer. **heated** *adj* chauffé; (*argument*) passionné. **heater** *n* appareil de chauffage *m*. **heating** *n* chauffage *m*.
heath [hiːθ] *n* lande *f*.
heathen [ˈhiːðn] *n, adj* païen, -enne.
heather [ˈheðə] *n* bruyère *f*.
heave [hiːv] *v* (*lift*) lever avec effort; (*pull*)

tirer avec effort; (*sea*) se soulever; (*sigh*) pousser; (*retch*) avoir des haut-le-cœur. *n* (*sea*) houle *f*; haut-le-cœur *m invar*; effort *m*.
heaven [ˈhevn] *n* ciel *m*. **heavenly** *adj* céleste; (*excellent*) divin.
heavy [ˈhevi] *adj* lourd; (*rain*) fort; (*cold*) gros, grosse. **heavyweight** *nm, adj* poids lourd. **heaviness** *n* lourdeur *f*.
Hebrew [ˈhiːbruː] *n* (*people*) Hébreu *m*, (*language*) hébreu *m*. *adj* hébreu, hébraïque.
heckle [ˈhekl] *v* chahuter; interrompre. **heckler** *n* interrupteur, -trice *m, f*. **heckling** *n* interpellations *f pl*.
hectare [ˈhektɑː] *n* hectare *m*.
hectic [ˈhektik] *adj* mouvementé, très bousculé.
hedge [hedʒ] *n* haie *f*. *v* entourer d'une haie; (*be evasive*) répondre à côté; (*bet*) couvrir.
hedgehog [ˈhedʒhɒg] *n* hérisson *m*.
heed [hiːd] *v* faire attention à. *n* attention *f*. **heedless** *adj* étourdi, insouciant.
heel [hiːl] *n* talon *m*. *v* (*shoe*) remettre un talon à.
hefty [ˈhefti] *adj* (*person*) costaud; (*heavy*) lourd; (*large*) gros, grosse.
heifer [ˈhefə] *n* génisse *f*.
height [hait] *n* hauteur *f*; (*person*) taille *f*; (*aircraft*) altitude *f*; (*of success, etc.*) sommet *m*, point culminant *m*. **heighten** *v* augmenter; (*make higher*) relever.
heir [eə] *n* héritier *m*. **heiress** *n* héritière *f*. **heirloom** *n* héritage *m*.
held [held] *V* **hold**[1].
helicopter [ˈhelikɒptə] *n* hélicoptère *m*.
hell [hel] *n* enfer *m*. **go to hell!** (*impol*) va te faire voir! **hell for leather** au triple galop. **hellish** *adj* infernal.
hello [həˈlou] *interj* bonjour! (*coll*) salut! (*phone*) allô!
helm [helm] *n* barre *f*. **be at the helm** tenir la barre.
helmet [ˈhelmit] *n* casque *m*.
help [help] *n* aide *f*, secours *m*. *interj* au secours! *v* aider; (*at meal, etc.*) servir; (*prevent oneself from*) s'empêcher de. **can I help you?** (*in shop*) vous désirez? **help yourself!** servez-vous! **it can't be helped!** tant pis! **helper** *n* aide *m, f*. **helpful** *adj* utile, efficace. **helping** *n* portion *f*. **helpless** *adj* impuissant.
Helsinki [helˈsiŋki] *n* Helsinki.

hem [hem] *n* ourlet *m*. *v* ourler.
hemisphere ['hemi₁sfiə] *n* hémisphère *m*.
hemp [hemp] *n* (*plant*) chanvre *m*; (*drug*) haschish *m*.
hen [hen] *n* poule *f*; femelle *f*. **henhouse** *n* poulailler *m*. **hen party** réunion de femmes *f*. **henpecked** *adj* mené par le bout du nez.
hence [hens] *adv* (*therefore*) d'où; (*from now*) d'ici. **henceforth** *adv* désormais.
henna ['henə] *n* henné *m*.
her [hə:] *pron* elle; (*direct object*) la; (*indirect object*) lui. *adj* son, sa; (*pl*) ses.
herald ['herəld] *n* héraut *m*. *v* annoncer. **heraldic** *adj* héraldique. **heraldry** *n* héraldique *f*.
herb [hə:b] *n* herbe *f*. **herbal** *adj* d'herbes.
herd [hə:d] *n* troupeau *m*. *v* mener. **herd together** s'attrouper.
here [hiə] *adv* ici. **hereafter** *adv* ci-après. **here and now** en ce moment même. **here and there** ça et là. **here goes!** allons-y! **here is/are** voici. **here, there, and everywhere** un peu partout.
hereditary [hi'redətəri] *adj* héréditaire.
heredity [hi'redəti] *n* hérédité *f*.
heresy ['herəsi] *n* hérésie *f*. **heretic** *n* hérétique *m*, *f*. **heretical** *adj* hérétique.
heritage ['heritidʒ] *n* héritage *m*.
hermit ['hə:mit] *n* ermite *m*.
hernia ['hə:niə] *n* hernie *f*.
hero ['hiərou] *n* héros *m*. **heroine** *n* héroïne *f*. **hero-worship** *n* culte du héros *m*. **heroic** *adj* héroïque. **heroism** *n* héroïsme *m*.
heroin ['herouin] *n* héroïne *f*.
heron ['herən] *n* héron *m*.
herring ['heriŋ] *n* hareng *m*.
hers [hə:z] *pron* le sien, la sienne.
herself [hə:'self] *pron* se; (*emphatic*) elle-même. **by herself** toute seule.
hesitate ['heziteit] *v* hésiter. **hesitant** *adj* hésitant. **hesitation** *n* hésitation *f*.
heterosexual [hetərə'sekʃuəl] *n*, *adj* hétérosexuel, -elle.
hexagon ['heksəgən] *n* hexagone *m*. **hexagonal** *adj* hexagonal.
heyday ['heidei] *n* (*of person*) apogée *m*; (*of thing*) âge d'or *m*.
hiatus [hai'eitəs] *n* lacune *f*.
hibernate ['haibəneit] *v* hiberner. **hibernation** *n* hibernation *f*.
hiccup ['hikʌp] *n* hoquet *m*. **have hiccups** avoir le hoquet. *v* hoqueter.

hid [hid] *V* **hide**¹.
***hide**¹ [haid] *v* (se) cacher. **hide-and-seek** *n* cache-cache *m*. **hide-out** *n* cachette *f*.
hide² [haid] *n* peau *f*; (*leather*) cuir *m*.
hidden ['hidn] *V* **hide**¹.
hideous ['hidiəs] *adj* hideux.
hiding¹ ['haidiŋ] *n* **be in hiding** se tenir caché. **go into hiding** se cacher. **hiding place** cachette *f*.
hiding² ['haidiŋ] *n* (*beating*) correction *f*.
hierarchy ['haiərɑ:ki] *n* hiérarchie *f*. **hierarchical** *adj* hiérarchique.
hi-fi ['hai₁fai] *n* hi-fi *f invar*; (*system*) chaîne hi-fi *f*.
high [hai] *adj* haut; (*speed*) grand; (*price, etc.*) élevé. *adv* (en) haut. **highly** *adv* (*very*) fort; (*recommend*) chaudement.
highbrow ['haibrau] *n*, *adj* intellectuel, -elle.
high chair *n* chaise haute *f*.
high-frequency [₁hai'fri:kwənsi] *adj* de haute fréquence.
high-heeled [₁hai'hi:ld] *adj* à hauts talons.
high jump *n* saut en hauteur *m*.
highland ['hailənd] *n* région montagneuse *f*. **the Highlands** (*Scotland*) les Highlands *m pl*.
highlight ['hailait] *v* mettre en lumière. *n* (*art*) rehaut *m*; (*hair*) reflet *m*; (*of evening, etc.*) clou *m*.
Highness ['hainis] *n* Altesse *f*.
high-pitched [₁hai'pitʃd] *adj* aigu, -uë.
high-rise block *n* tour *f*.
high-speed [₁hai'spi:d] *adj* ultra-rapide.
high-spirited [₁hai'spiritid] *adj* plein d'entrain. **high spirits** entrain *m*.
high street *n* rue principale *f*.
highway ['haiwei] *n* grande route *f*; voie publique *f*. **highway code** code de la route *m*. **highwayman** *n* voleur de grand chemin *m*.
hijack ['haidʒak] *v* détourner. *n* détournement *m*.
hike [haik] *n* excursion à pied *f*. *v* excursionner à pied. **hiker** *n* excursionniste à pied *m*, *f*. **hiking** *n* randonnées à pied *f pl*.
hilarious [hi'leəriəs] *adj* (*merry*) hilare; (*funny*) désopilant. **hilarity** *n* hilarité *f*.
hill [hil] *n* colline *f*; (*slope*) côte *f*. **hillside** *n* flanc de coteau *m*. **hilly** *adj* accidenté.
him [him] *pron* lui; (*direct object*) le.
himself [him'self] *pron* se; (*emphatic*) lui-même. **by himself** tout seul.

hind [haind] *adj* postérieur, -e; de derrière. **hindsight** *n* sagesse rétrospective *f*.
hinder ['hində] *v* gêner, entraver. **hindrance** *n* gêne *f*, entrave *f*.
Hindu [hin'duː] *n* Hindou, -e *m, f. adj* hindou. **Hinduism** *n* hindouisme *m*.
hinge [hindʒ] *n* charnière *f*; (*door*) gond *m. v* **hinge on** dépendre de.
hint [hint] *n* allusion *f*; (*tip*) conseil *m*; (*trace*) nuance *f. v* laisser entendre, insinuer.
hip [hip] *n* hanche *f*.
hippopotamus [hipə'potəməs] *n* hippopotame *m*.
hire [haiə] *v* louer; (*person*) engager. **hire out** louer. *n* location *f*; (*boat*) louage *m*. **for hire** à louer. **hire purchase** achat à crédit *m*.
his [hiz] *adj* son, sa; (*pl*) ses. *pron* le sien, la sienne.
hiss [his] *v* siffler. *n* sifflement *m*.
history ['histəri] *n* histoire *f*. **historian** *n* historien, -enne *m, f*. **historic** *adj* historique.
*hit [hit] *n* coup *m*; succès *m*, coup réussi *m*; (*slang: song*) tube *m. v* frapper; (*bump*) (se) heurter; (*reach*) atteindre. **hit-or-miss** *adv* au petit bonheur.
hitch [hitʃ] *n* (*obstacle*) anicroche *f. v* (*lift*) remonter; (*fasten*) accrocher. **hitch-hike** *v* faire du stop. **hitch-hiker** *n* auto-stoppeur, -euse *m, f*. **hitch-hiking** *n* auto-stop *m*.
hitherto [ˌhiðə'tuː] *adv* jusqu'ici.
hive [haiv] *n* ruche *f*.
hoard [hɔːd] *n* réserve *f*; trésor *m. v* amasser.
hoarding ['hɔːdiŋ] *n* (*advertising*) panneau d'affichage *m*; (*fence*) palissade *f*.
hoarse [hɔːs] *adj* enroué, rauque. **hoarsely** *adv* d'une voix rauque. **hoarseness** *n* enrouement *m*.
hoax [houks] *n* canular *m*.
hobble ['hobl] *v* clopiner; (*horse*) entraver.
hobby ['hobi] *n* passe-temps *m*.
hock¹ [hok] *n* jarret *m*.
hock² [hok] *n* vin du Rhin *m*.
hockey ['hoki] *n* hockey *m*. **hockey stick** crosse de hockey *f*.
hoe [hou] *n* houe *f. v* biner.
hog [hog] *n* porc *m. v* (*coll*) accaparer, monopoliser.
hoist [hoist] *v* hisser. *n* treuil *m*; (*for goods*) monte-charge *m invar*.

*hold¹ [hould] *n* prise *f*; influence *f*. **get hold of** saisir. *v* tenir; contenir; (*have*) avoir. **holdall** *n* fourre-tout *m invar*. **hold back** (se) retenir. **hold forth** pérorer. **hold on** (*wait*) attendre; maintenir en place; (*grip*) tenir bon. **hold out** tendre; (*resist*) tenir bon. **hold up** (*raise*) lever; (*support*) soutenir; (*delay*) retarder. **hold-up** *n* retard *m*; (*traffic*) bouchon *m*; (*robbery*) hold-up *m invar*. **holder** *n* (*person*) détenteur, -trice *m, f*; (*for object*) support *m*.
hold² [hould] *n* (*naut*) cale *f*.
hole [houl] *n* trou *m*; (*rabbit*) terrier *m. v* (se) trouer.
holiday ['holədi] *n* vacances *f pl*; (*day off*) jour de congé *m*. **holiday-maker** *n* vacancier, -ère *m, f*. **holiday resort** villégiature *f*.
Holland ['holənd] *n* Hollande *f*.
hollow ['holou] *adj, adv* creux. *n* creux *m*; (*in ground*) dépression *f. v* creuser.
holly ['holi] *n* houx *m*. **hollyhock** *n* rose trémière *f*.
holster ['houlstə] *n* étui de revolver *m*.
holy ['houli] *adj* saint. **holiness** *n* sainteté *f*.
homage ['homidʒ] *n* hommage *m*. **pay homage to** rendre hommage à.
home [houm] *n* maison *f*, foyer *m*. **at home** chez soi. **make oneself at home** faire comme chez soi. *adv* à la maison; (*right in*) à fond. **go home** rentrer. *adj* familial; domestique; (*not foreign*) intérieur, -e, national. **homeless** *adj* sans abri. **homely** *adj* simple, confortable; (*US: ugly*) laid.
home address *n* domicile permanent *m*; adresse personnelle *f*.
homecoming ['houmˌkʌmiŋ] *n* retour *m*.
home-grown [houm'groun] *adj* du jardin.
home help *n* aide ménagère *f*.
homeland ['houmland] *n* patrie *f*.
home-made [houm'meid] *adj* fait à la maison.
Home Office *n* ministère de l'Intérieur *m*.
home rule *n* autonomie *f*.
homesick ['houmsik] *adj* nostalgique. **homesickness** *n* mal du pays *m*; nostalgie *f*.
homework ['houmwəːk] *n* devoirs *m pl*.
homicide ['homisaid] *n* homicide *m*. **homicidal** *adj* homicide.

homogeneous [homə'dʒiːniəs] *adj* homogène.

homosexual [homə'sekʃuəl] *n, adj* homosexuel, -elle. **homosexuality** *n* homosexualité *f.*

honest ['onist] *adj* honnête; sincère; franc, franche. **honesty** *n* honnêteté *f*; sincérité *f.*

honey ['hʌni] *n* miel *m.* **honeycomb** *n* rayon de miel *m.* **honeymoon** *n* lune de miel *f.* **honeysuckle** *n* chèvrefeuille *m.*

honour ['onə] *n* honneur *m. v* honorer. **honorary** *adj* honoraire. **honourable** *adj* honorable.

hood [hud] *n* capuchon *m*; (*car roof*) capote *f*; (*US: car bonnet*) capot *m.*

hoof [huːf] *n* sabot *m.*

hook [huk] *n* crochet *m*; (*on dress*) agrafe *f*; (*fishing*) hameçon *m. v* accrocher; agrafer; (*fishing*) prendre. **hooked** *adj* crochu.

hooligan ['huːligən] *n* voyou *m.* **hooliganism** *n* vandalisme *m.*

hoop [huːp] *n* cerceau *m*; (*for barrel*) cercle *m.*

hoot [huːt] *v* (*owl*) hululer; (*car*) klaxonner; (*boo*) huer. *n* hululement *m*; coup de klaxon *m*; huée *f.* **hooter** *n* klaxon *m*; (*factory*) sirène *f.*

hop[1] [hop] *v* sauter à cloche-pied; (*jump*) sauter, sautiller. *n* saut *m*, sautillement *m*; (*coll: dance*) sauterie *f.*

hop[2] [hop] *n* (*bot*) houblon *m.*

hope [houp] *n* espoir *m. v* espérer. **hopeful** *adj* plein d'espoir; encourageant. **hopeless** *adj* désespéré; (*coll: bad*) nul.

horde [hoːd] *n* horde *f.*

horizon [hə'raizn] *n* horizon *m.*

horizontal [hori'zontl] *adj* horizontal. *n* horizontale *f.*

hormone ['hoːmoun] *n* hormone *f.*

horn [hoːn] *n* corne *f*; (*music*) cor *m*; (*car, etc.*) klaxon *m.*

hornet ['hoːnit] *n* frelon *m.*

horoscope ['horəskoup] *n* horoscope *m.*

horrible ['horibl] *adj* horrible, affreux.

horrid ['horid] *adj* méchant, vilain.

horrify ['horifai] *v* horrifier. **horrific** *adj* horrifique.

horror ['horə] *n* horreur *f. adj* (*story, film, etc.*) d'épouvante.

horse [hoːs] *n* cheval *m.*

horseback ['hoːsbak] *n* **on horseback** à cheval.

horse-box ['hoːsboks] *n* fourgon à chevaux *m.*

horse chestnut *n* (*nut*) marron d'Inde *m*; (*tree*) marronnier d'Inde *m.*

horse-drawn ['hoːsdroːn] *adj* à chevaux.

horsefly ['hoːsflai] *n* taon *m.*

horsehair ['hoːsheə] *n* crin *m.*

horseman ['hoːsmən] *n* cavalier *m.*

horsepower ['hoːs,pauə] *n* cheval-vapeur *m.*

horseradish ['hoːs,radiʃ] *n* raifort *m.*

horseshoe ['hoːʃʃuː] *n* fer à cheval *m.*

horsewoman ['hoːs,wumən] *n* cavalière *f.*

horticulture ['hoːtikʌltʃə] *n* horticulture *f.* **horticultural** *adj* horticole.

hose [houz] *n* tuyau *m*; (*mot*) durite *f*; (*stockings*) bas *m pl. v* arroser au jet.

hosiery ['houziəri] *n* bas *m pl*; (*business*) bonneterie *f.*

hospitable [ho'spitəbl] *adj* hospitalier.

hospital ['hospitl] *n* hôpital *m.* **hospitalize** *v* hospitaliser.

hospitality [,hospi'taliti] *n* hospitalité *f.*

host[1] [houst] *n* hôte *m.* **hostess** *n* hôtesse *f.*

host[2] [houst] *n* (*crowd*) foule *f.*

hostage ['hostidʒ] *n* otage *m.*

hostel ['hostəl] *n* foyer *m.* **youth hostel** auberge de jeunesse *f.*

hostile ['hostail] *adj* hostile. **hostility** *n* hostilité *f.*

hot [hot] *adj* chaud; (*curry, etc.*) fort; (*temper*) violent. **be hot** (*person*) avoir chaud; (*weather*) faire chaud. **hot dog** hot-dog *m.* **hot-house** *n* serre *f.* **hotplate** *n* chauffe-plats *m invar.* **hot-tempered** *adj* emporté. **hot-water bottle** bouillotte *f.*

hotel [hou'tel] *n* hôtel *m.*

hound [haund] *n* chien de meute *m. v* chasser, s'acharner sur.

hour ['auə] *n* heure *f.* **hourglass** *n* sablier *m.* **hourly** *adj, adv* toutes les heures.

house [haus; *v* hauz] *n* maison *f*; (*theatre*) salle *f. v* loger.

houseboat ['hausbout] *n* péniche aménagée *f.*

housebound ['hausbaund] *adj* confiné chez soi.

housecoat ['hauskout] *n* peignoir *m.*

household ['haushould] *n* maison *f*, ménage *m.*

housekeeper ['haus,kiːpə] *n* gouvernante *f.* **housekeeping** *n* (*work*) ménage *m*; (*money*) argent du ménage *m.*

housemaid ['hausmeid] n bonne f.
house-to-house adj, adv porte à porte.
house-trained ['haustreind] adj propre.
house-warming ['haus͵wɔːmiŋ] n **have a house-warming (party)** pendre la crémaillère.
housewife ['hauswaif] n ménagère f.
housework ['hauswɜːk] n ménage m.
housing ['hauziŋ] n logement m. **housing estate** cité f.
hovel ['hovəl] n taudis m.
hover ['hovə] v planer; (person) rôder.
hovercraft n aéroglisseur m.
how [hau] adv comment, comme. **how are you?** comment allez-vous? **how do you do?** bonjour; (on introduction) enchanté. **how much?** combien?
however [hau'evə] conj cependant. adv de quelque manière que.
howl [haul] v hurler. n hurlement m.
hub [hʌb] n moyeu m; pivot m. **hubcap** n (mot) enjoliveur m.
huddle ['hʌdl] v se blottir. n petit groupe m.
hue [hjuː] n teinte f.
huff [hʌf] n **in a huff** froissé.
hug [hʌg] v étreindre. n étreinte f.
huge [hjuːdʒ] adj énorme.
hulk [hʌlk] n épave f, carcasse f; (derog: person) mastodonte m. **hulking** adj balourd.
hull [hʌl] n (naut) coque f.
hum [hʌm] v bourdonner; (tune) fredonner; (engine) vrombir. n bourdonnement m; vrombissement m. **humming-bird** n oiseau-mouche m.
human ['hjuːmən] nm, adj humain. **human being** être humain m.
humane [hjuː'mein] adj humain.
humanity [hjuː'manəti] n humanité f. **humanitarian** n(m+f), adj humanitaire.
humble ['hʌmbl] adj humble. v humilier.
humdrum ['hʌmdrʌm] adj monotone.
humid ['hjuːmid] adj humide. **humidity** n humidité f.
humiliate [hjuː'milieit] v humilier. **humiliation** n humiliation f.
humility [hjuː'miləti] n humilité f.
humour ['hjuːmə] n humour m; (mood) humeur f. v ménager. **humorist** n humoriste m, f. **humorous** adj humoristique.
hump [hʌmp] n bosse f. **humpbacked** adj (bridge) en dos d'âne. v arrondir, voûter.

hunch [hʌntʃ] v arrondir, voûter. n pressentiment m. **hunchback** n bossu, -e m, f. **hunchbacked** adj bossu.
hundred ['hʌndrəd] nm, adj cent. **hundreds** pl n (coll) centaines f pl. **hundredth** n(m+f), adj centième.
hung [hʌŋ] V **hang**.
Hungary ['hʌŋgəri] n Hongrie f. **Hungarian** nm, adj hongrois; n (people) Hongrois, -e m, f.
hunger ['hʌŋgə] n faim f. v avoir faim. **be hungry** avoir faim. **hungrily** adv avidement.
hunt [hʌnt] n chasse f; (search) recherche f. v chasser; chercher. **hunting** n chasse f. **huntsman** n chasseur m.
hurdle ['hɜːdl] n obstacle m; (sport) haie f.
hurl [hɜːl] v jeter, précipiter. **hurl abuse** lancer des injures.
hurricane ['hʌrikən] n ouragan m.
hurry ['hʌri] n hâte f. **be in a hurry** être pressé. v (faire) se dépêcher, (se) presser. **hurried** adj précipité, pressé. **hurriedly** adv précipitamment.
***hurt** [hɜːt] v faire mal (à), blesser. n mal m. adj blessé.
husband ['hʌzbənd] n mari m.
hush [hʌʃ] n silence m. interj chut! v faire taire. **hush up** (news) étouffer. **hushed** adj étouffé.
husk [hʌsk] n (wheat) balle f; (rice, maize) enveloppe f; (nut) écale f. v (grain) vanner; (rice, maize) décortiquer; écaler.
husky ['hʌski] adj enroué. **huskily** adv d'une voix rauque. **huskiness** n enrouement m.
hussar [hə'zaɪ] n hussard m.
hustle ['hʌsl] v (se) bousculer. n bousculade f. **hustle and bustle** tourbillon m.
hut [hʌt] n hutte f.
hutch [hʌtʃ] n clapier m.
hyacinth ['haiəsinθ] n jacinthe f.
hybrid ['haibrid] nm, adj hybride.
hydraulic [hai'drɔːlik] adj hydraulique.
hydrocarbon [͵haidrou'kaːbən] n hydrocarbure m.
hydro-electric [͵haidroui'lektrik] adj hydro-électrique.
hydrofoil ['haidroufoil] n hydrofoil m.
hydrogen ['haidrədʒən] n hydrogène m.
hyena [hai'iːnə] n hyène f.
hygiene ['haidʒiːn] n hygiène f. **hygienic** adj hygiénique.

hymn [him] *n* hymne *f.* **hymn-book** *n* livre de cantiques *m.*

hyphen ['haifən] *n* trait d'union *m.*

hypnosis [hip'nousis] *n* hypnose *f.* **under hypnosis** en état d'hypnose. **hypnotic** *adj* hypnotique. **hypnotism** *n* hypnotisme *m.* **hypnotist** *n* hypnotiseur, -euse *m, f.* **hypnotize** *v* hypnotiser.

hypochondria [haipə'kondriə] *n* hypochondrie *f.* **hypochondriac** *n(m+f)*, *adj* hypochondriaque.

hypocrisy [hi'pokrəsi] *n* hypocrisie *f.* **hypocrite** *n* hypocrite *m, f.* **hypocritical** *adj* hypocrite.

hypodermic [haipə'dəɪmik] *adj* hypodermique. *n* seringue hypodermique *f.*

hypothesis [hai'poθəsis] *n, pl* **-ses** hypothèse *f.* **hypothetical** *adj* hypothétique.

hysterectomy [histə'rektəmi] *n* hystérectomie *f.*

hysteria [his'tiəriə] *n* hystérie *f.* **hysterical** *adj* hystérique; (*laughter, crying*) convulsif. **hysterics** *pl n* (*crying*) crise de nerfs *f sing*; (*laughter*) crise de rire *f sing.*

I

I [ai] *pron* je; (*emphatic*) moi.

ice [ais] *n* glace *f*; (*on road*) verglas *m.* **iceberg** *n* iceberg *m.* **ice-cold** *adj* glacé. **ice cream** glace *f.* **ice cube** glaçon *m.* **ice rink** patinoire *f.* **ice-skate** *n* patin à glace *m.* **ice-skating** *n* patinage sur glace *m.* *v* (*chill*) rafraîchir; (*cake*) glacer. **ice over** *or* **up** (*lake*) geler; (*windscreen, etc.*) givrer. **iced** *adj* glacé; (*champagne*) frappé; (*melon*) rafraîchi. **icing** *n* glaçage *m.* **icing sugar** sucre glace *m.* **icy** *adj* glacial; (*road*) verglacé.

Iceland ['aislənd] *n* Islande *f.* **Icelander** *n* Islandais, -e *m, f.* **Icelandic** *nm, adj.* islandais.

icicle ['aisikl] *n* glaçon *m.*

icon ['aikon] *n* icône *f.*

idea [ai'diə] *n* idée *f.*

ideal [ai'diəl] *nm, adj* idéal. **idealist** *n* idéaliste *m, f.* **idealistic** *adj* idéaliste.

identical [ai'dentikəl] *adj* identique. **identical twins** vrais jumeaux *m pl*, vraies jumelles *f pl.*

identify [ai'dentifai] *v* identifier. **identify with** s'identifier à *or* avec. **identification** *n* identification *f*; (*papers*) pièce d'identité *f.*

identity [ai'dentiti] *n* identité *f.* **identity card** carte d'identité *f.* **identity parade** séance d'identification *f.*

ideology [aidi'olədʒi] *n* idéologie *f.*

idiom ['idiəm] *n* (*expression*) idiotisme *m*; (*language*) idiome *m.* **idiomatic** *adj* idiomatique.

idiosyncrasy [,idiə'siŋkrəsi] *n* particularité *f.*

idiot ['idiət] *n* idiot, -e *m, f.* **idiotic** *adj* idiot.

idle ['aidl] *adj* (*doing nothing*) désœuvré; (*lazy*) oisif; (*machine*) en repos; (*talk, etc.*) oiseux. *v* fainéanter; (*engine*) tourner au ralenti. **idleness** *n* désœuvrement *m*; (*laziness*) paresse *f.*

idol ['aidl] *n* idole *f.* **idolatry** *n* idolâtrie *f.* **idolize** *v* idolâtrer.

idyllic [i'dilik] *adj* idyllique.

if [if] *conj* si. **as if** comme si. **if not** sinon. **if so** s'il en est ainsi.

ignite [ig'nait] *v* (*light*) mettre le feu à; (*catch fire*) prendre feu.

ignition [ig'niʃən] *n* ignition *f*; (*mot*) allumage *m.* **ignition key** clef de contact *f.* **ignition switch** contact *m.* **turn on the ignition** mettre le contact.

ignorant ['ignərənt] *adj* ignorant. **ignorance** *n* ignorance *f.*

ignore [ig'noɪ] *v* (*remark, etc.*) ne pas relever; (*person*) faire semblant de ne pas reconnaître; (*rule*) ne pas respecter.

ill [il] *adj* (*sick*) malade; (*bad*) mauvais. *nm, adv* mal. **ill-at-ease** *adj* mal à l'aise. **ill-bred** *or* **ill-mannered** *adj* mal élevé. **ill-gotten gains** biens mal acquis *m pl.* **ill-treat** *v* maltraiter. **illness** *n* maladie *f.*

illegal [i'liɡəl] *adj* illégal.

illegible [i'ledʒəbl] *adj* illisible.

illegitimate [,ili'dʒitimit] *adj* illégitime. **illegitimacy** *n* illégitimité *f.*

illicit [i'lisit] *adj* illicite.

illiterate [i'litərit] *n, adj* illettré, -e. **illiteracy** *n* analphabétisme *m.*

illogical [i'lodʒikəl] *adj* illogique.

illuminate [i'luːmiˌneit] *v* éclairer; (*building*) illuminer. **illumination** *n* éclairage *m*; illumination *f.*

illusion [i'luːʒən] *n* illusion *f*.

illustrate ['iləˌstreit] *v* illustrer. **illustration** *n* illustration *f*. **illustrator** *n* illustrateur, -trice *m, f*.

illustrious [i'lʌstriəs] *adj* illustre.

image ['imidʒ] *n* image *f*; (*public personality*) image de marque *f*; (*double*) portrait vivant *m*. **imagery** *n* images *f pl*.

imagine [i'madʒin] *v* (s')imaginer. **imaginary** *adj* imaginaire. **imagination** *n* imagination *f*. **imaginative** *adj* plein d'imagination.

imbalance [im'baləns] *n* déséquilibre *m*.

imbecile ['imbəˌsiːl] *n* imbécile *m, f*.

imitate ['imiˌteit] *v* imiter. **imitation** *n* imitation *f*.

immaculate [i'makjulit] *adj* impeccable; (*rel*) immaculé.

immaterial [ˌiməˈtiəriəl] *adj* insignifiant, indifférent.

immature [ˌiməˈtjuə] *adj* pas mûr. **be immature** (*person*) manquer de maturité. **immaturity** *n* manque de maturité *m*.

immediate [i'miːdiət] *adj* immédiat. **immediately** *adv* tout de suite; directement.

immense [i'mens] *adj* immense.

immerse [i'məːs] *v* immerger, plonger. **immersion** *n* immersion *f*. **immersion heater** chauffe-eau électrique *m invar*.

immigrate ['imiˌgreit] *v* immigrer. **immigrant** *n* immigrant, -e *m, f*. **immigration** *n* immigration *f*.

imminent ['iminənt] *adj* imminent.

immobile [i'moubail] *adj* immobile. **immobilize** *v* immobiliser.

immoral [i'morəl] *adj* immoral. **immorality** *n* immoralité *f*.

immortal [i'moːtl] *adj* immortel. **immortality** *n* immortalité *f*. **immortalize** *v* immortaliser.

immovable [i'muːvəbl] *adj* fixe; inflexible.

immune [i'mjuːn] *adj* immunisé. **immunity** *n* immunité *f*. **immunization** *n* immunisation *f*. **immunize** *v* immuniser.

imp [imp] *n* diablotin *m*.

impact ['impakt] *n* impact *m*.

impair [im'peə] *v* détériorer, abîmer.

impale [im'peil] *v* empaler.

impart [im'paːt] *v* communiquer; (*give*) donner.

impartial [im'paːʃəl] *adj* impartial. **impartiality** *n* impartialité *f*.

impasse [am'paːs] *n* impasse *f*.

impassive [im'pasiv] *adj* impassible.

impatient [im'peiʃənt] *adj* impatient. **get impatient** s'impatienter. **impatience** *n* impatience *f*.

impeach [im'piːtʃ] *v* accuser; (*question*) mettre en doute. **impeachment** *n* accusation *f*; (*US*) procédure d'impeachment *f*.

impeccable [im'pekəbl] *adj* impeccable.

impede [im'piːd] *v* empêcher, gêner.

impediment [im'pedimənt] *n* obstacle *m*. **speech impediment** défaut d'élocution *m*.

impel [im'pel] *v* pousser, obliger.

impending [im'pendiŋ] *adj* imminent; menaçant.

imperative [im'perətiv] *adj* urgent, impérieux. *n* impératif *m*.

imperfect [im'pəːfikt] *adj* imparfait; défectueux. *n* imparfait *m*.

imperial [im'piəriəl] *adj* impérial; majestueux. **imperialism** *n* impérialisme *m*.

impersonal [im'pəːsənl] *adj* impersonnel.

impersonate [im'pəːsəˌneit] *v* se faire passer pour; (*theatre*) imiter. **impersonation** *n* imitation *f*.

impertinent [im'pəːtinənt] *adj* impertinent. **impertinence** *n* impertinence *f*.

impervious [im'pəːviəs] *adj* imperméable; (*to criticism, etc.*) fermé.

impetuous [im'petjuəs] *adj* impétueux.

impetus ['impətəs] *n* impulsion *f*, élan *m*.

impinge [im'pindʒ] *v* **impinge on** empiéter sur; affecter.

implement ['implimənt; *v* 'impliment] *n* instrument *m*. **implements** *pl n* matériel *m sing*. *v* exécuter.

implication [impliˈkeiʃən] *n* insinuation *f*, implication *f*.

implicit [im'plisit] *adj* implicite; absolu.

implore [im'ploː] *v* implorer. **imploring** *adj* suppliant.

imply [im'plai] *v* (laisser) supposer; suggérer; insinuer. **implied** *adj* implicite, tacite.

impolite [impəˈlait] *adj* impoli.

import [im'poːt] *n* (*comm*) importation *f*; sens *m*; importance *f*. *v* (*comm*) importer; signifier.

importance [im'poːtəns] *n* importance *f*. **important** *adj* important.

impose [im'pouz] *v* imposer; (*fine, etc.*) infliger. **impose on** abuser de. **imposition** *n* imposition *f*.

impossible [im'posəbl] *nm, adj* impossible.

impostor [im'pɒstə] n imposteur m.
impotent ['impətənt] adj impuissant.
impotence n impuissance f.
impound [im'paund] v confisquer.
impoverish [im'pɒvəriʃ] v appauvrir.
impregnate ['impreg,neit] v imprégner.
impregnation n imprégnation f.
impress [im'pres] v impressionner; (print) imprimer. **impression** n impression f. **impressive** adj impressionnant.
imprint [im'print; n 'imprint] v imprimer. n empreinte f.
imprison [im'prizn] v emprisonner. **imprisonment** n emprisonnement m.
improbable [im'prɒbəbl] adj improbable; (story, etc.) invraisemblable.
impromptu [im'promptjuː] adv, adj impromptu.
improper [im'propə] adj indécent; malhonnête; incorrect.
improve [im'pruːv] v (s')améliorer; perfectionner. **improvement** n amélioration f; progrès m.
improvise ['imprə,vaiz] v improviser. **improvisation** n improvisation f.
impudent ['impjudənt] adj impudent. **impudence** n impudence f.
impulse ['impʌls] n impulsion f. **impulsive** adj impulsif; irréfléchi.
impure [im'pjuə] adj impur. **impurity** n impureté f.
in [in] prep dans, en; (town) à. adv (inside) dedans; (at home) chez soi.
inability [,inə'biləti] n incapacité f.
inaccessible [,inak'sesəbl] adj inaccessible.
inaccurate [in'akjurit] adj inexact. **inaccuracy** n inexactitude f.
inactive [in'aktiv] adj inactif, peu actif. **inaction** n inaction f. **inactivity** n inactivité f.
inadequate [in'adikwit] adj insuffisant. **inadequacy** n insuffisance f.
inadvertent [,inəd'vɜːtənt] adj inattentif. **inadvertently** adv par inadvertance.
inane [in'ein] adj inepte. **inanity** n ineptie f.
inanimate [in'animit] adj inanimé.
inarticulate [,inaː'tikjulit] adj (sound) inarticulé; (person) incapable de s'exprimer.
inasmuch [,inəz'mʌtʃ] adv **inasmuch as** attendu que.
inaudible [in'ɔːdəbl] adj inaudible.
inaugurate [i'nɔːgjuˌreit] v inaugurer.

inaugural adj inaugural. **inauguration** n inauguration f.
inborn [,in'bɔːn] adj inné; congénital.
incapable [in'keipəbl] adj incapable.
incendiary [in'sendiəri] adj incendiaire. **incendiary device** dispositif incendiaire m.
incense[1] ['insens] n encens m.
incense[2] [in'sens] v courroucer, exaspérer. **incensed by** outré de.
incentive [in'sentiv] n objectif m, stimulant m.
incessant [in'sesənt] adj incessant.
incest ['insest] n inceste m. **incestuous** adj incestueux.
inch [intʃ] n pouce m. **inch by inch** petit à petit. v **inch forward** avancer petit à petit.
incident ['insidənt] n incident m; épisode m. **incidental** adj accessoire; accidental. **incidental music** musique de fond f. **incidentally** adv (by the way) à propos.
incinerator [in'sinə,reitə] n incinérateur m. **incinerate** v incinérer. **incineration** n incinération f.
incite [in'sait] v pousser, inciter.
incline [in'klain] v (s')incliner. **be inclined to** incliner à. n pente f. **inclination** n inclination f; (hill) inclinaison f.
include [in'kluːd] v inclure, comprendre. **including** prep y compris. **inclusion** n inclusion f. **inclusive** adj inclus.
incognito [,inkog'niːtou] adv incognito.
incoherent [,inkə'hiərənt] adj incohérent. **incoherently** adv sans cohérence.
income ['inkʌm] n revenu m. **income tax** impôt sur le revenu m. **private income** rente f.
incompatible [inkəm'patəbl] adj incompatible. **incompatibility** n incompatibilité f.
incompetent [in'kompitənt] adj incompétent. **incompetence** n incompétence f.
incomplete [,inkəm'pliːt] adj incomplet, -ète.
incomprehensible [in,kɒmpri'hensəbl] adj incompréhensible.
inconceivable [inkən'siːvəbl] adj inconcevable.
incongruous [in'koŋgruəs] adj incongru; peu approprié.
inconsiderate [,inkən'sidərit] adj inconsidéré; (person) sans égards.
inconsistent [,inkən'sistənt] adj inconsistant. **inconsistency** n inconsistance f.

incontinence [in'kɒntinəns] *n* incontinence *f*. **incontinent** *adj* incontinent.
inconvenience [inkən'viːnjəns] *n* inconvénient *m*; (*trouble*) dérangement *m*. *v* déranger. **inconvenient** *adj* inopportun,
incommode.
incorporate [in'kɔːpəˌreit] *v* incorporer,
contenir; (*comm*) fusionner.
incorrect [inkə'rekt] *adj* incorrect.
increase [in'kriːs] *v* augmenter;
(s')intensifier. *n* augmentation *f*. **increasing** *adj* croissant. **increasingly** *adv* de
plus en plus.
incredible [in'kredəbl] *adj* incroyable.
incredulous [in'kredjuləs] *adj* incrédule.
incredulity *n* incrédulité *f*.
increment ['iŋkrəmənt] *n* augmentation *f*.
incriminate [in'krimineit] *v* incriminer.
incriminating *adj* compromettant; (*evidence, etc*.) à conviction.
incubate ['iŋkjuˌbeit] *v* incuber, couver.
incubation *n* incubation *f*. **incubator** *n*
couveuse *f*.
incur [in'kəː] *v* encourir; contracter; (*risk*)
courir.
incurable [in'kjuərəbl] *adj* incurable.
indecent [in'diːsnt] *adj* indécent. **indecency** *n* indécence *f*.
indeed [in'diːd] *adv* en effet, vraiment.
indefinite [in'definit] *adj* indéfini,
indéterminé.
indelible [in'deləbl] *adj* indélébile; (*memory, etc*.) ineffaçable.
indemnity [in'demnəti] *n* indemnité *f*.
indent [in'dent] *v* denteler; (*printing*)
renfoncer. **indentation** *n* dentelure *f*;
renfoncement *m*.
independent [indi'pendənt] *adj*
indépendant. **independence** *n*
indépendance *f*.
index ['indeks] *n* index *m*, catalogue *m*;
(*ratio*) indice *m*. **index finger** index *m*.
index-linked *adj* indexé. *v* classer; (*book*)
mettre un index à.
India ['indjə] *n* Inde *f*. **Indian** *n* Indien,
-enne *m*, *f*; *adj* indien. **Indian ink** encre
de Chine *f*.
indicate ['indikeit] *v* indiquer. **indication** *n*
indication *f*, signe *m*. **indicative** *nm*, *adj*
indicatif. *v* indicator *n* indicateur *m*; (*mot*)
clignotant *m*.
indict [in'dait] *v* accuser. **indictment** *n*
mise en accusation *f*.
indifferent [in'difrənt] *adj* indifférent;

(*derog*) médiocre. **indifference** *n* indifffér-
ence *f*.
indigenous [in'didʒinəs] *adj* indigène.
indigestion [indi'dʒestʃən] *n* dyspepsie *f*,
indigestion *f*.
indignant [in'dignənt] *adj* indigné. **get
indignant** s'indigner. **indignantly** *adv* avec
indignation. **indignation** *n* indignation *f*.
indignity [in'dignəti] *n* indignité *f*.
indirect [indi'rekt] *adj* indirect.
indiscreet [indi'skriːt] *adj* indiscret, -ète.
indiscretion *n* indiscrétion *f*.
indiscriminate [indi'skriminit] *adj* fait au
hasard; (*blind*) aveugle.
indispensable [indi'spensəbl] *adj* indispensable.
indisposed [indi'spouzd] *adj* (*ill*) indisposé; (*unwilling*) peu disposé. **indisposition** *n* indisposition *f*.
individual [indi'vidjuəl] *adj* individuel;
original. *n* individu *m*. **individuality** *n*
individualité *f*.
indoctrinate [in'doktriˌneit] *v* endoctriner.
indoctrination *n* endoctrination *f*.
indolent ['indələnt] *adj* indolent. **indolence** *n* indolence *f*.
indoor ['indɔː] *adj* d'intérieur; (*swimming
pool, etc*.) couvert. **indoors** *adv* à
l'intérieur, à la maison.
induce [in'djuːs] *v* persuader; provoquer;
(*med: labour*) déclencher. **inducement** *n*
encouragement *m*; (*incentive*) motif *m*.
indulge [in'dʌldʒ] *v* satisfaire; (*give way
to*) céder à. **indulge in** se livrer à. **indulgence** *n* indulgence *f*; satisfaction *f*.
indulgent *adj* indulgent.
industry ['indəstri] *n* industrie *f*; zèle *m*.
industrial *adj* industriel. **industrial action**
action revendicative *f*. **industrialize** *v*
industrialiser. **industrious** *adj* indus-
trieux.
inebriated [i'niːbrieitid] *adj* ivre.
inedible [in'edibl] *adj* non comestible.
inefficient [ini'fiʃnt] *adj* inefficace;
incompétent. **inefficiency** *n* inefficacité *f*;
incompétence *f*.
inept [i'nept] *adj* inepte.
inequality [ini'kwɒləti] *n* inégalité *f*.
inert [i'nəːt] *adj* inerte. **inertia** *n* inertie *f*.
inevitable [in'evitəbl] *adj* inévitable.
inexpensive [inik'spensiv] *adj* pas cher.
inexperienced [inik'spiəriənst] *adj*
inexpérimenté.
infallible [in'faləbl] *adj* infaillible.

infamous ['infəməs] *adj* ınfâme. **infamy** *n* infamie *f*.

infancy ['infənsi] *n* petite enfance *f*; (*of idea, etc.*) enfance *f*.

infant ['infənt] *n* bébé *m*; enfant en bas âge *m, f.* **infantile** *adj* enfantin, infantile.

infantry ['infəntri] *n* infanterie *f.*

infatuate [in'fatjueit] *v* **be infatuated with** (*person*) être entiché de; (*idea*) être engoué de. **infatuation** *n* engouement *m*.

infect [in'fekt] *v* infecter. **infection** *n* infection *f.* **infectious** *adj* infectieux, contagieux.

infer [in'fəː] *v* déduire. **inference** *n* déduction *f.*

inferior [in'fiəriə] *n(m+f), adj* inférieur, -e. **inferiority** *n* infériorité *f.*

infernal [in'fəːnl] *adj* infernal.

infest [in'fest] *v* infester. **infestation** *n* infestation *f.*

infidelity [ˌinfi'deliti] *n* infidélité *f.*

infiltrate [in'filˌtreit] *v* (s')infiltrer. **infiltration** *n* infiltration *f*; (*pol*) noyautage *m*.

infinite ['infinit] *nm, adj* infini. **infinity** *n* infinité *f*; (*maths*) infini *m*.

infinitive [in'finitiv] *nm, adj* infinitif.

infirm [in'fəːm] *adj* infirme. **infirmity** *n* infirmité *f.*

inflame [in'fleim] *v* (s')enflammer. **inflammable** *adj* inflammable. **inflammation** *n* inflammation *f.*

inflate [in'fleit] *v* gonfler; (*prices*) faire monter. **inflation** *n* (*econ*) inflation *f*; (*of tyre, etc.*) gonflement *m*.

inflection [in'flekʃən] *n* inflexion *f*; (*word ending*) désinence *f.*

inflict [in'flikt] *v* infliger. **infliction** *n* infliction *f.*

influence ['influəns] *n* influence *f. v* influencer. **influential** *adj* influent.

influenza [ˌinflu'enzə] *n* grippe *f.*

influx ['inflʌks] *n* flot *m*, afflux *m*.

inform [in'fɔːm] *v* informer. **informative** *adj* instructif. **informer** *n* dénonciateur, -trice *m, f.*

informal [in'fɔːml] *adj* familier; dénué de formalité; (*unofficial*) officieux.

information [ˌinfə'meiʃən] *n* renseignements *m pl.*

infra-red [ˌinfrə'red] *adj* infrarouge.

infringe [in'frindʒ] *v* enfreindre. **infringe on** empiéter sur. **infringement** *n* infraction *f.*

infuriate [in'fjuəriˌeit] *v* rendre furieux. **infuriating** *adj* exaspérant.

ingenious [in'dʒiːnjəs] *adj* ingénieux. **ingenuity** *n* ingéniosité *f.*

ingot ['iŋgət] *n* lingot *m*.

ingredient [in'griːdjənt] *n* ingrédient *m*.

inhabit [in'habit] *v* habiter. **inhabitant** *n* habitant, -e *m, f.*

inhale [in'heil] *v* inhaler; (*smoke*) avaler; (*perfume*) aspirer.

inherent [in'hiərənt] *adj* inhérent.

inherit [in'herit] *v* hériter (de). **inheritance** *n* héritage *m*; succession *f.*

inhibit [in'hibit] *v* inhiber, gêner. **inhibition** *n* inhibition *f.*

inhuman [in'hjuːmən] *adj* inhumain. **inhumanity** *n* inhumanité *f.*

iniquity [i'nikwəti] *n* iniquité *f.*

initial [i'niʃl] *adj* initial, premier. *n* initiale *f. v* parafer.

initiate [i'niʃiˌeit] *v* initier; inaugurer; commencer. **initiation** *n* initiation *f*; commencement *m*; inauguration *f.*

initiative [i'niʃiətiv] *n* initiative *f.*

inject [in'dʒekt] *v* injecter. **injection** *n* injection *f*, piqûre *f.*

injure ['indʒə] *v* blesser. **injury** *n* blessure *f.*

injustice [in'dʒʌstis] *n* injustice *f.*

ink [iŋk] *n* encre *f.* **ink-well** *n* encrier *m. v* encrer.

inkling ['iŋkliŋ] *n* soupçon *m*.

inland ['inlənd] *adv* in'land] *adj* intérieur, -e. **Inland Revenue** fisc *m. adv* à l'intérieur.

in-laws ['inˌlɔːz] *pl n* (*coll*) beaux-parents *m pl*, belle-famille *f sing.*

inlay [ˌin'lei] *v* incruster; marqueter. *n* incrustation *f*; marqueterie *f.*

inlet ['inlet] *n* crique *f.*

inmate ['inmeit] *n* occupant, -e *m, f*; (*prison*) détenu, -e *m, f*; hospitalisé, -e *m, f.*

inn [in] *n* auberge *f.* **innkeeper** *n* aubergiste *m, f.*

innate [ˌi'neit] *adj* inné.

inner ['inə] *adj* intérieur, -e; (*thoughts, etc.*) intime. **inner tube** chambre à air *f.*

innocent ['inəsnt] *adj* innocent. **innocence** *n* innocence *f.*

innocuous [i'nɔkjuəs] *adj* inoffensif.

innovation [inə'veiʃən] *n* innovation *f.*

innuendo [ˌinju'endou] *n* insinuation *f.*

innumerable [i'njuːmərəbl] *adj* innombrable.

inoculate [i'nokju,leit] *v* inoculer. **inoculation** *n* inoculation *f*.

inorganic [,inoɪ'ganik] *adj* inorganique.

input ['input] *n* (*elec*) énergie *f*; (*tech*) consommation *f*; (*computer*) input *m*.

inquest ['inkwest] *n* enquête *f*.

inquire [in'kwaiə] *v* s'informer (de), demander. **inquiring** *adj* (*mind*) curieux; (*look*) interrogateur, -trice. **inquiry** *n* (*official*) enquête *f*; (*individual*) demande de renseignements *f*. **inquiry desk** renseignements *m pl*.

inquisition [,inkwi'ziʃən] *n* investigation *f*. **the Inquisition** l'Inquisition *f*.

inquisitive [in'kwizətiv] *adj* curieux.

insane [in'sein] *adj* (*med*) aliéné; (*crazy*) fou, folle. **insanity** *n* aliénation *f*; folie *f*.

insatiable [in'seiʃəbl] *adj* insatiable.

inscribe [in'skraib] *v* inscrire, graver. **inscription** *n* inscription *f*.

insect ['insekt] *n* insecte *m*. **insecticide** *n* insecticide *m*.

insecure [,insi'kjuə] *adj* (*future*, *etc*.) incertain; (*person*) anxieux; (*structure*) peu solide. **insecurity** *n* insécurité *f*.

inseminate [in'semineit] *v* inséminer. **insemination** *n* insémination *f*.

insensitive [in'sensətiv] *adj* insensible. **insensitivity** *n* insensibilité *f*.

inseparable [in'sepərəbl] *adj* inséparable.

insert [in'səɪt; *n* 'insəɪt] *v* insérer. *n* insertion *f*; (*page*) encart *m*. **insertion** *n* insertion *f*.

inshore [,in'ʃoɪ] *adj* côtier.

inside [,in'said] *adv* dedans. *prep* à l'intérieur de. *adj* intérieur, -e. *n* dedans *m*, intérieur *m*. **inside out** à l'envers.

insidious [in'sidiəs] *adj* insidieux.

insight ['insait] *n* perspicacité *f*.

insignificant [,insig'nifikənt] *adj* insignifiant. **insignificance** *n* insignifiance *f*.

insincere [,insin'siə] *adj* hypocrite; faux, fausse.

insinuate [in'sinjueit] *v* insinuer. **insinuation** *n* insinuation *f*.

insipid [in'sipid] *adj* insipide.

insist [in'sist] *v* insister; affirmer. **insistence** *n* insistance *f*. **insistent** *adj* insistant. **insistently** *adv* avec insistance.

insolent ['insələnt] *adj* insolent. **insolence** *n* insolence *f*.

insoluble [in'soljubl] *adj* insoluble.

insomnia [in'somniə] *n* insomnie *f*. **insomniac** *n*(*m*+*f*), *adj* insomniaque.

inspect [in'spekt] *v* inspecter, examiner. **inspection** *n* inspection *f*; examen *m*. **inspector** *n* inspecteur, -trice *m*, *f*.

inspire [in'spaiə] *v* inspirer. **inspiration** *n* inspiration *f*.

instability [,instə'biləti] *n* instabilité *f*.

install [in'stoɪl] *v* installer. **installation** *n* installation *f*.

instalment [in'stoɪlmənt] *n* (*comm*) acompte *m*; (*of serial*) épisode *m*.

instance [in'stəns] *n* exemple *m*, cas *m*. **for instance** par exemple.

instant ['instənt] *adj* immédiat; (*comm*) courant; (*coffee*) soluble. *n* instant *m*. **instantaneous** *adj* instantané. **instantly** *adv* sur-le-champ.

instead [in'sted] *adv* à la place, plutôt. **instead of** au lieu de.

instep ['instep] *n* (*anat*) cou-de-pied *m*; (*shoe*) cambrure *f*.

instigate ['instigeit] *v* inciter; provoquer. **instigation** *n* instigation *f*. **instigator** *n* instigateur, -trice *m*, *f*.

instil [in'stil] *v* insuffler, inculquer.

instinct [in'stiŋkt] *n* instinct *m*. **instinctive** *adj* instinctif.

institute ['institjuɪt] *v* instituer, fonder. *n* institut *m*. **institution** *n* institution *f*; (*school*, *home*) établissement *m*.

instruct [in'strʌkt] *v* instruire; (*order*) charger. **instruction** *n* instruction *f*. **instructions** *pl n* directives *f pl*; (*comm*) indications *f pl*; (*for use*) mode d'emploi *m sing*. **instructive** *adj* instructif. **instructor** *n* professeur *m*; (*skiing*) moniteur, -trice *m*, *f*.

instrument ['instrəmənt] *n* instrument *m*. **instrumental** *adj* (*music*) instrumental. **be instrumental in** contribuer à.

insubordinate [,insə'boɪdənət] *adj* insubordonné. **insubordination** *n* insubordination *f*.

insufficient [,insə'fiʃənt] *adj* insuffisant.

insular ['insjulə] *adj* insulaire; (*outlook*) borné.

insulate ['insjuleit] *v* isoler. **insulation** *n* isolation *f*; (*against cold*) calorifugeage *m*; (*material*) isolant *m*.

insulin ['insjulin] *n* insuline *f*.

insult [in'sʌlt; *n* 'insʌlt] *v* insulter. *n* insulte *f*.

insure [in'ʃuə] *v* (faire) assurer. **insurance** *n* assurance *f*. **insurance certificate** (*mot*) carte d'assurance *f*.

intact [in'takt] *adj* intact.

intake ['inteik] *n* (*tech*) adduction *f*; (*school*) admission *f*; (*food*) consommation *f*.

intangible [in'tandʒəbl] *adj* intangible.

integral ['intigrəl] *adj* intégral; (*part*) intégrant. *n* intégrale *f*.

integrate ['intigreit] *v* intégrer. **integration** *n* intégration *f*.

integrity [in'tegrəti] *n* intégrité *f*.

intellect ['intilekt] *n* intellect *m*, intelligence *f*. **intellectual** *n*, *adj* intellectuel, -elle.

intelligent [in'telidʒənt] *adj* intelligent. **intelligence** *n* intelligence *f*; (*information*) renseignements *m pl*. **intelligence test** test d'aptitude intellectuelle *m*.

intelligible [in'telidʒəbl] *adj* intelligible.

intend [in'tend] *v* avoir l'intention (de). **intended** *adj* intentionnel; projeté.

intense [in'tens] *adj* intense; (*person*) véhément. **intensify** *v* (s')intensifier. **intensity** *n* intensité *f*; véhémence *f*. **intensive** *adj* intensif. **intensive care** service de réanimation *m*.

intent¹ [in'tent] *n* intention *f*.

intent² [in'tent] *adj* attentif; résolu; absorbé.

intention [in'tenʃən] *n* intention *f*. **intentional** *adj* intentionnel, voulu.

inter [in'təː] *v* enterrer. **interment** *n* enterrement *m*.

interact [,intər'akt] *v* agir réciproquement. **interaction** *n* interaction *f*.

intercede [,intə'siːd] *v* intercéder.

intercept [,intə'sept] *v* intercepter. **interception** *n* interception *f*.

interchange [,intə'tʃeindʒ] *n* échange *m*; (*motorway*) échangeur *m*. *v* échanger. **interchangeable** *adj* interchangeable.

intercom ['intə,kom] *n* interphone *m*.

intercourse ['intəkoːs] *n* relations *f pl*; (*sexual*) rapports *m pl*.

interest ['intrist] *n* intérêt *m*; (*comm*) intérêts *m pl*. *v* intéresser. **be interested in** s'intéresser à.

interfere [,intə'fiə] *v* s'immiscer. **interfere with** (*plans*) contrecarrer; (*work*) empiéter sur; (*meddle*) tripoter. **interference** *n* intrusion *f*; (*radio*) parasites *m pl*. **interfering** *adj* importun.

interim ['intərim] *n* intérim *m*. *adj* provisoire, intérimaire.

interior [in'tiəriə] *adj* intérieur, -e. *n* intérieur *m*.

interjection [,intə'dʒekʃən] *n* interjection *f*.

interlude ['intəluːd] *n* intervalle *m*; (*theatre*) intermède *m*; (*musical*) interlude *m*.

intermediate [,intə'miːdiət] *adj* intermédiaire.

interminable [in'təːminəbl] *adj* interminable.

intermission [,intə'miʃən] *n* interruption *f*; (*cinema*) entracte *m*.

intermittent [,intə'mitənt] *adj* intermittent. **intermittently** *adv* par intermittence.

intern [in'təːn] *v* interner. **internment** *n* internement *m*.

internal [in'təːnl] *adj* interne, intérieur, -e. **internal combustion engine** moteur à explosion *m*.

international [,intə'naʃənl] *adj* international.

interpose [,intə'pouz] *v* intervenir; (*remark, etc.*) intercaler.

interpret [in'təːprit] *v* interpréter. **interpretation** *n* interprétation *f*. **interpreter** *n* interprète *m*, *f*.

interrogate [in'terəgeit] *v* interroger. **interrogation** *n* interrogation *f*; (*police*) interrogatoire *m*. **interrogator** *n* interrogateur, -trice *m*, *f*.

interrogative [,intə'rogətiv] *adj* interrogateur, -trice; (*gramm*) interrogatif. *n* interrogatif *m*.

interrupt [,intə'rʌpt] *v* interrompre. **interruption** *n* interruption *f*.

intersect [,intə'sekt] *v* (se) couper; (*math*) (s')intersecter. **intersection** *n* croisement *m*; intersection *f*.

intersperse [,intə'spəːs] *v* parsemer.

interval ['intəvəl] *n* intervalle *m*; (*theatre*) entracte *m*.

intervene [,intə'viːn] *v* intervenir, survenir. **intervention** *n* intervention *f*.

interview ['intəvjuː] *n* entrevue; (*press, radio, etc.*) interview *f*. *v* interviewer.

intestine [in'testin] *n* intestin *m*. **intestinal** *adj* intestinal.

intimate¹ ['intimət] *adj* intime; (*detailed*) approfondi. **intimacy** *n* intimité *f*.

intimate² ['intimeit] *v* faire connaître; suggérer. **intimation** *n* annonce *f*; suggestion *f*.

intimidate [in'timideit] *v* intimider. **intimidation** *n* intimidation *f*.

into ['intu] *prep* dans, en.

intolerable [in'tɔlərəbl] *adj* intolérable.
intolerant [in'tɔlərənt] *adj* intolérant.
intolerance *n* intolérance *f*.
intonation [ˌintə'neiʃən] *n* intonation *f*.
intoxicate [in'tɔksikeit] *v* enivrer. **intoxicated** *adj* ivre. **intoxication** *n* ivresse *f*.
intransitive [in'transitiv] *nm, adj* intransitif.
intravenous [ˌintrə'viːnəs] *adj* intraveineux.
intrepid [in'trepid] *adj* intrépide.
intricate ['intriket] *adj* complexe, compliqué. **intricacy** *n* complexité *f*, complication *f*.
intrigue ['intriːg; *v* in'triːg] *n* intrigue *f*. *v* intriguer.
intrinsic [in'trinsik] *adj* intrinsèque.
introduce [ˌintrə'djuːs] *v* présenter, introduire. **introduction** *n* introduction *f*, présentation *f*. **introductory** *adj* préliminaire.
introspective [ˌintrə'spektiv] *adj* introspectif. **introspection** *n* introspection *f*.
introvert ['intrəˌvəːt] *n* introverti, -e *m, f*.
intrude [in'truːd] *v* s'imposer, s'immiscer. **intruder** *n* intrus, -e *m, f*. **intrusion** *n* intrusion *f*.
intuition [ˌintjuːˈiʃən] *n* intuition *f*. **intuitive** *adj* intuitif.
inundate ['inʌndeit] *v* inonder. **inundation** *n* inondation *f*.
invade [in'veid] *v* envahir. **invader** *n* envahisseur, -euse *m, f*. **invasion** *n* invasion *f*.
invalid[1] ['invəlid] *n(m+f)*, *adj* malade; *(disabled)* infirme, invalide.
invalid[2] [in'valid] *adj* non valide.
invaluable [in'valjuəbl] *adj* inestimable.
invariable [in'veəriəbl] *adj* invariable.
invective [in'vektiv] *n* invective *f*.
invent [in'vent] *v* inventer. **invention** *n* invention *f*. **inventor** *n* inventeur, -trice *m, f*.
inventory ['invəntri] *n* inventaire *m*.
invert [in'vəːt] *v* intervertir, renverser. **inverted commas** guillemets *m pl*. **inversion** *n* inversion *f*, renversement *m*.
invertebrate [in'vəːtibrət] *nm, adj* invertébré.
invest [in'vest] *v* investir, placer. **investment** *n* investissement *m*, placement *m*. **investor** *n* actionnaire *m, f*.
investigate [in'vestigeit] *v* examiner; *(crime)* enquêter sur. **investigation** *n* investigation *f*.

invigorating [in'vigəreitiŋ] *adj* vivifiant, tonifiant.
invincible [in'vinsəbl] *adj* invincible.
invisible [in'vizəbl] *adj* invisible.
invite [in'vait] *v* inviter. **invitation** *n* invitation *f*. **inviting** *adj* engageant, tentant.
invoice ['invois] *n* facture *f*. *v* facturer.
invoke [in'vouk] *v* invoquer. **invocation** *n* invocation *f*.
involuntary [in'vɔləntəri] *adj* involontaire.
involve [in'vɔlv] *v* impliquer, mêler; *(entail)* entraîner. **involved** *adj* compliqué. **involvement** *n* rôle *m*; problème *m*.
inward ['inwəd] *adj* vers l'intérieur; *(thoughts)* intime. **inwardly** *adv* secrètement. **inwards** *adv* vers l'intérieur.
iodine ['aiədiːn] *n* iode *m*.
ion ['aiən] *n* ion *m*.
irate [ai'reit] *adj* furieux.
Ireland ['aiələnd] *n* Irlande *f*. **Irish** *nm, adj* irlandais. **Irish Sea** mer d'Irlande *f*. **the Irish** les Irlandais *m pl*.
iris ['aiəris] *n* iris *m*.
irk [əːk] *v* contrarier. **irksome** *adj* ennuyeux.
iron ['aiən] *n* fer *m*. **Iron Curtain** rideau de fer *m*. **ironmonger's** *n* quincaillerie *f*. *v* repasser. **iron out** faire disparaître. **ironing** *n* repassage *m*. **ironing board** planche à repasser *f*.
irony ['aiərəni] *n* ironie *f*. **ironic** *adj* ironique.
irrational [i'raʃənl] *adj* pas rationnel, déraisonnable; *(math)* irrationnel.
irregular [i'regjulə] *adj* irrégulier. **irregularity** *n* irrégularité *f*.
irrelevant [i'reləvənt] *adj* sans rapport, hors de propos.
irreparable [i'repərəbl] *adj* irréparable.
irresistible [ˌiri'zistəbl] *adj* irrésistible.
irrespective [ˌiri'spektiv] *adj* **irrespective of** sans tenir compte de.
irresponsible [ˌiri'spɔnsəbl] *adj* irréfléchi.
irrevocable [i'revəkəbl] *adj* irrévocable.
irrigate ['irigeit] *v* irriguer. **irrigation** *n* irrigation *f*.
irritate ['iriteit] *v* irriter. **irritable** *adj* irritable. **irritation** *n* irritation *f*.
is [iz] *V* **be**.
Islam ['izlaːm] *n* Islam *m*. **Islamic** *adj* islamique.

island ['ailənd] *n* île *f; (in road)* refuge *m.*

isolate ['aisəleit] *v* isoler. **isolation** *n* isolement *m.*

issue ['iʃuː] *n* question *f;* résultat *m; (copy)* numéro *m; (stamps, etc.)* émission *f. v* distribuer; émettre; *(writ, etc.)* lancer.

isthmus ['isməs] *n* isthme *m.*

it [it] *pron (subject)* il, elle; *(direct object)* le, la; *(indirect object)* lui. **it is** c'est, il est.

italic [i'talik] *adj* italique. **italics** *pl n* italique *m sing.*

Italy ['itəli] *n* Italie *f.* **Italian** *nm, adj* italien; *(people)* Italien, -enne *m, f.*

itch [itʃ] *n* démangeaison *f. v* démanger.

item ['aitəm] *n* article *m;* question *f.*

itinerary [ai'tinərəri] *n* itinéraire *m.*

its [its] *adj* son, sa; *(pl)* ses. *pron* le sien, la sienne.

itself [it'self] *pron* se; *(emphatic)* lui-même, elle-même. **by itself** en soi; *(alone)* tout seul.

ivory ['aivəri] *n* ivoire *m.* **Ivory Coast** Côte d'Ivoire *f.*

ivy ['aivi] *n* lierre *m.*

J

jab [dʒab] *v* enfoncer. *n* coup de pointe *m; (coll: injection)* piqûre *f.*

jack [dʒak] *n (mot)* cric *m; (cards)* valet *m. v* **jack up** soulever avec un cric.

jackal ['dʒakɔːl] *n* chacal *m.*

jackdaw ['dʒakdɔː] *n* choucas *m.*

jacket ['dʒakit] *n (man's)* veston *m; (woman's)* jaquette *f; (of book)* couverture *f.* **jacket potato** pomme de terre au four *f.*

jackpot ['dʒakpot] *n* gros lot *m.*

jade [dʒeid] *nm* jade.

jaded ['dʒeidid] *adj* épuisé.

jagged ['dʒagid] *adj* déchiqueté.

jaguar ['dʒagjuə] *n* jaguar *m.*

jail *or* **gaol** [dʒeil] *n* prison *f. v* emprisonner. **jailer** *n* geôlier, -ère *m, f.*

jam[1] [dʒam] *v* (se) coincer; *(cram)* entasser; *(block)* encombrer. *n* embouteillage *m.*

jam[2] [dʒam] *n* confiture *f.*

janitor ['dʒanitə] *n* portier *m.*

January ['dʒanjuəri] *n* janvier *m.*

Japan [dʒə'pan] *n* Japon *m.* **Japanese** *nm, adj* japonais. **the Japanese** les Japonais *m pl.*

jar[1] [dʒaː] *n* pot *m,* bocal *m.*

jar[2] [dʒaː] *v (sound)* grincer; *(knock)* cogner; *(shake)* ébranler; *(irritate)* agacer.

jargon ['dʒaːgən] *n* jargon *m.*

jasmine ['dʒazmin] *n* jasmin *m.*

jaundice ['dʒɔːndis] *n* jaunisse *f.*

jaunt [dʒɔːnt] *n (coll)* balade *f.*

jaunty ['dʒɔːnti] *adj* enjoué, vif.

javelin ['dʒavəlin] *n* javelot *m.*

jaw [dʒɔː] *n* mâchoire *f.* **jawbone** *n* maxillaire *m.*

jay [dʒei] *n* geai *m.*

jazz [dʒaz] *n* jazz *m.*

jealous ['dʒeləs] *adj* jaloux, -ouse. **jealousy** *n* jalousie *f.*

jeans [dʒiːnz] *pl n* blue-jean *m sing.*

jeep [dʒiːp] *n* jeep *f.*

jeer [dʒiə] *v* railler, huer. *n* raillerie *f,* huée *f.*

jelly ['dʒeli] *n* gelée *f.* **jellyfish** *n* méduse *f.*

jeopardize ['dʒepədaiz] *v* mettre en danger. **jeopardy** *n* danger *m,* péril *m.*

jerk [dʒəːk] *n* saccade *f,* secousse *f. v* tirer brusquement; donner une secousse à. **jerky** *adj* saccadé. **jerkily** *adv* par saccades.

jersey ['dʒəːzi] *n* tricot *m.* **Jersey** *n* Jersey *f.*

jest [dʒest] *n* plaisanterie *f. v* plaisanter. **jester** *n* bouffon *m.*

jet[1] [dʒet] *n* jet *m.* **jet lag** décalage horaire *m.* **jet-propelled** *adj* à réaction.

jet[2] [dʒet] *n* jais *m.*

jetty ['dʒeti] *n* jetée *f.*

Jew [dʒuː] *n* Juif, Juive *m, f.* **Jewish** *adj* juif.

jewel ['dʒuːəl] *n* bijou *(pl* -oux) *m.* **jeweller** *n* bijoutier *m.* **jeweller's** *n* bijouterie *f.* **jewellery** *n* bijoux *m pl.*

jig [dʒig] *n* gigue *f. v* danser la gigue; sautiller.

jigsaw ['dʒigsɔː] *n (puzzle)* puzzle *m; (saw)* scie à chantourner *f.*

jilt [dʒilt] *v* laisser tomber.

jingle ['dʒiŋgl] *n* tintement *m; (verse)* petit couplet *m. v* (faire) tinter.

jinx [dʒiŋks] *n (coll)* porte-guigne *m.* **jinxed** *adj* ensorcelé.

job [dʒob] *n* travail (*pl* -aux) *m*; poste *m*. **jobcentre** *n* agence pour l'emploi *f*. **job lot** lot d'articles divers *m*.

jockey ['dʒoki] *n* jockey *m*.

jocular ['dʒokjulə] *adj* jovial; facétieux.

jodhpurs ['dʒodpəz] *pl n* culotte de cheval *f sing*.

jog [dʒog] *n* (*jerk*) secousse *f*; (*with elbow*) coup de coude *m*. **jogtrot** *n* petit trot *m*. *v* secouer; (*elbow*) pousser; (*memory*) rafraîchir. **jogging** *n* footing *m*. **go jogging** faire du footing.

join [dʒoin] *v* (se) joindre, (s')unir; devenir membre (de), s'inscrire (à); (*roads, rivers, etc.*) (se) rejoindre. **join in** participer (à). **join up** assembler; (*mil*) s'engager. **joiner** *n* menuisier *m*.

joint [dʒoint] *n* jointure *f*; (*anat*) articulation *f*; (*of meat*) rôti *m*; (*slang: place*) boîte *f*. *adj* commun. **jointly** *adv* en commun.

joist [dʒoist] *n* solive *f*.

joke [dʒouk] *n* plaisanterie *f*; (*trick*) farce *f*. *v* plaisanter. **joker** *n* blagueur, -euse *m*, *f*; (*cards*) joker *m*.

jolly ['dʒoli] *adj* enjoué. *adv* (*coll*) drôlement. **jollity** *n* gaieté *f*.

jolt [dʒoult] *v* cahoter. *n* secousse *f*, cahot *m*; choc *m*.

jostle ['dʒosl] *v* (se) bousculer. *n* bousculade *f*.

jot [dʒot] *v* **jot down** noter. *n* iota *m*. **jotter** *n* bloc-notes *m*.

journal ['dʒəɪnl] *n* revue *f*; (*comm*) livre de comptes *m*; (*diary*) journal *m*. **journalism** *n* journalisme *m*. **journalist** *n* journaliste *m*, *f*.

journey ['dʒəɪni] *n* voyage *m*; (*distance*) trajet *m*. *v* voyager.

jovial ['dʒouviəl] *adj* jovial. **joviality** *n* jovialité *f*.

joy [dʒoi] *n* joie *f*; plaisir *m*. **joyful** *or* **joyous** *adj* joyeux.

jubilant ['dʒuːbilənt] *adj* débordant de joie. **be jubilant** jubiler. **jubilation** *n* jubilation *f*.

jubilee ['dʒuːbiliː] *n* jubilé *m*.

Judaism ['dʒuːdeiˌizəm] *n* judaïsme *m*.

judge [dʒʌdʒ] *n* juge *m*. *v* juger. **judging by** à en juger par. **judgment** *n* jugement *m*; discernement *m*.

judicial [dʒuːˈdiʃəl] *adj* judiciaire.

judicious [dʒuːˈdiʃəs] *adj* judicieux.

judo ['dʒuːdou] *n* judo *m*.

jug [dʒʌg] *n* cruche *f*; (*for milk*) pot *m*; (*slang: prison*) taule *f*.

juggernaut ['dʒʌgənoɪt] *n* (*lorry*) mastodonte *m*.

juggle ['dʒʌgl] *v* jongler. **juggler** *n* jongleur, -euse *m*, *f*. **jugglery** *n* jonglerie *f*.

jugular ['dʒʌgjulə] *nf*, *adj* jugulaire.

juice [dʒuːs] *n* jus *m*. **juicy** *adj* juteux.

jukebox ['dʒuːkboks] *n* juke-box *m*.

July [dʒuˈlai] *n* juillet *m*.

jumble ['dʒʌmbl] *v* brouiller. *n* mélange *m*, fouillis *m*. **jumble sale** vente de charité *f*.

jump [dʒʌmp] *n* saut *m*; (*start*) sursaut *m*. *v* sauter; sursauter. **jump at** (*offer, etc.*) sauter sur. **jumped-up** *adj* (*derog*) parvenu. **jumpy** *adj* (*coll*) nerveux.

jumper ['dʒʌmpə] *n* pull *m*.

junction ['dʒʌŋktʃən] *n* jonction *f*; (*roads*) bifurcation *f*; (*rail*) embranchement *m*.

juncture ['dʒʌŋktʃə] *n* conjoncture *f*. **at this juncture** à ce moment-là.

June [dʒuːn] *n* juin *m*.

jungle ['dʒʌŋgl] *n* jungle *f*.

junior ['dʒuːnjə] *adj* (*younger*) cadet -ette; (*lower rank*) subalterne. *n* cadet -ette *m*, *f*; (*clerk*) petit commis *m*; (*in names*) fils *m*.

juniper ['dʒuːnipə] *n* genévrier *m*. **juniper berry** baie de genièvre *f*.

junk¹ [dʒʌŋk] *n* bric-à-brac *m invar*; (*coll: rubbish*) camelote *f*. **junk-shop** *n* brocanteur *m*.

junk² [dʒʌŋk] *n* (*boat*) jonque *f*.

junta ['dʒʌntə] *n* junte *f*.

jurisdiction [dʒuərisˈdikʃən] *n* juridiction *f*.

jury ['dʒuəri] *n* jury *m*. **juror** *n* juré femme juré *m*, *f*.

just [dʒʌst] *adv* juste; simplement. **have just** venir de: *il vient de partir*. *adj* juste.

justice ['dʒʌstis] *n* justice *f*. **Justice of the Peace** juge de paix *m*.

justify ['dʒʌstifai] *v* justifier. **justifiable** *adj* justifiable. **justification** *n* justification *f*.

jut [dʒʌt] *v* **jut out** saillir, dépasser.

jute [dʒuːt] *n* jute *m*.

juvenile ['dʒuːvənail] *n* adolescent, -e *m*, *f*. *adj* juvénile. **juvenile delinquent** mineur délinquant, mineure délinquante *m*, *f*.

juxtapose [ˌdʒʌkstəˈpouz] *v* juxtaposer. **juxtaposition** *n* juxtaposition *f*.

K

kaftan ['kaftan] n kaftan m.

kaleidoscope [kə'laidəskoup] n kaléido-scope m.

kangaroo [kaŋgə'ruː] n kangourou m.

karate [kə'raːti] n karaté m.

kayak ['kaiak] n kayak m.

kebab [ki'bab] n kébab m.

keel [kiːl] n quille f. v keel over (naut) chavirer; (coll: faint) tomber dans les pommes.

keen [kiːn] adj vif; enthousiaste; (sharp) aiguisé; (sight, judgment) pénétrant. **keenly** adv vivement, profondément; avec enthousiasme. **keenness** n finesse f; intensité f; enthousiasme m.

*keep [kiːp] v garder; (observe, maintain) tenir; (support) entretenir; (remain) rester; (food, etc.) se garder. **keep-fit** n culture physique f. **keep on** continuer. **keep out!** (on notice) défense d'entrer! **keepsake** n souvenir m. **keep up with** suivre; aller aussi vite que. **keeper** n gardien, -enne m, f.

keg [keg] n tonnelet m.

kennel ['kenl] n niche f. **kennels** pl n chenil m sing.

kept [kept] V keep.

kerb [kəːb] n bordure du trottoir f.

kernel ['kəːnl] n (nut) amande f; (seed) graine m.

kerosene ['kerəsiːn] n kérosène m.

ketchup ['ketʃəp] n ketchup m.

kettle ['ketl] n bouilloire f. **kettledrum** n timbale f.

key [kiː] n clef f; (piano) touche f; (music) ton m. **keyboard** n clavier m. **keyhole** n trou de serrure m. **key-ring** n porte-clefs m invar. adj clef. v key up surexciter.

khaki ['kaːki] nm, adj kaki.

kick [kik] n coup de pied m; (gun) recul m. v donner un coup de pied (à). **kick off** (football) donner le coup d'envoi; (coll: party, etc.) démarrer. **kick-off** n coup d'envoi m; (coll) démarrage m. **kick out** (coll) flanquer dehors.

kid¹ [kid] n (goat, leather) chevreau m; (coll: child) gosse m, f.

kid² [kid] v (coll) faire marcher.

kidnap ['kidnap] v kidnapper. **kidnapper** n kidnappeur, -euse m, f. **kidnapping** n enlèvement m.

kidney ['kidni] n (anat) rein m; (as food) rognon m. **kidney bean** haricot rouge m. **kidney machine** rein artificiel m.

kill [kil] v tuer. **killjoy** n rabat-joie m invar. **killer** n tueur, -euse m, f; assassin m. **killing** n meurtre m; massacre m.

kiln [kiln] n four m.

kilo ['kiːlou] n kilo m.

kilogram ['kiləgram] n kilogramme m.

kilometre ['kiləmiːtə] n kilomètre m.

kilt [kilt] n kilt m.

kin [kin] n parents m pl. **kinship** n parenté f.

kind¹ [kaind] adj aimable, gentil, -ille. **kind-hearted** adj bon, bonne. **kindness** n bonté f. gentillesse f.

kind² [kaind] n genre m; (brand) marque f. **in kind** en nature.

kindergarten ['kindəgaːtn] n jardin d'enfants m.

kindle ['kindl] v (s')allumer, (s')enflammer.

kindred ['kindrid] n parents m pl. adj (related) apparenté; similaire. **kindred spirit** âme sœur f.

kinetic [kin'etik] adj cinétique.

king [kiŋ] n roi m; (draughts) dame f. **kingfisher** n martin-pêcheur m. **kingdom** n royaume m; (plant, animal) règne m.

kink [kiŋk] n (rope) entortillement m; (hair) crêpelure f. v s'entortiller. **kinky** adj crêpelé; bizarre.

kiosk ['kiːosk] n kiosque m.

kipper ['kipə] n hareng fumé m.

kiss [kis] v (s')embrasser. n baiser m. **kiss of life** bouche à bouche m.

kit [kit] n (equipment) matériel m; (sport) affaires f pl; (tools, first-aid, etc.) trousse f; (do-it-yourself) kit m. v kit out équiper.

kitchen ['kitʃin] n cuisine f. **kitchen sink** évier m.

kite [kait] n cerf-volant m; (bird) milan m.

kitten ['kitn] n chaton m.

kitty ['kiti] n cagnotte f.

kleptomania [kleptə'meiniə] n kleptomanie f. **kleptomaniac** n(m + f). adj kleptomane.

knack [nak] n tour de main m, truc m. **get the knack of** attraper le tour de main pour.

knapsack ['napsak] n sac à dos m.

knead [niːd] v pétrir.

knee [niː] *n* genou (*pl* -oux) *m*. **kneecap** *n* rotule *f*.
***kneel** [niːl] *v* s'agenouiller.
knelt [nelt] *V* **kneel.**
knew [njuː] *V* **know.**
knickers ['nikəz] *pl n* culotte *f* *sing*; (*briefs*) slip *m* *sing*.
knife [naif] *n* couteau *m*. *v* donner un coup de couteau à.
knight [nait] *n* chevalier *m*. *v* faire chevalier. **knighthood** *n* titre de chevalier *m*. **get a knighthood** être fait chevalier.
knit [nit] *v* tricoter. **knit together** lier; (*bone*) se souder. **knitting** *n* tricot *m*. **knitting machine** tricoteuse *f*. **knitting needle** aiguille à tricoter *f*.
knob [nob] *n* bouton *m*; (*of butter*) noix *f*. **knobbly** ['nobli] *adj* noueux.
knock [nok] *n* coup *m*. *v* frapper; (*bump*) heurter. **knock down** abattre; (*mot*) renverser. **knock knees** genoux cagneux *m pl*. **knock out** (*stun*) assommer; (*from contest*) éliminer. **knockout** *n* (*boxing*) knock-out *m*. **knock over** renverser. **knocker** *n* marteau de porte *m*.
knot [not] *n* nœud *m*. *v* nouer.
***know** [nou] *v* (*facts*) savoir; (*places, people*) connaître; (*recognize*) reconnaître. **know-all** *n* (*coll*) je-sais-tout *m, f*. **know-how** *n* (*coll*) technique *f*. **know how to** savoir. **knowing** *adj* fin; (*look*) entendu.
knowledge ['nolidʒ] *n* connaissance *f*, savoir *m*. **knowledgeable** *adj* bien informé.
known [noun] *V* **know.**
knuckle ['nʌkl] *n* articulation du doigt *f*.

L

label ['leibl] *n* étiquette *f*. *v* étiqueter.
laboratory [lə'borətəri] *n* laboratoire *m*.
labour ['leibə] *n* travail (*pl* -aux) *m*; (*workers*) main-d'œuvre *f*. **Labour** *nm, adj* (*pol*) travailliste. **labour pains** douleurs de l'accouchement *f pl*. **labour-saving device** appareil ménager *m*. *v* peiner. **laborious** *adj* laborieux. **labourer** *n* ouvrier *m*.
laburnum [lə'bəːnəm] *n* cytise *m*.
labyrinth ['labərinθ] *n* labyrinthe *m*.

lace [leis] *n* dentelle *f*; (*for shoe*) lacet *m*. *v* lacer; (*drink*) arroser.
lacerate ['lasəreit] *v* lacérer. **laceration** *n* (*act*) lacération *f*; (*tear*) déchirure *f*.
lack [lak] *n* manque *m*. **for lack of** faute de. *v* manquer (de).
lackadaisical [,lakə'deizikəl] *adj* apathique; indolent.
lacquer ['lakə] *n* laque *f*. *v* laquer.
lad [lad] *n* (*coll*) gars *m*.
ladder ['ladə] *n* échelle *f*. *v* (*stocking*) filer. **ladderproof** *adj* indémaillable.
laden ['leidn] *adj* chargé.
ladle ['leidl] *n* louche *f*.
lady ['leidi] *n* dame *f*. **ladies** *n* (*sign*) dames *f*. **ladies and gentlemen!** mesdames, messieurs! **ladybird** *n* coccinelle *f*. **lady-in-waiting** *n* dame d'honneur *f*.
lag[1] [lag] *v* traîner. *n* retard *m*; (*time difference*) décalage *m*.
lag[2] [lag] *v* calorifuger. **lagging** *n* calorifuge *m*.
lager ['laːgə] *n* bière blonde *f*.
lagoon [lə'guːn] *n* lagune *f*.
laid [leid] *V* **lay**[1].
lain [lein] *V* **lie**[1].
lair [leə] *n* tanière *f*.
laity ['leiəti] *n* laïcs *m pl*.
lake [leik] *n* lac *m*.
lamb [lam] *n* agneau *m*.
lame [leim] *adj* boîteux; (*excuse, etc.*) faible. **be lame** boîter. *v* estropier. **lamely** *adv* maladroitement. **lameness** *n* boîterie *f*; faiblesse *f*.
lament [lə'ment] *n* lamentation *f*. *v* se lamenter, pleurer. **lamentable** *adj* lamentable; regrettable.
laminate ['lamineit] *v* laminer. **laminated** *adj* laminé; (*glass*) feuilleté; (*windscreen*) en verre feuilleté.
lamp [lamp] *n* lampe *f*. **lamppost** *n* réverbère *m*. **lampshade** *n* abat-jour *m* *invar*.
lance [laːns] *n* lance *f*. *v* (*blister, etc.*) ouvrir.
land [land] *n* terre *f*; (*country*) pays *m*. **landlady** *n* propriétaire *f*; (*boarding house*) patronne *f*. **landlord** *n* propriétaire *m*; (*pub*) patron *m*. **landmark** *n* point de repère *m*. **landscape** *n* paysage *m*. *v* (*boat*) débarquer; (*aircraft*) atterrir; (*fall*) tomber. **landing** *n* débarquement *m*; atterrissage *m*; (*between floors*) palier *m*. **landing stage** débarcadère *m*.

lane [lein] *n* chemin *m*; (*on motorway, etc.*) voie *f*; (*line of traffic*) file *f*.

language ['laŋgwidʒ] *n* (*means of expression*) langage *m*; (*of a nation*) langue *f*.

languish ['laŋgwiʃ] *v* languir.

lanky ['laŋki] *adj* dégingandé.

lantern ['lantən] *n* lanterne *f*.

Laos ['laɪos] *n* Laos *m*.

lap¹ [lap] *n* (*sport*) tour de piste *m*. *v* (*wrap*) enrouler. **lap over** se chevaucher.

lap² [lap] *v* (*drink*) laper; (*waves*) clapoter.

lap³ [lap] *n* genoux *m pl*.

lapel [lə'pel] *n* revers *m*.

Lapland ['lapland] *n* Laponie *f*. **Lapp** *nm, adj* lapon; *n* (*people*) Lapon, -e *m, f*.

lapse [laps] *n* (*fault*) défaillance *f*; (*time*) intervalle *m*; (*of custom*) disparition *f*. *v* (*expire*) se périmer; (*fall*) tomber; (*commit fault*) faire un écart.

larceny ['laɪsəni] *n* vol simple *m*.

larch [laɪtʃ] *n* mélèze *m*.

lard [laɪd] *n* saindoux *m*.

larder ['laɪdə] *n* garde-manger *m invar*.

large [laɪdʒ] *adj* grand; gros, grosse. **at large** en liberté; en général. **large-scale** *adj* à grande échelle; fait sur une grande échelle.

lark¹ [laɪk] *n* (*bird*) alouette *f*.

lark² [laɪk] (*coll*) *n* blague *f*. *v* **lark around** faire le petit fou, faire la petite folle.

larva ['laɪvə] *n, pl* **larvae** larve *f*.

larynx ['lariŋks] *n* larynx *m*. **laryngitis** *n* laryngite *f*.

laser ['leizə] *n* laser *m*.

lash [laʃ] *n* coup de fouet *m*; (*thong*) mèche *f*; (*of eye*) cil *m*. *v* (*whip*) fouetter; (*rain, etc.*) cingler; attacher. **lash out** envoyer un coup; (*coll: money*) lâcher. **lashing** *n* flagellation *f*. **lashings of** (*coll*) des tas de.

lass [las] *n* jeune fille *f*.

lassitude ['lasitjuɪd] *n* lassitude *f*.

lasso [la'suɪ] *n* lasso *m*. *v* prendre au lasso.

last¹ [laɪst] *adj* dernier. **last-minute** *adj* de dernière minute. **last night** (*evening*) hier soir. *adv* en dernier; finalement; la dernière fois. *n* dernier, -ière *m, f*. **at last** enfin. **lastly** *adv* pour terminer.

last² [laɪst] *v* durer. **last out** *v* (*person*) tenir; (*money, food, etc.*) faire. **lasting** *adj* durable.

latch [latʃ] *n* loquet *m*. *v* fermer au loquet.

late [leit] *adj* en retard; récent; (*former*) ancien; (*dead*) feu. *adv* (*not on time*) en retard; (*not early*) tard. **lately** *adv* récemment. **lateness** *n* retard *m*. **later** *adj* plus tard. **see you later!** à tout à l'heure! **latest** *adj* (*most recent*) dernier. **at the latest** au plus tard.

latent ['leitənt] *adj* latent.

lateral ['latərəl] *adj* latéral.

lathe [leið] *n* tour *m*.

lather ['laɪðə] *n* mousse *f*. *v* (*apply soap*) savonner; (*foam*) mousser.

Latin ['latin] *nm, adj* latin.

latitude ['latitjuɪd] *n* latitude *f*.

latrine [lə'triɪn] *n* latrine *f*.

latter ['latə] *adj* dernier, deuxième. **the latter** celui-ci, celle-ci *m, f*.

lattice ['latis] *n* treillis *m*; (*frame*) treillage *m*.

laugh [laɪf] *v* rire. **laugh at** rire de; se moquer de. *n* rire *m*; éclat de rire *m*. **laughable** *adj* ridicule. **it's no laughing matter** il n'y a pas de quoi rire. **laughing-stock** *n* risée *f*. **laughter** *n* rires *m pl*.

launch¹ [loɪntʃ] *v* lancer. **launching** *n* lancement *m*.

launch² [loɪntʃ] *n* vedette *f*; (*of warship*) chaloupe *f*.

launder ['loɪndə] *v* blanchir. **launderette** *n* laverie automatique *f*. **laundry** *n* (*clothes, etc.*) linge *m*; (*place*) blanchisserie *f*.

laurel ['lorəl] *n* laurier *m*.

lava ['laɪvə] *n* lave *f*.

lavatory ['lavətəri] *n* toilettes *f pl*, cabinets *m pl*.

lavender ['lavində] *n* lavande *f*.

lavish ['laviʃ] *adj* prodigue; somptueux. *v* prodiguer.

law [loɪ] *n* loi *f*; (*profession*) droit *m*; justice *f*. **law-abiding** *adj* respectueux des lois. **lawsuit** *n* procès *m*. **lawful** *adj* légal, légitime. **lawyer** *n* avocat *m*.

lawn [loɪn] *n* pelouse *f*. **lawn-mower** *n* tondeuse *f*.

lax [laks] *adj* relâché. **laxity** *n* relâchement *m*.

laxative ['laksətiv] *nm, adj* laxatif.

*lay¹ [lei] *v* poser; (*eggs*) pondre. **layabout** *n* fainéant, -e *m, f*. **lay-by** *n* petite aire de stationnement *f*. **lay off** (*workers*) licencier. **lay on** (*provide*) fournir. **layout** *n* (*of house, etc.*) disposition *f*; (*of page*) mise en page *f*. **lay the table** mettre la table.

lay² [lei] *adj* laïque. **layman** *n* profane *m*.
lay³ [lei] *V* lie¹.
layer ['leiə] *n* couche *f*. *v* (*hair*) couper en dégradé.
lazy ['leizi] *adj* paresseux. **laze around** paresser. **laziness** *n* paresse *f*.
*****lead¹** [liːd] *v* mener, conduire; être à la tête de; (*sport*) être en tête. **lead on** (*tease*) faire marcher; (*encourage*) amener. **lead up to** conduire à; précéder. *n* (*sport*) tête *f*; exemple *m*; (*clue*) piste *f*; (*for dog*) laisse *f*; rôle principal *m*; (*elec*) fil *m*. **leader** *n* chef *m*; guide *m*; (*newspaper*) éditorial *m*. **leadership** *n* direction *f*. **leading** *adj* principal; majeur, -e.
lead² [led] *n* plomb *m*; (*pencil*) mine *f*.
leaf [liːf] *n* feuille *f*; page *f*; (*of table*) rallonge *f*, rabat *m*. *v* **leaf through** feuilleter. **leaflet** *n* prospectus *m*.
league [liːg] *n* ligue *f*; (*sport*) championnat *m*.
leak [liːk] *n* fuite *f*. *v* fuir; (*information*) divulguer. **leakage** *n* fuite *f*.
*****lean¹** [liːn] *v* (se) pencher; (*support*) (s')appuyer. *n* inclinaison *f*. **leaning** *n* penchant *m*.
lean² [liːn] *nm, adj* maigre. **leanness** *n* maigreur *f*.
leant [lent] *V* lean¹.
*****leap** [liːp] *n* saut *m*, bond *m*. **by leaps and bounds** à pas de géant. *v* sauter, bondir. **leap-frog** *n* saute-mouton *m*. **leap year** année bissextile *f*.
leapt [lept] *V* leap.
*****learn** [ləːn] *v* apprendre. **learned** *adj* savant. **learner** *n* débutant, -e *m, f*. **learning** *n* érudition *f*.
learnt [ləːnt] *V* learn.
lease [liːs] *n* bail *m*. *v* louer à bail. **leasehold** *adj* loué à bail.
leash [liːʃ] *n* laisse *f*.
least [liːst] *adj* (*amount*) le moins de; (*smallest*) le moindre, la moindre. *pron, adv* le moins. **at least** au moins.
leather ['leðə] *n* cuir *m*. **leathery** *adj* coriace; (*skin*) parcheminé.
*****leave¹** [liːv] *v* laisser; (*go away from*) quitter; (*depart*) partir. **be left** rester. **leave out** omettre, exclure. **left-luggage office** consigne *f*. **left-overs** *pl n* restes *m pl*.
leave² [liːv] *n* permission *f*; (*holiday*) congé *m*.
lecherous ['letʃərəs] *adj* lubrique. **lecher** *n* débauché *m*. **lechery** *n* luxure *f*.

lectern ['lektən] *n* lutrin *m*.
lecture ['lektʃə] *n* conférence *f*; réprimande *f*. **lecture theatre** amphithéâtre *m*. *v* faire un cours; réprimander. **lecturer** *n* conférencier, -ère *m, f*; (*university*) maître assistant *m*.
led [led] *V* lead¹.
ledge [ledʒ] *n* rebord *m*, saillie *f*.
ledger ['ledʒə] *n* grand livre *m*.
lee [liː] *n* abri *m*; (*naut*) côté sous le vent *m*. **leeward** *adj, adv* sous le vent.
leech [liːtʃ] *n* sangsue *f*.
leek [liːk] *n* poireau *m*.
leer [liə] *v* lorgner. *n* regard mauvais *m*.
leeway ['liːwei] *n* (*naut*) dérive *f*; liberté d'action *f*.
left¹ [left] *V* leave¹.
left² [left] *nf, adj* gauche. *adv* à gauche. **left-hand** *adj* à gauche. **left-handed** *adj* gaucher. **left-wing** *adj* de gauche.
leg [leg] *n* (*person*) jambe *f*; (*animal*) patte *f*; (*pork, chicken*) cuisse *f*; (*lamb*) gigot *m*; (*furniture*) pied *m*.
legacy ['legəsi] *n* legs *m*.
legal ['liːgəl] *adj* légal; judiciaire. **legality** *n* légalité *f*. **legalize** *v* légaliser.
legend ['ledʒənd] *n* légende *f*. **legendary** *adj* légendaire.
legible ['ledʒəbl] *adj* lisible. **legibility** *n* lisibilité *f*.
legion ['liːdʒən] *n* légion *f*.
legislate ['ledʒisleit] *v* faire des lois, légiférer. **legislation** *n* législation *f*.
legitimate [lə'dʒitimət] *adj* légitime. **legitimacy** *n* légitimité *f*.
leisure ['leʒə] *n* loisir *m*.
lemon ['lemən] *n* (*fruit*) citron *m*; (*tree*) citronnier *m*. *adj* (*colour*) citron *invar*. **lemonade** *n* limonade *f*. **lemon sole** limande-sole *f*. **lemon tea** thé au citron *m*.
*****lend** [lend] *v* prêter.
length [lenθ] *n* longueur *f*; (*time*) durée *f*; (*piece*) morceau *m*. **lengthen** *v* (s')allonger, rallonger. **lengthy** *adj* long, longue.
lenient ['liːniənt] *adj* indulgent. **leniency** *n* indulgence *f*.
lens [lenz] *n* lentille *f*; (*camera*) objectif *m*; (*spectacles*) verre *m*; (*eye*) cristallin *m*. **lens hood** parasoleil *m*.
lent [lent] *V* lend.
Lent [lent] *n* Carême *m*.

lentil ['lentil] *n* lentille *f.*
Leo ['liːou] *n* Lion *m.*
leopard ['lepəd] *n* léopard *m.*
leotard ['liːətaːd] *n* collant *m.*
leper ['lepə] *n* lépreux, -euse *m, f.* **leprosy** *n* lèpre *f.* **leprous** *adj* lépreux.
lesbian ['lezbiən] *n* lesbienne *f. adj* lesbien. **lesbianism** *n* lesbianisme *m.*
less [les] *nm, adv, prep* moins. *adj* moins de. **less and less** de moins en moins. **lessen** *v* diminuer. **lesser** *adj* moindre.
lesson ['lesn] *n* leçon *f.* cours *m.*
lest [lest] *conj* de peur que.
***let** [let] *v* laisser; (*rent out*) louer. **let down** (*lower*) descendre; (*disappoint*) décevoir; (*dress*) rallonger. **let-down** *n* déception *f.* **let in** faire entrer. **let out** faire sortir; (*shout, cry*) laisser échapper; (*clothes*) élargir.
lethal ['liːθəl] *adj* mortel.
lethargy ['leθədʒi] *n* léthargie *f.* **lethargic** *adj* léthargique.
letter ['letə] *n* lettre *f.* **letter-box** *n* boîte aux lettres *f.*
lettuce ['letis] *n* laitue *f.*
leukaemia [luːˈkiːmiə] *n* leucémie *f.*
level ['levl] *n* niveau *m*; (*road, rail*) palier *m. adj* (*flat*) plat; horizontal; (*spoonful*) ras; (*equal*) à égalité. **be level with** être au niveau de; être à la hauteur de. **level crossing** passage à niveau *m.* **level-headed** *adj* équilibré. *v* niveler.
lever ['liːvə] *n* levier *m.*
levy ['levi] *n* taxation *f,* taxe *f. v* prélever, imposer.
lewd [luːd] *adj* obscène.
liable ['laiəbl] *adj* sujet, -ette; (*law*) responsable. **be liable to** risquer de. **liability** *n* responsabilité *f*; handicap *m.*
liaison [liːˈeizon] *n* liaison *f.*
liar ['laiə] *n* menteur, -euse *m, f.*
libel ['laibəl] *n* (*act*) diffamation *f*; (*writing*) libelle *m. v* diffamer; (*insult*) calomnier. **libellous** *adj* diffamatoire.
liberal ['libərəl] *adj* libéral; généreux. **Liberal** *n, adj* (*pol*) libéral, -e.
liberate ['libəreit] *v* libérer. **liberation** *n* libération *f.*
liberty ['libəti] *n* liberté *f.* **at liberty** en liberté, libre.
Libra ['liːbrə] *n* Balance *f.*
library ['laibrəri] *n* bibliothèque *f.* **librarian** *n* bibliothécaire *m, f.*
libretto [liˈbretou] *n* livret *m.*
lice [lais] *V* louse.

licence ['laisəns] *n* permis *m*; (*comm*) licence *f.* **license** *v* donner une licence à; autoriser. **be licensed** (*shop, etc.*) détenir une licence. **licensee** *n* (*pub*) patron, -onne *m, f.*
lichen ['laikən] *n* lichen *m.*
lick [lik] *n* coup de langue *m. v* lécher.
lid [lid] *n* couvercle *m.*
lido ['liːdou] *n* complexe balnéaire *m.*
***lie¹** [lai] *v* s'allonger, se coucher; (*be lying*) être allongé, être couché; (*be*) être. **lie around** traîner. **lie down** s'allonger, se coucher. **lie in** faire la grasse matinée.
lie² [lai] *n* mensonge *m. v* mentir.
Liechtenstein ['liktənˌstain] *n* Liechtenstein *m.*
lieutenant [ləfˈtenənt] *n* lieutenant *m.*
life [laif] *n* vie *f.* **lifeless** *adj* sans vie, inanimé.
lifebelt ['laifbelt] *n* bouée de sauvetage *f.*
lifeboat ['laifbout] *n* canot de sauvetage *m*; (*on ship*) chaloupe de sauvetage *f.*
lifeguard ['laifgaːd] *n* surveillant de baignade *m.*
life insurance *n* assurance-vie *f.*
life-jacket *n* gilet de sauvetage *m.*
lifeline ['laiflain] *n* main courante *f*; (*diver's*) corde de sécurité *f.*
lifelong ['laifloŋ] *adj* de toujours.
life-saving *n* sauvetage *m.*
life story *n* biographie *f.*
lifetime ['laiftaim] *n* vie *f*; éternité *f.*
lift [lift] *n* ascenseur *m.* **give someone a lift** prendre quelqu'un en voiture. *v* (se) lever, soulever.
ligament ['ligəmənt] *n* ligament *m.*
***light¹** [lait] *n* lumière *f*; (*mot*) feu *m. adj* clair. **light bulb** ampoule *f.* **lighthouse** *n* phare *m.* **light meter** photomètre *m.* **light-year** *n* année-lumineuse *f. v* (*set fire to*) allumer; (*room, etc.*) éclairer. **lighten** *v* (s')éclaircir. **lighter** *n* (*for cigarette*) briquet *m.* **lighting** *n* éclairage *m.*
light² [lait] *adj* léger. **light-headed** *adj* étourdi. **light-hearted** *adj* gai, joyeux. **lightweight** *adj* léger; (*boxing*) poids léger. **lighten** *v* alléger. **lightness** *n* légèreté *f.*
***light³** [lait] *v* **light upon** tomber sur.
lightning ['laitniŋ] *n* éclair *m*, foudre *f.* **lightning conductor** paratonnerre *m.*
like¹ [laik] *adj* semblable. *prep* comme. **be** *or* **look like** ressembler à. **liken** *v* comparer. **likeness** *n* ressemblance *f*; forme *f*; portrait *m.* **likewise** *adv* également.

like² [laik] v aimer; (want) vouloir. **likeable** adj sympathique. **liking** n goût m.

likely ['laikli] adj probable; plausible. **be likely to** risquer de. adv probablement. **likelihood** n probabilité f.

lilac ['lailək] nm, adj lilas.

lily ['lili] n lis m. **lily-of-the-valley** n muguet m.

limb [lim] n membre m.

limbo ['limbou] n (rel) limbes m pl; oubli m.

lime¹ [laim] n chaux f. **limestone** n pierre à chaux f.

lime² [laim] n (fruit) lime f; (tree) limettier m; (linden) tilleul m. **lime green** nm, adj vert jaune. **lime juice** jus de citron vert m.

limelight ['laim,lait] n **in the limelight** en vedette.

limerick ['limərik] n poeme hun cristique m.

limit ['limit] n limite f. v limiter. **limitation** n limitation f. **limitless** adj illimité.

limousine ['limə,ziːn] n limousine f.

limp¹ [limp] v boîter.

limp² [limp] adj mou, molle. **limpness** n mollesse f.

limpet ['limpit] n patelle f.

line¹ [lain] n ligne f; corde f; (of poem) vers m; (row) rangée f, file f. v régler; (wrinkle) rider. **line up** (s')aligner. **linear** adj linéaire.

line² [lain] v (clothes) doubler; (brakes) garnir.

linen ['linin] n lin m; (sheets, etc.) linge m. **linen basket** panier à linge m.

liner ['lainə] n liner m.

linger ['lingə] v (person) s'attarder; (pain, memory, etc.) persister; (dawdle) traîner.

lingerie ['læʒəri] n lingerie f.

linguist ['lingwist] n linguiste m, f. **linguistic** adj linguistique. **linguistics** n linguistique f.

lining ['lainiŋ] n (clothes) doublure f; (brakes) garniture f.

link [liŋk] n lien m, liaison f; (of chain) maillon m. v lier.

linoleum [li'nouliəm] n linoléum m. **lino** n (coll) lino m.

linseed ['lin,siːd] n graines de lin f pl. **linseed oil** huile de lin f.

lint [lint] n tissu ouaté m.

lion ['laiən] n lion m. **lioness** n lionne f.

lip [lip] n lèvre f; (edge) bord m. **lip-read** v lire sur les lèvres. **lipstick** n rouge à lèvres m.

liqueur [li'kjuə] n liqueur f.

liquid ['likwid] nm, adj liquide. **liquidate** v liquider. **liquidation** n liquidation f. **liquidizer** n centrifugeuse f.

liquor ['likə] n spiritueux m.

liquorice ['likəris] n réglisse f.

lira ['liərə] n lire f.

Lisbon ['lizbən] n Lisbonne.

lisp [lisp] v zézayer.

list¹ [list] n liste f. v cataloguer, énumérer.

list² [list] v (naut) gîter. n inclinaison f.

listen ['lisn] v écouter. **listener** n auditeur, -trice m, f.

listless ['listlis] adj sans énergie; indolent, apathique.

lit [lit] V **light¹**, **light³**.

litany ['litəni] n litanie f.

literacy ['litərəsi] n degré d'alphabétisation m. **be literate** savoir lire et écrire.

literal ['litərəl] adj littéral.

literary ['litərəri] adj littéraire.

literature ['litrətʃə] n littérature f; (brochures) documentation f.

litigation [liti'geiʃən] n litige m.

litre ['liːtə] n litre m.

litter ['litə] n détritus m pl; (zool) portée f; (bedding) litière f. **litter-bin** n boîte à ordures f. v joncher; (make untidy) mettre en désordre.

little ['litl] adj (small) petit; (not much) peu de. nm, adv peu. **little by little** peu à peu.

liturgy ['litədʒi] n liturgie f. **liturgical** adj liturgique.

live¹ [liv] v vivre; habiter. **live down** faire oublier. **live on** vivre de.

live² [laiv] adj vivant; (broadcast) en direct; (coal) ardent; (wire) sous tension. adv en direct.

livelihood ['laivlihud] n gagne-pain m invar.

lively ['laivli] adj vif, plein d'entrain. **liveliness** n vivacité f, entrain m.

liven ['laivn] v **liven up** égayer, (s')animer.

liver ['livə] n foie m.

livestock ['laivstok] n bétail m.

livid ['livid] adj livide; furieux.

living ['liviŋ] adj vivant, en vie. n vie f. **living room** salle de séjour f.

lizard ['lizəd] n lézard m.

load [loud] n charge f; (weight) poids m; (coll) tas m. v charger. **loaded** adj chargé;

(*dice*) pipé; (*question*) insidieux; (*slang: rich*) bourré de fric.
loaf[1] [louf] *n* pain *m*.
loaf[2] [louf] *v* **loaf around** fainéanter. **loafer** *n* (*coll*) flemmard, -e *m, f*.
loan [loun] *n* prêt *m*. *v* prêter.
loathe [louð] *v* détester. **loathing** *n* dégoût *m*. **loathsome** *adj* détestable.
lob [lob] *v* lancer; (*tennis*) lober. *n* lob *m*.
lobby ['lobi] *n* vestibule *m*, foyer *m*; groupe de pression *m*. *v* faire pression (sur).
lobe [loub] *n* lobe *m*.
lobster ['lobstə] *n* homard *m*.
local ['loukəl] *adj* local; du pays. *n* (*coll: pub*) café du coin *m*. **the locals** (*coll: people*) les gens du coin. **locality** *n* (*region*) environs *m pl*; (*place*) lieu *m*. **localize** *v* localiser. **locally** *adv* localement; (*nearby*) dans les environs.
locate [lə'keit] *v* (*find*) repérer, localiser; situer. **location** *n* emplacement *m*; (*cinema*) tournage *m*. **on location** en extérieur.
lock[1] [lok] *n* serrure *f*; (*canal*) écluse *f*. **locksmith** *n* serrurier *m*. **lock, stock, and barrel** en bloc. **under lock and key** sous clef. *v* fermer à clef; (*tech*) (se) bloquer. **lock away** mettre sous clef. **lock in** enfermer. **lock out** enfermer dehors. **lock up** tout fermer; (*jewels, etc.*) enfermer.
lock[2] [lok] *n* (*of hair*) mèche *f*; (*curl*) boucle *f*.
locker ['lokə] *n* casier *m*.
locket ['lokit] *n* médaillon *m*.
locomotive [,loukə'moutiv] *n* locomotive *f*. *adj* locomotif. **locomotion** *n* locomotion *f*.
locust ['loukəst] *n* locuste *f*.
lodge [lodʒ] *n* loge *f*; (*small house*) maison de gardien *f*. *v* (se) loger; (*report*) présenter. **lodge a complaint** porter plainte. **lodger** *n* locataire *m, f*; (*boarder*) pensionnaire *m, f*. **lodgings** *pl n* (*room*) chambre *f sing*; (*flatlet*) logement *m sing*.
loft [loft] *n* grenier *m*. **lofty** *adj* haut, élevé; (*haughty*) hautain.
log [log] *n* bûche *f*. **logbook** *n* registre *m*; (*naut*) livre de bord *m*; (*aero*) carnet de vol *m*; (*mot*) carnet de route *m*. **log cabin** cabane en rondins *f*. *v* noter.
logarithm ['logəriðəm] *n* logarithme *m*.
loggerheads ['logəhedz] *pl n* **at loggerheads** en désaccord.
logic ['lodʒik] *n* logique *f*. **logical** *adj* logique.

loins [loins] *pl n* reins *m pl*. **loin chop** côte première *f*. **loincloth** *n* pagne *m*.
loiter ['loitə] *v* traîner.
lollipop ['loli,pop] *n* sucette *f*.
London ['lʌndən] *n* Londres *m*.
lonely ['lounli] *adj* seul, solitaire. **loneliness** *n* solitude *f*.
long[1] [loŋ] *adj* long, longue. *adv* longtemps. **as long as** pourvu que. **long-distance** *adj* (*race*) de fond; (*phone*) interurbain. **long-playing record** 33 tours *m invar*. **long-range** *adj* à longue portée; (*weather forecast*) à long terme. **long-sighted** *adj* hypermétrope; (*having foresight*) prévoyant. **long-sleeved** *adj* à manches longues. **long-standing** *adj* de longue, date. **long-term** *adj* à long terme. **long-winded** *adj* (*person*) intarissable; (*speech*) interminable.
long[2] [loŋ] *v* avoir très envie. **long for** désirer ardemment. **longing** *n* désir *m*, envie *f*.
longevity [lon'dʒevəti] *n* longévité *f*.
longitude ['londʒitjuːd] *n* longitude *f*. **longitudinal** *adj* longitudinal.
loo [luː] *n* (*coll*) cabinets *m pl*.
look [luk] *n* regard *m*; (*glance*) coup d'œil *m*; air *m*, allure *f*. *v* regarder; sembler, avoir l'air. **look after** s'occuper de; (*possessions*) prendre soin de. **look at** regarder. **look down on** mépriser. **look for** chercher. **look forward to** attendre avec impatience. **look out** faire attention. **look out of** regarder par. **look up** lever les yeux; (*word, etc.*) chercher; s'améliorer.
loom[1] [luːm] *v* apparaître indistinctement; menacer.
loom[2] [luːm] *n* métier à tisser *m*.
loop [luːp] *n* boucle *f*. *v* boucler; former une boucle. **loop the loop** (*aero*) faire un looping.
loophole ['luːphoul] *n* (*in law, etc.*) lacune *f*, échappatoire *f*.
loose [luːs] *adj* lâche; (*knot*) desserré; (*tooth*) branlant. **come loose** se desserrer; branler. **get loose** s'échapper. **let loose** lâcher. **loose change** petite monnaie *f*. **loose chippings** gravillons *m pl*. **loose covers** housses *f pl*. **loose-leaf** *adj* à feuilles volantes. *v* (*free*) lâcher; (*undo*) défaire. **loosely** *adv* lâchement; approximativement. **loosen** *v* relâcher; (se) desserrer; (se) défaire.

loot [luːt] n butin m. v piller. **looter** n pillard m. **looting** n pillage m.

lop [lop] v couper.

lopsided [,lop'saidid] adj de travers.

lord [loːd] n seigneur m; (as title) lord m.

lorry ['lori] n camion m. **lorry-driver** n camionneur m, routier m.

***lose** [luːz] v perdre; (watch, clock) retarder. **loser** n perdant, -e m, f. **lost property** objets trouvés m pl.

loss [los] n perte f. **be at a loss** être embarrassé.

lost [lost] V **lose**.

lot [lot] n (destiny) sort m; (auction) lot m. **a lot** beaucoup. **lots of** beaucoup de. **quite a lot of** pas mal de. **the lot** tout m.

lotion ['louʃən] n lotion f.

lottery ['lotəri] n loterie f.

lotus ['loutəs] n lotus m.

loud [laud] adj fort, sonore; (gaudy) voyant. adv fort. **loud hailer** porte-voix m invar. **loud-mouthed** adj braillard. **loud-speaker** n haut-parleur m. **loudly** adv fort. **loudness** n force f.

lounge [laundʒ] n salon m. **lounge suit** complet-veston m. v (on bed) se prélasser; (idle) paresser, flâner. **lounger** n (bed) lit de plage m.

louse [laus] n, pl **lice** pou (pl poux) m. **lousy** adj pouilleux; (slang: bad) moche, dégueulasse.

lout [laut] n rustre m.

love [lʌv] n amour m; (tennis) zéro m. **fall in love** tomber amoureux. **love affair** liaison f. **make love** faire l'amour. **with love from** (in letter) affectueusement. v aimer. **lovable** adj adorable. **lover** n amant m; (enthusiast) amateur m. **loving** adj affectueux.

lovely ['lʌvli] adj charmant, agréable.

low [lou] adj bas, basse; faible. adv bas. **low-cut** adj décolleté. **lowland** n plaine f. **low-lying** adj à basse altitude. **low-paid** adj mal payé. **lowly** adj humble, modeste.

lower ['louə] adj inférieur, -e. v baisser; (on rope) descendre.

loyal ['loiəl] adj loyal, fidèle. **loyalty** n loyauté f; fidélité f.

lozenge ['lozindʒ] n pastille f.

lubricate ['luːbrikeit] v lubrifier; (mot) graisser. **lubricant** nm, adj lubrifiant. **lubrication** n lubrification f; graissage m.

lucid ['luːsid] adj lucide. **lucidity** n lucidité f.

luck [lʌk] n chance f, hasard m. **bad luck** malchance f, malheur m. **good luck** bonne chance f, bonheur m. **lucky** adj heureux; (charm) porte-bonheur m invar. **be lucky** avoir de la chance.

lucrative ['luːkrətiv] adj lucratif.

ludicrous ['luːdikrəs] adj ridicule.

lug [lʌg] v traîner.

luggage ['lʌgidʒ] n bagages m pl. **luggage label** étiquette à bagages f. **luggage rack** porte-bagages m invar.

lukewarm ['luːkwoːm] adj tiède.

lull [lʌl] n arrêt m; (storm) accalmie f. v apaiser.

lullaby ['lʌlə,bai] n berceuse f.

lumbago [lʌm'beigou] n lumbago m.

lumber[1] ['lʌmbə] n (wood) bois de charpente m; (junk) bric-à-brac m invar. **lumberjack** n bûcheron m. **lumber yard** chantier de scierie m. v **lumber with** (coll) coller à.

lumber[2] ['lʌmbə] v marcher pesamment.

luminous ['luːminəs] adj lumineux.

lump [lʌmp] n morceau m, masse f; (med) grosseur f. **lump sum** somme globale f. **lumpy** adj grumeleux.

lunacy ['luːnəsi] n folie f, démence f.

lunar ['luːnə] adj lunaire.

lunatic ['luːnətik] n, adj fou, folle; dément, -e. **lunatic asylum** asile d'aliénés m.

lunch [lʌntʃ] n déjeuner m. v déjeuner.

lung [lʌŋ] n poumon m.

lunge [lʌndʒ] v faire un mouvement brusque en avant. n coup en avant m.

lurch[1] [ləːtʃ] v (person) vaciller, tituber; (car, ship) faire une embardée. n vacillement m; embardée f.

lurch[2] [ləːtʃ] n **leave in the lurch** faire faux bond à.

lure [luə] v attirer par la ruse. n attrait m; (decoy) leurre m.

lurid ['luərid] adj affreux, horrible; à sensation.

lurk [ləːk] v (person) se tapir; (danger) menacer; (doubt) persister. **lurking** adj vague.

luscious ['lʌʃəs] adj succulent.

lush [lʌʃ] adj luxuriant, riche.

lust [lʌst] n (sexual) luxure f; (for power, etc.) soif f. v **lust after** convoiter; avoir soif de. **lusty** adj vigoureux.

lustre ['lʌstə] n lustre m.

lute [luːt] n luth m.

Luxembourg ['lʌksəm,bəːg] *n* Luxembourg *m.*
luxury ['lʌkʃəri] *n* luxe *m.* **luxuriant** *adj* luxuriant. **luxurious** *adj* luxueux.
lynch [lintʃ] *v* lyncher.
lynx [links] *n* lynx *m invar.*
lyre [laiə] *n* lyre *f.*
lyrical ['lirikəl] *adj* lyrique.
lyrics ['liriks] *pl n* paroles *f pl.* **lyricist** *n* parolier, -ère *m, f.*

M

mac [mak] *n* (*coll*) imper *m.*
macabre [mə'kaːbr] *adj* macabre.
macaroni [makə'rouni] *n* macaroni *m.*
mace[1] [meis] *n* (*staff*) masse *f*; (*club*) massue *f.*
mace[2] [meis] *n* (*spice*) macis *m.*
machine [mə'ʃiːn] *n* machine *f.* **machine-gun** *n* mitrailleuse *f.* **machinery** *n* machinerie *f*; mécanisme *m.*
mackerel ['makrəl] *n* maquereau *m.*
mackintosh ['makin,toʃ] *n* imperméable *m.*
mad [mad] *adj* fou, folle; (*angry*) furieux. **madden** *v* rendre fou; exaspérer. **madly** *adv* follement, éperdument. **madness** *n* folie *f.*
madam ['madəm] *n* madame *f.*
Madrid [mə'drid] *n* Madrid.
made [meid] *V* make.
Madeira [mə'diərə] *n* (*place*) Madère *f*; (*wine*) madère *m.*
magazine [,magə'ziːn] *n* revue *f*, magazine *m*; (*mil*) magasin *m.*
maggot ['magət] *n* ver *m.*
magic ['madʒik] *n* magie *f. adj also* **magical** magique. **magician** *n* magicien, -enne *m, f.*
magistrate ['madʒistreit] *n* magistrat *m.*
magnanimous [mag'naniməs] *adj* magnanime. **magnanimity** *n* magnanimité *f.*
magnate ['magneit] *n* magnat *m.*
magnet ['magnət] *n* aimant *m.* **magnetic** *adj* magnétique. **magnetism** *n* magnétisme *m.* **magnetize** *v* magnétiser.
magnificent [mag'nifisnt] *adj* magnifique. **magnificence** *n* magnificence *f.*
magnify ['magnifai] *v* grossir. **magnifying**

glass loupe *f.* **magnification** *n* grossissement *m.*
magnitude ['magnitjuːd] *n* ampleur *f.*
magnolia [mag'nouliə] *n* magnolia *m.*
magpie ['magpai] *n* pie *f.*
mahogany [mə'hogəni] *n* acajou *m.*
maid [meid] *n* bonne *f.* **old maid** vieille fille *f.*
maiden ['meidən] *n* jeune fille *f. adj* (*first*) premier. **maiden aunt** tante célibataire *f.* **maiden name** nom de jeune fille *m.*
mail [meil] *n* (*letters*) courrier *m*; (*service*) poste *f.* **mail-bag** *n* sac postal *m.* **mailbox** *n* (*US*) boîte aux lettres *f.* **mailman** *n* (*US*) facteur *m.* **mail order** vente par correspondence *f. v* envoyer par la poste. **mailing list** liste d'adresses *f.*
maim [meim] *v* estropier.
main [mein] *adj* principal. **main course** plat principal *m.* **mainland** *n* continent *m.* **main-line station** gare de grande ligne *f.* **main road** grande route *f.* **mainstay** *n* soutien *m. n* (*gas, water*) conduite *f.* **in the main** en général. **mains** *n* (*elec*) secteur *m.*
maintain [mein'tein] *v* maintenir; (*car, family*) entretenir; continuer. **maintenance** *n* maintien *m*; entretien *m*; (*alimony*) pension alimentaire *f.*
maisonette [meizə'net] *n* duplex *m.*
maize [meiz] *n* maïs *m.*
majesty ['madʒəsti] *n* majesté *f.* **majestic** *adj* majestueux.
major ['meidʒə] *adj* majeur, -e. *n* (*mil*) commandant *m.*
majority [mə'dʒoriti] *n* majorité *f.* **be in the majority** être majoritaire.
*make [meik] *n* marque *f. v* faire; rendre; obliger; arriver à. **make believe** faire semblant. **make out** (*draw up*) dresser; discerner; prétendre. **makeshift** *adj* de fortune. **make up** inventer; (*face*) (se) maquiller; composer; assembler. **make-up** *n* maquillage *m.* **make up for** compenser. **maker** *n* fabricant *m.* **making** *n* fabrication *f.*
maladjusted [malə'dʒʌstid] *adj* inadapté.
malaria [mə'leəriə] *n* malaria *m.*
male [meil] *nm, adj* mâle.
malevolent [mə'levələnt] *adj* malveillant. **malevolence** *n* malveillance *f.* **malevolently** *adv* avec malveillance.
malfunction [mal'fʌŋkʃən] *n* mauvaise fonction *f. v* mal fonctionner.

Mali ['maːli] *n* Mali *m*.
malice ['malis] *n* malice *f*. **malicious** *adj* méchant, malveillant.
malignant [mə'lignənt] *adj* malfaisant; (*med*) malin, -igne. **malignancy** *n* malfaisance *f*; malignité *f*.
malinger [mə'lingə] *v* faire le malade. **malingerer** *n* faux malade, fausse malade *m, f*.
mallet ['malit] *n* maillet *m*.
malnutrition [malnjuˈtriʃən] *n* sous-alimentation *f*.
malt [moːlt] *n* malt *m*.
Malta ['moːltə] *n* Malte *f*. **Maltese** *nm, adj* maltais. **the Maltese** les Maltais.
maltreat [mal'triːt] *v* maltraiter. **maltreatment** *n* mauvais traitement *m*.
mammal ['maməl] *n* mammifère *m*.
mammoth ['maməθ] *n* mammouth *m. adj* géant.
man [man] *n, pl* **men** homme *m. v* armer. **manhood** *n* âge d'homme *m*. **manly** *adj* viril.
manage ['manidʒ] *v* (*business, etc.*) gérer, administrer; (*cope*) se débrouiller. **manage to** réussir à. **manageable** *adj* maniable. **management** *n* gestion *f*, administration *f*, direction *f*; (*not workers*) cadres *m pl*. **manager** *n* directeur *m*, gérant *m*. **manageress** *n* directrice *f*, gérante *f*. **managerial** *adj* directorial. **managing director** directeur général *m*.
mandarin ['mandərin] *n* mandarin *m*. **mandarin orange** (*fruit*) mandarine *f*; (*tree*) mandarinier *m*.
mandate ['mandeit] *n* mandat *m*. **mandatory** *adj* obligatoire; (*power, etc.*) mandataire.
mandolin ['mandəlin] *n* mandoline *f*.
mane [mein] *n* crinière *f*.
mange [meindʒ] *n* gale *f*. **mangy** *adj* galeux; (*coll*) minable, miteux.
manger ['meindʒə] *n* mangeoire *f*; (*rel*) crèche *f*.
mangle[1] ['mangl] *n* (*wringer*) essoreuse *f. v* essorer.
mangle[2] ['mangl] *v* mutiler, estropier.
mango ['mangou] *n* (*fruit*) mangue *f*; (*tree*) manguier *m*.
manhandle [man'handl] *v* maltraiter; (*goods*) manutentionner.
manhole ['manhoul] *n* trou d'homme *m*.
mania ['meiniə] *n* manie *f*. **maniac** *n* (*psych*) maniaque *m, f*; (*coll: madman*) fou, folle *m, f*; (*coll: enthusiast*) mordu *m*.
manicure ['manikjuə] *n* soin des mains *m. v* (*nails*) faire. **manicurist** *n* manucure *m, f*.
manifest ['manifest] *adj* manifeste. *v* manifester. **manifestation** *n* manifestation *f*.
manifesto [mani'festou] *n* manifeste *m*.
manifold ['manifould] *adj* divers; multiple. *n* **exhaust manifold** (*mot*) collecteur d'échappement *m*.
manipulate [mə'nipjuleit] *v* manipuler; manœuvrer. **manipulation** *n* manipulation *f*; manœuvre *f*.
mankind [,man'kaind] *n* le genre humain *m*.
man-made [,man'meid] *adj* synthétique; artificiel.
manner ['manə] *n* manière *f*; attitude *f*; sorte *f*. **manners** *pl n* manières *f pl*.
mannerism ['manə,rizəm] *n* trait particulier *m*.
manoeuvre *or* US **maneuver** [mə'nuːvə] *n* manœuvre *f. v* manœuvrer.
manor ['manə] *n* manoir *m*.
manpower ['man,pauə] *n* main-d'œuvre *m*; force physique *f*.
mansion ['manʃən] *n* (*country*) château *m*; (*town*) hôtel particulier *m*.
manslaughter [,man,slɔːtə] *n* homicide involontaire *m*.
mantelpiece ['mantlpiːs] *n* cheminée *f*.
mantle ['mantl] *n* (*of snow*) manteau *m*; (*cloak*) cape *f*; (*of gas lamp*) manchon *m*.
manual ['manjuəl] *nm, adj* manuel. **manually** *adv* à la main.
manufacture [manju'faktʃə] *n* fabrication *f*; (*clothes*) confection *f. v* fabriquer; confectionner. **manufacturer** *n* fabricant *m*.
manure [mə'njuə] *n* fumier *m*; (*artificial*) engrais *m. v* fumer.
manuscript ['manjuskript] *nm, adj* manuscrit.
many ['meni] *adj* beaucoup de, un grand nombre de. *pron* beaucoup, un grand nombre. **as many** autant (de). **how many** combien (de). **so many** tant (de). **too many** trop (de).
map [map] *n* carte *f*; (*of town*) plan *m. v* faire la carte de. **map out** tracer.
maple ['meipl] *n* érable *m*.
mar [maː] *v* gâter.
marathon ['marəθən] *nm, adj* marathon.

marble ['maɪbl] *n* marbre *m*; *(toy)* bille *f*.
v marbrer.

march [maɪtʃ] *n* marche *f*. *v* marcher au
pas. **march-past** défilé *m*.

March [maɪtʃ] *n* mars *m*.

marchioness [ˌmaɪʃə'nes] *n* marquise *f*.

mare [meə] *n* jument *f*.

margarine [ˌmaɪdʒə'riɪn] *n* margarine *f*.

margin ['maɪdʒin] *n* marge *f*. **marginal** *adj*
marginal. **marginally** *adv* de très peu.

marguerite [ˌmaɪgə'riɪt] *n* marguerite *f*.

marigold ['marigould] *n* souci *m*.

marijuana [mari'waɪnə] *n* marihuana *f*.

marina [mə'riɪnə] *n* marina *f*.

marinade [ˌmari'neid] *n* marinade *f*. *v*
mariner.

marine [mə'riɪn] *adj* *(animal, plant)*
marin; *(products)* de mer; maritime. *n*
(naut) marine marchande *f*; *(mil)* fusilier
marin *m*.

marital ['maritl] *adj* conjugal, matrimonial.

maritime ['maritaim] *adj* maritime.

marjoram ['maɪdʒərəm] *n* marjolaine *f*.

mark[1] [maɪk] *n* marque *f*; *(school)* note *f*,
point *m*; *(model)* série *f*. **marksman** *n*
bon tireur *m*. *v* marquer; *(school)* corriger, noter. **marked** *adj* marqué, sensible. **marking** *n* correction *f*; *(of animal)*
marque *f*.

mark[2] [maɪk] *n* *(currency)* mark *m*.

market ['maɪkit] *n* marché *m*. **market day**
jour de marché *m*. **market gardening** culture maraîchère *f*. **market place** place du
marché *f*. **market research** étude de
marché *f*. **market value** valeur marchande *f*. *v* vendre. **marketing** *n* com-
mercialisation *f*.

marmalade ['maɪmɔleid] *n* confiture
d'orange *f*.

maroon[1] [mə'ruɪn] *adj* bordeaux *invar*.

maroon[2] [mə'ruɪn] *v* abandonner.

marquee [maɪ'kiɪ] *n* grande tente *f*; *(circus)* chapiteau *m*.

marquess *or* **marquis** ['maɪkwis] *n* marquis *m*.

marquetry ['maɪkətri] *n* marqueterie *f*.

marriage ['maridʒ] *n* mariage *m*. **by marriage** par alliance. **marriage certificate**
extrait d'acte de mariage *m*. **marriage
guidance counsellor** conseiller conjugal,
conseillère conjugale *m, f*. **marriage
licence** dispense de bans *f*.

marrow ['marou] *n* *(of bone)* moelle *f*;
(vegetable) courge *f*.

marry ['mari] *v* se marier; *(husband, wife)*
épouser; *(priest, vicar)* marier. **married**
adj marié; conjugal. **get married** se
marier. **married name** nom de femme
mariée *m*.

Mars [maɪz] *n* Mars *f*. **Martian** *n* Martien, -enne; *adj* martien.

marsh [maɪʃ] *n* marais *m*. **marshland** *n*
marécage *m*. **marshmallow** *n* guimauve *f*.
marshy *adj* marécageux.

marshal ['maɪʃəl] *n* *(mil)* maréchal *m*;
(sports, etc.) membre du service d'ordre
m. *v* rassembler.

martial ['maɪʃəl] *adj* martial.

martin ['maɪtin] *n* martinet *m*.

martyr ['maɪtə] *n* martyr, -e *m, f*. *v*
martyriser. **martyrdom** *n* martyre *m*.

marvel ['maɪvəl] *n* merveille *f*. *v* s'étonner
(de).

marvellous ['maɪvələs] *adj* merveilleux.

marzipan [maɪzi'pan] *n* pâte d'amandes *f*.

mascara [ma'skaɪrə] *n* mascara *m*.

mascot ['maskət] *n* mascotte *f*.

masculine ['maskjulin] *nm, adj* masculin.
masculinity *n* masculinité *f*.

mash [maʃ] *v* écraser; *(potatoes)* faire en
purée. **mashed potatoes** purée *f sing*. *n*
(animal feed) pâtée *f*; purée *f*.

mask [maɪsk] *n* masque *m*. *v* masquer.
masking tape papier-cache adhésif *m*.

masochist ['masəkist] *n* masochiste *m, f*.
masochism *n* masochisme *m*. **masochistic**
adj masochiste.

mason ['meisn] *n* maçon *m*. **masonry** *n*
maçonnerie *f*.

masquerade [maskə'reid] *n* *(pretence)*
mascarade *f*. *v* **masquerade as** se faire
passer pour.

mass[1] [mas] *n* masse *f*. **mass hysteria** hystérie collective *f*. **mass media** media *m pl*.
mass-produce *v* fabriquer en série. **mass
production** fabrication en série *f*. *v* (se)
masser.

mass[2] [mas] *n* *(rel)* messe *f*.

massacre ['masəkə] *n* massacre *m*. *v* massacrer.

massage ['masaɪʒ] *n* massage *m*. *v* masser.
masseur *n* masseur *m*. **masseuse** *n* masseuse *f*.

massive ['masiv] *adj* massif, énorme.

mast [maɪst] *n* *(naut)* mât *m*; *(radio, etc.)*
pylône *m*.

master ['maɪstə] *n* maître *m*; *(teacher)*
professeur *m*. **master copy** original *m*.
master key passe-partout *m invar*. **mas-**

terpiece *n* chef-d'œuvre *m.* **master plan**
stratégie d'ensemble *f. v* maîtriser;
surmonter; *(learn, understand)* posséder
à fond. **masterly** *adj* magistral. **mastery** *n*
maîtrise *f,* domination *f; (skill)* virtuosité
f.

mastermind ['maːstəˌmaind] *n* cerveau *m.*
v diriger.

masturbate ['mastəbeit] *v* se masturber.
masturbation *n* masturbàtion *f.*

mat [mat] *n (floor)* tapis *m; (door)* paillasson *m; (table)* dessous-de-plat *m invar;*
(cloth) napperon *m.* **matted** *adj (hair)*
emmêle; *(cloth)* feutrè.

match[1] [matʃ] *n* allumette *f.* **matchbox** *n*
boîte à allumettes *f.*

match[2] [matʃ] *n (sport)* match *m,* partie *f;*
(equal) égal, -e *m, f. v* égaler; *(clothes)*
s'assortir à, aller bien ensemble; *(pair)*
s'apparier. **matchless** *adj* sans égal.

mate [meit] *n* mâle, femelle *m, f;*
camarade *m, f;* aide *f; (coll: friend)*
copain, -ine *m, f. v* (s')accoupler.

material [mə'tiəriəl] *n (fabric)* tissu *m;*
(substance) matière *f; (for book, etc.)*
matériaux *m pl.* **materials** *n pl* fournitures *f pl. adj* matériel. **materialist** *n*
matérialiste *m, f.* **materialistic** *adj* matérialiste. **materialize** *v* se matérialiser.

maternal [mə'təːnl] *adj* maternel.

maternity [mə'təːnəti] *n* maternité *f.*
maternity clothes vêtements de grossesse
m pl. **maternity hospital** maternité *f.*

mathematics [maθə'matiks] *n* mathématiques *f pl.* **mathematical** *adj* mathématique. **mathematician** *n* mathématicien,
-enne *m, f.* **maths** *n (coll)* maths *f pl.*

matinee ['matinei] *n* matinée *f.* **matinée
coat** veste de bébé *f.*

matins ['matinz] *n* matines *f pl.*

matriarch ['meitriaːk] *n* matrone *f.* **matriarchal** *adj* matriarcal.

matrimony ['matriməni] *n* mariage *m.*
matrimonial *adj* matrimonial.

matrix ['meitriks] *n* matrice *f.*

matron ['meitrən] *n* matrone *f; (hospital)*
infirmière en chef *f; (school)* infirmière *f;*
(home) directrice *f.*

matt [mat] *adj* mat.

matter ['matə] *n (substance)* matière *f;*
affaire *f;* contenu *m.* **as a matter of fact** à
vrai dire. **matter-of-fact** *adj (tone)* neutre;
(person) terre à terre. **what's the matter?**
qu'est-ce qu'il y a? *v* importer. **it doesn't
matter** ça ne fait rien.

mattress ['matris] *n* matelas *m.*

mature [mə'tjuə] *adj* mûr. *v* mûrir. **maturity** *n* maturité *f.*

maudlin ['moːdlin] *adj* larmoyant.

maul [moːl] *v* mutiler, malmener.

mausoleum [moːsə'liəm] *n* mausolée *m.*

mauve [mouv] *nm, adj* mauve.

maxim ['maksim] *n* maxime *f.*

maximum ['maksiməm] *nm, adj* maximum.

*may [mei] *v* pouvoir.

May [mei] *n* mai *m.* **May Day** le Premier
mai.

maybe ['meibi] *adv* peut-être.

mayday ['meidei] *n* mayday *m.*

mayonnaise [ˌmeiə'neiz] *n* mayonnaise *f.*

mayor [meə] *n* maire *m.*

maze [meiz] *v* labyrinthe *m.*

me [miː] *pron* moi; *(direct object)* me.

mead [miːd] *n (drink)* hydromel *m.*

meadow ['medou] *n* pré *m.*

meagre ['miːgə] *adj* maigre.

meal[1] [miːl] *n (food)* repas *m.* **make a
meal of** *(labour)* faire tout un plat de.

meal[2] [miːl] *n (flour)* farine *f.*

*mean[1] [miːn] *v (signify)* vouloir dire;
avoir l'intention (de); destiner.

mean[2] [miːn] *n (not generous)* avare;
(unkind) mesquin; *(poor)* minable. **meanness** *n* avarice *f;* mesquinerie *f.*

mean[3] [miːn] *n* milieu *m; (math)* moyenne
f. adj moyen.

meander [mi'andə] *v (river)* serpenter;
(person) errer. *n* méandre *m.*

meaning ['miːniŋ] *n* sens *m,* signification
f. **meaningful** *adj* significatif. **meaningless**
adj dénué de sens; *(senseless)* insensé.

means [miːnz] *n (way)* moyen *m; (wealth)*
moyens *m pl.* **by all means** certainement.
by means of au moyen de. **by no means**
pas du tout. **means test** enquête sur les
ressources *f.*

meant [ment] *V* **mean**[1].

meanwhile ['miːnwail] *adv* en attendant.

measles ['miːzlz] *n* rougeole *f.*

measure ['meʒə] *n* mesure *f.* **made to
measure** fait sur mesure. *v* mesurer. **measurement** *n* mesure *f.*

meat [miːt] *n* viande *f.* **meatball** *n*
boulette de viande *f.* **meat pie** pâté en
croûte *m.*

mechanic [mi'kanik] *n* mécanicien *m.*
mechanical *adj* mécanique. **mechanics** *pl*
n mécanisme *m sing; (sing: science)*

mécanique *f.* **mechanism** *n* mécanisme *m.*
mechanize *v* mécaniser.
medal ['medl] *n* médaille *f.* **medallist** *n* médaillé, -e *m, f.*
meddle ['medl] *v* (*interfere*) se mêler (de); toucher (à). **meddlesome** *adj* indiscret, -ète.
media ['miːdiə] *pl n* media *m pl.*
mediate ['miːdieit] *v* s'entremettre; servir de médiateur. **mediation** *n* médiation *f.* **mediator** *n* médiateur, -trice *m, f.*
medical ['medikəl] *adj* médical. **medical officer** médecin du travail *m.* **medical school** école de médecine *f. n* visite médicale *f.* examen médical *m.* **medicate** *v* médicamenter. **medicated** *adj* (*shampoo, etc.*) médical.
medicine ['medsən] *n* (*science*) médecine *f;* (*drug*) médicament *m.* **medicine chest** pharmacie *f.* **medicinal** *adj* médicinal.
medieval [medi'iːvəl] *adj* médiéval.
mediocre [miːdi'oukə] *adj* médiocre. **mediocrity** *n* médiocrité *f.*
meditate ['mediteit] *v* méditer. **meditation** *n* méditation *f.* **meditative** *adj* méditatif.
Mediterranean [meditə'reiniən] *adj* méditerranéen. *n* Méditerranée *f.*
medium ['miːdiəm] *n* milieu *m;* (*means*) moyen *m;* (*spirits*) médium *m.* **happy medium** juste milieu *m. adj* moyen. **medium-dry** *adj* (*wine*) demi-sec. **medium wave** (*radio*) onde moyenne *f.*
medley ['medli] *n* mélange *m;* (*music*) pot-pourri *m.*
meek [miːk] *adj* doux, douce. **meekness** *n* douceur *f.*
*meet [miːt] *v* (se) rencontrer; (*by arrangement*) (se) retrouver; (*gather*) se réunir; (*expenses, etc.*) faire face à. **meeting** *n* réunion *f,* assemblée *f;* (*appointment*) rendez-vous *m.*
megaphone ['megəfoun] *n* porte-voix *m invar.*
melancholy ['melənkəli] *n* mélancolie *f. adj also* **melancholic** mélancolique.
mellow ['melou] *adj* moelleux, velouté; (*matured*) mûr. *v* mûrir; se velouter; (*person*) s'adoucir.
melodrama ['melədraːmə] *n* mélodrame *m.* **melodramatic** *adj* mélodramatique. **melodramatically** *adv* d'un air mélodramatique.
melody ['melədi] *n* mélodie *f.* **melodious** *adj* mélodieux.

melon ['melən] *n* melon *m.*
melt [melt] *v* (se) fondre. **melting** *n* fusion *f.*
member ['membə] *n* membre *m.* **membership** *n* adhésion *f.* **membership card** carte d'adhérent *f.* **membership fee** cotisation *f.*
membrane ['membrein] *n* membrane *f.* **membranous** *adj* membraneux.
memento [mə'mentou] *n* souvenir *m.*
memo ['memou] *n* (*coll*) note *f.*
memoirs ['memwaːz] *pl n* mémoires *m pl.*
memorable ['memərəbl] *adj* mémorable.
memorandum [memə'randəm] *n* mémorandum *m,* note *f.*
memorial [mi'moːriəl] *n* monument *m,* mémorial *m. adj* commémoratif.
memory ['meməri] *n* (*faculty*) mémoire *f;* (*thing remembered*) souvenir *m.* **memorize** *v* apprendre par cœur.
men [men] *V* **man**.
menace ['menis] *n* menace *f. v* menacer.
menagerie [mi'nadʒəri] *n* ménagerie *f.*
mend [mend] *v* raccommoder, réparer. *n* raccommodage *m.* **be on the mend** s'améliorer. **mending** *n* raccommodage *m.*
menial ['miːniəl] *adj* (*task*) de domestique; (*person*) servile.
meningitis [menin'dʒaitis] *n* méningite *f.*
menopause ['menəpoiz] *n* ménopause *f.*
menstrual ['menstruəl] *adj* menstruel. **menstruate** *v* avoir ses règles. **menstruation** *n* menstruation *f.*
mental ['mentl] *adj* mental; (*coll: mad*) timbré. **mental arithmetic** calcul mental *m.* **mental home** *or* **hospital** clinique psychiatrique *f.* **mentality** *n* mentalité *f.* **mentally** *adv* mentalement.
menthol ['menθəl] *n* menthol *m.*
mention ['menʃən] *v* mentionner. **don't mention it!** il n'y a pas de quoi! **not to mention** sans compter. *n* mention *f.*
menu ['menjuː] *n* menu *m.*
mercantile ['məːkəntail] *adj* marchand; commercial.
mercenary ['məːsinəri] *nm, adj* mercenaire.
merchandise ['məːtʃəndaiz] *n* marchandises *f pl.* **merchandizing** *n* techniques marchandes *f pl.*
merchant ['məːtʃənt] *n* négociant *m,* commerçant *m.* **merchant navy** marine marchande *f.*

mercury ['mɔːkjuri] *n* mercure *m.*
mercy ['mɜːsi] *n* pitié *f*, merci *f*; (*rel*) miséricorde *f.* **at the mercy of** à la merci de. **merciful** *adj* miséricordieux. **merciless** *adj* impitoyable.
mere [miə] *adj* simple. **it's a mere formality** ce n'est qu'une formalité.
merge [mɜːdʒ] *v* se mêler; (*comm*) fusionner; unifier. **merger** *n* fusion *f.*
meridian [mə'ridiən] *nm, adj* méridien.
meringue [mə'ran] *n* meringue *f.*
merit ['merit] *n* mérite *m. v* mériter.
mermaid ['mɜːmeid] *n* sirène *f.*
merry ['meri] *adj* gai, joyeux; (*coll*: *drunk*) éméché. **merry-go-round** *n* manège *m.* **merriment** *n* gaieté *f*; hilarité *f.*
mesh [meʃ] *n* maille *f*; (*network*) réseau *m*; (*gears*) engrenage *m.*
mesmerize ['mezməraiz] *v* hypnotiser.
mess [mes] *n* désordre *m*, gâchis *m*; (*dirt*) saleté *f*; (*mil*) mess *m.* **make a mess of** gâcher. *v* **mess up** salir; gâcher, mettre en désordre. **messy** *adj* en désordre; sale.
message ['mesidʒ] *n* message *m*; (*errand*) course *f.* **messenger** *n* messager, -ère *m, f.*
met [met] *V* **meet.**
metabolism [mi'tabəlizm] *n* métabolisme *m.*
metal ['metl] *n* métal *m.* **metallic** *adj* métallique. **metallurgist** *n* métallurgiste *m.* **metallurgy** *n* métallurgie *f.*
metamorphosis [metə'mɔːfəsis] *n* métamorphose *f.*
metaphor ['metəfə] *n* métaphore *f.* **metaphorical** *adj* métaphorique.
metaphysics [metə'fiziks] *n* métaphysique *f.* **metaphysical** *adj* métaphysique.
meteor ['miːtiə] *n* météore *m.* **meteoric** *adj* météorique; (*rapid*) fulgurant. **meteorite** *n* météorite *m.*
meteorology [miːtiə'rolədʒi] *n* météorologie *f.* **meteorological** *adj* météorologique. **meteorologist** *n* météorologue *m, f.*
meter ['miːtə] *n* compteur *m.*
methane ['miːθein] *n* méthane *m.*
method ['meθəd] *n* méthode *f.* **methodical** *adj* méthodique.
Methodist ['meθədist] *n* méthodiste *m, f.* **Methodism** *n* méthodisme *m.*
methylated spirits ['meθileitid] *n* alcool à brûler *m.*

meticulous [mi'tikjuləs] *adj* méticuleux.
metre ['miːtə] *n* mètre *m.* **metric** *adj* métrique.
metronome ['metrənoum] *n* métronome *m.*
metropolis [mə'tropəlis] *n* métropole *m.* **metropolitan** *adj* métropolitain.
mew [mjuː] *v* miauler. *n* miaulement *m.*
mice [mais] *V* **mouse.**
microbe ['maikroub] *n* microbe *m.*
microfilm ['maikrə,film] *n* microfilm *m.*
microphone ['maikrəfoun] *n* microphone *m.*
microscope ['maikrəskoup] *n* microscope *m.* **microscopic** *adj* microscopique.
microwave ['maikrəweiv] *n* micro-onde *f.*
mid [mid] *adj* du milieu. **mid-June, July, etc.** mi-juin, juillet, etc.
mid-air [,mid'eə] *n* **in mid-air** en plein ciel.
midday [,mid'dei] *n* midi *m.*
middle ['midl] *n* milieu *m.* **in the middle** au milieu. *adj* du milieu. **middle-aged** *adj* d'un certain âge. **the Middle Ages** le moyen âge *m sing.* **middle-class** *adj* bourgeois. **Middle East** Moyen-Orient *m.* **middleman** *n* intermédiaire *m.* **middle-of-the-road** *adj* modéré. **middle-sized** *adj* de grandeur moyenne. **middling** *adj* comme ci comme ça.
midge [midʒ] *n* moucheron *m.*
midget ['midʒit] *n* nain, -e *m, f.*
midnight ['midnait] *n* minuit *m.*
midriff ['midrif] *n* diaphragme *m*; (*waist*) taille *f.*
midst [midst] *n* milieu *m.* **in our midst** parmi nous. **in the midst of** au milieu de.
midstream [,mid'striːm] *n* **in midstream** au milieu du courant.
midsummer ['mid,sʌmə] *n* cœur de l'été *m.* **Midsummer Day** la Saint-Jean *f.*
midway [,mid'wei] *adv, adj* à mi-chemin.
midweek [,mid'wiːk] *n* milieu de la semaine *m.*
midwife ['midwaif] *n* sage-femme *f.* **midwifery** *n* obstétrique *f.*
midwinter [,mid'wintə] *n* milieu de l'hiver *m.*
might¹ [mait] *V* **may.**
might² [mait] *n* puissance *f.*
mighty ['maiti] *adj* puissant; vaste. *adv* (*coll*) rudement.
migraine ['miːgrein] *n* migraine *f.*

migrate [mai'greit] *v* émigrer. **migration** *n* migration *f*.

mike [maik] *n* (*coll: microphone*) micro *m*.

mild [maild] *adj* doux, douce. **mildness** *n* douceur *f*.

mildew ['mildjuː] *n* (*vine*) mildiou *m*; (*plants*) rouille *f*; (*cloth*) moisissure *f*.

mile [mail] *n* mille *m*. **mileage** *n* distance en milles *f*; (*petrol*) consommation aux cent *f*. **mileometer** *n* compteur de milles *m*. **milestone** *n* borne *f*; (*of life, etc.*) jalon *m*.

militant ['militənt] *n, adj* militant, -e.

military ['militəri] *adj* militaire.

milk [milk] *n* lait *m*. **milk chocolate** chocolat au lait *m*. **milkman** *n* laitier *m*. **milk shake** lait parfumé fouetté *m*. *v* traire. **milking** *n* traite *f*. **milky** *adj* laiteux.

mill [mil] *n* moulin *m*; (*larger*) minoterie *f*; (*factory*) usine *f*. **like a millpond** comme un lac. **millstone** *n* meule *f*; (*burden*) boulet *m*. *v* moudre. **mill round** grouiller autour de. **miller** *n* meunier *m*.

millennium [mi'leniəm] *n* millénaire *m*. **the millennium** le millénium *m*.

millet ['milit] *n* millet *m*.

milligram ['mili,gram] *n* milligramme *m*.

millilitre ['mili,liːtə] *n* millilitre *m*.

millimetre ['mili,miːtə] *n* millimètre *m*.

milliner ['milinə] *n* modiste *f*. **millinery** *n* modes *f pl*.

million ['miljən] *n* million *m*. **millionaire** *n* millionnaire *m*. **millions of** des milliers de. **millionth** *n*(*m+f*), *adj* millionième.

mime [maim] *n* mime *m*. *v* mimer.

mimic ['mimik] *n* imitateur, -trice *m, f*. *v* imiter. **mimicry** *n* imitation *f*; (*zool*) mimétisme *m*.

minaret [minə'ret] *n* minaret *m*.

mince [mins] *n* (*meat*) hachis *m*. **mincemeat** *n* hachis de fruit secs, de pommes et de graisse *m*. **mince pie** tarte anglaise au mincemeat *f*. *v* hacher; (*walk*) marcher à petits pas maniérés. **mince words** mâcher ses mots. **mincer** *n* hachoir *m*. **mincing** *adj* affecté.

mind [maind] *n* esprit *m*. **bear in mind** tenir compte de. **go out of one's mind** perdre la tête. **have a good mind to** avoir bien envie de. **in mind** dans l'idée. **make up one's mind** décider. **read someone's mind** lire la pensée de quelqu'un. **to my mind** à mon avis. *v* (*look out*) faire attention (à), prendre garde (à); (*look after*) garder. **do you mind?** cela ne vous fait rien? **I don't mind** ça m'est égal. **never mind** ça ne fait rien.

mine¹ [main] *pron* le mien, la mienne.

mine² [main] *n* mine *f*. **minefield** *n* champ de mines *m*. **mineshaft** *n* puits de mine *m*. **minesweeper** *n* dragueur de mines. *m*. *v* extraire; (*mil*) miner. **miner** *n* mineur *m*. **mining** *n* exploitation minière *f*. **mining town** ville minière *f*.

mineral ['minərəl] *nm, adj* minéral. **minerals** *pl n* (*drinks*) boissons gazeuses *f pl*.

mingle ['mingl] *v* (se) mêler (à).

miniature ['minitʃə] *n* miniature *f*; (*bottle*) mini-bouteille *f*. *adj* miniature; minuscule.

minim ['minim] *n* blanche *f*.

minimum ['miniməm] *nm, adj* minimum. **minimal** *adj* minime. **minimize** *v* minimiser.

minister ['ministə] *n* ministre *m*. **ministerial** *adj* ministériel. **ministry** *n* ministère *m*.

mink [mink] *n* vison *m*.

minor ['mainə] *adj* mineur, -e; (*unimportant*) petit, secondaire. *n* mineur, -e *m, f*.

minority [mai'noriti] *n* minorité *f*. **in the minority** en minorité. *adj* minoritaire.

minstrel ['minstrəl] *n* ménestrel *m*.

mint¹ [mint] *n* (*bot*) menthe *f*.

mint² [mint] *n* Monnaie *f*. **in mint condition** à l'état neuf. *v* battre.

minuet [minju'et] *n* menuet *m*.

minus ['mainəs] *prep* moins. **minus quantity** quantité négative *f*. **minus sign** moins *m*.

minute¹ ['minit] *n* minute *f*. **minutes** *pl n* compte rendu *m sing*. *v* (*meeting*) rédiger le compte rendu de.

minute² [mai'njuːt] *adj* (*tiny*) minuscule; (*detailed*) minutieux.

miracle ['mirəkl] *n* miracle *m*. **miraculous** *adj* miraculeux.

mirage ['miraːʒ] *n* mirage *m*.

mirror ['mirə] *n* miroir *m*, glace *f*; (*mot*) rétroviseur *m*. **mirror image** image invertie *f*. *v* refléter.

mirth [məːθ] *n* hilarité *f*.

misadventure [misəd'ventʃə] *n* mésaventure *f*. **death by misadventure** mort accidentelle *f*.

misanthropist [miz'anθrəpist] *n* misanthrope *m, f*. **misanthropic** *adj* misanthrope. **misanthropy** *n* misanthropie *f*.

misapprehension [misəpri'henʃən] *n* malentendu *m*.

misbehave [misbi'heiv] *v* se conduire mal.

miscalculate [mis'kalkjuleit] *v* mal calculer; se tromper.

miscarriage [mis'karidʒ] *n* (*med*) fausse couche *f*; (*plans, etc.*) insuccès *m*. **miscarriage of justice** erreur judiciaire *f*.

miscellaneous [misə'leiniəs] *adj* divers.

mischief ['mistʃif] *n* malice *f*; (*of child*) sottises *f pl*; (*damage*) mal *m*. **get into mischief** faire des sottises. **make mischief** semer la discorde. **mischievous** *adj* espiègle, malicieux.

misconception [miskən'sepʃən] *n* idée fausse *f*.

misconduct [mis'kondʌkt] *n* inconduite *f*.

misconstrue [miskən'struː] *v* mal interpréter.

misdeed [mis'diːd] *n* méfait *m*.

misdemeanour [misdi'miːnə] *n* incartade *f*; (*law*) infraction *f*.

miser ['maizə] *n* avare *m, f*. **miserly** *adj* avare.

miserable ['mizərəbl] *adj* (*sad*) malheureux; pitoyable; (*wretched*) misérable; dérisoire.

misery ['mizəri] *n* (*sadness*) tristesse *f*; (*wretchedness*) misère *f*; (*coll: person*) grincheux, -euse *m, f*.

misfire [mis'faiə] *v* rater; (*mot*) avoir des ratés.

misfit ['misfit] *n* inadapté, -e *m, f*.

misfortune [mis'foːtʃən] *n* malheur *m*.

misgiving [mis'giviŋ] *n* doute *m*, appréhension *f*.

misguided [mis'gaidid] *adj* malencontreux.

mishap ['mishap] *n* mésaventure *f*.

misinterpret [misin'təːprit] *v* mal interpréter. **misinterpretation** *n* interprétation erronée *f*.

misjudge [mis'dʒʌdʒ] *v* mal évaluer; (*person*) méjuger.

***mislay** [mis'lei] *v* égarer.

***mislead** [mis'liːd] *v* tromper. **misleading** *adj* trompeur, -euse.

misnomer [mis'noumə] *n* nom mal approprié *m*.

misogynist [mi'sodʒənist] *n* misogyne *m, f*. **misogyny** *n* misogynie *f*.

misplace [mis'pleis] *v* mal placer; (*lose*) égarer.

misprint ['misprint] *n* coquille *f*.

miss¹ [mis] *v* manquer; (*long for*) regretter. **miss out** sauter; omettre. *n* coup manqué *m*. **missing** *adj* absent, manquant.

miss² [mis] *n* mademoiselle *f*; (*abbrev*) Mlle.

misshapen [miʃ'ʃeipən] *adj* difforme.

missile ['misail] *n* projectile *m*; (*mil*) missile *m*.

mission ['miʃən] *n* mission *f*. **missionary** *n* missionnaire *m, f*.

mist [mist] *n* (*weather*) brume *f*; (*on glass*) buée *f*. *v* **mist over** or **up** (s')embuer. **misty** *adj* brumeux; embué.

***mistake** [mi'steik] *n* erreur *f*, faute *f*. **by mistake** par erreur. **make a mistake** faire une faute, se tromper. *v* mal interpréter; ne pas reconnaître; confondre. **mistaken** *adj* erroné. **be mistaken** se tromper, faire erreur.

mistletoe ['misltou] *n* gui *m*.

mistress ['mistris] *n* maîtresse *f*; (*teacher*) professeur *m*.

mistrust [mis'trʌst] *n* méfiance *f*. *v* se méfier de.

***misunderstand** [misʌndə'stand] *v* mal comprendre. **misunderstanding** *n* méprise *f*.

misuse [mis'juːs; *v* mis'juːz] *n* abus *m*, usage impropre *m*. *v* abuser de; employer improprement.

mitigate ['mitigeit] *v* atténuer.

mitre ['maitə] *n* (*rel*) mitre *f*; (*carpentry*) onglet *m*. *v* tailler à onglet.

mitten ['mitn] *n* moufle *f*.

mix [miks] *v* (se) mélanger; (*cookery*) préparer; (*salad*) remuer. **mix up** mélanger; confondre; (*person*) embrouiller. **mix-up** *n* confusion *f*. **mixed** *adj* mixte; assorti. **mixed feelings** sentiment contraires *m pl*. **mixed grill** assortiment de grillades *m*. **mixer** *n* (*cookery*) mixer *m*; (*cement*) malaxeur *m*. **mixture** *n* mélange *m*.

moan [moun] *v* gémir; (*coll: complain*) rouspéter. *n* gémissement *m*; (*complaint*) plainte *f*.

moat [mout] *n* douves *f pl*.

mob [mob] *n* cohue *f*.

mobile ['moubail] *nm, adj* mobile. **mobility** *n* mobilité *f*. **mobilize** *v* mobiliser.

moccasin ['mokəsin] *n* mocassin *m*.

mock [mok] *v* se moquer (de); ridiculiser. *adj* faux, fausse; simulé. **mockery** *n* moquerie *f*; travestissement *m*. **mocking** *adj* moqueur, -euse.

mode [moud] *n* mode *m*.
model ['modl] *n* modèle *m*; (*fashion*) mannequin *m*. *adj* modèle; en miniature. *v* modeler; être mannequin; poser.
moderate ['modərət; *v* 'modəreit] *n*, *adj* modéré, -e. *v* (se) modérer. **moderately** *adv* modérément; (*fairly*) plus ou moins. **moderation** *n* modération *f*. **in moderation** modérément.
modern ['modən] *adj* moderne. **modern languages** langues vivantes *f pl*. **modernization** *n* modernisation *f*. **modernize** *v* moderniser.
modest ['modist] *adj* modeste. **modesty** *n* modestie *f*.
modify ['modifai] *v* modifier; modérer. **modification** *n* modification *f*.
modulate ['modjuleit] *v* moduler. **modulation** *n* modulation *f*.
module ['modjuːl] *n* module *m*.
mohair ['mouheə] *n* mohair *m*.
moist [moist] *adj* moite, humide. **moisten** *v* humecter. **moisture** *n* humidité *f*. **moisturize** *v* humidifier; (*skin*) hydrater.
molasses [mə'lasiz] *n* mélasse *f*.
mold (*US*) *V* **mould**.
mole[1] [moul] *n* (*on skin*) grain de beauté *m*.
mole[2] [moul] *n* (*zool*) taupe *f*. **molehill** *n* taupinière *f*.
molecule ['molikjuːl] *n* molécule *f*. **molecular** *adj* moléculaire.
molest [mə'lest] *v* molester; (*law*) attenter à la pudeur de.
mollusc ['moləsk] *n* mollusque *m*.
molt (*US*) *V* **moult**.
molten ['moultən] *adj* en fusion.
moment ['moumənt] *n* moment *m*, instant *m*. **at the moment** en ce moment. **momentary** *adj* momentané. **momentous** *adj* considérable.
Monaco ['monəkou] *n* Monaco *f*.
monarch ['monək] *n* monarque *m*. **monarchist** *n* monarchiste *m*, *f*. **monarchy** *n* monarchie *f*.
monastery ['monəstəri] *n* monastère *m*. **monastic** *adj* monastique.
Monday ['mʌndi] *n* lundi *m*.
money ['mʌni] *n* argent *m*, monnaie *f*. **get one's money back** être remboursé. **get one's money's worth** en avoir pour son argent. **money-box** *n* tirelire *f*. **moneylender** *n* prêteur sur gages *m*. **moneymaking** *adj* lucratif.

mongol ['mongəl] *n*, *adj* (*med*) mongolien, -enne. **mongolism** *n* mongolisme *m*.
mongrel ['mʌngrəl] *n* (*dog*) chien bâtard *m*.
monitor ['monitə] *n* (*device*) moniteur *m*. *v* contrôler.
monk [mʌŋk] *n* moine *m*.
monkey ['mʌŋki] *n* singe *m*. *v* **monkey around** perdre son temps; faire l'idiot.
monogamy [mə'nogəmi] *n* monogamie *f*. **monogamous** *adj* monogame.
monogram ['monəgram] *n* monogramme *m*.
monologue ['monəlog] *n* monologue *m*.
monopolize [mə'nopəlaiz] *v* monopoliser. **monopoly** *n* monopole *m*.
monosyllable ['monəsiləbl] *n* monosyllabe *m*. **monosyllabic** *adj* (*word*) monosyllabe; (*reply*) monosyllabique.
monotone ['monətoun] *n* ton monocorde *m*. **monotonous** *adj* monotone. **monotony** *n* monotonie *f*.
monsoon [mon'suːn] *n* mousson *f*.
monster ['monstə] *n* monstre *m*. **monstrosity** *n* monstruosité *f*. **monstrous** *adj* monstrueux; colossal.
month [mʌnθ] *n* mois *m*.
monthly ['mʌnθli] *adj* mensuel. *adv* mensuellement, tous les mois.
monument ['monjument] *n* monument *m*. **monumental** *adj* monumental.
mood[1] [muːd] *n* humeur *f*. **be in the mood for** avoir envie de, être d'humeur à. **moody** *adj* maussade.
mood[2] [muːd] *n* (*gramm*) mode *m*.
moon [muːn] *n* lune *f*. **moonbeam** *n* rayon de lune *m*. **moonlight** *n* clair de lune *m*. **moonlighting** *n* (*coll*) travail noir *m*.
moor[1] [muə] *n* lande *f*. **moorhen** *n* poule d'eau *f*.
moor[2] [muə] *v* amarrer, mouiller.
mop [mop] *n* (*floor*) balai laveur *m*; (*dishes*) lavette *f*. **mop of hair** tignasse *f*. *v* essuyer. **mop up** éponger.
mope [moup] *v* se morfondre.
moped ['mouped] *n* cyclomoteur *m*.
moral ['morəl] *adj* moral. **moral support** soutien moral *m*. *n* (*fable*) morale *f*. **morals** *pl n* moralité *f sing*. **moralist** *n* moraliste *m*, *f*. **morality** *n* moralité *f*. **moralize** *v* moraliser.
morale [mə'raːl] *n* moral *m*.
morbid ['moːbid] *adj* morbide.
more [moi] *adj* (*larger number*) plus de; (*in addition*) encore de. *pron*, *adv* plus,

davantage; encore. **all the more** d'autant plus. **and what's more** et qui plus est. **even more** encore plus. **more and more** de plus en plus. **once more** une fois de plus.

moreover [mɔːˈrouvə] *adv* de plus; (*besides*) d'ailleurs.

morgue [mɔːg] *n* morgue *f*.

Mormon [ˈmɔːmən] *n, adj* mormon, -e.

morning [ˈmɔːniŋ] *n* matin *m*, matinée *f*. **morning dress** habit *m*. **morning sickness** nausées matinales *f pl*.

Morocco [məˈrokou] *n* Maroc *m*. **Moroccan** *n* Marocain, -e *m, f*; *adj* marocain.

moron [ˈmɔːron] *n* crétin, -e *m, f*. **moronic** *adj* crétin.

morose [məˈrous] *adj* morose.

morphine [ˈmɔːfiːn] *n* morphine *f*.

Morse code [mɔːs] *n* morse *m*.

morsel [ˈmɔːsəl] *n* petit morceau *m*.

mortal [ˈmɔːtl] *nm, adj* mortel. **mortality** *n* mortalité *f*.

mortar [ˈmɔːtə] *n* mortier *m*.

mortgage [ˈmɔːgidʒ] *n* (*loan*) emprunt-logement *m*; (*law*) hypothèque *f*. *v* hypothéquer.

mortify [ˈmɔːtifai] *v* mortifier. **mortification** *n* mortification *f*.

mortuary [ˈmɔːtʃuəri] *n* morgue *f*.

mosaic [məˈzeiik] *n* mosaïque *f*.

Moscow [ˈmoskou] *n* Moscou.

mosque [mosk] *n* mosquée *f*.

mosquito [məˈskiːtou] *n* moustique *m*. **mosquito net** moustiquaire *f*.

moss [mos] *n* mousse *f*. **mossy** *adj* moussu.

most [moust] *adj* le plus de; (*majority*) la plupart de. *pron* le plus; la plupart. *adv* le plus; (*very*) bien, fort. **at most** au maximum. **make the most of** profiter de; utiliser au mieux. **mostly** *adv* surtout, pour la plupart; en général.

motel [mouˈtel] *n* motel *m*.

moth [moθ] *n* papillon de nuit *m*. **clothes moth** mite *f*. **mothball** *n* boule de naphtaline *f*. **moth-eaten** *adj* mité.

mother [ˈmʌðə] *n* mère *f*. **mother-in-law** *n* belle-mère *f*. **mother-of-pearl** *n* nacre *f*. **Mother's Day** la fête des Mères *f*. **mother-to-be** *n* future maman *f*. *v* dorloter. **motherhood** *n* maternité *f*. **motherly** *adj* maternel.

motion [ˈmouʃən] *n* mouvement *m*; (*proposal*) motion *f*. **set in motion** mettre en marche. *v* faire signe. **motionless** *adj* immobile.

motivate [ˈmoutiveit] *v* motiver; (*person*) pousser. **motivation** *n* motivation *f*.

motive [ˈmoutiv] *n* motif *m*; (*law*) mobile *m*. *adj* moteur, -trice.

motor [ˈmoutə] *n* moteur *m*. **motorbike** *n* (*coll*) moto *f*. **motorboat** *n* canot automobile *m*. **motorcyclist** *n* motocycliste *m, f*. **motor racing** course automobile *f*. **motorway** *n* autoroute *f*. **motorist** *n* automobiliste *m, f*. **motorize** *v* motoriser.

mottled [ˈmotld] *adj* tacheté.

motto [ˈmotou] *n* devise *f*.

mould¹ or *US* **mold** [mould] *n* (*shape*) moule *m*. *v* mouler; modeler.

mould² or *US* **mold** [mould] *n* (*fungus*) moisissure *f*. **mouldy** *adj* moisi; (*coll*: *nasty*) moche. **go mouldy** moisir.

moult or *US* **molt** [mould] *v* muer. *n* mue *f*.

mound [maund] *n* (*natural*) tertre *m*; (*artificial*) remblai *m*; (*heap*) tas *m*; (*burial*) tumulus *m*.

mount¹ [maunt] *v* monter (sur). **mount up** s'accumuler. *n* monture *f*; (*for painting*) carton de montage *m*; (*for machine*) support *m*.

mount² [maunt] *n* mont *m*.

mountain [ˈmauntən] *n* montagne *f*. **mountaineer** *n* alpiniste *m, f*. **mountaineering** *n* alpinisme *m*. **mountainous** *adj* montagneux; énorme.

mourn [mɔːn] *v* pleurer. **mournful** *adj* (*person*) mélancolique; (*sound*) lugubre. **mourning** *n* deuil *m*.

mouse [maus] *n, pl* **mice** souris *f*. **mousetrap** *n* souricière *f*. **mousy** *adj* timide; (*hair*) châtain clair *invar*.

mousse [muːs] *n* mousse *f*.

moustache [məˈstaːʃ] *n* moustache *f*.

mouth [mauθ] *n* bouche *f*; (*dog, cat, etc.*) gueule *f*; (*river*) embouchure *f*. **mouth organ** harmonica *m*. **mouthpiece** *n* bec *m*; (*spokesman*) porte-parole *m invar*. **mouthwash** *n* eau dentifrice *f*. **mouth-watering** *adj* appétissant. *v* dire du bout des lèvres. **mouthful** *n* bouchée *f*.

move [muːv] *n* mouvement *m*; (*house*) déménagement *m*; (*game*) coup *m*; (*step*) pas *m*. *v* bouger, (se) déplacer, (se) mouvoir; (*emotionally*) émouvoir; proposer; déménager; (*act*) agir. **move back** reculer; (faire) retourner. **move forward** (faire) avancer. **move in** emménager.

move out déménager. **move over** (s')écarter; (*to make room*) se pousser. **move up** (faire) monter. **movable** *adj* mobile. **movement** *n* mouvement *m*. **moving** *adj* émouvant; mobile; (*pavement, etc.*) roulant.

movie ['muːvi] (*US*) *n* film *m*. **go to the movies** (*coll*) aller au ciné.

*****mow** [mou] *v* (*lawn*) tondre. **mow down** faucher.

mown [moun] *V* mow.

Mr ['mɪstə] *n* Monsieur *m*; (*abbrev*) M.

Mrs ['mɪsiz] *n* Madame *f*; (*abbrev*) Mme.

much [mʌtʃ] *adj* beaucoup de. *pron, adv* beaucoup. **as much** autant (que). **how much** combien (de). **much as** bien que. **so much** tant (de). **too much** trop (de).

muck [mʌk] *n* (*manure*) fumier *m*; (*dirt*) saleté *f*. *v* **muck about** (*coll*) perdre son temps. **muck in** (*slang*) mettre la main à la pâte. **muck out** nettoyer. **mucky** *adj* sale.

mucus ['mjuːkəs] *n* mucus *m*. **mucous** *adj* muqueux.

mud [mʌd] *n* boue *f*. **mudguard** *n* garde-boue *m invar*. **muddy** *adj* boueux.

muddle ['mʌdl] *n* désordre *m*; confusion *f*. *v* brouiller; confondre.

muff [mʌf] *n* manchon *m*.

muffle ['mʌfl] *v* assourdir. **muffle up** emmitoufler. **muffler** *n* cache-nez *m invar*; (*US: mot*) silencieux *m*.

mug [mʌg] *n* chope *f*; (*slang: fool*) poire *f*. *v* agresser. **mugging** *n* agression *f*.

muggy ['mʌgi] *adj* mou, molle.

mulberry ['mʌlbəri] *n* (*fruit*) mûre *f*; (*bush*) mûrier *m*.

mule[1] [mjuːl] *n* (*animal*) mulet, mule *m*, *f*. **mulish** *adj* têtu.

mule[2] [mjuːl] *n* (*slipper*) mule *f*.

multicoloured [,mʌlti'kʌləd] *adj* multicolore.

multilingual [,mʌlti'lingwəl] *adj* polyglotte.

multiple ['mʌltipl] *nm, adj* multiple. **multiple sclerosis** sclérose en plaques *f*.

multiply ['mʌltiplai] *v* (se) multiplier. **multiplication** *n* multiplication *f*.

multiracial [,mʌlti'reiʃəl] *adj* multiracial.

multi-storey [,mʌlti'stɔːri] *adj* à étages.

multitude ['mʌltitjuːd] *n* multitude *f*.

mumble ['mʌmbl] *v* marmotter. *n* marmottement *m*.

mummy[1] ['mʌmi] *n* (*corpse*) momie *f*.

mummification *n* momification *f*. **mummify** *v* momifier.

mummy[2] ['mʌmi] *n* (*coll: mother*) maman *f*.

mumps [mʌmps] *n* oreillons *m pl*.

munch [mʌntʃ] *v* mastiquer.

mundane [mʌn'dein] *adj* mondain, banal.

municipal [mju'nisipəl] *adj* municipal. **municipality** *n* municipalité *f*.

mural ['mjuərəl] *adj* mural. *n* peinture murale *f*.

murder ['mɜːdə] *n* meurtre *m*. *v* assassiner. **murderer** *n* meurtrier, -ère *m*, *f*. **murderous** *adj* meurtrier.

murky ['mɜːki] *adj* sombre; (*water*) trouble.

murmur ['mɜːmə] *n* murmure *m*. *v* murmurer.

muscle ['mʌsl] *n* muscle *m*. **muscular** *adj* musculaire; (*person*) musclé.

muse [mjuːz] *v* méditer, songer. *n* muse *f*.

museum [mju'ziəm] *n* musée *m*.

mushroom ['mʌʃrum] *n* champignon *m*.

music ['mjuːzik] *n* musique *f*. **music centre** chaîne compacte stéréo *f*. **music hall** music-hall *m*. **music stand** pupitre à musique *m*. **musical** *adj* musical; (*gifted*) musicien. **musical box** boîte à musique *f*. **musical (comedy)** comédie musicale *f*. **musical instrument** instrument de musique *m*. **musician** *n* musicien, -enne *m*, *f*.

musk [mʌsk] *n* musc *m*.

musket ['mʌskit] *n* mousquet *m*. **musketeer** *n* mousquetaire *m*.

Muslim ['mʌzlim] *n, adj* musulman, -e.

muslin ['mʌzlin] *n* mousseline *f*.

mussel ['mʌsl] *n* moule *f*.

*****must** [mʌst] *v* devoir. *n* (*coll*) chose indispensable *f*.

mustard ['mʌstəd] *n* moutarde *f*. **mustard pot** moutardier *m*.

muster ['mʌstə] *v* (se) rassembler, (se) réunir. *n* assemblée *f*. **pass muster** être acceptable.

musty ['mʌsti] *adj* de moisi. **smell musty** sentir le moisi.

mute [mjuːt] *adj* muet, -ette. *n* muet, -ette *m*, *f*; (*music*) sourdine *f*. *v* assourdir.

mutilate ['mjuːtileit] *v* mutiler. **mutilation** *n* mutilation *f*.

mutiny ['mjuːtini] *n* mutinerie *f*; révolte *f*. *v* se mutiner; se révolter. **mutinous** *adj* mutiné; rebelle.

mutter ['mʌtə] *n* marmonner. *n* marmonnement *m*.

mutton ['mʌtn] *n* mouton *m*.

mutual ['mjuːtʃuəl] *adj* mutuel; commun.

muzzle ['mʌzl] *n* (*nose*) museau *m*; (*device*) muselière *f*; (*gun*) bouche *f*. *v* museler.

my [mai] *adj* mon, ma; (*pl*) mes.

myself [mai'self] *pron* me; (*emphatic*) moi-même. **by myself** tout seul.

mystery ['mistəri] *n* mystère *m*. **mysterious** *adj* mystérieux.

mystic ['mistik] *n* mystique *m, f*. *adj also* **mystical** mystique; occulte; surnaturel. **mysticism** *n* mysticisme *m*.

mystify ['mistifai] *v* rendre perplexe, mystifier.

mystique [mi'stiːk] *n* mystique *f*.

myth [miθ] *n* mythe *m*. **mythical** *adj* mythique. **mythological** *adj* mythologique. **mythology** *n* mythologie *f*.

N

nag [nag] *v* harceler.

nail [neil] *n* clou *m*; (*anat*) ongle *m*. **bite one's nails** se ronger les ongles. **nailbrush** *n* brosse à ongles *f*. **nail-file** *n* lime à ongles *f*. **nail polish** vernis à ongles *m*. **nail-scissors** *pl n* ciseaux à ongles *m pl*. *v* clouer.

naive [nai'iːv] *adj* naïf. **naivety** *n* naïveté *f*.

naked ['neikid] *adj* nu; dénudé. **nakedness** *n* nudité *f*.

name [neim] *n* nom *m*. **my name is . . .** je m'appelle . . . . **namesake** *n* homonyme *m*. **what's your name?** comment vous appelez-vous? *v* nommer, appeler; donner un nom à. **nameless** *adj* sans nom; anonyme; inexprimable. **namely** *adv* à savoir.

nanny ['nani] *n* bonne d'enfants *f*.

nap[1] [nap] *n* petit somme *m*. *v* sommeiller. **catch napping** prendre à l'improviste.

nap[2] [nap] *n* (*of cloth*) poil *m*.

nape [neip] *n* nuque *f*.

napkin ['napkin] *n* serviette *f*.

nappy ['napi] *n* couche *f*.

narcotic [naːˈkotik] *nm, adj* narcotique.

narrate [nə'reit] *v* raconter. **narration** *n*

narration *f*. **narrator** *n* narrateur, -trice *m, f*.

narrative ['narətiv] *n* narration *f*. *adj* narratif.

narrow ['narou] *adj* étroit. **narrow-minded** *adj* borné. *v* (se) rétrécir. **narrow down** se ramener. **narrowly** *adv* (*only just*) de justesse; strictement.

nasal ['neizəl] *adj* nasal; (*voice*) nasillard. **nasalize** *v* nasaliser.

nasturtium [nə'stəːʃəm] *n* capucine *f*.

nasty ['naːsti] *adj* (*unpleasant*) mauvais, vilain; (*unkind*) méchant.

nation ['neiʃən] *n* nation *f*. **national** *n, adj* national. **national anthem** hymne national *m*. **nationalism** *n* nationalisme *m*. **nationalist** *n* nationaliste *m, f*. **nationality** *n* nationalité *f*. **nationalization** *n* nationalisation *f*. **nationalize** *v* nationaliser.

native ['neitiv] *adj* (*town*) natal; (*language*) maternel; indigène; inné. *n* autochtone *m, f*; indigène *m, f*.

nativity [nə'tivəti] *n* nativité *f*. **nativity play** miracle de la Nativité *m*.

natural ['natʃərəl] *adj* naturel. **naturalism** *n* naturalisme *m*. **naturalist** *n* naturaliste *m, f*. **naturally** *adv* naturellement; de nature.

nature ['neitʃə] *n* nature *f*. **nature study** histoire naturelle *f*. **nature trail** circuit forestier éducatif *m*.

naughty ['noːti] *adj* méchant. **naughtiness** *n* désobéissance *f*.

nausea ['noːziə] *n* nausée *f*. **nauseate** *v* écœurer.

nautical ['noːtikəl] *adj* nautique.

naval ['neivəl] *adj* naval; maritime. **naval officer** officier de marine *m*.

nave [neiv] *n* nef *f*.

navel ['neivəl] *n* nombril *m*. **navel orange** navel *f*.

navigate ['navigeit] *v* naviguer; (*steer*) diriger. **navigable** *adj* navigable. **navigation** *n* navigation *f*. **navigator** *n* navigateur *m*.

navy ['neivi] *n* marine *f*. **navy blue** bleu marine.

near [niə] *adv* près, proche. *prep* près de. *adj* proche. *v* approcher (de). **draw near** s'approcher (de). **in the near future** dans un proche avenir. **nearly** *adv* presque. **not nearly** loin de.

nearby [niə'bai] *adj* proche. *adv* près.

neat [niːt] *adj* net, nette; soigné; (*drink*) sec, sèche. **neaten** *v* ajuster; (*tidy*) ranger.

neatly *adv* avec soin; *(with skill)* habilement. **neatness** *n* netteté *f.*

necessary ['nesisəri] *adj* nécessaire. **if necessary** s'il le faut. **it is necessary** il faut. **necessitate** *v* nécessiter. **necessity** *n* nécessité *f*, chose nécessaire *f.*

neck [nek] *n* cou *m*; *(of shirt, etc.)* encolure *f*; *(of bottle, vase)* col *m*. **neck and neck** à égalité. **necklace** *n* collier *m*. **neckline** *n* encolure *f*. *v (slang)* se peloter.

nectar ['nektə] *n* nectar *m.*

née [nei] *adj* née.

need [niːd] *n* besoin *m*. *v* avoir besoin de; demander. **needless** *adj* inutile. **needy** *nm, adj* nécessiteux.

needle ['niːdl] *n* aiguille *f*. **needlework** *n* travaux d'aiguille *m pl*. *v (coll)* asticoter.

negative ['negətiv] *adj* négatif. *n (gramm)* négation *f*; *(photo)* négatif *m*; *(reply)* réponse négative *f.*

neglect [ni'glekt] *v* négliger. *n* manque de soins *m*. **in a state of neglect** à l'abandon. **neglected** *adj* abandonné. **negligible** *adj* négligeable.

negligée ['negliʒei] *n* négligé *m.*

negligence ['neglidʒəns] *n* négligence *f*. **negligent** *adj* négligent.

negotiate [ni'gouʃieit] *v* négocier; *(obstacle)* franchir. **negotiable** *adj* négociable; franchissable. **negotiation** *n* négociation *f.*

Negro ['niːgrou] *nm, adj* nègre. **Negress** *n* négresse *f.*

neigh [nei] *v* hennir. *n* hennissement *m.*

neighbour ['neibə] *n* voisin, -e *m, f.* **neighbourhood** *n* voisinage *m*. **neighbouring** *adj* avoisinant. **neighbourly** *adj* (de) bon voisin.

neither ['naiðə] *adv* ni. **neither ... nor ...** ni ... ni .... *conj* ni, non plus. *adj, pron* ni l'un ni l'autre.

neon ['niːon] *n* néon *m.*

nephew ['nefjuː] *n* neveu *m.*

nepotism ['nepətizəm] *n* népotisme *m.*

nerve [nəːv] *n* nerf *m*; courage *m*; *(coll: cheek)* toupet *m*. **get on someone's nerves** taper sur les nerfs à quelqu'un. **lose one's nerve** *(coll)* se dégonfler. **nerve-racking** *adj* éprouvant. **nerves** *pl n (coll: before performance)* trac *m sing*. **nervous** *adj* nerveux; *(apprehensive)* inquiet, -ète. **nervous breakdown** dépression nerveuse *f.*

nest [nest] *n* nid *m*. **nest egg** pécule *m*. **nest of tables** table gigogne *f*. *v* nicher.

nestle ['nesl] *v* se nicher, se blottir.

net¹ [net] *n* filet *m*. **netball** *n* netball *m*. **net curtains** voilage *m sing*. **network** *n* réseau *m*. *v* prendre au filet.

net² [net] *adj* net.

Netherlands ['neðələndz] *pl n* **the Netherlands** les Pays-Bas *m pl.*

nettle ['netl] *n* ortie *f*. **nettle-rash** *n* urticaire *f*. *v* agacer.

neuralgia [nju'raldʒə] *n* névralgie *f.*

neurosis [nju'rousis] *n* névrose *f*. **neurotic** *adj* névrosé.

neuter ['njuːtə] *nm, adj* neutre. *v* châtrer.

neutral ['njuːtrəl] *adj* neutre. *n (mot)* point mort *m*. **in neutral** au point mort. **neutrality** *n* neutralité *f*. **neutralize** *v* neutraliser.

never ['nevə] *adj* (ne...) jamais. **never-ending** *adj* sans fin.

nevertheless [nevəðə'les] *adv* néanmoins, malgré tout.

new [njuː] *adj* nouveau, -elle; *(brand-new)* neuf; *(fresh)* frais, fraîche.

new-born ['njuːbɔːn] *adj* nouveau-né.

newcomer ['njuːkʌmə] *n* nouveau venu, nouvelle venue *m, f.*

New Delhi *n* New Delhi.

new-fangled ['njuːfaŋgəld] *adj* nouveau genre.

new-laid [njuː'leid] *adj (egg)* du jour.

newly-weds ['njuːliwedz] *pl n* nouveaux mariés *m pl.*

news [njuːz] *n* nouvelles *f pl*; *(press, TV, etc.)* informations *f pl*, actualités *f pl*. **newsagent** *n* marchand, -e de journaux *m, f*. **newsletter** *n* bulletin *m*. **newspaper** *n* journal *m*. **newsreader** *n* speaker, -erine *m, f.*

newt [njuːt] *n* triton *m.*

New Testament *n* Nouveau Testament *m.*

New Year *n* nouvel an *m*. **Happy New Year!** bonne année! **New Year's Day** le jour de l'an *m*. **New Year's Eve** la Saint-Sylvestre *f.*

New Zealand [njuː'ziːlənd] *n* Nouvelle-Zélande *f*. **New Zealander** *n* Néo-Zélandais, -e *m, f.*

next [nekst] *adj* prochain, suivant; *(adjoining)* voisin. *adv* ensuite. *n* prochain, -e *m, f*. **the next day** le lendemain. **next-door** *adj* voisin, d'à

côté. **next-of-kin** n plus proche parent m.
next to à côté de.
nib [nib] n plume f.
nibble ['nibl] v grignoter, mordiller.
nice [nais] adj beau, belle; agréable;
(kind) gentil, -ille; (food) bon, bonne.
nicely adv bien.
niche [nitʃ] n niche f.
nick [nik] n (notch) encoche f; (cut)
entaille f; (slang: prison) taule f. **in the
nick of time** juste à temps. v entailler;
(slang: steal) piquer; (slang: arrest) pincer.
nickel ['nikl] n nickel m; (US: coin) pièce
de cinq cents f.
nickname ['nikneim] n surnom m. v
surnommer.
Nicosia [nikə'siə] n Nicosie.
nicotine ['nikətiːn] n nicotine f.
niece [niːs] n nièce f.
niggle ['nigl] v tatillonner. **niggling** adj
(detail) insignifiant; (doubt) insinuant;
(pain) persistant.
night [nait] n nuit f; (evening) soir m.
night after night des nuits durant. **work
nights** être de nuit.
night-club ['naitklʌb] n boîte de nuit f.
nightdress ['naitdres] n chemise de nuit f.
nightfall ['naitfɔːl] n tombée du jour f.
nightie ['naiti] n (coll) nuisette f.
nightingale ['naitiŋgeil] n rossignol m.
night-life ['naitlaif] n vie nocturne f.
night-light ['naitlait] n veilleuse f.
nightly ['naitli] adj de tous les soirs. adv
tous les soirs.
nightmare ['naitmeə] n cauchemar m.
night-school ['naitˌskuːl] n cours du soir
m pl.
night-time ['naitˌtaim] n nuit f.
night-watchman [nait'wotʃmən] n veilleur
de nuit m.
nil [nil] n rien m; (sport) zéro m.
nimble ['nimbl] adj agile; (mind) vif. **nimbleness** n agilité f.
nine [nain] nm, adj neuf. **dressed up to
the nines** sur son trente et un. **ninth**
n(m+f), adj neuvième.
nineteen [nain'tiːn] nm, adj dix-neuf.
nineteenth n(m+f), adj dix-neuvième.
ninety ['nainti] nm, adj quatre-vingt-dix.
ninetieth n(m+f), adj quatre-vingt-dixième.
nip¹ [nip] v pincer; (bite) donner un coup
de dent à; (coll: go quickly) faire un saut.

nip in the bud tuer dans l'œuf. n pinçon
m; (bite) morsure f. **nippy** adj (cold)
piquant; (quick) preste.
nip² [nip] n (drop) goutte f.
nipple ['nipl] n mamelon m; (mot) grais-
seur m.
nit [nit] n lente f; (coll) crétin, -e m, f.
nitrogen ['naitrədʒən] n azote m.
no [nou] adv non; (with comparative) ne
... pas. adj aucun, point de, pas de; (on
sign) défense de, interdit. **no-claims
bonus** bonification pour non-sinistre f.
no more or longer ne ... plus.
noble ['noubl] nm, adj noble. **nobleness or
nobility** n noblesse f.
nobody ['noubodi] pron (ne ...) personne. n (insignificant person) rien du
tout m.
nocturnal [nok'təːnəl] adj nocturne.
nod [nod] v faire un signe de tête;
(affirmative) faire signe que oui. **nod off**
s'endormir. n signe de tête m.
noise [noiz] n bruit m; (loud) tapage m.
noiseless adj silencieux. **noisy** adj
bruyant.
nomad ['noumad] n nomade m, f. **nomadic** adj nomade.
nominal ['nominl] adj nominal; (in name
only) de nom.
nominate ['nomineit] v proposer;
(appoint) nommer. **nomination** n proposition de candidat f; nomination f.
nonchalant ['nonʃələnt] adj nonchalant.
nonchalance n nonchalance f.
nonconformist [nonkən'fɔːmist] n(m+f),
adj non-conformiste.
nondescript ['nondiskript] adj quelconque.
none [nʌn] pron aucun.
nonentity [non'entəti] n nullité f.
nonetheless [ˌnʌnðə'les] adv néanmoins.
non-existent [nonig'zistənt] adj non-existant.
non-fiction [non'fikʃən] n littérature non-
romanesque f.
non-resident [non'rezidənt] n (hotel) client, -e de passage m, f.
nonsense ['nonsəns] n absurdités f pl, sottises f pl. **nonsensical** adj absurde.
non-smoker [non'smoukə] n (person)
non-fumeur m; (rail) compartiment
"non-fumeurs" m.
non-stop [non'stop] adj sans arrêt; (train,
flight) direct. adv sans arrêt.

noodles ['nuːdlz] *pl n* nouilles *f pl*.
noon [nuːn] *n* midi *m*.
no-one ['nouwʌn] *pron* (ne...) personne.
noose [nuːs] *n* nœud coulant *m*; (*hangman's*) corde *f*.
nor [noː] *conj* ni.
norm [noːm] *n* norme *f*.
normal ['noːməl] *adj* normal. *n* normale *f*.
north [noːθ] *n* nord *m*. *adj also* **northerly, northern** nord *invar*; au *or* du nord. *adv* au nord. **northbound** *adj* nord *invar*.
north-east *nm*, *adj* nord-est. **north-west** *nm*, *adj* nord-ouest.
Norway ['noːwei] *n* Norvège *f*. **Norwegian** *nm*, *adj* norvégien; *n* (*people*) Norvégien, -enne *m*, *f*.
nose [nouz] *n* nez *m*. **blow one's nose** se moucher. **have a nosebleed** saigner du nez. **nosebag** *n* musette mangeoire *f*. **nose-dive** *n* piqué *m*. **nose to tail** (*cars*) pare-choc contre pare-choc. *v* **nose out** flairer. **nosy** *adj* (*coll*) fouinard.
nostalgia [no'staldʒə] *n* nostalgie *f*. **nostalgic** *adj* nostalgique.
nostril ['nostrəl] *n* narine *f*; (*horse, etc.*) naseau *m*.
not [not] *adv* (ne...) pas; non. **I hope not** j'espère que non. **not at all** pas du tout; (*acknowledging thanks*) de rien.
notable ['noutəbl] *adj* notable. **notably** *adv* notamment.
notary ['noutəri] *n* notaire *m*.
notch [notʃ] *n* entaille *f*; (*belt*) cran *m*; (*wheel, saw*) dent *f*. *v* encocher; cranter; denteler.
note [nout] *n* note *f*; (*short letter*) mot *m*; (*money*) billet *m*. **notebook** *n* carnet *m*. **notepaper** *n* papier à lettres *m*. **noteworthy** *adj* notable. *v* noter; (*notice*) remarquer. **noted** *adj* célèbre.
nothing ['nʌθiŋ] *pron* (ne...) rien; (*with adjective*) rien de. *n* zéro *m*; (*void*) néant *m*. **nothing but** rien que.
notice ['noutis] *n* (*poster*) affiche *f*; (*in newspaper*) annonce *f*; (*warning*) préavis *m*, délai *m*; (*dismissal*) congé *m*; (*resignation*) démission *f*. **notice-board** *n* panneau d'affichage *m*. **take no notice of** ne tenir aucun compte de. *v* s'apercevoir de, remarquer. **noticeable** *adj* perceptible; évident.
notify ['noutifai] *v* (*make known*) notifier, signaler; (*inform*) aviser. **notification** *n* avis *m*, annonce *f*.
notion ['nouʃən] *n* idée *f*.

notorious [nou'toːriəs] *adj* notoire. **notoriety** *n* notoriété *f*.
notwithstanding [notwiθ'standiŋ] *prep* malgré. *adv* néanmoins.
nougat ['nuːgɑː] *n* nougat *m*.
nought [noːt] *n* zéro *m*.
noun [naun] *n* nom *m*.
nourish ['nʌriʃ] *v* nourrir. **nourishment** *n* nourriture *f*.
novel¹ ['novəl] *n* roman *m*. **novelist** *n* romancier, -ère *m*, *f*.
novel² ['novəl] *adj* nouveau, -elle; original. **novelty** *n* nouveauté *f*; innovation *f*.
November [nə'vembə] *n* novembre *m*.
novice ['novis] *n* novice *m*, *f*.
now [nau] *adv* maintenant; (*immediately*) tout de suite. **from now on** à partir de maintenant. **nowadays** *adv* de nos jours. **now and then** de temps en temps. **up to now** jusqu'ici.
nowhere ['nouweə] *adv* nulle part.
noxious ['nokʃəs] *adj* nocif.
nozzle ['nozl] *n* ajutage *m*.
nuance ['njuːãs] *n* nuance *f*.
nuclear ['njuːkliə] *adj* nucléaire.
nucleus ['njuːkliəs] *n* noyau *m*; (*of cell*) nucléus *m*.
nude ['njuːd] *n*, *adj* nu, -e. **in the nude** nu. **nudist** *n* nudiste *m*, *f*. **nudity** *n* nudité *f*.
nudge [nʌdʒ] *v* pousser du coude. *n* coup de coude *m*.
nugget ['nʌgit] *n* pépite *f*.
nuisance ['njuːsns] *n* (*thing*) ennui *m*; (*person*) peste *f*. **be a nuisance** embêter. **what a nuisance!** (*coll*) quelle barbe!
null [nʌl] *adj* nul, nulle. **null and void** nul et non avenu.
numb [nʌm] *adj* engourdi; (*with fear*) transi. *v* engourdir; transir. **numbness** *n* engourdissement *m*.
number ['nʌmbə] *n* nombre *m*; (*of house, page, etc.*) numéro *m*. **number plate** plaque de police *f*. *v* compter; (*house, etc.*) numéroter.
numeral ['njuːmərəl] *n* chiffre *m*.
numerate ['njuːmərət] *adj* **be numerate** savoir compter. **numeracy** *n* notions de calcul *f pl*. **numerator** *n* numérateur *m*.
numerical [njuːˈmerikl] *adj* numérique. **in numerical order** dans l'ordre numérique.
numerous ['njuːmərəs] *adj* nombreux.
nun [nʌn] *n* religieuse *f*.
nurse [nəːs] *n* infirmier, -ère *m*, *f*. *v* (*med*) soigner; (*cradle*) bercer; (*hope*) nourrir. **nursing home** clinique *f*.

nursery ['nɜɪsəri] n (room) nursery f; crèche f; (trees, etc.) pépinière f. **nursery rhyme** comptine f. **nursery school** école maternelle f. **nursery slopes** (skiing) pentes pour débutants f pl.

nurture ['nɜɪtʃə] v (rear) élever; (feed) nourrir.

nut [nʌt] n (bot) noix f; (tech) écrou m. **in a nutshell** en un mot. **nutcase** n (slang) dingue m, f. **nutcracker** n casse-noix m invar. **nutmeg** n muscade f.

nutrient ['njuːtriənt] n substance nutritive f.

nutrition [nju'trifən] n nutrition f. **nutritional** adj alimentaire. **nutritious** adj nutritif.

nuzzle ['nʌzl] v (dog) renifler; (pig) fouiner.

nylon ['nailon] n nylon m.

nymph [nimf] n nymphe f.

O

oak [ouk] n chêne m.

oar [oɪ] n rame f. **oarsman** n rameur m.

oasis [ou'eisis] n oasis f.

oath [ouθ] n (law) sermon m; (expletive) juron m. **take the oath** prêter serment.

oats [outs] pl n avoine f sing. **oatmeal** n flocons d'avoine m pl.

obedient [ə'biːdiənt] adj obéissant. **obedience** n obéissance f.

obelisk ['obəlisk] n obélisque m.

obese [ə'biːs] adj obèse. **obesity** n obésité f.

obey [ə'bei] v obéir (à).

obituary [ə'bitjuəri] n nécrologie f.

object ['obʒikt; v əb'ʒekt] n objet m; (gramm) complément m; (aim) but m. v élever une objection (contre); protester. **objection** n objection f. **objectionable** adj insupportable. **objective** nm, adj objectif.

oblige [ə'blaidʒ] v obliger. **be obliged to** (have to) être obligé de; (be grateful) être reconnaissant à. **obligation** n obligation f. devoir m. **obligatory** adj obligatoire.

oblique [ə'bliːk] adj oblique; indirect.

obliterate [ə'blitəreit] v effacer. **obliteration** n effacement m.

oblivion [ə'bliviən] n oubli m. **oblivious** adj inconscient.

oblong ['oblon] adj oblong, -ongue. n rectangle m.

obnoxious [əb'nokʃəs] adj odieux, détestable.

oboe ['oubou] n hautbois m. **oboist** n hautboïste m, f.

obscene [əb'siːn] adj obscène. **obscenity** n obscénité f.

obscure [əb'skjuə] adj obscur. v obscurcir; (hide) cacher. **obscurity** n obscurité f.

observe [əb'zɜɪv] v observer; remarquer. **observant** adj observateur, -trice. **observation** n observation f. **observatory** n observatoire m. **observer** n observateur, -trice m, f.

obsess [əb'ses] v obséder. **obsession** n obsession f.

obsolescent [obsə'lesnt] adj obsolescent. **obsolescence** n obsolescence f. **built-in obsolescence** désuétud · calculée f.

obsolete ['obsəliːt] adj dépassé, désuet, -ète.

obstacle ['obstəkl] n obstacle m.

obstetrics [ob'stetriks] n obstétrique f. **obstetrician** n obstétricien, -enne m, f.

obstinate ['obstinət] adj obstiné, têtu. **obstinacy** n obstination f.

obstruct [əb'strʌkt] v obstruer; (hinder) entraver. **obstruction** n obstruction f; obstacle m.

obtain [əb'tein] v obtenir, procurer.

obtrusive [əb'truːsiv] adj importun. **obtrusion** n intrusion f.

obtuse [əb'tjuːs] adj obtus.

obverse ['obvɜɪs] n (coin) face f; (statement, etc.) contrepartie f. adj de face; correspondant.

obvious ['obviəs] adj évident.

occasion [ə'keiʒən] n occasion f; (event) événement m. v occasionner. **occasional** adj intermittent. **occasionally** adv de temps en temps.

occult ['okʌlt] adj occulte. n **the occult** le surnaturel.

occupy ['okjupai] v occuper. **occupant or occupier** n occupant, -e m, f. **occupation** n occupation f; profession f; (trade) métier m. **occupational hazard** risque du métier m. **occupational therapy** ergothérapie f.

occur [ə'kɜɪ] v (happen) se produire, avoir lieu; (be found) se trouver; (come to mind) venir à l'esprit (de). **occurrence** n événement m.

ocean ['ouʃən] *n* océan *m*. **oceanic** *adj* océanique.

ochre ['oukə] *n* (*colour*) ocre *m*; (*substance*) ocre *f*.

o'clock [ə'klɔk] *adv* **one o'clock** une heure. **two/three/etc. o'clock** deux/trois/etc. heures.

octagon ['ɔktəgən] *n* octogone *m*. **octagonal** *adj* octogonal.

octane ['ɔktein] *n* octane *m*. **octane number** indice d'octane *m*.

octave ['ɔktiv] *n* octave *f*.

October [ɔk'toubə] *n* octobre *m*.

octopus ['ɔktəpəs] *n* pieuvre *f*.

oculist ['ɔkjulist] *n* oculiste *m, f*.

odd [ɔd] *adj* bizarre, étrange; (*number*) impair; (*from pair*) déparié. **odd jobs** menus travaux *m pl*. **odd man out** exception *f*. **oddity** *n* (*person*) excentrique *m, f*; (*thing*) curiosité *f*; (*oddness*) singularité *f*. **oddment** *n* fin de série *f*.

odds [ɔdz] *pl n* (*betting*) cote *f sing*; chances *f pl*. **be at odds with** ne pas être d'accord avec. **it makes no odds** ça ne fait rien. **odds and ends** bouts *m pl*, restes *m pl*.

ode [oud] *n* ode *f*.

odious ['oudiəs] *adj* odieux.

odour ['oudə] *n* odeur *f*. **odourless** *adj* inodore.

oesophagus [iː'sɔfəgəs] *n* œsophage *m*.

of [ɔv] *prep* de. **of it** *or* **them** en: *j'en ai deux.*

off [ɔf] *adj* absent; (*light*) éteint; (*gas, water, etc.*) coupé; (*cancelled*) annulé; (*food*) mauvais. **a day off** un jour de congé. *prep* de, sur; (*distant*) éloigné de.

offal ['ɔfəl] *n* abats *m pl*.

off chance ['ɔftʃɑːns] *n* **on the off chance (that)** (*coll*) au cas où.

off-colour [ɔf'kʌlə] *adj* **be off-colour** ne pas être dans son assiette.

offend [ə'fend] *v* offenser, offusquer. **offence** *n* (*law*) délit *m*. **take offence** se froisser. **offender** *n* délinquant, -e *m, f*; contrevenant, -e *m, f*. **offensive** *adj* offensant; déplaisant.

offer ['ɔfə] *n* offre *f*. *v* offrir, proposer. **offering** *n* offre *f*.

offhand [ɔf'hand] *adj* (*casual*) désinvolte; brusque. *adv* à l'improviste.

office ['ɔfis] *n* (*place*) bureau *m*; (*post*) fonction *f*. **take office** entrer en fonctions. **officer** *n* officier *m*; (*police*) agent *m*.

official [ə'fiʃəl] *adj* officiel. *n* officiel *m*, fonctionnaire *m, f*; employé, -e *m, f*.

officious [ə'fiʃəs] *adj* empressé.

offing ['ɔfiŋ] *n* **in the offing** en vue; (*naut*) au large.

off-licence ['ɔflaisns] *n* magasin de vins et spiritueux *m*.

off-peak [ɔf'piːk] *adj, adv* aux heures creuses.

off-putting ['ɔf,putiŋ] *adj* (*coll*) peu engageant.

off-season [ɔf'siːzn] *n* morte-saison *f*. *adv, adj* hors-saison.

offset [ɔf'set; *n* 'ɔfset] *v* contrebalancer. *n* (*printing*) offset *m*.

offshore [ɔf'ʃɔː] *adj* (*breeze*) de terre; (*waters*) côtier.

offside [ɔf'said] *n* (*mot: right*) côté droit *m*; (*mot: left*) côté gauche *m*; (*sport*) hors-jeu *m invar*.

offspring ['ɔfspriŋ] *n* progéniture *f*; résultat *m*.

offstage ['ɔfsteidʒ] *adv, adj* dans les coulisses.

off-the-cuff [ɔfðə'kʌf] *adv, adj* au pied levé.

off-white [ɔf'wait] *nm, adj* blanc cassé *invar*.

often ['ɔfn] *adv* souvent. **as often as not** le plus souvent. **every so often** de temps en temps.

ogre ['ougə] *n* ogre *m*. **ogress** *n* ogresse *f*.

oil [ɔil] *n* huile *f*; pétrole *m*. *v* graisser. **oily** *adj* huileux; (*hands, clothes*) graisseux; (*food*) gras, grasse; (*manners*) onctueux.

oilcan ['ɔilkan] *n* burette à huile *f*; (*storage*) bidon à huile *m*.

oilfield ['ɔilfiːld] *n* gisement pétrolifère *m*.

oil-fired [ɔil'faiəd] *adj* à mazout.

oil-painting ['ɔil,peintiŋ] *n* peinture à l'huile *f*.

oil pump *n* pompe à huile *f*.

oil refinery *n* raffinerie *f*.

oil rig *n* (*at sea*) plate-forme pétrolière *f*; (*on land*) derrick *m*.

oilskin ['ɔil,skin] *n* toile cirée *f*. **oilskins** *pl n* ciré *m sing. adj* en toile cirée.

oil-slick ['ɔilslik] *n* nappe de pétrole *f*.

oil-tanker ['ɔil,taŋkə] *n* (*ship*) pétrolier *m*; (*lorry*) camion-citerne *m*.

oil-well ['ɔilwel] *n* puits de pétrole *m*.

ointment ['ɔintmənt] *n* onguent *m*, pommade *f*.

O.K. [ou'kei] *interj* d'accord!
old [ould] *adj* vieux, vieille; âgé; (*former*)
ancien. **he is nine years old** il a neuf ans.
how old is he? quel âge a-t-il? **old age**
vieillesse *f.* **old-age pensioner** retraité, -e
m, f. **old-fashioned** *adj* démodé, vieux jeu
invar. **old maid** vieille fille *f.* **old master**
(*painting*) tableau de maître *m.* **Old Testament** Ancien Testament *m.* **old wives'
tale** conte de bonne femme *m.*
olive ['oliv] *n* (*fruit*) olive *f*; (*tree*) olivier
m. **olive green** *nm, adj* vert olive. **olive oil**
huile d'olive *f.*
Olympic [ə'limpik] *adj* olympique.
Olympic Games Jeux olympiques *m pl.*
omelette ['omlit] *n* omelette *f.*
omen ['oumən] *n* présage *m*, augure *m.*
ominous ['ominəs] *adj* menaçant, sinistre.
omit [ou'mit] *v* omettre. **omission** *n* omission *f.*
omnipotent [om'nipətənt] *adj* omnipotent.
on [on] *prep* sur, à. *adj* (*elec*) allumé;
(*tap*) ouvert. **oncoming** *adj* (*traffic*) qui
approche. **onlooker** *n* spectateur, -trice
m, f. **onset** *n* début *m*; attaque *f.* **onshore**
adj du large. **onslaught** *n* attaque *f.*
onward(s) *adj, adv* en avant. **from now
onwards** désormais.
once [wʌns] *adv* une fois; (*formerly*) jadis.
conj une fois que. **at once** tout de suite.
once again encore une fois. **once and for
all** une fois pour toutes.
one [wʌn] *n, adj* un, une, -e. *pron* un; (*impersonal*) on. **be one up** avoir l'avantage
sur. **one-armed bandit** machine à sous *f.*
one by one un à un. **one-man band**
homme-orchestre *m.* **one-sided** *adj* inégal, partial. **one-way** *adj* à sens unique.
that one celui-là, celle-là *m, f.* **this one**
celui-ci, celle-ci *m, f.* **which one** lequel,
laquelle *m, f.*
oneself [wʌn'self] *pron* se; (*emphatic*) soi-
même. **by oneself** tout seul.
onion ['ʌnjən] *n* oignon *m.*
only ['ounli] *adj* seul, unique. **only child**
enfant unique *m.* *adv* seulement; (ne...)
que. *conj* mais.
onus ['ounəs] *n* responsabilité *f.*
onyx ['oniks] *n* onyx *m.*
ooze [uːz] *v* suinter, exsuder.
opal ['oupəl] *n* opale *f.*
opaque [ə'paik] *adj* opaque; obscur. **opacity** *n* opacité *f*; obscurité *f.*
open ['oupən] *v* (s')ouvrir. *adj* ouvert;

(*meeting*) public, -ique; (*question*) non
résolu. **open-air** *adj* de *or* en plein air.
open-minded *adj* sans parti pris. **open-
mouthed** *adj, adv* bouche bée. **open-plan**
adj sans cloisons.
opening ['oupəniŋ] *n* ouverture *f*; (*door,
window*) embrasure *f*; (*ceremony*) inauguration *f*; (*opportunity*) occasion *f. adj*
inaugural; préliminaire. **opening time**
l'heure d'ouverture *f.*
opera ['opərə] *n* opéra *m.* **opera glasses**
jumelles de théâtre *f pl.* **opera house**
opéra *m.* **opera singer** chanteur, -euse
d'opéra *m, f.* **operatic** *adj* d'opéra. **operetta** *n* opérette *f.*
operate ['opəreit] *v* opérer; (*machine*)
(faire) marcher. **operable** *adj* opérable.
operating theatre salle d'opération *f.*
operation *n* opération *f*; marche *f*, fonctionnement *m.* **in operation** en service;
en application. **operational** *adj* opéra-
tionnel. **operative** *adj* en vigueur; (*med*)
opératoire. **the operative word** le mot
clef. **operator** *n* opérateur, -trice *m, f*;
(*phone*) standardiste *m, f.*
ophthalmic [of'θalmik] *adj* (*nerve*)
ophtalmique; (*surgeon*) ophtalmologique.
opinion [ə'pinjən] *n* opinion *f.* **in my
opinion** à mon avis. **opinion poll** sondage
d'opinion *m.*
opium ['oupiəm] *n* opium *m.*
opponent [ə'pounənt] *n* adversaire *m, f.*
opportune [opə'tjuːn] *adj* opportun.
opportunity [opə'tjuːnəti] *n* occasion *f*,
chance *f.*
oppose [ə'pouz] *v* s'opposer à. **opposed**
adj opposé. **as opposed to** par opposition
à. **opposition** *n* opposition *f.*
opposite ['opəzit] *adj* opposé; d'en face.
the opposite sex l'autre sexe *m. prep* en
face de. *n* opposé *m*, contraire *m.*
oppress [ə'pres] *v* opprimer; (*heat, etc.*)
oppresser. **oppression** *n* oppression *f.*
oppressive *adj* tyrannique; (*tax, etc.*)
oppressif; (*heat*) accablant. **oppressor** *n*
oppresseur *m.*
opt [opt] *v* opter. **opt out** se retirer;
choisir de ne pas participer.
optical ['optikl] *adj* optique. **optical illusion** illusion d'optique *f.* **optician** *n*
opticien, -enne *m, f.*
optimism ['optimizəm] *n* optimisme *m.*
optimist *n* optimiste *m, f.* **optimistic** *adj*
optimiste.

optimum ['optiməm] *nm, adj* optimum.

option ['opʃən] *n* option *f*, choix *m*. **optional** *adj* facultatif.

opulent ['opjulənt] *adj* opulent; abondant. **opulence** *n* opulence *f*; abondance *f*.

or [oɪ] *conj* ou; (*negative*) ni. **or else** ou bien; (*threat*) sinon.

oracle ['orəkl] *n* oracle *m*.

oral ['oɪrəl] *nm, adj* oral.

orange ['orindʒ] *n* (*fruit*) orange *f*; (*tree*) oranger *m*; (*colour*) orange *m*. *adj* (*colour*) orange; (*flavour*) d'orange. **orangeade** *n* orangeade *f*.

orator ['orətə] *n* orateur, -trice *m, f*. **orate** *v* discourir. **oration** *or* **oratory** *n* discours *m*.

orbit ['oɪbit] *n* orbite *f*. *v* orbiter.

orchard ['oɪtʃəd] *n* verger *m*.

orchestra ['oɪkəstrə] *n* orchestre *m*. **orchestral** *adj* orchestral. **orchestrate** *v* orchestrer. **orchestration** *n* orchestration *f*.

orchid ['oɪkid] *n* orchidée *f*.

ordain [oɪ'dein] *v* (*rel*) ordonner; (*fate*) décréter. **ordination** *n* ordination *f*.

ordeal [oɪ'diːl] *n* supplice *m*.

order ['oɪdə] *n* ordre *m*; (*comm*) commande *f*. **in order to** pour. **out of order** en panne. *v* ordonner; commander.

orderly ['oɪdəli] *adj* rangé; méthodique; en ordre. *n* (*mil*) planton *m*; (*med*) garçon de salle *m*.

ordinal ['oɪdinl] *adj* ordinal.

ordinary ['oɪdənəri] *adj* ordinaire, normal; (*average*) moyen. *n* ordinaire *m*. **out of the ordinary** hors du commun, insolite.

ore [oɪ] *n* minerai *m*.

oregano [ori'gaɪnou] *n* origan *m*.

organ ['oɪgən] *n* organe *m*; (*music*) orgue *m*. **organist** *n* organiste *m, f*.

organic [oɪ'ganik] *adj* organique; fondamental.

organism ['oɪgənizəm] *n* organisme *m*.

organize ['oɪgənaiz] *v* organiser. **organization** *n* organisation *f*. **organizer** *n* organisateur, -trice *m, f*.

orgasm ['oɪgazəm] *n* orgasme *m*.

orgy ['oɪdʒi] *n* orgie *f*.

oriental [oɪri'entl] *adj* oriental, d'Orient.

orientate ['oɪriənteit] *v* orienter. **orientation** *n* orientation *f*.

orifice ['orifis] *n* orifice *m*.

origin ['oridʒin] *n* origine *f*. **originate** *v*

être l'auteur de. **originate from** (*person*) être originaire de; (*thing*) provenir de; (*idea*) émaner de. **originator** *n* auteur *m*.

original [ə'ridʒinl] *adj* (*first*) originel; (*idea, play, etc.*) original. *n* original *m*. **originally** *adv* originairement, à l'origine.

ornament ['oɪnəmənt] *n* (*decoration*) ornement *m*; (*vase, etc.*) bibelot *m*. *v* orner, décorer. **ornamental** *adj* ornemental, décoratif.

ornate [oɪ'neit] *adj* très orné.

ornithology [oɪni'θolədʒi] *n* ornithologie *f*. **ornithological** *adj* ornithologique. **ornithologist** *n* ornithologiste *m, f*.

orphan ['oɪfən] *n, adj* orphelin, -e. *v* rendre orphelin. **be orphaned** devenir orphelin. **orphanage** *n* orphelinat *m*.

orthodox ['oɪθədoks] *adj* orthodoxe.

orthopaedic [oɪθə'piːdik] *adj* orthopédique.

oscillate ['osileit] *v* osciller; fluctuer. **oscillation** *n* oscillation *f*.

Oslo ['ozlou] *n* Oslo.

ostensible [o'stensəbl] *adj* prétendu. **ostensibly** *adv* en apparence.

ostentatious [osten'teiʃəs] *adj* prétentieux; exagéré. **ostentation** *n* ostentation *f*.

osteopath ['ostiəpaθ] *n* ostéopathe *m, f*.

ostracize ['ostrəsaiz] *n* frapper d'ostracisme.

ostrich ['ostritʃ] *n* autruche *f*.

other ['ʌðə] *pron, adj* autre. *adv* autrement.

otherwise ['ʌðəwaiz] *adv, conj* autrement.

Ottawa ['otəwə] *n* Ottawa.

otter ['otə] *n* loutre *f*.

***ought** [oɪt] *v* devoir.

our [auə] *pron* nous. *adj* notre; (*pl*) nos.

ours [auəz] *pron* le nôtre, la nôtre.

ourselves [auə'selvz] *pron* nous; (*emphatic*) nous-mêmes. **by ourselves** tout seuls.

oust [aust] *v* évincer.

out [aut] *adj* (*flower*) en fleur; (*light, etc.*) éteint. *adv* dehors. **out loud** tout haut. **out of** en dehors de, hors de; (*through*) par; (*from*) de, sur; (*without*) sans.

outboard ['autboɪd] *n* hors-bord *m*.

outbreak ['autbreik] *n* début *m*, déclenchement *m*.

outbuilding ['autbildiŋ] *n* appentis *m*, dépendance *f*.

outburst ['autbəɪst] *n* explosion *f*, accès *m*.

outcast ['autkɑɪst] *n* exilé, -e *m, f*; proscrit, -e *m, f*.

outcome ['autkʌm] *n* issue *f*; conséquence *f*.

outcry ['autkrai] *n* tollé *m*.

*outdo [aut'duɪ] *v* surpasser.

outdoor ['autdoɪ] *adj* de *or* en plein air. **outdoors** *adv* dehors.

outer ['autə] *adj* extérieur, -e. **outer space** espace cosmique *m*.

outfit ['autfit] *n* (*clothes*) tenue *f*; équipement *m*; (*coll*) équipe *f*.

outgoing ['autgouiŋ] *adj* (*person*) ouvert; (*tide*) descendant; (*train, mail, etc.*) en partance. **outgoings** *pl n* dépenses *f pl*.

*outgrow [aut'grou] *v* devenir trop grand pour; perdre *or* abandonner en grandissant.

outhouse ['authaus] *n* appentis *m*.

outing ['autiŋ] *n* sortie *f*, excursion *f*.

outlandish [aut'landiʃ] *adj* exotique; bizarre.

outlaw ['autloɪ] *n* hors-la-loi *m invar*. *v* proscrire.

outlay ['autlei] *n* frais *m pl*, dépenses *f pl*.

outlet ['autlit] *n* sortie *f*; (*comm*) débouché *m*; (*for emotions, etc.*) exutoire *m*.

outline ['autlain] *n* contour *m*; (*summary*) esquisse *f*. *v* délinéer; esquisser *or* exposer à grands traits.

outlive [aut'liv] *v* survivre à.

outlook ['autluk] *n* perspective *f*; attitude *f*.

outlying ['autlaiiŋ] *adj* périphérique; (*distant*) écarté.

outnumber [aut'nʌmbə] *v* surpasser en nombre.

out-of-date [autəv'deit] *adj* (*ticket, etc.*) périmé; (*clothes*) démodé.

outpatient ['autpeiʃənt] *n* malade en consultation externe *m, f*.

outpost ['autpoust] *n* avant-poste *m*.

output ['autput] *n* production *f*, rendement *m*; (*elec*) puissance fournie *f*.

outrage ['autreidʒ] *n* scandale *m*. *v* outrager.

outrageous [aut'reidʒəs] *adj* scandaleux, outrageant.

outright [aut'rait; *adj* 'autrait] *adv* complètement; catégoriquement; franchement. *adj* complet, -ète; franc, franche; (*winner*) incontesté; (*sale*) au comptant.

outset ['autset] *n* début *m*.

outside [aut'said; *adj* 'autsaid] *adv* dehors,

à l'extérieur. *prep* à l'extérieur de, hors de; (*beyond*) en dehors de. *n* extérieur *m*, dehors *m*. *adj* extérieur, -e. **outsider** *n* étranger, -ère *m, f*; (*horse*) outsider *m*.

outsize ['autsaiz] *adj* (*clothes*) grande taille *invar*; énorme.

outskirts ['autskəɪtz] *pl n* (*town*) faubourgs *m pl*; (*forest*) lisière *f sing*.

outspoken [aut'spoukən] *adj* carré. **be outspoken** avoir son franc-parler. **outspokenness** *n* franc-parler *m*.

outstanding [aut'standiŋ] *adj* exceptionnel; mémorable; (*debt*) impayé.

outstrip [aut'strip] *v* devancer.

outward ['autwəd] *adj* vers l'extérieur; (*appearance*) extérieur, -e. **outward bound** en partance. **outwardly** *adv* en apparence. **outwards** *adv* vers l'extérieur.

outweigh [aut'wei] *v* l'emporter sur.

outwit [aut'wit] *v* se montrer plus malin que; (*dodge*) dépister.

oval ['ouvəl] *nm, adj* ovale.

ovary ['ouvəri] *n* ovaire *m*.

ovation [ou'veiʃən] *n* ovation *f*.

oven ['ʌvn] *n* four *m*. **oven glove** gant isolant *m*. **ovenproof** *adj* allant au four. **oven-ready** *adj* prêt à cuire.

over ['ouvə] *adv* (par-)dessus; (*remaining*) en plus. *adj* fini. *prep* sur, par-dessus; (*above*) au-dessus de; (*during*) au cours de; (*more than*) plus de. **over and over again** à maintes reprises. **over here** ici. **over there** là-bas.

overall ['ouvərɔɪl] *adj* global; total. *n* blouse *f*. **overalls** *pl n* salopette *f sing*.

overbalance [ouvə'baləns] *v* basculer; perdre l'équilibre.

overbearing [ouvə'beəriŋ] *adj* autoritaire.

overboard ['ouvəbɔɪd] *adv* (*fall*) à la mer; (*throw*) par-dessus bord. **go overboard** (*coll*) s'emballer.

overcast [ouvə'kaɪst] *adj* couvert.

overcharge [ouvə'tʃaɪdʒ] *v* faire payer un prix excessif; (*elec*) surcharger.

overcoat ['ouvəkout] *n* pardessus *m*.

*overcome [ouvə'kʌm] *v* surmonter, triompher de. **be overcome by** succomber à.

overcrowded [ouvə'kraudid] *adj* surpeuplé, surchargé. **overcrowding** *n* surpeuplement *m*.

*overdo [ouvə'duɪ] *v* exagérer; (*overcook*) trop cuire.

overdose ['ouvədous] *n* surdose *f*.

overdraft ['ouvədrɑːft] *n* découvert *m*.

***overdraw** [ouvə'drɔː] *v* dépasser son crédit. **overdrawn** *adj* à découvert.

overdue [ouvə'djuː] *adj (payment)* arriéré; *(train, bus)* en retard.

overestimate [ouvə'estimeit] *v* surestimer; exagérer.

overexpose [ouvəik'spouz] *v* surexposer. **overexposure** *n* surexposition *f*.

overflow [ouvə'flou; *n* 'ouvəflou] *v* déborder. *n* débordement *m*; *(of sink)* trop-plein *m*; *(excess)* excédent *m*.

overgrown [ouvə'groun] *adj* envahi, recouvert.

***overhang** [ouvə'haŋ; *n* 'ouvəhaŋ] *v* surplomber; faire saillie. *n* surplomb *m*. **overhanging** *adj* en saillie, en surplomb.

overhaul [ouvə'hɔːl] *v* réviser. *n* révision *f*.

overhead [ouvə'hed] *adv* au-dessus; dans le ciel. *adj* aérien. **overheads** *pl n* frais généraux *m pl*.

***overhear** [ouvə'hiə] *v* surprendre, entendre par hasard.

overheat [ouvə'hiːt] *v* surchauffer; *(mot)* chauffer.

overjoyed [ouvə'dʒoid] *adj* ravi.

overland [ouvə'land] *adj, adv* par voie de terre.

overlap ['ouvəlap; *v* ouvə'lap] *n* chevauchement *m*. *v* se chevaucher.

***overlay** [ouvə'lei; *n* 'ouvəlei] *v* recouvrir. *n* revêtement *m*.

overleaf [ouvə'liːf] *adv* au verso.

overload [ouvə'loud; *n* 'ouvəloud] *v* surcharger. *n* surcharge *f*.

overlook [ouvə'luk] *v* *(miss)* oublier; *(house, etc.)* donner sur; *(ignore)* laisser passer.

overnight [ouvə'nait] *adv* jusqu'au lendemain, pendant la nuit; *(suddenly)* du jour au lendemain. *adj (journey)* de nuit; *(stay)* d'une nuit; *(sudden)* soudain.

overpower [ouvə'pauə] *v* subjuguer; dominer. **overpowering** *adj* irrésistible; suffocant.

overrated [ouvə'reitid] *adj* surfait.

***override** [ouvə'raid] *v* passer outre à, outrepasser; annuler. **overriding** *adj* prépondérant.

overrule [ouvə'ruːl] *v* annuler; rejeter.

***overrun** [ouvə'rʌn] *v* envahir; *(go beyond)* dépasser.

overseas [ouvə'siːz] *adv* outre-mer. *adj* d'outre-mer; *(trade)* extérieur, -e.

overseer [ouvə'siə] *n* contremaître *m*.

overshadow [ouvə'ʃadou] *v* ombrager; *(render insignificant)* éclipser.

***overshoot** [ouvə'ʃuːt] *v* dépasser.

oversight ['ouvəsait] *n* omission *f*. **through an oversight** par négligence.

***oversleep** [ouvə'sliːp] *v* dormir trop longtemps, se réveiller tard.

overspill ['ouvəspil] *n* excédent de population *m*.

overt [ou'vɔːt] *adj* déclaré. **overtly** *adv* ouvertement.

***overtake** [ouvə'teik] *v* *(pass)* doubler, dépasser; *(catch up)* rattraper.

***overthrow** [ouvə'θrou; *n* 'ouvəθrou] *v* renverser, vaincre. *n* chute *f*.

overtime ['ouvətaim] *n* heures supplémentaires *f pl*.

overtone ['ouvətoun] *n* note *f*, sous-entendu *m*.

overture ['ouvətjuə] *n* ouverture *f*.

overturn [ouvə'tɔːn] *v* (se) renverser; *(car)* capoter.

overweight [ouvə'weit] *adj* trop lourd. **be overweight** peser trop.

overwhelm [ouvə'welm] *v* accabler; *(flood)* submerger; *(conquer)* écraser. **overwhelmed** *adj* bouleversé, confus, accablé. **overwhelming** *adj* accablant; irrésistible; dominant.

overwork [ouvə'wɔːk] *n* surmenage *m*. *v* (se) surmener.

overwrought [ouvə'rɔːt] *adj* excédé.

ovulation [ovju'leiʃn] *n* ovulation *f*.

owe [ou] *v* devoir. **owing** *adj* dû, due. **owing to** à cause de.

owl [aul] *n* hibou *m*.

own [oun] *adj* propre. **get one's own back** prendre sa revanche. **on one's own** tout seul. *v* posséder. **own up** avouer. **owner** *n* propriétaire *m, f*. **ownership** *n* possession *f*.

ox [oks] *n, pl* **oxen** bœuf *m*. **oxtail** *n* queue de bœuf *f*.

oxygen ['oksidʒən] *n* oxygène *m*.

oyster ['oistə] *n* huître *f*.

P

pace [peɪs] *n* pas *m*. **keep pace with** marcher de pair avec. *v* arpenter. **pace up and down** faire les cent pas.

Pacific [pəˈsɪfɪk] *nm, adj* Pacifique.

pacify [ˈpasɪfaɪ] *v* calmer, pacifier. **pacific** *adj* pacifique. **pacifism** *n* pacifisme *m*. **pacifist** *n*(*m*+*f*). *adj* pacifiste.

pack [pak] *n* (*group*) bande *f*; (*hounds*) meute *f*; (*cards*) jeu *m*; (*packet*) paquet *m*. **packhorse** *n* cheval de charge *m*. *v* emballer; (*cram*) tasser, bourrer; (*suitcase*) faire; (*for holiday*) faire ses bagages. **packed lunch** panier-repas *m*. **packing** *n* emballage *m*.

package [ˈpakɪdʒ] *n* paquet *m*. *adj* (*deal, contract*) global; (*holiday, tour*) organisé. *v* emballer.

packet [ˈpakɪt] *n* paquet *m*; (*sweets*) sachet *m*.

pact [pakt] *n* pacte *m*.

pad[1] [pad] *n* bourrelet *m*; (*writing*) bloc *m*; (*ink*) tampon encreur *m*. *v* rembourrer, capitonner. **pad out** (*speech, essay*) délayer. **padding** *n* bourre *f*; délayage *m*.

pad[2] [pad] *v* aller à pas feutrés.

paddle[1] [ˈpadl] *n* (*canoe*) pagaie *f*; (*of waterwheel*) aube *f*. **paddle boat** *or* **steamer** bateau à aubes *m*. *v* pagayer.

paddle[2] [ˈpadl] *v* barboter. **paddling pool** petite piscine *f*.

paddock [ˈpadək] *n* enclos *m*; (*racing*) paddock *m*.

paddy-field [ˈpadɪfiːld] *n* rizière *f*.

padlock [ˈpadlok] *n* cadenas *m*. *v* cadenasser.

paediatric [piːdɪˈatrɪk] *adj* de pédiatrie; infantile. **paediatrician** *n* pédiatre *m, f*. **paediatrics** *n* pédiatrie *f*.

pagan [ˈpeɪgən] *n, adj* païen, -enne.

page[1] [peɪdʒ] *n* (*book*) page *f*.

page[2] [peɪdʒ] *n also* **page-boy** (*hotel*) groom *m*; (*court*) page *m*. *v* (*person*) faire appeler.

pageant [ˈpadʒənt] *n* spectacle historique *m*. **pageantry** *n* apparat *m*.

paid [peɪd] *V* **pay**.

pail [peɪl] *n* seau *m*.

pain [peɪn] *n* douleur *f*. **pain-killer** *n* calmant *m*. **pains** *pl n* (*trouble*) peine *f sing*. **painstaking** *adj* assidu, soigné. *v* peiner. **painful** *adj* douloureux; (*distressing*) pénible. **painless** *adj* sans douleur; (*easy*) inoffensif.

paint [peɪnt] *n* peinture *f*. **paintbox** *n* boîte de couleurs *f*. **paintbrush** *n* pinceau *m*. **paints** *pl n* couleurs *f pl*. **paint-stripper** *n* décapant *m*. **paintwork** *n* peintures *f pl*. *v* peindre; (*describe*) dépeindre. **painter** *n* peintre *m*. **painting** *n* peinture *f*; (*picture*) tableau *m*.

pair [peə] *n* paire *f*; couple *m*. *v* (*socks, etc.*) appareiller; (*mate*) (s')accoupler. **pair off** (*people*) s'arranger deux par deux.

pal [pal] *n* (*coll*) copain, copine *m, f*.

palace [ˈpaləs] *n* palais *m*. **palatial** *adj* grandiose.

palate [ˈpalɪt] *n* palais *m*. **palatable** *adj* acceptable.

pale [peɪl] *adj* pâle; (*unnaturally*) blême. *v* pâlir; devenir blême. **paleness** *n* pâleur *f*.

palette [ˈpalɪt] *n* palette *f*.

pall[1] [poːl] *v* perdre son charme (pour).

pall[2] [poːl] *n* drap mortuaire *m*; (*smoke*) voile *m*; (*snow*) manteau *m*.

pallid [ˈpalɪd] *adj* blafard.

palm[1] [paːm] *n* (*of hand*) paume *f*. *v* **palm off** (*coll*) refiler (à). **palmist** *n* chiromancien, -enne *m, f*. **palmistry** *n* chiromancie *f*.

palm[2] [paːm] *n* (*tree*) palmier *m*. **Palm Sunday** dimanche des Rameaux *m*.

palpitate [ˈpalpɪteɪt] *v* palpiter. **palpitation** *n* palpitation *f*.

paltry [ˈpoːltrɪ] *adj* misérable.

pamper [ˈpampə] *v* dorloter, choyer.

pamphlet [ˈpamflɪt] *n* brochure *f*.

pan [pan] *n* casserole *f*.

pancake [ˈpankeɪk] *n* crêpe *f*. **Pancake Tuesday** mardi gras *m*.

pancreas [ˈpaŋkrɪəs] *n* pancréas *m*. **pancreatic** *adj* pancréatique.

panda [ˈpandə] *n* panda *m*.

pandemonium [pandɪˈmouniəm] *n* tohu-bohu *m*.

pander [ˈpandə] *v* **pander to** se plier à.

pane [peɪn] *n* vitre *f*, carreau *m*.

panel [ˈpanl] *n* panneau *m*; (*dress*) panneau *m*; jury *m*; (*radio, TV*) invités *m pl*. *v* lambrisser. **panellist** *n* invité, -e *m, f*; membre d'un jury *m*. **panelling** *n* panneaux *m pl*.

pang [paŋ] *n* serrement de cœur *m*; (*conscience*) remords *m pl*; (*hunger*) tiraillement d'estomac *m*.

panic [ˈpanɪk] *n* panique *f*. **panic-stricken** *adj* affolé. *v* (s')affoler.

panorama [panəˈraːmə] *n* panorama *m*. **panoramic** *adj* panoramique.

pansy ['panzi] *n* pensée *f.*

pant [pant] *v* haleter. *n* halètement *m.*

panther ['panθə] *n* panthère *f.*

pantomime ['pantəmaim] *n* spectacle de Noël *m*; (*mime*) pantomime *f.*

pantry ['pantri] *n* garde-manger *m invar.*

pants [pants] *pl n* slip *m sing*; (*coll: trousers*) pantalon *m sing.*

papal ['peipl] *adj* papal, du Pape.

paper ['peipə] *n* papier *m*; (*news*) journal *m*; (*exam*) épreuve *f*; article *m.* **paperback** *n* livre de poche *m.* **paper bag** pochette *f.* **paper-boy** *n* livreur de journaux *m.* **paper-clip** *n* trombone *m.* **paper-knife** *n* coupe-papier *m invar.* **paper-mill** *n* papeterie *f.* **paper shop** (*coll*) marchand de journaux *m.* **paperweight** *n* presse-papiers *m invar.* **paperwork** *n* écritures *f pl*; (*derog*) paperasserie *f. v* (*room*) tapisser.

paprika ['paprikə] *n* paprika *m.*

par [pa:] *n* pair *m.* **be on a par with** aller de pair avec. **feel under par** ne pas se sentir en forme.

parable ['parəbl] *n* parabole *f.*

parachute ['parəʃu:t] *n* parachute *m. v* descendre en parachute; parachuter. **parachutist** *n* parachutiste *m, f.*

parade [pə'reid] *n* défilé *m*; (*ceremony*) parade *f. v* défiler; (*display*) faire étalage de.

paradise ['parədais] *n* paradis *m.*

paradox ['parədoks] *n* paradoxe *m.* **paradoxical** *adj* paradoxal.

paraffin ['parəfin] *n* paraffine *f*; (*fuel*) pétrole *m.*

paragraph ['parəgra:f] *n* paragraphe *m.* **start a new paragraph** aller à la ligne.

parallel ['parəlel] *nm, adj* parallèle. **parallelogram** *n* parallélogramme *m.*

paralyse ['parəlaiz] *v* paralyser. **paralysis** *n* paralysie *f*; immobilisation *f.* **paralytic** *adj* paralytique; (*slang: drunk*) ivre mort.

paramilitary [,parə'militəri] *adj* paramilitaire.

paramount ['parəmaunt] *adj* souverain, suprême.

paranoia [,parə'noiə] *n* paranoïa *f.* **paranoid** *adj* paranoïde.

parapet ['parəpit] *n* parapet *m.*

paraphernalia [,parəfə'neiliə] *n* attirail *m.*

paraphrase ['parəfreiz] *n* paraphrase *f. v* paraphraser.

paraplegic [,parə'pli:dʒik] *n(m+f),* *adj* paraplégique.

parasite ['parəsait] *n* parasite *m.* **parasitic** *adj* parasite.

parasol ['parəsol] *n* ombrelle *f.*

paratrooper ['parə,tru:pə] *n* parachutiste *m.*

parcel ['pa:sl] *n* colis *m*; (*portion*) parcelle *f.* **parcel office** bureau de messageries *m.* **parcel post** service de colis postaux *m. v also* **parcel up** emballer.

parch [pa:tʃ] *v* (*land*) dessécher; (*person*) altérer. **be parched** (*coll*) mourir de soif.

parchment ['pa:tʃmənt] *n* parchemin *m.*

pardon ['pa:dn] *n* pardon *m*; (*law*) grâce *f. v* pardonner; gracier. *interj* pardon? **pardon?**

pare [peə] *v* réduire; (*fruit*) peler.

parent ['peərənt] *n* père, mère *m, f.* **parents** parents *m pl.* **parental** *adj* des parents. **parenthood** *n* paternité *f,* maternité *f.*

parenthesis [pə'renθəsis] *n* parenthèse *f.* **in parenthesis** entre parenthèses.

Paris ['paris] *n* Paris.

parish ['pariʃ] *n* paroisse *f*; (*civil*) commune *f.* **parish church** église paroissiale *f.* **parishioner** *n* paroissien, -enne *m, f.*

parity ['pariti] *n* parité *f.*

park [pa:k] *n* jardin public *m*; (*of mansion*) parc *m. v* (se) garer. **parking** *n* stationnement *m.* **parking lot** (*US*) parking *m.* **parking meter** parcomètre *m.* **parking ticket** procès-verbal *m.*

parliament ['pa:ləmənt] *n* parlement *m.* **parliamentary** *adj* parlementaire.

parlour ['pa:lə] *n* petit salon *m.*

parochial [pə'roukiəl] *adj* paroissial; (*derog*) de clocher.

parody ['parədi] *n* parodie *f. v* parodier.

parole [pə'roul] *n* (*law*) liberté conditionnelle *f.*

paroxysm ['parəksizəm] *n* paroxysme *m*; (*anger*) accès *m*; (*joy*) transport *m.*

parrot ['parət] *n* perroquet *m.* **parrot fashion** comme un perroquet.

parsley ['pa:sli] *n* persil *m.*

parsnip ['pa:snip] *n* panais *m.*

parson ['pa:sn] *n* pasteur *m.* **parson's nose** croupion *m.* **parsonage** *n* presbytère *m.*

part [pa:t] *n* partie *f*; (*behalf*) part *f,* parti *m*; rôle *m*; épisode *m.* **part exchange** reprise en compte *f.* **part-time** *adj, adv* à mi-temps, à temps partiel. *v* (se) séparer; se quitter. **part one's hair** se faire une raie. **part with** se défaire de. **parting** *n* séparation *f*; (*hair*) raie *f*. **partly** *adv* partiellement.

*partake [paːˈteik] *v* **partake of** prendre.

partial [ˈpaːʃəl] *adj* partiel; (*biased*) partial. **be partial to** avoir un faible pour. **partiality** *n* partialité *f*; (*liking*) prédilection *f*.

participate [paːˈtisipeit] *v* participer. **participant** *n* participant, -e *m, f*. **participation** *n* participation *f*.

participle [ˈpaːtisipl] *n* participe *m*.

particle [ˈpaːtikl] *n* particule *f*; (*dust, etc.*) grain *m*.

particular [pəˈtikjulə] *adj* particulier; méticuleux; (*choosy*) pointilleux. *n* détail *m*. **in particular** en particulier. **particularity** *n* particularité *f*.

partisan [paːtiˈzan] *n* partisan *m*.

partition [paːˈtiʃən] *n* (*in room*) cloison *f*; division *f*, partage *m*. *v* cloisonner; diviser, partager.

partner [ˈpaːtnə] *n* (*comm*) associé, -e *m, f*; (*sport*) partenaire *m, f*; (*dancing*) cavalier, -ère *m, f*; (*marriage*) époux, -ouse *m, f*. *v* être l'associé de; être le partenaire de; danser avec. **partnership** *n* association *f*. **go into partnership** s'associer.

partridge [ˈpaːtridʒ] *n* perdrix *f*; (*cookery*) perdreau *m*.

party [ˈpaːti] *n* (*pol*) parti *m*; (*law*) partie *f*; groupe *m*; (*celebration*) réunion *f*, fête *f*, soirée *f*. **party line** (*phone*) ligne commune à deux abonnés *f*; (*pol*) ligne du parti *f*.

pass [paːs] *v* passer; (*go beyond*) dépasser; (*exam*) être reçu à. **pass away** *or* **on** (*die*) s'éteindre. **pass out** s'évanouir. **pass round** faire passer; distribuer. *n* (*permit*) laissez-passer *m invar*; (*exam*) moyenne *f*; (*mountain*) col *m*; (*sport*) passe *f*.

passage [ˈpasidʒ] *n* passage *m*; voyage *m*; (*corridor*) couloir *m*.

passenger [ˈpasindʒə] *n* passager, -ère *m, f*; (*train*) voyageur, -euse *m, f*.

passer-by [ˌpaːsəˈbai] *n* passant, -e *m, f*.

passion [ˈpaʃən] *n* passion *f*. **passionate** *adj* passionné.

passive [ˈpasiv] *nm, adj* passif. **passiveness** *n* passivité *f*.

Passover [ˈpaːsouvə] *n* Pâque des Juifs *f*.

passport [ˈpaːspoːt] *n* passeport *m*.

password [ˈpaːswəːd] *n* mot de passe *m*.

past [paːst] *nm, adj* passé. *prep* (*time*) plus de; (*beyond*) au delà de; (*in front of*) devant. **ten past four** quatre heures dix. *adv* devant. **go past** passer.

pasta [ˈpastə] *n* pâtes *f pl*.

paste [peist] *n* pâte *f*; (*meat*) pâté *m*; (*glue*) colle *f*; (*jewellery*) strass *m*. *v* coller.

pastel [ˈpastəl] *n* pastel *m*.

pasteurize [ˈpastʃəraiz] *v* pasteuriser. **pasteurization** *n* pasteurisation *f*.

pastime [ˈpaːstaim] *n* passe-temps *m invar*.

pastoral [ˈpaːstərəl] *adj* pastoral.

pastry [ˈpeistri] *n* pâte *f*; (*cake*) pâtisserie *f*. **puff pastry** pâte feuilletée *f*. **shortcrust pastry** pâte brisée *f*.

pasture [ˈpaːstʃə] *n* pâture *f*, pâturage *m*. *v* paître.

pasty[1] [ˈpeisti] *adj* pâteux; (*face*) terreux.

pasty[2] [ˈpasti] *n* petit pâté *m*.

pat [pat] *v* tapoter; caresser. *n* petite tape *f*; caresse *f*; (*of butter*) noix *f*.

patch [patʃ] *n* morceau *m*; (*of colour*) tache *f*; (*on clothes*) pièce *f*; (*of land*) parcelle *f*. **patchwork** *n* patchwork *m*. *v* rapiécer. **patchy** *adj* inégal.

patent [ˈpeitənt] *adj* patent. **patent leather** cuir verni *m*. *n* brevet *m*. *v* faire breveter. **patently** *adv* manifestement.

paternal [pəˈtəːnl] *adj* paternel. **paternity** *n* paternité *f*.

path [paːθ] *n* sentier *m*; (*garden*) allée *f*; (*of river*) cours *m*; (*of missile, etc.*) trajectoire *f*.

pathetic [pəˈθetik] *adj* pitoyable.

pathology [pəˈθolədʒi] *n* pathologie *f*. **pathological** *adj* pathologique. **pathologist** *n* pathologiste *m, f*.

patient [ˈpeiʃənt] *adj* patient. *n* malade *m f*; client, -e *m, f*. **patience** *n* patience *f*; (*game*) réussite *f*.

patio [ˈpatiou] *n* patio *m*.

patriarchal [ˈpeitriaːkəl] *adj* patriarcal.

patriot [ˈpatriət] *n* patriote *m, f*. **patriotic** *adj* (*deed*) patriotique; (*person*) patriote. **patriotism** *n* patriotisme *m*.

patrol [pəˈtroul] *n* patrouille *f*. **patrol car** voiture de police *f*. *v* patrouiller (dans).

patron [ˈpeitrən] *n* (*arts*) protecteur, -trice *m, f*; (*charity*) patron, -onne *m, f*; (*shop*) client, -e *m, f*. **patron saint** saint patron *m*, sainte patronne *m, f*. **patronage** patronage *m*. **patronize** *v* (*comm*) se fournir chez. **patronizing** *adj* condescendant.

patter[1] ['patə] v (footsteps) trottiner; (rain) crépiter. n petit bruit m; crépitement m.

patter[2] ['patə] n (comedian, etc.) bavardage m; (salesman) boniment m.

pattern ['patən] n dessin m, motif m; (sewing) patron m; modèle f. v modeler. **patterned** adj à motifs.

paunch [pɔintʃ] n panse f.

pauper ['pɔipə] n indigent, -e m, f.

pause [pɔiz] n pause f; silence m. v faire une pause, s'arrêter un instant; hésiter.

pave [peiv] v paver. **pave the way** préparer le chemin. **pavement** n trottoir m; (US) chaussée f. **paving** n pavage m, dallage m. **paving stone** pavé m.

pavilion [pə'viljən] n pavillon m.

paw [pɔi] n patte f. v donner un coup de patte à; (coll: person) tripoter.

pawn[1] [pɔin] v mettre en gage. n gage m. **pawnbroker** n prêteur, -euse sur gages m, f. **pawnshop** n mont-de-piété m.

pawn[2] [pɔin] n pion m.

*****pay** [pei] v payer; (attention, compliment) faire. **pay back** rembourser. **pay in** verser. **pay off** (debt) régler; (be worthwhile) rapporter. n paie f. **pay-day** n jour de paie m. **pay rise** augmentation de salaire f. **pay-roll** n registre du personnel m. **pay-slip** n feuille de paie f. **payable** adj payable. **payee** n bénéficiaire m, f. **payment** n paiement m; récompense f.

pea [pii] n petit pois m.

peace [piis] n paix f. **peacemaker** n pacificateur, -trice m, f. **peace offering** cadeau de réconciliation m. **peaceful** adj paisible.

peach [piitʃ] n (fruit) pêche f; (tree) pêcher m.

peacock ['piikok] n paon m.

peak [piik] n pic m; sommet m; (on cap) visière f. **peak hours** heures d'affluence f pl, heures de pointe f pl.

peal [piil] n (bells) carillon m; (thunder) coup m; (laughter) éclat m. v carillonner; (thunder) gronder; éclater.

peanut ['piinʌt] n cacahouète f.

pear [peə] n (fruit) poire f; (tree) poirier m.

pearl [pəil] n perle f; nacre f. v perler. **pearly** adj nacré.

peasant ['peznt] n paysan, -anne m, f.

peat [piit] n tourbe f.

pebble ['pebl] n caillou m; (on beach) galet m. **pebbledash** n crépi moucheté m. **pebbly** adj cailouteux.

peck [pek] v becqueter, picorer; donner un coup de bec à. n coup de bec m; (coll: kiss) bise f.

peckish ['pekiʃ] adj feel peckish (coll) avoir la dent.

peculiar [pi'kjuːljə] adj bizarre; particulier. **peculiarity** n bizarrerie f; particularité f.

pedal ['pedl] n pédale f. v pédaler.

pedantic [pi'dantik] adj pédant.

peddle ['pedl] v colporter; (drugs) faire le trafic de.

pedestal ['pedistl] n piédestal m.

pedestrian [pi'destriən] n piéton m. **pedestrian crossing** passage clouté m. **pedestrian precinct** zone piétonnière f. adj (style) prosaïque.

pedigree ['pedigrii] n pedigree m; (of person) ascendance f. adj de pure race.

pedlar ['pedlə] n colporteur m.

peel [piil] v (se) peler, éplucher. **peel off** (covering, etc.) décoller. n pelure f, épluchure f; (orange) écorce f; (candied) écorce confite f. **peeler** n éplucheur m. **peelings** pl n pelures f pl, épluchures f pl.

peep [piip] n coup d'œil m. v jeter un coup d'œil, regarder furtivement. **peeping Tom** voyeur m. **peep out** se montrer.

peer[1] [piə] v regarder d'un air interrogateur. **peer at** scruter du regard.

peer[2] [piə] n pair m. **peerage** n pairie f. **peerless** adj sans pareil.

peevish ['piiviʃ] adj grincheux, maussade.

peg [peg] n cheville f; (washing) pince f; (coat, hat) patère f; (tent) piquet m. **off the peg** adj prêt-à-porter. v cheviller; (prices) stabiliser.

pejorative [pə'dʒorətiv] adj péjoratif.

Peking [pii'kiŋ] n Pékin.

pelican ['pelikən] n pélican m.

pellet ['pelit] n boulette f; (for gun) plomb m.

pelmet ['pelmit] n (wood) lambrequin m; (fabric) cantonnière f.

pelt[1] [pelt] v bombarder; (coll: rain) tomber des cordes; (coll: run) galoper. n **at full pelt** à toute vitesse.

pelt[2] [pelt] n peau f; fourrure f.

pelvis ['pelvis] n bassin m. **pelvic** adj pelvien.

pen[1] [pen] n plume f, stylo m. **penfriend** n correspondant, -e m, f. **penknife** n canif m. **pen-name** n pseudonyme m.

pen¹ [pen] *n* (*enclosure*) parc *m*. *v* parquer.

penal ['piːnl] *adj* pénal. **penal colony** colonie pénitentiaire *f*. **penalize** *v* pénaliser. **penalty** *n* pénalité *f*, peine *f*; (*sport*) pénalisation *f*.

penance ['penəns] *n* pénitence *f*.

pencil ['pensl] *n* crayon *m*. **pencil-case** *n* trousse *f*. **pencil-sharpener** *n* taille-crayon *m*. *v* crayonner.

pendant ['pendənt] *n* pendentif *m*.

pending ['pendiŋ] *adj* pendant, en suspens. *prep* en attendant; durant.

pendulum ['pendjuləm] *n* pendule *m*.

penetrate ['penitreit] *v* pénétrer. **penetrable** *adj* pénétrable. **penetration** *n* pénétration *f*.

penguin ['peŋgwin] *n* pingouin *m*.

penicillin [peni'silin] *n* pénicilline *f*.

peninsula [pə'ninsjulə] *n* péninsule *f*. **peninsular** *adj* péninsulaire.

penis ['piːnis] *n* pénis *m*.

penitent ['penitənt] *n*, *adj* pénitent, -e. **penitence** *n* pénitence *f*.

pennant ['penənt] *n* banderole *f*.

penniless ['peniləs] *adj* sans le sou.

pension ['penʃən] *n* pension *f*; (*from company*) retraite *f*. **pension book** livret de retraite *m*. **pension scheme** caisse de retraite *f*. *v* pensionner. **pension off** mettre à la retraite. **pensioner** *n* retraité, -e *m*, *f*.

pensive ['pensiv] *adj* pensif.

pentagon ['pentəgən] *n* pentagone *m*. **pentagonal** *adj* pentagonal.

penthouse ['penthaus] *n* appentis *m*. **penthouse flat** appartement de grand standing *m*.

pent-up [,pent'ʌp] *adj* refoulé.

penultimate [pi'nʌltimit] *adj* avant-dernier.

people ['piːpl] *n* peuple *m*. *pl n* gens *m pl*, *f pl*; personnes *f pl*; (*inhabitants*) peuple *m sing*; (*coll*) famille *f sing*. *v* peupler.

pepper ['pepə] *n* (*spice*) poivre *m*; (*vegetable*) poivron *m*. **peppercorn** *n* grain de poivre *m*. **peppermint** *n* (*flavour*) menthe *f*; (*sweet*) pastille de menthe *f*. **pepperpot** *n* poivrier *m*. *v* poivrer. **peppery** *adj* poivré.

per [pəː] *prep* par. **per cent** pour cent. **percentage** *n* pourcentage *m*.

perceive [pə'siːv] *v* percevoir; (*notice*) remarquer.

perceptible [pə'septibl] *adj* perceptible. **perceptibly** *adv* sensiblement.

perception [pə'sepʃən] *n* perception *f*; sensibilité *f*; perspicacité *f*. **perceptive** *adj* percepteur, -trice; perspicace.

perch [pəːtʃ] *n* perchoir *m*. *v* (se) percher.

percolate ['pəːkəleit] *v* passer. **percolator** *n* cafetière à pression *f*.

percussion [pə'kʌʃən] *n* percussion *f*.

perennial [pə'reniəl] *adj* perpétuel; (*plant*) vivace. *n* plante vivace *f*.

perfect ['pəːfikt] *v* pə'fekt] *nm*, *adj* parfait. *v* achever, mettre au point. **perfection** *n* perfection *f*; (*perfecting*) perfectionnement *m*. **perfectionist** *n* perfectionniste *m*, *f*.

perforate ['pəːfəreit] *v* perforer. **perforation** *n* perforation *f*.

perform [pə'fɔːm] *v* accomplir, exécuter; (*theatre*) jouer, donner; (*machine*) marcher. **performance** *n* (*theatre*) représentation *f*, séance *f*; (*of individual*) interprétation *f*; (*sport*) performance *f*; (*of car*) fonctionnement *m*; exécution *f*; (*coll: fuss*) histoire *f*. **performer** *n* artiste *m*, *f*.

perfume ['pəːfjuːm] *n* parfum *m*. *v* parfumer.

perhaps [pə'haps] *adv* peut-être.

peril ['peril] *n* péril *m*. **perilous** *adj* périlleux.

perimeter [pə'rimitə] *n* périmètre *m*.

period ['piəriəd] *n* période *f*, époque *f*; (*school*) cours *m*; (*menstrual*) règles *f pl*. **periodic** *adj* périodique. **periodical** *nm*, *adj* périodique.

peripheral [pə'rifərəl] *adj* périphérique. **periphery** *n* périphérie *f*.

periscope ['periskoup] *n* périscope *m*.

perish ['periʃ] *v* périr; (*rubber, food*) se détériorer. **be perished** (*coll*) crever de froid. **perishable** *adj* périssable.

perjure ['pəːdʒə] *v* **perjure oneself** se parjurer; (*law*) faire un faux serment. **perjurer** *n* parjure *m*, *f*. **perjury** *n* parjure *m*, faux serment *m*.

perk [pəːk] *v* **perk up** (se) ragaillardir. **perky** *adj* vif, éveillé.

perm [pəːm] *n* permanente *f*. **have a perm** se faire faire une permanente.

permanent ['pəːmənənt] *adj* permanent. **permanence** *n* permanence *f*. **permanently** *adv* en permanence, à titre définitif.

permeate ['pəːmieit] *v* pénétrer; (*spread*)

se répandre (dans). **permeable** *adj* perméable.

permit [pə'mit; *n* 'pəːmit] *v* permettre. *n* permis *m*; autorisation écrite *f*. **permissible** *adj* permis; acceptable. **permission** *n* permission *f*; autorisation *f*. **permissive** *adj* tolérant; laxiste.

permutation [pəːmjuː'teiʃən] *n* permutation *f*.

pernicious [pə'niʃəs] *adj* (*med*) pernicieux; nuisible.

perpendicular [ˌpəːpen'dikjulə] *nf*, *adj* perpendiculaire.

perpetrate ['pəːpitreit] *v* perpétrer. **perpetration** *n* perpétration *f*. **perpetrator** *n* auteur *m*, coupable *m*, *f*.

perpetual [pə'petʃuəl] *adj* perpétual.

perpetuate [pə'petʃueit] *v* perpétuer. **perpetuation** *n* perpétuation *f*.

perplex [pə'pleks] *v* rendre perplexe; compliquer. **perplexed** *adj* perplexe. **perplexing** *adj* embarrassant. **perplexity** *n* perplexité *f*; complexité *f*.

persecute ['pəːsikjuːt] *v* persécuter; tourmenter. **persecution** *n* persécution *f*.

persevere [ˌpəːsi'viə] *v* persévérer. **perseverance** *n* persévérance *f*. **persevering** *adj* persévérant.

persist [pə'sist] *v* persister. **persistence** *n* persistance *f*. **persistent** *adj* continuel; (*person*) persévérant, obstiné.

person ['pəːsn] *n* personne *f*. **personal** *adj* personnel. **personality** *n* personnalité *f*. **personally** *adv* personnellement; en personne.

personify [pə'sonifai] *v* personnifier. **personification** *n* personnification *f*.

personnel [pəːsə'nel] *n* personnel *m*.

perspective [pə'spektiv] *n* perspective *f*.

perspire [pə'spaiə] *v* transpirer. **perspiration** *n* transpiration *f*, sueur *f*.

persuade [pə'sweid] *v* persuader. **persuasion** *n* persuasion *f*. **persuasive** *adj* persuasif; convaincant.

pert [pəːt] *adj* impertinent; (*hat*) coquin.

pertain [pə'tein] *v* se rapporter. **pertinent** *adj* pertinent, approprié.

perturb [pə'təːb] *v* perturber.

peruse [pə'ruːz] *v* lire attentivement. **perusal** *n* lecture attentive *f*.

pervade [pə'veid] *v* pénétrer dans, s'étendre dans.

perverse [pə'vəːs] *adj* pervers; obstiné; contrariant. **perversity** *n* perversité *f*; obstination *f*.

pervert [pə'vəːt; *n* 'pəːvəːt] *v* pervertir, dénaturer. *n* perverti sexuel, pervertie sexuelle *m*, *f*. **perversion** *n* perversion *f*.

pessimism ['pesimizəm] *n* pessimisme *m*. **pessimist** *n* pessimiste *m*, *f*. **pessimistic** *adj* pessimiste.

pest [pest] *n* animal familier *m*; (*coll*: *person*) casse-pieds *m*. **pesticide** *n* pesticide *m*.

pester ['pestə] *v* harceler.

pet [pet] *n* animal familier *m*; (*coll*: *favourite*) chouchou, -oute *m*, *f*; (*as endearment*) chou *m*. *adj* favori, -ite. *v* (*coll*) chouchouter; (*slang: sexually*) (se) peloter.

petal ['petl] *n* pétale *m*.

petition [pə'tiʃən] *n* pétition *f*. *v* pétitionner, adresser une pétition à.

petrify ['petrifai] *v* pétrifier de peur.

petrol ['petrəl] *n* essence *f*. **petrol pump** pompe d'essence *f*. **petrol station** station-service *f*. **petrol tank** réservoir d'essence *m*.

petroleum [pə'trouliəm] *n* pétrole *m*.

petticoat ['petikout] *n* jupon *m*; (*slip*) combinaison *f*.

petty ['peti] *adj* mesquin, petit; insignifiant. **petty cash** petite monnaie *f*. **petty officer** second maître *m*. **pettiness** *n* mesquinerie *f*; insignifiance *f*.

petulant ['petjulənt] *adj* irritable. **petulance** *n* irritabilité *f*.

pew [pjuː] *n* banc d'église *m*.

pewter ['pjuːtə] *n* étain *m*.

phantom ['fantəm] *n* fantôme *m*.

pharmacy ['faːməsi] *n* pharmacie *f*. **pharmaceutical** *adj* pharmaceutique. **pharmacist** *n* pharmacien, -enne *m*, *f*.

pharynx ['fariŋks] *n* pharynx *m*. **pharyngitis** *n* pharyngite *f*.

phase [feiz] *n* phase *f*. *v* **phase in** introduire progressivement. **phase out** retirer progressivement.

pheasant ['feznt] *n* faisan *m*.

phenomenon [fə'nomənən] *n*, *pl* -ena phénomène *m*. **phenomenal** *adj* phénoménal.

phial ['faiəl] *n* fiole *f*.

philanthropy [fi'lanθrəpi] *n* philanthropie *f*. **philanthropic** *adj* philanthropique. **philanthropist** *n* philanthrope *m*, *f*.

philately [fi'latəli] *n* philatélie *f*. **philatelist** *n* philatéliste *m*, *f*.

philosophy [fi'losəfi] *n* philosophie *f*. **philosopher** *n* philosophe *m*, *f*. **philosophical** *adj* philosophique; (*resigned*) philosophe. **philosophize** *v* philosopher.

phlegm [flem] *n* flegme *m*.

phlegmatic [fleg'matik] *adj* flegmatique.

phobia ['foubiə] *n* phobie *f*.

phone [foun] (*coll*) *n* téléphone *m*. *v* téléphoner (à).

phonetic [fə'netik] *adj* phonétique. **phonetics** *n* phonétique *f*.

phoney ['founi] *adj* (*coll*) faux, fausse.

phosphate ['fosfeit] *n* phosphate *m*.

phosphorescence [fosfə'resəns] *n* phosphorescence *f*. **phosphorescent** *adj* phosphorescent.

phosphorus ['fosfərəs] *n* phosphore *m*. **phosphorous** *adj* phosphoreux.

photo ['foutou] *n* (*coll*) photo *f*.

photocopy ['foutou,kopi] *n* photocopie *f*. *v* photocopier. **photocopier** *n* photocopieur *m*. **photocopying** *n* reprographie *f*.

photogenic [,foutou'dʒenik] *adj* photogénique.

photograph ['foutəgraɪf] *n* photographie *f*. **photograph album** album de photos *m*. *v* photographier. **photographer** *n* photographe *m*, *f*. **photographic** *adj* photographique. **photography** *n* photographie *f*.

phrase [freiz] *n* expression *f*; (*gramm*) locution *f*; (*music*) phrase *f*. **phrase-book** *n* recueil d'expressions *m*. *v* exprimer.

physical ['fizikəl] *adj* physique. *n* (*coll*) examen médical *m*.

physician [fi'ziʃən] *n* médecin *m*.

physics ['fiziks] *n* physique *f*. **physicist** *n* physicien, -enne *m*, *f*.

physiology [,fizi'olədʒi] *n* physiologie *f*. **physiological** *adj* physiologique. **physiologist** *n* physiologiste *m*, *f*.

physiotherapy [,fiziou'θerəpi] *n* kinésithérapie *f*. **physiotherapist** *n* kinésithérapeute *m*, *f*.

physique [fi'ziːk] *n* constitution *f*; (*appearance*) physique *m*.

piano [pi'anou] *n* piano *m*. **pianist** *n* pianiste *m*, *f*.

piccolo ['pikəlou] *n* piccolo *m*.

pick¹ [pik] *n* choix *m*; (*best*) meilleur, -e *m*, *f*. **take one's pick** faire son choix. *v* choisir; (*fruit*, *flowers*) cueillir; (*lock*) crocheter. **pick at** (*food*) chipoter. **pick-**

me-up *n* (*coll*) remontant *m*. **pick out** choisir; distinguer; (*highlight*) rehausser.

pickpocket *n* pick-pocket *m*. **pick up** ramasser; (*collect*) passer prendre; s'améliorer; (*learn*) apprendre; (*coll: arrest*) cueillir.

pick² [pik] *n* (*tool*) pioche *f*.

picket ['pikit] *n* piquet *m*. **picket line** cordon de piquet de grève *m*. *v* organiser un piquet de grève; mettre un piquet de grève.

pickle ['pikl] *v* conserver dans du vinaigre. **pickles** *pl n* pickles *m pl*.

picnic ['piknik] *n* pique-nique *m*. *v* pique-niquer. **picnicker** *n* pique-niqueur, -euse *m*, *f*.

pictorial [pik'toːriəl] *adj* en images; illustré.

picture ['piktʃə] *n* image *f*; (*painting*) tableau *m*. **picture frame** cadre *m*. **picture rail** cimaise *f*. **pictures** *pl n* (*coll*) cinéma *m*. **picture window** fenêtre panoramique *f*. *v* (s')imaginer; décrire.

picturesque [piktʃə'resk] *adj* pittoresque.

pidgin ['pidʒən] *n* pidgin *m*. **pidgin French** petit-nègre *m*.

pie [pai] *n* tourte *f*, pâté en croûte *m*.

piece [piːs] *n* morceau *m*; (*item*) pièce *f*. **piecemeal** *adv* par bribes, petit à petit. **piecework** *n* travail à la pièce *m*. *v* **piece together** rassembler.

pier [piə] *n* jetée *f*; (*landing-stage*) appontement *m*.

pierce [piəs] *v* percer, transpercer. **piercing** *adj* perçant; glacial.

piety ['paiəti] *n* piété *f*.

pig [pig] *n* cochon *m*. **pigheaded** *adj* entêté. **pig-iron** *n* saumon de fonte *m*. **pigskin** *n* peau de porc *f*. **pigsty** *n* porcherie *f*. **pigtail** *n* natte *f*.

pigeon ['pidʒən] *n* pigeon *m*. **pigeon-hole** *n* casier *m*.

pigment ['pigmənt] *n* pigment *m*. **pigmentation** *n* pigmentation *f*. **pigmented** *adj* pigmenté.

pike [paik] *n* (*fish*) brochet *m*.

pilchard ['piltʃəd] *n* pilchard *m*.

pile¹ [pail] *n* (*heap*) pile *f*, tas *m*. **piles of** (*coll*) des masses de. *v* empiler, entasser. **pile up** (s')amonceler. **pile-up** *n* carambolage *m*.

pile² [pail] *n* (*post*) pieu *m*.

pile³ [pail] *n* (*of carpet*, *etc.*) poils *m pl*.

piles [pailz] *pl n* (*med*) hémorroïdes *f pl*.

pilfer ['pilfə] (*coll*) v chaparder. **pilfering** n chapardage m.

pilgrim ['pilgrim] n pèlerin m. **pilgrimage** n pèlerinage m.

pill [pil] n pilule f.

pillage ['pilidʒ] n pillage m. v piller.

pillar ['pilə] n pilier m. colonne f. **pillar-box** n boîte aux lettres f.

pillion ['piljən] n siège arrière m.

pillow ['pilou] n oreiller m. **pillowcase** n taie d'oreiller f.

pilot ['pailət] n pilote m. **pilot-light** n veilleuse f. **pilot scheme** projet-pilote m. v piloter.

pimento [pi'mentou] n piment m.

pimp [pimp] n souteneur m.

pimple ['pimpl] n bouton m. **pimply** adj boutonneux.

pin [pin] n épingle f; (*tech*) goupille f; (*elec: in plug*) fiche f. **have pins and needles** avoir des fourmis. **pin-ball** n flipper m. **pincushion** n pelote à épingles f. **pin money** argent de poche m. **pinpoint** v mettre le doigt sur. **pin-stripe** n rayure très fine f. v épingler. **pin down** coincer. **pin up** (*notice*) afficher. **pin-up** n pin-up f invar.

pinafore ['pinəfo:] n (*apron*) tablier m. **pinafore dress** robe-chasuble f.

pincers ['pinsəz] pl n (*tool*) tenailles f pl; (*of crab*) pinces f pl.

pinch [pintʃ] n pincement m; (*of salt*) pincée f. **at a pinch** au besoin. v pincer; (*shoes, etc.*) serrer; (*coll: steal*) chiper.

pine¹ [pain] n pin m. **pine-cone** n pomme de pin f.

pine² [pain] v languir. **pine for** désirer ardemment.

pineapple ['painapl] n ananas m.

ping-pong ['piŋpoŋ] n ping-pong m. **ping-pong ball** balle de ping-pong f.

pinion¹ ['pinjən] n aileron m. v lier.

pinion² ['pinjən] n (*tech*) pignon m.

pink [piŋk] n (*colour*) rose m; (*flower*) œillet m. adj rose.

pinnacle ['pinəkl] n pinacle m.

pioneer [,paiə'niə] n pionnier m; explorateur, -trice m, f.

pious ['paiəs] adj pieux.

pip¹ [pip] n (*seed*) pépin m.

pip² [pip] n (*phone, etc.*) top m. **the pips** le bip-bip m sing.

pipe [paip] n (*water, etc.*) tuyau m; tube m; (*for smoking*) pipe f; (*music*) pipeau m. **pipe-cleaner** n cure-pipe m. **pipeline** n pipeline m. **in the pipeline** en route. v transporter par tuyau. **pipe down** (*coll*) mettre la sourdine. **piping** n tuyauterie f; (*sewing*) passepoil m.

piquant ['pi:kənt] adj piquant. **piquancy** n (*taste*) goût piquant m; (*of story*) piquant m.

pique [pi:k] n dépit m. v dépiter.

pirate ['paiərət] n pirate m; (*comm*) contrefacteur m. v contrefaire. piller. **piracy** n piraterie f; contrefaçon f; pillage m.

pirouette [piru'et] n pirouette f. v pirouetter.

Pisces ['paisi:z] n Poissons m pl.

piss [pis] (*impol*) v pisser. n pisse f. **piss off!** fous-moi le camp! **pissed** adj (*drunk*) bituré. **be pissed off** en avoir marre.

pistachio [pi'staːʃiou] n pistache f.

pistol ['pistl] n pistolet m.

piston ['pistən] n piston m.

pit [pit] n fosse f; mine f; (*hole*) trou m; (*theatre*) orchestre m. v trouer, grêler. **pit one's wits against** se mesurer avec.

pitch¹ [pitʃ] n (*throw*) lancement m; degré m; (*music*) ton m; (*sport*) terrain m. v lancer; (*music*) donner le ton de; (*tent*) dresser; (*fall*) tomber. **pitchfork** n fourche à foin f.

pitch² [pitʃ] n poix f. **pitch-black** adj noir ébène invar.

pitfall ['pitfo:l] n piège m.

pith [piθ] n (*of orange*) peau blanche f; (*of plant*) moelle f; essence f. **pithy** adj concis, piquant.

pittance ['pitəns] n maigre revenu m.

pituitary [pi'tju:itəri] adj pituitaire.

pity ['piti] n pitié f; (*shame*) dommage m. **take pity on** avoir pitié de. **what a pity!** quel dommage! v plaindre. **piteous** adj pitoyable. **pitiful** adj pitoyable; (*bad*) lamentable. **pitiless** adj sans pitié. **pitying** adj compatissant.

pivot ['pivət] n pivot m. v (faire) pivoter.

placard ['plakaːd] n affiche f. v placarder.

placate [plə'keit] v calmer.

place [pleis] n endroit m, lieu m; (*seat, position*) place f. **all over the place** partout. **out of place** déplacé; (*remark*) hors de propos. **take place** avoir lieu. v placer, mettre; situer; (*order*) passer.

placenta [plə'sentə] n placenta m.

placid ['plasid] adj placide. **placidity** n placidité f.

plagiarize ['pleidʒəraiz] v plagier. **plagiarism** n plagiat m. **plagiarist** n plagiaire m, f.

plague [pleig] n peste f; (nuisance) fléau m. v harceler, tourmenter.

plaice [pleis] n carrelet m.

plaid [plad] n tissu écossais m. adj écossais.

plain [plein] adj clair; simple; (not patterned) uni; sans beauté; (utter) pur. **plain-clothes** adj en civil. n plaine f.

plaintiff ['pleintif] n demandeur, -eresse m, f.

plaintive ['pleintiv] adj plaintif.

plait [plat] n natte f, tresse f. v natter, tresser.

plan [plan] n plan m, projet m. v projeter; organiser; préparer à l'avance. **planning** n planification f; (comm) planning m. **planning permission** permis de construire m.

plane¹ [plein] n (level) plan m; (coll: aeroplane) avion m. adj plan.

plane² [plein] n (tool) rabot. v raboter.

planet ['planit] n planète f. **planetarium** n planétarium m. **planetary** adj planétaire.

plank [plaŋk] n planche f.

plankton ['plaŋktən] n plancton m.

plant [plaint] n (bot) plante f; (tech) matériel m, installation f; (factory) usine f. v planter; (hide) cacher. **plantation** n plantation f.

plaque [plaik] n plaque f.

plasma ['plazmə] n plasma m.

plaster ['plaistə] n plâtre m; (for wound) sparadrap m. **plaster of Paris** plâtre de moulage m. v plâtrer; couvrir. **plasterer** n plâtrier m.

plastic ['plastik] nm, adj plastique. **plastic surgery** chirurgie esthétique f.

plate [pleit] n (dish) assiette f; (of metal) plaque f; (in book) gravure f. v plaquer; (silver) argenter; (gold) dorer. **plateful** n assiettée f.

plateau ['platou] n plateau m.

platform ['platfoɪm] n plate-forme f; (in hall) estrade f, tribune f; (rail) quai m. **platform-soled** adj (shoes) à semelles compensées. **platform ticket** billet de quai m.

platinum ['platinəm] n platine f.

platonic [plə'tonik] adj platonique.

platoon [plə'tuɪn] n (mil) section f.

plausible ['plɔɪzəbl] adj plausible; (person) convaincant. **plausibility** n plausibilité f.

play [plei] n jeu m; (theatre) pièce f. v jouer. **player** n joueur, -euse m, f. **playful** adj enjoué. **playfulness** n enjouement m, badinage m.

play-back ['pleibak] n réécoute f. **play back** v réécouter.

playboy ['pleiboi] n playboy m.

playground ['pleigraund] n cour de récréation f.

play-group ['pleigruɪp] n garderie f.

playing card n carte à jouer f.

playing field n terrain de sport m.

playmate ['pleimeit] n camarade m, f.

play-pen ['pleipen] n parc m.

plaything ['plei θiŋ] n jouet m.

playtime ['pleitaim] n récréation f.

playwright ['pleirait] n dramaturge m.

plea [pliɪ] n appel m; (law) argument m; excuse f.

plead [pliɪd] v supplier, implorer; (law) plaider; (as excuse) alléguer.

pleasant ['pleznt] adj agréable.

please [plitz] v plaire (à). **please oneself** faire comme on veut. adv s'il vous plaît. **pleased** adj content. **pleasing** adj plaisant.

pleasure ['pleʒə] n plaisir m. **pleasure boat** bateau de plaisance m. **pleasurable** adj agréable.

pleat [pliɪt] n pli m. v plisser.

plectrum ['plektrəm] n plectre m.

pledge [pledʒ] n gage m; promesse f. v engager; promettre.

plenty ['plenti] n abondance f. **plenty of** bien assez de. **plentiful** adj abondant, copieux.

pleurisy ['pluərisi] n pleurésie f.

pliable ['plaiəbl] adj flexible; (person) souple. **pliability** n flexibilité f; souplesse f.

pliers ['plaiəz] pl n pinces f pl, tenailles f pl.

plight [plait] n état critique m, crise f.

plimsoll ['plimsəl] n tennis m.

plod [plod] v marcher d'un pas lourd; (coll: work) bûcher. **plod on** persévérer. **plodder** n (coll) bûcheur m.

plonk [ploŋk] n (coll) vin ordinaire m.

plop [plop] n ploc m. v faire ploc.

plot¹ [plot] n (story, etc) intrigue f; (conspiracy) complot m. v comploter; (route) déterminer.

plot² [plot] n (land) terrain m, lotissement m.

plough [plau] *n* charrue *f.* *v* labourer; (*furrow*) creuser. **ploughing** *n* labour *m.*

pluck [plʌk] *n* courage *m.* *v* (*music*) pincer; (*fruit*) cueillir; (*fowl*) plumer; (*eyebrows*) épiler. **pluck out** arracher. **pluck up courage** prendre son courage à deux mains. **plucky** *adj* courageux.

plug [plʌg] *n* (*stopper*) bouchon *m,* tampon *m;* (*sink, bath*) bonde *f;* (*elec*) fiche *f;* (*mot*) bougie *f.* *v* boucher. **plug in** (se) brancher.

plum [plʌm] *n* (*fruit*) prune *f;* (*tree*) prunier *m.* *adj* (*colour*) lie de vin *invar.* **plum pudding** pudding *m.*

plumage ['pluːmidʒ] *n* plumage *m.*

plumb [plʌm] *n* plomb *m.* **plumbline** *n* fil à plomb *m.* *adj* vertical. *adv* en plein. *v* sonder. **plumb in** faire le raccordement de. **plumber** *n* plombier *m.* **plumbing** *n* plomberie *f.*

plume [pluːm] *n* plume *f;* (*smoke*) panache *m.* *v* lisser.

plummet ['plʌmit] *n* plomb *m.* *v* plonger; (*price, etc.*) dégringoler.

plump¹ [plʌmp] *adj* grassouillet, -ette, potelé. **plumpness** *n* rondeur *f.*

plump² [plʌmp] *v* tomber lourdement. **plump for** se décider pour.

plunder ['plʌndə] *v* piller. *n* (*loot*) butin *m.* **plunderer** *n* pillard *m.* **plundering** *n* pillage *m.*

plunge [plʌndʒ] *n* plongeon *m;* (*fall*) chute *f.* **take the plunge** se jeter à l'eau. *v* plonger; (*rush*) se jeter; (*fall*) tomber.

pluperfect [pluːˈpəfikt] *n* plus-que-parfait *m.*

plural ['pluərəl] *nm, adj* pluriel.

plus [plʌs] *nm, prep* plus. *adj* positif.

plush [plʌʃ] *n* peluche *f.* *adj* pelucheux; (*coll*) rupin.

ply¹ [plai] *v* (*tool*) manier; (*trade*) exercer; (*with questions, etc.*) presser; (*ship, etc.*) faire la navette.

ply² [plai] *n* (*wood*) feuille *f;* (*wool*) fil *m;* (*rope*) brin *m.* **plywood** *n* contre-plaqué *m.*

pneumatic [njuˈmatik] *adj* pneumatique. **pneumatic drill** marteau-piqueur *m.*

pneumonia [njuˈmouniə] *n* pneumonie *f.*

poach¹ [poutʃ] *v* braconner. **poacher** *n* braconnier *m.* **poaching** *n* braconnage *m.*

poach² [poutʃ] *v* (*egg*) pocher.

pocket ['pokit] *n* poche *f.* **pocket-money** *n* argent de poche *m.* *v* empocher.

pod [pod] *n* cosse *f.*

podgy ['podʒi] *adj* (*coll*) rondelet.

poem ['pouim] *n* poème *m.*

poet ['pouit] *n* poète *m.* **poetess** *n* poétesse *f.* **poetic** *adj* poétique. **poetry** *n* poésie *f.*

poignant ['poinjənt] *adj* poignant.

point [point] *n* point *m;* (*sharp end*) pointe *f;* (*decimal*) virgule *f;* (*elec: socket*) prise *f;* (*meaning*) sens *m.* **beside the point** hors de propos. **come to the point** en venir au fait. **make a point of** ne pas manquer de. **point-blank** *adv* (*shoot*) à bout portant; (*refuse*) tout net; (*demand*) de but en blanc. **what's the point?** à quoi bon? *v* indiquer; (*aim*) pointer, braquer. **point out** (*show*) montrer; (*say*) signaler. **pointed** *adj* pointu; (*remark*) lourd de sens. **pointless** *adj* inutile.

poise [poiz] *n* équilibre *m;* (*of body*) port *m;* calme *m,* assurance *f.* *v* tenir en équilibre. **be poised** être en équilibre; être suspendu.

poison ['poizən] *n* poison *m.* *v* empoisonner. **poisoning** *n* empoisonnement *m.* **poisonous** *adj* toxique; (*animal*) venimeux; (*plant*) vénéneux.

poke [pouk] *n* poussée *f,* coup *m.* *v* pousser, enfoncer; (*fire*) tisonner. **poker** *n* tisonnier *m.*

poker ['poukə] *n* (*cards*) poker *m.* **poker-faced** *adj* au visage impassible.

Poland ['poulənd] *n* Pologne *f.* **Pole** *n* Polonais, -e *m, f.* **Polish** *nm, adj* polonais.

polar ['poulə] *adj* polaire. **polar bear** ours blanc *m.* **polarize** *v* polariser.

pole¹ [poul] *n* perche *f;* (*fixed*) poteau *m,* mât *m.* **pole-vault** *n* saut à la perche *m.*

pole² [poul] *n* (*geog, elec*) pôle *m.* **pole star** étoile polaire *f.*

police [pəˈliːs] *n* police *f,* gendarmerie *f.* **the police force** la police *f,* les gendarmes *m pl.* **policeman** *n* agent de police *m,* gendarme *m.* **police station** poste de police *m,* gendarmerie *f.* **policewoman** *n* femme-agent *f.*

policy¹ ['poləsi] *n* politique *f;* ligne *f,* règle *f.*

policy² ['poləsi] *n* (*insurance*) police *f.*

polio ['pouliou] *n* polio *f.*

polish ['poliʃ] *n* (*shoes*) cirage *m;* (*floor, etc.*) cire *f;* (*shine*) poli *m.* *v* polir; cirer, faire briller. **polish off** finir. **polish up** perfectionner.

polite [pə'lait] *adj* poli. **politeness** *n* politesse *f*.

politics ['politiks] *n* politique *f*. **political** *adj* politique. **politician** *n* homme politique, femme politique *m, f*.

polka ['polkə] *n* polka *f*.

poll [poul] *n* vote *m*; élection *f*; (*survey*) sondage *m*. *v* voter. **polling booth** isoloir *m*. **polling day** jour des élections *m*. **polling station** bureau de vote *m*.

pollen ['polən] *n* pollen *m*. **pollinate** *v* féconder. **pollination** *n* pollinisation *f*.

pollute [pə'luːt] *v* polluer. **pollution** *n* pollution *f*.

polo ['poulou] *n* polo *m*. **polo-neck** *n* col roulé *m*.

polyester [,poli'estə] *n* polyester *m*.

polygamy [pə'ligəmi] *n* polygamie *f*. **polygamous** *adj* polygame.

polygon ['poligən] *n* polygone *m*.

polystyrene [,poli'staiəriːn] *n* polystyrène *m*.

polytechnic [,poli'teknik] *n* Institut Universitaire de Technologie *m*.

polythene ['poliθiːn] *n* polyéthylène *m*. **polythene bag** sac en plastique *m*.

pomegranate ['pomigranit] *n* (*fruit*) grenade *f*; (*tree*) grenadier *m*.

pomp [pomp] *n* pompe *f*. **pompous** *adj* pompeux.

pond [pond] *n* étang *m*; (*artificial*) bassin *m*.

ponder ['pondə] *v* réfléchir (à), méditer.

pony ['pouni] *n* poney *m*. **pony-tail** *n* queue de cheval *f*. **pony-trekking** *n* randonnée équestre *f*.

poodle ['puːdl] *n* caniche *m*.

poof [puːf] *n* (*derog*) tante *f*, tapette *f*.

pool¹ [puːl] *n* (*liquid*) flaque *f*; (*swimming*) piscine *f*.

pool² [puːl] *n* (*money*) cagnotte *f*; (*things*) fonds commun *m*; (*ideas*) réservoir *m*; (*comm*) pool *m*. *v* mettre en commun; unir.

poor [puə] *adj* pauvre; médiocre; faible.

poorly ['puəli] *adj* malade. *adv* pauvrement; (*badly*) mal.

pop¹ [pop] *n* pan *m*, bruit sec *m*; (*drink*) boisson gazeuse *f*. **popcorn** *n* pop-corn *m*. *v* (*balloon*) crever; (*cork*) (faire) sauter. **pop in** entrer en passant.

pop² [pop] *nm, adj* (*music, etc.*) pop *invar*.

pope [poup] *n* pape *m*.

poplar ['poplə] *n* peuplier *m*.

poplin ['poplin] *n* popeline *f*.

poppy ['popi] *n* pavot *m*, coquelicot *m*.

popular ['popjulə] *adj* populaire. **popularity** *n* popularité *f*. **popularize** *v* populariser.

population [,popju'leiʃən] *n* population *f*. **populate** *v* peupler.

porcelain ['poislin] *n* porcelaine *f*.

porch [poitʃ] *n* porche *m*.

porcupine ['poikjupain] *n* porc-épic *m*.

pore¹ [poi] *n* (*anat*) pore *m*.

pore² [poi] *v* **pore over** s'absorber dans.

pork [poik] *n* porc *m*.

pornography [poi'nogrəfi] *n* pornographie *f*. **pornographic** *adj* pornographique.

porous ['poirəs] *adj* poreux.

porpoise ['poipəs] *n* marsouin *m*.

porridge ['poridʒ] *n* porridge *m*.

port¹ [poit] *n* (*harbour*) port *m*.

port² [poit] *n* (*naut: left*) bâbord *m*.

port³ [poit] *n* (*wine*) porto *m*.

portable ['poitəbl] *adj* portatif.

portent ['poitent] *n* présage *m*.

porter ['poitə] *n* (*rail, etc.*) porteur *m*; (*in flats, etc.*) concierge *m, f*, portier *m*.

portfolio [poit'fouliou] *n* serviette *f*; (*pol*) portefeuille *f*.

porthole ['poithoul] *n* hublot *m*.

portion ['poiʃən] *n* portion *f*; partie *f*.

portrait ['poitrət] *n* portrait *m*.

portray [poi'trei] *v* peindre; représenter. **portrayal** *n* peinture *f*; représentation *f*.

Portugal ['poitjugl] *n* Portugal *m*. **Portuguese** *nm, adj* portugais. **the Portuguese** les Portugais.

pose [pouz] *n* pose *f*. *v* poser. **pose as** se faire passer pour.

posh [poʃ] *adj* chic *invar*.

position [pə'ziʃən] *n* position *f*, place *f*; situation *f*. *v* placer, mettre en place.

positive ['pozətiv] *adj* positif; catégorique, réel; sûr, certain.

possess [pə'zes] *v* posséder. **possession** *n* possession *f*. **possessive** *nm, adj* possessif.

possible ['posəbl] *adj* possible. **possibility** *n* possibilité *f*. **possibly** *adv* (*perhaps*) peut-être.

post¹ [poust] *n* (*pole*) poteau *m*. *v* afficher.

post² [poust] *n* (*sentry, job*) poste *m*. *v* poster; (*send*) affecter. **posting** *n* affectation *f*.

post³ [poust] *n* (*mail*) poste *f*; (*letters*) courrier *m*. **post-box** *n* boîte aux lettres *f*.

postcard *n* carte postale *f*. **post-code** *n* code postal *m*. **postman** *n* facteur *m*.

postmark *n* cachet de la poste *m*. **post-marked** *adj* timbré. **post office** poste *f*. *v* envoyer par la poste, poster. **postage** *n* tarifs postaux *m pl*. **postage stamp** timbre-poste *m*. **postal** *adj* postal, par la poste. **postal order** mandat *m*.

poster ['poustə] *n* affiche *f*; (*as decoration*) poster *m*. **poster paint** gouache *f*.

posterior [po'stiəriə] *adj* postérieur, -e. *n* (*coll*) derrière *m*.

posterity [po'sterəti] *n* postérité *f*.

postgraduate [poust'gradjuit] *adj* de troisième cycle. *n* étudiant, -e de troisième cycle *m, f*.

posthumous ['postjuməs] *adj* posthume.

post-mortem [poust'moːtəm] *n* autopsie *f*.

postpone [pous'poun] *v* remettre, ajourner. **postponement** *n* ajournement *m*.

postscript ['pousskript] *n* post-scriptum *m*.

postulate ['postjuleit; *n* 'postjulət] *v* postuler, poser comme principe. *n* postulat *m*.

posture ['postʃə] *n* posture *f*; attitude *f*.

pot [pot] *n* pot *m*; (*for cooking*) marmite *f*. **pot-roast** *n* rôti braisé *m*. **pots and pans** batterie de cuisine *f sing*. **take pot luck** manger à la fortune du pot. *v* mettre en pot.

potassium [pə'tasjəm] *n* potassium *m*.

potato [pə'teitou] *n* pomme de terre *f*.

potent ['poutənt] *adj* puissant; (*drink*) fort.

potential [pə'tenʃəl] *adj* potentiel; possible. *n* (*phys, elec, etc.*) potentiel *m*; (*promise*) potentialités *f pl*.

pot-hole ['pothoul] *n* (*in road*) fondrière *f*; (*underground*) caverne *f*, grotte *f*. **pot-holer** *n* spéléologue *m, f*. **pot-holing** *n* spéléologie *f*.

potion ['pouʃən] *n* potion *f*.

potter[1] ['potə] *v* (*coll*) bricoler.

potter[2] ['potə] *n* potier *m*. **potter's wheel** tour de potier *m*.

pottery ['potəri] *n* (*place, craft*) poterie *f*; (*things made*) poteries *f pl*.

potty ['poti] *n* (*coll*) pot de bébé *m*.

pouch [pautʃ] *n* petit sac *m*; (*kangaroo*) poche *f*; (*tobacco*) blague *f*.

poultice ['poultis] *n* cataplasme *m*.

poultry ['poultri] *n* volaille *f*.

pounce [pauns] *v* bondir, sauter. *n* bond *m*.

pound[1] [paund] *v* battre, piler, pilonner, marteler.

pound[2] [paund] *n* livre *f*.

pour [poɪ] *v* verser; (*flow copiously*) couler à flots, ruisseler; (*rain*) tomber à verse; (*people, etc.*) affluer.

pout [paut] *n* moue *f*. *v* faire la moue.

poverty ['povəti] *n* pauvreté *f*.

powder ['paudə] *n* poudre *f*. **powder puff** houppette *f*. **powder room** toilettes pour dames *f pl*. *v* poudrer; pulvériser. **powdery** *adj* poudreux.

power ['pauə] *n* (*authority, capacity*) pouvoir *m*; (*energy, force*) puissance *f*; faculté *f*. **power cut** coupure de courant *f*. **power station** centrale électrique *f*. *v* faire marcher. **powerful** *adj* puissant. **powerless** *adj* impuissant.

practicable ['praktikəbl] *adj* praticable.

practical ['praktikəl] *adj* pratique. **practical joke** farce *f*.

practice ['praktis] *n* pratique *f*; (*training*) entraînement *m*; (*medicine, etc.*) exercice *m*; clientèle *f*.

practise ['praktis] *v* pratiquer; s'entraîner (à); (*music*) travailler, s'exercer (à); (*doctor, lawyer*) exercer.

practitioner [prak'tiʃənə] *n* praticien, -enne *m, f*.

pragmatic [prag'matik] *adj* pragmatique; dogmatique.

Prague [praig] *n* Prague.

prairie ['preəri] *n* plaine *f*, prairie *f*.

praise [preiz] *v* louer. **praiseworthy** *adj* louable.

pram [pram] *n* voiture d'enfant *f*.

prance [prains] *v* caracoler.

prank [praŋk] *n* frasque *f*; (*joke*) farce *f*.

prattle ['pratl] *v* jaser, babiller; (*chat*) jacasser. *n* babil *m*; jacasserie *f*.

prawn [proɪn] *n* crevette rose *f*. **prawn cocktail** salade de crevettes *f*.

pray [prei] *v* prier. **prayer** *n* prière *f*. **prayer-book** *n* livre de messe *m*.

preach [priɪtʃ] *v* prêcher. **preacher** *n* prédicateur *m*. **preaching** *n* prédication *f*.

precarious [pri'keəriəs] *adj* précaire.

precaution [pri'koɪʃən] *n* précaution *f*. **take precautions** prendre ses précautions.

precede [pri'siːd] *v* précéder. **precedence** *n* préséance *f*; priorité *f*. **precedent** *n* précédent *m*.

precinct ['priɪsiŋkt] *n* enceinte *f*; limite *f*; (*shopping*) zone commerciale *f*.

precious ['preʃəs] *adj* précieux.

precipice ['presipis] *n* précipice *m*.

precipitate [pri'sipiteit; *adj* pri'sipitət] *v* (*hasten*) hâter; (*throw*) précipiter. *adj* irréfléchi. **precipitation** *n* précipitation *f*.

précis ['preisi] *n* précis *m*, résumé *m*.

precise [pri'sais] *adj* précis; méticuleux. **precision** *n* précision *f*.

preclude [pri'kluːd] *v* écarter; prévenir; exclure.

precocious [pri'kouʃəs] *adj* précoce. **precocity** *n* précocité *f*.

preconceive [,priːkən'siːv] *v* préconcevoir. **preconception** *n* idée préconçue *f*.

precursor [,priː'kəːsə] *n* (*person*) précurseur *m*; (*thing*) annonce *f*.

predator ['predətə] *n* prédateur *m*. **predatory** *adj* rapace, de prédateur.

predecessor ['priːdisesə] *n* prédécesseur *m*.

predestine [pri'destin] *v* prédestiner. **predestination** *n* prédestination *f*.

predicament [pri'dikəmənt] *n* situation difficile *f*.

predicate ['predikət] *n* prédicat *m*. *v* affirmer.

predict [pri'dikt] *v* prédire. **predictable** *adj* prévisible. **prediction** *n* prédiction *f*.

predominate [pri'domineit] *v* prédominer. **predominance** *n* prédominance *f*. **predominant** *adj* prédominant.

pre-eminent [priː'eminənt] *adj* prééminent. **pre-eminence** *n* prééminence *f*.

preen [priːn] *v* lisser. **preen oneself** se pomponner.

prefabricate [priː'fabrikeit] *v* préfabriquer. **prefab** *n* (*coll*) maison préfabriquée *f*.

preface ['prefis] *n* (*book*) préface *f*; (*speech*) introduction *f*. *v* faire précéder.

prefect ['priːfekt] *n* (*school*) élève chargé de la discipline *m*.

prefer [pri'fəː] *v* préférer, aimer mieux. **preferable** *adj* préférable. **preference** *n* préférence *f*. **preferential** *adj* préférentiel.

prefix ['priːfiks] *n* préfixe *m*. *v* préfixer.

pregnant ['pregnənt] *adj* (*woman*) enceinte; (*animal*) pleine. **pregnancy** *n* (*woman*) grossesse *f*; (*animal*) gestation *f*.

prehistoric [,priːhi'storik] *adj* préhistorique.

prejudice ['predʒədis] *n* préjugé *m*. *v* prévenir; (*damage*) nuire à. **prejudiced** *adj* de parti pris.

preliminary [pri'liminəri] *adj* pré-

liminaire; premier. **preliminaries** *pl n* préliminaires *m pl*.

prelude ['preljuːd] *n* prélude *m*.

premarital [priː'maritl] *adj* avant le mariage.

premature [premə'tʃuə] *adj* prématuré.

premeditate [priː'mediteit] *v* préméditer. **premeditation** *n* préméditation *f*.

premier ['premiə] *adj* premier. *n* premier ministre *m*.

première ['premieə] *n* première *f*.

premise ['premis] *n* prémisse *f*. **premises** *pl n* lieux *m pl*, locaux *m pl*.

premium ['priːmiəm] *n* prime *f*. **premium bond** bon à lots *m*.

premonition [,premə'niʃən] *n* prémonition *f*.

preoccupied [priː'okjupaid] *adj* préoccupé. **preoccupation** *n* préoccupation *f*.

prepare [pri'peə] *v* (se) préparer. **preparation** *n* préparation *f*. **preparations** *pl n* préparatifs *m pl*. **preparatory** *adj* préparatoire; préliminaire. **preparatory school** école primaire privée *f*.

preposition [,prepə'ziʃən] *n* préposition *f*.

preposterous [pri'postərəs] *adj* absurde, ridicule.

prerogative [pri'rogətiv] *n* prérogative *f*.

prescribe [pri'skraib] *v* prescrire. **prescription** *n* (*med*) ordonnance *f*; prescription *f*.

presence ['prezns] *n* présence *f*.

present¹ ['preznt] *adj* présent; actuel. *n* présent *m*. **at present** actuellement. **presently** *adv* tout à l'heure.

present² [pri'zent] *v* présenter; (*film, play*) donner; (*gift*) offrir; (*medal*) remettre. *n* cadeau *m*. **presentable** *adj* présentable. **presentation** *n* présentation *f*; (*of gift, medal*) remise *f*. **presenter** *n* présentateur, -trice *m, f*.

preserve [pri'zəːv] *v* conserver; (*from harm*) préserver. **preserved** *adj* en conserve. **preserves** *pl n* conserves *f pl*; (*jam*) confiture *f sing*. **preservation** *n* conservation *f*; préservation *f*. **preservative** *n* agent de conservation *m*.

preside [pri'zaid] *v* présider.

president ['prezidənt] *n* président *m*. **presidency** *n* présidence *f*. **presidential** *adj* présidentiel.

press [pres] *n* presse *f*; (*wine, cider*) pressoir *m*. **press conference** conférence de presse *f*. **press release** communiqué de presse *m*. *v* appuyer (sur), presser; (*iron*) repasser; insister. **press for** faire pression pour. **press-gang** v faire pression sur. **press on** continuer. **press-stud** n boutonpression m. **press-up** n traction f. **pressing** adj urgent.

pressure ['preʃə] n pression f. **pressurecooker** n autocuiseur m. **pressure gauge** manomètre m. **pressurize** v (cabin, etc.) pressuriser; (force) contraindre.

prestige [pre'stiːʒ] n prestige m. **prestigious** adj prestigieux.

presume [pri'zjuːm] v présumer. **presumption** n présomption f. **presumptuous** adj présomptueux.

pretend [pri'tend] v faire semblant; (claim) prétendre. **pretence** n feinte f, prétexte m; (claim) prétention f. **pretension** n prétention f. **pretentious** adj prétentieux.

pretext ['priːtekst] n prétexte m.

pretty ['priti] adj joli. adv assez.

prevail [pri'veil] v prévaloir, prédominer. **prevail upon** persuader. **prevailing** adj (wind) dominant; courant, actuel. **prevalent** adj répandu.

prevent [pri'vent] v empêcher. **prevention** n prévention f. **preventive** adj préventif.

preview ['priːvjuː] n avant-première f.

previous ['priːviəs] adj précédent. **previously** adv auparavant.

prey [prei] n proie f. **be a prey to** être en proie à. v **prey on** (animal) faire sa proie de; (fear) ronger.

price [prais] n prix m. **price-list** n tarif m. v fixer le prix de; marquer le prix de. **priceless** adj inestimable.

prick [prik] n piqûre f. v piquer. **prick up one's ears** dresser l'oreille.

prickle ['prikl] n piquant m. v piquer; (sensation) picoter. **prickly** adj hérissé.

pride [praid] n orgueil m; (satisfaction) fierté f. v **pride oneself on** être fier de.

priest [priːst] n prêtre m. **priesthood** n prêtrise f.

prim [prim] adj guindé.

primary ['praiməri] adj (first) primaire, premier; principal. **primary school** école primaire f.

primate ['praimət] n (zool) primate m; (rel) primat m.

prime [praim] adj principal; excellent, de premier choix; (math) premier. **prime minister** premier ministre m. v préparer; (for painting) apprêter. **primer** n apprêt m; (book) premier livre m.

primitive ['primitiv] adj primitif.

primrose ['primrouz] n primevère f.

prince [prins] n prince m. **princely** adj princier. **princess** n princesse f.

principal ['prinsəpəl] adj principal. n (school) directeur, -trice m, f.

principle ['prinsəpəl] n principe m. **on principle** par principe.

print [print] n (mark) empreinte f; (type) caractères m pl; (art) gravure f; (phot) épreuve f. **out of print** épuisé. v imprimer; (phot) tirer. **print-out** n listage m. **printed matter** imprimés m pl. **printer** n imprimeur m. **printing** n impression f; (phot) tirage m. **printing press** presse typographique f.

prior ['praiə] adj antérieur, -e. **prior to** antérieurement à. **priority** n priorité f.

prise [praiz] v **prise off/open** enlever/ouvrir en faisant levier; forcer.

prism ['prizm] n prisme m.

prison ['prizn] n prison f. **prisoner** n prisonnier, -ère m, f.

private ['praivət] adj privé; confidentiel; (lesson, car, etc.) particulier; personnel. n simple soldat m. **privacy** n intimité f, solitude f. **privately** adv en privé; à titre personnel.

privet ['privət] n troène m.

privilege ['privəlidʒ] n privilège m. **privileged** adj privilégié.

prize [praiz] n prix m. **prizewinner** n lauréat, -e m, f. adj primé. v priser.

probable ['probəbl] adj probable; (believable) vraisemblable. **probability** n probabilité f. **probably** adv probablement.

probation [prə'beiʃən] n (law) mise à l'épreuve f, liberté surveillée f. **on probation** (job) engagé à l'essai. **probationary** adj d'essai.

probe [proub] n sonde f; enquête f. v sonder, explorer.

problem ['probləm] n problème m. **problem child** enfant difficile m, f. **problem page** courrier du cœur m. **problematic** adj problématique.

proceed [prə'siːd] v aller, continuer, avancer. **proceed to** se mettre à. **proceeds** pl n produit m sing. **procedure** n procédure f. **proceedings** pl n cérémonie f sing; (law) mesures f pl.

process ['prouses] n processus m; (method) procédé m. **in the process of** en train de, au cours de. v traiter; (phot) développer; (admin) s'occuper de.

procession [prə'seʃən] n cortège m, défilé m.

proclaim [prə'kleim] v proclamer; démontrer. **proclamation** n proclamation f.

procreate ['proukrieit] v procréer. **procreation** n procréation f.

procure [prə'kjuə] v obtenir; (prostitute) procurer.

prod [prod] n petit coup m. v pousser doucement; (rouse) aiguillonner.

prodigal ['prodigəl] adj prodigue.

prodigy ['prodidʒi] n prodige m. **prodigious** adj prodigieux.

produce [prə'djuɪs; n 'prodjuɪs] v produire; (theatre) mettre en scène. n produits m pl. **producer** n producteur, -trice m, f; metteur en scène m. **product** n produit m. **production** n production f; mise en scène f. **productive** adj productif; fécond. **productivity** n productivité f.

profane [prə'fein] adj profane. v profaner. **profanity** n (oath) juron m.

profess [prə'fes] v professer, affirmer, déclarer.

profession [prə'feʃən] n profession f. **professional** n, adj professionnel, -elle.

professor [prə'fesə] n professeur m. **professorship** n chaire f.

proficient [prə'fiʃənt] adj compétent. **proficiency** n compétence f.

profile ['proufail] n profil m; (biographical sketch) portrait m.

profit ['profit] n profit m, bénéfice m. **profit-making** adj à but lucratif. v **profit by** or **from** tirer profit de. **profitable** adj rentable; (useful) fructueux.

profound [prə'faund] adj profond. **profoundly** adv profondément.

profuse [prə'fjuɪs] adj abondant, profus. **profusely** adv abondamment, à profusion. **profusion** n abondance f, profusion f.

programme ['prougram] n programme m; (broadcast) émission f. v programmer. **programmer** n programmeur, -euse m, f. **programming** n programmation f.

progress ['prougres] n progrès m. **in progress** en cours. **make progress** faire des progrès. v progresser, avancer. **progression** n progression f. **progressive** adj progressif; (outlook, etc.) progressiste.

prohibit [prə'hibit] v interdire, défendre;

(prevent) empêcher. **prohibition** n prohibition f.

project ['prodʒekt; v prə'dʒekt] n projet m; opération f; (school) dossier m. v projeter; (protrude) faire saillie. **projectile** n projectile m. **projecting** adj saillant. **projection** n projection f; saillie f. **projector** n projecteur m.

proletarian [proulə'teəriən] n prolétaire m. adj prolétarien. **proletariat** n prolétariat m.

proliferate [prə'lifəreit] v proliférer. **proliferation** n prolifération f.

prolific [prə'lifik] adj prolifique.

prologue ['proulog] n prologue m.

prolong [prə'loŋ] v prolonger. **prolongation** n (time) prolongation f; (space) prolongement m.

promenade [promə'naid] n promenade f.

prominent ['prominənt] adj proéminent; important; (striking) frappant. **prominence** n proéminence f; importance f.

promiscuous [prə'miskjuəs] adj léger, immoral; (person) de mœurs faciles. **promiscuity** n promiscuité f.

promise ['promis] n promesse f. v promettre. **promising** adj prometteur, -euse.

promontory ['promontəri] n promontoire m.

promote [prə'mout] v promouvoir; (comm) lancer. **promotion** n promotion f; lancement m.

prompt [prompt] adj rapide, prompt; ponctuel. v pousser, inciter; (theatre) souffler. **prompter** n souffleur, -euse m, f.

prone [proun] adj enclin; (lying) prostré.

prong [proŋ] n dent f.

pronoun ['prounaun] n pronom m.

pronounce [prə'nauns] v prononcer. **pronouncement** n déclaration f. **pronunciation** n prononciation f.

proof [pruɪf] n preuve f; (of book, photo, etc.) épreuve f. **proof-read** v corriger les épreuves de. **proof-reading** n correction des épreuves f. adj (resistant) à l'épreuve de.

prop[1] [prop] n support m. v (lean) appuyer; (support) étayer; (financially) soutenir.

prop[2] [prop] n (coll: theatre) accessoire m.

propaganda [propə'gandə] n propagande f.

propagate ['propəgeit] v (se) propager. **propagation** n propagation f.

propel [prə'pel] v propulser; (*push*) pousser. **propeller** n hélice f. **propelling pencil** porte-mine m *invar*.

proper ['propə] adj convenable, correct; (*real*) véritable. **proper noun** nom propre m. **properly** adv comme il faut.

property ['propəti] n propriété f; (*possessions*) biens m pl.

prophecy ['profəsi] n prophétie f. **prophesy** v prédire, prophétiser.

prophet ['profit] n prophète m. **prophetic** adj prophétique.

proportion [prə'poːʃən] n proportion f; part f. **out of proportion** mal proportionné; hors de proportion. v proportionner. **proportional** adj proportionnel.

propose [prə'pouz] v proposer; (*marriage*) faire sa demande; (*intend*) se proposer (de). **proposal** n proposition f; demande en mariage f; projet m. **proposition** n proposition f; affaire f.

proprietor [prə'praiətə] n propriétaire m, f.

propriety [prə'praiəti] n bienséance f; (*correctness*) justesse f.

propulsion [prə'pʌlʃən] n propulsion f.

prose [prouz] n prose f; (*translation*) thème m.

prosecute ['prosikjuːt] v poursuivre. **prosecution** n poursuites judiciaires f pl; (*side*) partie plaignante f.

prospect ['prospekt; v prə'spekt] n perspective f. **prospects** pl n (*of job, etc.*) avenir m sing. v prospecter. **prospective** adj futur; possible.

prospectus [prə'spektəs] n prospectus m.

prosper ['prospə] v prospérer. **prosperity** n prospérité f. **prosperous** adj prospère.

prostitute ['prostitjuːt] n prostituée f. v prostituer. **prostitution** n prostitution f.

prostrate ['prostreit; v pro'streit] adj prosterné, prostré; (*lying*) à plat ventre. v (*overcome*) accabler. **prostrate oneself** se prosterner. **prostration** n prosternation f; (*exhaustion*) prostration f.

protagonist [prou'tagənist] n protagoniste m.

protect [prə'tekt] v protéger. **protection** n protection f. **protective** adj protecteur, -trice; de protection.

protein ['proutiːn] n protéine f.

protest ['proutest; v prə'test] n protestation f. v protester. **protester** n (*on march*) manifestant, -e m, f.

Protestant ['protistənt] n, adj protestant, -e m, f.

protocol ['proutəkol] n protocole m.

prototype ['proutətaip] n prototype m.

protractor [prə'traktə] n rapporteur m.

protrude [prə'truːd] v dépasser, avancer. **protruding** adj saillant, en saillie.

proud [praud] adj fier; orgueilleux.

prove [pruːv] v prouver; se révéler.

proverb ['provɜːb] n proverbe m. **proverbial** adj proverbial.

provide [prə'vaid] v fournir, pourvoir. **provided that** pourvu que.

provident ['providənt] adj prévoyant. **providence** n providence f.

province ['provins] n province f; domaine m. **the provinces** la province f sing. **provincial** adj provincial.

provision [prə'viʒən] n (*supply*) provision f; (*providing*) fourniture f; (*of contract, law, etc.*) disposition f. **make provision for** pourvoir aux besoins de. **provisions** pl n provisions f pl. **provisional** adj provisoire.

proviso [prə'vaizou] n stipulation f, condition f.

provoke [prə'vouk] v provoquer. **provocation** n provocation f. **provocative** adj provocant.

prow [prau] n proue f.

prowess ['prauis] n prouesse f.

prowl [praul] v rôder. **prowler** n rôdeur, -euse m, f.

proximity [prok'siməti] n proximité f.

proxy ['proksi] n procuration f. **by proxy** par procuration.

prude [pruːd] n prude f. **prudish** adj prude.

prudent ['pruːdənt] adj prudent. **prudence** n prudence f.

prune[1] [pruːn] n (*fruit*) pruneau m.

prune[2] [pruːn] v tailler, élaguer.

pry [prai] v être indiscret. **pry into** fourrer son nez dans. **prying** adj fureteur, -euse.

psalm [saːm] n psaume m.

pseudonym ['sjuːdənim] n pseudonyme m.

psychedelic [ˌsaikə'delik] adj psychédélique.

psychiatry [sai'kaiətri] n psychiatrie f. **psychiatric** adj psychiatrique. **psychiatrist** n psychiatre m, f.

psychic ['saikik] adj métapsychique; (*psych*) psychique.

psychoanalysis [ˌsaikouəˈnaləsis] *n* psychanalyse *f*. **psychoanalyse** *v* psychanalyser. **psychoanalyst** *n* psychanalyste *m*, *f*.

psychology [saiˈkolədʒi] *n* psychologie *f*. **psychological** *adj* psychologique. **psychologist** *n* psychologue *m*, *f*.

psychopath [ˈsaikəpæθ] *n* psychopathe *m*, *f*. **psychopathic** *adj* psychopathe.

psychosis [saiˈkousis] *n* psychose *f*. **psychotic** *n*(*m* + *f*), *adj* psychotique.

psychosomatic [ˌsaikəsəˈmatik] *adj* psychosomatique.

psychotherapy [ˌsaikəˈθerəpi] *n* psychothérapie *f*.

pub [pʌb] *n* pub *m*. **pub-crawl** *n* tournée des bistrots *f*.

puberty [ˈpjuːbəti] *n* puberté *f*.

pubic [ˈpjuːbik] *adj* pubien.

public [ˈpʌblik] *adj* public, -ique. *n* public *m*.

publican [ˈpʌblikən] *n* patron de bistrot *m*.

publication [ˌpʌbliˈkeiʃən] *n* publication *f*.

public bar *n* bar *m*.

public conveniences *pl n* toilettes *f pl*.

public footpath *n* sentier public *m*.

public holiday *n* jour férié *m*.

publicity [pʌbˈlisəti] *n* publicité *f*.

publicize [ˈpʌblisaiz] *v* rendre public; (*advertise*) faire de la publicité pour.

public library *n* bibliothèque municipale *f*.

public relations *pl n* relations publiques *f pl*. **public relations officer** *n* public-relations *m*.

public school *n* collège secondaire privé *m*.

public speaking *n* art oratoire *m*.

public-spirited *adj* be **public-spirited** faire preuve de civisme.

public transport *n* transport en commun *m*.

publish [ˈpʌbliʃ] *v* publier. **publisher** *n* éditeur, -trice *m*, *f*. **publishing** *n* édition *f*; publication *f*. **publishing house** maison d'édition *f*.

pucker [ˈpʌkə] *v* (se) plisser; (*sewing*) (faire) goder. *n* (*sewing*) faux pli *m*.

pudding [ˈpudiŋ] *n* dessert *m*.

puddle [ˈpʌdl] *n* flaque d'eau *f*.

puerile [ˈpjuərail] *adj* puéril.

puff [pʌf] *n* bouffée *f*, souffle *m*; (*cake*) feuilleté *m*; (*for powder*) houppe *f*. **puff sleeves** manches bouffantes *f pl*. *v* souffler. **puff out** *or* **up** (se) gonfler. **puffy** *adj* gonflé.

pull [pul] *n* traction *f*; attraction *f*; (*action*) coup *m*. *v* tirer; (*trigger*) presser; (*muscle*) se déchirer. **pull away** démarrer, s'éloigner. **pull down** baisser, descendre; démolir. **pull off** enlever; (*deal*) conclure; (*trick*) réussir. **pull oneself together** se reprendre. **pull out** (*car, etc.*) déboîter; (*extract*) arracher; (*mil*) retirer. **pull to pieces** démolir. **pull up** (*car, etc.*) s'arrêter; (*socks, etc.*) remonter.

pulley [ˈpuli] *n* poulie *f*.

pullover [ˈpulˌouvə] *n* pull *m*.

pulp [pʌlp] *n* pulpe *f*. *v* réduire en pulpe. **pulpy** *adj* pulpeux.

pulpit [ˈpulpit] *n* chaire *f*.

pulsate [pʌlˈseit] *v* battre, palpiter; (*music*) vibrer. **pulsation** *n* pulsation *f*, battement *m*.

pulse [pʌls] *n* (*med*) pouls *m*; (*phys, elec*) vibration. *v* battre, palpiter.

pulverize [ˈpʌlvəraiz] *v* pulvériser. **pulverization** *n* pulvérisation *f*.

pump [pʌmp] *n* pompe *f*. *v* pomper. **pump up** gonfler.

pumpkin [ˈpʌmpkin] *n* citrouille *f*.

pun [pʌn] *n* calembour *m*.

punch[1] [pʌntʃ] *n* coup de poing *m*. **punch line** astuce *f*. *v* donner un coup de poing à.

punch[2] [pʌntʃ] *n* (*drink*) punch *m*.

punch[3] [pʌntʃ] *n* (*tool*) poinçonneuse *f*; perforateur *m*. *v* poinçonner; perforer.

punctual [ˈpʌŋktʃuəl] *adj* ponctuel, à l'heure. **punctuality** *n* ponctualité *f*, exactitude *f*.

punctuate [ˈpʌŋktʃueit] *v* ponctuer. **punctuation** *n* ponctuation *f*.

puncture [ˈpʌŋktʃə] *n* (*tyre*) crevaison *f*; (*leather, skin*) piqûre *f*. **have a puncture** crever. *v* crever; piquer.

pungent [ˈpʌndʒənt] *adj* âcre, piquant; (*remark*) mordant. **pungency** *n* âcreté *f*; mordant *m*.

punish [ˈpʌniʃ] *v* punir. **punishment** *n* punition *f*.

punt[1] [pʌnt] *n* (*boat*) bachot *m*.

punt[2] [pʌnt] *v* (*bet*) parier; (*cards*) ponter. **punter** *n* parieur, -euse *m*, *f*; ponte *m*.

puny [ˈpjuːni] *adj* chétif.

pupil[1] [ˈpjuːpl] *n* élève *m*, *f*.

pupil[2] [ˈpjuːpl] *n* (*eye*) pupille *f*.

puppet ['pʌpit] *n* marionnette *f*.
puppy ['pʌpi] *n* chiot *m*.
purchase ['pɜːtʃəs] *n* achat *m*. *v* acheter.
pure ['pjuə] *adj* pur. **purify** *v* épurer, purifier. **purity** *n* pureté *f*.
purée ['pjuərei] *n* purée *f*.
purgatory ['pɜːgətəri] *n* purgatoire *m*.
purge [pɜːdʒ] *n* purge *f*. *v* purger. **purgative** *nm, adj* purgatif.
puritan ['pjuəritən] *n, adj* puritain, -e. **puritanical** *adj* puritain.
purl [pɜːl] *n* maille à l'envers *f*. *v* tricoter à l'envers.
purple ['pɜːpl] *nm, adj* pourpre, violet.
purpose ['pɜːpəs] *n* (*aim*) but *m*; (*use*) usage *m*. **on purpose** exprès. **purposeful** *adj* résolu. **purposely** *adv* exprès.
purr [pɜː] *v* ronronner. *n* ronronnement *m*.
purse [pɜːs] *n* porte-monnaie *m invar*, bourse *f*. *v* **purse one's lips** se pincer les lèvres.
purser ['pɜːsə] *n* commissaire du bord *m*.
pursue [pə'sjuː] *v* poursuivre; (*seek*) rechercher. **pursuer** *n* poursuivant, -e *m, f*. **pursuit** *n* poursuite *f*; recherche *f*; occupation *f*.
pus [pʌs] *n* pus *m*.
push [puʃ] *n* poussée *f*. **push-chair** *n* poussette *f*. *v* pousser; (*press*) appuyer (sur). **be pushed for** être à court de.
*put [put] *v* mettre, poser; (*say*) dire, exprimer; (*case, etc.*) présenter. **put across** faire comprendre, communiquer. **put away** ranger. **put back** remettre. **put down** déposer; noter; attribuer; (*kill*) faire piquer. **put off** retarder, renvoyer à plus tard; (*distract*) dérouter. **put on** mettre. **put out** (*fire*) éteindre; (*bother*) déranger; (*annoy*) contrarier. **put up** (*tent*) dresser; construire; augmenter; loger; (*picture*) mettre. **put-up job** (*coll*) coup monté *m*. **put up with** supporter.
putrid ['pjuːtrid] *adj* putride.
putt [pʌt] *n* putt *m*. *v* putter. **putting** *n* putting *m*.
putty ['pʌti] *n* mastic *m*.
puzzle ['pʌzl] *n* énigme *f*; (*game*) casse-tête *m invar*. *v* rendre perplexe. **puzzle out** comprendre; éclaircir. **puzzled** *adj* perplexe. **puzzling** *adj* curieux.
pyjamas [pə'dʒɑːməz] *pl n* pyjama *m sing*.
pylon ['pailən] *n* pylône *m*.
pyramid ['pirəmid] *n* pyramide *f*.
python ['paiθən] *n* python *m*.

Q

quack[1] [kwak] *n* (*duck*) coin-coin *m*. *v* faire coin-coin.
quack[2] [kwak] *n* charlatan *m*.
quadrangle ['kwodraŋgl] *n* cour *f*; (*math*) quadrilatère *m*.
quadrant ['kwodrənt] *n* quadrant *m*.
quadrilateral [kwodrə'latərəl] *nm, adj* quadrilatère.
quadruped ['kwodruped] *nm, adj* quadrupède.
quadruple [kwod'ruːpl] *nm, adj* quadruple. *v* quadrupler.
quadruplet ['kwodruːplit] *n* quadruplé, -e *m, f*.
quagmire ['kwagmaiə] *n* bourbier *m*.
quail[1] [kweil] *n* (*bird*) caille *f*.
quail[2] [kweil] *v* perdre courage.
quaint [kweint] *adj* au charme vieillot; bizarre; pittoresque.
quake [kweik] *v* trembler.
qualify ['kwolifai] *v* qualifier; obtenir son diplôme; (*modify*) mitiger. **qualification** *n* capacité *f*; réserve *f*. **qualifications** *pl n* titres *m pl*, diplômes *m pl*. **qualified** *adj* qualifié, diplômé; mitigé.
quality ['kwoləti] *n* qualité *f*.
qualm [kwɑːm] *n* scrupule *m*; appréhension *f*; nausée *f*.
quandary ['kwondəri] *n* embarras *m*, dilemme *m*.
quantify ['kwontifai] *v* déterminer la quantité de.
quantity ['kwontəti] *n* quantité *f*.
quarantine ['kworəntiːn] *n* quarantaine *f*. *v* mettre en quarantaine.
quarrel ['kworəl] *n* querelle *f*. *v* se disputer. **quarrelsome** *adj* querelleur, -euse.
quarry[1] ['kwori] *n* (*stone*) carrière *f*. *v* extraire; exploiter (une carrière).
quarry[2] ['kwori] *n* proie *f*; (*game*) gibier *m*.
quarter ['kwoːtə] *n* quart *m*; (*of year*) trimestre *m*; (*of town*) quartier *m*. **quarter-final** *n* quart de finale *m*. **quartermaster** *n* (*naut*) maître de manœuvre *m*. **quarter past two** deux heures et quart. **quarters** *pl n* (*mil*) quartiers *m pl*. **quarter to two** deux heures moins le quart. *v* diviser en quatre; (*mil*) caserner. **quarterly** *adj* trimestriel.

quartet [kwɔr'tet] n quatuor m.
quartz [kwɔrts] n quartz m.
quash [kwɔʃ] v annuler; rejeter; (riot) étouffer.
quaver ['kweivə] n (music) croche f; tremblement m. v chevroter.
quay [kiː] n quai m.
queasy ['kwiːzi] adj (stomach) délicat. **feel queasy** avoir mal au cœur. **queasiness** n mal au cœur m.
queen [kwiːn] n reine f; (cards) dame f. **Queen Mother** reine mère f.
queer [kwiə] adj étrange; suspect; (slang) homosexuel. n (slang) pédé m.
quell [kwel] v réprimer.
quench [kwentʃ] v (fire) éteindre; (hope) réprimer. **quench one's thirst** se désaltérer.
query ['kwiəri] n question f. n mettre en doute.
quest [kwest] n quête f.
question ['kwestʃən] n question f; doute m. **it's out of the question** il n'en est pas question. **question mark** point d'interrogation m. v interroger; mettre en doute. **questionable** adj douteux. **questioning** n interrogation f. **questionnaire** n questionnaire m.
queue [kjuː] n queue f, file f. **queue-jumper** n resquilleur, -euse m, f. v faire la queue.
quibble ['kwibl] n chicane f. v chicaner.
quick [kwik] adj rapide, prompt. **quicksand** n sable mouvant m. **quickstep** n fox m. **quick-tempered** adj prompt à s'emporter. **quick-witted** adj à l'esprit vif. n vif m. **quicken** v (s')accélérer; stimuler. **quickly** adv vite, sans tarder.
quid [kwid] n (coll) livre f.
quiet ['kwaiət] adj tranquille; (subdued) doux, douce; (voice) bas, basse. n also **quietness** silence m; tranquillité f. **quieten** v calmer. **quietly** adv silencieusement, doucement.
quill [kwil] n penne f; (pen) plume d'oie f; (of porcupine) piquant m.
quilt [kwilt] n édredon piqué m. v ouater, ouatiner.
quince [kwins] n (fruit) coing m; (tree) cognassier m.
quinine [kwi'niːn] n quinine f.
quinsy ['kwinzi] n amygdalite purulente f.
quintet [kwin'tet] n quintette m.
quintuplet [kwin'tuːplit] n quintuplé, -e m, f.

quirk [kwɔːk] n bizarrerie f.
*quit [kwit] v (leave) quitter; (give up) se rendre, renoncer. **quits** adj quitte.
quite [kwait] adv complètement, tout; (fairly) plutôt, assez.
quiver[1] ['kwivə] v trembler, frémir. n frémissement m, tremblement m.
quiver[2] ['kwivə] n (for arrows) carquois m.
quiz [kwiz] n quiz m, jeu-concours m. v interroger.
quizzical ['kwizikl] adj moqueur, -euse; amusant; bizarre.
quorum ['kwɔrəm] n quorum m.
quota ['kwoutə] n quota m; (share) quotepart f.
quote [kwout] v citer; (reference number) rappeler; (comm) indiquer. **quotation** n citation f; (comm) devis m. **quotation marks** guillemets m pl.

R

rabbi ['rabai] n rabbin m.
rabbit ['rabit] n lapin m.
rabble ['rabl] n cohue f; (derog) populace f.
rabies ['reibiːz] n rage f. **rabid** adj enragé.
race[1] [reis] n (sport) course f. **racecourse** n champ de courses m. **racehorse** n cheval de course m. v (person) faire une course avec; (horse) faire courir; (rush) courir; (pulse) être très rapide. **racing car** voiture de course f. **racing driver** coureur automobile m.
race[2] [reis] n race f. **racial** adj racial. **racialism** or **racism** n racisme m. **racialist** or **racist** n(m+f), adj raciste.
rack [rak] n (bottles) casier m; (food) râtelier m; (shelves) étagère f; (torture) chevalet m. v torturer. **rack one's brains** se creuser la tête.
racket[1] ['rakit] n (sport) raquette f.
racket[2] ['rakit] n (noise) tapage m, vacarme m; (scheme) combine f, escroquerie f.
radar ['reidɑː] n radar m. **radar trap** piège radar m.
radial ['reidiəl] adj radial. **radial tyre** pneu à carcasse radiale m.

radiant ['reidiənt] *adj* radieux, rayonnant.
radiance *n* éclat *m*, rayonnement *m*.
radiate ['reidieit] *v* irradier, rayonner; (*heat*) émettre. **radiation** *n* (*heat*) rayonnement *m*; (*light*) irradiation *f*; (*radioactive*) radiation *f*. **radiator** *n* radiateur *m*.
radical ['radikəl] *nm, adj* radical.
radio ['reidiou] *n* radio *f*, poste *m*. **radio contact** contact radio *m*. **radio station** poste émetteur *m*. **radio wave** onde hertzienne *f*. *v* appeler par radio; signaler par radio.
radioactive [reidiou'aktiv] *adj* radioactif. **radioactivity** *n* radioactivité *f*.
radiography [reidi'ogrəfi] *n* radiographie *f*. **radiographer** *n* radiologue *m*, *f*.
radiology [reidi'olədʒi] *n* radiologie *f*. **radiologist** *n* radiologue *m*, *f*.
radiotherapy [reidiou'θerəpi] *n* radiothérapie *f*.
radish ['radiʃ] *n* radis *m*.
radium ['reidiəm] *n* radium *m*.
radius ['reidiəs] *n* rayon *m*.
raffia ['rafiə] *n* raphia *m*.
raffle ['rafl] *n* loterie *f*. *v* mettre en loterie.
raft [raift] *n* radeau *m*.
rafter ['raiftə] *n* chevron *m*.
rag¹ [rag] *n* (*piece*) loque *f*; (*for cleaning*) chiffon *m*; (*derog: newspaper*) torchon *m*. **rag doll** poupée de chiffon *f*. **rag-and-bone man** chiffonnier *m*. **rags** *pl n* haillons *m pl*. **ragged** *adj* (*clothes*) en loques; (*edge*) déchiqueté.
rag² [rag] (*coll*) *v* taquiner. *n* blague *f*.
rage [reidʒ] *n* rage *f*. **be all the rage** faire fureur. *v* (*person*) être furieux; (*storm*) faire rage. **raging** *adj* (*person*) furieux; (*pain*) atroce; (*storm*) déchaîné.
raid [reid] *n* raid *m*; (*police*) descente *f*; (*bandits*) razzia *f*. *v* faire un raid dans; faire une descente dans; razzier; (*orchard*) marauder dans; (*larder*) dévaliser. **raider** *n* pillard *m*.
rail [reil] *n* (*bar*) garde-fou *m*, balustrade *f*; (*for curtains*) tringle *m*; (*for train*) rail *m*. **by rail** par train. **railway** *or US* **railroad** chemin de fer *m*; (*track*) voie ferrée *f*.
railings ['reiliŋz] *pl n* grille *f sing*.
rain [rein] *n* pluie *f*. **rainbow** *n* arc-en-ciel *m*. **raincoat** *n* imperméable *m*. **raindrop** *n* goutte de pluie *f*. **rainfall** *n* hauteur des précipitations *f*. *v* pleuvoir. **rainy** *adj* pluvieux.

raise [reiz] *v* lever; augmenter; (*build, rear*) élever; (*question*) soulever; (*money*) se procurer.
raisin ['reizən] *n* raisin sec *m*.
rake [reik] *n* râteau *m*. *v* (*ground*) ratisser; (*leaves*) râteler. **rake in** (*coll*) amasser.
rally ['rali] *n* rassemblement *m*; (*mot*) rallye *m*; (*tennis*) échange *m*. *v* (se) rallier; (*get better*) aller mieux. **rally round** venir en aide.
ram [ram] *n* belier *m*. *v* enfoncer; (*pack in*) tasser; (*car*) emboutir.
ramble ['rambl] *n* randonnée *f*. *v* faire une randonnée. **ramble on** discourir.
ramp [ramp] *n* rampe *f*.
rampage [ram'peidʒ] *n* **be on the rampage** se déchaîner.
rampant ['rampənt] *adj* (*plant*) exubérant; (*heraldry*) rampant. **be rampant** sévir.
rampart ['rampait] *n* rempart *m*.
ramshackle ['ramʃakl] *adj* délabré.
ran [ran] *V* **run**.
ranch [raintʃ] *n* ranch *m*.
rancid ['ransid] *adj* rance. **go rancid** rancir.
rancour ['raŋkə] *n* rancœur *f*.
random ['randəm] *n* **at random** au hasard. *adj* fait au hasard. **random sample** échantillon prélevé au hasard *m*.
rang [raŋ] *V* **ring²**.
range [reindʒ] *n* (*scope*) portée *f*; (*mountains*) chaîne *f*; (*extent*) étendue *f*; gamme *f*; choix *m*; (*stove*) fourneau *m*; (*mil*) champ de tir *m*. *v* ranger; (*extend*) s'étendre; (*roam*) parcourir.
rank¹ [raŋk] *n* rang *m*. **the rank and file** la masse *f*; (*mil*) les hommes de troupe *m pl*. *v* compter, (se) classer.
rank² [raŋk] *adj* (*smell*) fétide; (*plants*) exubérant; flagrant.
rankle ['raŋkl] *v* rester sur le cœur.
ransack ['ransak] *v* saccager; (*search*) fouiller.
ransom ['ransəm] *n* rançon *f*. **hold to ransom** rançonner. *v* racheter.
rap [rap] *v* frapper. *n* petit coup sec *m*.
rape [reip] *n* viol *m*. *v* violer. **rapist** *n* violeur *m*.
rapid ['rapid] *adj* rapide. **rapids** *pl n* rapides *m pl*. **rapidity** *n* rapidité *f*.
rapier ['reipiə] *n* rapière *f*.
rapport [ra'poi] *n* rapport *m*.
rapture ['raptʃə] *n* ravissement *m*, extase *f*. **go into raptures over** s'extasier sur.

rare¹ ['reə] *adj* rare. **rarity** *n* rareté *f*.

rare² ['reə] *adj* (*meat*) saignant.

rascal ['raɪskəl] *n* polisson, -onne *m, f*; (*rogue*) coquin *m*.

rash¹ [raʃ] *adj* imprudent. **rashness** *n* imprudence *f*.

rash² [raʃ] *n* (*med*) éruption *f*.

rasher ['raʃə] *n* mince tranche *f*.

raspberry ['raɪzbəri] *n* (*fruit*) framboise *f*; (*bush*) framboisier *m*.

rat [rat] *n* rat *m*. **rat poison** mort-aux-rats *m*. **rat race** foire d'empoigne *f*.

rate [reit] *n* taux *m*; (*speed*) train *m*. **at any rate** en tout cas. **ratepayer** *n* contribuable *m, f*. **rates** *pl n* impôts locaux *m pl*. *v* évaluer; considérer; se classer.

rather ['raɪðə] *adv* plutôt; (*fairly*) assez, un peu. **I would rather** ... j'aimerais mieux . . . .

ratify ['ratifai] *v* ratifier. **ratification** *n* ratification *f*.

ratio ['reiʃiou] *n* proportion *f*, raison *f*.

ration ['raʃən] *n* ration *f*. *v* rationner. **rationing** *n* rationnement *m*.

rational ['raʃənl] *adj* raisonnable, rationnel, logique. **rationale** *n* raisonnement *m*. **rationalize** *v* justifier après coup; (*organize*) rationaliser.

rattle ['ratl] *n* bruit *m*, fracas *m*; (*chains, etc*.) cliquetis *m*; (*toy*) hochet *m*. *v* faire du bruit; (*objects*) (faire) s'entrechoquer; (faire) cliqueter; (*coll*) déconcerter.

raucous ['rɔːkəs] *adj* rauque.

ravage ['ravidʒ] *n* ravage *m*. *v* ravager.

rave [reiv] *v* délirer, divaguer; s'extasier (sur). **raving** *adj* délirant; furieux.

raven ['reivən] *n* corbeau *m*.

ravenous ['ravənəs] *adj* vorace. **be ravenous** avoir un faim de loup.

ravine [rə'viːn] *n* ravin *m*.

ravish ['raviʃ] *v* ravir.

raw [rɔː] *adj* cru; (*unprocessed*) brut; novice; (*sore*) à vif. **raw deal** (*coll*) sale coup *m*. **raw edge** bord coupé *m*. **raw materials** matières premières *f pl*.

ray [rei] *n* rayon *m*.

rayon [reiɒn] *n* rayonne *f*.

razor ['reizə] *n* rasoir *m*. **razor blade** lame de rasoir *f*.

reach [riːtʃ] *v* atteindre, arriver à; (*extend*) s'étendre. **reach out** étendre le bras. *n* portée *f*. **out of reach** hors de portée. **within reach** à portée.

react [ri'akt] *v* réagir. **reaction** *n* réaction

f. **reactionary** *n(m+f)*, *adj* réactionnaire. **reactor** *n* réacteur *m*.

*read [riːd] *v* lire; étudier. **reader** *n* lecteur, -trice *m, f*; (*anthology*) recueil de textes *m*. **reading** *n* lecture *f*.

readjust [riːə'dʒʌst] *v* rajuster, (se) réadapter. **readjustment** *n* réadaptation *f*, rajustement *m*.

ready ['redi] *adj* prêt; prompt. **get ready** (se) préparer. **ready cash** argent liquide *m*. **ready-made** *adj* tout fait, tout prêt. **readily** *adv* volontiers. **readiness** *n* empressement *m*.

real [riəl] *adj* réel, vrai. **realism** *n* réalisme *m*. **realist** *n* réaliste *m, f*. **realistic** *adj* réaliste. **reality** *n* réalité *f*. **really** *adv* vraiment.

realize ['riəlaiz] *v* se rendre compte de; (*make real*) réaliser. **realization** *n* prise de conscience *f*; réalisation *f*.

realm [relm] *n* domaine *m*; (*kingdom*) royaume *m*.

reap [riːp] *v* moissonner; (*profit*) récolter. **reaping** *n* moisson *f*. **reaping machine** moissonneuse *f*.

reappear [riːə'piə] *v* réapparaître. **reappearance** *n* réapparition *f*.

rear¹ [riə] *nm, adj* arrière. **bring up the rear** fermer la marche. **rear-admiral** *n* contre-amiral *m*. **rearguard** *n* arrière-garde *f*. **rear-view mirror** rétroviseur *m*.

rear² [riə] *n* (*family*) élever; (*lift up*) dresser; (*horse, etc*.) se cabrer.

rearrange [riːə'reindʒ] *v* réarranger. **rearrangement** *n* réarrangement *m*.

reason ['riːzn] *n* raison *f*. *v* raisonner. **reasonable** *adj* raisonnable. **reasoning** *n* raisonnement *m*.

reassure [riə'ʃuə] *v* rassurer. **reassurance** *n* réconfort *m*. **reassuring** *adj* rassurant.

rebate ['riːbeit] *n* (*discount*) rabais *m*; remboursement *m*.

rebel ['rebl] *n(m+f)*, *adj* rebelle. *v* se rebeller. **rebellion** *n* rébellion *f*. **rebellious** *adj* rebelle; désobéissant.

rebound [ri'baund; *n* 'riːbaund] *v* rebondir. *n* rebond *m*; ricochet *m*.

rebuff [ri'bʌf] *n* rebuffade *f*. *v* repousser.

*rebuild [riː'bild] *v* rebâtir.

rebuke [ri'bjuːk] *n* reproche *m*. *v* réprimander.

recall [ri'kɔːl] *v* (se) rappeler. *n* rappel *m*.

recant [ri'kant] *v* (se) rétracter; (*rel*) abjurer.

recap ['riːkap] (*coll*) *v* faire un résumé (de). *n* récapitulation *f*.

recapture [riˈkaptʃə] *v* reprendre; (*atmosphere*) recréer. *n* arrestation *f*.

recede [riˈsiːd] *v* s'éloigner; (*tide*) descendre.

receipt [rəˈsiːt] *n* (*receiving*) réception *f*; (*slip of paper*) reçu *m*, accusé de réception *m*.

receive [rəˈsiːv] *v* recevoir. **receiver** *n* (*phone*) récepteur *m*; (*law*) administrateur judiciaire *m*.

recent ['riːsnt] *adj* récent. **recently** *adv* récemment.

receptacle [rəˈseptəkl] *n* récipient *m*.

reception [rəˈsepʃən] *n* réception *f*. **receptionist** *n* réceptionniste *m*, *f*.

recess [riˈses] *n* renfoncement *m*, alcôve *f*; (*pol, law*) vacances *f pl*; (*of mind*) recoin *m*.

recession [rəˈseʃən] *n* (*econ*) récession *f*; recul *m*.

recharge [riːˈtʃɑːdʒ] *v* recharger.

recipe ['resəpi] *n* recette *f*.

recipient [rəˈsipiənt] *n* (*letter*) destinataire *m*, *f*; (*cheque*) bénéficiaire *m*, *f*.

reciprocate [rəˈsiprəkeit] *v* retourner; offrir en retour. **reciprocating engine** moteur alternatif *m*. **reciprocal** *nf*, *adj* réciproque.

recite [rəˈsait] *v* réciter. **recital** *n* (*music*) récital *m*. **recitation** *n* récitation *f*.

reckless ['rekləs] *adj* insouciant; imprudent. **recklessness** *n* insouciance *f*; imprudence *f*.

reckon ['rekən] *v* compter, calculer; considérer, estimer; (*coll*) penser. **reckoning** *n* compte *m*, calcul *m*; estimation *f*.

reclaim [riˈkleim] *v* réclamer; (*land*) assécher, défricher; (*by-product*) récupérer. **reclamation** *n* réclamation *f*; assèchement *m*, défrichement *m*; récupération *f*.

recline [rəˈklain] *v* reposer; être allongé.

recluse [rəˈkluːs] *n* reclus, -e *m*, *f*.

recognize ['rekəgnaiz] *v* reconnaître. **recognition** *n* reconnaissance *f*. **recognizable** *adj* reconnaissable.

recoil [rəˈkoil; *n* riˈkoil] *v* reculer; (*spring*) se détendre. *n* recul *m*; détente *f*; dégoût *m*.

recollect [rekəˈlekt] *v* se souvenir (de). **recollection** *n* souvenir *m*.

recommence [riːkəˈmens] *v* recommencer.

recommend [rekəˈmend] *v* recommander,

conseiller. **recommendation** *n* recommandation *f*.

recompense ['rekəmpens] *n* récompense *f*; (*law*) dédommagement *m*. *v* récompenser; dédommager.

reconcile ['rekənsail] *v* réconcilier; (*ideas*) concilier; (*argument*) arranger. **reconcile oneself to** se résigner à. **reconciliation** *n* réconciliation *f*; conciliation *f*.

reconstruct [riːkənˈstrʌkt] *v* reconstruire; (*crime*) reconstituer. **reconstruction** *n* reconstruction *f*; reconstitution *f*.

record [rəˈkoːd; *n* 'rekoːd] *v* enregistrer. *n* disque *m*; (*sport, etc.*) record *m*; registre *m*, rapport *m*; dossier *m*. **record-player** *n* électrophone *m*. **record token** chèque-disque *m*. **recorded** *adj* enregistré. **by recorded delivery** avec avis de réception. **recorder** *n* (*music*) flûte à bec *f*. **recording** *n* enregistrement *m*.

recount [riˈkaunt] *v* raconter.

recoup [riˈkuːp] *v* récupérer.

recover [rəˈkʌvə] *v* (*get back*) retrouver, récupérer; (*get well*) se remettre, se rétablir. **recovery** *n* récupération *f*; (*from illness*) guérison *f*.

recreation [rekriˈeiʃən] *n* récréation *f*.

recruit [rəˈkruːt] *n* recrue *f*. *v* recruter. **recruitment** *n* recrutement *m*.

rectangle ['rektaŋgl] *n* rectangle *m*. **rectangular** *adj* rectangulaire.

rectify ['rektifai] *v* rectifier.

rectum ['rektəm] *n* rectum *m*.

recuperate [rəˈkjuːpəreit] *v* (*person*) se rétablir; (*get back*) récupérer. **recuperation** *n* rétablissement *m*; récupération *f*.

recur [riˈkəː] *v* se reproduire, se retrouver; (*illness*) réapparaître. **recurrence** *n* répétition *f*. **recurrent** *or* **recurring** *adj* périodique.

red [red] *n* rouge *m*. **in the red** à découvert. *adj* rouge; (*hair*) roux, rousse. **go red** rougir. **redcurrant** *n* groseille rouge *f*. **red-handed** *adv* en flagrant délit. **redhead** *n* roux, rousse *m*, *f*. **red-hot** *adj* chauffé au rouge. **Red Indian** *n* peau-rouge *m*, *f*. **red tape** paperasserie *f*.

redeem [rəˈdiːm] *v* racheter; (*from pawn*) dégager. **redemption** *n* rachat *m*; dégagement *m*; (*rel*) rédemption *f*. **beyond redemption** irréparable; irrémédiable.

redirect [riːdaiˈrekt] *v* (*letter, etc.*) faire suivre.

redress [rəˈdres] *v* redresser. *n* redressement *m*, réparation *f*.

reduce [rə'djuːs] v réduire; diminuer; (*lower*) abaisser. **reduction** n réduction f; (*comm*) remise f, rabais m.

redundant [rə'dʌndənt] adj superflu, redondant, en surnombre. **be made redundant** être licencié. **redundancy** n superfluité f; licenciement m.

reed [riːd] n (*bot*) roseau m; (*of wind instrument*) anche f.

reef [riːf] n récif m.

reek [riːk] v puer. n puanteur f.

reel[1] [riːl] n (*thread*) bobine f; (*film*) bande f. v **reel off** débiter.

reel[2] [riːl] v chanceler, tituber.

refectory [rə'fektəri] n réfectoire m.

refer [rə'fəɪ] v parler; faire allusion; s'appliquer; (*consult*) se reporter; (*pass*) soumettre. **reference** n référence f; allusion f; (*in book*) renvoi m. **reference book** ouvrage de référence m. **reference number** numéro de référence m.

referee [refə'riː] n arbitre m; (*job application*) répondant, -e m, f. v arbitrer.

referendum [refə'rendəm] n référendum m.

refill [riː'fil; n 'riːfil] v recharger. n recharge f, cartouche f.

refine [rə'fain] v affiner, raffiner. **refinement** n (*person*) raffinement m; (*refining*) raffinage m, affinage m; perfectionnement m. **refinery** n raffinerie f, affinerie f.

reflation [rə'fleiʃn] n (*econ*) relance f.

reflect [rə'flekt] v (*light*) refléter; (*mirror*) réfléchir; (*think*) penser; méditer. **reflection** n réflexion f; image f, reflet m. **reflector** n réflecteur m.

reflex ['riːfleks] nm, adj réflexe. **reflexive** adj réfléchi.

reform [rə'fɔːm] n réforme f. v (se) réformer. **reformation** n réforme f. **reformed** adj réformé; (*person*) amendé.

refract [rə'frakt] v réfracter. **refraction** n réfraction f.

refrain[1] [rə'frein] v s'abstenir.

refrain[2] [rə'frein] n refrain m.

refresh [rə'freʃ] v rafraîchir; (*rest*) reposer. **refresher course** cours de recyclage m. **refreshments** pl n rafraîchissements m pl.

refrigerator [rə'fridʒəreitə] n réfrigérateur m. **refrigerate** v réfrigérer. **refrigeration** n réfrigération f.

refuel [riː'fjuːəl] v (se) ravitailler.

refuge ['refjuːdʒ] n refuge m. **take refuge** se réfugier. **refugee** n réfugié, -e m, f.

refund [ri'fʌnd; n 'riːfʌnd] v rembourser. n remboursement m.

refuse[1] [rə'fjuːz] v refuser. **refusal** n refus m.

refuse[2] ['refjuːs] n détritus m pl, déchets m pl, ordures f pl.

refute [ri'fjuːt] v réfuter.

regain [ri'gein] v regagner; (*health*) recouvrer; (*consciousness*) reprendre.

regal ['riːgəl] adj royal.

regard [rə'gaːd] v regarder; considérer. **as regards** en ce qui concerne. n égard m, attention f; respect m, estime f. **regards** pl n (*in letter*) amitiés f pl. **regarding** prep quant à. **regardless** adv quand même. **regardless of** sans regarder à.

regatta [rə'gatə] n régate f.

regent ['riːdʒənt] n régent, -e m, f. **regency** n régence f.

regime [rei'ʒiːm] n régime m.

regiment ['redʒimənt] n régiment m. **regimental** adj régimentaire.

region ['riːdʒən] n région f. **regional** adj régional.

register ['redʒistə] n registre m. v (*record*) enregistrer; (*as member, etc.*) s'inscrire; (*birth, death*) déclarer; (*meter*) indiquer; (*letter*) recommander. **registrar** n officier de l'état civil m; (*med*) interne m, f. **registration** n enregistrement m, inscription f. **registration number** numéro d'immatriculation m. **registry office** bureau de l'état civil m.

regress [ri'gres] v régresser; reculer. **regression** n recul m; régression f.

regret [rə'gret] v regretter. n regret m. **regrettable** adj regrettable.

regular ['regjulə] adj régulier; habituel, normal. n habitué, -e m, f. **regularity** n régularité f.

regulate ['regjuleit] v régler.

regulation [regju'leiʃən] n règlement m. adj réglementaire.

rehabilitate [riːhə'biliteit] v réhabiliter; (*for work*) réadapter. **rehabilitation** n réhabilitation f; réadaptation f.

rehearse [rə'həːs] v répéter. **rehearsal** n répétition f.

rehouse [riː'hauz] v reloger.

reign [rein] n règne m. v régner.

reimburse [riːim'bəːs] v rembourser.

rein [rein] n rêne f; (*control*) bride f.

reincarnation [riːinkaɪ'neiʃən] n réincarnation f.

reindeer ['reindiə] *n* renne *m*.
reinforce [riːin'fɔːs] *v* renforcer. **reinforcement** *n* renforcement *m*. **reinforcements** *pl n* renforts *m pl*.
reinstate [riːin'steit] *v* réintégrer. **reinstatement** *n* réintégration *f*.
reinvest [riːin'vest] *v* réinvestir.
reissue [riː'iʃuː] *v* (*book*) rééditer; (*film*) ressortir. *n* réédition *f*.
reject [rə'dʒekt; *n* 'riːdʒekt] *v* refuser, rejeter. *n* pièce de rebut *f*. *adj* de rebut. **rejection** *n* refus *m*, rejet *m*.
rejoice [rə'dʒɔis] *v* (se) réjouir. **rejoicing** *n* réjouissance *f*.
rejoin [rə'dʃɔin] *v* rejoindre.
rejuvenate [rə'dʒuːvəneit] *v* rajeunir.
relapse [rə'laps] *n* rechute *f*. *v* rechuter.
relate [rə'leit] *v* raconter; (*be connected*) se rapporter; (*associate*) établir un rapport entre. **related** *adj* apparenté. **relating to** concernant.
relation [rə'leiʃn] *n* (*family*) parent, -e *m, f*; (*connection*) rapport *m*; (*business, etc.*) relation *f*. **relationship** *n* liens de parenté *m pl*; (*personal*) rapports *m pl*, relations *f pl*.
relative ['relətiv] *adj* relatif; respectif. *n* parent, -e *m, f*. **relatively** *adv* relativement; (*rather*) assez. **relativity** *n* relativité *f*.
relax [rə'laks] *v* (se) relâcher; (*person*) (se) détendre; (*rules*) modérer. **relaxation** *n* relâchement *m*; détente *f*, relaxation *f*. **relaxing** *adj* délassant, relaxant.
relay ['riːlei; *v* ri'lei] *n* relais *m*. **relay race** course de relais *f*. *v* relayer.
release [rə'liːs] *v* libérer; (*let go*) lâcher; (*record, film*) sortir. *n* libération *f*; sortie *f*.
relegate ['religeit] *v* reléguer. **relegation** *n* relégation *f*.
relent [rə'lent] *v* s'adoucir; revenir sur sa décision. **relentless** *adj* implacable.
relevant ['reləvənt] *adj* pertinent; approprié; significatif. **relevance** *n* rapport *m*; pertinence *f*.
reliable [ri'laiəbl] *adj* sérieux; (*machine*) solide. **reliability** *n* sérieux *m*; sûreté *f*; solidité *f*.
relic ['relik] *n* relique *f*.
relief [rə'liːf] *n* soulagement *m*; (*help*) secours *m*; (*geog, art*) relief *m*. *adj* supplémentaire.
relieve [rə'liːv] *v* soulager; (*help*) secourir;

(*take over*) relayer; (*take away*) débarrasser, décharger.
religion [rə'lidʒən] *n* religion *f*. **religious** *adj* religieux; scrupuleux.
relinquish [rə'liŋkwiʃ] *v* (*give up*) renoncer à, abandonner; (*let go*) lâcher.
relish ['reliʃ] *n* goût *m*, attrait *m*. *v* (*food, drink*) savourer; (*enjoy*) se délecter à.
relive [riː'liv] *v* revivre.
reluctant [rə'lʌktənt] *adj* peu disposé. **reluctance** *n* répugnance *f*. **reluctantly** *adv* à contrecœur.
rely [rə'lai] *v* **rely on** compter sur.
remain [rə'mein] *v* rester. **remainder** *n* reste *m*. **remains** *pl n* restes *m pl*.
remand [rə'maind] *v* renvoyer. *n* renvoi *m*. **on remand** en prévention.
remark [rə'maik] *n* remarque *f*; observation *f*. *v* remarquer; faire une remarque. **remarkable** *adj* remarquable.
remarry [riː'mari] *v* se remarier. **remarriage** *n* remariage *m*.
remedial [rə'miːdiəl] *adj* réparateur, -trice; (*teaching, class*) de rattrapage.
remedy ['remədi] *n* remède *m*. *v* remédier à.
remember [ri'membə] *v* se souvenir (de), se rappeler. **remembrance** *n* souvenir *m*.
remind [rə'maind] *v* rappeler. **reminder** *n* mémento *m*; (*comm*) lettre de rappel *f*.
reminiscence [remə'nisens] *n* réminiscence *f*. **reminiscent** *adj* qui rappelle.
remiss [rə'mis] *adj* négligent.
remission [rə'miʃn] *n* rémission *f*; (*law*) remise *f*.
remit [rə'mit] *v* (*law, rel*) remettre; (*money*) envoyer; (*lessen*) (se) relâcher. **remittance** *n* versement *m*, paiement *m*.
remnant ['remnənt] *n* reste *m*; (*fabric*) coupon *m*.
remorse [rə'mɔːs] *n* remords *m*. **remorseless** *adj* sans remords; implacable.
remote [rə'mout] *adj* lointain; isolé; vague. **remote control** télécommande *f*.
remould ['riːmould; *v* riː'mould] *n* pneu rechapé *m*. *v* remouler; rechaper.
remove [rə'muːv] *v* enlever; (*move house*) déménager. **removal** *n* enlèvement *m*; déménagement *m*.
remunerate [rə'mjuːnəreit] *v* rémunérer. **remuneration** *n* rémunération *f*. **remunerative** *adj* rémunérateur, -trice.
renaissance [rə'neisəns] *n* renaissance *f*.
rename [riː'neim] *v* rebaptiser.

render [rendə] v rendre; remettre; (*fat*) faire fondre. **rendering** or **rendition** n interprétation f.

rendezvous ['rondivuː] n rendez-vous m. v se retrouver.

renegade ['renigeid] n renégat, -e m, f.

renew [rə'njuː] v renouveler; remplacer. **renewal** renouvellement m; remplacement m; (*of subscription*) réabonnement m.

renounce [ri'nauns] v renoncer à, renier. **renunciation** n renonciation f, reniement m.

renovate ['renəveit] v rénover, remettre à neuf. **renovation** n rénovation f; remise à neuf f.

renown [rə'naun] n renommée f; renom m. **renowned** adj renommé.

rent [rent] n loyer m. v louer. **rental** n prix de location m.

reopen [riː'oupən] v rouvrir; (*recommence*) reprendre. **reopening** n réouverture f.

reorganize [riː'ɔɪgənaiz] v (se) réorganiser. **reorganization** n réorganisation f.

rep [rep] n (*coll*) représentant, -e m, f.

repair [ri'peə] v réparer. n réparation f. **beyond repair** irréparable. **in good/bad repair** en bon/mauvais état. **repairer** n réparateur, -trice m, f.

repartee [repɑ'tiː] n repartie f.

repatriate [riː'patrieit; n riː'patriət] v rapatrier. n rapatrié, -e m, f. **repatriation** n rapatriement m.

*repay [ri'pei] v rembourser; récompenser; (*debt*) s'acquitter de. **repayment** n remboursement m; récompense f.

repeal [rə'piːl] v abroger, annuler. n abrogation f, annulation f.

repeat [rə'piːt] v répéter; réciter; (*music*) reprendre. n répétition f; (*broadcast, music*) reprise f.

repel [rə'pel] v repousser. **repellent** adj repoussant.

repent [rə'pent] v se repentir (de). **repentance** n repentir m. **repentant** adj repentant.

repercussion [riːpə'kʌʃən] n répercussion f.

repertoire ['repətwaɪ] n répertoire m.

repertory ['repətəri] n théâtre de répertoire m. **repertory company** compagnie de répertoire f.

repetition [repə'tiʃn] n répétition f. **repeti-tive** adj (*person*) rabâcheur, -euse; (*work*) monotone.

replace [rə'pleis] v (*substitute*) remplacer; (*put back*) replacer. **replacement** n remplacement m; (*person*) remplaçant, -e m, f; replacement m.

replay [ri'plei; n 'riːplei] v rejouer. n match rejoué m.

replenish [rə'pleniʃ] v remplir. **replenishment** n remplissage m.

replica ['replikə] n (*picture*) réplique f; (*document*) fac-similé m.

reply [rə'plai] n réponse f. v répondre.

report [rə'pɔɪt] n rapport m, compte rendu m; (*press*) reportage m; bulletin scolaire m; détonation f. v rapporter; faire un reportage; (*notify*) signaler; se présenter. **reporter** n reporter m; journaliste m, f.

repose [rə'pouz] n repos m. v (se) reposer.

represent [reprə'zent] v représenter. **representation** n représentation f.

representative [reprə'zentətiv] adj représentatif. n représentant, -e m, f.

repress [rə'pres] v réprimer. **repression** n répression f. **repressive** adj répressif.

reprieve [rə'priːv] n sursis m; (*law*) grâce f. v accorder du répit à.

reprimand ['reprimaːnd] n réprimande f. v réprimander.

reprint [riː'print; n 'riːprint] v réimprimer. n réimpression f.

reprisal [rə'praizəl] n représailles f pl.

reproach [rə'proutʃ] n reproche m. v réprocher à. **reproachful** adj réprobateur, -trice.

reproduce [riːprə'djuːs] v (se) reproduire. **reproduction** n reproduction f. **reproductive** adj reproducteur, -trice.

reprove [rə'pruːv] v (*person*) blâmer; (*action*) reprouver. **reproof** n réprimande m.

reptile ['reptail] n reptile m.

republic [rə'pʌblik] n république f. **republican** n, adj républicain, -e.

repudiate [rə'pjuːdieit] v répudier; (*person*) renier. **repudiation** n répudiation f; reniement m.

repugnant [rə'pʌgnənt] adj répugnant. **repugnance** n répugnance f.

repulsion [rə'pʌlʃn] n répulsion f. **repulsive** adj répulsif, repoussant.

repute [rə'pjuːt] n réputation f. **reputable** adj honorable, de bonne réputation. **rep-**

utation n réputation f. **reputed** adj
réputé, censé.
request [ri'kwest] n demande f. v
demander. **request stop** arrêt facultatif
m.
requiem ['rekwiəm] n requiem m.
require [rə'kwaiə] v (need) demander,
avoir besoin de; (order) exiger. **require-
ment** n (need) exigence f; condition f.
requisition [ˌrekwi'ziʃən] n demande f;
réquisition f. v réquisitionner.
*****reread** [riː'riːd] v relire.
re-route [riː'ruːt] v dérouter.
*****rerun** [riː'rʌn; n 'riːrʌn] v (film) passer de
nouveau; (race) courir de nouveau. n
reprise f.
resale [riː'seil] n revente f.
rescue ['reskjuː] n sauvetage m; (help)
secours m; (freeing) délivrance f. v
sauver; secourir; délivrer. **rescuer** n
sauveteur m.
research [ri'səːtʃ] n recherche f. v faire
des recherches. **researcher** n chercheur,
-euse m, f.
*****resell** [riː'sel] v revendre.
resemble [rə'zembl] v ressembler à.
resemblance n ressemblance f.
resent [ri'zent] v s'offusquer de. **resentful**
adj rancunier. **resentment** n ressentiment
m.
reserve [rə'zəːv] v réserver. n réserve f;
(sport) remplaçant, -e m, f. **reservation** n
réserve f; (booking) réservation f.
reserved adj réservé; (person) renfermé.
reservoir ['rezəvwaː] n réservoir m.
reside [rə'zaid] v résider. **residence** n résidence f; (hostel) foyer m; (stay) séjour m.
resident n habitant, -e m, f; (in hotel)
pensionnaire m, f. **residential** adj résidentiel.
residue ['rezidjuː] n reste m; (chem)
résidu m. **residual** adj restant; résiduaire.
resign [rə'zain] v (from job) donner sa
démission (de), démissionner. **resign
oneself to** se résigner à. **resignation** n
démission f; résignation f. **resigned** adj
résigné.
resilient [rə'ziliənt] adj (rubber, etc.) élastique. **be resilient** (person) avoir du ressort. **resilience** n elasticité f; ressort m.
resin ['rezin] n résine f.
resist [rə'zist] v résister (à). **resistance** n
résistance f. **resistant** adj résistant.
*****resit** [riː'sit; n 'riːsit] v (exam) repasser. n
deuxième session f.

resolute ['rezəluːt] adj résolu.
resolution [ˌrezə'luːʃən] n résolution f.
resolve [rə'zolv] v (se) résoudre. n résolution f.
resonant ['rezənənt] adj sonore; (phys)
résonant. **resonance** n résonance f. **resonate** v résonner.
resort [rə'zoːt] n recours m, ressource f;
(place) station f, lieu de vacances m. **as a
last resort** en dernier ressort. v **resort to**
avoir recours à.
resound [rə'zaund] v retentir, résonner.
resounding adj sonore; (victory, etc.)
retentissant.
resource [rə'zoːs] n ressource f. **resourceful** adj ingénieux.
respect [rə'spekt] n respect m; (aspect)
égard m, rapport m. **pay one's respects**
présenter ses respects. **with respect to** en
ce qui concerne. v respecter. **respectable**
adj respectable; (dress, behaviour) convenable. **respectful** adj respectueux. **respective** adj respectif.
respiration [respə'reiʃn] n respiration f.
respite ['respait] n répit m.
respond [rə'spond] v répondre. **response** n
réponse f. **be responsive** réagir bien.
responsible [rə'sponsəbl] adj responsable;
digne de confiance. **responsibility** n
responsabilité f.
rest[1] [rest] n repos m; (music) silence m;
support m. v (se) reposer; (lean)
(s')appuyer; (land, put) (se) poser. **restful**
adj reposant. **restive** adj agité; impatient.
restless adj agité.
rest[2] [rest] n **the rest** (remaining part) le
reste m; (remaining ones) les autres m pl.
v rester.
restaurant ['restront] n restaurant m. **restaurant car** (on train) wagon-restaurant
m.
restore [rə'stoː] v rendre; (order, rights,
etc.) rétablir; (building, etc.) restaurer.
restoration n rétablissement m; restauration f.
restrain [rə'strein] v retenir; (temper, etc.)
contenir. **restraint** n contrainte f; (moderation) retenue f.
restrict [rə'strikt] v restreindre. **restricted**
adj restreint; confidentiel; (narrow)
étroit. **restriction** n restriction f; limitation f. **restrictive** adj restrictif.
result [rə'zʌlt] n résultat m; conséquence
f. v résulter. **result in** aboutir à. **resultant**
adj résultant.

resume [rə'zjuːm] v reprendre. **resumption** n reprise f.

résumé ['reizumei] n résumé m.

resurgence [ri'sɜːdʒəns] n réapparition f.

resurrect [rezə'rekt] v ressusciter; (coll) remettre en service. **resurrection** n résurrection f.

resuscitate [rə'sʌsəteit] v ranimer.

retail ['riːteil] n détail m. v (se) vendre au détail. **retailer** n détaillant, -e m, f.

retain [rə'tein] v (keep) garder; (hold) retenir.

retaliate [rə'talieit] v se venger. **retaliation** n revanche f. in retaliation par représailles.

retard [rə'taɪd] v retarder. **retarded** adj retardé; (mentally) arriéré.

reticent ['retisənt] adj réticent. **reticence** n réticence f.

retina ['retinə] n rétine f.

retinue ['retinjuː] n suite f.

retire [rə'taiə] v se retirer; (from work) prendre sa retraite; (go to bed) se coucher. **retired** adj retraité. **retirement** n retraite f.

retort[1] [rə'tɔːt] v rétorquer. n réplique f.

retort[2] [rə'tɔːt] n (chem) cornue f.

retrace [ri'treis] v reconstituer, retracer. **retrace one's steps** rebrousser chemin.

retract [rə'trakt] v (se) rétracter.

retreat [rə'triːt] n retraite f; (place) asile m. v se retirer; (mil) battre en retraite.

retrial [ri:'traiəl] n nouveau procès m.

retrieve [rə'triːv] v récupérer; sauver. **retrieval** n récupération f. **retriever** n (dog) retriever m.

retrograde ['retrəgreid] adj rétrograde.

retrospect ['retrəspekt] n **in retrospect** rétrospectivement. **retrospective** adj rétrospectif.

return [rə'tɜːn] v retourner; (come back) revenir; (give back) rendre; (pol) élire. n retour m; (ticket) aller et retour m; (from investments, etc.) rapport m; (tax) déclaration f. in return en revanche. in return for en récompense de.

reunite [riːjuː'nait] v (se) réunir. **reunion** n réunion f.

rev [rev] n (mot) n tour m. v **rev up** emballer.

reveal [rə'viːl] v révéler; laisser voir. **revealing** adj révélateur, -trice. **revelation** n révélation f.

revel ['revl] v se délecter (à). **revelry** n festivités f pl.

revenge [rə'vendʒ] n vengeance f. v venger.

revenue ['revinjuː] n revenu m.

reverberate [rə'vɔːbəreit] v (sound) retentir, (se) répercuter; (heat, light) (se) réverbérer. **reverberation** n répercussion f; réverbération f.

reverence ['revərəns] n vénération f. **revere** v révérer. **reverent** adj respectueux.

reverse [rə'vɔːs] adj contraire, opposé. n contraire m, opposé m; (coin) revers m; (page) verso m; (mot) marche arrière f. v renverser, retourner; (order) inverser; (mot) faire marche arrière. **reverse the charges** (phone) téléphoner en P.C.V. **reversal** n renversement m. **reversible** adj réversible.

revert [rə'vɔːt] v revenir, retourner.

review [rə'vjuː] n revue f; révision f; critique f. v passer en revue; réconsidérer; faire la critique de. **reviewer** n critique m.

revise [rə'vaiz] v réviser; corriger. **revision** n révision f.

revive [rə'vaiv] v ranimer; reprendre connaissance; (custom) rétablir; (trade) reprendre. **revival** n reprise f.

revoke [rə'vouk] v révoquer, revenir sur; (withdraw) retirer.

revolt [rə'voult] n révolte f. v (se) révolter. **revolting** adj dégoûtant.

revolution [revə'luːʃən] n révolution f. **revolutionary** n(m+f), adj révolutionnaire. **revolutionize** v révolutionner.

revolve [rə'volv] v (faire) tourner. **revolver** n revolver m. **revolving door** tambour m.

revue [rə'vjuː] n revue f.

revulsion [rə'vʌlʃən] n dégoût m.

reward [rə'wɔːd] n récompense f. v récompenser.

***rewind** [riː'waind] v (film, tape) réembobiner. **rewinding** n réembobinage m.

***rewrite** [riː'rait] v récrire; recopier.

Reykjavik ['reikjə,viːk] n Reykjavik.

rhesus ['riːsəs] n rhésus m. **rhesus negative/positive** rhésus négatif/positif.

rhetoric ['retərik] n rhétorique f. **rhetorical** adj rhétorique. **rhetorical question** question pour la forme f.

rheumatism ['ruːmətizəm] n rhumatisme m. **rheumatic** adj rhumatismal.

rhinoceros [rai'nosərəs] n rhinocéros m.

rhododendron [roudə'dendrən] n rhododendron m.

rhubarb ['ruːbɑːb] n rhubarbe f.

rhyme [raim] n rime f; (poetry) vers m pl. v (faire) rimer.

rhythm ['riðəm] n rythme m. **rhythmic** adj rythmique; (music) rythmé.

rib [rib] n côte f.

ribbon ['ribən] n ruban m. **in ribbons** en lambeaux.

rice [rais] n riz m. **rice paper** papier de riz m. **rice pudding** riz au lait m.

rich [ritʃ] adj riche. **riches** pl n richesses f pl. **richness** n richesse f.

rickety ['rikəti] adj branlant.

***rid** [rid] v débarrasser. **get rid of** se débarrasser de. **riddance** n débarras m.

ridden ['ridn] V **ride**.

riddle¹ ['ridl] n énigme f.

riddle² ['ridl] v cribler.

***ride** [raid] v monter; (horse) monter à cheval. n promenade f, tour m; (journey) trajet m. **rider** n (horse) cavalier, -ère m, f; (addition) annexe f. **riding** n équitation f. **riding school** manège m.

ridge [ridʒ] n (hills) faîte m; (roof) arête f; (on surface) strie f.

ridicule ['ridikjuːl] n ridicule m. v ridiculiser. **ridiculous** adj ridicule.

rife [raif] adj répandu.

rifle¹ ['raifl] n fusil m. **rifle range** champ de tir m.

rifle² ['raifl] v piller; (house, drawer) dévaliser.

rift [rift] n fissure f; division f.

rig [rig] n (naut) gréement m. **rig-out** n (coll) tenue f. v gréer; (falsify) truquer. **rigging** n gréement m; truquage m.

right [rait] adj (not left) droit; juste; approprié; (correct) bon, bonne. **be right** avoir raison. adv à droite; (straight) droit; (completely) tout à fait; (well) bien. n droite f; (entitlement) droit m; (good) bien m. v redresser. **right angle** angle droit m. **right-handed** adj droitier m. **right-of-way** n (public) droit de passage m; (mot) priorité f. **right-wing** adj (pol) de droite.

righteous ['raitʃəs] adj vertueux; juste.

rightful ['raitful] adj légitime.

rigid ['ridʒid] adj rigide; strict. **rigidity** n rigidité f.

rigmarole ['rigməroul] n (coll) comédie f; (speech) galimatias m.

rigour ['rigə] n rigueur f. **rigorous** adj rigoureux.

rim [rim] n bord m; (wheel) jante f.

rind [raind] n (fruit) peau f; (cheese) croûte f; (bacon) couenne f.

ring¹ [riŋ] n anneau m; (with gem) bague f; cercle m, rond m; (circus) piste f; (boxing) ring m. v entourer d'un cercle. **ringleader** n meneur m. **ring road** route de ceinture f.

***ring²** [riŋ] v (bell) sonner; téléphoner (à); résonner. **ring off** (phone) raccrocher. **ring up** (coll: phone) donner un coup de fil à. n sonnerie f; (coll: phone) coup de fil m.

rink [riŋk] n patinoire f.

rinse [rins] v rincer. n rinçage m.

riot ['raiət] n émeute f. v faire une émeute.

rip [rip] v (se) déchirer. **rip off** or **out** arracher. n déchirure f.

ripe [raip] adj mûr. **ripen** v mûrir. **ripeness** n maturité f.

ripple ['ripl] n ondulation f, ride f; (laughter) cascade f. v (se) rider, (faire) onduler.

***rise** [raiz] n (sun, etc.) lever m; (increase) hausse f; (in salary) augmentation f; (in importance) essor m. **give rise to** engendrer. v se lever, s'élever; augmenter, être en hausse; (rebel) se soulever. **rising** adj levant; en hausse; (anger) croissant.

risen ['rizn] V **rise**.

risk [risk] n risque m. **at risk** en danger. v risquer. **risky** adj risqué.

rissole ['risoul] n croquette f.

rite [rait] n rite m.

ritual ['ritʃuəl] nm, adj rituel.

rival ['raivəl] n, adj rival, -e. v rivaliser avec. **rivalry** n rivalité f.

river ['rivə] n rivière f; (larger) fleuve m. **riverside** n bord de l'eau m.

rivet ['rivit] n rivet m. v (tech) riveter; fixer, clouer. **riveting** adj fascinant.

Riviera [rivi'eərə] n **the Riviera** (French) la Côte d'Azur f; (Italian) la Riviera f.

road [roud] n route f; (to success, etc.) voie f, chemin m. **road-block** n barrage routier m. **road safety** sécurité routière f. **roadside** n bord de la route m. **road sign** panneau de signalisation m. **road-works** pl n travaux m pl.

roam [roum] v parcourir, errer.

roar [roː] v (lion) rugir; (crowd) hurler; (bull, wind) mugir; (engine) vrombir;

(*thunder*) gronder. **roar with laughter** éclater de rire. *n* rugissement *m*; hurlement *m*; mugissement *m*; vrombissement *m*; grondement *m*.

roast [roust] *v* (*meat*) rôtir; (*coffee, chestnuts*) griller. *nm, adj* rôti.

rob [rob] *v* voler, dévaliser. **robber** *n* voleur *m*. **robbery** *n* vol *m*.

robe [roub] *n* robe *f*. *v* revêtir.

robin ['robin] *n* rouge-gorge *m*.

robot ['roubot] *n* robot *m*.

robust [rə'bʌst] *adj* robuste, vigoureux, solide.

rock¹ [rok] *n* (*stone*) roche *f*; (*hard*) roc *m*; (*boulder*) rocher *m*. **rock bun** or **cake** rocher *m*. **rock-climbing** *n* varappe *f*. **rock-plant** *n* plante alpestre *f*. **rockery** *n* rocaille *f*. **rocky** *adj* rocheux, rocailleux.

rock² [rok] *v* (*sway*) bercer, (se) balancer; (*shake*) ébranler. *n* (*music*) rock *m*. **rocking-chair** *n* fauteuil à bascule *m*. **rocking-horse** *n* cheval à bascule *m*.

rocket ['rokit] *n* fusée *f*. *v* (*prices*) monter en flèche.

rod [rod] *n* (*wood*) baguette *f*; (*metal*) tringle *f*; (*fishing*) canne *f*.

rode [roud] *V* ride.

rodent ['roudənt] *n* rongeur *m*.

roe [rou] n (*hard*) œufs de poisson *m pl*; (*soft*) laitance *f*.

rogue [roug] *n* coquin, -e *m, f*. **roguish** *adj* espiègle.

role [roul] *n* rôle *m*.

roll [roul] *n* rouleau *m*; (*bread*) petit pain *m*; (*drums*) roulement *m*; (*register*) liste *f*. **roll-call** *n* appel *m*. *v* rouler. **roll in** (*coll*) affluer; (*coll: person*) s'amener. **roll over** (se) retourner. **roll up** rouler; (*sleeves*) retrousser. **roller** *n* rouleau *m*. **roller-coaster** *n* montagnes russes *f pl*. **roller-skate** *n* patin à roulettes *m*. **rolling-pin** *n* rouleau *m*.

romance [rou'mans] *n* (*love*) idylle f, amour *m*; (*story*) roman à l'eau de rose *m*. **Romance** *adj* (*language*) roman. **romantic** *n*(*m*+*f*), *adj* romantique.

Romania [ru:'meinjə] *n* Roumanie *f*. **Romanian** *n*(*m*) roumain; *n* (*people*) Roumain, -e *m, f*.

Rome [roum] *n* Rome. **Roman** *n* Romain, -e *m, f*; *adj* romain. **Roman Catholic** *n*(*m*+*f*), *adj* catholique. **Roman numeral** chiffre romain *m*.

romp [romp] *n* ébats *m pl*. *v* s'ébattre. **rompers** *pl n* barboteuse *f sing*.

roof [ru:f] *n, pl* **roofs** toit *m*. **roof of the mouth** voûte du palais *f*. **roof-rack** *n* galerie *f*.

rook [ruk] *n* (*bird*) corneille *f*. *v* (*slang*) rouler.

room [ru:m] *n* pièce *f*; (*larger*) salle *f*; (*hotel*) chambre *f*; (*space*) place *f*. **at room temperature** (*wine*) chambré. **roommate** *n* camarade de chambre *m, f*. **room service** service des chambres *m*. **roomy** *adj* spacieux.

roost [ru:st] *n* perchoir *m*. *v* (se) jucher. **rooster** *n* coq *m*.

root¹ [ru:t] *n* racine *f*; origine *f*. *v* (s')enraciner.

root² [ru:t] *v* fouiller. **root for** (*slang*) encourager. **root out** (*find*) dénicher.

rope [roup] *n* corde *f*. **know the ropes** être au courant. **rope-ladder** *n* échelle de corde *f*. *v* corder, lier. **rope in** (*coll*) embringuer. **ropy** *adj* (*coll*) pas fameux.

rosary ['rouzəri] *n* chapelet *m*.

rose¹ [rouz] *V* rise.

rose² [rouz] *n* rose *f*. **rose-bush** *n* rosier *m*. **rose garden** roseraie *f*. **rosewood** *n* bois de rose *m*. **rosy** *adj* rose.

rosemary ['rouzməri] *n* romarin *m*.

rosette [rou'zet] *n* rosette *f*; (*prize*) cocarde *f*.

rot [rot] *n* pourriture *f*, carie *f*; (*coll: rubbish*) bêtises *f pl*. *v* pourrir. **rotten** *adj* pourri; (*coll: bad*) moche, sale; (*coll: ill*) mal fichu.

rota ['routə] *n* liste *f*.

rotate [rou'teit] *v* (faire) tourner, (faire) pivoter; (*crops*) alterner. **rotary** *adj* rotatif. **rotation** *n* rotation *f*.

rotor ['routə] *n* rotor *m*.

rouge [ru:ʒ] *n* rouge *m*.

rough [rʌf] *adj* (*surface*) rugueux; (*coarse*) rude; brutal, dur; (*draft*) ébauché; approximatif. **rough-and-ready** *adj* rudimentaire. **rough copy** or **draft** brouillon *m*. *v* **rough it** (*coll*) vivre à la dure. **roughly** *adv* à peu près. **roughness** *n* rugosité *f*; rudesse *f*; brutalité *f*.

roulette [ru:'let] *n* roulette *f*.

round [raund] *adj* rond. *prep* autour de. *n* rond *m*; (*of bread*) tranche *f*; (*drinks, postman, etc.*) tournée *f*; (*game, competition*) partie *f*. **round-necked** *adj* (*pullover*) ras du cou. **round-shouldered** *adj* voûté. *v* arrondir. **round off** terminer. **round up** rassembler; (*figure*) arrondir.

roundabout ['raundəbaut] *n* (*mot*) rond-point *m*; (*fair*) manège *m*. *adj* détourné, indirect.

rouse [rauz] *v* éveiller; stimuler.

route [ruːt] *n* itinéraire *m*.

routine [ruːˈtiːn] *n* routine *f*; (*theatre*) numéro *m*. *adj* d'usage; ordinaire.

rove [rouv] *v* errer (dans), vagabonder.

row¹ [rou] *n* (*side by side*) rang *m*; (*queue*) file *f*; (*trees, figures*) rangée *f*.

row² [rou] *v* (*boat*) ramer. *n* promenade en canot *f*. **rowing** *n* (*sport*) aviron *m*; (*for fun*) canotage *m*. **rowing boat** canot *m*.

row³ [rau] *n* querelle *f*; (*noise*) tapage *m*. *v* se quereller.

rowdy ['raudi] *adj* chahuteur, -euse. **rowdiness** *n* tapage *m*.

royal ['roiəl] *adj* royal. **royal blue** bleu roi *invar*. **royalist** *n*(*m*+*f*). *adj* royaliste. **royalties** *pl n* droits d'auteur *m pl*. **royalty** *n* royauté *f*.

rub [rʌb] *n* frottement *m*; (*with duster*) coup de chiffon *m*. *v* frotter. **rub in** faire pénétrer; insister sur. **rub out** (s')effacer. **rub up the wrong way** prendre à rebrousse-poil. **rubbing** *n* (*brass, etc.*) frottis *m*.

rubber ['rʌbə] *n* caoutchouc *m*; (*eraser*) gomme *f*. **rubber band** élastique *m*. **rubber stamp** tampon *m*. **rubber tree** arbre à gomme *m*. **rubbery** *adj* caoutchouteux.

rubbish ['rʌbiʃ] *n* détritus *m pl*, ordures *f pl*; (*derog*) camelote *f*; (*nonsense*) bêtises *f pl*.

rubble ['rʌbl] *n* décombres *m pl*.

ruby ['ruːbi] *n* rubis *m*.

rucksack ['rʌksak] *n* sac à dos *m*.

rudder ['rʌdə] *n* gouvernail *m*.

rude [ruːd] *adj* impoli, grossier; (*sudden*) brusque; primitif. **rudeness** *n* impolitesse *f*, grossièreté *f*.

rudiment ['ruːdimənt] *n* rudiment *m*. **rudimentary** *adj* rudimentaire.

rueful ['ruːfəl] *adj* triste. **ruefully** *adv* avec regret.

ruff [rʌf] *n* (*dress*) fraise *f*; (*bird*) collier *m*.

ruffian ['rʌfiən] *n* voyou *m*.

ruffle ['rʌfl] *v* (*hair*) ébouriffer; (*surface*) agiter; (*clothes*) froisser; (*worry*) troubler.

rug [rʌg] *n* carpette *f*, petit tapis *m*; (*blanket*) couverture *f*.

rugby ['rʌgbi] *n* rugby *m*.

rugged ['rʌgid] *adj* (*cliff*) déchiqueté; (*landscape*) accidenté; (*person*) rude; (*determination*) acharné.

ruin ['ruːin] *n* ruine *f*. *v* ruiner.

rule [ruːl] *n* règle *f*; autorité *f*. **as a rule** normalement. *v* gouverner; régner; dominer; (*lines*) régler. **rule out** exclure. **ruler** *n* souverain, -e *m, f*; (*measuring*) règle *f*. **ruling** *n* décision *f*.

rum [rʌm] *n* rhum *m*.

rumble ['rʌmbl] *n* grondement *m*; (*stomach*) gargouillement *m*. *v* gronder; gargouiller.

rummage ['rʌmidʒ] *n* fouiller. *n* **rummage sale** vente de charité *f*.

rumour ['ruːmə] *n* rumeur *f*, bruit *m*.

rump [rʌmp] *n* (*animal*) croupe *f*; (*beef*) culotte *f*. **rump steak** romsteck *m*.

*****run** [rʌn] *n* course *f*; (*outing*) tour *m*; (*track*) piste *f*; séquence *f*, série *f*; (*demand*) ruée *f*. **in the long run** à la longue. *v* courir; (*flow*) couler; (*colour*) s'étaler; (*function*) marcher; (*organize*) diriger; passer. **run away** *v* se sauver. **runaway** *n, adj* fugitif, -ive. **run down** *v* (*car, etc.*) renverser; (*coll*) dénigrer. **run-down** *adj* (*coll*) à plat, surmené. **run in** (*mot*) roder. **run out** expirer, s'épuiser. **run over** (*car, etc.*) écraser. **runway** *n* piste *f*. **runner** *n* coureur *m*. **runner bean** haricot à rames *m*. **runner-up** *n* second, -e *m, f*. **running** *adj* (*water, etc.*) courant; (*in succession*) de suite. **running commentary** commentaire suivi *m*. **running costs** frais d'exploitation *m pl*.

rung¹ [rʌŋ] *V* **ring²**.

rung² [rʌŋ] *n* barreau *m*.

rupture ['rʌptʃə] *n* rupture *f*. *v* (se) rompre.

rural ['ruərəl] *adj* rural; de la campagne.

ruse [ruːz] *n* ruse *f*.

rush¹ [rʌʃ] *n* ruée *f*; hâte *f*. *v* se précipiter; (*do quickly*) dépêcher. **rush hour** heure de pointe *f*.

rush² [rʌʃ] *n* (*bot*) jonc *m*.

rusk [rʌsk] *n* biscotte *f*.

Russia ['rʌʃə] *n* Russie *f*. **Russian** *nm, adj* russe; *n* (*people*) Russe *m, f*.

rust [rʌst] *n* rouille *f*. *v* (se) rouiller. **rusty** *adj* rouillé.

rustic ['rʌstik] *adj* rustique.

rustle ['rʌsl] *v* (*leaves*) (faire) bruire; (*paper*) froisser. *n* bruissement *m*; froissement *m*.

rut [rʌt] *n* ornière *f.* **be in a rut** suivre l'ornière.

ruthless ['ruːθlis] *adj* impitoyable, sans pitié.

rye [rai] *n* seigle *m.*

S

sabbath ['sabəθ] *n* sabbat *m.*

sabbatical [sə'batikəl] *adj* sabbatique. *n* année sabbatique *f.*

sable ['seibl] *n* zibeline *f.*

sabotage ['sabətɑːʒ] *n* sabotage *m. v* saboter. **saboteur** *n* saboteur, -euse *m, f.*

sabre ['seibə] *n* sabre *m.*

saccharin ['sakərin] *n* saccharine *f.*

sachet ['safei] *n* sachet *m.*

sack [sak] *n* sac *m.* **get the sack** (*coll*) être sacqué. *v* (*coll*) sacquer.

sacrament ['sakrəmənt] *n* sacrement *m.*

sacred ['seikrid] *adj* sacré.

sacrifice ['sakrifais] *n* sacrifice *m. v* sacrifier.

sacrilege ['sakrəlidʒ] *n* sacrilège *m.* **sacrilegious** *adj* sacrilège.

sad [sad] *adj* triste. **sadden** *v* attrister. **sadly** *adv* tristement; (*very*) bien, fort; (*unfortunately*) fâcheusement. **sadness** *n* tristesse *f.*

saddle ['sadl] *n* selle *f.* **saddle-bag** *n* (*horse*) sacoche de selle *f*; (*bicycle*) sacoche de bicyclette *f. v* seller. **saddle with** (*coll*) coller à. **saddler** *n* sellier *m.* **saddlery** *n* sellerie *f.*

sadism ['seidizəm] *n* sadisme *m.* **sadist** *n* sadique *m, f.* **sadistic** *adj* sadique.

safari [sə'fɑːri] *n* safari *m.* **safari park** réserve *f.*

safe [seif] *adj* (*person*) en sécurité; (*toy, etc.*) sans danger; sûr; solide. **safe and sound** sain et sauf. **safe keeping** bonne garde *f.* **to be on the safe side** par précaution. *n* coffre-fort *m.* **safely** *adv* sans danger; en sûreté. **safety** *n* sécurité *f*; solidité *f.* **safety-belt** *n* ceinture de sécurité *f.* **safety first** la sécurité d'abord. **safety-pin** *n* épingle de sûreté *f.*

safeguard ['seifgɑːd] *n* sauvegarde *f. v* sauvegarder.

saffron ['safrən] *n* safran *m.*

sag [sag] *v* s'affaisser, fléchir. *n* affaissement *m*, fléchissement *m.*

saga ['sɑːgə] *n* saga *f.*

sage[1] [seidʒ] *nm, adj* (*wise*) sage.

sage[2] [seidʒ] *n* (*herb*) sauge *f.*

Sagittarius [sadʒi'teəriəs] *n* Sagittaire *m.*

sago ['seigou] *n* sagou *m*; (*pudding*) sagou au lait *m.*

said [sed] *V* **say.**

sail [seil] *n* voile *f*; (*trip*) tour en bateau *m*; (*windmill*) aile *f.* **sailcloth** *n* toile à voile *f.* **set sail** partir. *v* (*leave*) partir; (*cross*) traverser; (*boat*) piloter. **sail through** (*coll*) réussir haut la main. **sailing** *n* navigation *f*; (*sport, hobby*) voile *f.* **sailing boat** bateau à voiles *m.* **sailor** *n* marin *m.*

saint [seint] *n* saint, -e *m, f.*

sake [seik] *n* **for the sake of** pour l'amour de, par égard pour; pour le plaisir de.

salad ['saləd] *n* salade *f.* **salad cream** mayonnaise *f.* **salad dressing** vinaigrette *f.*

salami [sə'lɑːmi] *n* salami *m.*

salary ['saləri] *n* traitement *m*, salaire *m.* **salary scale** échelle des traitements *f.*

sale [seil] *n* vente *f*; (*reductions*) soldes *m pl.* **for sale** à vendre. **on sale** en vente. **sale-room** *n* salle des ventes *f.* **sales department** service des ventes *m.* **salesman** *n* (*shop*) vendeur *m*; représentant *m.* **salesmanship** *n* art de la vente *m.*

saline ['seilain] *adj* salin. **salinity** *n* salinité *f.*

saliva [sə'laivə] *n* salive *f.* **salivary** *adj* salivaire. **salivate** *v* saliver.

sallow ['salou] *adj* jaunâtre.

salmon ['samən] *n* saumon *m.*

salon ['salon] *n* salon *m.*

saloon [sə'luːn] *n* salle *f*, salon *m.* **saloon bar** bar *m.* **saloon car** conduite intérieure *f.*

salt [soːlt] *n* sel *m.* **salt-cellar** *n* salière *f. v* saler. **salty** *adj* salé.

salute [sə'luːt] *n* salut *m*; (*guns*) salve *f. v* saluer.

salvage ['salvidʒ] *n* sauvetage *m*; récupération *f. v* sauver; récupérer.

salvation [sal'veiʃən] *n* salut *m.* **Salvation Army** Armée du Salut *f.*

same [seim] *adj, pron* même. **all the same** quand même. **at the same time** en même temps.

sample ['sɑːmpl] *n* échantillon *m*; (*blood*) prélèvement *m. v* goûter.

sanatorium [sanə'tɔɪriəm] *n* sanatorium *m.*

sanctify ['saŋktifai] *v* sanctifier. **sanctification** *n* sanctification *f.*

sanctimonious [saŋkti'mouniəs] *adj* moralisateur, -trice.

sanction ['saŋkʃən] *n* sanction *f. v* sanctionner.

sanctity ['saŋktəti] *n* sainteté *f*; inviolabilité *f.*

sanctuary ['saŋktʃuəri] *n* sanctuaire *m*; (*refuge*) asile *m*; (*birds, etc.*) réserve *f.*

sand [sand] *n* sable *m.* **sandbank** *n* banc de sable *m.* **sand-castle** *n* château de sable *m.* **sandpaper** *n* papier de verre *m.* **sandstone** *n* grès *m. v* sabler; (*with sandpaper*) frotter au papier de verre. **sandy** *adj* sablonneux; (*beach*) de sable; (*hair*) couleur sable.

sandal ['sandl] *n* sandale *f.*

sandwich ['sanwidʒ] *n* sandwich *m.* **sandwich board** panneau publicitaire *m.* **sandwich course** cours de formation professionnelle *m.*

sane [sein] *adj* sain d'esprit; raisonnable. **sanity** *n* santé mentale *f.*

sang [saŋ] *V* **sing.**

sanitary ['sanitəri] *adj* sanitaire; hygiénique. **sanitary towel** serviette hygiénique *f.*

sank [saŋk] *V* **sink.**

sap [sap] *n* sève *f.*

sapphire ['safaiə] *n* saphir *m.*

sarcasm ['saɪkazəm] *n* sarcasme *m.* **sarcastic** *adj* sarcastique.

sardine [saɪ'diɪn] *n* sardine *f.*

Sardinia [saɪ'dinjə] *n* Sardaigne *f.* **Sardinian** *nm, adj* sarde; *the* (*people*) Sarde *m, f.*

sardonic [saɪ'donik] *adj* sardonique.

sash¹ [saʃ] *n* (*uniform*) écharpe *f*; (*dress*) large ceinture *f.*

sash² [saʃ] *n* (*frame*) chassis à guillotine *m.* **sash-window** *n* fenêtre à guillotine *f.*

sat [sat] *V* **sit.**

Satan ['seitən] *n* Satan *m.* **satanic** *adj* satanique.

satchel ['satʃəl] *n* cartable *m.*

satellite ['satəlait] *n* satellite *m.*

satin ['satin] *n* satin *m.*

satire ['sataiə] *n* satire *f.* **satirical** *adj* satirique. **satirize** *v* faire la satire de.

satisfy ['satisfai] *v* satisfaire; convaincre. **satisfaction** *n* satisfaction *f.* **satisfactory** *adj* satisfaisant.

saturate ['satʃəreit] *v* saturer; (*soak*) trem-

per. **saturation** *n* saturation *f.* **reach saturation point** arriver à saturation.

Saturday ['satədi] *n* samedi *m.*

sauce [sɔɪs] *n* sauce *f*; (*slang*) toupet *m.* **saucy** *adj* impertinent; coquin.

saucepan ['sɔɪspən] *n* casserole *f.*

saucer ['sɔɪsə] *n* soucoupe *f.*

sauerkraut ['sauəkraut] *n* choucroute *f.*

sauna [sɔɪnə] *n* sauna *m.*

saunter [sɔɪntə] *v* flâner, se balader. *n* flânerie *f*, balade *f.*

sausage ['sosidʒ] *n* saucisse *f.* **sausagemeat** *n* chair à saucisse *f.* **sausage roll** friand *m.*

savage ['savidʒ] *adj* féroce, brutal; primitif, sauvage. *n* sauvage *m, f. v* attaquer férocement. **savagery** *n* sauvagerie *f.*

save¹ [seiv] *v* sauver; (*put aside*) mettre de côté, garder; économiser, épargner. **savings** *pl n* économies *f pl.* **savings bank** caisse d'épargne *f.*

save² [seiv] *prep* sauf.

saviour ['seivjə] *n* sauveur *m.*

savour ['seivə] *v* savourer. *n* saveur *f.* **savoury** *adj* savoureux, appétissant; (*not sweet*) salé.

saw¹ [sɔɪ] *V* **see¹.**

*saw² [sɔɪ] *n* scie *f.* **sawdust** *n* sciure *f.* **sawmill** *n* scierie *f. v* scier.

sawn [sɔɪn] *V* **saw².**

saxophone ['saksəfoun] *n* saxophone *m.*

*say [sei] *v* dire. **saying** *n* dicton *m*, proverbe *m.*

scab [skab] *n* croûte *f*; (*derog: non-striker*) jaune *m. v* se cicatriser; (*derog*) faire le jaune.

scaffold ['skafəld] *n* échafaud *m.* **scaffolding** *n* échafaudage *m.*

scald [skɔɪld] *v* échauder, ébouillanter. *n* brûlure *f.* **scalding** *adj* brûlant.

scale¹ [skeil] *n* (*fish, etc.*) écaille *f*; (*deposit*) tartre *m.* **scaly** *adj* écailleux; entartré.

scale² [skeil] *n* échelle *f*; (*music*) gamme *f.* **scale drawing** dessin à l'échelle *m. v* escalader. **scale down** réduire (proportionnellement).

scales [skeilz] *pl n* balance *f sing.*

scallop ['skaləp] *n* coquille Saint-Jacques *f*; (*sewing*) feston *m.* **scallop shell** coquille *f. v* festonner.

scalp [skalp] *n* cuir chevelu *m. v* scalper.

scalpel ['skalpəl] *n* bistouri *m.*

scamper ['skampə] *v* (*child*) galoper; (*mouse*) trottiner.

scampi ['skæmpi] *n* langoustines *f pl.*
scan [skæn] *v* scruter; (*glance over*)
parcourir des yeux; (*poetry*) (se) scander.
scandal ['skændl] *n* scandale *m*; (*gossip*)
cancans *m pl.* **scandalize** *v* scandaliser.
scandalous *adj* scandaleux.
Scandinavia [,skændi'neivjə] *n*
Scandinavie *f.* **Scandinavian** *n*
Scandinave *m, f; adj* scandinave.
scant [skænt] *or* **scanty** *adj* insuffisant.
scapegoat ['skeipgout] *n* bouc émissaire
m.
scar [skɑː] *n* cicatrice *f;* (*from knife*)
balafre *f.* *v* marquer d'une cicatrice;
balafrer.
scarce [skeəs] *adj* peu abondant; rare.
scarcely *adv* à peine. **scarcity** *n* manque
m; rareté *f.*
scare [skeə] *n* peur *f;* alarme *f. v* effrayer.
be scared avoir peur. **scarecrow** *n*
épouvantail *m.*
scarf [skɑːf] *n* écharpe *f;* (*square*) foulard
m.
scarlet ['skɑːlit] *nf, adj* écarlate. **scarlet
fever** scarlatine *f.*
scathing ['skeiðiŋ] *adj* acerbe, cinglant.
scatter ['skætə] *v* éparpiller, répandre; (se)
disperser. **scatterbrained** *adj* écervelé.
scavenge ['skævindʒ] *v* fouiller. **scavenger**
n éboueur *m*; insecte *or* animal
nécrophage *m.*
scene [siːn] *n* scène *f;* (*place*) lieu *m*;
spectacle *m*, vue *f.*
scenery ['siːnəri] *n* paysage *m*; (*theatre*)
décor *m.*
scent [sent] *n* parfum *m*; (*track*) piste *f. v*
parfumer; (*smell*) flairer.
sceptic ['skeptik] *n* sceptique *m, f.* **sceptical** *adj* septique. **scepticism** *n* scepticisme *m.*
sceptre ['septə] *n* sceptre *m.*
schedule ['ʃedjuːl] *n* programme *m*; (*timetable*) horaire *m. v* prévoir.
scheme [skiːm] *n* plan *m*, projet *m*; (*plot*)
complot *m*; arrangement *m. v* combiner,
comploter.
schizophrenia [,skitsə'friːniə] *n*
schizophrénie *f.* **schizophrenic** *n(m+f),*
adj schizophrène.
scholar ['skɒlə] *n* érudit, -e *m, f;* (*pupil*)
écolier, -ère *m, f.* **scholarly** *adj* érudit.
scholarship *n* (*award*) bourse *f;* érudition
f.
scholastic [skə'læstik] *adj* scolaire; scolastique.

school¹ [skuːl] *n* école *f;* (*secondary*) collège *m*, lycée *m.* **schoolboy** *n* élève *m*,
écolier *m.* **school-days** *pl n* années d'école
f pl. **schoolgirl** *n* élève *f*, écolière *f.*
school-leaving age âge de fin de scolarité
m. **school year** année scolaire *f. v* dresser.
schooling *n* scolarité *f;* instruction *f;*
dressage *m.*
school² [skuːl] *n* (*of fish*) banc *m.*
schooner ['skuːnə] *n* schooner *m.*
sciatica [sai'ætikə] *n* sciatique *f.* **sciatic** *adj*
sciatique.
science ['saiəns] *n* science *f.* **science
fiction** *n* science-fiction *f.* **scientific** *adj*
scientifique. **scientist** *n* scientifique *m, f.*
scintillating ['sintileitiŋ] *adj* scintillant;
(*remark, etc.*) brillant.
scissors ['sizəz] *pl n* ciseaux *m pl.*
scoff¹ [skɒf] *v* se moquer.
scoff² [skɒf] *v* (*coll*) bouffer.
scold [skould] *v* attraper, gronder. **scolding** *n* gronderie *f.*
scone [skɒn] *n* petit pain au lait *m.*
scoop [skuːp] *n* pelle *f*, cuiller *f;* (*press*)
scoop *m. v* (*pick up*) ramasser; (*water*)
écoper; (*hole*) creuser.
scooter ['skuːtə] *n* scooter *m*; (*child's*)
trottinette *f.*
scope [skoup] *n* (*range*) étendue *f;* (*opportunity*) possibilité *f.*
scorch [skɔːtʃ] *n* brûlure légère *f. v* roussir, brûler.
score [skɔː] *n* (*sport*) score *m*; (*game*)
marque *f;* (*subject*) titre *m*; (*music*) partition *f;* (*twenty*) vingtaine *f;* (*cut*) rayure *f.*
scoreboard *n* tableau *m. v* marquer;
rayer, strier. **scorer** *n* marqueur *m.*
scorn [skɔːn] *n* mépris *m*, dédain *m. v*
mépriser, dédaigner. **scornful** *adj*
méprisant, dédaigneux.
Scorpio ['skɔːpiou] *n* Scorpion *m.*
scorpion ['skɔːpiən] *n* scorpion *m.*
Scotland ['skɒtlənd] *n* Ecosse *f.* **Scot** *n*
Ecossais, -e *m, f.* **Scotch** *n* whisky *m*,
scotch *m.* **Scottish** *or* **Scots** *adj* écossais.
scoundrel ['skaundrəl] *n* vaurien *m.*
scour¹ [skauə] *v* (*clean*) récurer. **scourer** *n*
(*powder*) poudre à récurer *f;* (*pad*) tampon abrasif *m.*
scour² [skauə] *v* (*search*) parcourir.
scourge [skɔːdʒ] *n* fléau *m.*
scout [skaut] *n* scout *m*, éclaireur *m.*
scoutmaster *n* chef scout *m.* **scouting** *n*
scoutisme *m.*

scowl [skaul] v se renfrogner. n mine renfrognée f.

scramble ['skrambl] v avancer avec difficulté; (rush) se bousculer; (eggs, phone) brouiller. n bousculade f.

scrap [skrap] n bout m, fragment m; (metal) ferraille f. **scrap-book** n album m. **scrap-merchant** n ferrailleur m. **scrap paper** brouillon m. **scraps** pl n restes m pl. v mettre au rebut; abandonner.

scrape [skreip] n (noise) grattement m; (graze) éraflure f. v gratter, racler; érafler. **scrape through** (exam) réussir de justesse.

scratch [skratʃ] v (for itch) (se) gratter; (with claw) griffer; (graze) érafler; (glass, record, etc.) rayer. n grattement m; éraflure f; rayure f; zéro m.

scrawl [skrɔːl] v gribouiller. n gribouillage m.

scream [skriːm] n cri aigu m, hurlement m. v crier, hurler.

screech [skriːtʃ] n cri strident m, hurlement m; (brakes) grincement m. v crier, hurler; grincer.

screen [skriːn] n (TV, film) écran m; (hospital, room) paravent m; masque m. **screen-play** n scénario m. **screen test** essai filmé m. v masquer, cacher; (film) projeter; protéger.

screw [skruː] n vis m. **screwdriver** n tournevis m. v visser. **screw up** (paper) chiffonner.

scribble ['skribl] v gribouiller, griffonner. **scribble out** raturer. n gribouillage m, griffonage m.

script [skript] n (play) texte m; (film) scénario m; (writing) script m.

scripture ['skriptʃə] n (school) instruction religieuse f; (holy) écriture sainte f.

scroll [skrəul] n rouleau m; manuscrit m; (arch) volute f.

scrounge [skraundʒ] (coll) v chiper, taper. **scrounger** n parasite m.

scrub¹ [skrʌb] n nettoyage m. v nettoyer à la brosse, frotter; (coll: cancel) annuler. **scrubbing brush** brosse dure f.

scrub² [skrʌb] n broussailles f pl.

scruff [skrʌf] n **by the scruff of the neck** par la peau du cou.

scruffy ['skrʌfi] adj négligé, débraillé. **scruffiness** n débraillé m.

scrum [skrʌm] n mêlée f.

scruple ['skruːpl] n scrupule m. **scrupulous** adj scrupuleux.

scrutiny ['skruːtəni] n examen minutieux m. **scrutinize** v scruter.

scuffle ['skʌfl] n bagarre f. v se bagarrer.

scull [skʌl] n aviron m, godille f. v ramer, godiller.

scullery ['skʌləri] n arrière-cuisine f.

sculpt [skʌlpt] v sculpter. **sculptor** n sculpteur m. **sculpture** n sculpture f.

scum [skʌm] n écume f; (derog) rebut m.

scurf [skəːf] n pellicules f pl.

scurvy ['skəːvi] n scorbut m.

scuttle¹ ['skʌtl] n (coal) seau à charbon m.

scuttle² ['skʌtl] v (naut) saborder.

scuttle³ ['skʌtl] v courir précipitamment.

scythe [saið] n faux f. v faucher.

sea [siː] n mer f.

sea bed n fond de la mer m.

seafaring ['siːfeəriŋ] adj marin.

seafood ['siːfuːd] n fruits de mer m pl.

sea front n bord de mer m.

seagull ['siːgʌl] n mouette f.

seahorse ['siːhɔːs] n hippocampe m.

seal¹ [siːl] n sceau m, cachet m. v sceller; (stick down) coller; (fate) décider. **sealing wax** cire à cacheter f.

seal² [siːl] n (zool) phoque m. **sealskin** n peau de phoque f.

sea-level n niveau de la mer m.

sea-lion n otarie f.

seam [siːm] n couture f; joint m; (coal) veine f.

seaman ['siːmən] n marin m.

séance ['seiãs] n séance de spiritisme f.

sear [siə] v flétrir; (burn) brûler. **searing** adj (pain) aigu, -guë.

search [səːtʃ] n recherche f; (of house, etc.) fouille f. **searchlight** n projecteur m. **search-party** n équipe de secours f. **search-warrant** n mandat de perquisition m. v fouiller, chercher. **searching** adj (look) pénétrant; (examination) rigoureux.

sea shell n coquillage m.

seashore ['siːʃɔː] n rivage m, plage f.

seasick ['siːsik] adj **be seasick** avoir le mal de mer. **seasickness** n mal de mer m.

seaside ['siːsaid] n bord de la mer m. **seaside resort** station balnéaire f.

season ['siːzn] n saison f. **season ticket** carte d'abonnement m. v (food) assaisonner; (wood) faire sécher. **seasonal** adj saisonnier. **seasoning** n assaisonnement m.

seat [siːt] *n* siège *m*; place *f*. **seat-belt** *n* ceinture de sécurité *f*. *v* (faire) asseoir; placer.

seaweed ['siːwiːd] *n* algue *f*.

seaworthy ['siːwɜːði] *adj* en état de naviguer.

secluded [si'kluːdid] *adj* à l'écart, retiré. **seclusion** *n* solitude *f*.

second[1] ['sekənd] *n* (*time*) seconde *f*. **second hand** trotteuse *f*.

second[2] ['sekənd] *n* deuxième *m, f*, second, -e *m, f*; (*comm*) article de second choix *m*. *adj, adv* deuxième, second. **on second thoughts** réflexion faite. **second-class** *adj* de deuxième classe; (*mail*) tarif réduit. **second-hand** *adj, adv* d'occasion. **second-rate** *adj* médiocre. **second to none** sans pareil. *v* appuyer (la motion de). **secondly** *adv* deuxièment, en second lieu.

secondary ['sekəndəri] *adj* secondaire.

secret ['siːkrit] *n* secret *m*. *adj* secret, -ète. **secrecy** *n* secret *m*. **secretive** *adj* réservé, dissimulé. **secretly** *adv* en secret.

secretary ['sekrətəri] *n* secrétaire *m, f*. **secretarial** *adj* de secrétariat, de secrétaire.

secrete [si'kriːt] *v* sécréter; (*hide*) cacher. **secretion** *n* sécrétion *f*.

sect [sekt] *n* secte *f*. **sectarian** *adj* sectaire.

section ['sekʃən] *n* section *f*, partie *f*.

sector ['sektə] *n* secteur *m*.

secular ['sekjulə] *adj* séculier, laïque.

secure [si'kjuə] *adj* solide; sûr, assuré; tranquille. *v* fixer; se procurer; garantir; assurer. **security** sécurité *f*; (*for loan*) caution *f*.

sedate [si'deit] *adj* posé, calme. **sedation** *n* sédation *f*. **sedative** *nm, adj* calmant.

sediment ['sedimənt] *n* (*geol*) sédiment *m*; (*wine, etc.*) dépôt *m*.

seduce [si'djuːs] *v* séduire. **seduction** *n* séduction *f*. **seductive** *adj* séduisant.

*see[1] [siː] *v* voir. **see to** s'occuper de. **see you later!** à tout à l'heure!

see[2] [siː] *n* évêché *m*.

seed [siːd] *n* graine *f*; (*source*) germe *m*, **seedless** *adj* sans pépins. **seedling** *n* semis *m*. **seedy** *adj* miteux; (*coll: ill*) mal fichu.

*seek [siːk] *v* chercher, rechercher; demander.

seem [siːm] *v* sembler, paraître. **seeming** *adj* apparent. **seemingly** *adv* apparemment; à ce qu'il paraît.

seen [siːn] *V* see[1].

seep [siːp] *v* suinter, filtrer. **seepage** *n* suintement *m*; (*leak*) fuite *f*.

seesaw ['siːsɔː] *n* bascule *f*. *v* osciller.

seethe [siːð] *v* bouillir, bouillonner. **seething** *adj* (*coll*) furibond.

segment ['segmənt] *n* segment *m*; (*orange, etc.*) quartier *m*.

segregate ['segrigeit] *v* séparer, isoler. **segregation** *n* ségrégation *f*.

seize [siːz] *v* saisir; (*with force*) s'emparer de. **seize up** (*tech*) se gripper; (*med*) s'ankyloser. **seizure** *n* saisie *f*; capture *f*; (*med*) crise *f*.

seldom ['seldəm] *adv* rarement.

select [sə'lekt] *v* selectionner, choisir. *adj* choisi; (*club, etc.*) fermé. **selection** *n* sélection *f*. **selective** *adj* sélectif.

self [self] *n* moi *m*.

self-adhesive *adj* auto-adhésif.

self-assured *adj* plein d'assurance. **self-assurance** *n* assurance *f*.

self-centred *adj* égocentrique.

self-coloured *adj* uni.

self-confident *adj* sûr de soi. **self-confidence** *n* confiance en soi *f*.

self-conscious *adj* gêné. **self-consciousness** *n* gêne *f*.

self-contained *adj* indépendant.

self-control *n* maîtrise de soi *f*. **self-controlled** *adj* maître de soi, maîtresse de soi.

self-defence *n* légitime défense *f*.

self-discipline *n* discipline personelle *f*.

self-employed *adj* **be self-employed** travailler à son compte.

self-evident *adj* qui va de soi.

self-explanatory *adj* évident en soi.

self-expression *n* expression libre *f*.

self-important *adj* suffisant. **self-importance** *n* suffisance *f*.

self-interest *n* intérêt personnel *m*.

selfish ['selfiʃ] *adj* égoïste. **selfishness** *n* égoïsme *m*.

selfless ['selflis] *adj* désintéressé.

self-opinionated *adj* opiniâtre.

self-pity *n* apitoiement sur soi-même *m*.

self-portrait *n* autoportrait *m*.

self-possessed *adj* assuré. **self-possession** *n* sang-froid *m*.

self-raising flour *n* farine à levure *f*.

self-respect *n* respect de soi *m*.

self-righteous *adj* pharisaïque. **self-righteousness** *n* pharisaïsme *m*.

self-sacrifice *n* abnégation *f*.

selfsame ['selfseim] *adj* même.
self-satisfied *adj* content de soi.
self-service *n* libre-service *m*.
self-sufficient *adj* indépendant. **self-sufficiency** *n* indépendance *f*.
self-taught *adj* autodidacte.
self-willed *adj* entêté.
*sell [sel] *v* (se) vendre; (*coll*) faire accepter. **sell off** solder, liquider. **seller** *n* vendeur, -euse *m, f*; marchand, -e *m, f*.
sellotape ® ['seləteip] *n* scotch ® *m. v* scotcher.
semantic [sə'mantik] *adj* sémantique. **semantics** *n* sémantique *f*.
semaphore ['seməfɔi] *n* signaux à bras *m pl*; (*rail*) sémaphore *m*.
semblance ['sembləns] *n* semblant *m*.
semen ['siimən] *n* sperme *m*, semence *f*.
semibreve ['semibriiv] *n* ronde *f*.
semicircle ['semisəikl] *n* demi-cercle *m*. **semicircular** *adj* demi-circulaire.
semicolon [,semi'koulən] *n* point-virgule *m*.
semi-conscious *adj* à demi conscient.
semi-detached house *n* maison jumelée *f*.
semifinal [semi'fainl] *n* demi-finale *f*.
seminar ['seminaɪ] *n* séminaire *m*.
semi-precious *adj* semi-précieux.
semiquaver ['semikweivə] *n* double croche *f*.
semitone ['semitoun] *n* demi-ton *m*.
semolina [,semə'liinə] *n* semoule *f*; (*pudding*) semoule au lait *f*.
senate ['senit] *n* sénat *m*. **senator** *n* sénateur *m*.
*send [send] *v* envoyer; rendre. **send back** renvoyer. **send for** faire venir; (*mail-order*) se faire envoyer.
senile ['siinail] *adj* sénile. **senility** *n* sénilité *f*.
senior ['siinjə] *adj* (*age*) aîné; (*rank*) supérieur, -e. *n* aîné, -e *m, f*; (*school*) grand, -e *m, f*. **seniority** *n* (*rank*) supériorité *f*; (*service*) ancienneté *f*; priorité d'âge *f*.
sensation [sen'seiʃən] *n* sensation *f*. **sensational** *adj* sensationnel; (*newspaper*) à sensation.
sense [sens] *n* sens *m*; sensation *f*; (*feeling*) sentiment *m*; (*wisdom*) bon sens *m*. **senses** *pl n* raison *f sing. v* sentir. **senseless** *adj* insensé; (*unconscious*) sans connaissance.

sensible ['sensəbl] *adj* sensé, raisonnable; (*clothes*) pratique.
sensitive ['sensitiv] *adj* sensible; susceptible; délicat. **sensitivity** *n* sensibilité *f*; susceptibilité *f*; délicatesse *f*.
sensual ['sensjuəl] *adj* sensuel. **sensuality** *n* sensualité *f*.
sensuous ['sensjuəs] *adj* sensuel.
sent [sent] *V* send.
sentence ['sentəns] *n* (*gramm*) phrase *f*; (*law*) condamnation *f. v* condamner.
sentiment ['sentimənt] *n* sentiment *m*; opinion *f*; sentimentalité *f*. **sentimental** *adj* sentimental.
sentry ['sentri] *n* sentinelle *f*.
separate ['sepərət; *v* 'sepəreit] *adj* séparé; indépendant; différent. *v* (se) séparer; diviser. **separation** *n* séparation *f*.
September [sep'tembə] *n* septembre *m*.
septic ['septik] *adj* septique; (*wound*) infecté. **go septic** s'infecter.
sequel ['siikwəl] *n* suite *f*, conséquence *f*.
sequence ['siikwəns] *n* ordre *m*; (*cards, music*) séquence *f*; (*series*) suite *f*.
sequin ['siikwin] *n* paillette *f*.
serenade [serə'neid] *n* sérénade *f*.
serene [sə'riin] *adj* serein. **serenity** *n* sérénité *f*.
serf [səif] *n* serf, serve *m, f*.
sergeant ['saidʒənt] *n* (*mil*) sergent *m*; (*police*) brigadier *m*. **sergeant-major** *n* sergent-major *m*.
serial ['siəriəl] *n* feuilleton *m. adj* de série. **serialize** *v* adapter en feuilleton; publier en feuilleton.
series ['siəriiz] *n* série *f*.
serious ['siəriəs] *adj* sérieux, grave. **seriousness** *n* sérieux *m*, gravité *f*.
sermon ['səimən] *n* sermon *m*.
serpent ['səipənt] *n* serpent *m*.
serrated [sə'reitid] *adj* dentelé.
servant ['səivənt] *n* domestique *m, f*.
serve [səiv] *v* servir. **it serves you right** c'est bien fait pour toi.
service ['səivis] *n* service *m*; (*mot*) révision *f*. **service area** (*mot*) aire de services *f*. **service charge** service *m*. **serviceman** *n* militaire *m*. **service station** (*mot*) station-service *f. v* réviser. **serviceable** *adj* pratique, commode.
serviette [,səivi'et] *n* serviette *f*. **serviette ring** rond de serviette *m*.
servile ['səivail] *adj* servile. **servility** *n* servilité *f*.

session ['seʃən] n séance f, session f.

*set [set] n jeu m, série f; collection f; (people) groupe m; (TV) poste m; (cinema) plateau m; (hair) mise en plis f; (tennis) set m. adj fixe. v (put) mettre; (clock) régler; fixer; (mount) monter; (jelly, etc.) prendre; (sun) se coucher; (type) composer. **set about** se mettre à. **setback** n contretemps m, revers m. **set off** (leave) partir; faire exploser; (enhance) mettre en valeur. **set out** partir; exposer. **set up** dresser; établir; s'installer. **setting** n cadre m; (gem) monture f; (sun) coucher m.

settee [se'tiː] n canapé m.

settle ['setl] v (problem, account, etc.) régler; calmer; (bird) se poser; (person) s'installer. **settle down** se calmer; s'installer. **settle up** (bill) régler. **settlement** n règlement m; accord m; colonie f.

seven ['sevn] nm, adj sept. **seventh** n(m+f), adj septième.

seventeen [sevn'tiːn] nm, adj dix-sept. **seventeenth** n(m+f), adj dix-septième.

seventy ['sevnti] nm, adj soixante-dix. **seventieth** n(m+f), adj soixante-dixième.

sever ['sevə] v (cease) rompre, cesser; (cut) couper.

several ['sevrəl] adj, pron plusieurs.

severe [sə'viə] adj sévère; (hard) dur; (illness) grave. **severity** n sévérité f; intensité f.

*sew [sou] v coudre. **sewing** n couture f. **sewing machine** machine à coudre f.

sewage ['sjuidʒ] n vidanges f pl. **sewage farm** champ d'épandage m.

sewer ['sjuə] n égout m.

sewn [soun] V sew.

sex [seks] n sexe m. **sexual** adj sexuel. **sexual intercourse** rapports sexuels m pl. **sexuality** n sexualité f.

sextet [seks'tet] n sextuor m.

shabby ['ʃabi] adj râpé, minable; (behaviour) mesquin.

shack [ʃak] n cabane f.

shade [ʃeid] n ombre f; nuance f; (lamp) abat-jour m invar. v ombrager; (painting) ombrer; (drawing) hachurer. **shady** adj ombragé; (dishonest) louche.

shadow ['ʃadou] n ombre f. **shadow cabinet** cabinet fantôme m. v (follow) filer. **shadowy** adj ombragé; indistinct.

shaft [ʃaːft] n (tool) manche m; (light) trait m; (lift) cage f; (mine, ventilation) puits m; (spear) hampe f.

shaggy ['ʃagi] adj hirsute.

*shake [ʃeik] n secousse f; tremblement m. v secouer; (bottle) agiter; trembler; (weaken) ébranler. **shake hands** serrer la main. **shake off** se débarrasser de. **shaky** adj tremblant; (weak, unsure) chancelant.

shaken ['ʃeikn] V shake.

shall [ʃal] aux translated by future tense.

shallot [ʃə'lot] n échalote f.

shallow ['ʃalou] adj peu profond; superficiel.

sham [ʃam] n imitation f; comédie f. adj faux, fausse; feint, simulé. v feindre, simuler; jouer la comédie.

shame [ʃeim] n honte f; (pity) dommage m. v faire honte à. **shamefaced** adj honteux; timide. **shameful** adj honteux. **shameless** adj éhonté; impudique.

shampoo [ʃam'puː] n shampooing m. v faire un shampooing à.

shamrock ['ʃamrok] n trèfle m.

shandy ['ʃandi] n panaché m.

shanty¹ ['ʃanti] n (hut) baraque f. **shanty town** bidonville m.

shanty² ['ʃanti] n chanson de marins f.

shape [ʃeip] n forme f. v façonner; prendre forme. **shapeless** adj informe. **shapely** adj bien fait, bien proportionné.

share [ʃeə] n part f; (comm) action f. **shareholder** n actionnaire m, f. v partager.

shark [ʃaːk] n requin m.

sharp [ʃaːp] adj aigu, -guë; (point) pointu; (edge) tranchant; (sudden) brusque; (outline) net, nette; (pain, wind) vif. n (music) dièse m. **sharpen** v aiguiser; (pencil) tailler; (outline) rendre plus net. **sharpness** n tranchant m; netteté f.

shatter ['ʃatə] v (se) fracasser; briser, ruiner. **shattered** adj bouleversé; (tired) éreinté. **shattering** adj bouleversant.

shave [ʃeiv] v (se) raser. **shaving** n (of wood, metal) copeau m. **shaving brush** blaireau m. **shaving cream** crème à raser f.

shawl [ʃoːl] n châle m.

she [ʃiː] pron elle. **she who** celle qui. n (coll) femelle f.

sheaf [ʃiːf] n (corn) gerbe f; (papers) liasse f; (arrows) faisceau m.

*shear [ʃiə] v tondre. **shears** pl n cisailles f pl.

sheath [ʃiːθ] *n* gaine *f*; (*sword*) fourreau *m*; (*scissors*) étui *m*. **sheathe** *v* rengainer; recouvrir.

*shed[1] [ʃed] *v* (*drop*) perdre; (*radiate*) répandre.

shed[2] [ʃed] *n* remise *f*, hutte *f*.

sheen [ʃiːn] *n* lustre *m*, éclat *m*.

sheep [ʃiːp] *n* mouton *m*. **sheep-dog** *n* chien de berger *m*. **sheepskin** *n* peau de mouton *f*. **sheepish** *adj* penaud.

sheer[1] [ʃiə] *adj* pur, absolu; (*cliff*) à pic; (*stockings*) extrêmement fin.

sheer[2] [ʃiə] *v* (*naut*) faire une embardée.

sheet [ʃiːt] *n* (*bed*) drap *m*; (*paper*) feuille *f*; (*ice, metal*) plaque *f*. **sheet lightning** éclair en nappe *m*. **sheet music** partitions *f pl*.

sheikh [ʃeik] *n* cheik *m*.

shelf [ʃelf] *n* rayon *m*, étagère *f*.

shell [ʃel] *n* coquille *f*; (*tortoise, crab*) carapace *f*; (*from beach*) coquillage *m*; (*mil*) obus *m*. **shellfish** *n* coquillage *m*; (*pl: as food*) fruits de mer *m pl*. *v* (*nut, shrimp*) décortiquer; (*peas*) écosser; (*mil*) bombarder.

shelter [ˈʃeltə] *n* abri *m*. *v* (s')abriter; protéger; (*lodge*) recueillir.

shelve [ʃelv] *v* (*project*) mettre en sommeil. **shelving** *n* rayonnage *m*.

shepherd [ˈʃepəd] *n* berger *m*. **shepherd's pie** hachis Parmentier *m*.

sheriff [ˈʃerif] *n* shérif *m*.

sherry [ˈʃeri] *n* xérès *m*.

shield [ʃiːld] *n* bouclier; (*screen*) écran *m*. *v* protéger.

shift [ʃift] *n* changement *m*; (*work*) poste *m*. **shift key** touche de majuscule *f*. **shift work** travail en équipe *m*. *v* déplacer, bouger; changer (de place). **shifty** *adj* louche.

shimmer [ˈʃimə] *v* miroiter, chatoyer. *n* miroitement *m*, chatoiement *m*.

shin [ʃin] *n* tibia *m*.

*shine [ʃain] *n* éclat *m*, brillant *m*. *v* briller. **shiny** *adj* brillant, reluisant.

shingle [ˈʃiŋgl] *n* galets *m pl*.

ship [ʃip] *n* bateau *m*; (*larger*) navire *m*. **shipbuilding** *n* construction navale *f*. **shipshape** *adj* bien rangé. **shipwreck** *n* naufrage *m*. **be shipwrecked** faire naufrage *m*. **shipyard** *n* chantier naval *m*. *v* transporter; (*send*) expédier; (*take on*) embarquer. **shipment** *n* cargaison *m*. **shipping** *n* navigation *f*.

shirk [ʃəːk] *v* esquiver. **shirker** *n* (*coll*) tire-au-flanc *m invar*.

shirt [ʃəːt] *n* chemise *f*. **in one's shirt sleeves** en bras de chemise. **shirtwaister** *n* robe chemisier *f*.

shit [ʃit] *nf, interj* (*vulgar*) merde.

shiver [ˈʃivə] *v* frissonner. *n* frisson *m*. **shivery** *adj* frissonnant; fiévreux.

shoal [ʃoul] *n* (*fish*) banc *m*.

shock [ʃok] *n* choc *m*; (*elec*) décharge *f*. **shock absorber** amortisseur *m*. **shockproof** *adj* anti-choc *invar*. **shock treatment** électrochoc *m*. *v* secouer, bouleverser; dégoûter; (*scandalize*) choquer. **shocking** *adj* affreux, atroce; scandaleux.

shod [ʃod] *V* shoe.

shoddy [ˈʃodi] *adj* de mauvaise qualité. **shoddiness** *n* mauvaise qualité *f*.

*shoe [ʃuː] *n* chaussure *f*, soulier *m*. **shoehorn** *n* chausse-pied *m*. **shoe-lace** *n* lacet de soulier *m*. **shoemaker** *n* cordonnier *m*. **shoe repairer's** cordonnerie *f*. *v* (*horse*) ferrer.

shone [ʃon] *V* shine.

shook [ʃuk] *V* shake.

*shoot [ʃuːt] *v* (*fire*) tirer, lancer; (*kill*) abattre; (*hit*) atteindre d'un coup de fusil; (*goal*) shooter; (*film*) tourner; (*go quickly*) aller en flèche. *n* (*bot*) pousse *f*. **shooting** *n* fusillade *f*; (*hunting*) chasse *f*.

shop [ʃop] *n* magasin *m*; (*smaller*) boutique *f*; (*in factory*) atelier *m*. **shop assistant** vendeur, -euse *m, f*. **shop-floor** *n* ouvriers *m pl*. **shopkeeper** *n* marchand, -e. **shoplifting** *n* vol à l'étalage *m*. **shopsoiled** *adj* défraîchi. **shop-steward** *n* délégué syndical *m*. **shop-window** *n* vitrine *f*. *v* faire ses courses. **shopping** *n* achats *m pl*. **go shopping** faire des courses. **shopping bag** sac à provisions *m*. **shopping centre** centre commercial *m*.

shore [ʃoɪ] *n* (*beach*) plage *f*; (*of sea*) rivage *m*; (*coast*) littoral *m*.

shorn [ʃoɪn] *V* shear.

short [ʃoɪt] *adj* court; bref, brève; insuffisant; brusque. **in short** en bref. **shortage** *n* manque *m*, pénurie *f*. **shorten** *v* raccourcir. **shortly** *adv* bientôt.

shortbread [ˈʃoɪtbred] *n* sablé *m*.

short-circuit *n* court-circuit *m*. *v* court-circuiter.

shortcoming [ˈʃoɪtkʌmiŋ] *n* défaut *m*.

short cut *n* raccourci *m*.

shorthand ['ʃɔːthand] n sténographie f.
  shorthand typist sténodactylo m, f.
short list n liste de candidats sélectionnés
  f.
short-lived [ʃɔːt'livd] adj de courte durée.
shorts [ʃɔːts] pl n short m sing.
short-sighted adj myope.
short story n nouvelle f.
short-tempered adj coléreux.
short-term adj à court terme.
short wave n ondes courtes f pl. adj à or
  sur ondes courtes.
shot¹ [ʃɔt] V shoot.
shot² [ʃɔt] n coup m; (lead) plomb m;
  (try) essai m; photo f. **shotgun** n fusil de
  chasse m.
should¹ [ʃud] aux translated by conditional
  tense.
should² [ʃud] aux translated by conditional
  tense of devoir.
shoulder ['ʃouldə] n épaule f; (road)
  accotement m. **shoulder-bag** n sac à
  bandoulière m. **shoulder-blade** n
  omoplate f. v endosser.
shout [ʃaut] n cri m. v crier.
shove [ʃʌv] n poussée f. v pousser.
shovel ['ʃʌvl] n pelle f. v pelleter.
*show [ʃou] n démonstration f; (flowers,
  etc.) exposition f; (theatre) spectacle m;
  apparence f; (ostentation) parade f. **show
  business** le monde du spectacle m. **show-
  case** n vitrine f. **show-down** n épreuve de
  force f. **show-jumping** n concours hippique m. **show-room** n salle d'exposition
  f. v montrer; (be visible) se voir. **show in**
  faire entrer. **show off** (coll) crâner. **show
  up** être visible; (coll: arrive) se pointer;
  (embarrass) faire honte à.
shower ['ʃauə] n (rain) averse f; (bath)
  douche f. **shower-proof** adj imperméable.
  v combler, accabler. **showery** adj
  pluvieux.
shown [ʃoun] V show.
shrank [ʃraŋk] V shrink.
shred [ʃred] n lambeau m; (small amount)
  grain m. v déchiqueter.
shrew [ʃruː] n (zool) musaraigne f; (woman) mégère f.
shrewd [ʃruːd] adj perspicace, astucieux.
shriek [ʃriːk] n hurlement m, cri perçant
  m. v hurler, crier.
shrill [ʃril] adj perçant; (whistle) strident.
shrimp [ʃrimp] n crevette f.
shrine [ʃrain] n châsse f; lieu saint m.

*shrink [ʃriŋk] v rétrécir; reculer.
  shrinkage n rétrécissement m.
shrivel ['ʃrivl] v se ratatiner, se flétrir.
shroud [ʃraud] n linceul m; (mist) voile
  m. v ensevelir.
Shrove Tuesday [ʃrouv] n mardi gras m.
shrub [ʃrʌb] n arbrisseau m, arbuste m.
  shrubbery n massif d'arbustes m.
shrug [ʃrʌg] v hausser (les épaules). n
  haussement d'épaules m.
shrunk [ʃrʌŋk] V shrink.
shudder ['ʃʌdə] n frisson m; (engine)
  vibration f. v frissonner, frémir; vibrer.
shuffle ['ʃʌfl] v traîner les pieds; (cards)
  battre. n battage m; réorganisation f.
shun [ʃʌn] v fuir, éviter.
shunt [ʃʌnt] v (rail) aiguiller, manœuvrer.
*shut [ʃʌt] v fermer. **shut in** enfermer,
  entourer. **shut up** (coll) se taire, faire
  taire.
shutter ['ʃʌtə] n (window) volet m; (phot)
  obturateur m.
shuttle ['ʃʌtl] n navette f. **shuttlecock** n
  volant m. **shuttle service** service de
  navette m.
shy [ʃai] adj timide. v (horse) se cabrer.
  shyness n timidité f.
Siamese [ˌsaiə'miːz] adj (cat, twin)
  siamois.
sick [sik] adj malade; (mind, humour)
  malsain. **be sick** vomir. **be sick of** (coll)
  avoir marre de. **feel sick** avoir mal au
  cœur. **sick bay** infirmerie f. **sicken** v
  écœurer. **sicken for** couver. **sickening** adj
  écœurant; (coll) agaçant. **sickly** adj (person) maladif; pâle; (cake) écœurant.
  sickness n maladie f; vomissements m pl.
sickle ['sikl] n faucille f.
side [said] n côté m; (hill, animal) flanc
  m; (edge) bord m; (team) équipe f; (in
  argument, etc.) camp m. v **side with** prendre parti pour.
sideboard ['saidbɔːd] n buffet m.
side-effect n effet secondaire m.
sidelight ['saidlait] n (mot) lanterne f.
sideline ['saidlain] n activité secondaire f;
  (sport) touche f.
sidelong ['saidlɔŋ] adj, adv de côté.
side-show n attraction f.
side-step v éviter.
side-street n petite rue f.
side-track v faire dévier.
sidewalk ['saidwɔːk] n (US) trottoir m.
sideways ['saidweiz] adj oblique. adv de
  côté; (walk) en crabe.

siding ['saidiŋ] n (rail) voie de garage f.

sidle ['saidl] v marcher de côté; avancer furtivement. **sidle up to** se glisser vers.

siege [siːdʒ] n siège m.

sieve [siv] n tamis m; (coal) crible m. v tamiser; cribler.

sift [sift] v (food) tamiser; (coal) cribler; (evidence) passer au crible. **sift out** dégager. **sifter** n (flour) saupoudreuse f.

sigh [sai] n soupir m. v soupirer.

sight [sait] n vue f; spectacle m; (on gun) mire f. **sight-read** v déchiffrer. **sightseeing** n tourisme m. v apercevoir.

sign [sain] n signe m; (notice) panneau m. **signpost** n poteau indicateur m. v signer.

signal ['signəl] n signal m. v faire signe (à); faire des signaux.

signature ['signətʃə] n signature f. **signature tune** indicatif musical m.

signify ['signifai] v signifier. **significance** n signification f. **significant** adj significatif; considérable.

silence ['sailəns] n silence m. v réduire au silence, faire taire. **silencer** n silencieux m. **silent** adj silencieux.

silhouette [silu'et] n silhouette f. v **be silhouetted against** se découper contre.

silk [silk] n soie f. **silkworm** n ver à soie m. **silky** adj soyeux.

sill [sil] n rebord m; (mot) bas de marche m.

silly ['sili] adj bête, idiot. **silliness** n sottise f.

silt [silt] n vase f. v **silt up** envaser.

silver ['silvə] n argent m; (cutlery, etc.) argenterie f; (change) monnaie f. adj d'argent; en argent. **silver birch** bouleau argenté m. **silver paper** papier d'argent m. **silversmith** n orfèvre m, f. v argenter. **silvery** adj argenté.

similar ['similə] adj semblable. **similarity** n ressemblance f.

simile ['siməli] n comparaison f.

simmer ['simə] v (faire) cuire à feu doux, mijoter; (anger) couver. **simmer down** (coll) se calmer.

simple ['simpl] adj simple. **simpleton** n nigaud, -e m, f. **simplicity** n simplicité f. **simplify** v simplifier. **simply** adv simplement; absolument.

simulate ['simjuleit] v simuler. **simulation** n simulation f.

simultaneous [siməl'teinjəs] adj simultané.

sin [sin] n péché m. v pécher. **sinful** adj

coupable; scandaleux. **sinner** n pécheur, -eresse m, f.

since [sins] prep, adv depuis. conj depuis que; (because) puisque.

sincere [sin'siə] adj sincère. **sincerity** n sincérité f.

sinew ['sinjuː] n tendon m.

***sing** [siŋ] v chanter. **singer** n chanteur, -euse m, f. **singing** n chant m.

singe [sindʒ] v brûler légèrement, roussir. n légère brûlure f.

single ['siŋgl] adj seul; (not double) simple; célibataire. **single bed** lit d'une personne m. **single file** file indienne f. **single-handed** adv tout seul; (sail) en solitaire. **single-minded** adj résolu. **single ticket** aller simple m. **single room** chambre à un lit f. n (ticket) aller simple m; (record) 45 tours m. **singles** n (sport) simple m. v **single out** distinguer; choisir.

singular ['siŋgjulə] nm, adj singulier.

sinister ['sinistə] adj sinistre.

***sink** [siŋk] v (go under) couler; (collapse) s'affaisser; (go down) baisser; (mine) creuser. **sink in** (idea, etc.) rentrer, pénétrer. n évier m. **sink unit** bloc-évier m.

sinuous ['sinjuəs] adj sinueux.

sinus ['sainəs] n sinus m invar. **sinusitis** n sinusite f.

sip [sip] n petite gorgée f. v boire à petites gorgées.

siphon ['saifən] n siphon m. v siphonner.

sir [səɪ] n monsieur m; (knight) sir m.

siren ['saiərən] n sirène f.

sirloin ['səːloin] n aloyau m.

sister ['sistə] n sœur f; religieuse f; (hospital) infirmière en chef f. **sister-in-law** n belle-sœur f.

***sit** [sit] v (s')asseoir; (clothes) tomber; (committee) être en séance; (exam) passer. **sit down** s'asseoir. **sit-in** n sit-in m invar. **sit up** se redresser; (stay up) ne pas se coucher. **sitting** n séance f; (meal) service m. **sitting room** salon m. **sitting tenant** locataire en place m, f.

site [sait] n emplacement m; (building) chantier m; camping m. v placer.

situation [sitju'eifən] n situation f; emploi m. **situate** v placer, situer.

six [siks] nm, adj six. **sixth** n(m+f), adj sixième. **sixth form** classes de première et terminale f pl.

sixteen [siks'tiːn] nm, adj seize. **sixteenth** n(m+f), adj seizième.

sixty ['siksti] *nm, adj* soixante. **sixtieth** *n(m+f), adj* soixantième.

size [saiz] *n* taille *f*; grandeur *f*, dimensions *f pl*; (*shoes*) pointure *f*. *v* **size up** mesurer, juger. **sizeable** *adj* assez grand.

sizzle ['sizl] *v* grésiller. *n* grésillement *m*.

skate¹ [skeit] *n* patin *m*. **skateboard** *n* planche à roulettes *f*. *v* patiner. **skater** *n* patineur, -euse *m, f*. **skating** *n* patinage *m*.

skate² [skeit] *n* (*fish*) raie *f*.

skeleton ['skelitn] *n* squelette *m*. *adj* (*staff, etc.*) squelettique. **skeleton key** passe-partout *m invar*.

sketch [sketʃ] *n* croquis *m*; (*rough*) ébauche *f*; (*theatre*) sketch *m*. *v* esquisser. **sketchy** *adj* incomplet, -ète.

skewer ['skjuə] *n* brochette *f*. *v* embrocher.

ski [skiː] *n* ski *m*. **ski-lift** *n* remonte-pente *m*, remontée mécanique *f*. *v* faire du ski. **skier** *n* skieur, -euse *m, f*. **skiing** *n* ski *m*.

skid [skid] *n* dérapage *m*. *v* déraper.

skill [skil] *n* habileté *f*; technique *f*. **skilful** *adj* habile. **skilled** *adj* habile, adroit; (*worker*) qualifié.

skim [skim] *v* (*milk*) écrémer; (*surface*) raser; (*reading*) parcourir.

skimp [skimp] *v* lésiner (sur), économiser. **skimpy** *adj* insuffisant, maigre.

skin [skin] *n* peau *f*. **skin-diving** *n* plongée sous-marine *f*. **skin-tight** *adj* collant. *v* (*animal*) dépouiller; (*fruit, vegetable*) éplucher. **skinny** *adj* maigrelet.

skip [skip] *n* petit saut *m*. *v* gambader; sauter à la corde; (*miss*) sauter. **skipping** *n* saut à la corde *m*. **skipping rope** corde à sauter *f*.

skipper ['skipə] *n* capitaine *m*.

skirmish ['skəːmiʃ] *n* escarmouche *f*.

skirt [skəːt] *n* jupe *f*. *v* contourner. **skirting board** plinthe *f*.

skittle ['skitl] *n* quille *f*. **skittles** *n* jeu de quilles *m*.

skull [skʌl] *n* crâne *m*. **skull and crossbones** tête de mort *f*.

skunk [skʌŋk] *n* mouffette *f*.

sky [skai] *n* ciel *m*. **sky-blue** *nm, adj* bleu ciel. **skylark** *n* alouette *f*. **skylight** *n* lucarne *f*. **skyline** *n* ligne d'horizon *f*. **skyscraper** *n* gratte-ciel *m invar*.

slab [slab] *n* bloc *m*, plaque *f*; (*paving*) dalle *f*; (*butcher's*) étal *m*.

slack [slak] *adj* (*loose*) lâche; (*trade*) faible; (*person*) négligent, peu sérieux. *n*

mou *m*. **slacken** *v* (se) relâcher; diminuer. **slacker** *n* (*coll*) flemmard, -e *m, f*.

slacks [slaks] *pl n* pantalon *m sing*.

slag [slag] *n* scories *f pl*. **slag heap** (*mining*) terril *m*.

slalom ['slaːləm] *n* slalom *m*.

slam [slam] *n* claquement *m*. *v* claquer. **slam on the brakes** freiner à mort.

slander ['slaːndə] *n* calomnie *f*; (*law*) diffamation *f*. *v* calomnier; diffamer. **slanderous** *adj* calomnieux; diffamatoire.

slang [slaŋ] *n* argot *m*.

slant [slaːnt] *n* inclinaison *f*; angle *m*. *v* (faire) pencher. **slanting** *adj* incliné, penché.

slap [slap] *n* claque *f*; (*on face*) gifle *f*. *v* donner une claque à; gifler; (*coll: put*) flanquer. **slapdash** *adj* (*person*) négligent; (*work*) bâclé. **slapstick** *n* grosse farce *f*. **slap-up meal** (*coll*) repas fameux *m*.

slash [slaʃ] *n* entaille *f*. *v* entailler, taillader; (*coll: prices*) casser.

slat [slat] *n* lame *f*; (*of blind*) lamelle *f*.

slate [sleit] *n* ardoise *f*. *v* ardoiser; (*coll: criticize*) éreinter.

slaughter ['sloːtə] *n* abattage *m*; (*people*) carnage *m*. **slaughterhouse** *n* abattoir *m*. *v* abattre; massacrer.

slave [sleiv] *n* esclave *m, f*. **slave-driver** *n* négrier, -ère *m, f*. *v* trimer. **slavery** *n* esclavage *m*.

sledge [sledʒ] *n* luge *f*; (*drawn by animal*) traîneau *m*.

sledgehammer ['sledʒhamə] *n* marteau de forgeron *m*.

sleek [sliːk] *adj* lisse, brillant.

*sleep [sliːp] *n* sommeil *m*. **go to sleep** s'endormir. **sleepwalker** *n* somnambule *m, f*. *v* dormir; (*spend the night*) coucher. **sleep in** faire la grasse matinée. **sleeper** *n* train-couchettes *m*; (*wooden beam*) traverse *f*. **sleeping-bag** *n* sac de couchage *m*. **sleeping-pill** *n* somnifère *m*. **sleepless night** nuit blanche *f*. **sleepy** *adj* endormi, somnolent.

sleet [sliːt] *n* neige fondue *f*.

sleeve [sliːv] *n* manche *f*; (*record*) pochette *f*. **sleeveless** *adj* sans manches.

sleigh [slei] *n* traîneau *m*.

slender ['slendə] *adj* svelte; fin; faible; maigre.

slept [slept] *V* **sleep**.

slice [slais] *n* tranche *f*; partie *f*. *v* couper en tranches.

slick [slik] *adj (derog)* facile, superficiel.
slid [slid] *V* **slide.**

*slide [slaid] *n* glissade *f;* (*chute*) toboggan *m;* (*microscope*) porte-objet *m;* (*phot*) diapositive *f;* (*hair*) barrette *f.*
slide-rule *n* règle à calcul *f. v* (se) glisser.

sliding *adj* glissant; (*door, etc.*) coulissant.

slight [slait] *adj* petit, faible; (*person*) mince. *v* offenser. *n* offense *f.* **slightest** *adj* moindre. **slightly** *adv* un peu.

slim [slim] *adj* mince; faible. *v* (faire) maigrir. **slimming** *adj* (*diet, etc.*) amaigrissant.

slime [slaim] *n* vase *f,* limon *m.* **slimy** *adj* visqueux.

*sling [slin] *n* (*med*) écharpe *f;* (*weapon*) fronde *f. v* lancer; suspendre.

*slink [slink] *v* **slink away** s'en aller furtivement.

slip [slip] *n* erreur *f;* (*of paper*) bout *m,* fiche *f;* (*underskirt*) combinaison *f.* **slip of the tongue** *or* **pen** lapsus *m. v* (se) glisser. **slip-knot** *n* nœud coulant *m.* **sliproad** *n* bretelle d'accès *f.* **slipshod** *adj* négligé, négligent. **slipway** *n* cale *f.*

slipper ['slipə] *n* pantoufle *f.*

slippery ['slipəri] *adj* glissant.

*slit [slit] *n* fente *f,* incision *f. v* fendre, inciser.

slither ['sliðə] *v* glisser, déraper.

slobber ['slobə] *v* baver. *n* bave *f.*

sloe [slou] *n* prunelle *f.*

slog [slog] *n* gros effort *m. v* travailler très dur; (*ball*) donner un grand coup à.

slogan ['slougən] *n* slogan *m.*

slop [slop] *v* (*spill*) répandre; (*overflow*) déborder.

slope [sloup] *n* inclinaison *f;* (*hill*) côte *f. v* être incliné. **sloping** *adj* en pente, incliné.

sloppy ['slopi] *adj* (*food*) liquide; (*dress*) négligé; (*garment*) mal ajusté; (*coll: work*) bâclé.

slot [slot] *n* fente *f.* **slot-machine** *n* (*vending*) distributeur automatique *m;* (*gambling*) machine à sous *f. v* (s')emboîter; (s')insérer.

slouch [slautʃ] *v* se tenir mal.

slovenly ['slʌvnli] *adj* négligé.

slow [slou] *adj* lent. *adv* lentement. **in slow motion** au ralenti. **slowcoach** *n* (*coll*) lambin, -e *m, f. v* **slow down** ralentir.

slug [slʌg] *n* (zool) limace *f;* (*bullet*) balle *f.*

sluggish ['slʌgiʃ] *adj* lent, paresseux.

sluice [sluːs] *n* écluse *f. v* laver à grande eau.

slum [slʌm] *n* taudis *m.* **slums** *pl n* quartiers pauvres *m pl.*

slumber ['slʌmbə] *n* sommeil paisible *m. v* dormir paisiblement.

slump [slʌmp] *n* baisse soudaine *f;* récession *f,* crise *f. v* s'effondrer.

slung [slʌŋ] *V* **sling.**

slunk [slʌŋk] *V* **slink.**

slur [sləː] *n* tache *f;* insulte *f;* (*music*) liaison *f. v* mal articuler; (*music*) lier.

slush [slʌʃ] *n* neige fondante *f.*

slut [slʌt] *n* souillon *f.*

sly [slai] *adj* rusé, sournois.

smack¹ [smak] *n* tape *f,* claque *f;* (*sound*) claquement *m. v* donner une tape *or* claque à.

smack² [smak] *v* **smack of** sentir. *n* léger goût *m.*

small [smoːl] *adj* petit; peu nombreux. **feel small** se sentir honteux. **small change** petite monnaie *f.* **smallholding** *n* petite ferme *f.* **smallpox** *n* variole *f.* **small talk** papotage *m. n* **small of the back** creux des reins *m.*

smart [smaːt] *adj* chic *invar,* élégant; intelligent, astucieux; rapide, vif. *v* brûler, piquer. **smarten up** devenir plus élégant; rendre plus élégant. **smartness** *n* élégance *f;* intelligence *f.*

smash [smaʃ] *n* (*sound*) fracas *m;* accident *m,* collision *f;* (*blow*) coup violent *m. v* (se) briser (en mille morceaux), (se) fracasser. **smashing** *adj* (*slang*) formidable.

smear [smiə] *n* tache *f. v* (se) salir, barbouiller.

*smell [smel] *n* odeur *f;* (*sense*) odorat *m. v* sentir; (*sniff*) flairer. **smelly** *adj* malodorant.

smelt [smelt] *V* **smell.**

smile [smail] *n* sourire *m. v* sourire.

smirk [sməːk] *n* petit sourire satisfait *m. v* sourire d'un air satisfait.

smock [smok] *n* blouse *f.* **smocking** *n* smocks *m pl.*

smog [smog] *n* brouillard enfumé *m.*

smoke [smouk] *n* fumée *f.* **smoke-screen** *n* paravent *m. v* fumer. **smoker** *n* fumeur, -euse *m, f.* **no smoking** défense de fumer. **smoky** *adj* enfumé.

smooth [smuːð] *adj* lisse; régulier; (*person*) doucereux. *v* lisser. **smooth out** faire disparaître. **smoothly** *adv* facilement, doucement; (*move*) sans secousses; sans incident.

smother ['smʌðə] *v* étouffer.

smoulder ['smouldə] *v* couver.

smudge [smʌdʒ] *n* tache *f.* *v* (s')étaler, (se) maculer.

smug [smʌg] *adj* suffisant.

smuggle ['smʌgl] *v* passer en contrabande; passer clandestinement. **smuggler** *n* contrebandier, -ère *m, f.* **smuggling** *n* contrebande *f.*

snack [snak] *n* casse-croûte *m invar.* **snack-bar** *n* snack-bar *m.*

snag [snag] *n* inconvénient *m*, obstacle caché *m*; (*in cloth*) accroc *m.* *v* accrocher.

snail [sneil] *n* escargot *m.*

snake [sneik] *n* serpent *m.* *v* serpenter.

snap [snap] *n* bruit sec *m*, claquement *m*, craquement *m*; photo *f.* *adj* subit, irréfléchi. **snapdragon** *n* gueule-de-loup *f.* **snapshot** *n* photo *f.* *v* (se) casser net; (faire) claquer; (*dog*) essayer de mordre; (*person*) parler d'un ton brusque.

snare [sneə] *n* piège *m.* *v* attraper.

snarl [snaːl] *n* grondement *m.* *v* gronder.

snatch [snatʃ] *n* fragment *m*; (*theft*) vol *m.* *v* saisir, arracher (à).

sneak [sniːk] *v* se faufiler; (*slang: school*) moucharder. **sneak in/out** entrer/sortir furtivement. *n* (*coll*) mouchard, -e *m, f.*

sneer [sniə] *v* ricaner. *n* ricanement *m.* **sneering** *adj* ricaneur, -euse.

sneeze [sniːz] *n* éternuement *m.* *v* éternuer.

sniff [snif] *n* reniflement *m.* *v* renifler; (*air, aroma*) humer.

snigger ['snigə] *n* petit rire moqueur *m.* *v* pouffer de rire.

snip [snip] *v* couper à petits coups.

snipe [snaip] *n* bécassine *f.* *v* canarder. **sniper** *n* canardeur *m.*

snivel ['snivl] *v* pleurnicher. **snivelling** *adj* pleurnicheur, -euse.

snob [snob] *n* snob *m, f.* **snobbish** *adj* snob *invar.*

snooker ['snuːkə] *n* jeu de billard *m.*

snoop [snuːp] *v* (*coll*) fureter, fourrer son nez.

snooty ['snuːti] *adj* (*coll*) hautain.

snooze [snuːz] *n* roupillon *m.* *v* piquer un roupillon.

snore [snoː] *n* ronflement *m.* *v* ronfler. **snoring** *n* ronflements *m pl.*

snorkel ['snoːkəl] *n* (*swimmer*) tuba *m*; (*submarine*) schnorchel *m.*

snort [snoːt] *n* (*person*) grognement *m*; (*animal*) ébrouement *m.* *v* grogner; s'ébrouer.

snout [snaut] *n* museau *m.*

snow [snou] *n* neige *f.* **snow-drift** *n* congère *f.* **snowdrop** *n* perce-neige *m.* **snowflake** *n* flocon de neige *m.* **snowman** *n* bonhomme de neige *m.* **snow-plough** *n* chasse-neige *m invar.* **snow-shoe** *n* raquette *f.* **snowstorm** *n* tempête de neige *f.* *v* neiger. **be snowed under with** être submergé de. **snowy** *adj* neigeux; de neige.

snowball ['snoubɔːl] *n* boule de neige *f.* *v* (*increase*) faire boule de neige.

snub [snʌb] *n* rebuffade *f.* *v* (*person*) snober; repousser.

snuff [snʌf] *n* tabac à priser. **snuffbox** *n* tabatière *f.* **take snuff** priser.

snug [snʌg] *adj* douillet, -ette, confortable.

snuggle ['snʌgl] *v* se blottir, se pelotonner.

so [sou] *adv* si, tellement, aussi; (*thus*) ainsi. *conj* donc. **and so on** et ainsi de suite. **if so** si oui. **is that so?** vraiment? ... **or so** à peu près .... **so as to** afin de. **so-called** *adj* soi-disant *invar.* **so much** or **many** tant (de). **so-so** *adj* (*coll*) comme ci comme ça. **so that** pour (que). **so what?** et alors?

soak [souk] *v* (faire) tremper. **soak in** pénétrer. **soak up** absorber. **soaking** *n* trempage *m.* **soaking wet** trempé.

soap [soup] *n* savon *m.* **soap-box** *n* tribune improvisée *f.* **soap-dish** *n* porte-savon *m.* **soap opera** (*coll*) mélo à épisodes *m.* **soap powder** lessive *f.* *v* savonner. **soapy** *adj* savonneux.

soar [soː] *v* monter en flèche; (*hope*) grandir.

sob [sob] *n* sanglot *m.* *v* sangloter.

sober ['soubə] *adj* sérieux; modéré; (*not drunk*) pas ivre. *v* **sober up** désenivrer.

soccer ['sokə] *n* football *m.*

sociable ['souʃəbl] *adj* sociable.

social ['souʃəl] *adj* social; (*life, etc.*) mondain. **social club** association amicale *f.* **social science** sciences humaines *f pl.* **social security** aide sociale *f.* **social work** assistance sociale *f.* **socialism** *n* social-

isme *m*. **socialist** *n(m+f)*. *adj* socialiste.
socialize *v* fréquenter des gens.
society [sə'saiəti] *n* société *f*.
sociology [sousi'olədʒi] *n* sociologie *f*.
sociological *adj* sociologique. **sociologist** *n* sociologue *m, f*.
sock [sok] *n* chaussette *f*.
socket ['sokit] *n* cavité *f*; (*elec*) prise de courant *f*.
soda ['soudə] *n* (*chem*) soude *f*; (*water*) eau de Seltz *f*.
sodden ['sodn] *adj* détrempé.
sofa ['soufə] *n* sofa *m*.
Sofia ['soufjə] *n* Sofia.
soft [soft] *adj* doux, douce; (*butter, clay, etc.*) mou, molle; (*coll*) stupide. **soft-boiled** *adj* (*egg*) à la coque. **soft drink** boisson non alcoolisée *f*. **soft toy** jouet de peluche *m*. **soften** *v* (s')adoucir; (se) ramollir. **softness** *n* douceur *f*; mollesse *f*.
soggy ['sogi] *adj* détrempé.
soil¹ [soil] *n* sol *m*, terre *f*.
soil² [soil] *v* salir.
solar ['soulə] *adj* solaire, du soleil.
sold [sould] *V* sell.
solder ['soldə] *n* soudure *f*. *v* souder. **soldering iron** fer à souder *m*.
soldier ['souldʒə] *n* soldat *m*. *v* **soldier on** persévérer.
sole¹ [soul] *adj* seul, unique; exclusif.
sole² [soul] *n* (*of shoe*) semelle *f*; (*of foot*) plante *f*. *v* ressemeler.
sole³ [soul] *n* (*fish*) sole *f*.
solemn ['soləm] *adj* solennel. **solemnity** *n* solennité *f*.
solicitor [sə'lisitə] *n* avocat *m*.
solicitude [sə'lisitjuːd] *n* sollicitude *f*.
solid ['solid] *adj* solide; (*not hollow*) plein; (*line*) continu. *n* solide *m*. **solids** *pl n* (*food*) aliments solides *m pl*. **solidarity** *n* solidarité *f*. **solidify** *v* (se) solidifier; (se) congeler.
solitary ['solitəri] *adj* solitaire; seul, unique.
solitude ['solitjuːd] *n* solitude *f*.
solo ['soulou] *n* solo *m*. *adj* solo *invar*; (*flight*) en solitaire. **soloist** *n* soliste *m, f*.
solstice ['solstis] *n* solstice *m*.
soluble ['soljubl] *adj* soluble.
solution [sə'luːʃən] *n* solution *f*.
solve [solv] *v* résoudre, trouver la solution de.
solvent ['solvənt] *adj* (*finance*) solvable. *n*

(*chem*) solvant *m*. **solvency** *n* solvabilité *f*.
sombre ['sombə] *adj* sombre, morne.
some [sʌm] *adj* du, de la; (*pl*) des; certains; (*unspecified*) quelque. *pron* quelques-uns; (*before verb*) en. *adv* environ. **somebody** *or* **someone** *pron* quelqu'un. **somehow** *adv* d'une façon ou d'une autre. **something** *pron* quelque chose. **sometime** *adv* un de ces jours. **sometimes** *adv* quelquefois. **somewhat** *adv* quelque peu. **somewhere** *adv* quelque part. **somewhere else** ailleurs.
somersault ['sʌməsɔːlt] *n* culbute *f*. *v* faire la culbute.
son [sʌn] *n* fils *m*. **son-in-law** *n* gendre *m*.
sonata [sə'nɑːtə] *n* sonate *f*.
song [soŋ] *n* chanson *f*; (*birds*) chant *m*.
sonic ['sonik] *adj* sonique. **sonic boom** détonation supersonique *f*.
sonnet ['sonit] *n* sonnet *m*.
soon [suːn] *adv* bientôt; (*early*) tôt. **as soon as** dès que. **sooner or later** tôt ou tard.
soot [sut] *n* suie *f*.
soothe [suːð] *v* calmer, apaiser. **soothing** *adj* apaisant; (*ointment*) lénitif.
sophisticated [sə'fistikeitid] *adj* raffiné; élégant; (*machinery*) sophistiqué.
sopping ['sopiŋ] *adj* trempé.
soprano [sə'prɑːnou] *n* soprano *m, f*.
sordid ['soːdid] *adj* sordide.
sore [soː] *adj* douloureux. **sore point** point délicat *m*. *n* plaie *f*. **sorely** *adv* (*bitterly*) amèrement; (*greatly*) fortement. **soreness** *n* endolorissement *m*.
sorrow ['sorou] *n* peine *f*, chagrin *m*. *v* se lamenter. **sorrowful** *adj* triste, affligé.
sorry ['sori] *adj* désolé; (*plight*) triste. **feel sorry for** plaindre. *interj* pardon!
sort [soːt] *n* sorte *f*, genre *m*; (*brand*) marque *f*. *v* trier, classer. **sort out** ranger; (*problem*) régler; arranger. **sorting office** bureau de tri *m*.
soufflé ['suːflei] *n* soufflé *m*.
sought [soːt] *V* seek.
soul [soul] *n* âme *f*. **soul-destroying** *adj* démoralisant. **soulful** *adj* expressif.
sound¹ [saund] *n* (*noise*) son *m*, bruit *m*. **sound barrier** mur du son *m*. **sound effects** bruitage *m sing*. **soundproof** *adj* insonorisé. **sound-track** *n* piste sonore *f*. *v* sonner, retentir; (*seem*) sembler.
sound² [saund] *adj* sain, solide; (*advice*,

etc.) sensé; (*sleep*) profond. **be sound asleep** être profondément endormi.
sound[3] [saund] *v* (*depth*) sonder.
soup [suːp] *n* soupe *f*, potage *m*. **soup-plate** *n* assiette creuse *f*.
sour [sauə] *adj* aigre, acide; (*person*) acerbe, revêche. *v* (s')aigrir.
source [sɔːs] *n* source *f*.
south [sauθ] *n* sud *m*. *adj also* **southerly**, **southern** sud *invar*; au *or* du sud. *adv* au sud; vers le sud. **southbound** *adj* sud *invar*. **south-east** *nm*, *adj* sud-est. **southwest** *nm*, *adj* sud-ouest.
souvenir [suːvə'niə] *n* souvenir *m*.
sovereign ['sovrin] *n*, *adj* souverain, -e.
***sow**[1] [sou] *v* semer, ensemencer.
sow[2] [sau] *n* truie *f*.
sown [soun] *V* **sow**[1].
soya ['sɔiə] *n* soja *m*. **soya bean** graine de soja *f*. **soy sauce** sauce au soja *f*.
spa [spaː] *n* station thermale *f*.
space [speis] *n* espace *m*, place *f*. **spaceman** *n* astronaute *m*. **spaceship** *n* engin spatial. *m*. *v* espacer. **spacious** *adj* spacieux.
spade[1] [speid] *n* bêche *f*, pelle *f*.
spade[2] [speid] *n* (*cards*) pique *m*.
spaghetti [spə'geti] *n* spaghetti *m pl*.
Spain [spein] *n* Espagne *f*. **Spaniard** *n* Espagnol, -e *m*, *f*. **Spanish** *nm*, *adj* espagnol.
span [span] *n* envergure *f*, portée *f*; (*bridge*) travée *f*; (*time*) espace *m*, durée *f*. *v* enjamber.
spaniel ['spanjəl] *n* épagneul *m*.
spank [spaŋk] *v* donner une fessée à. **spanking** *n* fessée *f*.
spanner ['spanə] *n* clef (à écrous) *f*.
spare [speə] *adj* de réserve, de trop. **spare part** (*mot*) pièce détachée *f*. **spare-rib** *n* (*cookery*) côtelette dans l'échine *f*. **spare room** chambre d'ami *f*. **spare time** temps libre *m*. **spare tyre** pneu de rechange *m*; (*coll*) bourrelet *m*. **spare wheel** roue de secours *f*. *v* se passer de; (*save*) épargner. **sparing** *adj* limité, modéré.
spark [spaːk] *n* étincelle *f*. **spark-plug** *n* bougie *f*. *v* jeter des étincelles. **spark off** provoquer.
sparkle ['spaːkl] *n* scintillement *m*; (*in eye*) étincelle *f*. *v* étinceler, scintiller. **sparkling** *adj* (*drink*) pétillant.
sparrow ['sparou] *n* moineau *m*.
sparse [spaːs] *adj* clairsemé. **sparsely** *adv* peu.

spasm ['spazəm] *n* spasme *m*; (*fit*) accès *m*. **spasmodic** *adj* (*med*) spasmodique; irrégulier.
spastic ['spastik] *n*, *adj* handicapé, -e moteur.
spat [spat] *V* **spit**[1].
spatial ['speiʃl] *adj* spatial.
spatula ['spatjulə] *n* spatule *f*.
spawn [spɔːn] *n* frai *m*. *v* frayer.
***speak** [spiːk] *v* parler. **speak up** parler fort. **speaker** *n* orateur *m*; (*loudspeaker*) haut-parleur *m*.
spear [spiə] *n* lance *f*; (*asparagus*) pointe *f*.
special ['speʃəl] *adj* spécial, particulier; extraordinaire. **specialist** *n* spécialiste *m*, *f*. **speciality** *n* spécialité *f*. **specialize** *v* se spécialiser.
species ['spiːʃiz] *n* espèce *f*.
specify ['spesifai] *v* spécifier. **specific** *adj* précis; (*science*) spécifique. **specification** *n* spécification *f*; stipulation *f*.
specimen ['spesimin] *n* spécimen *m*; (*urine*) échantillon *m*; (*blood*) prélèvement *m*.
speck [spek] *n* grain *m*; petite tache *f*. **speckle** *v* tacheter.
spectacle ['spektəkl] *n* spectacle *m*. **spectacles** *pl n* lunettes *f pl*. **spectacular** *adj* spectaculaire.
spectator [spek'teitə] *n* spectateur, -trice *m*, *f*.
spectrum ['spektrəm] *n* spectre *m*; (*range*) gamme *f*.
speculate ['spekjuleit] *v* spéculer; s'interroger. **speculation** *n* spéculation *f*; conjecture *f*. **speculative** *adj* spéculatif.
sped [sped] *V* **speed**.
speech [spiːtʃ] *n* (*faculty*) parole *f*; articulation *f*; (*address*) discours *m*. **speech day** distribution des prix *f*. **speech impediment** défaut d'élocution *m*. **speech therapy** orthophonie *f*. **speechless** *adj* muet.
***speed** [spiːd] *n* vitesse *f*; rapidité *f*. **speedboat** *n* vedette *f*. **speed limit** limitation de vitesse *f*. **speedometer** *n* compteur de vitesse *m*. *v* (*mot*) conduire trop vite. **speed along** aller à toute vitesse. **speed up** aller plus vite; accélérer. **speeding** *n* excès de vitesse *m*. **speedy** *adj* rapide.
***spell**[1] [spel] *v* épeler; (*write*) écrire; signifier. **spelling** *n* orthographe *f*.

spell² [spel] n (magic) charme m, formule magique f. **spellbound** adj subjugué, envoûté.

spell³ [spel] n période f; (turn) tour m.

spelt [spelt] V spell¹.

*spend [spend] v (money) dépenser; (time) passer. **spendthrift** n dépensier, -ère m, f. **spending** n dépenses f pl. **spending money** argent de poche m.

spent [spent] V spend.

sperm [spɜːm] n sperme m.

spew [spjuː] v vomir.

sphere [sfɪə] n sphère f; domaine m. **spherical** adj sphérique.

spice [spaɪs] n épice f. v épicer. **spicy** adj épicé.

spider ['spaɪdə] n araignée f.

spike [spaɪk] n pointe f.

*spill [spɪl] v renverser, (se) répandre.

spilt [spɪlt] V spill.

*spin [spɪn] n tournoiement m; (drying) essorage m; (coll: ride) balade f. v (wool, etc.) filer; (turn) (faire) tourner, tournoyer. **spin-dry** v essorer. **spin-dryer** n essoreuse f. **spin out** faire durer. **spinning** n filage m. **spinning top** toupie f. **spinning wheel** rouet m.

spinach ['spɪnɪdʒ] n (bot) épinard m; (cookery) épinards m pl.

spindle ['spɪndl] n (spinning) fuseau m, broche f; (tech) axe m, tige f. **spindly** adj grêle.

spine [spaɪn] n (anat) colonne vertébrale; épine f; (book) dos m. **spinal** adj spinal, vertébral. **spiny** adj épineux.

spinster ['spɪnstə] n célibataire f.

spiral ['spaɪərəl] adj en spirale. **spiral staircase** escalier tournant m. n spirale f.

spire ['spaɪə] n flèche f.

spirit ['spɪrɪt] n esprit m; courage m; alcool m. **spirit-level** n niveau à bulle m. **spirited** adj fougueux. **spiritual** adj spirituel. **spiritualism** n spiritisme m. **spiritualist** n spirite m, f.

*spit¹ [spɪt] n crachat m; salive f. v cracher.

spit² [spɪt] n (cookery) broche f; (geog) pointe f.

spite [spaɪt] n rancune f. **in spite of** malgré. v vexer. **spiteful** adj malveillant.

splash [splæʃ] n éclaboussement m; (sound) plouf m; (mark) éclaboussure f, tache f. v éclabousser.

spleen [spliːn] n (anat) rate f; mauvaise humeur f.

splendid ['splendɪd] adj splendide; excellent. **splendour** n splendeur f.

splice [splaɪs] v épisser.

splint [splɪnt] n éclisse f.

splinter ['splɪntə] n éclat m; (in finger) écharde f. v (se) fendre en éclats, (se) briser en éclats.

*split [splɪt] n fente f, fissure f. v (se) fendre; (se) diviser; (share) (se) partager. **split second** fraction de seconde f.

splutter ['splʌtə] v (person) bredouiller; (engine) bafouiller; (fire, fat, etc.) crépiter. n bredouillement m; bafouillage m; crépitement m.

*spoil [spɔɪl] v gâter; (damage) (s')abîmer. **spoil-sport** n trouble-fête m, f. **spoils** pl n butin m sing.

spoke¹ [spəʊk] V speak.

spoke² [spəʊk] n rayon m.

spoken ['spəʊkn] V speak.

spokesman ['spəʊksmən] n porte-parole m invar.

sponge [spʌndʒ] n éponge f; (cake) gâteau de Savoie m. **sponge bag** sac de toilette m. v éponger. **sponge on** vivre au crochets de. **spongy** adj spongieux.

sponsor ['spɒnsə] n personne (f) or organisme (m) qui assure le patronage; (for loan) répondant, -e m, f; (fund-raising) donateur, -trice m, f. v patronner. **sponsorship** n patronage m.

spontaneous [spɒn'teɪnjəs] adj spontané. **spontaneity** n spontanéité f.

spool [spuːl] n bobine f.

spoon [spuːn] n cuiller f. **spoonful** n cuillerée f.

sporadic [spə'rædɪk] adj sporadique.

sport [spɔːt] n sport m. **sports car** voiture de sport f. **sports jacket** veste sport f. **sportsman** n sportif m. **sportswoman** n sportive f. v exhiber. **sporting** adj sportif. **sportive** adj folâtre.

spot [spɒt] n (mark) tache f; (pimple) bouton m; (polka dot) pois m; (place) endroit m; (small amount) goutte f, grain m. **on the spot** sur le champ. **spot check** n contrôle intermittent m. **spotlight** n (rayon de) projecteur m. v tacher; (see) apercevoir. **spotless** adj immaculé. **spotted** adj tacheté; à pois. **spotty** adj boutonneux.

spouse [spaʊs] n (law) conjoint, -e m, f.

spout [spaʊt] n bec m; jet m. v (faire) jaillir; (coll: recite) débiter.

sprain [sprein] *n* entorse *f. v* fouler.

sprang [spraŋ] *V* **spring.**

sprawl [sproːl] *v* s'étaler, être affalé.

spray[1] [sprei] *n* gouttelettes *f pl*; *(from aerosol)* pulvérisation *f*; bombe *f*, aérosol *m. v (water)* asperger; vaporiser, pulvériser.

spray[2] [sprei] *n (flowers)* gerbe *f*; branche *f.*

*spread [spred] *n* propagation *f*, diffusion *f*; *(span)* envergure *f*; *(paste)* pâte *f*; *(coll: meal)* festin *m. v* (s')étaler, (s')étendre; (se) propager, (se) communiquer. **spread-eagled** *adj* vautré. **spread out** (s')étaler; se disperser.

spree [spriː] *n* fête *f.*

sprig [sprig] *n* brin *m.*

sprightly ['spraitli] *adj* alerte.

*spring [spriŋ] *n (leap)* bond *m*; *(coil)* ressort *m*; *(water)* source *f*; *(season)* printemps *m.* **spring-board** *n* tremplin *m.* **spring-cleaning** *n* grand nettoyage *m.* **spring onion** ciboule *f. v* bondir. **spring up** surgir, jaillir. **springy** *adj* souple.

sprinkle ['spriŋkl] *v* asperger; *(sugar, etc.)* saupoudrer. **sprinkler** *n (garden)* arroseur *m*; *(fire)* diffuseur *m.* **sprinkling** *n* aspersion *f*; légère couche *f.*

sprint [sprint] *n* sprint *m. v (sport)* sprinter; foncer un sprint.

sprout [spraut] *n* pousse *f*, germe *m.* **Brussels sprouts** choux de Bruxelles *m pl. v* pousser, germer.

spruce [spruːs] *v* **spruce up** faire beau *or* belle.

sprung [sprʌŋ] *V* **spring.**

spun [spʌn] *V* **spin.**

spur [spəː] *n* éperon *m.* **on the spur of the moment** sous l'impulsion du moment. *v* éperonner.

spurious ['spjuəriəs] *adj* faux, fausse.

spurn [spəːn] *v* repousser.

spurt [spəːt] *n (water)* jet *m*; *(energy)* sursaut *m*; effort soudain *m. v* jaillir.

spy [spai] *n* espion, -onne *m, f. v* espionner; *(see)* apercevoir. **spying** *n* espionnage *m.*

squabble ['skwobl] *n* chamaillerie *f. v* se chamailler.

squad [skwod] *n* escouade *f*, groupe *m.*

squadron ['skwodrən] *n (mil)* escadron *m*; *(naut)* escadrille *f.*

squalid ['skwolid] *adj* misérable, sordide; *(dirty)* sale.

squall [skwoːl] *n* rafale *f.*

squander ['skwondə] *v* gaspiller.

square [skweə] *n* carré *m*; *(on chessboard, grid)* case *f*; *(in town)* place *f. adj* carré; en ordre. *v* carrer; *(settle)* régler.

squash [skwoʃ] *n (sport)* squash *m*; *(drink)* sirop *m*; *(crush)* cohue *f. v* (s')écraser; *(together)* (se) serrer.

squat [skwot] *adj* ramassé, courtaud. *v* s'accroupir; *(in house)* faire du squattage. **squatter** *n* squatter *m.*

squawk [skwoːk] *v* pousser des gloussements. *n* gloussement *m*, cri rauque *m.*

squeak [skwiːk] *n* grincement *m*; *(mouse, etc.)* petit cri aigu *m. v* grincer; *(mouse)* vagir.

squeal [skwiːl] *n* cri aigu *m*; *(brakes)* grincement *m. v* pousser un cri aigu; grincer.

squeamish ['skwiːmiʃ] *adj* délicat, facilement dégoûté.

squeeze [skwiːz] *n* pression *f. v* presser, serrer; *(extract)* exprimer.

squid [skwid] *n* calmar *m.*

squiggle ['skwigl] *n* gribouillis *m. v* gribouiller.

squint [skwint] *n (med)* strabisme *m*; *(glance)* coup d'œil *m. v* loucher.

squirm [skwəːm] *v* se tortiller; *(person)* avoir un haut-le-corps.

squirrel ['skwirəl] *n* écureuil *m.*

squirt [skwəːt] *n* jet *m. v* (faire) jaillir; asperger.

stab [stab] *n* coup de couteau *m. v* poignarder; donner un coup de couteau à.

stabilize ['steibilaiz] *v* stabiliser. **stabilizer** *n* stabilisateur *m.*

stable[1] ['steibl] *n* écurie *f.*

stable[2] ['steibl] *adj* stable; solide; constant. **stability** *n* stabilité *f*; solidité *f.*

staccato [stə'kaːtou] *adv* staccato. *adj (voice, sounds, etc.)* saccadé.

stack [stak] *n (pile)* tas *m*; *(hay, etc.)* meule *f*; *(chimneys)* souche de cheminée *f.* **stacks of** *(coll)* un tas de. *v* empiler, entasser.

stadium ['steidiəm] *n* stade *m.*

staff [staːf] *n* personnel *m*; bâton *m.* **staff-room** *n (school)* salle des professeurs *f.*

stag [stag] *n* cerf *m.* **stag party** *(coll)* réunion entre hommes *f.*

stage [steidʒ] *n (theatre)* scène *f*; *(platform)* estrade *f*; *(point)* étape *f.* **stage fright** trac *m.* **stage-manager** *n* régisseur *m.* **stage name** nom de théâtre *m.* **stage whisper** aparté *m.* *v* monter; organiser.

stagger ['stagə] *v* chanceler; (*amaze*) stupéfier; (*payments, etc.*) échelonner. **staggering** *adj* renversant.

stagnant ['stagnənt] *adj* stagnant. **stagnate** *v* croupir, stagner. **stagnation** *n* stagnation *f.*

staid [steid] *adj* (*person*) posé; (*opinion*) pondéré.

stain [stein] *n* tache *f;* colorant *m.* **stain remover** détachant *m. v* tacher; (*wood*) teinter. **stained glass** verre coloré *m;* (*windows*) vitraux *m pl.* **stainless steel** acier inoxydable *m.*

stair [steə] *n* marche *f.* **staircase** *n* escalier *m.* **stairs** *pl n* escalier *m sing.*

stake[1] [steik] *n* (*post*) pieu *m;* (*for execution*) bûcher *m. v* jalonner.

stake[2] [steik] *n* (*betting*) enjeu *m;* intérêt *m.* **at stake** en jeu. *v* jouer.

stale [steil] *adj* (*bread*) rassis; (*air*) confiné; (*joke*) rebattu. **staleness** *n* manque de fraîcheur *f.*

stalemate ['steilmeit] *n* (*chess*) pat *m;* impasse *f.*

stalk[1] [stɔːk] *n* (*plant*) tige *f;* (*fruit*) queue *f.*

stalk[2] [stɔːk] *v* traquer. **stalk in/out** entrer/sortir avec raideur.

stall[1] [stɔːl] *n* (*market*) éventaire *m;* kiosque *m;* (*theatre*) fauteuil d'orchestre *m;* (*cowshed*) stalle *f.* **stalls** *pl n* orchestre *m sing. v* (*car, etc.*) caler.

stall[2] [stɔːl] *v* (*delay*) atermoyer. **stall off** tenir à distance.

stallion ['staljən] *n* étalon *m.*

stamina ['staminə] *n* vigueur *f.* résistance *f.*

stammer ['stamə] *n* bégaiement *m. v* bégayer.

stamp [stamp] *n* timbre *m;* (*mark*) cachet *m;* (*with foot*) trépignement *m.* **stamp-collecting** *n* philatélie *f. v* timbrer, tamponner; (*with foot*) taper du pied, trépigner.

stampede [stam'piːd] *n* débandade *f;* (*rush*) ruée *f. v* fuir à la débandade; se ruer.

*****stand** [stand] *n* position *f;* support *m;* (*comm*) étalage *m;* (*at exhibition*) stand *m. v* être debout; (*get up*) se lever; (*put*) mettre; (*tolerate*) supporter; (*be based*) reposer. **stand for** représenter; tolérer.

stand out ressortir. **standstill** *n* arrêt *m.* **come to a standstill** s'immobiliser, s'arrêter. **stand up for** défendre.

standard ['standəd] *n* norme *f.* critère *m.* niveau (voulu) *m;* (*flag*) étendard *m. adj* normal, ordinaire; (*comm*) standard *invar;* (*measure*) étalon *invar;* correct. **standard lamp** lampadaire *m.* **standardize** *v* standardiser.

standing ['standiŋ] *adj* debout; fixe; permanent. **standing order** (*bank*) virement automatique *m. n* importance *f.* standing *m;* durée *f.*

stank [staŋk] *V* **stink.**

stanza ['stanzə] *n* strophe *f.*

staple[1] [steipl] *n* (*papers*) agrafe *f;* (*tech*) crampon *m. v* agrafer; cramponner.

staple[2] [steipl] *adj* principal; de base.

star [staː] *n* étoile *f;* astérisque *m;* (*cinema, etc.*) vedette *f.* **starfish** *n* étoile de mer *f. v* étoiler; (*film*) avoir pour vedette; (*person*) être la vedette. **stardom** *n* célébrité *f.* **starry** *adj* étoilé.

starboard ['staːbəd] *n* tribord *m.*

starch [staːtʃ] *n* amidon *m. v* amidonner. **starchy** *adj* (*food*) féculent; (*person*) guindé.

stare [steə] *n* regard fixe *m. v* dévisager, regarder fixement.

stark [staːk] *adj* désolé, austère; (*stiff*) raide; (*utter*) pur. **stark naked** complètement nu.

starling ['staːliŋ] *n* étourneau *m.*

start [staːt] *n* commencement *m,* départ *m;* (*jump*) sursaut *m. v* commencer; (*clock, etc.*) mettre en marche; (*leave*) partir; (*car*) démarrer; sursauter. **starter** *n* (*sport*) starter *m;* (*mot*) démarreur *m;* (*meal*) hors-d'œuvre *m.*

startle ['staːtl] *v* faire sursauter. **startling** *adj* surprenant.

starve [staːv] *v* manquer de nourriture; (*to death*) (faire) mourir de faim; (*deliberately*) affamer; (*deprive*) priver. **starvation** *n* inanition *f.* famine *f.* **starving** *adj* affamé. **be starving** (*coll*) avoir une faim de loup.

state [steit] *n* état *m;* pompe *f.* **statesman** *n* homme d'Etat *m. v* déclarer; formuler; fixer. **stately** *adj* majestueux. **statement** *n* déclaration *f;* (*law*) déposition *f;* (*bank*) relevé *m.*

static ['statik] *adj* statique. *n* (*elec, radio, etc.*) parasites *m pl.*

station ['steiʃən] *n* (*rail*) gare *f*; (*radio, underground*) station *f*; (*position*) poste *m*; (*in life*) rang *m*. *v* poster, placer.
stationary ['steiʃənəri] *adj* stationnaire.
stationer ['steiʃənə] *n* papetier, -ère *m, f*.
stationer's *n* papeterie *f*. **stationery** *n* articles de bureau *m pl*; papier à lettres *m*.
statistics [stə'tistiks] *n* (*science*) statistique *f*. *pl n* statistiques *f pl*. **statistical** *adj* statistique.
statue ['statjuː] *n* statue *f*.
stature ['statʃə] *n* stature *f*; importance *f*, envergure *f*.
status ['steitəs] *n* situation *f*; prestige *m*.
statute ['statjuːt] *n* loi *f*. **statutory** *adj* statutaire; légal.
staunch [stoːntʃ] *adj* loyal, dévoué.
stay [stei] *n* séjour *m*. *v* rester; loger.
steadfast ['stedfaːst] *adj* ferme; constant.
steady ['stedi] *adj* stable, solide; constant, régulier. *v* maintenir; (*person*) reprendre son aplomb; (se) calmer. **steadily** *adv* fermement; progressivement; sans arrêt. **steadiness** *n* stabilité *f*; constance *f*.
steak [steik] *n* bifteck *m*; (*of pork, fish*) tranche *f*.
***steal** [stiːl] *v* voler. **stealing** *n* vol *m*.
stealthy ['stelθi] *adj* furtif.
steam [stiːm] *n* vapeur *f*. **steam-roller** *n* rouleau compresseur *m*. *v* fumer; (*cookery*) cuire à la vapeur. **steam up** se couvrir de buée.
steel [stiːl] *n* acier *m*. **steel wool** paille de fer *f*. **steelworks** *n* aciérie *f*. **steely** *adj* dur, d'acier.
steep¹ [stiːp] *adj* raide.
steep² [stiːp] *v* tremper.
steeple ['stiːpl] *n* clocher *m*. **steeplechase** *n* steeple *m*.
steer [stiə] *v* (*ship*) gouverner; (*car*) conduire; (*person*) guider. **steering** *n* conduite *f*. **steering-wheel** *n* volant *m*.
stem¹ [stem] *n* tige *f*; (*glass*) pied *m*. *v* **stem from** provenir de.
stem² [stem] *v* (*stop*) contenir, endiguer.
stench [stentʃ] *n* puanteur *f*.
stencil ['stensl] *n* pochoir *m*; (*typing*) stencil *m*.
step [step] *n* pas *m*; mesure *f*; (*stair*) marche *f*. **step-ladder** *n* escabeau *m*. *v* faire un pas; marcher. **step up** augmenter, intensifier.
stepbrother ['stepbrʌðə] *n* demi-frère *m*.

stepdaughter ['stepdoːtə] *n* belle-fille *f*.
stepfather ['stepfaːðə] *n* beau-père *m*.
stepmother ['stepmʌðə] *n* belle-mère *f*.
stepsister ['stepsistə] *n* demi-sœur *f*.
stepson ['stepsʌn] *n* beau-fils *m*.
stereo ['steriou] *nf, adj* stéréo. **stereophonic** *adj* stéréophonique.
stereotype ['steriotaip] *n* stéréotype *m*; (*printing*) cliché *m*. *v* stéréotyper; clicher.
sterile ['sterail] *adj* stérile. **sterility** *n* stérilité *f*. **sterilization** *n* stérilisation *f*. **sterilize** *v* stériliser.
sterling ['stoːliŋ] *n* livres sterling *f pl. adj* (*silver*) fin; (*character*) solide.
stern¹ [stoːn] *adj* sévère.
stern² [stoːn] *n* arrière *m*.
stethoscope ['steθəskoup] *n* stéthoscope *m*.
stew [stjuː] *n* ragoût *m*. *v* (*meat*) cuire en ragoût; (*fruit*) faire cuire.
steward ['stjuəd] *n* intendant *m*; (*plane, ship*) steward *m*. **stewardess** *n* hôtesse *f*.
stick¹ [stik] *n* bâton *m*; petite branche *f*; (*walking*) canne *f*.
***stick²** [stik] *v* (*stab*) planter, enfoncer; (*glue*) coller (*put*) mettre; (*get jammed*) être bloqué; (*slang: put up with*) supporter; (*stay*) rester. **stick out** sortir, (faire) dépasser. **stick up for** défendre. **sticky** *adj* poisseux, gluant.
stickler ['stiklə] *n* **be a stickler for** insister sur; être pointilleux sur.
stiff [stif] *adj* raide, rigide; (*hard to move*) dur; (*exam*) difficile; (*cool*) froid. **stiff neck** torticolis *m*. **stiffen** *v* (se) raidir; renforcer. **stiffness** *n* raideur *f*.
stifle ['staifl] *v* étouffer; (*smile, etc.*) réprimer. **stifling** *adj* suffocant.
stigma ['stigmə] *n* stigmate *m*.
stile [stail] *n* échalier *m*.
still¹ [stil] *adv* encore; (*anyway*) quand même; (*sit, stand*) sans bouger. *adj* calme, tranquille. **stillborn** *adj* mort-né. **still life** nature morte. *n* (*cinema*) photo *f*.
still² [stil] *n* alambic *m*; distillerie *f*.
stilt [stilt] *n* échasse *f*. **stilted** *adj* guindé.
stimulus ['stimjuləs] *n, pl* **-li** stimulus (*pl* -li) *m*; impulsion *f*, stimulant *m*. **stimulant** *nm, adj* stimulant. **stimulate** *v* stimuler. **stimulation** *n* stimulation *f*.
***sting** [stiŋ] *n* (*insect*) dard *m*; (*wound*) piqûre *f*; (*iodine*) brûlure. *v* piquer; brûler; (*whip*) cingler.

*stink [stiŋk] n puanteur f. v puer, empester.

stint [stint] n ration de travail f. v lésiner sur.

stipulate ['stipjuleit] v stipuler. **stipulation** n stipulation f.

stir [stəɪ] n agitation f, sensation f. v (tea, etc.) tourner; (move) agiter, remuer; exciter.

stirrup ['stirəp] n étrier m.

stitch [stitʃ] n (sewing) point m; (knitting) maille f; (med) point de suture m; (pain) point de côté m. v coudre; (med) suturer.

stoat [stout] n hermine f.

stock [stok] n réserve f; (farm) cheptel m; (cookery) bouillon m; (lineage) souche f. **stockbroker** n agent de change m. **Stock Exchange** Bourse f. **stockpile** v stocker. **stocks and shares** valeurs f pl. **stocktaking** n inventaire m. v approvisionner.

Stockholm ['stokhoum] n Stockholm.

stocking ['stokiŋ] n bas m. **in one's stocking feet** sans chaussures.

stocky ['stoki] adj trapu.

stodge [stodʒ] (coll) n aliment bourratif m. **stodgy** adj bourratif.

stoical ['stouikl] adj stoïque.

stoke [stouk] v (fire) garnir; (furnace) alimenter; (boiler) chauffer.

stole¹ [stoul] V steal.

stole² [stoul] n étole f.

stolen ['stoulən] V steal.

stomach ['stʌmək] n estomac m; (abdomen) ventre m. **stomach-ache** n mal à l'estomac m. v supporter.

stone [stoun] n pierre f; (of fruit) noyau m; (med) calcul m. **stone-cold** adj complètement froid. v lapider; dénoyauter. **stony** adj pierreux; dur.

stood [stud] V stand.

stool [stuːl] n tabouret m.

stoop [stuːp] v se pencher, se courber; avoir le dos voûté; (descend) s'abaisser (jusqu'à).

stop [stop] n arrêt m. v (s')arrêter; cesser; (block) boucher; (prevent) empêcher. **stop-press** n dernière heure f. **stop thief!** au voleur! **stop-watch** n chronomètre m. **stoppage** n arrêt m; obstruction f; (strike) grève f. **stopper** n bouchon m.

store [stoː] n provision f; (depot) entrepôt m; (shop) magasin m. v mettre en réserve; emmagasiner. **storage** n entreposage m. **storage space** espace de rangement m.

storey ['stoːri] n étage m.

stork [stoːk] n cigogne f.

storm [stoːm] n tempête f; (thunder) orage m. v (mil) prendre d'assaut; (wind, rain) faire rage; (person) fulminer. **stormy** adj orageux.

story ['stoːri] n histoire f.

stout [staut] adj gros, grosse; solide; intrépide. n stout m.

stove [stouv] n (cooker) fourneau m; (heater) poêle m.

stow [stou] v ranger. **stow away** voyager clandestinement. **stowaway** n passager clandestin, passagère clandestine m, f.

straddle ['stradl] v enfourcher, enjamber, être à califourchon (sur).

straggle ['stragl] v (plant) pousser au hasard; (hair) être en désordre; (village) s'étendre en longueur. **straggler** n traînard, -e m, f.

straight [streit] adj droit; en ordre; franc, franche. adv droit; (directly) tout droit. **straight ahead** tout droit. **straight away** tout de suite. **straightforward** adj simple; honnête. **straighten** v redresser; mettre en ordre.

strain¹ [strein] n tension f, effort m; (med) entorse f. v forcer, tendre fortement; (med) froisser, filtrer; s'efforcer, peiner. **strainer** n passoire f.

strain² [strein] n race f; tendance f.

strait [streit] n détroit m.

strand¹ [strand] n brin m, fibre f, fil m.

strand² [strand] v laisser en rade; (ship) échouer.

strange [streindʒ] adj étrange; (unfamiliar) inconnu. **stranger** n inconnu, -e m, f.

strangle ['straŋgl] v étrangler.

strap [strap] n lanière f, sangle f; (on garment) bretelle f. v attacher avec une sangle. **strapping** adj costaud.

strategy ['stratədʒi] n stratégie f. **strategic** adj stratégique.

stratum ['straɪtəm] n, pl -ta strate f, couche f.

straw [stroː] n paille f. **it's the last straw!** c'est le comble!

strawberry ['stroːbəri] n (fruit) fraise f; (plant) fraisier m.

stray [strei] n animal errant m. adj errant, perdu; isolé. v s'égarer, errer.

streak [striːk] n raie f; tendance f. v zébrer, strier.

stream [striːm] *n* ruisseau *m*; courant *m*; flot *m*, torrent *m*. **streamlined** *adj* (*aero*) fuselé; (*mot*) aérodynamique; (*efficient*) rationalisé. *v* ruisseler; (*school*) répartir par niveau. **streamer** *n* serpentin *m*.

street [striːt] *n* rue *f*.

strength [streŋθ] *n* force *f*. **strengthen** *v* fortifier; consolider; augmenter.

strenuous ['strenjuəs] *adj* ardu; vigoureux, acharné.

stress [stres] *n* pression *f*; accent *m*; tension *f*; insistance *f*; (*tech*) travail *m*. *v* insister sur; accentuer.

stretch [stretʃ] *n* (*action*) étirement *m*; (*distance*) étendue *f*; période *f*. *v* (s')étirer, (se) tendre; (*reach*) s'étendre. **stretcher** *n* brancard *m*.

stricken ['strikən] *adj* affligé.

strict [strikt] *adj* strict; exact. **strictly** *adv* strictement. **strictly speaking** à proprement parler. **strictness** *n* sévérité *f*; exactitude *f*.

*****stride** [straid] *n* grand pas *m*, enjambée *f*. *v* marcher à grands pas.

strident ['straidənt] *adj* strident.

strife [straif] *n* conflit *m*; querelles *f pl*.

*****strike** [straik] *n* (*industry*) grève *f*; (*hit*) coup *m*; (*oil, etc.*) découverte *f*. *v* (*hit*) frapper, heurter; faire grève; (*clock*) sonner; découvrir; (*match*) allumer, frotter. **striker** *n* gréviste *m, f*. **striking** *adj* frappant; en grève.

*****string** [striŋ] *n* ficelle *f*; (*violin, racket, etc.*) corde *f*. **string bag** filet à provisions *m*. **string quartet** quatuor à cordes *m*. **string vest** gilet de coton à grosses mailles *m*. *v* (*beads*) enfiler; (*hang*) suspendre. **stringy** *adj* filandreux.

stringent ['strindʒənt] *adj* rigoureux.

strip[1] [strip] *v* dépouiller; (*undress*) (se) déshabiller; (*bed*) défaire. **strip off** enlever. **strip-tease** *n* strip-tease *m*. **stripper** *n* strip-teaseuse *f*; (*paint*) décapant *m*.

strip[2] [strip] *n* bande *f*. **strip cartoon** bande dessinée *f*.

stripe [straip] *n* raie *f*, rayure *f*. **striped** *adj* rayé.

*****strive** [straiv] *v* s'efforcer (de).

strode [stroud] *V* **stride**.

stroke[1] [strouk] *n* coup *m*; (*swimming*) nage *f*; (*mark*) trait *m*; (*med*) attaque d'apoplexie *f*.

stroke[2] [strouk] *v* caresser. *n* caresse *f*.

stroll [stroul] *n* petite promenade *f*. tou*m*. *v* se promener nonchalamment flâner.

strong [stroŋ] *adj, adv* fort; solide **stronghold** *n* bastion *m*; (*mil*) forteresse *f*. **strong-minded** *adj* résolu. **strong-room** *n* chambre forte.

strove [strouv] *V* **strive**.

struck [strʌk] *V* **strike**.

structure ['strʌktʃə] *n* structure *f*; construction *f*. **structural** *adj* structural; de construction.

struggle ['strʌgl] *n* lutte *f*. *v* lutter; (*to escape*) se débattre. **struggle in/ou** entrer/sortir avec peine.

strum [strʌm] *v* (*guitar*) racler; (*piano*) tapoter (de).

strung [strʌŋ] *V* **string**.

strut[1] [strʌt] *v* se pavaner.

strut[2] [strʌt] *n* étai *m*, support *m*.

stub [stʌb] *n* bout *m*; (*tree*) souche *f*; (*cheque*) talon *m*. *v* (*toe, etc.*) cogner. **stub out** écraser.

stubble ['stʌbl] *n* chaume *m*.

stubborn ['stʌbən] *adj* obstiné, opiniâtre **stubbornness** *n* obstination *f*, opiniâtreté *f*.

stuck [stʌk] *V* **stick**[2].

stud[1] [stʌd] *n* clou (à grosse tête) *m*. *v* clouter. **studded with** parsemé de.

stud[2] [stʌd] *n* écurie *f*; (*farm*) haras *m*. **b at stud** étalonner.

student ['stjuːdənt] *n* étudiant, -e *m, f* (*trainee*) stagiaire *m, f*.

studio ['stjuːdiou] *n* studio *m*.

study ['stʌdi] *n* étude *f*; (*room*) bureau *m* *v* étudier, faire des études. **studious** *ad* studieux.

stuff [stʌf] *n* choses *f pl*; substance *f* (*fabric*) étoffe *f*. *v* rembourrer; (*cram* bourrer; (*thrust*) fourrer; (*cookery* farcir; (*animal*) empailler. **stuffing** *n* bourre *f*, farce *f*; paille *f*. **stuffy** *adj* ma ventilé; (*person*) collet monté *invar*.

stumble ['stʌmbl] *v* trébucher.

stump [stʌmp] *n* (*tree*) souche *f*; (*limb* moignon *m*; (*pencil, etc.*) bout *m*; (*crick et*) piquet *m*. *v* (*sport*) mettre hors jeu (*coll*) coller, faire sécher.

stun [stʌn] *v* étourdir; (*amaze* abasourdir. **stunning** *adj* stupéfiant; (*col* sensationnel.

stung [stʌŋ] *V* **sting**.

stunk [stʌŋk] *V* **stink**.

stunt¹ [stʌnt] v retarder (la croissance de).
stunted adj rabougri.
stunt² [stʌnt] n tour de force m; (aero) acrobatie f; (trick, publicity) truc m. **stunt man** cascadeur m.
stupid ['stjuːpid] adj stupide. **stupidity** n stupidité f.
stupor ['stjuːpə] n stupeur f.
sturdy ['stəːdi] adj robuste, vigoureux. **sturdiness** n robustesse f, vigueur f.
sturgeon ['stəːdʒən] n esturgeon m.
stutter ['stʌtə] n bégaiement m. v bégayer.
sty [stai] n porcherie f.
style [stail] n style m; (dress) mode f; (hair) coiffure f; (type) genre m. v créer; (call) appeler. **stylish** adj élégant, chic invar.
stylus ['stailəs] n (tool) style m; (record player) pointe de lecture f.
suave [swaːv] adj doucereux.
subconscious [sʌb'konʃəs] nm, adj subconscient.
subcontract [sʌbkən'trakt] v sous-traiter. **subcontractor** n sous-traitant m.
subdivide [sʌbdi'vaid] v (se) subdiviser. **subdivision** n subdivision f.
subdue [səb'djuː] v (riot) subjuguer; (feelings) contenir; (light) adoucir. **subdued** adj contenu; faible; (voice) bas, basse; (lighting) tamisé.
subject ['sʌbdʒikt; v səb'dʒekt] n sujet m; (school) matière f; (people) sujet, -ette m, f. adj, adv subject to sujet à; à condition de; exposé à. v soumettre; exposer. **subjection** n sujétion f. **subjective** adj subjectif.
subjunctive [səb'dʒʌŋktiv] nm, adj subjonctif.
sublet [sʌb'let] v sous-louer.
sublime [sə'blaim] nm, adj sublime.
submarine ['sʌbməriːn] n sous-marin m.
submerge [səb'məːdʒ] v submerger. **submersion** n submersion f.
submit [səb'mit] v (se) soumettre. **submission** n soumission f. **submissive** adj soumis.
subnormal [sʌb'nɔːməl] adj au-dessous de la normale; (person) arriéré.
subordinate [sə'bɔːdinət] adj subalterne; (gramm) subordonné. n subalterne m, f; subordonné, -e m, f. v subordonner. **subordination** n subordination f.
subscribe [səb'skraib] v **subscribe to** souscrire à; (newspaper) s'abonner à. **subscriber** n souscripteur, -trice m, f;

abonné, -e m, f. **subscription** n souscription f; (club) cotisation f; abonnement m.
subsequent ['sʌbsikwənt] adj ultérieur, -e, suivant; résultant.
subservient [səb'səːviənt] adj subalterne; (derog) obséquieux.
subside [səb'said] v (land) s'affaisser; (flood) baisser; (wind) se calmer. **subsidence** n affaissement m.
subsidiary [səb'sidiəri] adj subsidiaire, accessoire. n (comm) filiale f.
subsidize ['sʌbsidaiz] v subventionner. **subsidy** n subvention f.
subsist [səb'sist] v subsister. **subsistence** n subsistance f.
substance ['sʌbstəns] n substance f. **substantial** adj important, substantiel.
substandard [sʌb'standəd] adj de qualité inférieure.
substitute ['sʌbstitjuːt] n (person) remplaçant, -e m, f; (thing) succédané m. v substituer, remplacer. **substitution** n substitution f.
subtitle ['sʌbtaitl] n sous-titre m. v sous-titrer.
subtle ['sʌtl] adj subtil. **subtlety** n subtilité f.
subtract [səb'trakt] v soustraire. **subtraction** n soustraction f.
suburb ['sʌbəːb] n faubourg m. **suburbs** pl n banlieue f sing. **suburban** adj suburbain.
subvert [səb'vəːt] v bouleverser; corrompre. **subversion** n subversion f. **subversive** adj subversif.
subway ['sʌbwei] n passage souterrain m; (US) métro m.
succeed [sək'siːd] v réussir; (follow) succéder à. **succeeding** adj suivant; à venir. **success** n succès m, réussite f. **successful** adj couronné de succès, qui a réussi. **successfully** adv avec succès. **succession** n succession f. **successive** adj successif, consécutif. **successor** n successeur m.
succinct [sək'siŋkt] adj succinct.
succulent ['sʌkjulənt] adj succulent.
succumb [sə'kʌm] v succomber.
such [sʌtʃ] adj tel, pareil; (so much) tant (de). **such as** tel que. adv si, tellement; (as) aussi. pron (those) ceux, celles; tel, telle.
suck [sʌk] v sucer; (baby) téter. **suck up to** (slang) faire de la lèche à.

sucker ['sʌkə] n (*bot*) surgeon m; (*device*) ventouse f; (*slang: person*) poire f.
suction ['sʌkʃən] n succion f.
sudden ['sʌdən] adj soudain, subit; imprévu. **all of a sudden** tout à coup.
suds [sʌdz] pl n mousse de savon f sing.
sue [suː] v poursuivre en justice.
suede [sweid] n daim m.
suet ['suːit] n graisse de rognon f.
suffer ['sʌfə] v souffrir; (*undergo*) subir, éprouver; tolérer. **suffering** n souffrance f.
sufficient [sə'fiʃənt] adj assez de, suffisant. **suffice** v suffire (à). **sufficiently** adv suffisamment.
suffix ['sʌfiks] n suffixe m.
suffocate ['sʌfəkeit] v suffoquer, étouffer. **suffocation** n suffocation f; (*med*) asphyxie f.
sugar ['ʃugə] n sucre m. **sugar-basin** n sucrier m. **sugar-beet** n betterave sucrière f. **sugar-cane** n canne à sucre f. **sugar-lump** n morceau de sucre m. v sucrer. **sugared almond** dragée f. **sugary** adj sucré.
suggest [sə'dʒest] v suggérer. **suggestion** n suggestion f; soupçon m. **suggestive** adj suggestif.
suicide ['suːisaid] n suicide m; (*person*) suicidé, -e m, f. **commit suicide** se suicider. **suicidal** adj suicidaire.
suit [suːt] n (*man's*) costume m; (*woman's*) tailleur m; (*law*) procès m; (*cards*) couleur f. **suitcase** n valise f. v convenir à, aller à. **suitable** adj qui convient; approprié.
suite [swiːt] n suite f; (*furniture*) mobilier m.
sulk [sʌlk] v bouder. n bouderie f. **sulky** adj boudeur, -euse.
sullen ['sʌlən] adj maussade, renfrogné. **sullenness** n maussaderie f.
sulphur ['sʌlfə] n soufre m. **sulphuric** adj sulfurique.
sultan ['sʌltən] n sultan m.
sultana [sʌl'tɑːnə] n raisin sec de Smyrne m.
sultry ['sʌltri] adj étouffant, lourd; sensuel.
sum [sʌm] n somme f; (*math*) calcul m. v **sum up** résumer, récapituler; (*person*) jauger.
summarize ['sʌməraiz] v résumer, récapituler. **summary** n résumé m.
summer ['sʌmə] n été m. **summer holidays** grandes vacances f pl. **summer-house** n pavillon m.
summit ['sʌmit] n sommet m.
summon ['sʌmən] v faire venir, convoquer, mander. **summon up** rassembler, faire appel à.
summons ['sʌmənz] n sommation f; (*law*) assignation f. v assigner.
sump [sʌmp] n (*mot*) carter m.
sumptuous ['sʌmptʃuəs] adj somptueux.
sun [sʌn] n soleil m. v **sun oneself** se chauffer au soleil. **sunny** adj ensoleillé.
sunbathe ['sʌnbeið] v prendre un bain de soleil. **sunbathing** n bains de soleil m pl.
sunbeam ['sʌnbiːm] n rayon de soleil m.
sunburn ['sʌnbəːn] n (*tan*) bronzage m; (*pain*) coup de soleil m. **sunburnt** adj bronzé; brûlé.
Sunday ['sʌndi] n dimanche m.
sundial ['sʌndaiəl] n cadran solaire m.
sundry ['sʌndri] adj divers. **all and sundry** n'importe qui. **sundries** pl n articles divers m pl.
sunflower ['sʌnflauə] n tournesol m.
sung [sʌŋ] V **sing**.
sun-glasses ['sʌnglaːsiz] pl n lunettes de soleil f pl.
sunk [sʌŋk] V **sink**.
sunlight ['sʌnlait] n soleil m.
sunrise ['sʌnraiz] n lever du soleil m.
sunset ['sʌnset] n coucher du soleil m.
sunshine ['sʌnʃain] n soleil m. **sunshine roof** (*mot*) toit ouvrant m.
sunstroke ['sʌnstrouk] n insolation f.
sun-tan ['sʌntan] n bronzage m. **sun-tan lotion/oil** lotion/huile solaire f.
super ['suːpə] adj (*coll*) formidable.
superannuation [ˌsuːpərʌnju'eiʃən] n retraite f; (*payments*) versements pour la pension m pl.
superb [suː'pəːb] adj superbe.
supercilious [ˌsuːpə'siliəs] adj hautain.
superficial [ˌsuːpə'fiʃəl] adj superficiel.
superfluous [suː'pəːfluəs] adj superflu.
superhuman [suːpə'hjuːmən] adj surhumain.
superimpose [ˌsuːpərim'pouz] v superposer. **superimposed** adj (*phot, etc.*) en surimpression.
superintendent [ˌsuːpərin'tendənt] n directeur, -trice m, f; (*police*) commissaire m.
superior [suːpiəriə] n, adj supérieur, -e.
superiority n supériorité f.

superlative [suː'pəːlətiv] *adj* suprême, sans pareil; (*gramm*) superlatif. *n* superlatif *m*.

supermarket ['suːpəˌmaːkit] *n* supermarché *m*.

supernatural [ˌsuːpə'natʃərəl] *nm, adj* surnaturel.

supersede [ˌsuːpə'siːd] *v* remplacer, supplanter.

supersonic [ˌsuːpə'sonik] *adj* supersonique.

superstition [suːpə'stiʃən] *n* superstition *f*. **superstitious** *adj* superstitieux.

supervise ['suːpəvaiz] *v* surveiller, diriger. **supervision** *n* surveillance *f*, direction *f*. **supervisor** *n* surveillant, -e *m, f*; (*comm*) chef de rayon *m*.

supper ['sʌpə] *n* souper *m*; (*evening meal*) dîner *m*.

supple ['sʌpl] *adj* souple. **suppleness** *n* souplesse *f*.

supplement ['sʌpləmənt] *n* supplément *m*. *v* augmenter, ajouter à. **supplementary** *adj* supplémentaire.

supply [sə'plai] *n* (*stock*) provision *f*; (*fuel, etc.*) alimentation *f*. **supplies** *pl n* provisions *f pl*; matériel *m sing*. *v* fournir; alimenter.

support [sə'poːt] *n* appui *m*, soutien *m*. *v* supporter, soutenir; (*financially*) subvenir aux besoins de. **supporter** *n* partisan, -e *m, f*; (*sport*) supporter *m*.

suppose [sə'pouz] *v* supposer. **supposed** *adj* prétendu; présumé. **be supposed to** être censé, devoir. **supposedly** *adv* soi-disant. **supposing** *conj* si, à supposer que. **supposition** *n* supposition *f*.

suppress [sə'pres] *v* supprimer, réprimer; (*yawn, etc.*) étouffer. **suppression** *n* suppression *f*, répression *f*; étouffement *m*.

supreme [su'priːm] *adj* suprême. **supremacy** *n* suprématie *f*.

surcharge ['səːtʃaːdʒ] *n* surcharge *f*, surtaxe *f*.

sure [ʃuə] *adj* sûr, certain. **make sure** s'assurer; (*check*) vérifier. **sure enough** effectivement, en effet. **sure-footed** *adj* au pied sûr. **surely** *adv* sûrement.

surety ['ʃuərəti] *n* caution *f*.

surf [səːf] *n* ressac *m*; (*foam*) écume *f*. **surf-board** *n* planche de surf *f*. **surf-boarder** *n* surfeur, -euse *m, f*. **surf-boarding** *or* **surfing** *n* surf *m*. *v* surfer.

surface ['səːfis] *n* surface *f*. **on the surface**

en apparence. *v* (*road*) revêtir; (*swimmer, etc.*) revenir à la surface, faire surface.

surfeit ['səːfit] *n* excès *m*.

surge [səːdʒ] *n* vague *f*, montée *f*. *v* déferler.

surgeon ['səːdʒən] *n* chirurgien *m*. **surgery** *n* (*skill*) chirurgie *f*; (*place*) cabinet *m*; (*time*) consultation *f*. **surgical** *adj* chirurgical.

surly ['səːli] *adj* revêche.

surmount [sə'maunt] *v* surmonter.

surname ['səːneim] *n* nom de famille *m*.

surpass [sə'paːs] *v* surpasser, dépasser.

surplus ['səːpləs] *n* surplus *m*, excédent *m*. *adj* en surplus.

surprise [sə'praiz] *n* surprise *f*. *adj* inattendu. *v* surprendre, étonner.

surrealism [sə'riəlizəm] *n* surréalisme *m*. **surrealist** *n(m + f)*, *adj* surréaliste. **surrealistic** *adj* surréaliste.

surrender [sə'rendə] *v* (se) rendre; (*documents*) remettre; renoncer à, abandonner. *n* reddition *f*; remise *f*; renonciation *f*.

surreptitious [ˌsʌrəp'tiʃəs] *adj* subreptice, furtif.

surround [sə'raund] *v* entourer, encercler. *n* bordure *f*. **surrounding** *adj* environnant. **surroundings** *pl n* alentours *m pl*; (*setting*) cadre *m sing*.

survey ['səːvei; *v* sə'vei] *n* vue générale *f*; enquête *f*; (*land*) levé *m*; (*house*) inspection *f*. *v* passer en revue; inspecter; (*land*) arpenter. **surveying** *n* arpentage *m*. **surveyor** *n* (*land*) géomètre *m*; (*house*) expert *m*.

survive [sə'vaiv] *v* survivre (à). **survival** *n* survie *f*; (*relic*) survivance *f*. **survivor** *n* survivant, -e *m, f*.

susceptible [sə'septəbl] *adj* sensible.

suspect ['sʌspekt; *v* sə'spekt] *n, adj* suspect, -e. *v* soupçonner.

suspend [sə'spend] *v* suspendre. **suspender** *n* jarretelle *f*. **suspender belt** porte-jarretelles *m invar*. **suspenders** *pl n* (*US*) bretelles *f pl*. **suspense** *n* incertitude *f*; (*book, film*) suspense *m*. **in suspense** en suspens. **suspension** *n* suspension *f*. **suspension bridge** pont suspendu *m*.

suspicion [sə'spiʃən] *n* soupçon *m*. **suspicious** *adj* soupçonneux; suspect.

sustain [sə'stein] *v* soutenir; (*suffer*) subir.

swab [swob] *n* (*mop*) serpillière *f*; (*med: sample*) prélèvement *m*; (*med: pad*) tampon *m*. *v* nettoyer.

swagger ['swagə] *n* air important *m*. *v* plastronner; (*boast*) se vanter.

swallow[1] ['swolou] *v* avaler. **swallow up** engloutir. *n* avalement *m*; (*amount*) gorgée *f*.

swallow[2] ['swolou] *n* (*bird*) hirondelle *f*.

swam [swam] *V* **swim**.

swamp [swomp] *n* marais *m*. *v* inonder, submerger. **swampy** *adj* marécageux.

swan [swon] *n* cygne *m*.

swank [swaŋk] (*coll*) *n* esbroufe *f*. *v* faire de l'esbroufe. **swank about** se vanter de.

swap *or* **swop** [swop] *n* troc *m*; double *m*. *v* échanger.

swarm [swoːm] *n* essaim *m*; (*ants*) fourmillement *m*. *v* essaimer; fourmiller. **swarm in/out** entrer/sortir en masse.

swarthy ['swoːði] *adj* basané.

swat [swot] *v* écraser.

sway [swei] *n* balancement *m*, oscillation *f*. *v* (se) balancer, osciller; influencer.

swear [sweə] *v* jurer. **swear in** assermenter. **swear-word** *n* juron *m*.

sweat [swet] *n* sueur *f*. *v* suer. **sweater** *n* tricot *m*.

swede [swiːd] *n* rutabaga *m*.

Sweden ['swiːdn] *n* Suède *f*. **Swede** *n* Suédois, -e *m*, *f*. **Swedish** *nm*, *adj* suédois.

sweep [swiːp] *n* (*chimney*) ramoneur *m*; coup de balai *m*; grand geste *m*; (*curve*) grande courbe *f*. *v* balayer; ramoner. **sweep in/out** entrer/sortir rapidement *or* majestueusement. **sweeping** *adj* large; radical. **sweeping statement** généralisation hâtive *f*.

sweet [swiːt] *adj* doux, douce; (*taste*) sucré; (*kind*) gentil, -ille; (*attractive*) mignon, -onne. *n* bonbon *m*; dessert *m*. **sweetbread** *n* ris de veau *m*. **sweet corn** maïs sucré *m*. **sweetheart** *n* bien-aimé, -e *m*, *f*. **sweet pea** pois de senteur *m*. **sweetshop** *n* confiserie *f*. **sweeten** *v* sucrer. **sweetly** *adj* (*sing*) mélodieusement; (*smile*) gentiment. **sweetness** *n* goût sucré *m*; douceur *f*.

swell [swel] *n* (*sea*) houle *f*. *v* (se) gonfler, (s')enfler, grossir. **swelling** *n* enflure *f*.

swelter ['sweltə] *v* étouffer de chaleur. **sweltering** *adj* étouffant.

swept [swept] *V* **sweep**.

swerve [swoːv] *v* dévier; (*car*, *ship*) faire une embardée. *n* embardée *f*.

swift [swift] *adj* prompt, rapide. *n* (*bird*) martinet *m*. **swiftness** *n* rapidité *f*.

swill [swil] *v* laver à grande eau, rincer. *n* (*for pigs*) pâtée *f*.

swim [swim] *v* nager; (*cross*) traverser à la nage. *n* baignade *f*. **swimmer** *n* nageur, -euse *m*, *f*. **swimming** *n* nage *f*, natation *f*. **swimming baths** *or* **pool** piscine *f*. **swimming costume** maillot de bain *m*.

swindle ['swindl] *n* escroquerie *f*. *v* escroquer. **swindler** *n* escroc *m*.

swine [swain] *n* pourceau; (*impol*) salaud *m*.

swing [swiŋ] *n* balancement *m*; (*pol*) revirement *m*; rythme *m*; (*in playground*) balançoire *f*. **be in full swing** battre son plein. **swing-door** *n* porte battante *f*. *v* (se) balancer, (faire) osciller; (*turn*) virer; influencer.

swipe [swaip] (*coll*) *n* grand coup *m*. *v* (*hit*) frapper à toute volée; (*take*) calotter.

swirl [swoːl] *n* tourbillon *m*, volute *f*. *v* tourbillonner.

swish [swiʃ] *n* bruissement *m*, sifflement *m*. *v* bruire, siffler.

Swiss [swis] *adj* suisse. **Swiss roll** gâteau roulé *m*. **the Swiss** les Suisses.

switch [switʃ] *n* bouton électrique *m*, interrupteur *m*; changement *m*; (*stick*) baguette *f*. **switchboard** *n* standard *m*. *v* changer, échanger; (*rail*) aiguiller. **switch off** éteindre. **switch on** allumer.

Switzerland ['switsələnd] *n* Suisse *f*.

swivel ['swivl] *v* (faire) pivoter. *n* pivot *m*.

swollen ['swoulən] *V* **swell**.

swoop [swuːp] *n* descente (en piqué) *f*. **at one fell swoop** d'un seul coup. *v* fondre, piquer.

swop *V* **swap**.

sword [soːd] *n* épée *f*. **swordfish** *n* espadon *m*.

swore [swoː] *V* **swear**.

sworn [swoːn] *V* **swear**.

swot [swot] (*coll*) *n* bûcheur, -euse *m*, *f*. *v* bûcher, potasser. **swotting** *n* bachotage *m*.

swum [swʌm] *V* **swim**.

swung [swʌŋ] *V* **swing**.

sycamore ['sikəmoː] *n* sycomore *m*.

syllable ['siləbl] *n* syllabe *f*. **syllabic** *adj* syllabique.

syllabus ['siləbəs] *n* programme *m*.

symbol ['simbl] *n* symbole *m*. **symbolic**

adj symbolique. **symbolism** *n* symbolisme *m*. **symbolize** *v* symboliser.

symmetry ['simitri] *n* symétrie *f*. **symmetrical** *adj* symétrique.

sympathy ['simpəθi] *n* compassion *f*; solidarité *f*. **sympathetic** *adj* compatissant, bien disposé. **sympathize with** *v* compatir à, plaindre.

symphony ['simfəni] *n* symphonie *f*. **symphonic** *adj* symphonique.

symposium [sim'pouziəm] *n* symposium *m*.

symptom ['simptəm] *n* symptôme *m*. **symptomatic** *adj* symptomatique.

synagogue ['sinəgog] *n* synagogue *f*.

synchromesh ['siŋkroumeʃ] *n* synchronisation *f*.

synchronize ['siŋkrənaiz] *v* synchroniser. **synchronization** *n* synchronisation *f*.

syncopate ['siŋkəpeit] *v* syncoper. **syncopation** *n* syncope *f*.

syndicate ['sindikit] *n* syndicat *m*.

syndrome ['sindroum] *n* syndrome *m*.

synonym ['sinənim] *n* synonyme *m*. **synonymous** *adj* synonyme.

synopsis [si'nopsis] *n, pl* **-ses** résumé *m*.

syntax ['sintaks] *n* syntaxe *f*.

synthesis ['sinθisis] *n, pl* **-ses** synthèse *f*. **synthesize** *v* synthétiser. **synthetic** *adj* synthétique.

syphilis ['sifilis] *n* syphilis *f*.

syringe [si'rindʒ] *n* seringue *f*. *v* seringuer.

syrup ['sirəp] *n* sirop *m*; (*golden*) mélasse raffinée *f*. **syrupy** *adj* sirupeux.

system ['sistəm] *n* système *m*; méthode *f*. **systematic** *adj* systématique.

T

tab [tab] *n* étiquette *f*, patte *f*. **keep tabs on** (*coll*) avoir à l'œil.

tabby ['tabi] *n* chat tigré *m*.

table ['teibl] *n* table *f*. **table-cloth** *n* nappe *f*. **table-mat** *n* dessous-de-plat *m invar*. **table salt** sel fin *m*. **tablespoon** *n* cuiller de service *f*. **tablespoonful** *n* cuillerée à soupe *f*. **table tennis** ping-pong *m*.

table d'hôte [taːblə'dout] *adj* à prix fixe.

tablet ['tablit] *n* (*pill*) comprimé *m*; (*stone*) plaque *f*; (*soap*) pain *m*.

taboo [ta'buː] *nm, adj* tabou. *v* proscrire.

tabulate ['tabjuleit] *v* mettre sous forme de table, classifier.

tacit ['tasit] *adj* tacite.

taciturn ['tasitəːn] *adj* taciturne.

tack [tak] *n* (*nail*) broquette *f*; (*sewing*) point de bâti *m*; (*naut*) bord *m*. *v* clouer; bâtir; faire un bord. **tacking** *n* bâtissage *m*.

tackle ['takl] *n* (*lifting*) appareil de levage *m*; équipement *m*; (*sport*) plaquage *m*. *v* s'attaquer à; plaquer.

tact [takt] *n* tact *m*. **tactful** *adj* plein de tact, discret, -ète. **tactless** *adj* peu délicat, indiscret, -ète.

tactics ['taktiks] *pl n* tactique *f sing*. **tactical** *adj* tactique.

tadpole ['tadpoul] *n* têtard *m*.

taffeta ['tafitə] *n* taffetas *m*.

tag [tag] *n* étiquette *f*, patte *f*; (*shoelace*) ferret *m*. *v* **tag along** (*coll*) suivre; traîner derrière.

tail [teil] *n* queue *f*; (*shirt*) pan *m*. **tail-end** *n* bout *m*, fin *f*. **tails** *pl n* (*coin*) pile *f sing*. *v* (*coll*) suivre.

tailor ['teilə] *n* tailleur *m*. *v* façonner; adapter.

taint [teint] *v* infecter, polluer. *n* infection *f*; corruption *f*; (*moral*) tache *f*.

***take** [teik] *v* prendre; (*exam*) passer; accepter; contenir; (*accompany*) emmener. **take after** ressembler à. **take away** emporter; soustraire. **take-away** *adj* (*food*) à emporter. **take in** prendre; (*dress*) reprendre; (*understand*) saisir; inclure, couvrir; (*coll: deceive*) rouler. **take off** (*aero*) décoller; (*clothes, etc.*) enlever. **take-off** *n* décollage *m*; pastiche *m*. **take out** sortir; (*insurance*) prendre. **take-over** *n* rachat *m*.

taken ['teikn] *V* take.

talcum powder ['talkəm] *n* talc *m*.

tale [teil] *n* conte *m*, histoire *f*. **tell tales** (*coll*) cafarder.

talent ['talənt] *n* talent *m*. **talented** *adj* talentueux, doué.

talk [toːk] *n* propos *m pl*; conversation *f*; (*lecture*) exposé *m*. *v* parler; (*chat*) causer. **talk about** parler de. **talk into** persuader de. **talk over** discuter. **talkative** *adj* bavard.

tall [toːl] *adj* grand; (*high*) haut. **tallboy** *n* commode *f*. **tallness** *n* grande taille *f*; hauteur *f*.

tally ['tali] *n* compte *m. v* s'accorder.
talon ['talən] *n* serre *f.*
tambourine [tambə'riːn] *n* tambourin *m.*
tame [teim] *adj* apprivoisé; (*not exciting*) insipide. *v* apprivoiser; (*lion*) dompter.
tamper ['tampə] *v* **tamper with** toucher à; falsifier.
tampon ['tampon] *n* tampon *m.*
tan [tan] *n* bronzage *m. adj* ocre. *v* (*hide*) tanner; (*sun*) bronzer, hâler.
tandem ['tandəm] *n* tandem *m.*
tangent ['tandʒənt] *n* tangente *f.* **go off at a tangent** partir dans une digression.
tangerine [tandʒə'riːn] *nf, adj* mandarine.
tangible ['tandʒəbl] *adj* tangible.
tangle ['taŋgl] *n* enchevêtrement *m,* confusion *f. v* (s')enchevêtrer, (s')embrouiller.
tank [taŋk] *n* réservoir *m;* (*mil*) char *m.*
tanker *n* (*lorry*) camion-citerne *m;* (*ship*) pétrolier *m.*
tankard ['taŋkəd] *n* chope *f.*
tantalize ['tantəlaiz] *v* tourmenter. **tantalizing** *adj* terriblement tentant.
tantamount ['tantəmaunt] *adj* **tantamount to** équivalent à.
tantrum ['tantrəm] *n* crise de colère *f.* **throw a tantrum** piquer une colère.
tap[1] [tap] *n* petit coup *m.* **tap-dance** *n* claquettes *f pl.* **tap-dancer** *n* danseur, -euse de claquettes *m, f. v* frapper légèrement, tapoter.
tap[2] [tap] *n* robinet *m. v* (*barrel*) percer; (*tree*) inciser; (*phone*) mettre sur écoute; exploiter.
tape [teip] *n* ruban *m,* bande *f;* (*recording*) bande magnétique *f.* **tape-measure** *n* mètre à ruban *m.* **tape-recorder** *n* magnétophone *m.* **tapeworm** *n* ténia *m. v* (*record*) enregistrer; attacher.
taper ['teipə] *n* bougie fine *f. v* (s')effiler. **tapered** *adj* fuselé.
tapestry ['tapəstri] *n* tapisserie *f.*
tapioca [tapi'oukə] *n* tapioca *m.*
tar [taː] *n* goudron *m. v* goudronner.
tarantula [tə'rantjulə] *n* tarentule *f.*
target ['taːgit] *n* cible *f;* objectif *m.*
tariff ['tarif] *n* tarif *m.*
tarmac ® ['taːmak] *n* macadam goudronné *m.*
tarnish ['taːniʃ] *v* (se) ternir. *n* ternissure *f.*
tarpaulin [taː'poːlin] *n* bâche *f,* prélart *m.*
tarragon ['tarəgən] *n* estragon *m.*
tart[1] [taːt] *adj* aigrelet, acerbe.

tart[2] [taːt] *n* tarte *f;* (*small*) tartelette *f;* (*slang*) poule *f.*
tartan ['taːtən] *n* tartan *m. adj* écossais.
tartar ['taːtə] *n* tartre *m.*
task [taːsk] *n* tâche *f.*
tassel ['tasəl] *n* gland *m.*
taste [teist] *n* goût *m. v* goûter; (*wine*) déguster. **taste of** avoir un goût de. **tasteful** *adj* de bon goût. **tasteless** *adj* (*flavourless*) sans saveur; insipide; (*in bad taste*) de mauvais goût. **tasty** *adj* savoureux.
tattered ['tatəd] *adj* en lambeaux.
tattoo[1] [tə'tuː] *v* tatouer. *n* tatouage *m.*
tattoo[2] [tə'tuː] *n* parade militaire *f;* (*drumming*) battements *m pl.*
tatty ['tati] *adj* (*coll*) fatigué, défraîchi.
taught [toːt] *V* **teach.**
taunt [toːnt] *n* raillerie *f. v* railler. **taunting** *adj* railleur, -euse.
Taurus ['toːrəs] *n* Taureau *m.*
taut [toːt] *adj* tendu. **tautness** *n* tension *f.*
tawny ['toːni] *adj* fauve.
tax [taks] *n* impôt *m,* taxe *f.* **tax-free** *adj* exempt d'impôts. **tax haven** refuge fiscal *m.* **taxpayer** *n* contribuable *m, f.* **tax return** déclaration de revenus *f. v* imposer, taxer; (*patience*) mettre à l'épreuve. **taxable** *adj* imposable. **taxation** *n* taxation *f;* (*taxes*) impôts *m pl.*
taxi ['taksi] *n* taxi *m.* **taxi-driver** *n* chauffeur de taxi *m.* **taxi rank** station de taxis *f. v* (*aero*) rouler lentement.
tea [tiː] *n* thé *m;* (*snack*) goûter *m.* **tea-bag** ['tiːbag] *n* sachet de thé *m.*
teacake ['tiːkeik] *n* petit pain brioché *m.*
tea-cosy ['tiːkouzi] *n* couvre-théière *m.*
tea-leaf ['tiːliːf] *n* feuille de thé *f.*
teapot ['tiːpot] *n* théière *f.*
tea-room ['tiːruːm] *n* salon de thé *m.*
tea-set ['tiːset] *n* service à thé *m.*
teaspoon ['tiːspuːn] *n* petite cuiller *f.* **teaspoonful** *n* cuillerée à café *f.*
tea-towel ['tiːtauəl] *n* torchon *m.*
tea-urn ['tiːəːn] *n* fontaine à thé *f.*
***teach** [tiːtʃ] *v* apprendre, enseigner. **teacher** professeur *m;* (*primary school*) instituteur, -trice *m, f.* **teaching** *n* enseignement *m.*
teak [tiːk] *n* teck *m.*
team [tiːm] *n* équipe *f;* (*horses*) attelage *m.* **team-member** *n* équipier, -ère *m, f.* **team spirit** esprit d'équipe *m.* **team-work** *n* collaboration *f.*

*tear¹ [teə] *n* déchirure *f. v* (se) déchirer;
(*snatch*) arracher. **tear along/out**
filer/sortir à toute allure.

tear² [tiə] *n* larme *f.* **burst into tears** fondre en larmes. **tear-gas** *n* gaz
lacrymogène *m.* **tearful** *adj* larmoyant.

tease [tiːz] *v* taquiner. **teasing** *n*
taquineries *f pl.*

teat [tiːt] *n* tétine *f.*

technique [tek'niːk] *n* technique *f.* **technical** *adj* technique. **technicality** *n* détail
technique *m.* **technician** *n* technicien,
-enne *m, f.* **technological** *adj* technologique. **technology** *n* technologie *f.*

teddy bear ['tedi‚beə] *n* nounours *m.*

tedious ['tiːdiəs] *adj* ennuyeux.

tee [tiː] *n* tee *m. v* **tee off** partir du tee.

teem [tiːm] *v* (*swarm*) grouiller; (*rain*)
pleuvoir à verse.

teenage ['tiːneidʒ] *adj* adolescent. **teen-
ager** *n* adolescent, -e *m, f.* **teens** *pl n*
adolescence *f sing.*

teeth [tiːθ] *V* tooth.

teethe [tiːð] *v* faire ses dents. **teething** *n*
dentition *f.* **teething troubles** difficultés
de croissance *f pl.*

teetotaller [tiː'toutələ] *n* personne qui ne
boit jamais d'alcool *f.*

telecommunications [‚telikəmjuːni-
'keiʃənz] *pl n* télécommunications
f pl.

telegram ['teligram] *n* télégramme *m.*

telegraph ['teligraːf] *n* télégraphe *m.* **telegraph pole** poteau télégraphique *m. v*
télégraphier. **telegraphic** *adj*
télégraphique.

telepathy [tə'lepəθi] *n* télépathie *f.* **telepathic** *adj* télépathique.

telephone ['telifoun] *n* téléphone *m.* **telephone box** cabine téléphonique *f.* **telephone call** coup de téléphone *m.* **telephone directory** annuaire *m.* **telephone
number** numéro de téléphone *m. v* téléphoner. **telephonist** *n* téléphoniste *m, f.*

telescope ['teliskoup] *n* télescope *m.* **telescopic** *adj* télescopique.

television ['teliviʒən] *n* télévision *f.* **televise** *v* téléviser.

telex ['teleks] *n* télex *m.*

*tell [tel] *v* dire; (*story*) raconter; (*know*)
savoir. **tell off** (*coll*) gronder.

temper ['tempə] *n* tempérament *m,*
humeur *f;* (*anger*) colère *f.* **lose one's
temper** se mettre en colère. *v* tempérer.

temperament ['tempərəmənt] *n* tempérament *m.* **temperamental** *adj* capricieux.

temperate ['tempərət] *adj* tempéré.

temperature ['temprətʃə] *n* température *f.*

tempestuous [tem'pestjuəs] *adj* orageux.

template ['templət] *n* patron *m.*

temple¹ ['templ] *n* (*rel*) temple *m.*

temple² ['templ] *n* (*anat*) tempe *f.*

tempo ['tempou] *n* tempo *m.*

temporary ['tempərəri] *adj* temporaire;
provisoire; (*secretary*) intérimaire.

tempt [tempt] *v* tenter. **temptation** *n* tentation *f.*

ten [ten] *nm, adj* dix. **tenth** *n(m+f), adj*
dixième.

tenacious [tə'neiʃəs] *adj* tenace. **tenacity** *n*
ténacité *f.*

tenant ['tenənt] *n* locataire *m, f.* **tenancy**
n location *f.*

tend¹ [tend] *v* avoir tendance, incliner.
tendency *n* tendance *f.*

tend² [tend] *v* (*look after*) garder, soigner.

tender¹ ['tendə] *adj* tendre; délicat;
(*heart, bruise*) sensible. **tenderize** *v* attendrir. **tenderness** *n* tendresse *f;* (*meat*)
tendreté *f.*

tender² ['tendə] *v* offrir; (*comm*) faire une
soumission. *n* soumission *f.* **legal tender**
cours légal *m.*

tendon ['tendən] *n* tendon *m.*

tendril ['tendril] *n* vrille *f.*

tenement ['tenəmənt] *n* logement *m.* **tenement block** bâtiment *m.*

tennis ['tenis] *n* tennis *m.* **tennis-court** *n*
court de tennis *m.*

tenor ['tenə] *n* (*music*) ténor *m;* sens *m;*
(*wording*) teneur *f.*

tense¹ [tens] *adj* tendu, crispé. *v* tendre.
tension *n* tension *f.*

tense² [tens] *n* temps *m.*

tent [tent] *n* tente *f.*

tentacle ['tentəkl] *n* tentacule *m.*

tentative ['tentətiv] *adj* hésitant; expérimental; provisoire.

tenterhooks ['tentəhuks] *pl n* **be on tenterhooks** être sur des charbons ardents.

tenuous ['tenjuəs] *adj* ténu.

tepid ['tepid] *adj* tiède. **tepidness** *n* tiédeur
f.

term [tɜːm] *n* terme *m;* (*school*) trimestre
m. **terms** *pl n* (*comm*) conditions *f pl.*
come to terms with faire face à. **on
good/bad terms** en bons/mauvais
termes. *v* appeler.

terminal ['tɜːminəl] adj terminal. n terminus m invar; (elec) borne f.

terminate ['tɜːmineit] v (se) terminer. termination n fin f.

terminology [tɜːmi'nolədʒi] n terminologie f.

terminus ['tɜːminəs] n terminus m invar.

terrace ['terəs] n terrasse f; (houses) rangée de maisons f.

terrain [tə'rein] n terrain m.

terrestrial [tə'restriəl] adj terrestre.

terrible ['terəbl] adj terrible; atroce; abominable. terribly adv (coll: very) drôlement.

terrier ['teriə] n terrier m.

terrify ['terifai] v terrifier. terrific adj (coll: excellent) formidable; (coll: extreme) énorme, terrible.

territory ['teritəri] n territoire m. territorial adj territorial.

terror ['terə] n terreur f. terrorism n terrorisme m. terrorist n(m+f), adj terroriste. terrorize v terroriser.

terse [tɜːs] adj laconique.

test [test] n essai m; (physical, mental) épreuve f; analyse f; (school) interrogation f. test card (TV) mire f. test case (law) conflit-test m. test drive n essai de route m. test flight vol d'essai m. test-tube n éprouvette f. v essayer, mettre à l'essai; mettre à l'épreuve; analyser; mesurer.

testament ['testəmənt] n testament m.

testicle ['testikl] n testicule m.

testify ['testifai] v témoigner, porter témoignage.

testimony ['testiməni] n témoignage m; déclaration f. testimonial n recommandation f.

tetanus ['tetənəs] n tétanos m.

tether ['teðə] n longe f. v attacher.

text [tekst] n texte m. textbook n manuel m. textual adj textuel.

textile ['tekstail] nm, adj textile.

texture ['tekstjuə] n contexture f; (wood, paper, etc.) grain m.

Thames [temz] n the Thames la Tamise f.

than [ðən] conj que, de.

thank [θaŋk] v remercier. thank you merci. thanks pl n remerciements m pl. thanksgiving n action de grâce f. thanks to grâce à. thankful adj reconnaissant. thankless adj ingrat.

that [ðat] adj ce, cette; (emphatic) ce ...

-là, cette ... -là: ce livre-là. pron cela, ça; ce; (that one) celui-là, celle-là; (who, which) qui, que, lequel, laquelle; (when) où. that is c'est-à-dire. conj que.

thatch [θatʃ] n chaume m. thatched cottage chaumière f.

thaw [θɔː] v (faire) dégeler, (faire) fondre. n dégel m.

the [ðə] art le, la; (pl) les.

theatre ['θiətə] n théâtre m. theatrical adj théâtral.

theft [θeft] n vol m.

their [ðeə] adj leur.

theirs [ðeəz] pron le leur, la leur.

them [ðem] pron eux, elles; (direct object) les; (indirect object) leur.

theme [θiːm] n thème m. thematic adj thématique.

themselves [ðəm'selvz] pron se; (emphatic) eux-mêmes, elles-mêmes. by themselves tout seuls.

then [ðen] adv alors; (next) ensuite, puis; (in that case) en ce cas. n (that time) ce moment-là, cette époque-là.

theology [θi'olədʒi] n théologie f. theologian n théologien, -enne m, f. theological adj théologique.

theorem ['θiərəm] n théorème m.

theory ['θiəri] n théorie f. theoretical adj théorique.

therapy ['θerəpi] n thérapie f, thérapeutique f. therapeutic adj thérapeutique. therapist n thérapeute m, f.

there [ðeə] adv y, là. thereabouts adv environ; (place) par là. thereby adv de cette façon. there is or are il y a; (showing) voilà. thereupon adv sur ce.

therefore ['ðeəfɔː] adv donc.

thermal ['θɜːməl] adj thermal; (phys) thermique. n courant ascendant m.

thermodynamics [θɜːmoudai'namiks] n thermodynamique f.

thermometer [θə'momitə] n thermomètre m.

thermonuclear [θɜːmou'njukliə] adj thermonucléaire.

thermos ® ['θɜːməs] n thermos ® m.

thermostat ['θɜːməstat] n thermostat m. thermostatic adj thermostatique.

these [ðiːz] adj ces; (emphatic) ces ... -ci: ces robes-ci. pron ce; ceux-ci, celles-ci.

thesis ['θiːsis] n, pl -ses thèse f.

they [ðei] pron ils, elles; (emphatic) eux, elles; (impersonal) on.

thump

thick [θik] adj épais, -aisse; (stupid) bête. **thick-skinned** adj peu sensible. **thicken** v (s')épaissir. **thickness** n épaisseur f.

thief [θiːf] n voleur, -euse m, f.

thigh [θai] n cuisse f.

thimble ['θimbl] n dé à coudre m.

thin [θin] adj mince, fin; (person) maigre; (liquid) peu épais, -aisse; (hair) clairsemé. v (s')éclaircir; (dilute) délayer. **thinness** n minceur f; maigreur f.

thing [θiŋ] n chose f. **things** pl n affaires f pl. **thingumajig** n (coll) machin m.

***think** [θiŋk] v penser; imaginer. **I think so** je pense que oui. **think about** penser à. **think over** réfléchir à.

third [θəːd] adj troisième. n troisième m, f; (fraction) tiers m; (musique) tierce f. **third party** (law) tiers m. **third-party insurance** assurance au tiers f. **third-rate** adj de qualité très inférieure. **Third World** Tiers-Monde m.

thirst [θəːst] n soif. v avoir soif. **be thirsty** avoir soif.

thirteen [θəːˈtiːn] nm, adj treize. **thirteenth** n(m+f), adj treizième.

thirty ['θəːti] nm, adj trente. **thirtieth** n(m+f), adj trentième.

this [δis] adj ce, cette; (emphatic) ce ... -ci, cette ... -ci: *cette maison-ci*. pron ceci, ce; (this one) celui-ci, celle-ci.

thistle ['θisl] n chardon m.

thong [θoŋ] n lanière f.

thorn [θoɪn] n épine f.

thorough ['θʌrə] adj profond; minutieux. **thoroughbred** n (horse) pur-sang m invar; bête de race f. **thoroughfare** n voie publique f. **thoroughly** adv à fond; (completely) tout à fait. **thoroughness** n minutie f.

those [δouz] adj ces; (emphatic) ces ... -là: *ces chaises-là*. pron ce; ceux-là, celles-là.

though [δou] conj bien que. adv pourtant. **as though** comme si.

thought [θoɪt] V think. n pensée f; idée f; opinion f; considération f. **thoughtful** adj pensif; sérieux; (considerate) prévenant, gentil, -ille. **thoughtless** adj étourdi; irréfléchi.

thousand ['θauzənd] nm, adj mille. **thousandth** n(m+f), adj millième.

thrash [θraʃ] v rosser, battre violemment; (sport, etc.) battre à plates coutures. **thrash about** se débattre. **thrash out** (problem, etc.) débattre de. **thrashing** n correction f.

thread [θred] n fil m; (screw) pas m. v enfiler; faire passer. **threadbare** adj usé, râpé.

threat [θret] n menace f. **threaten** v menacer.

three [θriː] nm, adj trois. **three-dimensional** adj à trois dimensions. **three-point turn** demi-tour en trois manœuvres m.

thresh [θreʃ] v battre. **threshing machine** batteuse f.

threshold ['θreʃould] n seuil m.

threw [θruː] V throw.

thrift [θrift] n économie f. **thrifty** adj économe.

thrill [θril] n frisson m. v transporter. **thriller** n roman or film à suspense m. **thrilling** adj palpitant.

thrive [θraiv] v se développer bien, pousser bien; prospérer. **thriving** adj robuste; prospère.

throat [θrout] n gorge f. **clear one's throat** s'éclaircir la voix. **throaty** adj guttural.

throb [θrob] n (heart) pulsation f; (engine) vibration f. v palpiter; vibrer; (pain) lanciner.

thrombosis [θrom'bousis] n thrombose f.

throne [θroun] n trône m.

throng [θroŋ] n foule f, multitude f. v affluer, se presser.

throttle ['θrotl] v étrangler. n (tech) papillon des gaz m; (mot) accélérateur m.

through [θruː] prep par; (place) à travers; (time) pendant. adv à travers. adj direct. **no through road** impasse f. **throughout** prep (place) partout dans; (time) pendant.

***throw** [θrou] n jet m. v jeter, lancer; (hurl) projeter. **throw away** jeter; (waste) gâcher, gaspiller. **throw out** rejeter; expulser. **throw up** vomir.

thrown [θroun] V throw.

thrush [θrʌʃ] n grive f.

***thrust** [θrʌst] n poussée f; coup m. v pousser brusquement, enfoncer; imposer.

thud [θʌd] n bruit sourd m. v faire un bruit sourd.

thumb [θʌm] n pouce m. v also **thumb through** feuilleter. **thumb a lift** (coll) faire du stop.

thump [θʌmp] n bruit lourd m; (blow) grand coup m. v cogner (à or sur); (heart) battre fort; (person) assener un coup à.

thunder ['θʌndə] n tonnerre m; (noise) fracas m. **thunderstorm** n orage m. **thunderstruck** adj abasourdi. v tonner. **thundery** adj orageux.

Thursday ['θəːzdi] n jeudi m.

thus [ðʌs] adv ainsi.

thwart [θwɔːt] v contrecarrer, contrarier.

thyme [taim] n thym m.

thyroid ['θairoid] nf, adj thyroïde.

tiara [ti'aːrə] n diadème m.

tick[1] [tik] n (mark) coche f; (sound) tic-tac m; (coll) instant m. v cocher; faire tic-tac. **tick off** (coll: scold) attraper. **tick over** (mot) tourner au ralenti.

tick[2] [tik] n (insect) tique f.

ticket ['tikit] n billet m; (bus) ticket m; (library) carte f; (label) étiquette f. **ticket collector** contrôleur m. **ticket office** guichet m.

tickle ['tikl] v chatouiller. n chatouillement m. **ticklish** adj chatouilleux.

tide [taid] n marée f. **tide-mark** n ligne de marée haute f; (of dirt) ligne de crasse f. v **tide over** dépanner.

tidy ['taidi] adj en ordre, bien rangé; (writing, appearance) net, nette. v ranger. **tidily** adv soigneusement. **tidiness** n propreté f.

tie [tai] n attache f; (neck) cravate f; (link) lien m; (draw) égalité f, match nul m. v attacher; lier; (ribbon, etc.) nouer; faire match nul.

tier [tiə] n étage m; (seating) gradin m.

tiger ['taigə] n tigre m.

tight [tait] adj raide, serré, étroit; (seal) étanche; (coll: drunk) soûl; (coll: mean) radin. **tight-fisted** adj avare. **tightrope** n corde raide f. **tightrope walker** funambule m, f. adv also **tightly** bien; hermétiquement. **tighten** v (se) resserrer; (rope) (se) tendre; (control) renforcer. **tights** pl n collant m sing.

tile [tail] n (roof) tuile f; (wall, floor) carreau m. v couvrir de tuiles; carreler.

till[1] [til] V until.

till[2] [til] n caisse f.

till[3] [til] v labourer.

tiller ['tilə] n (naut) barre du gouvernail f.

tilt [tilt] n inclinaison f. v pencher, incliner.

timber ['timbə] n bois d'œuvre m. **timbered** adj (house) en bois.

time [taim] n temps m; (clock) heure f; (occasion) fois f; époque f; moment m; (music) mesure f. **a long time** longtemps.

a short time peu de temps. **at the same time** à la fois. **from time to time** de temps en temps. **in time** à temps; (music) en mesure. **on time** à l'heure. **time bomb** bombe à retardement f. **time-sheet** n feuille de présence f. **time-switch** n minuteur m. **timetable** n (rail) horaire m; (school) emploi du temps m. **time zone** fuseau horaire m. v fixer; (runner, etc.) chronométrer; (programme, etc.) minuter. **timeless** adj éternel. **timely** adj à propos. **timer** n (cooking) compte-minutes m invar.

timid ['timid] adj timide, craintif. **timidity** n timidité f.

timpani ['timpəni] pl n timbales f pl.

tin [tin] n étain m; (can) boîte f; (baking) moule m; (roasting) plat m. **tin foil** papier d'étain m. **tin-opener** n ouvre-boîtes m. **tin soldier** soldat de plomb m. v mettre en boîte. **tinny** adj métallique.

tinge [tindʒ] n teinte f. v teinter.

tingle ['tiŋgl] v picoter. n picotement m.

tinker ['tiŋkə] n romanichel, -elle m, f. v bricoler.

tinkle ['tiŋkl] v (faire) tinter. n tintement m.

tinsel ['tinsəl] n clinquant m.

tint [tint] n teinte f; (hair) shampooing colorant m. v teinter.

tiny ['taini] adj tout petit, minuscule.

tip[1] [tip] n (end) bout m, pointe f. **on tiptoe** sur la pointe des pieds. v mettre un embout à.

tip[2] [tip] v (se) pencher, incliner; (overturn) (se) renverser; (pour) verser, déverser. n (rubbish) dépotoir m.

tip[3] [tip] n (hint) suggestion f, conseil m; (money) pourboire m. v donner un pourboire (à). **tip off** (warn) prévenir. **tip-off** n (coll) tuyau m.

tipsy ['tipsi] adj (coll) éméché.

Tirana [ti'raːnə] n Tirana.

tire[1] ['taiə] v (se) fatiguer. **tire out** épuiser. **tired** adj fatigué; las, lasse. **be tired of** en avoir assez de. **tiredness** n fatigue f. **tiresome** adj ennuyeux.

tire[2] (US) V tyre.

tissue ['tiʃuː] n tissu m; (handkerchief) mouchoir en papier m. **tissue paper** papier de soie m.

title ['taitl] n titre m; (law) droit m. **title-deed** n titre de propriété m. **title-page** n page de titre f. v intituler. **titled** adj titré.

titter ['titə] *n* gloussement *m. v* glousser.

to [tu] *prep* à; (*home, shop*) chez; (*in order to*) pour. **ten to four** quatre heures moins dix. **to-do** *n* (*coll*) histoire *f.*

toad [toud] *n* crapaud *m.* **toadstool** *n* champignon vénéneux *m.*

toast [toust] *n* pain grillé *m*; (*speech*) toast *m.* **toast-rack** *n* porte-toast *m. v* griller; porter un toast à. **toaster** *n* grille-pain *m invar.*

tobacco [tə'bakou] *n* tabac *m.* **tobacconist's** *n* tabac *m.*

toboggan [tə'bogən] *n* toboggan *m.*

today [tə'dei] *nm, adv* aujourd'hui.

toddler ['todlə] *n* petit, -e qui commence à marcher *m, f.*

toe [tou] *n* orteil *m.* **toe-nail** *n* ongle du pied *m. v* **toe the line** obéir, se plier.

toffee ['tofi] *n* caramel *m.* **toffee-apple** *n* pomme caramélisée *f.*

together [tə'geðə] *adv* ensemble; (*simultaneously*) à la fois.

toil [toil] *n* dur travail *m. v* travailler dur.

toilet ['toilit] *n* toilettes *f pl*, cabinets *m pl.* **toilet-paper** *n* papier hygiénique *m.* **toilet water** eau de toilette *f.*

token ['toukən] *n* marque *f*; (*disc*) jeton *m*; (*voucher*) bon *m.* **as a token of** en gage de. *adj* symbolique.

Tokyo ['toukiou] *n* Tokio.

told [tould] *V* tell.

tolerate ['toləreit] *v* tolérer, supporter. **tolerable** *adj* tolérable; passable. **tolerance** *or* **toleration** *n* tolérance *f.* **tolerant** *adj* tolérant.

toll¹ [toul] *n* péage *m.* **toll-gate** *n* barrière de péage *f.*

toll² [toul] *v* sonner.

tomato [tə'maitou] *n* tomate *f.*

tomb [tuim] *n* tombeau *m.* **tombstone** *n* pierre tombale *f.*

tomorrow [tə'morou] *nm, adv* demain. **the day after tomorrow** après-demain.

ton [tʌn] *n* tonne *f.*

tone [toun] *n* ton *m*; (*phone*) tonalité *f*; classe *f*; sonorité *f. v* (*colour*) s'harmoniser. **tone down** baisser, adoucir.

tongs [toŋz] *pl n* pinces *f pl*, pincettes *f pl.*

tongue [tʌŋ] *n* langue *f.* **tongue-tied** *adj* muet, -ette.

tonic ['tonik] *adj* tonique. *n* (*med*) tonique *m*; (*music*) tonique *f.*

tonight [tə'nait] *n, adv* cette nuit; (*evening*) ce soir.

tonsil ['tonsil] *n* amygdale *f.* **tonsillitis** *n* amygdalite *f.*

too [tuː] *adv* trop; (*also*) aussi; (*moreover*) en plus.

took [tuk] *V* take.

tool [tuːl] *n* outil *m.* **tool-shed** *n* cabane à outils *f.*

tooth [tuːθ] *n, pl* **teeth** dent *f.* **toothache** *n* mal de dents *m.* **have toothache** avoir mal aux dents. **tooth-brush** *n* brosse à dents *f.* **toothpaste** *n* dentifrice *m.* **toothpick** *n* cure-dent *m.* **toothless** *adj* édenté.

top¹ [top] *n* haut *m*; sommet *m*; (*lid*) couvercle *m*; surface *f*, dessus *m*; (*list*) tête *f.* **at the top of one's voice** à tue-tête. *adj* du haut; (*first*) premier; (*last*) dernier. **top hat** haut-de-forme *m.* **top-heavy** *adj* trop lourd du haut. **top secret** ultra-secret, -ète. **topside** *n* (*meat*) gîte *m.* **topsoil** *n* couche arable *f. v* surmonter; (*exceed*) dépasser. **top up** remplir, rajouter.

top² [top] *n* (*toy*) toupie *f.*

topaz ['toupaz] *n* topaze *f.*

topic ['topik] *n* sujet *m.* **topical** *adj* d'actualité.

topography [tə'pogrəfi] *n* topographie *f.* **topographical** *adj* topographique.

topple ['topl] *v* (faire) basculer, (faire) tomber.

topsy-turvy [topsi'təivi] *adj, adv* sens dessus dessous.

torch [toitʃ] *n* (*electric*) lampe de poche *f*; (*burning*) torche *f.*

tore [toi] *V* tear¹.

torment ['toiment; *v* toi'ment] *n* supplice *m. v* tourmenter.

torn [toin] *V* tear¹.

tornado [toi'neidou] *n* tornade *f.*

torpedo [toi'piidou] *n* torpille *f. v* torpiller.

torrent ['torənt] *n* torrent *m.* **torrential** *adj* torrentiel.

torso ['toisou] *n* torse *m*; (*sculpture*) buste *m.*

tortoise ['toitəs] *n* tortue *f.* **tortoise-shell** *n* écaille *f.*

tortuous ['toitʃuəs] *adj* tortueux.

torture ['toitʃə] *n* torture *f. v* torturer. **torturer** *n* tortionnaire *m.*

toss [tos] *n* lancement *m*; (*coin*) coup de pile ou face *m. v* lancer; (*pancake*) faire sauter; (s')agiter; (*coin*) jouer à pile ou face.

tot¹ [tɒt] *n* (*child*) petit enfant *m*; (*drink*) goutte *f*.

tot² [tɒt] *v* **tot up** additionner.

total ['təʊtəl] *nm, adj* total. *v* (*add up*) totaliser; (*add up to*) s'élever à. **totalitarian** *n*(*m*+*f*), *adj* totalitaire.

totter ['tɒtə] *v* chanceler.

touch [tʌtʃ] *n* toucher *m*; contact *m*; (*artist's*) touche *f*. *v* toucher (à), se toucher. **touchy** *adj* susceptible; délicat.

tough [tʌf] *adj* dur; (*strong*) résistant; (*struggle*) acharné. **toughen** *v* rendre plus solide; (*person*) (s')endurcir. **toughness** *n* dureté *f*; résistance *f*.

toupee ['tuːpeɪ] *n* postiche *m*.

tour [tʊə] *n* voyage *m*; (*of town, museum, etc.*) visite *f*; (*by musicians, etc.*) tournée *f*. *v* visiter. **touring** *or* **tourism** *n* tourisme *m*. **tourist** *n* touriste *m, f*. **tourist's guide** guide touristique *f*.

tournament ['tʊənəmənt] *n* tournoi *m*.

tousled ['taʊzld] *adj* échevelé.

tow [təʊ] *n* remorque *f*. *v* remorquer; (*trailer*) tirer. **tow-path** *n* chemin de halage *m*. **tow-rope** *n* remorque *f*.

towards [tə'wɔːdz] *prep* vers; (*attitude*) envers.

towel ['taʊəl] *n* serviette *f*; (*for hands*) essuie-mains *m*. **towel-rail** *n* porte-serviettes *m invar*. **towelling** *n* tissu éponge *m*.

tower ['taʊə] *n* tour *f*. **tower block** immeuble-tour *m*. *v* **tower over** dominer. **towering** *adj* imposant.

town [taʊn] *n* ville *f*. **town centre** centre de la ville *m*. **town hall** hôtel de ville *m*. **town planning** urbanisme *m*.

toxic ['tɒksik] *adj* toxique.

toy [tɔɪ] *n* jouet *m*. *adj* petit, miniature; d'enfant. *v* **toy with** jouer avec; (*idea*) caresser.

trace [treis] *n* trace *f*. *v* tracer; (*find*) retrouver; (*through paper*) décalquer. **tracing** *n* calque *m*. **tracing paper** papier-calque *m invar*.

track [trak] *n* (*marks*) trace *f*; (*path*) chemin *m*; (*sport*) piste *f*; (*rail*) voie *f*. **track suit** survêtement *m*. *v* suivre la trace de. **track down** traquer. **tracker** *n* traqueur *m*.

tract¹ [trakt] *n* (*region*) étendue *f*; (*anat*) système *m*.

tract² [trakt] *n* (*treatise*) tract *m*.

tractor ['traktə] *n* tracteur *m*.

trade [treid] *n* commerce *m*; (*job*) métier *m*. **trademark** *n* marque *f*. **tradesman** *n*

commerçant *m*. **trade union** syndicat *m*. **trade-unionist** *n* syndicaliste *m, f*. *v* faire le commerce (de); commercer (avec); échanger. **trade in** faire reprendre. **trader** *n* commerçant, -e *m, f*; négociant, -e *m, f*.

tradition [trə'diʃən] *n* tradition *f*. **traditional** *adj* traditionnel.

traffic ['trafik] *n* (*mot*) circulation *f*; (*aero, naut, etc.*) trafic *m*; commerce *m*. **traffic jam** embouteillage *m*. **traffic-light** *n* feu *m*. **traffic warden** contractuel, -elle *m, f*.

tragedy ['tradʒədi] *n* tragédie *f*. **tragic** *adj* tragique.

trail [treil] *n* traînée *f*; (*tracks*) trace *f*; (*path*) sentier *m*. *v* (*drag*) traîner; (*follow*) suivre la piste de. **trailer** *n* (*mot*) remorque *f*; film publicitaire *m*.

train [trein] *n* train *m*; (*series*) suite *f*; (*of dress*) traîne *f*. *v* (*teach*) former; (*learn*) recevoir sa formation; (*sport*) (s')entraîner; (*animal*) dresser. **trainee** *n* stagiaire *m, f*. **trainer** *n* (*sport*) entraîneur, -euse *m, f*; (*animal*) dresseur, -euse *m, f*; (*shoe*) chaussure de sport *f*. **training** *n* formation *f*; entraînement *m*; dressage *m*.

trait [treit] *n* trait *m*.

traitor ['treitə] *n* traître, -esse *m, f*.

tram [tram] *n* tram *m*.

tramp [tramp] *n* (*person*) clochard, -e *m, f*; (*hike*) randonnée *f*; (*sound*) martèlement des pas *m*. *v* marcher d'un pas lourd.

trample ['trampl] *v* piétiner, fouler aux pieds.

trampoline ['trampəliːn] *n* tremplin *m*.

trance [trɑːns] *n* transe *f*.

tranquil ['traŋkwil] *adj* tranquille. **tranquillity** *n* tranquillité *f*. **tranquillize** *v* tranquilliser. **tranquillizer** *n* tranquillisant *m*.

transact [tran'zakt] *v* traiter, régler. **transaction** *n* (*econ*) transaction *f*; (*comm*) opération *f*.

transcend [tran'send] *v* transcender; surpasser. **transcendental** *adj* transcendantal.

transcribe [tran'skraib] *v* transcrire. **transcription** *n* transcription *f*.

transept ['transept] *n* transept *m*.

transfer [trans'fəː; *n* 'transfəː] *v* transférer, être transféré. *n* transfert *m*; (*picture*) décalcomanie *f*. **not transferable** personnel.

transfixed [trans'fikst] *adj* cloué sur place.

transform [trans'fɔːm] *v* transformer. **transformation** *n* transformation *f*. **transformer** *n* (*elec*) transformateur *m*.

transfuse [trans'fjuːz] *v* transfuser. **transfusion** *n* transfusion *f*.

transient ['tranziənt] *adj* transitoire.

transistor [tran'zistə] *n* transistor *m*. **transistorize** *v* transistoriser.

transit ['transit] *n* transit *m*. **in transit** en transit.

transition [tran'ziʃən] *n* transition *f*. **transitional** *adj* de transition.

transitive ['transitiv] *adj* transitif.

transitory ['transitəri] *adj* transitoire.

translate [trans'leit] *v* traduire. **translation** *n* traduction *f*; (*school*) version *f*. **translator** *n* traducteur, -trice *m*, *f*.

translucent [trans'luːsnt] *adj* translucide. **translucence** *n* translucidité *f*.

transmit [tranz'mit] *v* transmettre; (*broadcast*) émettre. **transmission** *n* transmission *f*. **transmitter** *n* transmetteur *m*; émetteur *m*.

transparent [trans'peərənt] *adj* transparent. **transparency** (*phot*) diapositive *f*; transparence *f*.

transplant [trans'plaɪnt; *n* 'transplaɪnt] *v* transplanter. *n* transplantation *f*.

transport ['transpɔːt; *v* trans'pɔːt] *n* transport *m*. *v* transporter. **transportation** *n* transport *m*.

transpose [trans'pouz] *v* transposer. **transposition** *n* transposition *f*.

transverse ['tranzvɔːs] *adj* transversal.

transvestite [tranz'vesteit] *n* travesti, -e *m*, *f*.

trap [trap] *n* piège *m*. **trapdoor** *n* trappe *f*. *v* prendre au piège; bloquer.

trapeze [trə'piːz] *n* trapèze *m*. **trapeze artist** trapéziste *m*, *f*.

trash [traʃ] *n* (*worthless*) camelote *f*; (*waste*) ordures *f pl*. **trash can** (*US*) poubelle *f*.

trauma ['trɔːmə] *n* traumatisme *m*; (*med*) trauma *m*. **traumatic** *adj* traumatisant; (*med*) traumatique.

travel ['travl] *v* voyager; (*go*) aller; (*cover*) parcourir. *n* voyage *m*. **travel agency** agence de voyages *f*. **travel brochure** dépliant touristique *m*. **travel-sickness** *n* mal de la route. **traveller** *n* voyageur, -euse *m*, *f*; (*comm*) représentant *m*. **traveller's cheque** chèque de voyage *m*.

travesty ['travəsti] *n* simulacre *m*, parodie *f*.

trawler ['trɔːlə] *n* chalutier *m*. **trawling** *n* chalutage *m*.

tray [trei] *n* plateau *m*. **tray-cloth** *n* napperon *m*.

treachery ['tretʃəri] *n* traîtrise *f*. **treacherous** *adj* traître, -esse.

treacle ['triːkl] *n* mélasse *f*.

*tread [tred] *n* (bruit de) pas *m*; (*tyre*) chape *f*. *v* marcher. **tread on** mettre le pied sur; (*crush*) écraser du pied.

treason ['triːzn] *n* trahison *f*.

treasure ['treʒə] *n* trésor *m*. *v* tenir beaucoup à; garder précieusement. **treasurer** *n* trésorier, -ère *m*, *f*. **treasury** *n* trésorerie *f*.

treat [triːt] *v* traiter; (*med*) soigner. *n* plaisir *m*. **treatment** *n* traitement *m*.

treatise ['triːtiz] *n* traité *m*.

treaty ['triːti] *n* traité *m*.

treble ['trebl] *adj* triple; de soprano. *n* soprano *m*. *v* tripler. *adv* trois fois plus.

tree [triː] *n* arbre *m*.

trek [trek] *v* cheminer. *n* randonnée *f*.

trellis ['trelis] *n* treillis *m*, treillage *m*. *v* treillisser.

tremble ['trembl] *v* trembler, frémir. *n* tremblement *m*, frémissement *m*.

tremendous [trə'mendəs] *adj* énorme; (*terrible*) épouvantable; (*coll*: excellent) formidable.

tremor ['tremə] *n* tremblement *m*.

trench [trentʃ] *n* tranchée *f*.

trend [trend] *n* tendance *f*; mode *f*; direction *f*. **trendy** *adj* (*coll*) à la mode, dans le vent.

trespass ['trespəs] *v* s'introduire sans permission. *n* entrée non autorisée *f*. **trespasser** *n* intrus, -e *m*, *f*. **trespassers will be prosecuted** défense d'entrer sous peine de poursuites.

trestle ['tresl] *n* tréteau *m*. **trestle table** table à tréteaux *f*.

trial ['traiəl] *n* (*law*) procès *m*; (*test*) essai *m*; (*trouble*) épreuve *f*. **by trial and error** par tâtonnements. *adj* d'essai.

triangle ['traiangl] *n* triangle *m*. **triangular** *adj* triangulaire.

tribe [traib] *n* tribu *f*. **tribal** *adj* tribal. **tribesman** *n* membre d'une tribu *m*.

tribunal [trai'bjuːnl] *n* tribunal *m*.

tributary ['tribjutəri] *n* affluent *m*. *adj* tributaire.

tribute ['tribjuːt] *n* tribut *m*.
trick [trik] *n* tour *m*; ruse *f*; (*cards*) levée *f*. **do the trick** (*coll*) faire l'affaire. **trick photograph** photographie truquée *f*. **trick question** question-piège *f*. *v* attraper. **trickery** *n* ruse *f*. **tricky** *adj* délicat, difficile.
trickle ['trikl] *n* filet *m*. *v* couler, dégouliner.
tricycle ['traisikl] *n* tricycle *m*.
trifle ['traifl] *n* bagatelle *f*; (*sweet*) diplomate *m*. *v* **trifle with** traiter à la légère. **trifling** *adj* insignifiant.
trigger ['trigə] *n* détente *f*, gâchette *f*. *v* déclencher, provoquer.
trigonometry [trigə'nomətri] *n* trigonométrie *f*.
trill [tril] *n* trille *m*. *v* triller.
trim [trim] *adj* net, nette; (*tidy*) bien tenu. **in trim** en forme. *v* tailler légèrement; (*hair*) rafraîchir; (*decorate*) garnir. **trimmings** *pl n* garnitures *f pl*; accessoires *m pl*.
trinket ['triŋkit] *n* bibelot *m*.
trio ['triːou] *n* trio *m*.
trip [trip] *n* voyage *m*; (*stumble*) faux pas *m*; (*slang: drugs*) trip *m*. *v* trébucher. **trip up** (faire) trébucher; (*on purpose*) faire un croche-pied à.
tripe [traip] *n* tripes *f pl*; (*coll*) bêtises *f pl*.
triple ['tripl] *nm, adj* triple. *v* tripler. *adv* trois fois plus.
triplet ['triplit] *n* (*music*) triolet *m*; (*poetry*) tercet *m*; (*person*) triplé, -e *m, f*.
tripod ['traipod] *n* trépied *m*.
trite [trait] *adj* banal. **triteness** *n* banalité *f*.
triumph ['traiʌmf] *n* triomphe *m*. *v* triompher. **triumphant** *adj* triomphant. **triumphantly** *adv* triomphalement.
trivial ['triviəl] *adj* insignifiant; banal. **trivia** or **trivialities** *pl n* bagatelles *f pl*.
trod [trod] *V* **tread**.
trodden ['trodn] *V* **tread**.
trolley ['troli] *n* chariot *m*; (*shopping*) poussette *f*; (*tea*) table roulante *f*.
trombone [trom'boun] *n* trombone *m*.
troop [truːp] *n* bande *f*, troupe *f*. **troops** *pl n* (*mil*) troupes *f pl*. *v* **troop in/out** entrer/sortir en bande. **trooping the colour** le salut au drapeau.
trophy ['troufi] *n* trophée *m*.
tropic ['tropik] *n* tropique *m*. **tropical** *adj* tropical.

trot [trot] *n* trot *m*. **on the trot** (*coll*) de suite. *v* trotter. **trotter** *n* pied de porc *m*.
trouble ['trʌbl] *n* ennui *m*; (*bother*) peine *f*; difficulté *f*. **be in trouble** avoir des ennuis. **that's the trouble!** c'est ça l'ennui! **troublemaker** *n* fauteur, -trice de troubles *m, f*. **troublesome** *adj* fatigant, gênant. *v* (*bother*) (se) déranger; (*upset*) affliger, gêner; (*worry*) inquiéter.
trough [trof] *n* (*drinking*) abreuvoir *m*; (*food*) auge *f*; dépression *f*, creux *m*.
trousers ['trauzəz] *pl n* pantalon *m sing*; (*short*) culottes *f pl*. **trouser-suit** *n* tailleur-pantalon *m*.
trout [traut] *n* truite *f*.
trowel ['trauəl] *n* truelle *f*; (*gardening*) déplantoir *m*.
truant ['truːənt] *n* **play truant** faire l'école buissonnière. **truancy** *n* absence non autorisée *f*.
truce [truːs] *n* trêve *f*. **call a truce** faire trêve.
truck [trʌk] *n* camion *m*; (*rail*) wagon *m*. **truck-driver** *n* camionneur *m*.
trudge [trʌdʒ] *v* se traîner, marcher péniblement.
true [truː] *adj* vrai; exact; (*accurate*) fidèle; réel; (*straight*) droit; (*note*) juste. **truly** *adv* vraiment. **well and truly** bel et bien.
truffle ['trʌfl] *n* truffe *f*.
trump [trʌmp] *n* atout *m*. **turn up trumps** (*coll*) faire des merveilles. *v* couper.
trumpet ['trʌmpit] *n* trompette *f*. *v* (*elephant*) barrir. **trumpeter** *n* trompettiste *m, f*.
truncate [trʌŋ'keit] *v* tronquer.
truncheon ['trʌntʃən] *n* matraque *f*; (*police*) bâton *m*.
trunk [trʌŋk] *n* tronc *m*; (*elephant*) trompe *f*; (*case*) malle *f*; (*mot*) coffre *m*. **trunk call** communication interurbaine *f*. **trunk road** route nationale *f*. **trunks** *pl n* slip de bain *m sing*.
truss [trʌs] *n* (*hay*) botte *f*; (*fruit*) grappe *f*; (*med*) bandage herniaire *m*. *v* trousser.
trust [trʌst] *n* confiance *f*; charge *f*; (*comm*) trust *m*; (*law*) fidéicommis *m*. **trustworthy** *adj* digne de confiance. *v* avoir confiance en, se fier à; (*hope*) espérer. **trustee** *n* (*law*) fidéicommissaire *m*; (*of school*) administrateur, -trice *m, f*. **trusting** *adj* confiant. **trusty** *adj* fidèle.

truth [truːθ] n verité f. **truthful** adj véridique. **truthfulness** n véracité f.

try [trai] n essai m. v essayer; juger; (strain) mettre à l'épreuve; tester. **try on** essayer. **trying** adj pénible.

tsar [zaɪ] n tsar m.

T-shirt ['tiːʃəɪt] n T-shirt m.

tub [tʌb] n cuve f, baquet m; (bath) tub m.

tuba ['tjuːbə] n tuba m.

tube [tjuːb] n tube m; (rail) métro m. **tubeless** adj (tyre) sans chambre à air.

tuber ['tjuːbə] n tubercule m.

tuberculosis   [tjubəːkjuˈlousis]   n tuberculose f.

tuck [tʌk] n (sewing) rempli m. **tuck-shop** n (school) boutique à provisions f. v mettre. **tuck in** (flap) rentrer; (bedclothes) border; (coll: eat) boulotter. **tuck up** (in bed) border; (skirt) remonter.

Tuesday ['tjuːzdi] n mardi m.

tuft [tʌft] n touffe f; (feathers) huppe f.

tug [tʌg] n saccade f; (boat) remorqueur m. **tug-of-war** n lutte à la corde f. v tirer; remorquer.

tuition [tjuˈiʃən] n cours m pl.

tulip ['tjuːlip] n tulipe f.

tumble ['tʌmbl] n chute f, culbute f. v culbuter, dégringoler; (knock over) faire tomber, renverser. **tumbledown** adj en ruines. **tumble-dryer** n séchoir à air chaud m. **tumble out** tomber en vrac. **tumbler** n verre droit m.

tummy ['tʌmi] n (coll) ventre m.

tumour ['tjuːmə] n tumeur f.

tumult ['tjuːmʌlt] n tumulte m. **tumultuous** adj tumultueux.

tuna ['tjuːnə] n also **tunny** thon m.

tune [tjuːn] n air m. **in tune** accordé; (sing) juste. **out of tune** désaccordé; (sing) faux. v régler; (music) accorder. **tuneful** adj mélodieux. **tuner** n (person) accordeur m; (radio) radio-préamplificateur m. **tuning** n réglage m; accord m. **tuning fork** diapason m.

tunic ['tjuːnik] n tunique f.

tunnel ['tʌnl] n tunnel m. v percer un tunnel.

turban ['təːbən] n turban m.

turbine ['təːbain] n turbine f.

turbot ['təːbət] n turbot m.

turbulent ['təːbjulənt] adj turbulent. **turbulence** n turbulence f.

tureen [təˈriːn] n soupière f.

turf [təːf] n gazon m; (sport) turf m. **turf accountant** bookmaker m. v gazonner. **turf out** (coll: thing) bazarder; (coll: person) flanquer à la porte.

turkey ['təːki] n dindon m; (cookery) dinde f.

Turkey ['təːki] n Turquie f. **Turk** n Turc, Turque m. f. **Turkish** nm, adj turc, turque. **Turkish bath** bain turc m. **Turkish delight** loukoum m.

turmeric ['təːmərik] n curcuma m.

turmoil ['təːmoil] n agitation f, trouble m.

turn [təːn] n tour m; (in road) tournant m, virage m; (med) crise f; (theatre) numéro m. **do a good turn** rendre un service (à). v (faire) tourner; (se) retourner; changer. **turn away** (se) détourner; refuser, rejeter. **turn down** rejeter; (lower) baisser. **turn off** fermer, éteindre. **turn on** allumer, brancher; attaquer. **turn out** (end up) s'avérer; (light) éteindre; (empty) vider; (expel) mettre à la porte. **turnover** n (comm) roulement m; (cookery) chausson m. **turnstile** n tourniquet m. **turntable** n (record-player) platine f; (trains, etc.) plaque tournante f. **turn up** arriver; (be found) être trouvé; (raise) mettre plus fort, monter. **turning** n (side road) route latérale f; (bend) coude m. **turning point** tournant m, moment décisif m.

turnip ['təːnip] n navet m.

turpentine ['təːpəntain] n térébenthine f.

turquoise ['təːkwoiz] n (stone) turquoise f; (colour) turquoise m. adj (colour) turquoise invar.

turret ['tʌrit] n tourelle f.

turtle ['təːtl] n tortue marine f. **turn turtle** chavirer. **turtle-neck** n (jumper) col montant m.

tusk [tʌsk] n défense f.

tussle ['tʌsl] n lutte f. v se battre.

tutor ['tjuːtə] n (private) précepteur, -trice m. f; (university) directeur, -trice d'études m, f. v donner des cours particuliers (à).

tuxedo [tʌkˈsiːdou] n smoking m.

tweed [twiːd] n tweed m.

tweezers ['twiːzəz] pl n pinces fines f pl.

twelve [twelv] nm, adj douze. **twelfth** n(m+f), adj douzième. **Twelfth Night** la fête des Rois f.

twenty ['twenti] nm, adj vingt. **twentieth** n(m+f), adj vingtième.

twice [twais] *adv* deux fois.
twiddle ['twidl] *v* tripoter. **twiddle one's thumbs** se tourner les pouces.
twig [twig] *n* brindille *f.*
twilight ['twailait] *n* crépuscule *m.*
twin [twin] *n, adj* jumeau, -elle. **twin beds** lits jumeaux *m pl.* **twin town** ville jumelée *f. v* jumeler.
twine [twain] *n* ficelle *f. v* (*weave*) tresser; (s')enrouler; serpenter.
twinge [twindʒ] *n* (*pain*) élancement *m;* (*sadness*) pincement *m;* remords *m.*
twinkle ['twiŋkl] *v* scintiller, briller. *n* scintillement *m;* (*eyes*) pétillement *m.*
twirl [twɔːl] *v* (faire) tournoyer. *n* tournoiement *m.*
twist [twist] *n* torsion *f;* (*med*) entorse *f;* (*in wire, etc.*) tortillon *m;* (*in road*) tournant *m;* (*story*) coup de théâtre *m. v* (s')entortiller, tordre; (*turn*) tourner; (*road*) serpenter.
twit [twit] *n* (*slang*) idiot, -e *m, f.*
twitch [twitʃ] *n* tic *m;* (*pull*) coup sec *m. v* se convulser; avoir un tic; tirer d'un coup sec.
twitter ['twitə] *v* gazouiller. *n* gazouillement *m.*
two [tuː] *nm, adj* deux. **two-faced** *adj* hypocrite. **two-legged** *adj* bipède. **two-time** *v* (*coll*) doubler.
tycoon [tai'kuːn] *n* magnat *m.*
type [taip] *n* type *m;* (*sort*) genre *m.* **typesetting** *n* composition *f.* **typewriter** *n* machine à écrire *f. v* taper (à la machine). **typical** *adj* typique. **typing** *n* dactylo *f.* **typist** *n* dactylo *m, f.*
typhoid ['taifoid] *n* typhoïde *f.*
typhoon [tai'fuːn] *n* typhon *m.*
tyrant ['tairənt] *n* tyran *m.* **tyrannical** *adj* tyrannique. **tyranny** *n* tyrannie *f.*
tyre *or US* **tire** ['taiə] *n* pneu *m.*

U

ubiquitous [juː'bikwitəs] *adj* omniprésent.
udder ['ʌdə] *n* pis *m,* mamelle *f.*
ugly ['ʌgli] *adj* laid, vilain; répugnant. **ugliness** *n* laideur *f.*
ulcer ['ʌlsə] *n* ulcère *m.*
ulterior [ʌl'tiəriə] *adj* ultérieur, -e. **ulterior motive** arrière-pensée *f.*

ultimate ['ʌltimət] *adj* ultime; final; suprême. **ultimately** *adv* à la fin; (*basically*) en fin de compte. **ultimatum** *n* ultimatum *m.*
ultraviolet [ʌltrə'vaiələt] *adj* ultra-violet.
umbilical [ʌm'bilikəl] *adj* ombilical.
umbrage ['ʌmbridʒ] *n* ombrage *m.* **take umbrage** prendre ombrage.
umbrella [ʌm'brelə] *n* parapluie *m.*
umpire ['ʌmpaiə] *n* arbitre *m. v* arbitrer.
umpteen [ʌmp'tiːn] (*coll*) *adj* je ne sais combien (de). **umpteenth** *adj* énième.
unable [ʌn'eibl] *adj* incapable. **be unable to** (*lack means*) ne pas pouvoir; (*lack knowledge*) ne pas savoir.
unabridged [ʌnə'bridʒd] *adj* intégral.
unacceptable [ʌnək'septəbl] *adj* inacceptable; inadmissible.
unaccompanied [ʌnə'kumpənid] *adj* non accompagné; (*music*) sans accompagnement, seul.
unadulterated [ʌnə'dʌltəreitid] *adj* pur.
unaided [ʌn'eidid] *adj* sans aide.
unanimous [juː'naniməs] *adj* unanime. **unanimity** *n* unanimité *f.*
unarmed [ʌn'aːmd] *adj* (*combat*) sans armes; (*person*) non armé.
unattached [ʌnə'tatʃt] *adj* libre; indépendant.
unattractive [ʌnə'traktiv] *adj* peu attrayant, déplaisant.
unauthorized [ʌn'oːθəraizd] *adj* non autorisé.
unavoidable [ʌnə'voidəbl] *adj* inévitable.
unaware [ʌnə'weə] *adj* inconscient. **be unaware of** ignorer. **unawares** *adv* à l'improviste.
unbalanced [ʌn'balənst] *adj* mal équilibré; (*mentally*) déséquilibré.
unbearable [ʌn'beərəbl] *adj* insupportable.
unbelievable [ʌnbi'liːvəbl] *adj* incroyable.
***unbend** [ʌn'bend] *v* redresser; (*person*) se détendre. **unbending** *adj* inflexible.
unbiased [ʌn'baiəst] *adj* impartial.
unbreakable [ʌn'breikəbl] *adj* incassable.
unbridled [ʌn'braidld] *adj* débridé.
unbutton [ʌn'butn] *v* déboutonner.
uncalled-for [ʌn'koːldfoː] *adj* injustifié; déplacé.
uncanny [ʌn'kani] *adj* étrange, troublant.
uncertain [ʌn'səːtn] *adj* incertain. **uncertainty** *n* incertitude *f.*

uncle [ˈʌŋkl] *n* oncle *m.*
uncomfortable [ʌnˈkʌmfətəbl] *adj* inconfortable; mal à l'aise.
uncommon [ʌnˈkomən] *adj* rare.
uncompromising [ʌnˈkomprəmaiziŋ] *adj* intransigeant.
unconditional [ʌnkənˈdiʃənl] *adj* inconditionnel.
unconscious [ʌnˈkonʃəs] *adj* (*med*) sans connaissance; (*unaware*) inconscient.
unconventional [ʌnkənˈvenʃənl] *adj* peu conventionnel.
uncooked [ʌnˈkukt] *adj* non cuit.
uncouth [ʌnˈkuːθ] *adj* grossier.
uncover [ʌnˈkʌvə] *v* découvrir.
uncut [ʌnˈkʌt] *adj* non coupé, non taillé.
undecided [ʌndiˈsaidid] *adj* indécis.
undeniable [ʌndiˈnaiəbl] *adj* indéniable, incontestable.
under [ˈʌndə] *adv* au-dessous. *prep* sous; au dessous de; (*less*) moins de; (*according to*) selon.
underarm [ˈʌndəraim] *adj, adv* par en-dessous.
undercharge [ʌndəˈtʃɑidʒ] *v* ne pas faire payer assez à.
underclothes [ˈʌndəklouðz] *pl n* sous-vêtements *m pl.*
undercoat [ˈʌndəkout] *n* couche de fond *f.*
undercover [ʌndəˈkʌvə] *adj* secret, -ète.
undercut [ʌndəˈkʌt] *v* vendre moins cher que.
underdeveloped [ʌndədiˈveləpt] *adj* sous-développé.
underdog [ˈʌndədog] *n* (*loser*) perdant *m*; (*oppressed*) opprimé *m.*
underdone [ʌndəˈdʌn] *adj* (*meat*) saignant; pas assez cuit.
underestimate [ʌndəˈestimeit] *v* sous-estimer. **underestimation** *n* sous-estimation *f.*
underfoot [ʌndəˈfut] *adv* sous les pieds.
****undergo** [ʌndəˈgou] *v* subir, éprouver.
undergraduate [ʌndəˈgradjuət] *n* étudiant, -e *m, f.*
underground [ʌndəˈgraund; *adj*, ˈʌndəgraund] *adv* sous terre; clandestinement. *adj* sous terre, souterrain; clandestin. *n* (*rail*) métro *m.*
undergrowth [ˈʌndəgrouθ] *n* broussailles *f pl.*
underhand [ʌndəˈhand] *adj* en sous-main, sournois.

****underlie** [ʌndəˈlai] *v* être à la base de. **underlying** *adj* sous-jacent.
underline [ʌndəˈlain] *v* souligner. **underlining** *n* soulignage *m.*
undermine [ʌndəˈmain] *v* saper, miner.
underneath [ʌndəˈniːθ] *prep* sous, au-dessous de. *nm, adv* dessous. *adj* d'en dessous.
underpaid [ʌndəˈpeid] *adj* sous-payé.
underpants [ˈʌndəpants] *pl n* caleçon *m sing.*
underpass [ˈʌndəpais] *n* (*cars*) passage inférieur *m*; (*people*) passage souterrain *m.*
underprivileged [ʌndəˈprivilidʒd] *adj* défavorisé.
underrate [ʌndəˈreit] *v* sous-estimer.
underskirt [ˈʌndəskɔit] *n* jupon *m.*
understaffed [ʌndəˈstaift] *adj* à court de personnel.
understand [ʌndəˈstand] *v* comprendre; (*imply*) sous-entendre. **understandable** *adj* compréhensible. **understanding** *n* compréhension *f*; (*agreement*) accord *m.*
understate [ʌndəˈsteit] *n* minimiser. **make an understatement** ne pas assez dire. **that's an understatement!** c'est peu dire!
understudy [ˈʌndəstʌdi] *n* doublure *f. v* doubler.
****undertake** [ʌndəˈteik] *v* entreprendre, se charger de. **undertaker** *n* ordonnateur des pompes funèbres *m.* **undertaking** *n* entreprise *f*; promesse *f.*
undertone [ˈʌndətoun] *n* **in an undertone** à demi-voix.
underwater [ʌndəˈwɔitə] *adj* sous-marin. *adv* sous l'eau.
underwear [ˈʌndəweə] *n* sous-vêtements *m pl.*
underweight [ʌndəˈweit] *adj* (*goods*) d'un poids insuffisant; (*person*) trop maigre.
underworld [ˈʌndəwɔild] *n* (*criminal*) milieu *m*; (*hell*) enfers *m pl.*
****underwrite** [ʌndəˈrait] *v* garantir; (*insurance*) souscrire.
undesirable [ʌndiˈzaiərəbl] *adj* peu souhaitable. *n* indésirable *m, f.*
****undo** [ʌnˈduː] *v* défaire; (*destroy*) détruire. **come undone** se défaire. **undoing** *n* ruine *f.*
undoubted [ʌnˈdautid] *adj* indubitable.
undress [ʌnˈdres] *v* (se) déshabiller.
undue [ʌnˈdjuː] *adj* indu. **unduly** *adv* trop.
undulate [ˈʌndjuleit] *v* onduler. **undulating** *adj* onduleux. **undulation** *n* ondulation *f.*

unearth [ʌn'ɔıθ] v déterrer. **unearthly** adj
surnaturel; (coll: hour) impossible, indu.

uneasy [ʌn'iızi] adj mal à l'aise; troublé;
anxieux.

uneducated [ʌn'edjukeitid] adj sans éducation.

unemployed [ʌnem'ploid] adj en
chômage. **the unemployed** les chômeurs
m pl. **unemployment** n chômage m.

unenthusiastic [ʌnenθjuızi'astik] adj peu
enthusiaste.

unequal [ʌn'iıkwəl] adj inégal.

uneven [ʌn'iıvn] adj inégal; (number)
impair.

uneventful [ʌni'ventfəl] adj peu mouvementé.

unexpected [ʌneks'pektid] adj inattendu.

unfailing [ʌn'feiliŋ] adj inépuisable;
infaillible.

unfair [ʌn'feə] adj injuste. **unfairness** n
injustice f.

unfaithful [ʌn'feiθfəl] adj infidèle. **unfaithfulness** n infidélité f.

unfamiliar [ʌnfə'miljə] adj peu familier,
inconnu.

unfasten [ʌn'faısn] v défaire, ouvrir.

unfavourable [ʌn'feivərəbl] adj
défavorable.

unfinished [ʌn'finiʃt] adj inachevé; à finir.

unfit [ʌn'fit] adj inapte, impropre; (ill)
souffrant.

unfold [ʌn'fould] v déplier; exposer;
(story, countryside) se dérouler.

unforeseen [ʌnfɔr'siın] adj imprévu.

unforgivable [ʌnfə'givəbl] adj impardon-
nable.

unfortunate [ʌn'fɔrtʃənət] adj
malheureux, fâcheux.

unfounded [ʌn'faundid] adj sans fondement; injustifié.

unfriendly [ʌn'frendli] adj froid; hostile.

unfurnished [ʌn'fɔıniʃd] adj non meublé.

ungainly [ʌn'geinli] adj gauche.

ungrateful [ʌn'greitfəl] adj ingrat.

unhappy [ʌn'hapi] adj triste, malheureux.
unhappiness n tristesse f.

unhealthy [ʌn'helθi] adj malsain; (person)
maladif.

unheard-of [ʌn'hɔıdov] adj inouï, sans
précédent.

unhurt [ʌn'hɔıt] adj indemne, sain et sauf.

unhygienic [ʌnhai'dʒiınik] adj non
hygiénique.

unicorn ['juınikɔın] n licorne f.

unidentified [ʌnai'dentifaid] adj non
identifié. **unidentified flying object**
(UFO) objet volant non identifié
(OVNI) m.

uniform ['juınifɔım] nm, adj uniforme.
uniformity n uniformité f.

unify ['juınifai] v unifier. **unification** n unification f.

unilateral [juını'latərəl] adj unilatéral.

unimaginative [ʌni'madʒinətiv] adj peu
imaginatif.

unimportant [ʌnim'pɔıtnt] adj peu important.

uninhabited [ʌnin'habitid] adj inhabité.

uninhibited [ʌnin'hibitid] adj sans inhibi-
tions.

unintentional [ʌnin'tenʃənl] adj
involontaire.

uninterested [ʌn'intristid] adj indifférent.
uninteresting adj inintéressant.

union ['juınjən] n union f; (trade) syndicat m.

unique [ju'niık] adj unique.

unisex ['juıni,seks] adj (coll) unisexe.

unison ['juınisn] n unisson m. **in unison**
en chœur.

unit ['juınit] n unité f; bloc m, groupe m.

unite [ju'nait] v (s')unir, unifier. **united**
adj uni. **United Kingdom** Royaume-Uni
m. **United Nations** Nations Unies f pl.
United States of America Etats-Unis m
pl.

unity ['juıniti] n unité f.

universe ['juınivɔıs] n univers m. **universal**
adj universel.

university [juıni'vɔısəti] n université f. adj
universitaire.

unjust [ʌn'dʒʌst] adj injuste.

unkempt [ʌn'kempt] adj débraillé; (hair)
mal peigné.

unkind [ʌn'kaind] adj peu aimable,
méchant, cruel. **unkindness** n méchanceté
f.

unknown [ʌn'noun] nm, adj inconnu.

unlawful [ʌn'lɔıfəl] adj illégal, illégitime.

unless [ʌn'les] conj à moins que.

unlike [ʌn'laik] adj dissemblable, différent prep à la différence de.

unlikely [ʌn'laikli] adj peu probable;
(story) invraisemblable.

unlimited [ʌn'limitid] adj illimité.

unload [ʌn'loud] v décharger; (get rid of)
se défaire de.

unlock [ʌn'lok] v ouvrir.

unlucky [ʌn'lʌki] *adj* malchanceux, malheureux; (*number, etc.*) qui porte malheur.

unmarried [ʌn'marid] *adj* célibataire.

unnatural [ʌn'natʃərəl] *adj* anormal; contre nature.

unnecessary [ʌn'nesəsəri] *adj* inutile; superflu.

unnerving [ʌn'nɜːviŋ] *adj* déconcertant.

unnoticed [ʌn'noutist] *adj* inaperçu. **go unnoticed** passer inaperçu.

unobtainable [ʌnəb'teinəbl] *adj* impossible à obtenir.

unobtrusive [ʌnəb'truːsiv] *adj* discret, -ète.

unoccupied [ʌn'okjupaid] *adj* inoccupé, (*seat*) libre.

unofficial [ʌnə'fiʃəl] *adj* officieux, non officiel.

unorthodox [ʌn'ɔːθədoks] *adj* peu orthodoxe.

unpack [ʌn'pak] *v* (*case*) défaire (sa valise); (*contents*) déballer (ses affaires).

unpaid [ʌn'peid] *adj* impayé, non acquitté; (*worker*) non retribué.

unpleasant [ʌn'pleznt] *adj* désagréable, déplaisant.

unpopular [ʌn'popjulə] *adj* impopulaire.

unprecedented [ʌn'presidentid] *adj* sans précédent.

unpredictable [ʌnprə'diktəbl] *adj* imprévisible; incertain.

unqualified [ʌn'kwolifaid] *adj* non qualifié, non diplômé; (*absolute*) sans réserve.

unravel [ʌn'ravəl] *v* (s')effiler; (*mystery*) débrouiller.

unreal [ʌn'riəl] *adj* irréel.

unreasonable [ʌn'riːzənəbl] *adj* déraisonnable; excessif.

unrelenting [ʌnri'lentiŋ] *adj* implacable.

unreliable [ʌnri'laiəbl] *adj* sur qui on ne peut compter; (*machine*) peu fiable; (*source*) douteux.

unrest [ʌn'rest] *n* agitation *f*.

unruly [ʌn'ruːli] *adj* indiscipliné.

unsafe [ʌn'seif] *adj* dangereux.

unsatisfactory [ʌnsatis'faktəri] *adj* peu satisfaisant.

unscrew [ʌn'skruː] *v* (se) dévisser.

unscrupulous [ʌn'skruːpjuləs] *adj* sans scrupules, malhonnête.

unselfish [ʌn'selfiʃ] *adj* non égoïste, désintéressé.

unsettle [ʌn'setl] *v* perturber. **unsettled** *adj* perturbé; incertain; instable.

unsightly [ʌn'saitli] *adj* disgracieux.

unskilled [ʌn'skild] *adj* inexperimenté. **unskilled worker** manœuvre *m*.

unsound [ʌn'saund] *adj* peu solide; (*health*) précaire; (*reasoning*) mal fondé.

unspeakable [ʌn'spiːkəbl] *adj* indescriptible.

unspecified [ʌn'spesifaid] *adj* non spécifié.

unstable [ʌn'steibl] *adj* instable.

unsteady [ʌn'stedi] *adj* instable, mal assuré.

unstuck [ʌn'stʌk] *adj* **come unstuck** se décoller.

unsuccessful [ʌnsək'sesfəl] *adj* infructueux; (*candidate*) réfusé; (*marriage*) malheureux. **unsuccessfully** *adv* sans succès.

unsuitable [ʌn'suːtəbl] *adj* qui ne convient pas; inopportun; peu approprié.

unsure [ʌn'ʃuə] *adj* incertain.

untangle [ʌn'taŋgl] *v* démêler.

untidy [ʌn'taidi] *adj* négligé, débraillé; (*writing*) brouillon; (*room*) en désordre. **untidiness** *n* débraillé *m*; désordre *m*.

untie [ʌn'tai] *v* défaire.

until [ən'til] *prep* jusqu'à; (*before*) avant. *conj* jusqu'à ce que.

untoward [ʌntə'wɔːd] *adj* fâcheux.

untrue [ʌn'truː] *adj* faux, fausse; inexact.

unusual [ʌn'juːʒuəl] *adj* insolite; bizarre; exceptionnel.

unwanted [ʌn'wontid] *adj* superflu; non désiré.

unwell [ʌn'wel] *adj* indisposé, souffrant.

unwilling [ʌn'wiliŋ] *adj* peu disposé. **unwillingly** *adv* à contrecœur.

*unwind [ʌn'waind] *v* (se) dérouler; (*relax*) se détendre.

unwise [ʌn'waiz] *adj* imprudent.

unworthy [ʌn'wɜːði] *adj* indigne.

unwrap [ʌn'rap] *v* défaire.

up [ʌp] *adv* en haut, en l'air; (*standing*) debout; (*out of bed*) levé; terminé. **up there** là-haut. **up to** jusqu'à. *prep* dans, sur. **go up** monter. *n* **ups and downs** hauts et bas *m pl*.

upbringing ['ʌpbriŋiŋ] *n* éducation *f*.

update [ʌp'deit] *v* mettre à jour.

upheaval [ʌp'hiːvl] *n* bouleversement *m*; (*domestic*) branle-bas *m*; (*pol*) perturbation *f*.

uphill [ʌp'hil] *adj* qui monte; *(struggle)* pénible. *adv* **go uphill** monter.

***uphold** [ʌp'hould] *v* soutenir, maintenir.

upholster [ʌp'houlstə] *v* rembourrer. **upholstery** *n* tapisserie *f*; *(material)* rembourrage *m*; *(in car)* garniture *f*.

upkeep ['ʌpkiːp] *n* entretien *m*.

uplift [ʌp'lift] *v* élever.

upon [ə'pon] *prep* sur.

upper ['ʌpə] *adj* supérieur, -e, du dessus. **upper-class** *adj* aristocratique. **uppermost** *adj* le plus haut; en dessus.

upright ['ʌprait] *adj, adv* droit. *n* montant *m*.

uprising ['ʌpraiziŋ] *n* soulèvement *m*.

uproar ['ʌprɔɪ] *n* tumulte *m*, vacarme *m*. **uproarious** *adj* tumultueux; hilarant.

uproot [ʌp'ruːt] *v* déraciner.

***upset** [ʌp'set] *n* 'ʌpset] *v* *(knock over)* renverser; *(plans, etc.)* déranger; *(person)* faire de la peine à, contrarier. *adj (angry)* fâché; *(sad)* peiné; *(stomach)* dérangé. *n* désordre *m*; dérangement *m*; chagrin *m*.

upshot ['ʌpʃot] *n* résultat *m*.

upside down [ʌpsai'daun] *adv, adj* sens dessus dessous, à l'envers.

upstairs [ʌp'steəz] *adv* en haut. **go upstairs** monter (l'escalier). *adj* du dessus, d'en haut.

upstream [ʌp'striːm; *adj* 'ʌpstriːm] *adv* vers l'amont, en amont; *(swim)* contre le courant. *adj* d'amont.

uptight ['ʌptait] *adj (coll)* crispé.

up-to-date [ʌptə'deit] *adj* moderne.

upward ['ʌpwəd] *adj* ascendant. **upwards** *adv* vers le haut, en montant.

uranium [ju'reiniəm] *n* uranium *m*.

urban ['əːbən] *adj* urbain.

urchin ['əːtʃin] *n* polisson, -onne *m, f*.

urge [əːdʒ] *n* désir ardent *m*, forte envie *f*. *v* pousser, conseiller vivement.

urgent ['əːdʒənt] *adj* urgent; insistant. **urgency** *n* urgence *f*; insistance *f*. **urgently** *adv* d'urgence.

urine ['juːrin] *n* urine *f*. **urinate** *v* uriner.

urn [əːn] *n* urne *f*.

us [ʌs] *pron* nous.

usage ['juːzidʒ] *n* usage *m*.

use [juːs; *v* juːz] *n* usage *m*, emploi *m*. **it's no use** ça ne sert à rien. *v* se servir de, employer. **use up** user, consommer, épuiser. **used** *adj (car)* d'occasion. **be used to** être habitué à. **get used to** s'habituer à. **useful** *adj* utile. **useless** *adj* inutile. **user** *n* usager *m*.

usher ['ʌʃə] *n* *(law)* huissier *m*; *(church)* placeur *m*. *v* **usher in** introduire; inaugurer. **usherette** *n* ouvreuse *f*.

usual ['juːzuəl] *adj* habituel. **as usual** comme d'habitude. **usually** *adv* d'habitude, généralement.

usurp [ju'zəːp] *v* usurper.

utensil [ju'tensl] *n* ustensile *m*.

uterus ['juːtərəs] *n* utérus *m*.

utility [ju'tiləti] *n* utilité *f*. *adj* utilitaire.

utilize ['juːtilaiz] *v* utiliser.

utmost ['ʌtmoust] *adj* le plus grand; suprême; extrême. *n* plus haut point. **do one's utmost** faire tout son possible.

utter[1] ['ʌtə] *v* proférer; *(cry)* pousser.

utter[2] ['ʌtə] *adj* complet, -ète; pur; *(fool)* fini.

U-turn ['juːtəːn] *n* demi-tour *m*.

V

vacant ['veikənt] *adj* vacant, libre; *(stare)* vague. **vacancy** *n* *(room)* chambre à louer *f*; *(job)* vacance *f*. **no vacancies** complet.

vacate [vei'keit] *v* quitter.

vacation [və'keiʃn] *n* vacances *f pl*.

vaccine ['vaksiːn] *n* vaccin *m*. **vaccinate** *v* vacciner. **vaccination** *n* vaccination *f*.

vacillate ['vasileit] *v* vaciller. **vacillation** *n* indécision *f*, vacillation *f*.

vacuum ['vakjum] *n* vide *m*; *(phys)* vacuum *m*. **vacuum cleaner** aspirateur *m*. **vacuum flask** bouteille thermos ® *f*. **vacuum-packed** *adj* emballé sous vide. *v* passer à l'aspirateur.

vagina [və'dʒainə] *n* vagin *m*. **vaginal** *adj* vaginal.

vagrant ['veigrənt] *n, adj* vagabond, -e. **vagrancy** *n* vagabondage *m*.

vague [veig] *adj* vague, flou, imprécis.

vain [vein] *adj* vain, inutile, futile; *(conceited)* vaniteux. **in vain** en vain.

valiant ['valiənt] *adj* courageux.

valid ['valid] *adj* valide, valable. **validity** *n* validité *f*; force *f*.

Valletta [və'letə] *n* La Valette.

valley ['vali] *n* vallée *f*; *(smaller)* vallon *m*.

value ['valjuː] *n* valeur *f*. *v* évaluer; apprécier, tenir à. **valuable** *adj* de valeur, précieux. **valuables** *pl n* objets de valeur *m pl*. **valuation** *n* évaluation *f*, expertise *f*.

valve [valv] *n* soupape *f*, valve *f*.

vampire ['vampaiə] *n* vampire *m*.

van [van] *n* camionnette *f*; (*rail*) fourgon *m*.

vandal ['vandl] *n* vandale *m*, *f*. **vandalism** *n* vandalisme *m*. **vandalize** *v* saccager.

vanilla [və'nilə] *n* vanille *f*.

vanish ['vaniʃ] *v* disparaître.

vanity ['vanəti] *n* vanité *f*. **vanity case** sac de toilette *m*.

vapour ['veipə] *n* vapeur *f*. **vaporize** *v* vaporiser.

varicose veins ['varikous] *pl n* varices *f pl*.

variety [və'raiəti] *n* variété *f*; quantité *f*. **variety show** spectacle de variétés *m*.

various ['veəriəs] *adj* divers.

varnish ['vaɪniʃ] *n* vernis *m*. *v* vernir.

vary ['veəri] *v* varier, changer. **vary from** différer de. **variable** *nf*, *adj* variable. **variant** *n* variante *f*. **variation** *n* variation *f*.

vase [vaɪz] *n* vase *m*.

vasectomy [və'sektəmi] *n* vasectomie *f*.

vast [vaɪst] *adj* vaste. **vastness** *n* immensité *f*.

vat [vat] *n* cuve *f*.

Vatican ['vatikən] *n* Vatican *m*. **Vatican City** la Cité du Vatican *f*.

vault[1] [voɪlt] *n* (*cellar*) cave *f*; (*tomb*) caveau *m*; (*bank*) coffre-fort *m*; (*arch*) voûte *f*.

vault[2] [voɪlt] *v* sauter. *n* saut *m*. **vaulting horse** cheval d'arçons *m*.

veal [viɪl] *n* veau *m*.

veer [viə] *v* tourner, virer.

vegetable ['vedʒtəbl] *n* légume *m*. *adj* végétal. **vegetable garden** potager *m*. **vegetarian** *n, adj* végétarien, -enne. **vegetation** *n* végétation *f*.

vehement ['viːəmənt] *adj* ardent; violent. **vehemence** *n* ardeur *f*; violence *f*. **vehemently** *adv* avec passion; avec violence.

vehicle ['viəkl] *n* véhicule *m*.

veil [veil] *n* voile *m*. *v* voiler.

vein [vein] *n* veine *f*.

velocity [və'losəti] *n* vélocité *f*.

velvet ['velvit] *n* velours *m*. **velvety** *adj* velouteux, velouté.

vending machine ['vendiŋ] *n* distributeur automatique *m*.

veneer [və'niə] *n* placage *m*; (*superficiality*) vernis *m*. *v* plaquer.

venerate ['venəreit] *v* vénérer. **venerable** *adj* vénérable. **veneration** *n* vénération *f*.

venereal disease [və'niəriəl] *n* maladie vénérienne *f*.

Venetian blind [və'niːʃən] *n* store vénitien *m*.

vengeance ['vendʒəns] *n* vengeance *f*. **with a vengeance** (*coll*) pour de bon.

venison ['venisn] *n* venaison *f*.

venom ['venəm] *n* venin *m*. **venomous** *adj* venimeux.

vent [vent] *n* orifice *m*, trou *m*. **give vent to** donner libre cours à. *v* décharger.

ventilate ['ventileit] *v* ventiler, aérer. **ventilation** *n* aération *f*, ventilation *f*.

ventriloquist [ven'triləkwist] *n* ventriloque *m*, *f*.

venture ['ventʃə] *n* aventure *f*; entreprise (risquée) *f*. *v* (se) risquer, (se) hasarder.

venue ['venjuɪ] *n* lieu de rendez-vous *m*.

veranda [və'randə] *n* véranda *f*.

verb [vəɪb] *n* verbe *m*. **verbal** *adj* verbal.

verdict ['vəɪdikt] *n* verdict *m*.

verge [vəɪdʒ] *n* bord *m*. **on the verge of** sur le point de; à deux doigts de. *v* **verge on** approcher de, frôler.

verify ['verifai] *v* vérifier. **verification** *n* vérification *f*.

vermin ['vəɪmin] *n* animaux nuisibles *m pl*; (*insects, people*) vermine *f*.

vermouth ['vəɪməθ] *n* vermouth *m*.

vernacular [və'nakjulə] *adj* vernaculaire. *n* langue vernaculaire *f*.

versatile ['vəɪsətail] *adj* aux talents variés; (*mind*) souple. **versatility** *n* variété de talents *f*; souplesse *f*.

verse [vəɪs] *n* (*stanza*) strophe *f*; (*poetry*) vers *m pl*; (*bible*) verset *m*.

version ['vəɪʃən] *n* version *f*.

versus ['vəɪsəs] *prep* contre.

vertebra ['vəɪtibrə] *n, pl* **-brae** vertèbre *f*. **vertebral** *adj* vertébral. **vertebrate** *nm, adj* vertébré.

vertical ['vəɪtikl] *adj* vertical. *n* verticale *f*.

vertigo ['vəɪtigou] *n* vertige *m*.

very ['veri] *adv* très, fort, bien; (*absolutely*) tout. **very much** beaucoup. *adj* (*exact*) même; (*extreme*) tout; (*mere*) seul.

vessel ['vesl] *n* vaisseau *m*.

vest [vest] *n* tricot de corps *m*; (*US*) gilet *m*.

vestibule ['vestibjuɪl] *n* vestibule *m*.

vestige ['vestidʒ] *n* vestige *m*; grain *m*.

vestry ['vestri] *n* sacristie *f*.

vet [vet] (*coll*) *n* vétérinaire *m*, *f*. *v* examiner de près.

veteran ['vetərən] *n* vétéran *m*. **veteran car** voiture d'époque *f*. **war veteran** ancien combattant *m*.

veterinary ['vetərinəri] *adj* vétérinaire. **veterinary surgeon** vétérinaire *m, f*.

veto ['viːtou] *n* veto *m*. *v* mettre son veto à.

vex [veks] *v* contrarier, fâcher. **vexation** *n* ennui *m*.

via [vaiə] *prep* par, via.

viable ['vaiəbl] *adj* viable. **viability** *n* viabilité *f*.

viaduct ['vaiədʌkt] *n* viaduc *m*.

vibrate [vai'breit] *v* vibrer. **vibration** *n* vibration *f*.

vicar ['vikə] *n* pasteur *m*. **vicarage** *n* presbytère *m*.

vicarious [vi'keəriəs] *adj* délégué; indirect.

vice[1] [vais] *n* (*evil*) vice *m*; (*fault*) défaut *m*.

vice[2] [vais] *n* (*tool*) étau *m*.

vice-chancellor [vais'tʃaɪnsələ] *n* vice-chancelier *m*; (*university*) recteur *m*.

vice-consul [vais'konsl] *n* vice-consul *m*.

vice-president [vais'prezidənt] *n* vice-president, -e *m, f*.

vice versa [vaisi'vəːsə] *adv* vice versa.

vicinity [vi'sinəti] *n* environs *m pl*, alentours *m pl*.

vicious ['viʃəs] *adj* (*remark*) méchant; (*attack*) brutal; (*animal*) vicieux. **vicious circle** cercle vicieux *m*. **viciousness** *n* méchanceté *f*; brutalité *f*.

victim ['viktim] *n* victime *f*. **victimize** *v* prendre pour victime.

victory ['viktəri] *n* victoire *f*. **victorious** *adj* victorieux.

video-tape ['vidiouteip] *n* bande de magnétoscope *f*. *v* enregistrer sur magnétoscope.

vie [vai] *v* lutter, rivaliser.

Vienna [vi'enə] *n* Vienne.

view [vjuɪ] *n* vue *f*. **in view of** étant donné, vu. **viewfinder** *n* viseur *m*. **viewpoint** *n* point de vue *m*. **with a view to** dans l'intention de, afin de. *v* visiter; considérer; regarder. **viewer** *n* (*TV*) téléspectateur, -trice *m, f*; (*slides*) visionneuse *f*.

vigil ['vidʒil] *n* veille *f*. **vigilance** *n* vigilance *f*. **vigilant** *adj* vigilant.

vigour ['vigə] *n* vigueur *f*. **vigorous** *adj* vigoureux.

vile [vail] *adj* vil; abominable.

villa ['vilə] *n* villa *f*; (*country*) maison de campagne *f*.

village ['vilidʒ] *n* village *m*. **villager** *n* villageois, -e *m, f*.

villain ['vilən] *n* scélérat *m*. **villainy** *n* infamie *f*.

vindictive [vin'diktiv] *adj* vindicatif.

vine [vain] *n* vigne *f*. **vineyard** *n* vignoble *m*.

vinegar ['vinigə] *n* vinaigre *m*.

vintage ['vintidʒ] *n* (*year*) année *f*; (*harvest*) vendange *f*. **vintage car** voiture d'époque *f*. **vintage wine** grand vin *m*.

vinyl ['vainil] *n* vinyle *m*.

viola [vi'oulə] *n* alto *m*.

violate ['vaiəleit] *v* violer. **violation** *n* violation *f*.

violence ['vaiələns] *n* violence *f*. **violent** *adj* violent.

violet ['vaiəlit] *n* (*flower*) violette *f*; (*colour*) violet *m*. *adj* violet, -ette.

violin [vaiə'lin] *n* violon *m*. **violinist** *n* violoniste *m, f*.

viper ['vaipə] *n* vipère *f*.

virgin ['vəːdʒin] *nf, adj* vierge. **virginity** *n* virginité *f*.

Virgo ['vəːgou] *n* Vierge *f*.

virile ['virail] *adj* viril. **virility** *n* virilité *f*.

virtually ['vəːtʃuəli] *adv* en fait, pratiquement.

virtue ['vəːtʃuɪ] *n* vertu *f*; mérite *m*. **by virtue of** en vertu de. **virtuous** *adj* vertueux.

virus ['vaiərəs] *n* virus *m*.

visa ['viːzə] *n* visa *m*.

viscount ['vaikaunt] *n* vicomte *m*. **viscountess** *n* vicomtesse *f*.

visible ['vizəbl] *adj* visible. **visibility** *n* visibilité *f*.

vision ['viʒən] *n* vision *f*. **visionary** *n*(*m+f*), *adj* visionnaire.

visit ['vizit] *n* visite *f*; (*stay*) séjour *m*. *v* (*call on*) aller voir, rendre visite à; (*stay with*) faire un séjour chez; (*place*) aller à; (*go round*) visiter. **visitor** *n* visiteur, -euse *m, f*.

visor ['vaizə] *n* visière *f*.

visual ['viʒuəl] *adj* visuel. **visualize** *v* se représenter.

vital ['vaitl] *adj* vital. **vitality** *n* vitalité *f*. **vitally** *adv* absolument.

vitamin ['vitəmin] *n* vitamine *f*.

vivacious [vi'veiʃəs] *adj* vif, enjoué. **vivacity** *n* vivacité *f*.

vivid ['vivid] *adj* vif, éclatant; (*description*) vivant. **vividness** *n* vivacité *f*, éclat *m*, clarté *f*.

vivisection [vivi'sekʃən] *n* vivisection *f.*
vixen ['viksn] *n* renarde *f.*
vocabulary [və'kabjuləri] *n* vocabulaire *m*; glossaire *m.*
vocal ['voukəl] *adj* vocal. **vocalist** *n* chanteur, -euse *m, f.*
vocation [vou'keiʃən] *n* vocation *f.* **vocational** *adj* professionnel.
vociferous [və'sifərəs] *adj* bruyant.
vodka ['vodkə] *n* vodka *f.*
voice [vois] *n* voix *f. v* exprimer.
void [void] *n* vide *m. adj* vide; (*law*) nul, nulle. *v* évacuer.
volatile ['volətail] *adj* (*chem*) volatil; (*person*) versatile; (*situation*) explosif.
volcano [vol'keinou] *n* volcan *m.* **volcanic** *adj* volcanique.
volley ['voli] *n* volée *f*; torrent *m.* **volleyball** *n* volley *m. v* (*sport*) renvoyer une volée.
volt [voult] *n* volt *m.* **voltage** *n* voltage *m*, tension *f.*
volume ['voljum] *n* volume *m.*
volunteer [volən'tiə] *n* volontaire *m, f. v* s'offrir; offrir *or* fournir spontanément. **voluntary** *adj* volontaire; (*unpaid*) bénévole.
voluptuous [və'lʌptʃuəs] *adj* voluptueux. **voluptuousness** *n* volupté *f.*
vomit ['vomit] *n* vomissement *m. v* vomir.
voodoo ['vuːduː] *nm, adj* vaudou.
voracious [və'reiʃəs] *adj* vorace; avide. **voracity** *n* voracité *f.*
vote [vout] *n* vote *m*, voix *f.* **vote of thanks** discours de remerciement *m. v* voter; élire. **voter** *n* électeur, -trice *m, f.*
vouch [vautʃ] *v* **vouch for** se porter garant de, garantir.
voucher ['vautʃə] *n* bon *m*; (*receipt*) reçu *m.*
vow [vau] *n* vœu *m. v* jurer, vouer.
vowel ['vauəl] *n* voyelle *f.*
voyage ['voiidʒ] *n* voyage (par mer) *m. v* traverser, voyager (par mer).
vulgar ['vʌlgə] *adj* vulgaire, grossier. **vulgarity** *n* vulgarité *f*, grossièreté *f.*
vulnerable ['vʌlnərəbl] *adj* vulnérable.
vulture ['vʌltʃə] *n* vautour *m.*

W

wad [wod] *n* tampon *m*; (*papers*) liasse *f.*
wadding *n* bourre *f*, rembourrage *m*, ouate *f.*
waddle ['wodl] *v* se dandiner. *n* dandinement *m.*
wade [weid] *v* avancer dans l'eau.
wafer ['weifə] *n* gaufrette *f.* **wafer-thin** *adj* mince comme du papier à cigarette.
waft [woft] *n* (*carry*) porter; (*float*) flotter. *n* bouffée *f.*
wag [wag] *v* agiter, remuer. *n* remuement *m.*
wage [weidʒ] *n* salaire *m. v* **wage war** faire la guerre.
wager ['weidʒə] *n* pari *m. v* parier.
waggle ['wagl] *v* agiter, frétiller.
wagon ['wagən] *n* chariot *m*; (*rail*) wagon *m.*
waif [weif] *n* enfant abandonné *m.*
wail [weil] *n* gémissement *m*, vagissement *m. v* gémir, vagir.
waist [weist] *n* taille *f*, ceinture *f.* **waistband** *n* ceinture *f.* **waistcoat** *n* gilet *m.* **waistline** *n* taille *f.*
wait [weit] *n* attente *f.* **lie in wait for** guetter. *v* attendre; servir. **waiter** *n* garçon *m.* **waiting** *n* attente *f.* **waiting-list** *n* liste d'attente *f.* **waiting-room** *n* salle d'attente *f.* **waitress** *n* serveuse *f.*
waive [weiv] *v* renoncer à, abandonner.
wake¹ [weik] *n* sillage *m.*
*wake² [weik] *v also* **wake up** (se) réveiller.
Wales [weilz] *n* pays de Galles *m.*
walk [woːk] *n* promenade *f*; (*gait*) démarche *f. v* (faire) marcher; (*go on foot*) aller à pied; (*for pleasure*) se promener; (*distance*) faire à pied. **walkout** *n* grève surprise *f.* **walkover** *n* walkover *m*, victoire facile *f.* **walker** *n* promeneur, -euse *m, f.* **walking** *n* marche à pied *f.* **walking-stick** *n* canne *f.*
wall [woːl] *n* mur *m*, muraille *f. v* entourer d'un mur.
wallet ['wolit] *n* portefeuille *m.*
wallflower ['woːlflauə] *n* giroflée *f.* **be a wallflower** faire tapisserie.
wallop ['woləp] (*coll*) *n* coup *m*, beigne *f. v* cogner, rosser. **walloping** *adj* sacré.
wallow ['wolou] *v* se vautrer.
wallpaper ['woːlpeipə] *n* papier peint *m. v* tapisser.
walnut ['woːlnʌt] *n* (*nut*) noix *f*; (*tree, wood*) noyer *m.*

walrus ['wɔɪlrəs] n morse m.
waltz [wɔɪlts] n valse f. v valser.
wan [wɒn] adj pâle.
wand [wɒnd] n baguette f.
wander ['wɒndə] v errer; (stray) s'égarer. n tour m.
wane [weɪn] v décroître; diminuer.
wangle ['waŋgl] (coll) n combine f. v resquiller, se débrouiller pour avoir.
want [wɒnt] n (lack) manque m; (need) besoin m. **for want of** faute de. v vouloir, désirer; (ask for) demander; (need) avoir besoin de. **wanted** adj (police) recherché.
wanton ['wɒntən] adj (woman) dévergondé; (cruelty, etc.) gratuit. **wantonness** n dévergondage m; gratuité f.
war [wɔɪ] n guerre f. **be on the war-path** chercher la bagarre. **war-dance** n danse guerrière f. **warfare** n guerre f. **war memorial** monument aux morts m. **warship** n navire de guerre m. **wartime** n temps de guerre m.
warble ['wɔɪbl] n gazouillis m. v gazouiller. **warbler** n oiseau chanteur m.
ward [wɔɪd] n (hospital) salle f; section électorale f; (law) pupille m, f. v **ward off** parer.
warden ['wɔɪdn] n directeur, -trice m, f; gardien, -enne m, f.
warder ['wɔɪdə] n gardien de prison m. **wardress** n gardienne de prison f.
wardrobe ['wɔɪdroub] n garde-robe f; (theatre) costumes m pl.
warehouse ['weəhaus] n entrepôt m. v entreposer.
warm [wɔɪm] adj chaud; (welcome, etc.) chaleureux. v (se) chauffer. **warm up** s'échauffer. **warming-pan** n bassinoire f. **warmth** n chaleur f; cordialité f.
warn [wɔɪn] v prévenir, avertir. **warning** n avertissement m; (written) avis m. **warning light** voyant avertisseur m.
warp [wɔɪp] v (se) voiler, gauchir; pervertir; débaucher. n voilure f; (cloth) chaîne f.
warrant ['wɒrənt] n (police) mandat m; justification f; (voucher) bon m. v justifier; garantir. **warranty** n garantie f.
warren ['wɒrən] n garenne f.
warrior ['wɒriə] n guerrier, -ère m, f.
Warsaw ['wɔɪsɔɪ] n Varsovie.
wart [wɔɪt] n verrue f.
wary ['weəri] adj prudent, précautionneux.
was [wɒz] V **be**.

wash [wɒʃ] n (clothes) lavage m; (face, etc.) toilette f; (paint) badigeon m, lavis m. v (se) laver. **wash-basin** n lavabo m. **wash off** or **out** (faire) partir au lavage. **wash-out** n (slang) fiasco m. **wash-room** n toilettes f pl. **wash up** faire la vaisselle. **washable** adj lavable. **washing** n lessive f. **washing-machine** n machine à laver f. **washing-powder** n lessive f. **washing-up** n vaisselle f.
washer ['wɒʃə] n rondelle f.
Washington ['wɒʃɪŋtən] n Washington.
wasp [wɒsp] n guêpe f.
waste [weist] n gaspillage m; (time) perte f; (scrap) déchets m pl; désert m. adj de rebut; (lost) perdu; (extra) superflu. **waste disposal unit** broyeur d'ordures m. **waste land** terrain vague m. **waste paper** vieux papiers m pl. **waste-paper basket** corbeille f. v gaspiller; perdre. **waste away** dépérir. **wasteful** adj gaspilleur, -euse; peu économique.
watch [wɒtʃ] n (time) montre f; garde f; surveillance f; (naut) quart m. **keep watch** faire le guet. **watch-dog** n chien de garde m. **watch-strap** n bracelet de montre m. v regarder; surveiller; faire attention (à); guetter. **watchful** adj vigilant.
water ['wɔɪtə] n eau f. v (plant, etc.) arroser; (eyes) larmoyer. **water down** couper d'eau. **watery** adj aqueux; (tea, etc.) trop faible; pâle; insipide.
water-biscuit n craquelin m.
water-closet n cabinets m pl.
water-colour n aquarelle f.
watercress ['wɔɪtəkres] n cresson m.
waterfall ['wɔɪtəfɔɪl] n chute d'eau f.
water-ice n sorbet m.
watering-can n arrosoir m.
water-lily n nénuphar m.
waterlogged ['wɔɪtəlogd] adj (land) détrempé; (wood) imprégné d'eau.
water-main n conduite principale d'eau f.
watermark ['wɔɪtəmaɪk] n (paper) filigrane m; (tide) laisse de haute mer f.
water-melon n melon d'eau m.
water-pistol n pistolet à eau m.
waterproof ['wɔɪtəpruːf] nm, adj imperméable. v imperméabiliser.
water-rate n taxe sur l'eau f.
watershed ['wɔɪtəʃed] n moment critique m; (geog) ligne de partage des eaux f.
water-ski v faire du ski nautique. n ski nautique m. **water-skiing** n ski nautique m.

watertight ['wɔːtətait] *adj* étanche; (*excuse, etc.*) inattaquable.

water-way *n* voie navigable *f*.

waterworks ['wɔːtəwɜːks] *n* système hydraulique *m*.

watt [wɔt] *n* watt *m*.

wave [weiv] *n* (*sea*) vague *f*; (*hair*) ondulation *f*; (*phys, radio, etc.*) onde *f*; geste de la main *m*. **waveband** *n* bande de fréquences *f*. **wavelength** *n* longueur d'ondes *f*. *v* agiter, brandir; faire signe de la main; onduler. **wavy** *adj* (*hair*) ondulé; (*line*) onduleux.

waver ['weivə] *v* vaciller; trembler; (*weaken*) lâcher pied.

wax[1] [waks] *n* cire *f*. **waxwork** *n* personnage en cire *m*. **waxworks** *n* musée de cire *m*. *v* cirer. **waxy** *adj* cireux.

wax[2] [waks] *v* croître.

way [wei] *n* (*path*) chemin *m*, voie *f*; (*manner*) façon *f*, manière *f*; passage *m*; distance *f*; direction *f*, sens *m*. **be in the way** gêner. **by the way** à propos. **give way** céder; laisser la priorité. **on the way** en route. **this way** par ici. **under way** en cours, en marche. **way in** entrée *f*. **way out** sortie *f*.

*waylay [wei'lei] *v* arrêter au passage.

wayside ['weisaid] *n* bord de la route. *adj* au bord de la route.

wayward ['weiwəd] *adj* capricieux, rebelle.

we [wiː] *pron* nous.

weak [wiːk] *adj* faible. **weaken** *v* faiblir, (s')affaiblir. **weakling** *n* gringalet *m*. **weakness** *n* faiblesse *f*; point faible *m*; (*liking*) faible *m*.

wealth [welθ] *n* richesse *f*; abondance *f*. **wealthy** *adj* riche.

wean [wiːn] *v* (*baby*) sevrer. **wean off** détourner de.

weapon ['wepən] *n* arme *f*.

wear [weə] *n* usage *m*; (*deterioration*) usure *f*; (*clothes*) vêtements *m pl*. **wear and tear** usure *f*. *v* porter; (s')user. **wear off** passer, se dissiper. **wear out** épuiser.

weary ['wiəri] *adj* las, lasse. *v* (se) lasser. **wearily** *adv* avec lassitude. **weariness** *n* lassitude *f*.

weasel ['wiːzl] *n* belette *f*.

weather ['weðə] *n* temps *m*. **weather-beaten** *adj* hâlé. **weathercock** *n* girouette *f*. **weather forecast** prévisions météorologiques *f pl*. *v* (*survive*) réchapper à.

weave [wiːv] *v* tisser; entrelacer;

(*through traffic, etc.*) se faufiler. *n also* **weaving** tissage *m*.

web [web] *n* (*spider*) toile *f*; (*on feet*) palmure *f*; (*cloth*) tissu *m*. **web-footed** *adj* palmipède.

wedding ['wediŋ] *n* mariage *m*; noces *f pl*. **wedding-dress** *n* robe de mariée *f*. **wedding-ring** *n* alliance *f*.

wedge [wedʒ] *n* cale *f*, coin *m*. *v* caler; (*push in*) enfoncer; (*jam*) coincer.

Wednesday ['wenzdi] *n* mercredi *m*.

weed [wiːd] *n* mauvaise herbe *f*. **weedkiller** *n* désherbant *m*. *v* désherber. **weeding** *n* désherbage *m*.

week [wiːk] *n* semaine *f*. **a week today/tomorrow** aujourd'hui/demain en huit. **weekday** *n* jour de semaine *m*. **weekend** *n* week-end *m*.

weekly ['wiːkli] *adv* chaque semaine, tous les huit jours. *nm, adj* hebdomadaire.

*weep [wiːp] *v* pleurer. **weeping willow** saule pleureur *m*.

weigh [wei] *v* peser. **weighbridge** *n* pont-bascule *m*. **weight** *n* poids *m*. **lose weight** maigrir. **put on weight** grossir. **weight-lifting** *n* haltérophilie *f*. **weighting** *n* indemnité *f*. **weightlessness** *n* apesanteur *f*.

weir [wiə] *n* barrage *m*.

weird [wiəd] *adj* surnaturel; bizarre. **weirdness** *n* étrangeté *f*.

welcome ['welkəm] *adj* opportun. **be welcome** être le bienvenu. **you're welcome!** (*acknowledging thanks*) il n'y a pas de quoi! *n* accueil *m*. *v* accueillir; souhaiter la bienvenue à; (*news, etc.*) se réjouir de.

weld [weld] *v* souder. *n* soudure *f*. **welder** *n* soudeur *m*. **welding** *n* soudage *m*.

welfare ['welfeə] *n* bien *m*. **Welfare State** Etat-providence *m*. **welfare work** travail social *m*.

well[1] [wel] *n* puits *m*. *v* **well up** monter.

well[2] [wel] *adj, adv* bien. **as well** aussi.

well-behaved *adj* sage, obéissant.

well-being *n* bien-être *m*.

well-bred *adj* bien élevé.

well-built *adj* solide.

well-informed *adj* bien informé; instruit.

wellington ['weliŋtən] *n* botte de caoutchouc *f*.

well-known *adj* célèbre.

well-meaning *adj* bien intentionné.

well-nigh *adv* presque.

well-off *adj* riche, aisé.

well-paid adj bien payé.
well-spent adj (time) bien employé.
well-spoken adj poli. **be well-spoken** avoir une élocution soignée.
well-timed adj opportun.
well-to-do adj aisé, riche.
well-trodden adj battu.
well-worn adj usagé.
Welsh [welʃ] nm, adj gallois. **the Welsh** les Gallois m pl.
went [went] V go.
wept [wept] V weep.
were [wəɪ] V be.
west [west] n ouest m. **the West** l'Occident m. adj also **westerly** occidental; ouest invar; à or de l'ouest. adv à l'ouest, vers l'ouest. **westbound** adj ouest invar.
western ['westən] adj ouest invar; de l'ouest; occidental. n (film) western m.
wet [wet] adj mouillé; (damp) humide; (soaked) trempé; (weather) pluvieux. **wet blanket** rabat-joie m invar. **wet suit** combinaison de plongée f. n pluie f. v mouiller.
whack [wak] (coll) n grand coup m. v donner un grand coup à.
whale [weil] n baleine f.
wharf [woɪf] n quai m.
what [wot] pron (subject) (qu'est-ce) qui; (object) (qu'est-ce) que; (after prep) quoi; (relative) ce qui, ce que. adj quel, quelle. interj quoi!
whatever [wot'evə] pron tout ce que, quoi que. adj, adv quel que soit. **none whatever** pas le moindre.
wheat [wiit] n blé m, froment m.
wheel [wiil] n roue f. **wheelbarrow** n brouette f. **wheelchair** n fauteuil roulant m. v pousser, rouler; (turn) tournoyer.
wheeze [witz] n respiration bruyante f. v respirer bruyamment. **wheezy** adj poussif, asthmatique.
whelk [welk] n buccin m.
when [wen] adv quand. conj quand, lorsque; (relative) où, que. **whenever** conj chaque fois que.
where [weə] adv où. conj (là) où. **whereabouts** adv où. **whereas** conj alors que. **whereupon** adv sur quoi. **wherever** conj où que; (anywhere) là où; (everywhere) partout où.
whether ['weðə] conj si.
which [witʃ] pron lequel, laquelle; (the one that) celui qui or que, celle qui or

que; (relative) (ce) qui, (ce) que. adj quel, quelle.
whichever [witʃ'evə] pron (quel que soit) celui qui or que, (quelle que soit) celle qui or que. adj n'importe quel; quel que soit ... que.
whiff [wif] n bouffée f, odeur f.
while [wail] conj pendant que; (as long as) tant que. n quelque temps. v **while away** passer.
whim [wim] n caprice m.
whimper ['wimpə] n faible geignement m. v pleurnicher, geindre faiblement.
whimsical ['wimzikl] adj capricieux; étrange.
whine [wain] n gémissement m; (siren, etc.) plainte f. v gémir; (complain) se lamenter.
whip [wip] n fouet m. **whip-round** n (coll) collecte f. v fouetter. **whip away/out** enlever/sortir brusquement. **whipping** n correction f.
whippet ['wipit] n whippet m.
whirl [wəɪl] n tourbillon m. v (faire) tourbillonner. **whirlpool** n tourbillon m. **whirlwind** n tornade f, trombe f.
whirr [wəɪ] n (wings) bruissement m; (machinery) vrombissement m. v bruire; vrombir.
whisk [wisk] n (cookery) fouet m. v fouetter; (snatch) enlever brusquement.
whisker ['wiskə] n poil m. **whiskers** pl n moustaches f pl.
whisky ['wiski] n whisky m.
whisper ['wispə] v chuchoter. n chuchotement m.
whist [wist] n whist m. **whist drive** tournoi de whist m.
whistle ['wisl] n sifflet m; (sound) sifflement m. v siffler.
Whit [wit] n also **Whitsun** la Pentecôte f. adj de Pentecôte.
white [wait] adj blanc, blanche. **white elephant** objet superflu m. n blanc m; (person) Blanc, Blanche m, f. **whiten** v blanchir. **whiteness** n blancheur f.
whitewash ['waitwoʃ] n blanc de chaux m. v blanchir à la chaux; (cover up) justifier, blanchir.
whiting ['waitiŋ] n merlan m.
whittle ['witl] v tailler au couteau. **whittle down** (expenses, etc.) rogner.
whizz [wiz] n sifflement m. **whizz-kid** (coll) petit prodige m. v aller comme une flèche.

who [hu:] *pron* (qui est-ce) qui. **whoever** *pron* quiconque; qui que ce soit qui *or* que.

whole [houl] *n* totalité *f*; tout *m*. **on the whole** dans l'ensemble. *adj* entier; intact. **wholehearted** *adj* sans réserve. **wholeheartedly** *adv* de tout cœur. **wholemeal** *adj* (*flour*) brut; (*bread*) complet, -ète. **wholesome** *adj* sain.

wholesale ['houlseil] *n* vente en gros *f*. *adj* de gros; en masse, en bloc. *adv* en gros; en masse.

whom [hu:m] *pron* qui; (*relative*) que, lequel, laquelle. **of whom** dont.

whooping cough ['hu:piŋ] *n* coqueluche *f*.

whore [ho:] *n* (*derog*) putain *f*.

whose [hu:z] *pron* à qui. *adj* à qui, de qui; (*relative*) dont.

why [wai] *adv, conj* pourquoi. *interj* tiens!

wick [wik] *n* mèche *f*.

wicked ['wikid] *adj* mauvais, méchant, vilain. **wickedness** *n* méchanceté *f*.

wicker ['wikə] *n* osier *m*.

wicket ['wikit] *n* (*cricket*) guichet *m*.

wide [waid] *adj* large; grand; vaste. *adv* loin du but. **wide awake** bien éveillé. **widespread** *adj* répandu. **widely** *adv* largement; (*much*) beaucoup; généralement; radicalement. **widen** *v* (s')élargir.

widow ['widou] *n* veuve *f*. **be widowed** devenir veuf *or* veuve. **widower** *n* veuf *m*.

width [widθ] *n* largeur *f*.

wield [wi:ld] *v* manier; brandir; exercer.

wife [waif] *n* femme *f*, épouse *f*.

wig [wig] *n* perruque *f*.

wiggle ['wigl] *v* tortiller; agiter, remuer. **wiggly** *adj* (*line*) ondulé.

wild [waild] *adj* sauvage; violent; (*unrestrained*) fou, folle. **like wildfire** comme une traînée de poudre. **wildlife** *n* faune *f*. **wildly** *adv* violemment; fiévreusement; follement.

wilderness ['wildənəs] *n* désert *m*; région sauvage *f*.

wilful ['wilfəl] *adj* (*stubborn*) entêté; volontaire; prémédité.

will[1] [wil] *aux translated by future tense.*

will[2] [wil] *v* vouloir; léguer. *n* volonté *f*; testament *m*. **against one's will** à contrecœur. **willpower** *n* volonté *f*.

willing ['wiliŋ] *adj* de bonne volonté. **be willing to** être disposé à, vouloir bien. **willingly** *adv* volontiers. **willingness** *n* bonne volonté *f*, empressement *m*.

willow ['wilou] *n* saule *m*. **willow-pattern** *n* motif chinois *m*. **willowy** *adj* svelte.

wilt [wilt] *v* (se) faner, (se) dessécher; (*person*) s'affaiblir.

wily ['waili] *adj* rusé, malin, -igne.

***win** [win] *n* victoire *f*. *v* gagner. **winner** *n* gagnant, -e *m, f*. **winning** *adj* gagnant; (*smile, etc.*) charmeur, -euse. **winnings** *pl n* gains *m pl*.

wince [wins] *v* tressaillir; grimacer. *n* tressaillement *m*; grimace *f*.

winch [wintʃ] *n* treuil *m*. *v* **winch up/down** monter/descendre au treuil.

wind[1] [wind] *n* vent *m*; (*breath*) souffle *m*; (*med*) vents *m pl*. *v* couper le souffle à. **windy** *adj* (*place*) battu par les vents; (*day*) de vent.

***wind**[2] [waind] *v* enrouler; (*clock, etc.*) remonter; serpenter. **wind up** (se) terminer; (*comm*) liquider; (*clock, etc.*) remonter. **winder** *n* remontoir *m*. **winding** *adj* sinueux.

wind-break *n* pare-vent *m invar*.

windfall ['windfo:l] *n* fruit abattu par le vent *m*; (*surprise*) aubaine *f*.

wind instrument *n* instrument à vent *m*.

windlass ['windləs] *n* guindeau *m*.

windmill ['wind,mil] *n* moulin à vent *m*.

window ['windou] *n* fenêtre *f*; (*car*) vitre *f*; (*shop*) vitrine *f*; (*cashier's*) guichet *m*. **window-box** *n* jardinière *f*. **window-cleaner** *n* laveur, -euse de vitres *m, f*. **window-dresser** *n* étalagiste *m, f*. **window-shopping** *n* lèche-vitrine *m*. **window-sill** *n* (*inside*) appui de fenêtre *m*; (*outside*) rebord de fenêtre *m*.

windpipe ['windpaip] *n* (*anat*) trachée *f*.

windshield ['windʃi:ld] *n* pare-brise *m invar*. **windshield wiper** essuie-glace *m invar*.

wind-sock *n* manche à air *f*.

windswept ['windswept] *adj* venteux, balayé par le vent.

wind tunnel *n* tunnel aérodynamique *m*.

wine [wain] *n* vin *m*. **wineglass** *n* verre à vin *m*. **wine list** carte des vins *f*. **winetasting** *n* dégustation *f*. **wine waiter** sommelier *m*.

wing [wiŋ] *n* aile *f*. **wing commander** lieutenant-colonel *m*. **wing-mirror** *n* rétroviseur de côté *m*. **wings** *pl n* (*theatre*) coulisses *f pl*. **wingspan** *n* envergure *f*.

wink [wiŋk] *n* clin d'œil. *v* faire un clin d'œil; (*light*) clignoter.

winkle ['wiŋkl] n bigorneau m. v **winkle out** extirper.

winter ['wintə] n hiver m. v hiverner. **wintry** adj d'hiver.

wipe [waip] n coup de torchon m. v essuyer. **wipe out** effacer; anéantir.

wire [waiə] n fil m; télégramme m. **wire-brush** n brosse métallique f. **wire-cutters** pl n cisaille f sing. **wireless** n T.S.F. f. **wire netting** treillis métallique m. v télégraphier. **wiring** n installation électrique f. **wiry** adj (hair) dru; (person) noueux.

wisdom ['wizdəm] n sagesse f; prudence f. **wisdom tooth** dent de sagesse f.

wise [waiz] adj sage; prudent; (learned) savant.

wish [wiʃ] v souhaiter, désirer. n souhait m, vœu m; désir m. **wishbone** n bréchet m.

wisp [wisp] n brin m; (hair) fine mèche f; (smoke) mince volute f. **wispy** adj fin.

wistful ['wistfəl] adj nostalgique, mélancolique. **wistfully** adv avec nostalgie or mélancolie.

wit [wit] n esprit m, intelligence f; (person) homme d'esprit, femme d'esprit m, f. **be at one's wits' end** ne plus savoir que faire.

witch [witʃ] n sorcière f. **witchcraft** n sorcellerie f. **witch-doctor** n sorcier m. **witch-hunt** n chasse aux sorcières f.

with [wið] prep avec; (having) à; (because of) de; (despite) malgré.

*__withdraw** [wið'drɔː] v (se) retirer. **withdrawal** n retrait m, retraction f; (med) manque m. **withdrawn** adj renfermé.

wither ['wiðə] v (se) flétrir, (se) faner. **withered** adj flétri; desséché; (limb) atrophié. **withering** adj (look) méprisant; (remark) cinglant.

*__withhold** [wið'hould] v (keep back) retenir; (put off) remettre; refuser; (hide) cacher.

within [wi'ðin] adv dedans, à l'intérieur. prep à l'intérieur de; dans; (less than) (à) moins de.

without [wi'ðaut] prep sans. adv à l'extérieur.

*__withstand** [wið'stand] v résister à.

witness ['witnis] n (person) témoin m; (evidence) témoignage m. v (accident, etc.) être le témoin de; (document) attester l'authenticité de. **witness to** témoigner de.

witty ['witi] adj spirituel. **witticism** n mot d'esprit m.

wizard ['wizəd] n magicien m.

wobble ['wobl] v (faire) trembler, (faire) osciller, (faire) branler. **wobbly** adj bancal.

woke [wouk] V **wake²**.

woken ['woukn] V **wake²**.

wolf [wulf] n loup m. **wolfhound** n chien-loup m. **wolf-whistle** n sifflement admiratif m. v **wolf down** engloutir.

woman ['wumən] n, pl **women** femme f. **Women's Lib** (coll) M.L.F. m. **womanhood** n féminité f. **womanly** adj féminin.

womb [wuːm] n utérus m.

won [wʌn] V **win**.

wonder ['wʌndə] n émerveillement m; miracle m, merveille f. **no wonder** (ce n'est) pas étonnant. v se demander; (muse) songer; (marvel) s'émerveiller. **wonderful** adj merveilleux.

wood [wud] n bois m. **wooden** adj de or en bois; (stiff) raide. **woody** adj boisé; (stem) ligneux.

woodcock ['wudkɔk] n bécasse f.

woodcut ['wudkʌt] n gravure sur bois f.

woodland ['wudlənd] n région boisée f.

wood-louse n, pl **-lice** cloporte m.

woodpecker ['wudpekə] n pic m.

wood-pigeon n ramier m.

wood-shed n bûcher m.

wood-wind n (music) bois m pl.

woodwork ['wudwəːk] n menuiserie f.

woodworm ['wudwəːm] n vers du bois m.

wool [wul] n laine f. **woollen** adj de or en laine. **woolly** adj laineux; (ideas) confus.

word [wəːd] n mot m, parole f. **be word-perfect** in savoir sur le bout des doigts. **in other words** autrement dit. v formuler, rédiger. **wording** n termes m pl. **wordy** adj verbeux.

wore [wɔː] V **wear**.

work [wəːk] n travail m, œuvre f, ouvrage m. **out of work** en chômage. **work-force** n main d'œuvre f. **workman** n ouvrier m. **workmanship** n maîtrise f. **work permit** permis de travail m. **works** n usine f. **workshop** n atelier m. **work-to-rule** n grève du zèle f. v travailler; (machine, etc.) (faire) marcher; exploiter. **work out** résoudre; (plan) élaborer; calculer. **worker** n travailleur, -euse m, f. **working-class** adj ouvrier. **workings** pl n mécanisme m.

world [wɜːld] *n* monde *m*. **First/Second World War** Première/Deuxième guerre mondiale *f*. **world-wide** *adj* mondial. **worldly** *adj* terrestre; matérialiste.

worm [wɜːm] *n* ver *m*.

worn [wɔːn] *V* **wear**.

worry ['wʌri] *n* souci *m*. *v* (s')inquiéter; (*sheep*) harceler. **don't worry!** ne vous en faites pas! **worried** *adj* inquiet, -ète.

worse [wɜːs] *adj* pire, plus mauvais. *adv* plus mal. **get worse** empirer, se détériorer. **to make matters worse** pour comble de malheur. *n* pire *m*. **worsen** *v* empirer, se détériorer.

worship ['wɜːʃip] *n* adoration *f*; culte *m*. *v* adorer, vénérer; faire ses dévotions.

worst [wɜːst] *adj* le pire, la pire, les plus mauvais, la plus mauvaise. *adv* le plus mal. *n* pire *m*. **at worst** au pis aller.

worsted ['wustid] *n* worsted *m*.

worth [wɜːθ] *n* valeur *f*. *adj* **be worth** valoir. **be worth it** valoir la peine. **worthwhile** *adj* qui en vaut la peine; utile; notable. **worthless** *adj* qui ne vaut rien. **worthy** *adj* digne; (*effort, cause*) louable.

would [wud] *aux translated by conditional or imperfect tense*.

wound[1] [waund] *V* **wind**[2].

wound[2] [wuːnd] *n* blessure *f*. *v* blesser.

wove [wouv] *V* **weave**.

woven ['wouvn] *V* **weave**.

wrangle ['raŋgl] *n* dispute *f*. *v* se disputer.

wrap [rap] *v* envelopper; (*parcel*) emballer. **wrapper** *n* papier *m*. **wrapping** *n* emballage *m*. **wrapping paper** papier d'emballage *m*; (*fancy*) papier cadeau *m*.

wreath [riːθ] *n* guirlande *f*, couronne *f*.

wreck [rek] *n* (*ship*) naufrage *m*; (*car*) voiture accidenté *f*; (*person*) épave *f*. *v* démolir, détruire; (*hopes, etc.*) ruiner, briser. **wreckage** *n* débris *m pl*.

wren [ren] *n* roitelet *m*.

wrench [rentʃ] *n* (*tool*) clef à écrous *f*; mouvement de torsion *m*; (*emotional*) déchirement *m*. *v* tirer violemment, arracher; (*med*) tordre.

wrestle ['resl] *v* lutter. **wrestle with** (*problem*) se débattre avec. **wrestler** *n* lutteur, -euse *m*, *f*; catcheur, -euse *m*, *f*. **wrestling** *n* lutte *f*, catch *m*.

wretch [retʃ] *n* malheureux, -euse *m*, *f*; misérable *m*, *f*. **wretched** *adj* misérable; (*coll: annoying*) maudit.

wriggle ['rigl] *v* (se) tortiller, remuer; (*fish*) frétiller.

***wring** [riŋ] *v* tordre; (*wet clothes*) essorer. **wringer** *n* essoreuse *f*. **wringing wet** trempé.

wrinkle ['riŋkl] *n* ride *f*; (*in cloth*) pli *m*. *v* rider; (se) plisser.

wrist [rist] *n* poignet *m*. **wrist-watch** *n* montre-bracelet *f*.

writ [rit] *n* acte judiciaire *m*. **issue a writ against** assigner.

***write** [rait] *v* écrire. **writer** *n* auteur *m*, écrivain *m*. **writing** *n* écriture *f*. **in writing** par écrit. **writing-case** *n* correspondancier *m*. **writing-pad** *n* bloc-notes *m*. **writing-paper** *n* papier à lettres *m*.

writhe [raið] *v* se tordre, frémir.

written ['ritn] *V* **write**.

wrong [roŋ] *adj* (*bad*) mal; erroné; incorrect, faux, fausse; (*end, side, etc.*) mauvais. **be wrong** avoir tort, se tromper; (*amiss*) ne pas aller. *adv* mal. *n* mal *m*, tort *m*; injustice *f*. **wrongful** *adj* injustifié.

wrought iron [ˌrɔːtˈaiən] *n* fer forgé *m*.

wrote [rout] *V* **write**.

wrung [rʌŋ] *V* **wring**.

wry [rai] *adj* désabusé.

X

xenophobia [ˌzenəˈfoubiə] *n* xénophobie *f*. **xenophobic** *adj* xénophobe.

Xerox ® ['ziəroks] *n* (*machine*) photocopieuse *f*; (*copy*) photocopie *f*. *v* photocopier.

Xmas ['krisməs] *V* **Christmas**.

X-ray ['eksrei] *n* (*photo*) radio *f*; (*ray*) rayon X *m*. **have an X-ray** se faire radiographier. *v* radiographier.

xylophone ['zailəfoun] *n* xylophone *m*.

Y

yacht [jot] *n* yacht *m*. **yachting** *n* yachting *m*.

yank [jaŋk] *n* coup sec *m*. *v* tirer d'un coup sec.

yap [jap] *v* japper. *n* jappement *m*.

yard [jɑɪd] *n* cour *f*; (*site*) chantier *m*.

yarn [jɑɪn] *n* fil *m*; (*tale*) histoire *f*.

yawn [jɔɪn] *v* bâiller; (*hole*) s'ouvrir. *n* bâillement *m*.

year [jiə] *n* an *m*, année *f*. **yearly** *adj* annuel.

yearn [jɜɪn] *v* languir (après), aspirer (à). **yearning** *n* désir ardent *m*, envie *f*.

yeast [jiɪst] *n* levure *f*.

yell [jel] *n* hurlement *m*. *v* hurler.

yellow ['jelou] *nm, adj* jaune. *v* jaunir.

yelp [jelp] *v* glapir, japper. *n* glapissement *m*, jappement *m*.

yes [jes] *adv* oui; (*after negative*) si. *n* oui *m invar*.

yesterday ['jestədi] *nm, adv* hier. **the day before yesterday** avant-hier *m*.

yet [jet] *adv* encore; (*already*) déjà. *conj* cependant, toutefois.

yew [juɪ] *n* if *m*.

yield [jiɪld] *v* produire, rapporter; céder. *n* production *f*, rapport *m*.

yodel ['joudl] *v* jodler. *n* tyrolienne *f*.

yoga ['jougə] *n* yoga *m*.

yoghurt ['jogət] *n* yaourt *m*.

yoke [jouk] *n* joug *m*; (*dress*) empièce-ment *m*. *v* accoupler.

yolk [jouk] *n* jaune *m*.

yonder ['jondə] *adv* là-bas.

you [juɪ] *pron* (*subject: fam*) tu; (*subject: fml*) vous; (*after prep*) toi, vous; (*before verb*) te, vous; (*impersonal*) on.

young [jʌŋ] *adj* jeune. *pl n* (*people*) jeunes *m pl*; (*animals*) petits *m pl*. **youngster** *n* jeune *m*.

your [jɔɪ] *adj* (*fam*) ton, ta, (*pl*) tes; (*pl or fml*) votre, (*pl*) vos; (*impersonal*) son, sa, (*pl*) ses. **yours** *pron* (*fam*) le tien, la tienne; (*pl or fml*) le vôtre, la vôtre.

yourself [jəˈself] *pron* (*fam*) te; (*pl or fml*) vous; (*impersonal*) se; (*emphatic*) toi-même, vous-même, soi-même. **by yourself** tout seul.

youth [juɪθ] *n* jeunesse *f*; (*boy*) jeune homme *m*. **youth hostel** auberge de la jeunesse *f*.

yo-yo ['joujou] *n* yo-yo *m*.

Yugoslavia [juɪgou'slaɪviə] *n* Yougoslavie *f*. **Yugoslav** *adj* yougoslave; *n* Yougos-lave *m, f*. **Yugoslavian** *adj* yougoslave.

Z

Zaire [zɑɪˈiɪə] *n* Zaïre *m*.

zany ['zeini] *adj* (*coll*) toqué.

zeal [ziɪl] *n* zèle *m*. **zealous** *adj* zélé; dévoué.

zebra ['zebrə] *n* zèbre *m*. **zebra crossing** passage pour piétons *m*.

zero ['ziərou] *n* zéro *m*.

zest [zest] *n* entrain *m*; saveur *f*.

zigzag ['zigzag] *n* zigzag *m*. *v* zigzaguer.

zinc [ziŋk] *n* zinc *m*.

zip [zip] *n* fermeture éclair   *f*. **zip code** (*US*) code postal *m*. *v* **zip up** (se) fermer avec une fermeture éclair.

zodiac ['zoudiak] *n* zodiaque *m*.

zone [zoun] *n* zone *f*. *v* diviser en zones.

zoo [zuɪ] *n* zoo *m*.

zoology [zou'olədʒi] *n* zoologie *f*. **zoologi-cal** *adj* zoologique. **zoologist** *n* zoologiste *m, f*.

zoom [zuɪm] *n* vrombissement *m*. **zoom lens** zoom *m*. *v* vrombir. **zoom past/through** (*coll*) passer/traverser en trombe.

French–Anglais

A

à [a] *prep* (*vers*) to; (*position*) at; (*ville*) in; (*d'après*) according to; (*transport*) by; (*pour*) for.

abaisser [abese] *v* lower. **s'abaisser** *v* fall; (*personne*) humble oneself. **abaissement** *nm* fall; (*personne*) subservience; degradation.

abandon [abɑ̃dɔ̃] *nm* desertion; renunciation, giving up; neglect. **à l'abandon** in a state of neglect. **avec abandon** without constraint.

abandonner [abɑ̃dɔne] *v* abandon, give up. **s'abandonner à** give way to, indulge in.

abasourdir [abazurdir] *v* stun. **abasourdissement** *nm* stupefaction.

abat-jour *nm invar* lampshade.

abats [aba] *nm pl* offal *sing*; (*volaille*) giblets *pl*.

abattoir [abatwar] *nm* abattoir.

***abattre** [abatrə] *v* pull *or* knock down; (*arbre*) fell; (*tuer*) kill; (*affaiblir*) weaken. **s'abattre** fall, collapse. **abattement** *nm* depression, low spirits *pl*; (*fatigue*) exhaustion; (*rabais*) reduction. **abattu** *adj* exhausted; feeble; depressed.

abbaye [abei] *nf* abbey.

abbé [abe] *nm* abbot. **abbesse** *nf* abbess.

abcès [apsɛ] *nm* abscess.

abdiquer [abdike] *v* abdicate. **abdication** *nf* abdication.

abdomen [abdɔmɛn] *nm* abdomen. **abdominal** *adj* abdominal.

abeille [abɛj] *nf* bee.

abhorrer [abɔre] *v* abhor.

abîme [abim] *nm* abyss, gulf.

abîmer [abime] *v* spoil, damage.

abject [abʒɛkt] *adj* despicable, abject.

abnégation [abnegasjɔ̃] *nf* self-denial.

aboiement [abwamɑ̃] *nm* bark.

abois [abwa] *nm pl* **aux abois** at bay.

abolir [abɔlir] *v* abolish. **abolition** *nf* abolition.

abominable [abɔminablə] *adj* abominable. **abomination** *nf* abomination. **avoir en abomination** loathe.

abonder [abɔ̃de] *v* abound, be plentiful. **abondance** *nf* abundance; (*richesse*) wealth. **abondant** *adj* plentiful, profuse; (*cheveux*) thick; (*repas*) copious.

s'abonner [abɔne] *v* subscribe. **abonné, -e** *nm, nf* subscriber; (*gaz, etc.*) consumer. **abonnement** *nm* subscription; (*rail, sport, etc.*) season ticket.

abord [abɔr] *nm* manner; access. **abords** *nm pl* surroundings *pl*. **au premier abord** at first sight. **d'abord** *adv* (at) first.

aborder [abɔrde] *v* approach; (*arriver à*) reach; (*problème, etc.*) tackle. **abordable** *adj* reasonable; approachable; accessible.

aborigène [abɔriʒɛn] *n(m+f)* aborigine. *adj* aboriginal.

aboutir [abutir] *v* succeed. **aboutir à** end up in *or* at, come to. **aboutissement** *nm* result; success.

aboyer [abwaje] *v* bark.

abrasif [abrazif] *nm, adj* abrasive. **abrasion** *nf* abrasion.

abréger [abreʒe] *v* shorten; (*texte*) abridge. **abrégé** *nm* summary.

abreuver [abrœve] *v* (*animal*) water; (*tremper*) soak; (*inonder*) shower, swamp. **s'abreuver** *v* quench one's thirst.

abréviation [abrevjɑsjɔ̃] *nf* abbreviation.

abri [abri] *nm* shelter; protection. **à l'abri** sheltered, safe.

abricot [abriko] *nm* apricot. **abricotier** *nm* apricot (tree).

abriter [abrite] *v* shelter; (*du soleil*) shade. **s'abriter** *v* take cover.

abroger [abrɔʒe] v repeal. **abrogation** nf repeal.

abrutir [abrytir] v exhaust, daze, stupefy.

absent [apsɑ̃], **-e** nm, nf absentee. adj absent; (qui manque) missing. **absence** nf absence.

abside [apsid] nf apse.

absinthe [apsɛ̃t] nf absinthe.

absolu [apsɔly] nm, adj absolute.

absorber [apsɔrbe] v absorb; (temps, etc.) occupy, take up. **absorbant** adj absorbing; (matière) absorbent. **absorption** nf absorption.

***absoudre** [apsudrə] v absolve. **absolution** nf absolution.

***s'abstenir** [apstənir] v abstain, refrain. **abstention** nf abstention. **abstinence** nf abstinence.

abstrait [apstrɛ] adj abstract. nm abstract; abstract art; abstract artist. **abstraction** nf abstraction; abstract idea. **faire abstraction de** disregard.

absurde [apsyrd] nm, adj absurd. **absurdité** nf absurdity.

abus [aby] nm abuse; over-use, over-indulgence. **abuser de** v abuse, misuse; exploit; over-use, over-indulge. **abusif** adj excessive; improper.

académie [akademi] nf academy; school. **académique** adj academic.

acajou [akaʒu] nm mahogany.

acariâtre [akarjatrə] adj sour-tempered.

accabler [akɑble] v overwhelm, overcome; (questions, injures) shower. **accablant** adj overwhelming; (chaleur, travail) exhausting. **accablement** nm exhaustion; depression.

accaparer [akapare] v monopolize; (absorber) take up completely.

accéder [aksede] v **accéder à** (lieu) reach, get to; attain; (désirs) comply with.

accélérer [akselere] v accelerate, speed up. **accélérateur** nm accelerator. **accélération** nf acceleration.

accent [aksɑ̃] nm accent; emphasis, stress; tone.

accentuer [aksɑ̃tɥe] v accent; emphasize, accentuate; intensify.

accepter [aksɛpte] v accept; (être d'accord) agree. **acceptable** adj acceptable; satisfactory. **acceptation** nf acceptance.

accès [aksɛ] nm access, approach; (crise) fit, bout. **accessible** adj accessible; (personne) approachable.

accessoire [akseswar] adj secondary; additional. nm accessory.

accident [aksidɑ̃] nm accident, mishap. **accidenté** adj (terrain) uneven. **accidentel** adj accidental.

acclamer [aklame] v acclaim, cheer. **acclamations** nf pl cheers pl.

acclimater [aklimate] v acclimatize. **s'acclimater** v adapt (oneself), become acclimatized.

accommoder [akɔmɔde] v adapt; (cuisine) prepare. **s'accommoder de** put up with.

accompagner [akɔ̃paɲe] v accompany. **accompagnement** nm accompaniment.

accomplir [akɔ̃plir] v accomplish, carry out, achieve; complete. **accomplissement** nm accomplishment, fulfilment; completion.

accord [akɔr] nm agreement; harmony; (musique) chord. **d'accord** (fam) O.K. **être d'accord** agree.

accordéon [akɔrdeɔ̃] nm accordion.

accorder [akɔrde] v grant, give; (musique) tune. **s'accorder** v agree; match, be in harmony.

accotement [akɔtmɑ̃] nm (auto) shoulder, verge. **accotement stabilisé** hard shoulder.

accoucher [akuʃe] v give birth. **accouchement** nm childbirth, delivery. **accoucheuse** nf midwife.

accouder [akude] v **s'accouder à** or **sur** lean one's elbows on.

***accourir** [akurir] v rush up, hurry.

accoutumer [akutyme] v accustom. **s'accoutumer à** get used to.

accroc [akro] nm tear; (tache) blot; (anicroche) hitch.

accrocher [akrɔʃe] v catch; (tableau, etc.) hang; (voiture) bump into. **s'accrocher à** cling to. **accrocheur, -euse** adj persistent; (affiche, etc.) eye-catching, catchy.

***accroître** [akrwatrə] v increase. **accroissement** nm increase.

s'accroupir [akrupir] v squat, crouch.

***accueillir** [akœjir] v (aller chercher) welcome; receive; meet; (loger) accommodate. **accueil** nm reception, welcome.

accumuler [akymyle] v accumulate. **accumulateur** nm accumulator. **accumulation** nf accumulation.

accuser [akyze] v accuse, blame; accentuate; (montrer) show. **accuser réception de** acknowledge receipt of. **accusation** nf accusation. **accusé, -e** *nm, nf* accused, defendant.

acerbe [asɛrb] *adj* caustic.

acharner [aʃarne] *v* **s'acharner à** *or* **sur** try desperately to, work furiously at. **s'acharner contre** hound, set oneself against. **acharné** *adj* relentless; determined, set; (*combat*) fierce. **acharnement** *nm* relentlessness; determination; fierceness.

achat [aʃa] *nm* purchase. **faire des achats** go shopping.

acheminer [aʃmine] *v* forward, dispatch; transport. **s'acheminer vers** head for.

acheter [aʃte] *v* buy. **acheteur, -euse** *nm, nf* buyer.

achever [aʃve] *v* finish. **s'achever** end. **achevé** *adj* downright; accomplished. **achèvement** *nm* completion.

acide [asid] *nm, adj* acid. **acidité** *nf* acidity.

acier [asje] *nm* steel. **acier inoxydable** stainless steel. **aciérie** *nf* steelworks.

acné [akne] *nf* acne.

acompte [akɔ̃t] *nm* (*arrhes*) deposit, down payment; (*versement partiel*) instalment.

acoustique [akustik] *adj* acoustic. *nf* acoustics *pl*.

***acquérir** [akerir] *v* acquire; (*gagner*) win, gain. **acquéreur** *nm* purchaser.

acquiescer [akjese] *v* acquiesce, assent; approve. **acquiescement** *nm* acquiescence; approval.

acquis [aki] *adj* acquired; established. *nm* experience.

acquisition [akizisjɔ̃] *nf* acquisition.

acquit [aki] *nm* receipt.

acquitter [akite] *v* acquit; pay. **s'acquitter de** (*dette*) discharge; (*promesse, tâche*) fulfil. **acquittement** *nm* acquittal; payment; discharge; fulfilment.

âcre [akrə] *adj* acrid. **âcreté** *nf* acridity.

acrimonie [akrimɔni] *nf* acrimonie. **acrimonieux** *adj* acrimonious.

acrobate [akrɔbat] *n(m+f)* acrobat. **acrobatie** *nf* acrobatics. **acrobatique** *adj* acrobatic.

acrylique [akrilik] *adj* acrylic.

acte[1] [akt] *nm* action, act; (*jur*) deed, certificate. **acte de décès/mariage/naissance** death/marriage/birth certificate.

acte[2] [akt] *nm* (*théâtre*) act.

acteur [aktœr] *nm* actor. **actrice** *nf* actress.

actif [aktif] *adj* active. *nm* credit.

action [aksjɔ̃] *nf* action, act, deed; (*comm*) share. **actionnaire** *n(m+f)* shareholder.

activer [aktive] *v* speed up; (*chim*) activate. **activiste** *n(m+f)* activist. **activité** *nf* activity. **être en activité** function, be in operation.

actuaire [aktɥɛr] *n(m+f)* actuary.

actualité [aktɥalite] *nf* topicality; current events *pl*. **les actualités** the news *sing*.

actuel [aktɥɛl] *adj* current, present; (*livre, etc.*) topical. **actuellement** *adv* at the moment.

acupuncture [akypɔ̃ktyr] *nf* acupuncture.

adapter [adapte] *v* adapt, fit. **adaptable** *adj* adaptable. **adaptateur** *nm* adapter. **adaptation** *nf* adaptation.

addenda [adɛ̃da] *nm* addenda.

additif [aditif] *nm* additive; (*clause*) rider. **additionner** [adisjɔne] *v* add (up). **addition** *nf* addition; (*facture*) bill. **additionnel** *adj* additional.

adénoïde [adenɔid] *adj* adenoidal. **végétations adénoïdes** *nf pl* adenoids *pl*.

adhérer [adere] *v* adhere, stick. **adhérer à** (*pneu, etc.*) grip; support; (*parti*) join, be a member of. **adhérence** *nf* adhesion; grip. **adhérent, -e** *nm, nf* adherent, member. **adhésif, -ve** *nm, adj* adhesive. **adhésion** *nf* support; membership.

adieu [adjø] *nm* farewell. *interj* goodbye! **faire ses adieux** say goodbye.

adjacent [adʒasɑ̃] *adj* adjacent.

adjectif [adʒɛktif] *nm* adjective. *adj* adjectival.

adjoint, -e *nm, nf* assistant.

adjudication [adʒydikasjɔ̃] *nf* sale by auction. **offrir par adjudication** put up for tender.

adjuger [adʒyʒe] *v* auction; (*contrat, etc.*) award. **une fois, deux fois, trois fois, adjugé!** going, going, gone!

***admettre** [admɛtrə] *v* admit; receive; (*candidat*) pass; accept; suppose.

administrer [administre] *v* administer; (*gérer*) manage, run. **administrateur, -trice** *nm, nf* administrator; director. **administratif** *adj* administrative. **administration** *nf* administration; management, government.

admirer [admire] *v* admire. **admirable** *adj* admirable. **admirateur, -trice** *nm, nf* admirer. **admiration** *nf* admiration.

admission [admisjɔ̃] *nf* admission, admittance; entry; acceptance. **admissible** *adj* admissible; acceptable; *(candidat)* eligible.

adolescence [adɔlesɑ̃s] *nf* adolescence. **adolescent, -e** *n, adj* adolescent.

adonner [adɔne] *v* **s'adonner à** devote oneself to; *(boisson, etc.)* take to.

adopter [adɔpte] *v* adopt. **adoptif** *adj* *(enfant)* adopted; *(parent)* adoptive. **adoption** *nf* adoption.

adorer [adɔre] *v* adore; *(rel)* worship. **adorable** *adj* adorable; delightful. **adorateur, -trice** *nm, nf* worshipper. **adoration** *nf* adoration; worship.

adosser [adose] *v* **adosser à** *or* **contre** lean *or* stand against.

adoucir [adusir] *v* soften; sweeten; ease, soothe.

adrénaline [adrenalin] *nf* adrenalin.

adresse[1] [adrɛs] *nf* skill, dexterity.

adresse[2] [adrɛs] *nf* address. **adresser** *v* address, direct. **s'adresser à** apply to; *(parler)* speak to.

adroit [adrwa] *adj* skilful, deft, clever.

adulation [adylɑsjɔ̃] *nf* adulation.

adulte [adylt] *n(m+f)*, *adj* adult.

adultère [adyltɛr] *adj* adulterous. *nm* adultery.

*advenir [advənir] *v* happen. **advenir de** become of.

adverbe [advɛrb] *nm* adverb. **adverbial** *adj* adverbial.

adverse [advɛrs] *adj* opposing, adverse. **adversité** *nf* adversity.

aérer [aere] *v* air; *(terre)* aerate. **aérateur** *nm* ventilator. **aération** *nf* airing; ventilation; aeration.

aérien [aerjɛ̃] *adj* aerial, air. *nm* aerial.

aérodynamique [aerɔdinamik] *adj* aerodynamic, streamlined. *nf* aerodynamics.

aéroglisseur [aerɔglisør] *nm* hovercraft.

aéronautique [aerɔnotik] *adj* aeronautical. *nf* aeronautics.

aéroport [aerɔpɔr] *nm* airport.

aéroporté [aerɔpɔrte] *adj* airborne.

aérosol [aerɔsɔl] *nm* aerosol.

affable [afablə] *adj* affable. **affabilité** *nf* affability.

affaiblir [afeblir] *v* weaken. **s'affaiblir** grow weaker; *(son)* fade; *(tempête)* die down. **affaiblissement** *nm* weakening.

affaire [afɛr] *nf* affair, matter, business; transaction, deal. **affaires** *nf pl* *(com-*

merce) business *sing*; *(effets personnels)* things *pl*, belongings *pl*. **avoir affaire à** have to deal with. **faire l'affaire** do nicely, come in handy. **occupe-toi de tes affaires!** mind your own business! **affairé** *adj* busy.

s'affaisser [afese] *v* sink, subside; *(personne)* collapse. **affaissement** *nm* subsidence.

affamer [afame] *v* starve. **affamé** *adj* starving, ravenous.

affecter[1] [afɛkte] *v* feign; *(adopter)* take on, assume. **affectation** *nf* affectation.

affecter[2] [afɛkte] *v* allocate, assign; *(nommer)* appoint. **affectation** *nf* allocation; appointment.

affecter[3] [afɛkte] *v* affect, touch, move.

affection [afɛksjɔ̃] *nf* affection; *(méd)* ailment. **affectionner** *v* be fond of. **affectueux** *adj* affectionate.

affiche [afiʃ] *nf* poster, bill. **afficher** *v* stick up; *(péj)* flaunt, display.

affilier [afilje] *v* affiliate. **affiliation** *nf* affiliation.

affiner [afine] *v* refine.

affinité [afinite] *nf* affinity.

affirmer [afirme] *v* assert, affirm. **affirmatif** *adj* affirmative; positive. **affirmation** *nf* assertion. **affirmative** *nf* affirmative.

affliction [afliksjɔ̃] *nf* affliction.

affliger [afliʒe] *v* distress. **être affligé de** be afflicted with.

affluence [aflyɑ̃s] *nf* crowd.

affoler [afɔle] *v* throw into a panic, terrify. **s'affoler** panic. **affolant** *adj* alarming. **affolé** *adj* panic-stricken. **affolement** *nm* panic.

affranchir [afrɑ̃ʃir] *v* *(lettre)* stamp; *(timbre)* frank; *(libérer)* free, emancipate.

affréter [afrete] *v* charter, hire.

affreux [afrø] *adj* dreadful, horrible, ghastly.

affronter [afrɔ̃te] *v* confront, face, brave.

afin [afɛ̃] *prep* **afin de** so as to, in order to. **afin que** so that, in order that.

Afrique [afrik] *nf* Africa. **africain** *adj* African. **Africain, -e** *nm, nf* African.

agacer [agase] *v* irritate, annoy. **agacement** *nm* irritation, annoyance.

âge [ɑʒ] *nm* age. **quel âge avez-vous?** how old are you? **âgé** *adj* old, elderly. **âgé de quatre ans** four years old.

agence [aʒɑ̃s] *nf* agency, office, bureau.

agenda [aʒɛ̃da] *nm* diary.

s'agenouiller [aʒnuje] v kneel (down).
agent [aʒɑ̃] nm agent; policeman; officer. **agent de change** stockbroker. **agent immobilier** estate agent.
agglomération [aglɔmerɑsjɔ̃] nf built-up area, town; conglomeration.
aggraver [agrave] v aggravate, worsen; (redoubler) increase. **aggravation** nf aggravation, worsening; increase.
agile [aʒil] adj agile, nimble. **agilité** nf agility.
agir [aʒir] v act. **s'agir de** be a matter or question of, be about.
agiter [aʒite] v shake, wave, flap; trouble; debate, discuss. **s'agiter** fidget, get restless. **agitation** nf agitation; restlessness. **agité** adj troubled; restless; (mer) rough.
agneau [aɲo] nm lamb.
agnostique [agnɔstik] n(m+f), adj agnostic.
agoniser [agɔnize] v be dying. **agonie** nf mortal agony; (déclin) death throes pl. **à l'agonie** at death's door.
agrafe [agraf] nf hook; (papiers) staple. **agrafer** v hook, fasten; staple. **agrafeuse** nf stapler.
agrandir [agrɑ̃dir] v enlarge; (développer) expand, extend. **agrandissement** nm (phot) enlargement; expansion, extension.
agréable [agreablə] adj pleasant.
agréer [agree] v accept. **agréer à** please. **agrément** nm charm, pleasantness.
agression [agresjɔ̃] nf aggression; attack. **agressif** adj aggressive.
agricole [agrikɔl] adj agricultural.
agriculture [agrikyltyr] nf agriculture.
agrumes [agrym] nm pl citrus fruits pl.
aguets [agɛ] nm pl **aux aguets** on the look-out.
ahurir [ayrir] v astound. **ahurissement** nm stupefaction.
aide [ɛd] nf help, aid, assistance. n(m+f) assistant. **à l'aide!** help! **à l'aide de** with the help of. **venir en aide à** come to the assistance of.
aider [ede] v help, aid, assist.
aïeux [ajø] nm pl forefathers pl.
aigle [ɛglə] nm eagle.
aiglefin [ɛgləfɛ̃] nm haddock.
aigre [ɛgrə] adj sour; (son) shrill; (froid) bitter. **aigre-doux, -douce** adj bittersweet; (cuisine) sweet and sour. **aigreur** nf sourness.

aigrir [egrir] v embitter, sour.
aigu, -uë [egy] adj acute, sharp; (son) high-pitched.
aiguille [egɥij] nf needle; (horloge) hand. **travail à l'aiguille** nm needlework.
aiguillon [egɥijɔ̃] nm (insecte) sting; (plante) thorn; stimulus. **aiguillonner** v spur on.
aiguiser [egize] v sharpen; stimulate.
ail [aj] nm, pl **aulx** garlic.
aile [ɛl] nf wing; (moulin) sail. **ailé** adj winged.
ailleurs [ajœr] adv elsewhere. **d'ailleurs** adv besides. **par ailleurs** otherwise.
aimable [ɛmablə] adj kind, nice.
aimant [ɛmɑ̃] nm magnet. **aimanter** v magnetize.
aimer [eme] v like; (d'amour) love. **aimer mieux** prefer.
aine [ɛn] nf groin.
aîné [ene], **-e** adj elder, eldest. nm, nf eldest child; senior.
ainsi [ɛ̃si] adv in this way, thus, so. **ainsi que** just as, as well as. **et ainsi de suite** and so on. **pour ainsi dire** as it were.
air[1] [ɛr] nm air; atmosphere.
air[2] [ɛr] nm (apparence) air, look. **avoir l'air de** look or seem like.
air[3] [ɛr] nm (musique) tune, air; (opéra) aria.
aire [ɛr] nf area.
aise [ɛz] nf pleasure, joy. **à l'aise** at ease, comfortable. **mal à l'aise** ill at ease, uncomfortable. adj glad. **aisance** nf ease; (richesse) affluence. **aisé** adj easy.
aisselle [ɛsɛl] nf armpit.
ajonc [aʒɔ̃] nm gorse.
ajourner [aʒurne] v adjourn, postpone. **ajournement** nm adjournment, postponement.
ajouter [aʒute] v add. **s'ajouter à** add to.
ajuster [aʒyste] v adjust, fit; adapt.
alarme [alarm] nf alarm. **alarmer** v alarm. **alarmiste** n(m+f), adj alarmist.
Albanie [albani] nf Albania. **albanais** nm, adj Albanian. **Albanais, -e** nm, nf Albanian.
albatros [albatros] nm albatross.
album [albɔm] nm album. **album à colorier** colouring book.
alcali [alkali] nm alkali. **alcalin** adj alkaline.
alchimie [alʃimi] nf alchemy. **alchimiste** nm alchemist.

alcool [alkɔl] *nm* alcohol. **alcool à brûler** methylated spirits. **alcoolique** *n(m+f)*, *adj* alcoholic. **alcoolisme** *nm* alcoholism.

alcôve [alkov] *nf* alcove.

aléatoire [aleatwar] *adj* uncertain, chancy.

alentour [alɑ̃tur] *adv* around. **alentours** *nm pl* surroundings *pl*, neighbourhood *sing*.

alerte [alert] *adj* agile, alert, brisk. *nf* alert, alarm, warning. **alerter** *v* alert, notify, warn.

algèbre [alʒɛbrə] *nf* algebra. **algèbrique** *adj* algebraic.

Alger [alʒe] *n* Algiers.

Algérie [alʒeri] *nf* Algeria. **algérien** *adj* Algerian. **Algérien, -enne** *nm*, *nf* Algerian.

algue [alg] *nf* seaweed.

alias [aljɑs] *adv* alias.

alibi [alibi] *nm* alibi.

aliéner [aljene] *v* alienate; (*droits, etc.*) give up. **aliénation** *nf* alienation; (*méd*) derangement. **aliéné, -e** *nm*, *nf* insane person.

aligner [aliɲe] *v* align, line up. **alignement** *nm* alignment.

aliment [alimɑ̃] *nm* food. **alimentation** *nf* feeding; (*comm*) foodstuffs *pl*. **alimenter** *v* feed, supply.

alinéa [alinea] *nm* paragraph.

aliter [alite] *v* confine to bed. **alité** *adj* bedridden.

allaiter [alete] *v* (*femme*) (breast-)feed; (*animal*) suckle. **allaitement** *nm* (breast-) feeding; suckling.

allée [ale] *nf* path.

alléger [aleʒe] *v* alleviate; (*poids*) lighten, make lighter. **allégement** *nm* alleviation.

allégorie [alegɔri] *nf* allegory. **allégorique** *adj* allegorical.

allègre [alɛgrə] *adj* cheerful, lively. **allégresse** *nf* elation.

alléguer [alege] *v* allege; (*excuse*) put forward. **allégation** *nf* allegation.

alléluia [aleluja] *nm, interj* hallelujah.

Allemagne [almaɲ] *nf* Germany. **allemand** *nm*, *adj* German. **Allemand, -e** *nm*, *nf* German.

*****aller** [ale] *v* go; (*futur*) be going to. **aller à** (*style*) suit; (*mesure*) fit. **aller chercher** fetch. **aller de soi** be obvious. **allez-y!** go on! **allons! come on! allons-y!** let's go! **ça va** all right. **comment allez-vous?** how are

you? **s'en aller** go away. *nm* (*trajet*) outward journey; (*billet*) single. **aller-retour** *nm* return.

allergie [alɛrʒi] *nf* allergy. **allergique** *adj* allergic.

allier [alje] *v* ally; unite, combine. **alliage** *nm* alloy. **alliance** *nf* alliance; union; (*bague*) wedding ring; combination. **allié, -e** *nm*, *nf* ally.

alligator [aligatɔr] *nm* alligator.

allitération [aliterasjɔ̃] *nf* alliteration.

allô [alo] *interj* hello!

allocation [alɔkasjɔ̃] *nf* allocation; (*somme*) allowance. **allocation de chômage** unemployment benefit. **allocations familiales** family allowance *sing*.

allocution [alɔkysjɔ̃] *nf* short speech.

allonger [alɔ̃ʒe] *v* lengthen; (*étendre*) stretch out; (*cuisine*) thin. **allonger le cou** crane one's neck.

allouer [alwe] *v* allocate, allot.

allumer [alyme] *v* light; (*lampe, etc.*) turn on. **allumage** *nm* lighting, (*auto*) ignition. **allumette** *nf* match.

allure [alyr] *nf* (*vitesse*) speed, pace; (*démarche*) walk, bearing; air, appearance. **à toute allure** at full speed.

allusion [alyzjɔ̃] *nf* allusion. **faire allusion à** allude to.

almanach [almana] *nm* almanac.

aloi [alwa] *nm* **de bon aloi** respectable, worthy. **de mauvais aloi** of doubtful reputation *or* quality.

alors [alɔr] *adv* then; so; in that case. **alors même que** even if *or* though. **alors que** while.

alouette [alwɛt] *nf* lark.

alourdir [alurdir] *v* make heavy, weigh down.

aloyau [alwajo] *nm* sirloin.

alphabet [alfabɛ] *nm* alphabet. **alphabétique** *adj* alphabetical.

alpinisme [alpinismə] *nm* mountaineering. **alpiniste** *n(m+f)* mountaineer.

altercation [altɛrkasjɔ̃] *nf* altercation.

altérer [altere] *v* (*donner soif*) make thirsty; falsify; (*abîmer*) spoil, debase. **altération** *nf* deterioration; falsification.

alterner [altɛrne] *v* alternate. **alternance** *nf* alternation. **alternatif** *adj* alternate; (*élec*) alternating. **alternative** *nf* alternative.

Altesse [altɛs] *nf* Highness.

altier [altje] *adj* haughty.

altitude [altityd] *nf* altitude, height.

alto [alto] *nm* viola.

aluminium [alyminjɔm] *nm* aluminium.

amabilité [amabilite] *nf* kindness.

amadouer [amadwe] *v* coax, cajole.

amaigrir [amegrir] *v* make thin *or* thinner. **amaigrissant** *adj* (*régime*) slimming. **amaigrissement** *nm* thinness; slimming.

amalgamer [amalgame] *v* combine; (*métal*) amalgamate.

amande [amɑ̃d] *nf* almond. **amandier** *nm* almond (tree).

amant [amɑ̃] *nm* lover.

amarrer [amare] *v* (*naut*) moor; (*fixer*) make fast. **amarrage** *nm* mooring.

amas [amɑ] *nm* heap, mass. **amasser** *v* amass, accumulate.

amateur [amatœr] *nm* (*non-professionnel*) amateur; enthusiast. **d'amateur** *adj* amateurish.

ambassade [ɑ̃basad] *nf* embassy; mission. **ambassadeur, -drice** *nm, nf* ambassador.

ambiance [ɑ̃bjɑ̃s] *nf* atmosphere.

ambidextre [ɑ̃bidɛkstrə] *adj* ambidextrous.

ambigu, -uë [ɑ̃bigy] *adj* ambiguous. **ambiguïté** *nf* ambiguity.

ambition [ɑ̃bisjɔ̃] *nf* ambition. **ambitieux** *adj* ambitious.

ambivalent [ɑ̃bivalɑ̃] *adj* ambivalent. **ambivalence** *nf* ambivalence.

ambre [ɑ̃brə] *nm* amber.

ambulance [ɑ̃bylɑ̃s] *nf* ambulance. **ambulancier** *nm* ambulance man.

ambulant [ɑ̃bylɑ̃] *adj* itinerant, travelling.

âme [ɑm] *nf* soul.

améliorer [ameljɔre] *v* improve. **amélioration** *nf* improvement.

aménager [amenaʒe] *v* fit out *or* up; (*parc*) lay out; develop. **aménagement** *nm* fitting-out; development.

amender [amɑ̃de] *v* amend. **amende** *nf* fine.

amener [amne] *v* bring; cause.

amer [amɛr] *adj* bitter. **amertume** *nf* bitterness.

Amérique [amerik] *nf* America. **américain** *adj* American. **Américain, -e** *nm, nf* American.

améthyste [ametist] *nf, adj* amethyst.

ameublement [amœbləmɑ̃] *nm* furnishing; (*meubles*) furniture.

ami [ami], **-e** *nm, nf* friend. *adj* friendly.

amiable [amjablə] *adj* amicable.

amiante [amjɑ̃t] *nm* asbestos.

amibe [amib] *nf* amoeba.

amical [amikal] *adj* friendly. **amicale** *nf* association.

amidon [amidɔ̃] *nm* starch. **amidonner** *v* starch.

amiral [amiral] *nm* admiral.

amitié [amitje] *nf* friendship. **amitiés** *nf pl* best wishes *pl*. **prendre en amitié** befriend.

ammoniaque [amɔnjak] *nf* ammonia.

amnésie [amnezi] *nf* amnesia.

amnistie [amnisti] *nf* amnesty.

amoindrir [amwɛ̃drir] *v* reduce, weaken, diminish.

amollir [amɔlir] *v* soften, weaken.

amonceler [amɔ̃sle] *v* pile up, accumulate. **amoncellement** *nm* heap; accumulation.

amont [amɔ̃] *nm* **d'amont** *adj* (*eau*) upstream; (*pente*) uphill. **en amont** *adv* upstream; uphill.

amoral [amɔral] *adj* amoral.

amorcer [amɔrse] *v* bait; (*commencer*) begin. **amorce** *nf* bait; beginning.

amorphe [amɔrf] *adj* (*roche*) amorphous; (*personne*) passive, lifeless.

amortir [amɔrtir] *v* absorb, cushion, deaden; (*dette*) pay off. **amortisseur** *nm* shock absorber.

amour [amur] *nm* love. **amour-propre** *nm* pride, self-esteem. **amoureux** *adj* (*personne*) in love; (*tendre*) loving.

ampère [ɑ̃pɛr] *nm* amp.

amphétamine [ɑ̃fetamin] *nf* amphetamine.

amphibie [ɑ̃fibi] *adj* amphibious. *nm* amphibian.

amphithéâtre [ɑ̃fiteatrə] *nm* amphitheatre; (*université*) lecture theatre.

ample [ɑ̃plə] *adj* ample, full. **ampleur** *nf* (*importance*) scale, extent; fullness.

amplifier [ɑ̃plifje] *v* develop, expand; (*son*) amplify. **amplificateur** *nm* amplifier.

ampoule [ɑ̃pul] *nf* (*élec*) bulb; (*méd*) blister.

amputer [ɑ̃pyte] *v* amputate; (*texte, etc.*) reduce drastically.

Amsterdam [amsterdam] *n* Amsterdam.

amuser [amyze] *v* amuse. **s'amuser** enjoy oneself, have fun. **amusement** *nm* entertainment, amusement; pastime.

amygdale [amidal] *nf* tonsil. **amygdalite** *nf* tonsillitis.

an [ɑ̃] *nm* year. **avoir 15 ans** be 15 years old.

anachronisme [anakrɔnisn ə] *nm* anachronism.

anagramme [anagram] *nf* aɪ ɪgram.

anal [anal] *adj* anal.

analogie [analɔʒi] *nf* analogy.

analphabète [analfabɛt] *adj* illiterate. **analphabétisme** *nm* illiteracy.

analyser [analize] *v* analyse; (*méd*) test. **analyse** *nf* analysis; test. **analytique** *adj* analytical.

ananas [anana] *nm* pineapple.

anarchie [anarʃi] *nf* anarchy. **anarchiste** *n(m+f)* anarchist.

anatomie [anatɔmi] *nf* anatomy.

ancêtre [ɑ̃sɛtrə] *n(m+f)* ancestor.

anchois [ɑ̃ʃwa] *nm* anchovy.

ancien [ɑ̃sjɛ̃], **-enne** *adj* (*vieux*) ancient; (*d'autrefois*) former. *nm, nf* elder; (*élève*) old boy, old girl. **ancienneté** *nf* seniority; great age.

ancre [ɑ̃krə] *nf* anchor. **ancrer** *v* anchor.

Andorre [ɑ̃dɔr] *nm* Andorra.

âne [ɑn] *nm* donkey, ass.

anéantir [aneɑ̃tir] *v* annihilate; destroy; (*accabler*) overwhelm. **anéanti** *adj* (*fatigué*) exhausted; overwhelmed. **anéantissement** *nm* annihilation; destruction; exhaustion.

anecdote [anɛkdɔt] *nf* anecdote.

anémie [anemi] *nf* anaemia. **anémique** *adj* anaemic.

anémone [anemɔn] *nf* anemone.

anesthésier [anɛstezje] *v* anaesthetize. **anesthésique** *nm, adj* anaesthetic. **anesthésiste** *n(m+f)* anaesthetist.

ange [ɑ̃ʒ] *nm* angel.

angélique¹ [ɑ̃ʒelik] *adj* angelic.

angélique² [ɑ̃ʒelik] *nf* angelica.

angine [ɑ̃ʒin] *nf* sore throat. **angine de poitrine** angina.

angle [ɑ̃glə] *nm* angle; (*coin*) corner. **angle droit** right angle.

Angleterre [ɑ̃glətɛr] *nf* England. **anglais** *nm, adj* English. **les Anglais** the English.

anglican [ɑ̃glikɑ̃], **-e** *n, adj* Anglican.

angoisse [ɑ̃gwas] *nf* anguish, distress; (*peur*) dread. **angoissant** *adj* harrowing. **angoissé** *adj* anguished, distressed.

anguille [ɑ̃gij] *nf* eel.

anguleux [ɑ̃gylø] *adj* angular, bony.

anicroche [anikrɔʃ] *nf* (*fam*) hitch, snag.

animal¹ [animal] *nm* animal.

animal² [animal] *adj* animal.

animer [anime] *v* animate; (*discussion, etc.*) lead; (*pousser*) drive, impel; (*soirée, etc.*) liven up. **s'animer** come to life, liven up. **animateur, -trice** *nm, nf* compère; (*cinéma*) animator. **animation** *nf* animation; liveliness. **animé** *adj* busy, lively.

animosité [animozite] *nf* animosity.

anis [ani] *nm* aniseed.

annales [anal] *nf pl* annals *pl*.

anneau [ano] *nm* ring; (*chaîne*) link.

année [ane] *nf* year. **année bissextile** leap year. **année-lumière** *nf* light year.

annexer [anɛkse] *v* annex. **annexe** *nf* annexe.

annihiler [aniile] *v* destroy, ruin, annihilate. **annihilation** *nf* annihilation, destruction, ruin.

anniversaire [anivɛrsɛr] *nm* (*naissance*) birthday; (*événement*) anniversary. **anniversaire de mariage** (wedding) anniversary.

annoncer [anɔ̃se] *v* announce; (*prédire*) forecast, foreshadow; indicate. **s'annoncer** approach. **s'annoncer bien** look promising. **annonce** *nf* announcement; sign, indication; (*publicité*) advertisement.

annoter [anɔte] *v* annotate. **annotation** *nf* annotation.

annuaire [anɥɛr] *nm* annual, yearbook; telephone directory.

annuel [anɥɛl] *adj* annual.

annuler [anyle] *v* (*rendre nul*) nullify; (*mariage*) annul; (*commande, etc.*) cancel. **annulation** *nf* nullification; annulment; cancellation.

anode [anɔd] *nf* anode.

anodin [anɔdɛ̃] *adj* insignificant, trivial; (*sans danger*) harmless.

anomalie [anɔmali] *nf* anomaly.

anonyme [anɔnim] *adj* anonymous; impersonal. **anonymat** *nm* anonymity.

anormal [anɔrmal] *adj* abnormal.

anse [ɑ̃s] *nf* handle; (*géog*) cove.

antagonist [ɑ̃tagɔnist] *n(m+f)* antagonist. *adj* antagonistic. **antagonisme** *nm* antagonism.

antarctique [ɑ̃tarktik] *adj* antarctic. **l'Antarctique** *nm* the Antarctic.

antenne [ɑ̃tɛn] *nf* antenna; (*TV, radio*) aerial. **sur** *or* **à l'antenne** on the air.

antérieur, -e [ɑ̃terjœr] *adj* previous; (*patte, membre*) front, fore. **antérieur à** prior to.

anthologie [ãtɔlɔʒi] *nf* anthology.
anthropologie [ãtrɔpɔlɔʒi] *nf* anthropology. **anthropologique** *adj* anthropological. **anthropologiste** *n(m+f)* anthropologist.
antiaérien [ãtiaerjɛ̃] *adj* anti-aircraft; (*abri*) air-raid.
antialcoolique [ãtialkɔlik] *adj* against alcohol *or* alcoholism. **ligue antialcoolique** *nf* temperance league.
antibiotique [ãtibjɔtik] *nm, adj* antibiotic.
antichoc [ãtiʃɔk] *adj* shockproof.
anticiper [ãtisipe] *v* anticipate. **anticipation** *nf* anticipation. **par anticipation** in advance.
anticonceptionnel [ãtikɔ̃sɛpsjɔnɛl] *adj* contraceptive.
anticorps [ãtikɔr] *nm* antibody.
anticyclone [ãtisiklon] *nm* anticyclone.
antidater [ãtidate] *v* backdate.
antidote [ãtidɔt] *nm* antidote.
antigel [ãtiʒɛl] *nm* antifreeze.
antihistaminique [ãtiistaminik] *nm, adj* antihistamine.
antilope [ãtilɔp] *nf* antelope.
antipathique [ãtipatik] *adj* unpleasant.
antique [ãtik] *adj* antique, ancient. **antiquaire** *n(m+f)* antique dealer. **antiquité** *nf* antiquity. **antiquités** *nf pl* (*meubles, etc.*) antiques *pl*.
antisémite [ãtisemit] *adj* anti-Semitic. *n(m+f)* anti-Semite. **antisémitisme** *nm* anti-Semitism.
antiseptique [ãtisɛptik] *nm, adj* antiseptic.
antisocial [ãtisɔsjal] *adj* antisocial.
antithèse [ãtitɛz] *nf* antithesis. **antithétique** *adj* antithetical.
antonyme [ãtɔnim] *nm* antonym.
antre [ãtrə] *nm* den.
anus [anys] *nm* anus.
anxiété [ãksjete] *nf* anxiety. **anxieux** *adj* anxious.
août [u] *nm* August.
apaiser [apeze] *v* calm, soothe; (*soif*) quench. **s'apaiser** die down; calm down; be satisfied.
aparté [aparte] *nm* aside.
apathie [apati] *nf* apathy. **apathique** *adj* apathetic.
apercevoir [apɛrsəvwar] *v* see; (*brièvement*) catch sight of. **s'apercevoir de** notice. **aperçu** *nm* outline; (*coup d'œil*) glimpse.
apéritif [aperitif] *nm* aperitif.

aphrodisiaque [afrɔdizjak] *nm, adj* aphrodisiac.
aplanir [aplanir] *v* level; (*problèmes*) smooth away, iron out.
aplatir [aplatir] *v* flatten. **s'aplatir devant** grovel to. **aplati** *adj* flat.
aplomb [aplɔ̃] *nm* self-assurance; balance, equilibrium. **d'aplomb** *adv* (*stable*) steady; (*vertical*) straight down.
apogée [apɔʒe] *nm* peak, apogee.
apologie [apɔlɔʒi] *nf* apologia, defence.
apostrophe [apɔstrɔf] *nf* apostrophe; (*interpellation*) rude remark.
apôtre [apotrə] *nm* apostle.
*apparaître [aparɛtrə] *v* appear; seem.
apparat [apara] *nm* pomp. **d'apparat** *adj* ceremonial.
appareil [aparɛj] *nm* device, apparatus, appliance; (*TV, radio*) set; (*fam*) phone; (*dents*) brace; (*fracture*) splint; (*anat*) system. **à l'appareil** (*téléphone*) speaking. **appareil-photo** *nm* camera. **appareil à sous** slot machine.
apparence [aparãs] *nf* appearance; semblance. **en apparence** apparently. **apparent** *adj* obvious; visible.
apparenter [aparãte] *v* **s'apparenter à** ally oneself with; marry into; (*ressembler*) be similar to.
apparition [aparisjɔ̃] *nf* appearance; vision, apparition.
appartement [apartəmã] *nm* flat; (*hôtel*) suite.
*appartenir [apartənir] *v* **appartenir à** belong to; (*impersonnel*) be up to.
appât [apa] *nm* (*pêche*) bait; lure. **appâter** *v* lure; (*piège*) bait.
appeler [aple] *v* call; summon, send for; telephone. **en appeler à/de** appeal to/against. **s'appeler** be called. **comment vous appelez-vous?** what is your name? **appel** *nm* appeal; (*cri*) call; (*école*) register. **faire appel** appeal.
appendice [apɛ̃dis] *nm* appendix. **appendicite** *nf* appendicitis.
appentis [apãti] *nm* lean-to; (*toit*) sloping roof.
appétit [apeti] *nm* appetite. **appétissant** *adj* appetizing.
applaudir [aplodir] *v* applaud. **s'applaudir** congratulate oneself. **applaudissements** *nm pl* applause *sing*.
appliquer [aplike] *v* apply. **applicable** *adj* applicable. **application** *nf* application. **appliqué** *adj* industrious.

appointements [apwɛtmɑ̃] *nm pl* salary *sing.*

apporter [apɔrte] *v* bring.

apposer [apoze] *v* affix.

apprécier [apresje] *v* appreciate; value, assess. **appréciable** *adj* appreciable. **appréciation** *nf* assessment.

appréhender [apreɑ̃de] *v* apprehend; (*craindre*) dread. **appréhensif** *adj* apprehensive. **appréhension** *nf* apprehension.

*apprendre [aprɑ̃drə] *v* learn; (*enseigner*) teach; (*aviser*) inform (of).

apprenti [aprɑ̃ti], **-e** *nm, nf* apprentice; (*débutant*) beginner. **apprentissage** *nm* apprenticeship.

apprivoiser [aprivwaze] *v* tame. **apprivoisé** *adj* tame.

approbation [aprɔbasjɔ̃] *nf* approval. **approbateur, -trice** *adj* approving.

approcher [aprɔʃe] *v* approach, draw *or* go near; (*objet*) move near. **s'approcher de** come *or* go near to, approach. **approche** *nf* approach.

approfondir [aprɔfɔ̃dir] *v* deepen; (*étudier*) go into. **approfondi** *adj* thorough.

approprier [aprɔprije] *v* suit, adapt. **s'approprier** appropriate. **s'approprier à** be appropriate to, suit. **approprié** *adj* appropriate.

approuver [apruve] *v* approve (of).

approvisionner [aprɔvizjɔne] *v* supply.

approximatif [aprɔksimatif] *adj* approximate. **approximation** *nf* approximation.

appui [apᶣi] *nm* support. **appui-bras** *nm* armrest.

appuyer [apᶣije] *v* press; support; (*poser*) lean, rest. **appuyer sur** press; rest on; stress, accentuate. **s'appuyer sur** rely on.

âpre [ɑprə] *adj* pungent, acrid; (*cruel*) bitter; (*dur*) grim; (*rude*) harsh.

après [aprɛ] *prep* after. *adv* afterwards. **après-demain** *adv* the day after tomorrow. **après-midi** *nm* afternoon. **après-rasage** *nm* after-shave. **d'après** (*selon*) according to; (*suivant*) next, following.

à-propos [aprɔpo] *nm* aptness.

apte [aptə] *adj* **apte à** capable of, fit for. **aptitude** *nf* aptitude, ability.

aquarelle [akwarɛl] *nf* watercolour.

aquarium [akwarjɔm] *nm* aquarium.

aquatique [akwatik] *adj* aquatic.

aqueduc [akdyk] *nm* aqueduct.

aqueux [akø] *adj* aqueous.

arable [arablə] *adj* arable.

arachide [araʃid] *nf* peanut.

araignée [areɲe] *nf* spider.

arbitrer [arbitre] *v* arbitrate; (*sport*) referee, umpire. **arbitrage** *nm* arbitration. **arbitraire** *adj* arbitrary. **arbitre** *nm* judge; (*sport*) referee, umpire.

arbre [arbrə] *nm* tree; (*tech*) shaft. **arbre à cames** camshaft. **arbre de Noël** Christmas tree. **arbre généalogique** family tree.

arbrisseau [arbriso] *nm* shrub.

arbuste [arbyst] *nm* bush.

arc [ark] *nm* arc; (*arme*) bow; arch. **arc-en-ciel** *nm* rainbow.

arcade [arkad] *nf* archway. **arcades** *nf pl* arcade *sing*, arches *pl*.

archaïque [arkaik] *adj* archaic.

arche¹ [arʃ] *nf* arch.

arche² [arʃ] *nf* (*rel*) ark.

archéologie [arkeɔlɔʒi] *nf* archaeology. **archéologique** *adj* archaeological. **archéologue** *n(m+f)* archaeologist.

archet [arʃɛ] *nm* bow.

archevêque [arʃəvɛk] *nm* archbishop.

archi- [arʃi] *prefix* tremendously, utterly. **archiplein** *adj* (*fam*) chock-a-block.

archiduc [arʃidyk] *nm* archduke.

archipel [arʃipɛl] *nm* archipelago.

architecte [arʃitɛkt] *nm* architect. **architectural** *adj* architectural. **architecture** *nf* architecture.

archives [arʃiv] *nf pl* archives *pl*.

arctique [arktik] *adj* arctic. **l'arctique** *nm* the Arctic.

ardent [ardɑ̃] *adj* burning; passionate; ardent.

ardeur [ardœr] *nf* ardour; passion.

ardoise [ardwaz] *nf* slate.

ardu [ardy] *adj* arduous.

arène [arɛn] *nf* arena.

arête [arɛt] *nf* fishbone; (*bord*) ridge; (*cube*) edge.

argent [arʒɑ̃] *nm* money; (*métal*) silver. **argent comptant** cash. **argent de poche** pocket money. **argent liquide** ready money. **argenté** *adj* silvery, silvered. **argenterie** *nf* silverware.

argile [arʒil] *nf* clay.

argot [argo] *nm* slang. **argotique** *adj* slang.

argument [argymɑ̃] *nm* argument. **argumenter** *v* argue, reason.

aride [arid] *adj* arid, dry. **aridité** *nf* aridity.

aristocratie [aristɔkrasi] *nf* aristocracy.
aristocrate *n(m+f)* aristocrat. **aristocratique** *adj* aristocratic.
arithmétique [aritmetik] *nf* arithmetic. *adj* arithmetical.
arme [arm] *nf* weapon, arm. **armes** *nf pl* coat of arms *sing*.
armée [arme] *nf* army. **armée de l'air** air force. **Armée du Salut** Salvation Army.
armer [arme] *v* arm; equip; reinforce; (*fusil*) cock.
armoire [armwar] *nf* cupboard.
armure [armyr] *nf* armour.
arôme [arom] *nm* aroma; fragrance.
arpenter [arpɑ̃te] *v* (*terrain*) measure; pace up and down. **arpentage** *nm* surveying.
arquer [arke] *v* curve; arch. **arqué** *adj* curved; arched. **avoir les jambes arquées** be bow-legged.
arracher [araʃe] *v* snatch; (*extraire*) pull up *or* out; (*déchirer*) tear off *or* out. **d'arrache-pied** *adv* relentlessly.
arranger [arɑ̃ʒe] *v* arrange; (*régler*) settle; be convenient; (*réparer*) fix. **s'arranger** manage; (*se mettre d'accord*) come to an agreement; (*situation*) work out. **arrangement** *nm* arrangement; agreement.
arrérages [areraʒ] *nm pl* arrears *pl*.
arrestation [arɛstasjɔ̃] *nf* arrest.
arrêt [arɛ] *nm* stop; stopping; judgment. **arrêt d'autobus** bus stop. **arrêt du cœur** cardiac arrest. **arrêt de mort** death sentence.
arrêté [arete] *adj* firm, fixed. *nm* order, decree.
arrêter [arete] *v* stop; (*abandonner*) give up; (*police*) arrest; fix, decide on. **s'arrêter (de)** stop.
arrhes [ar] *nf pl* deposit *sing*.
arrière [arjɛr] *nm* rear, back; (*naut*) stern. **en arrière** backwards; (*derrière*) behind. *adj* rear, back. **arrière-goût** *nm* aftertaste. **arrière-pensée** *nf* ulterior motive. **arrière-plan** *nm* background. **arriéré** *adj* (*comm*) overdue, in arrears; (*personne, pays*) backward.
arriver [arive] *v* arrive; (*se passer*) happen. **arriver à** reach; (*réussir à*) manage. **j'arrive!** I'm coming! **arrivée** *nf* arrival.
arrogance [arɔgɑ̃s] *nf* arrogance. **arrogant** *adj* arrogant.
arrondir [arɔ̃dir] *v* round (off), make rounded. **arrondi** *adj* round.

arrondissement [arɔ̃dismɑ̃] *nm* district.
arroser [aroze] *v* water, spray; (*fam: repas*) wash down. **arrosoir** *nm* watering-can.
arsenal [arsɔnal] *nm* arsenal.
arsenic [arsɔnik] *nm* arsenic.
art [ar] *nm* art; (*adresse*) skill. **arts ménagers** domestic science *sing*.
artère [artɛr] *nf* artery. **artériel** *adj* arterial.
arthrite [artrit] *nf* arthritis. **arthritique** *adj* arthritic.
artichaut [artiʃo] *nm* globe artichoke.
article [artikl] *nm* article, item. **article réclame** special offer. **articles de Paris** fancy goods *pl*. **articles de toilette** toiletries *pl*.
articuler [artikyle] *v* articulate. **articulation** *nf* (*anat*) joint; articulation. **articulation du doigt** knuckle. **articulé** *adj* articulate; jointed.
artifice [artifis] *nm* device, trick, artifice.
artificiel [artifisjɛl] *adj* artificial.
artillerie [artijri] *nf* artillery.
artisan [artizɑ̃] *nm* craftsman, artisan.
artiste [artist] *n(m+f)* artist; (*théâtre*) performer. **artistique** *adj* artistic.
as [ɑs] *nm* ace.
asbeste [asbɛst] *nm* asbestos.
ascendant [asɑ̃dɑ̃] *adj* upward, rising. *nm* influence, ascendancy. **ascendance** *nf* ancestry.
ascenseur [asɑ̃sœr] *nm* elevator.
ascension [asɑ̃sjɔ̃] *nf* ascent.
Asie [azi] *nf* Asia. **asiatique** *adj* Asian. **Asiatique** *n(m+f)* Asian.
asile [azil] *nm* refuge, asylum, sanctuary; (*vieillards*) home.
aspect [aspɛ] *nm* aspect; appearance, look.
asperge [aspɛrʒ] *nf* asparagus.
asperger [aspɛrʒe] *v* spray, sprinkle.
asphalte [asfalt] *nm* asphalt.
asphyxie [asfiksi] *nf* suffocation, asphyxia.
aspirer [aspire] *v* inhale; (*liquide*) suck up. **aspirer à** aspire to, long for. **aspirant, -e** *nm, nf* candidate. **aspirateur** *nm* vacuum cleaner. **aspiration** *nf* aspiration.
aspirine [aspirin] *nf* aspirin.
***assaillir** [asajir] *v* assail, attack.
assainir [asenir] *v* clean up; purify.
assaisonner [asɛzɔne] *v* season. **assaisonnement** *nm* seasoning.

assassiner [asasine] v murder; (pol) assassinate. **assassin, -e** nm, nf murderer; assassin. **assassinat** nm murder; assassination.

assaut [aso] nm assault, attack. **prendre d'assaut** take by storm.

assembler [asãble] v assemble. **assemblage** nm assembling, assembly. **assemblée** nf assembly, meeting.

assentiment [asãtimã] nm assent.

***asseoir** [aswar] v sit; establish. **s'asseoir** (chaise, etc.) sit down; (lit) sit up.

assez [ase] adv enough; (plutôt) rather, fairly. **en avoir assez de** be fed up with.

assidu [asidy] adj assiduous; regular.

assiéger [asjeʒe] v besiege, beset.

assiette [asjɛt] nf plate; (cavalier) seat. **assiette creuse** soup dish. **assiette plate** dinner plate. **ne pas être dans son assiette** be off-colour.

assigner [asiɲe] v assign, allot, allocate; (jur) summons. **assignation** nf assignation; summons.

assimiler [asimile] v assimilate, absorb. **assimiler à** liken to. **assimilation** nf assimilation.

assis [asi] adj sitting, seated.

assises [asiz] nf pl assizes pl.

assister [asiste] v assist. **assister à** attend, witness. **assistance** nf (aide) assistance; (assemblée) audience, attendance. **assistant, -e** nm, nf assistant.

associer [asɔsje] v associate, combine. **s'associer** join together; (comm) form a partnership. **association** nf association; partnership. **associé, -e** nm, nf associate; partner.

assombrir [asɔ̃brir] v darken; (personne) make gloomy. **assombri** adj gloomy, sombre.

assommer [asɔme] v knock out; (fam) bore stiff.

assortir [asɔrtir] v (couleurs, etc.) match; accompany; (comm) supply. **assorti** adj assorted; matched. **assortiment** nm assortment; arrangement; (vaisselle, etc.) set.

assoupir [asupir] v numb, dull, deaden. **s'assoupir** (s'endormir) doze off. **assoupissement** nm drowsiness.

assourdir [asurdir] v deafen; (amortir) muffle.

assujettir [asyʒetir] v subject, subjugate; (fixer) secure.

assumer [asyme] v assume, take on.

assuré [asyre], **-e** adj assured; certain, sure. nm, nf insured person, policyholder.

assurer [asyre] v assure; (maison, etc.) insure; maintain, provide; (rendre sûr) secure, ensure. **s'assurer** make sure, check; insure oneself. **assurance** nf assurance; self-confidence; (contrat) insurance.

astérisque [asterisk] nm asterisk.

asthme [asmə] nm asthma. **asthmatique** adj asthmatic.

astre [astrə] nm star.

***astreindre** [astrɛ̃drə] v force, compel.

astringent [astrɛ̃ʒã] nm, adj astringent.

astrologie [astrɔlɔʒi] nf astrology. **astrologique** adj astrological. **astrologue** nm astrologer.

astronaute [astronot] n(m+f) astronaut.

astronomie [astronomi] nf astronomy. **astronome** nm astronomer. **astronomique** adj astronomical.

astucieux [astysjø] adj shrewd. **astuce** nf shrewdness; (truc) trick.

asymétrique [asimetrik] adj asymmetric.

atelier [atəlje] nm workshop; (art) studio.

athée [ate] adj atheistic. n(m+f) atheist. **athéisme** nm atheism.

Athènes [atɛn] n Athens. **athénien** adj Athenian. **Athénien, -enne** nm, nf Athenian.

athlète [atlɛt] n(m+f) athlete. **athlétique** adj athletic. **athlétisme** nm athletics.

atlantique [atlãtik] adj Atlantic. **l'Atlantique** nm the Atlantic (Ocean).

atlas [atlɑs] nm atlas.

atmosphère [atmɔsfɛr] nf atmosphere. **atmosphérique** adj atmospheric.

atome [atom] nm atom. **atomique** adj atomic.

atout [atu] nm trump; (avantage) asset, trump card.

âtre [ɑtrə] nm hearth.

atroce [atrɔs] adj atrocious, dreadful. **atrocité** nf atrocity.

s'attabler [atable] v sit (down) at table.

attacher [ataʃe] v attach; (lier) tie up, fasten. **s'attacher** (fermeture) fasten, do up. **attachant** adj engaging. **attache** nf fastener, string; (lien) tie. **à l'attache** tied up. **attaché** nm attached.

attaquer [atake] v attack; (problème) tackle; (travail) set about. **s'attaquer à** attack. **attaque** nf attack.

attarder [atarde] *v* make late. **s'attarder** *v* linger.

***atteindre** [atɛ̃drə] *v* reach; *(balle, etc.)* hit; *(maladie)* affect. **être atteint de** be suffering from. **atteinte** *nf* attack.

atteler [atle] *v* harness. **s'atteler à** get down to.

attenant [atnɑ̃] *adj* adjoining.

attendre [atɑ̃drə] *v* wait (for); *(compter sur)* expect. **faire attendre** keep waiting. **s'attendre à** expect. **en attendant** meanwhile.

attendrir [atɑ̃drir] *v* *(personne)* move; *(viande)* tenderize. **s'attendrir sur** feel sorry for. **attendrissant** *adj* touching, moving. **attendrissement** *nm* emotion; pity. **attendrisseur** *nm* tenderizer.

attendu [atɑ̃dy] *adj* long-awaited; expected. *prep* considering. **attendu que** seeing that.

attentat [atɑ̃ta] *nm* murder attempt; attack; *(jur)* violation; offence.

attente [atɑ̃t] *nf* wait, waiting; expectation.

attention [atɑ̃sjɔ̃] *nf* attention, care. **avec attention** carefully. **faire attention** take care. **faire attention à** pay attention to. *interj* watch out! careful! **attentif** *adj* attentive; *(scrupuleux)* careful; *(prévenant)* thoughtful.

atténuer [atenɥe] *v* tone down, lighten; *(douleur)* alleviate; *(faute)* mitigate. **s'atténuer** die down, subside.

atterrer [atere] *v* appal.

atterrir [aterir] *v* land. **atterrissage** *nm* landing.

attester [atɛste] *v* testify to, attest.

attirail [atiraj] *nm* *(fam)* gear.

attirer [atire] *v* attract; *(appâter)* lure, entice; cause. **attirance** *nf* attraction; lure. **attirant** *adj* attractive.

attiser [atize] *v* poke, stir up.

attitré [atitre] *adj* accredited; regular.

attitude [atityd] *nf* attitude.

attraction [atraksjɔ̃] *nf* attraction.

attrait [atrɛ] *nm* appeal, attraction.

attraper [atrape] *v* catch, get; *(tromper)* take in; *(gronder)* tell off. **attrape** *nf* trick.

attrayant [atrɛjɑ̃] *adj* appealing, attractive.

attribuer [atribɥe] *v* attribute; allocate, accord, award. **s'attribuer** claim. **attribut** *nm* attribute.

attrister [atriste] *v* sadden.

s'attrouper [atrupe] *v* flock together.

au [o] *contraction of* à le.

aubaine [obɛn] *nf* godsend, windfall.

aube[1] [ob] *nf* *(du jour)* dawn.

aube[2] [ob] *nf* *(bateau)* paddle; *(moulin)* vane.

aubépine [obepin] *nf* hawthorn.

auberge [obɛrʒ] *nf* inn. **auberge de la jeunesse** youth hostel. **aubergiste** *nm* innkeeper, landlord.

aubergine [obɛrʒin] *nf* aubergine.

aucun [okœ̃] *adj, pron* any. **ne ... aucun** not any, no, none. **aucunement** *adv* in no way, not in the least.

audace [odas] *nf* audacity, daring. **audacieux** *adj* daring, bold, audacious.

au-delà [odla] *nm, adv* beyond.

au-dessous [odəsu] *adv* below, underneath.

au-dessus [odəsy] *adv* above, over.

au-devant [odəvɑ̃] *adv* ahead. **aller au-devant de** anticipate; *(personne)* go and meet.

audible [odiblə] *adj* audible.

audience [odjɑ̃s] *nf* audience, hearing.

auditeur [oditœr], **-trice** *nm, nf* listener.

audition [odisjɔ̃] *nf* *(essai)* audition; recital; *(ouïe)* hearing.

auditoire [oditwar] *nm* audience.

auge [oʒ] *nf* trough.

augmenter [ɔgmɑ̃te] *v* increase. **augmentation** *nf* increase, rise.

aujourd'hui [oʒurdɥi] *adv* today. **aujourd'hui en huit** a week today.

aulx [o] *V* ail.

aumône [omon] *nf* alms; charity. **aumônier** *nm* chaplain.

auparavant [oparavɑ̃] *adv* before, previously.

auprès [oprɛ] *prep* **auprès de** next to, close to; compared with; in the opinion of.

auquel [okɛl] *contraction of* à lequel.

aura [ora] *nf* aura.

auréole [oreol] *nf* halo.

Aurigny [oriɲi] *nf* Alderney.

aurore [oror] *nf* dawn, daybreak.

aussi [osi] *adv* too, also; *(comparaison)* as; *(si)* so. **aussi bien** just as well. *conj* therefore.

aussitôt [osito] *adv* straight away. **aussitôt que** as soon as.

austère [ɔstɛr] *adj* austere. **austérité** *nf* austerity.

Australie [ɔstrali] *nf* Australia. **australien** *adj* Australian. **Australien, -enne** *nm, nf* Australian.

autant [otɑ̃] *adv* as much, so much. **autant de** as much, as many; (*tant*) so much, so many. **autant que** as much as. **autant que possible** as far as possible. **d'autant plus** all the more.

autel [ɔtɛl] *nm* altar.

auteur [otœr] *nm* author, writer; (*musique*) composer.

authentique [ɔtɑ̃tik] *adj* authentic, genuine. **authenticité** *nf* authenticity.

autistique [ɔtistik] *adj* autistic.

auto [oto] *nf* car. **auto-école** *nf* driving school. **auto-stop** *nm* hitch-hiking. **faire de l'auto-stop** hitch-hike. **auto-stoppeur, -euse** *nm, nf* hitch-hiker.

autobiographie [ɔtɔbjɔgrafi] *nf* autobiography. **autobiographique** *adj* autobiographical.

autobus [ɔtɔbys] *nm* bus.

autocar [ɔtɔkar] *nm* coach.

autodidacte [ɔtɔdidakt] *adj* self-taught.

autographe [ɔtɔgraf] *nm* autograph.

automatique [ɔtɔmatik] *adj* automatic. **automation** *or* **automatisation** *nf* automation. **automatiser** *v* automate.

automne [ɔtɔn] *nm* autumn. **automnal** *adj* autumnal.

automobile [ɔtɔmɔbil] *nf* motor car. **l'automobile** *nf* the motor industry; (*sport*) motoring. **automobiliste** *n(m+f)* motorist.

autonome [ɔtɔnɔm] *adj* autonomous. **autonomie** *nf* autonomy.

autopont [ɔtɔpɔ̃] *nm* flyover.

autopsie [ɔtɔpsi] *nf* post-mortem.

autoriser [ɔtɔrize] *v* authorize, give permission. **autorisation** *nf* authorization, permission. **autorisé** *adj* authorized; official.

autorité [ɔtɔrite] *nf* authority. **autoritaire** *n(m+f)*, *adj* authoritarian.

autoroute [ɔtɔrut] *nf* motorway.

autour [otur] *adv* around. *prep* **autour de** around.

autre [otrə] *adj* other; different. **autre chose** something else. **autre part** somewhere else. **d'autre part** on the other hand. *pron* another. **d'autres** others. **rien/personne d'autre** nothing/nobody else.

autrefois [otrəfwa] *adv* in the past. **d'autrefois** of the past.

autrement [otrəmɑ̃] *adv* differently, in another way; (*sinon*) otherwise. **autrement dit** in other words, that is.

Autriche [otriʃ] *nf* Austria. **autrichien** *adj* Austrian. **Autrichien, -enne** *nm, nf* Austrian.

autruche [otryʃ] *nf* ostrich.

autrui [otrɥi] *pron* others.

auvent [ovɑ̃] *nm* awning, canopy.

aux [o] *contraction of* **à les**.

auxiliaire [ɔksiljɛr] *adj* auxiliary, secondary. *n(m+f)* assistant, auxiliary.

auxquels, auxquelles [okɛl] *contractions of* **à lesquels, à lesquelles**.

aval [aval] *nm* **d'aval** (*eau*) downstream; (*pente*) downhill. **en aval** *adv* downstream; downhill.

avalanche [avalɑ̃ʃ] *nf* avalanche; torrent, flood.

avaler [avale] *v* swallow.

avancer [avɑ̃se] *v* advance; move *or* bring forward; (*accélérer*) speed up; make progress; (*montre*) gain. **avance** *nf* advance; lead. **à l'avance** in advance, beforehand. **d'avance** in advance. **en avance** (*heure*) early; ahead. **avancement** *nm* promotion; progress.

avant [avɑ̃] *prep* before. *adv* before; (*mouvement*) forward. *nm* front; (*naut*) bow. **avant tout** above all. **d'avant** *adj* previous. **en avant** (*mouvement*) forward; (*position*) ahead.

avantage [avɑ̃taʒ] *nm* advantage. **avantageux** *adj* worthwhile.

avant-bras *nm invar* forearm.

avant-coureur *nm* forerunner.

avant-dernier, -ère *n, adj* last but one.

avant-garde *nf* avant-garde. **d'avant-garde** *adj* avant-garde.

avant-goût *nm* foretaste.

avant-hier *adv* the day before yesterday.

avant-poste *nm* outpost.

avant-première *nf* preview.

avant-propos *nm invar* foreword.

avant-veille *nf* two days before.

avare [avar] *adj* miserly. *n(m+f)* miser. **avarice** *nf* avarice.

avarie [avari] *nf* damage. **avarié** *adj* rotting, damaged.

avec [avɛk] *prep* with.

avènement [avɛnmɑ̃] *nm* advent; (*roi*) accession.

avenir [avnir] *nm* future. **à l'avenir** from now on.

Avent [avã] *nm* Advent.
aventure [avãtyr] *nf* adventure; (*entreprise*) venture. **à l'aventure** at random, aimlessly. **s'aventurer** *v* venture. **aventureux** *adj* adventurous; risky. **aventurier** *nm* adventurer.
avenue [avny] *nf* avenue.
s'avérer [avere] *v* prove to be, turn out to be.
averse [avɛrs] *nf* shower.
aversion [avɛrsjɔ̃] *nf* aversion, loathing. **avoir en aversion** loathe.
avertir [avɛrtir] *v* warn; (*renseigner*) inform. **avertissement** *nm* warning; notice.
aveu [avø] *nm* confession, admission.
aveugle [avœglə] *adj* blind. *n*(*m+f*) blind person. **aveugler** *v* blind; (*éblouir*) dazzle. **s'aveugler sur** shut one's eyes to. **à l'aveuglette** blindly.
aviateur [avjatœr] *nm* airman. **aviation** *nf* aviation, flying; (*mil*) air force.
avide [avid] *adj* eager, avid; (*cupide*) greedy. **avidité** *nf* eagerness; greed.
avilir [avilir] *v* degrade, debase.
avion [avjɔ̃] *nm* aeroplane. **par avion** by airmail.
aviron [avirɔ̃] *nm* oar; (*sport*) rowing. **faire de l'aviron** row.
avis [avi] *nm* opinion; (*conseil*) advice; notice. **à mon avis** in my opinion. **avis au lecteur** foreword.
aviser [avize] *v* inform, notify; (*apercevoir*) notice. **aviser à** see to. **s'aviser de** realize suddenly; (*oser*) dare to. **avisé** *adj* sensible.
avocat[1] [avɔka], **-e** *nm, nf* (*jur*) barrister; advocate.
avocat[2] [avɔka] *nm* avocado (pear). **avocatier** *nm* avocado (tree).
avoine [avwan] *nf* oats *pl*.
***avoir**[1] [avwar] *v* have; (*obtenir*) get; (*être*) be. **il y a** there is *or* are; (*temps écoulé*) ago. **il n'y a pas de quoi** don't mention it. **qu'est-ce qu'il y a?** what's the matter?
avoir[2] [avwar] *nm* assets *pl*; (*comm*) credit.
avoisiner [avwazine] *v* border on, be close to. **avoisinant** *adj* neighbouring, nearby.
avorter [avɔrte] *v* abort; (*projet*) fail. **se faire avorter** have an abortion. **avortement** *nm* abortion. **avorteur, -euse** *nm, nf* abortionist.

avouer [avwe] *v* confess, admit. **avoué** *nm* solicitor.
avril [avril] *nm* April.
axe [aks] *nm* axis; (*tech*) axle.
azalée [azale] *nf* azalea.
azote [azɔt] *nf* nitrogen.

B

babiller [babije] *v* (*personne*) chatter; (*ruisseau*) babble; (*oiseau*) twitter. **babillage** *nm* chatter; babble; twitter. **babillard, -e** *nm, nf* chatterbox.
babines [babin] *nf pl* lips *pl*, chops *pl*.
bâbord [babɔr] *nm* (*naut*) port (side).
babouin [babwɛ̃] *nm* baboon.
bac [bak] *nm* ferry-boat; (*récipient*) tub, tray, sink.
baccalauréat [bakalɔrea] *nm* examination equivalent to A-levels.
bâche [baʃ] *nf* canvas cover. **bâche goudronnée** tarpaulin.
bâcler [bakle] *v* hurry through; (*travail*) botch. **bâclé** *adj* slapdash.
bactérie [bakteri] *nf* bacterium (*pl* -ria).
badigeonner [badiʒɔne] *v* (*mur*) distemper, whitewash; (*méd*) paint. **badigeon** *nm* distemper, whitewash.
badiner [badine] *v* banter; (*avec négatif*) treat lightly, trifle with. **badinage** *nm* banter.
bafouiller [bafuje] *v* splutter; (*bredouiller*) stammer.
bagage [bagaʒ] *nm* bag, piece of luggage. **bagages** *nm pl* luggage *sing*. **bagages à main** hand baggage *sing*.
bagarre [bagar] *nf* fight. (**se**) **bagarrer** *v* (*fam*) fight, scrap.
bagatelle [bagatɛl] *nf* trifle; (*objet*) trinket.
bagne [baɲ] *nm* hard labour.
bagnole [baɲɔl] *nf* (*fam*) old banger.
bague [bag] *nf* ring.
baguette [bagɛt] *nf* stick; (*musique*) baton; (*pour manger*) chopstick; (*pain*) thin French loaf; (*magique*) wand.
bahut [bay] *nm* chest; (*argot*) school.
bai [bɛ] *adj* bay.
baie[1] [bɛ] *nf* (*géog*) bay.

baie² [bɛ] *nf* (*bot*) berry.
baigner [beɲe] *v* bathe; (*bébé*) bath; (*tremper*) soak. **se baigner** (*mer, piscine*) go swimming; (*se laver*) have a bath. **baignade** *nf* bathe, bathing. **baigneur, -euse** *nm, nf* bather. **baignoire** *nf* bath.
bail [baj] *nm, pl* **baux** lease.
bâiller [bɑje] *v* yawn; (*couture, col, etc.*) gape; (*porte*) be ajar. **bâillement** *nm* yawn.
bâillonner [bɑjɔne] *v* gag. **bâillon** *nm* gag.
bain [bɛ̃] *nm* (*baignoire*) bath; (*piscine, mer*) swim, bathe. **bain de foule** walkabout. **bain de mousse** bubble bath. **prendre un bain de soleil** sunbathe.
baïonnette [bajɔnɛt] *nf* bayonet.
baiser [beze] *nm* kiss. *v* (*embrasser*) kiss; (*vulgaire*) screw.
baisser [bese] *v* (*mettre plus bas*) lower; (*décliner*) fall, drop. **se baisser** bend down. **baisse** *nf* fall, drop.
bal [bal] *nm, pl* **bals** dance, ball; (*lieu*) dance hall. **bal costumé** fancy-dress ball.
balader [balade] (*fam*) *v* trail round. **se balader** go for a walk; (*en voiture*) go for a drive. **balade** *nf* walk; drive.
balafrer [balafre] *v* gash. **balafre** *nf* gash; (*cicatrice*) scar. **balafré** *adj* scarred.
balai [balɛ] *nm* broom, brush. **balai mécanique** carpet sweeper.
balance [balɑ̃s] *nf* scales *pl*; (*comm*) balance. **Balance** *nf* Libra.
balancer [balɑ̃se] *v* swing, rock; (*compte*) balance; (*argot*) chuck (out). **se balancer** sway, swing. **balancier** *nm* pendulum. **balançoire** *nf* swing; (*bascule*) seesaw.
balayer [baleje] *v* sweep.
balbutier [balbysje] *v* stammer, mumble.
balcon [balkɔ̃] *nm* balcony; (*théâtre*) dress circle.
baldaquin [baldakɛ̃] *nm* canopy.
baleine [balɛn] *nf* whale.
balise [baliz] *nf* beacon; (*flottante*) buoy.
balistique [balistik] *adj* ballistic. *nf* ballistics.
balivernes [balivɛrn] *nf pl* nonsense *sing*.
ballade [balad] *nf* ballad.
ballant [balɑ̃] *adj* dangling.
balle [bal] *nf* (*projectile*) bullet; (*sport*) ball.
ballet [balɛ] *nm* ballet. **ballerine** *nf* ballerina.
ballon [balɔ̃] *nm* balloon; (*sport*) ball.
ballotter [balɔte] *v* jolt, toss *or* shake about.

balnéaire [balneɛr] *adj* bathing. **station balnéaire** *nf* seaside resort.
balustrade [balystrad] *nf* handrail.
bambou [bɑ̃bu] *nm* bamboo.
banal [banal] *adj* banal, commonplace. **banalité** *nf* banality; (*propos*) platitude.
banane [banan] *nf* banana. **bananier** *nm* banana (tree).
banc [bɑ̃] *nm* bench, seat; (*géol*) layer, bed. **banc d'église** pew. **banc de sable** sandbank. **banc des accusés** dock.
bancal [bɑ̃kal] *adj* wobbly, shaky; (*personne*) bandy-legged.
bandage [bɑ̃daʒ] *nm* bandage.
bande¹ [bɑ̃d] *nf* strip, band; (*magnétophone*) tape; (*méd*) bandage. **bande dessinée** comic strip. **bande sonore** sound-track.
bande² [bɑ̃d] *nf* band, group, gang.
bandeau [bɑ̃do] *nm* (*ruban*) headband; (*yeux*) blindfold.
bander [bɑ̃de] *v* bandage; (*tendre*) stretch. **bander les yeux à** blindfold.
bandit [bɑ̃di] *nm* bandit, thief; (*escroc*) crook.
banlieue [bɑ̃ljø] *nf* suburbs *pl*.
banne [ban] *nf* (*magasin*) awning; (*manne*) hamper.
bannière [banjer] *nf* banner.
bannir [banir] *v* banish. **banni, -e** *nm, nf* exile. **bannissement** *nm* banishment.
banque [bɑ̃k] *nf* bank; (*métier*) banking. **banquier** *nm* banker.
banqueroute [bɑ̃krut] *nf* bankruptcy. **faire banqueroute** go bankrupt. **banqueroutier, -ère** *nm, nf* bankrupt.
banquet [bɑ̃kɛ] *nm* banquet.
banquette [bɑ̃kɛt] *nf* seat.
baptême [batɛm] *nm* baptism, christening.
baptiser [batize] *v* baptize, christen.
bar [bar] *nm* bar.
baragouiner [baragwine] *v* (*fam*) gabble, talk gibberish. **baragouin** *nm* gibberish.
baraque [barak] *nf* stand, stall; (*abri*) shed; (*fam: maison*) place.
baratte [barat] *nf* churn. **baratter** *v* churn.
barbare [barbar] *adj* barbarous, barbaric. *nm* barbarian. **barbarie** *nf* barbarity.
barbe [barb] *nf* beard. **barbe à papa** candy floss. **quelle barbe!** (*fam*) what a drag!
barbecue [barbəkju] *nm* barbecue.

barbelé [barbəle] *adj* **fil de fer barbelé** barbed wire.

barbier [barbje] *nm* barber.

barbiturique [barbityrik] *nm* barbiturate.

barboter [barbɔte] *v* paddle, splash about; (*fam*) pinch. **barboteuse** *nf* rompers *pl*.

barbouiller [barbuje] *v* smear, daub; (*écrire*) scribble. **barbouillis** *nm* daub; scribble.

barbu [barby] *adj* bearded. *nm* bearded man.

barème [barɛm] *nm* list, scale, table.

bariolé [barjɔle] *adj* gaudy, multicoloured.

baromètre [barɔmɛtrə] *nm* barometer.

baron [barɔ̃] *nm* baron. **baronne** *nf* baroness. **baronnet** *nm* baronet.

baroque [barɔk] *adj* weird, strange; (*arch*) baroque. *nm* baroque.

barque [bark] *nf* small boat.

barrage [baraʒ] *nm* (*rivière*) dam; barrier; barricade.

barre [bar] *nf* bar, rod; (*trait*) stroke; (*naut*) helm, tiller.

barreau [baro] *nm* (*échelle*) rung; (*cage, jur*) bar.

barrer [bare] *v* bar, obstruct; (*rayer*) cross (out); (*naut*) steer.

barrette [barɛt] *nf* hair-slide.

barricade [barikad] *nf* barricade. **barricader** *v* barricade.

barrière [barjɛr] *nf* (*porte*) gate; (*clôture*) fence; (*obstacle*) barrier.

baryton [baritɔ̃] *nm*, *adj* baritone.

bas¹, basse [ba, bas] *adj* low. *adv* low; (*parler*) in a low voice. *nm* bottom. **en bas** down below; (*maison*) downstairs. **basse** *nf* bass.

bas² [ba] *nm* stocking.

basculer [baskyle] *v* fall over, topple; (*renverser*) tip up or out. **bascule** *nf* (*jeu*) see-saw. **cheval/fauteuil à bascule** *nm* rocking-horse/chair.

base [baz] *nf* base; (*fondement*) basis. **de base** basic.

base-ball [bɛzbol] *nm* baseball.

baser [baze] *v* base.

basilic [bazilik] *nm* basil.

basket-ball [baskɛtbol] *nm* basketball.

bassin [basɛ̃] *nm* pond, pool; (*géog*) basin; (*anat*) pelvis; (*naut*) dock.

basson [basɔ̃] *nm* bassoon.

bastille [bastij] *nf* fortress.

bataclan [bataklɑ̃] *nm* (*fam*) junk.

bataille [batɑj] *nf* battle, fight. **bataillon** *nm* battalion.

bâtard [batar], **-e** *n*, *adj* bastard.

bateau [bato] *nm* boat. **bateau à voiles** sailing boat. **bateau de sauvetage** lifeboat.

bâtiment [batimɑ̃] *nm* building; (*naut*) ship.

bâtir [batir] *v* build; (*couture*) tack. **bâti** *nm* frame; tacking.

bâton [batɔ̃] *nm* stick.

battant [batɑ̃] *nm* flap; (*porte*) door; (*cloche*) clapper.

batte [bat] *nf* (*sport*) bat.

battement [batmɑ̃] *nm* beat, beating; interval, pause. **battement de paupières** blink.

batterie [batri] *nf* battery; (*musique*) percussion, drums.

***battre** [batrə] *v* beat; (*parcourir*) scour; (*cartes*) shuffle. **battre des mains** clap. **battre son plein** be at its height. **se battre** fight.

baux [bo] *V* **bail**.

bavard [bavar], **-e** *adj* talkative. *nm*, *nf* (*fam*) chatterbox.

bavarder [bavarde] *v* chatter; (*papoter*) gossip. **bavardage** *nm* chatter; gossip.

baver [bave] *v* dribble, slobber. **bave** *nf* dribble, slobber. **bavette** *nf* bib.

béant [beɑ̃] *adj* gaping, wide open.

béat [bea] *adj* smug; (*sourire*) blissful.

beau [bo], **belle** *adj* beautiful, fine, lovely. **bel et bien** well and truly. **de plus belle** all the more. **beauté** *nf* beauty.

beaucoup [buku] *adv* (very) much, a great deal, a lot; (*personnes*) many. **de beaucoup** by far.

beau-fils *nm* son-in-law; (*remariage*) stepson.

beau-frère *nm* brother-in-law.

beau-père *nm* father-in-law; (*remariage*) stepfather.

beaux-arts [bozar] *nm pl* fine arts *pl*.

bébé [bebe] *nm* baby.

bec [bɛk] *nm* beak; (*plume*) nib; (*carafe*) lip; (*théière*) spout.

bécane [bekan] *nf* (*fam*) bike.

bécasse [bekas] *nf* woodcock. **bécassine** *nf* snipe.

bêcher [beʃe] *v* dig. **bêche** *nf* spade.

becqueter [bɛkte] *v* peck.

bedaine [bədɛn] *nf* (*fam*) paunch.

bée [be] *adj* **bouche bée** open-mouthed.
beffroi [befrwa] *nm* belfry.
bégayer [begeje] *v* stammer, stutter.
bégueule [begœl] *nf* prude. *adj* prudish.
béguin [begɛ̃] *nm* bonnet. **avoir le béguin pour** (*fam*) have a crush on, take a fancy to.
beige [bɛʒ] *nm, adj* beige.
beignet [bɛɲɛ] *nm* fritter; (*soufflé*) doughnut.
bel [bɛl] *form of* **beau** *used before vowel or mute h.*
bêler [bele] *v* bleat.
belette [bəlɛt] *nf* weasel.
Belgique [bɛlʒik] *nf* Belgium. **belge** *adj* Belgian. **belge** *n(m+f)* Belgian.
Belgrade [bɛlgrad] *n* Belgrade.
bélier [belje] *nm* ram. **Bélier** *nm* Aries.
belle [bɛl] *V* **beau.**
belle-fille *nf* daughter-in-law; (*remariage*) stepdaughter.
belle-mère *nf* mother-in-law; (*remariage*) stepmother.
belle-sœur *nf* sister-in-law.
bémol [bemɔl] *nm* flat.
bénédicité [benedisite] *nm* grace.
bénédiction [benediksjɔ̃] *nf* blessing.
bénéfice [benefis] *nm* (*comm*) profit; advantage, benefit. **bénéficiaire** *n(m+f)* beneficiary; (*chèque*) payee. **bénéficier de** *v* benefit from; (*jouir de*) enjoy; (*obtenir*) get.
bénévole [benevɔl] *adj* voluntary, unpaid.
bénin, -igne [benɛ̃, -iɲ] *adj* mild, slight; (*tumeur*) benign.
bénir [benir] *v* bless. **bénit** *adj* consecrated, holy.
béquille [bekij] *nf* crutch.
bercer [bɛrse] *v* rock; (*apaiser*) lull. **se bercer** delude oneself. **berceau** *nm* cradle. **berceuse** *nf* lullaby.
berger [bɛrʒe] *nm* shepherd; (*chien*) sheepdog. **berger allemand** alsatian. **bergère** *nf* shepherdess.
Berlin [bɛrlɛ̃] *n* Berlin.
Berne [bɛrn] *n* Bern.
besogne [bəzɔɲ] *nf* work.
besoin [bəzwɛ̃] *nm* need. **au besoin** if necessary. **avoir besoin de** need.
bétail [betaj] *nm* livestock; (*bovins*) cattle.
bête [bɛt] *nf* animal, creature, beast. **bête à bon dieu** ladybird. **bête noire** pet hate. **faire la bête** act stupid. *adj* stupid. **bêtise** *nf* stupidity; (*erreur*) blunder; (*action*) silly thing. **dire des bêtises** talk nonsense.

béton [betɔ̃] *nm* concrete. **bétonner** *v* concrete.
betterave [bɛtrav] *nf* beet. **betterave rouge** beetroot. **betterave sucrière** sugar beet.
beugler [bøgle] *v* bellow; (*radio*) blare; (*vache*) low.
beurre [bœr] *nm* butter. **beurrer** *v* butter.
bévue [bevy] *nf* blunder.
biais [bjɛ] *nm* (*détour*) expedient, device; (*aspect*) angle; (*couture*) bias; (*oblique*) slant. **de biais** at an angle; indirectly. **en biais** diagonally, at an angle.
bibelot [biblo] *nm* trinket, knick-knack.
biberon [bibrɔ̃] *nm* feeding bottle. **élevé au biberon** bottle-fed.
Bible [biblə] *nf* Bible. **biblique** *adj* biblical.
bibliographie [biblijɔgrafi] *nf* bibliography.
bibliothécaire [biblijɔtekɛr] *n(m+f)* librarian.
bibliothèque [biblijɔtɛk] *nf* library; (*meuble*) bookcase.
biceps [bisɛps] *nm* biceps.
biche [biʃ] *nf* doe.
bicyclette [bisiklɛt] *nf* bicycle; (*sport*) cycling. **aller à bicyclette** cycle.
bidon [bidɔ̃] *nm* can, tin.
bien [bjɛ̃] *adv* well; (*très*) very; (*beaucoup*) very much; (*plutôt*) rather; certainly, indeed; (*tout à fait*) properly, carefully. *adj* good; (*beau*) nice. *nm* good; possession. **bien de** much. **bien que** although. **biens** *nm pl* goods *pl*; property *sing.*
bien-aimé [bjɛ̃neme], **-e** *n, adj* beloved.
bien-être [bjɛ̃nɛtrə] *nm* well-being.
bienfaisant [bjɛ̃fəzɑ̃] *adj* beneficial; (*personne*) kind. **bienfaisance** *nf* charity.
bienfaiteur [bjɛ̃fɛtœr] *nm* benefactor. **bienfaitrice** *nf* benefactress.
bienheureux [bjɛ̃nœrø] *adj* (*rel*) blessed; happy.
biennal [bjenal] *adj* biennial.
bienséance [bjɛ̃seɑ̃s] *nf* propriety. **bienséant** *adj* proper, seemly.
bientôt [bjɛ̃to] *adv* soon. **à bientôt!** see you!
bienveillance [bjɛ̃vejɑ̃s] *nf* kindness, benevolence. **bienveillant** *adj* benevolent, kindly.
bienvenu [bjɛ̃vny], **-e** *adj* well-chosen. *nm, nf* welcome person *or* thing. **être le bienvenu** be welcome. **bienvenue** *nf* welcome.

bocal

bière[1] [bjɛr] *nf* (*boisson*) beer. **bière (à la) pression** draught beer. **bière blonde** lager.

bière[2] [bjɛr] *nf* coffin.

biffer [bife] *v* cross out.

bifocal [bifɔkal] *adj* bifocal. **lunettes bifocales** *nf pl* bifocals *pl*.

bifteck [biftɛk] *nm* steak.

bifurcation [bifyrkɑsjɔ̃] *nf* fork, branching off. **bifurquer** *v* fork, branch off.

bigame [bigam] *adj* bigamous. *n(m+f)* bigamist. **bigamie** *nf* bigamy.

bigorneau [bigɔrno] *nm* winkle.

bigot [bigo], **-e** *adj* bigoted. *nm, nf* bigot.

bigoudi [bigudi] *nm* curler, roller.

bijou [biʒu] *nm, pl* **-oux** jewel. **bijouterie** *nf* jewellery; (*boutique*) jeweller's. **bijoutier**, **-ère** *nm, nf* jeweller.

bikini [bikini] *nm* bikini.

bilan [bilɑ̃] *nm* assessment; consequence; (*comm*) balance sheet. **bilan de santé** check-up.

bile [bil] *nf* bile. **se faire de la bile** get worried.

bilingue [bilɛ̃g] *adj* bilingual.

billard [bijar] *nm* billiards; billiard table.

bille [bij] *nf* marble; billiard ball.

billet [bijɛ] *nm* ticket; note. **billet de banque** banknote.

billot [bijo] *nm* block.

binaire [binɛr] *adj* binary.

biner [bine] *v* hoe. **binette** *nf* hoe.

biographie [bjɔgrafi] *nf* biography. **biographe** *n(m+f)* biographer. **biographique** *adj* biographical.

biologie [bjɔlɔʒi] *nf* biology. **biologique** *adj* biological. **biologiste** *n(m+f)* biologist.

bis [bis] *nm, interj* encore. *adv* (*musique*) repeat.

bisannuel [bizanɥɛl] *adj* biennial.

biscornu [biskɔrny] *adj* irregular; (*bizarre*) peculiar.

biscotte [biskɔt] *nf* rusk.

biscuit [biskɥi] *nm* biscuit; (*gâteau*) sponge cake.

bise[1] [biz] *nf* (*vent*) north wind.

bise[2] [biz] *nf* kiss.

bistouri [bisturi] *nm* scalpel.

bistro [bistro] *nm* pub, café.

bizarre [bizar] *adj* strange, odd. **bizarrerie** *nf* strangeness, oddness.

blafard [blafar] *adj* pale, wan.

blague [blag] *nf* joke; (*farce*) trick. **sans blague?** really? **blaguer** (*fam*) *v* (*taquiner*) tease; (*plaisanter*) be joking.

blaireau [blɛro] *nm* badger; (*brosse*) shaving brush.

blâmer [blɑme] *v* blame; reprimand. **blâme** *nm* blame, reprimand.

blanc, blanche [blɑ̃, blɑ̃ʃ] *nm, adj* (*couleur*) white; (*page, etc.*) blank. **blanc cassé** off-white. **blancheur** *nf* whiteness.

blanchir [blɑ̃ʃir] *v* whiten; (*mur*) whitewash; (*toile*) bleach; (*linge*) launder; (*devenir blanc*) go *or* turn white. **blanchisserie** *nf* laundry.

blasé [blaze] *adj* blasé. **être blasé de** be bored with.

blason [blazɔ̃] *nm* coat of arms; heraldry.

blasphémer [blasfeme] *v* blaspheme. **blasphématoire** *adj* blasphemous. **blasphème** *nm* blasphemy.

blatte [blat] *nf* cockroach.

blé [ble] *nm* wheat, corn.

blêmir [blemir] *v* turn *or* go pale. **blême** *adj* pallid, wan.

blessé [blese], **-e** *adj* wounded. *nm, nf* casualty.

blesser [blese] *v* hurt, injure, wound. **blessure** *nf* wound.

blet, blette [blɛ, blɛt] *adj* overripe.

bleu [blø] *adj* blue. *nm* blue; (*meurtrissure*) bruise; (*vêtement*) overalls *pl*; (*débutant*) beginner. **bleu marine** navy blue. **bleu roi** royal blue.

bleuet [bløɛ] *nm* cornflower.

blindé [blɛde] *adj* armoured, reinforced.

bloc [blɔk] *nm* (*pierre, bois*) block; (*papier*) pad; group; (*d'éléments*) unit. **à bloc** fully, properly. **en bloc** outright.

blocage [blɔkaʒ] *nm* (*prix, etc.*) freeze; (*blocaille*) rubble.

blocus [blɔkys] *nm* blockade. **faire le blocus de** blockade.

blond [blɔ̃] *adj* fair, blond; (*sable*) golden. **blonde** *nf* blonde.

bloquer [blɔke] *v* block, jam, wedge; group together; (*salaires, etc.*) freeze.

se blottir [blɔtir] *v* snuggle up.

blouse [bluz] *nf* overall; (*chemisier*) blouse.

blue-jean [bludʒin] *nm* jeans *pl*.

bluff [blœf] *nm* (*fam*) bluff. **bluffer** *v* bluff.

bobine [bɔbin] *nf* spool, reel, bobbin; (*élec*) coil. **bobiner** *v* wind.

bocage [bɔkaʒ] *nm* grove; (*géog*) bocage.

bocal [bɔkal] *nm* jar; (*poissons*) bowl.

bock [bɔk] *nm* glass of beer.
bœuf [bœf] *nm* (*animal*) bullock, ox; (*viande*) beef.
bohème [bɔɛm] *n(m+f)*, *adj* bohemian.
*boire [bwar] *v* drink; absorb.
bois [bwa] *nm* wood; (*cerf*) antler; (*musique*) wood-wind instrument. **bois de chauffage** firewood. **de** *or* **en bois** wooden. **boisé** *adj* wooded, woody. **boiserie** *nf* panelling.
boisson [bwasɔ̃] *nf* drink. **boisson alcoolisée** alcoholic drink.
boîte [bwat] *nf* box; (*métal*) tin, can. **boîte à lettres** pillar-box. **boîte à ordures** dustbin. **boîte de nuit** night-club. **boîte de vitesses** gearbox.
boiter [bwate] *v* limp. **boiteux** *adj* lame; (*meuble*) wobbly; (*projet*) shaky.
bol [bɔl] *nm* bowl.
bombarder [bɔ̃barde] *v* bombard; bomb. **bombardier** *nm* (*avion*) bomber.
bombe [bɔ̃b] *nf* bomb; aerosol, spray. **bombe atomique** atom bomb.
bomber [bɔ̃be] *v* bulge, stick out; (*route*) camber. **bombé** *adj* rounded, bulging. **bombement** *nm* bulge; camber.
bon [bɔ̃], **bonne** *adj* good; (*agréable*) nice; (*gentil*) kind; (*valable*) valid; (*correct*) right. **à quoi bon?** what's the use? **bon à** *or* **pour** fit for. **de bonne heure** early. **pour de bon** for good. *nm* good person; good part. *interj* right!
bon² [bɔ̃] *nm* form; coupon, voucher; (*titre*) bond.
bon anniversaire *interj* happy birthday!
bonasse [bɔnas] *adj* meek.
bonbon [bɔ̃bɔ̃] *nm* sweet. **bonbon à la menthe** mint.
bond [bɔ̃] *nm* leap, bound; (*balle*) bounce.
bonde [bɔ̃d] *nf* plug, stopper.
bondé [bɔ̃de] *adj* packed, crammed.
bondir [bɔ̃dir] *v* leap (up), jump (up); (*balle*) bounce; (*sursauter*) start.
bon enfant *adj invar* good-natured.
bonheur [bɔnœr] *nm* happiness; joy; (*chance*) luck. **au petit bonheur** haphazardly. **par bonheur** fortunately.
bonhomie [bɔnɔmi] *nf* good nature.
bonhomme [bɔnɔm] *nm* (*fam*) chap, bloke. **bonhomme de neige** (*fam*) snowman. *adj invar* good-natured.
boni [bɔni] *nm* profit.
bonjour [bɔ̃ʒur] *nm*, *interj* hello; (*matin*) good morning; (*après-midi*) good afternoon.
bon marché *adj invar* cheap.
Bonn [bɔn] *n* Bonn.
bonne [bɔn] *V* **bon¹**. *nf* maid.
bonne année *interj* happy New Year!
bonne-maman *nf* (*fam*) granny, grandma.
bonnet [bɔnɛ] *nm* hat, bonnet; (*soutien-gorge*) cup. **bonnet d'âne** dunce's cap. **bonnet de bain** bathing cap. **bonneterie** *nf* hosiery.
bon-papa *nm* (*fam*) grand-dad, grandpa.
bon sens *nm* common sense.
bonsoir [bɔ̃swar] *nm*, *interj* good evening; (*en se couchant*) goodnight.
bonté [bɔ̃te] *nf* kindness, goodness.
bord [bɔr] *nm* edge, side; (*verre*) rim. **à bord** on board, aboard. **à ras bord** to the brim. **au bord de** (*lac*, etc.) by, alongside; (*larmes*, *ruine*) on the verge *or* brink of. **au bord de la mer** at the seaside. **bord du trottoir** kerb. **bordure** *nf* edge, border.
bordeaux [bɔrdo] *nm* Bordeaux. **bordeaux rouge** claret. *adj invar* maroon.
bordel [bɔrdɛl] *nm* brothel.
border [bɔrde] *v* edge; (*rue*) line; (*lit*) tuck in.
bordereau [bɔrdəro] *nm* note, slip; (*relevé*) statement.
borgne [bɔrɲə] *adj* one-eyed; (*louche*) shady.
borner [bɔrne] *v* limit; (*terrain*) mark out. **se borner à** content oneself with, confine oneself to. **borne** *nf* limit; (*kilométrique*) milestone. **sans bornes** limitless. **borné** *adj* narrow-minded; limited.
bosquet [bɔskɛ] *nm* copse.
bosse [bɔs] *nf* bump, lump; (*bossu*) hump. **avoir la bosse de** (*fam*) be good at, have a flair for.
bosseler [bɔsle] *v* emboss; (*déformer*) dent. **bosselé** *adj* dented, battered; (*sol*) bumpy. **bosselure** *nf* dent.
bossu [bɔsy], **-e** *adj* hunchbacked. *nm*, *nf* hunchback.
bot [bo] *adj* **pied bot** club foot.
botanique [bɔtanik] *adj* botanical. *nf* botany. **botaniste** *n(m+f)* botanist.
botte¹ [bɔt] *nf* boot. **botte de caoutchouc** wellington, gumboot. **bottillon** *nm* bootee.
botte² [bɔt] *nf* bunch, bundle.
botte³ [bɔt] *nf* (*escrime*) thrust.
botter [bɔte] *v* put boots on; (*fam*, *sport*) kick.

Bottin ® [bɔtɛ̃] *nm* directory.

bouc [buk] *nm* goat. **bouc émissaire** scapegoat.

boucaner [bukane] *v* (*viande*) cure; (*peau*) tan.

bouche [buʃ] *nf* mouth. **bouche à bouche** *nm invar* kiss of life. **bouchée** *nf* mouthful.

boucher[1] [buʃe] *v* block; (*bouteille*) cork; (*trou*) plug, fill up. **boucher le passage** be in the way. **bouché** *adj* (*temps*) cloudy; (*argot*) stupid, thick.

boucher[2] [buʃe] *nm* butcher. **boucherie** *nf* butcher's.

bouchon [buʃɔ̃] *nm* stopper, top; (*liège*) cork; (*évier*) plug; (*auto*) traffic jam.

boucler [bukle] *v* (*fermer*) buckle, fasten up; complete; (*cheveux*) curl. **boucler la boucle** (*aéro*) loop the loop; come full circle; complete. **boucle** *nf* buckle; curl; (*ruban, etc.*) loop. **boucle d'oreille** earring. **bouclé** *adj* curly.

bouclier [buklije] *nm* shield.

bouddhisme [budismə] *nm* Buddhism. **bouddhiste** *n*(*m*+*f*), *adj* Buddhist.

bouder [bude] *v* sulk. **boudeur, -euse** *adj* sulky.

boudin [budɛ̃] *nm* black pudding.

boue [bu] *nf* mud.

bouée [bwe] *nf* buoy. **bouée de sauvetage** lifebuoy.

boueux [bwø] *adj* muddy. *nm* dustman.

bouffer [bufe] *v* puff out; (*fam*) eat. **bouffant** *adj* (*manche*) full; (*pantalon, etc.*) baggy. **bouffe** *nf* (*argot*) grub. **bouffée** *nf* puff; (*vent*) gust; (*parfum*) whiff.

bouffir [bufir] *v* puff up. **bouffi** *adj* bloated, swollen; (*yeux*) puffy. **bouffissure** *nf* puffiness.

bouffon, -onne [bufɔ̃, -ɔn] *adj* comical. *nm* buffoon, clown. **bouffonnerie** *nf* clowning.

bouger [buʒe] *v* move, stir.

bougie [buʒi] *nf* candle; (*auto*) spark plug. **bougeoir** *nm* candlestick.

bouillir [bujir] *v* boil. **bouilloire** *nf* kettle. **bouillon** [bujɔ̃] *nm* broth, stock; (*bulle*) bubble. **bouillon cube** stock cube. **bouillonner** [bujɔne] *v* bubble, foam, seethe.

bouillotte [bujɔt] *nf* hot-water bottle.

boulanger [bulɑ̃ʒe] *nm* baker. **boulangerie** *nf* baker's, bakery.

boule [bul] *nf* ball. **boule de neige** snowball. **boules** *nf pl* (*jeu*) bowls *sing*.

bouleau [bulo] *nm* birch.

bouledogue [buldɔg] *nm* bulldog.

boulet [bulɛ] *nm* cannon-ball.

boulette [bulɛt] *nf* pellet.

boulevard [bulvar] *nm* boulevard.

bouleverser [bulvɛrse] *v* (*renverser*) turn upside down; disrupt, change completely; (*personne*) overwhelm, distress deeply. **bouleversement** *nm* upheaval.

boulon [bulɔ̃] *nm* bolt. **boulonner** *v* bolt.

boulot[1], **-otte** [bulo, -ɔt] *adj* plump.

boulot[2] [bulo] *nm* (*fam*) work.

boulotter [bulɔte] *v* (*fam*) eat.

bouquet[1] [bukɛ] *nm* bouquet, bunch; (*arbres*) clump. **c'est le bouquet!** that's the last straw!

bouquet[2] [bukɛ] *nm* (*crevette*) prawn.

bouquin [bukɛ̃] *nm* (*fam*) book. **bouquiniste** *nm* second-hand bookseller.

bourbe [burb] *nf* mire, mud. **bourbeux** *adj* miry, muddy.

bourdon [burdɔ̃] *nm* bumble-bee; (*musique*) drone.

bourdonner [burdɔne] *v* hum, buzz. **bourdonnement** *nm* buzz, hum.

bourg [bur] *nm* market town.

bourgeois [burʒwa], **-e** *adj* middle-class; (*péj*) bourgeois, conventional. *nm, nf* middle-class person. **bourgeoisie** *nf* middle class.

bourgogne [burgɔɲ] *nm* burgundy.

bourgeon [burʒɔ̃] *nm* bud. **bourgeonner** *v* bud.

bourrade [burad] *nf* thump, prod.

bourrage [buraʒ] *nm* stuffing, filling.

bourrasque [burask] *nf* gust of wind.

bourre [bur] *nf* stuffing, wadding.

bourreau [buro] *nm* torturer; executioner.

bourrelet [burlɛ] *nm* (*porte, etc.*) draught excluder; (*chair*) roll.

bourrer [bure] *v* stuff, cram.

bourriche [buriʃ] *nf* hamper.

bourru [bury] *adj* surly, gruff.

bourse [burs] *nf* purse; (*d'étudiant*) grant. **la Bourse** the Stock Exchange.

boursoufler [bursufle] *v* puff up. **se boursoufler** (*peinture*) blister. **boursouflé** *adj* puffy, swollen; blistered; (*style*) turgid. **boursouflure** *nf* puffiness; blister; turgidity.

bousculer [buskyle] *v* jostle; (*heurter*) bump into; (*renverser*) knock over. **bousculade** *nf* hustle, crush; (*hâte*) rush.

bousiller [buzije] (*fam*) *v* (*travail*) botch; (*abîmer*) wreck.
boussole [busɔl] *nf* compass.
bout [bu] *nm* end, tip; (*morceau*) piece, bit. **à bout** at the end of one's tether. **à bout de souffle** out of breath. **à bout portant** point-blank. **au bout de** at the end of; (*après*) after. **au bout du compte** all things considered. **de bout en bout** from start to finish. **jusqu'au bout** to the (bitter) end.
bouteille [butɛj] *nf* bottle. **en bouteille** bottled.
boutique [butik] *nf* shop. **boutiquier, -ère** *nm, nf* shopkeeper.
bouton [butɔ̃] *nm* button; (*élec*) switch; (*porte*) handle; (*fleur*) bud; (*méd*) pimple. **bouton de col** collar stud. **bouton de manchette** cuff-link. **bouton d'or** buttercup. **bouton-pression** *nm* press stud. **boutonner** *v* button. **boutonneux** *adj* pimply. **boutonnière** *nf* buttonhole.
bouture [butyr] *nf* cutting. **faire des boutures** take cuttings.
bouvier [buvje] *nm* herdsman.
bovin [bɔvɛ̃] *adj* bovine. **bovins** *nm pl* cattle *pl*.
boxer [bɔkse] *v* box. **boxe** *nf* boxing. **boxeur** *nm* boxer.
boyau [bwajo] *nm* gut; passageway. **boyaux** *nm pl* entrails *pl*.
boycotter [bɔjkɔte] *v* boycott. **boycottage** *nm* boycott.
bracelet [braslɛ] *nm* bracelet; (*montre*) strap. **bracelet-montre** *nm* wristwatch.
braconner [brakɔne] *v* poach. **braconnage** *nm* poaching. **braconnier** *nm* poacher.
braguette [bragɛt] *nf* (*pantalon*) fly.
braille [brɑj] *nm* braille.
brailler [brɑje] *v* bawl, yell.
***braire** [brɛr] *v* bray.
braise [brɛz] *nf* embers *pl*.
braiser [breze] *v* braise.
brancard [brɑ̃kar] *nm* stretcher; (*bras*) shaft.
branche [brɑ̃ʃ] *nf* branch.
brancher [brɑ̃ʃe] *v* plug in, connect up.
brandir [brɑ̃dir] *v* brandish.
branle-bas [brɑ̃lba] *nm invar* bustle, commotion.
branler [brɑ̃le] *v* be shaky *or* unsteady; (*dent*) be loose. **branle** *nm* swing. **mettre en branle** set in motion, get moving.
braquer [brake] *v* aim, point; (*auto*) turn (the wheel).

bras [bra] *nm* arm; (*tech*) handle; (*travailleur*) worker. **bras dessus, bras dessous** arm in arm. **en bras de chemise** in shirt sleeves.
brasero [brazero] *nm* brazier.
brasier [brazje] *nm* inferno.
brasse [bras] *nf* breast-stroke. **brasse papillon** butterfly.
brassée [brase] *nf* armful.
brasser [brase] *v* stir, mix; (*bière*) brew. **brasserie** *nf* brewery; (*café*) brasserie.
brave [brav] *adj* good, nice; brave, courageous.
braver [brave] *v* brave, defy, stand up to.
bravoure [bravur] *nf* bravery.
break [brɛk] *nm* estate car.
brebis [brəbi] *nf* ewe, sheep. **brebis galeuse** black sheep.
brèche [brɛʃ] *nf* breach, gap.
bredouiller [brəduje] *v* stammer, mumble. **bredouille** *adj* empty-handed.
bref, brève [brɛf, brɛv] *adj* brief, short. **(en) bref** in short.
breloque [brəlɔk] *nf* charm.
Bretagne [brətaɲ] *nf* Brittany.
bretelle [brətɛl] *nf* strap. **bretelles** *nf pl* braces *pl*.
breuvage [brœvaʒ] *nm* drink, beverage.
brevet [brəvɛ] *nm* certificate, diploma; (*d'invention*) patent. **breveter** *v* patent.
bribe [brib] *nf* scrap, snatch, bit.
bricoler [brikɔle] *v* potter about, do odd jobs; (*réparer*) mend. **bricolage** *nm* do-it-yourself; makeshift repair. **bricoleur** *nm* handyman.
brider [bride] *v* bridle, restrain. **bride** *nf* bridle, rein; (*bonnet*) string, strap. **à bride abattue** (*fam*) flat out. **tenir en bride** keep a tight rein on.
bridge [bridʒ] *nm* bridge.
brièvement [brijɛvmɑ̃] *adv* briefly. **brièveté** *nf* brevity.
brigade [brigad] *nf* brigade; (*police*) squad; (*équipe*) team.
brigand [brigɑ̃] *nm* (*péj*) crook; (*enfant*) rascal. **brigandage** *nm* (armed) robbery.
brigue [brig] *nf* intrigue. **briguer** *v* covet, crave; solicit.
brillant [brijɑ̃] *adj* brilliant; (*luisant*) shiny, bright; outstanding, excellent. *nm* brilliance; shine, brightness.
briller [brije] *v* shine, sparkle.
brin [brɛ̃] *nm* sprig; (*herbe*) blade; (*fil*) strand. **un brin de** a bit of.

brindille [brɛ̃dij] nf twig.
brioche [brijɔʃ] nf bun.
brique [brik] nf brick.
briquet [brikɛ] nm cigarette lighter.
brise [briz] nf breeze.
briser [brize] v break, smash; (espérance, rebelle) crush. **brise-lames** nm invar breakwater.
britannique [britanik] adj British. **les Britanniques** the British.
broc [bro] nm pitcher.
brocanter [brɔkɑ̃te] v deal in second-hand goods. **brocante** nf second-hand goods pl; (commerce) second-hand trade. **brocanteur, -euse** nm, nf second-hand dealer.
broche [brɔʃ] nf (bijou) brooch; (cuisine) spit; (tech) pin.
broché [brɔʃe] adj **livre broché** paperback book.
brochet [brɔʃɛ] nm pike.
brochette [brɔʃɛt] nf (broche) skewer; (plat) kebab.
brochure [brɔʃyr] nf brochure, booklet.
brocoli [brɔkɔli] nm broccoli.
broder [brɔde] v embroider. **broder sur** elaborate on. **broderie** nf embroidery.
broncher [brɔ̃ʃe] v (cheval) stumble. **sans broncher** (sans peur) without flinching; (sans faute) without faltering.
bronchite [brɔ̃ʃit] nf bronchitis.
bronzer [brɔ̃ze] v tan; (métal) bronze. **bronzage** nm suntan. **bronze** nm bronze.
brosser [brɔse] v brush. **brosse** nf brush; (cheveux) crew-cut. **brosse à cheveux/dents/ongles** hair/tooth/nailbrush.
brouette [bruɛt] nf wheelbarrow.
brouhaha [bruaa] nm hubbub.
brouillard [brujar] nm fog. **il fait du brouillard** it's foggy.
brouiller [bruje] v (troubler) blur; (mêler) mix or muddle up. **se brouiller** become confused; (se fâcher) fall out. **brouille** nf quarrel.
brouillon, -onne [brujɔ̃, -ɔn] adj untidy; unsystematic. nm rough copy.
broussailles [brusɑj] nf pl undergrowth sing. scrub sing. **broussailleux** adj bushy.
brouter [brute] v graze.
broyer [brwaje] v grind, crush.
bru [bry] nf daughter-in-law.
bruiner [brɥine] v drizzle. **bruine** nf drizzle.

bruire [brɥir] v rustle; (eau) murmur. **bruissement** nm rustle; murmur.
bruit [brɥi] nm noise; rumour; (histoires) fuss. **bruitage** nm sound effects pl.
brûler [bryle] v burn. **brûlant** adj burning, scorching; (objet) red hot; (liquide) boiling hot. **brûlure** nf burn.
brume [brym] nf mist. **brumeux** adj misty.
brun [brœ̃] adj brown, dark. nm brown. **brune** nf brown ale; (femme) brunette.
brunir [brynir] v darken; (peau) tan, get sunburnt.
brusque [brysk] adj brusque, abrupt. **brusquerie** nf brusqueness, abruptness.
brut [bryt] adj crude, raw, rough; (comm) gross. **brute** nf brute.
brutal [brytal] adj rough, brutal; (franc) blunt, plain. **brutalité** nf brutality.
brutaliser [brytalize] v bully, ill-treat.
Bruxelles [brysɛl] n Brussels.
bruyant [brɥijɑ̃] adj noisy.
bruyère [bryjɛr] nf heather.
Bucarest [bykarɛst] n Bucharest.
buccin [byksɛ̃] nm whelk.
bûche [byʃ] nf log; (fam) blockhead.
bûcher¹ [byʃe] nm (remise) woodshed; (supplice) stake.
bûcher² [byʃe] v (fam) swot.
bucheron [byʃrɔ̃] nm woodcutter, lumberjack.
Budapest [bydapɛst] n Budapest.
budget [bydʒɛ] nm budget.
buée [bɥe] nf steam, condensation. **couvert de buée** misted up.
buffet [byfɛ] nm buffet; (meuble) sideboard. **buffet de cuisine** dresser.
buffle [byflə] nm buffalo.
buisson [bɥisɔ̃] nm bush.
bulbe [bylbə] nm bulb. **bulbeux** adj bulbous.
Bulgarie [bylgari] nf Bulgaria. **bulgare** nm, adj Bulgarian. **Bulgare** nm, nf Bulgarian.
bulle [byl] nf bubble; (méd) blister.
bulletin [byltɛ̃] nm bulletin; ticket; certificate; (école) report. **bulletin de vote** ballot paper. **bulletin météorologique** weather report.
bungalow [bœ̃galo] nm bungalow; (motel) chalet.
bureau [byro] nm (meuble) desk; (cabinet) study; (lieu) office; (section) department. **bureau de location** booking office. **bureau**

de poste post office. **bureau de vote** polling station.

bureaucratie [byrokrasi] *nf* bureaucracy. **bureaucrate** *n(m+f)* bureaucrat. **bureaucratique** *adj* bureaucratic.

buriner [byrine] *v* engrave.

burlesque [byrlɛsk] *adj* comical, ludicrous.

buste [byst] *nm* bust, chest.

but [by] *nm* goal, aim. **de but en blanc** point-blank, suddenly.

buter [byte] *v* stumble; (*sport*) score a goal; (*mur*) prop up. **se buter à** bump into. **buté** *adj* stubborn.

butin [bytɛ̃] *nm* booty, spoils.

butoir [bytwar] *nm* buffer.

butte [byt] *nf* mound. **être en butte à** be exposed to.

buvard [byvar] *nm* blotting paper.

buvette [byvɛt] *nf* refreshment bar.

buveur [byvœr], **-euse** *nm, nf* drinker.

byzantin [bizɑ̃tɛ̃] *adj* Byzantine.

C

c' [s] *V* **ce²**.

ça [sa] *informal contraction of* **cela**.

çà [sa] *adv* **çà et là** here and there.

cabale [kabal] *nf* cabal.

cabane [kaban] *nf* hut, shed, cabin. **cabane à outils** toolshed. **cabane en rondins** log cabin.

cabaret [kabarɛ] *nm* night-club, cabaret.

cabillaud [kabijo] *nm* fresh cod.

cabine [kabin] *nf* cabin; (*réduit*) cubicle, booth. **cabine de bain** beach hut. **cabine téléphonique** telephone box.

cabinet [kabinɛ] *nm* (*bureau*) office; (*médecin, dentiste*) surgery; (*meuble, pol*) cabinet. **cabinet de débarras** box-room. **cabinet de toilette** toilet. **cabinet de travail** study.

câble [kablə] *nm* cable. **câbler** *v* cable.

cabosser [kabɔse] *v* dent.

se cabrer [kabre] *v* rear up; rebel.

cabriole [kabrijɔl] *nf* caper; (*danse*) cabriole; (*culbute*) somersault. **cabrioler** *v* caper about.

cacahouette [kakawɛt] *nf* peanut.

cacao [kakao] *nm* cocoa.

cachemire [kaʃmir] *nm* cashmere.

cacher [kaʃe] *v* hide, conceal. **cache-cache** *nm invar* hide-and-seek. **cache-col** *or* **cache-nez** *nm invar* scarf. **se cacher de** hide from.

cachet [kaʃɛ] *nm* seal, stamp; (*comprimé*) tablet; style. **cachet de la poste** postmark. **cacheter** *v* seal.

cachette [kaʃɛt] *nf* hiding-place. **en cachette** on the quiet, secretly.

cachot [kaʃo] *nm* dungeon.

cactus [kaktys] *nm invar* cactus (*pl* -ti).

cadavre [kadavrə] *nm* corpse; (*animal*) carcass. **cadavéreux** *or* **cadavérique** *adj* deathly.

cadeau [kado] *nm* present, gift.

cadenas [kadna] *nm* padlock. **cadenasser** *v* padlock.

cadence [kadɑ̃s] *nf* rhythm; (*musique*) cadence; (*vitesse*) rate. **cadencé** *adj* rhythmic.

cadet, -ette [kadɛ, -ɛt] *adj* younger, youngest. *nm, nf* (*famille*) youngest child; junior.

cadran [kadrɑ̃] *nm* dial, face. **cadran solaire** sundial.

cadre [kadrə] *nm* frame; (*milieu*) setting; (*formulaire*) space; scope, limits *pl*; context; (*responsable*) executive. **les cadres** management *sing*.

cadrer [kadre] *v* tally, conform; (*phot*) centre.

caduc, -uque [kadyk] *adj* (*feuilles*) deciduous; (*jur*) null and void; (*périmé*) outmoded.

cafard [kafar] *nm* (*insecte*) cockroach; (*tristesse*) depression; (*mouchard*) sneak. **avoir le cafard** be down in the dumps. **cafarder** *v* sneak, tell tales.

café [kafe] *nm* coffee; (*lieu*) café. **café au lait** white coffee. **café noir** *or* **nature** black coffee. **café soluble** instant coffee.

caféine [kafein] *nf* caffeine.

cafetière [kaftjɛr] *nf* coffee-pot.

cage [kaʒ] *nf* cage; (*tech*) casing. **cage à poules** hen-coop.

cagneux [kaɲø] *adj* knock-kneed.

cagnotte [kaɲɔt] *nf* kitty.

cagoule [kagul] *nf* hood.

cahier [kaje] *nm* notebook, exercise book.

cahin-caha [kaɛ̃kaa] *adv* (*fam*) so-so.

cahot [kao] *nm* jolt, bump. **cahotant** *or* **cahoteux** *adj* bumpy. **cahoter** *v* jolt.

caille [kaj] *nf* quail.

cailler [kaje] v (lait) curdle; (sang) clot. **caillé** nm curds pl. **caillot** nm clot.

caillou [kaju] nm, pl -**oux** stone, pebble. **caillouteux** adj stony, pebbly.

caisse [kɛs] nf box, case; (argent) cash-box, till; (guichet) cash-desk; (tambour) drum. **caisse d'épargne** savings bank. **caissier, -ère** nm, nf cashier.

cajoler [kaʒɔle] v coax, cajole; (câliner) make a fuss of.

cake [kɛk] nm fruit cake.

calamité [kalamite] nf calamity, disaster.

calcaire [kalkɛr] adj chalky; (eau) hard. nm limestone.

calcium [kalsjɔm] nm calcium.

calculer [kalkyle] v calculate, work out. **calcul** nm calculation, sum; arithmetic.

cale[1] [kal] nf (naut) hold; (plan incliné) slipway. **cale sèche** dry dock.

cale[2] [kal] nf wedge.

caleçon [kalsɔ̃] nm underpants pl. **caleçon de bain** bathing trunks pl.

calembour [kalɑ̃bur] nm pun.

calendrier [kalɑ̃drije] nm calendar; (programme) timetable, schedule.

calepin [kalpɛ̃] nm notebook.

caler [kale] v wedge; prop up, support; (moteur) stall; (fam) give up.

calfeutrer [kalføtre] v stop up; (pièce) draughtproof.

calibre [kalibrə] nm calibre; (qualité) grade; (grosseur) size; (instrument) gauge. **calibrer** v gauge; grade.

califourchon [kalifurʃɔ̃] nm **à califourchon** astride.

câlin [kalɛ̃] adj cuddly; tender. nm cuddle. **câliner** v fondle, cuddle. **câlinerie** nf tenderness; caress.

calleux [kalø] adj callous.

calmant [kalmɑ̃] adj soothing. nm tranquillizer; (analgésique) pain-killer.

calmar [kalmar] nm squid.

calme [kalmə] adj quiet, calm, peaceful. nm stillness, peace, calmness.

calmer [kalme] v calm, soothe. **se calmer** calm down; (diminuer) ease, subside.

calomnier [kalɔmnje] v slander; (par écrit) libel. **calomnie** nf slander; libel. **calomnieux** adj slanderous; libellous.

calorie [kalɔri] nf calorie.

calorifuger [kalɔrifyʒe] v lag, insulate. **calorifugeage** nm lagging, insulation.

calquer [kalke] v trace; copy exactly. **calque** nm tracing; exact copy. **papier-calque** nm tracing paper.

calvitie [kalvisi] nf baldness.

camarade [kamarad] n(m+f) companion, friend. **camarade de jeu** playmate.

cambrer [kɑ̃bre] v arch, bend. **se cambrer** arch one's back. **cambrure** nf curve, arch.

cambrioler [kɑ̃brijɔle] v break into, burgle. **cambriolage** nm burglary. **cambrioleur** nm burglar.

camée [kame] nm cameo.

caméléon [kameleɔ̃] nm chameleon.

camelote [kamlɔt] nf (fam) junk.

caméra [kamera] nf cine-camera.

Cameroun [kamrun] nm Cameroon.

camion [kamjɔ̃] nm truck. **camion-citerne** nm tanker. **camionnette** nf van. **camionneur** nm truck driver.

camoufler [kamufle] v camouflage; (cacher) conceal; disguise. **camouflage** nm camouflage.

camp [kɑ̃] nm camp; (parti) side. **camp de concentration** concentration camp.

campagne [kɑ̃paɲ] nf country, countryside; (pol, mil, etc.) campaign. **campagnard, -e** n, adj rustic.

camper [kɑ̃pe] v camp. **se camper** plant oneself. **campeur, -euse** nm, nf camper. **camping** nm camping; (lieu) campsite.

campus [kɑ̃pys] nm campus.

Canada [kanada] nm Canada. **canadien** adj Canadian. **Canadien, -enne** nm, nf Canadian.

canaille [kanɑj] adj coarse. nf scoundrel, rogue.

canal [kanal] nm channel; (artificiel, anat) canal. **canaliser** v channel.

canapé [kanape] nm sofa, settee; (cuisine) canapé.

canard [kanar] nm duck; false report; (musique) false note. **canardeau** nm duckling. **canardière** nf duck-pond.

canari [kanari] nm canary.

cancan [kɑ̃kɑ̃] nm gossip. **cancaner** v gossip. **cancanier, -ère** nm, nf gossip, scandalmonger.

cancer [kɑ̃sɛr] nm cancer. **Cancer** nm Cancer. **cancérigène** adj carcinogenic.

cancre [kɑ̃krə] nm (fam) dunce.

candeur [kɑ̃dœr] nf naivety.

candidat [kɑ̃dida] -**e** nm, nf candidate, applicant.

candide [kɑ̃did] adj naive, ingenuous.

cane [kan] nf (female) duck. **caneton** nm duckling.

canevas [kanva] *nm* (*toile*) canvas; (*ébauche*) framework.
caniche [kaniʃ] *nm* poodle.
canif [kanif] *nm* penknife.
canin [kanɛ̃] *adj* canine.
caniveau [kanivo] *nm* gutter.
canne [kan] *nf* cane; walking stick. **canne à pêche** fishing rod. **canne à sucre** sugar cane.
canneler [kanle] *v* flute. **cannelure** *nf* groove.
cannelle [kanɛl] *nf* cinnamon.
canoë [kanɔe] *nm* canoe. **faire du canoë** go canoeing.
canon¹ [kanɔ̃] *nm* gun, cannon; (*tube*) barrel.
canon² [kanɔ̃] *nm* canon; model.
cañon [kaɲɔ̃] *nm* canyon.
canoniser [kanɔnize] *v* canonize.
canot [kano] *nm* boat, dinghy. **canot automobile** motor boat. **canot de sauvetage** lifeboat. **canot pneumatique** rubber dinghy. **canotage** *nm* boating, rowing. **faire du canotage** go boating *or* rowing. **canotier** *nm* boater.
cantatrice [kɑ̃tatris] *nf* singer.
cantine [kɑ̃tin] *nf* canteen.
canton [kɑ̃tɔ̃] *nm* canton, district; section.
cantonnier [kɑ̃tɔnje] *nm* road-mender.
canular [kanylar] *nm* hoax. **faire un canular à** hoax, play a hoax on.
caoutchouc [kautʃu] *nm* rubber. **caoutchouc mousse** foam rubber. **caoutchouteux** *adj* rubbery.
cap [kap] *nm* cape; headland.
capable [kapablə] *adj* capable, able.
capacité [kapasite] *nf* capacity; ability.
cape [kap] *nf* cape, cloak.
capitaine [kapitɛn] *nm* captain.
capital [kapital] *adj* major, chief; fundamental. *nm* capital; fund. **capitale** *nf* capital (letter); capital (city). **capitaliser** *v* amass, accumulate. **capitalisme** *nm* capitalism. **capitaliste** *n*(*m*+*f*), *adj* capitalist.
capiteux [kapitø] *adj* heady; (*femme*) alluring.
capitonner [kapitɔne] *v* pad. **capitonnage** *nm* padding. **capitonné de** lined with.
caporal [kapɔral] *nm* corporal.
capot [kapo] *nm* (*auto*) bonnet *or* US hood.
capote [kapɔt] *nf* (*auto*) hood; (*manteau*) greatcoat.

câpre [kɑprə] *nf* caper.
caprice [kapris] *nm* whim, caprice. **capricieux** *adj* capricious, temperamental.
Capricorne [kaprikɔrn] *nm* Capricorn.
capsule [kapsyl] *nf* capsule; (*pistolet*) cap.
capter [kapte] *v* win, gain; (*émission*) pick up.
captieux [kapsjø] *adj* specious.
captif [kaptif], **-ive** *n*, *adj* captive. **captivité** *nf* captivity.
captiver [kaptive] *v* captivate, fascinate.
capuchon [kapyʃɔ̃] *nm* hood; (*stylo*) cap.
capucine [kapysin] *nf* nasturtium.
caquet [kakɛ] *nm* cackle. **caqueter** *v* cackle.
car¹ [kar] *nm* coach.
car² [kar] *conj* because, for.
carabine [karabin] *nf* rifle.
caractère [karaktɛr] *nm* character, nature. **caractériser** *v* characterize. **caractéristique** *nf*, *adj* characteristic.
carafe [karaf] *nf* carafe, decanter.
caramboler [karɑ̃bɔle] *v* collide with. **carambolage** *nm* pile-up.
caramel [karamɛl] *nm* caramel; (*dur*) toffee.
carapace [karapas] *nf* shell.
carat [kara] *nm* carat.
caravane [karavan] *nf* caravan.
carbone [karbɔn] *nm* carbon.
carboniser [karbɔnize] *v* (*forêt*) burn to the ground; (*cuisine*) burn to a cinder. **carbonisé** *adj* charred.
carburant [karbyrɑ̃] *nm* fuel.
carburateur [karbyratœr] *nm* carburettor.
carcasse [karkas] *nf* carcass; (*charpente*) frame.
cardiaque [kardjak] *adj* cardiac. **être cardiaque** have heart trouble, suffer from heart disease.
cardinal [kardinal] *nm*, *adj* cardinal.
carême [karɛm] *nm* fast. **Carême** *nm* Lent.
carence [karɑ̃s] *nf* deficiency.
carène [karɛn] *nf* hull.
caresser [karese] *v* caress, stroke; (*projet*) toy with. **caresse** *nf* caress.
cargaison [kargɛzɔ̃] *nf* cargo.
caricaturer [karikatyre] *v* caricature. **caricature** *nf* caricature.
carier [karje] *v* decay. **carie** *nf* tooth decay.

carillon [karijɔ̃] *nm* chime. **carillonner** *v* chime, ring. **carillonneur** *nm* bell-ringer.

carnage [karnaʒ] *nm* carnage.

carnassier [karnasje] *adj* carnivorous. *nm* carnivore.

carnaval [karnaval] *nm* carnival.

carnet [karnɛ] *nm* notebook. **carnet de chèques** chequebook. **carnet de billets/timbres** book of tickets/stamps.

carnivore [karnivɔr] *adj* carnivorous. *nm* carnivore.

carotte [karɔt] *nf* carrot.

carpette [karpɛt] *nf* rug.

carquois [karkwa] *nm* quiver.

carré [kare] *adj* square; *(franc)* straight, forthright. *nm* square. **carrément** *adv* bluntly, straight.

carreau [karo] *nm* (*mur, sol*) tile; *(vitre)* pane; *(tissu)* check; *(papier)* square; *(cartes)* diamond.

carrefour [karfur] *nm* crossroads.

carreler [karle] *v* tile; *(papier)* square. **carrelage** *nm* tiling.

carrelet [karlɛ] *nm* plaice.

carrer [kare] *v* square. **se carrer** ensconce oneself.

carrière[1] [karjɛr] *nf* (*pierre*) quarry.

carrière[2] [karjɛr] *nf* (*profession*) career.

carrosse [karɔs] *nm* coach. **carrosserie** *nf* (*auto*) body, bodywork.

carrure [karyr] *nf* build; stature.

cartable [kartablə] *nm* schoolbag, satchel.

carte [kart] *nf* card; *(géog)* map; menu. **carte à jouer** playing card. **carte de crédit** credit card. **carte des vins** wine list. **carte d'identité** identity card. **carte postale** postcard.

cartilage [kartilaʒ] *nm* cartilage; *(viande)* gristle. **cartilagineux** *adj* cartilaginous; gristly.

carton [kartɔ̃] *nm* cardboard; *(boîte)* box.

cartouche [kartuʃ] *nf* cartridge; *(cigarettes)* carton.

carvi [karvi] *nm* caraway.

cas [kɑ] *nm* case; situation. **au cas où** in case. **cas limite** borderline case. **cas urgent** emergency. **en aucun cas** under no circumstances. **en tout cas** in any case. **faire cas de** attach importance to.

cascade [kaskad] *nf* waterfall; torrent. **cascadeur** *nm* stuntman.

case [kaz] *nf* (*papier, échiquier*) square; compartment; hut.

caser [kaze] *v* find a place for; fix up;

(fam) put. **se caser** settle down; find a job.

caserne [kazɛrn] *nf* barracks. **caserne de pompiers** fire station.

casier [kazje] *nm* compartment; *(courrier)* pigeon-hole; *(fermant à clef)* locker; *(bouteilles)* rack. **casier judiciaire** police record.

casino [kazino] *nm* casino.

casque [kask] *nm* helmet; *(à écouteurs)* headphones *pl*.

casquette [kaskɛt] *nf* cap.

casse [kɑs] *nf* breakage, damage. **mettre à la casse** scrap.

casser [kase] *v* break; *(jur)* annul, quash. **casse-cou** *nm invar (fam)* reckless person. **casse-croûte** *nm invar* snack. **casse-noisettes** *nm invar* nutcracker. **casse-pieds** *n(m+f) invar (fam)* nuisance. **cassable** *adj* breakable. **cassant** *adj* brittle; brusque, abrupt. **cassure** *nf* break.

casserole [kasrɔl] *nf* saucepan.

cassette [kasɛt] *nf* casket; *(magnétophone)* cassette.

cassis [kasis] *nm* blackcurrant.

cassonade [kasɔnad] *nf* brown sugar.

caste [kast] *nf* caste.

castor [kastɔr] *nm* beaver.

cataloguer [kataloge] *v* catalogue, list. **catalogue** *nm* catalogue, list.

catalyseur [katalizœr] *nm* catalyst.

catamaran [katamarɑ̃] *nm* catamaran.

cataphote [katafɔt] *nm* reflector; *(route)* cat's-eye.

cataplasme [kataplasmə] *nm* poultice.

cataracte [katarakt] *nf* cataract.

catarrhe [katar] *nm* catarrh.

catastrophe [katastrɔf] *nf* disaster, catastrophe.

catch [katʃ] *nm* wrestling. **catcheur, -euse** *nm, nf* wrestler.

catéchisme [kateʃismə] *nm* catechism. **aller au catéchisme** go to Sunday school.

catégoriser [kategɔrize] *v* categorize. **catégorie** *nf* category. **catégorique** *adj* categorical.

cathédrale [katedral] *nf* cathedral.

cathode [katɔd] *nf* cathode.

catholique [katɔlik] *n(m+f)*, *adj* Catholic. **catholicisme** *nm* Catholicism.

cauchemar [koʃmar] *nm* nightmare. **cauchemardesque** *adj* nightmarish.

cause [koz] *nf* cause; *(jur)* case, brief. **à cause de** because of. **en cause** in question. **pour cause de** on account of.

causer¹ [koze] v (occasionner) cause.
causer² [koze] v (bavarder) chat, talk.
causant adj (fam) talkative. **causerie** nf chat, talk.
caustique [kostik] adj caustic.
cauteleux [kotlø] adj wily.
caution [kosjɔ̃] nf guarantee; (jur) bail; support. **sous caution** on bail.
cautionnement [kosjɔnmɑ̃] nm guarantee.
cavalerie [kavalri] nf cavalry.
cavalier [kavalje], **-ère** adj offhand. nm, nf (cheval) rider; (bal) partner. nm escort; (échecs) knight.
cave¹ [kav] nf cellar.
cave² [kav] adj hollow, sunken.
caveau [kavo] nm vault.
caverne [kavɛrn] nf cave. **caverneux** adj cavernous.
caviar [kavjar] nm caviar.
cavité [kavite] nf cavity.
ce¹ [sə], **cette** adj (ci) this; (là) that.
ce² [sə], **c'** pron it; (homme) he; (femme) she. **ce que** or **qui** what, which.
ceci [səsi] pron this.
cécité [sesite] nf blindness.
céder [sede] v give up or in; (fléchir, succomber) give way.
cédille [sedij] nf cedilla.
cèdre [sɛdrə] nm cedar.
*ceindre [sɛ̃drə] v encircle; (mettre) put on.
ceinture [sɛ̃tyr] nf belt; (gaine) girdle; (écharpe) sash; (anat) waist. **ceinture de sécurité** seat or safety belt.
cela [səla] pron that; it. **cela** or **ça ne fait rien** it doesn't matter.
célèbre [selɛbrə] adj famous. **célébrité** nf celebrity.
célébrer [selebre] v celebrate. **célébration** nf celebration.
celer [sle] v conceal.
céleri [sɛlri] nm celery.
céleste [selɛst] adj celestial, heavenly.
célibataire [selibatɛr] adj single. nm bachelor, single man. nf single girl or woman. **celibat** nm celibacy.
cellule [selyl] nf cell.
celte [sɛlt] adj also **celtique** Celtic. **Celte** n(m+f) Celt.
celui, celle [səlчi, sɛl] pron the one. **celui-ci, celle-ci** this one; (dernier) the latter. **celui-là, celle-là** that one; (premier) the former.
cendre [sɑ̃drə] nf ash. **cendrier** nm ashtray.

cène [sɛn] nf (rel) Communion. **la Cène** the Last Supper.
censé [sɑse] adj supposed.
censeur [sɑsœr] nm censor; critic; (lycée) deputy head.
censurer [sɑsyre] v (film, etc.) censor; (critiquer) censure. **censure** nf censorship; censure.
cent [sɑ] nm, adj a hundred. **faire les cent pas** pace up and down. **pour cent** per cent. **une centaine (de)** about a hundred. **centième** n(m+f), adj hundredth.
centenaire [sɑtnɛr] adj hundred-year-old. n(m+f) centenarian. nm centenary.
centigrade [sɑtigrad] adj centigrade.
centime [sɑtim] nm centime.
centimètre [sɑtimɛtrə] nm centimetre; (ruban) tape measure.
central [sɑtral] adj central. nm telephone exchange. **centrale** nf power station.
centraliser [sɑtralize] v centralize. **centralisation** nf centralization.
centre [sɑtrə] nm centre. **centre commercial** shopping centre. **centre-ville** nm town centre.
cep [sɛp] nm stock.
cependant [səpɑdɑ̃] conj however, nevertheless.
céramique [seramik] nf, adj ceramic. **la céramique** ceramics.
cerceau [sɛrso] nm hoop.
cercle [sɛrklə] nm circle; club; (étendue) range. **cercle vicieux** vicious circle.
cercueil [sɛrkœj] nm coffin.
céréale [sereal] nf cereal.
cérébral [serebral] adj cerebral; mental.
cérémonie [seremɔni] nf ceremony. **faire des cérémonies** stand on ceremony; (fam) make a fuss. **sans cérémonie** informal, informally. **cérémonieux** adj ceremonious, formal.
cerf [sɛr] nm stag. **cerf-volant** nm kite.
cerise [səriz] nf cherry. **cerisier** nm cherry (tree).
cerner [sɛrne] v encircle, surround. **avoir les yeux cernés** have rings under one's eyes.
certain [sɛrtɛ̃] adj certain; definite. **certains** pron, adj some, certain. **certainement** adv certainly; most probably.
certes [sɛrt] adv indeed, most certainly; admittedly.
certifier [sɛrtifje] v certify; (signature) witness; assure. **certificat** nm certificate.

certitude [sɛrtityd] *nf* certainty.
cerveau [sɛrvo] *nm* brain; *(intelligence)* mind; *(personne)* mastermind.
cervelle [sɛrvɛl] *nf* brains *pl.*
Cervin [sɛrvɛ̃] *nm* Matterhorn.
ces [se] *adj (ci)* these; *(là)* those.
cesse [sɛs] *nf* **sans cesse** continually; incessantly.
cesser [sese] *v* stop, cease. **faire cesser** put a stop to.
cet [sɛt] *form of* ce¹ *used before vowel or mute h.*
cette [sɛt] *V* ce¹.
ceux, celles [sø, sɛl] *pron* the ones, those. **ceux-ci, celles-ci** these; *(derniers)* the latter. **ceux-là, celles-là** those; *(premiers)* the former.
chacal [ʃakal] *nm, pl* **-als** jackal.
chacun [ʃakœ̃] *pron* each; *(tout le monde)* everyone.
chagrin [ʃagrɛ̃] *adj* despondent; morose. *nm* sorrow, grief.
chagriner [ʃagrine] *v* distress, worry.
chahut [ʃay] *nm* rumpus. **chahuteur, -euse** *n, adj* rowdy.
chaîne [ʃɛn] *nf* chain; *(montagnes)* range; *(usine)* production line; *(TV)* channel.
chair [ʃɛr] *nf* flesh. **chair à saucisse** sausage-meat. **chair de poule** goose-flesh.
chaire [ʃɛr] *nf (rel)* pulpit; *(université)* chair.
chaise [ʃɛz] *nf* chair.
chaland [ʃalɑ̃] *nm* barge.
châle [ʃal] *nm* shawl.
chalet [ʃalɛ] *nm* chalet.
chaleur [ʃalœr] *nf* heat, warmth; fervour. **chaleureux** *adj* warm.
chaloupe [ʃalup] *nf* launch. **chaloupe de sauvetage** lifeboat.
chalumeau [ʃalymo] *nm (tech)* blowlamp; *(musique)* pipe.
chalut [ʃaly] *nm* trawl. **pêcher au chalut** trawl. **chalutier** *nm* trawler.
se chamailler [ʃamaje] *v (fam)* squabble. **chamailleur, -euse** *adj* quarrelsome.
chambellan [ʃɑ̃belɑ̃] *nm* chamberlain.
chambranle [ʃɑ̃brɑ̃l] *nm* frame; *(cheminée)* mantelpiece.
chambre [ʃɑ̃brə] *nf* room; *(à coucher)* bedroom; *(tech, admin)* chamber; *(pol)* house. **chambre d'ami** spare room. **chambre d'enfants** nursery. **chambre noire** dark-room. **chambrer** *v (vin)* bring to room temperature; *(personne)* corner.
chameau [ʃamo] *nm* camel.

chamois [ʃamwa] *nm* chamois. *adj invar* buff.
champ [ʃɑ̃] *nm* field. **champ d'aviation** airfield. **champ de courses** racecourse. **champ de foire** fairground.
champagne [ʃɑ̃paɲ] *nm* champagne.
champêtre [ʃɑ̃pɛtr] *adj* rural.
champignon [ʃɑ̃piɲɔ̃] *nm* mushroom; *(vénéneux)* toadstool; *(terme générique)* fungus; *(fam)* accelerator.
champion, -onne [ʃɑ̃pjɔ̃, -ɔn] *nm, nf* champion. *adj (fam)* first-rate. **championnat** *nm* championship.
chance [ʃɑ̃s] *nf* luck; *(possibilité)* chance. **avoir de la chance** be lucky. **pas de chance!** hard luck! **chanceux** *adj* lucky.
chanceler [ʃɑ̃sle] *v* totter, falter. **chancelant** *adj* unsteady, shaky.
chancelier [ʃɑ̃səlje] *nm* chancellor.
chandail [ʃɑ̃daj] *nm* sweater.
chandelle [ʃɑ̃dɛl] *nf* candle. **chandelier** *nm* candlestick.
changer [ʃɑ̃ʒe] *v* change; exchange; *(modifier)* alter. **change** *nm* exchange; *(taux)* exchange rate. **changeant** *adj* changeable. **changement** *nm* change; alteration.
chanoine [ʃanwan] *nm* canon.
chanson [ʃɑ̃sɔ̃] *nf* song.
chant [ʃɑ̃] *nm* singing; *(chanson)* song. **chant de Noël** Christmas carol.
chanter [ʃɑ̃te] *v* sing. **faire chanter** blackmail. **chantage** *nm* blackmail. **chanteur, -euse** *nm, nf* singer.
chantier [ʃɑ̃tje] *nm* yard, site; *(route)* roadworks *pl.* **chantier naval** shipyard.
chantonner [ʃɑ̃tɔne] *v* hum, croon.
chanvre [ʃɑ̃vrə] *nm* hemp.
chaos [kao] *nm* chaos.
chape [ʃap] *nf (pneu)* tread; *(rel)* cope.
chapeau [ʃapo] *nm* hat. **chapeau melon** bowler hat.
chapelain [ʃaplɛ̃] *nm* chaplain.
chapelet [ʃaplɛ] *nm* rosary.
chapelle [ʃapɛl] *nf* chapel.
chapelure [ʃaplyr] *nf* breadcrumbs *pl.*
chaperon [ʃaprɔ̃] *nm* chaperon. **chaperonner** *v* chaperon.
chapitre [ʃapitrə] *nm* chapter; subject.
chaque [ʃak] *adj* every, each.
char [ʃar] *nm (mil)* tank; *(carnaval)* float.
charabia [ʃarabja] *nm (fam)* gibberish.
charbon [ʃarbɔ̃] *nm* coal. **charbon de bois** charcoal. **charbonnage** *nm* coal-mining. **charbonnier** *nm* coalman.

charcuterie [ʃarkytri] *nf* (*magasin*) pork butcher's, delicatessen; (*viande*) cooked pork meats. **charcutier, -ère** *nm, nf* pork butcher.

chardon [ʃardɔ̃] *nm* thistle.

chardonneret [ʃardɔnrɛ] *nm* goldfinch.

charger [ʃarʒe] *v* load; (*mil, élec*) charge. **charger de** ask to, put in charge of. **se charger de** see to, take care of. **charge** *nf* load; charge; responsibility; (*frais*) expense. **à charge de** on condition that. **chargé** *adj* loaded, laden; (*rempli, occupé*) full, heavy. **chargement** *nm* loading.

chariot [ʃarjo] *nm* trolley; (*charrette*) wagon; (*tech*) carriage.

charité [ʃarite] *nf* charity; (*gentillesse*) kindness.

charivari [ʃarivari] *nm* hullabaloo.

charlatan [ʃarlatɑ̃] *nm* charlatan; (*médecin*) quack.

charmer [ʃarme] *v* charm, enchant. **charmant** *adj* charming, delightful. **charme** *nm* charm; (*magique*) spell.

charnel [ʃarnɛl] *adj* carnal.

charnière [ʃarnjɛr] *nf* hinge.

charnu [ʃarny] *adj* fleshy.

charpente [ʃarpɑ̃t] *nf* framework, structure; (*carrure*) build. **charpenté** *adj* built.

charrette [ʃarɛt] *nf* cart.

charrue [ʃary] *nf* plough.

charte [ʃart] *nf* charter.

chasse [ʃas] *nf* hunting, hunt; (*au fusil*) shooting; (*poursuite*) chase; (*d'eau*) flush. **tirer la chasse** pull the chain.

châsse [ʃas] *nf* shrine.

chasser [ʃase] *v* hunt; (*au fusil*) shoot; (*faire partir*) drive out, chase away; (*dissiper*) dispel. **chasse-neige** *nm invar* snowplough. **chasseur** *nm* hunter; (*hôtel*) page.

châssis [ʃasi] *nm* frame; (*auto*) chassis.

chaste [ʃast] *adj* chaste. **chasteté** *nf* chastity.

chat, chatte [ʃa, ʃat] *nm, nf* cat. **chaton** *nm* (*zool*) kitten; (*bot*) catkin.

châtaigne [ʃɑtɛɲ] *nf* chestnut. **châtaignier** *nm* chestnut (tree).

châtain [ʃatɛ̃] *adj* chestnut, auburn.

château [ʃɑto] *nm* castle; (*manoir*) mansion.

châtier [ʃatje] *v* punish; refine. **châtiment** *nm* punishment.

chatouiller [ʃatuje] *v* tickle. **chatouille-**ment *nm* tickle. **chatouilleux** *adj* ticklish; (*irritable*) touchy, sensitive.

chatoyer [ʃatwaje] *v* glisten, shimmer, sparkle. **chatoiement** *nm* glistening, shimmer, sparkle.

châtrer [ʃatre] *v* castrate.

chaud [ʃo] *adj* warm, hot. *nm* heat, warmth. **avoir chaud** be warm *or* hot. **chaudière** *nf* boiler.

chauffer [ʃofe] *v* warm (up), heat (up); (*moteur*) overheat. **chauffe-eau** *nm invar* water-heater. **chauffe-plats** *nm invar* hotplate. **chauffage** *nm* heating. **chauffage central** central heating.

chauffeur [ʃofœr] *nm* driver; (*privé*) chauffeur.

chaume [ʃom] *nm* stubble; (*toit*) thatch. **chaumière** *nf* thatched cottage.

chaussée [ʃose] *nf* road; causeway.

chausser [ʃose] *v* (*mettre*) put (shoes) on; (*marchand*) supply with shoes; (*chaussure*) fit. **chausse-pied** *nm* shoehorn. **chaussette** *nf* sock. **chausson** *nm* slipper. **chaussure** *nf* shoe, boot; footwear.

chauve [ʃov] *adj* bald. **chauve-souris** *nf* bat.

chauvin [ʃovɛ̃], **-e** *nm, nf* chauvinist. *adj* chauvinistic. **chauvinisme** *nm* chauvinism.

chaux [ʃo] *nf* lime. **blanchir à la chaux** whitewash.

chavirer [ʃavire] *v* capsize, overturn.

chef [ʃɛf] *nm* head; (*patron*) boss; (*tribu*) chief; (*révolte, etc.*) leader; (*cuisine*) chef. **chef d'équipe** foreman; (*sport*) captain. **chef de gare** station-master. **chef de train** guard. **chef-d'œuvre** *nm* masterpiece. **chef d'orchestre** conductor. **chef-lieu** *nm* county town.

cheik [ʃɛk] *nm* sheik.

chelem [ʃlɛm] *nm* (*cartes*) slam.

chemin [ʃəmɛ̃] *nm* way, path; (*campagne*) lane. **chemin de fer** railway. **chemin faisant** on the way. **se mettre en chemin** set off.

chemineau [ʃəmino] *nm* tramp.

cheminée [ʃəmine] *nf* chimney; (*foyer*) fireplace; (*encadrement*) mantelpiece; (*paquebot*) funnel.

cheminer [ʃəmine] *v* walk; (*péniblement*) trudge along; (*eau, sentier*) make its way.

chemise [ʃəmiz] *nf* shirt; (*dossier*) folder; (*tech*) lining, jacket. **chemise de nuit** nightdress. **chemisier** *nm* blouse.

chenal [ʃənal] *nm* channel; canal.

chêne [ʃɛn] *nm* oak.

chenille [ʃənij] *nf* caterpillar.

chèque [ʃɛk] *nm* check. **chèque-cadeau** *nm* gift token. **chèque de voyage** traveller's check. **chèque en blanc** blank check. **chéquier** *nm* check book.

cher [ʃɛr] *adj* dear; (*coûteux*) expensive. *adv* dearly. **coûter/payer cher** cost/pay a lot. **cherté** *nf* high price *or* cost.

chercher [ʃɛrʃe] *v* look for, seek. **chercher à** try to. **chercheur, -euse** *nm, nf* researcher.

chéri [ʃeri] -e *adj* beloved. *nm, nf* darling.

chérir [ʃerir] *v* cherish.

hérubin [ʃerybɛ̃] *nm* cherub.

chétif [ʃetif] *adj* (*enfant, etc.*) puny; (*repas, etc.*) meagre.

cheval [ʃəval] *nm* horse; (*auto*) horsepower. **à cheval** on horseback; (*chaise, etc.*) astride, straddling. **cheval à bascule** rocking horse. **cheval de course** racehorse.

chevalerie [ʃəvalri] *nf* chivalry. **chevaleresque** *adj* chivalrous.

chevalet [ʃəvalɛ] *nm* (*peinture*) easel; (*menuiserie*) trestle; (*violon*) bridge.

chevalier [ʃəvalje] *nm* knight. **chevalière** *nf* signet ring.

chevaucher [ʃəvoʃe] *v* be astride, straddle; (*tuile, pan*) overlap.

chevelu [ʃəvly] *adj* long-haired, hairy. **chevelure** *nf* (head of) hair.

chevet [ʃəvɛ] *nm* bedside.

cheveu [ʃəvø] *nm* hair. **cheveux** *nm pl* hair *sing*. **tiré par les cheveux** farfetched.

cheville [ʃəvij] *nf* ankle; (*fiche*) peg, pin.

chèvre [ʃɛvr] *nf* goat. **chevreau** *nm* kid.

chèvrefeuille [ʃɛvrəfœj] *nm* honeysuckle.

chevron [ʃəvrɔ̃] *nm* rafter; (*motif*) chevron.

chevroter [ʃəvrɔte] *v* quaver.

chez [ʃe] *prep* at *or* to the house of; (*avec*) with, in, among; (*docteur, etc.*) at, to; (*adresse*) care of, c/o. **chez soi** at home. **faites comme chez vous!** make yourself at home!

chic [ʃik] *nm* style. **avoir le chic pour** have the knack of. *adj invar* smart; (*fam*) nice, decent. *interj* great! terrific!

chicaner [ʃikane] *v* quibble. **chicanerie** *nf* quibbling.

chiche [ʃiʃ] *adj* niggardly, paltry, mean.

chicorée [ʃikɔre] *nf* (*salade*) endive; (*café*) chicory.

chien [ʃjɛ̃] *nm* dog. **chien d'aveugle** guide dog. **chien de berger** sheepdog. **chien de garde** guard dog. **entre chien et loup** in the twilight. **temps de chien** *nm* filthy weather. **chienne** *nf* bitch.

chiffon [ʃifɔ̃] *nm* rag; (*de papier*) scrap; (*à poussière*) duster.

chiffonner [ʃifɔne] *v* crumple, crease; (*fam*) bother, worry.

chiffre [ʃifr] *nm* figure; total; code. **chiffre d'affaires** turnover.

chiffrer [ʃifre] *v* code; (*évaluer*) assess; (*pages*) number. **se chiffrer à** add up to.

chignon [ʃiɲɔ̃] *nm* bun.

chimère [ʃimɛr] *nf* dream, fancy. **chimérique** *adj* fanciful; imaginary.

chimie [ʃimi] *nf* chemistry. **chimique** *adj* chemical. **chimiste** *n(m+f)* chemist.

chimpanzé [ʃɛ̃pɑ̃ze] *nm* chimpanzee.

Chine [ʃin] *nf* China. **chinois** *nm, adj* Chinese. **les Chinois** the Chinese.

chiot [ʃjo] *nm* puppy.

chiper [ʃipe] *v* (*fam*) pinch.

chipoter [ʃipote] (*fam*) *v* haggle, quibble; (*manger*) pick at.

chips [ʃip] *nm pl* potato chips *pl*.

chiquenaude [ʃiknod] *nf* flick, flip.

chiromancie [kiromɑ̃si] *nf* palmistry. **chiromancien, -enne** *nm, nf* palmist.

chirurgie [ʃiryrʒi] *nf* surgery. **chirurgical** *adj* surgical. **chirurgien** *nm* surgeon.

chlore [klɔr] *nm* chlorine. **chlorer** *v* chlorinate.

chloroforme [klɔrɔfɔrm] *nm* chloroform. **chloroformer** *v* chloroform.

chlorophylle [klɔrɔfil] *nf* chlorophyll.

choc [ʃɔk] *nm* shock; impact, crash; (*conflit*) clash.

chocolat [ʃɔkɔla] *nm* chocolate. **chocolat à croquer** plain chocolate. **chocolat au lait** milk chocolate. **chocolat en poudre** drinking chocolate. *adj invar* chocolate-coloured.

chœur [kœr] *nm* chorus; (*chanteurs*) choir. **en chœur** in chorus.

*****choir** [ʃwar] *v* fall.

choisir [ʃwazir] *v* choose, select. **choisi** *adj* chosen; (*raffiné*) select.

choix [ʃwa] *nm* choice, selection. **de choix** choice.

choléra [kɔlera] *nm* cholera.

cholestérol [kɔlesterɔl] *nm* cholesterol.

chômer [ʃome] *v* be idle; (*travailleur*) be unemployed; (*usine, etc.*) be at a standstill. **chômage** *nm* unemployment. **au**

chômage unemployed. **mettre au chômage** make redundant. **chômeur, -euse** *nm, nf* unemployed person.

chope [ʃɔp] *nf* tankard.

choquer [ʃɔke] *v* shock, appal; (*offusquer*) offend; (*commotionner*) shake up; (*heurter*) knock, clink. **se choquer** be shocked.

choral [kɔral] *adj* choral. *nm* chorale. **chorale** *nf* choral society, choir.

chorégraphie [kɔregrafi] *nf* choreography. **chorégraphe** *n(m+f)* choreographer.

chose [ʃoz] *nf* thing. *nm* (*fam*) thingumajig. **être tout chose** (*fam*) feel peculiar.

chou [ʃu] *nm, pl* **choux** cabbage; (*ruban*) rosette; (*cuisine*) puff. **chou de Bruxelles** Brussels sprout. **chou-fleur** *nm* cauliflower.

choucas [ʃuka] *nm* jackdaw.

chouchou, -oute [ʃuʃu, -ut] *nm, nf* (*fam*) pet.

choucroute [ʃukrut] *nf* sauerkraut.

chouette[1] [ʃwɛt] *adj, interj* (*fam*) smashing, great.

chouette[2] [ʃwɛt] *nf* owl.

choyer [ʃwaje] *v* pamper; cherish.

chrétien [kretjɛ̃] *adj* Christian. **Chrétien, -enne** *nm, nf* Christian.

christianisme [kristjanismə] *nm* Christianity.

chromatique [krɔmatik] *adj* chromatic.

chrome [krom] *nm* chromium, chrome. **chromé** *adj* chromium-plated.

chromosome [krɔmozom] *nm* chromosome.

chronique[1] [krɔnik] *adj* chronic.

chronique[2] [krɔnik] *nf* chronicle; (*journal*) column.

chronologique [krɔnɔlɔʒik] *adj* chronological.

chronométrer [krɔnɔmetre] *v* time. **chronomètre** *nm* stopwatch.

chrysalide [krizalid] *nf* chrysalis.

chrysanthème [krizɑ̃tɛm] *nm* chrysanthemum.

chuchoter [ʃyʃɔte] *v* whisper. **chuchotement** *nm* whisper.

chuinter [ʃɥɛ̃te] *v* hiss softly; (*chouette*) hoot.

chut [ʃyt] *interj* hush!

chute [ʃyt] *nf* fall; (*ruine*) collapse, downfall. **chute d'eau** waterfall.

Chypre [ʃipr] *n* Cyprus.

ci [si] *adv* this; here. **ci-après** *adv* below. **ci-contre** *adv* opposite. **ci-dessous** below.

ci-dessus *adv* above. **ci-devant** *adv* formerly. **ci-inclus** *adj* enclosed. **ci-joint** *adj* enclosed, attached.

cible [sibl] *nf* target.

ciboule [sibul] *nf* spring onion. **ciboulette** *nf* chive.

cicatrice [sikatris] *nf* scar.

cidre [sidr] *nm* cider.

ciel [sjɛl] *nm, pl* **ciels** *or* **cieux** sky; (*rel*) heaven.

cierge [sjɛrʒ] *nm* candle.

cigale [sigal] *nf* cicada.

cigare [sigar] *nm* cigar. **cigarette** *nf* cigarette.

cigogne [sigɔɲ] *nf* stork.

cil [sil] *nm* eyelash.

cime [sim] *nf* peak; (*montagne*) summit; (*arbre*) top.

ciment [simɑ̃] *nm* cement. **cimenter** *v* cement.

cimetière [simtjɛr] *nm* cemetery, graveyard.

cinéaste [sineast] *n(m+f)* film-maker.

cinéma [sinema] *nm* cinema.

cinétique [sinetik] *adj* kinetic. *nf* kinetics.

cingler [sɛ̃gle] *v* lash, whip. **cinglant** *adj* biting; (*pluie*) driving. **cinglé** *adj* (*fam*) mad, crazy.

cinq [sɛ̃k] *nm, adj* five. **cinquième** *n(m+f), adj* fifth.

cinquante [sɛ̃kɑ̃t] *nm, adj* fifty. **cinquantième** *n(m+f), adj* fiftieth.

cintrer [sɛ̃tre] *v* arch; bend. **cintre** *nm* arch; (*vêtements*) coat-hanger.

cirage [siraʒ] *nm* shoe polish.

*circoncire [sirkɔ̃sir] *v* circumcize. **circoncision** *nf* circumcision.

circonférence [sirkɔ̃ferɑ̃s] *nf* circumference.

circonflexe [sirkɔ̃flɛks] *adj* circumflex.

circonscription [sirkɔ̃skripsjɔ̃] *nf* district; (*électorale*) constituency.

*circonscrire [sirkɔ̃skrir] *v* confine; (*math*) circumscribe.

circonspect [sirkɔ̃spɛkt] *adj* circumspect, cautious.

circonstance [sirkɔ̃stɑ̃s] *nf* circumstance, occasion. **de circonstance** appropriate.

circuit [sirkɥi] *nm* circuit; (*excursion*) tour.

circuler [sirkyle] *v* circulate; (*voiture, piéton*) go, move along. **circulaire** *nf, adj* circular. **circulation** *nf* circulation; (*auto*) traffic.

cirer [sire] *v* polish. **cire** *nf* wax; (*meubles*) polish. **ciré** *nm* oilskin. **cireux** *adj* waxy.

cirque [sirk] *nm* circus.

cisaille [sizaj] *nf* shears *pl*.

ciseau [sizo] *nm* chisel. **ciseaux** *nm pl* scissors *pl*.

ciseler [sizle] *v* chisel, carve.

cité [site] *nf* city, town. **cité universitaire** halls of residence *pl*.

citer [site] *v* quote, cite; (*jur*) summon. **citation** *nf* quotation; summons.

citerne [sitern] *nf* tank.

cithare [sitar] *nf* zither.

citoyen [sitwajɛ̃] **-enne** *nm, nf* citizen.

citron [sitrɔ̃] *nm, adj* lemon. **citron pressé** lemon juice. **citronnade** *nf* lemon squash. **citronnier** *nm* lemon tree.

citrouille [sitruj] *nf* pumpkin.

civette [sivɛt] *nf* chive.

civière [sivjɛr] *nf* stretcher.

civil [sivil] *adj* civil; civilian. *nm* civilian. **en civil** in plain clothes.

civiliser [sivilize] *v* civilize. **civilisation** *nf* civilization.

civique [sivik] *adj* civic.

clair [klɛr] *adj* clear; (*lumineux*) light, bright; (*sauce, tissu*) thin; (*couleur*) pale; (*evident*) plain. *adv* clearly. *nm* light. **clair de lune** moonlight.

clairière [klɛrjɛr] *nf* clearing.

clairon [klɛrɔ̃] *nm* bugle.

clairsemé [klɛrsəme] *adj* scattered, sparse.

clairvoyant [klɛrvwajɑ̃] *adj* perceptive, clear-sighted.

clameur [klamœr] *nf* clamour.

clan [klɑ̃] *nm* clan.

clandestin [klɑ̃dɛstɛ̃] *adj* secret, clandestine, underground.

clapier [klapje] *nm* hutch.

clapoter [klapote] *v* lap. **clapotement** or **clapotis** *nm* lapping.

claquemurer [klakmyre] *v* coop up, shut away.

claquer [klake] *v* (*son*) bang, snap, crack; (*gifler*) slap; (*fam: fatiguer*) tire out; (*fam: mourir*) die. **claque** *nf* slap. **claquement** *nm* bang, snap, crack.

clarifier [klarifje] *v* clarify. **clarification** *nf* clarification.

clarinette [klarinɛt] *nf* clarinet.

clarté [klarte] *nf* brightness, clearness; (*lumière*) light; (*netteté*) clarity.

classe [klas] *nf* class; (*salle*) classroom;

(*école*) school. **aller en classe** go to school. **faire la classe** teach. **sans classe** classless.

classer [klase] *v* class, classify; (*ranger*) file; (*élève, fruits*) grade. **classement** *nm* classification; filing; grading. **classeur** *nm* file; (*meuble*) filing cabinet.

classifier [klasifje] *v* classify. **classification** *nf* classification.

classique [klasik] *adj* classic; (*art, musique, etc.*) classical; (*habituel*) usual. *nm* (*ouvrage*) classic; (*auteur*) classicist.

claustrophobie [klostrofɔbi] *nf* claustrophobia.

clavecin [klavsɛ̃] *nm* harpsichord.

clavicule [klavikyl] *nf* collarbone.

clavier [klavje] *nm* keyboard.

clef *or* **clé** [kle] *nf* key; (*tech*) spanner; (*musique*) clef. **clef de contact** ignition key. **sous clef** under lock and key.

clémence [klemɑ̃s] *nf* clemency; (*temps*) mildness. **clément** *adj* lenient; mild.

clerc [klɛr] *nm* clerk.

clergé [klɛrʒe] *nm* clergy.

clérical [klerikal] *adj* clerical.

cliché [kliʃe] *nm* cliché; (*phot*) negative.

client [klijɑ̃] **-e** *nm, nf* customer, client; (*hôtel*) guest; (*médecin*) patient. **clientèle** *nf* clientèle; (*magasin*) customers *pl*; (*médecin*) practice; (*comm*) custom.

cligner [kliɲe] *v* **cligner les yeux** blink; (*fermer à demi*) screw up one's eyes. **clignement** *nm* blink.

clignoter [kliɲote] *v* (*yeux*) blink; (*étoile*) twinkle; (*vaciller*) flicker; (*signal*) flash. **clignotant** *nm* (*auto*) indicator.

climat [klima] *nm* climate. **climatique** *adj* climatic.

climatiser [klimatize] *v* air-condition. **climatisation** *nf* air-conditioning. **climatiseur** *nm* air-conditioner.

clin [klɛ̃] *nm* **clin d'œil** wink.

clinique [klinik] *adj* clinical. *nf* nursing home.

clinquant [klɛ̃kɑ̃] *adj* flashy. *nm* tinsel.

cliqueter [klikte] *v* rattle, clatter; (*métal*) clink, jingle. **cliquetis** *nm* clatter; clink, jingle.

clitoris [klitɔris] *nm* clitoris.

clochard [klɔʃar] **-e** *nm, nf* (*fam*) tramp.

cloche [klɔʃ] *nf* bell; cover.

clocher[1] [klɔʃe] *nm* church tower, steeple.

clocher[2] [klɔʃe] *v* (*fam*) be wrong.

cloison [klwazɔ̃] *nf* partition; barrier.

cloître [klwatrə] *nm* cloister.
clopiner [klɔpine] *v* hobble along. **clopin-clopant** *adv* hobbling. **entrer/sortir clopin-clopant** hobble in/out.
cloporte [klɔpɔrt] *nm* wood-louse (*pl* -lice).
*clore [klɔr] *v* close, end, conclude.
clos [klo] *adj* closed, enclosed. *nm* enclosed field; vineyard.
clôture [klotyr] *nf* (*fermeture*) closure, closing; (*enceinte*) fence.
clou [klu] *nm* nail; (*chaussée*) stud; (*méd*) boil; (*théâtre*) star turn. **clou de girofle** clove.
clouer [klue] *v* nail down, pin down. **cloué au lit** confined to bed. **cloué sur place** rooted to the spot.
clouter [klute] *v* stud.
clovisse [klɔvis] *nf* clam.
clown [klun] *nm* clown.
club [klœb] *nm* club.
coaguler [kɔagyle] *v* congeal; (*sang*) coagulate; (*lait*) curdle.
coalition [kɔalisjɔ̃] *nf* coalition.
coasser [kɔase] *v* croak. **coassement** *nm* croak.
cobaye [kɔbaj] *nm* guinea-pig.
cobra [kɔbra] *nm* cobra.
cocarde [kɔkard] *nf* rosette.
cocasse [kɔkas] *adj* comical.
coccinelle [kɔksinɛl] *nf* ladybird.
cocher[1] [kɔʃe] *v* (*crayon*) tick; (*entaille*) notch.
cocher[2] [kɔʃe] *nm* coachman.
cochon, -onne [kɔʃɔ̃, -ɔn] *nm* pig. **cochon d'Inde** guinea-pig. *adj* (*argot*) dirty. **cochonnerie** (*fam*) *nf* rubbish; (*saleté*) filth; (*tour*) dirty trick.
cocktail [kɔktɛl] *nm* cocktail; cocktail party.
cocon [kɔkɔ̃] *nm* cocoon.
cocotier [kɔkɔtje] *nm* coconut palm.
cocotte[1] [kɔkɔt] *nf* (*poule*) hen; (*péj: femme*) tart.
cocotte[2] [kɔkɔt] *nf* casserole.
code [kɔd] *nm* code. **code de la route** highway code. **se mettre en code** (*auto*) dip one's headlights.
cœur [kœr] *nm* heart; courage; (*fruit*) core. **avoir mal au cœur** feel sick. **de bon cœur** willingly. **parler à cœur ouvert** have a heart-to-heart.
coexister [kɔɛgziste] *v* coexist. **coexistence** *nf* coexistence.

coffre [kɔfrə] *nm* chest; (*auto*) trunk. **coffre-fort** *nm* safe.
cognac [kɔɲak] *nm* cognac.
cogner [kɔɲe] *v* hit, knock; (*plus fort*) hammer, bang.
cohabiter [kɔabite] *v* live together.
cohérent [kɔerɑ̃] *adj* coherent, consistent. **cohérence** *nf* coherence, consistency.
cohue [kɔy] *nf* crowd.
coiffer [kwafe] *v* (*mettre*) put (a hat) on; cover. **coiffer quelqu'un** do someone's hair. **se coiffer** do one's hair. **se coiffer de** put on; (*péj*) become infatuated with. **coiffeur** *nm* hairdresser; (*hommes*) barber. **coiffeuse** *nf* hairdresser; (*meuble*) dressing table. **coiffure** *nf* hair-style; (*métier*) hairdressing.
coin [kwɛ̃] *nm* corner; (*lieu*) spot, area. **au coin du feu** by the fireside. **du coin local**.
coincer [kwɛ̃se] *v* wedge, jam.
coïncider [kɔɛ̃side] *v* coincide. **coïncidence** *nf* coincidence.
coin-coin [kwɛ̃kwɛ̃] *nm*, *interj* quack.
coing [kwɛ̃] *nm* quince.
col [kɔl] *nm* (*vêtement*) collar; (*géog*) pass; (*vase*) neck. **col roulé** polo-neck.
coléoptère [kɔleɔptɛr] *nm* beetle.
colère [kɔlɛr] *nf* anger, rage. **en colère** angry. **coléreux** *adj* quick-tempered.
colimaçon [kɔlimasɔ̃] *nm* snail. **en colimaçon** spiral.
colin [kɔlɛ̃] *nm* hake.
colique [kɔlik] *nf* stomach-ache; colic; diarrhoea.
colis [kɔli] *nm* parcel. **par colis postal** by parcel post.
collaborer [kɔlabɔre] *v* collaborate. **collaborateur, -trice** *nm*, *nf* collaborator; (*journal*) contributor. **collaboration** *nf* collaboration; contribution.
collant [kɔlɑ̃] *nm* (*bas*) tights *pl*; (*acrobate*) leotard. *adj* sticky; (*vêtement*) close-fitting, clinging.
colle [kɔl] *nf* glue, paste; (*fam: question*) poser.
collectif [kɔlɛktif] *adj* collective; (*hystérie*) mass; (*billet*) group. **collectivité** *nf* group; community.
collection [kɔlɛksjɔ̃] *nf* collection.
collectionner [kɔlɛksjɔne] *v* collect. **collectionneur, -euse** *nm*, *nf* collector.
collège [kɔlɛʒ] *nm* secondary school; college. **collégien** *nm* schoolboy. **collégienne** *nf* schoolgirl.

collègue [kɔlɛg] *n(m+f)* colleague.
coller [kɔle] *v* stick, cling.
collet [kɔlɛ] *nm* (*piège*) snare; (*tech*) collar, neck. **collet monté** prim, strait-laced.
collier [kɔlje] *nm* (*femme*) necklace; (*animal*) collar.
colline [kɔlin] *nf* hill.
collision [kɔlizjɔ̃] *nf* collision; (*conflit*) clash.
colombe [kɔlɔ̃b] *nf* dove. **colombier** *nm* dovecote.
colonel [kɔlɔnɛl] *nm* colonel.
colonie [kɔlɔni] *nf* colony. **colonie de vacances** holiday camp for children. **colonial** *nm*, *adj* colonial. **coloniser** *v* colonize.
colonne [kɔlɔn] *nf* column; (*arch*) pillar. **colonne vertébrale** spine.
colorer [kɔlɔre] *v* colour; (*tissu*) dye; (*bois*) stain. **coloration** *nf* colouring. **coloré** *adj* colourful; (*teint*) ruddy. **colorier** *v* colour in.
coloris [kɔlɔri] *nm* colour, colouring.
colosse [kɔlɔs] *nm* giant, colossus. **colossal** *adj* colossal.
colporter [kɔlpɔrte] *v* peddle. **colporteur, -euse** *nm*, *nf* pedlar.
coma [kɔma] *nm* coma.
combat [kɔ̃ba] *nm* fight, combat; (*sport*) match.
***combattre** [kɔ̃batrə] *v* fight, combat.
combien [kɔ̃bjɛ̃] *adv* (*quantité*) how much; (*nombre*) how many. **combien de temps** how long. **le combien sommes-nous?** what date is it?
combinaison [kɔ̃binezɔ̃] *nf* combination; (*sous-vêtement*) slip; (*astuce*) device, scheme.
combiner [kɔ̃bine] *v* combine; (*élaborer*) devise, plan. **combine** *nf* (*truc*) trick; (*péj*) scheme. **combiné** *nm* (*chim*) compound; (*téléphone*) receiver.
comble¹ [kɔ̃blə] *nm* height, climax, peak; (*toit*) roof timbers *pl*. **c'est le comble!** that's the last straw! **pour comble to cap it all.**
comble² [kɔ̃blə] *adj* packed.
combler [kɔ̃ble] *v* fill; (*déficit*) make good; (*désir*) fulfil.
combustible [kɔ̃bystiblə] *adj* combustible. *nm* fuel. **combustion** *nf* combustion.
comédie [kɔmedi] *nf* comedy, play; (*fam*) fuss. **comédie musicale** musical. **jouer la comédie** put on an act. **comédien** *nm*

comedian; actor; comedy actor. **comédienne** *nf* comedienne; actress; comedy actress.
comestible [kɔmɛstiblə] *adj* edible. **comestibles** *nm pl* food *sing*.
comète [kɔmɛt] *nf* comet.
comique [kɔmik] *adj* comic; (*drôle*) comical. *nm* comedy; (*artiste*) comic.
comité [kɔmite] *nm* committee, board.
commander [kɔmɑ̃de] *v* order; command; control. **commandant** *nm* commander; (*mil*) major; (*naut*) captain. **commande** *nf* order; control. **de commande** affected, forced. **fait sur commande** made to order. **commandement** *nm* command; (*rel*) commandment.
commanditer [kɔmɑ̃dite] *v* finance.
comme [kɔm] *conj* as; (*tel que*) like, such as. *adv* how. **comme ça** like that. **comme ci comme ça** so-so. **comme si** as if, as though. **comme il faut** properly. ... **comme tout** as ... as can be.
commémorer [kɔmemɔre] *v* commemorate. **commémoratif** *adj* commemorative, memorial. **commémoration** *nf* commemoration.
commencer [kɔmɑ̃se] *v* begin, start. **commencement** *nm* beginning, start.
comment [kɔmɑ̃] *adv* how. **comment allez-vous?** how are you? **comment s'appelle-t-il?** what's his name? *interj* what.
commenter [kɔmɑ̃te] *v* comment on; (*sport*) give a commentary on. **commentaire** *nm* comment; (*exposé*) commentary. **commentateur, -trice** *nm*, *nf* (*sport*) commentator; (*journal*) correspondent.
commérage [kɔmeraʒ] *nm* gossip.
commerçant [kɔmɛrsɑ̃], **-e** *adj* commercial; (*rue*) shopping. *nm*, *nf* shopkeeper, tradesman.
commerce [kɔmɛrs] *nm* trade, commerce, business. **commercial** *adj* commercial. **commerciale** *nf* van.
***commettre** [kɔmɛtrə] *v* commit.
commis [kɔmi] *nm* assistant; (*bureau*) clerk.
commissaire [kɔmisɛr] *nm* commissioner; (*surveillant*) steward. **commissaire de police** police superintendant. **commissaire-priseur** *nm* auctioneer.
commissariat [kɔmisarja] *nm* police station.

commission [kɔmisjɔ̃] *nf* commission; message; (*course*) errand; committee. **commissions** *nf pl* shopping.

commissionnaire [kɔmisjɔnɛr] *nm* messenger; (*livreur*) delivery man; (*hôtel*) commissionnaire; (*comm*) agent.

commode [kɔmɔd] *adj* handy, convenient; (*facile*) easy; (*personne*) easygoing. *nf* chest of drawers. **commodité** *nf* convenience.

commotion [kɔmosjɔ̃] *nf* shock. **commotion cérébrale** concussion. **commotionner** *v* shock, shake.

commun [kɔmœ̃] *adj* common; (*partagé*) shared, communal. **hors du commun** out of the ordinary. **peu commun** uncommon.

communauté [kɔmynote] *nf* community; (*cohabitation*) commune.

commune [kɔmyn] *nf* district, borough; parish. **communal** *adj* local; council.

communiant [kɔmynjɑ̃], **-e** *nm, nf* communicant.

communication [kɔmynikasjɔ̃] *nf* communication; message; telephone call. **communication interurbaine/en PCV/avec préavis** trunk/reverse-charge/personal call.

communion [kɔmynjɔ̃] *nf* communion.

communiquer [kɔmynike] *v* communicate; pass on; transmit. **se communiquer** spread; (*personne*) be communicative.

communisme [kɔmynismə] *nm* communism. **communiste** *n(m+f)*, *adj* communist.

compact [kɔ̃pakt] *adj* compact; dense.

compagnie [kɔ̃paɲi] *nf* company. **compagnon, compagne** *nm, nf* companion.

comparer [kɔ̃pare] *v* compare. **comparable** *adj* comparable. **comparaison** *nf* comparison. **comparatif** *nm, adj* comparative.

compartiment [kɔ̃partimɑ̃] *nm* compartment.

compas [kɔ̃pa] *nm* compass; (*math*) pair of compasses.

compassion [kɔ̃pasjɔ̃] *nf* compassion, sympathy.

compatible [kɔ̃patiblə] *adj* compatible. **compatibilité** *nf* compatibility.

compatir [kɔ̃patir] *v* sympathize. **compatissant** *adj* compassionate, sympathetic.

compenser [kɔ̃pɑ̃se] *v* compensate (for). **compensation** *nf* compensation.

compère [kɔ̃pɛr] *nm* accomplice.

compétent [kɔ̃petɑ̃] *adj* competent. **compétence** *nf* competence.

compétition [kɔ̃petisjɔ̃] *nf* competition; event, race. **compétiteur, -trice** *nm, nf* competitor. **compétitif** *adj* competitive.

compiler [kɔ̃pile] *v* compile. **compilation** *nf* compilation.

complaisance [kɔ̃plɛzɑ̃s] *nf* kindness; servility; indulgence; self-satisfaction. **complaisant** *adj* kind; servile; indulgent; self-satisfied.

complément [kɔ̃plemɑ̃] *nm* complement. **complémentaire** *adj* complementary; additional.

complet, -ète [kɔ̃plɛ, -ɛt] *adj* complete; (*plein*) full. *nm* suit.

compléter [kɔ̃plete] *v* complete; (*augmenter*) supplement, add to.

complexe [kɔ̃plɛks] *nm, adj* complex. **complexité** *nf* complexity.

complication [kɔ̃plikasjɔ̃] *nf* complication.

complice [kɔ̃plis] *n(m+f)* accomplice. *adj* knowing. **être complice de** be a party to. **complicité** *nf* complicity.

compliment [kɔ̃plimɑ̃] *nm* compliment. **compliments** *nm pl* congratulations *pl*. **complimenter** *v* compliment; congratulate.

compliquer [kɔ̃plike] *v* complicate. **se compliquer** get complicated.

complot [kɔ̃plo] *nm* plot. **comploter** *v* plot.

comporter [kɔ̃pɔrte] *v* consist of; (*impliquer*) entail; include. **se comporter** behave, perform. **comportement** *nm* behaviour, performance.

composer [kɔ̃poze] *v* compose, make up; (*numéro*) dial. **composer avec** come to terms with. **se composer de** consist of. **composé** *nm, adj* compound. **compositeur, -trice** *nm, nf* composer. **composition** *nf* composition.

compote [kɔ̃pɔt] *nf* stewed fruit.

compréhensif [kɔ̃preɑ̃sif] *adj* understanding. **compréhension** *nf* understanding, comprehension.

*comprendre [kɔ̃prɑ̃drə] *v* understand; consist of, comprise; include. **se faire comprendre** make oneself understood. **compris** *adj* included. **tout compris** all inclusive. **y compris** including.

compresse [kɔ̃prɛs] *nf* compress.

compression [kɔ̃presjɔ̃] *nf* compression; *(réduction)* cut-back.

comprimer [kɔ̃prime] *v* compress; *(réduire)* cut back; *(contenir)* hold back.

***compromettre** [kɔ̃prɔmɛtrə] *v* compromise; *(santé, etc.)* jeopardize. **compromis** *nm* compromise.

comptable [kɔ̃tablə] *adj* accounts; *(responsable)* accountable.

compte [kɔ̃t] *nm* account; number; *(calcul)* count. **compte à rebours** countdown. **compte rendu** report, review. **tenir compte de** take into account.

compter [kɔ̃te] *v* count; *(escompter)* reckon; pay; *(facturer)* charge for. **comptant** *nm, adv* cash.

compteur [kɔ̃tœr] *nm* meter. **compteur de vitesse** speedometer. **compteur kilométrique** milometer.

comptine [kɔ̃tin] *nf* nursery rhyme.

comptoir [kɔ̃twar] *nm* counter; bar.

comte [kɔ̃t] *nm* count. **comtesse** *nf* countess.

comté [kɔ̃te] *nm* county.

concave [kɔ̃kav] *adj* concave.

concéder [kɔ̃sede] *v* concede, grant.

concentrer [kɔ̃sɑ̃tre] *v* concentrate. **concentration** *nf* concentration. **concentré** *nm* concentrate, extract.

concentrique [kɔ̃sɑ̃trik] *adj* concentric.

concept [kɔ̃sɛpt] *nm* concept.

conception [kɔ̃sɛpsjɔ̃] *nf* conception; idea.

concerner [kɔ̃sɛrne] *v* concern.

concert [kɔ̃sɛr] *nm* concert. **de concert** together, in unison.

concerté [kɔ̃sɛrte] *adj* concerted.

concertina [kɔ̃sɛrtina] *nm* concertina.

concerto [kɔ̃sɛrto] *nm* concerto.

concession [kɔ̃sesjɔ̃] *nf* concession.

***concevoir** [kɔ̃səvwar] *v* conceive; *(comprendre)* understand; *(rédiger)* express.

concierge [kɔ̃sjɛrʒ] *n(m+f)* caretaker. **conciergerie** *nf* caretaker's lodge.

concilier [kɔ̃silje] *v* reconcile; *(attirer)* win, gain.

concis [kɔ̃si] *adj* concise.

***conclure** [kɔ̃klyr] *v* conclude. **concluant** *adj* conclusive. **conclusion** *nf* conclusion.

concombre [kɔ̃kɔ̃brə] *nm* cucumber.

concorder [kɔ̃kɔrde] *v* agree, tally. **concordance** *nf* agreement. **concorde** *nf* concord.

***concourir** [kɔ̃kurir] *v* compete; converge.

concours [kɔ̃kur] *nm* competition; *(examen)* competitive examination; aid.

concret, -ète [kɔ̃krɛ, -ɛt] *adj* concrete.

concurrence [kɔ̃kyrɑ̃s] *nf* competition. **faire concurrence à** compete with. **concurrent, -e** *nm, nf* competitor; *(examen)* candidate. **concurrentiel** *adj* competitive.

condamner [kɔ̃dane] *v* condemn; *(jur)* sentence; *(porte, etc.)* block up. **condamnation** *nf* condemnation; sentence.

condenser [kɔ̃dɑ̃se] *v* condense. **condensation** *nf* condensation.

condescendre [kɔ̃desɑ̃drə] *v* condescend. **condescendance** *nf* condescension.

condition [kɔ̃disjɔ̃] *nf* condition; *(comm)* term; *(rang)* station. **à condition** on approval. **à condition de** provided that. **conditionnel** *nm, adj* conditional.

conditionner [kɔ̃disjɔne] *v* condition; *(emballer)* package. **conditionnement** *nm* conditioning; packaging.

condoléances [kɔ̃dɔleɑ̃s] *nf pl* condolences *pl.*

conducteur [kɔ̃dyktœr], **-trice** *nm, nf* driver; *(chef)* leader. *nm (élec)* conductor. **conduction** *nf* conduction.

***conduire** [kɔ̃dɥir] *v* *(véhicule)* drive; *(emmener)* take; *(guider)* lead; *(élec)* conduct; *(diriger)* run. **se conduire** behave. **conduit** *nm* duct, pipe. **conduite** *nf* driving; running; behaviour. conduct; pipe. **conduite d'eau/de gaz** water/gas main. **conduite intérieure** saloon car.

cône [kon] *nm* core.

confectionner [kɔ̃fɛksjɔne] *v* make. **confection** *nf* making; clothing industry. **de confection** ready-made, off-the-peg.

confédéré [kɔ̃federe] *adj* confederate. **confédération** *nf* confederation.

conférer [kɔ̃fere] *v* confer; compare. **conférence** *nf* conference; *(exposé)* lecture. **conférencier, -ère** *nm, nf* lecturer.

confesser [kɔ̃fese] *v* confess. **confession** *nf* confession.

confetti [kɔ̃feti] *nm* confetti.

confiance [kɔ̃fjɑ̃s] *nf* confidence, trust. **avec confiance** confidently. **avoir confiance en** trust. **confiance en soi** self-confidence. **de confiance** trustworthy. **confiant** *adj* confident.

confidence [kɔ̃fidɑ̃s] *nf* confidence, personal secret. **confidentiel** *adj* confidential.

confier [kɔ̃fje] *v* confide. **se confier à** (*se livrer*) confide in; (*se fier*) put one's trust in.

confiner [kɔ̃fine] *v* confine. **confiner à** border on. **confins** *nm pl* borders *pl*.

*****confire** [kɔ̃fir] *v* preserve.

confirmer [kɔ̃firme] *v* confirm. **confirmation** *nf* confirmation.

confiserie [kɔ̃fizri] *nf* confectionery; (*magasin*) confectioner's, sweet-shop. **confiseur, -euse** *nm, nf* confectioner.

confisquer [kɔ̃fiske] *v* confiscate. **confiscation** *nf* confiscation.

confit [kɔ̃fi] *adj* candied.

confiture [kɔ̃fityr] *nf* jam. **confiture d'oranges** marmalade.

conflit [kɔ̃fli] *nm* conflict, clash.

confluer [kɔ̃flye] *v* join, converge. **confluence** *nf* mingling. **confluent** *nm* confluence.

confondre [kɔ̃fɔ̃drə] *v* mix up, confuse; (*ennemi*) confound; (*étonner*) astound; join, meet. **se confondre** merge. **se confondre en excuses/remerciements** apologize/thank profusely. **confondu** *adj* overwhelmed.

conforme [kɔ̃fɔrm] *adj* **conforme à** true to; in accordance with; in keeping with. **conformément à** in accordance with.

conformer [kɔ̃fɔrme] *v* model. **se conformer à** conform to. **conformité** *nf* conformity; similarity.

confort [kɔ̃fɔr] *nm* comfort. **confortable** *adj* comfortable.

confrère [kɔ̃frɛr] *nm* colleague.

confronter [kɔ̃frɔ̃te] *v* confront; compare. **confrontation** *nf* confrontation; comparison.

confus [kɔ̃fy] *adj* confused; (*honteux*) ashamed. **confusion** *nf* confusion; (*honte*) embarrassment.

congé [kɔ̃ʒe] *nm* holiday, leave; (*renvoi*) notice. **prendre congé** take one's leave.

congédier [kɔ̃ʒedje] *v* dismiss.

congeler [kɔ̃ʒle] *v* freeze. **congélateur** *nm* freezer.

congestion [kɔ̃ʒɛstjɔ̃] *nf* congestion. **congestionné** *adj* congested; (*visage*) flushed.

congrès [kɔ̃grɛ] *nm* congress.

conifère [kɔnifɛr] *nm* conifer.

conlque [kɔnik] *adj* conical.

conjoint [kɔ̃ʒwɛ̃], **-e** *nm, nf* spouse. *adj* joint.

conjonction [kɔ̃ʒɔ̃ksjɔ̃] *nf* conjunction.

conjugal [kɔ̃ʒygal] *adj* conjugal.

conjuguer [kɔ̃ʒyge] *v* conjugate; combine. **conjugaison** *nf* conjugation.

connaissance [kɔnɛsɑ̃s] *nf* knowledge; (*personne*) acquaintance; (*conscience*) consciousness. **sans connaissance** unconscious.

connaisseur [kɔnɛsœr], **-euse** *adj* expert. *nm, nf* connoisseur.

*****connaître** [kɔnɛtrə] *v* know; be acquainted or familiar with; (*éprouver*) experience. **faire connaître** make known.

connu [kɔny] *adj* known; (*répandu, fameux*) well-known.

*****conquérir** [kɔ̃kerir] *v* conquer.

conquête [kɔ̃kɛt] *nf* conquest.

consacrer [kɔ̃sakre] *v* consecrate; (*dédier*) devote, dedicate. **consacré** *adj* consecrated, hallowed; accepted, established. **consécration** *nf* consecration.

conscience [kɔ̃sjɑ̃s] *nf* consciousness; (*morale*) conscience. **avoir conscience de** be aware of. **consciencieux** *adj* conscientious. **conscient** *adj* conscious.

conscription [kɔ̃skripsjɔ̃] *nf* conscription. **conscrit** [kɔ̃skri] *nm* conscript.

consécutif [kɔ̃sekytif] *adj* consecutive.

conseil [kɔ̃sɛj] *nm* advice; (*organisme*) board, council. **conseil d'administration** board of directors. **conseil de guerre** court-martial. **conseiller, -ère** *nm, nf* adviser; councillor.

conseiller [kɔ̃seje] *v* recommend; advise.

*****consentir** [kɔ̃sɑ̃tir] *v* consent, agree. **consentement** *nm* consent.

conséquence [kɔ̃sekɑ̃s] *nf* consequence, result. **conséquent** *adj* logical; consistent. **par conséquent** consequently.

conservateur [kɔ̃sɛrvatœr], **-trice** *adj* conservative. *nm, nf* (*musée*) curator; (*pol*) Conservative.

conservatoire [kɔ̃sɛrvatwar] *nm* academy, school.

conserve [kɔ̃sɛrv] *nf* **en conserve** tinned, canned. **mettre en conserve** can.

conserver [kɔ̃sɛrve] *v* keep, retain, conserve; (*aliments, etc.*) preserve. **conservation** *nf* preservation.

considérer [kɔ̃sidere] *v* consider; regard; respect. **considérable** *adj* considerable. **considération** *nf* consideration; reflection; respect.

consigner [kɔ̃siɲe] *v* (*par écrit*) record; (*en dépôt*) deposit; (*soldat*) confine to barracks. **consignation** *nf* deposit; (*comm*) consignment. **consigne** *nf* orders *pl*; (*bagages*) left-luggage office; (*comm*) deposit. **consigné** *adj* (*bouteille, etc.*) returnable.

consister [kɔ̃siste] *v* consist. **consister en** consist of. **consistance** *nf* consistency. **consistant** *adj* solid.

consoler [kɔ̃sɔle] *v* console. **consolation** *nf* consolation.

consolider [kɔ̃sɔlide] *v* strengthen, consolidate. **consolidation** *nf* strengthening, consolidation.

consommer [kɔ̃sɔme] *v* consume; use; (*manger*) eat; (*mariage*) consummate. **consommateur, -trice** *nm*, *nf* consumer; (*café*) customer. **consommation** *nf* consumption; (*café*) drink; consummation. **consommé** *nm* consommé.

consonne [kɔ̃sɔn] *nf* consonant.

conspirer [kɔ̃spire] *v* conspire. **conspirateur, -trice** *nm*, *nf* conspirator. **conspiration** *nf* conspiracy.

conspuer [kɔ̃spɥe] *v* shout down.

constant [kɔ̃stɑ̃] *adj* constant. **constamment** *adv* constantly. **constance** *nf* constancy.

constater [kɔ̃state] *v* note, notice; (*consigner*) record, certify. **constatation** *nf* observation.

constellation [kɔ̃stelasjɔ̃] *nf* constellation.

consterner [kɔ̃stɛrne] *v* dismay. **consternation** *nf* consternation, dismay.

constipation [kɔ̃stipasjɔ̃] *nf* constipation. **constipé** *adj* constipated.

constituer [kɔ̃stitɥe] *v* constitute; (*fonder*) put together, set up; (*jur*) appoint. **constituent** *adj* constituent. **constitution** *nf* constitution; composition.

construction [kɔ̃stryksjɔ̃] *nf* construction; (*bâtiment*) building. **constructif** *adj* constructive.

***construire** [kɔ̃strɥir] *v* construct; build.

consul [kɔ̃syl] *nm* consul. **consulat** *nm* consulate.

consulter [kɔ̃sylte] *v* consult. **consultation** *nf* consultation.

consumer [kɔ̃syme] *v* consume; destroy.

contact [kɔ̃takt] *nm* contact; (*auto*) ignition.

contagieux [kɔ̃taʒjø] *adj* contagious, infectious. **contagion** *nf* contagion.

contaminer [kɔ̃tamine] *v* contaminate. **contamination** *nf* contamination.

conte [kɔ̃t] *nm* tale, story. **conte de fée** fairy tale.

contempler [kɔ̃tɑ̃ple] *v* contemplate. **contemplatif** *adj* contemplative. **contemplation** *nf* contemplation.

contemporain [kɔ̃tɑ̃pɔrɛ̃], **-e** *n*, *adj* contemporary.

contenance [kɔ̃tnɑ̃s] *nf* capacity; attitude. **faire bonne contenance** put on a brave face.

***contenir** [kɔ̃tnir] *v* contain; (*récipient*) hold.

content [kɔ̃tɑ̃] *adj* pleased, happy; satisfied, content.

contenter [kɔ̃tɑ̃te] *v* satisfy. **se contenter de** content oneself with. **contentement** *nm* contentment, satisfaction.

contenu [kɔ̃tny] *adj* restrained. *nm* content; (*récipient*) contents *pl*.

conter [kɔ̃te] *v* recount, relate. **conteur, -euse** *nm*, *nf* storyteller.

contester [kɔ̃tɛste] *v* contest, dispute; protest. **contestable** *adj* questionable. **contestation** *nf* dispute.

contexte [kɔ̃tɛkst] *nm* context.

contigu, -uë [kɔ̃tigy] *adj* adjacent, adjoining.

continent [kɔ̃tinɑ̃] *nm* continent. **continental** *adj* continental.

contingent [kɔ̃tɛ̃ʒɑ̃] *nm* contingent; quota; (*part*) share.

continuer [kɔ̃tinɥe] *v* continue. **continu** *adj* continuous. **continuel** *adj* continual; continuous. **continuité** *nf* continuity; continuation.

contourner [kɔ̃turne] *v* skirt round, bypass; (*façonner*) shape; (*déformer*) twist.

contraception [kɔ̃trasɛpsjɔ̃] *nf* contraception. **contraceptif** *nm*, *adj* contraceptive.

contracter¹ [kɔ̃trakte] *v* (*raidir*) tense, contract. **contraction** *nf* contraction.

contracter² [kɔ̃trakte] *v* contract; (*dette*) incur; (*alliance*) enter into.

contractuel [kɔ̃traktɥɛl], **-elle** *adj* contractual. *nm*, *nf* traffic warden.

contradiction [kɔ̃tradiksjɔ̃] *nf* contradiction; debate, argument. **contradictoire** *adj* contradictory.

***contraindre** [kɔ̃trɛ̃drə] *v* force, compel. **contrainte** *nf* constraint.

contraire [kɔ̃trɛr] *adj* contrary; opposite; conflicting. *nm* opposite. **au contraire** on the contrary.

contrarier [kɔ̃trarje] *v* (*irriter*) annoy; (*gêner*) thwart. **contrariant** *adj* tiresome; (*personne*) contrary.

contraster [kɔ̃traste] v contrast. **contraste** nm contrast.

contrat [kɔ̃tra] nm contract, agreement.

contravention [kɔ̃travɑ̃sjɔ̃] nf (amende) fine; (procès-verbal) parking ticket; (jur) contravention.

contre [kɔ̃trə] prep against; (protection) from; (échange) for; (rapport) to. **par contre** on the other hand.

contre-amiral nm rear admiral.

contre-attaque nf counter-attack. **contre-attaquer** v counter-attack.

contre-avion adj anti-aircraft.

contrebande [kɔ̃trəbɑ̃d] nf contraband; (activité) smuggling. **faire la contrebande de** smuggle. **contrebandier, -ère** nm, nf smuggler.

contrebasse [kɔ̃trəbas] nf double bass.

contre-boutant nm buttress.

contrecarrer [kɔ̃trəkare] v thwart.

contrecœur [kɔ̃trəkœr] adv **à contrecœur** grudgingly.

contrecoup [kɔ̃trəku] nm repercussions pl.

*__contredire__ [kɔ̃trədir] v contradict.

contrée [kɔ̃tre] nf region.

contrefaçon [kɔ̃trəfasɔ̃] nf forgery, counterfeit, imitation.

*__contrefaire__ [kɔ̃trəfɛr] v counterfeit, forge; disguise; imitate. **contrefait** adj deformed.

contre-interrogatoire nm cross-examination.

contremaître [kɔ̃trəmɛtrə] nm foreman.

contremander [kɔ̃trəmɑ̃de] v cancel.

contre-manifestation nf counter-demonstration.

contre-pied nm opposite.

contre-plaqué nm plywood.

contrepoids [kɔ̃trəpwa] nm counterbalance.

contre-poil adv **à contre-poil** the wrong way.

contrepoison [kɔ̃trəpwazɔ̃] nm antidote.

contresens [kɔ̃trəsɑ̃s] nm misinterpretation. **à contresens** the wrong way. **à contresens de** against.

contretemps [kɔ̃trətɑ̃] nm hitch. **à contretemps** at an inconvenient time.

contre-torpilleur nm destroyer.

*__contrevenir__ [kɔ̃trəvnir] v contravene.

contrevent [kɔ̃trəvɑ̃] nm shutter.

contre-voie adv **à contre-voie** (rail) on the wrong side.

contribuer [kɔ̃tribɥe] v contribute. **contribuable** n(m+f) taxpayer. **contribution** nf contribution. **contributions** nf pl (à l'état) taxes pl; (à la commune) rates pl; (bureau) tax office sing.

contrôler [kɔ̃trole] v control; (vérifier) check; (argent, or) hallmark. **contrôle** nm control; check, inspection; list; hallmark. **contrôleur** nm inspector; bus conductor; ticket collector.

controverse [kɔ̃trɔvɛrs] nf controversy.

contusion [kɔ̃tyzjɔ̃] nf bruise. **contusionner** v bruise.

*__convaincre__ [kɔ̃vɛ̃krə] v convince, persuade; (jur) convict.

convalescence [kɔ̃valesɑ̃s] nf convalescence. **convalescent, -e** nm, nf convalescent.

*__convenir__ [kɔ̃vnir] v suit; (être utile) be convenient; (être approprié) be suitable; (avouer) acknowledge; admit; (s'accorder) agree on. **convenable** adj fitting, suitable, appropriate; decent, acceptable, proper. **convenance** nf convenience; preference. **les convenances** propriety sing. **convenu** adj agreed.

convention [kɔ̃vɑ̃sjɔ̃] nf convention; (accord) understanding; (pacte) agreement. **conventionnel** adj conventional.

converger [kɔ̃vɛrze] v converge.

convers [kɔ̃vɛr] adj lay.

conversation [kɔ̃vɛrsasjɔ̃] nf conversation.

conversion [kɔ̃vɛrsjɔ̃] nf conversion.

convertir [kɔ̃vɛrtir] v convert. **converti, -e** nm, nf convert. **convertible** adj convertible.

convexe [kɔ̃vɛks] adj convex.

conviction [kɔ̃viksjɔ̃] nf conviction.

convier [kɔ̃vje] v invite, urge.

convive [kɔ̃viv] n(m+f) guest.

convocation [kɔ̃vɔkasjɔ̃] nf summons.

convoi [kɔ̃vwa] nm convoy.

convoiter [kɔ̃vwate] v covet. **convoitise** nf lust.

convoquer [kɔ̃vɔke] v (assemblée) convene; (personne) summon.

convulsion [kɔ̃vylsjɔ̃] nf convulsion. **convulsif** adj convulsive.

coopérer [kɔɔpere] v cooperate. **coopératif** adj cooperative. **coopération** nf cooperation. **coopérative** nf cooperative.

coordination [kɔɔrdinasjɔ̃] nf coordination.

coordonner [kɔɔrdɔne] v coordinate.

copain, copine [kɔpɛ̃, kɔpin] *nm, nf (fam)* pal, mate.

Copenhague [kɔpənag] *n* Copenhagen.

copier [kɔpje] *v* copy. **copie** *nf* copy; *(examen)* paper.

copieux [kɔpjø] *adj* copious.

copuler [kɔpyle] *v* copulate. **copulation** *nf* copulation.

coq [kɔk] *rm* cock.

coque [kɔk] *nf* shell; *(mollusque)* cockle; *(bateau)* hull.

coquelicot [kɔkliko] *nm* poppy.

coqueluche [kɔklyʃ] *nf* whooping cough.

coquet, -ette [kɔke, -ɛt] *adj* flirtatious; clothes-conscious; charming; *(fam: somme)* tidy.

coquetier [kɔktje] *nm* egg-cup.

coquille [kɔkij] *nf* shell; *(récipient)* scallop; *(erreur)* misprint. **coquille Saint-Jacques** scallop. **coquillage** *nm* shellfish.

coquin, -e [kɔkɛ̃, -e] *adj* mischievous, naughty. *nm, nf* rascal.

cor [kɔr] *nm (musique)* horn; *(méd)* corn. **cor anglais** cor anglais. **cor d'harmonie** French horn.

corail [kɔraj] *nm, pl* **-aux** coral.

corbeau [kɔrbo] *nm* crow.

corbeille [kɔrbɛj] *nf* basket. **corbeille à papier** wastepaper basket.

corbillard [kɔrbijar] *nm* hearse.

cordages [kɔrdaʒ] *nm pl* ropes *pl*, rigging *sing*.

corde [kɔrd] *nf* rope; *(musique, raquette)* string; *(tissu)* thread. **corde à linge** clothes-line. **corde à sauter** skipping-rope. **corde raide** tightrope. **cordes vocales** vocal cords *pl*.

corder [kɔrde] *v* twist; *(raquette)* string.

cordon [kɔrdɔ̃] *nm* cord, string; *(soldats, police)* cordon. **cordonnier** *nm* cobbler.

coriace [kɔrjas] *adj* tough.

corne [kɔrn] *nf* horn. **corne de brume** fog-horn.

corneille [kɔrnɛj] *nf* crow.

cornemuse [kɔrnəmyz] *nf* bagpipes *pl*.

cornet [kɔrne] *nm (papier, glace)* cone, cornet. **cornet à pistons** cornet.

cornichon [kɔrniʃɔ̃] *nm* gherkin.

Cornouailles [kɔrnwaj] *nf* Cornwall.

cornu [kɔrny] *adj* horned.

corporation [kɔrpɔrasjɔ̃] *nf* guild, corporate body.

corporel [kɔrpɔrel] *adj* corporal.

corps [kɔr] *nm* body; *(mil)* corps; *(cadavre)* corpse. **corps à corps** *adv* hand-to-hand. **le corps enseignant/médical** the teaching/medical profession.

corpulent [kɔrpylɑ̃] *adj* stout, corpulent.

corpuscule [kɔrpyskyl] *nm* corpuscle.

correct [kɔrekt] *adj* correct, accurate, right. **correction** *nf* correction; *(châtiment)* thrashing; accuracy.

correspondant [kɔrespɔ̃dɑ̃], **-e** *adj* corresponding. *nm, nf* correspondent. **correspondance** *nf* correspondence; *(transport)* connection.

correspondre [kɔrespɔ̃drə] *v* correspond; connect. **correspondre à** fit, agree with, suit.

corrida [kɔrida] *nf* bullfight.

corridor [kɔridɔr] *nm* corridor.

corriger [kɔriʒe] *v* correct; *(punir)* thrash.

corroborer [kɔrɔbɔre] *v* corroborate. **corroboration** *nf* corroboration.

corroder [kɔrɔde] *v* corrode. **corrodant** *adj* corrosive.

corrompre [kɔrɔ̃prə] *v* corrupt; *(eau, aliments)* taint; *(soudoyer)* bribe. **corrompu** *adj* corrupt.

corruption [kɔrypsjɔ̃] *nf* corruption; bribery; decomposition.

corsage [kɔrsaʒ] *nm* bodice.

corrosion [kɔrozjɔ̃] *nf* corrosion. **corrosif** *adj* corrosive; *(ironie, etc.)* scathing.

Corse [kɔrs] *nf* Corsica. *n(m+f)* Corsican. **corse** *nm, adj* Corsican.

corset [kɔrse] *nm* corset.

cortège [kɔrtɛʒ] *nm* procession.

corvée [kɔrve] *nf* chore; *(mil)* fatigue.

cosmétique [kɔsmetik] *adj* cosmetic.

cosmique [kɔsmik] *adj* cosmic.

cosmopolite [kɔsmɔpɔlit] *adj* cosmopolitan.

cosmos [kɔsmos] *nm* cosmos.

cosse [kɔs] *nf* pod, hull.

cossu [kɔsy] *adj* well-off, opulent.

costaud [kɔsto] *adj* strong, sturdy.

costume [kɔstym] *nm* costume, dress; *(complet)* suit.

cote [kɔt] *nf* rating, popularity; *(comm)* quotation; *(courses)* odds *pl*; mark.

côte [kot] *nf (anat, tricot)* rib; *(pente)* slope, hill; *(littoral)* coast, coastline.

côté [kote] *nm* side; way, direction. **à côté** *(maison, pièce)* next door; *(près)* nearby. **à côté de** beside; compared to. **de côté** sideways; aside.

coteau [kɔto] *nm* hill, slope.

côtelette [kotlɛt] *nf* chop, cutlet.

coter [kɔte] *v* rate, mark; (*comm*) quote.

côtier [kotje] *adj* coastal, inshore.

se cotiser [kɔtize] *v* subscribe; (*groupe*) club together. **cotisant, -e** *nm, nf* (*club*) subscriber; (*pension*) contributor. **cotisation** *nf* subscription; contribution; collection.

coton [kɔtɔ̃] *nm* cotton. **coton à broder/repriser** embroidery/darning thread.

côtoyer [kotwaje] *v* skirt, run alongside; (*frôler*) be close to, be verging on.

cou [ku] *nm* neck. **cou-de-pied** *nm* instep.

couchant [kuʃɑ̃] *adj* setting. *nm* west; sunset.

couche [kuʃ] *nf* layer; (*peinture*) coat; (*bébé*) nappy. **couches** *nf pl* (*méd*) confinement *sing.*

coucher [kuʃe] *v* lay down; (*loger*) put up; (*séjourner*) sleep; (*mettre au lit*) put to bed. **se coucher** go to bed; (*s'étendre*) lie down; (*soleil*) set. *nm* **coucher du soleil** sunset. **couché** *adj* lying down; in bed; (*penché*) sloping. **couchette** *nf* couchette, berth.

coucou [kuku] *nm* cuckoo.

coude [kud] *nm* elbow; (*rivière, tuyau*) bend.

*coudre [kudr] *v* sew, stitch.

coudrier [kudrije] *nm* hazel tree.

couenne [kwan] *nf* rind.

couic [kwik] *interj* squeak!

couler [kule] *v* run, flow; (*fuir*) leak; (*bateau*) sink; (*verser*) pour. **se couler** slip. **coulant** *adj* smooth, flowing. **coulé** *nm* (*musique*) slur. **coulée** *nf* casting.

couleur [kulœr] *nf* colour; (*cartes*) suit; (*peinture*) paint.

couleuvre [kulœvrə] *nf* grass snake.

coulisse [kulis] *nf* runner, slide. **coulisses** *nf pl* wings *pl.* **dans les coulisses** behind the scenes. **porte à coulisse** *nf* sliding door.

couloir [kulwar] *nm* corridor; (*voie*) lane; (*pol*) lobby.

coup [ku] *nm* blow, knock; (*pinceau, plume*) stroke; (*bruit*) sound; (*essai*) try; (*tour*) trick. **à coup sûr** definitely. **après coup** afterwards. **du coup** suddenly. **du premier coup** first time. **tout à coup** suddenly.

coupable [kupablə] *adj* guilty. *n(m+f)* culprit.

coup de bec *nm* peck.

coup de coude *nm* nudge.

coup de feu *nm* shot.

coup de fil *nm* (*fam*) phone call.

coup de froid *nm* chill.

coup de main *nm* (helping) hand.

coup d'envoi *nm* kick-off.

coup de pied *nm* kick.

coup de poing *nm* punch.

coup de soleil *nm* sunburn.

coup de sonnette *nm* ring.

coup de téléphone *nm* telephone call.

coup de vent *nm* gust.

coup d'œil *nm* glance.

coupe¹ [kup] *nf* (*dessert*) dish; (*boire*) goblet; (*sport*) cup.

coupe² [kup] *nf* cut, cutting. **coupe transversale** cross section.

couper [kupe] *v* cut; (*eau, élec, etc.*) cut off; (*traverser*) cross; (*voyage*) break; (*vin*) dilute, blend. **coupe-papier** *nm* paper knife. **coupant** *adj* sharp. **coupure** *nf* cut; (*journal*) cutting; (*courant*) power cut.

couple [kuplə] *nm* couple, pair. **coupler** *v* couple.

couplet [kuplɛ] *nm* verse.

coupon [kupɔ̃] *nm* coupon; (*reste*) remnant.

cour [kur] *nf* court; (*bâtiment*) yard, courtyard; (*école*) playground; (*gare*) forecourt; (*femme*) courtship. **cour de ferme** farmyard. **faire la cour (à)** court.

courage [kuraʒ] *nm* courage; spirit, will. **perdre courage** lose heart. **courageux** *adj* brave, courageous.

couramment [kuramɑ̃] *adv* fluently; commonly.

courant [kurɑ̃] *adj* (*normal*) ordinary, standard; (*fréquent*) common; (*actuel*) current. *nm* current; movement; course. **au courant** well-informed, up to date. **courant d'air** draught.

courbature [kurbatyr] *nf* ache. **courbaturé** *adj* aching, stiff.

courbe [kurb] *adj* curved. *nf* curve.

courber [kurbe] *v* bend, curve. **se courber** bend down; (*saluer*) bow.

courge [kurʒ] *nf* marrow. **courgette** *nf* courgette.

*courir [kurir] *v* run; (*sport*) race; (*aller vite*) rush, speed; (*chasser*) hunt; (*parcourir*) roam. **coureur, -euse** *nm, nf* runner; (*sport*) competitor. **coureur automobile** racing driver.

couronner [kurɔne] v crown; (*ceindre*) encircle; award a prize to. **couronne** nf crown; (*fleurs*) wreath. **couronnement** nm coronation.

courrier [kurje] nm mail, letters pl; (*journal*) column, page.

courroie [kurwa] nf belt, strap. **courroie de ventilateur** fan belt.

courroux [kuru] nm wrath.

cours [kur] nm course; (*monnaie*) currency; (*leçon*) class. **au cours de** during. **avoir cours** be current. **cours du change** exchange rate. **en cours** in progress.

course [kurs] nf run, running; (*épreuve*) race; (*achat*) shopping, errand; (*voyage*) journey. **faire des courses** go shopping.

court¹ [kur] adj, adv short. **à court de** short of. **court-circuit** nm short-circuit.

court² [kur] nm tennis court.

courtier [kurtje], **-ère** nm, nf broker.

courtisan [kurtizɑ̃] nm courtier; (*flatteur*) sycophant.

courtois [kurtwa] adj courteous.

cousin¹ [kuzɛ̃], **-e** nm, nf cousin. **cousin germain** first cousin.

cousin² [kuzɛ̃] nm gnat.

coussin [kusɛ̃] nm cushion. **coussinet** nm pad; (*tech*) bearing.

cousu [kuzy] adj sewn, stitched.

coût [ku] nm cost.

couteau [kuto] nm knife. **couteau à découper** carving knife. **couteau de poche** pocket knife. **couteau-éplucheur** nm peeler.

coutellerie [kutɛlri] nf cutlery.

coûter [kute] v cost. **coûte que coûte** at all costs. **coûter cher** be expensive. **coûteux** adj expensive.

coutume [kutym] nf custom. **coutumier** adj customary.

couture [kutyr] nf sewing; (*confection*) dressmaking; (*suite de points*) seam. **couturier** nm fashion designer. **couturière** nf dressmaker.

couvent [kuvɑ̃] nm convent.

couver [kuve] v (*feu, haine*) smoulder; (*émeute*) brew; (*poule*) brood, sit on; (*œufs*) hatch. **couvée** nf brood, clutch. **couveuse** nf incubator.

couvercle [kuvɛrklə] nm lid, cover, top.

couvert [kuvɛr] adj covered; (*ciel*) overcast. nm place setting; (*restaurant*) cover charge; (*abri*) cover, shelter. **mettre le couvert** lay the table.

couverture [kuvɛrtyr] nf cover; (*lit*) blanket. **couverture chauffante** electric blanket.

*****couvrir** [kuvrir] v cover; (*cacher*) conceal. **se couvrir** (*vêtements*) wrap up; (*chapeau*) put on one's hat; (*ciel*) cloud over. **couvre-feu** nm curfew. **couvre-lit** nm bedspread.

crabe [krab] nm crab.

crac [krak] interj crack!

cracher [kraʃe] v spit (out). **crachat** nm spit, spittle. **crachement** nm spitting.

crachiner [kraʃine] v drizzle. **crachin** nm drizzle.

craie [krɛ] nf chalk.

*****craindre** [krɛ̃drə] v fear, be afraid (of). **crainte** [krɛ̃t] nf fear. **craintif** adj timid.

cramoisi [kramwazi] adj crimson.

crampe [krɑ̃p] nf cramp.

cramponner [krɑ̃pɔne] v clamp; (*fam*) cling to. **se cramponner à** clutch, cling to. **crampon** nm clamp; (*chaussure*) stud.

cran [krɑ̃] nm notch; (*fusil*) catch; (*cheveux*) wave; (*fam*) guts pl.

crâne [krɑn] nm skull, head.

crâner [krane] (*fam*) v show off. **craneur, -euse** nm, nf show-off.

crapaud [krapo] nm toad.

crapuleux [krapylø] adj (*vie*) dissolute; (*action*) villainous.

craquer [krake] v crack; (*neige*) crunch; (*parquet*) creak; (*bas, pantalon*) rip. **craquement** nm crack, creak.

crasse [kras] nf grime, filth. **crasseux** adj grimy, filthy.

cratère [kratɛr] nm crater.

cravate [kravat] nf tie.

crawl [krol] nm crawl. **dos crawlé** nm backstroke.

crayon [krɛjɔ̃] nm pencil; (*dessin*) pencil sketch. **crayon de couleur** crayon.

crayonner [krɛjɔne] v jot down, scribble; (*dessin*) sketch.

créance [kreɑ̃s] nf debt, claim. **créancier, -ère** nm, nf creditor.

créateur [kreatœr] **-trice** adj creative. nm, nf creator.

création [kreasjɔ̃] nf creation.

créature [kreatyr] nf creature.

crèche [krɛʃ] nf crèche; (*rel*) crib.

crédit [kredi] nm credit; bank; trust. **créditer** v credit. **créditeur, -trice** adj credit.

crédule [kredyl] adj gullible. **crédulité** nf gullibility.

créer [kree] v create.
crémaillère [kremajɛr] nf (tech) rack. **pendre la crémaillère** have a house-warming party.
crématoire [krematwar] nm crematorium. **crémation** nf cremation.
crème [krɛm] nf, adj cream. **crème anglaise** custard. **crème à raser** shaving cream. **crème patissière** confectioner's custard. **crémerie** nf dairy. **crémeux** adj creamy.
crénelé [krɛnle] adj notched; (bordure) scalloped; (mur) crenellated.
crêpe¹ [krɛp] nf (cuisine) pancake. **crêperie** nf pancake shop or café.
crêpe² [krɛp] nm (tissu) crepe.
crépiter [krepite] v crackle.
crépuscule [krepyskyl] nm twilight.
cresson [krɛsɔ̃] nm cress.
crête [krɛt] nf ridge, crest; (coq) comb; (mur) top.
creuser [krøze] v dig (out), hollow (out); (problème) go into thoroughly.
creux [krø] adj hollow; (vide) empty; (visage) gaunt; (jours) slack. **heures creuses** off-peak periods pl. nm hollow; slack period. **creux des reins** small of the back.
crevaison [krəvɛzɔ̃] nf puncture.
crevasser [krəvase] v crack; (mains) chap. **crevasse** nf crack, crevice.
crever [krəve] v burst; (pneu) puncture; (fam: fatiguer) wear out; (fam: mourir) die.
crevette [krəvɛt] nf shrimp; (rose) prawn.
cri [kri] nm cry, shout.
criailler [kriaje] v squawk, screech; (bébé) bawl; (rouspéter) grumble.
criard [krijar] adj yelling, squawking; (couleur) garish; (son) piercing.
cribler [krible] v sift; (percer) riddle. **crible** nm sieve, riddle. **passer au crible** examine closely. **criblé de** riddled with; covered with; (dettes) crippled with.
cric [krik] nm jack. **soulever au cric** jack up.
cricket [krikɛt] nm cricket.
cri-cri [krikri] nm (grillon) cricket.
criée [krije] nf auction.
crier [krije] v shout, cry, scream; (oiseau) call; (grincer) squeak, squeal.
crime [krim] nm crime. **criminel, -elle** n, adj criminal.
crin [krɛ̃] nm hair, horsehair. **crinière** nf mane; (personne) mop of hair.
crique [krik] nf creek.

criquet [krikɛ] nm locust.
crise [kriz] nf crisis; (accès) attack, fit; (pénurie) shortage. **crise cardiaque** heart attack. **crise de foie** bilious attack. **piquer une crise** (fam) fly off the handle.
crisper [krispe] v tense, clench; (plisser) shrivel up. **se crisper** become tense, clench. **crispation** nf contraction; (nervosité) tension; (spasme) twitch. **crispé** adj nervous, tense, on edge.
crisser [krise] v (gravier) crunch; (freins) screech; (soie) rustle. **crisser des dents** grind one's teeth.
cristal [kristal] nm crystal. **cristal taillé** cut glass. **cristallin** adj crystalline; (son) crystal-clear.
cristalliser [kristalize] v crystallize. **cristallisation** nf crystallization.
critère [kritɛr] nm criterion.
critique [kritik] adj critical; crucial. nf criticism; (analyse) critique, review. n(m+f) critic. **critiquer** v criticize.
croasser [krɔase] v caw. **croassement** nm caw.
croc [kro] nm fang, tooth; (grappin) hook. **faire un croc-en-jambe à** trip up.
croche [krɔʃ] nf quaver.
crochet [krɔʃɛ] nm hook; (technique) crochet; detour; (véhicule) swerve. **crochets** nm pl square brackets pl. **faire du crochet** crochet. **vivre aux crochets de** sponge on, live off.
crochu [krɔʃy] adj hooked.
crocodile [krɔkɔdil] nm crocodile.
crocus [krɔkys] nm crocus.
***croire** [krwar] v believe, think. **croire à** or **en** believe in.
croisade [krwazad] nf crusade.
croiser [krwaze] v cross; pass; (naut) cruise. **croisé** adj double-breasted. **croisement** nm crossing; (carrefour) crossroads. **croisière** nf cruise.
croissance [krwasɑ̃s] nf growth, development.
croissant [krwasɑ̃] nm crescent; (pain) croissant. adj growing, increasing, rising.
***croître** [krwatrə] v grow, increase; (rivière, vent) rise.
croix [krwa] nf cross. **croix gammée** swastika.
croquer [krɔke] v crunch, munch; (salade, fruit) be crisp; (dessiner) sketch. **croquant** adj crisp, crunchy. **croque-monsieur** nm invar toasted cheese and ham sandwich.

croquet [krɔkɛ] *nm* croquet.
croquis [krɔki] *nm* sketch.
crosse [krɔs] *nf (sport)* club, stick; *(fusil)* butt; *(rel)* crook.
crotter [krɔte] *v* dirty, make muddy, soil. **crotte** *nf* droppings *pl*, dung.
crouler [ˌrule] *v* collapse; *(délabré)* be tumbledown; *(empire, etc.)* totter. **croulant** *adj* crumbling, tumbledown.
croupe [krup] *nf* rump, hindquarters *pl*; *(colline)* hilltop. **monter en croupe** ride pillion.
croupir [krupir] *v* stagnate; *(personne)* wallow. **croupi** *adj* stagnant.
croustiller [krustije] *v* be crisp *or* crunchy; *(pain)* be crusty. **croustillant** *adj* crisp, crunchy; crusty; *(grivois)* spicy.
croûte [krut] *nf (pain)* crust; *(fromage)* rind; *(plaie)* scab. **croûton** *nm* crust; *(cuisine)* crouton.
croyable [krwajablə] *adj* credible.
croyance [krwajɑ̃s] *nf* belief. **croyant, -e** *nm, nf* believer.
cru[1] [kry] *adj* raw, crude; *(lumière)* harsh; *(franc)* blunt.
cru[2] [kry] *nm (vignoble)* vineyard; *(vin)* vintage, wine.
cruauté [kryote] *nf* cruelty.
cruche [kryʃ] *nf* jug, pitcher.
crucifier [krysifje] *v* crucify. **crucifixion** *nf* crucifixion.
crucifix [krysifi] *nm* crucifix.
crudité [krydite] *nf* crudeness; harshness. **crudités** *nf pl* coarse remarks *pl*; *(cuisine)* salads *pl*.
crue [kry] *nf* swelling, rising.
cruel [kryɛl] *adj* cruel.
crûment [krymɑ̃] *adv* bluntly.
crustacé [krystase] *nm* shellfish. **crustacés** *nm pl (cuisine)* seafood *sing*.
crypte [kript] *nf* crypt.
cube [kyb] *nm* cube; *(d'enfant)* block, brick. *adj* cubic. **cubique** *adj* cubic.
***cueillir** [kœjir] *v* pick, gather; *(attraper)* catch.
cuiller [kᵁijɛr] *nf* spoon. **cuiller à café** teaspoon. **cuiller de service** tablespoon. **cuillerée** *nf* spoonful. **cuillerée à soupe** tablespoonful.
cuir [kᵁir] *nm* leather; *(avant tannage)* hide. **cuir chevelu** scalp. **cuir suédé** suede. **cuir verni** patent leather.
cuirasse [kᵁiras] *nf* armour; *(chevalier)* breastplate.

cuirassé [kᵁirase] *adj* armoured. *nm* battleship.
***cuire** [kᵁir] *v* cook; *(pain)* bake; *(porcelaine)* fire; *(brûler)* smart. **à cuire** *adj* cooking. **cuire à feu doux** simmer. **cuire à l'eau** boil. **cuire au four** *(viande)* roast; *(pain)* bake.
cuisant [kᵁizɑ̃] *adj* burning, stinging; *(regret)* bitter.
cuisine [kᵁizin] *nf (pièce)* kitchen; *(art)* cookery, cooking. **faire la cuisine** cook. **cuisinier** *nm* cook. **cuisinière** *nf (personne)* cook; *(fourneau)* cooker.
cuisse [kᵁis] *nf* thigh; *(cuisine)* leg.
cuit [kᵁi] *adj* cooked, ready. **cuit à point** done to a turn.
cuivre [kᵁivrə] *nm* copper. **cuivre jaune** brass.
cul [ky] *nm* bottom; *(vulgaire)* arse.
culasse [kylas] *nf* cylinder head.
culbuter [kylbyte] *v* somersault; *(tomber)* tumble, topple; *(renverser)* knock over. **culbute** *nf* somersault; tumble, fall; *(fam: banque, etc.)* collapse.
culinaire [kylinɛr] *adj* culinary.
culminer [kylmine] *v* culminate, reach its highest point.
culot [kylo] *nm* cap, base; *(fam)* cheek.
culotte [kylɔt] *nf* short trousers *pl*; *(slip)* pants *pl*.
culpabilité [kylpabilite] *nf* guilt.
culte [kylt] *nm* cult, worship.
cultiver [kyltive] *v* cultivate. **cultivateur, -trice** *nm, nf* farmer. **cultivé** *adj* cultured.
culture [kyltyr] *nf (champ, etc.)* cultivation; *(esprit)* culture. **culturel** *adj* cultural.
cupide [kypid] *adj* greedy. **cupidité** *nf* greed.
cure [kyr] *nf* cure; course of treatment.
curé [kyre] *nm* parish priest.
curer [kyre] *v* clean out; *(nez)* pick. **cure-dent** *nm* toothpick. **cure-pipe** *nm* pipe cleaner.
curieux [kyrjø], **-euse** *adj* curious; interested, keen; *(indiscret)* inquisitive. *nm* strange thing. *nm, nf* inquisitive person.
curiosité [kyrjozite] *nf* curiosity; inquisitiveness; *(d'une ville, etc.)* strange sight or feature; *(bibelot)* curio.
curry [kyri] *nm* curry. **au curry** curried.
cuver [kyve] *v* ferment. **cuve** *nf* vat, tank. **cuvée** *nf* vintage. **cuvette** *nf* basin.
cycle[1] [siklə] *nm (révolution)* cycle.

cycle² [siklə] *nm* (*bicyclette*) cycle. **cycl-isme** *nm* cycling. **cycliste** *n(m+f)* cyclist.

cyclomoteur [siklɔmɔtœr] *nm* moped.

cyclone [siklon] *nm* cyclone.

cygne [siɲ] *nm* swan.

cylindre [silɛ̃drə] *nm* cylinder; roller. **cylindrique** *adj* cylindrical.

cymbale [sɛ̃bal] *nf* cymbal.

cynique [sinik] *adj* cynical. *nm* cynic.

cyprès [siprɛ] *nm* cypress.

cypriote [siprijɔt] *adj* Cypriot. **Cypriote** *n(m+f)* Cypriot.

D

d' [d] *V* de.

dactylographier [daktilɔgrafje] *v* type. **dactylo** *nf* typist. **dactylographie** *nf* typing.

dague [dag] *nm* dagger.

daigner [deɲe] *v* condescend, deign.

daim [dɛ̃] *nm* (*animal*) deer; (*cuir*) suede.

dais [dɛ] *nm* canopy.

daller [dale] *v* pave. **dallage** *nm* paving. **dalle** *nf* (*pierre*) slab; (*trottoir*) paving stone.

daltonien [daltɔnjɛ̃] *adj* colour-blind. **daltonisme** *nm* colour-blindness.

damas [dama] *nm* damask. **prune de Damas** *nf* damson.

dame [dam] *nf* lady; (*cartes*) queen. **dames** *nf pl* (*jeu*) draughts *sing*.

damier [damje] *nm* draughtboard.

damner [dane] *v* damn. **damnation** *nf* damnation. **damné** *adj* (*fam*) confounded.

se dandiner [dãdine] *v* waddle. **dandinement** *nm* waddle.

Danemark [danmark] *nm* Denmark.

danger [dãʒe] *nm* danger. **mettre en danger** endanger. **sans danger** *adv* safely. **dangereux** *adj* dangerous.

danois [danwa] *nm, adj* Danish. **Danois, -e** *nm, nf* Dane.

dans [dã] *prep* in; into.

danser [dãse] *v* dance. **danse** *nf* dance; (*art*) dancing. **danseur, -euse** *nm, nf* dancer.

dard [dar] *nm* sting.

darder [darde] *v* (*lancer*) shoot; (*dresser*) point.

dater [date] *v* date. **date** *nf* date. **date limite** deadline.

datte [dat] *nf* date. **dattier** *nm* date palm.

daube [dob] *nf* stew, casserole.

dauphin [dofɛ̃] *nm* dolphin.

davantage [davãtaʒ] *adv* (*plus*) more, any more; (*plus longtemps*) longer, any longer.

de [də], **d'** *prep* of; from. **de/du/de la/des** some, any.

dé [de] *nm* dice. **couper en dés** dice. **dé à coudre** thimble.

débâcle [debaklə] *nf* collapse; (*mil*) rout; (*glace*) breaking up.

déballer [debale] *v* unpack. **déballage** *nm* unpacking.

se débander [debãde] *v* disperse, scatter. **débandade** *nf* scattering. **à la débandade** in disorder.

débarbouiller [debarbuje] *v* wash. **se débarbouiller** wash one's face.

débarcadère [debarkadɛr] *nm* landing stage.

débardeur [debardœr] *nm* docker.

débarquer [debarke] *v* land; (*navire*) disembark; (*décharger*) unload. **débarquement** *nm* landing; unloading.

débarras [debara] *nm* lumber room. **bon débarras!** good riddance!

débarrasser [debarase] *v* rid; (*table*) clear. **se débarrasser de** get rid of.

débat [deba] *nm* debate; discussion.

***débattre** [debatrə] *v* debate; discuss. **se débattre** struggle.

débaucher [deboʃe] *v* lead astray; (*ouvriers*) lay off, make redundant. **débauche** *nf* debauchery. **débauché** *adj* debauched.

débile [debil] *adj* weak, feeble.

débit¹ [debi] *nm* (*comm*) turnover; (*fluide*) flow, output; (*élocution*) delivery. **débit de boissons** bar. **débit de tabac** tobacconist's.

débit² [debi] *nm* debit.

débiter¹ [debite] *v* (*comm*) retail; (*fluide*) produce; recite; (*couper*) cut up.

débiter² [debite] *v* debit.

déblai [deblɛ] *nm* clearing. **déblais** *nm pl* rubble *sing*, debris *sing*.

déblayer [debleje] *v* clear.

déboîter [debwate] *v* (*méd*) dislocate; (*séparer*) disconnect; (*auto*) pull out. **déboîtement** *nm* dislocation.

débonnaire [debɔner] *adj* easy-going.
déborder [debɔrde] *v* (*liquide*) overflow; (*dépasser*) go beyond, jut out; (*drap*) untuck. **débordant** *adj* exuberant, unbounded. **débordé de** (*fam*) snowed under with. **débordement** *nm* overflowing; outburst.
déboucher[1] [debuʃe] *v* (*tuyau*) unblock; (*bouteille*) uncork.
déboucher[2] [debuʃe] *v* emerge. **débouché** *nm* opening; (*comm*) outlet.
débourser [deburse] *v* pay out. **débours** *nm* outlay.
debout [dəbu] *adv, adj* standing. **être debout** stand. **se mettre debout** stand up.
déboutonner [debutɔne] *v* unbutton.
débraillé [debrɑje] *adj* slovenly, untidy. *nm* slovenliness.
débrancher [debrɑ̃ʃe] *v* disconnect; (*appareil électrique*) unplug.
débrayer [debreje] *v* (*auto*) let out the clutch; (*fam*) knock off work.
débris [debri] *nm pl* fragments *pl*; (*restes*) remains *pl*; debris *sing*.
débrouiller [debruje] *v* sort out; (*fils*) disentangle. **se débrouiller** manage, cope.
début [deby] *nm* beginning. **au début** at first. **débuts** *nm pl* début *sing*. **débutant, -e** *nm, nf* beginner. **débuter** *v* start.
deçà [dəsa] *adv* **en deçà de** on this side of.
décade [dekad] *nf* decade.
décadent [dekadɑ̃] *adj* decadent. **décadence** *nf* decadence.
décaler [dekale] *v* shift; (*avancer*) bring forward; (*reculer*) put back. **décalage** *nm* gap; (*temps*) interval; (*concepts*) discrepancy; (*horaire, etc.*) change.
décamper [dekɑ̃pe] *v* (*fam*) clear off.
décanter [dekɑ̃te] *v* (*liquide*) allow to settle; (*verser*) decant. **se décanter** settle; (*idées*) become clear. **décanteur** *nm* decanter.
décapotable [dekapɔtablə] *adj* (*voiture*) convertible.
décéder [desede] *v* die. **décédé, -e** *n, adj* deceased.
déceler [desle] *v* detect; reveal.
décembre [desɑ̃brə] *nm* December.
décent [desɑ̃] *adj* decent; (*acceptable*) proper. **décence** *nf* decency.
déception [desɛpsjɔ̃] *nf* disappointment.
décerner [desɛrne] *v* award.
décès [desɛ] *nm* decease.

*decevoir [desvwar] *v* disappoint.
déchaîner [deʃene] *v* (*colère, etc.*) unleash; (*enthousiasme*) rouse. **se déchaîner** (*personne*) rage; (*tempête*) break out. **déchaînement** *nm* fury.
décharger [deʃarʒe] *v* discharge; (*bagages*) unload; (*tirer*) fire. **décharger de** relieve of, release from. **décharge** *nf* discharge; (*arme*) volley of shots; (*ordures*) rubbish tip.
décharné [deʃarne] *adj* bony, emaciated.
se déchausser [deʃose] *v* take one's shoes off. **déchaussé** *adj* barefooted.
déchéance [deʃeɑ̃s] *nf* decline; degeneration; (*pol*) deposition.
déchet [deʃɛ] *nm* (*reste*) scrap; (*comm*) waste. **déchets** *nm pl* rubbish, waste.
déchiffrer [deʃifre] *v* decipher, decode; (*musique*) sight-read.
déchiqueter [deʃikte] *v* tear to pieces, shred. **déchiqueté** *adj* jagged.
déchirer [deʃire] *v* tear. **déchirant** *adj* heartrending. **déchirure** *nf* tear.
*déchoir [deʃwar] *v* (*se dégrader*) demean oneself; decline.
décibel [desibɛl] *nm* decibel.
décider [deside] *v* decide; persuade; determine. **se décider** (*personne*) make up one's mind; (*question*) be settled. **décidé** *adj* determined; settled. **décidément** *adv* undoubtedly.
décimal [desimal] *adj* decimal. **décimale** *nf* decimal.
décisif [desizif] *adj* decisive.
décision [desizjɔ̃] *nf* decision.
déclarer [deklare] *v* declare, announce; (*naissance*) register. **déclaration** *nf* declaration; (*discours*) statement; (*aveu*) admission; registration.
déclencher [deklɑ̃ʃe] *v* (*mécanisme*) release, activate; (*attaque*) launch; (*entraîner*) trigger off.
déclin [deklɛ̃] *nm* decline; (*jour*) close; (*lune*) wane.
décliner [dekline] *v* decline. **déclinaison** *nf* declension.
décoiffé [dekwafe] *adj* dishevelled.
décoller [dekɔle] *v* unstick; (*avion*) take off. **se décoller** come unstuck. **décollage** *nm* take-off.
décolorer [dekɔlɔre] *v* fade; (*cheveux*) bleach.
décombres [dekɔ̃brə] *nm pl* rubble *sing*.
décommander [dekɔmɑ̃de] *v* cancel.

décomposer [dekɔ̃poze] v split up; (visage) distort. **se décomposer** decompose.
décomposition nf decomposition.

décompte [dekɔ̃t] nf deduction; (compte) breakdown. **décompter** v deduct.

déconcerter [dekɔ̃sɛrte] v disconcert.

décongeler [dekɔ̃ʒle] v thaw out.

déconseiller [dekɔ̃seje] v advise against. **déconseillé** adj inadvisable.

décontracter [dekɔ̃trakte] v relax. **décontraction** nf relaxation.

déconvenue [dekɔ̃vny] nf disappointment.

décor [dekɔr] nm scenery; (maison) décor; (cadre) setting.

décorer [dekɔre] v decorate. **décorateur**, -trice nm, nf decorator. **décoratif** adj decorative. **décoration** nf decoration.

découper [dekupe] v cut out or up. **se découper** stand out.

décourager [dekuraʒe] v discourage. **découragement** nm discouragement.

décousu [dekuzy] adj disjointed; (couture) undone.

découvert [dekuvɛr] adj uncovered; (terrain) exposed, open. nm overdraft, deficit. **découverte** nf discovery.

*****découvrir** [dekuvrir] v (trouver) discover, find out; (exposer) uncover.

décrasser [dekrase] v clean.

décret [dekrɛ] nm decree. **décréter** v decree, order.

*****décrire** [dekrir] v describe.

décrocher [dekrɔʃe] v take down; (téléphone) pick up (the receiver).

*****décroître** [dekrwatrə] v decrease, decline, (lune) wane. **décroissance** nf decrease, decline.

dédaigner [dedɛɲe] v despise, scorn. **dédaigneux** adj scornful, contemptuous.

dédain [dedɛ̃] nm contempt, scorn.

dédale [dedal] nm maze.

dedans [dədɑ̃] adv inside, indoors. nm inside.

dédicace [dedikas] nf dedication. **dédicacer** v sign, autograph.

dédier [dedje] v dedicate.

se *dédire [dedir] v go back on (one's word); retract.

dédit [dedi] nm forfeit; retraction.

dédommager [dedɔmaʒe] v compensate. **dédommagement** nm compensation.

déduction [dedyksjɔ̃] nf deduction; conclusion.

*****déduire** [dedɥir] v (comm) deduct; (conclure) deduce.

déesse [deɛs] nf goddess.

*****défaillir** [defajir] v weaken, fail (s'évanouir) faint. **défaillance** n (faiblesse) weakness; (incapacité) failure faint.

*****défaire** [defɛr] v (couture, nœud) undo (valise) unpack; (construction) dismantle **se défaire** come undone or apart. s **défaire de** get rid of.

défaite [defɛt] nf defeat.

défalquer [defalke] v deduct.

défaut [defo] nm fault, flaw, defect (manque) lack. **faire défaut** be lacking (jur) default.

défection [defɛksjɔ̃] nf desertion, defec tion.

défectueux [defɛktɥø] adj defective faulty.

défendre [defɑ̃drə] v (protéger) defend (interdire) forbid.

défense [defɑ̃s] nf defence. **défense d** **fumer/stationner** no smoking/parking **défense d'entrer** keep out.

déférer [defere] v defer; (jur) hand ove **déférence** nf deference. **déférent** adj def erential.

défi [defi] nm challenge; (bravade) defi ance.

déficeler [defisle] v untie.

déficit [defisit] nm deficit.

défier [defje] v defy, challenge. **se défi** **de** distrust. **défiance** nf distrust. **défian** adj distrustful.

défigurer [defigyre] v disfigure, spoil (verité) distort; (monument) deface **défiguration** nf distortion; disfiguremen

défilé [defile] nm procession; (géog gorge, pass.

définir [definir] v define. **défini** adj defi nite. **définitif** adj final, definitive. **défini** **tion** nf definition; (mots croisés) clue.

défoncer [defɔ̃se] v smash in, break up

déformer [defɔrme] v deform, distor (métal, etc.) bend or put out of shap **déformation** nf deformation, distortion.

défraîchi [defreʃi] adj faded.

défricher [defriʃe] v clear. **défricher le te** **rain** prepare the ground.

défunt [defœ̃], -e n, adj deceased.

dégager [degaʒe] v clear; (libérer) free (exhaler) give off. **dégagé** adj clea (allure) casual.

dégarnir [degarnir] v strip, clear, empty. **dégarni** adj bare.

dégât [dega] nm damage.

dégel [deʒɛl] nm thaw. **dégeler** v thaw (out).

dégénérer [deʒenere] v degenerate. **dégénéré** adj degenerate. **dégénérescence** nf degeneration, degeneracy.

dégivrer [deʒivre] v defrost, de-ice. **dégivreur** nm defroster, de-icer.

dégonfler [degɔ̃fle] v deflate. **se dégonfler** go down; (fam) back out. **dégonflé** adj (pneu) flat; (fam) chicken.

dégorger [degɔrʒe] v discharge, pour out; (déboucher) clear out.

dégouliner [deguline] v trickle, drip. **dégoulinade** nf trickle.

dégourdir [degurdir] v warm up. **se dégourdir** stretch one's legs. **dégourdi** adj (fam) smart, bright.

dégoûter [degute] v disgust. **dégoût** nm disgust.

dégoutter [degute] v drip.

dégrader [degrade] v degrade, debase; (mur, monument) deface, damage. **se degrader** debase oneself, deteriorate. **dégradation** nf degradation.

dégrafer [degrafe] v unfasten.

dégraisser [degrese] v remove the fat or grease from. **dégraissage** nm cleaning.

degré [dəgre] nm degree; stage.

dégringoler [degrɛ̃gɔle] v tumble (down). **dégringolade** nf tumble.

dégriser [degrize] v sober up.

déguenillé [dɛgnije] adj ragged.

déguerpir [degerpir] v (fam) clear off.

dégueulasse [degœlas] adj (argot) lousy, rotten, revolting.

déguiser [degize] v disguise. **se déguiser** (en) dress up (as). **déguisé** adj in disguise; (travesti) in fancy dress. **déguisement** nm disguise; fancy dress.

déguster [degyste] v taste, sample; savour, enjoy. **dégustation** nf wine-tasting.

dehors [dəɔr] adv outside, outdoors. **en dehors** de outside; (sauf) apart from. nm outside; appearance.

déjà [deʒa] adv already; (encore) yet.

déjeuner [deʒœne] v have lunch. nm lunch.

delà [dəla] adv **au delà** beyond. **en delà** beyond, outside. **par delà** beyond. prep **au delà de** beyond, over.

délabré [delabre] adj dilapidated, falling down; (vêtements) ragged.

délai [delɛ] nm delay; time limit, deadline. **à bref délai** at short notice; (bientôt) very soon.

délaisser [delese] v abandon; neglect; (jur) relinquish. **délaissement** nm desertion; neglect.

délasser [delase] v refresh, relax. **délassement** nm relaxation.

délavé [delave] adj faded, washed-out.

délayer [deleje] v mix; dilute, thin down; (péj) spin out.

déléguer [delege] v delegate. **délégation** nf delegation. **délégué, -e** nm, nf delegate.

délibérer [delibere] v deliberate, confer, consider. **délibération** nf deliberation; resolution. **délibéré** adj deliberate; resolute.

délicat [delika] adj delicate; refined; scrupulous; sensitive; (difficile) fussy. **délicatesse** nf delicacy; tact; refinement.

délice [delis] nm delight. **délicieux** adj delightful; (goût) delicious.

délier [delje] v untie, loosen. **délié** adj agile; fine, slender.

délinquant [delɛ̃kɑ̃], **-e** n, adj delinquent. **délinquance** nf delinquency.

délire [delir] nm delirium; frenzy. **avoir le délire** be delirious. **délirer** v be delirious.

délit [deli] nm offence.

délivrer [delivre] v (libérer) free; (débarrasser) relieve; (livrer) issue. **délivrance** nf release; relief; issue.

déloyal [delwajal] adj disloyal; (procédé) unfair. **déloyauté** nf disloyalty; unfairness.

delta [dɛlta] nm delta.

déluge [delyʒ] nm deluge, flood; (pluie) downpour.

déluré [delyre] adj smart, resourceful.

se démailler [demaje] v (bas) ladder; (tricot) unravel.

demain [dəmɛ̃] adv tomorrow. **à demain!** see you tomorrow! **demain en huit** a week tomorrow.

demander [dəmɑ̃de] v ask for; enquire, ask; (médecin, etc.) send for; (avoir besoin de) require, need. **se demander** wonder. **demande** nf request; (emploi) application; (remboursement) claim; (comm) demand. **demandé** adj in demand.

démanger [demɑ̃ʒe] v itch. **démangeaison** nf itch.

démaquiller [demakije] v remove make-up from. **démaquillant** nm make-up remover.

démarche [demarʃ] nf gait; procedure, step; approach.

démarrer [demare] v (auto) start; (partir) move off. **bien démarrer** get off to a good start. **démarreur** nm (auto) starter.

démêler [demele] v untangle. **démêlé** nm dispute.

démembrer [demãbre] v dismember, carve up.

déménager [demenaʒe] v move (house). **déménagement** nm removal, move. **déménageur** nm removal man.

démence [demãs] nf madness.

se démener [dɛmne] v struggle; make an effort.

***démentir** [demãtir] v refute, deny, contradict. **démenti** nm denial.

démesuré [demazyre] adj immoderate; enormous.

***démettre** [demɛtrə] v dislocate; (renvoyer) dismiss. **se démettre** resign.

demeurer [dəmœre] v (rester) remain; (habiter) live. **au demeurant** for all that. **demeure** nf residence. **à demeure** permanent.

demi [dəmi], **-e** n, adj half. **à demi** adv half.

demi-bouteille nf half-bottle.

demi-cercle nm semicircle. **en demi-cercle** semicircular.

demi-douzaine nf half-dozen. **une demi-douzaine** half-a-dozen.

demi-finale nf semifinal. **demi-finaliste** n(m + f) semifinalist.

demi-frère nm half-brother.

demi-heure nf half-hour. **une demi-heure** half an hour.

demi-pension nf half-board.

demi-sœur nf half-sister.

démission [demisjɔ̃] nf resignation; abdication. **donner sa démission** hand in one's notice. **démissionner** v resign.

demi-tarif nm half-price; (transport) half-fare.

demi-teinte nf half-tone.

demi-tour nm about-turn; (auto) U-turn.

démocratie [demɔkrasi] nf democracy. **démocrate** n(m + f) democrat. **démocratique** adj democratic.

démodé [demɔde] adj old-fashioned.

demoiselle [dəmwazɛl] nf young lady. **demoiselle d'honneur** bridesmaid.

démolir [demɔlir] v demolish; destroy. **démolition** nf demolition.

démon [demɔ̃] nm demon.

démonter [demɔ̃te] v dismantle, take apart; disconcert.

démontrer [demɔ̃tre] v demonstrate. **démonstratif** adj demonstrative. **démonstration** nf demonstration.

démoraliser [demɔralize] v demoralize. **se démoraliser** lose heart. **démoralisation** nf demoralization.

démordre [demɔrdrə] v give up. **ne pas démordre de** stick to.

démunir [demynir] v deprive, divest. **démuni de** without.

dénaturer [denatyre] v distort. **dénaturé** adj unnatural.

dénégation [denegasjɔ̃] nf denial.

dénicher [deniʃe] (fam) v discover; (personne) track down; (objet) unearth.

dénigrer [denigre] v denigrate, run down.

dénivellation [denivɛlasjɔ̃] nf unevenness; (pente) slope; (auto) ramp.

dénombrer [denɔ̃bre] v count; enumerate.

dénominateur [denɔminatœr] nm denominator.

dénommer [denɔme] v name.

dénoncer [denɔ̃se] v denounce; (coupable) give away; (révéler) expose.

dénoter [denɔte] v denote, indicate.

dénouer [denwe] v (nœud) undo; (intrigue) untangle, resolve. **se dénouer** come undone; be resolved. **dénouement** nm outcome; (théâtre) dénouement.

denrée [dãre] nf foodstuff.

dense [dãs] adj dense; compact.

densité [dãsite] nf density.

dent [dã] nf tooth (pl teeth); (fourche) prong; (roue) cog. **avoir la dent** (fam) be peckish. **avoir une dent contre** have a grudge against. **du bout des dents** half-heartedly. **en dents de scie** serrated. **faire ses dents** teethe. **dentaire** adj dental.

denteler [dãtle] v indent. **dentelé** adj jagged.

dentelle [dãtɛl] nf lace.

dentier [dãtje] nm denture.

dentifrice [dãtifris] nm toothpaste.

dentiste [dãtist] n(m + f) dentist.

dénuder [denyde] v strip, bare. **dénudé** adj bare; (crâne) bald.

dénué [denᶣe] adj **dénué de** devoid of, lacking in.

déodorant [deɔdɔrɑ̃] *nm, adj* deodorant.

dépanner [depane] *v* fix, repair. **dépannage** *nm* repairing. **service de dépannage** *nm* breakdown service. **dépanneuse** *nf* breakdown lorry.

dépaqueter [depakte] *v* unpack.

dépareillé [depareje] *adj* (*objet*) odd; (*collection*) incomplete.

départ [depar] *nm* departure; (*début*) start.

département [departəmɑ̃] *nm* department.

départir [departir] *v* assign. **se départir de** abandon, depart from.

dépasser [depase] *v* pass; (*auto*) overtake; exceed, go beyond; (*clou, rocher, etc.*) stick out. **dépassé** *adj* outmoded; (*fam*) out of one's depth. **dépassement** *nm* overtaking.

dépaysé [depeize] *adj* disorientated. **sentir dépaysé** not feel at home.

dépêcher [depeʃe] *v* dispatch. **se dépêcher** hurry. **dépêche** *nf* dispatch; telegram.

***dépeindre** [depɛ̃dr] *v* depict.

dépendance [depɑ̃dɑ̃s] *nf* dependence, dependency; subordination; (*bâtiment*) outbuilding. **dépendant de** (*employé*) answerable to; dependent on.

dépendre[1] [depɑ̃drə] *v* **dépendre de** depend on, be dependent on; (*employé*) be answerable to; (*appartenir*) belong to.

dépendre[2] [depɑ̃drə] *v* take down.

dépens [depɑ̃] *nm pl* costs *pl.* **aux dépens de** at the expense of.

dépenser [depɑ̃se] *v* (*argent*) spend; (*consumer*) use (up). **se dépenser** exert oneself. **dépense** *nf* expenditure, expense; consumption. **dépensier** *adj* extravagant. **être dépensier** be a spendthrift.

dépérir [deperir] *v* decline; (*personne*) waste away; (*plante*) wither.

dépêtrer [depetre] *v* extricate, free.

dépister [depiste] *v* (*découvrir*) detect, track down; (*détourner*) throw off the scent.

dépit [depi] *nm* vexation, resentment. **en dépit de** in spite of.

déplacer [deplase] *v* move, shift; (*air, eau, etc.*) displace. **se déplacer** move (around); (*voyager*) travel. **déplacé** *adj* uncalled-for; out of place. **déplacement** *nm* displacement; moving, movement; travel.

***déplaire** [deplɛr] *v* **déplaire à** be disliked by, displease. **se déplaire** be unhappy, dislike it. **déplaisant** *adj* unpleasant. **déplaisir** *nm* displeasure.

déplantoir [deplɑ̃twar] *nm* trowel.

déplier [deplije] *v* unfold, open out. **dépliant** *nm* leaflet, folder.

déplorer [deplɔre] *v* regret, deplore. **déplorable** *adj* deplorable.

déployer [deplwaje] *v* spread out; (*troupes*) deploy; (*étaler*) display.

se déplumer [deplyme] *v* moult.

déporter [depɔrte] *v* deport. **déportation** *nf* deportation.

déposer[1] [depoze] *v* set *or* put down; (*argent, sédiment*) deposit; (*admin*) file, register; (*roi*) depose. **déposant, -e** *nm, nf* depositor. **déposition** *nf* deposition.

dépositaire [depoziter] *n(m + f)* guardian; agent.

dépôt [depo] *nm* deposit; (*train, autobus*) depot; (*entrepôt*) warehouse; (*garde*) trust.

dépouiller [depuje] *v* strip; (*examiner*) peruse, study. **se dépouiller de** shed. **dépouille** *nf* skin, hide. **dépouillé** *adj* bare.

dépourvu [depurvy] *adj* **dépourvu de** devoid of, lacking in, without. *nm* **au dépourvu** unprepared.

dépraver [deprave] *v* deprave. **dépravation** *nf* depravity.

déprécier [depresje] *v* depreciate; (*dénigrer*) belittle. **dépréciation** *nf* depreciation.

dépression [depresjɔ̃] *nf* depression.

déprimer [deprime] *v* depress.

depuis [dəpɥi] *prep* since, from. *adv* ever since.

députation [depytasjɔ̃] *nf* deputation.

député [depyte] *nm* member of parliament; (*envoyé*) delegate.

déraciner [derasine] *v* (*détruire*) eradicate; (*arbre*) uproot. **déracinement** *nm* eradication.

dérailler [deraje] *v* be derailed. **déraillement** *nm* derailment.

déraisonnable [derɛzɔnablə] *adj* unreasonable.

déranger [derɑ̃ʒe] *v* disturb; (*coiffure*) ruffle; (*gêner*) trouble; (*routine*) upset. **se déranger** put oneself out; move aside. **dérangement** *nm* trouble; disorder.

déraper [derape] *v* skid. **dérapage** *nm* skid.

derechef [dərəʃɛf] *adv* once more.
dérégler [deregle] *v* disturb, unsettle, upset. **se dérégler** go wrong. **déréglé** *adj* out of order; *(mœurs)* dissolute; upset. **déréglement** *nm* disturbance; dissoluteness.
dérision [derizjɔ̃] *nf* derision, mockery. **dérisoire** *adj* derisory.
dériver[1] [derive] *v* derive; *(rivière)* divert. **dérivation** *nf* derivation; diversion. **dérivé** *nm* derivative, by-product.
dériver[2] [derive] *v* drift. **dérive** *nf* drift. **à la dérive** adrift.
dernier [dɛrnje], **-ère** *adj* last; *(plus récent)* latest; *(extrême)* utmost; *(pire)* bottom; *(ultime)* top. *nm, nf* last. **ce dernier, cette dernière** the latter. **dernièrement** *adv* recently.
dérober [derɔbe] *v (cacher)* hide; *(voler)* steal. **se dérober** shy away; *(échapper)* slip away; *(s'effondrer)* give way. **dérobé** *adj* secret. **à la dérobée** secretly.
déroger [derɔʒe] *v* **déroger à** *(jur)* go against; *(s'abaisser)* lower oneself.
dérouler [derule] *v* unroll, unwind. **se dérouler** *(fil)* unwind, unroll; develop, progress; *(se passer)* take place.
dérouter [derute] *v (avion)* divert; disconcert. **déroute** *nf* rout. **déroutement** *nm* diversion.
derrière [dɛrjɛr] *prep* behind. *adv* behind, at the back. *nm* back, rear; *(fam)* behind.
des [de] *contraction of* **de les**.
dès [dɛ] *prep* from, since. **dès lors** from then on, from that moment. **dès que** as soon as.
désabuser [dezabyze] *v* disillusion. **désabusé** *adj* disenchanted. **désabusement** *nm* disillusionment.
désaccord [dezakɔr] *nm* discord, conflict, disagreement; *(contradiction)* discrepancy.
désaffecter [dezafɛkte] *v* close down. **désaffecté** *adj* disused.
désagréable [dezagreablə] *adj* unpleasant.
désagréger [dezagreʒe] *v* disintegrate, break up. **désagrégation** *nf* disintegration.
désagrément [dezagremɑ̃] *nm* annoyance, trouble.
se désaltérer [dezaltere] *v* quench one's thirst. **désaltérant** *adj* thirst-quenching.
désappointer [dezapwɛte] *v* disappoint.
désapprobation [dezaprɔbasjɔ̃] *nf* disapproval. **désapprobateur, -trice** *adj* disapproving.
désapprouver [dezapruve] *v* disapprove of.
désarmer [dezarme] *v* disarm.
désarroi [dezarwa] *nm* confusion.
désassorti [dezasɔrti] *adj* unmatching.
désastre [dezastrə] *nm* disaster. **désastreux** *adj* disastrous.
désavantage [dezavɑ̃taʒ] *nm* disadvantage, handicap.
désaveu [dezavø] *nm* disavowal, repudiation; retraction.
désavouer [dezavwe] *v* disown, repudiate. **se désavouer** retract.
désaxé [dezakse] *adj* unbalanced.
descendant [desɑ̃dɑ̃], **-e** *adj* downward, descending. *nm, nf* descendant.
descendre [desɑ̃drə] *v* go down, come down; *(transport)* get out or off; *(tomber)* fall; *(baisser)* lower; *(porter)* take down. **descendre de** be descended from.
descente [desɑ̃t] *nf* descent; raid; *(pente)* downward slope. **descente de lit** bedside rug.
description [dɛskripsjɔ̃] *nf* description. **descriptif** *adj* descriptive.
désemparer [dezɑ̃pare] *v (naut)* disable. **sans désemparer** without stopping. **désemparé** *adj* bewildered; *(navire, avion)* crippled.
désencombrer [dezɑ̃kɔ̃bre] *v* clear.
désenfler [dezɑ̃fle] *v* go down, become less swollen.
désengager [dezɑ̃gaʒe] *v* free, release; *(mil)* disengage.
désenivrer [dezɑ̃nivre] *v* sober up.
déséquilibré [dezekilibre] *adj* unbalanced.
désert [dezɛr] *adj* deserted. *nm* desert. **déserter** [dezɛrte] *v* desert. **déserteur** *nm* deserter. **désertion** *nf* desertion.
désespérer [dezɛspere] *v* despair, lose hope; *(désoler)* drive to despair. **désespérant** *adj* maddening. **désespéré** *adj* desperate.
désespoir [dezɛspwar] *nm* despair.
déshabiller [dezabije] *v* undress. **déshabillé** *nm* negligee.
désherber [dezɛrbe] *v* weed. **désherbage** *nm* weeding. **désherbant** *nm* weed-killer.
déshériter [dezerite] *v* disinherit; *(désavantager)* deprive.
déshonneur [dezɔnœr] *nm* disgrace, dishonour.

déshonorer [dezɔnɔre] v disgrace, dishonour.
déshydrater [dezidrate] v dehydrate.
déshydratation nf dehydration.
désigner [deziɲe] v designate; (montrer)
point out; (nommer) name, appoint.
désignation nf designation; appointment.
désillusionner [dezilyzjɔne] v disillusion.
désillusion nf disillusionment.
désinfecter [dezɛ̃fɛkte] v disinfect.
désinfectant nm, adj disinfectant.
désinfection nf disinfection.
désintégrer [dezɛ̃tegre] v split or break
up. **se désintégrer** disintegrate.
désintégration nf disintegration.
désintéressé [dezɛ̃terese] adj disinterested, unselfish. **désintéressement** nm
unselfishness.
désinvolte [dezɛ̃vɔlt] adj casual. **avec
désinvolture** casually.
désirer [dezire] v desire, want. **désir** nm
desire, wish. **désirable** adj desirable.
désireux de anxious to.
désobéir [dezɔbeir] v disobey. **désobéissance** nf disobedience. **désobéissant** adj
disobedient.
désodorisant [dezɔdɔrizɑ̃] nm, adj deodorant.
désœuvré [dezœvre] adj idle.
désœuvrement nm idleness.
désoler [dezɔle] v distress, upset; devastate. **désolation** nf distress, grief; devastation. **désolé** sorry, distressed; (endroit)
desolate.
désopilant [dezɔpilɑ̃] adj hilarious.
désordonné [dezɔrdɔne] adj disorderly,
untidy, muddled.
désordre [dezɔrdrə] nm disorder, untidiness; confusion. **désordres** nm pl distur-
bances pl.
désorganiser [dezɔrganize] v disorganize,
disrupt. **désorganisation** nf disorganiza-
tion.
désorienter [dezɔrjɑ̃te] v disorientate,
bewilder.
désormais [dezɔrmɛ] adv in future, from
now on.
désosser [dezɔse] v bone.
desquels, desquelles [dekɛl] contractions
of **de lesquels, de lesquelles**.
dessécher [deseʃe] v dry out, parch;
(feuille) wither; (aliments) dehydrate;
(amaigrir) emaciate.
dessein [desɛ̃] nm intention, plan. **à des-**

sein intentionally. **avoir des desseins sur**
have designs on.
desserrer [desere] v loosen, release. **desserrer les dents** open one's mouth,
speak. **desserré** adj loose.
dessert [desɛr] nm dessert, sweet.
*desservir[1] [desɛrvir] v clear the table;
(nuire) harm, do a disservice to.
*desservir[2] [desɛrvir] v (transport) serve;
(porte) lead into.
dessin [desɛ̃] nm drawing; (motif) pattern; (contour) outline. **dessin animé** cartoon (film). **dessin humoristique** cartoon.
dessinateur, -trice nm, nf draughtsman;
designer; cartoonist.
dessiner [desine] v draw; design. **se
dessiner** stand out; become apparent.
dessous [dəsu] adv under, below. nm bottom, underside. **avoir le dessous** get the
worst of it. **dessous de plat** table mat.
dessous de verre coaster.
dessus [dəsy] adv above, over, on top. nm
top. **avoir le dessus** have the upper hand.
dessus de lit bedspread.
destin [destɛ̃] nm fate, destiny.
destination [destinasjɔ̃] nf destination. **à
destination de** bound for.
destiner [destine] v destine; intend.
destinée nf fate, destiny.
destituer [destitɥe] v dismiss. **destitution**
nf dismissal, discharge.
destruction [destryksjɔ̃] nf destruction.
destructif adj destructive.
désuet, -ète [desɥɛ, -ɛt] adj outdated.
désuétude nf disuse. **tomber en désuétude**
become obsolete.
désunir [dezynir] v divide, disunite.
détacher[1] [detaʃe] v (dénouer) untie,
undo; (ôter) remove; separate. **se détacher** come undone; come off or away; (ressortir) stand out. **se détacher de**
renounce. **détachable** adj detachable.
détachement nm detachment.
détacher[2] [detaʃe] v clean, remove stains
from. **détachant** nm stain remover.
détail [detaj] nm detail; (facture) breakdown; (comm) retail.
détailler [detaje] v explain in detail; (articles) sell separately; (comm) retail. **détaillant, -e** nm, nf retailer. **détaillé** adj
detailed.
détective [detɛktiv] nm **détective privé**
private detective.
*déteindre [detɛ̃drə] v (au soleil) fade;
(au lavage) run.

détendre [detɑ̃drə] v release, loosen. **se détendre** relax.

*détenir [dɛtnir] v have, hold; (*prisonnier*) detain. **détenteur, -trice** nm, nf holder. **détenu, -e** nm, nf prisoner.

détente [detɑ̃t] nf relaxation; (*élan*) spring; (*gâchette*) trigger.

détergent [detɛrʒɑ̃] nm, adj detergent.

détériorer [deterjɔre] v damage. **se détériorer** deteriorate. **détérioration** nf damage; deterioration.

déterminer [detɛrmine] v determine; fix; decide. **se déterminer** make up one's mind. **détermination** nf determination; resolution. **déterminé** adj determined; specific.

déterrer [detere] v dig up, unearth.

détester [detɛste] v hate, detest. **détestable** adj loathsome.

détoner [detɔne] v detonate. **détonant** nm, adj explosive. **détonateur** nm detonator.

détonner [detɔne] v clash, be out of place; (*musique*) go out of tune.

détour [detur] nm detour; (*courbe*) bend. **sans détours** straight out.

détourner [deturne] v divert; (*regard*) turn away; (*avion*) hijack; (*argent*) embezzle. **détourné** adj indirect, roundabout. **détournement** nm diversion; hijacking; embezzlement.

détraqué [detrake] adj broken down, out of order; (*temps*) unsettled; (*fam: personne*) crazy.

détremper [detrɑ̃pe] v soak; dilute, mix with water.

détresse [detrɛs] nf distress.

détritus [detritys] nm pl rubbish sing, refuse sing.

*détruire [detrɥir] v destroy; ruin.

dette [dɛt] nf debt.

deuil [dœj] nm mourning; (*perte*) bereavement.

deux [dø] adj two; (*quelques*) a couple of; (*épelant*) double. nm two. **deux-points** nm invar colon. (**tous**) **les deux** both. **tous les deux jours** every other day. **deuxième** n(m + f), adj second.

dévaler [devale] v rush or hurtle down.

dévaliser [devalize] v burgle, rob.

dévaluer [devalɥe] v devalue. **dévaluation** nf devaluation.

devancer [dəvɑ̃se] v forestall; (*question, etc.*) anticipate; (*coureur*) get ahead of, leave behind. **devancier, -ère** nm, nf precursor.

devant [dəvɑ̃] prep in front of, before. adv in front, ahead. nm front. **aller au-devant de** anticipate.

devanture [dəvɑ̃tyr] nf (*étalage*) window, display; (*façade*) shop front. **à la devanture** in the window.

dévaster [devaste] v devastate. **dévastation** nf devastation.

développer [devlɔpe] v develop; (*industrie, etc.*) expand. **se développer** develop, spread. **développement** nm development; expansion.

*devenir [dəvnir] v become.

dévergondé [devɛrgɔ̃de] adj shameless; licentious.

déverser [devɛrse] v pour out. **déversoir** nm overflow.

dévêtir [devetir] v undress.

dévier [devje] v deviate, veer off course; divert. **déviation** nf deviation; diversion.

deviner [dəvine] v guess; (*énigme*) solve. **devinette** nf riddle.

devis [dəvi] nm estimate.

dévisager [devizaʒe] v stare at.

devise [dəviz] nf motto; (*comm*) slogan. **devises** nf pl currency sing.

dévisser [devise] v unscrew.

dévoiler [devwale] v unveil; reveal, disclose.

*devoir [dəvwar] v have to, must; (*argent, etc.*) owe. nm duty; (*école*) homework.

dévorer [devɔre] v devour; consume.

dévot [devo], **-e** adj devout, pious. nm, nf pious person. **dévotion** nf devoutness.

se dévouer [devwe] v devote oneself; sacrifice oneself. **dévouement** nm devotion.

dextérité [dɛksterite] nf skill, dexterity.

diabète [djabɛt] nm diabetes. **diabétique** n(m + f), adj diabetic.

diable [djablə] nm devil. **diablerie** nf mischief. **diabolique** adj diabolical.

diablotin [djablɔtɛ̃] nm (*enfant*) imp; (*pétard*) cracker.

diadème [djadɛm] nm diadem; (*bijou*) tiara.

diagnostiquer [djagnɔstike] v diagnose. **diagnostic** nm diagnosis.

diagonal [djagɔnal] adj diagonal. **diagonale** nf diagonal.

dialecte [djalɛkt] nm dialect.

dialogue [djalɔg] nm dialogue, conversation.

diamant [djamɑ̃] nm diamond.

diamètre [djamɛtrə] *nm* diameter. **diamétralement opposé** diametrically opposed.

diaphragme [djafragmə] *nm* diaphragm.

diapositive [djapozitiv] *nf* slide, transparency.

diapré [djapre] *adj* mottled.

diarrhée [djare] *nf* diarrhoea.

dictateur [diktatœr] *nm* dictator. **dictature** *nf* dictatorship.

dicter [dikte] *v* dictate. **dictée** *nf* dictation.

dictionnaire [diksjɔnɛr] *nm* dictionary.

dicton [diktɔ̃] *nm* saying.

dièse [djɛz] *nm*, *adj* sharp.

diesel [djezɛl] *nm* diesel.

diète [djɛt] *nf* diet.

dieu [djø] *nm* god.

diffamer [difame] *v* slander; (*par écrit*) libel. **diffamation** *nf* slander; libel. **diffamatoire** *adj* slanderous; libellous.

différence [diferɑ̃s] *nf* difference. **à la différence de** unlike. **différent** *adj* different.

différencier [diferɑ̃sje] *v* differentiate. **différenciation** *nf* differentiation.

différend [diferɑ̃] *nm* disagreement, difference of opinion.

différentiel [diferɑ̃sjɛl], **-elle** *n*, *adj* differential.

différer [difere] *v* differ; (*renvoyer*) defer, postpone.

difficile [difisil] *adj* difficult. **difficulté** *nf* difficulty.

difforme [difɔrm] *adj* deformed. **difformité** *nf* deformity.

diffuser [difyze] *v* diffuse, spread; (*émission*) broadcast.

digérer [diʒere] *v* digest.

digestion [diʒɛstjɔ̃] *nf* digestion.

digitale [diʒital] *nf* **digitale pourprée** foxglove.

digne [diɲ] *adj* worthy; (*grave*) dignified. **dignité** *nf* dignity.

dique [dig] *nf* dyke.

dilapider [dilapide] *v* squander; (*détourner*) embezzle.

dilater [dilate] *v* dilate, distend. **se dilater** swell, expand. **dilatation** *nf* dilation.

dilemme [dilɛm] *nm* dilemma.

diluer [dilɥe] *v* dilute. **dilution** *nf* dilution.

dimanche [dimɑ̃ʃ] *nm* Sunday. **dimanche des Rameaux** Palm Sunday.

dimension [dimɑ̃sjɔ̃] *nf* dimension, size, measurement.

diminuer [diminɥe] *v* diminish, reduce,

decrease. **diminutif** *nm*, *adj* diminutive. **diminution** *nf* reduction, decrease.

dinde [dɛd] *nf* turkey. **dindon** *nm* turkey.

dîner [dine] *v* have dinner, dine. *nm* dinner. **dineur, -euse** *nm*, *nf* diner.

dingue [dɛ̃g] (*fam*) *adj* barmy, crazy. *n(m+f)* nutcase.

dinosaure [dinozɔr] *nm* dinosaur.

diocèse [djɔsɛz] *nm* diocese.

diphtongue [diftɔ̃g] *nf* diphthong.

diplomate [diplɔmat] *adj* diplomatic. *n(m+f)* diplomat. *nm* (*cuisine*) trifle. **diplomatie** *nf* diplomacy. **diplomatique** *adj* diplomatic.

diplôme [diplom] *nm* diploma; examination.

diplômé [diplome], **-e** *adj* qualified. *nm*, *nf* holder of a diploma.

*dire [dir] *v* say, tell. **c'est-à-dire** that is. **vouloir dire** mean.

direct [dirɛkt] *adj* direct, straight, immediate. *nm* fast train, express. **directement** *adv* directly, straight, immediately.

directeur [dirɛktœr] *nm* director; (*responsable*) manager; (*école*) headmaster. **directeur général** managing director. **directrice** *nf* director; manageress; headmistress.

direction [dirɛksjɔ̃] *nf* direction; (*gestion*) management; (*auto*) steering.

diriger [diriʒe] *v* direct; (*gérer*) run, manage; (*arme*) point, aim; steer. **se diriger** find one's way. **se diriger vers** head for.

discerner [disɛrne] *v* discern; distinguish.

disciple [disiplə] *nm* disciple.

discipline [disiplin] *nf* discipline. **disciplinaire** *adj* disciplinary. **discipliner** *v* discipline, control.

discontinu [diskɔ̃tiny] *adj* discontinuous; intermittent.

discorde [diskɔrd] *nf* discord, dissension. **discordant** *adj* discordant.

discothèque [diskɔtɛk] *nf* record collection; (*club*) discotheque.

discours [diskur] *nm* speech.

discréditer [diskredite] *v* discredit. **discrédit** *nm* discredit.

discret, -ète [diskrɛ, -ɛt] *adj* discreet; quiet, sober; (*quantité*) discrete. **discrétion** *nf* discretion. **avec discrétion** discreetly. **discrétionnaire** *adj* discretionary.

discrimination [diskriminasjɔ̃] *nf* discrimination.

discussion [diskysjɔ̃] *nf* discussion; (*querelle*) argument.

discuter [diskyte] v discuss; question, dispute; (*protester*) argue. **discutable** adj debatable; questionable.

disette [dizɛt] nf scarcity, shortage.

disgrâce [disgrɑs] nf disgrace. **disgracié** adj in disgrace.

disgracieux [disgrasjø] adj inelegant; (*laid*) unsightly.

disloquer [dislɔke] v (*méd*) dislocate; (*désunir*) dismantle; (*briser*) break up; (*dissoudre*) disperse. **dislocation** nf dislocation.

*disparaître [disparɛtrə] v disappear, vanish. **faire disparaître** get rid of, remove. **disparition** nf disappearance.

disparate [disparat] adj disparate, illassorted. **disparité** nf disparity.

disparu [dispary], -e adj vanished; (*époque*) bygone; (*mort*) dead; (*mil, etc.*) missing. nm, nf dead person; missing person.

dispendieux [dispɑ̃djø] adj extravagant, expensive.

dispenser [dispɑ̃se] v dispense; exempt. **se dispenser de** avoid, get out of. **dispense** nf exemption.

disperser [dispɛrse] v disperse, scatter.

disponible [dispɔniblə] adj available, free. **disponibilité** nf availability.

dispos [dispo] adj alert, in good form.

disposer [dispoze] v arrange, lay out; (*engager*) dispose, incline. **disposer de** have at one's disposal. **se disposer à** be about to, prepare to. **disposition** nf arrangement; disposal; (*humeur*) mood; tendancy; aptitude; (*jur*) clause.

dispositif [dispozitif] nm device; plan of action.

disputer [dispyte] v fight, contest; (*fam*) tell off. **se disputer** quarrel; fight over. **dispute** nf quarrel.

disqualifier [diskalifje] v disqualify; (*discréditer*) dishonour. **disqualification** nf disqualification.

disque [disk] nm disc; (*musique*) record.

dissemblable [disɑ̃blablə] adj dissimilar, different. **dissemblance** nf dissimilarity.

disséminer [disemine] v scatter.

dissentiment [disɑ̃timɑ̃] nm disagreement.

disséquer [diseke] v dissect.

dissident [disidɑ̃], -e n, adj dissident. **dissidence** nf dissidence, rebellion.

dissimuler [disimyle] v conceal; disguise. **dissimulation** nf dissimulation.

dissiper [disipe] v dispel, disperse; (*gaspiller*) waste, squander. **dissipation** nf dissipation; dispersal.

dissocier [disɔsje] v dissociate. **dissociation** nf dissociation.

*dissoudre [disudrə] v dissolve.

dissuader [disɥade] v dissuade. **dissuasion** nf dissuasion.

distance [distɑ̃s] nf distance. **distant** adj distant.

distiller [distile] v distil. **distillerie** nf distillery.

distinct [distɛ̃] adj distinct. **distinctif** adj distinctive. **distinction** nf distinction.

distinguer [distɛ̃ge] v distinguish; honour. **distingué** adj distinguished; eminent.

distraction [distraksjɔ̃] nf absent-mindedness, lack of attention; (*détente*) recreation, entertainment.

*distraire [distrɛr] v distract; (*divertir*) entertain. **se distraire** amuse oneself. **distrait** adj absent-minded.

distribuer [distribɥe] v distribute; arrange; (*cartes*) deal; (*courrier*) deliver. **distributeur** nm distributor. **distributeur automatique** slot machine. **distribution** nf distribution; arrangement; delivery; (*acteurs*) cast.

divaguer [divage] v ramble.

divan [divɑ̃] nm divan.

diverger [divɛrʒe] v diverge. **divergence** nf divergence.

divers [divɛr] adj diverse; different; (*plusieurs*) various, several. **diversité** nf diversity, variety.

divertir [divɛrtir] v amuse, entertain. **divertissement** nm amusement, entertainment.

dividende [dividɑ̃d] nm dividend.

divin [divɛ̃] adj divine. **divinité** nf divinity.

diviser [divize] v divide. **divisible** adj divisible. **division** nf division; discord.

divorcer [divɔrse] v get divorced. **divorce** nm divorce. **divorcé, -e** nm, nf divorcee.

divulguer [divylge] v divulge, disclose.

dix [dis] nm, adj ten. **dixième** n(m+f), adj tenth.

dix-huit [dizɥit] nm, adj eighteen. **dix-huitième** n(m+f), adj eighteenth.

dix-neuf [diznœf] nm, adj nineteen. **dix-neuvième** n(m+f), adj nineteenth.

dix-sept [disɛt] nm, adj seventeen. **dix-septième** n(m+f), adj seventeenth.

dizaine [dizɛn] *nf* **une dizaine** (**de**) about ten.

docile [dɔsil] *adj* docile.

docte [dɔktə] *adj* learned.

docteur [dɔktœr] *nm* doctor.

doctrine [dɔktrin] *nf* doctrine.

document [dɔkymɑ̃] *nm* document. **documentaire** *nm, adj* documentary. **documentation** *nf* documentation, information, research. **documenter** *v* document, research.

dodu [dɔdy] *adj* (*fam*) plump, chubby.

dogmatique [dɔgmatik] *adj* dogmatic.

dogme [dɔgmə] *nm* dogma.

doigt [dwa] *nm* finger. **doigt de pied** toe. **doigté** *nm* (*musique*) fingering; tact.

doit [dwa] *nm* debit.

doléances [dɔleɑ̃s] *nf pl* complaints *pl*.

dollar [dɔlar] *nm* dollar.

domaine [dɔmɛn] *nm* domain; property, estate; sphere, field.

dôme [dom] *nm* dome.

domestique [dɔmɛstik] *n(m+f)* servant. *adj* domestic.

domestiquer [dɔmɛstike] *v* domesticate. **domestication** *nf* domestication.

domicile [dɔmisil] *nm* home, place of residence; address.

dominer [dɔmine] *v* dominate; surpass; (*contrôler*) master; prevail; (*donner sur*) overlook. **dominant** *adj* dominant, main. **dominateur, -trice** *adj* domineering. **domination** *nf* domination.

dominion [dɔminjɔn] *nm* dominion.

domino [dɔmino] *nm* domino.

dommage [dɔmaʒ] *nm* harm, damage. **dommages-intérêts** *nm pl* damages *pl*. **quel dommage!** what a pity!

dompter [dɔ̃te] *v* tame; subdue; master. **dompteur, -euse** *nm, nf* tamer.

don [dɔ̃] *nm* gift; talent; (*argent*) donation. **faire don de** donate. **donateur, -trice** *nm, nf* donor.

donc [dɔk] *conj* so, then, thus. **dis donc I** say; tell me. **tais-toi donc!** do be quiet!

donner [dɔne] *v* give; (*cartes*) deal; produce. **donner dans** fall into. **donner pour** present as, make out to be. **donner sur** overlook, open onto. **se donner à** devote oneself to. **donne** *nf* (*cartes*) deal. **donné** *adj* given. **étant donné que** seeing that. **données** *nf pl* data *pl*, facts *pl*. **donneur, -euse** *nm, nf* dealer; (*méd*) donor.

dont [dɔ̃] *pron* whose; (*objet*) of which; (*personne*) of whom.

dorénavant [dɔrenavɑ̃] *adv* from now on.

dorer [dɔre] *v* gild; (*cuisine*) brown; (*peau*) tan. **doré** *adj* gilt; (*blé, etc.*) golden.

dorloter [dɔrlote] *v* pamper, cosset.

***dormir** [dɔrmir] *v* sleep, be asleep. **dormir à poings fermés** sleep soundly.

dortoir [dɔrtwar] *nm* dormitory.

dorure [dɔryr] *nf* gilt, gilding.

dos [do] *nm* back; (*livre*) spine.

dose [doz] *nf* dose, dosage.

dossier [dosje] *nm* file; (*siège*) back.

dot [dɔt] *nf* dowry.

doter [dɔte] *v* endow; equip.

douane [dwan] *nf* customs *pl*. **exempté de douane** duty-free. **douanier, -ère** *nm, nf* customs officer.

double [dublə] *adj, adv* double. *nm* double; copy; duplicate.

doubler [duble] *v* double; (*école*) repeat; (*film*) dub; (*acteur*) stand in for; (*revêtir*) line; (*auto*) overtake. **doubler le pas** speed up. **doublage** *nm* dubbing; lining. **doublure** *nf* lining; (*acteur*) stand-in, understudy.

douceur [dusœr] *nf* softness; (*clémence*) mildness; (*goût, son, etc.*) sweetness; (*personne*) gentleness.

douche [duʃ] *nf* shower.

douer [dwe] *v* endow. **doué** *adj* gifted, talented.

douille [duj] *v* socket; cartridge case.

douillet, -ette [dujɛ, -ɛt] *adj* cosy, soft.

douleur [dulœr] *nf* pain; (*chagrin*) sorrow, distress. **douloureux** *adj* painful; distressing.

douter [dute] *v* **douter de** doubt. **se douter de** suspect. **doute** *nm* doubt. **mettre en doute** question. **sans doute** doubtless. **douteux** *adj* doubtful; uncertain; (*péj*) dubious.

douve [duv] *nf* moat, ditch.

Douvres [duvrə] *n* Dover.

doux, douce [du, dus] *adj* soft; (*clément, pas fort*) mild; (*agréable, sucré*) sweet; (*personne, pente*) gentle.

douze [duz] *nm, adj* twelve. **douzaine** *nf* dozen. **douzième** *n(m+f), adj* twelfth.

doyen, -enne [dwajɛ̃, -ɛn] *nm, nf* dean; senior member.

drachme [drakmə] *nf* drachma.

dragée [draʒe] *nf* sugared almond.

dragon [dragɔ̃] *nm* dragon.

draguer [drage] *v* dredge, drag.

dramatiser [dramatize] *v* dramatize. **dramatique** *adj* dramatic.

dramaturge [dramatyrʒ] *nm, nf* dramatist, playwright.

drame [dram] *nm* drama.

drap [dra] *nm* sheet.

drapeau [drapo] *nm* flag.

draper [drape] *v* drape. **draperie** *nf* drapery. **drapier** *nm* draper.

dresser [drese] *v* put up, erect; (*liste*, *plan*) draw up; (*lever*) raise; (*animal*) train. **dresser l'oreille** prick up one's ears. **se dresser** stand (up); rise (up). **dressage** *nm* training. **dressoir** *nm* dresser.

drogue [drɔg] *nf* drug. **drogué, -e** *nm, nf* drug addict. **se droguer** take drugs.

droit¹ [drwa] *adj* (*côté*) right; (*ligne*) straight; (*vertical*) upright; honest. *adv* straight. **droitier** *adj* right-handed.

droit² [drwa] *nm* right; (*taxe*) duty; (*d'entrée, etc.*) fee, charge; (*jur*) law. **droits d'auteur** royalties *pl*. **droit de passage** right of way.

droite [drwat] *nf* right, right-hand side.

drôle [drol] *adj* funny. **drôlement** *adv* (*fam*) terribly, awfully.

dromadaire [drɔmadɛr] *nm* dromedary.

dru [dry] *adj* thick, dense. *adv* thick and fast; (*pluie*) heavily.

du [dy] *contraction of* **de le**.

dû, due [dy] *adj* owing, due. *nm* due.

duc [dyk] *nm* duke. **duchesse** *nf* duchess.

duel [dᶣɛl] *nm* duel.

dûment [dymɑ̃] *adv* duly.

dune [dyn] *nf* dune.

Dunkerque [dœ̃kɛrk] *n* Dunkirk.

duo [dᶣo] *nm* duet.

duper [dype] *v* dupe, deceive.

duquel [dykɛl] *contraction of* **de lequel**.

dur [dyr] *adj* hard, stiff, tough; (*pénible*) harsh. *adv* (*fam*) hard. **à la dure** rough. **durcir** *v* harden. **dureté** *nf* hardness.

durer [dyre] *v* last. **durable** *adj* lasting. **durant** *prep* during, for. **durée** *nf* duration, length; (*ampoule, pile, etc.*) life.

duvet [dyvɛ] *nm* down; sleeping-bag.

dynamique [dinamik] *adj* dynamic, *nf* dynamics. **dynamisme** *nm* dynamism.

dynamite [dinamit] *nf* dynamite.

dynamo [dinamo] *nf* dynamo.

dynastie [dinasti] *nf* dynasty.

dysenterie [disɑ̃tri] *nf* dysentery.

dyslexie [dislɛksi] *nf* dyslexia. **dyslexique** *n(m+f)*, *adj* dyslexic.

dyspepsie [dispɛpsi] *nf* dyspepsia.

E

eau [o] *nf* water. **eau de Javel** bleach. **eau de vie** brandy. **eau douce** fresh water. **eau gazeuse** soda water. **eau minérale** mineral water. **eau potable** drinking water. **eau salée** salt water. **faire eau** leak. **prendre l'eau** leak.

ébahir [ebair] *v* astound. **ébahi** *adj* flabbergasted, dumbfounded. **ébahissement** *nm* astonishment.

ébats [eba] *nm pl* frolics *pl*.

ébaucher [ebofe] *v* sketch out, outline. **s'ébaucher** take shape. **ébauche** *nf* outline, rough draft.

ébène [ebɛn] *nf* ebony.

éberlué [ebɛrlᶣe] *adj* astounded, flabbergasted.

éblouir [ebluir] *v* dazzle. **éblouissement** *nm* dazzle; (*méd*) dizzy turn.

éboulement [ebulmɑ̃] *nm* landslide.

ébouriffer [eburife] *v* tousle, ruffle; (*fam*) amaze.

ébranler [ebrɑ̃le] *v* shake; (*affaiblir*) weaken. **s'ébranler** move off. **ébranlement** *nm* (*choc*) shock; weakening.

ébrécher [ebrefe] *v* chip, nick; (*fortune*) break into. **ébréchure** *nf* chip, nick.

ébrouer [ebrue] *v* snort; (*s'agiter*) shake oneself. **ébrouement** *nm* snort.

ébullition [ebylisjɔ̃] *nf* boiling point; (*agitation*) turmoil. **en ébullition** boiling; (*ville, personne*) seething.

écailler [ekaje] *v* scale. **s'écailler** flake, peel. **écaille** *nf* scale; (*peinture*) flake; (*de tortue*) tortoise-shell. **écailleux** *adj* scaly; flaky.

écaler [ekale] *v* shell. **écale** *nf* shell.

écarlate [ekarlat] *nf, adj* scarlet.

écarquiller [ekarkije] *v* open wide.

écart [ekar] *nm* gap; difference; (*contradiction*) discrepancy; (*faute*) lapse. **à l'écart** on one side; (*isolé*) out of the way; (*distant*) aloof. **à l'écart de** well away from. **faire le grand écart** do the splits. **faire un écart** (*cheval*) shy; (*auto*) swerve.

écarter [ekarte] v separate, open; (exclure) dismiss; (éloigner) push aside, lead away from. **s'écarter** (séparer) part; (s'éloigner) move away; deviate, wander. **écarté** adj remote.

ecclésiastique [eklezjastik] adj ecclesiastical. nm ecclesiastic.

écervelé [esɛrvəle], **-e** adj scatterbrained. nm, nf scatterbrain.

échafaud [eʃafo] nm scaffold. **échafaudage** nm scaffolding.

échalier [eʃalje] nm stile.

échalote [eʃalɔt] nf shallot.

échancré [eʃɑ̃kre] adj (robe) V-necked, with a scooped neckline; (côte) indented; (feuille) serrated.

échanger [eʃɑ̃ʒe] v exchange. **échange** nm exchange. **échangeable** adj exchangeable.

échantillon [eʃɑ̃tijɔ̃] nm sample.

échapper [eʃape] v escape. **échapper à** escape (from). **laisser échapper** let out, let slip. **échappatoire** nf loophole, way out. **échappement** nm (auto) exhaust.

écharde [eʃard] nf splinter.

écharpe [eʃarp] nf scarf; (méd) sling; (maire) sash.

échasse [eʃɑs] nf stilt.

échauder [eʃode] v scald; (laver) wash in hot water; (théière) warm.

échauffer [eʃofe] v make hot; (moteur) overheat; excite. **s'échauffer** (sport) warm up; (s'animer) become heated. **échauffement** nm overheating; warm-up.

échéance [eʃeɑ̃s] nf expiry date; date of payment; term. **échéant** adj due, payable. **le cas échéant** if the case arises.

échec [eʃɛk] nm failure; (revers) setback; (jeu) check. **échec et mat** checkmate. **échecs** nm pl (jeu) chess sing.

échelle [eʃɛl] nf ladder; (carte, etc.) scale.

échelon [eʃlɔ̃] nm rung; step, grade; (niveau) level.

échelonner [eʃlɔne] v space or spread out; (vacances, etc.) stagger.

échevelé [eʃəvle] adj dishevelled; (effréné) wild.

échine [eʃin] nf spine.

échiquier [eʃikje] nm chessboard.

écho [eko] nm echo.

***échoir** [eʃwar] v fall due; expire.

échouer [eʃwe] v fail; (naut) run aground; (aboutir) end up. **faire échouer** foil, thwart.

éclabousser [eklabuse] v splash. **éclaboussure** nf splash; (tache) stain, smear.

éclair [eklɛr] nm flash; (temps) lightning; (cuisine) éclair.

éclaircir [eklɛrsir] v lighten; (soupe, plantes) thin; (question, mystère) explain, clarify. **s'éclaircir** (temps) clear up; thin out, become thin. **éclaircie** nf bright interval, break. **éclaircissement** nm clarification.

éclairer [eklere] v light up; (problème, texte) throw light on; (personne) enlighten. **s'éclairer** light up; (rue, maison, etc.) be lit. **éclairage** nm lighting. **éclaireur** nm scout. **éclaireuse** nf guide.

éclat [ekla] nm brightness; splendour, glamour; fragment, splinter; (rire, colère) burst; (scandale) fuss.

éclater [eklate] v (pneu) burst; (bombe) explode; (briser) break up, shatter; (guerre) break out. **éclater de rire** burst out laughing. **faire éclater** blow up. **éclatant** adj bright; (fort) loud; (victoire) resounding.

éclipse [eklips] nf eclipse. **éclipser** v eclipse.

éclisse [eklis] nf splint.

éclopé [eklɔpe] adj lame.

***éclore** [eklɔr] v hatch; (fleur) open out. **éclosion** nf hatching; (apparition) birth, dawn.

écluse [eklyz] nf lock.

écœurer [ekœre] v nauseate, sicken; disgust. **écœurant** adj disgusting; (gâteau) sickly. **écœurement** nm nausea; disgust; discouragement.

école [ekɔl] nf school. **école de secrétariat** secretarial college. **école maternelle** nursery school. **école normale** college of education. **faire l'école buissonnière** play truant. **écolier** nm schoolboy. **écolière** nf schoolgirl.

écologie [ekɔlɔʒi] nf ecology. **écologique** adj ecological.

***éconduire** [ekɔ̃dɥir] v dismiss; reject.

économe [ekɔnɔm] adj thrifty. **économie** nf economy; (science) economics; (épargne) saving. **faire des économies** save. **économique** adj economic.

économiser [ekɔnɔmize] v economize, save. **économiste** n(m + f) economist.

écoper [ekɔpe] v bale out.

écorcer [ekɔrse] v peel; (arbre) bark. **écorce** nf peel; bark.

écorcher [ekɔrʃe] v (animal) skin; (égratigner) graze, scratch; (frotter) chafe;

(*fam: estamper*) fleece. **écorchure** *nf* graze, scratch.

écorné [ekɔrne] *adj* (*livre*) dog-eared.

Écosse [ekɔs] *nf* Scotland. **écossais** *adj* Scottish, Scots; (*whisky*) Scotch; (*tissu*) tartan. **Écossais, -e** *nm*, *nf* Scot.

écot [eko] *nm* share.

écouler [ekule] *v* get rid of; (*comm*) move, sell. **s'écouler** (*liquide*) flow, ooze; pass; sell. **écoulement** *nm* flow; (*méd*) discharge; passing.

écourter [ekurte] *v* shorten.

écouter [ekute] *v* listen (to). **écouter aux portes** eavesdrop.

écouteur, -euse [ekutœr, -øz] *nm*, *nf* listener; eavesdropper. *nm* (*telephone*) receiver. **écouteurs** *nm pl* headphones *pl*.

écran [ekrɑ̃] *nm* screen.

écraser [ekraze] *v* crush; (*voiture*) run over; (*accabler*) overcome. **s'écraser** (*voiture, avion*) crash. **se faire écraser** get run over. **écrasant** *adj* overwhelming; (*poids*) crushing; (*travail*) gruelling.

écrémer [ekreme] *v* cream, skim.

écrevisse [ekrəvis] *nf* crayfish.

s'écrier [ekrije] *v* exclaim.

écrin [ekrɛ̃] *nm* jewel case.

***écrire** [ekrir] *v* write. **écrit** *nm* writing; (*examen*) written paper. **par écrit** in writing. **écriteau** *nm* notice. **écritoire** *nf* writing case. **écriture** *nf* writing; (*comm*) entry.

écrivain [ekrivɛ̃] *nm* writer.

écrou [ekru] *nm* nut.

s'écrouler [ekrule] *v* collapse, crumble, fall (down). **écroulement** *nm* collapse, fall.

écru [ekry] *adj* raw; (*toile*) unbleached.

écu [eky] *nm* shield.

écueil [ekœj] *nm* reef; (*piège*) pitfall.

écuelle [ekɥɛl] *nf* bowl.

écumer [ekyme] *v* skim; (*mousser*) foam, froth; pillage, scour. **écume** *nf* foam, froth; (*crasse*) scum. **écumeux** *adj* frothy.

écureuil [ekyrœj] *nm* squirrel.

écurie [ekyri] *nf* stable.

écuyer [ekɥije], **-ère** *nm* rider.

eczéma [ɛgzema] *nm* eczema.

édenté [edɑ̃te] *adj* toothless.

édifice [edifis] *nm* building; structure. **édifier** [edifje] *v* edify; construct, build.

Edimbourg [edɛ̃bur] *n* Edinburgh.

édit [edi] *nm* edict.

éditer [edite] *v* publish; (*annoter*) edit. **éditeur, -trice** *nm*, *nf* publisher; editor.

édition *nf* publishing; edition. **éditorial** *nm* leading article.

édredon [edrədɔ̃] *nm* eiderdown.

éducation [edykasjɔ̃] *nf* education; (*familiale*) upbringing. **éducatif** *adj* educational.

éduquer [edyke] *v* educate; (*élever*) bring up.

effacer [efase] *v* erase, obliterate. **s'effacer** fade, wear away; (*s'écarter*) step aside. **effacé** *adj* faded; (*personne*) retiring.

effarer [efare] *v* alarm. **effarement** *nm* alarm.

effaroucher [efaruʃe] *v* scare; shock. **s'effaroucher** take fright; be shocked.

effectif [efɛktif] *adj* effective, actual, real. *nm* size, strength.

effectuer [efɛktɥe] *v* carry out, make, execute.

efféminé [efemine] *adj* effeminate.

effervescence [efɛrvesɑ̃s] *nf* effervescence; agitation, turmoil.

effet [efɛ] *nm* effect; impression; (*comm*) bill. **effets** *nm pl* things *pl*, clothes *pl*. **en effet** indeed.

s'effeuiller [efœje] *v* shed its leaves.

efficace [efikas] *adj* effective; (*personne*) efficient. **efficacité** *nf* effectiveness; efficiency.

effigie [efiʒi] *nf* effigy.

effiler [efile] *v* (*amincir*) taper; (*forme*) streamline; (*étoffe*) fray.

effleurer [eflœre] *v* touch lightly.

s'effondrer [efɔ̃dre] *v* collapse, cave in. **effondrement** *nm* collapse.

s'efforcer [eforse] *v* try hard, do one's best.

effort [efor] *nm* effort; (*tech*) stress.

effrayer [efreje] *v* frighten.

effréné [efrene] *adj* wild, frantic.

effriter [efrite] *v* crumble.

effroi [efrwa] *nm* terror. **effroyable** *adj* appalling.

effronté [efrɔ̃te] *adj* insolent, cheeky; (*ehonté*) brazen. **effronterie** *nf* insolence.

égal [egal], **-e** *adj* equal; (*constant*) even. **ça m'est égal** I don't mind. *nm*, *nf* equal. **également** *adv* equally; (*aussi*) also. **égaler** *v* equal, match. **égalité** *nf* equality; evenness.

égaliser [egalize] *v* equalize; (*sol*) level out.

égard [egar] *nm* respect, consideration. **à l'égard de** (*envers*) towards; concerning. **avoir égard à** take into account.

égarer [egare] v lead astray; (*perdre*) mislay. **s'égarer** get lost. **égaré** adj lost; (*animal*) stray; (*isolé*) remote; (*éperdu*) distraught.

égayer [egeje] v brighten up; (*divertir*) amuse.

église [egliz] nf church.

égocentrique [egɔsɑ̃trik] adj self-centred.

égoïste [egɔist] adj selfish. **égoïsme** nm selfishness.

égorger [egɔrʒe] v cut the throat of.

égout [egu] nm sewer, drain.

égoutter [egute] v drain; (*linge*) drip. **égouttoir** nm draining board.

égratigner [egratiɲe] v scratch, scrape. **égratignure** nf scratch.

égrener [egrəne] v (*écosser*) shell; (*raisins*) pick off; (*chapelet*) say.

éhonté [eɔ̃te] adj shameless, brazen.

éjaculer [eʒakyle] v ejaculate. **éjaculation** nf ejaculation.

éjecter [eʒɛkte] v eject.

élaborer [elabɔre] v work out, elaborate.

élaguer [elage] v prune. **élagage** nm pruning.

élan [elɑ̃] nm rush, surge; (*vitesse*) momentum; vigour, spirit.

s'élancer [elɑ̃se] v rush, dash. **élancé** adj slender. **élancement** nm sharp pain.

élargir [elarʒir] v widen, stretch; (*jur*) release.

élastique [elastik] adj elastic; flexible. nm elastic; rubber band.

élection [elɛksjɔ̃] nf election; choice. **élection partielle** by-election.

électoral [elɛktɔral] adj electoral. **électorat** nm electorate.

électricité [elɛktrisite] nf electricity. **électricien** nm electrician.

électrique [elɛktrik] adj electric.

électriser [elɛktrize] v electrify.

électrocuter [elɛktrɔkyte] v electrocute. **électrocution** nf electrocution.

électrode [elɛktrɔd] nf electrode.

électronique [elɛktrɔnik] adj electronic. nf electronics.

électrophone [elɛktrɔfɔn] nm record player.

élégant [elegɑ̃] adj elegant. **élégance** nf elegance.

élégie [eleʒi] nf elegy.

élément [elemɑ̃] nm element; fact; (*préfabriqué*) unit. **éléments** nm pl rudiments pl. **élémentaire** adj elementary, basic.

éléphant [elefɑ̃] nm elephant.

élevage [ɛlvaʒ] nm breeding, rearing; farm. **faire l'élevage de** breed, rear.

élévation [elevasjɔ̃] nf elevation; (*action*) raising; erection.

élève [elɛv] n(m+f) pupil, student.

élever [ɛlve] v raise; (*enfant*) bring up; (*animal*) rear, breed; erect. **s'élever** rise, go up. **s'élever à** add up to. **élevé** adj high, lofty. **bien/mal élevé** well-/ill-mannered.

elfe [ɛlf] nm elf.

éligible [eliʒiblə] adj eligible.

éliminer [elimine] v eliminate. **élimination** nf elimination.

*élire [elir] v elect.

élite [elit] nf elite.

elle [ɛl] pron (*sujet: personne*) she; (*objet: personne*) her; (*chose, animal*) it. **elle-même** pron herself; itself. **elles** pron (*sujet*) they; (*objet*) them. **elles-mêmes** pron themselves.

ellipse [elips] nf ellipse. **elliptique** adj elliptical.

élocution [elɔkysjɔ̃] nf elocution, diction. **défaut d'élocution** nm speech impediment.

éloge [elɔʒ] nm praise. **faire l'éloge de** praise.

éloigner [elwaɲe] v remove; move or take away; (*ajourner*) postpone. **s'éloigner** go away. **éloigné** adj distant, far. **éloignement** nm distance; removal; absence; postponement.

éloquent [elɔkɑ̃] adj eloquent. **éloquence** nf eloquence.

élu [ely], **-e** adj elected, chosen. nm, nf elected member or representative.

éluder [elyde] v evade, elude.

émaciation [emasjasjɔ̃] nf emaciation. **émacié** adj emaciated.

émail [emaj] nm, pl **-aux** enamel. **émailler** v enamel; (*parsemer*) dot.

émanciper [emɑ̃sipe] v emancipate, liberate. **émancipation** nf emancipation, liberation.

emballer [ɑ̃bale] v pack, wrap; (*fam*) thrill. **s'emballer** (*moteur*) race; (*cheval*) bolt; (*fam*) get worked up. **emballage** nm packing, wrapping; (*comm*) package.

embarcadère [ɑ̃barkadɛr] nm landing stage, pier.

embardée [ɑ̃barde] nf swerve. **faire une embardée** swerve.

embargo [ɑ̃bargo] nm embargo.
embarquer [ɑ̃barke] v embark, board; (*cargaison*) load. **s'embarquer dans** (*fam*) get involved in. **embarquement** nm boarding; loading.
embarras [ɑ̃bara] nm obstacle; (*gêne*) embarrassment; (*situation difficile*) predicament; dilemma. **faire des embarras** make a fuss.
embarrasser [ɑ̃barase] v hinder, hamper; put in a predicament. **s'embarrasser** be troubled; (*s'emmêler*) get tangled up. **embarrassant** adj awkward. **embarrassé** adj embarrassed, ill-at-ease; confused.
embaucher [ɑ̃boʃe] v take on, hire.
embaumer [ɑ̃bome] v embalm; perfume; (*sentir bon*) be fragrant.
embellir [ɑ̃belir] v make attractive; embellish. **embellissement** nm embellishment.
embêter [ɑ̃bete] (*fam*) v bother, annoy. **s'embêter** be fed up. **embêtement** nm nuisance, annoyance.
emblée [ɑ̃ble] adv **d'emblée** straight away.
emblème [ɑ̃blɛm] nm emblem.
emboîter [ɑ̃bwate] v fit together.
embouchure [ɑ̃buʃyr] nf (*fleuve*) mouth; (*musique*) mouthpiece.
embouteiller [ɑ̃buteje] v block. **embouteillage** nm traffic jam.
emboutir [ɑ̃butir] v crash into.
embrancher [ɑ̃brɑ̃ʃe] v join up. **embranchement** nm branch; junction.
embraser [ɑ̃braze] v set ablaze. **s'embraser** blaze up, flare up. **embrasement** nm blaze.
embrasser [ɑ̃brase] v embrace; (*donner un baiser*) kiss.
embrayer [ɑ̃breje] v (*auto*) let in the clutch. **embrayage** nm clutch.
embrouiller [ɑ̃bruje] v muddle (up); (*ficelle*) tangle (up).
embryon [ɑ̃brijɔ̃] nm embryo.
embuscade [ɑ̃byskad] nf ambush.
éméché [emeʃe] adj tipsy.
émeraude [ɛmrod] nf, adj emerald.
émerger [emɛrʒe] v emerge.
émerveiller [emɛrveje] v fill with wonder. **s'émerveiller de** marvel at. **émerveillement** nm wonder.
*émettre [emɛtrə] v give out, emit; (*TV, radio*) transmit, broadcast; (*monnaie, etc.*) issue. **émetteur** nm transmitter.
émeu [emø] nm emu.

émeute [emøt] nf riot.
émietter [emjete] v crumble; split up, disperse.
émigrer [emigre] v emigrate; (*oiseau*) migrate. **émigrant, -e** nm, nf emigrant. **émigration** nf emigration.
éminent [eminɑ̃] adj eminent.
émission [emisjɔ̃] nf (*radio, TV*) programme, broadcast; emission; issue.
emmagasiner [ɑ̃magazine] v store (up). **emmagasinage** nm storage.
emmancher [ɑ̃mɑ̃ʃe] v put a handle on; (*fam*) make a start (on). **emmanchure** [ɑ̃mɑ̃ʃyr] nf armhole.
emmêler [ɑ̃mele] v tangle; confuse, muddle.
emménager [ɑ̃menaʒe] v move in.
emmener [ɑ̃mne] v take (away). (*équipe*) lead.
emmitoufler [ɑ̃mitufle] v muffle up.
émoi [emwa] nm agitation, commotion.
émonder [emɔ̃de] v prune.
émotion [emosjɔ̃] nf emotion; (*peur*) fright. **émotif** or **émotionnel** adj emotional.
émousser [emuse] v blunt, dull. **émoussé** adj blunt.
*émouvoir [emuvwar] v move, affect; (*indigner*) rouse; (*troubler*) upset. **émouvant** adj (*compassion*) moving, touching; (*admiration*) stirring.
empailler [ɑ̃paje] v stuff.
empaqueter [ɑ̃pakte] v pack, wrap up. **empaquetage** nm packing.
emparer [ɑ̃pare] v **s'emparer de** seize, take possession of.
empâter [ɑ̃pate] v thicken, fatten.
empêcher [ɑ̃peʃe] v prevent, stop. **n'empêche (que)** all the same.
empereur [ɑ̃prœr] nm emperor.
empeser [ɑ̃pɔze] v starch.
empester [ɑ̃pɛste] v stink.
s'empêtrer [ɑ̃petre] v get entangled or involved.
empiéter [ɑ̃pjete] v encroach.
s'empiffrer [ɑ̃pifre] v (*fam*) stuff oneself.
empiler [ɑ̃pile] v pile, stack.
empire [ɑ̃pir] nm empire; influence.
empirer [ɑ̃pire] v worsen.
empirique [ɑ̃pirik] adj empirical.
emplacement [ɑ̃plasmɑ̃] nm site.
emplâtre [ɑ̃plɑtrə] nm plaster.
emplette [ɑ̃plɛt] nf purchase. **faire des emplettes** do some shopping.

emplir [ɑ̃plir] v fill.

emploi [ɑ̃plwa] nm use; (poste) job, employment. **emploi du temps** timetable, schedule.

employer [ɑ̃plwaje] v use; (ouvrier) employ. **s'employer à** apply oneself to. **employé, -e** nm, nf employee; (bureau) clerk. **employeur, -euse** nm, nf employer.

empoigner [ɑ̃pwaɲe] v grasp, grab; (lecture, etc.) grip.

empoisonner [ɑ̃pwazɔne] v poison; (empester) stink; (fam) annoy, aggravate. **empoisonnement** nm poisoning; (fam) bother.

emporter [ɑ̃pɔrte] v take (away); (entraîner) carry away or along; (gagner) win. **l'emporter sur** get the better of. **s'emporter** lose one's temper. **emporté** adj angry; (personne) quick-tempered. **emportement** nm anger.

s'empourprer [ɑ̃purpre] v flush, turn crimson.

*empreindre [ɑ̃prɛ̃drə] v imprint; (marquer) stamp, tinge.

empreinte [ɑ̃prɛ̃t] nf impression; mark, stamp; (animal) track. **empreinte de pas** footprint. **empreinte digitale** fingerprint.

s'empresser [ɑ̃prese] v (se hâter) hurry; (s'affairer) bustle around. **empressé** adj attentive; (péj) over-zealous. **empressement** nm attentiveness; (hâte) eagerness.

emprisonner [ɑ̃prizɔne] v imprison. **emprisonnement** nm imprisonment.

emprunter [ɑ̃prœ̃te] v borrow; derive. **emprunt** nm loan. **d'emprunt** (nom) assumed. **emprunté** adj ill-at-ease, awkward.

ému [emy] adj moved, touched; excited; emotional.

emulsion [emylsjɔ̃] nf emulsion.

en[1] [ɑ̃] prep in; (à) to; (transport) by; (comme) as; (composition) made of; (durée) while, when.

en[2] [ɑ̃] pron of it or them; (lieu) from there; (cause) about it; (des) some, any.

encadrer [ɑ̃kadre] v frame; (entourer) surround; (instruire) train. **encadrement** nm frame; training.

encaisser [ɑ̃kese] v collect; (chèque) cash. **encaisse** nf cash in hand.

enceinte[1] [ɑ̃sɛ̃t] adj pregnant.

enceinte[2] [ɑ̃sɛ̃t] nf enclosure; (mur) surrounding wall; (palissade) fence.

encens [ɑ̃sɑ̃] nm incense.

encercler [ɑ̃sɛrkle] v surround, encircle.

enchaîner [ɑ̃ʃene] v chain up; (lier) link together; continue, carry on. **enchaînement** nm series, chain.

enchanter [ɑ̃ʃɑ̃te] v enchant; (ravir) delight. **enchanté** adj delighted; (salutation) pleased to meet you. **enchantement** nm enchantment; magic; delight.

enchère [ɑ̃ʃɛr] nf bid. **enchères** nf pl auction sing.

enchérir [ɑ̃ʃerir] v **enchérir sur** (comm) bid higher than; (dépasser) go further than. **enchérisseur, -euse** nm, nf bidder.

enchevêtrer [ɑ̃ʃəvetre] v entangle; confuse, muddle.

enclin [ɑ̃klɛ̃] adj inclined, prone.

*enclore [ɑ̃klɔr] v enclose, shut in.

enclos [ɑ̃klo] nm enclosure; (chevaux) paddock.

enclume [ɑ̃klym] nf anvil.

encoche [ɑ̃kɔʃ] nf notch.

encoignure [ɑ̃kɔɲyr] nf corner.

encolure [ɑ̃kɔlyr] nf neck; (comm) collar size.

encombrer [ɑ̃kɔ̃bre] v clutter, obstruct; (ligne téléphonique) block. **s'encombrer de** load oneself with. **encombrant** adj cumbersome. **sans encombre** without mishap. **encombrement** nm congestion; clutter.

encontre [ɑ̃kɔ̃trə] prep **à l'encontre de** against, counter to; contrary to.

encore [ɑ̃kɔr] adv (toujours) still; (de nouveau) again; (en plus) more; (aussi) also; (même) even. **pas encore** not yet.

encorner [ɑ̃kɔrne] v gore.

encourager [ɑ̃kuraʒe] v encourage. **encouragement** nm encouragement.

*encourir [ɑ̃kurir] v incur.

encrasser [ɑ̃krase] v clog (up); (salir) dirty.

encre [ɑ̃krə] nf ink.

encroûter [ɑ̃krute] v encrust. **s'encroûter** (fam) get into a rut.

encyclopédie [ɑ̃siklɔpedi] nf encyclopedia.

endémique [ɑ̃demik] adj endemic.

s'endetter [ɑ̃dete] v get into debt. **endetté** adj in debt.

endiablé [ɑ̃djable] adj boisterous, wild.

s'endimancher [ɑ̃dimɑ̃ʃe] v put on one's Sunday best.

endive [ɑ̃div] nf endive; chicory.

endoctriner [ɑ̃dɔktrine] v indoctrinate. **endoctrination** nf indoctrination.

endolori [ãdɔlɔri] *adj* painful.
endommager [ãdɔmaʒe] *v* damage. **endommagement** *nm* damage.
*endormir [ãdɔrmir] *v* send to sleep; (*douleur*) deaden. **s'endormir** *v* fall asleep. **endormi** *adj* asleep.
endosser [ãdose] *v* (*vêtement*) put on; (*chèque, etc.*) endorse. **endossement** *nm* endorsement.
endroit [ãdrwa] *nm* place; (*roman, film, etc.*) point, part. **à l'endroit** (*vêtement*) the right side out; (*objet*) the right way round.
*enduire [ãdɥir] *v* coat. **enduit** *nm* coating.
endurcir [ãdyrsir] *v* harden.
endurer [ãdyre] *v* endure. **endurance** *nf* endurance.
énergie [enɛrʒi] *nf* energy; (*fermeté*) spirit, force. **énergique** *adj* energetic; forceful.
énerver [enɛrve] *v* irritate. **s'énerver** get excited.
enfant [ãfã] *n(m+f)* child (*pl* children). **enfant unique** only child. **enfance** *nf* childhood; (*bébé*) infancy. **enfantin** *adj* childlike; (*puéril*) childish.
enfanter [ãfãte] *v* give birth (to).
enfer [ãfɛr] *nm* hell.
enfermer [ãfɛrme] *v* shut up *or* in; (*sous clef*) lock up.
enfiler [ãfile] *v* thread; (*fam: vêtement*) slip on; (*rue, etc.*) take.
enfin [ãfɛ̃] *adv* at last, finally; (*bref*) in short; (*après tout*) after all.
enflammer [ãflame] *v* (*allumer*) set fire to; (*irriter*) inflame. **s'enflammer** catch fire; (*colère, désir*) flare up. **enflammé** *adj* blazing; inflamed.
enfler [ãfle] *v* swell. **enflé** *adj* swollen. **enflure** *nf* swelling.
enfoncer [ãfɔ̃se] *v* (*clou, etc.*) drive in; (*porte*) break down. **s'enfoncer** sink, plunge.
enfouir [ãfwir] *v* bury.
*enfreindre [ãfrɛ̃drə] *v* infringe.
*s'enfuir [ãfɥir] *v* run away.
engager [ãgaʒe] *v* engage; (*lier*) bind; (*entraîner*) involve; (*clef, etc.*) insert. **s'engager** (*promettre*) commit oneself, undertake; (*mil*) enlist. **engagement** *nm* (*promesse*) agreement; enlistment; (*acteur*) engagement.
engelure [ãʒlyr] *nf* chilblain.
engendrer [ãʒãdre] *v* generate, create.

engin [ãʒɛ̃] *nm* machine; (*outil*) tool.
englober [ãglɔbe] *v* include.
engloutir [ãglutir] *v* (*navire*) swallow up; (*manger*) gulp down.
engorger [ãgɔrʒe] *v* block.
engouffrer [ãgufre] *v* engulf; (*fam: manger*) wolf down. **s'engouffrer** rush.
engourdir [ãgurdir] *v* numb; (*esprit*) dull. **engourdi** *adj* numb. **engourdissement** *nm* numbness.
engrais [ãgrɛ] *nm* fertilizer; (*organique*) manure.
engraisser [ãgrese] *v* (*animal*) fatten up (*terre*) fertilize.
engrenage [ãgrənaʒ] *nm* (*tech*) gearing (*enchaînement*) chain.
engueuler [ãgœle] (*fam*) *v* shout at **s'engueuler** have a row. **engueulade** *n* shouting at; (*dispute*) row.
enhardir [ãardir] *v* embolden. **s'enhardir** become bolder.
énigme [enigmə] *nf* (*mystère*) enigma (*devinette*) riddle, puzzle. **énigmatique** *ad* enigmatic.
enivrer [ãnivre] *v* intoxicate. **s'enivrer** ge drunk. **enivrement** *nm* intoxication.
enjamber [ãʒãbe] *v* step over; (*pont* straddle. **enjambée** *nf* stride.
enjeu [ãʒø] *nm* stake.
enjôler [ãʒole] *v* coax.
enjoliveur [ãʒɔlivœr] *nm* (*auto*) hub cap
enjoué [ãʒwe] *adj* jolly, playful. **enjoue ment** *nm* jollity, playfulness.
enlacer [ãlase] *v* entwine. **s'enlacer** (*fils* intertwine; (*amants*) embrace.
enlaidir [ãledir] *v* (*déparer*) make ugly (*personne*) become ugly.
enlever [ãlve] *v* remove, take off *or* away kidnap. **s'enlever** come off. **enlèvemen** *nm* kidnapping; removal.
enliser [ãlize] *v* get stuck. **s'enliser** sink
ennemi [ɛnmi], **-e** *nm, nf* enemy. *adj* hos tile. **être ennemi de** be opposed to.
ennui [ãnɥi] *nm* boredom; (*difficulté* trouble.
ennuyer [ãnɥije] *v* (*lasser*) bore (*inquiéter*) worry; (*importuner*) bothe (*agacer*) annoy. **s'ennuyer** be bore **ennuyeux** *adj* boring, annoying.
énoncer [enɔ̃se] *v* state.
enorgueillir [ãnɔrgœjir] *v* make prouc **s'enorgueillir de** boast about.
énorme [enɔrm] *adj* enormous. **énorm ment** *adv* tremendously. **énormément d** a tremendous amount of.

s'enquérir [ãkerir] v inquire. **s'enquérir de** ask after.

enquête [ãkɛt] nf inquiry; (police) investigation; (sondage) survey; (mort) inquest. **enquêter** v investigate.

enraciné [ãrasine] adj deep-rooted, entrenched.

enragé [ãraʒe], **-e** nm, nf (fam) fanatic. adj furious; (fam) mad keen. **enrager** v be furious.

enrayer [ãreje] v (maladie) check; (machine) jam. **s'enrayer** jam.

enregistrer [ãrʒistre] v register; (son) record. **enregistrement** nm registration; recording.

s'enrhumer [ãryme] v catch a cold. **être enrhumé** have a cold.

enrichir [ãriʃir] v enrich. **enrichissement** nm enrichment.

enrôler [ãrole] v enrol; (mil) enlist. **enrôlé** nm recruit. **enrôlement** nm enrolment; enlistment.

enroué [ãrwe] adj hoarse.

enseigne [ãsɛɲ] nf sign; (mil, naut) ensign.

enseigner [ãseɲe] v teach. **enseignant, -e** nm, nf teacher. **enseignement** nm education; teaching.

ensemble [ãsãblə] adv together. nm whole; unity; (groupe) set; (vêtements) outfit. **dans l'ensemble** on the whole. **d'ensemble** overall.

ensemencer [ãsmãse] v sow.

ensevelir [ãsəvlir] v bury; (cacher) shroud, hide.

ensoleillé [ãsɔleje] adj sunny.

ensorceler [ãsɔrsəle] v bewitch, cast a spell on.

ensuite [ãsɥit] adv then, next; afterwards.

*s'ensuivre [ãsɥivrə] v follow.

entaille [ãtaj] nf cut, gash, notch. **entailler** v cut, gash, notch.

entamer [ãtame] v start (on), open; (couper) cut into.

entasser [ãtase] v pile up; amass; (serrer) cram.

entendre [ãtãdrə] v hear; (écouter) listen to; (comprendre) understand; intend, mean. **entendre parler de** hear of. **s'entendre** agree; (s'accorder) get on. **entendu** adj agreed; understood. **bien entendu** of course.

entente [ãtãt] nf understanding; (accord) agreement; harmony.

enterrer [ãtere] v bury. **enterrement** nm burial; (cérémonie) funeral.

en-tête nm heading. **papier à lettres à en-tête** nm headed notepaper.

entêté [ãtete] adj stubborn. **entêtement** nm stubbornness.

enthousiaste [ãtuzjast] n(m+f) enthusiast. adj enthusiastic. **enthousiasme** nm enthusiasm. **s'enthousiasmer** v be enthusiastic.

enticher [ãtiʃe] v **s'enticher de** become infatuated with.

entier [ãtje] adj entire, whole; intact; absolute. **en entier** totally. **tout entier** entirely, completely.

entité [ãtite] nf entity.

entonnoir [ãtɔnwar] nm funnel.

entorse [ãtɔrs] nf sprain, twist.

entortiller [ãtɔrtije] v twist, wind; (fam: enjôler) get round. **s'entortiller** twist; get entangled.

entourer [ãture] v surround. **entourage** nm circle, entourage; (bordure) surround.

entracte [ãtrakt] nm interval, interlude.

entrailles [ãtraj] nf pl entrails pl.

entrain [ãtrɛ̃] nm spirit, gusto.

entraîner [ãtrene] v carry along; (causer) bring about; (athlète) train; (influencer) lead. **entraînement** nm training; force, impetus. **entraîneur, -euse** nm, nf trainer, coach.

entraver [ãtrave] v hinder; (animal) shackle. **entrave** nf hindrance; shackle.

entre [ãtrə] prep between; (parmi) among; (dans) in.

entrebâillé [ãtrəbaje] adj ajar.

s'entrechoquer [ãtrəʃɔke] v knock together; (verres) clink.

entrecouper [ãtrəkupe] v interrupt, intersperse. **s'entrecouper** intersect.

s'entrecroiser [ãtrəkrwaze] v (fils) intertwine; (lignes) intersect.

entrée [ãtre] nf entry, entrance; (accès) admission; (début) outset; (cuisine) first course, entrée.

entrefaites [ãtrəfɛt] nf pl **sur ces entrefaites** at that moment.

entrefilet [ãtrəfilɛ] nm paragraph; (journal) item.

entremets [ãtrəmɛ] nm dessert.

*s'entremettre [ãtrəmɛtrə] v intervene. **entremise** nf intervention.

entrepôt [ãtrəpo] nm warehouse.

*entreprendre [ãtrəprãdrə] v undertake;

(*commencer*) begin, embark upon.
entreprenant *adj* enterprising.
entrepreneur, -euse [ɑ̃trəprənœr, -øz] *nm, nf* contractor. **entrepreneur de pompes funèbres** undertaker.
entreprise [ɑ̃trəpriz] *nf* firm; enterprise, venture.
entrer [ɑ̃tre] *v* enter, go *or* come in. **faire entrer** (*personne*) show in; (*objet*) put in. **laisser entrer** let in.
entre-temps *adv* meanwhile.
*****entretenir** [ɑ̃trətnir] *v* maintain; (*famille*) support; (*sentiment*) keep alive. **s'entretenir** converse; support oneself. **entretien** *nm* maintenance, upkeep; (*subsistance*) keep; discussion, conversation; interview.
*****entrevoir** [ɑ̃trəvwar] *v* make out, glimpse.
entrevue [ɑ̃trəvy] *nf* meeting; interview.
entrouvert [ɑ̃truvɛr] *adj* half-open.
envahir [ɑ̃vair] *v* invade; (*occuper*) overrun. **envahissement** *nm* invasion. **envahisseur, -euse** *nm, nf* invader.
envelopper [ɑ̃vlɔpe] *v* wrap; (*entourer*) envelop, shroud. **enveloppe** *nf* envelope; (*emballage*) wrapping, covering.
envenimer [ɑ̃vnime] *v* poison; aggravate. **s'envenimer** fester.
envergure [ɑ̃vɛrgyr] *nf* scope, range; (*ailes*) wingspan; calibre.
envers[1] [ɑ̃vɛr] *prep* towards, to.
envers[2] [ɑ̃vɛr] *nm* wrong side; (*médaille*) reverse. **à l'envers** (*vêtement*) inside out; (*dessus dessous*) upside down; (*devant derrière*) back to front.
envier [ɑ̃vje] *v* envy. **enviable** *adj* enviable. **envie** *nf* desire; envy; (*anat*) birthmark. **avoir envie de** want, fancy. **envieux** *adj* envious.
environ [ɑ̃virɔ̃] *adv* about. **environs** *nm pl* surroundings *pl*, vicinity *sing*.
environnement [ɑ̃virɔnmɑ̃] *nm* environment.
envisager [ɑ̃vizaʒe] *v* envisage; consider.
envoi [ɑ̃vwa] *nm* sending; (*colis*) parcel, consignment.
s'envoler [ɑ̃vɔle] *v* fly away; (*avion*) take off; disappear, vanish.
*****envoyer** [ɑ̃vwaje] *v* send. **envoyer chercher** send for. **envoyé, -e** *nm, nf* messenger; (*pol*) envoy; (*journal*) correspondent.
enzyme [ɑ̃zim] *nm* enzyme.

épagneul [epaɲœl] *nm* spaniel.
épais, -aisse [epɛ, -ɛs] *adj* thick. **épaisseur** *nf* thickness; (*neige, nuit*) depth. **épaissir** *v* thicken.
épancher [epɑ̃ʃe] *v* (*sentiments*) pour out; (*colère*) vent.
épandre [epɑ̃drə] *v* spread.
s'épanouir [epanwir] *v* blossom, open out; (*visage*) light up. **épanoui** *adj* (*fleur*) in full bloom; (*sourire*) radiant.
épargner [eparɲe] *v* save, spare. **épargne** *nf* saving.
éparpiller [eparpije] *v* scatter, disperse.
épars [epar] *adj* scattered.
épater [epate] (*fam*) *v* amaze, stagger. **épatement** *nm* amazement.
épaule [epol] *nf* shoulder.
épave [epav] *nf* wreck, ruin; (*débris*) wreckage.
épée [epe] *nf* sword.
épeler [eple] *v* spell.
éperdu [epɛrdy] *adj* distraught, frantic; passionate.
éperon [eprɔ̃] *nm* spur. **éperonner** *v* spur on.
éphémère [efemɛr] *adj* ephemeral, short-lived.
épi [epi] *nm* (*blé*) ear; (*cheveux*) tuft.
épice [epis] *nf* spice.
épicier [episje], **-ère** *nm, nf* grocer. **épicerie** *nf* grocer's; (*aliments*) groceries *pl*.
épidémie [epidemi] *nf* epidemic. **épidémique** *adj* epidemic; contagious.
épier [epje] *v* spy on; (*guetter*) watch for.
épilepsie [epilɛpsi] *nf* epilepsy. **épileptique** *n*(*m+f*), *adj* epileptic.
épiler [epile] *v* remove hair from; (*sourcils*) pluck.
épilogue [epilɔg] *nm* epilogue; conclusion.
épinards [epinar] *nm pl* spinach *sing*.
épine [epin] *nf* (*plante*) thorn; (*animal*) spine, quill. **épine dorsale** backbone. **épineux** *adj* thorny; (*situation*) tricky.
épingle [epɛ̃glə] *nf* pin. **épingle à cheveux** hairpin. **épingle de nourrice** or **sûreté** safety-pin. **épingler** *v* pin.
Épiphanie [epifani] *nf* Twelfth Night, Epiphany.
épique [epik] *adj* epic.
épiscopal [episkɔpal] *adj* episcopal.
épisode [epizɔd] *nm* episode. **épisodique** *adj* episodic, occasional; secondary, minor.

épitaphe [epitaf] *nf* epitaph.

éploré [eplɔre] *adj* tearful, in tears.

éplucher [eplyʃe] *v* (*légumes*) peel; (*salade*) clean; (*texte*) examine closely. **éplucheur** *nm* peeler. **épluchures** *nf pl* peelings *pl.*

épointé [epwɛte] *adj* blunt.

éponger [epɔ̃ʒe] *v* mop (up). **éponge** *nf* sponge.

épopée [epɔpe] *nf* epic.

époque [epɔk] *nf* time; (*passé*) age, era; (*géol*) period.

épouser [epuze] *v* marry. **épouse** *nf* wife.

épousseter [epuste] *v* dust. **époussetage** *nm* dusting.

épouvanter [epuvɑ̃te] *v* terrify, appal. **épouvantable** *adj* dreadful, terrible. **épouvantail** *nm* scarecrow. **épouvante** *nf* terror, dread. **film d'épouvante** *nm* horror film.

époux [epu] *nm* husband.

*__**éprendre**__ [eprɑ̃dre] *v* **s'éprendre de** fall in love with.

épreuve [eprœv] *nf* test; (*peine*) ordeal; (*sport*) event; (*texte*) proof; (*phot*) print.

éprouver [epruve] *v* feel, experience; (*subir*) suffer; test. **éprouvette** *nf* test tube.

épuiser [epɥize] *v* exhaust; use up. **épuisé** *adj* worn out; (*comm*) sold out. **épuisement** *nm* exhaustion.

épurer [epyre] *v* purify, refine. **épuration** *nf* purification, refinement.

équateur [ekwatœr] *nm* equator. **équatorial** *adj* equatorial.

équation [ekwɑsjɔ̃] *nf* equation.

équerre [ekɛr] *nf* set square. **en équerre** at right angles.

équestre [ekɛstrə] *adj* equestrian.

équilatéral [ekɥilateral] *adj* equilateral.

équilibre [ekilibrə] *nm* balance; (*mental, tech*) equilibrium; harmony. **en équilibre** balanced. **équilibré** *adj* well-balanced. **équilibrer** *v* balance; counterbalance.

équinoxe [ekinɔks] *nm* equinox.

équiper [ekipe] *v* equip, fit out. **équipage** *nm* crew; equipment. **équipe** *nf* team; (*usine*) shift. **équipement** *nm* equipment.

équitable [ekitablə] *adj* fair.

équitation [ekitɑsjɔ̃] *nf* riding.

équité [ekite] *nf* equity.

équivalent [ekivalɑ̃] *nm, adj* equivalent.

*__**équivaloir**__ [ekivalwar] *v* be equivalent.

équivoque [ekivɔk] *adj* ambiguous; (*louche*) dubious. *nf* ambiguity; doubt.

érable [erablə] *nm* maple.

érafler [erɑfle] *v* scratch, graze. **éraflure** *nf* scratch, graze.

éraillé [erɑje] *adj* scratched; (*voix*) hoarse, rasping.

ère [ɛr] *nf* era.

érection [erɛksjɔ̃] *nf* erection.

éreinter [erɛ̃te] *v* exhaust; (*fam: critiquer*) slate.

ergoter [ɛrgɔte] *v* quibble.

ériger [eriʒe] *v* establish, set up; (*monument*) erect.

ermite [ɛrmit] *nm* hermit.

éroder [erɔde] *v* erode. **érosif** *adj* erosive. **érosion** *nf* erosion.

érotique [erɔtik] *adj* erotic.

errer [ɛre] *v* wander, stray.

erreur [ɛrœr] *nf* mistake, error.

éruption [erypsjɔ̃] *nf* eruption. **entrer en éruption** erupt.

ès [ɛs] *prep* in the. **licencié ès lettres/sciences** *nm* Bachelor of Arts/Science.

escabeau [ɛskabo] *nm* stool; (*échelle*) step-ladder.

escadron [ɛskadrɔ̃] *nm* squadron.

escalader [ɛskalade] *v* climb, scale. **escalade** *nf* climbing.

escale [ɛskal] *nf* stop; (*naut*) port of call.

escalier [ɛskalje] *nm* staircase, stairs. **escalier de secours** fire escape. **escalier roulant** escalator. **escalier tournant** spiral staircase.

escalope [ɛskalɔp] *nf* escalope.

escamoter [ɛskamɔte] *v* (*esquiver*) dodge, evade; (*carte, etc.*) make disappear; (*fam*) pinch. **escamoteur, -euse** *nm, nf* conjuror.

escarbille [ɛskarbij] *nf* smut.

escargot [ɛskargo] *nm* snail.

escarmouche [ɛskarmuʃ] *nf* skirmish.

escarpé [ɛskarpe] *adj* steep.

escient [esjɑ̃] *nm* **à bon escient** advisedly. **à mauvais escient** ill-advisedly.

esclandre [ɛsklɑ̃drə] *nm* scene.

esclave [ɛsklav] *nm* slave. **esclavage** *nm* slavery.

escompter [ɛskɔ̃te] *v* discount; (*attendre*) expect, count on. **escompte** *nm* discount.

escorte [ɛskɔrt] *nf* escort. **escorter** *v* escort.

escrime [ɛskrim] *nf* fencing. **faire de l'escrime** fence.

escroc [ɛskro] nm swindler.

escroquer [ɛskrɔke] v swindle. **escroquerie** nf swindle, fraud.

espace [ɛspas] nm space. **espacer** v space out.

espadon [ɛspadɔ̃] nm swordfish.

Espagne [ɛspaɲ] nf Spain. **espagnol** nm, adj Spanish. **Espagnol, -e** nm, nf Spaniard.

espèce [ɛspɛs] nf sort, kind; (bot, zool) species. **espèces** nf pl cash sing.

espérer [ɛspere] v hope (for). **espérer en** trust in. **espérance** nf hope, expectation.

espiègle [ɛspjɛglə] adj mischievous. **espièglerie** nf mischief.

espion, -onne [ɛspjɔ̃, -ɔn] nm, nf spy. **espionnage** nm espionage. **espionner** v spy on.

esplanade [ɛsplanad] nf esplanade.

espoir [ɛspwar] nm hope.

esprit [ɛspri] nm spirit; (pensée) mind; (humour) wit. **avoir l'esprit large/étroit** be broad-/narrow-minded.

esquimau, -aude [ɛskimo, -od] nm, adj Eskimo. **Esquimau, -aude** nm, nf Eskimo.

esquisser [ɛskise] v sketch, outline. **esquisse** nf sketch, outline.

esquiver [ɛskive] v dodge, evade. **s'esquiver** slip away.

essai [ɛse] nm try, attempt; (produit, voiture) trial, test; (littéraire) essay. **à l'essai** on trial.

essaim [ɛsɛ̃] nm swarm. **essaimer** v swarm; (se disperser) scatter, spread.

essayer [ɛseje] v try; test; (vêtement) try on.

essence [ɛsɑ̃s] nf (carburant) gasoline; (extrait) oil, essence.

essentiel [ɛsɑ̃sjɛl] adj essential. nm main thing, essentials pl. **l'essentiel de** the best part of.

essieu [ɛsjø] nm axle.

essor [ɛsɔr] nm development, expansion; (oiseau) flight.

essorer [ɛsɔre] v wring (out); (machine) spin-dry. **essoreuse** nf spin-dryer; (à rouleaux) mangle.

essoufflé [ɛsufle] adj breathless, out of breath.

essuyer [ɛsɥije] v wipe; (sécher) dry; (subir) suffer. **essuie-glace** nm windscreen wiper. **essuie-mains** nm hand towel. **essuie-pieds** doormat.

est [ɛst] nm east. adj invar east; (région) eastern; (direction) eastward.

estaminet [ɛstaminɛ] nm tavern.

estamper [ɛstɑ̃pe] v stamp; (fam) diddle. **estampe** nf engraving, print.

estampille [ɛstɑ̃pij] nf stamp.

esthétique [ɛstetik] adj aesthetic. **esthéticien, -enne** nm, nf beautician.

estimer [ɛstime] v estimate; value; respect, esteem; consider. **estime** nf esteem, respect.

estivant [ɛstivɑ̃], **-e** nm, nf holiday-maker.

estomac [ɛstɔma] nm stomach.

estomper [ɛstɔ̃pe] v blur.

estrade [ɛstrad] nf platform.

estragon [ɛstragɔ̃] nm tarragon.

estropier [ɛstrɔpje] v cripple. **estropié, -e** nm, nf cripple.

estuaire [ɛstɥɛr] nm estuary.

esturgeon [ɛstyrʒɔ̃] nm sturgeon.

et [e] conj and.

étable [etablə] nf cowshed.

établir [etablir] v establish, set up; (liste, plan) draw up. **s'établir** become established; (s'installer) settle. **établissement** nm establishment.

étage [etaʒ] nm floor, storey; (gâteau) tier. **étagère** nf shelf; (meuble) set of shelves.

étai [etɛ] nm stay, prop.

étain [etɛ̃] nm tin; (alliage) pewter.

étaler [etale] v spread (out); (comm) display; parade, flaunt. **s'étaler** stretch out. **étalage** nm display; (vitrine) shop window. **étalagiste** n(m+f) window-dresser.

étalon¹ [etalɔ̃] nm (cheval) stallion.

étalon² [etalɔ̃] nm standard.

étancher [etɑ̃ʃe] v stem, staunch; make watertight. **étanche** adj watertight. **étanche à l'air** airtight.

étang [etɑ̃] nm pond.

étape [etap] nf stage; (arrêt) stop.

état [eta] nm state; condition; (comm) statement. **état-major** nm (mil) staff; (comm) senior management.

États-Unis [etazyni] nm pl United States sing.

étau [eto] nm (tech) vice.

étayer [eteje] v support, prop up.

été [ete] nm summer.

***éteindre** [etɛ̃drə] v extinguish; (lampe, radio, etc.) switch or turn off; (calmer) quench. **s'éteindre** (feu, etc.) go out; (mourir) die out. **éteint** adj dull, faded; feeble; (disparu) extinct.

étendard [etãdar] *nm* standard.

étendre [etãdrə] *v* extend, expand; (*étaler*) spread (out), stretch out; dilute. **étendu** *adj* vast, extensive. **étendue** *nf* (*terre*) expanse, area; (*pouvoir*) scope, extent.

éternel [etɛrnɛl] *adj* eternal; perpetual. **éternité** [etɛrnite] *nf* eternity.

éternuer [etɛrnɥe] *v* sneeze. **éternuement** *nm* sneeze.

éther [etɛr] *nm* ether.

éthique [etik] *adj* ethical. *nf* ethics *pl*.

ethnique [ɛtnik] *adj* ethnic.

étinceler [etɛ̃sle] *v* sparkle, glitter. **étincelle** *nf* spark. **étincellement** *nm* sparkle, gleam.

étiquette [etikɛt] *nf* label; (*protocole*) etiquette. **étiqueter** *v* label.

étirer [etire] *v* stretch.

étoffe [etɔf] *nf* material. **avoir l'étoffe de** have the makings of.

étoile [etwal] *nf* star. **étoile de mer** starfish.

étole [etɔl] *nf* stole.

étonner [etɔne] *v* surprise, amaze. **étonnement** *nm* surprise, amazement.

étouffer [etufe] *v* stifle, suffocate; (*bruit*) muffle; (*sentiments, révolte*) suppress. **étouffement** *nm* suffocation; suppression.

étourdir [eturdir] *v* stun, daze; (*altitude, etc.*) make dizzy; (*douleur*) deaden; (*bruit*) deafen. **étourderie** *nf* thoughtlessness. **étourdi** *adj* scatterbrained, thoughtless. **étourdissement** *nm* dizzy spell.

étourneau [eturno] *nm* starling.

étrange [etrãʒ] *adj* strange.

étranger [etrãʒe], **-ère** *adj* foreign; (*inconnu*) strange, unfamiliar. *nm* foreign country. **à l'étranger** abroad. *nm*, *nf* foreigner; stranger.

étrangler [etrãgle] *v* strangle, choke. **étranglement** *nm* strangulation.

étrave [etrav] *nf* stem.

***être** [ɛtrə] *v* be. **être à** belong to. *nm* being; (*âme*) soul. **être humain** *nm* human being.

***étreindre** [etrɛ̃drə] *v* embrace; (*serrer*) grasp, grip. **étreinte** *nf* embrace; grasp, grip.

étrenne [etrɛn] *nf* New Year's gift.

étrier [etrije] *nm* stirrup.

étriqué [etrike] *adj* narrow, cramped, tight.

étroit [etrwa] *adj* narrow; (*vêtement*) tight; (*intime*) close; strict. **étroitesse** *nf* narrowness; tightness.

étude [etyd] *nf* study.

étudier [etydje] *v* study; examine. **étudiant, -e** *nm*, *nf* student.

étui [etɥi] *nm* case.

étymologie [etimɔlɔʒi] *nf* etymology. **étymologique** *adj* etymological.

eucalyptus [økaliptys] *nm* eucalyptus.

Eucharistie [økaristi] *nf* Eucharist.

eunuque [ønyk] *nm* eunuch.

euphémisme [øfemismə] *nm* euphemism. **euphémique** *adj* euphemistic.

euphorie [øfɔri] *nf* euphoria. **euphorique** *adj* euphoric.

Europe [ørɔp] *nf* Europe. **européen** *adj* European. **Européen, -enne** *nm*, *nf* European.

euthanasie [øtanazi] *nf* euthanasia.

eux [ø] *pron* (*sujet*) they; (*objet*) them. **eux-mêmes** *pron* themselves.

évacuer [evakɥe] *v* evacuate. **évacuation** *nf* evacuation. **évacué -e** *nm*, *nf* evacuee.

s'évader [evade] *v* escape.

évaluer [evalɥe] *v* (*bijou*) value; (*dégâts*) assess; estimate.

évangélique [evãʒelik] *adj* evangelical. **évangéliste** *nm* evangelist.

évangile [evãʒil] *nm* gospel.

s'évanouir [evanwir] *v* (*personne*) faint; (*disparaître*) vanish. **évanouissement** *nm* loss of consciousness; disappearance.

évaporer [evapore] *v* evaporate. **évaporation** *nf* evaporation.

évasé [evaze] *adj* flared.

évasion [evazjɔ̃] *nf* escape. **évasif** *adj* evasive.

éveiller [eveje] *v* arouse, awaken. **éveil** *nm* alert, alarm. **en éveil** on the alert. **éveillé** *adj* alert; awake.

événement [evɛnmã] *nm* event.

éventail [evãtaj] *nm* fan.

éventer [evãte] *v* fan, air; discover. **s'éventer** go flat or stale. **éventé** *adj* stale, flat.

éventrer [evãtre] *v* tear open; (*taureau*) gore.

éventuel [evãtɥɛl] *adj* possible. **éventualité** *nf* possibility, eventuality.

évêque [evɛk] *nm* bishop.

s'évertuer [evɛrtɥe] *v* strive, do one's utmost.

évidence [evidãs] *nf* evidence; (*fait*) obvious fact. **en évidence** conspicuous.

évidemment *adv* obviously, of course.

évident *adj* obvious, evident.

évider [evide] *v* hollow out.

évier [evje] *nm* sink.

évincer [evɛ̃se] *v* oust.

éviter [evite] *v* avoid. **évitable** *adj* avoidable.

évocateur, -trice [evɔkatœr, -tris] *adj* evocative.

évoluer [evɔlчe] *v* evolve, develop; move about, manoeuvre. **évolution** *nf* evolution, development; movement, manoeuvre.

évoquer [evɔke] *v* evoke, recall.

exacerber [ɛgzasɛrbe] *v* exacerbate.

exact [ɛgzakt] *adj* exact; correct; (*vrai*) true; precise, accurate; punctual. **exactitude** *nf* exactness; precision; accuracy; punctuality.

exagérer [ɛgzaʒere] *v* exaggerate; (*abuser*) go too far. **exagération** *nf* exaggeration.

exalter [ɛgzalte] *v* excite; (*glorifier*) exalt. **exaltation** *nf* great excitement. **exalté** *adj* excited, elated; (*imagination*) vivid; fanatical.

examen [ɛgzamɛ̃] *nm* examination; test.

examiner [ɛgzamine] *v* examine.

exaspérer [ɛgzaspere] *v* exasperate, aggravate. **exaspération** *nf* exasperation.

exaucer [ɛgzose] *v* grant.

excaver [ɛkskave] *v* excavate. **excavation** *nf* excavation.

excéder [ɛksede] *v* exceed; exasperate. **excédent** *nm* surplus, excess.

excellent [ɛksɛlɑ̃] *adj* excellent. **excellence** *nf* excellence. **Excellence** *nf* Excellency.

exceller [ɛksele] *v* excel.

excentrique [ɛksɑ̃trik] *n(m+f)*, *adj* eccentric. **excentricité** *nf* eccentricity.

excepter [ɛksɛpte] *v* exclude. **excepté** *prep* except. **exception** *nf* exception. **exceptionnel** *adj* exceptional.

excès [ɛksɛ] *nm* excess; surplus. **excès de vitesse** (*auto*) speeding. **excessif** *adj* excessive.

exciter [ɛksite] *v* excite; (*provoquer*) arouse; stimulate; (*encourager*) urge. **s'exciter** (*fam*) get worked up. **excitation** *nf* excitement; stimulation.

s'exclamer [ɛksklame] *v* exclaim. **exclamation** *nf* exclamation.

*****exclure** [ɛksklyr] *v* exclude; (*chasser*) expel. **exclusif** *adj* exclusive; sole. **exclusion** *nf* exclusion; expulsion.

excommunier [ɛkskɔmynje] *v* excommunicate. **excommunication** *nf* excommunication.

excréter [ɛkskrete] *v* excrete. **excrément** *nm* excrement. **excrétion** *nf* excretion.

excursion [ɛkskyrsjɔ̃] *nf* excursion, trip.

excuser [ɛkskyze] *v* excuse; pardon, forgive. **excusez-moi** I'm sorry. **s'excuser** apologize. **excuse** *nf* excuse. **excuses** *nf pl* apology *sing*.

exécrer [ɛgzekre] *v* loathe. **exécrable** *adj* atrocious.

exécuter [ɛgzekyte] *v* execute, perform, carry out. **exécutif** *adj* executive. **exécution** *nf* execution.

exemplaire [ɛgzɑ̃plɛr] *adj* exemplary. *nm* copy; specimen.

exemple [ɛgzɑ̃plə] *nm* example. **par exemple** for example; (*surprise*) indeed, really.

exempt [ɛgzɑ̃] *adj* exempt, free. **exempter** *v* exempt. **exemption** *nf* exemption.

exercer [ɛgzɛrse] *v* exercise; practise; (*force*) exert; (*entraîner*) train. **s'exercer** practise.

exercice [ɛgzɛrsis] *nm* exercise; practice; (*mil*) drill.

exhaler [ɛgzale] *v* exhale; (*odeur*) give off; (*soupir*) utter.

exhiber [ɛgzibe] *v* exhibit, show, display. **exhibition** *nf* exhibition; show. **exhibitionniste** *n(m+f)*, *adj* exhibitionist.

exiger [ɛgziʒe] *v* demand, insist; (*nécessiter*) need, require. **exigences** *nf pl* demands *pl*, requirements *pl*.

exigu, -uë [ɛgzigy] *adj* cramped.

exiler [ɛgzile] *v* exile, banish. **exil** *nm* exile.

exister [ɛgziste] *v* exist; (*être*) be. **existence** *nf* existence. **existentialisme** *nm* existentialism.

exorbitant [ɛgzɔrbitɑ̃] *adj* exorbitant.

exorciser [ɛgzɔrsize] *v* exorcize. **exorcisme** *nm* exorcism. **exorciste** *nm* exorcist.

exotique [ɛgzɔtik] *adj* exotic.

expansion [ɛkspɑ̃sjɔ̃] *nf* expansion. **expansif** *adj* expansive.

expatrier [ɛkspatrije] *v* expatriate. **expatrié, -e** *n*, *adj* expatriate.

expédier [ɛkspedje] *v* send, dispatch; (*fam*) dispose of. **expédient** *nm*, *adj* expedient. **expéditeur, -trice** *nm*, *nf* sender. **expédition** *nf* dispatch; (*paquet*) consignment; (*voyage*) expedition.

expérience [ɛksperjɑ̃s] *nf* experience; (*scientifique*) experiment.
expérimenter [ɛksperimɑ̃te] *v* experiment; test, try out. **expérimental** *adj* experimental. **expérimenté** *adj* experienced.
expert [ɛksper] *nm, adj* expert. **expert-comptable** *nm* chartered accountant.
expier [ɛkspje] *v* atone for. **expiation** *nf* atonement.
expirer [ɛkspire] *v* expire; (*air*) breathe out. **expiration** *nf* expiry.
explication [ɛksplikasjɔ̃] *nf* explanation; (*texte*) analysis, commentary. **explicatif** *adj* explanatory.
explicite [ɛksplisit] *adj* explicit.
expliquer [ɛksplike] *v* explain; (*texte*) analyse.
exploit [ɛksplwa] *nm* exploit.
exploiter [ɛksplwate] *v* exploit; operate, run.
explorer [ɛksplɔre] *v* explore; examine. **explorateur, -trice** *nm, nf* explorer. **exploration** *nf* exploration.
exploser [ɛksploze] *v* explode. **explosif** *nm, adj* explosive. **explosion** *nf* explosion.
exporter [ɛkspɔrte] *v* export. **exportation** *nf* export.
exposer [ɛkspoze] *v* expose; exhibit, display; (*expliquer*) explain. **exposant, -e** *nm, nf* exhibitor. **exposé** *nm* talk, account. **exposition** *nf* exhibition; (*à l'air, etc.*) exposure; (*maison*) aspect.
exprès [ɛksprɛ] *adj invar* express. *adv* on purpose; specially.
express [ɛksprɛs] *nm* fast train.
expression [ɛksprɛsjɔ̃] *nf* expression. **expressif** *adj* expressive.
exprimer [ɛksprime] *v* express.
expulser [ɛkspylse] *v* expel; (*locataire*) evict. **expulsion** *nf* expulsion; eviction.
exquis [ɛkski] *adj* exquisite, delightful.
extase [ɛkstaz] *nf* ecstasy. **extasié** *adj* ecstatic.
extension [ɛkstɑ̃sjɔ̃] *nf* extension, expansion.
exténuer [ɛkstenɥe] *v* exhaust.
extérieur, -e [ɛksterjœr] *adj* outer, external, outside; (*étranger*) foreign. *nm* exterior, outside. **à l'extérieur** outside. **en extérieur** on location.
exterminer [ɛkstermine] *v* exterminate. **extermination** *nf* extermination.
externe [ɛkstern] *adj* external. **pour**

l'usage externe for external use only. *n(m+f)* day pupil. **externat** *nm* day school.
extinction [ɛkstɛ̃ksjɔ̃] *nf* extinction. **extincteur** *nm* extinguisher.
extirper [ɛkstirpe] *v* eradicate; (*arracher*) pull out.
extorquer [ɛkstɔrke] *v* extort. **extorsion** *nf* extortion.
extra [ɛkstra] *adj invar* first-rate, top-quality; (*fam*) fantastic. *adv* extra.
extraction [ɛkstraksjɔ̃] *nf* extraction.
extrader [ɛkstrade] *v* extradite. **extradition** *nf* extradition.
***extraire** [ɛkstrɛr] *v* extract; (*charbon*) mine; (*pierre*) quarry. **extrait** *nm* extract.
extraordinaire [ɛkstraɔrdinɛr] *adj* extraordinary; exceptional.
extravagant [ɛkstravagɑ̃] *adj* extravagant; (*prix*) excessive; (*idée*) crazy. **extravagance** *nf* extravagance.
extraverti [ɛkstraverti], **-e** *n, adj* extrovert.
extrême [ɛkstrɛm] *nm* extreme. *adj* extreme; (*loin*) far; intense; (*suprême*) utmost. **Extrême-Orient** *nm* Far East. **extrémiste** *n(m+f)*, *adj* extremist. **extrémité** *nf* end, tip; limit. **extrémités** *nf pl* (*anat*) extremities *pl*.
exubérant [ɛgzyberɑ̃] *adj* exuberant. **exubérance** *nf* exuberance.

F

fable [fɑblə] *nf* fable.
fabricant [fabrikɑ̃] *nm* manufacturer. **fabrication** *nf* manufacture.
fabriquer [fabrike] *v* manufacture, make; (*mensonge*) fabricate. **fabrique** *nf* factory.
fabuleux [fabyløʏ] *adj* fabulous.
fac [fak] *nf* (*argot*) university, college.
façade [fasad] *nf* façade, front.
face [fas] *nf* face; (*côté*) side. **de face** frontal. **en face (de)** opposite. **face à** facing. **faire face à** face.
facétie [fasesi] *nf* joke, trick. **facétieux** *adj* mischievous; humorous.
facette [fasɛt] *nf* facet.
fâcher [fɑʃe] *v* make angry. **se fâcher** get angry; (*se brouiller*) fall out. **fâché** *adj*

angry; (*désolé*) sorry. **fâcheux** *adj* unfortunate; (*ennuyeux*) annoying.

facile [fasil] *adj* easy; (*spontané*) ready.

faciliter [fasilite] *v* facilitate, make easier. **facilité** *nf* ease, easiness; aptitude; tendency. **facilités** *nf pl* facilities *pl*.

façon [fasɔ̃] *nf* way, manner; (*robe*) cut. **de façon à** so as to. **de toute façon** anyway. **façons** *nf pl* (*conduite*) behaviour *sing*; (*chichis*) fuss *sing*.

façonner [fasɔne] *v* shape, form; (*fabriquer*) manufacture, make.

fac-similé [faksimile] *nm* facsimile.

facteur [faktœr] *nm* factor; postman.

factice [faktis] *adj* artificial, false.

faction [faksjɔ̃] *nf* faction; guard, sentry.

facture [faktyr] *nf* bill; (*comm*) invoice. **facturer** *v* invoice; (*compter*) charge for.

facultatif [fakyltatif] *adj* optional; (*arrêt*) request.

faculté [fakylte] *nf* faculty; (*pouvoir*) power; (*droit*) right; (*argot*) university, college.

fadaises [fadɛz] *nf pl* nonsense *sing*.

fade [fad] *adj* insipid, dull.

fagot [fago] *nm* bundle of sticks.

fagoter [fagɔte] *v* (*péj*) rig out.

faible [fɛblə] *adj* weak, feeble; (*petit*) low, small, slight. *nm* (*personne*) weakling; (*penchant*) weakness. **faiblesse** *nf* weakness.

faiblir [feblir] *v* weaken, fail.

faïence [fajɑ̃s] *nf* earthenware.

faillible [fajiblə] *adj* fallible. **faillibilité** *nf* fallibility.

***faillir** [fajir] *v* fail. **faillir faire** almost do, narrowly miss doing. **failli, -e** *n, adj* bankrupt. **faillite** *nf* bankruptcy; (*chute*) collapse. **faire faillite** go bankrupt.

faim [fɛ̃] *nf* hunger. **avoir faim** be hungry.

fainéant [fɛneɑ̃], **-e** *adj* lazy, idle. *nm, nf* idler. **fainéantise** *nf* idleness.

***faire** [fɛr] *v* make; do; (*mesurer, temps*) be; (*sport, théâtre*) play; (*paraître*) look; (*dire*) say. **ça ne fait rien** it doesn't matter. **faire faire** have done. **faire-part** *nm invar* announcement. **faire voir** show. **se faire à** get used to.

faisable [fəzablə] *adj* feasible.

faisan [fəzɑ̃] *nm* pheasant.

faisceau [fɛso] *nm* bundle; (*rayon*) beam.

fait¹ [fɛ] *nm* fact; event; act. **au fait** (*à propos*) by the way; (*au courant*) informed. **en fait** in fact. **fait divers** news item.

fait² [fɛ] *adj* made; done; (*mûr*) ripe. **c'est bien fait pour toi!** it serves you right!

faîte [fɛt] *nm* summit, top.

faix [fɛ] *nm* burden.

falaise [falɛz] *nf* cliff.

***falloir** [falwar] *v* be necessary. **il faut le faire** it must be done. **s'en falloir (de)** be lacking.

falsifier [falsifje] *v* falsify, alter. **falsification** *nf* falsification.

famé [fame] *adj* **mal famé** disreputable.

fameux [famø] *adj* famous; first-rate, excellent; (*rude*) real. **pas fameux** not so good.

familial [familjal] *adj* family, domestic.

familiariser [familjarize] *v* familiarize. **familiarité** *nf* familiarity.

familier [familje] *adj* familiar; (*amical*) informal; (*mot*) colloquial. *nm* regular visitor.

famille [famij] *nf* family.

famine [famin] *nf* famine.

fanal [fanal] *nm* lantern.

fanatique [fanatik] *adj* fanatical. *n(m+f)* fanatic.

faner [fane] *v* make hay. **se faner** fade, wither.

fanfare [fɑ̃far] *nf* fanfare, flourish; (*orchestre*) brass band.

fanfaron, -onne [fɑ̃farɔ̃, -ɔn] *adj* boastful.

fange [fɑ̃ʒ] *nf* mire.

fantaisie [fɑ̃tezi] *nf* fantasy, fancy; (*caprice*) whim; extravagance; imagination.

fantastique [fɑ̃tastik] *adj* fantastic; (*bizarre*) weird, uncanny.

fantoche [fɑ̃tɔʃ] *nm* puppet.

fantôme [fɑ̃tom] *nm* ghost, phantom. **cabinet fantôme** *nm* shadow cabinet.

faon [fɑ̃] *nm* fawn.

farce¹ [fars] *nf* joke, prank; (*théâtre*) farce. **farceur, -euse** *nm, nf* practical joker.

farce² [fars] *nf* stuffing.

farcir [farsir] *v* stuff.

fard [far] *nm* make-up.

fardeau [fardo] *nm* burden.

farder [farde] *v* make up; disguise.

farfouiller [farfuje] *v* (*fam*) rummage about.

farine [farin] *nf* flour. **farine d'avoine** oatmeal. **farine de maïs** cornflour. **farineux** *adj* floury.

farouche [faruʃ] *adj* fierce; timid; savage, wild; unsociable.

fart [far] *nm* wax. **farter** *v* wax.

fascicule [fasikyl] *nm* volume; part, instalment.

fasciner [fasine] *v* fascinate. **fascination** *nf* fascination.

fascisme [fasismə] *nm* fascism. **fasciste** *n(m+f)*, *adj* fascist.

faste [fast] *nm* splendour.

fastidieux [fastidjø] *adj* tedious.

fastueux [fastɥø] *adj* sumptuous, luxurious.

fatal [fatal] *adj* fatal; inevitable. **fatalité** *nf* fate.

fatiguer [fatige] *v* tire, strain; (*agacer*) annoy. **se fatiguer** get tired. **fatigant** *adj* tiring; (*agaçant*) tiresome. **fatigue** *nf* fatigue, tiredness.

fatras [fatra] *nm* jumble.

faubourg [fobur] *nm* suburb.

faucher [foʃe] *v* mow, cut; (*fam*) pinch, nick. **fauché** *adj* (*fam*) broke, hard up.

faucon [fokɔ̃] *nm* falcon; hawk.

faufiler [fofile] *v* tack. **se faufiler** thread *or* edge one's way.

faune [fon] *nm* fauna.

fausser [fose] *v* distort, alter; (*courber*) bend, buckle. **fausser compagnie à** slip away from.

fausset [fosɛ] *nm* falsetto.

faute [fot] *nf* fault; mistake, error; (*jur*) offence. **faute de** for lack of. **fautif** *adj* at fault, guilty; incorrect.

fauteuil [fotœj] *nm* armchair; (*théâtre*) seat. **fauteuil à bascule** rocking chair. **fauteuil roulant** wheelchair.

fauve [fov] *adj* tawny, fawn. *nm* wild animal; (*couleur*) fawn.

faux¹, fausse [fo, fos] *adj* false; (*incorrect*) wrong; (*argent, etc.*) fake, forged. **fausse alerte** false alarm. **fausse couche** miscarriage. **faux-filet** *nm* sirloin. **faux pli** crease. *adv* out of tune. *nm* falsehood; forgery. **à faux** wrongly. **fausseté** *nf* falseness, falsity.

faux² [fo] *nf* scythe.

faveur [favœr] *nf* favour. **billet de faveur** *nm* complimentary ticket. **en faveur de** on behalf of. **favorable** *adj* favourable.

favori, -ite [favɔri, -it] *n*, *adj* favourite. **favoriser** *v* favour.

fébrile [febril] *adj* feverish. **fébrilité** *nf* feverishness.

fécond [fekɔ̃] *adj* fertile; prolific. **fécondité** *nf* fertility.

fécule [fekyl] *nf* starch. **féculent** *adj* starchy.

fédérer [federe] *v* federate. **fédéral** *adj* federal. **fédération** *nf* federation.

fée [fe] *nf* fairy. **féerique** *adj* magical.

***feindre** [fɛ̃drə] *v* feign. **feindre de** pretend.

fêler [fele] *v* crack. **fêlure** *nf* crack.

féliciter [felisite] *v* congratulate. **félicitations** *nf pl* congratulations *pl*.

félin [felɛ̃] *adj* feline.

femelle [fəmɛl] *nf*, *adj* female.

féminin [feminɛ̃] *adj* feminine, female. *nm* feminine. **féminisme** *nm* feminism. **féministe** *n(m+f)*, *adj* feminist. **féminité** *nf* femininity.

femme [fam] *nf* woman; (*épouse*) wife. **femme de chambre** chambermaid. **femme de ménage** cleaner.

fémur [femyr] *nm* femur.

fendre [fɑ̃drə] *v* split, crack.

fenêtre [fənɛtrə] *nf* window. **fenêtre à guillotine** sash window. **fenêtre en saillie** bay window.

fenouil [fənuj] *nm* fennel.

fente [fɑ̃t] *nf* crack, fissure; (*interstice*) slit; slot.

féodal [feɔdal] *adj* feudal.

fer [fɛr] *nm* iron. **fer à cheval** horseshoe. **fer à repasser** iron. **fer-blanc** *nm* tin. **fer forgé** wrought iron.

férié [ferje] *adj* **jour férié** *nm* public holiday.

ferme¹ [fɛrm] *adj* firm; (*solide*) steady. *adv* hard. **fermeté** *nf* firmness; steadiness.

ferme² [fɛrm] *nf* farm; (*maison*) farmhouse. **fermier** *nm* farmer. **fermière** *nf* farmer's wife.

fermenter [fɛrmɑ̃te] *v* ferment. **ferment** *nm* ferment. **fermentation** *nf* fermentation.

fermer [fɛrme] *v* close, shut; (*boucher*) block; (*gaz, eau, etc.*) turn off. **fermer à clef** lock. **fermeture** *nf* (*vêtement, sac, etc.*) fastener, catch; (*action*) closing. **fermeture à glissière** zip.

féroce [ferɔs] *adj* ferocious, fierce. **férocité** *nf* ferocity.

ferraille [fɛrɑj] *nf* scrap iron.

ferré [fɛre] *adj* (*canne*) steel-tipped; (*soulier*) hobnailed. **voie ferrée** *nf* railway track *or* line.

ferroviaire [fɛrɔvjɛr] *adj* railway.
fertile [fɛrtil] *adj* fertile. **fertilisation** *nf* fertilization. **fertiliser** *v* fertilize. **fertilité** *nf* fertility.
fervent [fɛrvɑ̃] *adj* fervent. **ferveur** *nf* fervour.
fesser [fese] *v* spank. **fesse** *nf* buttock. **fesses** *nf pl* bottom *sing.* **fessée** *nf* spanking.
festin [fɛstɛ̃] *nm* feast.
festival [fɛstival] *nm* festival.
feston [fɛstɔ̃] *nm* festoon; (*couture*) scallop. **festonner** *v* festoon; scallop.
fête [fɛt] *nf* festival; (*congé*) holiday; (*rel*) feast day; (*foire*) fair; celebration. **fête des Mères** Mothers' Day. **fête foraine** funfair.
fêter [fete] *v* celebrate.
fétiche [fetiʃ] *nm* fetish; mascot.
fétide [fetid] *adj* fetid.
feu¹ [fø] *nm* fire; (*lumière, lampe*) light; (*cuisine*) ring, burner; (*chaleur*) heat. **feu d'artifice** firework. **feu de joie** bonfire. **feu de position** sidelight. **feux** *nm pl* (*auto*) traffic lights *pl.*
feu² [fø] *adj* late, deceased.
feuille [fœj] *nf* leaf; (*papier, etc.*) sheet; form; (*bulletin*) slip. **feuillage** *nm* foliage. **feuillet** *nm* (*livre*) leaf, page. **feuilleter** [fœjte] *v* leaf *or* skim through. **pâte feuilletée** *nf* puff pastry. **feuilleton** [fœjtɔ̃] *nm* serial.
feutre [føtrə] *nm* felt; (*stylo*) felt-tip pen. **feutré** *adj* muffled.
fève [fɛv] *nf* broad bean.
février [fevrije] *nm* February.
fiacre [fjakrə] *nm* cab.
fiancé [fjɑ̃se] *adj* engaged. *nm* fiancé. **fiancée** *nf* fiancée.
se fiancer [fjɑ̃se] *v* get engaged. **fiançailles** *nf pl* engagement *sing.*
fiasco [fjasko] *nm* fiasco.
fibre [fibrə] *nf* fibre.
ficeler [fisle] *v* tie up. **ficelle** *nf* string.
ficher¹ [fiʃe] *v* (*enfoncer*) stick, drive in; (*mettre en fiche*) file. **fiche** *nf* (*cheville*) peg; (*élec*) pin; index card; form, slip. **fichier** *nm* file.
ficher² [fiʃe] (*fam*) *v* do, be up to; (*donner*) give; (*mettre*) put. **ficher le camp** clear off. **se ficher de** (*se moquer*) make fun of; (*être indifférent*) not care about. **fichu** *adj* (*mauvais*) rotten; (*perdu*) done for; capable, likely.

fiction [fiksjɔ̃] *nf* fiction. **fictif** *adj* fictitious; false; imaginary.
fidèle [fidɛl] *adj* faithful; loyal; (*habituel*) regular. *n(m+f)* (*rel*) believer; regular. **fidélité** *nf* faithfulness; loyalty; (*conjugale*) fidelity.
fiel [fjɛl] *nm* gall.
fiente [fjɑ̃t] *nm* droppings *pl.*
fier¹ [fjɛr] *adj* proud. **fierté** *nf* pride.
fier² [fje] *v* **se fier à** trust.
fièvre [fjɛvrə] *nf* fever. **fievreux** *adj* feverish.
figer [fiʒe] *v* congeal, clot, coagulate; (*paralyser*) freeze, stiffen.
figue [fig] *nf* fig. **figuier** *nm* fig tree.
figure [figyr] *nf* figure; (*visage*) face; (*image*) picture.
figurer [figyre] *v* represent; appear. **se figurer** imagine. **figurant, -e** *nm, nf* (*cinéma*) extra; (*théâtre*) walk-on; (*pantin*) puppet. **figuré** *adj* figurative.
fil [fil] *nm* thread; (*élec*) wire; (*linge, pêche*) line; (*bois*) grain; (*tranchant*) edge; current. **fil à plomb** plumbline. **fil de fer** wire.
filament [filamɑ̃] *nm* filament; (*fil*) thread.
file [fil] *nf* line; (*auto*) lane; (*d'attente*) queue. **à la file** in single file; one after the other.
filer [file] *v* spin; prolong, draw out; (*liquide, sable*) flow, run; (*bas*) ladder; (*fam: courir*) fly, dash; (*fam: s'en aller*) slip away.
filet¹ [filɛ] *nm* streak; (*eau*) trickle; (*fumée*) wisp.
filet² [filɛ] *nm* (*viande, etc.*) fillet.
filet³ [filɛ] *nm* (*sport, pêche*) net; (*bagages*) rack. **filet à provisions** string bag.
filial [filjal] *adj* filial. **filiale** *nf* subsidiary company.
filigrane [filigran] *nm* (*papier*) watermark; (*argent, verre, etc.*) filigree.
fille [fij] *nf* girl; (*opposé à fils*) daughter. **fillette** *nf* little girl.
filleul [fijœl] *nm* (*garçon*) godson; (*enfant*) godchild. **filleule** *nf* goddaughter.
film [film] *nm* film. **film fixe** filmstrip. **filmer** *v* film.
filou [filu] *nm* rogue.
filouter [filute] (*fam*) *v* diddle; (*tricher*) cheat; (*voler*) filch.
fils [fis] *nm* son; (*après nom*) junior.

filtrer [filtre] *v* filter. **filtre** *nm* filter; (*cigarette*) filter-tip.

fin¹ [fɛ̃] *adj* fine; (*mince*) thin; (*vue*) sharp; (*personne*) shrewd, astute; (*aliments*) choice; (*habile*) expert. **fines herbes** *nf pl* mixed herbs *pl*.

fin² [fɛ̃] *nf* end; (*but*) purpose. **en fin de compte** in the end. **fin de série** oddment. **final** [final] *adj* final. **finale** *nf* (*sport*) final. **finalement** *adv* in the end, finally. **finaliste** *n(m+f)* finalist.

finance [finɑ̃s] *nf* finance. **financer** *v* finance.

financier [finɑ̃sje] *adj* financial. *nm* financier.

finaud [fino] *adj* wily.

finesse [finɛs] *nf* fineness; (*vue*) sharpness; (*broderie*) delicacy; subtlety.

finir [finir] *v* finish, end; (*arrêter*) stop. **fini** *adj* finished; (*terminé*) over; (*complet*) utter.

Finlande [fɛ̃lɑ̃d] *nf* Finland. **finlandais** *adj* Finnish. **Finlandais, -e** *nm*, *nf* Finn. **finnois** *nm*, *adj* Finnish. **Finnois, -e** *nm*, *nf* Finn, Finnish speaker.

fioriture [fjorityr] *nf* flourish.

firme [firm] *nf* firm.

fisc [fisk] *nm* Inland Revenue. **fiscal** *adj* tax, fiscal.

fission [fisjɔ̃] *nf* fission.

fissure [fisyr] *nf* crack, fissure.

fixer [fikse] *v* fix; decide, settle; arrange, set. **fixation** *nf* fixation; (*attache*) fastening; (*ski*) binding. **fixe** *adj* fixed, set.

flacon [flakɔ̃] *nm* bottle.

flageller [flaʒele] *v* flog. **flagellation** *nf* flogging.

flagrant [flagrɑ̃] *adj* blatant, glaring. **prendre en flagrant délit** catch red-handed.

flairer [flere] *v* smell, sniff (at); (*discerner*) sense, scent. **flair** *nm* sense of smell; intuition.

flamand [flamɑ̃] *nm*, *adj* Flemish. **les Flamands** the Flemish.

flamant [flamɑ̃] *nm* flamingo.

flambeau [flɑ̃bo] *nm* torch; candlestick.

flamber [flɑ̃be] *v* blaze; (*cheveux*) singe. **flambée** *nf* blaze; (*colère, etc.*) outburst.

flamboyant [flɑ̃bwajɑ̃] *adj* blazing, fiery.

flamme [flam] *nf* flame; (*ardeur, éclat*) fire. **flammèche** *nf* spark.

flan [flɑ̃] *nm* (*cuisine*) egg custard; (*tech*) mould.

flanc [flɑ̃] *nm* side, flank.

flanelle [flanɛl] *nf* flannel.

flâner [flane] *v* stroll; (*péj*) dawdle.

flanquer [flɑ̃ke] *v* flank; (*fam*) fling, chuck.

flaque [flak] *nf* pool. **flaque d'eau** puddle.

flasque [flask] *adj* flaccid, flabby, limp; (*personne*) spineless.

flatter [flate] *v* flatter; encourage; (*caresser*) stroke. **se flatter** delude oneself. **se flatter de** pride oneself on. **flatterie** *nf* flattery. **flatteur, -euse** *adj* flattering.

flatulence [flatylɑ̃s] *nf* flatulence.

fléau [fleo] *nm* scourge; (*fam*) plague.

flèche [flɛʃ] *nf* arrow; (*église*) spire. **monter en flèche** soar, rocket. **fléchette** *nf* dart.

fléchir [fleʃir] *v* bend, sag; (*personne*) yield.

flegme [flɛgmə] *nm* composure. **flegmatique** *adj* phlegmatic.

flet [flɛ] *nm* flounder.

flétan [fletɑ̃] *nm* halibut.

flétrir¹ [fletrir] *v* (*faner*) wither, fade.

flétrir² [fletrir] *v* condemn; (*marquer*) brand. **flétrissure** *nf* (*tache*) stain, blemish; brand.

fleur [flœr] *nf* flower; (*arbre*) blossom; (*meilleur*) prime. **à fleur de** just above, on the surface of. **fleuriste** *n(m+f)* florist.

fleurir [flœrir] *v* flower, bloom; blossom; flourish, prosper; decorate with flowers. **fleuri** *adj* flowery; (*plante*) in flower; (*teint*) florid.

fleuve [flœv] *nm* river.

flexible [flɛksiblə] *adj* flexible.

flibustier [flibystje] *nm* buccaneer, pirate.

flic [flik] *nm* (*fam*) copper, policeman.

flirter [flœrte] *v* flirt. **flirteur, -euse** *nm*, *nf* flirt.

flocon [flokɔ̃] *nm* flake.

floral [floral] *adj* floral.

flore [flor] *nf* flora.

florissant [florisɑ̃] *adj* flourishing; (*santé*) blooming.

flot [flo] *nm* flood, stream. **à flot** afloat. **à flots** in torrents.

flotter [flote] *v* float; (*brume*) drift; (*parfum*) waft; (*drapeau*) flutter, fly; hesitate. **flottabilité** *nf* buoyancy. **flottable** *adj* buoyant. **flottant** *adj* floating; (*vêtement*) loose; irresolute. **flotte** *nf* fleet. **flotteur** *nm* float.

flou [flu] *adj* blurred; vague.

fluctuer [flyktЧe] *v* fluctuate. **fluctuation** *nf* fluctuation.

fluet, -ette [flyɛ, -ɛt] *adj* slender.

fluide [flЧid] *nm, adj* fluid. **fluidité** *nf* fluidity, flow.

fluorescent [flyɔresɑ̃] *adj* fluorescent. **fluorescence** *nf* fluorescence.

flûte [flyt] *nf* flute; (*pain*) long thin loaf. **flûte à bec** recorder. **flûtiste** *n(m+f)* flautist.

flux [fly] *nm* flood; (*méd*) flow; (*phys*) flux.

fluxion [flyksjɔ̃] *nf* inflammation, swelling. **fluxion dentaire** gumboil. **fluxion de poitrine** pneumonia.

focal [fɔkal] *adj* focal.

fœtus [fetys] *nm* foetus. **fœtal** *adj* foetal.

foi [fwa] *nf* faith; (*parole*) word.

foie [fwa] *nm* liver.

foin [fwɛ̃] *nm* hay.

foire [fwar] *nf* fair.

fois [fwa] *nf* time. **à la fois** at once. **des fois** (*fam*) sometimes. **deux fois** twice. **une fois** once.

foisonner [fwazɔne] *v* abound. **à foison** in abundance.

fol [fɔl] *form of* **fou** *used before vowel or mute h.*

folâtre [fɔlɑtrə] *adj* playful, lively.

folie [fɔli] *nf* (*méd*) madness; (*bêtise*) folly; (*dépense*) extravagance.

folklore [fɔlklɔr] *nm* folklore. **folklorique** *adj* folk; (*fam*) weird, outlandish.

folle [fɔl] *V* **fou.**

follet, -ette [fɔlɛ, -ɛt] *adj* scatter-brained.

follicule [fɔlikyl] *nm* follicle.

foncer [fɔ̃se] *v* charge, rush; (*fam*) tear along; (*puits*) sink; (*couleur*) go darker. **foncé** *adj* dark.

foncier [fɔ̃sje] *adj* land; fundamental.

fonction [fɔ̃ksjɔ̃] *nf* function; post, office. **faire fonction de** act as. **fonctionnaire** *n(m+f)* civil servant. **fonctionnel** *adj* functional.

fonctionner [fɔ̃ksjɔne] *v* function, work, operate.

fond [fɔ̃] *nm* bottom; (*pièce*) back; (*tableau*) background; (*essentiel*) heart, core; (*profondeur*) depth; (*lie*) sediment. **à fond** thoroughly. **au fond** deep down, basically. **de fond** basic.

fondamental [fɔ̃damɑ̃tal] *adj* fundamental, basic.

fondant [fɔ̃dɑ̃] *adj* melting. *nm* fondant.

fonder [fɔ̃de] *v* found; base; (*foyer*) start,

set up; justify. **se fonder sur** (*idée*) be based on; (*personne*) go on. **fondateur, -trice** *nm, nf* founder. **fondation** *nf* foundation. **fondement** *nm* foundation, base, grounds *pl.*

fonderie [fɔ̃dri] *nf* foundry.

fondre [fɔ̃drə] *v* melt; (*dans l'eau*) dissolve; (*statue, etc.*) cast; (*couleur*) merge. **fondre sur** swoop down on.

fondrière [fɔ̃drjɛr] *nf* pothole, rut.

fonds [fɔ̃] *nm* fund, collection; (*comm*) business. *nm pl* funds *pl.*

fontaine [fɔ̃tɛn] *nf* fountain.

fonts [fɔ̃] *nm pl* **fonts baptismaux** font *sing.*

football [futbol] *nm* football. **footballeur** *nm* footballer.

footing [futiŋ] *nm* jogging. **faire du footing** go jogging.

for [fɔr] *nm* **dans son for intérieur** in one's heart of hearts.

forain [fɔrɛ̃] *nm* (*marchand*) stallholder; fairground entertainer.

forçat [fɔrsa] *nm* convict.

force [fɔrs] *nf* force, strength. **à force de** by dint of.

forcené [fɔrsəne], **-e** *adj* (*fou*) deranged; (*acharné*) frenzied. *nm, nf* fanatic, maniac.

forceps [fɔrsɛps] *nm* forceps *pl.*

forcer [fɔrse] *v* force; (*claquer*) strain, overdo. **forcé** *adj* forced; inevitable. **forcément** *adv* inevitably, of course. **pas forcément** not necessarily.

forer [fɔre] *v* drill, bore. **foreuse** *nf* drill.

forêt [fɔre] *nf* forest. **forestier** *nm* forester.

forfait¹ [fɔrfɛ] *nm* (*sport*) withdrawal; serious crime. **déclarer forfait** withdraw.

forfait² [fɔrfɛ] *nm* fixed price; contract. **forfaitaire** *adj* inclusive.

forger [fɔrʒe] *v* forge; create, form; (*mot*) coin; (*inventer*) contrive, concoct. **forge** *nf* forge. **forgeron** *nm* blacksmith.

se formaliser [fɔrmalize] *v* take offence.

format [fɔrma] *nm* format, size.

former [fɔrme] *v* form; make up; (*éduquer*) train; develop. **formalité** *nf* formality. **formation** *nf* formation; training. **forme** *nf* form; (*contour*) shape. **être en forme** be fit. **formel** *adj* formal; definite.

formidable [fɔrmidablə] *adj* tremendous; (*fam*) incredible, fantastic.

formuler [fɔrmyle] *v* formulate; (*sentiment*) express; (*ordonnance*) draw up.

formulaire *nm* form. **formule** *nf* formula; expression; system, method; form.

fort [fɔr] *adj* strong; (*gros*) large; (*bruit*) loud; (*grand*) great; (*violent*) hard; (*doué*) good, able. *adv* loudly; hard; (*très*) very, most; (*beaucoup*) greatly, very much. *nm* strong point, forte; (*forteresse*) fort; (*milieu*) height, depths *pl*.

forteresse [fɔrtərɛs] *nf* fortress, stronghold.

fortifier [fɔrtifje] *v* fortify, strengthen. **fortification** *nf* fortification.

fortuit [fɔrtɥi] *adj* fortuitous, chance.

fortune [fɔrtyn] *nf* fortune; (*chance*) luck. **de fortune** makeshift. **fortuné** *adj* (*riche*) wealthy; (*heureux*) fortunate.

fosse [fos] *nf* pit; (*tombe*) grave. **fossé** *nm* ditch; (*écart*) gulf. **fossette** *nf* dimple. **fossoyeur** *nm* gravedigger.

fossile [fosil] *nm* fossil. *adj* fossilized.

fou [fu], **folle** *adj* mad; (*fam*) terrific, tremendous. **avoir le fou rire** have the giggles. *nm*, *nf* lunatic.

foudre [fudrə] *nf* lightning. **coup de foudre** love at first sight.

foudroyer [fudrwaje] *v* strike (down). **foudroyant** *adj* (*vitesse*, *attaque*) lightning; violent; (*succès*) thundering.

fouet [fwɛ] *nm* whip; (*cuisine*) whisk. **fouetter** *v* whip.

fougère [fuʒɛr] *nf* fern.

fougue [fug] *nf* ardour, spirit. **fougueux** *adj* fiery, spirited.

fouiller [fuje] *v* search; (*creuser*) dig, excavate. **fouiller dans** rummage in, go through. **fouille** *nf* excavation; search.

fouillis [fuji] *nm* jumble, muddle.

fouir [fwir] *v* dig, burrow.

foulard [fular] *nm* scarf.

foule [ful] *nf* crowd, mob.

fouler [fule] *v* trample, tread; (*méd*) sprain. **foulure** *nf* sprain.

four [fur] *nm* oven; (*usine*) furnace; (*poterie*) kiln.

fourbe [furb] *adj* deceitful, treacherous. **fourberie** *nf* deceit, treachery.

fourche [furʃ] *nf* fork; (*foin*) pitchfork; (*anat*) crotch. **fourcher** *v* split. **fourchette** *nf* fork. **fourchu** *adj* forked; (*pied*) cloven.

fourgon [furgɔ̃] *nm* coach, wagon, van.

fourmi [furmi] *nf* ant. **avoir des fourmis** have pins and needles. **fourmilier** *nm* anteater. **fourmilière** *nf* ant-hill.

fourmiller [furmije] *v* swarm.

fourneau [furno] *nm* furnace; (*cuisine*) stove.

fournir [furnir] *v* supply, provide. **fourni** *adj* bushy, thick. **fournisseur** *nm* tradesman, stockist; (*comm*) supplier. **fournitures** *nf pl* supplies *pl*.

fourrer [fure] *v* (*cuisine*) stuff, fill; (*vêtement*) line with fur; (*fam*) shove, stick. **fourreau** *nm* sheath. **fourre-tout** *nm invar* (*pièce*) lumber room; (*sac*) holdall. **fourreur** *nm* furrier. **fourrure** *nf* fur.

***foutre** [futrə] (*impol*) *v* do. **fous-moi le camp!** bugger off! **se foutre de** not give a damn about. **va te faire foutre!** fuck off! **foutaise** *nf* rubbish.

foyer [fwaje] *nm* home; (*âtre*) hearth; (*jeunes*) hostel; (*théâtre*) foyer; (*phys*) focus; (*infection*, *etc.*) seat, centre.

fracas [fraka] *nm* crash, din.

fracasser [frakase] *v* smash, shatter.

fraction [fraksjɔ̃] *nf* fraction.

fracturer [fraktyre] *v* fracture, break. **fracture** *nf* fracture.

fragile [fraʒil] *adj* fragile, delicate, frail. **fragilité** *nf* fragility, frailty.

fragment [fragmɑ̃] *nm* fragment, bit.

frai [frɛ] *nm* spawn.

frais¹, **fraîche** [frɛ, frɛʃ] *adj* fresh; (*froid*) cool; (*nouveau*) new. **fraîcheur** *nf* freshness; coolness.

frais² [frɛ] *nm pl* costs *pl*, expenses *pl*.

fraise¹ [frɛz] *nf* (*fruit*) strawberry. **fraisier** *nm* strawberry plant.

fraise² [frɛz] *nf* (*col*) ruff; (*dentiste*) drill.

framboise [frɑ̃bwaz] *nf* raspberry. **framboisier** *nm* raspberry bush.

franc¹ [frɑ̃] *nm* franc.

franc², **franche** [frɑ̃, frɑ̃ʃ] *adj* frank, candid; (*libre*) free; (*péj*) utter, downright; (*net*) clear. **franc-parler** *nm invar* outspokenness.

France [frɑ̃s] *nf* France. **français** *nm*, *adj* French. **les Français** the French.

franchir [frɑ̃ʃir] *v* (*obstacle*) clear, get over; (*traverser*) cross; pass.

franchise [frɑ̃ʃiz] *nf* frankness; exemption; (*bagages*) allowance.

franco [frɑ̃ko] *adv* post-free, carriage-paid.

frange [frɑ̃ʒ] *nf* fringe.

frapper [frape] *v* hit, strike; (*glacer*) chill, ice; (*porte*) knock.

fraternel [fratɛrnɛl] *adj* brotherly, fraternal. **fraternité** *nf* brotherhood, fraternity.

fraterniser [fratɛrnize] v fraternize.
fraude [frod] nf fraud, cheating. **passer en fraude** smuggle in. **frauder** v defraud, cheat. **frauduleux** adj fraudulent.
frayer [freje] v clear, open up; (poisson) spawn. **frayer avec** mix or associate with.
fredaine [frədɛn] nf mischief.
fredonner [frədɔne] v hum.
frein [frɛ̃] nm brake; (cheval) bit. **frein à main** handbrake. **mettre le frein à** curb, check. **freiner** v slow down; (auto) brake; (contrarier) check.
frêle [frɛl] adj frail, flimsy.
frelon [frəlɔ̃] nm hornet.
frémir [fremir] v shudder, tremble; (de froid) shiver. **frémissement** nm shudder, shiver.
frêne [frɛn] nm ash.
frénésie [frenezi] nf frenzy. **frénétique** adj frenzied, frenetic.
fréquence [frekɑ̃s] nf frequency. **fréquent** adj frequent.
fréquenter [frekɑ̃te] v frequent; (amis, etc.) go around with, see often.
frère [frɛr] nm brother; (moine) friar.
fresque [frɛsk] nf fresco.
fret [frɛ] nm freight.
fréter [frete] v charter.
frétiller [fretije] v wriggle; (queue) wag.
friable [frijablə] adj crumbly.
friand [frijɑ̃] adj **friand de** fond of, partial to. **friandise** nf sweet, delicacy.
fricoter [frikɔte] v (fam) cook up.
friction [friksjɔ̃] nf friction. **frictionner** v rub.
frigide [friʒid] adj frigid. **frigidité** nf frigidity.
frigo [frigo] nm (fam) fridge.
frileux [frilø] adj sensitive to cold, chilly.
friper [fripe] v crumple.
fripon, -onne [fripɔ̃, -ɔn] adj cheeky, mischievous. nm, nf (fam) rascal.
***frire** [frir] v fry.
frise [friz] nf frieze.
friser [frize] v curl; (frôler) skim; (approcher) verge on. **frisé** adj curly.
frisquet, -ette [friskɛ, -ɛt] adj chilly.
frissonner [frisɔne] v tremble, shudder; (de froid) shiver; (feuillage) rustle. **frisson** nm shiver.
frit [fri] adj fried. **frites** nf pl chips pl. **friteuse** nf chip pan, deep-fryer. **friture** nf frying; fried food.
frivole [frivɔl] adj frivolous. **frivolité** nf frivolity.

froid [frwa] adj cold. nm cold. **avoid froid** be cold. **froideur** nf coldness.
froisser [frwase] v crumple, crease; (personne) offend. **se froisser** take offence.
frôler [frole] v brush against, skim.
fromage [frɔmaʒ] nm cheese. **fromage blanc** cream cheese. **fromage maigre** cottage cheese.
froment [frɔmɑ̃] nm wheat.
froncer [frɔ̃se] v gather. **froncer les sourcils** frown. **fronce** nm gather. **froncement de sourcils** nm frown.
fronde [frɔ̃d] nf sling.
front [frɔ̃] nm front; (anat) forehead. **de front** head-on; (côte à côte) abreast. **faire front à** face up to. **frontal** adj frontal.
frontière [frɔ̃tjɛr] nf frontier, border.
frotter [frɔte] v rub; (nettoyer) scrub; (allumette) strike.
fructueux [fryktɥø] adj fruitful, profitable.
frugal [frygal] adj frugal. **frugalité** nf frugality.
fruit [frɥi] nm fruit. **fruits de mer** seafood sing. **fruits secs** dried fruit sing.
fruste [fryst] adj unpolished, crude.
frustrer [frystre] v frustrate. **frustration** nf frustration.
fugace [fygas] adj fleeting.
fugitif [fyʒitif], **-ive** nm, nf fugitive. adj runaway; (fugace) fleeting.
***fuir** [fɥir] v run away, escape; (éviter) shun, avoid; (gaz, liquide) leak. **fuite** nf escape, flight; leak.
fumer [fyme] v smoke; (vapeur) steam. **fumée** nf smoke; steam. **fumeur, -euse** nm, nf smoker.
fumier [fymje] nf dung, manure.
funambule [fynɑ̃byl] n(m+f) tightrope walker.
funèbre [fynɛbrə] adj funeral; (lugubre) mournful, gloomy.
funérailles [fyneraj] nf pl funeral sing.
funeste [fynɛst] adj disastrous; fatal, deadly.
fur [fyr] nm **au fur et à mesure** as, as soon as, as fast as.
furet [fyrɛ] nm ferret.
fureter [fyrte] v ferret about; (fouiller) rummage.
fureur [fyrœr] nf fury, rage; passion, mania. **furibond** adj furious, mad. **furie** nf fury; mania. **furieux** adj furious.

garder

furoncle [fyrɔ̃klə] *nm* boil.

furtif [fyrtif] *adj* furtive.

fusée [fyze] *nf* rocket; (*mine*) fuse; (*tech*) spindle.

fusil [fyzi] *nm* gun, rifle. **fusil de chasse** shotgun. **fusiller** *v* shoot.

fusion [fyzjɔ̃] *nf* fusion; (*métal, glace*) melting.

fusionner [fyzjɔne] *v* merge, amalgamate.

fustiger [fystiʒe] *v* censure.

fût [fy] *nm* (*arbre*) bole; (*tonneau*) barrel; (*colonne*) shaft.

futaie [fytɛ] *nf* forest, plantation of timber trees.

futaille [fytaj] *nf* barrel.

futile [fytil] *adj* futile; (*frivole*) trivial. **futilité** *nf* futility; triviality.

futur [fytyr] *adj* future, prospective. **future maman** *nf* mother-to-be. **futur mari** *nm* husband-to-be. *nm* future.

fuyant [fɥijɑ̃] *adj* elusive; (*menton, etc.*) receding.

G

gâcher [gaʃe] *v* (*gaspiller*) waste; (*gâter*) spoil; (*travail*) botch. **gâchis** *nm* mess; waste.

gâchette [gaʃɛt] *nf* trigger.

gaffe [gaf] *nf* (*impair*) blunder; (*naut*) boat-hook.

gage [gaʒ] *nm* guarantee, security; (*preuve*) proof, evidence; (*jeu*) forfeit. **gages** *nm pl* wages *pl*. **gager** *v* wager; guarantee.

gagner [gaɲe] *v* (*toucher, mériter*) earn; (*être vainqueur*) win; (*obtenir*) gain; (*arriver à*) reach. **gagnant, -e** *nm, nf* winner.

gai [ge] *adj* cheerful, gay, merry. **gaieté** *nf* gaiety, cheerfulness.

gaillard [gajar] *adj* strong; (*alerte*) lively, sprightly; (*grivois*) ribald. *nm* strapping fellow. **gaillardise** *nf* ribald remark.

gain [gɛ̃] *nm* gain; (*salaire*) earnings *pl*. **gains** *nm pl* profits *pl*; (*jeu*) winnings *pl*.

gaine [gɛn] *nf* sheath; (*vêtement*) girdle. **gainer** *v* sheathe, cover.

galant [galɑ̃] *adj* gallant; courteous; romantic. **galanterie** *nf* gallantry.

galaxie [galaksi] *nf* galaxy.

galbe [galbə] *nm* curve.

gale [gal] *nf* mange, scabies. **galeux** *adj* mangy; (*sordide*) squalid, seedy.

galère [galɛr] *nf* galley.

galerie [galri] *nf* gallery; (*auto*) roof rack.

galet [galɛ] *nm* pebble. **galets** *nm pl* shingle *sing*.

galette [galɛt] *nf* (*crêpe*) pancake; biscuit; (*gâteau*) cake.

galion [galjɔ̃] *nm* galleon.

Galles [gal] *nf pl* **pays de Galles** *nm* Wales. **gallois** *nm, adj* Welsh. **les Gallois** the Welsh.

gallon [galɔ̃] *nm* gallon.

galon [galɔ̃] *nm* braid; (*mil*) stripe.

galop [galo] *nm* gallop. **petit galop** canter. **galoper** *v* gallop.

galvaniser [galvanize] *v* galvanize.

gambader [gɑ̃bade] *v* gambol, leap about. **gambade** *nf* leap, caper.

gamin [gamɛ̃], **-e** *adj* playful; (*puéril*) childish. *nm, nf* (*fam*) kid.

gamme [gam] *nf* scale; (*série*) range.

gangrène [gɑ̃grɛn] *nf* gangrene.

gangster [gɑ̃gstɛr] *nm* gangster.

gant [gɑ̃] *nm* glove. **gant de toilette** facecloth, flannel.

garage [garaʒ] *nm* garage. **garagiste** *nm* garage owner; garage mechanic.

garant [garɑ̃], **-e** *nm, nf* (*personne*) guarantor; (*chose*) guarantee. **se porter garant de** stand bail for.

garantir [garɑ̃tir] *v* guarantee; assure; protect. **garantie** *nf* guarantee.

garce [gars] *nf* (*impol*) bitch.

garçon [garsɔ̃] *nm* boy; (*magasin*) assistant; (*restaurant*) waiter; (*célibataire*) bachelor. **garçon d'honneur** best man.

garde [gard] *nf* guard; (*jur*) custody; (*surveillance*) care. **garde-à-vous!** (*mil*) attention! **prendre garde** be careful, take care. *nm* guard; (*château*) warden. **garde du corps** bodyguard.

garder [garde] *v* (*surveiller*) look after, guard; (*conserver, retenir*) keep. **garde-boue** *nm invar* fender. **garde-chasse** *nm* gamekeeper. **garde-feu** *nm invar* fireguard. **garde-fou** *nm* railing, parapet. **garde-manger** *nm invar* pantry, larder. **garde-nappe** *nm* tablemat. **garde-robe** *nf* wardrobe. **se garder de** beware of, be careful not to. **garderie** *nf* crèche, day nursery.

gardien [gardjɛ̃], **-enne** *nm, nf* guard; (*prison*) warder; (*château*) warden; (*zoo*) keeper; (*musée*) attendant; (*défenseur*) guardian. **gardien de but** goalkeeper. **gardien de nuit** night watchman.

gare¹ [gar] *nf* station. **gare routière** bus station.

gare² [gar] *interj* look out! beware!

garenne [garɛn] *nf* rabbit warren.

garer [gare] *v* (*voiture*) park: (*bateau*) dock. **se garer** park; (*piéton*) move aside. **se garer de** avoid.

se gargariser [gargarize] *v* gargle. **gargarisme** *nm* gargle.

gargouiller [garguje] *v* gurgle; (*intestin*) rumble. **gargouille** *nf* gargoyle.

garnir [garnir] *v* (*remplir*) fill, stock; (*équiper*) fit; (*doubler*) line; cover; decorate; (*cuisine*) garnish. **garnison** *nm* garrison. **garniture** *nf* fittings *pl*; (*cuisine*) garnish, trimmings *pl*; (*légumes*) vegetables *pl*; lining.

gars [gɑ] *nm* (*fam*) lad.

gaspiller [gaspije] *v* waste. **gaspillage** *nm* waste. **gaspilleur, -euse** *adj* wasteful.

gastrique [gastrik] *adj* gastric.

gastronomie [gastrɔnɔmi] *nf* gastronomy. **gastronomique** *adj* gastronomic.

gâteau [gɑto] *nm* cake; (*dessert*) gâteau. **petit gâteau** (**sec**) biscuit.

gâter [gɑte] *v* spoil, ruin. **se gâter** go bad *or* off; take a turn for the worse.

gauche [goʃ] *adj* left; (*maladroit*) awkward, clumsy. *nf* left, left-hand side. **gaucher** *adj* left-handed. **gaucherie** *nf* awkwardness, clumsiness.

gauchir [goʃir] *v* warp; (*fausser*) distort.

gaz [gɑz] *nm invar* gas. **gazeux** *adj* gaseous; (*boisson*) fizzy.

gaze [gɑz] *nf* gauze.

gazéifier [gazeifje] *v* aerate.

gazelle [gazɛl] *nf* gazelle.

gazon [gɑzɔ̃] *nm* lawn; (*motte*) turf.

gazouiller [gazuje] *v* (*oiseau*) chirp; (*bébé*) gurgle; (*ruisseau*) babble.

géant [ʒeɑ̃] *adj* gigantic, giant. *nm* giant.

*****geindre** [ʒɛ̃drə] *v* groan, moan, whine.

gel [ʒɛl] *nm* frost.

gélatine [ʒelatin] *nf* gelatine.

geler [ʒəle] *v* freeze, be frozen. **gelé** *adj* frozen; (*membre*) frostbitten. **gelée** *nf* frost; (*cuisine*) jelly. **gelure** *nf* frostbite.

gélignite [ʒelignit] *nf* gelignite.

Gémeaux [ʒemo] *nm pl* Gemini *sing*.

gémir [ʒemir] *v* groan, moan, whine;

(*grincer*) creak. **gémissement** *nm* groan, moan.

gemme [ʒɛm] *nf* gem.

gencive [ʒɑ̃siv] *nf* gum.

gendarme [ʒɑ̃darm] *nm* policeman.

gendre [ʒɑ̃drə] *nm* son-in-law.

gène [ʒɛn] *nm* gene.

gêne [ʒɛn] *nf* trouble, bother; embarrassment; (*physique*) discomfort; financial difficulties *pl*.

généalogie [ʒenealɔʒi] *nf* genealogy. **généalogique** *adj* genealogical.

gêner [ʒene] *v* bother, embarrass; (*obstacle*) hamper; inconvenience. **se gêner** put oneself out. **gênant** *adj* embarrassing, awkward. **gêné** *adj* embarrassed, uncomfortable; short of money.

général [ʒeneral] *nm, adj* general. **en général** in general, usually. **général de brigade** brigadier. **généralisation** *nf* generalization. **généraliser** *v* generalize. **généraliste** *nm* general practitioner.

génération [ʒenerasjɔ̃] *nf* generation.

génératrice [ʒeneratris] *nf* generator.

généreux [ʒenerø] *adj* generous. **générosité** *nf* generosity.

générique [ʒenerik] *adj* generic. *nm* (*cinéma*) credits *pl*.

génétique [ʒenetik] *adj* genetic. *nf* genetics.

génie [ʒeni] *nm* genius; spirit. **le génie** (*mil*) the Engineers. **génial** *adj* brilliant, inspired.

genièvre [ʒənjɛvrə] *nm* (*arbre*) juniper; (*fruit*) juniper berry; (*boisson*) gin.

génital [ʒenital] *adj* genital. **organes génitaux** *nm pl* genitals *pl*.

genou [ʒənu] *nm, pl* **-oux** knee. **à genoux** kneeling.

genre [ʒɑ̃r] *nm* kind, sort; (*gramm*) gender; (*art, etc.*) genre; family, genus. **le genre humain** mankind.

gens [ʒɑ̃] *nm pl* people *pl*.

gentiane [ʒɑ̃sjan] *nf* gentian.

gentil, -ille [ʒɑ̃ti, -ij] *adj* nice; (*personne*) kind; (*sage*) good. **gentillesse** *nf* kindness; favour. **gentiment** *adv* nicely; kindly.

génuflexion [ʒenyflɛksjɔ̃] *nf* genuflexion.

géographie [ʒeɔgrafi] *nf* geography. **géographe** *n(m + f)* geographer. **géographique** *adj* geographical.

geôle [ʒol] *nf* jail. **geôlier, -ère** *nm, n* jailer.

géologie [ʒeɔlɔʒi] *nf* geology. **géologique** *adj* geological. **géologue** *n(m+f)* geologist.

géométrie [ʒeɔmetri] *nf* geometry. **géomètre** *nm* surveyor. **géométrique** *adj* geometrical.

géranium [ʒeranjɔm] *nm* geranium.

gerbe [ʒɛrb] *nf* sheaf, bundle; *(fleurs)* spray; *(eau, étincelles)* shower.

gercer [ʒɛrse] *v* chap, crack. **gerçure** *nf* crack.

gérer [ʒere] *v* manage. **gérance** *nf* management. **gérant** *nm* manager. **gérante** *nf* manageress.

gériatrie [ʒerjatri] *nf* geriatrics. **gériatrique** *adj* geriatric.

germanique [ʒɛrmanik] *adj* Germanic.

germer [ʒɛrme] *v* germinate; *(plante)* sprout, shoot. **germe** *nm* germ; *(source)* seed. **germination** *nf* germination.

gérondif [ʒerɔ̃dif] *nm* gerund, gerundive.

***gésir** [ʒezir] *v* lie, be lying.

geste [ʒɛst] *nm* gesture; act, deed.

gesticuler [ʒɛstikyle] *v* gesticulate. **gesticulation** *nf* gesticulation.

gestion [ʒɛstjɔ̃] *nf* management, administration.

geyser [ʒɛzɛr] *nm* geyser.

ghetto [ɡeto] *nm* ghetto.

gibet [ʒibɛ] *nm* gallows.

gibier [ʒibje] *nm* game.

giboulée [ʒibule] *nf* shower.

gicler [ʒikle] *v* spurt, squirt. **giclée** *nf* spurt, squirt.

gifler [ʒifle] *v* slap in the face. **gifle** *nf* slap in the face.

gigantesque [ʒiɡɑ̃tɛsk] *adj* gigantic, immense.

gigot [ʒiɡo] *nm* leg of lamb.

gigue [ʒiɡ] *nf* jig.

gilet [ʒilɛ] *nm* waistcoat; cardigan. **gilet de sauvetage** life-jacket.

gin [dʒin] *nm* gin.

gingembre [ʒɛ̃ʒɑ̃brə] *nm* ginger.

girafe [ʒiraf] *nf* giraffe.

girofle [ʒirɔflə] *nm* clove.

giron [ʒirɔ̃] *nm* lap.

girouette [ʒirwɛt] *nf* weathercock.

gisement [ʒizmɑ̃] *nm* deposit.

gitan [ʒitɑ̃] *adj* gipsy. **Gitan, -e** *nm, nf* gipsy.

gîte [ʒit] *nm* shelter.

givre [ʒivrə] *nm* hoar-frost. **givrer** *v* ice up.

glabre [ɡlabrə] *adj* hairless; *(rasé)* clean-shaven.

glacer [ɡlase] *v* freeze; *(boissons, etc.)* chill; *(cuisine)* glaze; *(gâteau)* ice. **glaçage** *nm* icing. **glace** *nf* ice; *(crème)* ice cream; mirror; *(vitre)* window; *(verre)* glass. **glacé** *adj* frozen, icy; *(boisson)* iced. **glacial** *adj* icy, frosty. **glacière** *nf* icebox. **glaçon** *nm* icicle; *(boisson)* ice cube.

glacier [ɡlasje] *nm* glacier. **glaciation** *nf* glaciation.

glaise [ɡlɛz] *nf* clay.

gland [ɡlɑ̃] *nm* acorn; *(ornement)* tassel.

glande [ɡlɑ̃d] *nf* gland. **glandulaire** *adj* glandular.

glaner [ɡlane] *v* glean.

glapir [ɡlapir] *v* yelp, squeal.

glisser [ɡlise] *v* slide, slip; *(voilier, patineur)* glide; *(véhicule)* skid. **se glisser** slip, creep. **glissade** *nf* slide, slip; skid. **glissant** *adj* slippery. **glissière** *nf* groove, channel. **à glissière** sliding. **glissoire** *nf* slide.

globe [ɡlɔb] *nm* globe. **globe oculaire** eyeball. **global** *adj* global, overall, total.

gloire [ɡlwar] *nf* glory; *(renommée)* fame; distinction, credit. **glorieux** *adj* glorious. **glorifier** [ɡlɔrifje] *v* glorify. **se glorifier de** glory in. **glorification** *nf* glorification.

glossaire [ɡlɔsɛr] *nm* glossary.

glouglouter [ɡluɡlute] *v* *(eau)* gurgle; *(dindon)* gobble. **glouglou** *nm* gurgling; gobbling.

glousser [ɡluse] *v* *(poule)* cluck; *(personne)* chuckle. **gloussement** *nm* cluck; chuckle.

glouton, -onne [ɡlutɔ̃, -ɔn] *adj* greedy. *nm, nf* glutton. **gloutonnerie** *nf* gluttony, greed.

gluant [ɡlyɑ̃] *adj* sticky.

glucose [ɡlykoz] *nm* glucose.

glycine [ɡlisin] *nf* wisteria.

gnome [ɡnom] *nm* gnome.

go [ɡo] *adv* *(fam)* **tout de go** straight; *(dire)* straight out.

gobelet [ɡɔblɛ] *nm* beaker; *(verre)* tumbler; *(papier)* cup.

gober [ɡɔbe] *v* swallow whole; *(mensonge)* swallow, believe. **se gober** fancy oneself.

godasse [ɡɔdas] *nf* *(fam)* shoe.

godet [ɡɔdɛ] *nm* pot, jar.

godiche [ɡɔdiʃ] *adj* awkward, oafish.

goéland [ɡɔelɑ̃] *nm* seagull.

goélette [ɡɔelɛt] *nf* schooner.

gogo [gɔgo] *adv* **à gogo** (*fam*) galore.
golf [gɔlf] *nm* golf; (*terrain*) golf course.
golfeur, -euse *nm, nf* golfer.
golfe [gɔlf] *nm* gulf, bay.
gommer [gɔme] *v* (*effacer*) erase, rub out; (*coller*) gum. **gomme** *nf* eraser, rubber; gum. **gommeux** *adj* sticky.
gond [gɔ̃] *nm* hinge.
gondole [gɔ̃dɔl] *nf* gondola. **gondolier, -ère** *nm, nf* gondolier.
gonfler [gɔ̃fle] *v* swell; (*d'air*) inflate. **gonflé** *adj* swollen; (*yeux*) puffy; (*ventre*) bloated. **gonflement** *nm* swelling; inflation.
gong [gɔ̃] *nm* gong.
gorge [gɔrʒ] *nf* (*gosier*) throat; (*poitrine*) breast; (*défilé*) gorge; (*rainure*) groove. **gorgée** *nf* mouthful. **petite gorgée** sip. **se gorger** *v* gorge.
gorille [gɔrij] *nm* gorilla.
gosier [gozje] *nm* throat.
gosse [gɔs] *n(m+f)* (*fam*) kid.
gothique [gɔtik] *nm* Gothic.
goudron [gudrɔ̃] *nm* tar. **goudronner** *v* tar.
gouffre [gufrə] *nm* abyss.
goulot [gulo] *nm* neck.
goulu [guly] *adj* greedy.
gourde [gurd] *nf* gourd; (*bidon*) flask; (*fam*) clot.
gourmand [gurmɑ̃] *adj* greedy. **gourmandise** *nf* greed.
gourmet [gurmɛ] *nm* gourmet.
gousse [gus] *nf* pod. **gousse d'ail** clove of garlic.
goût [gu] *nm* taste; (*penchant*) liking; style. **de bon/mauvais goût** in good/bad taste.
goûter [gute] *v* taste; savour, enjoy. **goûter à** taste, sample. *nm* afternoon tea.
goutte [gut] *nf* drop; (*méd*) gout. **goutte-à-goutte** *nm invar* (*méd*) drip. **tomber goutte à goutte** drip. **gouttière** *nf* gutter.
gouvernail [guvɛrnaj] *nm* rudder; (*barre*) helm.
gouverner [guvɛrne] *v* govern, rule; control; (*naut*) steer. **gouvernante** *nf* housekeeper; (*des enfants*) governess. **gouvernement** *nm* government. **gouverneur** *nm* governor.
grâce [grɑs] *nf* grace; favour; charm; pardon, mercy. **de bonne grâce** willingly. **grâce à** thanks to. **gracieux** *adj* graceful; amiable, kindly.
gracile [grasil] *adj* slender.

grade [grad] *nm* grade; (*échelon*) rank; (*titre*) degree.
gradin [gradɛ̃] *nm* terrace, step; (*théâtre*) tier.
graduer [gradɥe] *v* increase gradually; (*exercices*) grade; (*règle, etc.*) graduate. **graduel** *adj* gradual; progressive.
graffiti [grafiti] *nm pl* graffiti *pl*.
grain [grɛ̃] *nm* grain; (*café*) bean; (*collier*) bead. **grain de beauté** mole. **grain de poivre** peppercorn. **grain de raisin** grape.
graine [grɛn] *nf* seed.
graisser [grese] *v* grease. **graisse** *nf* fat, grease. **graisse de rognon** suet. **graisse de viande** dripping. **graisseux** *adj* greasy, fatty.
grammaire [gramɛr] *nf* grammar. **grammatical** *adj* grammatical.
gramme [gram] *nm* gram.
grand [grɑ̃], **-e** *adj* large, big; (*personne*) tall; (*intense, important*) great; (*principal*) main; (*réception, etc.*) grand. *nm, adj* senior *or* older pupil. **grandeur** *nf* greatness; (*dimension*) size.
grand-chose *n(m+f)* *invar* much.
Grande-Bretagne *nf* Great Britain.
grande ligne *nf* (*rail*) main line.
grandes vacances *nf pl* summer holidays *pl*.
grandiose [grɑ̃djoz] *adj* grand, imposing.
grandir [grɑ̃dir] *v* grow; (*augmenter*) increase; exaggerate; (*grossir*) magnify; (*hausser*) make taller.
grand magasin *nm* department store.
grand-mère *nf* grandmother.
grand ouvert *adj* wide open.
grand-parent *nm* grandparent.
grand-père *nm* grandfather.
grand-route *nf* main road.
grand-voile *nf* mainsail.
grange [grɑ̃ʒ] *nf* barn.
granit [granit] *nm* granite.
graphique [grafik] *adj* graphic. *nm* graph.
grappe [grap] *nf* cluster. **grappe de raisin** bunch of grapes.
gras, grasse [grɑ, grɑs] *adj* fat; (*graisseux*) greasy; (*épais*) thick; rich. **faire la grasse matinée** have a lie-in. *nm* fat. **grassouillet, -ette** *adj* (*fam*) plump, podgy.
gratifier [gratifje] *v* present, give, favour. **gratification** *nf* bonus.
gratin [gratɛ̃] *nm* **au gratin** topped with breadcrumbs or grated cheese.

gratitude [gratityd] *nf* gratitude.

gratter [grate] *v* scratch, scrape. **gratte-ciel** *nm invar* skyscraper.

gratuit [gratᵁi] *adj* free; (*injustifié*) gratuitous.

grave [grav] *adj* serious, grave; (*digne*) solemn; (*son*) deep, low. **gravité** *nf* gravity, seriousness.

graver [grave] *v* engrave; (*disque*) cut. **graver à l'eau-forte** etch. **graveur** *nm* engraver. **gravure** *nf* engraving; (*illustration*) plate; (*réproduction*) print.

gravier [gravje] *nm* gravel.

gravir [gravir] *v* climb.

gré [gre] *nm* (*volonté*) will; (*goût*) taste, liking.

Grèce [grɛs] *nf* Greece. **grec, grecque** *nm, adj* Greek. **Grec, Grecque** *nm, nf* Greek.

gréer [gree] *v* rig. **gréement** *nm* rigging.

greffer [grefe] *v* graft; (*organe*) transplant. **greffe** *nf* graft; transplant.

greffier [grefje] *nm* clerk of the court.

grégaire [gregɛr] *adj* gregarious.

grêle¹ [grɛl] *adj* spindly, lanky; (*son*) shrill.

grêle² [grɛl] *nf* hail. **grêler** *v* hail. **grêlon** *nm* hailstone.

grelotter [grɔlɔte] *v* shiver; (*tinter*) jingle.

grenade¹ [grɔnad] *nf* (*fruit*) pomegranate. **grenadier** *nm* pomegranate tree.

grenade² [grɔnad] *nf* grenade. **grenade à main** hand grenade. **grenadier** *nm* grenadier.

grenier [grɔnje] *nm* attic, loft.

grenouille [grɔnuj] *nf* frog.

grès [grɛ] *nm* sandstone.

grésiller [grezije] *v* sizzle; (*phone, radio*) crackle.

grève¹ [grɛv] *nf* (*rivière*) bank; (*mer*) shore.

grève² [grɛv] *nf* strike. **faire grève** be on strike. **grève de la faim** hunger strike. **grève du zèle** work-to-rule. **grève perlée** go-slow. **se mettre en grève** strike, go on strike. **gréviste** *n(m+f)* striker.

grever [grɔve] *v* burden, put a strain on.

gribouiller [gribuje] *v* scribble; (*dessiner*) doodle. **gribouillage** *nm* scribble; doodle.

grief [grijɛf] *nm* grievance. **grièvement blessé** seriously injured.

griffer [grife] *v* scratch. **griffe** *nf* claw; signature.

griffonner [grifɔne] *v* scribble. **griffonnage** *nm* scribble.

grignoter [griɲɔte] *v* nibble (at).

gril [gril] *nm* grill pan.

grille [grij] *nf* grid; (*claire-voie*) grille; (*prison*) bars *pl*; (*clôture*) gate; (*égout*) grating.

griller [grije] *v* grill; (*pain*) toast; (*brûler*) burn, scorch. **grille-pain** *nm invar* toaster. **grillade** *nm* grill.

grillon [grijɔ̃] *nm* cricket.

grimacer [grimase] *v* grimace, pull a face; (*sourire*) grin. **grimace** *nf* grimace.

grimer [grime] *v* (*théâtre*) make up. **grimage** *nm* make-up.

grimper [grɛ̃pe] *v* climb (up).

grincer [grɛ̃se] *v* (*métal*) grate; (*bois*) creak. **grincer des dents** gnash one's teeth.

grincheux [grɛ̃ʃø] *adj* grumpy.

grippe [grip] *nf* flu, influenza. **prendre en grippe** take a sudden dislike to.

gris [gri] *adj* grey; (*morne*) dull; (*ivre*) drunk. *nm* grey. **griser** *v* intoxicate. **se griser** get drunk. **grisonner** *v* go grey.

grive [griv] *nf* thrush.

grivois [grivwa] *adj* saucy.

Groënland [grɔɛnlɑ̃d] *nm* Greenland. **Groënlandais, -e** *nm, nf* Greenlander.

grogner [grɔɲe] *v* (*chien*) growl; (*cochon*) grunt; (*grommeler*) grumble. **grognement** *nm* growl, grunt.

groin [grwɛ̃] *nm* snout.

grommeler [grɔmle] *v* mutter, grumble.

gronder [grɔ̃de] *v* (*enfant*) scold; (*train, orage*) rumble; (*chien*) growl.

gros, grosse [gro, gros] *adj* big, large; (*personne*) fat; (*épais*) thick, heavy; (*important*) great; (*rude*) coarse. **gros lot** *nm* jackpot. **gros plan** *nm* close-up. **gros titre** *nm* headline. *nm* fat man; (*principal*) main part, bulk; (*comm*) wholesale. **en gros** wholesale; broadly, roughly. **grosse** *nf* fat woman; (*comm*) gross.

groseille [grozɛj] *nf* (*rouge*) red currant; (*blanche*) white currant. **groseille à maquereau** gooseberry. **groseillier** *nm* currant bush.

grossier [grosje] *adj* coarse, rough, crude. **grossièreté** *nf* coarseness, crudeness.

grossir [grosir] *v* swell, grow; (*personne*) put on weight; (*augmenter*) increase; exaggerate; (*agrandir*) enlarge, magnify.

grotesque [grɔtɛsk] *adj* grotesque; (*risible*) ludicrous. *nm* grotesque.

grotte [grɔt] *nf* cave; (*artificielle*) grotto.

grouiller [gruje] v mill about. **grouiller de** be swarming or crawling with.

grouper [grupe] v group, put together. **groupe** nm group.

grue [gry] nf crane.

grumeau [grymo] nm lump.

se grumeler [grymle] v go lumpy; (lait) curdle. **grumeleux** adj lumpy.

gué [ge] nm ford. **passer à gué** ford.

guenille [gənij] nf rag.

guépard [gepar] nm cheetah.

guêpe [gɛp] nf wasp. **guêpier** nm wasp's nest; (piège) trap.

guère [gɛr] adv hardly, scarcely; not much.

guérilla [gerija] nf guerrilla warfare. **guérillero** nm guerilla.

guérir [gerir] v (maladie) cure; (blessure) heal; (malade) get better. **guérison** nf recovery.

Guernesey [gɛrnəzɛ] nf Guernsey.

guerre [gɛr] nf war; (stratégie) warfare. **en guerre** at war. **guerre mondiale** world war. **guerrier, -ère** nm, nf warrior.

guerroyer [gɛrwaje] v wage war.

guet [gɛ] nm watch. **faire le guet** be on the look-out. **guet-apens** nm ambush, trap.

guetter [gete] v watch (for); (menace) lie in wait for.

gueuler [gœle] v (argot) bawl, yell. **gueule** nf mouth; (fam: figure) face. **gueule de bois** (fam) hangover. **gueule-de-loup** nf snapdragon.

gueux [gø], **gueuse** nm, nf beggar.

gui [gi] nm mistletoe.

guichet [giʃɛ] nm window, counter; (théâtre) box office; (gare) ticket office; (porte) hatch, grille.

guide [gid] nm guide; (livre) guidebook. nf rein; (jeune fille) girl guide. **guider** v guide.

guidon [gidɔ̃] nm handlebars pl.

guigne [giɲ] nf (fam) bad luck.

guillemets [gijmɛ] nm pl inverted commas pl, quotation marks pl. **entre guillemets** in inverted commas.

guilleret, -ette [gijrɛ, -ɛt] adj perky, lively; (propos) saucy.

guillotine [gijɔtin] nf guillotine. **guillotiner** v guillotine.

guimauve [gimov] nf marshmallow.

guindé [gɛ̃de] v (air) stiff; (style) stilted.

Guinée [gine] nf Guinea.

guingois [gɛ̃gwa] adv **de guingois** (fam) askew, lop-sided.

guirlande [girlɑ̃d] nf garland. **guirlande de Noël** tinsel. **guirlande électrique** or **lumineuse** fairy lights pl.

guise [giz] nf **à sa guise** as one pleases. **en guise de** by way of.

guitare [gitar] nf guitar. **guitariste** n(m + f) guitarist.

gymnase [ʒimnaz] nm gymnasium. **gymnaste** n(m + f) gymnast. **gymnastique** nf (sport) gymnastics; exercises pl.

gynécologie [ʒinekɔlɔʒi] nf gynaecology. **gynécologique** adj gynaecological. **gynécologue** n(m + f) gynaecologist.

gypse [ʒips] nm gypsum.

gyroscope [ʒirɔskɔp] nm gyroscope.

H

habile [abil] adj skilful, clever; (malin) cunning. **habileté** nf skill, cleverness.

habiller [abije] v dress, clothe; cover. **s'habiller** get dressed. **s'habiller en** dress up as. **habillement** nm clothing; outfit.

habit [abi] nm (costume) dress, outfit; (soirée) formal dress; (rel) habit. **habits** nm pl clothes pl.

habiter [abite] v live (in). **habitable** adj habitable. **habitant, -e** nm, nf inhabitant; (maison) occupant. **habitat** nm habitat. **habitation** nf residence, home; (logement) housing.

habitude [abityd] nf habit; custom. **avoir l'habitude de** be used to. **comme d'habitude** as usual. **d'habitude** usually.

habituer [abitɥe] v accustom. **s'habituer à** get used to. **habitué** nm regular. **habituel** adj usual, habitual.

hâbleur, -euse ['ablœr, -øz] adj boastful. nm, nf braggart. **hablerie** nf bragging, boasting.

hacher ['aʃe] v chop; (menu) mince. **hache** nf axe. **haché** adj minced; (phrases) jerky. **hachette** nf hatchet. **hachis** nm mince. **hachis Parmentier** cottage pie. **hachoir** nm chopper; mincer.

hagard ['agar] adj wild, distraught.

haie ['ɛ] nf hedge; (sport) hurdle, fence; (rangée) line.

haillon [ˈɑjɔ̃] *nm* rag.

haine [ɛn] *nf* hatred.

*****haïr** [ˈair] *v* detest, hate.

Haïti [aiti] *nf* Haiti.

halage [ˈalaʒ] *nm* towing. **chemin de halage** *nm* towpath.

hâle [ˈɑl] *nm* sunburn, tan. **hâlé** *adj* sunburnt, tanned.

haleine [alɛn] *nf* breath. **hors d'haleine** out of breath. **reprendre haleine** get one's breath back.

haler [ˈale] *v* tow; *(ancre)* haul in.

haleter [ˈalte] *v* pant, gasp for breath. **haletant** *adj* panting, breathless.

hall [ˈol] *nm* hall.

halle [ˈal] *nf* covered market.

hallucination [alysinasjɔ̃] *nf* hallucination.

halte [ˈalt] *nf* stop, pause; *(rail)* halt. **faire halte** stop, halt. *interj* stop! halt!

haltérophilie [alterɔfili] *nf* weight-lifting.

hamac [ˈamak] *nm* hammock.

hameau [ˈamo] *nm* hamlet.

hameçon [amsɔ̃] *nm* hook.

hampe [ˈɑ̃p] *nf* pole, shaft.

hamster [ˈamstɛr] *nm* hamster.

hanche [ˈɑ̃ʃ] *nf* hip; *(cheval)* haunch.

handicaper [ˈɑ̃dikape] *v* handicap. **handicap** *nm* handicap. **handicapé, -e** *nm*, *nf* handicapped person. **handicapé moteur** spastic.

hangar [ˈɑ̃gar] *nm* shed; *(aéro)* hangar.

hanter [ˈɑ̃te] *v* haunt. **hantise** *nf* obsession.

happer [ˈape] *v* snatch, grab.

haras [ˈara] *nm* stud farm.

harassé [ˈarase] *adj* exhausted.

harceler [ˈarsəle] *v* harass, pester.

harde [ˈard] *nf* herd.

hardes [ˈard] *nf pl* old clothes *pl*.

hardi [ˈardi] *adj* bold, daring. **hardiesse** *nf* boldness; effrontery, audacity.

hareng [ˈarɑ̃] *nm* herring. **hareng fumé** kipper.

hargneux [ˈarɲø] *adj* aggressive.

haricot [ˈariko] *nm* bean. **haricot à rames** runner bean. **haricot beurre/blanc/rouge/vert** butter/haricot/kidney/French bean.

harmonica [armɔnika] *nm* harmonica.

harmonie [armɔni] *nf* harmony. **harmonieux** *adj* harmonious. **harmonique** *nm*, *adj* harmonic. **harmoniser** *v* harmonize.

harnacher [ˈarnaʃe] *v* harness.

harnais [ˈarnɛ] *nm* harness.

harpe [ˈarp] *nf* harp. **harpiste** *n(m+f)* harpist.

harpon [ˈarpɔ̃] *nm* harpoon.

hasard [ˈazar] *nm* chance, luck; risk, hazard; coincidence. **au hasard** at random. **par hasard** by accident. **hasarder** *v* risk. **hasardeux** *adj* risky, dangerous.

haschich [ˈaʃiʃ] *nm* hashish.

hâter [ˈate] *v* hasten, hurry. **hâte** *nf* haste, hurry; impatience. **à la hâte** hurriedly. **hâtif** *adj* hasty, hurried; precocious, early.

hausser [ˈose] *v* raise. **hausser les épaules** shrug one's shoulders. **hausse** *nf* rise, increase.

haut [ˈo] *adj* high; *(arbre, édifice)* tall; noble. *adv* high; *(fort)* loudly. *nm* top. **à haute voix** aloud. **de haut en bas** downwards; *(regarder)* up and down. **en haut** at the top; *(dessus)* above; *(maison)* upstairs. **haut-de-forme** *nm* top hat. **haut fourneau** blast furnace. **haut-parleur** *nm* loudspeaker.

hautain [ˈotɛ̃] *adj* haughty.

hautbois [ˈobwa] *nm* oboe. **hauboïste** *n(m+f)* oboist.

hauteur [ˈotœr] *nf* height; *(son)* pitch; nobility; *(arrogance)* haughtiness. **à la hauteur de** level with; equal to.

hâve [ˈav] *adj* haggard, gaunt.

havre [ˈavrə] *nm* haven.

havresac [ˈavrəsak] *nm* haversack.

Haye [ˈɛ] *nf* **La Haye** the Hague.

hebdomadaire [ɛbdɔmadɛr] *nm*, *adj* weekly.

héberger [eberʒe] *v* lodge, take in.

hébéter [ebete] *v* daze, numb. **hébétement** *nm* stupor.

hébraïque [ebraik] *adj* Hebrew.

hébreu [ebrø] *nm*, *adj* Hebrew. **Hebreu** *nm* Hebrew.

hectare [ɛktar] *nm* hectare.

hein [ˈɛ̃] *interj (fam)* eh?

hélas [ˈelas] *interj* alas!

héler [ˈele] *v* hail.

hélice [elis] *nf* propeller.

hélicoptère [elikɔptɛr] *nm* helicopter.

hémisphère [emisfɛr] *nm* hemisphere.

hémorragie [emɔraʒi] *nf* haemorrhage.

hémorroïdes [emɔrɔid] *nf pl* haemorrhoids *pl*.

henné [ˈene] *nm* henna.

hennir ['enir] *v* neigh. **hennissement** *nm* neigh.

héraldique [eraldik] *adj* heraldic. *nf* heraldry.

héraut ['ero] *nm* herald.

herbe [ɛrb] *nf* grass; (*cuisine*) herb. **en herbe** (*plante*) unripe; (*personne*) budding. **herbeux** *or* **herbu** *adj* grassy. **herbicide** *nm* weed-killer.

hérédité [eredite] *nf* heredity. **héréditaire** *adj* hereditary.

hérésie [erezi] *nf* heresy.

hérétique [eretik] *adj* heretical. *n(m + f)* heretic.

hérisser ['erise] *v* bristle, spike; (*personne*) ruffle. **se hérisser** stand on end, bristle up. **hérissé** *adj* bristly, prickly.

hérisson ['erisɔ̃] *nm* hedgehog.

hériter [erite] *v* inherit. **héritage** *nm* inheritance; (*civilisation*) heritage. **héritier** *nm* heir. **héritière** *nf* heiress.

hermétique [ɛrmetik] *adj* sealed; (*étanche*) watertight; (*à l'air*) airtight; impenetrable.

hermine [ɛrmin] *nf* ermine; (*animal*) stoat.

hernie ['ɛrni] *nf* hernia. **hernie discale** slipped disc.

héroïne[1] [erɔin] *nf* (*femme*) heroine.

héroïne[2] [erɔin] *nf* (*drogue*) heroin.

héroïsme [erɔismə] *nm* heroism. **héroïque** *adj* heroic.

héron ['erɔ̃] *nm* heron.

héros ['ero] *nm* hero.

hésiter [ezite] *v* hesitate. **hésitant** *adj* hesitant. **hésitation** *nf* hesitation.

hétéroclite [eterɔklit] *adj* sundry, assorted; (*personne*) eccentric.

hétérosexual [eterɔsɛksɥɛl] *adj* heterosexual.

hêtre ['ɛtrə] *nm* beech.

heure [œr] *nf* time; (*mesure*) hour. **à l'heure** on time. **deux/trois etc. heures** two/three etc. o'clock. **heure d'affluence** rush hour. **heures creuses** off-peak periods *pl.* **heures supplémentaires** overtime *sing.* **tout à l'heure** (*passé*) just now; (*futur*) shortly.

heureux [œrø] *adj* happy; fortunate, lucky.

heurter ['œrte] *v* strike, hit; (*sentiments, idées*) conflict with, go against. **se heurter** collide; (*s'opposer*) clash. **heurt** *nm* collision; clash. **sans heurts** smoothly. **heurtoir** *nm* door-knocker.

hexagone [ɛgzagɔn] *nm* hexagon. **hexagonal** *adj* hexagonal.

hiberner [ibɛrne] *v* hibernate. **hibernation** *nf* hibernation.

hibou ['ibu] *nm, pl* -oux *nm* owl.

hideux ['idø] *adj* hideous.

hier [jɛr] *adv* yesterday. **hier soir** yesterday evening, last night.

hiérarchie ['jerarʃi] *nf* hierarchy. **hiérarchique** *adj* hierarchical.

hilare [ilar] *adj* merry, mirthful. **hilarité** *nf* hilarity.

hindou [ɛ̃du] *adj* Hindu. **Hindou, -e** *nm, nf* Hindu. **hindouisme** *nm* Hinduism.

hippique [ipik] *adj* horse, equestrian. **concours hippique** *nm* show-jumping. **hippisme** *nm* (*courses*) horse-racing; (*équitation*) horse-riding.

hippocampe [ipɔkãp] *nm* sea-horse.

hippodrome [ipɔdrom] *nm* racecourse.

hippopotame [ipɔpɔtam] *nm* hippopotamus.

hirondelle [irɔ̃dɛl] *nf* swallow.

hisser ['ise] *v* hoist. **se hisser** heave *or* haul oneself up.

histoire [istwar] *nf* history; (*conte*) story; (*fam: affaire*) business. **histoires** *nf pl* (*fam*) fuss *sing*, trouble *sing*. **historien, -enne** *nm, nf* historian. **historique** *adj* historical; (*événement*) historic.

hiver [ivɛr] *nm* winter. **hivernal** *adj* winter; (*temps*) wintry.

hocher ['ɔʃe] *v* **hocher la tête** (*oui*) nod; (*non*) shake one's head. **hochement de tête** *nm* nod; shake of the head.

hochet ['ɔʃɛ] *nm* rattle.

hockey ['ɔkɛ] *nm* hockey.

Hollande ['ɔlãd] *nf* Holland. **hollandais** *nm, adj* Dutch. **les Hollandais** the Dutch.

homard ['ɔmar] *nm* lobster.

homicide [ɔmisid] *nm* murder. **homicide involontaire** manslaughter.

hommage [ɔmaʒ] *nm* homage, tribute; (*témoignage*) token. **hommages** *nm pl* respects *pl.*

homme [ɔm] *nm* man (*pl* men); (*espèce*) mankind. **homme à tout faire** odd-job man. **homme d'affaires** businessman. **homme de loi** lawyer. **homme d'État** statesman. **homme-grenouille** *nm* frogman. **homme politique** politician.

homogène [ɔmɔʒɛn] *adj* homogeneous.

homonyme [ɔmɔnim] *nm* homonym; (*personne*) namesake.

homosexuel [ɔmɔsɛksɥɛl], **-elle** *n*, *adj* homosexual. **homosexualité** *nf* homosexuality.

Hongrie ['ɔ̃gri] *nf* Hungary. **hongrois** *nm*, *adj* Hungarian. **Hongrois, -e** *nm*, *nf* Hungarian.

honnête [ɔnɛt] *adj* honest; decent; (*juste*) fair, reasonable. **honnêteté** *nf* honesty; decency; fairness.

honneur [ɔnœr] *nm* honour; (*mérite*) credit.

honorer [ɔnɔre] *v* honour; do credit to; respect. **honorable** *adj* honourable, worthy. **honoraire** *adj* honorary.

honte ['ɔ̃t] *nf* shame; (*déshonneur*) disgrace. **avoir honte** be ashamed. **faire honte à** put to shame. **honteux** *adj* (*penaud*) ashamed; (*scandaleux*) shameful, disgraceful.

hôpital [ɔpital] *nm* hospital.

hoquet ['ɔkɛ] *nm* hiccup. **avoir le hoquet** have hiccups. **hoqueter** *v* hiccup.

horaire [ɔrɛr] *adj* hourly. *nm* timetable.

horde ['ɔrd] *nf* horde.

horizon [ɔrizɔ̃] *nm* horizon; (*paysage*) landscape, view.

horizontal [ɔrizɔ̃tal] *adj* horizontal. **horizontale** *nf* horizontal.

horloge [ɔrlɔʒ] *nf* clock.

hormis ['ɔrmi] *prep* but, save.

hormone [ɔrmɔn] *nf* hormone.

horoscope [ɔrɔskɔp] *nm* horoscope.

horreur [ɔrœr] *nf* horror. **avoir horreur de** loathe, detest. **faire horreur à** disgust.

horrible [ɔriblə] *adj* horrible, dreadful. **horrifier** [ɔrifje] *v* horrify.

hors ['ɔr] *prep* except, apart from. **hors-bord** *nm invar* speedboat. **hors de** out of; (*dehors*) outside; (*loin de*) away from. **être hors de soi** be beside oneself. **hors d'œuvre** *nm invar* hors d'oeuvre, starter. **hors-jeu** *nm*, *adj invar* offside. **hors-la-loi** *nm invar* outlaw. **hors-taxe** *adv*, *adj invar* duty-free.

horticulture [ɔrtikyltyr] *nf* horticulture. **horticole** *adj* horticultural.

hospice [ɔspis] *nm* home.

hospitalier [ɔspitalje] *adj* (*service*) hospital; (*accueillant*) hospitable. **hospitalité** *nf* hospitality.

hostile [ɔstil] *adj* hostile.

hôte [ot] *nm* host. *n(m+f)* (*invité*) guest. **hôtesse** *nf* hostess. **hôtesse de l'air** air hostess.

hôtel [otɛl] *nm* hotel; (*particulier*) mansion. **hôtel de ville** town hall. **hôtel-Dieu** *nm* general hospital. **hôtelier, -ère** *nm*, *nf* hotelier.

houblon ['ublɔ̃] *nm* hop.

houe ['u] *nf* hoe.

houille ['uj] *nf* coal. **houille blanche** hydro-electric power. **houillère** *nf* coalmine.

houle ['ul] *nf* swell. **houleux** *adj* turbulent, stormy.

houppe ['up] *nf* tuft, tassel. **houppette** *nf* powder puff.

houspiller ['uspije] *v* scold, tell off.

housse ['us] *nf* cover.

houx ['u] *nm* holly.

hublot ['yblo] *nm* porthole.

huer ['ɥe] *v* boo; (*chouette*) hoot. **huées** *nf pl* boos *pl*.

huile ['ɥil] *nf* oil. **huile de coude** (*fam*) elbow grease. **huile de ricin** castor oil. **huile solaire** suntan oil. **huiler** *v* oil. **huileux** *adj* oily.

huis ['ɥi] *nm* **à huis clos** in camera.

huissier ['ɥisje] *nm* usher; (*jur*) bailiff.

huit ['ɥit] *nm*, *adj* eight. **huit jours** a week. ... **en huit** a week on ... . **huitaine** *nf* about eight; about a week. **huitième** *n(m+f)*, *adj* eighth.

huître ['ɥitrə] *nf* oyster.

humain [ymɛ̃] *adj* human; (*compatissant*) humane. *nm* human. **humanitaire** *adj* humanitarian. **humanité** *nf* humanity.

humble [œ̃blə] *adj* humble.

humecter [ymɛkte] *v* dampen, moisten.

humer ['yme] *v* smell; (*air*) inhale.

humeur [ymœr] *nf* mood, humour; temperament, temper; (*colère*) bad temper. **d'humeur égale** even-tempered.

humide [ymid] *adj* damp, moist; (*climat*) humid. **humidité** *nf* humidity; dampness, damp.

humilier [ymilje] *v* humiliate. **humiliation** *nf* humiliation. **humilité** *nf* humility, humbleness.

humour [ymur] *nm* humour; sense of humour. **humoriste** *n(m+f)* humorist. **humoristique** *adj* humorous.

huppe ['yp] *nf* crest.

hurler ['yrle] *v* yell, roar; (*chien*) howl. **hurlement** *nm* yell, roar; howl.

hussard ['ysar] *nm* hussar.

hutte ['yt] *nf* hut.

hybride [ibrid] *nm*, *adj* hybrid.

hydrate [idrat] *nm* **hydrate de carbone** carbohydrate.
hydraulique [idrolik] *adj* hydraulic.
hydro-électrique [idroelɛktrik] *adj* hydroelectric.
hydrofoil [idrofɔjl] *nm* hydrofoil.
hydrogène [idrɔʒɛn] *nm* hydrogen.
hydromel [idrɔmɛl] *nm* mead.
hydrophile [idrɔfil] *adj* absorbent.
hyène [jɛn] *nf* hyena.
hygiène [iʒjɛn] *nf* hygiene. **hygiénique** *adj* hygienic.
hymne [imnə] *nm* hymn. **hymne national** national anthem.
hypermétropie [ipɛrmetrɔpi] *nf* longsightedness. **hypermétrope** *adj* longsighted.
hypertension [ipɛrtɑ̃sjɔ̃] *nf* high blood pressure.
hypnose [ipnoz] *nf* hypnosis. **hypnotique** *adj* hypnotic. **hypnotiser** *v* hypnotize. **hypnotiseur** *nm* hypnotist. **hypnotisme** *nm* hypnotism.
hypocondrie [ipɔkɔ̃dri] *nf* hypochondria. **hypocondriaque** *n(m+f)*, *adj* hypochondriac.
hypocrite [ipɔkrit] *adj* hypocritical. *n(m+f)* hypocrite. **hypocrisie** *nf* hypocrisy.
hypodermique [ipɔdɛrmik] *adj* hypodermic.
hypotension [ipɔtɑ̃sjɔ̃] *nf* low blood pressure.
hypothéquer [ipɔteke] *v* mortgage. **hypothèque** *nf* mortgage.
hypothèse [ipɔtɛz] *nf* hypothesis. **hypothétique** *adj* hypothetical.
hystérectomie [iskerɛktɔmi] *nf* hysterectomy.
hystérie [isteri] *nf* hysteria. **hystérique** *adj* hysterical.

I

iceberg [ajsbɛrg] *nm* iceberg.
ici [isi] *adv* (*lieu*) here; (*temps*) now. **d'ici là** before then. **d'ici peu** before long. **par ici** this way.
icône [ikon] *nf* icon.
idéal [ideal] *nm*, *adj* ideal.

idéaliste [idealist] *adj* idealistic. *n(m+f)* idealist.
idée [ide] *nf* idea; (*esprit*) mind. **idée fixe** obsession. **idée lumineuse** brainwave.
identifier [idɑ̃tifje] *v* identify. **identification** *nf* identification.
identique [idɑ̃tik] *adj* identical. **identité** *nf* identity.
idéologie [ideɔlɔʒi] *nf* ideology.
idiome [idjom] *nm* idiom. **idiomatique** *adj* idiomatic.
idiosyncrasie [idjɔsɛ̃krazi] *nf* idiosyncrasy.
idiot [idjo], **-e** *adj* idiotic. *nm*, *nf* idiot. **idiotie** *nf* idiocy, stupidity; (*action, propos*) idiotic *or* stupid thing.
idiotisme [idjɔtismə] *nm* idiom.
idolâtrer [idɔlatre] *v* idolize. **idolâtrie** *nf* idolatry.
idole [idɔl] *nf* idol.
idyllique [idilik] *adj* idyllic.
if [if] *nm* yew.
igloo [iglu] *nm* igloo.
ignifuger [ignifyʒe] *v* fireproof. **ignifuge** *adj* fireproof.
ignorer [iɲɔre] *v* not know, be unaware of. **ignorance** *nf* ignorance. **ignorant** *adj* ignorant. **ignorant de** unaware of. **ignoré** *adj* unknown.
il [il] *pron* it; (*personne*) he. **il y a** (*sing*) there is; (*pl*) there are.
île [il] *nf* island. **les îles anglo-normandes** the Channel Islands.
illégal [ilegal] *adj* illegal. **illégalité** *nf* illegality.
illégitime [ileʒitim] *adj* illegitimate. **illégitimité** *nf* illegitimacy.
illettré [iletre], **-e** *n*, *adj* illiterate.
illicite [ilisit] *adj* illicit.
illimité [ilimite] *adj* unlimited, boundless.
illisible [iliziblə] *adj* (*écriture*) illegible; (*livre*) unreadable.
illogique [ilɔʒik] *adj* illogical.
illuminer [ilymine] *v* light up, illuminate. **illumination** *nf* illumination, lighting.
illusion [ilyzjɔ̃] *nf* illusion. **illusion d'optique** optical illusion.
illustre [ilystrə] *adj* illustrious.
illustrer [ilystre] *v* illustrate. **illustrateur**, **-trice** *nm*, *nf* illustrator. **illustration** *nf* illustration.
ils [il] *pron* they.
image [imaʒ] *nf* image; (*dessin*) picture; reflection.

imaginer [imaʒine] v imagine; *(inventer)* think up. **s'imaginer** imagine; *(croire)* think. **imaginatif** adj imaginative. **imagination** nf imagination.

imbécile [ɛ̃besil] adj stupid. n(m+f) imbecile.

imbiber [ɛ̃bibe] v saturate, impregnate, soak. **s'imbiber** absorb.

imbu [ɛ̃by] adj **imbu de** full of, steeped in.

imiter [imite] v imitate; copy; *(signature)* forge; *(ressembler)* look like; *(célébrité)* impersonate. **imitation** nf imitation; forgery; impersonation.

immaculé [imakyle] adj immaculate, spotless.

immanquable [ɛ̃mɑ̃kablə] adj inevitable; infallible.

immatriculer [imatrikyle] v register. **immatriculation** nf registration.

immédiat [imedja] adj immediate.

immense [imɑ̃s] adj vast, immense; *(espace)* boundless.

immerger [imɛrʒe] v immerse, submerge. **immersion** nf immersion, submersion.

immeuble [imœblə] nm building; *(appartements)* block of flats; *(bureaux)* office block.

immigrer [imigre] v immigrate. **immigrant, -e** nm, nf immigrant. **immigration** nf immigration.

imminent [iminɑ̃] adj imminent, impending.

immiscer [imise] v **s'immiscer dans** interfere with.

immobile [imɔbil] adj immobile, motionless, still. **immobilier** adj property. **immobiliser** v immobilize. **s'immobiliser** come to a standstill.

immonde [imɔ̃d] adj vile, foul; *(rel)* unclean. **immondices** nf pl refuse sing.

immoral [imɔral] adj immoral. **immoralité** nf immorality.

immortel [imɔrtɛl] adj immortal. **immortaliser** v immortalize. **immortalité** nf immortality.

immuniser [imynize] v immunize. **immunisation** nf immunization. **immunisé** adj immune. **immunité** nf immunity.

impact [ɛ̃pakt] nm impact.

impair [ɛ̃pɛr] adj odd, uneven. nm blunder.

imparfait [ɛ̃parfɛ] nm, adj imperfect.

impartial [ɛ̃parsjal] adj impartial, unbiased. **impartialité** nf impartiality.

impasse [ɛ̃pɑs] nf dead end, no through road; *(situation)* impasse, deadlock.

impassible [ɛ̃pasiblə] adj impassive.

impatience [ɛ̃pasjɑ̃s] nf impatience. **impatient** adj impatient; *(avide)* eager.

impatienter [ɛ̃pasjɑ̃te] v irritate. **s'impatienter** lose one's patience.

impeccable [ɛ̃pekablə] adj perfect, impeccable.

imper [ɛ̃pɛr] nm *(fam)* mac.

impératif [ɛ̃peratif] nm, adj imperative.

impératrice [ɛ̃peratris] nf empress.

impérial [ɛ̃perjal] adj imperial. **impériale** nf *(autobus)* top deck. **autobus à impériale** double-decker.

imperméable [ɛ̃pɛrmeablə] adj waterproof; *(roches)* impervious. nm raincoat. **imperméabiliser** v waterproof.

impersonnel [ɛ̃pɛrsɔnɛl] adj impersonal.

impertinent [ɛ̃pɛrtinɑ̃] adj impertinent. **impertinence** nf impertinence.

impétueux [ɛ̃petɥø] adj impetuous.

impitoyable [ɛ̃pitwajablə] adj merciless, ruthless.

implicite [ɛ̃plisit] adj implicit.

impliquer [ɛ̃plike] v imply; *(mêler)* involve.

implorer [ɛ̃plɔre] v implore.

impoli [ɛ̃pɔli] adj impolite.

impopulaire [ɛ̃pɔpylɛr] adj unpopular. **impopularité** nf unpopularity.

importer¹ [ɛ̃pɔrte] v *(comm)* import. **importation** nf import.

*importer² [ɛ̃pɔrte] v matter. **n'importe** never mind, it doesn't matter. **n'importe comment/où/quand/quel/qui/quoi** anyhow/anywhere/anytime/any/anybody/ anything. **importance** nf importance; *(grandeur)* size, extent. **important** adj important; considerable.

importuner [ɛ̃pɔrtyne] v bother, trouble.

imposer [ɛ̃poze] v impose; *(prescrire)* set; tax. **imposable** adj taxable. **imposant** adj imposing, impressive.

impossible [ɛ̃pɔsiblə] adj impossible.

imposteur [ɛ̃pɔstœr] nm impostor.

impôt [ɛ̃po] nm tax; taxation.

impotent [ɛ̃pɔtɑ̃], -e adj disabled, crippled. nm, nf disabled person. **impotence** nf disability.

imprécis [ɛ̃presi] adj imprecise.

imprégner [ɛ̃preɲe] v impregnate; *(air)* pervade. **s'imprégner de** absorb, soak up.

impression [ɛ̃presjɔ̃] *nf* impression; (*imprimerie*) printing. **impressionable** *adj* impressionable. **impressionnant** *adj* impressive. **impressionner** *v* impress; (*bouleverser*) upset.

imprévu [ɛ̃prevy] *adj* unexpected, unforeseen.

imprimer [ɛ̃prime] *v* print; (*cachet*) stamp; (*marquer*) imprint; publish. **imprimé** *nm* (*poste*) printed matter; (*tissu*) print. **imprimerie** *nf* printing; printing house *or* works. **imprimeur** *nm* printer.

improbable [ɛ̃prɔbablə] *adj* improbable, unlikely.

impromptu [ɛ̃prɔ̃pty] *adj, adv* impromptu.

improviser [ɛ̃prɔvize] *v* improvise. **improvisation** *nf* improvisation.

improviste [ɛ̃prɔvist] *nm* **à l'improviste** without warning, unexpectedly.

imprudent [ɛ̃prydɑ̃] *adj* unwise, foolish, careless. **imprudence** *nf* foolishness, carelessness.

impudent [ɛ̃pydɑ̃] *adj* impudent. **impudence** *nf* impudence.

impuissant [ɛ̃pɥisɑ̃] *adj* powerless; (*effort*) ineffectual; (*sexuellement*) impotent. **impuissance** *nf* impotence.

impulsion [ɛ̃pylsjɔ̃] *nf* impulse; impetus. **impulsif** *adj* impulsive.

impur [ɛ̃pyr] *adj* impure. **impureté** *nf* impurity.

imputer [ɛ̃pyte] *v* impute, attribute; (*frais*) charge.

inaccessible [inaksesiblə] *adj* inaccessible.

inactif [inaktif] *adj* inactive, idle.

inadapté [inadapte], **-e** *nm, nf* misfit. *adj* (*psychol*) maladjusted.

inadvertance [inadvɛrtɑ̃s] *nf* oversight. **par inadvertance** inadvertently.

inanimé [inanime] *adj* inanimate; (*personne*) unconscious.

inaperçu [inapɛrsy] *adj* unnoticed. **passer inaperçu** go unnoticed.

inappréciable [inapresjablə] *adj* invaluable; imperceptible.

inapte [inapt] *adj* incapable, unfit.

inarticulé [inartikyle] *adj* inarticulate.

inattendu [inatɑ̃dy] *adj* unexpected.

inaudible [inodiblə] *adj* inaudible.

inaugurer [inɔgyre] *v* inaugurate; (*plaque*) unveil; (*exposition*) open. **inaugural** *adj* inaugural; (*voyage*) maiden. **inauguration** *nf* inauguration; unveiling; opening. .

incapable [ɛ̃kapablə] *adj* incapable, unable.

incapacité [ɛ̃kapasite] *nf* incapacity; incompetence; inability; (*invalidité*) disability.

incendier [ɛ̃sɑ̃dje] *v* set fire to, burn. **incendiaire** *adj* incendiary. **incendie** *nm* fire. **incendie volontaire** arson.

incertain [ɛ̃sɛrtɛ̃] *adj* uncertain. **incertitude** *nf* uncertainty.

incessant [ɛ̃sɛsɑ̃] *adj* incessant. **incessamment** *adv* very soon.

inceste [ɛ̃sɛst] *nm* incest. **incestueux** *adj* incestuous.

incident [ɛ̃sidɑ̃] *adj* incidental. *nm* incident; (*anicroche*) setback, hitch. **incidemment** *adv* incidentally.

incinérer [ɛ̃sinere] *v* (*ordures*) incinerate; (*cadavre*) cremate. **incinérateur** *nm* incinerator. **incinération** *nf* incineration; cremation.

inciter [ɛ̃site] *v* incite, encourage.

incliner [ɛ̃kline] *v* slope, tilt; tend, be inclined. **s'incliner** bow. **inclinaison** *nm* slope, incline. **inclination** *nf* inclination.

***inclure** [ɛ̃klyr] *v* include; (*joindre*) enclose; insert. **inclus** *adj* enclosed; included, inclusive. **inclusion** *nf* inclusion; insertion. **inclusivement** *adv* inclusively.

incognito [ɛ̃kɔnito] *adv* incognito.

incohérent [ɛ̃kɔerɑ̃] *adj* incoherent.

incolore [ɛ̃kɔlɔr] *adj* colourless.

incommoder [ɛ̃kɔmɔde] *v* disturb, bother. **incommode** *adj* inconvenient, awkward; (*siège*) uncomfortable. **incommodité** *nf* inconvenience.

incompatible [ɛ̃kɔ̃patiblə] *adj* incompatible. **incompatibilité** *nf* incompatibility.

incompétent [ɛ̃kɔ̃petɑ̃] *adj* incompetent. **incompétence** *nf* incompetence; (*ignorance*) lack of knowledge.

incomplet, -ète [ɛ̃kɔ̃plɛ, -ɛt] *adj* incomplete.

inconcevable [ɛ̃kɔ̃svablə] *adj* inconceivable.

inconfort [ɛ̃kɔ̃fɔr] *nm* discomfort. **inconfortable** *adj* uncomfortable.

inconnu [ɛ̃kɔny], **-e** *adj* unknown; strange. *nm, nf* stranger. **l'inconnu** the unknown.

inconscience [ɛ̃kɔ̃sjɑ̃s] *nf* unconsciousness; (*folie*) thoughtlessness, rashness. **inconscient** *adj* unconscious; thoughtless, rash.

inconséquent [ɛ̃kɔ̃sekɑ̃] adj inconsistent; (irréfléchi) thoughtless.

inconstant [ɛ̃kɔ̃stɑ̃] adj fickle.

incontestable [ɛ̃kɔ̃tɛstablə] adj unquestionable, undeniable.

inconvenant [ɛ̃kɔ̃vnɑ̃] adj improper, unseemly.

inconvénient [ɛ̃kɔ̃venjɑ̃] nm disadvantage, drawback; risk.

incorporer [ɛ̃kɔrpɔre] v incorporate; mix.

incorrect [ɛ̃kɔrɛkt] adj incorrect; impolite.

incrédule [ɛ̃kredyl] adj incredulous. n(m+f) (rel) unbeliever. **incrédulité** nf incredulity.

incriminer [ɛ̃krimine] v incriminate.

incroyable [ɛ̃krwajablə] adj incredible.

incuber [ɛ̃kybe] v incubate, hatch. **incubation** nf incubation.

inculper [ɛ̃kylpe] v charge. **inculpation** nf charge.

inculte [ɛ̃kylt] adj uncultivated; (négligé) unkempt.

incurable [ɛ̃kyrablə] adj incurable.

Inde [ɛ̃d] nf India.

indécent [ɛ̃desɑ̃] adj indecent. **indécence** nf indecency.

indécis [ɛ̃desi] adj (irrésolu) indecisive; (hésitant) undecided; (douteux) unsettled; vague.

indéfini [ɛ̃defini] adj indefinite.

indemne [ɛ̃dɛmnə] adj unharmed, unhurt.

indemniser [ɛ̃dɛmnize] v compensate, reimburse. **indemnité** nf compensation, indemnity; (frais) allowance.

indépendant [ɛ̃depɑ̃dɑ̃] adj independent; (appartement) self-contained; (journaliste, etc.) freelance. **indépendance** nf independence.

index [ɛ̃dɛks] nm index; (aiguille) needle, pointer; (doigt) index finger.

indicatif [ɛ̃dikatif] adj indicative. nm (musical) signature tune; (téléphonique) dialling code; (gramm) indicative.

indication [ɛ̃dikasjɔ̃] nf indication; (renseignement) information; instruction; direction. **indicateur** nm indicator; (horaire) timetable; guide; gauge.

indice [ɛ̃dis] nm indication, sign; (clef) clue; index, rating.

indien [ɛ̃djɛ̃] adj Indian. **Indien, -enne** nm, nf Indian.

indifférent [ɛ̃diferɑ̃] adj indifferent; (sans importance) immaterial. **indifférence** nf indifference.

indigence [ɛ̃diʒɑ̃s] nf poverty. **indigent** adj poor, destitute.

indigène [ɛ̃diʒɛn] n(m+f), adj native.

indigestion [ɛ̃diʒɛstjɔ̃] nf indigestion.

indigne [ɛ̃diɲ] adj unworthy.

indigner [ɛ̃diɲe] v make indignant. **s'indigner** be indignant. **indignation** nf indignation. **indigné** adj indignant.

indiquer [ɛ̃dike] v indicate, show, point out.

indirect [ɛ̃dirɛkt] adj indirect.

indiscipliné [ɛ̃disipline] adj unruly.

indiscret, -ète [ɛ̃diskrɛ, -ɛt] adj indiscreet. **indiscrétion** nf indiscretion.

indispensable [ɛ̃dispɑ̃sablə] adj essential.

indisposé [ɛ̃dispoze] adj unwell.

individu [ɛ̃dividy] nm individual. **individualité** nf individuality. **individuel** adj individual; personal, private.

indolent [ɛ̃dɔlɑ̃] adj idle, indolent. **indolence** nf idleness, indolence.

indolore [ɛ̃dɔlɔr] adj painless.

*induire [ɛ̃dɥir] v infer. **induire en erreur** mislead.

indulgence [ɛ̃dylʒɑ̃s] nf indulgence, leniency. **indulgent** adj indulgent, lenient.

industrie [ɛ̃dystri] nf industry. **industrialiser** v industrialize. **industriel** adj industrial.

inébranlable [inebrɑ̃lablə] adj steadfast; solid.

inefficace [inefikas] adj (mesure) ineffective; (employé) inefficient.

inégal [inegal] adj (irrégulier) uneven; (différent) unequal. **inégalité** nf inequality; unevenness; difference.

inepte [inɛpt] adj inept.

inerte [inɛrt] adj inert, lifeless; passive, apathetic. **inertie** nf inertia; apathy.

inestimable [inɛstimablə] adj invaluable.

inévitable [inevitablə] adj inevitable; (accident) unavoidable.

inexact [inɛgzakt] adj inaccurate; unpunctual. **inexactitude** nf inaccuracy; unpunctuality.

inexpérimenté [inɛksperimɑ̃te] adj (personne) inexperienced; (produit) untested.

infaillible [ɛ̃fajiblə] adj infallible.

infâme [ɛ̃fɑm] adj infamous; (odieux) vile, despicable. **infamie** nf infamy.

infanterie [ɛ̃fɑ̃tri] nf infantry.

infarctus [ɛ̃farktys] nm infarctus **du myocarde** coronary thrombosis.

infatué [ɛ̃fatɥe] *adj* conceited, vain.
infécond [ɛ̃fekɔ̃] *adj* sterile, infertile.
infécondité *nf* sterility, infertility.
infect [ɛ̃fɛkt] *adj* vile, revolting.
infecter [ɛ̃fɛkte] *v* infect, contaminate.
s'infecter turn septic. **infectieux** *adj*
infectious. **infection** *nf* infection;
(*puanteur*) stench.
inférieur, -e [ɛ̃ferjœr] *adj* (*plus bas*) lower; (*qualité*) inferior; (*quantité*) smaller.
nm, nf inferior. **infériorité** *nf* inferiority.
infester [ɛ̃fɛste] *v* infest. **infestation** *nf*
infestation.
infidèle [ɛ̃fidɛl] *adj* unfaithful; (*inexact*)
inaccurate. **infidélité** *nf* unfaithfulness;
(*mari, femme*) infidelity; inaccuracy.
s'infiltrer [ɛ̃filtre] *v* infiltrate; (*liquide*)
percolate; (*lumière*) filter through. **infiltration** *nf* infiltration.
infime [ɛ̃fim] *adj* tiny, minute.
infini [ɛ̃fini] *adj* infinite; interminable. *nm*
infinity. **infinité** *nf* infinity; infinite
number. **infinitif** *nm, adj* infinitive.
infirme [ɛ̃firm] *adj* crippled, disabled;
(*vieillards*) infirm. *nm, nf* cripple, disabled person. **infirmerie** *nf* (*école*) sick
bay. **infirmier, -ère** *nm, nf* nurse.
infirmité *nf* disability; infirmity.
inflammable [ɛ̃flamablə] *adj* inflammable.
inflammation *nf* inflammation.
inflation [ɛ̃flɑsjɔ̃] *nf* inflation.
inflexion [ɛ̃flɛksjɔ̃] *nf* inflection; (*courbe*)
bend.
infliger [ɛ̃fliʒe] *v* inflict; impose.
influencer [ɛ̃flyɑ̃se] *v* influence. **influence**
nf influence. **influent** *adj* influential.
influer [ɛ̃flye] *v* **influer sur** have an influence on.
informe [ɛ̃fɔrm] *adj* shapeless.
informer [ɛ̃fɔrme] *v* inform. **s'informer**
inquire, find out. **information** *nf* information; (*jur*) inquiry. **informations** *nf pl*
news *sing*.
infortune [ɛ̃fɔrtyn] *nf* misfortune. **infor-
tuné** *adj* ill-fated, wretched.
infraction [ɛ̃fraksjɔ̃] *nf* offence; (*loi*)
infringement, breach.
infroissable [ɛ̃frwasablə] *adj* crease-resistant.
infuser [ɛ̃fyze] *v* (*thé*) brew, infuse.
ingénieur [ɛ̃ʒenjœr] *nm* engineer.
ingénieux [ɛ̃ʒenjø] *adj* ingenious. **ingéniosité** *nf* ingenuity.
ingénu [ɛ̃ʒeny] *adj* naïve, ingenuous.

s'ingérer [ɛ̃ʒere] *v* interfere, meddle.
ingérence *nf* interference.
ingrat [ɛ̃gra] *adj* ungrateful; (*tâche*)
thankless; (*déplaisant*) unattractive.
ingratitude *nf* ingratitude.
ingrédient [ɛ̃gredjɑ̃] *nm* ingredient.
inhabile [inabil] *adj* clumsy, inept.
inhabité [inabite] *adj* uninhabited, unoccupied.
inhaler [inale] *v* inhale.
inhérent [inerɑ̃] *adj* inherent.
inhiber [inibe] *v* inhibit. **inhibition** *nf*
inhibition.
inhumain [inymɛ̃] *adj* inhuman.
inimitié [inimitje] *nf* enmity.
initial [inisjal] *adj* initial. **initiale** *nf* initial.
initiative [inisjativ] *nf* initiative.
initier [inisje] *v* initiate. **initiation** *nf* initiation.
injecter [ɛ̃ʒɛkte] *v* inject. **injection** *nf*
injection.
injurier [ɛ̃ʒyrje] *v* abuse, insult. **injure** *nf*
abuse, insult. **injurieux** *adj* abusive,
insulting.
injuste [ɛ̃ʒyst] *adj* unjust, unfair. **injustice**
nf injustice, unfairness.
inné [ine] *adj* innate.
innocent [inosɑ̃], **-e** *adj* innocent. *nm, nf*
innocent (person); idiot, simpleton.
innocence *nf* innocence.
innovation [inovasjɔ̃] *nf* innovation.
inoccupé [inɔkype] *adj* unoccupied.
inoculer [inɔkyle] *v* inoculate. **inoculation**
nf inoculation.
inonder [inɔ̃de] *v* flood; (*tremper*) soak.
inondation *nf* flood.
inopiné [inɔpine] *adj* unexpected.
inouï [inwi] *adj* incredible, unheard-of.
inoxydable [inɔksidablə] *adj* stainless;
(*couteau, etc.*) stainless steel.
inquiéter [ɛ̃kjete] *v* worry, bother. **inquiet,
-ète** *adj* worried, anxious. **inquiétude** *nf*
worry, anxiety.
inquisition [ɛ̃kizisjɔ̃] *nf* inquisition.
inscription [ɛ̃skripsjɔ̃] *nf* inscription;
(*club, cours, etc.*) enrolment, registration.
*inscrire [ɛ̃skrir] *v* write down, enrol, register; (*graver*) inscribe.
insecte [ɛ̃sɛkt] *nm* insect. **insecticide** *nm*
insecticide.
insécurité [ɛ̃sekyrite] *nf* insecurity.
inséminer [ɛ̃semine] *v* inseminate. **insémination** *nf* insemination.

insensé [ɛ̃sɑ̃se] *adj* insane, crazy.
insensible [ɛ̃sɑ̃siblə] *adj* insensitive;
imperceptible. **insensibilité** *nf* insensitivity.
insérer [ɛ̃sere] *v* insert. **s'insérer dans** fit
into. **insertion** *nf* insertion.
insidieux [ɛ̃sidjø] *adj* insidious.
insigne [ɛ̃siɲ] *adj* distinguished, notable.
nm badge, insignia.
insignifiant [ɛ̃siɲifjɑ̃] *adj* insignificant.
insignifiance *nf* insignificance.
insinuer [ɛ̃sinɥe] *v* insinuate, imply.
s'insinuer dans worm one's way into.
insinuation *nf* insinuation.
insipide [ɛ̃sipid] *adj* insipid.
insister [ɛ̃siste] *v* insist. **insister sur** stress.
insistance *nf* insistence. **insistant** *adj*
insistent.
insolation [ɛ̃sɔlasjɔ̃] *nf* (*méd*) sunstroke;
(*temps*) sunshine.
insolent [ɛ̃sɔlɑ̃] *adj* insolent. **insolence** *nf*
insolence.
insolite [ɛ̃sɔlit] *adj* strange, unusual.
insomnie [ɛ̃sɔmni] *nf* insomnia.
insomniaque *n(m+f)*, *adj* insomniac.
insonore [ɛ̃sɔnɔr] *adj* soundproof. **insonoriser** *v* soundproof.
insouciant [ɛ̃susjɑ̃] *adj* carefree, happy-go-lucky.
inspecter [ɛ̃spɛkte] *v* inspect. **inspecteur,
-trice** *nm*, *nf* inspector. **inspection** *nf*
inspection.
inspirer [ɛ̃spire] *v* inspire; (*respirer*)
breathe in. **inspiration** *nf* inspiration.
instable [ɛ̃stablə] *adj* unstable. **instabilité**
nf instability.
installer [ɛ̃stale] *v* install; (*pièce*) fit out.
s'installer settle in (*or* down);
(*emménager*) move in, set up home.
installation *nf* installation. **installations** *nf*
pl fittings *pl*, facilities *pl*; (*usine*) plant
sing.
instant [ɛ̃stɑ̃] *nm* moment, instant. **à
l'instant** at this moment; (*passé*) a
moment ago. **par instants** at times. **pour
l'instant** for the time being. **instantané**
adj instantaneous; (*café*) instant.
instar [ɛ̃star] *nm* **à l'instar de** after the
fashion of.
instigation [ɛ̃stigasjɔ̃] *nf* instigation. **instigateur, -trice** *nm*, *nf* instigator.
instinct [ɛ̃stɛ̃] *nm* instinct. **instinctif** *adj*
instinctive.
instituer [ɛ̃stitɥe] *v* institute. **institut** *nm*
institute. **instituteur, -trice** *nm*, *nf* primary school teacher. **institution** *nf* institution; (*école*) private school.
instruction [ɛ̃stryksjɔ̃] *nf* education.
instructions *nf pl* instructions *pl*. **instructif** *adj* instructive.
***instruire** [ɛ̃strɥir] *v* teach, instruct; educate; inform.
instrument [ɛ̃strymɑ̃] *nm* instrument;
(*outil*) tool. **instrumental** *adj* instrumental.
insu [ɛ̃sy] *nm* **à l'insu de** unknown to. **à
mon insu** without my knowing it.
insubordonné [ɛ̃sybɔrdɔne] *adj*
insubordinate. **insubordination** *nf* insubordination.
insuccès [ɛ̃syksɛ] *nm* failure.
insuffisant [ɛ̃syfizɑ̃] *adj* inadequate;
(*quantité*) insufficient. **insuffisance** *nf*
inadequacy; insufficiency.
insulaire [ɛ̃sylɛr] *adj* insular. *n(m+f)*
islander.
insuline [ɛ̃sylin] *nf* insulin.
insulter [ɛ̃sylte] *v* insult. **insulte** *nf* insult.
insupportable [ɛ̃sypɔrtablə] *adj* unbearable, intolerable.
s'insurger [ɛ̃syrʒe] *v* rebel. **insurgé, -e** *nm*,
nf rebel. **insurrection** *nf* revolt.
intact [ɛ̃takt] *adj* intact.
intègre [ɛ̃tɛgrə] *adj* honest. **intégrité** *nf*
integrity.
intégrer [ɛ̃tegre] *v* integrate. **intégral** *adj*
complete, full; (*texte*) unabridged. **intégration** *nf* integration.
intellect [ɛ̃telɛkt] *nm* intellect. **intellectuel, -elle** *n*, *adj* intellectual.
intelligence [ɛ̃teliʒɑ̃s] *nf* intelligence;
(*compréhension*) understanding. **intelligent** *adj* intelligent, clever.
intelligible [ɛ̃teliʒiblə] *adj* intelligible.
intendant [ɛ̃tɑ̃dɑ̃] *nm* (*école*) bursar;
(*maison*) steward; (*mil*) quartermaster.
intense [ɛ̃tɑ̃s] *adj* intense. **intensif** *adj*
intensive. **intensifier** *v* intensify. **intensité**
nf intensity.
intention [ɛ̃tɑ̃sjɔ̃] *nf* intention. **à
l'intention de** for the benefit of, for. **avoir
l'intention de** intend to. **intentionnel** *adj*
intentional.
intercéder [ɛ̃tɛrsede] *v* intercede.
intercepter [ɛ̃tɛrsɛpte] *v* intercept;
(*boucher*) block, cut off. **interception** *nf*
interception.
***interdire** [ɛ̃tɛrdir] *v* forbid, ban. **interdiction** *nf* ban. **interdit** *adj* prohibited.

intéresser [ɛterese] v interest; concern. **s'intéresser à** be interested in. **intéressant** adj interesting; (offre, prix) attractive.
intérêt [ɛterɛ] nm interest; importance.
intérieur, -e [ɛterjœr] adj inner, internal, inside; (pol) domestic, home. nm interior, inside. **à l'intérieur** inside.
intérim [ɛterim] nm interim. **intérimaire** adj temporary.
interjection [ɛterʒɛksjɔ̃] nf interjection.
interloquer [ɛterlɔke] v dumbfound, take aback.
intermède [ɛtermɛd] nm interlude.
intermédiaire [ɛtermedjɛr] adj intermediate. n(m+f) go-between; (comm) middleman. **sans intermédiaire** directly.
interminable [ɛterminablə] adj endless, interminable.
intermittent [ɛtermitɑ̃] adj intermittent.
internat [ɛterna] nm boarding school.
international [ɛternasjɔnal] adj international.
interne [ɛtern] adj internal. n(m+f) boarder; (méd) houseman, intern. **internement** nm internment. **interner** v intern.
interpeller [ɛterpele] v (appeler) call out to; (apostropher) shout at; question.
interphone [ɛterfɔn] nm intercom.
interposer [ɛterpoze] v interpose. **s'interposer** intervene.
interpréter [ɛterprete] v interpret; (théâtre, musique) perform. **interprétation** nf interpretation. **interprète** n(m+f) interpreter; performer.
interroger [ɛterɔʒe] v question; examine; (police, etc.) interrogate. **interrogatif** nm, adj interrogative. **interrogation** nf questioning, interrogation; question; (école) test. **interrogatoire** nm questioning; (jur) cross-examination.
***interrompre** [ɛterɔ̃prə] v interrupt; (arrêter) break off.
interruption [ɛterypsjɔ̃] nf interruption. **interrupteur** nm switch.
interurbain [ɛteryrbɛ̃] adj (téléphone) long-distance.
intervalle [ɛterval] nm interval; space. **dans l'intervalle** in the meantime.
***intervenir** [ɛtervənir] v intervene; (survenir) take place, occur. **intervention** nf intervention.
intervertir [ɛtervertir] v invert, reverse.
interview [ɛtervju] nf interview.
intestin [ɛtestɛ̃] nm intestine. **intestins** nm

pl bowels pl. adj internal. **intestinal** adj intestinal.
intime [ɛtim] adj intimate; private, personal; (ami) close. n(m+f) close friend. **intimité** nf intimacy; privacy.
intimider [ɛtimide] v intimidate. **intimidation** nf intimidation.
intituler [ɛtityle] v entitle, call. **intitulé** nm title.
intolérable [ɛtɔlerablə] adj intolerable. **intolérance** nf intolerance. **intolérant** adj intolerant.
intonation [ɛtɔnasjɔ̃] nf intonation.
intoxiquer [ɛtɔksike] v poison. **intoxication** nf poisoning. **intoxiqué, -e** nm, nf addict.
intransitif [ɛtrɑ̃zitif] nm, adj intransitive.
intraveineux [ɛtravɛnø] adj intravenous.
intrépide [ɛtrepid] adj intrepid, bold.
intriguer [ɛtrige] v intrigue; (comploter) scheme. **intrigue** nf scheme; (film, livre, etc.) plot.
intrinsèque [ɛtrɛsɛk] adj intrinsic.
***introduire** [ɛtrɔdɥir] v introduce; insert; (faire entrer) show in. **s'introduire** get in. **introduction** nf introduction; insertion; admission.
introverti [ɛtrɔverti] -e adj introverted. nm, nf introvert.
intrus [ɛtry] -e nm, nf intruder. adj intrusive. **intrusion** nf intrusion.
intuition [ɛtɥisjɔ̃] nf intuition. **intuitif** adj intuitive.
inutile [inytil] adj useless; (effort) pointless; (superflu) needless.
invaincu [ɛvɛ̃ky] adj unbeaten.
invalide [ɛvalid] n(m+f) disabled person. adj disabled. **invalidité** nf disability.
invariable [ɛvarjablə] adj invariable.
invasion [ɛvazjɔ̃] nf invasion.
inventaire [ɛvɑ̃ter] nm inventory; (comm) stocktaking.
inventer [ɛvɑ̃te] v invent; (forger) make up; (imaginer) think up. **inventeur, -trice** nm, nf inventor. **invention** nf invention.
inverse [ɛvers] nm, adj opposite, reverse. **inversement** adv conversely. **inverser** v reverse, invert. **inversion** nf inversion.
invertébré [ɛvertebre] nm, adj invertebrate.
investigation [ɛvestigasjɔ̃] nf investigation.
investir [ɛvestir] v invest. **investissement** nm investment.

invisible [ɛ̃viziblə] *adj* invisible.

inviter [ɛ̃vite] *v* invite, ask. **invitation** *nf* invitation. **invité, -e** *nm, nf* guest.

involontaire [ɛ̃vɔlɔ̃tɛr] *adj* involuntary; unintentional.

invoquer [ɛ̃vɔke] *v* call upon; (*excuse*) put forward.

invraisemblable [ɛ̃vrɛsɑ̃blablə] *adj* unlikely, improbable; incredible.

iode [jɔd] *nm* iodine.

ion [jɔ̃] *nm* ion.

iris [iris] *nm* iris.

Irlande [irlɑ̃d] *nf* Ireland. **irlandais** *nm, adj* Irish. **les Irlandais** the Irish.

ironie [irɔni] *nf* irony. **ironique** *adj* ironic.

irrationnel [irasjɔnɛl] *adj* irrational.

irréel [ireɛl] *adj* unreal.

irréfléchi [irefleʃi] *adj* thoughtless, hasty.

irrégulier [iregylje] *adj* irregular. **irrégularité** *nf* irregularity.

irrésistible [irezistiblə] *adj* irresistible.

irrespect [irɛspɛ] *nm* disrespect. **irrespectueux** *adj* disrespectful.

irrévocable [irevɔkablə] *adj* irrevocable.

irriguer [irige] *v* irrigate. **irrigation** *nf* irrigation.

irriter [irite] *v* irritate; annoy. **irritable** *adj* irritable. **irritation** *nf* irritation.

irruption [irypsjɔ̃] *nf* **faire irruption** burst in.

Islam [islam] *nm* Islam. **islamique** *adj* Islamic.

Islande [islɑ̃d] *nf* Iceland. **islandais** *nm, adj* Icelandic. **Islandais, -e** *nm, nf* Icelander.

isoler [izɔle] *v* isolate; (*élec*) insulate. **isolation** *nf* insulation. **isolé** *adj* isolated, lonely, remote. **isolement** *nm* isolation. **isoloir** *nm* polling booth.

issu [isy] *adj* **issu de** descended from.

issue [isy] *nf* (*sortie*) exit; solution; (*fin*) outcome; (*eau*) outlet.

isthme [ismə] *nm* isthmus.

Italie [itali] *nf* Italy. **italien** *nm, adj* Italian. **Italien, -enne** *nm, nf* Italian.

italique [italik] *nm* italics *pl. adj* italic.

itinéraire [itinerɛr] *nm* itinerary, route.

ivoire [ivwar] *nm* ivory. **Côte d'Ivoire** *nf* Ivory Coast.

ivre [ivrə] *adj* drunk. **ivresse** *nf* drunkenness; ecstasy, exhilaration. **ivrogne** *n(m + f)* drunkard.

J

j' [ʒ] *V* **je.**

jabot [ʒabo] *nm* (*chemise*) jabot; (*zool*) crop.

jacasser [ʒakase] *v* chatter. **jacasse** *nf* magpie. **jacassement** *nm* chatter.

jachère [ʒaʃɛr] *nf* fallow.

jacinthe [ʒasɛ̃t] *nf* hyacinth. **jacinthe des bois** bluebell.

jade [ʒad] *nm* jade.

jadis [ʒadis] *adv* formerly, long ago.

jaguar [ʒagwar] *nm* jaguar.

jaillir [ʒajir] *v* gush forth, spurt out; (*rires, etc.*) burst out; (*surgir*) spring up. **jaillissement** *nm* spurt, gush.

jais [ʒɛ] *nm* jet.

jalonner [ʒalɔne] *v* mark out; (*border*) line.

jaloux, -ouse [ʒalu, -uz] *adj* jealous. **jalousie** *nf* jealousy; (*store*) blind.

jamais [ʒamɛ] *adv* ever; (*négatif*) never. **à tout jamais** for ever and ever. **ne ... jamais** never.

jambe [ʒɑ̃b] *nf* leg.

jambon [ʒɑ̃bɔ̃] *nm* ham.

jante [ʒɑ̃t] *nf* rim.

janvier [ʒɑ̃vje] *nm* January.

Japon [ʒapɔ̃] *nm* Japan. **japonais** *nm, adj* Japanese. **les Japonais** the Japanese.

japper [ʒape] *v* yap. **jappement** *nm* yap.

jaquette [ʒakɛt] *nf* jacket; (*homme*) morning coat.

jardin [ʒardɛ̃] *nm* garden. **jardin d'enfants** nursery school. **jardin maraîcher** market garden. **jardin public** park.

jardiner [ʒardine] *v* garden. **jardinage** *nm* gardening. **jardinier** *nm* gardener. **jardinière** *nf* gardener; (*caisse*) window box.

jargon [ʒargɔ̃] *nm* jargon.

jarret [ʒarɛ] *nm* (*anat*) back of the knee; (*zool*) hock; (*cuisine*) knuckle.

jarretelle [ʒartɛl] *nf* suspender *or US* garter.

jarretière [ʒartjɛr] *nf* garter.

jars [ʒar] *nm* gander.

jaser [ʒɑze] *v* chatter; (*médire*) gossip; (*ruisseau*) babble.

jasmin [ʒasmɛ̃] *nm* jasmine.

jatte [ʒat] *nf* bowl.

jauger [ʒoʒe] *v* measure, gauge; (*personne*) size up. **jauge** *nf* gauge; capacity.

jauge d'essence petrol gauge. jauge d'huile dipstick.

jaune [ʒon] adj yellow. nm yellow; (œuf) yolk; (péj) blackleg. jaunir v turn yellow. jaunisse nf jaundice.

javelot [ʒavlo] nm javelin.

jazz [dʒaz] nm jazz.

je [ʒə], j' pron I.

jean [dʒin] nm jeans pl.

jeep [ʒip] nf jeep.

jersey [ʒɛrzɛ] nm jersey, jumper. Jersey [ʒɛrzɛ] nf Jersey.

jet¹ [ʒɛ] nm (liquide) jet, spurt, stream; (lumière) beam; (pierre) throw; (fam: coup) go.

jet² [dʒɛt] nm (aéro) jet.

jetée [ʒəte] nf jetty; pier.

jeter [ʒəte] v throw.

jeton [ʒətɔ̃] nm token; (jeu) counter.

jeu [ʒø] nm play; game; (série) set; (casino) gambling. jeu de cartes (ensemble) pack of cards; (partie) card game. jeu de mots pun.

jeudi [ʒødi] nm Thursday. jeudi saint Maundy Thursday.

jeun [ʒœ̃] adv à jeun on an empty stomach.

jeune [ʒœn] adj young; (cadet) junior, younger. n(m+f) young person. jeunesse nf youth; (personnes) young people pl.

jeûner [ʒøne] v go without food; (rel) fast. jeûne nm fast.

joaillier [ʒɔaje], -ère nm, nf jeweller. joaillerie nf jewellery; (magasin) jeweller's.

jockey [ʒɔkɛ] nm jockey.

jodler [ʒɔdle] v yodel.

joie [ʒwa] nf joy, delight.

*joindre [ʒwɛ̃drə] v join; (unir) combine; (inclure) attach, enclose; (personne) contact.

joint [ʒwɛ̃] nm joint; (auto) gasket; (robinet) washer. adj joint. jointure nf joint.

joli [ʒɔli] adj pretty, nice. joliment adv nicely; (fam) pretty, jolly.

jonc [ʒɔ̃] nm (plante) rush; cane; (bracelet) bangle; (baque) ring.

joncher [ʒɔ̃ʃe] v strew, litter.

jonction [ʒɔ̃ksjɔ̃] nf junction.

jongler [ʒɔ̃gle] v juggle. jonglerie nf juggling, jugglery. jongleur, -euse nm, nf juggler.

jonquille [ʒɔ̃kij] nf daffodil.

joue [ʒu] nf cheek.

jouer [ʒwe] v play; (théâtre) act; (clef etc.) be loose; (casino) gamble; (argent) stake. jouer de use, make use of. se jouer de (tromper) deceive; (moquer) scoff at. jouet nm toy. joueur, -euse nm, nf player; gambler.

joufflu [ʒufly] adj chubby-cheeked.

joug [ʒu] nm yoke.

jouir [ʒwir] v jouir de enjoy. jouissance nf pleasure, delight; (jur) use.

jour [ʒur] nm day; (lumière) light; (ouverture) gap. de nos jours nowadays. jour de congé day off. jour férié bank holiday. jour ouvrable weekday. le jour de l'An New Year's day. quinze jours a fortnight. vivre au jour le jour live from hand to mouth. journée nf day.

journal [ʒurnal] nm newspaper; magazine, journal; (intime) diary. journalier adj daily; (banal) everyday. journalisme nm journalism. journaliste n(m+f) journalist.

jovial [ʒɔvjal] adj jovial, jolly. jovialité nf joviality, jollity.

joyau [ʒwajo] nm jewel, gem.

joyeux [ʒwajø] adj joyful, merry.

jubilé [ʒybile] nm jubilee.

jubiler [ʒybile] v (fam) be jubilant. jubilation nf jubilation.

jucher [ʒyʃe] v perch.

judaïsme [ʒydaismə] nm Judaism.

judiciaire [ʒydisjɛr] adj judicial.

judicieux [ʒydisjø] adj judicious.

judo [ʒydo] nm judo.

juger [ʒyʒe] v judge; (jur) try; consider decide. au jugé by guesswork. juge nm judge. juge de paix Justice of the Peace jugement nm judgment; (jur) sentence.

juif [ʒɥif] adj Jewish. Juif, Juive nm, nf Jew.

juillet [ʒɥijɛ] nm July.

juin [ʒɥɛ̃] nm June.

jumeau, -elle [ʒymo, -ɛl] adj twin; (maisons) semi-detached. nm, nf twin. vrais jumeaux, vraies jumelles identical twins. jumelles nf pl binoculars pl.

jumeler [ʒymle] v twin; join. jumelé adj double; twin.

jument [ʒymɑ̃] nf mare.

jungle [ʒɔ̃glə] nf jungle.

junte [ʒɔ̃t] nf junta.

jupe [ʒyp] nf skirt. jupon nm waist slip.

jurer [ʒyre] v swear, vow; (couleurs) clash. juré, -e nm, nf juror.

juridique [ʒyridik] *adj* legal. **juridiction** *nf* jurisdiction.

juron [ʒyrɔ̃] *nm* oath, curse.

jury [ʒyri] *nm* jury.

jus [ʒy] *nm* juice. **jus de viande** gravy.

jusant [ʒyzɑ̃] *nm* ebb.

jusque [ʒyskə] *prep* up to. **jusqu'à** up to; (*lieu*) as far as; (*temps*) until; (*même*) even. **jusqu'à ce que** until. **jusqu'au bout** to the bitter end. **jusqu'ici** so far; (*lieu*) up to here; (*temps*) until now. **jusqu'où?** how far?

juste [ʒyst] *adj* just, fair; exact, accurate, right; (*pertinent*) sound; (*musique*) in tune; (*trop petit*) tight, barely enough. *adv* just; exactly; accurately; in tune. **au juste** exactly. **tout juste** only just, barely; exactly. **justesse** *nf* accuracy; soundness.

justice [ʒystis] *nf* justice, fairness; (*pol*) law.

justifier [ʒystifje] *v* justify; prove. **justifiable** *adj* justifiable. **justification** *nf* justification; proof.

jute [ʒyt] *nm* jute.

juteux [ʒytø] *adj* juicy.

juvénile [ʒyvenil] *adj* young, youthful.

juxtaposer [ʒykstapoze] *v* juxtapose. **juxtaposition** *nf* juxtaposition.

K

kaki [kaki] *nm, adj* khaki.

kaléidoscope [kaleidɔskɔp] *nm* kaleidoscope.

kangourou [kɑ̃guru] *nm* kangaroo.

karaté [karate] *nm* karate.

kayak [kajak] *nm* kayak.

kermesse [kɛrmɛs] *nf* fair, bazaar.

kidnapper [kidnape] *v* kidnap. **kidnappeur, -euse** *nm, nf* kidnapper.

kilo [kilo] *nm* kilo.

kilogramme [kilɔgram] *nm* kilogram.

kilomètre [kilɔmɛtrə] *nm* kilometre. **kilométrage** *nm* mileage.

kilowatt [kilɔwat] *nm* kilowatt.

kimono [kimɔno] *nm* kimono.

kinésithérapie [kineziterapi] *nf* physiotherapy. **kinésithérapeute** *n(m+f)* physiotherapist.

kiosque [kjɔsk] *nm* kiosk; (*jardin*) summer-house.

kiwi [kiwi] *nm* kiwi.

klaxon ® [klaksɔn] *nm* horn. **klaxonner** *v* sound one's horn, hoot.

kleptomanie [klɛptɔmani] *nf* kleptomania. **kleptomane** *n(m+f)*, *adj* kleptomaniac.

kyste [kist] *nm* cyst.

L

l' [l] *V* **la**, **le**.

la [la], **l'** *art* the. *pron* (*personne*) her; (*animal, chose*) it.

là [la] *adv* there; (*ici*) here; (*temps*) then; (*cela*) that. **là-bas** *adv* over there. **là-dedans** *adv* inside, in it. **là-dessous** *adv* underneath. **là-dessus** *adv* on that; (*à ce sujet*) about that; (*alors*) at that point. **là-haut** up there.

laboratoire [labɔratwar] *nm* laboratory.

laborieux [labɔrjø] *adj* (*pénible*) laborious; (*diligent*) hard-working.

labourer [labure] *v* plough. **laboureur** *nm* ploughman.

labyrinthe [labirɛ̃t] *nm* labyrinth, maze.

lac [lak] *nm* lake.

lacer [lase] *v* lace (up). **lacet** *nm* lace; (*route*) sharp bend; (*piège*) snare. **en lacet** winding.

lacérer [lasere] *v* tear up; (*corps*) lacerate. **lacération** *nf* laceration.

lâche [lɑʃ] *adj* loose; (*personne*) cowardly. *n(m+f)* coward. **lâcheté** *nf* cowardice.

lâcher [lɑʃe] *v* release, let go (of); (*ceinture*) loosen; (*fam: abandonner*) give up, drop. **lâcher pied** give way. **lâcher prise** let go.

lacrymogène [lakrimɔʒɛn] *adj* **gaz lacrymogène** *nm* tear-gas.

lacté [lakte] *adj* milky.

lacune [lakyn] *nf* gap.

ladre [lɑdrə] *adj* mean. *n(m+f)* miser.

lagune [lagyn] *nf* lagoon.

laid [lɛ] *adj* ugly. **laideur** *nf* ugliness.

laine [lɛn] *nf* wool. **de laine** woollen. **laineux** *adj* woolly.

laïque [laik] *adj* lay, secular. *nm* layman. **laïques** *nm pl* laity *sing*.

laisse [lɛs] *nf* lead, leash.

laisser [lese] v˙ leave; let. **laisser-aller** nm invar carelessness. **laissez-passer** nm invar pass.

lait [lɛ] nm milk. **lait caillé** curds pl. **lait concentré** evaporated milk. **laiterie** nf dairy. **laiteux** adj milky. **laitier** nm milkman.

laiton [lɛtɔ̃] nm brass.

laitue [lety] nf lettuce.

lama [lama] nm llama.

lambeau [lãbo] nm scrap, shred.

lambrequin [lãbrəkɛ̃] nm pelmet.

lame [lam] nf (bande) strip; (tranchant) blade; (vague) wave.

se lamenter [lamãte] v lament, moan. **lamentable** adj lamentable, awful; (cri) pitiful. **lamentation** nf lament.

lampadaire [lãpadɛr] nm standard lamp.

lampe [lãp] nf lamp, light. **lampe de poche** torch.

lamper [lãpe] (fam) v swig. **lampée** nf swig.

lance [lãs] nf spear.

lancer [lãse] v throw, hurl; (émettre) send out; (mettre en mouvement) launch. **lance-pierres** nm invar catapult. **se lancer** (sauter) leap; (se précipiter) dash. **se lancer dans** embark on.

lanciner [lãsine] v throb; obsess, torment.

landau [lãdo] nm pram.

lande [lãd] nf moor.

langage [lãgaʒ] nm language.

langouste [lãgust] nf crayfish. **langoustines** nf pl scampi pl.

langue [lãg] nf (anat) tongue; language.

languir [lãgir] v languish; (conversation) flag; (désirer) pine, long. **languissant** adj (personne) listless; (récit) dull.

lanière [lanjɛr] nf strap, thong.

lanterne [lãtɛrn] nf lantern; lamp, light; (auto) sidelight.

Laos [laɔs] nm Laos.

laper [lape] v lap (up).

lapin [lapɛ̃] nm rabbit.

Laponie [lapɔni] nf Lapland. **lapon** nm, adj Lapp. **Lapon, -e** nm, nf Lapp.

lapsus [lapsys] nm (parlé) slip of the tongue; (écrit) slip of the pen.

laque [lak] nf lacquer. **laquer** v lacquer.

laquelle [lakɛl] V **lequel**.

larcin [larsɛ̃] nm (vol) theft.

lard [lar] nm bacon; (gras) fat.

large [larʒ] adj wide, broad; generous. nm width; (place) space, room; (naut) open

sea. **largement** adv widely; generously; (de loin) greatly; (au moins) at least, easily. **largesse** nf generosity. **largeur** nf width, breadth.

larme [larm] nf tear.

larmoyer [larmwaje] v whimper; (yeux) water. **larmoyant** adj tearful.

larve [larv] nf larva, grub.

larynx [larɛ̃ks] nm larynx. **laryngite** nf laryngitis.

las, lasse [lɑ, lɑs] adj weary.

lascif [lasif] adj lascivious.

laser [lazɛr] nm laser.

lasser [lɑse] v weary. **se lasser de** grow tired of.

lasso [laso] nm lasso. **prendre au lasso** lasso.

latent [latã] adj latent.

latéral [lateral] adj lateral.

latin [latɛ̃] nm, adj Latin.

latitude [latityd] nf latitude.

laurier [lɔrje] nm laurel; (cuisine) bay leaves pl.

lavable [lavablə] adj washable.

lavabo [lavabo] nm washbasin. **lavabos** nm pl toilets pl.

lavage [lavaʒ] nm wash, washing. **lavage de cerveau** brainwashing.

lavande [lavãd] nf lavender.

lave [lav] nf lava.

laver [lave] v wash; (plaie) bathe. **lave-vaisselle** nm invar dishwasher. **se laver** have a wash. **laverie automatique** nf launderette. **lavette** nf dishcloth. **laveur de vitres** nm window-cleaner.

laxatif [laksatif] nm, adj laxative.

le [lə], **l'** art le pron (personne) him; (animal, chose) it.

lécher [leʃe] v lick. **faire du lèche-vitrines** go window-shopping.

leçon [ləsɔ̃] nf lesson.

lecteur, -trice [lɛktœr, -tris] nm, nf reader. **lecture** nf reading.

ledit, ladite [lədi, ladit] adj, pl **lesdits, lesdites** the aforementioned or aforesaid.

légal [legal] adj legal; official. **légaliser** v legalize. **légalité** nf legality.

légende [leʒãd] nf legend; (illustration) caption. **légendaire** adj legendary.

léger [leʒe] adj light; (petit) slight; agile; (licencieux) ribald. **à la légère** thoughtlessly; not seriously. **légèreté** nf lightness.

légiférer [leʒifere] v legislate.

légion [leʒjɔ̃] *nf* legion; vast number. **être légion** be numberless.

législation [leʒislasjɔ̃] *nf* legislation.

légitime [leʒitim] *adj* legitimate, lawful.

legs [lɛg] *nm* legacy.

léguer [lege] *v* bequeath.

légume [legym] *nm* vegetable.

Léman [lemɑ̃] *nm* **lac Léman** *nm* Lake Geneva.

lendemain [lɑ̃dmɛ̃] *nm* day after, next day; future. **le lendemain matin/soir** the next morning/evening.

lent [lɑ̃] *adj* slow. **lenteur** *nf* slowness.

lentille [lɑ̃tij] *nf* lentil; (*optique*) lens.

léopard [leɔpar] *nm* leopard.

lépreux [leprø], **-euse** *adj* leprous. *nm*, *nf* leper. **lèpre** *nf* leprosy.

lequel [ləkɛl], **laquelle** *pron*, *pl* **lesquels**, **lesquelles** which; (*personne*) who, whom.

les [le] *art* the. *pron* them.

lesbienne [lɛsbjɛn] *nf* lesbian.

léser [leze] *v* wrong; injure.

lésiner [lezine] *v* skimp.

lessive [lesiv] *nf* washing; (*substance*) washing powder.

lest [lɛst] *nm* ballast.

leste [lɛst] *adj* nimble, sprightly; risqué; (*cavalier*) offhand.

léthargie [letarʒi] *nf* lethargy. **léthargique** *adj* lethargic.

lettre [lɛtrə] *nf* letter. **au pied de la lettre** literally. **lettres** *nf pl* (*université*) arts *pl*; literature *sing*. **lettres de créance** credentials *pl*.

leu [lø] *nm* **à la queue leu leu** in single file.

leucémie [løsemi] *nf* leukaemia.

leur [lœr] *pron* them, to them. *adj* their. **le** *or* **la leur** theirs.

leurrer [lœre] *v* deceive, delude. **leurre** *nm* delusion; (*appât*) lure; (*piège*) trap.

levé [ləve] *nm* survey. *adj* raised.

lever [ləve] *v* raise, lift; (*impôts*) levy; (*séance*) close; (*cuisine*) rise. **se lever** rise, get up. *nm* rising. **lever du soleil** sunrise. **levée** *nf* raising; closing; (*poste*) collection; (*cartes*) trick.

levier [ləvje] *nm* lever. **levier de vitesse** gear lever.

lèvre [levrə] *nf* lip.

lévrier [levrije] *nm* greyhound.

levure [ləvyr] *nf* yeast.

lézard [lezar] *nm* lizard. **lézarde** *nf* crack. **lézarder** *v* crack; (*au soleil*) bask in the sun.

liaison [ljɛzɔ̃] *nf* (*d'affaires*) relationship; contact; (*rapport*) connection, link; (*amoureuse*) affair.

liasse [ljas] *nf* bundle, wad.

libelle [libɛl] *nm* libel; (*satire*) lampoon.

libellule [libelyl] *nf* dragonfly.

libéral [liberal], **-e** *adj* liberal; (*pol*) Liberal. *nm*, *nf* Liberal.

libérer [libere] *v* release, free, liberate. **libération** *nf* release, liberation.

liberté [libɛrte] *nf* freedom, liberty. **liberté conditionnelle** parole. **liberté sous caution** bail. **liberté surveillée** probation.

librairie [libreri] *nf* bookshop. **libraire** *n*(*m*+*f*) bookseller.

libre [librə] *adj* free. **libre-service** *nm* self-service shop *or* restaurant.

licence [lisɑ̃s] *nf* (*université*) degree; (*comm*) licence; permit. **licencié, -e** *nm*, *nf* graduate. **licencié ès lettres/sciences** Bachelor of Arts/Science.

licorne [likɔrn] *nf* unicorn.

licou [liku] *nm* halter.

lie [li] *nf* dregs *pl*.

Liechtenstein [liʃtɛnʃtajn] *nm* Liechtenstein.

liège [ljeʒ] *nm* cork.

lien [ljɛ̃] *nm* (*attache*) bond; (*liaison*) link; (*de famille, etc.*) tie.

lier [lje] *v* tie up, bind; (*relier*) link up; unite; (*cuisine*) thicken.

lierre [ljɛr] *nm* ivy.

lieu [ljø] *nm* place. **au lieu de** instead of. **avoir lieu** take place. **avoir lieu de** have good reason to. **donner lieu à** give rise to. **sur les lieux** at the scene, on the spot. **tenir lieu de** take the place of.

lieutenant [ljøtnɑ̃] *nm* lieutenant. **lieutenant-colonel** *nm* wing commander.

lièvre [ljevrə] *nm* hare.

ligament [ligamɑ̃] *nm* ligament.

ligne [lip] *nf* line; (*rangée*) row; (*silhouette*) figure. **à la ligne** new paragraph. **hors ligne** outstanding. **ligne d'horizon** skyline.

ligoter [ligɔte] *v* tie, bind.

ligue [lig] *nf* league.

lilas [lila] *nm*, *adj invar* lilac.

limace [limas] *nf* slug. **limaçon** *nm* snail.

limaille [limaj] *nf* filings *pl*.

limbe [lɛb] *nm* **les limbes** limbo *sing*. **dans les limbes** (*rel*) in limbo; (*projet*) in the air.

limer [lime] v file. **lime** nf file. **lime à ongles** nail-file.
limier [limje] nm bloodhound; (policier) sleuth.
limite [limit] nf limit; (pays) boundary. adj maximum. **cas limite** nm borderline case. **date limite** nf deadline.
limiter [limite] v limit, restrict; (frontière) border. **limitation** nf limitation, restriction.
limon [limɔ̃] nm silt.
limonade [limɔnad] nf lemonade.
lin [lɛ̃] nm flax.
linceul [lɛ̃sœl] nm shroud.
linéaire [lineɛr] adj linear.
linge [lɛ̃ʒ] nm linen; (lessive) washing; (sous-vêtements) underwear; (torchon) cloth. **lingerie** nf lingerie.
lingot [lɛ̃go] nm ingot.
linguistique [lɛ̃gɥistik] nf linguistics. adj linguistic. **linguiste** n(m+f) linguist.
linoléum [linɔleɔm] nm linoleum. **lino** nm (fam) lino.
lion [ljɔ̃] nm lion. **Lion** nm Leo. **lionceau** nm lion cub. **lionne** nf lioness.
liqueur [likœr] nf liqueur.
liquide [likid] nm, adj liquid. **liquidation** nf liquidation; (règlement) settlement. **liquider** v liquidate; settle.
*lire¹ [lir] v read.
lire² [lir] nf lira.
lis [lis] nm lily.
Lisbonne [lisbɔn] n Lisbon.
lisible [lizibl] adj (écriture) legible; (livre) readable. **lisibilité** nf legibility.
lisière [lizjɛr] nf edge; (tissu) selvage.
lisse [lis] adj smooth. **lisser** v smooth.
liste [list] nf list.
lit [li] nm bed; (couche) layer. **lit de camp** camp-bed. **lit d'enfant** cot. **lit d'une personne** single bed. **literie** nf bedding.
litanie [litani] nf litany.
litée [lite] nf litter.
litre [litrə] nm litre.
littéraire [literɛr] adj literary.
littéral [literal] adj literal.
littérature [literatyr] nf literature.
littoral [litɔral] adj coastal. nm coast.
livide [livid] adj pallid, livid.
livraison [livrɛzɔ̃] nm delivery; (revue) part, issue.
livre¹ [livrə] nm book. **livre à succès** best-seller. **livre de bord** logbook. **livre de poche** paperback. **livre d'images** picture book. **livre d'or** visitors' book.

livre² [livrə] nf pound.
livrer [livre] v deliver; (abandonner) hand over, give up. **se livrer** confide. **se livrer à** (s'adonner) indulge in; (se consacrer) devote oneself to.
livret [livrɛ] nm (musique) libretto; (carnet) booklet, record book.
lobe [lɔb] nm lobe.
local [lɔkal] adj local. nm premises pl. **localiser** v localize; (déterminer) locate; (limiter) confine. **localité** nf locality.
locataire [lɔkatɛr] n(m+f) tenant.
location [lɔkasjɔ̃] nf (maison) renting; (voiture, bateau) hiring. **bureau de location** nm booking office.
locomotive [lɔkɔmɔtiv] nf locomotive, engine.
locuste [lɔkyst] nf locust.
locution [lɔkysjɔ̃] nf phrase.
logarithme [lɔgaritmə] nm logarithm.
loger [lɔʒe] v lodge; accommodate, put up; (habiter) live. **se loger** find accommodation; (se coincer) get stuck. **loge** nf lodge; (artiste) dressing room; (spectateur) box. **logement** nm housing; accommodation, lodgings pl. **logeur** nm landlord. **logeuse** nf landlady.
logique [lɔʒik] nf logic. adj logical.
logis [lɔʒi] nm dwelling.
loi [lwa] nf law.
loin [lwɛ̃] adv far. **au loin** in the distance. **de loin** from a distance; (de beaucoup) by far. **plus loin** further.
lointain [lwɛ̃tɛ̃] adj distant, remote. nm (tableau) background. **au lointain** in the distance.
loir [lwar] nm dormouse.
loisir [lwazir] nm leisure, spare time.
lombric [lɔ̃brik] nm earthworm.
Londres [lɔ̃drə] n London.
long, longue [lɔ̃, lɔ̃g] adj long. **à long terme** long-term. **à longue portée** long-range. **de longue date** long-standing. **longue-vue** nf telescope. adv **en savoir/dire long** know/say a lot. nm length. **de long en large** back and forth. **le long de** along. nf **à la longue** at last, in the end. **longueur** nf length. **longueur d'onde** wavelength.
longer [lɔ̃ʒe] v border; (sentier, etc.) run alongside; (personne) walk along.
longévité [lɔ̃ʒevite] nf longevity.
longitude [lɔ̃ʒityd] nf longitude.

longtemps [lɔ̃tɑ̃] *adv* (for) a long time, (for) long.
loque [lɔk] *nf* rag.
loquet [lɔkɛ] *nm* latch.
lorgner [lɔrɲe] *v* (*fam*) peer at, eye up.
lors [lɔr] *adv* **dès lors** from then on. **lors de** at the time of. **lors même que** even if.
lorsque [lɔrskə] *conj* when.
losange [lɔzɑ̃ʒ] *nm* diamond.
lot [lo] *nm* (*assortiment*) set, batch; (*portion*) share; (*prix*) prize.
loterie [lɔtri] *nf* lottery, raffle.
lotion [losjɔ̃] *nf* lotion.
lotus [lɔtys] *nm* lotus.
louange [lwɑ̃ʒ] *nf* praise.
louche[1] [luʃ] *adj* dubious, shady. **loucher** *v* have a squint.
louche[2] [luʃ] *nf* ladle.
louer[1] [lwe] *v* (*exalter*) praise. **louable** *adj* praiseworthy.
louer[2] [lwe] *v* rent, hire.
loufoque [lufɔk] *adj* (*fam*) crazy.
loup [lu] *nm* wolf. **loup-cervier** *nm* lynx. **loup-garou** *nm* werewolf.
loupe [lup] *nf* magnifying glass.
louper [lupe] (*fam*) *v* bungle, make a mess of; (*occasion*) miss; (*examen*) fail.
lourd [lur] *adj* heavy; (*temps*) close; (*important*) serious; (*gauche*) clumsy. **lourdeur** *nf* heaviness.
loutre [lutrə] *nf* otter.
louveteau [luvto] *nm* wolf cub; cub scout.
loyal [lwajal] *adj* loyal; (*honnête*) fair. **loyauté** *nf* loyalty; fairness.
loyer [lwaje] *nm* rent.
lubie [lybi] *nf* whim, fad.
lubrifier [lybrifje] *v* lubricate. **lubrifiant** *nm* lubricant. **lubrification** *nf* lubrication.
lucarne [lykarn] *nf* skylight, dormer window.
lucide [lysid] *adj* lucid. **lucidité** *nf* lucidity.
lucratif [lykratif] *adj* lucrative, profitable.
lueur [lɥœr] *nf* glimmer, glow.
luge [lyʒ] *nf* sledge, toboggan.
lugubre [lygybrə] *adj* gloomy, dismal.
lui [lɥi] *pron* (*homme*) him, to him; (*femme*) her, to her; (*chose, animal*) it, to it; (*sujet*) he. **lui-même** *pron* himself; itself.
*****luire** [lɥir] *v* gleam, shine. **luisant** *nm* sheen, gloss.
lumbago [lɔ̃bago] *nm* lumbago.
lumière [lymjɛr] *nf* light.

lumineux [lyminø] *adj* luminous.
lundi [lœ̃di] *nm* Monday.
lune [lyn] *nf* moon. **lune de miel** honeymoon. **lunaire** *adj* lunar.
lunette [lynɛt] *nf* telescope. **lunettes** *nf pl* glasses *pl*. **lunettes de soleil** sunglasses *pl*. **lunettes protectrices** goggles *pl*.
lurette [lyrɛt] *nf* **il y a belle lurette** ages ago.
lustrer [lystre] *v* polish; make shiny. **lustre** *nm* lustre; (*appareil d'éclairage*) chandelier. **lustré** *adj* shiny.
luth [lyt] *nm* lute.
lutin [lytɛ̃] *nm* imp. *adj* impish, mischievous.
lutrin [lytrɛ̃] *nm* lectern.
lutter [lyte] *v* struggle, fight. **lutte** *nf* struggle, fight; (*sport*) wrestling. **lutteur, -euse** *nm, nf* fighter; wrestler.
luxe [lyks] *nm* luxury. **luxueux** *adj* luxurious.
Luxembourg [lyksɑ̃bur] *nm* Luxembourg.
luxure [lyksyr] *nf* lust. **luxurieux** *adj* lascivious.
lycée [lise] *nm* secondary school. **lycéen, -enne** *nm, nf* secondary school pupil.
lyncher [lɛ̃ʃe] *v* lynch.
lynx [lɛ̃ks] *nm* lynx.
lyre [lir] *nf* lyre.
lyrique [lirik] *adj* lyrical.

M

m' [m] *V* **me**.
ma [ma] *V* **mon**.
macabre [makabrə] *adj* macabre.
macaroni [makarɔni] *nm* macaroni.
macédoine [masedwan] *nf* (*fam*) jumble. **macédoine de fruits** fruit salad. **macédoine de légumes** mixed vegetables *pl*.
mâcher [maʃe] *v* chew, munch. **mâchoire** *nf* jaw.
machin [maʃɛ̃] (*fam*) *nm* thing, contraption; whatsit. **Machin** *nm* what's-his-name.
machine [maʃin] *nf* machine; (*rail, naut*) engine. **machine à coudre/laver** sewing/washing machine. **machine à écrire** typewriter. **machine à sous** slot machine. **machinal** *adj* mechanical, automatic. **machinerie** *nf* machinery.

macis [masi] *nm* mace.

maçon [masɔ̃] *nm* (*pierre*) mason; (*construction*) builder; (*briques*) bricklayer. **maçonner** *v* build. **maçonnerie** *nf* masonry; building.

maculer [makyle] *v* stain. **macule** *nf* smudge.

madame [madam] *nf*, *pl* **mesdames** madam. **Madame** *nf* (*suivi du nom de famille*) Mrs.

mademoiselle [madmwazɛl] *nf*, *pl* **mesdemoiselles** miss, young lady. **Mademoiselle** *nf* (*suivi du nom de famille*) Miss.

madère [madɛr] *nm* (*vin*) Madeira. **Madère** *nf* (*île*) Madeira.

Madrid [madrid] *n* Madrid.

madrier [madrije] *nm* beam.

magasin [magazɛ̃] *nm* shop; (*entrepôt*) warehouse; (*fusil*) magazine. **magasin à succursales multiples** chain store.

magazine [magazin] *nm* magazine.

magie [maʒi] *nf* magic. **magicien, -enne** *nm*, *nf* magician. **magique** *adj* magic, magical.

magistral [maʒistral] *adj* masterly, brilliant; authoritative.

magistrat [maʒistra] *nm* magistrate.

magnanime [maɲanim] *adj* magnanimous. **magnanimité** *nf* magnanimity.

magnat [magna] *nm* tycoon, magnate.

magnétiser [maɲetize] *v* magnetize. **magnétique** *adj* magnetic. **magnétisme** *nm* magnetism.

magnétophone [maɲetɔfɔn] *nm* tape-recorder.

magnifique [maɲifik] *adj* magnificent.

mai [mɛ] *nm* May.

maigre [mɛgrə] *adj* thin; (*viande*) lean; (*petit*) meagre, slight; (*médiocre*) poor. *nm* lean meat. **maigreur** *nf* thinness. **maigrir** *v* lose weight; (*exprès*) slim.

maille [mɑj] *nf* stitch; (*armure*) link; (*filet*) mesh. **maille filée** ladder.

maillet [majɛ] *nm* mallet.

maillot [majo] *nm* vest; (*sport*) jersey; (*danse*) leotard. **maillot de bain** (*homme*) swimming trunks *pl*; (*femme*) bathing costume.

main [mɛ̃] *nf* hand. **à la main** by hand. **en venir aux mains** come to blows. **fait main** handmade. **main-d'œuvre** *nf* labour, manpower. **sous la main** to or at hand.

maint [mɛ̃] *adj* many (a). **maintes fois** time and again.

maintenant [mɛ̃tnɑ̃] *adv* now.

***maintenir** [mɛ̃tnir] *v* maintain; support; (*garder*) keep. **se maintenir** hold one's own, keep up; continue, persist. **maintien** *nm* maintenance, upholding; (*posture*) deportment.

maire [mɛr] *nm* mayor. **mairie** *nf* town hall.

mais [mɛ] *conj* but. *nm* objection.

maïs [mais] *nm* maize or US corn.

maison [mɛzɔ̃] *nf* house; (*foyer*) home; firm, company; (*domestique*) household. *adj invar* home-made. **maison de repos** convalescent home. **maison de retraite** old people's home. **maison de santé** nursing home.

maître, -esse [mɛtrə, -ɛs] *adj* main, major. *nm* master. **être maître de** be in control of. **maître chanteur** blackmailer. **maître de chapelle** choirmaster. **maître d'hôtel** (*maison*) butler; (*hôtel*) head waiter. *nf* mistress.

maîtriser [metrize] *v* control, master, overcome. **maîtrise** *nf* mastery; control. **maîtrise de soi** self-control.

majesté [maʒɛste] *nf* majesty. **majestueux** *adj* majestic.

majeur, -e [maʒœr] *adj* major; (*principal*) main; (*jur*) of age.

majorité [maʒɔrite] *nf* majority. **être majoritaire** be in the majority.

majuscule [maʒyskyl] *nf*, *adj* capital.

mal [mal] *adv* badly; ill; (*incorrectement*) wrongly; with difficulty. **mal acquis** ill-gotten. **mal à l'aise** ill-at-ease. **mal comprendre** misunderstand. **mal élevé** ill-mannered. **mal interpréter** misinterpret. **pas mal** rather well, not badly. **pas mal de** (*fam*) quite a lot of. *adj invar* bad, wrong; (*malade*) ill; (*mal à l'aise*) uncomfortable. *nm* evil; (*douleur*) pain; (*maladie*) sickness; (*tristesse*) sorrow; difficulty, trouble; (*dommage*) harm. **avoir mal** be in pain, ache. **avoir mal à** have a pain in. **avoir mal aux dents/oreilles** have toothache/earache. **faire du mal à** hurt, harm. **mal de l'air** airsickness. **mal de mer** seasickness. **mal de tête** headache. **mal du pays** homesickness. **se faire mal** hurt oneself.

malade [malad] *adj* ill, sick. *n(m + f)* invalid, sick person; (*d'un médecin*) patient. **maladie** *nf* illness, disease. **maladif** *adj* sickly.

maladresse [maladrɛs] *nf* clumsiness, awkwardness; (*gaffe*) blunder.
maladroit [maladrwa] *adj* clumsy; (*indélicat*) tactless.
malaise [malɛz] *nm* discomfort; (*trouble*) uneasiness.
malappris [malapri] *adj* ill-mannered.
malaria [malarja] *nf* malaria.
malavisé [malavize] *adj* unwise, ill-advised.
malchance [malʃɑ̃s] *nf* misfortune, bad luck. **malchanceux** *adj* unlucky.
malcommode [malkɔmɔd] *adj* inconvenient; (*peu pratique*) unsuitable.
mâle [mɑl] *adj* male; virile. *nm* male.
malédiction [malediksjɔ̃] *nf* curse.
malentendu [malɑ̃tɑ̃dy] *nm* misunderstanding.
malfaisant [malfəzɑ̃] *adj* evil, harmful.
malgré [malgre] *prep* despite, in spite of.
malheur [malœr] *nm* misfortune; (*épreuve*) hardship; (*accident*) mishap. **malheureux** *adj* unfortunate; miserable.
malhonnête [malɔnɛt] *adj* dishonest; (*impoli*) rude. **malhonnêteté** *nf* dishonesty; rudeness.
Mali [mali] *nm* Mali.
malice [malis] *nf* mischief; (*malignité*) malice. **malicieux** *adj* mischievous.
malin, -igne [malɛ̃, -iɲ] *adj* cunning, shrewd; (*fam*) difficult; (*mauvais*) malicious; (*méd*) malignant.
malingre [malɛ̃grə] *adj* sickly, puny.
malle [mal] *nf* trunk; (*auto*) boot.
malmener [malmənə] *v* manhandle.
malotru [malɔtry], **-e** *nm, nf* uncouth person, lout.
malpropre [malprɔprə] *adj* dirty; (*travail*) slovenly; (*indélicat*) unsavoury. **malpropreté** *nf* dirtiness; (*propos*) unsavoury remark; (*acte*) low trick.
malsain [malsɛ̃] *adj* unhealthy.
malséant [malseɑ̃] *adj* unseemly.
malt [malt] *nm* malt.
Malte [malt] *nf* Malta. **maltais** *nm, adj* Maltese. **les Maltais** the Maltese.
maltraiter [maltrete] *v* ill-treat, manhandle; misuse.
malveillant [malvɛjɑ̃, -ɑ̃t] *adj* malevolent, malicious. **malveillance** *nf* malevolence.
maman [mamɑ̃] *nf* (*fam*) mummy, mum.
mamelle [mamɛl] *nf* (*femme*) breast; (*animal*) teat; (*pis*) udder. **mamelon** *nm* nipple.
mammifère [mamifɛr] *nm* mammal.

mammouth [mamut] *nm* mammoth.
manche[1] [mɑ̃ʃ] *nf* sleeve. **à manches courtes/longues** short-/long-sleeved. **la Manche** the English Channel. **manchette** *nf* cuff; (*journal*) headline. **manchon** *nm* muff.
manche[2] [mɑ̃ʃ] *nf* handle. **manche à balai** broomstick; (*aéro*) joystick.
manchot [mɑ̃ʃo] *adj* one-armed; (*sans bras*) armless. *nm* penguin.
mandarine [mɑ̃darin] *nf* mandarin, tangerine.
mandat [mɑ̃da] *nm* mandate; (*police*) warrant. **mandat-poste** *nm* postal order. **mandater** *v* commission; elect.
mandoline [mɑ̃dɔlin] *nf* mandolin.
manège [manɛʒ] *nm* (*fête foraine*) roundabout; (*équitation*) riding school; (*jeu*) game.
manette [manɛt] *nf* lever.
manger [mɑ̃ʒe] *v* eat; (*fortune*) squander. *nm* food. **mangeable** *adj* edible.
mangue [mɑ̃g] *nf* mango. **manguier** *nm* mango tree.
maniaque [manjak] *adj* fussy, fanatical. *n(m+f)* fanatic.
manie [mani] *nf* odd habit; (*obsession*) mania.
manier [manje] *v* handle. **maniable** *adj* manageable; easily influenced; (*accommodant*) amenable. **maniement** *nm* handling.
manière [manjɛr] *nf* way, manner; style. **de manière à** so as to. **d'une manière ou d'une autre** somehow or other. **manières** *nf pl* manners *pl*; behaviour *sing*. **maniéré** *adj* affected.
manifeste [manifɛst] *adj* obvious, evident. *nm* manifesto.
manifester [manifɛste] *v* show, indicate; (*pol*) demonstrate. **manifestant, -e** *nm, nf* demonstrator. **manifestation** *nf* demonstration; expression; appearance.
manipuler [manipyle] *v* manipulate; (*objet*) handle. **manipulation** *nf* manipulation; handling.
manivelle [manivɛl] *nf* crank.
manne [man] *nf* hamper.
mannequin [mankɛ̃] *nm* (*personne*) model; (*objet*) dummy.
manœuvre [manœvrə] *nf* manoeuvre, operation; (*intrigue*) scheme. *nm* labourer. **manœuvrer** *v* manoeuvre; (*machine*) operate.

manoir [manwar] *nm* manor house.

manquer [mɑ̃ke] *v* miss; (*rater*) make a mess of, botch; (*faire défaut*) be lacking; be absent; (*échouer*) fail. **manquer à** be missed by. **manquer de** lack. **manquer de faire** almost do. **ne pas manquer de** be sure to. **manque** *nm* lack, shortage; (*lacune*) gap; (*méd*) withdrawal.

mansarde [mɑ̃sard] *nf* attic.

manteau [mɑ̃to] *nm* coat.

manuel [manɥɛl] *nm, adj* manual.

manuscrit [manyskri] *adj* handwritten. *nm* manuscript.

manutention [manytɑ̃sjɔ̃] *nf* handling.

maquereau¹ [makro] *nm* (*poisson*) mackerel.

maquereau² [makro] *nm* (*argot*) pimp.

maquette [makɛt] *nf* model.

maquiller [makije] *v* make up; (*document, etc.*) fake. **maquillage** *nm* make-up.

maquis [maki] *nm* scrub, bush.

maraîcher [mareʃe], **-ère** *nm, nf* market gardener.

marais [marɛ] *nm* marsh.

marathon [maratɔ̃] *nm* marathon.

marbre [marbrə] *nm* marble.

marchand [marʃɑ̃], **-e** *nm, nf* (*boutiquier*) shopkeeper, tradesman; dealer, merchant. **marchand de journaux** newsagent. **marchand de légumes** greengrocer. **marchand de poissons** fishmonger. *adj* (*valeur*) market; (*navire*) merchant.

marchander [marʃɑ̃de] *v* haggle (over), bargain.

marchandise [marʃɑ̃diz] *nf* merchandise, goods *pl*.

marche [marʃ] *nf* walk, walking; (*mil, etc.*) march; (*machine, véhicule*) running; progress; (*escalier*) step. **marche arrière** reverse. **mettre en marche** start, set going.

marché [marʃe] *nm* market; (*contrat*) bargain, deal. **Marché commun** Common Market. **marché noir** black market.

marcher [marʃe] *v* walk; (*mil*) march; (*mettre le pied*) step, tread; (*fonctionner*) work.

mardi [mardi] *nm* Tuesday. **Mardi gras** Shrove Tuesday.

mare [mar] *nf* (*étang*) pond; (*flaque*) pool.

marécage [marekaʒ] *nm* marsh, bog. **marécageux** *adj* marshy.

maréchal [mareʃal] *nm* marshal, field marshal. **maréchal-ferrant** *nm* blacksmith.

marée [mare] *nf* tide. **marée noire** oil slick.

margarine [margarin] *nf* margarine.

marge [marʒ] *nf* margin. **marginal** *adj* marginal.

marguerite [margərit] *nf* daisy.

mari [mari] *nm* husband.

mariage [marjaʒ] *nm* marriage; (*cérémonie*) wedding.

marié [marje], **-e** *adj* married. *nm* bridegroom. *nf* bride.

marier [marje] *v* marry; (*couleurs, etc.*) blend. **se marier** get married.

marihuana [mariɥana] *nf* marijuana.

marin [marɛ̃] *adj* sea, marine. *nm* sailor.

marina [marina] *nf* marina.

marine [marin] *nf, adj invar* navy. **marine marchande** merchant navy.

mariner [marine] *v* marinade. **marinade** *nf* marinade.

marionnette [marjɔnɛt] *nf* puppet.

marital [marital] *adj* marital.

maritime [maritim] *adj* maritime; (*ville*) coastal; (*commerce, etc.*) shipping.

marjolaine [marʒɔlɛn] *nf* marjoram.

mark [mark] *nm* mark.

marmite [marmit] *nf* pot.

marmonner [marmɔne] *v* mumble, mutter.

marmot [marmo] *nm* (*fam*) kid, brat.

marmotter [marmɔte] *v* mumble, mutter.

Maroc [marɔk] *nm* Morocco. **marocain** *adj* Moroccan. **Marocain, -e** *nm, nf* Moroccan.

marotte [marɔt] *nf* hobby, craze.

marquer [marke] *v* mark; indicate, show; (*écrire*) write *or* note down; (*événement*) stand out. **marque** *nf* mark; (*comm*) brand, make; (*sport*) score. **de marque** (*produit*) high-class; (*personne*) distinguished, important. **marque de fabrique** trademark.

marqueterie [markətri] *nf* marquetry.

marquis [marki] *nm* marquis *or* marquess. **marquise** *nf* marchioness.

marraine [marɛn] *nf* godmother.

marre [mar] (*fam*) *adv* **en avoir marre** be fed up. **marrant** *adj* funny. **se marrer** *v* laugh.

marron [marɔ̃] *nm* chestnut; (*couleur*) brown. **marron d'Inde** horse-chestnut. *adj invar* brown. **marronnier** *nm* chestnut tree.

mars [mars] *nm* March.

Mars [mars] *nm* Mars. **martien, -enne** *n, adj* Martian.

marsouin [marswɛ̃] *nm* porpoise.

marsupial [marsypjal] *nm, adj* marsupial.

marteau [marto] *nm* hammer; *(porte)* knocker. **marteau-piqueur** *nm* pneumatic drill.

marteler [martəle] *v* hammer, pound.

martial [marsjal] *adj* martial, warlike.

martinet [martinɛ] *nm* swift.

martin-pêcheur [martɛ̃pɛʃœr] *nm* king-fisher.

martre [martrə] *nf* marten. **martre zibeline** sable.

martyr [martir], **-e** *nm, nf* martyr. **martyre** *nm* martyrdom; *(souffrance)* agony. **martyriser** *v* (*rel*) martyr; torture; *(bébé)* batter.

mascara [maskara] *nm* mascara.

mascarade [maskarad] *nf* masquerade.

mascotte [maskɔt] *nf* mascot.

masculin [maskylɛ̃] *nm, adj* masculine. **masculinité** *nf* masculinity.

masochiste [mazɔʃist] *n(m+f)* masochist. *adj* masochistic. **masochisme** *nm* masochism.

masquer [maske] *v* hide, mask. **masque** *nm* mask; air, façade. **masque de beauté** face-pack.

massacrer [masakre] *v* massacre; *(animaux)* slaughter; *(fam)* make a mess of. **massacre** *nm* massacre; slaughter.

masse[1] [mas] *nf* mass; *(élec)* earth.

masse[2] [mas] *nf* *(maillet)* sledge-hammer; *(bâton)* mace.

massepain [maspɛ̃] *nm* marzipan.

masser[1] [mase] *v* assemble, gather together.

masser[2] [mase] *v* massage. **massage** *nm* massage. **masseur** *nm* masseur. **masseuse** *nf* masseuse.

massif [masif] *adj* massive; solid, heavy. *nm* clump; *(géog)* massif.

massue [masy] *nf* club.

mastic [mastik] *nm* putty.

mastiquer[1] [mastike] *v* (*mâcher*) chew.

mastiquer[2] [mastike] *v* apply putty to.

mastodonte [mastɔdɔ̃t] *nm* *(camion)* juggernaut; *(personne)* colossus.

se masturber [mastyrbe] *v* masturbate. **masturbation** *nf* masturbation.

mat[1] [mat] *nm* checkmate. *adj invar* checkmated. **faire mât** checkmate.

mat[2] [mat] *adj* matt, dull.

mât [mɑ] *nm* (*naut*) mast; *(poteau)* pole.

match [matʃ] *nm* match. **match nul** draw.

matelas [matla] *nm* mattress. **matelas pneumatique** air-bed. **matelasser** *v* pad.

matelot [matlo] *nm* sailor.

se matérialiser [materjalize] *v* materialize.

matérialiste [materjalist] *adj* materialistic. *n(m+f)* materialist.

matériaux [materjo] *nm pl* material(s).

matériel [materjɛl] *adj* material. *nm* equipment, materials *pl*; *(tech)* plant.

maternel [maternɛl] *adj* maternal; *(soin, geste)* motherly. **école maternelle** *nf* nursery school. **maternité** *nf* maternity, motherhood; maternity hospital.

mathématique [matematik] *adj* mathematical. **mathématiques** *nf pl* mathematics *sing*. **mathématicien, -enne** *nm, nf* mathematician. **maths** *nf pl* (*fam*) maths *sing*.

matière [matjɛr] *nf* matter; subject; material. **matière grasse** fat. **matières premières** raw materials *pl*.

matin [matɛ̃] *nm* morning. **de bon matin** early in the morning. **matinal** *adj* morning, early. **matinée** *nf* morning; *(théâtre)* afternoon performance, matinée.

matois [matwa] *adj* wily, sly.

matraque [matrak] *nf* truncheon, cosh.

matriarcal [matrijarkal] *adj* matriarchal.

matrice [matris] *nf* matrix; *(utérus)* womb.

matrimonial [matrimɔnjal] *adj* matrimonial.

maturité [matyrite] *nf* maturity.

*maudire [modir] *v* curse.

mausolée [mozɔle] *nm* mausoleum.

maussade [mosad] *adj* sullen, morose; *(triste)* gloomy.

mauvais [movɛ] *adj* bad; *(erroné)* wrong; *(vilain)* wicked, evil; *(désagréable)* nasty, unpleasant. **mauvaise herbe** *nf* weed.

mauve [mov] *nm, adj* mauve.

maxime [maksim] *nf* maxim.

maximum [maksimɔm] *nm, adj* maximum.

mayonnaise [majɔnɛz] *nf* mayonnaise.

mazout [mazut] *nm* oil.

me [mə], **m'** *pron* me, to me; *(réfléchi)* myself.

méandre [meɑ̃drə] *nm* meander.

mec [mɛk] *nm* (*argot*) bloke.

mécanique [mekanik] *adj* mechanical. *nf* mechanics. **mécanicien, -enne** *nm, nf* mechanic; (*naut, aéro*) engineer. **mécaniser** *v* mechanize. **méchanisme** *nm* mechanism; mechanics *pl*.

méchant [meʃɑ̃] *adj* nasty; (*malveillant*) spiteful; (*enfant*) naughty; (*vilain*) wicked. **méchanceté** *nf* nastiness; (*propos*) spiteful remark.

mèche [mɛʃ] *nf* (*bougie*) wick; (*bombe*) fuse; (*cheveux*) lock; (*tech*) bit. **être de mèche avec** be in league with.

mécompte [mekɔ̃t] *nm* (*déception*) disappointment; (*erreur*) miscalculation.

mécontent [mekɔ̃tɑ̃] *adj* discontented, dissatisfied; (*contrarié*) annoyed. **mécontentement** *nm* dissatisfaction. **mécontenter** *v* displease, annoy.

médaille [medaj] *nf* medal.

médecin [mɛdsɛ̃] *nm* doctor. **médecine** *nf* medicine.

media [medja] *nm pl* mass media *pl*.

médiation [medjasjɔ̃] *nf* mediation. **médiateur, -trice** *nm, nf* mediator.

médical [medikal] *adj* medical.

médicament [medikamɑ̃] *nm* medicine.

médication [medikasjɔ̃] *nf* treatment, medication.

médicinal [medisinal] *adj* medicinal.

médiéval [medjeval] *adj* medieval.

médiocre [medjɔkrə] *adj* mediocre, poor. **médiocrité** *nf* mediocrity.

*médire [medir] *v* speak ill, malign. **médisance** *nf* scandal, gossip.

méditer [medite] *v* meditate, contemplate. **Méditerrané** [mediterane] *nf* Mediterranean (Sea). **méditerranéen** *adj* Mediterranean.

méduse [medyz] *nf* jellyfish.

méfait [mefɛ] *nm* misdemeanour. **méfaits** *nm pl* ravages *pl*, damage *sing*.

se méfier [mefje] *v* be careful, look out. **se méfier de** mistrust, be suspicious of; beware of. **méfiance** *nf* distrust. **méfiant** *adj* suspicious.

mégarde [megard] *nf* **par mégarde** accidentally, inadvertently.

mégère [meʒɛr] *nf* shrew.

mégot [mego] *nm* (*fam*) fag end.

meilleur, -e [mɛjœr] *adj, adv* better. **le meilleur, la meilleure** (the) best.

mélancolie [melɑ̃kɔli] *nf* melancholy. **mélancolique** *adj* melancholy, melancholic.

mélanger [melɑ̃ʒe] *v* mix (up); (*couleurs, etc.*) blend. **mélange** *nm* mixture; blend.

mélasse [melas] *nf* treacle.

mêler [mele] *v* mix, mingle; (*cartes*) shuffle; (*impliquer*) involve. **se mêler à** join, mingle with; get involved in. **se mêler de** meddle with, interfere in. **mêle-toi de tes affaires!** mind your own business! **mêlée** *nf* fray, mêlée; (*rugby*) scrum. **mêlée générale** free-for-all.

mélèze [melɛz] *nm* larch.

mélodie [melɔdi] *nf* melody. **mélodieux** *adj* melodious. **mélodique** *adj* melodic.

mélodrame [melɔdram] *nm* melodrama. **mélodramatique** *adj* melodramatic.

melon [məlɔ̃] *nm* melon; (*chapeau*) bowler.

membrane [mɑ̃bran] *nf* membrane.

membre [mɑ̃brə] *nm* (*anat*) limb; (*société*) member.

même [mɛm] *adj* (*semblable*) same; very. *pron* same. *adv* even. **de même** likewise. **quand même** all the same.

mémé [meme] *nf* (*fam*) granny, grandma.

mémento [memɛ̃to] *nm* (*agenda*) engagement diary; note.

mémoire[1] [memwar] *nf* memory.

mémoire[2] (*memwar*) *nm* memorandum; report; (*comm*) bill; (*exposé*) paper. **mémoires** *nm pl* memoirs *pl*.

mémorable [memɔrablə] *adj* memorable.

mémorandum [memɔrɑ̃dɔm] *nm* memorandum.

menacer [mənase] *v* threaten. **menaçant** *adj* menacing, threatening. **menace** *nf* threat.

ménage [menaʒ] *nm* (*entretien*) housekeeping, housework; married couple; (*communauté*) household. **ménager** *adj* household, domestic. **ménagère** *nf* (*femme*) housewife; (*couverts*) canteen of cutlery.

ménager [menaʒe] *v* spare; (*personne*) show consideration for; (*argent, etc.*) use sparingly *or* carefully; (*amener*) bring about; arrange. **ménagement** *nm* care, consideration.

mendier [mɑ̃dje] *v* beg (for). **mendiant, -e** *nm, nf* beggar. **mendicité** *nf* begging.

mener [məne] *v* lead; (*emmener*) take; (*enquête, conversation*) conduct; (*affaires, entreprise*) manage, run. **menées** *nf pl* intrigues *pl*. **meneur, -euse** *nm, nf* leader.

ménestrel [menɛstrɛl] *nm* minstrel.

méningite [menɛ̃ʒit] *nf* meningitis.
ménopause [menɔpoz] *nf* menopause.
menottes [mənɔt] *nf pl* handcuffs *pl.*
mensonge [mɑ̃sɔ̃ʒ] *nm* lie. **mensonger** *adj* false.
menstruel [mɑ̃stryɛl] *adj* menstrual. **menstruation** *nf* menstruation.
mensuel [mɑ̃sɥɛl] *adj* monthly. **mensuellement** *adv* monthly.
mensuration [mɑ̃syrɑsjɔ̃] *nf* measurement.
mental [mɑ̃tal] *adj* mental. **mentalité** *nf* mentality.
menteur, -euse [mɑ̃tœr, -øz] *adj* false; illusory; (*personne*) untruthful. *nm, nf* liar.
menthe [mɑ̃t] *nf* mint.
menthol [mɛ̃tɔl] *nm* menthol.
mention [mɑ̃sjɔ̃] *nf* mention; note; (*examen*) grade, class. **avec mention très bien** with distinction. **mentionner** *v* mention.
*mentir [mɑ̃tir] *v* lie.
menton [mɑ̃tɔ̃] *nm* chin.
menu [mⱥny] *adj* (*fin*) small, slight; (*peu important*) petty, minor. *adv* finely, small. *nm* menu.
menuisier [mⱥnɥizje] *nm* joiner, carpenter. **menuiserie** *nf* joinery, carpentry, woodwork.
se *méprendre [meprɑ̃drⱥ] *v* make a mistake.
mépris [mepri] *nm* contempt, scorn.
méprise [mepriz] *nf* mistake.
mépriser [meprize] *v* scorn, despise. **méprisable** *adj* contemptible. **méprisant** *adj* contemptuous.
mer [mɛr] *nf* sea; (*marée*) tide. **en mer** at sea.
mercenaire [mɛrsⱥnɛr] *nm, adj* mercenary.
mercerie [mɛrsⱥri] *nf* haberdashery.
merci [mɛrsi] *interj* thank you; (*refus*) no thank you. **merci beaucoup** *or* **bien** thank you very much. *nm* thank-you, thanks *pl. nf* mercy.
mercier [mɛrsje], **-ère** *nm, nf* haberdasher.
mercredi [mɛrkrⱥdi] *nm* Wednesday. **mercredi des Cendres** Ash Wednesday.
mercure [mɛrkyr] *nm* mercury.
merde [mɛrd] (*vulgaire*) *nf* shit. *interj* hell! shit!
mère [mɛr] *nf* mother.
méridien [meridjɛ̃] *nm, adj* meridian.
méridional [meridjɔnal] *adj* southern; from the south of France. **Méridional, -e** *nm, nf* Southerner.

meringue [mⱥrɛ̃g] *nf* meringue.
mériter [merite] *v* deserve, merit; (*exiger*) require; (*valoir*) be worth. **mérite** *nm* merit; (*respect*) credit; quality.
merlan [mɛrlɑ̃] *nm* whiting.
merle [mɛrl] *nm* blackbird.
merveille [mɛrvɛj] *nf* wonder, marvel. **à merveille** perfectly, marvellously. **merveilleux** *adj* wonderful, marvellous.
mes [me] *V* **mon.**
mésaventure [mezavɑ̃tyr] *nf* misadventure, misfortune.
mesquin [mɛskɛ̃] *adj* mean, stingy; (*étroit*) petty. **mesquinerie** *nf* meanness; pettiness.
message [mesaʒ] *nm* message. **messager, -ère** *nm, nf* messenger. **messageries** *nf pl* parcels service *sing.* **bureau de messageries** *nm* parcel office.
messe [mɛs] *nf* mass.
mesurer [mⱥzyre] *v* measure; (*évaluer*) assess; limit, ration. **mesure** *nf* measure; measurement; (*musique*) bar; (*cadence*) time; moderation. **à mesure que** as. **fait sur mesure** made-to-measure. **mesuré** *adj* measured; moderate; (*ton*) steady.
métabolisme [metabɔlismⱥ] *nm* metabolism.
métal [metal] *nm* metal. **métallique** *adj* metallic. **métallurgie** *nf* metallurgy. **métallurgiste** *nm* metallurgist; (*ouvrier*) metal-worker.
métamorphose [metamɔrfoz] *nf* metamorphosis.
métaphore [metafɔr] *nf* metaphor. **métaphorique** *adj* metaphorical.
métaphysique [metafizik] *adj* metaphysical. *nf* metaphysics.
météore [meteɔr] *nm* meteor. **météorique** *adj* meteoric. **météorite** *nm* meteorite.
météorologie [meteɔrɔlɔʒi] *nf* meteorology. **météorologique** *adj* meteorological, weather. **météorologue** *n(m + f)* meteorologist.
méthane [metan] *nm* methane.
méthode [metɔd] *nf* method. **méthodique** *adj* methodical.
méthodiste [metɔdist] *n(m + f), adj* Methodist. **méthodisme** *nm* Methodism.
méticuleux [metikyløʉ] *adj* meticulous.
métier [metje] *nm* job, trade, profession; technique, experience; (*machine*) loom.

métis, -isse [metis] *n, adj* half-caste, half-breed. **métisser** *v* cross.

métrage [metraʒ] *nm* length; measurement.

mètre [mɛtrə] *nm* metre; (*règle*) rule. **mètre à ruban** tape measure. **métrique** *adj* metric.

metro [metro] *nm* subway, tube.

métronome [metrɔnɔm] *nm* metronome.

métropole [metrɔpɔl] *nf* metropolis. **métropolitain** *adj* metropolitan.

mets [mɛ] *nm* dish.

***mettre** [mɛtrə] *v* put; (*vêtements*) put on, wear; (*temps*) take, spend; suppose. **se mettre à** start. **metteur en scène** *nm* (*théâtre*) producer; (*cinéma*) director.

meubler [mœble] *v* furnish; (*remplir*) fill (out). **meuble** *nm* piece of furniture. **meubles** *nm pl* furniture *sing*.

meugler [møgle] *v* moo, low. **meuglement** *nm* lowing.

meule[1] [møl] *nf* (*moudre*) millstone; (*aiguiser*) grindstone.

meule[2] [møl] *nf* stack, rick. **meule de foin** haystack.

meunier [mønje] *nm* miller.

meurtre [mœrtrə] *nm* murder.

meurtrier [mœrtrije], **-ère** *nm, nf* murderer. *adj* murderous, lethal.

meurtrir [mœrtrir] *v* bruise. **meurtrissure** *nf* bruise.

meute [møt] *nf* pack.

mi- [mi] *prefix* half-, mid-. **à mi-chemin** halfway. **à mi-corps** to the waist. **à mi-côte** halfway up *or* down. **à mi-temps** part-time. **à mi-voix** in an undertone. **mijanvier, mi-février, etc.** mid-January, mid-February, etc.

miche [miʃ] *nf* round loaf.

micro [mikro] *nm* (*fam*) mike.

microbe [mikrɔb] *nm* germ, microbe.

microfilm [mikrɔfilm] *nm* microfilm.

microphone [mikrɔfɔn] *nm* microphone.

microscope [mikrɔskɔp] *nm* microscope. **microscopique** *adj* microscopic.

microsillon [mikrɔsijɔ̃] *nm* long-playing record.

midi [midi] *nm* midday, noon; lunchtime; (*géog*) south. **le Midi** the South of France.

mie [mi] *nf* soft part of bread.

miel [mjɛl] *nm* honey. **mielleux** *adj* (*péj*) sugary, smooth.

mien [mjɛ̃], **mienne** *pron* **le mien, la mienne** mine.

miette [mjɛt] *nf* crumb.

mieux [mjø] *adj, adv* better. **le** *or* **la mieux** (the) best.

mièvre [mjɛvrə] *adj* mawkish, affected.

mignon, -onne [miɲɔ̃, -ɔn] *adj* sweet, dainty. *nm, nf* darling.

migraine [migrɛn] *nf* headache; (*méd*) migraine.

migration [migrasjɔ̃] *nf* migration.

mijoter [miʒɔte] *v* simmer; (*fam*) plot, cook up.

mildiou [mildju] *nm* mildew.

milieu [miljø] *nm* middle; environment; (*social*) circle, background. **au milieu de** in the middle of. **juste milieu** happy medium.

militaire [militɛr] *adj* military. *nm* soldier.

militant [militɑ̃], **-e** *n, adj* militant.

mille[1] [mil] *nm, adj invar* (a) thousand. **mille-pattes** *nm invar* centipede. **milliard** *nm* thousand million. **millième** *n(m+f)*, *adj* thousandth. **millier** *nm* thousand or so. **des milliers de** thousands *or* millions of.

mille[2] [mil] *nm* mile.

millénaire [milenɛr] *nm* millennium, thousand years. *adj* thousand-year-old, ancient.

milligramme [miligram] *nm* milligram.

millilitre [mililitrə] *nm* millilitre.

millimètre [milimɛtrə] *nm* millimetre.

million [miljɔ̃] *nm* million. **millionnaire** *n(m+f)* millionnaire. **millionième** *n(m+f)*, *adj* millionth.

mimer [mime] *v* mime; (*imiter*) mimic. **mime** *nm* mime; mimic.

minable [minablə] *adj* (*lieu*) seedy, shabby; miserable, wretched; (*fam: piètre*) pathetic, hopeless.

minauder [minode] *v* mince, simper.

mince [mɛ̃s] *adj* thin; (*svelte*) slim, slender; (*insignifiant*) slight, small. *adv* thinly. *interj* blast! drat! **minceur** *nf* thinness.

mine[1] [min] *nf* expression; look, appearance. **avoir bonne/mauvaise mine** look well/unwell. **faire mine de** pretend to, make as if to.

mine[2] [min] *nf* mine; (*crayon*) lead. **miner** *v* (*mil*) mine; (*saper*) undermine. **mineur** *nm* miner. **minier** *adj* mining.

minerai [minrɛ] *nm* ore.

minéral [mineral] *nm, adj* mineral.

mineur, -e [minœr] *n, adj* minor.

miniature [minjatyr] *nf, adj* miniature.

minime [minim] *adj* minimal; (*insignifiant*) trivial; (*piètre*) paltry. **minimiser** *v* minimize. **minimum** *nm, adj* minimum.

ministère [ministɛr] *nm* ministry; government. **ministériel** *adj* ministerial. **ministre** *nm* minister.

minorité [minɔrite] *nf* minority. **minoritaire** *adj* minority.

minuit [minɥi] *nm* midnight.

minuscule [minyskyl] *adj* minute, tiny; (*lettre*) small. *nf* small letter.

minute [minyt] *nf* minute; moment, instant.

minutieux [minysjø] *adj* meticulous, minute. **minutie** *nf* meticulousness; (*ouvrage*) minute detail.

mioche [mjɔʃ] *n(m+f)* (*fam*) kid, brat.

miracle [miraklə] *nm* miracle. **miraculeux** *adj* miraculous.

mirage [miraʒ] *nm* mirage.

mirer [mire] *v* mirror. **se mirer** be reflected.

miroir [mirwar] *nm* mirror.

miroiter [mirwate] *v* sparkle, gleam.

misanthrope [mizɑ̃trɔp] *n(m+f)* misanthropist. *adj* misanthropic. **misanthropie** *nf* misanthropy.

mise [miz] *nf* putting; (*enjeu*) stake; (*vêtements*) clothing. **être de mise** be acceptable. **mise en plis** set. **mise en scène** production. **miser** *v* stake, bet.

misérable [mizerablə] *adj* miserable; (*pitoyable*) wretched; (*pauvre*) destitute; (*minable*) paltry. *n(m+f)* wretch.

misère [mizɛr] *nf* (*malheur*) misery, misfortune; poverty. **faire des misères à** (*fam*) be nasty to.

miséricorde [mizerikɔrd] *nf* mercy. **miséricordieux** *adj* merciful.

misogyne [mizɔʒin] *n(m+f)* misogynist. **misogynie** *nf* misogyny.

missile [misil] *nm* missile.

mission [misjɔ̃] *nf* mission. **missionnaire** *n(m+f)* missionary.

mite [mit] *nf* clothes moth. **mité** *adj* moth-eaten. **miteux** *adj* seedy, shabby.

mitoyen [mitwajɛ̃] *adj* dividing, common. **mur mitoyen** *nm* party wall.

mitrailleuse [mitrajøz] *nf* machine gun.

mitre [mitrə] *nf* mitre.

mixte [mikst] *adj* mixed; (*école*) coeducational.

mobile [mɔbil] *adj* mobile, moving, movable. *nm* motive; (*art*) mobile. **mobiliser** *v* mobilize. **mobilité** *nf* mobility.

mobilier [mɔbilje] *adj* (*jur*) personal, movable. *nm* furniture.

mocassin [mɔkasɛ̃] *nm* moccasin.

moche [mɔʃ] (*fam*) *adj* (*mauvais*) rotten; (*laid*) ugly.

mode[1] [mɔd] *nf* fashion; style. **à la mode** fashionable.

mode[2] [mɔd] *nm* mode; method; (*gramm*) mood. **mode d'emploi** directions for use.

modeler [mɔdle] *v* model, shape, mould. **modèle** *nm, adj* model.

modérer [mɔdere] *v* moderate, restrain. **se modérer** control oneself. **modération** *nf* moderation; reduction. **modéré** *adj* moderate.

moderne [mɔdɛrn] *adj* modern. **modernisation** *nf* modernization. **moderniser** *v* modernize.

modeste [mɔdɛst] *adj* modest. **modestie** *nf* modesty.

modifier [mɔdifje] *v* modify. **modification** *nf* modification.

modique [mɔdik] *adj* modest, small.

module [mɔdyl] *nm* module.

moduler [mɔdyle] *v* modulate. **modulation** *nf* modulation.

moelle [mwal] *nf* (*anat*) marrow; pith. **moelle épinière** spinal cord. **moelleux** *adj* soft, smooth, mellow.

mœurs [mœr] *nf pl* morals *pl*; customs *pl*; habits *pl*; manners *pl*.

mohair [mɔɛr] *nm* mohair.

moi [mwa] *pron* me; (*sujet*) I. *nm* self, ego. **moi-même** *pron* myself.

moignon [mwaɲɔ̃] *nm* stump.

moindre [mwɛ̃drə] *adj* less; (*plus bas*) lower; (*inférieur*) poorer. **le** *or* **la moindre** the least, the slightest.

moine [mwan] *nm* monk.

moineau [mwano] *nm* sparrow.

moins [mwɛ̃] *nm, adv* less. **à moins de** barring, unless. **à moins que** unless. **au moins** at least. **du moins** at least. **le** *or* **la moins** (the) least. **moins de** less (than); (*heure*) before. *prep* minus. **six heures moins dix** ten to six.

mois [mwa] *nm* month. **au mois** by the month, monthly.

moisir [mwazir] *v* go mouldy. **moisi** *adj* mouldy. **sentir le moisi** smell musty. **moisissure** *nf* mould.

moisson [mwasɔ̃] *nf* harvest, crop. **mois-**

sonner v harvest, reap. **moissonneuse-batteuse** nf combine harvester.
moite [mwat] adj moist, clammy.
moitié [mwatje] nf half. **à moitié** half. **moitié moitié** half-and-half.
mol [mɔl] form of **mou** used before a vowel or mute h.
molécule [mɔlekyl] nf molecule. **moléculaire** adj molecular.
molester [mɔlɛste] v manhandle, maul.
mollasse [mɔlas] (fam) adj lethargic; (flasque) flabby.
molle [mɔl] V **mou**.
mollesse [mɔlɛs] nf softness; (manque de fermeté) limpness; lethargy, lifelessness.
mollet, -ette [mɔlɛ, -ɛt] adj soft; (œuf) soft-boiled. nm (anat) calf.
mollir [mɔlir] v soften; (vent) abate; (fléchir) yield; give way.
mollusque [mɔlysk] nm mollusc.
môme [mom] n(m+f) (fam) kid, brat.
moment [mɔmɑ̃] nm moment; time. **en ce moment** at the moment. **momentané** adj momentary, brief.
momie [mɔmi] nf mummy. **momification** nf mummification. **momifier** v mummify.
mon [mɔ̃], **ma** adj, pl **mes** my.
Monaco [mɔnako] nm Monaco.
monarque [mɔnark] nm monarch. **monarchie** nf monarchy. **monarchiste** n(m+f) monarchist.
monastère [mɔnastɛr] nm monastery. **monastique** adj monastic.
monceau [mɔ̃so] nm heap, pile.
monde [mɔ̃d] nm world; (gens) people; society, circle. **tout le monde** everybody.
mondain adj fashionable; society; refined; (rel) worldly. **mondial** adj worldwide.
monétaire [mɔnetɛr] adj monetary.
mongolien [mɔ̃gɔljɛ̃], **-enne** n, adj mongol. **mongolisme** nm mongolism.
moniteur, -trice [mɔnitœr, -tris] nm, nf (sport) instructor; (surveillant) supervisor.
monnaie [mɔnɛ] nf (devises) currency; (pièce) coin; (appoint) change. **monnayer** v mint; (tirer profit de) capitalize on.
monogamie [mɔnɔgami] nf monogamy. **monogame** adj monogamous.
monogramme [mɔnɔgram] nm monogram.
monologue [mɔnɔlɔg] nm monologue.
monopole [mɔnɔpɔl] nm monopoly. **monopoliser** v monopolize.

monosyllabe [mɔnɔsilab] nm monosyllable. **monosyllabique** adj monosyllabic.
monotone [mɔnɔtɔn] adj monotonous. **monotonie** nf monotony.
monseigneur [mɔ̃sɛɲœr] nm Your or His Grace, Your or His Lordship.
monsieur [məsjø] nm, pl **messieurs** gentleman; (titre) sir. **Monsieur** nm (suivi du nom de famille) Mr.
monstre [mɔ̃strə] nm monster. adj (fam) colossal. **monstrueux** adj monstrous. **monstruosité** nf monstrosity.
mont [mɔ̃] nm mount. **mont-de-piété** nm pawnshop.
montagne [mɔ̃taɲ] nf mountain. **montagnes russes** big dipper sing. **montagneux** adj mountainous.
montant [mɔ̃tɑ̃] adj upward, rising; (col, corsage) high. nm (portant) upright; (somme) total.
monter [mɔ̃te] v mount; go up, rise; ascend, climb; (porter) take up; (cheval) ride; (théâtre) put on, produce; assemble; equip. **monter à cheval/bicyclette** ride a horse/bicycle. **monter dans** or **en** get on or into. **se monter à** amount to. **montage** nm assembly; (cinéma) editing. **montée** nf ascent, climb; rise; (côte) hill. **monture** nf frame, setting, mount.
montre [mɔ̃trə] nf watch. **faire montre de** show, display. **montre-bracelet** nf wristwatch.
montrer [mɔ̃tre] v show. **se montrer** appear; prove to be.
monument [mɔnymɑ̃] nm monument. **momumental** adj monumental.
moquer [mɔke] v **se moquer de** make fun of; (mépriser) not care about. **moquerie** nf mockery.
moral [mɔral] adj moral. nm morale. **morale** or **moralité** nf morality; (mœurs) morals pl; (fable) moral. **moraliser** v moralize. **moraliste** n(m+f) moralist.
morbide [mɔrbid] adj morbid.
morceau [mɔrso] nm piece; (bout) bit; extract, passage.
mordre [mɔrdrə] v bite. **mordant** adj biting; (acerbe) scathing, cutting. **mordu** adj (fam) mad keen.
se morfondre [mɔrfɔ̃drə] v mope.
morgue[1] [mɔrg] nf morgue, mortuary.
morgue[2] [mɔrg] nf (arrogance) pride, haughtiness.

moribond [mɔribɔ̃] *adj* dying.

mormon [mɔrmɔ̃], **-e** *n, adj* Mormon.

morne [mɔrn] *adj* gloomy, dismal.

morose [mɔroz] *adj* sullen, morose.

morphine [mɔrfin] *nf* morphine.

mors [mɔr] *nm* bit.

morse[1] [mɔrs] *nm* (*zool*) walrus.

morse[2] [mɔrs] *nm* Morse code.

morsure [mɔrsyr] *nf* bite.

mort[1] [mɔr], **-e** *adj* dead. *nm, nf* dead person. **morte-saison** *nf* off season. **mort-né** *adj* stillborn.

mort[2] [mɔr] *nf* death. **mort-aux-rats** *nf* rat poison.

mortalité [mɔrtalite] *nf* mortality; (*taux*) death rate.

mortel [mɔrtɛl] *adj* mortal; fatal; (*poison, etc.*) lethal, deadly.

mortier [mɔrtje] *nm* mortar.

mortifier [mɔrtifje] *v* mortify. **mortification** *nf* mortification.

mortuaire [mɔrtᶣɛr] *adj* mortuary. **dépôt mortuaire** *nm* funeral parlour.

morue [mɔry] *nf* cod.

morveux [mɔrvø], **-euse** *nm, nf* (*argot*) kid, brat.

mosaïque [mɔzaik] *nf* mosaic.

Moscou [mɔsku] *n* Moscow.

mosquée [mɔske] *nf* mosque.

mot [mo] *nm* word; note; (*expression*) saying. **mot de passe** password. **mots croisés** crossword *sing*.

motel [mɔtɛl] *nm* motel.

moteur, -trice [mɔtœr, -tris] *nm* motor, engine. **moteur à explosion** internal combustion engine. **moteur à réaction** jet engine. *adj* (*anat*) motor; (*tech*) driving.

motif [mɔtif] *nm* motive, grounds *pl*; (*ornement, musique*) motif.

motion [mɔsjɔ̃] *nf* motion.

motiver [mɔtive] *v* motivate; justify; (*expliquer*) account for. **motivation** *nf* motivation.

moto [mɔto] *nf* (*fam*) motorbike. **motocycliste** *n*(*m*+*f*) motorcyclist.

motte [mɔt] *nf* lump; (*terre*) clod; (*gazon*) turf.

mou [mu], **molle** *adj* soft; (*sans fermeté*) limp; (*flasque*) flabby; feeble, weak; lethargic; (*temps*) muggy. *nm* softness. **avoir du mou** be slack.

mouche [muʃ] *nf* fly. **prendre la mouche** (*fam*) get in a huff. **moucheron** *nm* midge.

moucher [muʃe] *v* (*fam*) snub; (*chandelle*) snuff. **se moucher** blow one's nose.

moucheter [muʃte] *v* speckle. **moucheture** *nf* speck, spot.

mouchoir [muʃwar] *nm* handkerchief. **mouchoir en papier** tissue.

*****moudre** [mudrə] *v* grind.

moue [mu] *nf* pout. **faire la moue** pout, pull a face.

mouette [mwɛt] *nf* sea-gull.

mouffette [mufɛt] *nf* skunk.

moufle [muflə] *nf* mitten.

mouiller [muje] *v* wet; (*naut*) moor, anchor. **mouillage** *nm* mooring, anchorage. **mouillé** *adj* wet.

moule[1] [mul] *nm* mould.

moule[2] [mul] *nf* (*zool, cuisine*) mussel.

mouler [mule] *v* mould, cast; (*vêtements*) hug, fit closely.

moulin [mulɛ̃] *nm* mill. **moulin à café** coffee-mill. **moulin à paroles** (*fam*) chatterbox. **moulin à vent** windmill. **moulinet** *nm* (*pêche*) reel.

moulu [muly] *adj* ground.

*****mourir** [murir] *v* die.

mousquet [muskɛ] *nm* musket. **mousquetaire** *nm* musketeer.

mousse[1] [mus] *nf* (*bot*) moss; (*écume*) froth, foam; (*savon*) lather; (*cuisine*) mousse. **mousser** *v* froth, foam; lather; (*vin*) sparkle. **mousseux** *adj* frothy; sparkling. **moussu** *adj* mossy.

mousse[2] [mus] *nm* cabin boy.

mousseline [muslin] *nf* muslin.

mousson [musɔ̃] *nf* monsoon.

moustache [mustaʃ] *nf* moustache. **moustaches** *nf pl* (*animal*) whiskers *pl*.

moustique [mustik] *nm* mosquito.

moutarde [mutard] *nf* mustard.

mouton [mutɔ̃] *nm* sheep; (*cuisine*) mutton.

*****mouvoir** [muvwar] *v* drive, move. **se mouvoir** move. **mouvant** *adj* changing, shifting. **mouvement** *nm* movement; activity; impulse. **mouvementé** *adj* lively, eventful.

moyen [mwajɛ̃], **-enne** *adj* medium, average; middle. **moyen âge** *nm* Middle Ages *pl*. **Moyen-Orient** *nm* Middle East. *nm* means, way. **au moyen de** by means of. **moyens** *nm pl* means *pl*. **la moyenne** *nf* average.

moyennant [mwajɛnɑ̃] *prep* (in return) for.

moyeu [mwajø] *nm* hub.

muer [mɥe] v moult; (voix) break.
muet, -ette [mɥɛ, -ɛt] adj silent; (infirme) dumb. nm, nf mute, dumb person.
mufle [myflə] nm muzzle; (argot) lout.
mugir [myʒir] v bellow, roar; (vache) moo.
muguet [mygɛ] nm lily of the valley.
mule [myl] nf mule.
mulet [mylɛ] nm mule.
multicolore [myltikɔlɔr] adj multicoloured.
multiple [myltiplə] adj multiple, numerous, many. nm multiple.
multiplier [myltiplije] v multiply; (augmenter) increase. **multiplication** nf multiplication.
multitude [myltityd] nf multitude, vast number.
municipal [mynisipal] adj municipal; (conseil) local; (piscine, etc.) public. **municipalité** nf municipality; town council.
munir [mynir] v **munir de** provide with, equip with. **munitions** nf pl ammunition sing.
mur [myr] nm wall; barrier. **muraille** nf high wall.
mûr [myr] adj (fruit) ripe; (personne) mature.
mural [myral] adj mural. **peinture murale** nf mural.
mûre [myr] nf (ronce) blackberry; (mûrier) mulberry. **mûrier** nm mulberry bush; blackberry bush.
mûrir [myrir] v ripen; mature.
murmurer [myrmyre] v murmur. **murmure** nm murmur.
musc [mysk] nm musk.
muscade [myskad] nf nutmeg.
muscle [mysklə] nm muscle. **musclé** adj muscular.
museau [myzo] nm muzzle; (porc) snout.
musée [myze] nm museum; (d'art) art gallery.
museler [myzle] v muzzle. **muselière** nf muzzle.
muséum [myzeɔm] nm natural history museum.
musicien [myzisjɛ̃], -enne nm, nf musician. adj musical.
musique [myzik] nf music; (mil) band. **musical** adj musical.
musulman [myzylmɑ̃], -e n, adj Muslim.
mutiler [mytile] v mutilate; (personne)

maim. **mutilation** nf mutilation. **mutilé, -e** nm, nf disabled person.
mutin [mytɛ̃] adj mischievous. nm rebel.
se mutiner [mytine] v mutiny; rebel. **mutiné** adj mutinous. **mutinerie** nf mutiny; rebellion.
mutisme [mytismə] nm silence; (méd) dumbness.
mutuel [mytɥɛl] adj mutual.
myope [mjɔp] adj short-sighted. **myopie** nf short-sightedness.
myrtille [mirtij] nf bilberry.
mystère [mistɛr] nm mystery. **mystérieux** adj mysterious.
mystifier [mistifje] v fool, take in.
mystique [mistik] n(m+f) mystic. adj mystical, mystic. **mysticisme** nm mysticism.
mythe [mit] nm myth. **mythique** adj mythical. **mythologie** nf mythology. **mythologique** adj mythological.

N

n' [n] V ne.
nabot [nabo], -e adj tiny. nm, nf dwarf.
nacre [nakrə] nf mother-of-pearl. **nacré** adj pearly.
nager [naʒe] v swim; float; (naut) row. **nage** nf (action) swimming; (manière) stroke. **nage libre** freestyle. **nageoire** nf (poisson) fin; (phoque) flipper. **nageur, -euse** nm, nf swimmer.
naguère [nagɛr] adv not long ago; (autrefois) formerly.
naïf [naif], -ïve adj naive. nm, nf gullible fool. **naïveté** nf naivety.
nain [nɛ̃], -e n, adj dwarf.
naissance [nɛsɑ̃s] nf birth; source.
***naître** [nɛtrə] v be born; (surgir) arise, spring up. **faire naître** arouse; create.
nappe [nap] nf tablecloth; (eau) sheet; (brouillard) blanket. **nappe de pétrole** oil slick. **napperon** nm mat.
narcotique [narkɔtik] nm, adj narcotic.
narine [narin] nf nostril.
narquois [narkwa] adj mocking, derisive.
narrer [nare] v narrate. **narrateur, -trice** nm, nf narrator. **narratif** adj narrative. **narration** nf narration; (récit) narrative.

nasal [nazal] *adj* nasal. **nasaliser** *v* nasalize. **naseau** *nm* nostril. **nasillard** *adj* nasal.

natal [natal] *adj* native. **natalité** *nf* birth rate.

natation [natasjɔ̃] *nf* swimming.

natif [natif] -**ive** *n, adj* native.

nation [nɑsjɔ̃] *nf* nation. **national, -e** *n, adj* national. **nationalisation** *nf* nationalization. **nationaliser** *v* nationalize. **nationalisme** *nm* nationalism. **nationaliste** *n(m+f)* nationalist. **nationalité** *nf* nationality.

nativité [nativite] *nf* nativity.

natter [nate] *v* plait. **natte** *nf* (*cheveux*) plait; (*paille, etc.*) mat.

naturalisme [natyralismə] *nm* naturalism. **naturaliste** *n(m+f)* naturalist.

nature [natyr] *nf* nature. **en nature** in kind. **nature morte** still life. *adj invar* plain, neat.

naturel [natyrɛl] *adj* natural. *nm* disposition.

naufrage [nofraʒ] *nm* shipwreck; ruin. **naufragé** *adj* shipwrecked.

nausée [noze] *nf* nausea. **avoir la nausée** feel sick. **nauséabond** *adj* nauseating.

nautique [notik] *adj* nautical.

naval [naval] *adj* naval.

navet [navɛ] *nm* turnip; (*fam*) rubbish.

navette [navɛt] *nf* shuttle (service). **faire la navette** commute; go backwards and forwards.

naviguer [navige] *v* (*bateau*) sail; (*avion*) fly; (*piloter*) navigate. **navigateur** *nm* navigator. **navigation** *nf* navigation; traffic.

navire [navir] *nm* ship.

navrer [navre] *v* distress; (*irriter*) annoy. **navré** *adj* sorry; distressed.

ne [nə], **n'** *adv* not. **ne . . . guère** scarcely. **ne . . . jamais** never. **ne . . . pas** not. **ne . . . personne** nobody. **ne . . . plus** no longer. **ne . . . que** only. **ne . . . rien** nothing.

né [ne] *adj* born.

néanmoins [neãmwɛ̃] *adv* nevertheless, yet.

néant [neã] *nm* nothing, void.

nébuleux [nebylø] *adj* nebulous, vague; (*ciel*) cloudy.

nécessaire [nesesɛr] *adj* necessary; indispensable. *nm* essentials *pl*. **le nécessaire** what is needed. **nécessité** *nf* necessity. **nécessiter** *v* necessitate.

nécrologie [nekrɔlɔʒi] *nf* (*notice*) obituary; (*liste*) obituary column.

nectar [nɛktar] *nm* nectar.

néerlandais [neɛrlãdɛ] *nm, adj* Dutch. **les Néerlandais** the Dutch.

nef [nɛf] *nf* nave.

néfaste [nefast] *adj* (*nuisible*) harmful; (*funeste*) unlucky.

négatif [negatif] *nm, adj* negative.

négligé [negliʒe] *adj* neglected; (*tenue*) slovenly; (*travail*) careless. *nm* slovenliness; (*vêtement*) negligée.

négliger [negliʒe] *v* neglect; (*occasion*) miss. **négligeable** *adj* negligible. **négligence** *nf* negligence, carelessness. **négligent** *adj* negligent, careless.

négocier [negɔsje] *v* negotiate. **négoce** *nm* trade. **négociable** *adj* negotiable. **négociant, -e** *nm, nf* merchant. **négociation** *nf* negotiation.

nègre [nɛgrə] *nm, adj* Negro. **petit nègre** pidgin French. **négresse** *nf* Negress. **négrier** *nm* (*péj*) slave-driver.

neige [nɛʒ] *nf* snow. **neige fondue** sleet. **neiger** *v* snow. **neigeux** *adj* snowy.

nénuphar [nenyfar] *nm* water-lily.

néon [neɔ̃] *nm* neon.

néo-zélandais [neɔzelãdɛ] *adj* New Zealand. **Néo-Zélandais, -e** *nm, nf* New Zealander.

nerf [nɛr] *nm* nerve; spirit, energy. **nerveux** *adj* nervous; energetic, vigorous; (*musclé*) sinewy. **nervosité** *nf* nervousness; tension; irritability.

net, nette [nɛt] *adj* neat; (*propre*) clean; (*comm*) net; (*clair*) clear; distinct. *adv* net; frankly; (*sur le coup*) outright; (*s'arrêter*) dead. **netteté** *nf* neatness; clearness.

nettoyer [nɛtwaje] *v* clean. **nettoyer à sec** dry-clean. **nettoyage** *nm* cleaning.

neuf¹ [nœf] *nm, adj* nine. **neuvième** *n(m+f), adj* ninth.

neuf² [nœf] *adj* new. **à neuf** as good as new.

neutre [nøtrə] *nm, adj* neutral; (*genre*) neuter. **neutraliser** *v* neutralize. **neutralité** *nf* neutrality.

neveu [nəvø] *nm* nephew.

névralgie [nevralʒi] *nf* neuralgia.

névrose [nev '] *nf* neurosis. **névrosé** *adj* neurotic.

nez [ne] *nm* nose; flair; (*figure*) face.

ni [ni] *conj* nor, or. **ni . . . ni . . .** neither . . . nor . . . .

niais [njɛ], **-e** adj simple, silly. nm, nf simpleton. **niaiserie** nf silliness; (propos) foolish talk.

nicher [niʃe] v nest. **niche** nf niche; (chien) kennel. **nichée** nf brood.

nickel [nikɛl] nm nickel.

Nicosie [nikɔsi] n Nicosia.

nicotine [nikɔtin] nf nicotine.

nid [ni] nm nest. **nid de poule** pot-hole.

nièce [njɛs] nf niece.

nier [nje] v deny.

nigaud [nigo], **-e** adj silly, simple. nm, nf simpleton.

nimbe [nɛ̃b] nm halo.

nitouche [nituʃ] nf **sainte nitouche** hypocrite. **faire la sainte nitouche** look as if butter wouldn't melt in one's mouth.

niveau [nivo] nm level; (degré) standard. **niveau à bulle** spirit level. **niveau de vie** standard of living.

niveler [nivle] v level, even out.

noble [nɔblə] nm, adj noble. **noblesse** nf nobleness, nobility.

noce [nɔs] nf wedding. **faire la noce** (fam) live it up.

nocif [nɔsif] adj noxious, harmful.

nocturne [nɔktyrn] adj nocturnal.

Noël [nɔɛl] nm Christmas.

nœud [nø] nm knot; (de ruban) bow; (lien) bond; (rail, route) junction. **nœud coulant** slip-knot. **nœud papillon** bow tie.

noir [nwar] adj black; (obscur) dark; (profond) deep. nm black; darkness. **Noir** nm black man. **noire** nf crotchet. **Noire** nf black woman. **noircir** v blacken; darken.

noisette [nwazɛt] nf hazelnut. adj invar hazel. **noisetier** nm hazel tree.

noix [nwa] nf walnut. **noix de beurre** knob of butter. **noix de coco** coconut.

nom [nɔ̃] nm name; (gramm) noun. **nom de baptême** Christian name. **nom de famille** surname. **nom de jeune fille** maiden name. **nom d'emprunt** assumed name. **nom de théâtre** stage name. **nom propre** proper noun.

nomade [nɔmad] adj nomadic. n(m+f) nomad.

nombre [nɔ̃brə] nm number. **nombreux** adj numerous.

nombril [nɔ̃bri] nm navel.

nominal [nɔminal] adj nominal.

nomination [nɔminasjɔ̃] nf appointment, nomination.

nommer [nɔme] v name; (désigner) appoint.

non [nɔ̃] adv no; (pas) not. **non plus** neither. nm invar no.

nonchalant [nɔ̃ʃalɑ̃] adj nonchalant. **nonchalance** nf nonchalance.

non-conformiste [nɔ̃kɔ̃fɔrmist] n(m+f), adj nonconformist.

non-existant [nɔnɛgzistɑ̃] adj non-existent.

nonobstant [nɔnɔpstɑ̃] prep, adv notwithstanding.

nord [nɔr] nm north. adj invar north; (région) northern; (direction) northward. **nord-est** nm, adj invar north-east. **nord-ouest** nm, adj invar north-west.

normal [nɔrmal] adj normal. **normale** nf norm, normal.

norme [nɔrm] nf norm; standard.

Norvège [nɔrvɛʒ] nf Norway. **norvégien** nm, adj Norwegian. **Norvégien, -enne** nm, nf Norwegian.

nos [no] V **notre**.

nostalgie [nɔstalʒi] nf nostalgia. **nostalgique** adj nostalgic.

notable [nɔtablə] adj notable.

notaire [nɔtɛr] nm notary.

notamment [nɔtamɑ̃] adv notably, in particular.

notation [nɔtasjɔ̃] nf notation; (devoir) marking.

noter [nɔte] v (écrire) note down; (remarquer) notice, note; (devoir) mark. **note** nf note; mark; (compte) bill.

notice [nɔtis] nf note; instructions pl.

notifier [nɔtifje] v notify. **notification** nf notification.

notion [nɔsjɔ̃] nf notion.

notoire [nɔtwar] adj well-known; (criminal) notorious. **notoriété** nf fame; notoriety. **notoriété publique** common knowledge.

notre [nɔtrə] adj, pl **nos** our.

nôtre [notrə] pron **le** or **la nôtre** ours.

nouer [nwe] v tie, knot; (amitié, etc.) strike up; (intrigue) build up. **noueux** adj knotty, gnarled.

nouilles [nuj] nf pl noodles pl.

nounou [nunu] nf (fam) nanny.

nounours [nunurs] nm (fam) teddy.

nourrice [nuris] nf nurse. **nourricier** adj nutritive.

nourrir [nurir] v feed, nourish; (espoir, etc.) nurse, harbour. **nourrisson** nm infant. **nourriture** nf food, nourishment.

nous [nu] *pron (sujet)* we; *(objet)* us, to us; *(réfléchi)* ourselves, each other. **nous-mêmes** *pron* ourselves.

nouveau, -elle [nuvo, -ɛl] *adj* new; fresh. **à nouveau** afresh. **de nouveau** again. **nouveau-né** *adj* newborn. **Nouveau Testament** *nm* New Testament. **nouveau venu, nouvelle venue** *nm, nf* newcomer. **nouveaux-mariés** *nm pl* newly-weds *pl*. **nouvel an** *nm* New Year. **Nouvelle-Zélande** *nf* New Zealand. *nf* piece of news; *(récit)* short story. **nouvelles** *nf pl* news *sing*. **nouveauté** *nf* novelty; change; *(mode)* fashion.

nouvel [nuvɛl] *form of* **nouveau** *used before a vowel or mute h.*

novateur, -trice [nɔvatœr, -tris] *adj* innovative. *nm, nf* innovator.

novembre [nɔvɑ̃brə] *nm* November.

novice [nɔvis] *adj* inexperienced. *n(m+f)* novice.

noyau [nwajo] *nm (fruit)* stone; nucleus; *(tech)* core; small group.

noyer¹ [nwaje] *nm (arbre, bois)* walnut.

noyer² [nwaje] *v* drown; *(auto)* flood; *(submerger)* swamp. **noyade** *nf* drowning.

nu [ny] *adj* bare; *(sans vêtements)* naked; *(style)* plain. *nm* nude. **mettre à nu** expose, lay bare. **nu-pieds** *adv* barefoot.

nuage [nʮaʒ] *nm* cloud. **nuageux** *adj* cloudy.

nuance [nʮɑ̃s] *nf* nuance; *(couleur)* shade; slight difference. **nuancer** *v* shade.

nucléaire [nykleɛr] *adj* nuclear.

nudité [nydite] *nf* nudity; *(dénuement)* bareness. **nudiste** *n(m+f)* nudist.

nue [ny] *nf* **porter aux nues** praise to the skies. **tomber des nues** be flabbergasted.

nuée [nʮe] *nf* cloud; *(multitude)* horde.

***nuire** [nʮir] *v* **nuire à** harm. **nuisible** *adj* harmful. **animal** *or* **insecte nuisible** *nm* pest.

nuit [nʮi] *nf* night; *(obscurité)* darkness. **cette nuit** *(passé)* last night; *(futur)* tonight. **nuit blanche** sleepless night.

nul, nulle [nyl] *adj (aucun)* no; *(résultat)* nil; *(personne)* useless. **nul et non avenu** null and void. **nulle part** nowhere. *pron* no-one. **nullement** *adv* not at all.

numéral [nymeral] *nm* numeral.

numérique [nymerik] *adj* numerical.

numéro [nymero] *nm* number; *(journal)* issue. **numéro minéralogique** *(auto)* registration number.

numéroter [nymerɔte] *v* number.

nuptial [nypsjal] *adj* bridal, nuptial.

nuque [nyk] *nf* nape of the neck.

nutrition [nytrisjɔ̃] *nf* nutrition. **nutritif** *adj* nutritious, nourishing.

nylon [nilɔ̃] *nm* nylon.

nymphe [nɛ̃f] *nf* nymph.

O

oasis [ɔazis] *nf* oasis.

obéir [ɔbeir] *v* **obéir à** obey. **obéissance** *nf* obedience. **obéissant** *adj* obedient.

obélisque [ɔbelisk] *nm* obelisk.

obèse [ɔbɛz] *adj* obese. **obésité** *nf* obesity.

objecter [ɔbʒɛkte] *v* object; *(raison)* put forward; *(prétexter)* plead. **objection** *nf* objection.

objectif [ɔbʒɛktif] *adj* objective. *nm* objective; *(appareil-photo)* lens.

objet [ɔbʒɛ] *nm* object; *(but)* purpose; subject. **objets trouvés** lost property *sing*.

obliger [ɔbliʒe] *v* oblige; force, compel. **obligation** *nf* obligation; *(devoir)* duty. **obligatoire** *adj* compulsory; *(fam)* inevitable.

oblique [ɔblik] *adj* oblique. **regard oblique** *nm* sidelong glance.

oblitérer [ɔblitere] *v* cancel.

oblong, -ongue [ɔblɔ̃, -ɔ̃g] *adj* oblong.

obscène [ɔpsɛn] *adj* obscene. **obscénité** *nf* obscenity.

obscur [ɔpskyr] *adj* obscure; *(sombre)* dark; humble. **obscurité** *nf* obscurity; darkness.

obscurcir [ɔpskyrsir] *v* obscure; darken.

obséder [ɔpsede] *v* obsess, haunt. **obsédant** *adj* obsessive, haunting. **obsédé, -e** *nm, nf (fam)* fanatic.

obsèques [ɔpsɛk] *nf pl* funeral *sing*.

observateur, -trice [ɔpsɛrvatœr, -tris] *nm, nf* observer. *adj* observant.

observer [ɔpsɛrve] *v* observe; *(regarder)* watch; *(remarquer)* notice. **observation** *nf* observation; remark. **observatoire** *nm* observatory.

obsession [ɔpsesjɔ̃] *nf* obsession.

obstacle [ɔpstaklə] *nm* obstacle; *(hippisme)* fence.

obstétrique [ɔpstetrik] *nf* obstetrics.

s'obstiner [ɔpstine] v insist. **s'obstiner à** persist obstinately in. **obstination** nf obstinacy. **obstiné** adj obstinate.

obstruer [ɔpstrye] v obstruct, block. **obstruction** nf obstruction.

*obtenir [ɔptǝnir] v obtain, get; (atteindre) achieve.

obturateur [ɔptyratœr] nm (phot) shutter.

obtus [ɔbty] adj obtuse.

obus [ɔby] nm shell.

occasion [ɔkazjɔ̃] nf opportunity, chance; (circonstance) occasion; cause; (comm) bargain; (marché) second-hand market. **d'occasion** second-hand. **occasionnel** adj casual; (fortuit) chance. **occasionner** v cause.

occident [ɔksidɑ̃] nm west. **occidental** adj western.

occulte [ɔkylt] adj occult; secret, hidden.

occuper [ɔkype] v occupy. **s'occuper de** attend to, take care of. **occupant, -e** nm, nf occupant, occupier. **occupation** nf occupation. **occupé** adj busy; (téléphone, toilettes) engaged; (mil) occupied.

océan [ɔseɑ̃] nm ocean. **océanique** adj oceanic.

ocre [ɔkrǝ] nf ochre. nm (couleur) ochre.

octane [ɔktan] nm octane.

octave [ɔktav] nf octave.

octobre [ɔktɔbrǝ] nm October.

octogone [ɔktɔgɔn] nm octagon. **octogonal** adj octagonal.

octroyer [ɔktrwaje] v grant.

oculiste [ɔkylist] n(m+f) oculist.

ode [ɔd] nf ode.

odeur [ɔdœr] nf odour, smell; (agréable) fragrance, scent. **odorant** adj sweet-smelling. **odorat** nm sense of smell.

odieux [ɔdjø] adj obnoxious, odious.

œil [œj] nm, pl **yeux** eye; (expression) look. **œil poché** black eye. **œillade** nf wink. **œillères** nf pl blinkers pl. **œillet** nm carnation; (trou) eyelet.

œsophage [ezɔfaʒ] nm oesophagus.

œuf [œf] nm egg. **œuf à la coque** boiled egg. **œuf du jour** new-laid egg. **œuf dur** hard-boiled egg. **œuf mollet** soft-boiled egg. **œuf poché** poached egg. **œufs brouillés** scrambled eggs pl. **œuf sur le plat** fried egg.

œuvre [œvrǝ] nf work; (tâche) task; charity. **œuvre d'art** work of art.

offenser [ɔfɑ̃se] v offend. **s'offenser** take offence. **offensant** adj offensive. **offense** nf insult; (rel) trespass. **offensive** nm (mil) offensive.

office [ɔfis] nm office; bureau, agency; (rel) service. **faire office de** act as. **officiel, -elle** n, adj official. **officier** nm officer. **officieux** adj unofficial.

officine [ɔfisin] nf dispensary.

*offrir [ɔfrir] v offer; present; (cadeau) give. **s'offrir** treat oneself to. **offrande** nf offering. **offre** nf offer; (enchères) bid; (comm) tender.

offusquer [ɔfyske] v offend.

ogre [ɔgrǝ] nm ogre. **ogresse** nf ogress.

oie [wa] nf goose.

oignon [ɔɲɔ̃] nm (légume) onion; (bot) bulb.

*oindre [wɛ̃drǝ] v anoint.

oiseau [wazo] nm bird.

oisif [wazif] adj idle. **oisiveté** nf idleness.

oison [wazɔ̃] nm gosling.

olive [ɔliv] nf olive. **olivier** nm olive tree.

olympique [ɔlɛ̃pik] adj Olympic.

ombrage [ɔ̃braʒ] nm shade. **prendre ombrage** take umbrage. **ombrager** v shade. **ombrageux** adj touchy.

ombre [ɔ̃brǝ] nf shadow; (ombrage) shade; obscurity, dark. **ombrer** v shade.

omelette [ɔmlɛt] nf omelette.

*omettre [ɔmɛtrǝ] v omit. **omission** nf omission.

omnibus [ɔmnibys] nm slow train.

omnipotent [ɔmnipɔtɑ̃] adj omnipotent.

omoplate [ɔmɔplat] nf shoulder blade.

on [ɔ̃] pron one, (les gens) they, people; (tu, vous) you; (nous) we; (quelqu'un) someone. **on demande ...** ... wanted. **on-dit** nm invar rumour, hearsay.

oncle [ɔ̃klǝ] nm uncle.

onde [ɔ̃d] nf wave. **grandes ondes** long wave(s). **ondes courtes/moyennes** short/medium wave(s). **sur les ondes** on the air.

ondoyer [ɔ̃dwaje] v ripple, wave. **ondoyant** adj undulating; (flamme) wavering; (forme) supple.

onduler [ɔ̃dyle] v undulate; (cheveux) be wavy. **ondulant** adj undulating; (pouls) uneven. **ondulation** nf undulation. **ondulé** adj (cheveux) wavy. **onduleux** adj wavy; (movement) sinuous.

ongle [ɔ̃glǝ] nm nail; (animal) claw.

onguent [ɔ̃gɑ̃] nm ointment.

onyx [ɔniks] nm onyx.

onze [ɔ̃z] nm, adj eleven. **onzième** n(m+f), adj eleventh.

opale [ɔpal] *nf* opal.

opaque [ɔpak] *adj* opaque. **opacité** *nf* opacity.

opéra [ɔpera] *nm* opera; (*édifice*) opera house. **opérette** *nf* operetta.

opérer [ɔpere] *v* operate; (*accomplir*) carry out; (*effectuer*) bring about; (*faire*) make; (*agir*) act, work. **se faire opérer** have an operation. **opérateur, -trice** *nm, nf* operator. **opération** *nf* operation; (*comm*) deal; (*tech*) process. **salle d'opération** *nf* operating theatre.

ophtalmique [ɔftalmik] *adj* ophthalmic.

s'opiniâtrer [ɔpinjɑtre] *v* persist stubbornly. **opiniâtre** *adj* stubborn, obstinate; persistent. **opiniâtreté** *nf* stubbornness, obstinacy.

opinion [ɔpinjɔ̃] *nf* opinion.

opium [ɔpjɔm] *nm* opium.

opportun [ɔpɔrtœ̃] *adj* opportune; appropriate. **opportunité** *nf* timeliness.

opposé [ɔpoze] *adj* opposite; conflicting, opposing; contrasting. **opposé à** opposed to. *nm* opposite.

opposer [ɔpoze] *v* place opposite; contrast. **s'opposer à** oppose. **opposition** *nf* opposition; conflict; contrast. **par opposition à** as opposed to.

opprimer [ɔprime] *v* oppress.

opprobre [ɔprɔbrə] *nm* disgrace.

opter [ɔpte] *v* opt, choose. **option** *nf* option.

opticien [ɔptisjɛ̃], **-enne** *nm, nf* optician.

optimiste [ɔptimist] *n(m+f)* optimist. *adj* optimistic. **optimisme** *nm* optimism.

optimum [ɔptimɔm] *nm, adj* optimum.

optique [ɔptik] *adj* optical, optic. *nf* optics.

opulent [ɔpylɑ̃] *adj* wealthy, rich, opulent. **opulence** *nf* richness, opulence.

or¹ [ɔr] *nm* gold. **d'or** golden.

or² [ɔr] *conj* now.

oracle [ɔraklə] *nm* oracle.

orage [ɔraʒ] *nm* storm. **orageux** *adj* stormy.

oraison [ɔrɛzɔ̃] *nf* prayer.

oral [ɔral] *nm, adj* oral.

orange [ɔrɑ̃ʒ] *nf* orange. *nm, adj invar* (*couleur*) orange. **oranger** *nm* orange tree.

orateur, -trice [ɔratœr, -tris] *nm, nf* orator, speaker.

orbite [ɔrbit] *nf* orbit. **orbiter** *v* orbit.

orchestre [ɔrkɛstrə] *nm* orchestra; (*danse, jazz*) band; (*théâtre*) stalls *pl*. **orchestral**

adj orchestral. **orchestration** *nf* orchestration. **orchestrer** *v* orchestrate.

orchidée [ɔrkide] *nf* orchid.

ordinaire [ɔrdinɛr] *adj* ordinary; common; (*habituel*) usual. *nm* ordinary.

ordinal [ɔrdinal] *adj* ordinal.

ordinateur [ɔrdinatœr] *nm* computer.

ordonner [ɔrdɔne] *v* order; arrange, organize; (*méd*) prescribe; (*rel*) ordain. **ordonnance** *nf* order; prescription; organization. **ordonné** *adj* orderly, tidy.

ordre [ɔrdrə] *nm* order. **de premier/deuxième ordre** first-/second-rate. **en ordre** tidy. **ordre du jour** agenda.

ordure [ɔrdyr] *nf* dirt, filth. **ordures** *nf pl* rubbish *sing*, refuse *sing*; obscenities *pl*.

oreille [ɔrɛj] *nf* ear; (*ouïe*) hearing. **oreiller** *nm* pillow. **oreillons** *nm pl* mumps *sing*.

ores [ɔr] *adv* **d'ores et déjà** already, here and now.

orfèvre [ɔrfɛvrə] *nm* (*argent*) silversmith; (*or*) goldsmith.

organe [ɔrgan] *nm* organ; instrument; (*porte-parole*) spokesman, mouthpiece.

organique [ɔrganik] *adj* organic.

organiser [ɔrganize] *v* organize. **organisateur, -trice** *nm, nf* organizer. **organisation** *nf* organization. **organisme** *nm* organism; (*institution*) body.

organiste [ɔrganist] *n(m+f)* organist.

orgasme [ɔrgasmə] *nm* orgasm.

orge [ɔrʒ] *nf* barley.

orgie [ɔrʒi] *nf* orgy; (*excès*) profusion.

orgue [ɔrg] *nm* organ.

orgueil [ɔrgœj] *nm* pride, arrogance. **orgueilleux** *adj* proud, arrogant.

orient [ɔrjɑ̃] *nm* east. **oriental** *adj* eastern, oriental.

orienter [ɔrjɑ̃te] *v* orientate; direct; (*disposer*) position, adjust. **orienter vers** turn towards. **s'orienter** find one's bearings. **orientation** *nf* orientation; direction; positioning; (*maison, jardin*) aspect. **orientation professionnelle** careers guidance.

origan [ɔrigɑ̃] *nm* oregano.

origine [ɔriʒin] *nf* origin. **à l'origine** originally. **originaire** *adj* original; native. **original** *nm, adj* original; (*péj*) eccentric. **originalité** *nf* originality; eccentricity. **originel** *adj* original.

orme [ɔrm] *nm* elm.

ornement [ɔrnəmɑ̃] *nm* ornament. **orne-**

mental *adj* ornamental. **ornementation** *nf* ornamentation.

orner [ɔrne] *v* decorate; embellish. **orné** *adj* ornate.

ornière [ɔrnjɛr] *nf* rut.

ornithologie [ɔrnitɔlɔʒi] *nf* ornithology. **ornithologique** *adj* ornithological. **ornithologiste** *n(m+f)* ornithologist.

orphelin [ɔrfəlɛ̃], **-e** *n*, *adj* orphan. **orphelinat** *nm* orphanage.

orteil [ɔrtɛj] *nm* toe.

orthodoxe [ɔrtɔdɔks] *adj* orthodox.

orthographe [ɔrtɔgraf] *nf* spelling. **orthographier** *v* spell.

orthopédique [ɔrtɔpedik] *adj* orthopaedic.

orthophonie [ɔrtɔfɔni] *nf* (*méd*) speech therapy. **orthophoniste** *n(m+f)* speech therapist.

ortie [ɔrti] *nf* nettle.

os [ɔs] *nm* bone. **os à moelle** marrowbone. **trempé jusqu'aux os** soaked to the skin.

osciller [ɔsile] *v* oscillate; (*se balancer*) rock, swing; (*hésiter*) waver; (*prix, etc.*) fluctuate. **oscillation** *nf* oscillation; fluctuation.

oser [oze] *v* dare. **osé** *adj* bold, daring.

osier [ozje] *nm* wicker. **en osier** wickerwork.

ossature [ɔsatyr] *nf* (*corps*) frame; framework; (*visage*) bone structure.

osseux [ɔsø] *adj* bony.

ostentation [ɔstɑ̃tasjɔ̃] *nf* ostentation.

ostraciser [ɔstrasize] *v* ostracize. **ostracisme** *nm* ostracism.

otage [ɔtaʒ] *nm* hostage.

otarie [ɔtari] *nf* sea-lion.

ôter [ote] *v* take away *or* off, remove.

ou [u] *conj* or. **ou bien** or else. **ou ... ou ...** either ... or ....

où [u] *adv* where; (*temps*) when.

ouate [wat] *nf* cotton wool; (*rembourrage*) wadding. **ouater** *v* quilt.

oublier [ublije] *v* forget. **oubli** *nm* oblivion; lapse of memory; omission, oversight.

ouest [wɛst] *nm* west. *adj invar* west; (*région*) western; (*direction*) westward.

oui [wi] *adv*, *nm* yes.

*ouïr [wir] *v* hear. **ouï-dire** *nm invar* hearsay. **ouïe** *nf* hearing.

ouragan [uragɑ̃] *nm* hurricane.

ourdir [urdir] *v* (*complot*) hatch.

ourler [urle] *v* hem. **ourlet** *nm* hem.

ours [urs] *nm* bear. **ours blanc** polar bear.

outil [uti] *nm* tool, implement. **outillage** *nm* set of tools; equipment. **outiller** *v* provide with tools; equip.

outrager [utraʒe] *v* outrage; insult. **outrage** *nm* insult. **outrage à la pudeur** indecent behaviour. **outrage à magistrat** contempt of court.

outrance [utrɑ̃s] *nf* excess.

outre [utrə] *prep* as well as. **en outre** moreover, besides. **outre-mer** *adv* overseas.

outrer [utre] *v* outrage; exaggerate. **outré** *adj* excessive, overdone; outraged.

ouvert [uvɛr] *adj* open. **ouvertement** *adv* openly, overtly. **ouverture** *nf* opening; (*musique, avance*) overture.

ouvrable [uvrablə] *adj* **jour ouvrable** weekday.

ouvrage [uvraʒ] *nm* work, piece of work.

ouvreuse [uvrøz] *nf* usherette.

ouvrier [uvrije], **-ère** *adj* labour, industrial; working-class. *nm*, *nf* worker.

*ouvrir [uvrir] *v* open; (*gaz, robinet, etc.*) turn on. **ouvre-boîte** *nm invar* tin-opener. **ouvre-bouteille** *nm invar* bottle-opener.

ovaire [ɔvɛr] *nm* ovary.

ovale [ɔval] *nm*, *adj* oval.

ovation [ɔvasjɔ̃] *nf* ovation.

ovulation [ɔvylasjɔ̃] *nf* ovulation.

oxygène [ɔksiʒɛn] *nm* oxygen.

P

pacage [pakaʒ] *nm* pasture.

pacifier [pasifje] *v* pacify. **pacifique** *adj* peaceful, peaceable. **pacifisme** *nm* pacifism. **pacifiste** *n(m+f)*, *adj* pacifist. **Pacifique** [pasifik] *nm*, *adj* Pacific.

pacte [paktə] *nm* pact, treaty.

pagaie [pagɛ] *nf* paddle. **pagayer** *v* paddle.

pagaïe [pagaj] *nf* mess; (*cohue*) chaos.

page¹ [paʒ] *nf* (*livre*) page. **à la page** up-to-date.

page² [paʒ] *nm* (*garçon*) page.

pagode [pagɔd] *nf* pagoda.

paie [pɛ] *nf* pay. **paiement** *nm* payment.

païen [pajɛ̃], **-enne** *n*, *adj* pagan, heathen.

paillasson [pajasɔ̃] *nm* doormat.

paille [pɑj] *nf* straw; (*défaut*) flaw. **paille de fer** steel wool. **paillette** *nf* speck; (*savon*) flake; (*ornement*) sequin; flaw.

pain [pɛ̃] *nm* bread; (*miche*) loaf; (*savon*) bar. **pain bis/complet** brown/wholemeal bread. **pain de mie** sandwich loaf. **pain d'épice** gingerbread. **pain grillé** toast. **petit pain** roll.

pair¹ [pɛr] *nm* peer. **au pair** *adj* au pair. **pairie** *nf* peerage.

pair² [pɛr] *adj* even.

paire [pɛr] *nf* pair.

paisible [peziblə] *adj* peaceful, quiet.

*paître [pɛtrə] *v* graze.

paix [pɛ] *nf* peace.

palace [palas] *nm* luxury hotel.

palais¹ [palɛ] *nm* palace. **palais de justice** law courts *pl*.

palais² [palɛ] *nm* (*anat*) palate.

pâle [pɑl] *adj* pale; (*faible*) faint, weak. **paleur** *nf* paleness.

palefrenier [palfrənje] *nm* groom.

palette [palɛt] *nf* palette; (*aube*) paddle.

palier [palje] *nm* landing; (*étape*) stage.

pâlir [palir] *v* turn pale; (*couleur, etc.*) fade; (*lumière*) grow dim.

palissade [palisad] *nf* fence.

palmarès [palmarɛs] *nm* prize list.

palme [palmə] *nf* palm leaf; (*nageur*) flipper. **palmé** *adj* (*patte*) webbed. **palmier** *nm* palm tree. **palmipède** *adj* web-footed.

palombe [palɔ̃b] *nf* wood-pigeon.

palourde [palurd] *nf* clam.

palper [palpe] *v* feel, finger.

palpiter [palpite] *v* (*cœur*) beat; (*violemment*) pound, throb; (*frémir*) quiver. **palpitant** *adj* thrilling. **palpitation** *nf* palpitation.

paludisme [palydismə] *nm* malaria.

pâmer [pame] *v* **se pâmer de** be overcome with.

pamphlet [pɑ̃flɛ] *nm* lampoon.

pamplemousse [pɑ̃pləmus] *nm* grapefruit.

pan [pɑ̃] *nm* piece; (*côté*) side. **pan de chemise** shirt-tail.

panache [panaʃ] *nm* plume; gallantry.

panaché [panaʃe] *adj* multicoloured; mixed, motley. *nm* shandy. **panacher** *v* vary; (*mélanger*) blend.

panais [panɛ] *nm* parsnip.

pancarte [pɑ̃kart] *nf* sign; (*manifestation*) placard.

pancréas [pɑ̃kreas] *nm* pancreas. **pancréatique** *adj* pancreatic.

panda [pɑ̃da] *nm* panda.

paner [pane] *v* coat with breadcrumbs.

panier [panje] *nm* basket. **panier à salade** salad shaker; (*fam*) police van, Black Maria. **panier-repas** *nm* packed lunch.

panique [panik] *nf* panic.

panne [pan] *nf* breakdown, failure. **être en panne** break down. **être en panne de** run out of.

panneau [pano] *nm* panel; (*écriteau*) sign. **panneau d'affichage** notice-board. **panneau de signalisation** road sign. **panneau-réclame** *nm* hoarding.

panoplie [panɔpli] *nf* outfit.

panorama [panɔrama] *nm* panorama. **panoramique** *adj* panoramic.

panse [pɑ̃s] *nf* paunch.

panser [pɑ̃se] *v* (*plaie*) dress; bandage; (*cheval*) groom. **pansement** *nm* dressing; bandage; (*sparadrap*) plaster.

pantalon [pɑ̃talɔ̃] *nm* trousers *pl*; pair of trousers.

pantelant [pɑ̃tlɑ̃] *adj* panting; (*cœur*) throbbing.

panthère [pɑ̃tɛr] *nf* panther.

pantomime [pɑ̃tɔmim] *nf* mime.

pantoufle [pɑ̃tuflə] *nf* slipper.

paon [pɑ̃] *nm* peacock.

papa [papa] *nm* (*fam*) dad, daddy.

pape [pap] *nm* pope. **papal** *adj* papal. **papauté** *nf* papacy.

papeterie [papetri] *nf* stationery; (*magasin*) stationer's; (*fabrique*) paper mill. **papetier, -ère** *nm, nf* stationer.

papier [papje] *nm* paper.

papier à lettres *nm* notepaper.

papier à musique *nm* manuscript paper.

papier buvard *nm* blotting paper.

papier calque *nm* tracing paper.

papier d'aluminium *nm* kitchen foil.

papier de soie *nm* tissue paper.

papier de verre *nm* sandpaper.

papier hygiénique *nm* toilet paper.

papier millimétré *nm* graph paper.

papier peint *nm* wallpaper.

papillon [papijɔ̃] *nm* butterfly; (*police*) parking ticket. **papillon de nuit** moth.

paprika [paprika] *nm* paprika.

paquebot [pakbo] *nm* liner.

pâquerette [pakrɛt] *nf* daisy.

Pâques [pɑk] *nm* Easter.

paquet [pakɛ] *nm* packet, pack; (*colis*) parcel; (*tas*) pile, mass. **mettre en paquet** parcel up.

par [par] *prep* by; through; *(distribution)* per. **par-ci par-là** here and there; *(temps)* now and then. **par-dessous** *prep, adv* under. **par-dessus** *prep, adv* over. **par ici/là** this/that way.

parabole [parabɔl] *nf (rel)* parable; *(math)* parabola.

parachute [paraʃyt] *nm* parachute. **parachuter** *v* parachute. **parachutiste** *n(m+f)* parachutist; *(mil)* paratrooper.

parade [parad] *nf* parade; *(ostentation)* show. **faire parade de** show off, brag about.

paradis [paradi] *nm* paradise, heaven.

paradoxe [paradɔks] *nm* paradox. **paradoxal** *adj* paradoxical.

paraffine [parafin] *nf* paraffin (wax).

parages [paraʒ] *nm pl* vicinity *sing.* **dans les parages** round about, in the area.

paragraphe [paragraf] *nm* paragraph.

*paraître [parɛtrə] *v* appear; *(sembler)* seem; be visible, show; be published.

parallèle [paralɛl] *nm, adj* parallel. *nf* parallel line. **parallélogramme** *nm* parallelogram.

paralyser [paralize] *v* paralyse. **paralysie** *nf* paralysis. **paralytique** *adj* paralytic.

paramilitaire [paramiliter] *adj* paramilitary.

paranoïa [paranɔja] *nf* paranoia. **paranoïde** *adj* paranoid.

parapet [parapɛ] *nm* parapet.

paraphraser [parafraze] *v* paraphrase. **paraphrase** *nf* paraphrase.

paraplégique [parapleʒik] *n(m+f)*, *adj* paraplegic.

parapluie [paraplɥi] *nm* umbrella.

parasite [parazit] *nm* parasite. **parasites** *nm pl (radio)* interference *sing.* *adj* parasitic.

paratonnerre [paratɔnɛr] *nm* lightning conductor.

parc [park] *nm* park; *(château)* grounds *pl*; *(animal)* pen; *(bébé)* play-pen.

parcelle [parsɛl] *nf* fragment, bit. **parcelle de terre** plot of land.

parce que [parskə] *conj* because.

parchemin [parʃəmɛ̃] *nm* parchment. **parcheminé** *adj* wrinkled.

parcomètre [parkɔmɛtrə] *nm* parking meter.

*parcourir [parkurir] *v* travel through, cover; *(livre)* glance through.

parcours [parkur] *nm* distance; *(trajet)* journey; course; *(itinéraire)* route.

pardessus [pardəsy] *nm* overcoat.

pardon [pardɔ̃] *nm* forgiveness, pardon. **demander pardon** apologize. *interj (comment)* pardon; *(désolé)* sorry, excuse me. **pardonner** *v* forgive, pardon; excuse.

pareil, -eille [parɛj] *adj* the same, alike; *(tel)* such. *nm, nf* equal, peer.

parement [parmɑ̃] *nm* facing.

parent [parɑ̃], **-e** *nm, nf* relation. **parents** *nm pl (père, mère)* parents *pl.* **parenté** *nf* relationship.

parenthèse [parɑ̃tɛz] *nf* parenthesis; digression; *(signe)* bracket. **entre parenthèses** in brackets; incidentally.

parer[1] [pare] *v (orner)* adorn; *(robe)* trim; *(préparer)* dress.

parer[2] [pare] *v* ward off. **pare-balles** *adj invar* bulletproof. **pare-brise** *nm invar* windshield. **pare-chocs** *nm invar* bumper. **pare-étincelles** *nm invar* fireguard. **parer à** deal with; prepare for.

paresseux [parɛsø] *adj* lazy. **paresse** *nf* laziness.

parfait [parfɛ] *adj* perfect; complete; absolute.

parfois [parfwa] *adv* sometimes; occasionally.

parfum [parfœ̃] *nm* perfume, scent; *(glace)* flavour. **parfumer** *v* perfume; flavour.

pari [pari] *nm* bet. **parier** *v* bet.

Paris [pari] *n* Paris.

parité [parite] *nf* parity.

parjure [parʒyr] *adj* false. *nm* perjury, false witness. *n(m+f)* perjurer. **se parjurer** *v* perjure oneself, bear false witness.

parking [parkiŋ] *nm* car park.

parlement [parləmɑ̃] *nm* parliament. **parlementaire** *adj* parliamentary.

parler [parle] *v* talk, speak. **sans parler de** not to mention. **tu parles!** *(fam)* you're telling me! *nm* speech.

parmi [parmi] *prep* among.

parodie [parɔdi] *nf* parody. **parodier** *v* parodier.

paroi [parwa] *nf* wall; *(cloison)* partition; rock face; *(récipient)* inside surface.

paroisse [parwas] *nf* parish. **paroissial** *adj* parish. **salle paroissiale** *nf* church hall. **paroissien, -enne** *nm, nf* parishioner.

parole [parɔl] *nf* word; *(faculté)* speech; remark. **parolier, -ère** *nm, nf* lyricist.

paroxysme [parɔksismə] *nm* height, climax.

parquer [parke] *v* (*auto*) park; (*enfermer*) pen in; (*entasser*) pack in.

parquet [parkε] *nm* floor.

parrain [parε̃] *nm* godfather.

parsemer [parsəme] *v* scatter, sprinkle.

part [par] *nf* part; portion, share. **à part** (*de côté*) aside; separately; except for, apart from. **d'autre part** moreover. **de la part de** on behalf of. **faire part de** announce.

partager [partaʒe] *v* share; divide. **partage** *nm* share, portion; (*distribution*) sharing out; division.

partance [partɑ̃s] *nf* **en partance** outbound. **en partance pour** (bound) for.

partenaire [partənεr] *n*(*m + f*) partner.

parterre [partεr] *nm* border, flower-bed; (*théâtre*) stalls *pl*.

parti [parti] *nm* party, side; decision; (*mariage*) match. **parti pris** prejudice, bias. **prendre le parti de** stand up for. **prendre parti pour** side with. **tirer parti de** take advantage of, put to good use.

partial [parsjal] *adj* partial, biased. **partialité** *nf* partiality, bias.

participe [partisip] *nm* participle.

participer [partisipe] *v* **participer à** participate in, take part in; (*frais*) contribute to; (*profits, etc.*) share in. **participant, -e** *nm, nf* participant; (*concours*) entrant. **participation** *nf* participation; (*comm*) interest.

particularité [partikylarite] *nf* particularity, characteristic.

particule [partikyl] *nf* particle.

particulier [partikylje] *adj* particular; special, exceptional; (*étrange*) peculiar; private. *nm* person, individual.

partie [parti] *nf* part; (*sport, etc.*) game; (*droit, divertissement*) party. **faire partie de** belong to.

partiel [parsjεl] *adj* partial.

*****partir** [partir] *v* leave, go; (*fusil*) go off; (*commencer*) start. **à partir de** from.

partisan [partizɑ̃], **-e** *nm, nf* supporter, advocate. **être partisan de** be in favour of.

partition [partisjɔ̃] *nf* (*musique*) score.

partout [partu] *adv* everywhere. **partout où** wherever.

parure [paryr] *nf* finery; (*bijoux*) jewels *pl*; (*ensemble*) set; (*ornement*) trimming.

*****parvenir** [parvənir] *v* **parvenir à** reach, get to; (*réussir*) manage to, succeed in. **parvenu, -e** *nm, nf* (*péj*) upstart.

pas¹ [pɑ] *nm* step; (*vitesse*) pace; (*trace*) footprint; (*géog*) pass. **à pas de loup** stealthily. **pas de la porte** doorstep.

pas² [pɑ] *adv* not. **ne ... pas** not. **pas du tout** not at all. **pas mal de** (*fam*) quite a lot of.

passage [pɑsaʒ] *nm* passage; change, transition; (*traversée*) crossing. **passage à niveau** level crossing. **passage clouté** pedestrian crossing. **passage interdit** no thoroughfare. **passage souterrain** subway.

passager [pɑsaʒe], **-ère** *adj* passing, brief; (*oiseau*) migratory; (*rue*) busy. *nm, nf* passenger. **passager clandestin** stowaway.

passant [pɑsɑ̃], **-e** *nm, nf* passer-by.

passe [pɑs] *nf* pass. **en passe de** on the way to.

passé [pɑse] *adj* past; (*dernier*) last. *nm* past. *prep* after.

passe-partout *nm invar* skeleton key.

passeport [pɑspɔr] *nm* passport.

passer [pɑse] *v* pass; go past; (*aller*) go; (*franchir*) get through or over; (*examen*) sit, take; (*temps*) spend; (*film*) show; (*cuisine*) strain; (*traverser*) cross. **passer par** go through. **passer prendre** pick up, call for. **passer voir** call on. **se passer** happen, take place; (*finir*) be over. **se passer de** do without.

passerelle [pɑsrεl] *nf* (*pont*) foot-bridge; (*naut*) gangway.

passe-temps *nm invar* pastime.

passif [pɑsif] *nm, adj* passive. **passivité** *nf* passiveness.

passion [pɑsjɔ̃] *nf* passion.

passionné [pɑsjɔne], **-e** *adj* passionate. *nm, nf* fanatic.

passionner [pɑsjɔne] *v* fascinate. **se passionner pour** be mad keen on.

passoire [pɑswar] *nf* sieve; (*plus grande*) colander.

pastel [pastεl] *nm, adj invar* pastel.

pastèque [pastεk] *nf* water-melon.

pasteuriser [pastœrize] *v* pasteurize. **pasteurisation** *nf* pasteurization.

pastille [pastij] *nf* pastille.

pastis [pastis] *nm* (*boisson*) pastis; (*argot*) jam, fix.

pastoral [pastɔral] *adj* pastoral.

pat [pat] *nm* stalemate.

pataud [pato] *adj* clumsy.

patauger [patoʒe] *v* wade, splash; (*se perdre*) flounder.

pâte [pɑt] *nf* paste; cream; (*tarte*) pastry; (*à frire*) batter; (*gâteau*) mixture; (*pain*) dough. **pâte à modeler** plasticine ®. **pâte brisée** shortcrust pastry. **pâte dentifrice** toothpaste. **pâte feuilletée** puff pastry. **pâtes** *nf pl* pasta *sing*.

pâté [pɑte] *nm* (*cuisine*) pâté; (*encre*) blot; (*maisons*) block; (*sable*) sand-castle. **pâté en croûte** pie.

patelin [patlɛ̃] *nm* (*fam*) village.

patelle [patɛl] *nf* limpet.

patent [patɑ̃] *adj* patent, obvious.

patenté [patɑ̃te] *adj* licensed.

patère [patɛr] *nf* peg.

paternel [patɛrnɛl] *adj* paternal; (*bienveillant*) fatherly. **paternité** *nf* paternity.

pâteux [pɑtø] *adj* pasty; (*langue*) furred; (*voix*) husky.

pathétique [patetik] *adj* pathetic. *nm* pathos.

pathologie [patɔlɔʒi] *nf* pathology. **pathologique** *adj* pathological. **pathologiste** *n(m+f)* pathologist.

patient [pasjɑ̃], -e *n, adj* patient. **patience** *nf* patience. **patienter** *v* wait.

patin [patɛ̃] *nm* skate; (*luge*) runner. **patin à glace** ice-skate. **patin à roulettes** roller-skate. **patinage** *nm* skating. **patiner** *v* skate; (*auto*) spin. **patineur, -euse** *nm, nf* skater. **patinoire** *nf* ice rink.

patio [patjo] *nm* patio.

pâtir [pɑtir] *v* suffer.

pâtisserie [pɑtisri] *nf* (*magasin*) cake shop; (*gâteau*) pastry, cake; (*métier*) confectionery. **pâtissier, -ère** *nm, nf* confectioner.

patois [patwa] *nm* patois, dialect.

patrie [patri] *nf* homeland.

patrimoine [patrimwan] *nm* inheritance, heritage.

patriote [patrijɔt] *n(m+f)* patriot. *adj* patriotic. **patriotique** *adj* patriotic. **patriotisme** *nm* patriotism.

patron, -onne [patrɔ̃, -ɔn] *nm, nf* proprietor; employer; (*fam*) boss; (*protecteur*) patron; (*naut*) skipper. *nm* pattern. **patronage** *nm* patronage. **patronat** *nm* management. **patronner** *v* support, sponsor.

patrouille [patruj] *nf* patrol. **patrouiller** *v* patrol.

patte [pat] *nf* (*jambe*) leg; (*pied*) paw, foot; (*languette*) flap, tongue. **patte de derrière** hind leg. **patte de devant** foreleg. **patte de mouche** scrawl.

pâture [pɑtyr] *nf* pasture; (*nourriture*) food. **pâturage** *nm* pasture.

paume [pom] *nf* palm.

paupière [popjɛr] *nf* eyelid.

pause [poz] *nf* break, pause. **pause-café** *nf* coffee break.

pauvre [povr] *adj* poor; (*piètre*) weak. *n(m+f)* poor person. **pauvreté** *nf* poverty; poorness; weakness.

se pavaner [pavane] *v* strut about.

paver [pave] *v* pave; (*chaussée*) cobble. **pavé** *nm* paving stone; (*rond*) cobblestone.

pavillon [pavijɔ̃] *nm* pavilion; lodge; (*villa*) house; (*drapeau*) flag.

pavot [pavo] *nm* poppy.

payer [peje] *v* pay (for). **se payer** (*fam*) treat oneself to. **payable** *adj* payable.

pays [pei] *nm* country, land; region. **du pays** local. **les Pays-Bas** the Netherlands *pl*. **pays de Galles** Wales. **paysage** *nm* landscape; scenery. **paysan, -anne** *nm, nf* peasant.

péage [peaʒ] *nm* toll.

peau [po] *nf* skin; (*cuir*) hide; (*fruit*) peel. **peau de chamois** chamois leather. **peau de mouton** sheepskin. **Peau-Rouge** *n(m+f)* Red Indian.

pêche[1] [pɛʃ] *nf* (*fruit*) peach. **pêcher** *nm* peach tree.

pêche[2] [pɛʃ] *nf* fishing. **aller à la pêche** go fishing.

pécher [peʃe] *v* sin. **péché** *nm* sin. **pécheur, -eresse** *nm, nf* sinner.

pêcher [peʃe] *v* fish (for); (*attraper*) catch. **pêcheur** *nm* fisherman.

pédagogique [pedagɔʒik] *adj* educational.

pédaler [pedale] *v* pedal. **pédale** *nf* pedal.

pédant [pedɑ̃] *adj* pedantic.

pédéraste [pederast] *nm* homosexual. **pédé** *nm* (*argot*) queer. **pédérastie** *nf* homosexuality.

pédiatre [pedjatrə] *n(m+f)* paediatrician. **pédiatrie** *nf* paediatrics.

pédicure [pedikyr] *n(m+f)* chiropodist.

pedigree [pedigri] *nm* pedigree.

peigner [peɲe] *v* comb. **se peigner** comb one's hair. **mal peigné** dishevelled. **peigne** *nm* comb. **peignoir** *nm* dressing-gown.

*peindre [pɛ̃drə] *v* paint; (*décrire*) depict, portray.

peine [pɛn] *nf* effort, trouble; (*tristesse*) sorrow; difficulty; punishment. **à peine** scarcely, hardly.

peiner [pene] v (s'efforcer) labour, struggle; (affliger) grieve, distress.

peintre [pɛtrə] n(m+f) painter. **peinture** nf painting; (surface) paintwork; (matière) paint.

péjoratif [peʒɔratif] adj derogatory.

Pékin [pekɛ̃] n Peking.

pelage [pəlaʒ] nm coat, fur.

pêle-mêle [pɛlmɛl] adv pell-mell, any old how. nm invar jumble.

peler [pəle] v peel.

pèlerin [pɛlrɛ̃] nm pilgrim. **pèlerinage** nm pilgrimage. **pèlerine** nf cape.

pélican [pelikɑ̃] nm pelican.

pelle [pɛl] nf shovel; (d'enfant) spade. **pelle à ordures** dustpan. **pelleter** v shovel (up).

pelletier [pɛltje], -ère nm, nf furrier.

pellicule [pelikyl] nf film. **pellicules** nf pl dandruff sing.

pelote [pəlɔt] nf ball; (à épingles) pincushion.

se peloter [pəlɔte] v (fam) pet, neck.

peloton [pəlɔtɔ̃] nm small ball; group, squad.

pelotonner [pəlɔtɔne] v (laine) wind into a ball. **se pelotonner** curl up, snuggle up.

pelouse [pəluz] nf lawn.

peluche [pəlyʃ] nf plush, fur fabric; (poil, flocon) bit of fluff. **en peluche** fluffy. **pelucheux** adj fluffy.

pelure [pəlyr] nf peel, peeling.

pénal [penal] adj penal. **pénaliser** v penalize. **pénalité** nf penalty.

penaud [pəno] adj sheepish, contrite.

pencher [pɑ̃ʃe] v tilt, lean (over), slant. **se pencher** lean (over); (se baisser) bend (down). **penchant** nm tendency; (goût) liking. **penché** adj sloping.

pendant¹ [pɑ̃dɑ̃] adj hanging, drooping; (affaire) pending. nm counterpart, match.

pendant² [pɑ̃dɑ̃] prep during, for. **pendant que** conj while.

pendentif [pɑ̃dɑ̃tif] nm pendant.

pendiller [pɑ̃dije] v flap about.

pendre [pɑ̃drə] v hang; (s'affaisser) sag; (bras, jambes) dangle. **pendaison** nf hanging.

pendule [pɑ̃dyl] nf clock. nm pendulum.

pêne [pɛn] nm bolt.

pénétrer [penetre] v penetrate. **pénétrer dans** enter. **pénétrable** adj penetrable.

pénétrant adj piercing, penetrating;

(pluie) drenching; (esprit, personne) shrewd. **pénétration** nf penetration.

pénible [peniblə] adj hard, difficult; (fatigant) tiresome; (douloureux) painful.

péniche [peniʃ] nf barge.

pénicilline [penisilin] nf penicillin.

péninsule [penɛ̃syl] nf peninsula. **péninsulaire** adj peninsular.

pénis [penis] nm penis.

pénitent [penitɑ̃], -e n, adj penitent. **pénitence** nf penitence; (peine) penance; punishment.

penser [pɑ̃se] v think. **penser à** think of or about; (réfléchir) think over. **penser de** think of. **penser faire** be thinking of doing, expect to do. **pensée** nf thought; (bot) pansy. **pensif** adj pensive.

pension [pɑ̃sjɔ̃] nf (allocation) pension; (hôtel) guest house; (école) boarding school; (hébergement) board and lodging. **pension complète** full board. **pension de famille** boarding house. **pensionnaire** n(m+f) (école) boarder; (maison) lodger; (hôtel) resident. **pensionnat** nm boarding school.

pentagone [pɛtagɔn] nm pentagon. **pentagonal** adj pentagonal.

pente [pɑ̃t] nf slope. **en pente** sloping, on a slope.

Pentecôte [pɑ̃tkot] nf Whitsun. **lundi de Pentecôte** nm Whit Monday.

pénurie [penyri] nf shortage.

pépé [pepe] nm (fam) grandad, grandpa.

pépier [pepje] v chirp, tweet. **pépiement** nm chirping.

pépin [pepɛ̃] nm pip; (fam) snag, hitch. **pépinière** nf nursery.

pépite [pepit] nf nugget.

percepteur, -**trice** [persɛptœr, -tris] adj perceptive. nm tax collector.

perception [persɛpsjɔ̃] nf perception; (impôt, etc.) collection; (bureau) tax office. **perceptible** adj perceptible; payable. **perceptif** adj perceptive.

percer [perse] v pierce; (avec perceuse) drill, bore; penetrate; (abcès) burst; (mil, soleil) break through. **perce-neige** nm invar snowdrop. **perce-oreille** nm earwig. **percer des dents** cut one's teeth, be teething. **percée** nf opening, gap. **perceuse** nf drill.

*****percevoir** [persəvwar] v perceive; (impôt) collect.

perche¹ [perʃ] nf (poisson) perch.

perche² [pɛrʃ] nf pole.
percher [pɛrʃe] v perch. **perchoir** nm perch.
perclus [pɛrkly] adj paralysed.
percussion [pɛrkysjɔ̃] nf percussion.
perdre [pɛrdrə] v lose; (gaspiller) waste; (manquer) miss; (réservoir, etc.) leak; ruin. **se perdre** get lost; disappear; go to waste. **perdant, -e** nm, nf loser. **perdu** adj lost, wasted; missed; ruined; isolated.
perdrix [pɛrdri] nf partridge.
père [pɛr] nm father. **le père Noël** Father Christmas.
perfection [pɛrfɛksjɔ̃] nf perfection. **perfectionner** v improve, perfect. **perfectionniste** nm(n + f) perfectionist.
perfide [pɛrfid] adj treacherous, false. **perfidie** nf perfidy.
perforer [pɛrfɔre] v perforate; (poinçonner) punch. **perforation** nf perforation.
péril [peril] nm peril. **périlleux** adj perilous.
périmé [perime] adj out-of-date.
périmètre [perimɛtrə] nm perimeter; (zone) area.
période [perjɔd] nf period.
périodique [perjɔdik] adj periodic, periodical; (math, méd) recurring. nm periodical.
péripétie [peripesi] nf event, episode.
périphérique [periferik] adj peripheral. nm ring road. **périphérie** nf periphery; (ville) outskirts pl.
périr [perir] v perish, die. **périssable** adj perishable.
périscope [periskɔp] nm periscope.
périssoire [periswar] nf canoe.
perle [pɛrl] nf pearl; (grain) bead; (goutte) drop; (erreur) howler.
permanence [pɛrmanɑ̃s] nf permanence; (bureau) office. **en permanence** permanently; continuously. **être de permanence** be on duty. **permanent** adj permanent; continuous. **permanente** nf perm.
perméable [pɛrmeablə] adj permeable, pervious.
*permettre [pɛrmɛtrə] v allow, permit; (rendre possible) enable.
permis [pɛrmi] adj permitted. nm permit, licence. **permis de conduire** driving licence. **permis de construire** planning permission. **permis de séjour/travail** residence/work permit.

permission [pɛrmisjɔ̃] nf permission; (mil) leave.
permutation [pɛrmytasjɔ̃] nf permutation.
pernicieux [pɛrnisjø] adj pernicious; (nuisible) harmful.
pérorer [perɔre] v hold forth.
peroxyde [pɛrɔksid] nm peroxide.
perpendiculaire [pɛrpɑ̃dikylɛr] nf, adj perpendicular.
perpétrer [pɛrpetre] v perpetrate. **perpétration** nf perpetration.
perpétuer [pɛrpetɥe] v perpetuate, carry on. **se perpétuer** survive. **perpétuel** adj perpetual; constant; permanent. **perpétuité** nf perpetuity. **à perpétuité** for ever; (jur) for life.
perplexe [pɛrplɛks] adj perplexed, puzzled. **perplexité** nf perplexity, confusion.
perquisition [pɛrkizisjɔ̃] nf search. **perquisitionner** v search.
perron [pɛrɔ̃] nm steps pl.
perroquet [pɛrɔkɛ] nm parrot.
perruche [pɛryʃ] nf budgerigar.
perruque [pɛryk] nf wig.
persécuter [pɛrsekyte] v persecute; harass. **persécution** nf persecution.
persévérer [pɛrsevere] v persevere. **persévérance** nf perseverance. **persévérant** adj persevering.
persienne [pɛrsjɛn] nf shutter.
persifler [pɛrsifle] v mock. **persiflage** nm mockery.
persil [pɛrsi] nm parsley.
persister [pɛrsiste] v persist. **persister à** persist in. **persistance** nf persistence. **persistant** adj persistent. **à feuilles persistantes** (arbre, plante) evergreen.
personne [pɛrsɔn] nf person. pron anyone. **ne ... personne** nobody. **personnage** nm character; individual; celebrity, important person. **personnalité** nf personality.
personnel [pɛrsɔnɛl] adj personal. nm staff, personnel.
personnifier [pɛrsɔnifje] v personify. **personnification** nf personification, embodiment.
perspective [pɛrspɛktiv] nf perspective; view, angle; (éventualité) prospect.
perspicace [pɛrspikas] adj shrewd. **perspicacité** nf shrewdness, insight.
persuader [pɛrsɥade] v persuade; convince. **persuasif** adj persuasive. **persuasion** nf persuasion; (croyance) belief.

perte [pɛrt] *nf* loss; ruin; (*gaspillage*) waste. **à perte de vue** as far as the eye can see.

pertinent [pɛrtinɑ̃] *adj* pertinent, relevant; (*juste*) apt. **pertinence** *nf* pertinence, relevance; aptness.

perturbateur, -trice [pɛrtyrbatœr, -tris] *adj* disruptive. *nm, nf* troublemaker.

perturber [pɛrtyrbe] *v* disturb, disrupt; (*personne*) perturb. **perturbation** *nf* disturbance, disruption.

pervers [pɛrvɛr] *adj* perverse; depraved, perverted. **perversion** *nf* perversion. **perversité** *nf* perversity; depravity.

pervertir [pɛrvɛrtir] *v* pervert, corrupt. **perverti, -e** *nm, nf* pervert.

peser [pəze] *v* weigh; (*appuyer*) press. **pesant** *adj* heavy. **pesanteur** *nf* heaviness; (*phys*) gravity; (*poids*) weight.

pessimiste [pesimist] *adj* pessimistic. *n(m+f)* pessimist. **pessimisme** *nm* pessimism.

peste [pɛst] *nf* plague; (*personne*) nuisance, pest.

pet [pɛ] *nm* (*vulgaire*) fart.

pétale [petal] *nm* petal.

pétarader [petarade] *v* backfire.

pétard [petar] *nm* banger, firecracker; (*mil*) explosive charge; (*fam: tapage*) row, din.

péter [pete] *v* (*vulgaire*) fart; (*fam: casser*) bust; (*fam: exploser*) burst, go off.

pétiller [petije] *v* sparkle; (*champagne*) bubble; (*feu*) crackle. **pétillant** *adj* sparkling; bubbly.

petit [pəti], **-e** *adj* small, little; (*mince*) slim, thin; (*jeune*) young; (*court*) short; (*faible*) faint, slight; (*mesquin*) petty. **petit ami** *nm* boyfriend. **petit déjeuner** *nm* breakfast. **petite amie** *nf* girlfriend. **petite-fille** *nf* granddaughter. **petit-enfant** *nm* grandchild. **petit-fils** *nm* grandson. **petit gâteau** *nm* biscuit. **petit-pois** *nm* pea. *adv* **petit à petit** little by little. *nm, nf* young child; small person; (*animal*) young. **petitesse** *nf* smallness; pettiness.

pétrin [petrɛ̃] *nm* mess, fix.

pétrir [petrir] *v* knead; mould.

pétrole [petrɔl] *nm* oil, petroleum. **pétrole lampant** paraffin. **pétrolifère** *adj* oil-bearing. **gisement pétrolifère** *nm* oilfield.

pétrolier [petrɔlje] *adj* oil. *nm* tanker.

pétulant [petylɑ̃] *adj* vivacious. **pétulance** *nf* vivacity.

peu [pø] *nm* little. *adv* little; (*quantité*)

not much; (*nombre*) few; (*pas très*) not very. **à peu près** about; (*presque*) almost. **peu à peu** little by little.

peupler [pœple] *v* populate, fill. **peuple** *nm* people; nation; (*foule*) crowd. **peuplier** [pøplije] *nm* poplar.

peur [pœr] *nf* fear; fright. **avoir peur** be frightened *or* afraid. **faire peur à** frighten, scare. **peureux** *adj* fearful, timorous.

peut-être [pøtɛtrə] *adv* perhaps, maybe.

phallus [falys] *nm* phallus. **phallique** *adj* phallic. **phallocrate** *nm* (*fam*) male chauvinist pig.

phare [far] *nm* lighthouse; (*balise*) beacon; (*auto*) headlight. **phare antibrouillard** fog lamp.

pharmacie [farmasi] *nf* pharmacy; (*magasin*) chemist's; (*armoire*) medicine chest. **pharmaceutique** *adj* pharmaceutical. **pharmacien, -enne** *nm, nf* chemist, pharmacist.

pharynx [farɛ̃ks] *nm* pharynx. **pharyngite** *nf* pharyngitis.

phase [fɑz] *nf* phase; stage.

phénix [feniks] *nm* phoenix.

phénomène [fenɔmɛn] *nm* phenomenon (*pl* -ena); (*personne*) freak. **phénoménal** *adj* phenomenal.

philanthropie [filɑ̃trɔpi] *nf* philanthropy. **philanthrope** *n(m+f)* philanthropist. **philanthropique** *adj* philanthropic.

philatélie [filateli] *nf* philately. **philatéliste** *n(m+f)* philatelist.

philosophe [filɔzɔf] *adj* philosophical. *n(m+f)* philosopher. **philosophie** *nf* philosophy. **philosophique** *adj* philosophical.

phobie [fɔbi] *nf* phobia.

phonétique [fɔnetik] *adj* phonetic. *nf* phonetics.

phonographe [fɔnɔgraf] *nm* gramophone.

phoque [fɔk] *nm* seal.

phosphate [fɔsfat] *nm* phosphate.

phosphore [fɔsfɔr] *nm* phosphorus. **phosphoreux** *adj* phosphorous.

phosphorescence [fɔsfɔresɑ̃s] *nf* phosphorescence. **phosphorescent** *adj* phosphorescent; luminous.

photo [fɔto] *nf* photo.

photocopier [fɔtɔkɔpje] *v* photocopy. **photocopie** *nf* photocopy. **photocopieur** *nm* photocopier.

photogénique [fɔtɔʒenik] *adj* photogenic.

photographie [fɔtɔgrafi] *nf* (*image*) photograph; (*art*) photography. **photographe** *n(m+f)* photographer. **photographier** *v*

photograph, take a picture of.
photographique *adj* photographic.
phrase [frɑz] *nf* phrase; (*gramm*) sentence.
physiologie [fizjɔlɔʒi] *nf* physiology. **physiologique** *adj* physiological. **physiologiste** *n(m+f)* physiologist.
physique[1] [fizik] *adj* physical. *nm* physique.
physique[2] [fizik] *nf* physics. **physicien, -enne** *nm, nf* physicist.
piaffer [pjafe] *v* stamp, paw the ground.
piailler [pjaje] *v* (*fam*) squawk, screech.
piano [pjano] *nm* piano. **piano à queue** grand piano. **pianiste** *n(m+f)* pianist.
piauler [pjole] *v* whine; (*enfant*) whimper; (*oiseau*) cheep.
pic[1] [pik] *nm* (*oiseau*) woodpecker; (*instrument*) pick.
pic[2] [pik] *nm* (*cime*) peak. **à pic** sheer; (*arriver, tomber*) just at the right time.
piccolo [pikɔlo] *nm* piccolo.
picorer [pikɔre] *v* peck (at).
picoter [pikɔte] *v* (*yeux*) smart, sting; (*gorge*) tickle; (*peau*) prickle; (*picorer*) peck.
pie [pi] *nf* magpie.
pièce [pjɛs] *nf* piece; (*machine*) part; document; (*maison*) room; (*théâtre*) play; (*monnaie*) coin; (*couture*) patch. **à la pièce** separately. **pièce détachée** spare part.
pied [pje] *nm* foot; (*table*) leg; base; (*verre*) stem. **à pied** on foot. **au pied de la lettre** literally. **en pied** full-length. **être sur pied** be under way. **mettre les pieds dans le plat** put one's foot in it. **mettre sur pied** set up. **perdre pied** get out of one's depth. **pied bot** *adj* club-footed.
piédestal [pjedɛstal] *nm* pedestal.
piège [pjɛʒ] *nm* trap. **piéger** *v* trap; (*engin, etc.*) booby-trap. **lettre/voiture piégée** *nf* letter/car bomb.
pierre [pjɛr] *nf* stone. **pierre à briquet** flint. **pierre à chaux** limestone. **pierre d'achoppement** stumbling block. **pierre de gué** stepping stone. **pierre ponce** pumice stone. **pierre tombale** tombstone. **pierreux** *adj* stony.
piété [pjete] *nf* piety; devotion.
piétiner [pjetine] *v* (*fouler*) trample (on); (*trépigner*) stamp; make no progress.
piéton [pjetɔ̃] *nm* pedestrian.
piètre [pjɛtrə] *adj* paltry, very poor.
pieu [pjø] *nm* post; (*pointu*) stake.

pieuvre [pjœvrə] *nf* octopus.
pieux [pjø] *adj* pious, devout.
pigeon [piʒɔ̃] *nm* pigeon.
piger [piʒe] (*argot*) *v* cotton on, twig. **tu piges?** do you get it?
pigment [pigmɑ̃] *nm* pigment. **pigmentation** *nf* pigmentation.
pignon [piɲɔ̃] *nm* (*arch*) gable; (*tech*) pinion.
pile[1] [pil] *nf* (*tas*) pile; support; (*élec*) battery.
pile[2] [pil] *nf* (*pièce*) tails *pl*. **côté pile** *nm* reverse side. **pile ou face?** heads or tails? **tirer à pile ou face** toss up. *adv* (*fam*) dead, exactly.
piler [pile] *v* crush, pound.
pilier [pilje] *nm* pillar.
piller [pije] *v* pillage, plunder. **pillage** *nm* pillage, looting.
pilote [pilɔt] *nm* pilot; (*auto*) driver; guide. *adj* experimental. **piloter** *v* pilot; (*avion*) fly; drive; (*personne*) show round.
pilule [pilyl] *nf* pill.
piment [pimɑ̃] *nm* pimento; piquancy, spice. **piment doux** capsicum. **piment rouge** chilli. **pimenté** *adj* (*plat*) hot; (*récit*) spicy.
pimpant [pɛ̃pɑ̃] *adj* trim, smart.
pin [pɛ̃] *nm* pine.
pinacle [pinaklə] *nm* pinnacle.
pince [pɛ̃s] *nf* pliers *pl*; (*charbon, sucre*) tongs *pl*; (*levier*) crowbar; (*couture*) dart; (*crabe*) pincer, claw. **pince à épiler** eyebrow tweezers *pl*. **pince à linge** clothes peg. **pincé** *adj* stiff; (*sourire*) tight-lipped. **pincée** *nf* pinch. **pincer** *v* pinch, nip; (*serrer*) grip; (*musique*) pluck; (*fam*) catch.
pinceau [pɛ̃so] *nm* paintbrush.
pingouin [pɛ̃gwɛ̃] *nm* penguin.
ping-pong [piŋpɔ̃g] *nm* table tennis.
pinson [pɛ̃sɔ̃] *nm* chaffinch.
piocher [pjɔʃe] *v* dig with a pick; (*fam*) swot; (*cartes, etc.*) pick up. **pioche** *nf* pick, pickaxe.
pion [pjɔ̃] *nm* (*jeu*) piece; (*échecs*) pawn; student supervising schoolchildren.
pionnier [pjɔnje] *nm* pioneer.
pipe [pip] *nf* pipe.
piquant [pikɑ̃] *adj* (*tige*) prickly; (*goût*) hot, pungent; (*vin*) tart; (*mordant*) biting; (*sauce, détail*) piquant. *nm* prickle; (*hérisson*) spine; piquancy.
pique[1] [pik] *nf* (*arme*) pike. *nm* (*cartes*) spade.

pique² [pik] nf cutting remark.
pique-nique [piknik] nm picnic. **pique-niquer** v picnic. **pique-niqueur, -euse** nm, nf picnicker.
piquer [pike] v prick; sting; (insecte, serpent) bite; (aiguille, etc.) jab, stick; excite, arouse; (fam: voler) pinch; (moutarde, etc.) be hot or pungent; (avion, oiseau) swoop down. **piquer une colère** fly into a rage. **piquer une crise** throw a fit. **se faire piquer** have an injection. **se piquer** get stung; give oneself an injection; take offence. **piqué** adj (couture) quilted; (marqué) dotted, pitted; (fam) barmy. **piqûre** nf prick; sting; bite; injection; (couture) stitch; (trou) hole.
piquet [pike] nm post, stake; (tente) peg; (de grève) picket.
pirate [pirat] nm, adj pirate. **pirate de l'air** hijacker. **piraterie** nf piracy.
pire [pir] adj worse. **le** or **la pire** (the) worst.
pirouette [pirwɛt] nf pirouette. **pirouetter** v pirouette.
pis¹ [pi] nm udder.
pis² [pi] adj, adv worse. **de pis en pis** worse and worse. nm worst. **au pis aller** if the worst comes to the worst. **pis-aller** nm invar makeshift.
piscine [pisin] nf swimming pool; (publique) baths pl.
pissenlit [pisãli] nm dandelion.
pisser [pise] (vulgaire) v piss. **pisse** nf piss.
pistache [pistaʃ] nf pistachio.
piste [pist] nf track; (traces) trail; (aéro) runway; (ski) run; (police) lead. **piste cavalière** bridle-path. **piste sonore** soundtrack.
pistolet [pistɔlɛ] nm pistol, gun.
piston [pistɔ̃] nm piston; (musique) valve. **avoir du piston** (fam) have friends in the right places.
pitié [pitje] nf pity. **avoir pitié de** take pity on; (compâtir) feel sorry for. **piteux** adj pitiful, sorry; (honteux) shamefaced. **pitoyable** adj pitiful.
pitre [pitrə] nm clown.
pittoresque [pitɔrɛsk] adj picturesque.
pivot [pivo] nm pivot. **pivoter** v pivot, revolve, swivel round.
placage [plakaʒ] nm (bois) veneer; (pierre) facing.
placard [plakar] nm (armoire) cupboard;

(affiche) notice, placard. **placarder** v (affiche) stick up; (mur) placard.
place [plas] nf place; space; (siège) seat; (prix) fare; (ville) square; (emploi) job. **à la place de** instead of; (personne) on behalf of. **à ta** or **votre place** if I were you. **faire place à** give way to. **sur place** on the spot.
placenta [plasɛ̃ta] nm placenta.
placer [plase] v place, put; (argent) invest; (vendre) sell. **se placer** (debout) stand; (assis) sit; (avoir lieu) take place; find a job. **placement** nm investment. **placeur** nm usher.
placide [plasid] adj placid. **placidité** nf placidity.
plafond [plafɔ̃] nm ceiling.
plage [plaʒ] nf beach; (ville) seaside resort; (disque) track.
plagier [plaʒje] v plagiarize. **plagiaire** n(m + f) plagiarist. **plagiat** nm plagiarism.
plaider [plede] v plead.
plaie [plɛ] nf wound; (fam) nuisance.
***plaindre** [plɛ̃drə] v pity, feel sorry for. **se plaindre** moan, complain, grumble.
plaine [plɛn] nf plain.
plain-pied [plɛ̃pje] adv **de plain-pied avec** on the same level as.
plainte [plɛ̃t] nf complaint; (gémissement) moan. **plaintif** adj plaintive.
***plaire** [plɛr] v **plaire à** please; (convenir à) suit. **se plaire** be happy, enjoy oneself. **se plaire à** like, delight in. **s'il te** or **vous plaît** please.
plaisance [plɛzãs] nf **maison de plaisance** nf country house. **navigation de plaisance** nf boating; yachting.
plaisant [plɛzã] adj pleasant; amusing.
plaisanter [plɛzãte] v joke; (taquiner) tease. **plaisanterie** nf joke.
plaisir [plɛzir] nm pleasure. **faire plaisir à** please, make happy.
plan¹ [plã] adj flat, level, plane. nm plane, level; (cinéma) shot. **premier plan** foreground.
plan² [plã] nm plan; (carte) map.
planche [plãʃ] nf board, plank; (rayon) shelf. **faire la planche** float on one's back. **planche à dessin/repasser** drawing/ironing board. **planche à pain** breadboard.
plancher [plãʃe] nm floor.
plancton [plãktɔ̃] nm plankton.
planer [plane] v glide, hover; (monter) soar. **planer sur** (danger) hang over;

(regard) look down over. **planeur** nm glider.

planète [planɛt] nf planet. **planétaire** adj planetary. **planétarium** nm planetarium.

plant [plɑ̃] nm seedling, young plant; *(arbres)* plantation; *(légumes, fleurs)* bed.

plantation [plɑ̃tasjɔ̃] nf plantation; *(action)* planting.

plante¹ [plɑ̃t] nf *(bot)* plant. **plante grimpante** creeper.

plante² [plɑ̃t] nf *(anat)* sole of the foot.

planter [plɑ̃te] v plant; *(enfoncer)* drive or stick in; *(mettre)* put, stick; *(installer)* put or set up. **planter là** *(fam)* dump, ditch.

planton [plɑ̃tɔ̃] nm orderly.

plantureux [plɑ̃tyrø] adj copious, lavish.

plaque [plak] nf plate, sheet; *(pierre, chocolat)* slab; *(tache)* patch, blotch; *(commémorative)* plaque; *(insigne)* badge. **plaque chauffante** hotplate. **plaque minéralogique** or **d'immatriculation** number plate.

plaquer [plake] v *(bois)* veneer; *(métal)* plate; *(fam)* ditch, chuck; *(aplatir)* plaster down, flatten; *(sport)* tackle.

plasma [plasma] nm plasma.

plastique [plastik] nm, adj plastic.

plat [pla] adj flat; *(fade)* dull; *(cheveux)* straight. **à plat** flat. **plate-bande** nf flowerbed. **plate-forme** nf platform. nm flat part; *(cuisine)* dish; *(partie d'un repas)* course.

plateau [plato] nm tray; *(géog)* plateau; *(théâtre)* stage. **plateau à** or **de fromages** cheeseboard.

platine [platin] nm platinum.

platonique [platɔnik] adj *(amour)* platonic; vain, futile.

plâtrer [plɑtre] v plaster; *(méd)* set in plaster. **plâtre** nm plaster; *(méd, art)* plaster cast. **plâtrier** nm plasterer.

plausible [plozibl] adj plausible. **plausibilité** nf plausibility.

plectre [plɛktrə] nm plectrum.

plein [plɛ̃] adj full; complete; solid; *(animal)* pregnant. **en plein** ... at the height of ... , in the middle of ... . **en plein jour** in broad daylight. **plein air** nm open air. **pleine mer** nf open sea; *(marée)* high tide. adv full. nm **faire le plein** fill up.

pleurer [plœre] v cry; *(yeux)* water; lament, bemoan; *(mort)* mourn. **pleureur, -euse** adj tearful; *(enfant)* whining.

pleurnicher [plœrniʃe] v snivel, whine.

***pleuvoir** [pløvwar] v rain.

pli [pli] nm fold; *(faux)* crease; *(couture)* pleat; *(genou)* bend; envelope; *(forme)* shape; habit.

plier [plije] v fold; *(courber)* bend; *(céder)* yield, give way. **se plier à** submit to. **pliant** adj collapsible, folding.

plinthe [plɛ̃t] nf skirting board.

plisser [plise] v *(jupe, etc.)* pleat; *(rider)* pucker, crease.

plomb [plɔ̃] nm lead; *(chasse)* shot; *(élec)* fuse. **à plomb** straight down. **de plomb** leaden; *(sommeil)* heavy. **plombage** nm filling. **plomber** v weight; *(dent)* fill. **plomberie** nf plumbing. **plombier** nm plumber.

plonger [plɔ̃ʒe] v plunge, dive. **plonge** nf washing-up. **plongé dans** adj immersed in, buried in. **plongée** nf diving. **plongée sous-marine** skin-diving. **plongeoir** nm diving board. **plongeon** nm dive. **plongeur, -euse** nm, nf diver; *(restaurant)* washer-up.

plouf [pluf] nm, interj splash.

ployer [plwaje] v bend; *(plancher)* sag; *(céder)* give way.

pluie [plɥi] nf rain; *(averse)* shower.

plume [plym] nf *(oiseau)* feather; *(écrire)* pen; *(bec)* nib. **plumage** nm plumage. **plumer** v pluck; *(argot)* fleece.

plupart [plypar] nf **la plupart** most, the majority. **pour la plupart** mostly.

pluriel [plyrjɛl] nm, adj plural.

plus [ply] adv more. **de** or **en plus** on top extra, in addition, besides. **de plus en plus** more and more. **le** or **la plus** the most. **ne ... plus** no more; *(temps)* no longer. **plus de** more than, over. **plus-que-parfait** nm pluperfect. conj plus.

plusieurs [plyzjœr] adj several.

plutôt [plyto] adv rather.

pluvieux [plyvjø] adj rainy, wet.

pneu [pnø] nm tyre. **pneu réchapé** remould.

pneumatique [pnømatik] adj pneumatic *(canot, matelas)* inflatable.

pneumonie [pnømɔni] nf pneumonia.

pochard [poʃar], **-e** nm, nf *(argot)* drunk.

poche [poʃ] nf pocket; *(sac)* bag; *(zool)* pouch. **de poche** pocket; *(livre)* paper back. **pochette** nf pocket handkerchief envelope, case.

pocher [pɔʃe] v poach. **pocher un œil à** give a black eye to. **pochade** nf quick sketch. **pochoir** nm stencil.

poêle¹ [pwal] nf frying pan.

poêle² [pwal] nm stove.

poème [pɔɛm] nm poem. **poésie** nf poetry. **poète** nm poet. **poétesse** nf poetess. **poétique** adj poetic.

poids [pwa] nm weight. **poids lourd** heavyweight; (camion) lorry. **prendre du poids** put on weight.

poignant [pwaɲɑ̃] adj poignant, harrowing.

poignard [pwaɲar] nm dagger. **poignarder** v stab, knife.

poigne [pwaɲ] nf grip; (main) hand. **poignée** nf (valise, porte, etc.) handle; (quantité) handful. **poignée de main** handshake. **poignet** nm wrist; (vêtement) cuff.

poil [pwal] nm hair; (brosse) bristle; (tapis, tissu) pile. **à poil** (fam) naked. **poilu** adj hairy.

poinçon [pwɛ̃sɔ̃] nm awl; (or, etc.) die, stamp; (marque) hallmark. **poinçonner** v stamp; hallmark; (billet) punch.

*__poindre__ [pwɛ̃drə] v (jour) dawn; (aube) break; (plante) come up.

poing [pwɛ̃] nm fist.

point¹ [pwɛ̃] nm point; (marque) dot; (tache) spot; (ponctuation) full stop; (couture, tricot) stitch. **à point** just right; (bifteck) medium. **au point** (phot) in focus; perfect. **être sur le point de** be just about to. **mettre au point** perfect; (phot) focus; finalize. **point de côté** stitch. **point de mire** focal point. **point de suture** (méd) stitch. **point d'exclamation** exclamation mark. **point d'interrogation** question mark. **point du jour** daybreak. **point mort** (auto) neutral. **point noir** (visage) blackhead; (auto) black spot. **point virgule** semicolon.

point² [pwɛ̃] adv not. **ne ... point** not at all.

pointe [pwɛ̃t] nf point; (bout) tip; (maximum) peak; (soupçon) touch, dash. **sur la pointe des pieds** on tiptoe.

pointer¹ [pwɛ̃te] v (cocher) tick off; (braquer) aim, point; (employé) clock in or out. **pointeur** nm timekeeper.

pointer² [pwɛ̃te] v (piquer) stick; appear; (dresser) soar up.

pointillé [pwɛ̃tije] adj dotted. nm dotted line. **pointiller** v (art) stipple.

pointilleux [pwɛ̃tijø] adj particular.

pointu [pwɛ̃ty] adj pointed; (aigu) sharp; (péj) touchy, peevish.

pointure [pwɛ̃tyr] nf size.

poire [pwar] nf pear; (fam) mug. **poirier** nm pear tree.

poireau [pwaro] nm leek.

pois [pwa] nm pea; (point) dot, spot. **pois cassés** split peas pl. **pois chiche** chickpea. **pois de senteur** sweet pea.

poison [pwazɔ̃] nm poison.

poisseux [pwasø] adj sticky.

poisson [pwasɔ̃] nm fish. **poisson d'avril** April fool. **poisson rouge** goldfish. **Poissons** nm pl Pisces sing. **poissonnerie** nm fish shop. **poissonnier, -ère** nm, nf fishmonger.

poitrine [pwatrin] nf chest; (seins) bust; (cuisine) breast.

poivre [pwavrə] nm pepper. **poivre de Cayenne** Cayenne pepper. **poivré** adj peppery; (récit) spicy. **poivrer** v pepper. **poivrier** nm pepper-pot. **poivron** nm pepper.

poix [pwa] nf pitch.

polaire [pɔlɛr] adj polar.

polariser [pɔlarize] v polarize; attract; (concentrer) focus. **se polariser sur** be centred on.

pôle [pol] nm pole.

polémique [pɔlemik] adj controversial. nf controversy, argument.

poli¹ [pɔli] adj polite.

poli² [pɔli] adj polished. nm shine.

police¹ [pɔlis] nf police. **faire la police** keep order.

police² [pɔlis] nf (assurance) policy.

policier [pɔlisje] nm policeman; (roman) detective novel. adj police; detective.

polio [pɔljo] nf polio.

polir [pɔlir] v polish.

polisson, -onne [pɔlisɔ̃, -ɔn] nm, nf rascal. adj (enfant) naughty; (grivois) saucy. **polissonnerie** nf naughty trick; saucy remark or action.

politesse [pɔlitɛs] nf politeness, courtesy; polite remark or gesture.

politique [pɔlitik] adj political. nf (science) politics; (ligne de conduite) policy. **politicien, -enne** nm, nf politician.

polka [pɔlka] nf polka.

pollen [pɔlɛn] nm pollen. **pollinisation** nf pollination.

polluer [pɔlɥe] v pollute. **pollution** nf pollution.

Pologne [pɔlɔɲ] nf Poland. **polonais** nm, adj Polish. **Polonais, -e** nm, nf Pole.

poltron, -onne [pɔltrɔ̃, -ɔn] nm, nf coward. adj cowardly. **poltronnerie** nf cowardice.

polycopier [pɔlikɔpje] v duplicate, stencil.

polyester [pɔliɛstɛr] nm polyester.

polyéthylène [pɔlietilɛn] nm polythene.

polygame [pɔligam] adj polygamous. nm polygamist. **polygamie** nf polygamy.

polyglotte [pɔliglɔt] adj multilingual. n(m + f) polyglot.

polygone [pɔligɔn] nm polygon.

pommade [pɔmad] nf ointment.

pomme [pɔm] nf apple; (laitue, chou) heart; (arrosoir) rose. **pomme à couteau/cuire** eating/cooking apple. **pomme d'Adam** Adam's apple. **pomme de pin** pine cone. **pomme de terre** potato. **pommes frites** chips pl. **pommier** nm apple tree.

pommelé [pɔmle] adj (cheval) dappled.

pommette [pɔmɛt] nf cheekbone.

pompe¹ [pɔ̃p] nf pump. **pompe à incendie** fire engine. **pomper** v pump. **pompier** nm fireman. **pompiste** n(m + f) petrol pump attendant.

pompe² [pɔ̃p] nf pomp. **pompeux** adj pompous.

poncer [pɔ̃se] v rub down, sandpaper.

ponctuel [pɔ̃ktɥɛl] adj punctual; (assidu) meticulous. **ponctualité** nf punctuality; meticulousness.

ponctuer [pɔ̃ktɥe] v punctuate. **ponctuation** nf punctuation.

pondérer [pɔ̃dere] v balance. **pondéré** adj level-headed.

pondre [pɔ̃drə] v lay; (œuvre) produce.

poney [pɔnɛ] nm pony.

pont [pɔ̃] nm bridge; (naut) deck. **pont aérien** airlift. **pont-levis** nm drawbridge. **pont suspendu** suspension bridge. **pont tournant** swing bridge.

popeline [pɔplin] nf poplin.

populace [pɔpylas] nf rabble.

populaire [pɔpylɛr] adj popular; (république, etc.) people's, of the people. **populariser** v popularize. **popularité** nf popularity.

population [pɔpylasjɔ̃] nf population.

porc [pɔr] nm pig; (viande) pork. **porc-épic** nm porcupine.

porcelaine [pɔrsəlɛn] nf porcelain, china.

porche [pɔrʃ] nm porch.

porcherie [pɔrʃəri] nf pigsty.

pore [pɔr] nm pore. **poreux** adj porous.

pornographie [pɔrnɔgrafi] nf pornography. **pornographique** adj pornographic.

port¹ [pɔr] nm port; (bassin) harbour.

port² [pɔr] nm carriage; postage; (comportement) bearing; (casque, barbe, etc.) wearing.

porte [pɔrt] nf door; (aéro, jardin, écluse) gate; (embrasure) doorway. **mettre à la porte** throw out; (licencier) sack.

porte-avions nm invar aircraft carrier.

porte-bagages nm invar luggage rack.

porte-bébé nm carrycot.

porte-bonheur nm invar lucky charm.

porte-clefs nm invar key ring.

porte d'entrée nf front door.

porte-fenêtre nf French window.

portefeuille [pɔrtəfœj] nm wallet; (pol) portfolio.

portemanteau [pɔrtmɑ̃to] nm coat rack.

porte-mine nm propelling pencil.

porte-monnaie nm invar purse.

porte-parole nm invar spokesman.

porter [pɔrte] v carry; bear; (vêtement) wear; (amener) take; direct, turn; (comm) put down, enter; (ressentir) feel; (inciter) prompt, induce; (coup) strike home. **se porter bien/mal** be well/ill. **portable** adj wearable. **portatif** adj portable. **porté** adj inclined, prone. **portée** nf range, reach; (effet) significance, consequences pl; (animal) litter; (musique) stave. **porteur, -euse** nm, nf bearer; (valises) porter; messenger.

porte-serviettes nm invar towel rail.

porte-voix nm invar megaphone.

portière [pɔrtjɛr] nf door.

portion [pɔrsjɔ̃] nf portion; part.

porto [pɔrto] nm port.

portrait [pɔrtrɛ] nm portrait.

Portugal [pɔrtygal] nm Portugal. **portugais** nm, adj Portuguese. **les Portugais** the Portuguese.

poser [poze] v put, lay; set down; (question) ask; (tableau, étagères) put up; (art) pose. **se poser** alight, come down; (regard) rest; (question) crop up, arise. **se poser en** pose as. **pose** nf pose; (phot) exposure; affectation; laying; (chauffage, etc.) installation. **posé** adj sedate, staid; (allure) steady.

positif [pozitif] *adj* positive; real; definite.
position [pozisjɔ̃] *nf* position.
posséder [posede] *v* possess, have. **possessif** *nm, adj* possessive. **possession** *nf* possession.
possible [posiblə] *adj* possible; feasible; potential. **possibilité** *nf* possibility.
poste[1] [post] *nf* post; (*bureau*) post office. **mettre à la poste** post. **poste aérienne** air mail. **postal** *adj* postal.
poste[2] [post] *nm* post; (*emploi*) job; (*TV, radio*) set; (*téléphone*) extension. **poste de police** police station. **poste d'essence** petrol station.
poster [poste] *v* post.
postérieur, -e [posterjœr] *adj* (*temps*) later; (*espace*) back; (*pattes, etc.*) hind. *nm* (*fam*) behind.
postérité [posterite] *nf* posterity.
posthume [postym] *adj* posthumous.
postiche [postiʃ] *adj* false. *nm* hairpiece.
postscolaire [postskolɛr] *adj* **enseignement postscolaire** *nm* further education.
post-scriptum [postskriptom] *nm invar* postscript.
postuler [postyle] *v* (*emploi*) apply for; (*poser*) postulate. **postulant, -e** *nm, nf* applicant. **postulat** *nm* postulate.
posture [postyr] *nf* posture, position.
pot [po] *nm* pot; (*verre*) jar; (*lait*) jug; carton; (*fam: chance*) luck. **pot à bière** tankard. **pot-au-feu** *nm invar* stew. **pot-de-vin** *nm* bribe.
potable [potablə] *adj* drinkable; (*fam*) reasonable, decent.
potage [potaʒ] *nm* soup.
potager [potaʒe] *adj* vegetable; (*plante*) edible. *nm* vegetable garden.
potassium [potasjom] *nm* potassium.
poteau [poto] *nm* post. **poteau indicateur** signpost. **poteau télégraphique** telegraph pole.
potelé [potle] *adj* plump, chubby.
potence [potɑ̃s] *nf* (*gibet*) gallows; (*support*) bracket.
potentiel [potɑ̃sjɛl] *nm, adj* potential.
poterie [potri] *nf* pottery. **potier** *nm* potter.
potin [potɛ̃] *nm* din, racket. **potins** *nm pl* gossip *sing*. **potiner** *v* gossip.
potion [posjɔ̃] *nf* potion.
potiron [potirɔ̃] *nm* pumpkin.
pou [pu] *nm, pl* **poux** louse (*pl* lice).
poubelle [pubɛl] *nf* bin.

pouce [pus] *nm* thumb; (*orteil*) big toe; (*mesure*) inch.
poudre [pudrə] *nf* powder. **poudre à canon** gunpowder. **poudre de riz** face powder. **poudrer** *v* powder. **poudreux** *adj* dusty. **poudrier** *nm* powder compact.
pouffer [pufe] *v* snigger.
poulain [pulɛ̃] *nm* foal.
poule [pul] *nf* hen; (*cuisine*) fowl. **poulailler** *nm* henhouse. **poulet** *nm* chicken.
pouliche [puliʃ] *nf* filly.
poulie [puli] *nf* pulley.
poulpe [pulp] *nm* octopus.
pouls [pu] *nm* pulse.
poumon [pumɔ̃] *nm* lung.
poupe [pup] *nf* stern.
poupée [pupe] *nf* doll.
pour [pur] *prep* for; (*comme*) as; (*but*) to. **pour cent** per cent. **pour que** so that.
pourboire [purbwar] *nm* tip.
pourceau [purso] *nm* (*péj*) swine.
pourcentage [pursɑ̃taʒ] *nm* percentage.
pourchasser [purʃase] *v* pursue.
pourpre [purprə] *nm, adj* crimson, purple.
pourquoi [purkwa] *conj, adv* why.
pourrir [purir] *v* rot, decay; (*fruit*) go rotten *or* bad; (*gâter*) spoil. **pourri** *adj* rotten, bad. **pourriture** *nf* rot.
****poursuivre** [pursчivrə] *v* pursue; (*harceler*) hound; (*jur*) prosecute; continue, carry on. **poursuite** *nf* pursuit, chase. **poursuites** *nf pl* legal proceedings *pl*. **poursuivant, -e** *nm, nf* pursuer.
pourtant [purtɑ̃] *adv* yet, nevertheless.
pourtour [purtur] *nm* circumference; perimeter.
****pourvoir** [purvwar] *v* provide, equip, supply. **pourvoir à** provide for, cater for. **pourvoyeur, -euse** *nm, nf* supplier.
pourvu [purvy] *adj* **être pourvu de** (*personne*) be endowed with; (*chose*) be fitted *or* equipped with. **pourvu que** *conj* provided that, as long as.
pousser [puse] *v* push; (*stimuler, inciter*) drive, urge; continue, pursue; (*cri*) utter, let out; (*grandir*) grow. **pousser du coude** nudge. **pousse** *nf* growth; (*bot*) shoot. **poussé** *adj* advanced; elaborate; (*enquête*) exhaustive. **poussée** *nf* push, thrust; (*prix, pol*) upsurge. **poussette** *nf* push-chair.
poussière [pusjɛr] *nf* dust. **poussiéreux** *adj* dusty.

poussin [pusɛ̃] nm chick.

poutre [putrə] nf beam; (métal) girder.

***pouvoir** [puvwar] v can; (permission) may, be allowed to; (capacité) be able to; (possibilité) might, could. **n'en plus pouvoir** be tired out. **n'y rien pouvoir** be unable to do anything about it. **se pouvoir** be possible. nm power; (capacité) ability; influence.

pragmatique [pragmatik] adj pragmatic.

Prague [prag] n Prague.

prairie [preri] nf meadow, grassland; (Amérique) prairie.

praticable [pratikablə] adj practicable; feasible; (chemin) passable.

praticien [pratisjɛ̃], **-enne** nm, nf practitioner.

pratique¹ [pratik] adj practical; (commode) handy, convenient.

pratique² [pratik] nf practice.

pratiquer [pratike] v practise; (faire) make; (employer) use; (rel) go to church.

pré [pre] nm meadow.

préalable [prealablə] adj preliminary, prior. nm **au préalable** first.

préavis [preavi] nm (advance) notice.

précaire [preker] adj precarious.

précaution [prekosjɔ̃] nf precaution; (prudence) care, caution.

précédent [presedɑ̃] adj previous. nm precedent.

précéder [presede] v precede.

précepteur [preseptœr] nm tutor. **préceptrice** nf governess.

prêcher [preʃe] v preach. **prêche** nm sermon.

précieux [presjø] adj precious; affected.

précipice [presipis] nm precipice, chasm.

précipiter [presipite] v precipitate; (lancer) throw, hurl; (hâter) hasten, speed up. **se précipiter** rush. **précipitamment** adv hurriedly, hastily. **précipitation** nf precipitation; haste. **précipité** adj hurried, rapid; (décision) hasty; (fuite) headlong.

précis [presi] adj precise. nm précis, summary; (manuel) handbook. **précisément** adv precisely; exactly; just. **préciser** v specify, make clear; be more precise (about). **se préciser** become clear, take shape. **précision** nf precision; detail, point.

précoce [prekɔs] adj precocious; (fruit, etc.) early; (sénilité) premature. **précocité** nf precocity; earliness.

préconçu [prekɔ̃sy] adj preconceived.

préconiser [prekɔnize] v recommend; advocate.

précurseur [prekyrsœr] nm precursor.

prédateur, -trice [predatœr, -tris] nm predator. adj predatory.

prédécesseur [predesesœr] nm predecessor.

prédestiner [predestine] v predestine. **prédestination** nf predestination.

prédicat [predika] nm predicate.

prédicateur [predikatœr] nm preacher.

***prédire** [predir] v predict, foretell. **prédiction** nf prediction.

prédominer [predɔmine] v predominate, prevail. **prédominance** nf predominance. **prédominant** adj predominant, prevailing.

prééminent [preeminɑ̃] adj pre-eminent. **prééminence** nf pre-eminence.

préfabriqué [prefabrike] adj prefabricated.

préface [prefas] nf preface.

préfecture [prefɛktyr] nf prefecture. **préfecture de police** Paris police headquarters.

préférer [prefere] v prefer. **préférable** adj preferable. **préféré, -e** n, adj favourite. **préférence** nf preference. **préférentiel** adj preferential.

préfet [prefɛ] nm prefect, chief administrative officer of a French department. **préfet de police** chief of Paris police.

préfixe [prefiks] nm prefix. **préfixer** v prefix.

préhistorique [preistɔrik] adj prehistoric.

préjudice [preʒydis] nm harm, wrong; (matériel) loss. **au préjudice de** at the expense of. **préjudiciable** adj detrimental.

préjugé [preʒyʒe] nm prejudice.

prélever [prɛlve] v take; (argent) deduct. **prélèvement** nm taking; deduction. **faire un prélèvement de sang** take a blood sample.

préliminaire [preliminɛr] adj preliminary. **préliminaires** nm pl preliminaries pl.

prélude [prelyd] nm prelude.

prématuré [prematyre] adj premature.

préméditer [premedite] v premeditate. **préméditation** nf premeditation.

premier [prəmje], **-ère** adj first; (le plus bas) bottom; (le plus haut) top; (le plus important) greatest, foremost; (fondamental) basic; original. **premier ministre** nm prime minister. **premiers secours** nm pl first aid sing. nm first; (étage) first

floor. *nf* first; (*cinéma*) première; (*transport*) first class; (*lycée*) lower sixth form.

prémisse [premis] *nf* premise.

prémonition [premɔnisjɔ̃] *nf* premonition.

prenant [prənɑ̃] *adj* absorbing, fascinating.

***prendre** [prɑ̃drə] *v* take; (*aller chercher*) fetch, pick up; (*attraper*) catch; (*repas*) have; (*acheter*) buy; (*air*) assume, put on; (*manier*) handle; (*durcir*) set. **s'en prendre à** take it out on; blame; attack. **s'y prendre** set about it.

prénom [prenɔ̃] *nm* Christian name.

prénuptial [prenypsjal] *adj* premarital.

préoccuper [preɔkype] *v* (*absorber*) preoccupy; (*inquiéter*) worry. **se préoccuper de** be concerned with *or* about. **préoccupation** *nf* preoccupation; worry.

préparer [prepare] *v* prepare; (*faire*) make; (*apprêter*) get ready; (*réserver*) have in store. **préparatifs** *nm pl* preparations *pl*. **préparation** *nf* preparation. **préparatoire** *adj* preparatory.

préposé [prepoze], **-e** *nm, nf* employer, official; (*vestiaire*) attendant.

préposition [prepozisjɔ̃] *nf* preposition.

prérogative [prerɔgativ] *nf* prerogative.

près [prɛ] *adv* near, close. **à cela près** apart from that. **de près** closely. **près de** close to; (*presque*) almost.

présager [prezaʒe] *v* be an omen of; (*prédire*) predict. **présage** *nm* omen.

presbyte [presbit] *adj* long-sighted. **presbytie** *nf* long-sightedness.

***prescrire** [preskrir] *v* prescribe; order; stipulate. **prescription** *nf* prescription; order.

préséance [preseɑ̃s] *nf* precedence.

présence [prezɑ̃s] *nf* presence; (*bureau, école*) attendance.

présent [prezɑ̃] *nm, adj* present. **à présent** now. **d'à présent** of today, present-day.

présent² [prezɑ̃] *nm* present, gift.

présenter [prezɑ̃te] *v* present; introduce; (*exposer*) set out; turn. **se présenter** appear; (*occasion*) arise; (*élection*) stand; (*concours*) go in for; (*examen*) take. **présentable** *adj* presentable. **présentateur, -trice** *nm, nf* presenter. **présentation** *nf* presentation; introduction.

préserver [prezɛrve] *v* protect; save. **préservatif** *nm* condom. **préservation** *nf* preservation, protection.

président [prezidɑ̃] *nm* president;

(*comité*) chairman. **présidence** *nf* presidency. **présidentiel** *adj* presidential.

présider [prezide] *v* preside (over); (*débat*) chair.

présomption [prezɔ̃psjɔ̃] *nf* presumption. **présomptueux** *adj* presumptuous.

presque [prɛskə] *adv* almost, nearly; (*guère*) scarcely, hardly.

presqu'île [prɛskil] *nf* peninsula.

presser [prese] *v* press; (*serrer*) squeeze; (*hâter*) speed up, hurry; be urgent. **presse-papiers** *nm invar* paperweight. **se presser** hurry; squeeze up, crowd together. **pressant** *adj* urgent. **presse** *nf* press. **pressé** *adj* hurried, in a hurry; urgent. **pression** *nf* pressure. **à la pression** on draught. **pressoir** *nm* press. **pressuriser** *v* pressurize.

preste [prɛst] *adj* nimble.

prestidigitateur, -trice [prɛstidiʒitatœr, -tris] *nm, nf* conjuror. **prestidigitation** *nf* conjuring.

prestige [prɛstiʒ] *nm* prestige. **prestigieux** *adj* prestigious.

présumer [prezyme] *v* presume.

prêt¹ [prɛ] *adj* ready. **prêt-à-porter** *nm* ready-to-wear clothes *pl*.

prêt² [prɛ] *nm* loan; advance; (*action*) lending.

prétendre [pretɑ̃drə] *v* claim; intend, mean. **prétendant, -e** *nm, nf* candidate. **prétendu** *adj* so-called, alleged. **prétention** *nf* claim, pretension; (*vanité*) pretentiousness. **prétentieux** *adj* pretentious.

prêter [prete] *v* lend; attribute; (*offrir*) give; (*tissu*) stretch. **prête-nom** *nm* figurehead. **prêter attention à** pay attention to. **prêter serment** take an oath. **prêteur, -euse** *nm, nf* lender. **prêteur sur gages** pawnbroker.

prétexte [pretɛkst] *nm* pretext, excuse.

prêtre [prɛtrə] *nm* priest. **prêtrise** *nf* priesthood.

preuve [prœv] *nf* proof, evidence.

***prévaloir** [prevalwar] *v* prevail. **se prévaloir de** (*profiter*) take advantage of; (*se flatter*) pride oneself on.

***prévenir** [prevnir] *v* (*avertir*) warn; inform; anticipate; (*éviter*) avert; (*influencer*) prejudice. **prévenance** *nf* kindness, consideration. **prévenant** *adj* kind, considerate. **prévenu, -e** *n, adj* accused.

préventif [prevɑ̃tif] *adj* preventive. **prévention** *nf* prevention; (*jur*) custody; (*préjugé*) prejudice.

prévision [previzjɔ̃] *nf* prediction, forecast. **prévisions météorologiques** weather forecast *sing*. **prévisible** *adj* foreseeable.

*prévoir [prevwar] *v* anticipate; (*temps*) forecast; (*projeter*) plan; (*envisager*) allow; (*jur*) provide for. **prévoyance** *nf* foresight.

prier [prije] *v* pray; invite, ask; (*implorer*) beg. **je vous en prie** (*de rien*) don't mention it; (*faites donc*) please do. **prière** *nf* prayer; (*demande*) request, plea.

prieuré [prijœre] *nm* priory.

primaire [primɛr] *adj* primary.

prime[1] [prim] *nf* premium; bonus; (*cadeau*) free gift.

prime[2] [prim] *adj* first, earliest.

primer[1] [prime] *v* prevail over, outdo.

primer[2] [prime] *v* award a prize to.

primesautier [primsotje] *adj* impulsive.

primeurs [primœr] *nf pl* early fruit and vegetables *pl*.

primevère [primvɛr] *nf* primrose.

primitif [primitif] *adj* primitive; original.

primordial [primɔrdjal] *adj* primordial, essential.

prince [prɛ̃s] *nm* prince. **princesse** *nf* princess. **princier** *adj* princely.

principal [prɛ̃sipal] *adj* main, principal; (*employé*) chief, head. *nm* principal; main point.

principe [prɛ̃sip] *nm* principle. **par principe** on principle.

printanier [prɛ̃tanje] *adj* spring, spring-like.

printemps [prɛ̃tɑ̃] *nm* spring, springtime.

priorité [prijɔrite] *nf* priority; (*auto*) right of way.

pris [pri] *adj* (*place*) taken, occupied; (*mains*) full; (*personne*) busy, engaged.

prise [priz] *nf* hold, grip; capture; (*élec: à fiches*) plug; (*élec: à douilles*) socket. **en prise** (*auto*) in gear. **prise multiple** adapter.

priser [prize] *v* prize.

prisme [prismə] *nm* prism.

prison [prizɔ̃] *nf* prison, jail; imprisonment. **prisonnier, -ère** *nm, nf* prisoner.

privé [prive] *adj* private.

priver [prive] *v* deprive. **se priver** deny oneself. **se priver de** do without. **privation** *nf* deprivation.

privilège [privilɛʒ] *nm* privilege. **privilégié** *adj* privileged.

prix [pri] *nm* price, cost; (*récompense*) prize. **à tout prix** at all costs. **prix fixe** set price.

probable [prɔbablə] *adj* probable, likely. **probabilité** *nf* probability, likelihood.

probe [prɔb] *adj* honest. **probité** *nf* integrity.

problème [prɔblɛm] *nm* problem. **problématique** *adj* problematic.

procéder [prɔsede] *v* proceed. **procédé** *nm* process; conduct, behaviour. **procédure** *nf* procedure.

procès [prɔsɛ] *nm* (*jur*) trial; (*poursuite*) proceedings *pl*, lawsuit; (*affaire*) case. **procès-verbal** *nm* minutes *pl*, report.

procession [prɔsesjɔ̃] *nf* procession.

processus [prɔsesys] *nm* process.

prochain [prɔʃɛ̃] *adj* next; (*départ, etc.*) imminent; (*proche*) near, nearby. **prochainement** *adv* soon.

proche [prɔʃ] *adj* near, close; (*village, rue, etc.*) nearby. **proches** *nm pl* close relations *pl*.

proclamer [prɔklame] *v* proclaim, declare; announce. **proclamation** *nf* proclamation.

procréer [prɔkree] *v* procreate. **procréation** *nf* procreation.

procurer [prɔkyre] *v* (*fournir*) provide; (*donner*) give; (*apporter*) bring. **se procurer** get, obtain. **procuration** *nf* proxy; power of attorney. **procureur** *nm* public prosecutor, attorney.

prodige [prɔdiʒ] *nm* wonder, marvel; (*personne*) prodigy. **prodigieux** *adj* fantastic, prodigious, phenomenal.

prodigue [prɔdig] *adj* prodigal, extravagant; generous, lavish. **prodigalité** *nf* extravagance.

*produire [prɔdɥir] *v* produce. **se produire** happen. **producteur, -trice** *nm, nf* producer. **productif** *adj* productive. **production** *nf* production; (*produit*) product. **productivité** *nf* productivity. **produit** *nm* product. **produits** *nm pl* (*légumes, etc.*) produce *sing*; (*comm*) goods *pl*. **produits chimiques** chemicals *pl*. **produits de beauté** cosmetics *pl*.

proéminence [prɔeminɑ̃s] *nf* prominence. **proéminent** *adj* prominent.

profane [prɔfan] *adj* secular, profane. *n(m+f)* layman. **profaner** *v* desecrate, profane, debase.

professer [prɔfese] *v* profess, declare; (*enseigner*) teach.

professeur [prɔfesœr] *nm* teacher; (*université*) professor.

profession [prɔfɛsjɔ̃] *nf* profession; occupation.

professionnel [prɔfɛsjɔnɛl], **-elle** *adj* professional; (*formation*) vocational. *nm, nf* professional; (*ouvrier*) skilled worker.

profil [prɔfil] *nm* profile; contour, outline.

profit [prɔfi] *nm* profit; advantage, benefit. **tirer profit de** profit from. **profitable** *adj* beneficial.

profiter [prɔfite] *v* **profiter à** benefit, be beneficial to. **profiter de** take advantage of.

profond [prɔfɔ̃] *adj* deep; (*sentiment, remarque*) profound. **peu profond** shallow. **profondément** *adv* deeply; profoundly. **profondeur** *nf* depth.

profus [prɔfy] *adj* profuse. **profusion** *nf* profusion.

progéniture [prɔʒenityr] *nf* offspring.

programme [prɔgram] *nm* programme; (*scolaire*) curriculum, syllabus; (*ordinateur*) program. **programmation** *nf* programming. **programmer** *v* programme. **programmeur, -euse** *nm, nf* computer programmer.

progrès [prɔgrɛ] *nm* progress; advance, improvement.

progresser [prɔgrese] *v* progress; advance; make progress. **progressif** *adj* progressive. **progression** *nf* progression; progress. **progressiste** *n(m+f)*, *adj* progressive.

prohiber [prɔibe] *v* prohibit. **prohibition** *nf* prohibition.

proie [prwa] *nf* prey. **être en proie à** be a prey to; be a victim of.

projecteur [prɔʒɛktœr] *nm* projector; (*théâtre*) spotlight; (*monument, sport*) floodlight; (*pour chercher*) searchlight.

projectile [prɔʒɛktil] *nm* missile, projectile.

projection [prɔʒɛksjɔ̃] *nf* projection.

projet [prɔʒɛ] *nm* plan; (*ébauche*) draft. **projeter** *v* project; plan.

prolétariat [prɔletarja] *nm* proletariat. **prolétaire** *nm* proletarian. **prolétarien** *adj* proletarian.

proliférer [prɔlifere] *v* proliferate. **prolifération** *nf* proliferation.

prolifique [prɔlifik] *adj* prolific.

prologue [prɔlɔg] *nm* prologue.

prolonger [prɔlɔ̃ʒe] *v* prolong, extend. **se prolonger** go on, persist. **prolongation** *nf* prolongation. **prolongement** *nm* extension.

promener [prɔmne] *v* take for a walk. **se promener** go for a walk; (*errer*) wander. **promenade** *nf* walk, stroll; (*en voiture*) drive; (*à cheval*) ride.

promesse [prɔmɛs] *nf* promise.

*promettre [prɔmɛtr] *v* promise. **prometteur, -euse** *adj* promising.

promotion [prɔmosjɔ̃] *nf* promotion.

*promouvoir [prɔmuvwar] *v* promote.

prompt [prɔ̃] *adj* swift, prompt, quick. **promptitude** *nf* swiftness, promptness.

prône [pron] *nm* sermon.

pronom [prɔnɔ̃] *nm* pronoun.

prononcer [prɔnɔ̃se] *v* pronounce; (*dire*) utter;· (*discours*) deliver. **se prononcer** come to a decision; give an opinion. **prononciation** *nf* pronunciation.

propagande [prɔpagɑ̃d] *nf* propaganda.

propager [prɔpaʒe] *v* propagate, spread. **propagation** *nf* propagation.

prophète [prɔfɛt] *nm* prophet. **prophétie** *nf* prophecy. **prophétique** *adj* prophetic. **prophétiser** *v* prophesy.

propice [prɔpis] *adj* favourable.

proportion [prɔpɔrsjɔ̃] *nf* proportion. **proportionnel** *adj* proportional. **proportionner** *v* proportion, make proportional.

propos [prɔpo] *nm* purpose, intention; subject. *nm pl* talk sing; remarks *pl*. **à propos** by the way; (*arriver*) at the right time; (*remarque*) apt. **à propos de** concerning, about.

proposer [prɔpoze] *v* propose; suggest; offer. **se proposer de** intend to. **proposition** *nf* proposal, proposition; suggestion; (*gramm*) clause.

propre [prɔpr] *adj* (*pas sale*) clean; (*net*) neat; (*chien, chat*) house-trained; honest; (*possessif*) own; appropriate, suitable. **propre à** suitable for; (*coutume, etc.*) peculiar to. **proprement** *adv* cleanly; neatly; (*comme il faut*) properly; strictly. **à proprement parler** strictly speaking. **propreté** *nf* cleanness; neatness.

propriétaire [prɔprijetɛr] *nm* owner; (*hôtel*) proprietor; (*location*) landlord. *nf* owner; proprietress; landlady. **propriété** *nf* property; (*droit*) ownership; correctness, suitability.

propulser [prɔpylse] *v* propel. **propulseur** *nm* propeller. **propulsion** *nf* propulsion.

*proscrire [prɔskrir] v ban, prohibit; (*personne*) banish, exile. **proscrit, -e** *nm*, *nf* outlaw; exile.

prose [proz] *nf* prose.

prospectus [prɔspɛktys] *nm* leaflet, brochure.

prospérer [prɔspere] v thrive, flourish; (*personne*) prosper. **prospère** *adj* thriving, flourishing; prosperous. **prospérité** *nf* prosperity.

se prosterner [prɔstɛrne] v bow down, prostrate oneself; (*s'humilier*) grovel. **prosternation** *nf* prostration. **prosterné** *adj* prostrate.

prostituer [prɔstitɥe] v prostitute. **prostituée** *nf* prostitute. **prostitution** *nf* prostitution.

protagoniste [prɔtagɔnist] *nm* protagonist.

protecteur, -trice [prɔtɛktœr, -tris] *adj* protective. *nm*, *nf* protector; (*art*) patron. **protection** *nf* protection; patronage.

protéger [prɔteʒe] v protect; patronize, be a patron of.

protéine [prɔtein] *nf* protein.

protester [prɔtɛste] v protest; declare. **protestant, -e** *n*, *adj* Protestant. **protestation** *nf* protest.

protocole [prɔtɔkɔl] *nm* protocol; etiquette.

prototype [prɔtɔtip] *nm* prototype.

proue [pru] *nf* bow, prow.

prouesse [prues] *nf* prowess; (*acte*) feat.

prouver [pruve] v prove.

*provenir [prɔvnir] v **provenir de** come from; be the result of. **provenance** *nf* origin, source. **en provenance de** (coming) from.

proverbe [prɔvɛrb] *nm* proverb. **proverbial** *adj* proverbial.

providence [prɔvidɑ̃s] *nf* providence.

province [prɔvɛ̃s] *nf* province. **provincial** *adj* provincial.

proviseur [prɔvizœr] *nm* headmaster.

provision [prɔvizjɔ̃] *nf* stock, supply. **provisions** *nf pl* provisions *pl*, food *sing*.

provisoire [prɔvizwar] *adj* provisional, temporary.

provoquer [prɔvɔke] v provoke; cause; incite; (*duel*) challenge; (*colère, curiosité*) arouse. **provocant** *adj* provocative. **provocation** *nf* provocation.

proximité [prɔksimite] *nf* proximity.

prude [pryd] *nf* prude. *adj* prudish.

prudent [prydɑ̃] *adj* prudent; (*circonspect*) careful, cautious; (*sage*) sensible. **prudence** *nf* prudence; care, caution.

prune [pryn] *nf* plum. **pruneau** *nm* prune. **prunelle** *nf* (*bot*) sloe; (*anat*) pupil. **prunier** *nm* plum tree.

psaume [psom] *nm* psalm.

pseudonyme [psødɔnim] *nm* pseudonym.

psychanalyse [psikanaliz] *nf* psychoanalysis. **psychanalyser** v psychoanalyse. **psychanalyste** *n(m+f)* psychoanalyst.

psychédélique [psikedelik] *adj* psychedelic.

psychiatrie [psikjatri] *nf* psychiatry. **psychiatre** *n(m+f)* psychiatrist. **psychiatrique** *adj* psychiatric.

psychique [psiʃik] *adj* psychic.

psychologie [psikɔlɔʒi] *nf* psychology. **psychologique** *adj* psychological. **psychologue** *n(m+f)* psychologist.

psychopathe [psikɔpat] *n(m+f)* psychopath.

psychose [psikoz] *nf* psychosis. **psychotique** *n(m+f)*, *adj* psychotic.

psychosomatique [psikɔsɔmatik] *adj* psychosomatic.

psychothérapie [psikɔterapi] *nf* psychotherapy.

puanteur [pɥɑ̃tœr] *nf* stink.

puberté [pybɛrte] *nf* puberty.

pubien [pybjɛ̃] *nf* puberty.

public, -ique [pyblik] *adj* public. *nm* public; audience. **le grand public** the general public.

publicité [pyblisite] *nf* publicity; (*comm*) advertising; (*annonce*) advertisement. **publicitaire** *adj* advertising.

publier [pyblije] v publish. **publication** *nf* publication; publishing.

puce [pys] *nf* flea. **jeu de puce** *nm* tiddlywinks. **puceron** *nm* greenfly.

pucelle [pysɛl] *nf* virgin.

pudeur [pydœr] *nf* modesty, decency. **pudique** [pydik] *adj* modest; discreet.

puer [pɥe] v stink.

puéril [pɥeril] *adj* childish.

puis [pɥi] *adv* then.

puiser [pɥize] v draw. **puiser dans** dip into.

puisque [pɥiskə] *conj* since, seeing that, as.

puissance [pɥisɑ̃s] *nf* power; (*jur*) authority. **en puissance** potentially. **puissant** *adj* powerful.

puits [pɥi] *nm* well; (*mine*) shaft.

pull [pyl] *nm* (*fam*) jumper.

pulluler [pylyle] *v* swarm, teem. **pullulation** *nf* swarm, multitude.

pulpe [pylp] *nf* pulp. **pulpeux** *adj* pulpy.

pulsation [pylsɑsjɔ̃] *nf* beat, pulsation. **pulsation du cœur** heartbeat.

pulvériser [pylverize] *v* pulverize; (*liquide*) spray; demolish. **pulvérisateur** *nm* spray. **pulvérisation** *nf* pulverization; spraying; demolition.

punaise [pynɛz] *nf* (*zool*) bug; (*clou*) drawing-pin.

punch [pɔ̃ʃ] *nm* punch.

punir [pynir] *v* punish. **punition** *nf* punishment.

pupille[1] [pypij] *nf* (*anat*) pupil.

pupille[2] [pypij] *n*(*m+f*) ward.

pupitre [pypitrə] *nm* desk; (*rel*) lectern; music stand.

pur [pyr] *adj* pure; (*boisson*) neat; honest; (*absolu*) sheer. **pur-sang** *nm* thoroughbred. **pureté** *nf* purity.

purée [pyre] *nf* (*tomates, etc.*) purée; (*pommes de terre*) mashed potato.

purgatoire [pyrgatwar] *nm* purgatory.

purger [pyrʒe] *v* purge; (*tech*) flush out, drain. **purgatif** *nm, adj* purgative. **purge** *nf* purge.

purifier [pyrifje] *v* purify, cleanse. **purification** *nf* purification.

puritain [pyritɛ̃], **-e** *adj* puritanical. *nm, nf* puritan.

pus [py] *nm* pus.

pusillanime [pyzilanim] *adj* faint-hearted.

putain [pytɛ̃] *nf* (*argot*) whore.

putride [pytrid] *adj* putrid.

puzzle [pœzlə] *nm* jigsaw.

pygmée [pigme] *nm* pygmy.

pyjama [piʒama] *nm* pyjamas *pl.*

pylône [pilon] *nm* pylon.

pyramide [piramid] *nf* pyramid.

python [pitɔ̃] *nm* python.

Q

qu' [k] *V* que.

quadrant [kadrɑ̃] *nm* quadrant.

quadrilatère [kadrilatɛr] *nm* quadrilateral.

quadrillé [kadrije] *adj* squared.

quadrupède [kadrypɛd] *nm, adj* quadruped.

quadrupler [kadryple] *v* quadruple. **quadruple** *nm, adj* quadruple. **quadruplé, -e** *nm, nf* quadruplet.

quai [ke] *nm* quay; (*gare*) platform; (*rivière*) embankment.

qualifier [kalifje] *v* qualify; describe, call. **qualification** *nf* qualification; description, label.

qualité [kalite] *nf* quality; (*don*) skill; (*fonction*) position, capacity.

quand [kɑ̃] *conj, adv* when. **quand même** all the same, nevertheless.

quant [kɑ̃] *adv* **quant à** as for; regarding.

quantité [kɑ̃tite] *nf* quantity, amount; great number, great deal.

quarantaine [karɑ̃tɛn] *nf* quarantine. **mettre en quarantaine** quarantine.

quarante [karɑ̃t] *nm, adj* forty. **quarantième** *n*(*m+f*), *adj* fortieth.

quart [kar] *nm* quarter; (*naut*) watch. . . . **et quart** quarter past . . . . **moins le quart** quarter to . . . . **quart de finale** quarter-final. **quart d'heure** quarter of an hour.

quartier [kartje] *nm* quarter; (*ville*) district, area; (*portion*) piece. **du quartier** local. **quartier général** headquarters.

quartz [kwarts] *nm* quartz.

quasi [kazi] *adv* almost.

quatorze [katɔrz] *nm, adj* fourteen. **quatorzième** *n*(*m+f*), *adj* fourteenth.

quatre [katrə] *nm, adj* four. **à quatre pattes** on all fours. **quatrième** *n*(*m+f*), *adj* fourth.

quatre-vingt-dix *nm, adj* ninety. **quatre-vingt-dixième** *n*(*m+f*), *adj* ninetieth.

quatre-vingts *nm, adj* eighty. **quatre-vingtième** *n*(*m+f*), *adj* eightieth.

quatuor [kwatɥɔr] *nm* quartet.

que[1] [kə] *conj* that; (*but*) so that; (*comparaison*) than; (*aussi*) as. **ne . . . que** only. **que . . . que . . .** whether . . . or . . .

que[2] [kə] *adv* how.

que[3] [kə] *pron* that, which; (*temps*) when; (*personne*) that, whom; (*interrogatif*) what. **qu'est-ce que** or **qui** what.

quel [kɛl], **quelle** *pron, adj* what, which. **quel que** whatever; (*personne*) whoever.

quelconque [kɛlkɔ̃k] *adj* any, some; (*médiocre*) poor; ordinary.

quelque [kɛlkə] *adj, adv* some. **quelque chose** something. **quelquefois** *adv* sometimes. **quelque part** somewhere. **quelque peu** somewhat. **quelques** *adj* some, a few; (*peu de*) few. **quelques-uns, -unes** *pron* some, a few. **quelqu'un** *pron* somebody.

quémander [kemɑ̃de] *v* beg for.

querelle [kərɛl] *nf* quarrel. **se quereller** *v* quarrel. **querelleur, -euse** *adj* quarrelsome.

question [kɛstjɔ̃] *nf* question. **il n'en est pas question** it's out of the question. **questionnaire** *nm* questionnaire. **questionner** *v* question, interrogate.

quêter [kete] *v* collect money; (*chercher*) seek. **quête** *nf* collection; (*recherche*) quest, search. **en quête de** in search of. **faire la quête** collect for charity; (*rel*) take the collection.

queue [kø] *nf* tail; (*file*) queue; (*bout, fin*) end; (*liste*) bottom; (*fleur, fruit*) stalk; (*train*) rear; (*billard*) cue. **faire la queue** queue.

qui [ki] *pron* who; (*objet*) whom; (*chose*) which, that; (*quiconque*) whoever, anyone who. **à** *or* **de qui** (*possessif*) whose.

quiche [kiʃ] *nf* quiche.

quiconque [kikɔ̃k] *pron* whoever; (*personne*) anyone.

quignon [kiɲɔ̃] *nm* hunk of bread; (*croûton*) crust.

quille[1] [kij] *nf* (*jeu*) skittle; (*fam: jambe*) pin, leg. **jeu de quilles** skittles.

quille[2] [kij] *nf* (*naut*) keel.

quincaillerie [kɛ̃kɑjri] *nf* hardware; (*magasin*) hardware shop. **quincaillier, -ère** *nm, nf* ironmonger.

quinine [kinin] *nf* quinine.

quinte [kɛ̃t] *nf* coughing fit; (*musique*) fifth.

quintessence [kɛ̃tesɑ̃s] *nf* quintessence.

quintette [kɛ̃tɛt] *nm* quintet.

quintuplé [kɛ̃typle], **-e** *nm, nf* quintuplet.

quinze [kɛ̃z] *nm, adj* fifteen. **demain en quinze** a fortnight tomorrow. **quinze jours** a fortnight. **quinzaine** *nf* fortnight. **quinzième** *n(m+f), adj* fifteenth.

quiproquo [kiprɔko] *nm* mistake; (*malentendu*) misunderstanding.

quittance [kitɑ̃s] *nf* receipt.

quitter [kite] *v* leave; (*espoir*) give up. **ne quittez pas** (*téléphone*) hold the line. **se quitter** part. **quitte** *adj* quits, even; (*débarrassé*) clear, rid.

quoi [kwa] *pron* what. **à quoi bon?** what's the use? **avoir de quoi** have (the) means. **il n'y a pas de quoi** don't mention it. **quoi que** whatever.

quoique [kwakə] *conj* although.

quorum [kɔrɔm] *nm* quorum.

quote-part [kɔtpar] *nf* share, quota.

quotidien [kɔtidjɛ̃] *adj* daily; (*banal*) everyday. *nm* daily newspaper.

R

rabâcher [rabɑʃe] *v* harp on, keep repeating.

rabais [rabɛ] *nm* reduction, discount.

rabaisser [rabese] *v* belittle, disparage; reduce.

rabat [raba] *nm* flap.

*****rabattre** [rabatrə] *v* (*fermer*) close; (*faire retomber*) pull *or* turn down; (*drap*) fold back; reduce; deduct. **rabat-joie** *nm invar* spoilsport. **se rabattre** close; (*voiture*) cut in.

rabbin [rabɛ̃] *nm* rabbi.

rabot [rabo] *nm* plane. **raboter** *v* plane; (*fam*) scrape. **raboteux** *adj* uneven, rough.

rabougri [rabugri] *adj* stunted; (*ratatiné*) shrivelled.

racaille [rakaj] *nf* rabble.

raccommoder [rakɔmɔde] *v* mend; (*fam*) reconcile. **se raccommoder** (*fam*) make it up. **raccommodage** *nm* (*action*) mending; (*endroit*) mend. **raccommodement** *nm* (*fam*) reconciliation.

raccorder [rakɔrde] *v* join, link up, connect. **raccord** *nm* join, link.

raccourcir [rakursir] *v* shorten; get shorter. **raccourci** *nm* (*résumé*) summary; (*chemin*) short cut. **en raccourci** in miniature.

raccrocher [rakrɔʃe] *v* (*téléphone*) hang up, ring off; (*attraper*) grab, get hold of; (*tableau, etc.*) hang up again. **se raccrocher à** cling to; (*relier*) link with.

race [ras] *nf* race; (*animal*) breed; (*famille*) stock, blood. **de race** pedigree, thoroughbred. **racial** *adj* racial. **racisme** *nm* racialism, racism. **raciste** *n(m+f), adj* racialist, racist.

racheter [raʃte] v buy back; (dette) redeem; (otage) ransom; (péché) atone for; (faute) make up for. **rachat** nm redemption; ransom; atonement.

racine [rasin] nf root.

racler [rɑkle] v scrape. **se racler la gorge** clear one's throat. **raclée** nf (fam) thrashing.

racoler [rakɔle] v (prostituée) solicit; (vendeur) tout for.

raconter [rakɔ̃te] v tell, relate. **racontar** nm story, piece of gossip. **raconteur, -euse** nm, nf story-teller, narrator.

se racornir [rakɔrnir] v shrivel up; (durcir) become hard or tough.

radar [radar] nm radar.

rade [rad] nf harbour. **laisser en rade** leave stranded, abandon.

radeau [rado] nm raft.

radial [radjal] adj radial.

radiateur [radjatœr] nm radiator; (à gaz) heater. **radiateur électrique** electric fire. **radiateur soufflant** fan heater.

radiation [radjɑsjɔ̃] nf radiation.

radical [radikal] nm, adj radical.

radier [radje] v cross or strike off.

radieux [radjø] adj radiant.

radin [radɛ̃], **-e** (fam) adj stingy. nm, nf skinflint.

radio [radjo] nf radio; (méd) X-ray.

radioactif [radjoaktif] adj radioactive. **radioactivité** nf radioactivity.

radiodiffuser [radjɔdifyze] v broadcast. **radiodiffusion** nf broadcasting.

radiographie [radjɔgrafi] nf radiography. **radiographier** v X-ray.

radiologie [radjɔlɔʒi] nf radiology.

radiothérapie [radjɔterapi] nf radiotherapy.

radis [radi] nm radish.

radium [radjɔm] nm radium.

radoter [radɔte] v (péj) ramble on. **radotage** nm drivel.

radoucir [radusir] v soften. **se radoucir** (personne) calm down; (temps, voix) become milder.

rafale [rafal] nf gust, blast.

raffermir [rafɛrmir] v strengthen; (durcir) harden; (voix) steady. **se raffermir** grow stronger; harden; become steady.

raffiner [rafine] v refine. **raffinage** nm refining. **raffinement** nm refinement. **raffinerie** nf refinery.

raffoler [rafɔle] v **raffoler de** be very fond of.

raffut [rafy] nm (fam) row, racket.

rafistoler [rafistɔle] v patch up.

rafle [rɑflə] nf police raid. **rafler** v (fam) swipe.

rafraîchir [rafreʃir] v refresh; (visage) freshen up; (refroidir) cool; (vêtement, appartement, etc.) brighten up; (cheveux) trim. **rafraîchissements** nm pl refreshments pl.

rage [raʒ] nf rage; mania; (méd) rabies. **rage de dents** raging toothache. **rager** v fume, be furious. **rageur, -euse** adj hot-tempered.

ragots [rago] nm pl (fam) gossip sing.

ragoût [ragu] nm stew.

raide [rɛd] adj stiff; (cheveux) straight; (corde) tight; (pente) steep; (fam: histoire) far-fetched; (osé) daring. adv steeply. **raideur** nf stiffness; straightness; tightness; steepness. **raidir** v stiffen.

raie[1] [rɛ] nf line; (bande) stripe; (cheveux) parting; (éraflure) scratch.

raie[2] [rɛ] nf (poisson) skate, ray.

raifort [rɛfɔr] nm horse-radish.

rail [rɑj] nm rail.

railler [rɑje] v scoff at. **raillerie** nf mockery. **railleur, -euse** adj mocking.

rainure [renyr] nf groove; (plus courte) slot.

raisin [rɛzɛ̃] nm grape. **raisin de Corinthe** currant. **raisin de Smyrne** sultana. **raisin sec** raisin.

raison [rɛzɔ̃] nf reason; (math) ratio. **avoir raison** be right. **raisonnable** adj reasonable; (sensé) sensible. **raisonnement** nm reasoning; argument. **raisonner** v reason; (convaincre) reason with; argue.

rajeunir [raʒœnir] v rejuvenate; modernize; (rafraîchir) brighten up; (personne) look or feel younger.

rajuster [raʒyste] v readjust; rearrange, tidy.

ralenti [ralɑ̃ti] adj slow. nm (cinéma) slow motion; (auto) tick-over. **au ralenti** in slow motion. **tourner au ralenti** tick over, idle.

ralentir [ralɑ̃tir] v slow down.

rallier [ralje] v rally; unite; (gagner) win over. **se rallier à** join, side with.

rallonger [ralɔ̃ʒe] v lengthen, extend. **rallonge** nf extension; (table) leaf. **à rallonges** (fam: nom) double-barrelled.

ramasser [ramase] v pick up; collect; (récolter) gather. **ramassé** adj crouched, huddled up; (trapu) squat; compact.

rame[1] [ram] *nf* (*aviron*) oar. **ramer** *v* row.
rameur *nm* oarsman.

rame[2] [ram] *nf* train; (*papier*) ream.

rame[3] [ram] *nf* (*branche*) stick, stake.

rameau [ramo] *nm* branch.

ramener [ramne] *v* bring back; (*tirer*) draw, pull.

ramier [ramje] *nm* wood-pigeon.

se ramifier [ramifje] *v* branch out.

ramollir [ramɔlir] *v* soften; (*courage, etc.*) weaken. **ramolli** *adj* soft.

ramoner [ramɔne] *v* sweep. **ramoneur** *nm* chimney-sweep.

ramper [rɑ̃pe] *v* crawl, creep. **rampe** *nf* ramp; (*côte*) slope; (*balustrade*) handrail; (*escalier*) banister; (*théâtre*) footlights *pl*.

rancart [rɑ̃kar] *nm* **mettre au rancart** (*argot*) scrap, chuck out.

rance [rɑ̃s] *adj* rancid.

rançon [rɑ̃sɔ̃] *nf* ransom. **rançonner** *v* hold to ransom.

rancune [rɑ̃kyn] *nf* spite; grudge.

randonnée [rɑ̃dɔne] *nf* (*voiture*) drive; (*bicyclette*) ride; (*pied*) walk, hike.

rang [rɑ̃] *nm* (*rangée*) row; (*place*) rank.

ranger [rɑ̃ʒe] *v* arrange; (*à sa place*) put away; (*en ordre*) tidy up; (*compter*) rank. **se ranger** (*s'écarter*) step aside; (*voiture*) pull over; (*soldats, etc.*) line up; (*fam*) settle down. **se ranger à** go along with, fall in with. **rangé** *adj* orderly; settled. **rangée** *nf* row.

ranimer [ranime] *v* revive; (*feu, amour*) rekindle.

rapace [rapas] *adj* (*avide*) rapacious; (*oiseau*) predatory.

rapatrier [rapatrije] *v* repatriate. **rapatrié, -e** *nm, nf* repatriate. **rapatriement** *nm* repatriation.

râper [rɑpe] *v* (*cuisine*) grate; (*bois*) rasp. **râpe** *nf* grater; rasp. **râpé** *adj* grated; (*usé*) threadbare. **râpeux** *adj* rough.

rapetisser [raptise] *v* shorten; (*vêtement*) take up *or* in; look smaller; (*vieillard*) shrink; (*dénigrer*) belittle.

raphia [rafja] *nm* raffia.

rapide [rapid] *adj* fast, rapid, quick. *nm* express train. **rapides** *nm pl* rapids *pl*. **rapidité** *nf* speed, rapidity.

rapiécer [rapjese] *v* patch, mend.

rappeler [raple] *v* call back; (*faire souvenir*) remind, recall. **se rappeler** remember. **rappel** *nm* recall; reminder.

rapport [rapɔr] *nm* connection; relation-

ship; (*exposé*) report; revenue, yield; (*math*) ratio. **être en rapport avec** (*s'accorder*) be in keeping with; (*comm, etc.*) have dealings with. **par rapport à** in relation to; (*envers*) with regard to.

rapporter [rapɔrte] *v* bring back; (*revenu*) yield, bring in; report; (*argot*) tell tales, sneak. **se rapporter à** relate to, refer to. **s'en rapporter à** rely on. **rapporteur** *nm* (*fam*) sneak; (*géom*) protractor. **rapporteuse** *nf* (*fam*) sneak.

rapprocher [raprɔʃe] *v* bring together; (*approcher*) bring nearer; compare. **se rapprocher** come together; get closer, approach; be reconciled. **rapprochement** *nm* comparison; reconciliation; (*lien*) link, parallel.

raquette [rakɛt] *nf* racket.

rare [rar] *adj* rare; (*peu*) few; (*peu abondant*) scarce, sparse; exceptional. **rareté** *nf* rarity.

ras [ra] *adj* short; (*cheveux*) close-cropped. **à ras bords** to the brim. **au ras de** level with. **en avoir ras le bol** (*fam*) be fed up with.

raser [raze] *v* shave; (*effleurer*) skim, scrape; (*fam*) bore. **se raser** have a shave; (*fam*) be bored. **rasage** *nm* shaving. **raseur, -euse** *nm, nf* (*fam*) bore. **rasoir** *nm* razor; (*fam*) bore.

rassasier [rasazje] *v* satisfy. **se rassasier** eat one's fill. **se rassasier de** tire of.

rassembler [rasɑ̃ble] *v* collect, assemble, gather (together); (*remonter*) reassemble.

rassis [rasi] *adj* stale; (*personne*) composed, calm.

rassurer [rasyre] *v* reassure. **se rassurer** put one's mind at ease.

rat [ra] *nm* rat.

ratatiner [ratatine] *v* wrinkle, shrivel up.

râteau [rɑto] *nm* rake.

râtelier [rɑtəlje] *nm* rack; (*fam*) set of false teeth.

rater [rate] *v* (*fusil*) misfire; (*affaire*) go wrong; (*fam: manquer*) miss; (*fam: gâcher*) mess up; (*fam: échouer*) fail.

ratifier [ratifje] *v* ratify. **ratification** *nf* ratification.

ration [rasjɔ̃] *nf* ration.

rationaliser [rasjɔnalize] *v* rationalize. **rationnel** *adj* rational.

rationner [rasjɔne] *v* ration. **rationnement** *nm* rationing.

ratisser [ratise] *v* rake (up).

rattacher [rataʃe] v fasten again; join; (*relier*) link, relate.

rattraper [ratrape] v catch again; (*regagner, réparer*) make up for; (*rejoindre*) catch up with.

rature [ratyr] nf deletion, erasure.

rauque [rok] adj hoarse; (*cri*) raucous.

ravager [ravaʒe] v ravage, devastate. **ravages** nm pl ravages pl, devastation sing.

ravaler [ravale] v swallow; (*colère, larmes*) hold back; (*mur*) restore.

ravauder [ravode] v mend.

ravin [ravɛ̃] nm ravine, gully.

ravir [ravir] v delight; (*enlever*) carry off. **ravissant** adj delightful, beautiful. **ravissement** nm rapture.

se raviser [ravize] v change one's mind.

ravitailler [ravitaje] v (*carburant*) refuel; (*vivres, etc.*) provide with fresh supplies.

rayer [reje] v (*marquer*) line; (*érafler*) scratch; (*biffer*) cross out. **rayé** adj (*papier*) ruled, lined; (*tissu*) striped; scratched.

rayon[1] [rɛjɔ̃] nm ray, beam; (*roue*) spoke; (*cercle*) radius. **rayon X** X-ray.

rayon[2] [rɛjɔ̃] nm (*planche*) shelf; (*comm*) department; (*comptoir*) counter; (*miel*) honeycomb.

rayon[3] [rɛjɔ̃] nm row, drill.

rayonne [rɛjɔn] nf rayon.

rayonner [rɛjɔne] v radiate; (*briller*) shine (forth), be radiant. **rayonnant** adj radiant. **rayonnement** nm radiance; radiation; influence.

rayure [rɛjyr] nf (*bande*) stripe; (*éraflure*) scratch.

razzia [razja] nf raid.

réaction [reaksjɔ̃] nf reaction. **moteur à réaction** jet engine. **réacteur** nm reactor. **réactionnaire** n(m+f), adj reactionary.

réadapter [readapte] v readjust; (*méd*) rehabilitate. **réadaptation** nf readjustment; rehabilitation.

réagir [reaʒir] v react.

réaliser [realize] v realize; (*ambition*) fulfil; (*projet*) carry out; (*cinéma*) produce. **réalisateur, -trice** nm, nf director. **réalisation** nf realization; fulfilment; production.

réaliste [realist] adj realistic. n(m+f) realist. **réalisme** nm realism.

réalité [realite] nf reality.

*****réapparaître** [reaparɛtrə] v reappear. **réapparition** nf reappearance.

réarranger [rearɑ̃ʒe] v rearrange. **réarrangement** nm rearrangement.

rébarbatif [rebarbatif] adj forbidding, daunting.

rebattu [rəbaty] adj hackneyed.

rebelle [rəbɛl] adj rebellious; (*cheveux*) unruly; (*virus*) resistant. n(m+f) rebel. **se rebeller** v rebel. **rébellion** nf rebellion.

rebondir [rəbɔ̃dir] v bounce, rebound. **rebond** nm bounce, rebound; **rebondi** adj (*personne*) plump, portly; (*forme*) rounded.

rebord [rəbɔr] nm edge; (*plat, assiette*) rim; (*vêtement*) hem. **rebord de fenêtre** window ledge or sill.

rebours [rəbur] nm **à rebours** the wrong way; (*compter*) backwards. **à rebours de** against.

rebrousser [rəbruse] v brush up or back. **à rebrousse-poil** the wrong way. **prendre à rebrousse-poil** rub up the wrong way. **rebrousser chemin** turn back, retrace one's steps.

rebuffade [rəbyfad] nf rebuff.

rebut [rəby] nm scrap. **mettre au rebut** throw out, discard.

rebuter [rəbyte] v discourage, put off; (*répugner*) repel.

receler [rəsale] v (*secret*) conceal; (*malfaiteur*) harbour; (*objet volé*) receive.

recensement [rəsɑ̃smɑ̃] nm census.

récent [resɑ̃] adj recent; (*nouveau*) new. **récemment** adv recently.

récépissé [resepise] nm receipt.

récepteur, -trice [resɛptœr, -tris] adj receiving. nm receiver.

réception [resɛpsjɔ̃] nf reception; (*d'une lettre, etc.*) receipt. **réceptionniste** n(m+f) receptionist.

récession [resesjɔ̃] nf recession.

recette [rəsɛt] nf (*cuisine*) recipe; (*comm*) takings pl. **recettes** nf pl receipts pl, revenue sing.

*****recevoir** [rəsvwar] v receive; (*invité*) entertain; (*contenir*) take, hold. **être reçu (à) (examen)** pass. **receveur, -euse** nm, nf tax collector; bus conductor.

rechange [rəʃɑ̃ʒ] nm **de rechange** spare; alternative. **rechange de vêtements** change of clothes.

réchapper [reʃape] v **réchapper de** come through.

recharger [rəʃarʒe] v (*stylo, etc.*) refill; (*fusil, etc.*) reload; (*batterie*) recharge. **recharge** nf refill.

réchaud [reʃo] *nm* stove.
réchauffer [reʃofe] *v* warm up; (*cuisine*) reheat.
rêche [rɛʃ] *adj* rough, harsh.
rechercher [rəʃɛrʃe] *v* seek; (*chercher*) search for; (*viser*) strive for, pursue; (*s'informer*) inquire into. **recherche** *nf* search; pursuit; investigation; (*université*) research. **à la recherche de** in search of. **recherché** *adj* in demand; (*soigné*) meticulous; (*péj*) affected.
rechute [rəʃyt] *nf* relapse.
récif [resif] *nm* reef.
récipient [resipjɑ̃] *nm* container, receptacle.
réciproque [resiprɔk] *adj* reciprocal, mutual.
réciter [resite] *v* recite. **récit** *nm* story, account. **récital** *nm* recital. **récitation** *nf* recitation.
réclamer [reklame] *v* (*demander*) ask for, call for; (*protester*) complain; (*droit, etc.*) claim. **réclamation** *nf* complaint. **réclame** *nf* (*annonce*) advertisement; (*publicité*) advertising. **en réclame** on offer. **faire de la réclame** advertise.
reclus [rəkly], **-e** *nm, nf* recluse. *adj* cloistered.
recoin [rəkwɛ̃] *nm* nook, recess.
récolter [rekɔlte] *v* harvest; collect. **récolte** *nf* harvest, crop; collection.
recommander [rəkɔmɑ̃de] *v* recommend; (*conseiller*) advise; (*poste*) register. **recommandation** *nf* recommendation. **recommandé** *adj* recommended; advisable; registered. **en recommandé** by registered post; (*avec avis de réception*) recorded delivery.
recommencer [rəkɔmɑ̃se] *v* start again.
récompenser [rekɔ̃pɑ̃se] *v* reward. **récompense** *nf* reward.
réconcilier [rekɔ̃silje] *v* reconcile. **réconciliation** *nf* reconciliation.
***reconduire** [rəkɔ̃dɥir] *v* (*raccompagner*) take back; (*renouveler*) renew.
réconforter [rekɔ̃fɔrte] *v* comfort; (*remonter*) fortify. **réconfort** *nm* comfort.
***reconnaître** [rəkɔnɛtrə] *v* recognize; (*avouer*) admit, acknowledge; (*mil*) reconnoitre. **reconnaissable** *adj* recognizable. **reconnaissance** *nf* recognition; acknowledgement; (*mil*) reconnaissance; gratitude. **reconnaissant** *adj* grateful.
reconstituer [rəkɔ̃stitɥe] *v* (*crime*) recon-

struct; (*édifice*) restore. **reconstitution** *nf* reconstruction; restoration.
***reconstruire** [rəkɔ̃strɥir] *v* rebuild, reconstruct. **reconstruction** *nf* reconstruction.
record [rəkɔr] *nm* record.
recours [rəkur] *nm* recourse, resort. **avoir recours à** resort to.
***recouvrir** [rəkuvrir] *v* cover.
récréation [rekreasjɔ̃] *nf* recreation; (*école*) break.
recrue [rəkry] *nf* recruit.
recruter [rəkryte] *v* recruit. **recrutement** *nm* recruitment.
rectangle [rɛktɑ̃glə] *nm* rectangle, oblong. *adj* right-angled. **rectangulaire** *adj* rectangular, oblong.
rectifier [rɛktifje] *v* rectify, correct; adjust; (*rendre droit*) straighten.
rectitude [rɛktityd] *nf* rectitude.
rectum [rɛktɔm] *nm* rectum.
reçu [rəsy] *adj* accepted; (*candidat*) successful. *nm* receipt.
recueil [rəkœj] *nm* collection; (*poèmes*) anthology. **recueil d'expressions** phrasebook.
***recueillir** [rəkœjir] *v* collect, gather; (*réfugié*) take in; (*enregistrer*) record, take down. **se recueillir** collect one's thoughts. **recueillement** *nm* meditation. **recueilli** *adj* meditative.
reculer [rəkyle] *v* move back; (*fusil*) recoil; (*mil*) retreat; (*diminuer*) decline, subside; (*date, décision*) postpone. **reculer devant** (*hésiter*) shrink from. **recul** *nm* retreat; recoil; decline; postponement; distance. **reculé** *adj* remote. **à reculons** backwards.
récupérer [rekypere] *v* recover; (*ferraille, etc.*) salvage, retrieve; (*heures*) make up. **récupération** *nf* recovery; salvage.
récurer [rekyre] *v* scour.
rédacteur, -trice [redaktœr, -tris] *nm, nf* editor; (*article*) writer. **rédaction** *nf* (*contrat*) drafting; writing; editing; (*personnel*) editorial staff; (*école*) essay.
rédiger [rediʒe] *v* write; (*contrat*) draft, draw up.
***redire** [rədir] *v* repeat. **trouver à redire à** find fault with.
redondant [rədɔ̃dɑ̃] *adj* redundant, superfluous.
redoubler [rəduble] *v* increase, intensify; (*école*) repeat a year.

redouter [rədute] *v* dread, fear. **redoutable** *adj* formidable.

redresser [rədrese] *v* straighten (up); (*relever*) right, set upright; rectify. **se redresser** stand up straight.

***réduire** [redᶣir] *v* reduce. **se réduire à** amount to; limit oneself to. **se réduire en** be reduced to. **réduction** *nf* reduction.

réduit [redᶣi] *adj* small-scale, miniature; (*prix*) reduced. *nm* tiny room; (*recoin*) recess.

réel [reel] *adj* real. *nm* reality.

***refaire** [rəfɛr] *v* do *or* make again; (*pièce*, *meuble*) do up, renovate. **se refaire** recover.

réfectoire [refɛktwar] *nm* canteen, refectory.

référence [referɑ̃s] *nf* reference. **faire référence à** refer to.

référendum [referɛ̃dɔm] *nm* referendum.

référer [refere] *v* **se référer à** refer to; consult.

réfléchir [refleʃir] *v* reflect; (*penser*) think. **réfléchir à** think over *or* about. **réfléchi** *adj* (*personne*) thoughtful; (*action*) well thought out; (*gramm*) reflexive.

réflecteur [reflɛktœr] *nm* reflector.

reflet [rəflɛ] *nm* reflection; (*lumière*) light, glint.

refléter [rəflete] *v* reflect, mirror.

réflexe [reflɛks] *nm*, *adj* reflex.

réflexion [reflɛksjɔ̃] *nf* reflection; (*pensée*) thought; remark. **réflexion faite** on second thoughts.

reflux [rəfly] *nm* ebb.

réformer [reforme] *v* reform; (*mil*) discharge. **réforme** *nf* reform; (*rel*) reformation; discharge.

refouler [rəfule] *v* force back, repress.

réfracter [refrakte] *v* refract. **réfraction** *nf* refraction.

refrain [rəfrɛ̃] *nm* refrain.

réfrigérer [refriʒere] *v* refrigerate. **réfrigérateur** *nm* refrigerator. **réfrigération** *nf* refrigeration.

refroidir [rəfrwadir] *v* cool (down). **refroidissement** *nm* cooling; (*méd*) chill.

refuge [rəfyʒ] *nm* refuge; (*pour piétons*) traffic island.

se réfugier [refyʒje] *v* take refuge. **réfugié**, **-e** *nm*, *nf* refugee.

refuser [rəfyze] *v* refuse; (*client*) turn away. **être refusé (à)** (*examen*) fail. **refus** *nm* refusal.

réfuter [refyte] *v* refute.

regagner [rəgaɲe] *v* regain; (*argent*, *etc.*) win back; (*temps*) make up; (*lieu*) get back to.

regain [rəgɛ̃] *nm* renewal, revival.

régal [regal] *nm*, *pl* **-als** delight, treat. **régaler** *v* treat.

regarder [rəgarde] *v* look at; (*action*) watch; concern, regard. **regarder fixement** stare at, gaze at. **regard** *nm* look, glance; expression; (*égout*) manhole. **regard fixe** gaze, stare. **regard furieux** glare.

régate [regat] *nf* regatta.

régent [reʒɑ̃], **-e** *nm*, *nf* regent. **régence** *nf* regency.

régie [reʒi] *nf* state control.

régime [reʒim] *nm* regime; system; government; (*méd*) diet.

régiment [reʒimɑ̃] *nm* regiment. **régimentaire** *adj* regimental.

région [reʒjɔ̃] *nf* region, area. **régional** *adj* regional.

régir [reʒir] *v* govern. **régisseur** *nm* (*théâtre*) stage manager; (*gérant*) steward.

registre [rəʒistrə] *nm* register.

régler [regle] *v* settle; adjust, regulate; (*papier*) rule. **réglage** *nm* adjustment; (*moteur*, *TV*, *etc.*) tuning. **règle** *nf* rule; (*instrument*) ruler. **en règle** (*papiers*) in order. **règle à calcul** slide rule. **règles** *nf pl* (*méd*) period *sing*. **réglé** *adj* regular; (*papier*) lined. **règlement** *nm* settlement; (*règle*) rule. **réglementaire** *adj* regulation; statutory.

réglisse [reglis] *nf* liquorice.

régner [reɲe] *v* reign. **règne** *nm* reign; (*bot*, *zool*) kingdom.

regret [rəgrɛ] *nm* regret. **regrettable** *adj* regrettable. **regretter** *v* regret; (*personne*, *pays*, *etc.*) miss; (*être désolé*) be sorry; deplore.

régulier [regylje] *adj* regular; (*constant*) steady; (*égal*) even. **régularité** *nf* regularity; steadiness; evenness.

réhabiliter [reabilite] *v* rehabilitate; restore to favour. **réhabilitation** *nf* rehabilitation.

rehausser [rəose] *v* (*relever*) raise, make higher; (*beauté*, *goût*, *etc.*) enhance, bring out.

rein [rɛ̃] *nm* kidney. **reins** *nm pl* back *sing*.

réincarnation [reɛ̃karnasjɔ̃] *nf* reincarnation.

reine [rɛn] *nf* queen. **reine-claude** *nf* greengage.

réintégrer [reɛ̃tegre] *v* reinstate; return to. **réintégration** *nf* reinstatement; return.

rejeter [rɔʒte] *v* reject; (*relancer*) throw back; (*lave, déchets, etc.*) throw out; (*expulser*) cast out, expel. **se rejeter sur** fall back on. **rejet** *nm* rejection; expulsion; (*bot*) shoot.

*****rejoindre** [rɔʒwɛ̃drɔ] *v* rejoin; join; (*rattraper*) catch up with. **se rejoindre** meet.

réjouir [reʒwir] *v* delight, thrill. **se réjouir** be delighted; rejoice. **réjouissance** *nf* rejoicing. **réjouissant** *adj* amusing; (*nouvelle*) cheerful.

relâcher [rɔlɑʃe] *v* relax; (*desserrer*) loosen; (*libérer*) release. **relâche** *nf* rest, respite; (*théâtre*) closure; (*naut*) port of call. **relâché** *adj* loose; (*discipline*) lax.

relais [rɔlɛ] *nm* relay; (*usine*) shift.

relatif [rɔlatif] *adj* relative. **relativité** *nf* relativity.

relation [rɔlasjɔ̃] *nf* relationship; (*connaissance*) acquaintance, connection; (*récit*) account. **relations** *nf pl* relations *pl*.

relayer [rɔleje] *v* (*remplacer*) relieve, take over from; (*TV, radio*) relay. **se relayer** take turns.

reléguer [rɔlege] *v* relegate. **relégation** *nf* relegation.

relevé [rɔlve] *adj* raised, elevated; (*manches*) rolled-up; (*col*) turned-up; (*cuisine*) highly-seasoned. *nm* summary, list; (*facture*) bill. **relevé de compte** bank statement.

relever [rɔlve] *v* (*redresser*) pick up, stand up; (*remonter*) raise; (*manche*) roll up; (*chaussette*) pull up; (*col*) turn up; (*cuisine*) season; (*relayer*) relieve; (*faute*) find; (*notes*) take down. **relever de** be a matter for, be the concern of. **relève** *nf* relief. **relève de la garde** changing of the guard.

relief [rɔljɛf] *nm* relief. **en relief** in relief; (*en-tête*) embossed; (*phot*) three-dimensional. **mettre en relief** bring out, accentuate.

relier [rɔlje] *v* link, connect, (*livre*) bind.

religieux [rɔliʒjø] *adj* religious. *nm* monk. **religieuse** *nf* nun.

religion [rɔliʒjɔ̃] *nf* religion; (*foi*) faith.

relique [rɔlik] *nf* relic.

*****relire** [rɔlir] *v* re-read.

*****reluire** [rɔlᶣir] *v* shine, gleam. **reluisant** *adj* shiny.

remanier [rɔmanje] *v* revise, modify.

se remarier [rɔmarje] *v* remarry. **remariage** *nm* remarriage.

remarquer [rɔmarke] *v* notice; (*faire une remarque*) remark. **faire remarquer** point out. **remarquable** *adj* remarkable. **remarque** *nf* remark, comment.

remblai [rɑ̃blɛ] *nm* embankment.

rembourrer [rɑ̃bure] *v* stuff, pad. **rembourrage** *nm* stuffing, padding.

rembourser [rɑ̃burse] *v* repay; (*dépenses*) refund, reimburse. **remboursement** *nm* repayment; refund, reimbursement.

remède [rɔmɛd] *nm* remedy, cure. **remédier à** *v* remedy.

remercier [rɔmɛrsje] *v* thank. **remerciement** *nm* thanks *pl*.

*****remettre** [rɔmɛtrɔ] *v* put back; (*donner*) hand over; (*ajourner*) postpone; (*dette, péché*) remit. **se remettre** recover, get better.

réminiscence [reminisɑ̃s] *nf* reminiscence.

remise [rɔmiz] *nf* (*rabais*) discount; (*livraison*) delivery; (*grâce*) remission; (*resserre*) shed; (*ajournement*) postponement.

rémission [remisjɔ̃] *nf* remission.

remonter [rɔmɔ̃te] *v* go up (again); return, go back; (*cheval*) remount; (*relever*) raise; (*montre*) wind up; (*moral*) cheer up; (*machine, etc.*) reassemble. **remontant** *nm* tonic. **remontée** *nf* ascent, rise.

remords [rɔmɔr] *nm* remorse.

remorquer [rɔmɔrke] *v* tow. **remorque** *nf* towing; (*câble*) tow-rope; (*véhicule*) trailer. **en remorque** on tow. **remorqueur** *nm* tugboat.

remous [rɔmu] *nm* (*eau*) wash, swirl; (*air*) eddy; (*foule*) bustle; (*agitation*) stir.

rempart [rɑ̃par] *nm* rampart.

remplacer [rɑ̃plase] *v* replace; (*acteur, etc.*) stand in for; be a substitute for. **remplaçant, -e** *nm, nf* replacement; substitute; (*sport*) reserve; (*théâtre*) understudy. **remplacement** *nm* replacement; substitution.

rempli [rɑ̃pli] *adj* full. *nm* (*vêtement*) tuck.

remplir [rɑ̃plir] *v* fill; (*à nouveau*) refill; (*devoir*) fulfil; (*travail*) carry out.

remporter [rãpɔrte] *v* take away; (*victoire*) win; (*prix*) carry off.

remuer [rəmɥe] *v* move; (*tourner*) stir. **remue-ménage** *nm invar* commotion.

rémunérer [remynere] *v* remunerate, pay. **rémunérateur, -trice** *adj* remunerative, lucrative. **rémunération** *nf* remuneration.

renâcler [rənɑkle] *v* (*animal*) snort; (*personne*) grumble.

renaissance [rənɛsɑ̃s] *nf* rebirth.

renard [rənar] *nm* fox.

renchérir [rɑ̃ferir] *v* (*prix*) get more expensive; (*ajouter*) add, go further; (*péj*) go one better.

rencontrer [rɑ̃kɔ̃tre] *v* meet; (*trouver*) come across; (*obstacle*) come up against, encounter. **rencontre** *nf* meeting, encounter.

rendez-vous [rɑ̃devu] *nm invar* appointment; (*lieu*) meeting place. **donner rendez-vous à** make an appointment with.

se *rendormir [rɑ̃dɔrmir] *v* go back to sleep.

rendre [rɑ̃drə] *v* return, give back; (*achat*) take *or* send back; render; (*faire*) make; (*mil*) surrender; (*terre*) yield. **se rendre** surrender. **se rendre à** go to. **se rendre compte de** realize. **rendement** *nm* yield, output.

rêne [rɛn] *nf* rein.

renégat [rənega], **-e** *nm, nf* renegade.

renfermer [rɑ̃fɛrme] *v* contain. **renfermé** *adj* withdrawn. **sentir le renfermé** smell stuffy.

renforcer [rɑ̃fɔrse] *v* reinforce, strengthen; intensify. **renforcement** *nm* reinforcement, strengthening; intensification.

renfort [rɑ̃fɔr] *nm* reinforcement. **de** *or* **en renfort** extra, additional. **renforts** *nm pl* supplies *pl*.

se renfrogner [rɑ̃frɔɲe] *v* scowl. **renfrogné** *adj* sullen, sulky.

rengaine [rɑ̃gɛn] *nf* hackneyed expression.

renier [rənje] *v* renounce, deny; repudiate, disown; (*promesse*) go back on. **reniement** *nm* renunciation, denial; repudiation.

renifler [rənifle] *v* sniff. **reniflement** *nm* sniff.

renne [rɛn] *nm* reindeer.

renom [rənɔ̃] *nm* renown, fame. **renommé** *adj* renowned, famous. **renommée** *nf* renown, fame.

renoncer [rənɔ̃se] *v* **renoncer à** give up, renounce, abandon. **renonciation** *nf* renunciation.

renoncule [rənɔ̃kyl] *nf* buttercup.

renouer [rənwe] *v* tie again; (*conversation, etc.*) renew, resume.

renouveler [rənuvle] *v* renew. **se renouveler** recur. **renouvellement** *nm* renewal; recurrence.

rénover [renɔve] *v* renovate; (*méthodes, etc.*) reform. **rénovation** *nf* renovation; restoration.

renseigner [rɑ̃seɲe] *v* inform, give information to. **se renseigner** find out, make inquiries. **renseignements** *nm pl* information *sing*; inquiries *pl*; (*mil*) intelligence *sing*.

rente [rɑ̃t] *nf* pension, allowance. **rentes** *nf pl* private income *sing*. **rentable** *adj* profitable.

rentrer [rɑ̃tre] *v* return, go *or* come back; (*chez soi*) go home; (*entrer*) go in; (*à nouveau*) go back in; (*amener*) bring *or* take in. **rentrer dans** go into; (*voiture*) crash into; be included in. **rentrée** *nf* return; reopening; beginning of school term; (*acteur*) comeback.

renverser [rɑ̃vɛrse] *v* (*faire tomber*) knock over; (*mettre à l'envers*) turn upside down; (*gouvernement*) overthrow; (*inverser*) invert, reverse; (*fam*) stagger, astound. **se renverser** overturn. **renversé** *adj* upside down; inverted. **renversement** *nm* inversion, reversal; overthrow.

*renvoyer [rɑ̃vwaje] *v* send back; (*employé*) dismiss; (*élève*) expel; (*soldat*) discharge; refer; (*ajourner*) postpone; echo. **renvoi** *nm* dismissal; expulsion; discharge; cross-reference; postponement; (*rot*) belch.

réorganiser [reɔrganize] *v* reorganize. **réorganisation** *nf* reorganization.

repaire [rəpɛr] *nm* den.

répandre [repɑ̃drə] *v* (*renverser*) spill; (*disperser*) scatter; (*étendre*) spread; (*odeur, chaleur, etc.*) give off. **répandu** *adj* widespread.

*reparaître [rəparɛtrə] *v* reappear.

réparer [repare] *v* mend, repair; correct; (*compenser*) make up for. **réparation** *nf* repair; correction; compensation.

repartie [rəparti] *nf* repartee; (*riposte*) retort.

répartir [repartir] *v* share out, divide up; distribute; (*étaler*) spread. **répartition** *nf* distribution; allocation.

repas [rəpɑ] *nm* meal. **repas léger** snack.

repasser [rəpase] *v* (*frontière*) go back across; (*souvenir, trait*) go (back) over; (*examen*) resit; (*film, émission*) show again; (*au fer*) iron; (*couteau*) sharpen. **repassage** *nm* ironing; sharpening.

se *repentir [rəpɑ̃tir] *v* repent. **se repentir de** regret, be sorry for. *nm* repentance. **repentant** *adj* repentant.

répercussion [repɛrkysjɔ̃] *nf* repercussion.

répercuter [repɛrkyte] *v* echo; reflect. **se répercuter** reverberate.

repérer [rəpere] *v* locate; (*fam*) spot, discover. **repère** *nm* mark, marker; (*monument, etc.*) landmark.

répertoire [repɛrtwar] *nm* index, list; (*carnet*) notebook; (*théâtre*) repertory; (*chanteur*) repertoire.

répéter [repete] *v* repeat; (*théâtre*) rehearse. **répétiteur, -trice** *nm, nf* tutor. **répétition** *nf* repetition; rehearsal. **répétition générale** dress rehearsal.

répit [repi] *nm* respite.

replacer [rəplase] *v* replace, put back; (*employé*) find a new job for.

replier [rəplije] *v* fold up; (*mil*) withdraw. **se replier** curl up; (*se renfermer*) withdraw. **repli** *nm* fold; withdrawal.

réplique [replik] *nf* reply, retort; counterattack; (*théâtre*) line, cue; (*art*) replica. **répliquer** *v* reply, retort; (*se venger*) retaliate.

répondre [repɔ̃drə] *v* answer, reply; (*réagir*) respond. **répondre de** answer for.

réponse [repɔ̃s] *nf* answer, reply; (*réaction*) response.

reporter¹ [rəpɔrte] *v* (*ramener*) take back; (*différer*) put off, postpone; transfer; copy out. **se reporter à** refer to; (*penser*) think back to.

reporter² [rəpɔrtɛr] *nm* reporter. **reportage** *nm* report; (*sport*) commentary.

repos [rəpo] *nm* rest; pause; (*tranquillité*) peace.

reposer¹ [rəpoze] *v* rest; (*être étendu*) lie. **se reposer** rest; (*compter*) rely. **reposant** *adj* restful.

reposer² [rəpoze] *v* put back; (*question*) repeat, raise again.

repousser [rəpuse] *v* repulse, repel; (*écarter*) push away; reject; (*différer*) put off, postpone; (*cheveux, etc.*) grow again. **repoussant** *adj* repulsive.

*reprendre [rəprɑ̃drə] *v* take back; (*récupérer*) recover, get back; (*recommencer*) resume; (*attraper*) recapture; reprimand. **se reprendre** correct onself; (*se ressaisir*) pull oneself together.

représailles [rəprezɑj] *nf pl* reprisals *pl*, retaliation *sing*.

représenter [rəprezɑ̃te] *v* represent; (*art*) depict, portray; (*théâtre*) perform. **se représenter** imagine; (*survenir*) occur or arise again; (*à un examen*) resit. **représentant, -e** *nm, nf* representative. **représentatif** *adj* representative. **représentation** *nf* representation; performance.

répressif [represif] *adj* repressive. **répression** *nf* repression.

réprimande [reprimɑ̃d] *nf* reprimand. **réprimander** *v* reprimand.

réprimer [reprime] *v* repress, suppress.

reprise [rəpriz] *nf* (*recommencement*) resumption, renewal; (*film, émission*) repeat; (*affaires, etc.*) recovery; (*chaussette*) darn; (*fois*) occasion, time. **· à maintes reprises** many times. **repriser** *v* darn.

reprocher [rəprɔʃe] *v* reproach; criticize. **reproche** *nm* reproach.

reproduction [rəprɔdyksjɔ̃] *nf* reproduction.

*reproduire [rəprɔdᴵir] *v* reproduce. **se reproduire** recur.

réprouver [repruve] *v* reprove, condemn.

reptile [rɛptil] *nm* reptile.

républicain [repyblikɛ̃], **-e** *n, adj* republican.

république [repyblik] *nf* republic.

répudier [repydje] *v* repudiate, renounce. **répudiation** *nf* repudiation.

répugnant [repyɲɑ̃] *adj* repugnant, revolting. **répugnance** *nf* repugnance, loathing.

répulsif [repylsif] *adj* repulsive. **répulsion** *nf* repulsion.

réputation [repytasjɔ̃] *nf* reputation, repute. **réputé** *adj* reputable, renowned; (*prétendu*) reputed.

*requérir [rəkerir] *v* require, call for; (*solliciter*) request.

requête [rəkɛt] *nf* request, petition.

requiem [rekᴵijɛm] *nm invar* requiem.

requin [rəkɛ̃] *nm* shark.

requis [rəki] *adj* required, requisite.

réquisition [rekizisjɔ̃] *nf* requisition.
réquisitionner *v* requisition.
rescapé [rɛskape], **-e** *nm*, *nf* survivor.
réseau [rezo] *nm* network.
réserver [rezɛrve] *v* reserve; (*mettre de côté*) keep, save; (*destiner*) have in store. **réservation** *nf* reservation. **réserve** *nf* reserve; (*restriction*) reservation; (*provision*) stock; (*entrepôt*) storeroom.
réservoir [rezɛrvwar] *nm* tank; (*étang*) reservoir; (*poissons*) fishpond.
résider [rezide] *v* reside. **résidence** *nf* residence. **résidentiel** *adj* residential.
résidu [rezidy] *nm* residue.
se résigner [reziɲe] *v* resign oneself. **résignation** *nf* resignation.
résilier [rezilje] *v* terminate, cancel.
résille [rezij] *nf* net; (*coiffure*) hairnet.
résine [rezin] *nf* resin.
résister [reziste] *v* **résister à** resist, withstand. **résistance** *nf* resistance. **résistant** *adj* strong, robust.
résolu [rezɔly] *adj* resolute, determined. **résolution** *nf* resolution; solution.
résonner [rezɔne] *v* resonate, resound. **resonance** *nf* resonance.
*****résoudre** [rezudrə] *v* resolve; (*problème*) solve.
respect [rɛspɛ] *nm* respect. **respect de soi** self-respect. **respectable** *adj* respectable. **respecter** *v* respect. **respectif** *adj* respective. **respectueux** *adj* respectful.
respirer [rɛspire] *v* breathe. **respiration** *nf* breathing. **respiration artificielle** artificial respiration.
resplendir [rɛsplɑ̃dir] *v* beam, shine, gleam. **resplendissant** *adj* radiant.
responsable [rɛspɔ̃sablə] *adj* responsible. *n*(*m* + *f*) (*coupable*) culprit; (*dirigeant*) official. **responsabilité** *nf* responsibility.
resquiller [rɛskije] *v* get in without paying; jump the queue; (*carotter*) wangle.
se ressaisir [rəsezir] *v* pull oneself together.
ressembler [rəsɑ̃blə] *v* **ressembler à** resemble, be like. **se ressembler** be alike. **ressemblance** *nf* resemblance; similarity.
*****ressentir** [rəsɑ̃tir] *v* feel. **se ressentir de** (*personne*) feel the effects of; (*travail*) show the effects of. **ressentiment** *nm* resentment.
resserrer [rəsere] *v* tighten.
ressort[1] [rəsɔr] *nm* spring.
ressort[2] [rəsɔr] *nm* scope, province.

*****ressortir** [rəsɔrtir] *v* go *or* come out again; (*retirer*) bring *or* take out again; (*se détacher*) stand out. **ressortir de** be the result of.
ressource [rəsurs] *nf* resource; possibility; (*recours*) resort.
ressusciter [resysite] *v* revive; (*rel*, *péj*) resurrect.
restant [rɛstɑ̃] *adj* remaining. *nm* rest, remainder.
restaurant [rɛstɔrɑ̃] *nm* restaurant.
restaurer [rɛstɔre] *v* restore. **restauration** *nf* restoration.
rester [rɛste] *v* stay, remain; (*subsister*) be left; (*durer*) last. **en rester à** go no further than. **reste** *nm* rest, remainder; (*morceau*) piece left over. **du reste** moreover. **restes** *nm pl* remains *pl*; (*nourriture*) left-overs *pl*.
restituer [rɛstitɥe] *v* restore; (*rendre*) return.
*****restreindre** [rɛstrɛ̃drə] *v* restrict, limit. **restriction** [rɛstriksjɔ̃] *nf* restriction. **restrictif** *adj* restrictive.
résulter [rezylte] *v* result. **résultat** *nm* result.
résumer [rezyme] *v* summarize, sum up. **résumé** *nm* summary, résumé.
résurrection [rezyrɛksjɔ̃] *nf* resurrection.
rétablir [retablir] *v* restore; (*réintégrer*) reinstate. **se rétablir** (*malade*) recover. **rétablissement** *nm* recovery; restoration.
retard [rətar] *nm* delay; (*personne*) lateness; (*peuple*, *enfant*) backwardness. **en retard** late. **retardé** *adj* backward. **retarder** *v* delay; (*remettre*) put back; (*montre*) be slow.
*****retenir** [rətnir] *v* hold back; (*garder*) keep, retain; (*retarder*) detain; (*réserver*) book; (*contenir*) restrain.
retentir [rətɑ̃tir] *v* ring, resound, echo. **retentissement** *nm* repercussion; effect.
retenue [rətny] *nf* restraint, reserve; (*prélèvement*) deduction; (*école*) detention.
réticent [retisɑ̃] *adj* reticent; hesitant. **réticence** *nf* reservation.
rétif [retif] *adj* restive.
rétine [retin] *nf* retina.
retirer [rətire] *v* remove, withdraw. **se retirer** retire, withdraw.
retomber [rətɔ̃be] *v* fall (again); (*fusée*, *etc.*) land, come down; (*pendre*) hang down.

rétorquer [retɔrke] v retort.

retors [rətɔr] adj sly, wily.

retoucher [rətuʃe] v touch up; (vêtement) alter. **retouche** nf alteration.

retour [rətur] nm return. **être de retour** be back.

retourner [rəturne] v return; (renverser) turn over; (sens opposé) turn round.

rétracter [retrakte] v retract.

retrait [rətrɛ] nm withdrawal. **en retrait** set back.

retraite [rətrɛt] nf retreat; (vieux travailleur) retirement; pension. **prendre sa retraite** retire.

retraité [rətrete], **-e** adj retired. nm, nf pensioner.

retrancher [rətrɑ̃ʃe] v deduct, take away; (couper) cut out or off. **se retrancher** (mil) entrench oneself; take refuge.

rétrécir [retresir] v (tissu) shrink; (rue) narrow; (pupille) contract. **rétrécissement** nm shrinkage; contraction.

rétribuer [retribɥe] v pay. **rétribution** nf payment.

rétrograder [retrɔgrade] v regress, go backward; (officier) demote. **rétrogradation** nf regression; demotion. **rétrograde** adj retrograde, backward.

rétrospectif [retrɔspɛktif] adj retrospective. **rétrospectivement** adv in retrospect.

retrousser [rətruse] v (manche) roll up; (lèvre) curl up; (jupe, etc.) hitch up; (nez) turn up.

retrouver [rətruve] v find (again); (personne) meet, join; (santé) regain. **se retrouver** meet up, get together.

rétroviseur [retrɔvizœr] nm driving mirror.

réunir [reynir] v collect, gather (together); join; (ennemis, anciens amis) reunite. **se réunir** unite; (amis) get together. **réunion** nf (séance) meeting; reunion; collection.

réussir [reysir] v succeed. **réussir à** succeed in; (examen) pass; (air, nourriture) agree with. **réussi** adj successful. **réussite** nf success; (cartes) patience.

revanche [rəvɑ̃ʃ] nf revenge. **en revanche** (au contraire) on the other hand; (en retour) in return.

rêvasser [rɛvase] v daydream.

rêve [rɛv] nm dream.

revêche [rəvɛʃ] adj surly.

réveiller [reveje] v wake (up); (raviver) rouse, reawaken, revive. **se réveiller** wake up, awake. **réveil** nm waking; (à la réalité) awakening; (pendule) alarm clock. **réveillé** adj awake.

révéler [revele] v reveal. **révélateur, -trice** adj revealing. **révélation** nf revelation.

revendiquer [rəvɑ̃dike] v claim, demand. **revendication** nf claim, demand.

*__revenir__ [rəvnir] v come back, return. **revenir à** come to, amount to. **revenir à soi** come round. **revenir de** get over. **revenir sur** (promesse) go back on; (passé) go back over. **revenant, -e** nm, nf ghost. **revenu** nm income, revenue.

rêver [reve] v dream. **rêverie** nf daydream. **rêveur, -euse** adj dreamy.

réverbérer [reverbere] v reverberate, reflect. **réverbération** nf reverberation. **réverbère** nm street lamp.

révérence [reverɑ̃s] nf (homme) bow; (femme) curtsy; (respect) reverence. **faire une révérence** bow; curtsy.

revers [rəvɛr] nm back; (monnaie) reverse; (tissu) wrong side; (veste) lapel; (manche) cuff. **réversible** adj reversible.

*__revêtir__ [rəvetir] v assume, take on; (habiller) clothe; cover, coat. **revêtement** nm covering, coating; surface.

revirement [rəvirmɑ̃] nm sudden change, reversal.

réviser [revize] v revise; (examiner) review; (voiture, machine) service, overhaul. **révision** nf revision; review; service.

*__revivre__ [rəvivrə] v relive. **faire revivre** revive.

*__revoir__ [rəvwar] v see again; revise. **au revoir!** goodbye!

révolter [revɔlte] v revolt, outrage. **se révolter** revolt, rebel. **révolte** nf revolt, rebellion.

révolution [revɔlysjɔ̃] nf revolution. **révolutionnaire** n(m+f), adj revolutionary. **révolutionner** v revolutionize.

revolver [revɔlvɛr] nm gun, revolver.

révoquer [revɔke] v revoke; (destituer) dismiss.

revue [rəvy] nf review; (spectacle) revue; magazine; (mil) inspection.

rez-de-chaussée [redʃose] nm invar ground floor.

rhésus [rezys] nm rhesus. **rhésus négatif/positif** rhesus negative/positive.

rhétorique [retɔrik] nf rhetoric. adj rhetorical.

rhinocéros [rinɔserɔs] nm rhinoceros.
rhododendron [rɔdɔdɛ̃drɔ̃] nm rhododendron.
rhubarbe [rybarb] nf rhubarb.
rhum [rɔm] nm rum.
rhumatisme [rymatismə] nm rheumatism. **rhumatismal** adj rheumatic.
rhume [rym] nm cold. **rhume des foins** hay fever.
riant [rjɑ̃] adj cheerful, smiling.
ricaner [rikane] v snigger, sneer. **ricanement** nm snigger, sneer.
riche [riʃ] adj rich. n(m+f) rich person. **richesse** nf richness; (argent) wealth; abundance. **richesses** nf pl riches pl.
ride [rid] nf (peau) wrinkle; (eau) ripple. **rider** v wrinkle; ripple.
rideau [rido] nm curtain; (écran) screen. **rideau de fer** Iron Curtain.
ridicule [ridikyl] adj ridiculous. nm ridicule; absurdity. **ridiculiser** v ridicule.
rien [rjɛ̃] pron nothing; (quelque chose) anything. **ça ne fait rien** (fam) it doesn't matter. **de rien** (fam) not at all, you're welcome. **ne ... rien** nothing. nm nothing; (bagatelle) trivial thing; (goutte) touch, hint.
rigide [riʒid] adj rigid, stiff; strict. **rigidité** nf rigidity, stiffness; strictness.
rigole [rigɔl] nf channel; (d'écoulement) drain; (sillon) furrow.
rigoler [rigɔle] (fam) v (plaisanter) joke; (rire) laugh; (s'amuser) have fun. **rigolo, -ote** adj funny, comical.
rigoureux [rigurø] adj rigorous, (sévère) harsh; strict.
rigueur [rigœr] nf rigour; (sévérité) harshness; strictness; precision. **à la rigueur** if need be; possibly. **de rigueur** compulsory; (étiquette) the done thing.
rime [rim] nf rhyme. **rimer** v rhyme.
rincer [rɛ̃se] v rinse. **rinçage** nm rinse.
riposter [ripɔste] v retort; (contre-attaquer) retaliate. **riposte** nf retort.
rire [rir] v laugh; (plaisanter) joke; (s'amuser) have fun. **se rire de** laugh at. nm laugh; (éclat) laughter. **petit rire** chuckle. **petit rire nerveux** giggle.
ris [ri] nm **ris de veau** sweetbread.
risée [rize] nf ridicule; (personne) laughing stock.
risquer [riske] v risk. **risquer de** may well. **risque-tout** n(m+f) invar daredevil. **se risquer** venture. **risque** nm risk. **risqué** adj risky; (licencieux) risqué.

ristourne [risturn] nf rebate, refund.
rite [rit] nm rite.
rituel [rityɛl] nm, adj ritual.
rival [rival], **-e** n, adj rival. **rivaliser** [rivalize] v **rivaliser avec** rival, vie with. **rivalité** nf rivalry.
rive [riv] nf (mer) shore; (rivière) bank. **rivage** nm shore.
river [rive] v rivet; (lier) bind. **rivet** nm rivet.
rivière [rivjɛr] nf river.
rixe [riks] nf brawl.
riz [ri] nm rice. **riz au lait** rice pudding.
robe [rɔb] nf dress; (magistrat) robe; (professeur) gown; (peau) skin. **robe-chasuble** nf pinafore dress. **robe de chambre** dressing-gown. **robe de grossesse** maternity dress, smock. **robe de mariée** wedding dress. **robe du soir** evening dress.
robinet [rɔbinɛ] nm tap.
robot [rɔbo] nm robot.
robuste [rɔbyst] adj robust.
roc [rɔk] nm rock. **rocaille** nf (jardin) rockery.
roche [rɔʃ] nf rock. **rocher** nm rock; (gros bloc) boulder.
roder [rɔde] v (auto) run in. **en rodage** running in.
rôder [rode] v (en maraude) prowl; (au hasard) roam. **rôdeur, -euse** nm, nf prowler.
rogner [rɔɲe] v trim, clip; (dépense) whittle down.
rognon [rɔɲɔ̃] nm kidney.
rogue [rɔg] adj haughty, arrogant.
roi [rwa] nm king. **la fête des Rois** Twelfth Night.
roitelet [rwatlɛ] nm wren.
rôle [rol] nm role, part; (liste) roll.
romain [rɔmɛ̃] adj Roman. **Romain, -e** nm, nf Roman.
roman[1] [rɔmɑ̃] nm novel; (récit) story. **roman-feuilleton** nm serial. **roman policier** detective story. **romans** nm pl fiction sing. **romancier, -ère** nm, nf novelist.
roman[2] [rɔmɑ̃] adj (langue) Romance; (arch) Romanesque.
romanesque [rɔmanɛsk] adj (personne) romantic; (récit) fantastic; (amour) storybook.
romantique [rɔmɑ̃tik] n(m+f), adj romantic.

romarin [rɔmarɛ̃] *nm* rosemary.
Rome [rɔm] *n* Rome.
rompre [rɔ̃prə] *v* break. **rompu** *adj* broken; (*fatigué*) exhausted. **rompu à** experienced in.
romsteck [rɔmstɛk] *nm* rump steak.
ronce [rɔs] *nf* bramble; (*mûrier*) blackberry bush.
rond [rɔ̃] *adj* round; (*gras*) chubby, plump; (*fam*) drunk. **rond-de-cuir** *nm* clerk. **rond-point** *nm* roundabout. *nm* ring; (*tranche*) slice. **en rond** in a circle. **ronde** *nf* patrol, rounds *pl*; (*musique*) semibreve. **rondelle** *nf* washer; disc. **rondement** *adv* (*promptement*) briskly; frankly. **rondeur** *nf* roundness; plumpness. **rondin** *nm* log.
ronfler [rɔ̃fle] *v* snore; (*rugir*) roar; (*vrombir*) hum. **ronflement** *nm* snore; roar; hum.
ronger [rɔ̃ʒe] *v* gnaw at, eat into; (*malade*) sap. **se ronger les ongles** bite one's nails. **rongeur** *nm* rodent.
ronronner [rɔ̃rɔne] *v* purr. **ronron** *or* **ronronnement** *nm* purr.
roquet [rɔkɛ] *nm* ill-tempered little dog.
roquette [rɔkɛt] *nf* rocket.
rosaire [rozɛr] *nm* rosary.
rosbif [rɔsbif] *nm* roast beef.
rose [roz] *nf* rose. *nm* pink. *adj* pink; (*joues*) rosy. **roseraie** *nf* rose garden. **rosier** *nm* rose-bush.
roseau [rozo] *nm* reed.
rosée [roze] *nf* dew.
rosette [rozɛt] *nf* rosette; (*nœud*) bow.
rosser [rɔse] *v* thrash. **rossée** *nf* (*fam*) thrashing, hiding.
rossignol [rɔsiɲɔl] *nm* nightingale; (*fam*) piece of junk.
rot [ro] (*fam*) *nm* burp. **roter** *v* burp.
rotatif [rɔtatif] *adj* rotary.
rôtir [rotir] *v* roast. **rôti** *nm* joint, roast. **rôtisserie** *nf* steak-house.
rotor [rɔtɔr] *nm* rotor.
rotule [rɔtyl] *nf* kneecap.
rouage [rwaʒ] *nm* cog; part. **rouages** *nm pl* works *pl*.
roublard [rublar] *adj* (*fam*) crafty, wily.
roucouler [rukule] *v* coo. **roucoulement** *nm* coo.
roue [ru] *nf* wheel. **faire la roue** (*se pavaner*) strut about; (*gymnaste*) do a cart-wheel. **roue de secours** spare wheel.
roué [rwe] *adj* cunning.
rouge [ruʒ] *adj* red. **rouge-gorge** *nm* robin. *nm* red; (*fard*) rouge. **rouge à lèvres** lipstick. **rougeur** *nf* redness; (*visage*) flush, flushing; (*de gêne, honte*) blush, blushing.
rougeole [ruʒɔl] *nf* measles.
rougir [ruʒir] *v* go *or* turn red, redden; (*visage*) flush; (*de gêne, honte*) blush.
rouiller [ruje] *v* rust, go rusty. **rouille** *nf* rust. **rouillé** *adj* rusty.
rouleau [rulo] *nm* roller; (*papier, pellicule, tabac, etc.*) roll; (*parchemin*) scroll. **rouleau à pâtisserie** rolling pin. **rouleau compresseur** steam-roller. **rouleau de papier hygiénique** toilet roll.
rouler [rule] *v* roll; (*enrouler*) roll up; (*pousser*) wheel; (*aller*) go, run; (*conduire*) drive; (*fam: duper*) con, diddle. **roulant** *adj* moving; (*meuble*) on wheels; (*argot*) hilarious. **roulement** *nm* roll; movement; (*bruit*) rumble. **roulement à billes** ball bearings *pl*. **roulette** *nf* castor; (*jeu*) roulette.
roulotte [rulɔt] *nf* caravan.
Roumanie [rumani] *nf* Romania. **roumain** *nm*, *adj* Romanian. **Roumain, -e** *nm*, *nf* Romanian.
roupiller [rupije] (*fam*) *v* snooze. **roupillon** *nm* snooze.
rouquin [rukɛ̃], **-e** (*fam*) *nm*, *nf* redhead. *adj* red-haired.
rouspéter [ruspete] *v* (*fam*) moan, grumble.
roussir [rusir] *v* (*brûler*) scorch, singe; (*feuilles*) go brown. **rousseur** *nf* redness.
route [rut] *nf* road; (*chemin*) way; (*ligne*) route. **en route** on the way. **en route pour** bound for. **se mettre en route** set off. **routier** *adj* road.
routine [rutin] *nf* routine. **routinier** *adj* humdrum, routine.
***rouvrir** [ruvrir] *v* reopen.
roux, rousse [ru, rus] *adj* reddish-brown; (*cheveux*) red, auburn, ginger. *nm*, *nf* redhead.
royal [rwajal] *adj* royal; majestic, regal. **royaliste** *n(m + f)*, *adj* royalist. **royauté** *nf* royalty; monarchy.
royaume [rwajom] *nm* kingdom, realm. **Royaume-Uni** *nm* United Kingdom.
ruban [rybɑ̃] *nm* ribbon; band, tape.
rubéole [rybeɔl] *nf* German measles.
rubis [rybi] *nm* ruby.
rubrique [rybrik] *nf* (*article*) column; (*titre*) heading.

ruche [ryʃ] nf hive.

rude [ryd] adj (pénible, dur) hard, harsh; (surface) rough; (grossier) crude. **rudement** adv harshly; roughly; (fam) terribly, awfully. **rudesse** nf harshness; roughness; crudeness.

rudiment [rydimã] nm rudiment. **rudimentaire** adj rudimentary.

rudoyer [rydwaje] v treat roughly.

rue [ry] nf street. **rue à sens unique** one-way street. **ruelle** nf alley.

ruer [rᵱe] v kick out. **se ruer** dash, rush, hurl oneself. **se ruer sur** pounce on. **ruée** nf rush, stampede.

rugby [rygbi] nm rugby.

rugir [ryʒir] v roar. **rugissement** nm roar.

rugueux [rygø] adj rough. **rugosité** nf roughness.

ruine [rᵱin] nf ruin. **ruiner** v ruin.

ruisseau [rᵱiso] nm stream; (caniveau) gutter.

ruisseler [rᵱisle] v stream.

rumeur [rymœr] nf (nouvelle) rumour; (son) murmur, hum, hubbub.

rupture [ryptyr] nf rupture, break. **rupture de contrat** breach of contract.

rural [ryral] adj rural, country.

ruse [ryz] nf (procédé) trick, ruse; (art) cunning, guile. **ruses de guerre** tactics pl. **rusé** adj sly, cunning.

Russie [rysi] nf Russia. **russe** nm, adj Russian. **Russe** n(m+f) Russian.

rustique [rystik] adj rustic.

rustre [rystrə] nm lout.

rutabaga [rytabaga] nm swede.

rythme [ritmə] nm rhythm; (vitesse) rate. **rythmé** or **rythmique** adj rhythmic.

S

s' [s] V se, si¹.

sa [sa] V son¹.

sabbat [saba] nm sabbath.

sable¹ [sablə] nm sand. **sables mouvants** quicksands pl. **sabler** v sand. **sableux** or **sablonneux** adj sandy. **sablier** nm hourglass.

sable² [sablə] nm sable.

sablé [sable] nm shortbread.

saborder [saborde] v scuttle.

sabot [sabo] nm (chaussure) clog; (animal) hoof.

saboter [sabote] v sabotage. **sabotage** nm sabotage. **saboteur, -euse** nm, nf saboteur.

sabre [sabrə] nm sabre.

sac [sak] nm bag; (à charbon, etc.) sack. **sac à dos** rucksack. **sac à main** handbag. **sac à provisions** shopping bag. **sac de couchage** sleeping bag.

saccade [sakad] nf jerk. **par saccades** jerkily, in fits and starts. **saccadé** adj jerky.

saccager [sakaʒe] v wreck, devastate; (piller) ransack. **saccage** nm havoc.

saccharine [sakarin] nf saccharin.

sacerdoce [saserdɔs] nm priesthood.

sachet [saʃɛ] nm sachet; (bonbons) bag. **sachet de thé** tea-bag.

sacoche [sakɔʃ] nf bag; (cycliste) saddlebag; (écolier) satchel.

sacquer [sake] v (fam) v sack; (recaler) fail.

sacrement [sakrəmã] nm sacrament.

sacrer [sakre] v consecrate; (roi) crown; (fam) swear. **sacre** nm consecration; (roi) coronation. **sacré** adj sacred; (fam) blasted, damned.

sacrifier [sakrifje] v sacrifice. **sacrifice** nm sacrifice.

sacrilège [sakrileʒ] nm sacrilege. adj sacrilegious.

sacristie [sakristi] nf vestry.

sadique [sadik] adj sadistic. n(m+f) sadist. **sadisme** nm sadism.

safari [safari] nm safari.

safran [safrã] nm saffron.

saga [saga] nf saga.

sagace [sagas] adj shrewd. **sagacité** nf shrewdness.

sage [saʒ] adj wise, sensible; (enfant) good; moderate. **sage-femme** nf midwife. **sois sage!** be good! behave yourself! nm wise man, sage. **sagesse** nf wisdom; good behaviour; moderation.

Sagittaire [saʒitɛr] nm Sagittarius.

sagou [sagu] nm sago.

saigner [seɲe] v bleed. **saignant** adj bleeding; (viande) rare, underdone.

saillir [sajir] v jut out, protrude. **saillant** adj prominent, protruding; (frappant) outstanding. **saillie** nf projection; (boutade) witticism. **en saillie** overhanging.

sain [sɛ̃] adj healthy; (d'esprit) sane;

(*robuste*) sound. **sain et sauf** safe and sound.

saindoux [sɛ̃du] *nm* lard.

saint [sɛ̃], **-e** *adj* holy; pious, saintly. *nm*, *nf* saint. **Saint-Esprit** *nm* Holy Spirit. **Saint-Jean** *nm* Midsummer Day. **saint patron** patron saint. **Saint-Sylvestre** *nf* New Year's Eve. **sainteté** *nf* holiness, sanctity; saintliness.

saisir [sezir] *v* seize, take hold of; (*comprendre*) grasp; (*serrer*) grip. **saisie** *nf* seizure; capture. **saisissant** *adj* (*spectacle*) gripping; (*frappant*) striking; (*froid*) biting. **saisissement** *nm* (*frisson*) shiver; rush of emotion.

saison [sɛzɔ̃] *nf* season. **hors de saison** out of season; (*prix*) low-season. **saisonnier** *adj* seasonal.

salade [salad] *nf* salad; (*laitue*) lettuce; (*fam*) muddle.

salaire [salɛr] *nm* pay; (*à la semaine*) wages *pl*; (*au mois*) salary; (*récompense*) reward.

salami [salami] *nm* salami.

salaud [salo] *nm* (*impol*) bastard, sod.

sale [sal] *adj* dirty; (*fam*) nasty, lousy. **saleté** *nf* dirt; obscenity; (*sale tour*) dirty trick; (*fam: camelote*) rubbish.

saler [sale] *v* salt; (*fam*) do, overcharge. **salé** *adj* salty; salted; (*fam: grivois*) spicy; (*fam: sévère*) stiff, steep. **salière** *nf* salt-cellar.

salin [salɛ̃] *adj* saline. **salinité** *nf* salinity.

salir [salir] *v* dirty, soil; corrupt, sully. **se salir** get dirty; tarnish one's reputation.

salive [saliv] *nf* saliva. **salivaire** *adj* salivary. **saliver** *v* salivate.

salle [sal] *nf* room; hall; auditorium; (*hôpital*) ward. **salle à manger** dining room. **salle d'attente** waiting room. **salle de bain** bathroom. **salle de bal** ballroom. **salle de classe** classroom. **salle de séjour** living room. **salle des professeurs** staff-room. **salle d'opération** operating theatre.

saloperie [salɔpri] (*argot*) *nf* (*camelote*) rubbish; (*ordure*) muck; (*sale tour*) dirty trick.

salopette [salɔpɛt] *nf* (*ouvrier*) overalls *pl*; (*enfant, femme*) dungarees *pl*; (*ski*) salopette.

saltimbanque [saltɛ̃bɑ̃k] *n(m+f)* acrobat, member of travelling circus.

salubre [salybrə] *adj* healthy.

saluer [salɥe] *v* greet; (*mil*) salute; (*acteur*) bow; (*acclamer*) hail.

salut [saly] *nm* (*mil*) salute; (*salutation*) greeting; (*révérence*) bow; (*sécurité*) safety; (*rel*) salvation. *interj* (*fam: bonjour*) hi! (*fam: au revoir*) bye! **salutation** *nf* greeting.

salutaire [salytɛr] *adj* salutary, beneficial; profitable; (*sain*) healthy.

samedi [samdi] *nm* Saturday.

sanatorium [sanatɔrjɔm] *nm* sanatorium.

sanctifier [sɑ̃ktifje] *v* hallow, sanctify. **sanctification** *nf* sanctification.

sanction [sɑ̃ksjɔ̃] *nf* sanction; (*peine*) punishment, penalty. **sanctionner** *v* sanction; punish.

sanctuaire [sɑ̃ktɥer] *nm* sanctuary.

sandale [sɑ̃dal] *nf* sandal.

sandwich [sɑ̃dwitʃ] *nm* sandwich.

sang [sɑ̃] *nm* blood. **à sang chaud/froid** warm-/cold-blooded. **sang-froid** *nm invar* calmness, coolness. **sang-mêlé** *n(m+f)* invar half-caste.

sanglant [sɑ̃glɑ̃] *adj* bloody; (*visage, habit, etc.*) covered in blood; cruel.

sangle [sɑ̃glə] *nf* strap; (*selle*) girth. **sangler** *v* strap up.

sanglier [sɑ̃glije] *nm* boar.

sanglot [sɑ̃glo] *nm* sob. **sangloter** *v* sob.

sangsue [sɑ̃sy] *nf* leech.

sanguin [sɑ̃gɛ̃] *adj* blood; (*visage*) ruddy; (*tempérament*) fiery. **sanguinaire** *adj* bloodthirsty.

sanitaire [sanitɛr] *adj* sanitary.

sans [sɑ̃] *prep* without; but for. **sans-abri** *n(m+f)* invar homeless person. **sans ça** or else. **sans faute** without fail. **sans-gêne** *adj invar* offhand. **sans quoi** otherwise. **sans-souci** *adj invar* carefree.

sansonnet [sɑ̃sɔnɛ] *nm* starling.

santé [sɑ̃te] *nf* health. **à votre santé!** cheers!

saper [sape] *v* undermine, sap.

sapeur [sapœr] *nm* (*mil*) sapper. **sapeur-pompier** *nm* fireman.

saphir [safir] *nm* sapphire.

sapin [sapɛ̃] *nm* fir.

sarcasme [sarkasmə] *nm* sarcasm. **sarcastique** *adj* sarcastic.

sarcler [sarkle] *v* weed. **sarclage** *nm* weeding.

Sardaigne [sardɛɲ] *nf* Sardinia. **sarde** *nm*, *adj* Sardinian. **Sarde** *n(m+f)* Sardinian.

sardine [sardin] *nf* sardine.

sardonique [sardɔnik] *adj* sardonic.

Satan [satɑ̃] *nm* Satan. **satanique** *adj* satanic.

satellite [satelit] *nm* satellite.

satin [satɛ̃] *nm* satin.

satire [satir] *nf* satire. **faire la satire de** satirize. **satirique** *adj* satirical.

satisfaction [satisfaksjɔ̃] *nf* satisfaction.

***satisfaire** [satisfɛr] *v* satisfy. **satisfaire à** *(condition)* fulfil. **satisfaisant** *adj* satisfactory. **satisfait** *adj* satisfied.

saturer [satyre] *v* saturate. **saturation** *nf* saturation.

sauce [sos] *nf* sauce; *(jus de viande)* gravy.

saucée [sose] *nf (fam)* downpour.

saucisse [sosis] *nf* sausage. **saucisson** *nm* large sausage.

sauf [sof] *adj* unharmed; intact. *prep* except, but; *(à moins de)* unless.

sauge [soʒ] *nf* sage.

saugrenu [sogrəny] *adj* ludicrous.

saule [sol] *nm* willow.

saumon [somɔ̃] *nm* salmon.

saumure [somyr] *nf* brine.

sauna [sona] *nm* sauna.

saupoudrer [sopudre] *v* sprinkle. **saupoudreuse** *nf* dredger.

saut [so] *nm* jump, leap. **saut à la corde** skipping. **saut-de-lit** *nm invar* housecoat. **saut-de-mouton** *nm* flyover. **saut en hauteur/longueur** high/long jump. **saut périlleux** somersault.

sauter [sote] *v* jump, leap; explode; *(fusible)* blow; *(omettre)* skip. **faire sauter** *(mine, etc.)* blow up; *(crêpe)* toss. **saute-mouton** *nm* leapfrog. **saute** *nf* sudden change. **sauté** *adj* sauté. **sauterelle** *nf* grasshopper. **sauterie** *nf* party.

sautiller [sotije] *v* hop; *(enfant)* skip.

sauvage [sovaʒ] *adj* wild; *(brutal, primitif)* savage; unsociable. *n(m+f)* savage; recluse. **sauvagerie** *nf* savagery.

sauvegarder [sovgarde] *v* safeguard. **sauvegarde** *nf* safeguard.

sauver [sove] *v* save, rescue; *(récupérer)* salvage. **sauve-qui-peut** *nm invar* stampede. **se sauver** run away. **sauvetage** *nm* rescue; *(technique)* life-saving; salvage. **sauveur** *nm* saviour.

savant [savɑ̃] *adj* learned, scholarly; *(habile)* skilful; *(chien)* performing. *nm* scholar; scientist.

savate [savat] *(fam) nf* old shoe *or* slipper; *(maladroit)* clumsy oaf.

saveur [savœr] *nf (goût)* flavour; *(piment)* savour.

***savoir** [savwar] *v* know; *(être capable de)* know how to. **à savoir** namely, that is. **faire savoir à** inform. **sans le savoir** unknowingly. *nm* learning, knowledge.

savon [savɔ̃] *nm* soap. **savonner** *v* soap, lather. **savonneux** *adj* soapy.

savourer [savure] *v* savour. **savoureux** *adj* tasty; *(histoire)* spicy.

saxophone [saksofon] *nm* saxophone.

scabreux [skabrø] *adj* indecent, shocking; risky.

scandale [skɑ̃dal] *nm* scandal; scene, fuss. **scandaleux** *adj* scandalous. **scandaliser** *v* scandalize, shock.

Scandinavie [skɑ̃dinavi] *nf* Scandinavia. **scandinave** *adj* Scandinavian. **Scandinave** *n(m+f)* Scandinavian.

scaphandrier [skafɑ̃drije] *nm* diver.

scarlatine [skarlatin] *nf* scarlet fever.

sceau [so] *nm* seal; *(marque)* stamp.

scélérat [selera], **-e** *nm, nf* villain. *adj* wicked.

sceller [sele] *v* seal.

scénario [senarjo] *nm* scenario; *(dialogue, etc.)* screenplay.

scène [sɛn] *nf* scene; *(estrade, profession)* stage. **mettre en scène** present; *(pièce)* stage; *(film)* direct. **scénique** *adj* theatrical.

sceptique [sɛptik] *adj* sceptical. *n(m+f)* sceptic. **scepticisme** *nm* scepticism.

sceptre [sɛptrə] *nm* sceptre.

schéma [ʃema] *nm* diagram; *(résumé)* outline.

schizophrénie [skizofreni] *nf* schizophrenia. **schizophrène** *n(m+f)*, *adj* schizophrenic.

sciatique [sjatik] *nf* sciatica. *adj* sciatic.

scie [si] *nf* saw; *(péj: personne)* bore. **scie à découper** fretsaw. **scie à métaux** hacksaw.

sciemment [sjamɑ̃] *adv* knowingly.

science [sjɑ̃s] *nf* science; *(savoir)* knowledge. **science-fiction** *nf* science fiction.

scientifique [sjɑ̃tifik] *adj* scientific. *n(m+f)* scientist.

scintiller [sɛ̃tije] *v* sparkle, glitter; *(esprit)* scintillate.

scolaire [skɔlɛr] *adj* school, scholastic. **scolarité** *nf* schooling.

scooter [skutœr] *nm* scooter.

scorpion [skɔrpjɔ̃] *nm* scorpion. **Scorpion** *nm* Scorpio.

scotch¹ [skɔtʃ] *nm* (*boisson*) Scotch.
scotch² ® [skɔtʃ] *nm* sellotape ®.
scrupule [skrypyl] *nm* scruple. **sans scrupules** *adj* unscrupulous. **scrupuleux** *adj* scrupulous.
scruter [skryte] *v* scrutinize, examine.
scrutin [skrytɛ̃] *nm* (*vote*) ballot; (*élection*) poll.
sculpter [skylte] *v* sculpt. **sculpteur** *nm* sculptor. **sculpture** *nf* sculpture.
se [sə], **s'** *pron* (*réfléchi*) oneself; (*homme*) himself; (*femme*) herself; (*chose, animal*) itself; (*au pluriel*) themselves; (*réciproque*) each other.
séance [seɑ̃s] *nf* session; (*réunion*) meeting; (*théâtre*) performance.
séant [seɑ̃] *nm* (*fam*) behind, posterior. *adj* seemly.
seau [so] *nm* bucket.
sec, sèche [sɛk, sɛʃ] *adj* dry; (*raisin, etc.*) dried; (*maigre*) lean; (*dur*) hard, cold; (*bref*) curt; (*alcool*) neat. *nm* **à sec** dried-up; (*fam*) broke. **au sec** in a dry place. *nf* (*argot*) fag. *adv* hard. **sécheresse** *nf* dryness; hardness; coldness; curtness.
sécher [seʃe] *v* dry. **sèche-cheveux** *nm invar* hair-drier. **séchoir** *nm* drier. **séchoir à linge** clothes-horse.
second [səgɔ̃] *adj* second. *nm* second; (*étage*) second floor. **seconde** *nf* second; (*transport*) second class. **secondaire** *adj* secondary.
secouer [səkwe] *v* shake.
***secourir** [səkurir] *v* help.
secours [səkur] *nm* help, aid; (*mil*) relief. **au secours!** help! **de secours** (*de rechange*) spare; (*d'urgence*) emergency.
secousse [səkus] *nf* jolt, bump; shock; (*saccade*) jerk. **par secousses** jerkily.
secret, -ète [səkrɛ, -ɛt] *adj* secret; (*caché*) hidden. *nm* secret; (*silence, discrétion*) secrecy. **en secret** secretly, in secret.
secrétaire [səkretɛr] *n*(*m+f*) secretary. *nm* (*meuble*) writing desk.
sécréter [sekrete] *v* secrete. **sécrétion** *nf* secretion.
secte [sɛkt] *nf* sect. **sectaire** *adj* sectarian.
secteur [sɛktœr] *nm* sector; (*zone*) area; (*élec*) mains (supply).
section [sɛksjɔ̃] *nf* section; (*autobus*) fare stage.
séculaire [sekylɛr] *adj* a hundred years old; (*très vieux*) age-old; (*jeux, fête, etc.*) occurring once a century.
séculier [sekylje] *adj* secular.

sécurité [sekyrite] *nf* security; (*sûreté*) safety.
sédatif [sedatif] *nm, adj* sedative. **sédation** *nf* sedation.
sédiment [sedimɑ̃] *nm* sediment.
***séduire** [sedɥir] *v* seduce; (*attirer*) charm; (*plaire*) appeal to. **séduction** *nf* seduction; charm; appeal. **séduisant** *adj* seductive; appealing, attractive.
segment [sɛgmɑ̃] *nm* segment.
ségrégation [segregɑsjɔ̃] *nf* segregation.
seigle [sɛglə] *nm* rye.
seigneur [sɛɲœr] *nm* lord.
sein [sɛ̃] *nm* breast; (*milieu*) bosom.
séisme [seismə] *nm* earthquake; (*bouleversement*) upheaval.
seize [sɛz] *nm, adj* sixteen. **seizième** *n*(*m+f*), *adj* sixteenth.
séjour [seʒur] *nm* stay; (*demeure*) abode. **séjourner** *v* stay.
sel [sɛl] *nm* salt; (*esprit*) wit; (*piquant*) spice. **sel de cuisine/table** cooking/table salt.
sélection [selɛksjɔ̃] *nf* selection. **sélectif** *adj* selective.
sélectionner [selɛksjɔne] *v* select.
selle [sɛl] *nf* saddle. **seller** *v* saddle. **sellerie** *nf* saddlery; (*lieu*) harness room. **sellier** *nm* saddler.
selon [səlɔ̃] *prep* according to.
Seltz [sɛls] *nf* **eau de Seltz** soda water.
semaine [səmɛn] *nf* week.
sémantique [semɑ̃tik] *adj* semantic. *nf* semantics.
sémaphore [semafɔr] *nm* semaphore.
sembler [sɑ̃ble] *v* seem. **semblable** *adj* similar; (*tel*) such. **semblable à** like. **semblant** *nm* semblance. **faire semblant de** pretend.
semelle [səmɛl] *nf* sole. **semelle intérieure** insole. **semelles compensées** platform soles *pl*.
semence [səmɑ̃s] *nf* seed.
semer [səme] *v* sow; (*en dispersant*) scatter; (*parsemer*) sprinkle, dot.
semestre [səmɛstrə] *nm* half-year. **semestriel** *adj* half-yearly.
séminaire [seminɛr] *nm* (*université*) seminar; (*rel*) seminary.
semi-précieux *adj* semi-precious.
semoule [səmul] *nf* semolina.
sempiternel [sɛpitɛrnɛl] *adj* never-ending.
sénat [sena] *nm* senate. **sénateur** *nm* senator.

sénile [senil] *adj* senile. **sénilité** *nf* senility.

sens [sɑ̃s] *nm* sense; direction; (*signification*) meaning. **à sens unique** (*rue*) oneway. **bon sens** common sense. **dans le sens des aiguilles d'une montre** clockwise. **sens dessus dessous** upside down. **sens devant derrière** back to front. **sens interdit** no entry.

sensation [sɑ̃sasjɔ̃] *nf* sensation; (*impression*) feeling. **sensationnel** *adj* sensational; (*fam*) fantastic, terrific.

sensé [sɑ̃se] *adj* sensible.

sensible [sɑ̃siblə] *adj* sensitive; perceptible, noticeable; (*cœur*) tender; (*impressionnable*) susceptible. **sensibilité** *nf* sensitivity.

sensuel [sɑ̃sɥɛl] *adj* (*charnel*) sensual; (*esthétique*) sensuous. **sensualité** *nf* sensuality; sensuousness.

sentence [sɑ̃tɑ̃s] *nf* (*jur*) sentence; maxim.

sentier [sɑ̃tje] *nm* path.

sentiment [sɑ̃timɑ̃] *nm* feeling; (*péj*) sentiment. **sentimental** *adj* sentimental.

sentinelle [sɑ̃tinɛl] *nf* sentry.

****sentir** [sɑ̃tir] *v* feel; (*odeur*) smell; (*goût*) taste; (*pressentir*) sense; (*être conscient de*) be aware of.

****seoir** [swar] *v* be fitting. **seoir à** become.

séparer [separe] *v* separate; (*diviser*) part, split. **séparation** *nf* separation; parting; division. **séparé** *adj* separated; (*éloigné*) apart.

sept [sɛt] *nm, adj* seven. **septième** *n(m+f), adj* seventh.

septembre [sɛptɑ̃brə] *nm* September.

septentrional [sɛptɑ̃trijɔnal] *adj* northern.

septique [sɛptik] *adj* septic.

séquence [sekɑ̃s] *nf* sequence.

serein [sərɛ̃] *adj* serene, calm.

sérénade [serenad] *nf* serenade.

serf [sɛrf], **serve** *nm, nf* serf.

sergent [sɛrʒɑ̃] *nm* sergeant.

série [seri] *nf* series; (*ensemble*) set. **de série** standard. **fait en série** mass-produced. **hors série** (*machine*) custombuilt; (*qualité*) outstanding.

sérieux [serjø] *adj* serious; (*sage*) responsible; (*sûr*) reliable; (*grand*) considerable. *nm* seriousness. **prendre au sérieux** take seriously.

serin [sərɛ̃] *nm* canary.

seringue [sərɛ̃g] *nf* syringe.

serment [sɛrmɑ̃] *nm* oath.

sermon [sɛrmɔ̃] *nm* sermon.

serpent [sɛrpɑ̃] *nm* snake, serpent. **serpent à sonnettes** rattlesnake.

serpenter [sɛrpɑ̃te] *v* snake, wind.

serre [sɛr] *nf* greenhouse; (*contiguë à une maison*) conservatory; (*griffe*) talon. **serre chaude** hothouse.

serrer [sere] *v* grip; (*dents, poings*) clench; (*vêtement*) be tight; (*nœud, écrou*) tighten; (*rester près de*) keep close to; (*rapprocher*) close up. **serrer la main à** shake hands with. **se serrer** squeeze up, crowd together. **serré** *adj* tight; (*personnes*) packed, crowded; dense.

serrure [seryr] *nf* lock. **serrurier** *nm* locksmith.

servante [sɛrvɑ̃t] *nf* servant, maid.

serveur [sɛrvœr] *nm* (*restaurant*) waiter; (*bar*) barman. **serveuse** *nf* waitress; barmaid.

service [sɛrvis] *nm* service; (*travail*) duty; department; (*ensemble*) set. **être de service** be on duty. **service à thé** tea-set.

serviette [sɛrvjɛt] *nf* (*de toilette*) towel; (*de table*) serviette; (*cartable*) briefcase. **serviette hygiénique** sanitary towel.

servile [sɛrvil] *adj* servile. **servilité** *nf* servility.

****servir** [sɛrvir] *v* serve; (*dîneur, patron*) wait on; (*client*) attend to; aid. **servir à** be used for; (*être utile*) be useful for. **servir de** act as. **se servir** help oneself. **se servir de** use.

serviteur [sɛrvitœr] *nm* servant.

ses [se] *V* son¹.

session [sesjɔ̃] *nf* session.

seuil [sœj] *nm* threshold; (*porte*) doorway; (*dalle*) doorstep.

seul [sœl] *adj* only; (*sans compagnie*) alone; (*isolé*) lonely; (*unique*) single, sole. *adv* by oneself. **seulement** *adv* only.

sève [sɛv] *nf* sap.

sévère [sever] *adj* severe. **sévérité** *nf* severity.

sévir [sevir] *v* act ruthlessly; punish severely; (*régime, fléau*) rage.

sexe [sɛks] *nm* sex. **sexualité** *nf* sexuality. **sexuel** *adj* sexual, sex.

sextuor [sɛkstɥɔr] *nm* sextet.

shampooing [ʃɑ̃pwɛ̃] *nm* shampoo.

shérif [ʃerif] *nm* sheriff.

short [ʃɔrt] *nm* shorts *pl*.

si¹ [si], **s'** *conj* if.

si² [si] *adv* so; (*aussi*) as; (*oui*) yes. **si bien que** so that. **si ... que** however.

siamois [sjamwa] *adj* Siamese.

sidérer [sidere] *v* (*fam*) stagger, shatter.

siècle [sjɛklə] *nm* century; (*époque*) age.

siège [sjɛʒ] *nm* seat; (*organisation*) headquarters; (*épiscopal*) see; (*mil*) siege. **siège éjectable** ejector seat.

siéger [sjeʒe] *v* be located; (*tenir séance*) sit.

sien [sjɛ̃], **sienne** *pron* **le sien, la sienne** (*homme*) his; (*femme*) hers; (*chose, animal*) its own; (*réfléchi*) one's own.

sieste [sjɛst] *nf* siesta; (*petit somme*) nap.

siffler [sifle] *v* whistle; (*serpent, gaz*) hiss. **sifflement** *nm* whistle, hiss. **sifflet** *nm* whistle.

signal [siɲal] *nm* signal.

signaler [siɲale] *v* indicate; (*faire un signe*) signal; (*faire un exposé*) report. **se signaler** stand out, distinguish oneself. **signalement** *nm* description.

signature [siɲatyr] *nf* signature; (*action*) signing.

signe [siɲ] *nm* sign; mark. **faire signe à** beckon. **signet** *nm* bookmark.

signer [siɲe] *v* sign.

signifier [siɲifje] *v* mean, signify. **significatif** *adj* significant. **signification** *nf* significance, meaning.

silence [silɑ̃s] *nm* silence; pause; (*musique*) rest.

silencieux [silɑ̃sjø] *adj* silent. *nm* silencer.

silex [silɛks] *nm* flint.

silhouette [silwɛt] *nf* silhouette, outline; figure.

sillage [sijaʒ] *nm* wake.

sillon [sijɔ̃] *nm* furrow; (*disque*) groove. **sillonner** *v* furrow; (*traverser*) cross.

simagrée [simagre] *nf* pretence. **simagrées** *nf pl* fuss *sing*, play-acting *sing*.

simple [sɛ̃plə] *adj* simple; (*billet*) single. **simplement** *adv* simply; (*seulement*) merely, just. **simplicité** *nf* simplicity. **simplifier** *v* simplify.

simulacre [simylakrə] *nm* pretence, show.

simuler [simyle] *v* simulate; feign. **simulation** *nf* simulation. **simulé** *adj* simulated; feigned, sham.

simultané [simyltane] *adj* simultaneous.

sincère [sɛ̃sɛr] *adj* sincere; (*authentique*) genuine, true. **sincérité** *nf* sincerity.

singe [sɛ̃ʒ] *nm* monkey, ape.

singer [sɛ̃ʒe] *v* mimic, ape. **singeries** *nf pl* antics *pl*, clowning *sing*.

singulier [sɛ̃gylje] *adj* (*gramm*) singular; remarkable; uncommon. *nm* singular. **singularité** *nf* peculiarity. **singulièrement** *adv* remarkably; strangely; particularly.

sinistre [sinistrə] *adj* sinister. *nm* disaster; (*assurances*) damage, loss.

sinon [sinɔ̃] *conj* if not; (*autrement*) otherwise; (*sauf*) except, other than.

sinueux [sinɥø] *adj* winding; (*ligne*) sinuous.

sinus [sinys] *nm invar* (*anat*) sinus. **sinusite** *nf* sinusitis.

siphon [sifɔ̃] *nm* siphon. **siphonner** *v* siphon.

sirène [sirɛn] *nf* siren; (*mythologie*) mermaid.

sirop [siro] *nm* syrup; (*boisson*) squash, cordial. **sirupeux** *adj* syrupy.

siroter [sirɔte] *v* sip.

site [sit] *nm* site; (*environnement*) setting; (*tourisme*) beauty spot, place of interest.

sitôt [sito] *adv* immediately, no sooner. **sitôt que** as soon as.

situer [sitɥe] *v* situate, locate; (*par la pensée*) place. **situation** *nf* situation; position; (*emploi*) job.

six [sis] *nm, adj* six. **sixième** *n(m+f)*, *adj* sixth.

ski [ski] *nm* ski; (*sport*) skiing. **faire du ski** ski, go skiing. **ski nautique** water-skiing. **skieur, -euse** *nm, nf* skier.

slalom [slalɔm] *nm* slalom.

slip [slip] *nm* briefs *pl*, pants *pl*. **slip de bain** (*homme*) trunks *pl*.

slogan [slɔgɑ̃] *nm* slogan.

smoking [smɔkiŋ] *nm* dinner jacket.

snob [snɔb] *n(m+f)* snob. *adj* snobbish.

sobre [sɔbrə] *adj* temperate, abstemious; (*repas*) frugal; (*style*) sober. **sobriété** *nf* temperance; frugality; (*modération*) restraint; sobriety.

sobriquet [sɔbrikɛ] *nm* nickname.

sociable [sɔsjablə] *adj* sociable.

social [sɔsjal] *adj* social. **socialisme** *nm* socialism. **socialiste** *n(m+f)*, *adj* socialist.

société [sɔsjete] *nf* society; club; company. **société anonyme** limited company. **sociétaire** *n(m+f)* member.

sociologie [sɔsjɔlɔʒi] *nf* sociology. **sociologique** *adj* sociological. **sociologue** *n(m+f)* sociologist.

socle [sɔklə] *nm* base; pedestal.

socquette [sɔkɛt] *nf* ankle sock.
sœur [sœr] *nf* sister; (*rel*) nun.
sofa [sofa] *nm* sofa.
soi [swa] *pron* one, oneself. **aller de soi** be obvious, stand to reason. **soi-même** *pron* oneself.
soi-disant *adj invar* so-called. *adv* supposedly.
soie [swa] *nf* silk; (*poil*) bristle.
soif [swaf] *nf* thirst. **avoir soif** be thirsty.
soigner [swaɲe] *v* look after, take care of; (*malade*) treat. **soigné** *adj* neat, tidy; (*consciencieux*) carefully done. **soigneux** *adj* careful; (*soigné*) neat, tidy.
soin [swɛ̃] *nm* care.
soir [swar] *nm* evening. **ce soir** this evening, tonight. **soirée** *nf* evening; party; (*théâtre*) evening performance.
soit [swa] *adv* very well, so be it. *conj* whether; (*à savoir*) that is to say. **soit que** whether. **soit ... soit ...** either ... or
soixante [swasɑ̃t] *nm, adj* sixty. **soixantième** *n(m+f), adj* sixtieth.
soixante-dix *nm, adj* seventy. **soixante-dixième** *n(m+f), adj* seventieth.
soja [sɔʒa] *nm* soya.
sol [sɔl] *nm* ground; (*plancher*) floor; (*territoire*) soil.
solaire [sɔlɛr] *adj* solar; (*crème, etc.*) suntan.
soldat [sɔlda] *nm* soldier.
solde¹ [sɔld] *nf* pay.
solde² [sɔld] *nm* (*compte*) balance; (*vente*) sale; (*marchandises*) sale goods *pl*.
sole [sɔl] *nf* sole.
soleil [sɔlɛj] *nm* sun; (*lumière*) sunshine. **il fait du soleil** it's sunny.
solennel [sɔlanɛl] *adj* solemn; ceremonial. **solennité** *nf* solemnity; grand occasion.
solide [sɔlid] *adj* solid; (*sérieux, durable*) sound; robust, sturdy. *nm* solid. **solidarité** *nf* solidarity. **solidement** *adv* solidly; firmly. **solidifier** *v* solidify.
soliste [sɔlist] *n(m+f)* soloist.
solitaire [sɔlitɛr] *adj* solitary; deserted; (*seul, sans compagnie*) lonely. *n(m+f)* recluse. **solitairement** *adv* alone.
solitude [sɔlityd] *nf* solitude; loneliness.
solive [sɔliv] *nf* joist.
solliciter [sɔlisite] *v* appeal to; (*demander*) seek, request.
solo [sɔlo] *nm, adj invar* solo.
soluble [sɔlybl] *adj* soluble.
solution [sɔlysjɔ̃] *nf* solution.

solvable [sɔlvablə] *adj* solvent. **solvabilité** *nf* solvency.
sombre [sɔ̃brə] *adj* dark; (*morne*) sombre, gloomy.
sombrer [sɔ̃bre] *v* sink, founder.
sommaire [sɔmɛr] *adj* brief, basic. *nm* summary.
sommation [sɔmasjɔ̃] *nf* (*jur*) summons; demand.
somme¹ [sɔm] *nf* **bête de somme** *nf* beast of burden.
somme² [sɔm] *nm* nap, snooze. **faire un petit somme** have a nap.
somme³ [sɔm] *nf* sum, amount. **en somme** all in all; (*en résumé*) in short. **faire la somme de** add up. **somme toute** when all is said and done.
sommeil [sɔmɛj] *nm* sleep; (*envie de dormir*) sleepiness. **avoir sommeil** feel sleepy.
sommeiller [sɔmeje] *v* doze.
sommelier [sɔmalje] *nm* wine waiter.
sommer [sɔme] *v* (*jur*) summon.
sommet [sɔmɛ] *nm* summit, top.
somnambule [sɔmnãbyl] *n(m+f)* sleepwalker. **somnambulisme** *nm* sleep-walking.
somnifère [sɔmnifɛr] *nm* sleeping-pill.
somnoler [sɔmnɔle] *v* doze. **somnolent** *adj* sleepy, drowsy.
son¹ [sɔ̃], **sa** *adj, pl* **ses** (*homme*) his, (*femme*) her; (*chose, animal*) its; (*indéfini*) one's.
son² [sɔ̃] *nm* (*bruit*) sound.
son³ [sɔ̃] *nm* bran.
sonate [sɔnat] *nf* sonata.
sonder [sɔ̃de] *v* (*fouiller*) probe; (*naut*) sound; (*personne*) sound out; (*tech*) bore, drill. **sondage** *nm* probe; sounding; drilling; (*d'opinion*) poll. **sonde** *nf* probe; drill.
songer [sɔ̃ʒe] *v* (*rêver*) dream; reflect. **songer à** consider, think of. **songe** *nm* dream.
songeur, -euse [sɔ̃ʒœr, -øz] *adj* pensive. *nm, nf* dreamer.
sonique [sɔnik] *adj* sonic.
sonner [sɔne] *v* (*cloche, etc.*) ring; (*trompette, etc.*) sound; (*heure*) strike. **sonnerie** *nf* ringing; (*sonnette*) bell; (*pendule*) chimes *pl*. **sonnette** *nf* bell.
sonnet [sɔnɛ] *nm* sonnet.
sonore [sɔnɔr] *adj* resonant; (*rire, gifle, etc.*) resounding; (*film, onde, effet*) sound.

soprano [sɔprano] *n(m+f)* soprano.

sorcier [sɔrsje] *nm* sorcerer, wizard. **sorcière** *nf* witch. **sorcellerie** *nf* witchcraft, sorcery.

sordide [sɔrdid] *adj* sordid.

sort [sɔr] *nm* fate; (*condition*) lot; (*charme*) spell. **tirer au sort** draw lots.

sorte [sɔrt] *nf* sort, kind. **de la sorte** in that way. **de sorte que** so that. **en quelque sorte** in a way.

*sortir [sɔrtir] *v* go out; come out; (*quitter, partir*) leave; (*retirer*) take *or* bring out; (*film, disque*) release. **sortie** *nf* (*endroit, porte*) way out, exit; (*promenade*) outing; (*emportement*) outburst; publication; release. **sortie de secours** emergency exit.

sot, sotte [so, sɔt] *adj* silly, foolish. *nm, nf* fool. **sottise** *nf* silliness; silly thing.

sou [su] *nm* penny. **sans le sou** penniless.

soubresaut [subrəso] *nm* jolt, start.

souche [suʃ] *nf* (*arbre*) stump; (*talon*) stub; (*famille*) founder.

souci¹ [susi] *nm* (*bot*) marigold.

souci² [susi] *nm* (*tracas*) worry; (*préoccupation*) concern.

se soucier [susje] *v* **se soucier de** care about. **soucieux** *adj* concerned.

soucoupe [sukup] *nf* saucer.

soudain [sudɛ̃] *adj* sudden. *adv* suddenly.

soude [sud] *nf* soda.

souder [sude] *v* (*autogène*) weld; (*avec fil à souder*) solder; unite. **se souder** (*os*) knit together. **soudeur** *nm* welder; solderer. **soudure** *nf* welding; soldering; (*substance*) solder; (*endroit*) weld.

soudoyer [sudwaje] *v* bribe.

souffler [sufle] *v* blow; (*bougie*) blow out; (*se reposer*) get one's breath back; (*haleter*) puff, pant; (*dire*) whisper; (*théâtre*) prompt; (*fam: voler*) pinch; (*fam: étonner*) stagger. **souffle** *nm* blow, puff; (*respiration*) breathing; (*haleine*) breath; inspiration. **être à bout de souffle** be out of breath.

soufflet¹ [sufle] *nm* bellows *pl*; (*couture*) gusset.

soufflet² [sufle] *nm* (*gifle*) slap (in the face). **souffleter** *v* slap (in the face).

*souffrir [sufrir] *v* suffer; (*avoir mal*) be in pain; (*supporter*) endure, bear; (*permettre*) allow. **souffrance** *nf* suffering. **en souffrance** pending. **souffrant** *adj* suffering; (*malade*) unwell.

soufre [sufrə] *nm* sulphur.

souhait [swɛ] *nm* wish. **à souhait** to perfection, as well as one could wish. **souhaiter** *v* wish; (*espérer*) hope.

souiller [suje] *v* soil, dirty; (*réputation*) tarnish; (*profaner*) defile. **souillon** *nm* slut. **souillure** *nf* stain.

soûl [su] *adj* drunk. **tout son soûl** to one's heart's content. **soûlard, -e** *nm, nf* (*argot*) drunkard. **soûler** *v* intoxicate. **se soûler** get drunk.

soulager [sulaʒe] *v* relieve; (*conscience*) ease. **soulagement** *nm* relief.

soulever [sulve] *v* raise; (*lever*) lift; (*provoquer*) arouse, stir up. **soulèvement** *nm* uprising.

soulier [sulje] *nm* shoe.

souligner [suliɲe] *v* underline; accentuate, emphasize.

*soumettre [sumɛtrə] *v* (*dompter*) subject; (*présenter*) submit. **se soumettre** submit. **soumis** *adj* submissive. **soumission** *nf* submission; (*comm*) tender.

soupape [supap] *nf* valve.

soupçon [supsɔ̃] *nm* suspicion; (*ombre*) touch, hint; (*goutte*) drop. **soupçonner** *v* suspect. **soupçonneux** *adj* suspicious.

soupe [sup] *nf* soup.

soupente [supɑ̃t] *nf* cupboard (under the stairs).

souper [supe] *nm* supper. *v* have supper.

soupir [supir] *nm* sigh. **soupirer** *v* sigh.

soupirail [supiraj] *nm, pl* **-aux** basement window.

souple [suplə] *adj* supple; flexible; (*gracieux*) lithe. **souplesse** *nf* suppleness; flexibility; litheness.

source [surs] *nf* source; (*point d'eau*) spring.

sourcil [sursi] *nm* eyebrow.

sourd [sur], **-e** *adj* deaf; (*son, couleur*) muted; (*douleur*) dull; (*caché*) hidden. *nm, nf* deaf person.

sourd-muet, sourde-muette *adj* deaf and dumb. *nm, nf* deaf mute.

sourdine [surdin] *nf* mute.

souricière [surisjɛr] *nf* mousetrap.

*sourire [surir] *nm* smile. *v* smile.

souris [suri] *nf* mouse.

sournois [surnwa] *adj* underhand, deceitful; (*air*) shifty.

sous [su] *prep* under; (*temps*) within; (*pluie, soleil, etc.*) in.

sous-alimentation *nf* malnutrition.

*souscrire [suskrir] *v* subscribe; sign. **souscripteur, -trice** *nm, nf* subscriber. **souscription** *nf* subscription.

sous-développé *adj* underdeveloped.

sous-entendre *v* imply, infer.

sous-entendu *adj* understood. *nm* innuendo.

sous-estimer *v* underestimate, underrate. **sous-estimation** *nf* underestimation.

sous-jacent *adj* underlying.

sous-louer *v* sublet.

sous-marin *adj* underwater. *nm* submarine.

sous-payé *adj* underpaid.

sous-sol *nm* (*maison*) basement; (*terre*) subsoil.

sous-titre *nm* subtitle. **sous-titrer** *v* subtitle.

*soustraire [sustrɛr] *v* take away; (*math*) subtract; (*cacher*) shield. **se soustraire à** shirk, escape. **soustraction** *nf* subtraction.

sous-traiter *v* subcontract. **sous-traitant** *nm* subcontractor.

sous-vêtements *nm pl* underwear *sing*.

soutane [sutan] *nf* cassock.

*soutenir [sutnir] *v* support; (*faire durer*) sustain, keep up; (*résister à*) withstand; (*affirmer*) uphold. **soutenu** *adj* sustained; elevated.

souterrain [sutɛrɛ̃] *adj* underground. *nm* underground passage.

soutien [sutjɛ̃] *nm* support. **soutien de famille** breadwinner. **soutien-gorge** *nm* bra.

*souvenir [suvnir] *nm* memory; (*souvenance*) recollection; (*objet*) memento; (*pour touristes*) souvenir. *v* **se souvenir (de)** remember.

souvent [suvã] *adv* often. **peu souvent** seldom.

souverain [suvrɛ̃], **-e** *adj* supreme, sovereign. *nm, nf* sovereign.

soyeux [swajø] *adj* silky.

spacieux [spasjø] *adj* spacious.

spaghetti [spageti] *nm pl* spaghetti.

sparadrap [sparadra] *nm* sticking plaster.

spasme [spasmə] *nm* spasm. **spasmodique** *adj* spasmodic.

spatial [spasjal] *adj* spatial; (*voyage, engin, etc.*) space.

spatule [spatyl] *nf* spatula.

speaker, speakerine [spikœr, spikrin] *nm, nf* announcer.

spécial [spesjal] *adj* special; (*bizarre*)

peculiar. **spécialement** *adv* particularly, especially; (*exprès*) specially. **se spécialiser** *v* specialize. **spécialiste** *n(m+f)* specialist. **spécialité** *nf* speciality.

spécieux [spesjø] *adj* specious.

spécifier [spesifje] *v* specify, state. **spécification** *nf* specification. **spécifique** *adj* specific.

spécimen [spesimɛn] *nm* specimen; (*exemplaire*) sample copy.

spectacle [spɛktaklə] *nm* sight, spectacle; (*représentation*) show. **spectaculaire** *adj* spectacular.

spectateur, -trice [spɛktatœr, -tris] *nm, nf* onlooker; (*sport*) spectator. **spectateurs** *nm pl* (*théâtre*) audience *sing*.

spectre [spɛktrə] *nm* (*fantôme*) spectre; (*phys*) spectrum.

spéculer [spekyle] *v* speculate. **spéculatif** *adj* speculative. **spéculation** *nf* speculation.

spéléologie [speleɔlɔʒi] *nf* pot-holing. **spéléologue** *n(m+f)* pot-holer.

sperme [spɛrm] *nm* sperm.

sphère [sfɛr] *nf* sphere. **sphérique** *adj* spherical.

spinal [spinal] *adj* spinal.

spiral [spiral] *adj* spiral. **spirale** *nf* spiral.

spirite [spirit] *n(m+f)* spiritualist. **spiritisme** *nm* spiritualism.

spirituel [spiritɥɛl] *adj* spiritual; (*fin*) witty.

spiritueux [spiritɥø] *nm* (*liqueur*) spirit.

splendeur [splãdœr] *nf* splendour; glory. **splendide** *adj* splendid, magnificent.

spongieux [spɔ̃ʒjø] *adj* spongy.

spontané [spɔ̃tane] *adj* spontaneous. **spontanéité** *nf* spontaneity.

sporadique [spɔradik] *adj* sporadic.

sport [spɔr] *nm* sport. **de sport** sports.

sportif [spɔrtif] *adj* sports; competitive; (*personne*) athletic; (*attitude*) sporting. *nm* sportsman. **sportive** *nf* sportswoman.

square [skwar] *nm* square with public garden.

squelette [skɔlɛt] *nm* skeleton. **squelettique** *adj* skeletal; (*très maigre*) scrawny; (*exposé*) sketchy.

stabiliser [stabilize] *v* stabilize. **stabilisateur** *nm* stabilizer.

stable [stablə] *adj* stable. **stabilité** *nf* stability.

stade [stad] *nm* (*étape*) stage; (*sport*) stadium.

stage [staʒ] *nm* training period; training course. **stagiaire** *n(m+f)*, *adj* trainee, student.
stagnant [stagnɑ̃] *adj* stagnant. **stagnation** *nf* stagnation. **stagner** *v* stagnate.
stalle [stal] *nf* stall.
standard [stɑ̃dar] *nm* switchboard. *adj* standard. **standardiser** *v* standardize. **standardiste** *n(m+f)* switchboard operator.
starter [startɛr] *nm* (*auto*) choke; (*sport*) starter.
station [stɑsjɔ̃] *nf* station; (*halte*) stop; site; (*de vacances*) resort; posture. **station balnéaire** seaside resort. **station de taxis** taxi rank. **station-service** *nf* petrol station.
stationner [stasjɔne] *v* park. **stationnaire** *adj* stationary. **stationnement** *nm* parking.
statique [statik] *adj* static.
statistique [statistik] *nf* statistic; (*science*) statistics. *adj* statistical.
statue [staty] *nf* statue.
stature [statyr] *nf* stature.
statut [staty] *nm* status. **statuts** *nm pl* statutes, rules *pl*. **statutaire** *adj* statutory.
steeple [stiplə] *nm* steeplechase.
stencil [stɛnsil] *nm* stencil.
sténodactylo [stenɔdaktilo] *nf* (*personne*) shorthand typist; (*emploi*) shorthand typing.
sténographie [stenɔgrafi] *nf* shorthand.
stéréo [stereo] *nf*, *adj* stereo. **stéréophonique** [stereɔfɔnik] *adj* stereophonic.
stéréotype [stereɔtip] *nm* stereotype.
stérile [steril] *adj* sterile; (*terre*) barren; (*effort*) fruitless. **stérilet** *nm* (*méd*) coil. **stérilisation** *nf* sterilization. **stériliser** *v* sterilize. **stérilité** *nf* sterility; barrenness; fruitlessness.
stéthoscope [stetɔskɔp] *nm* stethoscope.
stigmate [stigmat] *nm* stigma; mark.
stimulant [stimylɑ̃] *adj* stimulating. *nm* stimulant; stimulus (*pl* -li).
stimuler [stimyle] *v* stimulate. **stimulation** *nf* stimulation.
stimulus [stimylys] *nm*, *pl* -li stimulus (*pl* -li).
stipuler [stipyle] *v* stipulate, specify. **stipulation** *nf* stipulation.
stock [stɔk] *nm* stock. **stocker** *v* stock; (*amasser*) stockpile.
Stockholm [stɔkɔlm] *n* Stockholm.

stoïque [stɔik] *adj* stoical. **stoïcisme** *nm* stoicism.
stop [stɔp] *interj* stop! *nm* (*panneau*) stop sign; (*feu*) brake light; (*fam*) hitch-hiking. **faire du stop** hitch-hike.
store [stɔr] *nm* blind; (*magasin*) awning.
strabisme [strabismə] *nm* squint.
strapontin [strapɔ̃tɛ̃] *nm* folding seat.
strate [strat] *nf* stratum (*pl* -ta).
stratégie [strateʒi] *nf* strategy. **stratégique** *adj* strategic.
strict [strikt] *adj* strict; (*tenue*) plain.
strident [stridɑ̃] *adj* strident, shrill.
strié [strije] *adj* streaked; (*en relief*) ridged.
strophe [strɔf] *nf* verse, stanza.
structure [stryktyr] *nf* structure. **structural** *adj* structural.
studieux [stydjø] *adj* studious.
studio [stydjo] *nm* studio; (*logement*) flatlet.
stupéfiant [stypefjɑ̃] *adj* astounding. *nm* drug, narcotic.
stupéfier [stypefje] *v* stun, astound. **stupéfaction** *nf* amazement. **stupéfait** *adj* astounded, dumbfounded.
stupeur [stypœr] *nf* amazement; (*méd*) stupor.
stupide [stypid] *adj* stupid, silly. **stupidité** *nf* stupidity.
style [stil] *nm* style.
stylo [stilo] *nm* pen. **stylo à bille** ball-point pen.
suaire [sɥer] *nm* shroud.
suant [sɥɑ̃] *adj* sweaty.
suave [sɥav] *adj* smooth; (*musique*, *etc*.) sweet. **suavité** *nf* smoothness; sweetness.
subalterne [sybaltern] *n(m+f)*, *adj* subordinate.
subconscient [sypkɔ̃sjɑ̃] *nm*, *adj* subconscious.
subdiviser [sybdivize] *v* subdivide. **subdivision** *nf* subdivision.
subir [sybir] *v* undergo; endure; suffer.
subit [sybi] *adj* sudden. **subitement** *adv* suddenly. **subito** *adv* (*fam*) suddenly, at once.
subjectif [sybʒektif] *adj* subjective.
subjonctif [sybʒɔ̃ktif] *nm*, *adj* subjunctive.
subjuguer [sybʒyge] *v* captivate.
sublime [syblim] *nm*, *adj* sublime.
submerger [sybmerʒe] *v* submerge; (*ennemi*, *émotion*) overwhelm; (*travail etc*.) swamp. **submersion** *nf* submersion.

subordonner [sybɔrdɔne] v subordinate.
subordination nf subordination.
subordonné, -e n, adj subordinate.
subreptice [sybrɛptis] adj surreptitious.
subsidiaire [sypsidjɛr] adj subsidiary.
subsister [sybziste] v survive, live; (rester) remain, subsist. **subsistance** nf subsistence, maintenance.
substance [sypstɑ̃s] nf substance. **substantiel** adj substantial.
substituer [sypstitɥe] v substitute. **substitution** nf substitution.
subtil [syptil] adj subtle. **subtilité** nf subtlety.
suburbain [sybyrbɛ̃] adj suburban.
*****subvenir** [sybvənir] v **subvenir à** meet, provide for.
subvention [sybvɑ̃sjɔ̃] nf grant, subsidy. **subventionner** v subsidize.
subversion [sybvɛrsjɔ̃] nf subversion. **subversif** adj subversive.
suc [syk] nm juice; essence, pith.
succédané [syksedane] nm substitute.
succéder [syksede] v **succéder à** succeed; (suivre) follow. **succès** nm success. **à succès** successful. **avec succès** successfully.
successeur nm successor. **successif** adj successive. **succession** nf succession.
succinct [syksɛ̃] adj succinct.
succion [syksjɔ̃] nf suction.
succomber [sykɔ̃be] v succumb, yield; (mourir) die.
succulent [sykylɑ̃] adj succulent, delicious.
succursale [sykyrsal] nf branch.
sucer [syse] v suck. **sucette** nf lollipop; (tétine) dummy.
sucre [sykrə] nm sugar. **sucre d'orge** barley sugar. **sucre en poudre** caster sugar. **sucre glace** icing sugar. **sucre semoule** granulated sugar. **sucré** adj sweet. **sucrer** v sweeten; (thé, café, etc.) put sugar in. **sucrier** nm sugar-basin.
sud [syd] nm south. adj invar south; (région) southern; (direction) southward. **sud-est** nm, adj invar south-east. **sud-ouest** nm, adj invar south-west.
suède [sɥɛd] nm suede.
Suède [sɥɛd] nf Sweden. **suédois** nm, adj Swedish. **Suédois, -e** nm, nf Swede.
suer [sɥe] v sweat. **sueur** nf sweat.
*****suffire** [syfir] v suffice, be enough or sufficient. **ça suffit** that will do, that's enough. **suffisant** adj sufficient; (résultat) satisfactory; (personne) self-important.

suffixe [syfiks] nm suffix.
suffoquer [syfɔke] v suffocate, choke. **suffocation** nf suffocation.
suffrage [syfraʒ] nm suffrage; (voix) vote; approbation, approval.
suggérer [sygʒere] v suggest. **suggestif** adj suggestive. **suggestion** nf suggestion.
se suicider [sɥiside] v commit suicide. **suicidaire** adj suicidal. **suicide** nm suicide. **suicidé, -e** nm, nf suicide.
suie [sɥi] nf soot.
suif [sɥif] nm tallow.
suinter [sɥɛ̃te] v ooze.
Suisse [sɥis] nf Switzerland. **les Suisses** the Swiss. **suisse** adj Swiss.
suite [sɥit] nf result, effect; succession, series; (musique, appartement) suite; (feuilleton) next episode, continuation; (roman, film) sequel; coherence, consistency. **de suite** in succession. **faire suite à** follow. **par la suite** afterwards, subsequently. **par suite** consequently. **suite à** (comm) further to. **tout de suite** at once, immediately.
suivant [sɥivɑ̃], **-e** adj next, following. nm, nf next (one). prep according to.
*****suivre** [sɥivrə] v follow; (cours) attend; (en classe) keep up (with). **faire suivre** forward. **suivi** adj consistent; regular; coherent.
sujet, -ette [syʒɛ, -ɛt] adj subject, liable, prone. nm subject; (d'examen) question. **au sujet de** about, concerning. **sujet de** cause for. nm, nf (personne) subject. **sujétion** nf subjection.
sultan [syltɑ̃] nm sultan.
superbe [sypɛrb] adj superb, magnificent.
supercherie [sypɛrʃəri] nf trick.
superficie [sypɛrfisi] nf surface area.
superficiel [sypɛrfisjɛl] adj superficial.
superflu [sypɛrfly] adj superfluous.
supérieur, -e [sypɛrjœr] adj upper; (hautain, meilleur) superior; (plus grand) greater; (plus haut) higher. nm, nf superior. **supériorité** nf superiority.
superlatif [sypɛrlatif] nm, adj superlative.
supermarché [sypɛrmarʃe] nm supermarket.
supersonique [sypɛrsɔnik] adj supersonic.
superstition [sypɛrstisjɔ̃] nf superstition. **superstitieux** adj superstitious.
suppléant [syplećɑ̃], **-e** adj temporary. nm, nf deputy; (professeur) supply teacher; (médecin) locum.

suppléer [syplee] *v* supply, provide; (*lacune*) fill in; (*manque*) make up (for); replace. **suppléer à** (*remédier*) make up for; (*remplacer*) substitute for.

supplément [syplemɑ̃] *nm* supplement; (*tarif*) extra charge; (*transport*) excess fare. **en supplément** extra. **supplémentaire** *adj* additional, extra, supplementary.

supplice [syplis] *nm* torture; torment. **dernier supplice** execution.

supplier [syplije] *v* implore, entreat.

support [sypɔr] *nm* support; (*moyen*) medium.

supporter [sypɔrte] *v* support; endure, bear; tolerate, put up with; (*résister à*) withstand. **supportable** *adj* bearable; tolerable.

supposer [sypoze] *v* suppose; imply. **supposition** *nf* supposition.

supprimer [syprime] *v* suppress; (*enlever*) remove; (*mot*) delete; abolish, do away with; (*train, etc.*) cancel. **suppression** *nf* suppression; removal; deletion; abolition; cancellation.

suprême [syprɛm] *adj* supreme. **suprématie** *nf* supremacy.

sur [syr] *prep* on; (*par-dessus*) over; (*au-dessus*) above; (*sujet*) about; (*proportion*) out of; (*mesure*) by; (*après*) after. **sur-le-champ** *adv* immediately.

sûr [syr] *adj* sure, certain; (*sans danger*) safe; (*sérieux*) reliable. **à coup sûr** definitely.

surabondance [syrabɔ̃dɑ̃s] *nf* overabundance. **surabondant** *adj* overabundant.

suranné [syrane] *adj* outdated, outmoded.

surcharger [syrʃarʒe] *v* overload. **surcharge** *nf* extra *or* excess load; (*surabondance*) surfeit; (*impôt*) surcharge. **surchauffer** [syrʃofe] *v* overheat.

surcroît [syrkrwa] *nm* excess; (*augmentation*) increase. **par surcroît** in addition.

surdité [syrdite] *nf* deafness.

surdose [syrdoz] *nf* overdose.

sureau [syro] *nm* elder. **baie du sureau** elderberry

surélever [syrelve] *v* raise, heighten.

surenchère [syrɑ̃ʃɛr] *nf* higher bid.

surestimer [syrɛstime] *v* overestimate.

sûreté [syrte] *nf* (*sécurité*) safety; (*précision*) reliability; guarantee.

surexposer [syrɛkspoze] *v* overexpose. **surexposition** *nf* overexposure.

surface [syrfas] *nf* surface; (*aire*) surface area. **faire surface** surface.

surfait [syrfɛ] *adj* overrated.

surgeler [syrʒəle] *v* deep-freeze.

surgir [syrʒir] *v* appear suddenly; (*jaillir*) spring up; (*problème, etc.*) arise.

surhumain [syrymɛ̃] *adj* superhuman.

surimpression [syrɛ̃presjɔ̃] *nf* superimposition. **en surimpression** superimposed.

surlendemain [syrlɑ̃dmɛ̃] *nm* next day but one. **le surlendemain** two days later.

surmener [syrmɛne] *v* overwork. **surmenage** *nm* overwork.

surmonter [syrmɔ̃te] *v* surmount; (*vaincre*) overcome; (*dôme, etc.*) top.

surnaturel [syrnatyrɛl] *nm, adj* supernatural.

surnom [syrnɔ̃] *nm* nickname. **surnommer** *v* nickname.

surnombre [syrnɔ̃brə] *nm* **en surnombre** too many.

surpasser [syrpase] *v* surpass.

surpeuplé [syrpœple] *adj* overpopulated, overcrowded. **surpeuplement** *nm* overpopulation, overcrowding.

surplomb [syrplɔ̃] *nm* overhang. **surplomber** *v* overhang.

surplus [syrply] *nm* surplus. **au surplus** moreover.

***surprendre** [syrprɑ̃drə] *v* surprise; discover, detect; (*prendre*) catch (out). **surpris** *adj* surprised. **surprise** *nf* surprise.

surréaliste [syrrealist] *adj* surrealistic. *n(m + f)* surrealist. **surréalisme** *nm* surrealism.

sursaut [syrso] *nm* start, jump. **sursauter** *v* start, jump.

***surseoir** [syrswar] *v* **surseoir à** defer, postpone. **sursis** *nm* reprieve.

surtaxer [syrtakse] *v* surcharge. **surtaxe** *nf* surcharge.

surtout [syrtu] *adv* above all; especially, particularly.

surveiller [syrveje] *v* (*garder, épier*) watch; (*contrôler*) supervise. **surveillance** *nf* watch; supervision. **surveillant, -e** *nm, nf* supervisor; (*prison*) warder; (*école*) person in charge of discipline.

***survenir** [syrvənir] *v* occur, take place; (*problème*) arise; (*personne*) arrive unexpectedly.

survêtement [syrvɛtmɑ̃] *nm* tracksuit.

***survivre** [syrvivrə] *v* survive. **survivre à** outlive. **survivance** *nf* survival. **survivant, -e** *nm, nf* survivor.

sus [sy] *adv* en sus in addition.
susceptible [sysɛptiblə] *adj* sensitive, touchy. susceptible à (*possible*) likely to; capable of.
susciter [sysite] *v* arouse; (*obstacles, etc.*) create.
susdit [sysdi] *adj* aforesaid.
suspect [syspɛkt], -e *adj* suspicious; (*douteux*) suspect. suspect de suspected of. *nm, nf* suspect.
suspendre [syspɑ̃drə] *v* suspend; (*fixer, accrocher*) hang (up). suspendu *adj* suspended; hanging.
suspens [syspɑ̃] *nm* en suspens (*projet, etc.*) in abeyance; in suspense; in suspension. suspense *nm* suspense.
suspension [syspɑ̃sjɔ̃] *nf* suspension.
susurrer [sysyre] *v* murmur.
suture [sytyr] *nf* suture. suturer *v* (*méd*) stitch (up).
svelte [svɛlt] *adj* slender.
sycomore [sikɔmɔr] *nm* sycamore.
syllabe [silab] *nf* syllable. syllabique *adj* syllabic.
sylvestre [silvɛstrə] *adj* forest, woodland. sylviculture *nf* forestry.
symbole [sɛ̃bɔl] *nm* symbol. symbolique *adj* symbolic; (*donation, contribution*) nominal. symboliser *v* symbolize. symbolisme *nm* symbolism.
symétrie [simetri] *nf* symmetry. symétrique *adj* symmetrical.
sympathie [sɛ̃pati] *nf* liking; affinity. sympathique *adj* nice, pleasant; (*personne*) likeable, friendly.
symphonie [sɛ̃fɔni] *nf* symphony. symphonique *adj* symphonic.
symposium [sɛ̃pozjɔm] *nm* symposium.
symptôme [sɛ̃ptɔm] *nm* symptom; sign. symptomatique *adj* symptomatic.
synagogue [sinagɔg] *nf* synagogue.
synchroniser [sɛ̃krɔnize] *v* synchronize. synchronisation *nf* synchronization.
syncoper [sɛ̃kɔpe] *v* (*musique*) syncopate. syncope *nf* syncopation; (*méd*) black-out, fainting fit.
syndicat [sɛ̃dika] *nm* syndicate; (*ouvrier*) union; association. syndicat d'initiative tourist information bureau. syndical *adj* union. syndicaliste *n(m+f)* trade unionist. syndiqué, -e *nm, nf* union member.
syndrome [sɛ̃drom] *nm* syndrome.
synonyme [sinɔnim] *nm* synonym. *adj* synonymous.
syntaxe [sɛ̃taks] *nf* syntax.

synthèse [sɛ̃tɛz] *nf* synthesis (*pl* -ses). synthétique *adj* synthetic. synthétiser *v* synthesize.
syphilis [sifilis] *nf* syphilis.
système [sistɛm] *nm* system. systématique *adj* systematic.

T

t' [t] *V* te.
ta [ta] *V* ton[1].
tabac [taba] *nm* tobacco; (*magasin*) tobacconist's. tabac à priser snuff. tabatière *nf* snuffbox.
table [tablə] *nf* table; tablet. faire table rase make a clean sweep. table basse coffee table. table des matières table of contents. table gigogne nest of tables. table roulante trolley.
tableau [tablo] *nm* picture; (*peinture*) painting; scene; (*support, panneau*) board; list; (*graphique*) table, chart. tableau de bord dashboard. tableau noir blackboard.
tablette [tablɛt] *nf* tablet; (*rayon*) shelf; (*chocolat*) bar.
tablier [tablije] *nm* apron.
tabou [tabu] *nm, adj* taboo.
tabouret [taburɛ] *nm* stool.
tache [taʃ] *nf* mark, spot; (*sang, vin, etc.*) stain; (*pâté*) blot. tache de rousseur or son freckle. tacher *v* mark; stain.
tâche [taʃ] *nf* task, work. tâcher *v* try, endeavour.
tacheté [taʃte] *adj* speckled, spotted.
tacite [tasit] *adj* tacit.
taciturne [tasityrn] *adj* taciturn.
tact [takt] *nm* tact. avoir du tact be tactful.
tactique [taktik] *nf* tactics *pl. adj* tactical.
taffetas [tafta] *nm* taffeta.
taie [tɛ] *nf* taie d'oreiller pillowcase.
taillade [tajad] *nf* slash, gash. taillader *v* slash, gash.
taille [tɑj] *nf* size; (*hauteur*) height; (*corps, vêtement*) waist; (*coupe*) cutting, cut; (*tranchant*) edge. à la taille de in keeping with. être de taille à be up to.
tailler [tɑje] *v* cut; (*bois*) carve; (*barbe, haie, etc.*) trim; (*crayon*) sharpen. taille-

crayon nm invar pencil sharpener. **tailleur** nm (personne) tailor; (costume) suit.

taillis [taji] nm copse.

*taire [tɛr] v conceal, hush up. **faire taire** silence. **se taire** be quiet.

talc [talk] nm talcum powder.

talent [talɑ̃] nm talent. **talentueux** adj talented.

talon [talɔ̃] nm heel; (chèque) stub; (pain) crust.

talonner [talɔne] v (suivre) follow closely; (harceler) hound; (cheval) spur on.

talus [taly] nm embankment.

tambour [tɑ̃bur] nm drum; (joueur) drummer. **tambourin** nm tambourine. **tambouriner** v drum.

tamis [tami] nm sieve. **tamiser** v sieve, sift; filter.

Tamise [tamiz] nf **la Tamise** the Thames.

tampon [tɑ̃pɔ̃] nm pad, wad; (pour boucher) plug; (pour règles) tampon; (timbre) stamp; (rail) buffer. **tamponner** v dab, mop; stamp; plug; (heurter) crash into.

tancer [tɑ̃se] v scold, reprimand.

tandem [tɑ̃dɛm] nm tandem; (couple) pair.

tandis [tɑ̃di] conj **tandis que** while; (contraste) whereas.

tangente [tɑ̃ʒɑ̃t] nf tangent.

tangible [tɑ̃ʒiblə] adj tangible.

tanguer [tɑ̃ge] v pitch, reel.

tanière [tanjɛr] nf den, lair.

tanner [tane] v tan; (fam) pester, annoy.

tan-sad [tɑ̃sad] nm pillion.

tant [tɑ̃] adv so much, so. **en tant que** as. **tant de** (quantité) so much; (nombre) so many; (qualité) such. **tant mieux** so much the better. **tant pis** too bad. **tant que** as long as, while. **tant s'en faut** far from it.

tante [tɑ̃t] nf aunt.

tantôt [tɑ̃to] adv this afternoon. **tantôt . . . tantôt . . .** sometimes . . . sometimes . . . .

taon [tɑ̃] nm horse-fly.

tapage [tapaʒ] nm (vacarme) uproar, din; (scandale) fuss. **tapageur, -euse** adj rowdy; (criard) showy, flashy.

taper [tape] v knock, hit; (battre) beat; (à la machine) type. **taper sur les nerfs de quelqu'un** get on someone's nerves. **tape** nf slap.

tapioca [tapjɔka] nm tapioca.

se tapir [tapir] v crouch; (se cacher) hide away.

tapis [tapi] nm carpet; (carpette) rug; (natte) mat; (table) cloth, covering. **tapis de sol** groundsheet. **tapis roulant** conveyor belt.

tapisser [tapise] v cover; (sol) carpet; (mur) paper. **tapisserie** nf tapestry; (papier peint) wallpaper. **tapissier** nm upholsterer; (maison) interior decorator.

tapoter [tapɔte] v pat, tap.

taquin [takɛ̃] adj teasing. **taquiner** v tease; (inquiéter) bother, worry. **taquinerie** nf teasing.

tard [tar] adv late.

tarder [tarde] v (différer) delay, put off; (être lent) take a long time, be long. **tardif** adj late; (remords, etc.) belated.

tarif [tarif] nm tariff, rate; (tableau) price list; (transport) fare.

tarir [tarir] v run dry, dry up.

tarte [tart] nf tart. **tartelette** nf tart. **tartine** nf slice of bread (and butter). **tartiner** v spread.

tartre [tartrə] nm tartar; (bouilloire) fur.

tas [tɑ] nm pile, heap; (fam: foule) crowd. **un tas de** (fam) loads of, lots of.

tasse [tɑs] nf cup. **tasse à thé/café** tea/coffee cup.

tasser [tɑse] v pack (down), cram. **se tasser** (se serrer) squeeze up; (s'affaisser) settle; (corps) shrink.

tâter [tɑte] v (palper) feel; (opinion, etc.) sound out; (essayer) try out.

tâtonner [tɑtɔne] v grop along or around, feel one's way. **par tâtonnements** by trial and error.

tâtons [tɑtɔ̃] adv **avancer à tâtons** feel one's way along. **chercher à tâtons** feel around for.

tatouer [tatwe] v tattoo. **tatouage** nm tattoo.

taudis [todi] nm slum.

taule [tol] nf (argot: prison) nick.

taupe [top] nf mole.

taureau [tɔro] nm bull. **Taureau** nm Taurus.

taux [to] nm rate; degree, level. **taux de change** exchange rate.

taxer [takse] v tax; (comm) fix the price of; accuse. **taxation** nf taxation. **taxe** nf tax; (douane) duty; fixed price.

taxi [taksi] nm taxi.

Tchécoslovaquie [tʃekɔslɔvaki] nf Czechoslovakia. **tchécoslovaque** nm, adj Czechoslovak. **Tchécoslovaque** n(m+f) Czechoslovak. **tchèque** *nm, adj* Czech. **Tchèque** *n(m+f)* Czech.

te [tə], **t'** *pron* you, to you; *(réfléchi)* yourself.

technique [tɛknik] *adj* technical. *nf* technique. **technicien, -enne** *nm, nf* technician. **technologie** *nf* technology. **technologique** *adj* technological.

teck [tɛk] *nm* teak.

***teindre** [tɛ̃drə] *v* dye; colour, tinge.

teint [tɛ̃] *adj* dyed. *nm* complexion, colouring. **teinte** *nf* shade, tint; colour; *(trace)* tinge, hint.

teinter [tɛ̃te] *v (verre)* tint; *(bois)* stain. **teinture** [tɛ̃tyr] *nf (substance)* dye; *(action)* dyeing. **teinturerie** *nf* cleaner's.

tel [tɛl], **telle** *adj* such (a), like, as. **tel que** such as, like. **tel quel** as it stands, as it is. *pron* one, someone.

télécommande [telekɔmɑ̃d] *nf* remote control.

télécommunications [telekɔmynikasjɔ̃] *nf pl* telecommunications *pl.*

télégramme [telegram] *nm* telegram.

télégraphier [telegrafje] *v* telegraph, cable. **télégraphe** *nm* telegraph. **télégraphique** *adj* telegraphic; *(poteau)* telegraph.

télépathie [telepati] *nf* telepathy. **télépathique** *adj* telepathic.

téléphérique [teleferik] *nm* cable-car.

téléphone [telefɔn] *nm* telephone, phone. **téléphoner** *v* telephone, phone. **téléphonique** *adj* telephone. **téléphoniste** *n(m+f)* telephonist.

télescope [teleskɔp] *nm* telescope. **télescopique** *adj* telescopic.

télésiège [telesjɛʒ] *nm* chair-lift.

téléski [teleski] *nm* ski-lift.

téléviser [televize] *v* televise. **télévision** *nf* television. **téléviseur** *nm* television set.

télex [telɛks] *nm* telex.

tellement [tɛlmɑ̃] *adv* so (much). **pas tellement** not (very) much.

téméraire [temerɛr] *adj* rash, reckless. **témérité** *nf* rashness, recklessness.

témoigner [temwaɲe] *v* testify; *(montrer)* show, reveal. **témoigner de** bear witness to. **témoignage** *nm* evidence, testimony; *(récit)* account; expression; *(cadeau)* token. **témoin** *nm* witness; evidence, testimony; *(sport)* baton.

tempe [tɑ̃p] *nf* temple.

tempérament [tɑ̃peramɑ̃] *nm* temperament, disposition; constitution. **achat à tempérament** *nm* hire purchase.

température [tɑ̃peratyr] *nf* temperature.

tempérer [tɑ̃pere] *v* temper; *(douleur)* soothe. **tempéré** *adj* temperate.

tempête [tɑ̃pɛt] *nf* storm. **tempétueux** *adj* stormy, tempestuous.

temple [tɑ̃plə] *nm* temple; Protestant church.

tempo [tɛmpo] *nm* tempo.

temporaire [tɑ̃pɔrɛr] *adj* temporary.

temporel [tɑ̃pɔrɛl] *adj* temporal, worldly.

temps [tɑ̃] *nm* time; *(météorologie)* weather; *(musique)* beat; *(gramm)* tense. **à temps** in time. **de temps en temps** now and again. **quel temps fait-il?** what's the weather like?

tenace [tənas] *adj* stubborn, persistent, tenacious. **ténacité** *nf* stubbornness, persistence, tenacity.

tenailles [tənɑj] *nf pl* pincers *pl.* **tenailler** *v* torture, torment.

tendance [tɑ̃dɑ̃s] *nf* tendency; *(évolution)* trend; *(opinions)* leanings *pl.* **avoir tendance à** tend to.

tendon [tɑ̃dɔ̃] *nm* tendon.

tendre[1] [tɑ̃drə] *v (raidir)* tighten; *(tirer sur)* stretch; *(muscle)* tense; *(poser)* set; *(tapisserie, etc.)* hang; *(présenter)* hold out. **tendre à** tend to; *(viser à)* aim at or to. **tendre le cou** crane one's neck. **tendre l'oreille** prick up one's ears. **tendu** *adj* taut, tight; tense; *(bras)* outstretched. **tendu de** hung with.

tendre[2] [tɑ̃drə] *adj* tender; soft, delicate. **tendresse** *nf* tenderness, affection. **tendreté** *nf* tenderness.

ténèbres [tenɛbrə] *nf pl* darkness *sing,* gloom *sing.* **ténébreux** *adj* dark, gloomy; obscure; mysterious.

***tenir** [tənir] *v* hold; *(garder)* keep; *(avoir)* have; *(magasin, etc.)* run; *(occuper)* take up; *(durer)* last. **se tenir** *(se conduire)* behave; *(debout)* stand. **se tenir à** hold on to. **se tenir à** *(vouloir)* be anxious to, insist on; *(aimer)* be fond of; *(résulter)* stem from. **tenir compte de** take into account. **tenir de** take after. **tenir pour** regard as.

tennis [tenis] *nm* tennis; tennis court. *nf pl* plimsolls *pl.*

ténor [tenɔr] *nm* tenor.

tension [tɑ̃sjɔ̃] *nf* tension; *(méd)* blood pressure; *(élec)* voltage.

tentacule [tɑ̃takyl] *nm* tentacle.

tente [tɑ̃t] *nf* tent.

tenter [tɑ̃te] *v* (*tentation*) tempt; (*tentative*) attempt. **tentation** *nf* temptation. **tentative** *nf* attempt.

tenture [tɑ̃tyr] *nf* hanging; (*rideau*) curtain.

tenu [təny] *adj* **bien tenu** neat, well-kept. **être tenu de** be obliged to. **mal tenu** untidy, neglected. **tenue** *nf* (*habillement*) dress; (*maintien*) posture; (*conduite*) manners *pl*; (*magasin, etc.*) running; control.

ténu [teny] *adj* fine; (*subtil*) tenuous.

térébenthine [terebɑ̃tin] *nf* turpentine.

tergiverser [tɛrʒivɛrse] *v* prevaricate.

terme [tɛrm] *nm* term; (*date limite*) deadline; (*loyer*) rent. **avant terme** prematurely.

terminaison [tɛrminɛzɔ̃] *nf* ending.

terminal [tɛrminal] *adj* terminal. **terminale** *nf* (*classe*) upper sixth.

terminer [tɛrmine] *v* end, finish, terminate.

terminologie [tɛrminɔlɔʒi] *nf* terminology.

terminus [tɛrminys] *nm* terminus.

ternir [tɛrnir] *v* tarnish, dull. **terne** *adj* dull, drab.

terrain [tɛrɛ̃] *nm* ground, land; (*sport*) pitch, field; (*parcelle*) plot, site. **terrain de jeu** playing field. **terrain vague** wasteland.

terrasse [tɛras] *nf* terrace.

terrasser [tɛrase] *v* overcome, overwhelm.

terre [tɛr] *nf* earth; (*sol*) ground; (*étendue, pays*) land. **à terre** ashore. **par terre** on the ground. **terre-à-terre** *adj invar* down-to-earth.

terrestre [tɛrɛstrə] *adj* earthly, terrestrial.

terreur [tɛrœr] *nf* terror.

terrible [tɛriblə] *adj* terrible, dreadful; (*fam*) terrific.

terrier [tɛrje] *nm* hole; (*lapin*) burrow; (*renard*) earth; (*race de chien*) terrier.

terrifier [tɛrifje] *v* terrify.

terrine [tɛrin] *nf* earthenware dish; pâté.

territoire [tɛritwar] *nm* territory. **territorial** *adj* territorial.

terroir [tɛrwar] *nm* soil.

terroriser [tɛrɔrize] *v* terrorize. **terrorisme** *nm* terrorism. **terroriste** *n*(*m*+*f*), *adj* terrorist.

tes [te] *V* **ton**[1].

tesson [tesɔ̃] *nm* piece of broken glass.

testament [tɛstamɑ̃] *nm* testament; (*jur*) will.

testicule [tɛstikyl] *nm* testicle.

tétanos [tetanos] *nm* tetanus.

têtard [tɛtar] *nm* tadpole.

tête [tɛt] *nf* head; (*visage*) face; (*devant*) front; (*haut*) top; (*esprit*) mind. **en tête** in front; at the top. **tenir tête à** stand up to. **tête-à-tête** *nm invar* private conversation.

tétine [tetin] *nf* teat; (*vache*) udder; (*sucette*) dummy.

têtu [tety] *adj* stubborn.

texte [tɛkst] *nm* text; passage; subject. **textuel** *adj* textual.

textile [tɛkstil] *nm, adj* textile.

texture [tɛkstyr] *nf* texture.

thé [te] *nm* tea. **théière** *nf* teapot.

théâtre [teatrə] *nm* theatre; drama. **théâtral** *adj* theatrical; dramatic.

thème [tɛm] *nm* theme; (*traduction*) prose. **thématique** *adj* thematic.

théologie [teɔlɔʒi] *nf* theology. **théologien, -enne** *nm, nf* theologian. **théologique** *adj* theological.

théorème [teɔrɛm] *nm* theorem.

théorie [teɔri] *nf* theory. **théorique** *adj* theoretical.

thérapeutique [terapøtik] *adj* therapeutic. *nf also* **thérapie** therapy. **thérapeute** *n*(*m*+*f*) therapist.

thermal [tɛrmal] *adj* thermal. **station thermale** *nf* spa.

thermique [tɛrmik] *adj* thermal, heat.

thermodynamique [tɛrmɔdinamik] *nf* thermodynamics.

thermomètre [tɛrmɔmɛtrə] *nm* thermometer.

thermonucléaire [tɛrmɔnykleɛr] *adj* thermonuclear.

thermos ® [tɛrmos] *nm* thermos flask ®.

thermostat [tɛrmɔsta] *nm* thermostat.

thésauriser [tezɔrize] *v* hoard (money).

thèse [tɛz] *nf* thesis.

thon [tɔ̃] *nm* tuna.

thym [tɛ̃] *nm* thyme.

thyroïde [tirɔid] *nf, adj* thyroid.

tiare [tjar] *nf* tiara.

tic [tik] *nm* tic, twitch; (*manie*) mannerism.

ticket [tikɛ] *nm* ticket.

tic-tac [tiktak] *nm* tick, ticking. **faire tic-tac** tick.

tiède [tjɛd] *adj* lukewarm, tepid; *(doux)* mild.

tien [tjɛ̃], **tienne** *pron* **le tien, la tienne** yours.

tiens [tjɛ̃] *interj* well! *(en donnant)* here! *(en expliquant)* look!

tiers, tierce [tjɛr, tjɛrs] *adj* third. **Tiers-Monde** *nm* Third World. *nm* third; *(jur)* third party. *nf (musique)* third.

tige [tiʒ] *nf* stem, stalk; *(métal)* rod.

tigre [tigrə] *nm* tiger. **tigré** *adj (tacheté)* spotted; *(rayé)* striped. **chat tigré** *nm* tabby cat.

tilleul [tijœl] *nm* lime tree.

timbale [tɛ̃bal] *nf* kettledrum; *(gobelet)* metal tumbler. **timbales** *nf pl* timpani *pl*.

timbre [tɛ̃brə] *nm* stamp; *(son)* tone; *(sonnette)* bell. **timbrer** *v* stamp; *(d'un cachet)* postmark.

timide [timid] *adj* timid; *(mal à l'aise)* shy. **timidité** *nf* timidity; shyness.

tintamarre [tɛ̃tamar] *nm* din.

tinter [tɛ̃te] *v* ring; *(clochette)* tinkle; *(clefs, monnaie, etc.)* jingle; *(verres)* chink.

tir [tir] *nm* firing; *(feu)* fire; *(sport)* shooting. **tir à l'arc** archery.

tirailler [tiraje] *v* tug *or* pull at; *(harceler)* plague; *(douleur)* gnaw *or* stab at. **tiraillement** *nm* pulling, tugging; conflict; stabbing *or* gnawing pain.

tirelire [tirlir] *nf* money-box.

tirer [tire] *v* pull, draw; extract, get out, take from; *(fusil)* fire, shoot; *(imprimer)* print. **se tirer de** *(s'échapper)* get out of; *(se débrouiller)* handle, cope with. **tire-bouchon** *nm* corkscrew. **tirage** *nm* printing; *(journal)* circulation; edition; *(loterie)* draw.

tiroir [tirwar] *nm* drawer. **tiroir-caisse** *nm* till.

tisane [tizan] *nf* herb tea.

tisonner [tizɔne] *v* poke. **tisonnier** *nm* poker.

tisser [tise] *v* weave. **tissage** *nm* weaving.

tissu [tisy] *nm* cloth, fabric, material; *(bot, anat)* tissue.

titre [titrə] *nm* title; *(diplôme)* qualification; *(bourse)* bond, security; *(droit)* right, claim. **à ce titre** as such. **à titre de** as, in the capacity of.

tituber [titybe] *v* stagger.

toast [tost] *nm* toast.

toboggan [tɔbɔgɑ̃] *nm* toboggan; *(glissière)* slide, chute.

toi [twa] *pron* you. **toi-même** *pron* yourself.

toile [twal] *nf* cloth; *(grosse)* canvas; linen; cotton; *(araignée)* web. **toile cirée** oilskin. **toile de fond** backcloth, backdrop.

toilette [twalɛt] *nf (soins de propreté)* wash; *(habillement)* outfit, clothes *pl*. **toilettes** *nf pl* toilet *sing*.

toison [twazɔ̃] *nf* fleece.

toit [twa] *nm* roof.

Tokio [tɔkjo] *n* Tokyo.

tôle [tol] *nf* metal sheet. **tôle ondulée** corrugated iron.

tolérer [tɔlere] *v* tolerate; endure, stand. **tolérable** *adj* tolerable. **tolérance** *nf* tolerance, toleration. **tolérant** *adj* tolerant.

tomate [tɔmat] *nf* tomato.

tombe [tɔ̃b] *nf* grave, tomb. **tombeau** *nm* tomb.

tomber [tɔ̃be] *v* fall; *(baisser)* drop; *(pendre)* hang. **laisser tomber** drop. **tomber juste** be exactly right. **tomber sur** come across. **tombée** *nf* fall.

tome [tɔm] *nm* volume.

ton[1] [tɔ̃], **ta** *adj*, *pl* **tes** your.

ton[2] [tɔ̃] *nm* tone; *(hauteur)* pitch; *(échelle musicale)* key.

tondre [tɔ̃drə] *v* clip; *(mouton)* shear; *(pelouse)* mow. **tondeuse** *nf* shears *pl*; clippers *pl*; lawn-mower. **tondu** *adj* closely-cropped.

tonifier [tɔnifje] *v* tone up, invigorate. **tonifiant** *adj* invigoratìng, bracing.

tonique [tɔnik] *nm* tonic. *nf (musique)* tonic.

tonne [tɔn] *nf* ton.

tonneau [tɔno] *nm* barrel.

tonner [tɔne] *v* thunder. **tonnerre** *nm* thunder.

topaze [tɔpaz] *nf* topaz.

toper [tɔpe] *v* agree. **tope-là!** *(fam)* it's a deal!

topographie [tɔpɔgrafi] *nf* topography. **topographique** *adj* topographical.

torche [tɔrʃ] *nf* torch.

torcher [tɔrʃe] *v (fam)* wipe.

torchon [tɔrʃɔ̃] *nm* cloth; *(à vaisselle)* tea towel; *(chiffon)* duster.

tordre [tɔrdrə] *v* twist; *(linge, cou)* wring; *(déformer)* distort. **se tordre de douleur/rire** be doubled up with pain/laughter. **tordu** *adj* twisted, crooked.

tornade [tɔrnad] *nf* tornado.
torpille [tɔrpij] *nf* torpedo. **torpiller** *v* torpedo.
torréfier [tɔrefje] *v* roast.
torrent [tɔrɑ̃] *nm* torrent. **torrentiel** *adj* torrential.
tors [tɔr] *adj* twisted, crooked.
torse [tɔrs] *nm* torso; (*poitrine*) chest.
tort [tɔr] *nm* wrong; fault; (*dommage*) harm. **à tort** wrongly. **avoir tort** be wrong.
torticolis [tɔrtikɔli] *nm* stiff neck.
tortiller [tɔrtije] *v* twist; (*cheveux, doigts*) twiddle; (*hanches*) wiggle. **se tortiller** wriggle; (*fumée*) curl.
tortue [tɔrty] *nf* tortoise. **tortue de mer** turtle.
tortueux [tɔrtЧø] *adj* (*chemin, etc.*) twisting, winding; (*oblique*) tortuous.
torturer [tɔrtyre] *v* torture. **torture** *nf* torture.
tôt [to] *adv* early, soon. **tôt ou tard** sooner or later.
total [tɔtal] *adj* total; complete, absolute. *nm* total. **totaliser** *v* total. **totalitaire** *adj* totalitarian. **totalité** *nf* whole. **la totalité de** all (of).
toucher [tuʃe] *v* touch; concern, affect; (*être contigu*) adjoin; (*frapper*) hit; contact, reach; (*pension, etc.*) draw; (*chèque*) cash; (*salaire*) get. **toucher à** touch; (*modifier*) meddle with; approach. *nm* touch. **touche** *nf* touch; (*piano*) key.
touffe [tuf] *nf* tuft; (*arbres, fleurs*) clump. **touffu** *adj* bushy, thick; (*roman*) complex.
toujours [tuʒur] *adv* always; (*encore*) still; (*en tout cas*) anyway.
toupet [tupɛ] *nm* (*cheveux*) quiff; (*fam*) nerve, cheek.
toupie [tupi] *nf* spinning-top.
tour[1] [tur] *nf* tower.
tour[2] [tur] *nm* turn; (*excursion*) trip; (*tourisme*) tour; (*poitrine, taille, etc.*) measurement; (*farce, ruse*) trick; (*tech*) lathe. **à tour de rôle** in turn. **faire le tour de** go round. **tour de main** knack. **tour de piste** lap.
tourbe [turb] *nf* peat.
tourbillon [turbijɔ̃] *nm* (*vent*) whirlwind; (*eau*) whirlpool; (*vie, plaisir, etc.*) whirl. **tourbillonner** *v* whirl, swirl.
tourelle [turɛl] *nf* turret.
tourisme [turism] *nm* (*industrie*) tour-

ism; (*activité*) sightseeing. **touriste** *n(m+f)* tourist. **touristique** *adj* tourist.
tourment [turmɑ̃] *nm* agony, torment. **tourmenter** *v* torment. **se tourmenter** fret, worry.
tourmente [turmɑ̃t] *nf* storm; (*pol*) upheaval.
tournant [turnɑ̃] *adj* (*pivotant*) revolving, swivel; (*escalier*) spiral; (*sinueux*) winding, twisting. *nm* bend; (*moment décisif*) turning point.
tourner [turne] *v* turn; (*film*) make, shoot; (*lait*) turn sour; (*disque, etc.*) revolve, go round; (*moteur*) run. **bien/mal tourner** turn out well/badly.
tourne-disque *nm* record player.
tournevis *nm* screwdriver. **tournée** *nf* round; tour.
tournesol [turnəsɔl] *nm* sunflower.
tourniquet [turnikɛ] *nm* (*barrière*) turnstile; (*méd*) tourniquet.
tournoi [turnwa] *nm* tournament.
tournoyer [turnwaje] *v* whirl, swirl.
tournure [turnyr] *nf* turn; turn of phrase; (*apparence*) shape, face.
tourte [turt] *nf* pie.
tourterelle [turtərɛl] *nf* turtle-dove.
Toussaint [tusɛ̃] *nf* All Saints' Day.
tousser [tuse] *v* cough.
tout [tu], **toute** *adj, pl* **tous, toutes** all; (*chaque*) every; (*n'importe quel*) any; (*total*) utmost, full. **de toute façon** in any case. **tous les deux** both. **tous risques** (*assurance*) fully comprehensive. *pron* everything, all. *nm* whole. **du tout** at all. **pas du tout** not at all. *adv* quite, completely; (*très*) very; (*quoique*) though, however. **tout à coup** suddenly. **tout à fait** quite, entirely. **tout à l'heure** (*futur*) presently; (*passé*) just now. **tout au plus/moins** at the very most/least. **tout de même** all the same. **tout de suite** at once. **tout en ... while ... tout fait** ready-made. **tout neuf** brand new. **tout-puissant** *adj* omnipotent.
toutefois [tutfwa] *adv* however.
toux [tu] *nf* cough.
toxique [tɔksik] *adj* toxic.
trac [trak] *nm* fit of nerves; (*théâtre*) stage fright.
tracas [traka] *nm* worry, bother. **tracasser** *v* worry, bother.
trace [tras] *nf* trace; mark, sign; (*chemin*) track, path; (*empreinte*) tracks *pl*, trail. **suivre à la trace** track.

racer [trase] v trace, draw; (chemin) mark out.

ract [trakt] nm pamphlet.

racteur [traktœr] nm tractor.

radition [tradisjɔ̃] nf tradition. **traditionnel** adj traditional.

***traduire** [traduir] v translate; express, convey. **traducteur, -trice** nm, nf translator. **traduction** nf translation.

rafic [trafik] nm traffic; (péj) dealings pl. **trafiquer** v traffic, trade illicitly.

ragédie [traʒedi] nf tragedy. **tragique** adj tragic.

rahir [trair] v betray; (forces, etc.) fail; (mal exprimer) misrepresent. **trahison** nf betrayal; (crime) treason.

rain [trɛ̃] nm train; (allure) pace; (file) line. **en train** under way. **être en train de** be in the middle of.

rain-train nm daily routine.

raîner [trene] v drag; (mots) drawl; (s'attarder) dawdle, lag behind; (pendre) trail; (s'éterniser) drag on; (être éparpillé) lie around. **se traîner** drag oneself, crawl. **traîneau** nm sledge, sleigh. **traînée** nf streak; (trace) trail.

traire [trɛr] v milk.

rait [trɛ] nm line; (caractéristique) trait; (visage) feature; (de lumière, satire, etc.) shaft; (gorgée) gulp. **d'un trait** at one go. **trait d'union** hyphen.

raiter [trete] v treat; (qualifier) call; (s'occuper de) deal with; (négocier) have dealings. **traité** nm (convention) treaty; (livre) treatise. **traitement** nm treatment; salary.

raître, -esse [trɛtrə, -ɛs] adj treacherous. nm, nf traitor. **traîtrise** nf treachery.

rajet [traʒɛ] nm (voyage) journey; distance.

rame [tram] nf (tissu) thread; (vie) texture, web. **tramer** v (combiner) plot; (tisser) weave.

ramway [tramwɛ] nm tram.

ranchant [trɑ̃ʃɑ̃] adj sharp; (personne) assertive. nm cutting edge.

rancher [trɑ̃ʃe] v cut, sever; resolve, settle; contrast sharply. **tranche** nf slice; section; (bord) edge. **tranché** adj clearcut, distinct. **tranchée** nf trench.

ranquille [trɑ̃kil] adj quiet; calm, peaceful; (esprit) easy, at rest. **laisser tranquille** leave alone. **tranquillisant** nm tranquillizer. **tranquilliser** v reassure. **tranquillité** nf peace, tranquillity.

transaction [trɑ̃zaksjɔ̃] nf transaction; compromise.

transatlantique [trɑ̃zatlɑ̃tik] adj transatlantic. nm (chaise) deckchair.

transcender [trɑ̃sɑ̃de] v transcend. **transcendantal** adj transcendental.

***transcrire** [trɑ̃skrir] v transcribe; copy out. **transcription** nf transcription; copy.

transe [trɑ̃s] nf trance. **transes** nf pl agony sing.

transept [trɑ̃sɛpt] nm transept.

transférer [trɑ̃sfere] v transfer. **transfert** nm transfer.

transformer [trɑ̃sfɔrme] v change, alter; (radicalement) transform; convert. **transformateur** nm transformer. **transformation** nf change; transformation; conversion.

transfuge [trɑ̃sfyʒ] n(m+f) renegade.

transfuser [trɑ̃sfyze] v transfuse. **transfusion** nf transfusion.

transiger [trɑ̃ziʒe] v come to an agreement, compromise.

transir [trɑ̃zir] v numb; (froid) chill to the bone; (peur) transfix. **transi** adj numb with cold; transfixed with fear.

transistor [trɑ̃zistɔr] nm transistor. **transistoriser** v transistorize.

transit [trɑ̃zit] nm transit. **en transit** in transit.

transitif [trɑ̃zitif] adj transitive.

transition [trɑ̃zisjɔ̃] nf transition. **de transition** transitional.

transitoire [trɑ̃zitwar] adj transient, transitory; provisional.

translucide [trɑ̃slysid] adj translucent. **translucidité** nf translucence.

***transmettre** [trɑ̃smɛtrə] v pass on; (tech) transmit. **transmetteur** nm transmitter. **transmission** nf transmission.

transparent [trɑ̃sparɑ̃] adj transparent.

transpirer [trɑ̃spire] v sweat, perspire; (secret) come to light. **transpiration** nf perspiration.

transplanter [trɑ̃splɑ̃te] v transplant. **transplantation** nf transplant.

transport [trɑ̃spɔr] nm transport; (marchandises) carriage, transportation. **transporter** v carry, convey; (avec un véhicule) transport; (exalter) carry away.

transposer [trɑ̃spoze] v transpose. **transposition** nf transposition.

transvaser [trɑ̃svaze] v decant.

transversal [trɑ̃svɛrsal] *adj* transverse.
trapèze [trapɛz] *nm* (*sport*) trapeze; (*géom*) trapezium. **trapéziste** *n*(*m+f*) trapeze artist.
trappe [trap] *nf* trapdoor.
trapu [trapy] *adj* squat, stocky.
traquer [trake] *v* track (down), hunt (out); (*harceler*) hound. **traquenard** *nm* trap; (*embûche*) pitfall.
trauma [troma] *nm* trauma. **traumatique** *adj* traumatic. **traumatisant** *adj* traumatic. **traumatisme** *nm* trauma.
travail [travaj] *nm*, *pl* -**aux** work; (*métier*, *tâche*) job; (*méd*, *ouvriers*) labour. **travaux d'aiguille** needlework *sing*.
travailler [travaje] *v* work; (*vin*) ferment; (*exercer*) practise, work at; (*agir sur*) work on; torment, distract. **travaillé** *adj* (*style*) polished; (*ornement*) intricate; (*façonné*) wrought.
travailleur, -euse [travajœr, -øz] *adj* hard-working. *nm*, *nf* worker.
travailliste [travajist] *adj* Labour. *n*(*m+f*) member of the Labour party. **les travaillistes** *nm pl* Labour *sing*.
travers [travɛr] *nm* failing, fault. **à travers** (*milieu*) through; (*surface*) across. **au travers** through. **de travers** (*pas droit*) crooked; (*mal*) wrong. **en travers** across.
traverser [travɛrse] *v* (*surface*) cross; (*milieu*) go through. **traverse** *nf* (*rail*) sleeper; (*tech*) strut, cross-piece. **traversée** *nf* crossing.
traversin [travɛrsɛ̃] *nm* bolster.
travestir [travɛstir] *v* dress up; (*vérité*) misrepresent. **se travestir** (*bal*) put on fancy dress; (*cabaret, psych*) dress up as a woman.
travesti [travɛsti], -**e** *adj* disguised; (*bal*) fancy-dress. *nm* fancy dress; (*cabaret*) drag artist. *nm*, *nf* (*psych*) transvestite.
trébucher [trebyʃe] *v* stumble. **faire trébucher** trip up. **trébuchant** *adj* staggering; (*voix*) halting.
trèfle [trɛflə] *nm* clover; (*cartes*) club.
treillis [treji] *nm* trellis, lattice. **treillis métallique** wire netting.
treize [trɛz] *nm*, *adj* thirteen. **treizième** *n*(*m+f*), *adj* thirteenth.
trembler [trɑ̃ble] *v* tremble, shake; (*de froid*) shiver; (*lumière*) flicker. **tremblement** *nm* tremble, tremor; shiver. **tremblement de terre** earthquake.
se trémousser [tremuse] *v* fidget, wriggle; (*se dandiner*) wiggle.

tremper [trɑ̃pe] *v* soak; (*plonger*) dip. **faire trempette** dunk one's bread *or* sugar.
tremplin [trɑ̃plɛ̃] *nm* spring-board; (*piscine*) diving-board.
trente [trɑ̃t] *nm*, *adj* thirty. **trentième** *n*(*m+f*), *adj* thirtieth.
trépas [trepɑ] *nm* death. **trépasser** *v* die, pass away.
trépider [trepide] *v* vibrate. **trépidation** *nf* vibration; (*agitation*) flurry.
trépied [trepje] *nm* tripod.
trépigner [trepiɲe] *v* stamp.
très [trɛ] *adv* very; (*devant un participe*) highly, very much.
trésor [trezɔr] *nm* treasure; (*source*) mine, wealth; (*endroit*) treasury; (*de l'état*) exchequer. **trésorerie** *nf* treasury; finances *pl*, funds *pl*. **trésorier, -ère** *nm*, *nf* treasurer.
*tressaillir [tresajir] *v* quiver; (*de peur*) shudder; (*de douleur*) wince; (*sursauter*) start; vibrate, shake. **tressaillement** *nm* quiver; shudder; start; vibration.
tresser [trese] *v* (*cheveux*) plait; (*guirlande*) weave; (*corde*) twist. **tresse** *nf* plait; (*cordon*) braid.
tréteau [treto] *nm* trestle.
treuil [trœj] *nm* winch.
trêve [trɛv] *nf* (*mil, pol*) truce; respite. **sans trêve** unceasingly, relentlessly.
tri [tri] *nm* sorting; selection. **faire le tri de** sort; select. **triage** *nm* sorting, selection.
triangle [trijɑ̃glə] *nm* triangle. **triangulaire** *adj* triangular.
tribord [tribɔr] *nm* starboard.
tribu [triby] *nf* tribe.
tribunal [tribynal] *nm* court, tribunal. **tribune** *nf* (*église*) gallery; (*stade*) stand; platform; (*journal, radio, etc.*) forum.
tribut [triby] *nm* tribute.
tributaire [tribytɛr] *adj* tributary.
tricher [triʃe] *v* cheat. **tricherie** *nf* cheating. **tricheur, -euse** *nm*, *nf* cheat.
tricot [triko] *nm* (*technique*) knitting; (*vêtement*) jumper. **tricot de corps** vest. **tricoter** *v* knit.
trictrac [triktrak] *nm* backgammon.
tricycle [trisiklə] *nm* tricycle.
trier [trije] *v* sort (out); select. **trier sur le volet** hand-pick.
trille [trij] *nm* trill. **triller** *v* trill.

trimballer [trɛ̃bale] *v* (*fam*) cart around.
trimestre [trimɛstrə] *nm* quarter; (*école*) term. **trimestriel** *adj* quarterly; end-of-term.
tringle [trɛ̃glə] *nf* rod.
trinquer [trɛ̃ke] *v* clink glasses.
trio [trijo] *nm* trio.
triompher [trijɔ̃fe] *v* triumph, win. **triompher de** overcome, conquer. **triomphant** *adj* triumphant. **triomphe** *nm* triumph.
tripes [trip] *nf pl* (*cuisine*) tripe *sing*; (*fam*) guts *pl*.
triple [triplə] *adj* triple, treble. *nm* **le triple** three times as much. **triplé, -e** *nm, nf* triplet. **tripler** *v* triple, treble.
tripoter [tripɔte] *v* fiddle with; (*fouiller*) rummage about; (*affaire*) be involved in.
triste [trist] *adj* sad, miserable; (*sombre*) dreary, dismal. **tristesse** *nf* sadness, sorrow; dreariness.
triton [tritɔ̃] *nm* newt.
trivial [trivjal] *adj* (*grossier*) coarse; (*ordinaire*) mundane. **trivialité** *nf* coarseness; coarse remark *or* detail; mundane nature.
troc [trɔk] *nm* exchange; (*système économique*) barter.
trognon [trɔɲɔ̃] *nm* core.
trois [trwɑ] *nm, adj* three. **à trois dimensions** three-dimensional. **trois-quarts** *nm pl* three quarters. **troisième** *n(m + f)*, *adj* third.
trombe [trɔ̃b] *nf* (*pluie*) downpour; (*tornade*) whirlwind.
trombone [trɔ̃bɔn] *nm* trombone; (*agrafe*) paper-clip.
trompe [trɔ̃p] *nf* (*éléphant*) trunk; (*musique*) horn.
tromper [trɔ̃pe] *v* deceive; (*par accident*) mislead; (*poursuivant*) elude; (*duper*) fool, trick. **se tromper** be wrong, make a mistake. **tromperie** *nf* deception, deceit. **trompeur, -euse** *adj* (*apparence*) deceptive, misleading; (*personne*) deceitful.
trompette [trɔ̃pɛt] *nf* trumpet. **trompettiste** *n(m + f)* trumpeter.
tronc [trɔ̃] *nm* trunk.
tronçon [trɔ̃sɔ̃] *nm* section.
trône [tron] *nm* throne.
tronquer [trɔ̃ke] *v* truncate; (*texte*) cut down; (*détails*) cut out.
trop [tro] *adv* too, too much. **de trop** (*quantité*) too much; (*nombre*) too many;

(*importun*) in the way. **trop de** too much; too many. **trop-plein** *nm* overflow. *nm* excess.
trophée [trɔfe] *nm* trophy.
tropique [trɔpik] *nm* tropic. **tropical** *adj* tropical.
troquer [trɔke] *v* exchange, swap; (*transaction commerciale*) barter.
trot [tro] *nm* trot; (*souris*) scamper. **trotter** *v* trot. **trottinette** *nf* scooter.
trottoir [trɔtwar] *nm* pavement.
trou [tru] *nm* hole; (*vide*) gap. **trou de serrure** keyhole. **trou d'homme** manhole.
trouble¹ [trublə] *adj* (*eau*) cloudy; (*vue*) blurred, misty; (*affaire*) shady.
trouble² [trublə] *nm* (*agitation*) turmoil; discord; embarrassment; (*inquiétude*) distress; (*méd*) disorder.
troubler [truble] *v* disturb, trouble; (*eau*) make cloudy. **se troubler** (*personne*) get flustered; (*eau*) become cloudy. **trouble-fête** *n(m + f)* invar spoilsport.
trouer [true] *v* make a hole in; pierce; (*parsemer*) dot. **trouée** *nf* gap; (*mil*) breach.
troupe [trup] *nf* (*mil*) troop; (*chanteurs, etc.*) troupe; band, group. **troupeau** *nm* herd; (*moutons*) flock.
trousse [trus] *nf* case, kit; (*sac*) bag. **trousseau** *nm* (*clefs*) bunch; (*mariée*) trousseau. **trousser** *v* truss.
trouver [truve] *v* find. **se trouver** be; (*se sentir*) feel; (*arriver*) happen. **trouvaille** *nf* find.
truc [tryk] *nm* trick; (*fam: combine*) knack; (*fam: chose*) thing; (*fam: machin*) whatsit, thingummy.
truelle [tryɛl] *nf* trowel.
truffe [tryf] *nf* truffle.
truie [trɥi] *nf* sow.
truite [trɥit] *nf* trout.
truquer [tryke] *v* rig, fix. **truquage** *nm* rigging, fixing; (*cinéma*) trick photography, special effects *pl*.
tsar [dzar] *nm* tsar.
tu [ty] *pron* you.
tuba [tyba] *nm* tuba.
tube [tyb] *nm* tube; pipe; (*fam: chanson, disque*) hit.
tuberculose [tybɛrkyloz] *nf* tuberculosis.
tuer [tɥe] *v* kill. **à tue-tête** at the top of one's voice. **tuerie** *nf* slaughter. **tueur, -euse** *nm, nf* killer.
tuile [tɥil] *nf* tile; (*fam*) blow.

tulipe [tylip] *nf* tulip.

tumeur [tymœr] *nf* tumour.

tumulte [tymylt] *nm* tumult, commotion. **tumultueux** *adj* turbulent, stormy.

tunique [tynik] *nf* tunic.

tunnel [tynɛl] *nm* tunnel.

turban [tyrbã] *nm* turban.

turbine [tyrbin] *nf* turbine.

turbot [tyrbo] *nm* turbot.

turbulent [tyrbylã] *adj* turbulent; (*agité*) boisterous, unruly. **turbulence** *nf* turbulence.

turf [tyrf] *nm* (*hippisme*) racing; (*terrain*) racecourse.

turquoise [tyrkwaz] *nf, adj invar* turquoise.

tutelle [tytɛl] *nf* (*surveillance*) supervision; protection; (*jur*) guardianship.

tuteur, -trice [tytœr, -tris] *nm, nf* guardian. *nm* stake.

tutoyer [tytwaje] *v* address as 'tu'. **tutoiement** *nm* use of the 'tu' form.

tuyau [tЧijo] *nm* pipe; (*d'arrosage*) hose; (*fam*) tip. **tuyau d'échappement** exhaust pipe.

tympan [tɛpã] *nm* eardrum.

type [tip] *nm* type; (*représentant*) classic example; (*fam*) bloke, chap.

typhoïde [tifɔid] *nf, adj* typhoid.

typhon [tifɔ̃] *nm* typhoon.

typique [tipik] *adj* typical.

tyran [tirã] *nm* tyrant. **tyrannie** *nf* tyranny. **tyrannique** *adj* tyrannical.

U

ulcérer [ylsere] *v* (*méd*) ulcerate; (*blesser*) wound, embitter. **ulcère** *nm* ulcer.

ultérieur, -e [ylterjœr] *adj* later, subsequent.

ultimatum [yltimatɔm] *nm* ultimatum.

ultime [yltim] *adj* ultimate, final.

ultrasonique [yltrasɔnik] *adj* ultrasonic.

ultraviolet, -ette [yltravjɔlɛ, -ɛt] *adj* ultraviolet.

un [œ̃], **une** *art* a, an. *n, adj, pron* one. **les uns** some. **l'un et l'autre** both. **l'un ou l'autre** either. **unième** *adj* first.

unanime [ynanim] *adj* unanimous. **unanimité** *nf* unanimity.

uni [yni] *adj* (*tissu, couleur*) plain; (*famille*) close; (*lisse*) smooth, even.

unifier [ynifje] *v* unify. **unification** *nf* unification.

uniforme [ynifɔrm] *adj* uniform; (*surface*) even. *nm* uniform. **uniformité** *nf* uniformity.

union [ynjɔ̃] *nf* union; association; combination.

unique [ynik] *adj* (*seul*) only; (*exceptionnel*) unique. **uniquement** *adv* only.

unir [ynir] *v* unite; combine; join. **unité** *nf* (*élément*) unit; (*cohésion*) unity.

unisexe [yniseks] *adj invar* unisex.

unisson [ynisɔ̃] *nm* unison. **à l'unisson** in unison.

univers [ynivɛr] *nm* universe. **universel** *adj* universal; (*outil*) all-purpose.

université [yniversite] *nf* university. **universitaire** *adj* university.

urbain [yrbɛ̃] *adj* urban, town. **urbanisme** *nm* town planning. **urbaniste** *n(m + f)* town planner.

urgent [yrʒã] *adj* urgent. **urgence** *nf* urgency; (*cas urgent*) emergency.

uriner [yrine] *v* urinate. **urine** *nf* urine. **urinoir** *nm* urinal.

urne [yrn] *nf* (*vase*) urn; (*pol*) ballot-box.

usage [yzaʒ] *nm* use; custom; (*gramm*) usage; (*politesse*) breeding. **usagé** *adj* (*usé*) worn, old; (*d'occasion*) secondhand, used.

user [yze] *v* wear out; (*consommer*) use. **user de** use, make use of. **usé** *adj* worn; (*banal*) hackneyed; (*râpé*) threadbare. **usure** *nf* wear.

usine [yzin] *nf* factory, works.

ustensile [ystãsil] *nm* implement; (*de cuisine*) utensil.

usuel [yzЧɛl] *adj* common, everyday; (*d'usage*) usual.

usurper [yzyrpe] *v* usurp. **usurpateur, -trice** *nm, nf* usurper. **usurpation** *nf* usurpation.

utérus [yterys] *nm* womb, uterus.

utile [ytil] *adj* useful. **utilité** *nf* use, usefulness.

utiliser [ytilize] *v* use, utilize. **utilisable** *adj* usable.

V

vacance [vakɑ̃s] *nf* vacancy. **vacances** *nf pl* holiday *sing*, vacation *sing*. **en vacances** on holiday. **vacant** *adj* vacant.

vacarme [vakarm] *nm* din, row.

vaccin [vaksɛ̃] *nm* vaccine. **vaccination** *nf* vaccination. **vacciner** *v* vaccinate.

vache [vaʃ] *nf* cow; (*argot*) bitch, swine. *adj* (*argot*) rotten. **vachement** *adv* (*argot*) bloody.

vaciller [vasije] *v* wobble, sway; (*flamme*) flicker; (*courage*) falter, fail. **vacillant** *adj* unsteady; flickering; (*santé*) shaky; indecisive.

va-et-vient [vaevjɛ̃] *nm invar* comings and goings *pl*; (*mécanisme*) movement to and fro.

vagabond [vagabɔ̃], **-e** *adj* (*errant*) roaming, restless; (*nomade*) wandering. *nm, nf* tramp, vagrant. **vagabondage** *nm* wandering; vagrancy. **vagabonder** *v* roam, wander.

vagin [vaʒɛ̃] *nm* vagina. **vaginal** *adj* vaginal.

vague¹ [vag] *adj* vague. *nm* vagueness. **regarder dans le vague** stare into space.

vague² [vag] *nf* wave; (*montée*) surge. **vague de chaleur** heat wave.

vaillant [vajɑ̃] *adj* brave, valiant; vigorous, robust.

vain [vɛ̃] *adj* vain; empty, futile. **en vain** in vain.

***vaincre** [vɛ̃krə] *v* conquer, defeat, overcome.

vainqueur [vɛ̃kœr] *nm* conqueror; (*sport*) winner. *adj* victorious.

vaisseau [vɛso] *nm* vessel; (*naut*) ship.

vaisselle [vɛsɛl] *nf* crockery, dishes *pl*; (*lavage*) washing-up. **faire la vaisselle** wash up.

val [val] *nm* valley.

valable [valablə] *adj* valid; (*notable*) worthwhile.

valet [valɛ] *nm* servant, valet; (*cartes*) jack. **valet d'écurie** groom. **valet de ferme** farm-hand.

valeur [valœr] *nf* value; (*qualité*) worth. **de valeur** valuable. **mettre en valeur** exploit; (*détail*) bring out, highlight. **objets de valeur** *nm pl* valuables *pl*. **valeurs** *nf pl* (*bourse*) securities *pl*.

valide [valid] *adj* (*billet*) valid; (*personne*) fit; able-bodied. **validité** *nf* validity.

valise [valiz] *nf* suitcase.

vallée [vale] *nf* valley.

***valoir** [valwar] *v* be worth; be valid, apply; (*équivaloir à*) be as good as; (*causer*) bring, earn. **faire valoir** exploit; (*caractéristique*) bring out, highlight. **il vaut mieux** it is better. **valoir la peine** be worth it.

valse [vals] *nf* waltz. **valser** *v* waltz.

valve [valv] *nf* valve.

vampire [vɑ̃pir] *nm* vampire.

vandale [vɑ̃dal] *n(m+f)* vandal. **vandalisme** *nm* vandalism.

vanille [vanij] *nf* vanilla.

vanité [vanite] *nf* vanity, conceit; futility. **vaniteux** *adj* vain, conceited.

vanter [vɑ̃te] *v* praise. **se vanter** boast. **se vanter de** pride oneself on. **vantard** *adj* boastful. **vantardise** *nf* boasting, boastfulness; (*propos*) boast.

vapeur [vapœr] *nf* vapour, steam. **bateau à vapeur** *nm* steamer. **cuire à la vapeur** steam. **vaporiser** *v* (*parfum*) spray; (*phys*) vaporize.

varice [varis] *nf* varicose vein.

varicelle [varisɛl] *nf* chicken-pox.

varier [varje] *v* vary. **variable** *nf, adj* variable. **variante** *nf* variant. **variation** *nf* variation. **variété** *nf* variety.

variole [varjɔl] *nf* smallpox.

Varsovie [varsɔvi] *n* Warsaw.

vase¹ [vɑz] *nm* vase.

vase² [vɑz] *nf* mud, sludge.

vaste [vast] *adj* vast, immense.

Vatican [vatikɑ̃] *nm* Vatican.

vau [vo] *nm* **à vau-l'eau** with the current; (*projets*, *etc.*) down the drain. **aller à vau-l'eau** be on the road to ruin.

vaudou [vodu] *nm, adj invar* voodoo.

vaurien [vorjɛ̃], **-enne** *nm, nf* good-for-nothing.

vautour [votur] *nm* vulture.

se vautrer [votre] *v* sprawl. **se vautrer dans** wallow in.

veau [vo] *nm* calf; (*cuisine*) veal.

vedette [vədɛt] *nf* (*cinéma, etc.*) star; (*bateau*) launch.

végétal [veʒetal] *adj* plant, vegetable.

végétation [veʒetasjɔ̃] *nf* vegetation. **végétations adénoïdes** adenoids *pl*.

véhément [veemɑ̃] *adj* vehement. **véhémence** *nf* vehemence.

véhicule [veikyl] *nm* vehicle.
veille [vɛj] *nf* (*garde*) watch, vigil; (*jour précédent*) eve, day before; (*état*) wakefulness. **veillée** *nf* evening; (*mort*) watch.
veiller *v* (*mort, malade*) sit up with, watch over; (*rester éveillé*) stay awake; be vigilant. **veiller à** attend to, see to. **veiller sur** watch over. **veilleuse** *nf* (*flamme*) pilot-light; (*lampe*) night-light.
veine [vɛn] *nf* vein; (*fam*) luck.
vélo [velo] *nm* (*fam*) bike.
vélocité [velɔsite] *nf* swiftness, nimbleness; (*vitesse*) velocity.
velours [vəlur] *nm* velvet. **velours côtelé** corduroy. **velouté** *adj* velvety, smooth.
velu [vəly] *adj* hairy.
venaison [vənɛzɔ̃] *nf* venison.
vendange [vɑ̃dɑ̃ʒ] *nf* grape harvest.
vendre [vɑ̃drə] *v* sell. **vendre la mèche** (*fam*) give the game away. **vendeur, -euse** *nm, nf* seller; (*magasin*) shop assistant.
vendredi [vɑ̃drədi] *nm* Friday. **vendredi saint** Good Friday.
vénéneux [venenø] *adj* poisonous.
vénérer [venere] *v* venerate, revere. **vénérable** *adj* venerable. **vénération** *nf* veneration.
vénérien [venerjɛ̃] *adj* venereal. **maladie vénérienne** venereal disease.
venger [vɑ̃ʒe] *v* avenge. **se venger** take one's revenge. **vengeance** *nf* vengeance, revenge.
venin [vənɛ̃] *nm* venom. **venimeux** *adj* venomous.
*****venir** [vənir] *v* come. **en venir à** come to, resort to. **faire venir** send for. **venir de** come from; (*suivi d'un infinitif*) have just.
vent [vɑ̃] *nm* wind. **dans le vent** (*fam*) trendy, fashionable. **il fait du vent** it is windy. **venteux** *adj* windswept.
vente [vɑ̃t] *nf* sale. **vente aux enchères** auction. **vente de charité** bazaar, jumble sale.
ventiler [vɑ̃tile] *v* ventilate. **ventilateur** *nm* fan, ventilator. **ventilation** *nf* ventilation.
ventouse [vɑ̃tuz] *nf* sucker, suction pad.
ventre [vɑ̃trə] *nm* stomach, belly.
ventriloque [vɑ̃trilɔk] *n(m+f)* ventriloquist.
venue [vəny] *nf* coming.
ver [vɛr] *nm* worm; (*larve*) grub; (*asticot*) maggot. **ver à soie** silkworm. **ver du bois** woodworm.
véranda [verɑ̃da] *nf* veranda.
verbe [verb] *nm* verb. **verbal** *adj* verbal.

verdict [vɛrdikt] *nm* verdict.
verdir [vɛrdir] *v* turn green. **verdure** *nf* greenery.
verge [vɛrʒ] *nf* rod; penis.
verger [vɛrʒe] *nm* orchard.
verglas [vɛrgla] *nm* black ice.
vergogne [vɛrgɔɲ] *nf* shame.
véridique [veridik] *adj* truthful.
vérifier [verifje] *v* check, verify; (*comptes*) audit; confirm, prove. **vérification** *nf* check, verification; auditing; confirmation.
vérité [verite] *nf* truth; (*sincérité*) truthfulness. **véritable** *adj* real, true, genuine.
vermeil, -eille [vɛrmɛj] *adj* bright red.
vermine [vɛrmin] *nf* vermin.
vermouth [vɛrmut] *nm* vermouth.
vernaculaire [vɛrnakylɛr] *adj* vernacular.
vernir [vɛrnir] *v* varnish. **verni** *adj* varnished; (*luisant*) glossy. **cuir verni** patent leather. **vernis** *nm* varnish; (*poterie*) glaze; (*éclat*) gloss; (*apparence*) veneer. **vernisser** *v* glaze.
vérole [verɔl] *nf* **petite vérole** smallpox.
verre [vɛr] *nm* glass; (*optique*) lens; (*boisson*) drink. **verres de contact** contact lenses *pl.*
verrou [vɛru] *nm* bolt.
verrouiller [vɛruje] *v* bolt.
verrue [vɛry] *nf* wart.
vers¹ [vɛr] *prep* towards; to; (*approximation*) about, around.
vers² [vɛr] *nm* line. *nm pl* verse *sing.*
versant [vɛrsɑ̃] *nm* side, slope.
verse [vɛrs] *nf* **à verse** in torrents. **il pleut à verse** it is pouring down.
Verseau [vɛrso] *nm* Aquarius.
verser [vɛrse] *v* pour; (*sang, larmes*) shed; pay; (*basculer*) overturn. **versement** *nm* payment; (*échelonné*) instalment.
version [vɛrsjɔ̃] *nf* version; (*traduction*) translation.
verso [vɛrso] *nm* back.
vert [vɛr] *adj* green; (*fruit*) unripe; (*propos*) spicy. *nm* green.
vertèbre [vɛrtɛbrə] *nf* vertebra (*pl* -brae). **vertébral** *adj* vertebral. **vertébré** *nm, adj* vertebrate.
vertical [vɛrtikal] *adj* vertical. **verticale** *nf* vertical.
vertige [vɛrtiʒ] *nm* vertigo, dizziness. **avoir le vertige** feel dizzy. **pris de vertige** dizzy, giddy. **vertigineux** *adj* breathtaking; (*hauteur*) giddy.

vertu [vɛrty] *nf* virtue. **vertueux** *adj* virtuous.

verve [vɛrv] *nf* vigour, zest; eloquence.

vessie [vesi] *nf* bladder.

veste [vɛst] *nf* jacket.

vestiaire [vestjɛr] *nm* cloakroom; (*piscine, etc.*) changing-room.

vestibule [vestibyl] *nm* hall, vestibule.

vestige [vɛstiʒ] *nm* vestige, remnant, trace.

veston [vɛstɔ̃] *nm* jacket.

vêtement [vɛtmɑ̃] *nm* garment. **vêtements** *nm pl* clothes *pl*, clothing *sing*.

vétéran [veterɑ̃] *nm* veteran.

vétérinaire [veterinɛr] *nm* vet. *adj* veterinary.

vétille [vetij] *nf* trifle.

*****vêtir** [vetir] *v* clothe, dress. **vêtu de** wearing.

veto [veto] *nm* veto. **mettre son veto à** veto.

vétuste [vetyst] *adj* ancient, decrepit. **vétusté** *nf* age, decay.

veuf [vœf] *adj* widowed. *nm* widower. **veuve** *nf* widow. **veuvage** *nm* widowhood.

veule [vøl] *adj* spineless, weak.

vexer [vɛkse] *v* upset, hurt. **vexant** *adj* hurtful; (*contrariant*) annoying.

via [vja] *prep* via.

viable [vjablə] *adj* viable. **viabilité** *nf* viability; (*chemin*) practicability.

viaduc [vjadyk] *nm* viaduct.

viager [vjaʒe] *adj* for life.

viande [vjɑ̃d] *nf* meat.

vibrer [vibre] *v* vibrate; (*voix*) quiver. **vibration** *nf* vibration.

vicaire [vikɛr] *nm* curate.

vice [vis] *nm* vice; fault.

vice-chancelier *nm* vice-chancellor.

vice-consul *nm* vice-consul.

vice-président, -e *nm, nf* (*état*) vice-president; (*réunion*) vice-chairman.

vice versa [viseversa] *adv* vice versa.

vicier [visje] *v* pollute, taint; (*jur*) invalidate.

vicieux [visjø] *adj* licentious, depraved; (*animal*) unruly; (*fautif*) incorrect.

vicomte [vikɔ̃t] *nm* viscount. **vicomtesse** *nf* viscountess.

victime [viktim] *nf* victim.

victoire [viktwar] *nf* victory. **victorieux** *adj* victorious.

vidange [vidɑ̃ʒ] *nf* emptying; (*auto*) oil change. **vidanges** *nf pl* sewage *sing*. **vidanger** *v* empty, drain.

vide [vid] *adj* empty; (*disponible*) vacant. *nm* emptiness; (*espace*) void; (*sans air*) vacuum; (*creux*) gap. **vider** *v* empty; (*bassin, etc.*) drain; (*quitter*) vacate; (*cuisine*) gut; (*fam: épuiser*) wear out; (*fam: expulser*) throw out.

vie [vi] *nf* life; (*moyens*) living.

vieil [vjɛj] *form of* **vieux** *used before a vowel or mute h.*

vieillir [vjejir] *v* age, grow old. **vieillard** *nm* old man. **vieillesse** *nf* old age.

Vienne [vjɛn] *n* Vienna.

vierge [vjɛrʒ] *nf* virgin. **Vierge** *nf* Virgo. *adj* (*terre, etc.*) virgin; (*papier*) blank.

vieux, vieille [vjø, vjɛj] *adj* old. **vieille fille** spinster. **vieux jeu** *adj invar* old-fashioned. *nm* old man. *nf* old woman.

vif [vif] *adj* lively; brusque; (*aigu*) sharp, keen; intense, vivid; (*fort*) strong, great; (*froid*) biting; (*éclat*) bright; (*allure*) brisk. *nm* quick.

vigile [viʒil] *nf* vigil. **vigilance** *nf* vigilance. **vigilant** *adj* vigilant.

vigne [viɲ] *nf* vi..e. **vignoble** *nm* vineyard.

vignette [viɲɛt] *nf* label; (*auto*) tax disc.

vigoureux [viguɾø] *adj* vigorous; robust, sturdy.

vigueur [vigœr] *nf* vigour; (*robustesse*) sturdiness; (*force*) strength. **entrer en vigueur** come into effect. **en vigueur** in force, current.

vil [vil] *adj* vile, base.

vilain [vilɛ̃] *adj* nasty; (*laid*) ugly; (*méchant*) mean, wicked.

vilebrequin [vilbrəkɛ̃] *nm* (*auto*) crankshaft; (*tech*) brace.

villa [villa] *nf* villa, detached house.

village [vilaʒ] *nm* village. **villageois, -e** *nm, nf* villager.

ville [vil] *nf* town; (*plus grande*) city. **ville d'eau** spa.

villégiature [vileʒatyr] *nf* holiday; (*lieu*) holiday resort.

vin [vɛ̃] *nm* wine. **grand vin** vintage wine.

vinaigre [vinɛgrə] *nm* vinegar. **vinaigrette** *nf* French dressing, vinaigrette.

vindicatif [vɛ̃dikatif] *adj* vindictive.

vingt [vɛ̃] *nm, adj* twenty. **vingtième** $n(m+f)$, *adj* twentieth.

vinyle [vinil] *nm* vinyl.

viol [vjɔl] *nm* rape.

violent [vjɔlɑ̃] *adj* violent; (*effort*) strenuous; (*fort*) strong, intense. **violence** *nf* violence.

violer [vjɔle] *v* violate; *(femme)* rape; *(loi, promesse)* break. **violation** *nf* violation.
violet, -ette [vjɔlɛ, -ɛt] *adj* purple, violet. *nm* purple. *nf* violet.
violon [vjɔlɔ̃] *nm* violin. **violoncelle** *nm* cello. **vio'oniste** *n(m+f)* violinist.
vipère [vipɛr] *nf* adder, viper.
virage [viraʒ] *nm* bend, turn.
virer [vire] *v* turn; change; *(argent)* transfer. **virement** *nm* transfer.
virginité [virʒinite] *nf* virginity.
virgule [virgyl] *nf* comma; *(math)* decimal point.
viril [viril] *adj* virile, manly; masculine. **virilité** *nf* virility.
virtuel [virtɥɛl] *adj* potential. **virtuellement** *adv* potentially; *(pratiquement)* virtually.
virus [virys] *nm* virus.
vis [vis] *nf* screw.
visa [viza] *nm* *(passeport)* visa; *(timbre)* stamp; *(de censure)* certificate.
visage [vizaʒ] *nm* face.
vis-à-vis [vizavi] *adv* opposite, face to face. *nm* **en vis-à-vis** opposite each other. *prep* **vis-à-vis de** opposite; *(comparaison)* beside, next to; *(envers)* towards.
viser [vize] *v* aim (at); *(remarque)* be directed at. **visée** *nf* aim; design.
visible [viziblə] *adj* visible; *(évident)* obvious. **visibilité** *nf* visibility.
visière [vizjɛr] *nf* *(casquette)* peak; *(armure)* visor.
vision [vizjɔ̃] *nf* vision; *(faculté)* eyesight. **visionnaire** *n(m+f)*, *adj* visionary.
visiter [vizite] *v* visit; *(ville, château)* go round; examine; *(fouiller)* search. **visite** *nf* visit; tour; inspection, examination. **rendre visite à** visit, call on. **visiteur, -euse** *nm*, *nf* visitor.
vison [vizɔ̃] *nm* mink.
visser [vise] *v* screw down *or* on.
visuel [vizɥɛl] *adj* visual.
vital [vital] *adj* vital. **vitalité** *nf* vitality, energy.
vitamine [vitamin] *nf* vitamin.
vite [vit] *adv* fast, quickly; *(tôt)* soon. *interj* quick! **vitesse** *nf* speed; *(auto)* gear; velocity.
vitrer [vitre] *v* put glass in, glaze. **vitrail** *nm*, *pl* **-aux** stained-glass window. **vitre** *nf* pane of glass; *(fenêtre)* window. **vitrine** *nf* *(magasin)* shop-window; *(armoire)* display cabinet, glass case.
vivace [vivas] *adj* *(plante)* hardy; *(foi,*

haine) undying. **vivacité** *nf* vivacity, liveliness; *(éclat)* brightness; *(mordant)* sharpness; intensity.
vivant [vivɑ̃] *adj* alive, living; *(vivace)* lively. *nm* living person; *(vie)* lifetime.
vivier [vivje] *nm* fish-pond.
vivifier [vivifje] *v* invigorate.
vivisection [vivisɛksjɔ̃] *nf* vivisection.
***vivre** [vivrə] *v* live, be alive. **vive ... !** *interj* long live ... ! three cheers for ... ! **vivre de** live on. *nm* board. **vivres** *nm pl* provisions *pl*.
vocabulaire [vɔkabylɛr] *nm* vocabulary.
vocal [vɔkal] *adj* vocal.
vocation [vɔkasjɔ̃] *nf* vocation, calling.
vodka [vɔdka] *nf* vodka.
vœu [vø] *nm* *(souhait)* wish; *(promesse)* vow.
vogue [vɔg] *nf* fashion, vogue. **en vogue** fashionable.
voguer [vɔge] *v* sail; *(pensées, etc.)* drift.
voici [vwasi] *prep* *(sing)* here is, this is; *(pl)* here are, these are. **voici ... que** it is ... since. **voici une heure** an hour ago.
voie [vwa] *nf* way, road; *(rail)* track, line; *(autoroute, etc.)* lane. **voie d'eau** leak. **voie ferrée** railway line. **voie publique** public highway. **voie sans issue** no through road.
voilà [vwala] *prep* *(sing)* there is, that is; *(pl)* there are, those are. **voilà ... que** it is ... since. **voilà une heure** an hour ago.
voile[1] [vwal] *nf* sail; *(sport)* sailing. **voilier** *nm* sailing ship *or* boat.
voile[2] [vwal] *nm* veil; *(tissu)* net.
voiler [vwale] *v* veil, shroud. **se voiler** mist over, grow hazy.
***voir** [vwar] *v* see. **aller voir** call on, visit. **faire voir** show. **n'avoir rien à voir avec** have nothing to do with. **se voir** show, be obvious.
voire [vwar] *adv* indeed.
voirie [vwari] *nf* *(voies)* highways *pl*; *(entretien)* highway maintenance; *(enlèvement des ordures)* refuse collection; *(dépotoir)* refuse dump.
voisin, -e *adj* neighbouring; *(adjacent)* adjoining; *(ressemblant)* akin. *nm*, *nf* neighbour. **voisinage** *nm* neighbourhood; proximity.
voiture [vwatyr] *nf* car; *(wagon)* coach, carriage. **voiture d'enfant** pram.
voix [vwa] *nf* voice; *(pol)* vote. **à voix basse/haute** in a low/loud voice. **être sans voix** be speechless.

vol¹ [vɔl] *nm* flight. **à vol d'oiseau** as the crow flies. **vol à voile** gliding. **vol libre** hang-gliding.

vol² [vɔl] *nm* theft. **vol à l'étalage** shoplifting. **vol à main armée** armed robbery.

volaille [vɔlɑj] *nf* poultry, fowl.

volant [vɔlɑ̃] *nm* (*auto*) steering wheel; (*tech*) flywheel; (*sport*) shuttlecock; (*robe*) flounce. *adj* flying.

volatil [vɔlatil] *adj* volatile.

volcan [vɔlkɑ̃] *nm* volcano. **volcanique** *adj* volcanic.

voler¹ [vɔle] *v* fly. **volée** *nf* flight; (*groupe*) flock, swarm; (*coups, sport*) volley.

voler² [vɔle] *v* (*chose*) steal; (*personne*) rob. **voleur, -euse** *nm, nf* thief. **au voleur!** stop thief!

volet [vɔlɛ] *nm* shutter; (*tech*) flap.

volière [vɔljɛr] *nf* aviary.

volontaire [vɔlɔ̃tɛr] *adj* voluntary; intentional; (*décidé*) headstrong, determined. *n(m + f)* volunteer.

volonté [vɔlɔ̃te] *nf* will; (*détermination*) willpower. **bonne volonté** goodwill, willingness. **volontiers** *adv* gladly, willingly.

volt [vɔlt] *nm* volt. **voltage** *nm* voltage.

volte-face [vɔltəfas] *nf invar* about-turn.

voltiger [vɔltiʒe] *v* flutter about.

volume [vɔlym] *nm* volume.

volupté [vɔlypte] *nf* sensual delight, voluptuousness. **voluptueux** *adj* voluptuous.

vomir [vɔmir] *v* vomit. **vomissement** *nm* vomiting; (*matière*) vomit.

vorace [vɔras] *adj* voracious. **voracité** *nf* voracity.

vos [vo] *V* **votre**.

voter [vɔte] *v* vote; (*loi*) pass. **vote** *nm* vote.

votre [vɔtrə] *adj, pl* **vos** your.

vôtre [votrə] *pron* **le** or **la vôtre** yours.

vouer [vwe] *v* (*promettre*) vow; (*consacrer*) devote; (*condamner*) doom.

*vouloir [vulwar] *v* want; (*essayer*) try; require, need. **en vouloir à** have a grudge against. **vouloir bien** be willing. **vouloir dire** mean. *nm* will.

vous [vu] *pron* you, to you; (*réfléchi*) yourselves, each other. **vous-mêmes** *pron* yourselves.

voûter [vute] *v* arch. **voûte** *nf* vault, arch. **voûté** *adj* arched; (*personne*) stooped.

vouvoyer [vuvwaje] *v* address as 'vous'. **vouvoiement** *nm* use of the 'vous' form.

voyage [vwajaʒ] *nm* (*course*) journey, trip; (*action*) travel, travelling; (*par mer, d'exploration*) voyage. **voyage de noces** honeymoon. **voyage organisé** package tour. **voyager** *v* travel. **voyageur, -euse** *nm, nf* traveller; passenger.

voyant [vwajɑ̃] *adj* gaudy, garish.

voyelle [vwajɛl] *nf* vowel.

voyou [vwaju] *nm* hooligan, lout.

vrai [vrɛ] *adj* true; real. *nm* truth. **à vrai dire** to tell the truth, in actual fact. **pour de vrai** (*fam*) for real. **vraiment** *adv* really.

vraisemblable [vrɛsɑ̃blablə] *adj* likely, probable; (*histoire*) convincing, plausible. **vraisemblance** *nf* likelihood, probability; plausibility.

vrille [vrij] *nf* (*bot*) tendril; (*tech*) gimlet; spiral.

vrombir [vrɔ̃bir] *v* hum. **vrombissement** *nm* humming.

vu [vy] *adj* **bien vu** highly regarded. **mal vu** poorly thought of. *prep* in view of. *conj* **vu que** seeing that. **vue** *nf* view; (*sens, spectacle*) sight; (*projet*) plan, design.

vulgaire [vylgɛr] *adj* (*grossier*) vulgar; (*banal*) common. **vulgarité** *nf* vulgarity.

vulnérable [vylnerablə] *adj* vulnerable.

W

wagon [vagɔ̃] *nm* (*marchandises*) truck, wagon; (*voyageurs*) carriage. **wagon-lit** *nm* sleeping-car. **wagon-restaurant** *nm* restaurant-car.

watt [wat] *nm* watt.

week-end [wikɛnd] *nm* weekend.

western [wɛstɛrn] *nm* western.

whisky [wiski] *nm* whisky.

whist [wist] *nm* whist.

X

xénophobe [ksenɔfɔb] *adj* xenophobic.
n(*m* + *f*) xenophobe. **xénophobie** *nf* xenophobia.
xérès [gzɛrɛs] *nm* sherry.
xylophone [ksilɔfɔn] *nm* xylophone.

Y

y [i] *adv* there. *pron* it, about it, to it, in
it. **n'y être pour rien** have nothing to do
with it.
yacht [jɔt] *nm* yacht.
yaourt [jaurt] *nm* yoghurt.
yeux [jø] *V* œil.
yoga [jɔga] *nm* yoga.
Yougoslavie [jugɔslavi] *nf* Yugoslavia.
yougoslave *adj* Yugoslav, Yugoslavian.
Yougoslave *n*(*m* + *f*) Yugoslav.
youyou [juju] *nm* dinghy.
yo-yo [jojo] *nm invar* yo-yo.

Z

zèbre [zɛbrə] *nm* zebra. **zébrer** *v* stripe.
zébrure *nf* stripe; (*d'un coup*) weal.
zèle [zɛl] *nm* zeal. **zélé** *adj* zealous.
zéro [zero] *nm* zero, nought.
zeste [zɛst] *nm* peel, zest.
zézayer [zezeje] *v* lisp. **zézaiement** *nm*
lisp.
zibeline [ziblin] *nf* sable.
zigzag [zigzag] *nm* zigzag. **zigzaguer** *v* zigzag.
zinc [zɛ̃g] *nm* zinc; (*fam*) bar, counter.
zodiaque [zɔdjak] *nm* zodiac.
zone [zɔn] *nf* zone, area.
zoo [zoo] *nm* zoo.
zoologie [zɔɔlɔʒi] *nf* zoology. **zoologique**
adj zoological